DISTRIBUTED SYSTEMS
Fourth edition

INTERNATIONAL COMPUTER SCIENCE SERIES

Consulting Editor **A D McGettrick** University of Strathclyde

SELECTED TITLES IN THE SERIES

Operating Systems *J Bacon and T Harris*

Programming Language Essentials *H E Bal and D Grune*

Programming in Ada 95 (2nd edn) *J G P Barnes*

Java Gently (3rd edn) *J Bishop*

Software Design (2nd edn) *D Budgen*

Concurrent Programming *A Burns and G Davies*

Real-Time Systems and Programming Languages: Ada 95, Real-Time Java and Real-Time POSIX (3rd edn) *A Burns and A Wellings*

Comparative Programming Languages (3rd edn) *L B Wilson and R G Clark, updated by R G Clark*

Database Systems: A Practical Approach to Design, Implementation, and Management (4th edn) *T Connolly and C Begg*

Fortran 90 Programming *T M R Ellis, I R Philips and T M Lahey*

Program Verification *N Francez*

Introduction to Programming using SML *M Hansen and H Rischel*

Functional *C P Hartel and H Muller*

Algorithms and Data Structures: Design, Correctness, Analysis (2nd edn) *J Kingston*

Introductory Logic and Sets for Computer Scientists *N Nissanke*

Human–Computer Interaction *J Preece et al.*

Algorithms: A Functional Programming Approach *F Rabhi and G Lapalme*

Ada 95 From the Beginning (3rd edn) *J Skansholm*

C++ From the Beginning (2nd edn) *J Skansholm*

Java From the Beginning (2nd edn) *J Skansholm*

Software Engineering (7th edn) *I Sommerville*

Miranda: The Craft of Functional Programming *S Thompson*

Haskell: The Craft of Functional Programming (2nd edn) *S Thompson*

Discrete Mathematics for Computer Scientists (2nd edn) *J K Truss*

Compiler Design *R Wilhelm and D Maurer*

Discover Delphi: Programming Principles Explained *S Williams and S Walmsley*

DISTRIBUTED SYSTEMS

CONCEPTS AND DESIGN

Fourth edition

GEORGE COULOURIS

JEAN DOLLIMORE

TIM KINDBERG

 ADDISON-WESLEY

Harlow, England • London • New York • Boston • San Francisco • Toronto • Sydney • Singapore • Hong Kong
Tokyo • Seoul • Taipei • New Delhi • Cape Town • Madrid • Mexico City • Amsterdam • Munich • Paris • Milan

Pearson Education Limited
Edinburgh Gate
Harlow
Essex CM20 2JE
England

and Associated Companies throughout the world

Visit us on the World Wide Web at:
www.pearsoned.co.uk

First published 1988
Second edition 1994
Third edition 2001
Fourth edition 2005

ISBN-13: 978-0-321-26354-4
ISBN-10: 0-321-26354-5

British Library Cataloguing-in-Publication Data
A catalogue record for this book is available from the British Library

Library of Congress Cataloging-in-Publication Data
Coulouris, George F.
  Distributed systems : concepts and design / George Coulouris, Jean Dollimore, Tim Kindberg.--4th ed.
    p. cm.
  Includes bibliographical references and index.
  ISBN 0-321-26354-5
    1. Electronic data processing--Distributed processing. I. Dollimore, Jean. II. Kindberg, Tim. III. Title

  QA76.9.D5C68 2005
  004'.36--dc22

                                                                    2005043613

10 9 8 7 6 5 4 3 2
10 09 08 07 06

Typeset by the authors using FrameMaker
Printed and bound in the United States of America

The publisher's policy is to use paper manufactured from sustainable forests.

CONTENTS

PREFACE

This fourth edition of our textbook appears at a time when the Internet and the Web are mature systems, supporting a wide variety of distributed applications on a scale far greater than could have been anticipated when our third edition was published almost five years ago.

The book aims to provide an understanding of the principles on which the Internet and other distributed systems are based, their architecture, algorithms and design. We begin with two conceptual overview chapters that outline the characteristics of distributed systems and the challenges that must be addressed in their design: scalability, heterogeneity, security and failure handling being the most significant. These chapters also develop abstract models for understanding process interaction, failure and security. They are followed by foundational chapters devoted to the study of networking, interprocess communication, remote invocation and middleware, operating system support and naming.

We then cover the well-established topics of security, data replication, group communication, distributed file systems, distributed transactions, CORBA, distributed shared memory and multimedia systems together with several new ones: Web Services, XML, the Grid, peer-to-peer, mobile and ubiquitous systems. Algorithms associated with all these topics are covered as they arise and also in separate chapters devoted to timing, coordination and agreement.

Purposes and readership

The book is intended for use in undergraduate and introductory postgraduate courses. It can equally be used for self-study. We take a top-down approach, addressing the issues to be resolved in the design of distributed systems and describing successful approaches in the form of abstract models, algorithms and detailed case studies of widely-used systems. We cover the field in sufficient depth and breadth to enable readers to go on to study most research papers in the literature on distributed systems.

We aim to make the subject accessible to students who have a basic knowledge of object oriented programming, operating systems and elementary computer architecture. The book includes coverage of those aspects of computer networks relevant to distributed systems, including the underlying technologies for the Internet, wide area, local area and wireless networks. Algorithms and interfaces are presented throughout the book in Java or, in a few cases, ANSI C. For brevity and clarity of presentation, a form of pseudo-code derived from Java/C is also used.

Organization of the book

The following diagram shows the book's chapters under six main topic areas. It is intended to provide a guide to the book's structure and to indicate recommended navigation routes for instructors wishing to provide, or readers wishing to achieve, understanding of the various subfields of distributed system design:

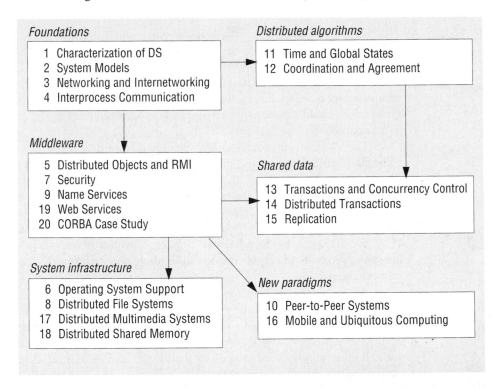

Foundations

1 Characterization of DS
2 System Models
3 Networking and Internetworking
4 Interprocess Communication

Distributed algorithms

11 Time and Global States
12 Coordination and Agreement

Middleware

5 Distributed Objects and RMI
7 Security
9 Name Services
19 Web Services
20 CORBA Case Study

Shared data

13 Transactions and Concurrency Control
14 Distributed Transactions
15 Replication

System infrastructure

6 Operating System Support
8 Distributed File Systems
17 Distributed Multimedia Systems
18 Distributed Shared Memory

New paradigms

10 Peer-to-Peer Systems
16 Mobile and Ubiquitous Computing

References

The existence of the World Wide Web has changed the way in which a book such as this can be linked to source material, including research papers, technical specifications and standards. Many of the source documents are now available on the Web; some are available only there. For reasons of brevity and readability, we employ a special form of reference to web material which loosely resembles a URL: references such as [www.omg.org] and [www.rsasecurity.com I] refer to documentation that is available only on the Web. They can be looked up in the reference list at the end of the book, but the full URLs are given only in an online version of the reference list at the book's web site: www.cdk4.net/refs where they take the form of clickable links. Both versions of the reference list include a more detailed explanation of this scheme.

Entirely new chapters:

10 Peer-to-Peer Systems	
16 Mobile and Ubiquitous Computing	Chapters from 10 onwards have new numbering in this edition.
19 Web Services	

Chapters to which new material has been added, but without structural changes:

1 Characterization of DS	Section 1.3.1: updated to introduce web services
2 System Models	Section 2.2.2: updated to introduce peer-to-peer
3 Networking and Internetworking	Many updates New Section 3.5.3: Case Study: Bluetooth
4 Interprocess Communication	New Section 4.3.3: XML
7 Security	Several updates New Section 7.6.4: weaknesses of WiFi
9 Name Services	Section 9.1.1: section on URIs updated
20 CORBA Case Study	Section 20.2.1: upgraded to Java 2 vn 1.4 Section 20.2.6: integration with web services

The remaining chapters have received only minor modifications.

Changes relative to the third edition

Before embarking on the writing of this new edition, we carried out a survey of teachers who used the third edition. From the results, we identified the new material required and the changes to be made. This led to our writing three entirely new chapters and making numerous insertions throughout the book. All the chapters have been changed to reflect new information that has become available about the systems described. However, to help teachers who used the third edition, we have left the structure of the existing chapters almost unchanged. The new chapters and those containing substantial changes are listed in the table above. The Mach case study chapter has been removed and is available from the book's web site, together with several smaller case studies that were removed from the second and third editions.

Acknowledgements

We are very grateful to the following teachers who participated in our survey: Kay Robbins, Kohei Honda, Stefan Leue and Ian Wakeman.

We would like to thank the following people who reviewed the new chapters or provided other substantial help: John Barton, Arne Glenstrup, Roy Logie, Friedemann Mattern, Christian Mortensen, Anthony Rowstron, Bo Sanden, Dave Scott, Ben Smyth, Mirjana Spasojevic, Salman Taherian, Andrew Twigg, Jim Waldo, Eiko Yoneki, Kan Zhang and Ben Zhao.

The Department of Computer Science, Queen Mary College, University of London, has hosted the companion web site for the third edition and has agreed to host the site for the fourth edition. We thank the department for its support and Keith Clarke and the systems team for their help in setting up and maintaining these sites.

Finally, we thank Simon Plumtree, Bridget Allen, Mary Lince and Owen Knight of Pearson Education/Addison-Wesley for essential support throughout the arduous process of getting the book into print.

Web site

As before, we shall maintain a web site with a wide range of material designed to assist teachers and readers. This web site can be accessed via either of the URLs:

www.cdk4.net   www.pearsoned.co.uk/coulouris

The web site includes:

Instructor's Guide: Comprising:

- Complete artwork of the book available as PowerPoint files.
- Solutions to the exercises (protected by a password available only to teachers).
- Chapter-by-chapter teaching hints.
- Suggested laboratory projects.

Reference list: The list of references that can be found at the end of the book is replicated at the web site. The web version of the reference list includes active links for material that is available online.

Errata list: A list of known errors in the book, with corrections for each one. As with the third edition, the errors will be corrected in new impressions and a separate errata list will be provided for each impression.

Supplementary material: We maintain a set of supplementary material for each chapter. This consists of source code for the programs in the book and relevant reading material that was present in previous editions of the book but was removed for reasons of space. References to this supplementary material appear in the book with links such as www.cdk4.net/ipc.

Links to web sites for courses using the book: The web site for the third edition contains links to 15 courses using our book, which make available a wealth of useful lecture notes, slides, exercises and laboratory projects. We hope to get permission from the teachers of these courses to put these references on the new web site. Other teachers are asked to notify us of their courses with web sites for inclusion in the list.

George Coulouris
Jean Dollimore
Tim Kindberg
London and Bristol, March 2005
<authors@cdk4.net>

CHARACTERIZATION OF DISTRIBUTED SYSTEMS

A distributed system is one in which components located at networked computers communicate and coordinate their actions only by passing messages. This definition leads to the following characteristics of distributed systems: concurrency of components, lack of a global clock and independent failures of components.

We give three examples of distributed systems:

- the Internet;

- an intranet, which is a portion of the Internet managed by an organization;

- mobile and ubiquitous computing.

The sharing of resources is a main motivation for constructing distributed systems. Resources may be managed by servers and accessed by clients or they may be encapsulated as objects and accessed by other client objects. The Web is discussed as an example of resource sharing and its main features are introduced.

The challenges arising from the construction of distributed systems are the heterogeneity of its components, openness, which allows components to be added or replaced, security, scalability – the ability to work well when the number of users increases – failure handling, concurrency of components and transparency.

1.1   Introduction

Networks of computers are everywhere. The Internet is one, as are the many networks of which it is composed. Mobile phone networks, corporate networks, factory networks, campus networks, home networks, in-car networks, all of these, both separately and in combination, share the essential characteristics that make them relevant subjects for study under the heading *distributed systems*. In this book we aim to explain the characteristics of networked computers that impact system designers and implementors and to present the main concepts and techniques that have been developed to help in the tasks of designing and implementing systems that are based on them.

We define a distributed system as one in which hardware or software components located at networked computers communicate and coordinate their actions only by passing messages. This simple definition covers the entire range of systems in which networked computers can usefully be deployed.

Computers that are connected by a network may be spatially separated by any distance. They may be on separate continents, in the same building or the same room. Our definition of distributed systems has the following significant consequences:

Concurrency: In a network of computers, concurrent program execution is the norm. I can do my work on my computer while you do your work on yours, sharing resources such as web pages or files when necessary. The capacity of the system to handle shared resources can be increased by adding more resources (for example. computers) to the network. We will describe ways in which this extra capacity can be usefully deployed at many points in this book. The coordination of concurrently executing programs that share resources is also an important and recurring topic.

No global clock: When programs need to cooperate they coordinate their actions by exchanging messages. Close coordination often depends on a shared idea of the time at which the programs' actions occur. But it turns out that there are limits to the accuracy with which the computers in a network can synchronize their clocks – there is no single global notion of the correct time. This is a direct consequence of the fact that the *only* communication is by sending messages through a network. Examples of these timing problems and solutions to them will be described in Chapter 11.

Independent failures: All computer systems can fail and it is the responsibility of system designers to plan for the consequences of possible failures. Distributed systems can fail in new ways. Faults in the network result in the isolation of the computers that are connected to it, but that doesn't mean that they stop running. In fact the programs on them may not be able to detect whether the network has failed or has become unusually slow. Similarly, the failure of a computer, or the unexpected termination of a program somewhere in the system (a *crash*) is not immediately made known to the other components with which it communicates. Each component of the system can fail independently, leaving the others still running. The consequences of this characteristic of distributed systems will be a recurring theme throughout the book.

The motivation for constructing and using distributed systems stems from a desire to share resources. The term 'resource' is a rather abstract one, but it best characterizes the range of things that can usefully be shared in a networked computer system. It extends

Figure 1.1   A typical portion of the Internet

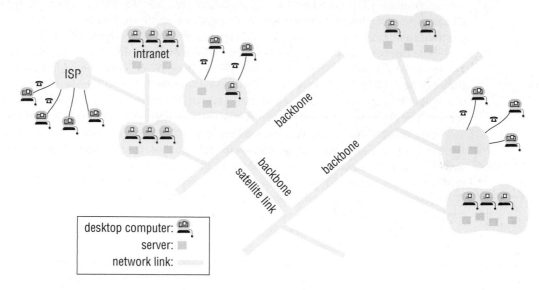

from hardware components such as disks and printers to software-defined entities such as files, databases and data objects of all kinds. It includes the stream of video frames that emerges from a digital video camera and the audio connection that a mobile phone call represents.

The purpose of this chapter is to convey a clear view of the nature of distributed systems and the challenges that must be addressed in order to ensure that they are successful. Section 1.2 gives some key examples of distributed systems, the components from which they are constructed and their purposes. Section 1.3 explores the design of resource-sharing systems in the context of the World Wide Web. Section 1.4 describes the key challenges faced by the designers of distributed systems: heterogeneity, openness, security, scalability, failure handling, concurrency and the need for transparency.

1.2   Examples of distributed systems

Our examples are based on familiar and widely used computer networks: the Internet, intranets and the emerging technology of networks based on mobile devices. They are designed to exemplify the wide range of services and applications that are supported by computer networks and to begin the discussion of the technical issues that underlie their implementation.

1.2.1   The Internet

The Internet is a vast interconnected collection of computer networks of many different types. Figure 1.1 illustrates a typical portion of the Internet. Programs running on the computers connected to it interact by passing messages, employing a common means of communication. The design and construction of the Internet communication mechanisms (the Internet protocols) is a major technical achievement, enabling a program running anywhere to address messages to programs anywhere else.

The Internet is also a very large distributed system. It enables users, wherever they are, to make use of services such as the World Wide Web, email and file transfer. (Indeed, the Web is sometimes incorrectly equated with the Internet). The set of services is open-ended – it can be extended by the addition of server computers and new types of service. The figure shows a collection of intranets – subnetworks operated by companies and other organizations. Internet Service Providers (ISPs) are companies that provide modem links and other types of connection to individual users and small organizations, enabling them to access services anywhere in the Internet as well as providing local services such as email and web hosting. The intranets are linked together by backbones. A backbone is a network link with a high transmission capacity, employing satellite connections, fibre optic cables and other high-bandwidth circuits.

Multimedia services are available in the Internet, enabling users to access audio and video data including music, radio and TV channels and to hold phone and video conferences. The capacity of the Internet to handle the special communication requirements of multimedia data is currently quite limited because it does not provide the necessary facilities to reserve network capacity for individual streams of data. Chapter 17 discusses the needs of distributed multimedia systems.

The implementation of the Internet and the services that it supports has entailed the development of practical solutions to many distributed system issues (including most of those defined in Section 1.4). We shall highlight those solutions throughout the book, pointing out their scope and their limitations where appropriate.

1.2.2   Intranets

An intranet is a portion of the Internet that is separately administered and has a boundary that can be configured to enforce local security policies. Figure 1.2 shows a typical intranet. It is composed of several local area networks (LANs) linked by backbone connections. The network configuration of a particular intranet is the responsibility of the organization that administers it and may vary widely – ranging from a LAN on a single site to a connected set of LANs belonging to branches of a company or other organization in different countries.

An intranet is connected to the Internet via a router, which allows the users inside the intranet to make use of services elsewhere such as the Web or email. It also allows the users in other intranets to access the services it provides. Many organizations need to protect their own services from unauthorized use by possibly malicious users elsewhere. For example, a company will not want secure information to be accessible to users in competing organizations, and a hospital will not want sensitive patient data to be revealed. Companies also want to protect themselves from harmful programs such as viruses entering and attacking the computers in the intranet and possibly destroying valuable data.

The role of a *firewall* is to protect an intranet by preventing unauthorized messages leaving or entering. A firewall is implemented by filtering incoming and outgoing messages, for example according to their source or destination. A firewall

Figure 1.2   A typical intranet

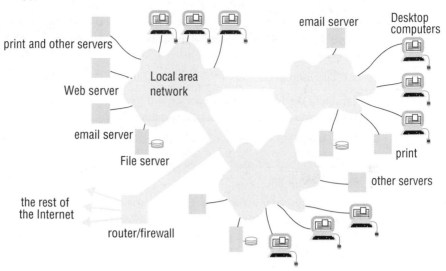

might for example allow only those messages related to email and web access to pass into or out of the intranet that it protects.

Some organizations do not wish to connect their internal networks to the Internet at all. For example, police and other security and law enforcement agencies are likely to have at least some internal networks that are isolated from the outside world. Some military organizations disconnect their internal networks from the Internet at times of war. But even those organizations will wish to benefit from the huge range of application and system software that employs Internet communication protocols. The solution that is usually adopted by such organizations is to operate an intranet as described above, but without the connections to the Internet. Such an intranet can dispense with the firewall; or, to put it another way, it has the most effective firewall possible – the absence of any physical connections to the Internet.

The main issues arising in the design of components for use in intranets are:

- File services are needed to enable users to share data; the design of these is discussed in Chapter 8.

- Firewalls tend to impede legitimate access to services – when resource sharing between internal and external users is required, firewalls must be complemented by the use of fine-grained security mechanisms; these are discussed in Chapter 7.

- The cost of software installation and support is an important issue. These costs can be reduced by the use of system architectures such as network computers and thin clients, described in Chapter 2.

1.2.3 Mobile and ubiquitous computing

Technological advances in device miniaturization and wireless networking have led increasingly to the integration of small and portable computing devices into distributed systems. These devices include:

- Laptop computers.

- Handheld devices, including personal digital assistants (PDAs), mobile phones, pagers, video cameras and digital cameras.

- Wearable devices, such as smart watches with functionality similar to a PDA.

- Devices embedded in appliances such as washing machines, hi-fi systems, cars and refrigerators.

The portability of many of these devices, together with their ability to connect conveniently to networks in different places, makes *mobile computing* possible. Mobile computing (also called *nomadic computing* [Kleinrock 1997]) is the performance of computing tasks while the user is on the move, or visiting places other than their usual environment. In mobile computing, users who are away from their 'home' intranet (the intranet at work, or their residence) are still provided with access to resources via the devices they carry with them. They can continue to access the Internet; they can continue to access resources in their home intranet; and there is increasing provision for users to utilize resources such as printers that are conveniently nearby as they move around. The latter is also known as *location-aware* or *context-aware computing*.

Ubiquitous computing [Weiser 1993] is the harnessing of many small, cheap computational devices that are present in users' physical environments, including the home, office and even natural settings. The term 'ubiquitous' is intended to suggest that small computing devices will eventually become so pervasive in everyday objects that they are scarcely noticed. That is, their computational behaviour will be transparently and intimately tied up with their physical function.

The presence of computers everywhere only becomes useful when they can communicate with one another. For example, it would be convenient for users to control their washing machine and their hi-fi system from a 'universal remote control' device in the home. Equally, the washing machine could page the user via a smart badge or watch when the washing is done.

Ubiquitous and mobile computing overlap, since the mobile user can in principle benefit from computers that are everywhere. But they are distinct, in general. Ubiquitous computing could benefit users while they remain in a single environment such as the home or a hospital. Similarly, mobile computing has advantages even if it involves only conventional, discrete computers and devices such as laptops and printers.

Figure 1.3 shows a user who is visiting a host organization. The figure shows the user's home intranet and the host intranet at the site that the user is visiting. Both intranets are connected to the rest of the Internet.

The user has access to three forms of wireless connection. Their laptop has a means of connecting to the host's wireless LAN. This network provides coverage of a few hundreds of metres (a floor of a building, say). It connects to the rest of the host intranet via a gateway. The user also has a mobile (cellular) telephone, which is connected to the Internet. The phone gives access to pages of simple information, which

Figure 1.3   Portable and handheld devices in a distributed system

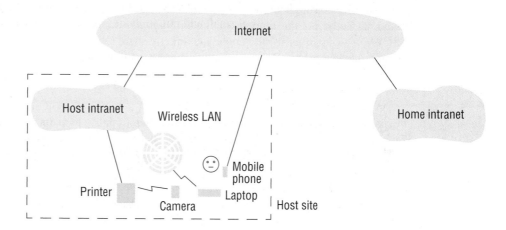

it presents on its small display. Finally, the user carries a digital camera, which can communicate over a personal area wireless network (with range up to about 10m) with a device such as a printer.

With a suitable system infrastructure, the user can perform some simple tasks in the host site using the devices they carry. While journeying to the host site, the user can fetch the latest stock prices from a web server using the mobile phone. During the meeting with their hosts, the user can show them a recent photograph by sending it from the digital camera directly to a suitably enabled printer in the meeting room. This requires only the wireless link between the camera and printer. And they can in principle send a document from their laptop to the same printer, utilizing the wireless LAN and wired Ethernet links to the printer.

Mobile and ubiquitous computing are a lively area of research and they are the subject of Chapter 16.

1.3   Resource sharing and the Web

Users are so accustomed to the benefits of resource sharing that they may easily overlook their significance. We routinely share hardware resources such as printers, data resources such as files, and resources with more specific functionality such as search engines.

Looked at from the point of view of hardware provision, we share equipment such as printers and disks to reduce costs. But of far greater significance to users is their sharing of the higher-level resources that play a part in their applications and in their everyday work and social activities. For example, users are concerned with sharing data in the form of a shared database or a set of web pages – not the disks and processors that those are implemented on. Similarly, users think in terms of shared resources such as a search engine or a currency converter, without regard for the server or servers that provide these.

In practice, patterns of resource sharing vary widely in their scope and in how closely users work together. At one extreme, a search engine on the Web provides a facility to users throughout the world, users who need never come into contact with one another directly. At the other extreme, in *computer-supported cooperative working* (CSCW), a group of users who cooperate directly share resources such as documents in a small, closed group. The pattern of sharing and the geographic distribution of particular users determines what mechanisms the system must supply to coordinate users' actions.

We use the term *service* for a distinct part of a computer system that manages a collection of related resources and presents their functionality to users and applications. For example, we access shared files through a file service; we send documents to printers through a printing service; we buy goods through an electronic payment service. The only access we have to the service is via the set of operations that it exports. For example, a file service provides *read*, *write* and *delete* operations on files.

The fact that services restrict resource access to a well-defined set of operations is in part standard software engineering practice. But it also reflects the physical organization of distributed systems. Resources in a distributed system are physically encapsulated within computers and can only be accessed from other computers by communication. For effective sharing, each resource must be managed by a program that offers a communication interface enabling the resource to be accessed and updated reliably and consistently.

The term *server* is probably familiar to most readers. It refers to a running program (a *process*) on a networked computer that accepts requests from programs running on other computers to perform a service and responds appropriately. The requesting processes are referred to as *clients*. Requests are sent in messages from clients to a server and replies are sent in messages from the server to the clients. When the client sends a request for an operation to be carried out, we say that the client *invokes an operation* upon the server. A complete interaction between a client and a server, from the point when the client sends its request to when it receives the server's response, is called a *remote invocation*.

The same process may be both a client and a server, since servers sometimes invoke operations on other servers. The terms 'client' and 'server' apply only to the roles played in a single request. In so far as they are distinct, clients are active and servers are passive; servers run continuously, whereas clients last only as long as the applications of which they form a part.

Note that by default the terms 'client' and 'server' refer to *processes* rather than the computers that they execute upon, although in everyday parlance those terms also refer to the computers themselves. Another distinction, which we shall discuss in Chapter 5, is that in a distributed system written in an object-oriented language, resources may be encapsulated as objects and accessed by client objects, in which case we speak of a *client object* invoking a method upon a *server object*.

Many, but certainly not all, distributed systems can be constructed entirely in the form of interacting clients and servers. The World Wide Web, email and networked printers all fit this model. We discuss alternatives to client-server systems in Chapter 2.

An executing web browser is an example of a client. The web browser communicates with a web server, to request web pages from it. We now examine the Web in more detail.

1.3.1   The World Wide Web

The World Wide Web [www.w3.org I, Berners-Lee 1991] is an evolving system for publishing and accessing resources and services across the Internet. Through commonly available web browsers, users retrieve and view documents of many types, listen to audio streams and view video streams, and interact with an unlimited set of services.

The Web began life at the European centre for nuclear research (CERN), Switzerland, in 1989 as a vehicle for exchanging documents between a community of physicists connected by the Internet [Berners-Lee 1999]. A key feature of the Web is that it provides a *hypertext* structure among the documents that it stores, reflecting the users' requirement to organize their knowledge. This means that documents contain *links* (or *hyperlinks*) – references to other documents and resources that are also stored in the Web.

It is fundamental to the user's experience of the Web that when he or she encounters a given image or piece of text within a document, this will frequently be accompanied by links to related documents and other resources. The structure of links can be arbitrarily complex and the set of resources that can be added is unlimited – the 'web' of links is indeed world-wide. Bush [1945] conceived of hypertextual structures over fifty years ago; it was with the development of the Internet that this idea could be manifested on a world-wide scale.

The Web is an *open* system: it can be extended and implemented in new ways without disturbing its existing functionality (see Section 1.4.2). First, its operation is based on communication standards and document standards that are freely published and widely implemented. For example, there are many types of browser, each in many cases implemented on several platforms; and there are many implementations of web servers. Any conformant browser can retrieve resources from any conformant server. So users have access to browsers on the majority of the devices that they use, from mobile phones to desktop computers.

Second, the Web is open with respect to the types of resource that can be published and shared on it. At its simplest, a resource on the Web is a web page or some other type of *content* that can be stored in a file and presented to the user, such as program files, media files, and documents in PostScript or Portable Document Format. If somebody invents, say, a new image-storage format, then images in this format can immediately be published on the Web. Users require a means of viewing images in this new format, but browsers are designed to accommodate new content-presentation functionality in the form of 'helper' applications and 'plug-ins'.

The Web has moved beyond these simple data resources to encompass services, such as electronic purchasing of goods. It has evolved without changing its basic architecture. The Web is based on three main standard technological components:

- The HyperText Markup Language (HTML) is a language for specifying the contents and layout of pages as they are displayed by web browsers.

- Uniform Resource Locators (URLs), which identify documents and other resources stored as part of the Web. Chapter 9 discusses other terms for web identifiers.

- A client-server system architecture, with standard rules for interaction (the HyperText Transfer Protocol – HTTP) by which browsers and other clients fetch documents and other resources from web servers. Figure 1.4 shows some web

Figure 1.4   Web servers and web browsers

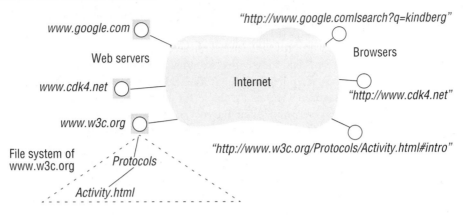

servers, and browsers making requests of them. It is an important feature that users may locate and manage their own web servers anywhere on the Internet.

We now discuss these components in turn, and in so doing explain the operation of browsers and web servers when a user fetches web pages and clicks on the links within them.

HTML ◊ The HyperText Markup Language [www.w3.org II] is used to specify the text and images that make up the contents of a web page, and to specify how they are laid out and formatted for presentation to the user. A web page contains such structured items as headings, paragraphs, tables and images. HTML is also used to specify links and which resources are associated with them.

Users either produce HTML by hand, using a standard text editor, or they can use an HTML-aware 'wysiwyg' editor that generates HTML from a layout that they create graphically. A typical piece of HTML text follows:

```
<IMG SRC = "http://www.cdk4.net/WebExample/Images/earth.jpg">         1
<P>                                                                   2
Welcome to Earth! Visitors may also be interested in taking a look at the   3
<A HREF = "http://www.cdk4.net/WebExample/moon.html">Moon</A>.        4
</P>                                                                  5
```

This HTML text is stored in a file that a web server can access – let us say the file *earth.html*. A browser retrieves the contents of this file from a web server – in this case a server on a computer called *www.cdk4.net*. The browser reads the content returned by the server and renders it into formatted text and images laid out on a web page in the familiar fashion. Only the browser – not the server – interprets the HTML text. But the server does inform the browser of the type of content it is returning, to distinguish it from, say, a document in PostScript. The server can infer the content type from the filename extension '.html'.

Note that the HTML directives, known as *tags*, are enclosed by angle brackets, such as *<P>*. Line 1 of the example identifies a file containing an image for presentation. Its URL is *http://www.cdk4.net/WebExample/Images/earth.jpg*. Lines 2 and 5 are directives to begin and end a paragraph, respectively. Lines 3 and 4 contain text to be displayed on the web page in the standard paragraph format.

Line 4 specifies a link in the web page. It contains the word 'Moon' surrounded by two related HTML tags *<A HREF...>* and *</A>*. The text between these tags is what appears in the link as it is presented on the web page. Most browsers are configured to show the text of links underlined by default, so what the user will see in that paragraph is:

Welcome to Earth! Visitors may also be interested in taking a look at the <u>Moon</u>.

The browser records the association between the link's displayed text and the URL contained in the *<A HREF...>* tag – in this case:

http://www.cdk4.net/WebExample/moon.html

When the user clicks on the text, the browser retrieves the resource identified by the corresponding URL and presents it to the user. In the example, the resource is an HTML file specifying a web page about the Moon.

URLs ◊ The purpose of a Uniform Resource Locator [www.w3.org III] is to identify a resource. Indeed, the term used in web architecture documents is Uniform Resource *Identifier* (URI) but in this book the better-known term URL will be used when no confusion can arise. Browsers examine URLs in order to access the corresponding resources. Sometimes the user types a URL into the browser. More commonly, the browser looks up the corresponding URL when the user clicks on a link or selects one of their 'bookmarks'; or when the browser fetches a resource embedded in a web page, such an image.

Every URL, in its full, absolute form, has two top-level components:

scheme : scheme-specific-identifier

The first component, the 'scheme', declares which type of URL this is. URLs are required to identify a variety of resources. For example, *mailto:joe@anISP.net* identifies a user's email address; *ftp://ftp.downloadIt.com/software/aProg.exe* identifies a file that is to be retrieved using the File Transfer Protocol (FTP) rather than the more commonly used protocol HTTP. Other examples of schemes are 'nntp' (used to specify a Usenet news group), and 'mid' (used to identify an email message).

The Web is open with respect to the types of resources it can be used to access, by virtue of the scheme designators in URLs. If somebody invents a useful new type of 'widget' resource – perhaps with its own addressing scheme for locating widgets and its own protocol for accessing them – then the world can start using URLs of the form *widget:...* . Of course, browsers must be given the capability to use the new 'widget' protocol, but this can be done by adding a plug-in.

HTTP URLs are the most widely used, for accessing resources using the standard HTTP protocol. An HTTP URL has two main jobs to do: to identify which web server maintains the resource, and to identify which of the resources at that server is required. Figure 1.4 shows three browsers issuing requests for resources managed by three web servers. The topmost browser is issuing a query to a search engine. The middle browser requires the default page of another web site. The bottommost browser requires a web page that is specified in full, including a path name relative to the server. The files for a given web server are maintained in one or more sub-trees (directories) of the server's file system, and each resource is identified by a path name relative to the server.

In general, HTTP URLs are of the following form:

http://servername [:port] [/pathName] [?query][#fragment]

– where items in square brackets are optional. A full HTTP URL always begins with the string 'http://' followed by a server name, expressed as a Domain Name System (DNS) name (see Section 9.2). The server's DNS name is optionally followed by the number of the 'port' on which the server listens for requests (see Chapter 4) – which is 80 by default. Then comes an optional path name of the server's resource. If this is absent then the server's default web page is required. Finally, the URL optionally ends in a query component – for example, when a user submits the entries in a form such as a search engine's query page – and/or a fragment identifier, which identifies a component of the resource.

Consider the URLs:

http://www.cdk4.net
http://www.w3.org/Protocols/Activity.html#intro
http://www.google.com/search?q=kindberg

These can be broken down as follows:

Server DNS name	Path name	Query	Fragment
www.cdk4.net	(default)	(none)	(none)
www.w3.org	Protocols/Activity.html	(none)	intro
www.google.com	search	q=kindberg	(none)

The first URL designates the default page supplied by *www.cdk4.net*. The next identifies a fragment of an HTML file whose path name is *Protocols/Activity.html* relative to the server *www.w3.org*. The fragment's identifier (specified after the '#' character in the URL) is *intro*, and a browser will search for that fragment identifier within the HTML text after it has downloaded the whole file. The third URL specifies a query to a search engine. The path identifies a program called 'search', and the string after the '?' character encodes a query string supplied as arguments to this program. We discuss URLs that identify programmatic resources in more detail when we consider more advanced features below.

Publishing a resource: While the Web has a clearly defined model for accessing a resource from its URL, the exact methods for publishing resources on the Web are dependent upon the web server implementation. The simplest method of publishing a resource on the Web is to place the corresponding file in a directory that the web server can access. Knowing the name of the server *S* and a path name for the file *P* that the server can recognize, the user then constructs the URL as *http://S/P*. The user puts this URL in a link from an existing document or distributes the URL to other users, for example by email.

There are certain path name conventions that servers recognize. For example, a path name beginning *~joe* is by convention in a subdirectory *public_html* of user joe's home directory. Similarly, a path name that ends in a directory name rather than a simple file conventionally refers to a file in that directory called *index.html*.

Huang *et al.* [2000] provide a model for inserting content into the Web with minimal human intervention. This is particularly relevant where users need to extract content from a variety of devices, such as cameras, for publication in web pages.

HTTP ◊ The HyperText Transfer Protocol [www.w3.org IV] defines the ways in which browsers and other types of client interact with web servers. Chapter 4 will consider HTTP in more detail, but here we outline its main features (restricting our discussion to the retrieval of resources in files):

Request-reply interactions: HTTP is a 'request-reply' protocol. The client sends a request message to the server containing the URL of the required resource. The server looks up the path name and, if it exists, sends back the file's contents in a reply message to the client. Otherwise, it sends back an error response such as the familiar '404 Not Found'.

Content types: Browsers are not necessarily capable of handling every type of content. When a browser makes a request, it includes a list of the types of content it prefers – for example, in principle it may be able to display images in 'GIF' format but not 'JPEG' format. The server may be able to take this into account when it returns content to the browser. The server includes the content type in the reply message so that the browser will know how to process it. The strings that denote the type of content are called MIME types, and they are standardized in RFC 1521 [Freed and Borenstein 1996]. For example, if the content is of type 'text/html' then a browser will interpret the text as HTML and display it; if the content is of type 'image/GIF' then the browser will render it as an image in 'GIF' format; if the content type is 'application/zip' then it is data compressed in 'zip' format, and the browser will launch an external helper application to decompress it. The set of actions that a browser will take for a given type of content is configurable, and readers may care to check these settings for their own browsers.

One resource per request: Clients specify one resource per HTTP request. If a web page contains nine images, say, then the browser will issue a total of ten separate requests to obtain the entire contents of the page. Browsers typically make several requests concurrently, to reduce the overall delay to the user.

Simple access control: By default, any user with network connectivity to a web server can access any of its published resources. If users wish to restrict access to a resource, then they can configure the server to issue a 'challenge' to any client that requests it. The corresponding user then has to prove that they have the right to access the resource, for example, by typing in a password.

Dynamic pages ◊ So far we have described how users can publish web pages and other content stored in files on the Web. However, much of the users' experience of the Web is that of interacting with services rather than retrieving data. For example, when purchasing an item at an online store, the user often fills out a *web form* to give their personal details or to specify exactly what they wish to purchase. A web form is a web page containing instructions for the user and input widgets such as text fields and check boxes. When the user submits the form (usually by pressing a button or the 'return' key), the browser sends an HTTP request to a web server, containing the values that the user has entered.

Since the result of the request depends upon the user's input, the server has to *process the user's input*. Therefore, the URL or its initial component designates a *program* on the server, not a file. If the user's input is reasonably short then it is usually sent as the *query* component of the URL, following a '?' character (otherwise it is sent as additional data in the request). For example, a request containing the following URL invokes a program called 'search' at www.google.com and specifies a query string of 'kindberg': *http://www.google.com/search?q=kindberg*.

That 'search' program produces HTML text as its output, and the user will see a listing of pages that contain the word 'kindberg'. (The reader may care to enter a query into their favourite search engine and notice the URL that the browser displays when the result is returned.) The server returns the HTML text that the program generates just as though it had retrieved it from a file. In other words, the difference between static content fetched from a file and content that is dynamically generated is transparent to the browser.

A program that web servers run to generate content for their clients is often referred to as a Common Gateway Interface (CGI) program. A CGI program may have any application-specific functionality, as long as it can parse the arguments that the client provides to it and produce content of the required type (usually HTML text). The program will often consult or update a database in processing the request.

Downloaded code: A CGI program runs at the server. Sometimes the designers of web services require some service-related code to run inside the browser, at the user's computer. For example, code written in Javascript [www.netscape.com] is often downloaded with a web form in order to provide better-quality interaction with the user than that supported by HTML's standard widgets. A Javascript-enhanced page can give the user immediate feedback on invalid entries (instead of forcing the user to check the values at the server, which would take much longer). Javascript can also be used to update parts of a web page's contents without fetching an entire new version of the page and re-rendering it.

Javascript has quite limited functionality. By contrast, an *applet* is an application that the browser automatically downloads and runs when it fetches a corresponding web page. Applets may access the network and provide customized user interfaces, using the facilities of the Java language [java.sun.com, Flanagan 2002]. For example, 'chat' applications are sometimes implemented as applets that run on the users' browsers, together with a server program. The applets send the users' text to the server, which in turn distributes it to all the applets for presentation to the user. We discuss applets in more detail in Section 2.2.3.

Web Services ◊ So far we have discussed the Web largely from the point of view of a user operating a browser. But programs other than browsers can be clients of the Web, too; indeed, programmatic access to web resources is commonplace.

However, by themselves, the HTML and HTTP standards are somewhat lacking for programmatic interoperation. First, there is an increasing need to exchange many types of structured data on the Web, but HTML is limited in that it is not extensible to applications beyond information browsing. HTML has a static set of structures such as paragraphs, and they are bound up with the way that the data is to be presented to users.

The Extensible Markup Language (XML) (see Section 4.3.3) has been designed as a way of representing data in standard, structured, application-specific forms. For example, XML is used to describe the capabilities of devices and to describe personal information held about users. XML is a meta-language for describing data, which makes data portable between applications.

Second, HTTP provides no structure for specifying the service-specific operations that can be invoked on web resources, or the operations' arguments and error responses For example, in the store at amazon.com, web service operations include one to order a book and another to check the current state of an order. The flip-side of that flexibility can be a lack of robustness in how software operates. Chapter 19 takes an in-depth look at the web services framework, which enables the designers of web services to specify to programmers exactly how clients must access them.

Discussion of the Web ◊ The Web's phenomenal success rests upon the relative ease with which many individual and organizational sources can publish resources, the suitability of its hypertext structure for organizing many types of information, and the openness of its system architecture. The standards upon which its architecture is based are simple and they were widely published at an early stage. They have enabled many new types of resource and service to be integrated.

The Web's success belies some design problems. First, its hypertext model is lacking in some respects. If a resource is deleted or moved, then so-called 'dangling' links to that resource may still remain, causing frustration for users. And there is the familiar problem of users getting 'lost in hyperspace'. Users often find themselves confused, following many disparate links, referencing pages from a disparate collection of sources, and of dubious reliability in some cases.

Search engines are an alternative to following links as a means of finding information on the Web, but these are notoriously imperfect at producing what the user specifically intends. One approach to this problem, exemplified in the Resource Description Framework [www.w3.org V], is to produce standard vocabularies, syntax and semantics for expressing metadata about the things in our world, and to encapsulate that metadata in corresponding web resources for programmatic access. Rather than searching for words that occur in web pages, programs can then, in principle, perform searches against the metadata to compile lists of related links based on semantic matching. Collectively, the web of linked metadata resources is what is meant by the *semantic web*.

As a system architecture the Web faces problems of scale. Popular web servers may experience many 'hits' per second, and as a result the response to users can be slow. Chapter 2 describes the use of caching in browsers and proxy servers to increase responsiveness, and the division of the server's load across clusters of computers. But the Web's client-server architecture means that it has no efficient means of keeping users up to date with the latest versions of pages. Users have to press their browser's 'reload' button to ensure that they have the latest information, and browsers are forced to communicate with servers to check whether a local copy of a resource is still valid.

Finally, a web page is not always a satisfactory user interface. The interface widgets defined for HTML are limited, and designers often include applets or many images in web pages to make them look and function more acceptably. There is a consequent increase in the download time.

1.4   Challenges

The examples in Section 1.2 are intended to illustrate the scope of distributed systems and to suggest the issues that arise in their design. Although distributed systems are to be found everywhere, their design is quite simple and there is still a lot of scope to develop more ambitious services and applications. Many of the challenges discussed in this section have already been met, but future designers need to be aware of them and to be careful to take them into account.

1.4.1   Heterogeneity

The Internet enables users to access services and run applications over a heterogeneous collection of computers and networks. Heterogeneity (that is, variety and difference) applies to all of the following:

- networks;
- computer hardware;
- operating systems;
- programming languages;
- implementations by different developers.

Although the Internet consists of many different sorts of network (illustrated in Figure 1.1), their differences are masked by the fact that all of the computers attached to them use the Internet protocols to communicate with one another. For example, a computer attached to an Ethernet has an implementation of the Internet protocols over the Ethernet, whereas a computer on a different sort of network will need an implementation of the Internet protocols for that network. Chapter 3 explains how the Internet protocols are implemented over a variety of different networks.

Data types such as integers may be represented in different ways on different sorts of hardware for example, there are two alternatives for the byte ordering of integers. These differences in representation must be dealt with if messages are to be exchanged between programs running on different hardware.

Although the operating systems of all computers on the Internet need to include an implementation of the Internet protocols, they do not necessarily all provide the same application programming interface to these protocols. For example, the calls for exchanging messages in UNIX are different from the calls in Windows.

Different programming languages use different representations for characters and data structures such as arrays and records. These differences must be addressed if programs written in different languages are to be able to communicate with one another.

Programs written by different developers cannot communicate with one another unless they use common standards, for example, for network communication and the representation of primitive data items and data structures in messages. For this to happen, standards need to be agreed and adopted – as have the Internet protocols.

Middleware ◊ The term *middleware* applies to a software layer that provides a programming abstraction as well as masking the heterogeneity of the underlying networks, hardware, operating systems and programming languages. The Common Object Request Broker (CORBA), which is described in Chapters 4, 5 and 20, is an example. Some middleware, such as Java Remote Method Invocation (RMI) (see Chapter 5) supports only a single programming language. Most middleware is implemented over the Internet protocols, which themselves mask the difference of the underlying networks. But all middleware deals with the differences in operating systems and hardware – how this is done is the main topic of Chapter 4.

In addition to solving the problems of heterogeneity, middleware provides a uniform computational model for use by the programmers of servers and distributed applications. Possible models include remote object invocation, remote event notification, remote SQL access and distributed transaction processing. For example, CORBA provides remote object invocation, which allows an object in a program running on one computer to invoke a method of an object in a program running on another computer. Its implementation hides the fact that messages are passed over a network in order to send the invocation request and its reply.

Heterogeneity and mobile code ◊ The term *mobile code* is used to refer to code that can be sent from one computer to another and run at the destination – Java applets are an example. Code suitable for running on one computer is not necessarily suitable for running on another because executable programs are normally specific both to the instruction set and to the host operating system. For example, executable files sent as email attachments by Windows/x86 users will not run on an x86 computer running Linux or a Macintosh computer running Mac OS X.

The *virtual machine* approach provides a way of making code executable on any hardware: the compiler for a particular language generates code for a virtual machine instead of a particular hardware order code for example, the Java compiler produces code for the Java virtual machine, which needs to be implemented once for each type of hardware to enable Java programs to run. However, the Java solution is not generally applicable to programs written in other languages.

1.4.2   Openness

The openness of a computer system is the characteristic that determines whether the system can be extended and re-implemented in various ways. The openness of distributed systems is determined primarily by the degree to which new resource-sharing services can be added and be made available for use by a variety of client programs.

Openness cannot be achieved unless the specification and documentation of the key software interfaces of the components of a system are made available to software developers. In a word, the key interfaces are *published*. This process is akin to the standardization of interfaces, but it often bypasses official standardization procedures, which are usually cumbersome and slow-moving.

However, the publication of interfaces is only the starting point for adding and extending services in a distributed system. The challenge to designers is to tackle the complexity of distributed systems consisting of many components engineered by different people.

The designers of the Internet protocols introduced a series of documents called 'Requests For Comments', or RFCs, each of which is known by a number. The specifications of the Internet communication protocols were published in this series in the early 1980s, followed by specifications for applications that run over them, such as file transfer, email and telnet by the mid-1980s. This practice has continued and forms the basis of the technical documentation of the Internet. This series includes discussions as well as the specifications of protocols. Copies can be obtained from [www.ietf.org]. Thus the publication of the original Internet communication protocols has enabled a variety of Internet systems and applications including the Web to be built. RFCs are not the only means of publication. For example, CORBA is published through a series of technical documents, including a complete specification of the interfaces of its services. See [www.omg.org].

Systems that are designed to support resource sharing in this way are termed *open distributed systems* to emphasize the fact that they are extensible. They may be extended at the hardware level by the addition of computers to the network and at the software level by the introduction of new services and the re-implementation of old ones, enabling application programs to share resources. A further benefit that is often cited for open systems is their independence from individual vendors.

To summarize:

- Open systems are characterized by the fact that their key interfaces are published.

- Open distributed systems are based on the provision of a uniform communication mechanism and published interfaces for access to shared resources.

- Open distributed systems can be constructed from heterogeneous hardware and software, possibly from different vendors. But the conformance of each component to the published standard must be carefully tested and verified if the system is to work correctly.

1.4.3 Security

Many of the information resources that are made available and maintained in distributed systems have a high intrinsic value to their users. Their security is therefore of considerable importance. Security for information resources has three components: confidentiality (protection against disclosure to unauthorized individuals); integrity (protection against alteration or corruption); and availability (protection against interference with the means to access the resources).

Section 1.1 pointed out that although the Internet allows a program in one computer to communicate with a program in another computer irrespective of its location, security risks are associated with allowing free access to all of the resources in an intranet. Although a firewall can be used to form a barrier around an intranet, restricting the traffic that can enter and leave, this does not deal with ensuring the appropriate use of resources by users within an intranet, or with the appropriate use of resources in the Internet, that are not protected by firewalls.

In a distributed system, clients send requests to access data managed by servers, which involves sending information in messages over a network. For example:

1. A doctor might request access to hospital patient data or send additions to that data.

2. In electronic commerce and banking, users send their credit card numbers across the Internet.

In both examples, the challenge is to send sensitive information in a message over a network in a secure manner. But security is not just a matter of concealing the contents of messages – it also involves knowing for sure the identity of the user or other agent on whose behalf a message was sent. In the first example, the server needs to know that the user is really a doctor and in the second example, the user needs to be sure of the identity of the shop or bank with which they are dealing. The second challenge here is to identify a remote user or other agent correctly. Both of these challenges can be met by the use of encryption techniques developed for this purpose. They are used widely in the Internet and are discussed in Chapter 7.

However, the following two security challenges have not yet been fully met:

Denial of service attacks: Another security problem is that a user may wish to disrupt a service for some reason. This can be achieved by bombarding the service with such a large number of pointless requests that the serious users are unable to use it. This is called a *denial of service* attack. From time to time, there have been several recent denial of service attacks on well-known web services. Currently such attacks are countered by attempting to catch and punish the perpetrators after the event, but that is not a general solution to the problem. Counter-measures based on improvements in the management of networks are under development and these will be touched on in Chapter 3.

Security of mobile code: Mobile code needs to be handled with care. Consider someone who receives an executable program as an electronic mail attachment: the possible effects of running the program are unpredictable; for example, it may seem to display an interesting picture but in reality it may access local resources, or perhaps be part of a denial of service attack. Some measures for securing mobile code are outlined in Chapter 7.

1.4.4 Scalability

Distributed systems operate effectively and efficiently at many different scales, ranging from a small intranet to the Internet. A system is described as *scalable* if it will remain effective when there is a significant increase in the number of resources and the number of users. The Internet provides an illustration of a distributed system in which the number of computers and services has increased dramatically. Figure 1.5 shows the increase in the number of computers in the Internet during the 24 years up to 2003, and Figure 1.6 shows the increasing number of computers and web servers during the ten-year history of the Web up to 2004, see [zakon.org].

The design of scalable distributed systems presents the following challenges:

Controlling the cost of physical resources: As the demand for a resource grows, it should be possible to extend the system, at reasonable cost, to meet it. For example, the frequency with which files are accessed in an intranet is likely to grow as the number of users and computers increases. It must be possible to add server computers to avoid the performance bottleneck that would arise if a single file server had to

Figure 1.5   Computers (with registered IP addresses) in the Internet

Date	Computers	Web servers
1979, Dec.	188	0
1989, July	130,000	0
1999, July	56,218,000	5,560,866
2003, Jan.	171,638,297	35,424,956

handle all file access requests. In general, for a system with n users to be scalable, the quantity of physical resources required to support them should be at most $O(n)$ – that is, proportional to n. For example, if a single file server can support 20 users, then two such servers should be able to support 40 users. Although that sounds an obvious goal, it is not necessarily easy to achieve in practice, as we show in Chapter 8.

Controlling the performance loss: Consider the management of a set of data whose size is proportional to the number of users or resources in the system, for example the table with the correspondence between the domain names of computers and their Internet addresses held by the Domain Name System, which is used mainly to look up DNS names such as www.amazon.com. Algorithms that use hierarchic structures scale better than those that use linear structures. But even with hierarchic structures an increase in size will result in some loss in performance: the time taken to access hierarchically structured data is $O(log\ n)$, where n is the size of the set of data. For a system to be scalable, the maximum performance loss should be no worse than this.

Figure 1.6   Computers vs. web servers in the Internet

Date	Computers	Web servers	Percentage
1993, July	1,776,000	130	0.008
1995, July	6,642,000	23,500	0.4
1997, July	19,540,000	1,203,096	6
1999, July	56,218,000	6,598,697	12
2001, July	125,888,197	31,299,592	25
2003, July		42,298,371	

one web server may be hosted at multiple sites

Preventing software resources running out: An example of lack of scalability is shown by the numbers used as Internet (IP) addresses (computer addresses in the Internet). In the late 1970s, it was decided to use 32 bits for this purpose, but as will be explained in Chapter 3 the supply of available Internet addresses is running out. For this reason, a new version of the protocol with 128-bit Internet addresses is being adopted and this will require modifications to many software components. To be fair to the early designers of the Internet, there is no correct solution to this problem. It is difficult to predict the demand that will be put on a system years ahead. Moreover, over-compensating for future growth may be worse than adapting to a change when we are forced to – larger Internet addresses will occupy extra space in messages and in computer storage.

Avoiding performance bottlenecks: In general, algorithms should be decentralized to avoid having performance bottlenecks. We illustrate this point with reference to the predecessor of the Domain Name System in which the name table was kept in a single master file that could be downloaded to any computers that needed it. That was fine when there were only a few hundred computers in the Internet, but it soon became a serious performance and administrative bottleneck. The Domain Name System removed this bottleneck by partitioning the name table between servers located throughout the Internet and administered locally – see Chapters 3 and 9.

Some shared resources are accessed very frequently; for example, many users may access the same Web page, causing a decline in performance. We shall see in Chapter 2 that caching and replication may be used to improve the performance of resources that are very heavily used.

Ideally, the system and application software should not need to change when the scale of the system increases, but this is difficult to achieve. The issue of scale is a dominant theme in the development of distributed systems. The techniques that have been successful are discussed extensively in this book. They include the use of replicated data (Chapter 15), the associated technique of caching (Chapters 2 and 8) and the deployment of multiple servers to handle commonly performed tasks, enabling several similar tasks to be performed concurrently.

1.4.5 Failure handling

Computer systems sometimes fail. When faults occur in hardware or software, programs may produce incorrect results or they may stop before they have completed the intended computation. We shall discuss and classify a range of possible failure types that can occur in the processes and networks that comprise a distributed system in Chapter 2.

Failures in a distributed system are partial – that is, some components fail while others continue to function. Therefore the handling of failures is particularly difficult. The following techniques for dealing with failures are discussed throughout the book:

Detecting failures: Some failures can be detected. For example, checksums can be used to detect corrupted data in a message or a file. Chapter 2 explains that is difficult or even impossible to detect some other failures such as a remote crashed server in the Internet. The challenge is to manage in the presence of failures that cannot be detected but may be suspected.

Masking failures: Some failures that have been detected can be hidden or made less severe. Two examples of hiding failures:

1. messages can be retransmitted when they fail to arrive;

2. file data can be written to a pair of disks so that if one is corrupted, the other may still be correct.

Just dropping a message that is corrupted is an example of making a fault less severe – it could be retransmitted. The reader will probably realize that the techniques described for hiding failures are not guaranteed to work in the worst cases; for example, the data on the second disk may be corrupted too, or the message may not get through in a reasonable time however often it is retransmitted.

Tolerating failures: Most of the services in the Internet do exhibit failures – it would not be practical for them to attempt to detect and hide all of the failures that might occur in such a large network with so many components. Their clients can be designed to tolerate failures, which generally involves the users tolerating them as well. For example, when a web browser cannot contact a web server, it does not make the user wait for ever while it keeps on trying – it informs the user about the problem, leaving them free to try again later. Services that tolerate failures are discussed in the paragraph on redundancy below.

Recovery from failures: Recovery involves the design of software so that the state of permanent data can be recovered or 'rolled back' after a server has crashed. In general, the computations performed by some programs will be incomplete when a fault occurs, and the permanent data that they update (files and other material stored in permanent storage) may not be in a consistent state. Recovery is described in Chapter 14.

Redundancy: Services can be made to tolerate failures by the use of redundant components. Consider the following examples:

1. There should always be at least two different routes between any two routers in the Internet.

2. In the Domain Name System, every name table is replicated in at least two different servers.

3. A database may be replicated in several servers to ensure that the data remains accessible after the failure of any single server; the servers can be designed to detect faults in their peers; when a fault is detected in one server, clients are redirected to the remaining servers.

The design of effective techniques for keeping replicas of rapidly changing data up-to-date without excessive loss of performance is a challenge. Approaches are discussed in Chapter 15.

Distributed systems provide a high degree of availability in the face of hardware faults. The *availability* of a system is a measure of the proportion of time that it is available for use. When one of the components in a distributed system fails, only the work that was using the failed component is affected. A user may move to another computer if the one that they were using fails; a server process can be started on another computer.

1.4.6 Concurrency

Both services and applications provide resources that can be shared by clients in a distributed system. There is therefore a possibility that several clients will attempt to access a shared resource at the same time. For example, a data structure that records bids for an auction may be accessed very frequently when it gets close to the deadline time.

The process that manages a shared resource could take one client request at a time. But that approach limits throughput. Therefore services and applications generally allow multiple client requests to be processed concurrently. To make this more concrete, suppose that each resource is encapsulated as an object and that invocations are executed in concurrent threads. In this case it is possible that several threads may be executing concurrently within an object, in which case their operations on the object may conflict with one another and produce inconsistent results. For example, if two concurrent bids at an auction are 'Smith: $122' and 'Jones: $111', and the corresponding operations are interleaved without any control, then they might get stored as 'Smith: $111' and 'Jones: $122'.

The moral of this story is that any object that represents a shared resource in a distributed system must be responsible for ensuring that it operates correctly in a concurrent environment. This applies not only to servers but also to objects in applications. Therefore any programmer who takes an implementation of an object that was not intended for use in a distributed system must do whatever is necessary to make it safe in a concurrent environment.

For an object to be safe in a concurrent environment, its operations must be synchronized in such a way that its data remains consistent. This can be achieved by standard techniques such as semaphores, which are used in most operating systems. This topic and its extension to collections of distributed shared objects are discussed in Chapters 6 and 13.

1.4.7 Transparency

Transparency is defined as the concealment from the user and the application programmer of the separation of components in a distributed system, so that the system is perceived as a whole rather than as a collection of independent components. The implications of transparency are a major influence on the design of the system software.

The ANSA Reference Manual [ANSA 1989] and the International Organization for Standardization's Reference Model for Open Distributed Processing (RM-ODP) [ISO 1992] identify eight forms of transparency. We have paraphrased the original ANSA definitions, replacing their migration transparency with our own mobility transparency, whose scope is broader:

Access transparency enables local and remote resources to be accessed using identical operations.

Location transparency enables resources to be accessed without knowledge of their physical or network location (for example, which building or IP address).

Concurrency transparency enables several processes to operate concurrently using shared resources without interference between them.

Replication transparency enables multiple instances of resources to be used to increase reliability and performance without knowledge of the replicas by users or application programmers.

Failure transparency enables the concealment of faults, allowing users and application programs to complete their tasks despite the failure of hardware or software components.

Mobility transparency allows the movement of resources and clients within a system without affecting the operation of users or programs.

Performance transparency allows the system to be reconfigured to improve performance as loads vary.

Scaling transparency allows the system and applications to expand in scale without change to the system structure or the application algorithms.

The two most important transparencies are access and location transparency; their presence or absence most strongly affects the utilization of distributed resources. They are sometimes referred to together as *network transparency*.

As an illustration of access transparency, consider a graphical user interface with folders, which is the same whether the files inside the folder are local or remote. Another example is an API for files that uses the same operations to access both local and remote files (see Chapter 8). As an example of a lack of access transparency, consider a distributed system that does not allow you to access files on a remote computer unless you make use of the ftp program to do so.

Web resource names or URLs are location-transparent because the part of the URL that identifies a web server domain name refers to a computer name in a domain, rather than to an Internet address. However, URLs are not mobility-transparent, because someone's personal web page cannot move to their new place of work in a different domain – all of the links in other pages will still point to the original page.

In general, identifiers such as URLs that include the domain names of computers prevent replication transparency. Although the DNS allows a domain name to refer to several computers, it picks just one of them when it looks up a name. Since a replication scheme generally needs to be able to access all of the participating computers, it would need to access each of the DNS entries by name.

As an illustration of the presence of network transparency, consider the use of an electronic mail address such as *Fred.Flintstone@stoneit.com*. The address consists of a user's name and a domain name. Note that although mail programs accept user names for local users, they do append the local domain name. Sending mail to such a user does not involve knowing their physical or network location. Nor does the procedure to send a mail message depend upon the location of the recipient. Thus electronic mail within the Internet provides both location and access transparency (that is, network transparency).

Failure transparency can also be illustrated in the context of electronic mail, which is eventually delivered, even when servers or communication links fail. The faults are masked by attempting to retransmit messages until they are successfully delivered, even if it takes several days. Middleware generally converts the failures of networks and processes into programming-level exceptions (see Chapter 5 for an explanation).

To illustrate mobility transparency, consider the case of mobile phones. Suppose that both caller and callee are travelling by train in different parts of a country, moving from one environment (cell) to another. We regard the caller's phone as the client and the callee's phone as a resource. The two phone users making the call are unaware of the mobility of the phones (the client and the resource) between cells.

Transparency hides and renders anonymous the resources that are not of direct relevance to the task in hand from users and application programmers. For example, it is generally desirable for similar hardware resources to be allocated interchangeably to perform a task – the identity of a processor used to execute a process is generally hidden from the user and remains anonymous. As pointed out in Section 1.2.3, this may not always be what is required: for example, a traveller who attaches a laptop computer to the local network in each office visited should make use of local services such as the send mail service, using different servers at each location. Even within a building, it is normal to arrange for a document to be printed at a particular, named printer: usually one that is near to the user.

1.5   Summary

Distributed systems are everywhere. The Internet enables users throughout the world to access its services wherever they may be located. Each organization manages an intranet, which provides local services and Internet services for local users and generally provides services to other users in the Internet. Small distributed systems can be constructed from mobile computers and other small computational devices that are attached to a wireless network.

Resource sharing is the main motivating factor for constructing distributed systems. Resources such as printers, files, web pages or database records are managed by servers of the appropriate type. For example, web servers manage web pages and other web resources. Resources are accessed by clients for example, the clients of web servers are generally called browsers.

The construction of distributed systems produces many challenges:

Heterogeneity: They must be constructed from a variety of different networks, operating systems, computer hardware and programming languages. The Internet communication protocols mask the difference in networks, and middleware can deal with the other differences.

Openness: Distributed systems should be extensible – the first step is to publish the interfaces of the components, but the integration of components written by different programmers is a real challenge.

Security: Encryption can be used to provide adequate protection of shared resources and to keep sensitive information secret when is transmitted in messages over a network. Denial of service attacks are still a problem.

Scalability: A distributed system is scalable if the cost of adding a user is a constant amount in terms of the resources that must be added. The algorithms used to access shared data should avoid performance bottlenecks and data should be structured hierarchically to get the best access times. Frequently accessed data can be replicated.

Failure handling: Any process, computer or network may fail independently of the others. Therefore each component needs to be aware of the possible ways in which the components it depends on may fail and be designed to deal with each of those failures appropriately.

Concurrency: The presence of multiple users in a distributed system is a source of concurrent requests to its resources. Each resource must be designed to be safe in a concurrent environment.

Transparency: The aim is to make certain aspects of distribution invisible to the application programmer so that they need only be concerned with the design of their particular application. For example, they need not be concerned with its location or the details of how its operations are accessed by other components, or whether it will be replicated or migrated. Even failures of networks and processes can be presented to application programmers in the form of exceptions – but they must be handled.

EXERCISES

1.1   Give five types of hardware resource and five types of data or software resource that can usefully be shared. Give examples of their sharing as it occurs in practice in distributed systems.   *pages 2*, 7–9

1.2   How might the clocks in two computers that are linked by a local network be synchronized without reference to an external time source? What factors limit the accuracy of the procedure you have described? How could the clocks in a large number of computers connected by the Internet be synchronized? Discuss the accuracy of that procedure.   *page 2*

1.3   A user arrives at a railway station that she has never visited before, carrying a PDA that is capable of wireless networking. Suggest how the user could be provided with information about the local services and amenities at that station, without entering the station's name or attributes. What technical challenges must be overcome?   *page 6*

1.4   What are the advantages and disadvantages of HTML, URLs and HTTP as core technologies for information browsing? Are any of these technologies suitable as a basis for client-server computing in general?   *page 9*

1.5   Use the World Wide Web as an example to illustrate the concept of resource sharing, client and server.

Resources in the World Wide Web and other services are named by URLs. What do the initials URL denote? Give examples of three different sorts of web resources that can be named by URLs.   *page 7*

1.6   Give an example of an HTTP URL.

List the main components of an HTTP URL, stating how their boundaries are denoted and illustrating each one from your example.

To what extent is an HTTP URL location transparent? *page 7*

1.7 A server program written in one language (for example C++) provides the implementation of a BLOB object that is intended to be accessed by clients that may be written in a different language (for example Java). The client and server computers may have different hardware, but all of them are attached to an internet. Describe the problems due to each of the five aspects of heterogeneity that need to be solved to make it possible for a client object to invoke a method on the server object. *page 16*

1.8 An open distributed system allows new resource sharing services such as the BLOB object in Exercise 1.7 to be added and accessed by a variety of client programs. Discuss in the context of this example, to what extent the needs of openness differ from those of heterogeneity. *page 17*

1.9 Suppose that the operations of the BLOB object are separated into two categories – public operations that are available to all users and protected operations that are available only to certain named users. State all of the problems involved in ensuring that only the named users can use a protected operation. Supposing that access to a protected operation provides information that should not be revealed to all users, what further problems arise? *page 18*

1.10 The INFO service manages a potentially very large set of resources, each of which can be accessed by users throughout the Internet by means of a key (a string name). Discuss an approach to the design of the names of the resources that achieves the minimum loss of performance as the number of resources in the service increases. Suggest how the INFO service can be implemented so as to avoid performance bottlenecks when the number of users becomes very large. *page 19*

1.11 List the three main software components that may fail when a client process invokes a method in a server object, giving an example of a failure in each case. Suggest how the components can be made to tolerate one another's failures. *page 21*

1.12 A server process maintains a shared information object such as the BLOB object of Exercise 1.7. Give arguments for and against allowing the client requests to be executed concurrently by the server. In the case that they are executed concurrently, give an example of possible 'interference' that can occur between the operations of different clients. Suggest how such interference may be prevented. *page 23*

1.13 A service is implemented by several servers. Explain why resources might be transferred between them. Would it be satisfactory for clients to multicast all requests to the group of servers as a way of achieving mobility transparency for clients? *page 23*

2

SYSTEM MODELS

An architectural model of a distributed system is concerned with the placement of its parts and the relationships between them. Examples include the client-server model and the peer-to-peer model. The client-server model can be modified by:

- the partition of data or replication at cooperating servers;
- the caching of data by proxy servers and clients;
- the use of mobile code and mobile agents;
- the requirement to add and remove mobile devices in a convenient manner.

Fundamental models are concerned with a more formal description of the properties that are common in all of the architectural models.

There is no global time in a distributed system, so the clocks on different computers do not necessarily give the same time as one another. All communication between processes is achieved by means of messages. Message communication over a computer network can be affected by delays, can suffer from a variety of failures and is vulnerable to security attacks. These issues are addressed by three models:

- The interaction model deals with performance and with the difficulty of setting time limits in a distributed system, for example for message delivery.

- The failure model attempts to give a precise specification of the faults that can be exhibited by processes and communication channels. It defines reliable communication and correct processes.

- The security model discusses the possible threats to processes and communication channels. It introduces the concept of a secure channel, which is secure against those threats.

2.1   Introduction

Systems that are intended for use in real-world environments should be designed to function correctly In the widest possible range of circumstances and in the face of many possible difficulties and threats (for some examples, see the box at the bottom of this page). The discussion and examples of Chapter 1 suggest that distributed systems of different types share important underlying properties and give rise to common design problems. In this chapter we bring out the common properties and design issues for distributed systems in the form of descriptive models. Each model is intended to provide an abstract, simplified but consistent description of a relevant aspect of distributed system design.

An architectural model defines the way in which the components of systems interact with one another and the way in which they are mapped onto an underlying network of computers. In Section 2.2, we describe the layered structure of distributed system software and the main architectural models that determine the locations and interactions of the components. We discuss variants of the client-server model, including those due to the use of mobile code. We consider the features of a distributed system to which mobile devices can be added or removed conveniently. Finally, we look at the general design requirements for distributed systems.

In Section 2.3, we introduce three fundamental models that help to reveal key problems for the designers of distributed systems. Their purpose is to specify the design issues, difficulties and threats that must be resolved in order to develop distributed systems that fulfil their tasks correctly, reliably and securely. The fundamental models provide abstract views of just those characteristics of distributed systems that affect their *dependability* characteristics – correctness, reliability and security.

Difficulties for and threats to distributed systems ◊ Here are some of the problems that the designers of distributed systems face:

Widely varying modes of use: The component parts of systems are subject to wide variations in workload – for example, some web pages are accessed several million times a day. Some parts of a system may be disconnected, or poorly connected some of the time – for example when mobile computers are included in a system. Some applications have special requirements for high communication bandwidth and low latency – for example, multimedia applications.

Wide range of system environments: A distributed system must accommodate heterogeneous hardware, operating systems and networks. The networks may differ widely in performance – wireless networks operate at a fraction of the speed of local networks. Systems of widely differing scales – ranging from tens of computers to millions of computers – must be supported.

Internal problems: Non-synchronized clocks, conflicting data updates, many modes of hardware and software failure involving the individual components of a system.

External threats: Attacks on data integrity and secrecy, denial of service.

2.2   Architectural models

The architecture of a system is its structure in terms of separately specified components. The overall goal is to ensure that the structure will meet present and likely future demands on it. Major concerns are to make the system reliable, manageable, adaptable and cost-effective. The architectural design of a building has similar aspects – it determines not only its appearance but also its general structure and architectural style (gothic, neo-classical, modern) provides a consistent frame of reference for the design.

In this section, we shall describe the main architectural models employed in distributed systems – the architectural styles of distributed systems. We build our architectural models around the concepts of process and object introduced in Chapter 1. An architectural model of a distributed system first simplifies and abstracts the functions of the individual components of a distributed system and then it considers:

- the placement of the components across a network of computers – seeking to define useful patterns for the distribution of data and workload;

- the interrelationships between the components – that is, their functional roles and the patterns of communication between them.

An initial simplification is achieved by classifying processes as *server processes*, *client processes* and *peer processes* – the latter being processes that cooperate and communicate in a symmetrical manner to perform a task. This classification of processes identifies the responsibilities of each and hence helps us to assess their workloads and to determine the impact of failures in each of them. The results of this analysis can then be used to specify the placement of the processes in a manner that meets performance and reliability goals for the resulting system.

Some more dynamic systems can be built as variations on the client-server model:

- The possibility of moving code from one process to another allows a process to delegate tasks to another process; for example, clients can download code from servers and run it locally. Objects and the code that accesses them can be moved to reduce access delays and minimize communication traffic.

- Some distributed systems are designed to enable computers and other mobile devices to be added or removed seamlessly, allowing them to discover the available services and to offer their services to others.

There are several widely used patterns for the allocation of work in a distributed system that have an important impact on the performance and effectiveness of the resulting system. The actual placement of the processes that make up a distributed system in a network of computers is also influenced by many detailed issues of performance, reliability, security and cost. The architectural models described here can provide only a somewhat simplified view of the more important patterns of distribution.

2.2.1   Software layers

The term *software architecture* referred originally to the structuring of software as layers or modules in a single computer and more recently in terms of services offered

Figure 2.1   Software and hardware service layers in distributed systems

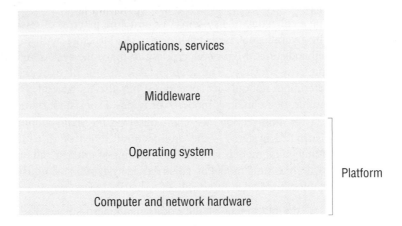

and requested between processes located in the same or different computers. This process- and service-oriented view can be expressed in terms of *service layers*. We introduce this view in Figure 2.1 and develop it in increasing detail in Chapters 3 to 6. A *server* is a process that accepts requests from other processes. A distributed service can be provided by one or more server processes, interacting with each other and with client processes in order to maintain a consistent system-wide view of the service's resources. For example, a network time service is implemented on the Internet based on the Network Time Protocol (NTP) by server processes running on hosts throughout the Internet that supply the current time to any client that requests it and adjust their version of the current time as a result of interactions with each other.

Figure 2.1 introduces the important terms *platform* and *middleware*, which we define as follows:

Platform ◊ The lowest-level hardware and software layers are often referred to as a *platform* for distributed systems and applications. These low-level layers provide services to the layers above them, which are implemented independently in each computer, bringing the system's programming interface up to a level that facilitates communication and coordination between processes. Intel x86/Windows, Intel x86/Solaris, PowerPC/Mac OS X, Intel x86/Linux are major examples.

Middleware ◊ Middleware was defined in Section 1.4.1 as a layer of software whose purpose is to mask heterogeneity and to provide a convenient programming model to application programmers. Middleware is represented by processes or objects in a set of computers that interact with each other to implement communication and resource-sharing support for distributed applications. It is concerned with providing useful building blocks for the construction of software components that can work with one another in a distributed system. In particular, it raises the level of the communication activities of application programs through the support of abstractions such as remote method invocation, communication between a group of processes, notification of events, the partitioning, placement and retrieval of shared data objects amongst cooperating computers, the replication of shared data objects and the transmission of multimedia data in real time. Group communication is introduced in Chapter 4 and dealt with in detail in Chapters 12 and 15. Event notification is described in Chapter 5. Chapter 10 describes approaches to sharing large sets of data objects amongst many computers. Data replication is discussed in Chapter 15 and multimedia systems in Chapter 17.

Remote procedure calling packages such as Sun RPC (Chapter 5) and group communication systems such as Isis (Chapter 15) were amongst the earliest instances of middleware. Object-oriented middleware products and standards are widely used. They include:

- CORBA;
- Java RMI;
- web services;
- Microsoft's Distributed Component Object Model (DCOM);
- the ISO/ITU-T's Reference Model for Open Distributed Processing (RM-ODP).

Java RMI, web services and CORBA are described in Chapters 5, 19 and 20; details on DCOM and RM-ODP can be found in Redmond [1997] and Blair and Stefani [1997].

Middleware can also provide services for use by application programs. They are infrastructural services, tightly bound to the distributed programming model that the middleware provides. For example, CORBA offers a variety of services that provide applications with facilities, which include naming, security, transactions, persistent storage and event notification. Some of the CORBA services are discussed in Chapter 20. The services in the top layer of Figure 2.1 are the domain-specific services that utilize the middleware – its communication operations and its own services.

Limitations of middleware: Many distributed applications rely entirely on the services provided by the available middleware to support their needs for communication and data sharing. For example, an application that is suited to the client-server model such as a database of names and addresses can rely on middleware that provides only remote method invocation.

Much has been achieved in simplifying the programming of distributed systems through the development of middleware support, but some aspects of the dependability of systems require support at the application level.

Consider the transfer of large electronic mail messages from the mail host of the sender to that of the recipient. At first sight this a simple application of the TCP data transmission protocol (discussed in Chapter 3). But consider the problem of a user who attempts to transfer a very large file over a potentially unreliable network. TCP provides some error detection and correction, but it cannot recover from major network interruptions. The mail transfer service adds another level of fault tolerance, maintaining a record of progress and resuming transmission using a new TCP connection if the original one breaks.

A classic paper by Saltzer, Reed and Clarke [Saltzer *et al.* 1984] makes a similar and valuable point about the design of distributed systems, which they call the 'the end-to-end argument'. To paraphrase their statement:

Figure 2.2   Clients invoke individual servers

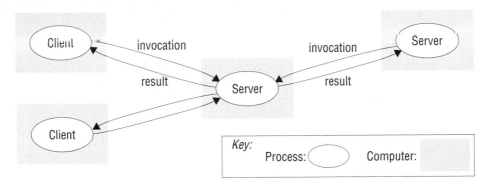

Some communication-related functions can be completely and reliably implemented only with the knowledge and help of the application standing at the end points of the communication system. Therefore, providing that function as a feature of the communication system itself is not always sensible. (An incomplete version of the function provided by the communication system may sometimes be useful as a performance enhancement.)

It can be seen that their argument runs counter to the view that all communication activities can be abstracted away from the programming of applications by the introduction of appropriate middleware layers.

The nub of their argument is that correct behaviour in distributed programs depends upon checks, error-correction mechanisms and security measures at many levels, some of which require access to data within the application's address space. Any attempt to perform the checks within the communication system alone will guarantee only part of the required correctness. The same work is therefore likely to be duplicated in application programs, wasting programming effort, and more importantly, adding unnecessary complexity and performing redundant computations.

There is not space to detail their arguments further here; the cited paper is strongly recommended – it is replete with illuminating examples. One of the original authors has recently pointed out that the substantial benefits that the use of the argument brought to the design of the Internet are placed at risk by recent moves towards the specialization of network services to meet current application requirements [www.reed.com].

2.2.2   System architectures

The division of responsibilities between system components (applications, servers and other processes) and the placement of the components on computers in the network is perhaps the most evident aspect of distributed system design. It has major implications for the performance, reliability and security of the resulting system. In this section, we outline the principal architectural models on which this distribution of responsibilities is based.

In a distributed system, processes with well-defined responsibilities interact with each other to perform a useful activity. In this section, our attention will focus on the placement of processes, illustrated in the manner of Figure 2.2, showing the disposition of processes (ellipses) in computers (light blue boxes). We use the terms 'invocation' and 'result' to label messages – they could equally be labelled as 'request' and 'reply'.

The two main types of architectural model are illustrated in Figure 2.2 and Figure 2.3 and described below.

Client-server ◊ This is the architecture that is most often cited when distributed systems are discussed. It is historically the most important and remains the most widely employed. Figure 2.2 illustrates the simple structure in which client processes interact with individual server processes in separate host computers in order to access the shared resources that they manage.

Servers may in turn be clients of other servers, as the figure indicates. For example, a web server is often a client of a local file server that manages the files in which the web pages are stored. Web servers and most other Internet services are clients of the DNS service, which translates Internet Domain Names to network addresses. Another web-related example concerns *search engines*, which enable users to look up summaries of information available on web pages at sites throughout the Internet. These summaries are made by programs called *web crawlers*, which run in the background at a search engine site using HTTP requests to access web servers throughout the Internet. Thus a search engine is both a server and a client: it responds to queries from browser clients and it runs web crawlers that act as clients of other web servers. In this example, the server tasks (responding to user queries) and the crawler tasks (making requests to other web servers) are entirely independent; there is little need to synchronize them and they may run concurrently. In fact, a typical search engine would normally include many concurrent threads of execution, some serving its clients and others running web crawlers. In Exercise 2.4, the reader is invited to consider the only synchronization issue that does arise for a concurrent search engine of the type outlined here.

Peer-to-peer ◊ In this architecture all of the processes involved in a task or activity play similar roles, interacting cooperatively as *peers* without any distinction between client and server processes or the computers that they run on. While the client-server model offers a direct and relatively simple approach to the sharing of data and other resources, it scales poorly. The centralization of service provision and management implied by placing a service at a single address does not scale well beyond the capacity of the computer that hosts the service and the bandwidth of its network connections.

In the next section we describe several variations on the client-server architecture that have evolved in response this problem, but none of them addresses the fundamental issue – the need to distribute shared resources much more widely in order to share the computing and communication loads incurred in accessing them amongst a much larger number of computers and network links.

The hardware capacity and operating system functionality of today's desktop computers exceeds that of yesterday's servers and the majority are equipped with always-on broadband network connections. The aim of the peer-to-peer architecture is to exploit the resources (both data and hardware) in a large number of participating computers for the fulfillment of a given task or activity. Peer-to-peer applications and systems have been successfully constructed that enable tens or hundreds of thousands of

Figure 2.3   A distributed application based on the peer-to-peer architecture

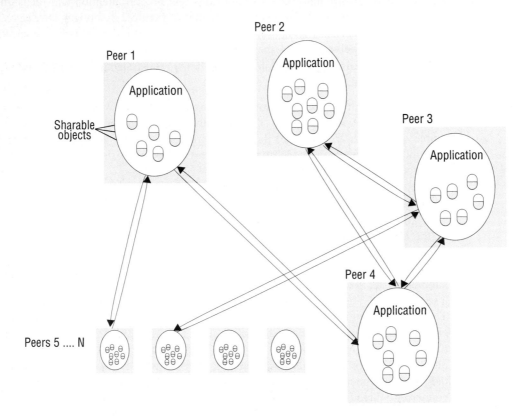

computers to provide access to data and other resources that they collectively store and manage. The earliest and most widely known instance is the Napster application for sharing digital music files. Although it became notorious for reasons other than its architecture, its demonstration of feasibility has resulted in the development of the architectural model in many valuable directions.

Figure 2.3 illustrates the form of a peer-to-peer application. Applications are composed of large numbers of peer processes running on separate computers and the pattern of communication between them depends entirely on application requirements. A large number of data objects are shared, an individual computer holds only a small part of the application database and the storage, processing and communication loads for access to objects are distributed across many computers and network links. Each object is replicated in several computers to further distribute the load and to provide resilience in the event of disconnection of individual computers (as is inevitable in the large, heterogeneous networks at which peer-to-peer systems are aimed). The need to place individual objects and retrieve them and to maintain replicas amongst many computers renders this architecture substantially more complex than the client server architecture.

The development of peer-to-peer applications and middleware to support them is described in depth in Chapter 10.

Figure 2.4   A service provided by multiple servers

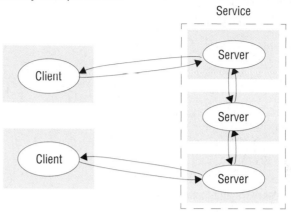

2.2.3 Variations

Several variations on the above models can be derived from the consideration of the following factors:

- the use of multiple servers and caches to increase performance and resilience;
- the use of mobile code and mobile agents;
- users' need for low-cost computers with limited hardware resources that are simple to manage;
- the requirement to add and remove mobile devices in a convenient manner.

Services provided by multiple servers ◊ Services may be implemented as several server processes in separate host computers interacting as necessary to provide a service to client processes (Figure 2.4). The servers may partition the set of objects on which the service is based and distribute them between themselves, or they may maintain replicated copies of them on several hosts. These two options are illustrated by the following examples.

The Web provides a common example of partitioned data in which each web server manages its own set of resources. A user can employ a browser to access a resource at any one of the servers.

An example of a service based on replicated data is the Sun NIS (Network Information Service), which is used by computers on a LAN when users log in. Each NIS server has its own replica of the password file containing a list of users' login names and encrypted passwords. Chapter 15 discusses techniques for replication in detail.

A more closely-coupled type of multiple-server architecture is the cluster, which is used for highly scalable web services such as search engines and online stores. A cluster is constructed from up to thousands of commodity processing boards (see Section 6.4.2). Service processing can be partitioned or replicated between them.

Figure 2.5   Web proxy server

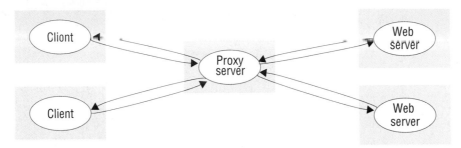

Proxy servers and caches ◊ A *cache* is a store of recently used data objects that is closer than the objects themselves. When a new object is received at a computer it is added to the cache store, replacing some existing objects if necessary. When an object is needed by a client process the caching service first checks the cache and supplies the object from there if an up-to-date copy is available. If not, an up-to-date copy is fetched. Caches may be collocated with each client or they may be located in a proxy server that can be shared by several clients.

Caches are used extensively in practice. Web browsers maintain a cache of recently visited web pages and other web resources in the client's local file system, using a special HTTP request to check with the original server that cached pages are up to date before displaying them. Web proxy servers (Figure 2.5) provide a shared cache of web resources for the client machines at a site or across several sites. The purpose of proxy servers is to increase availability and performance of the service by reducing the load on the wide-area network and web servers. Proxy servers can take on other roles; for example, they may be used to access remote web servers through a firewall.

Mobile code ◊ Chapter 1 introduced mobile code. Applets are a well-known and widely used example of mobile code – the user running a browser selects a link to an applet whose code is stored on a web server; the code is downloaded to the browser and runs there, as shown in Figure 2.6. An advantage of running the downloaded code locally is that it can give good interactive response since it does not suffer from the delays or variability of bandwidth associated with network communication.

Accessing services means running code that can invoke their operations. Some services are likely to be so standardized that we can access them with an existing and well-known application – the Web is the most common example of this, but even there, some web sites use functionality not found in standard browsers and require the downloading of additional code. The additional code may, for example, communicate with the server. Consider an application that requires that users should be kept up to date with changes as they occur at an information source in the server. This cannot be achieved by normal interactions with the web server, which are always initiated by the client. The solution is to use additional software that operates in a manner often referred to as a *push* model – one in which the server instead of the client initiates interactions.

For example, a stockbroker might provide a customized service to notify customers of changes in the prices of shares; to use the service, each customer would have to download a special applet that receives updates from the broker's server,

Figure 2.6   Web applets

a) client request results in the downloading of applet code

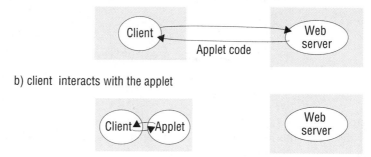

b) client interacts with the applet

displays them to the user and perhaps performs automatic buy and sell operations triggered by conditions set up by the customer and stored locally in the customer's computer.

Chapter 1 mentioned that mobile code is a potential security threat to the local resources in the destination computer. Therefore browsers give applets limited access to local resources using a scheme discussed in Section 7.1.1.

Mobile agents ◊ A mobile agent is a running program (including both code and data) that travels from one computer to another in a network carrying out a task on someone's behalf, such as collecting information, eventually returning with the results. A mobile agent may make many invocations to local resources at each site it visits – for example, accessing individual database entries. If we compare this architecture with a static client making remote invocations to some resources, possibly transferring large amounts of data, there is a reduction in communication cost and time through the replacement of remote invocations with local ones.

Mobile agents might be used to install and maintain software on the computers within an organization or to compare the prices of products from a number of vendors by visiting the site of each vendor and performing a series of database operations. An early example of a similar idea is the so-called worm program developed at Xerox PARC [Shoch and Hupp 1982], which was designed to make use of idle computers in order to carry out intensive computations.

Mobile agents (like mobile code) are a potential security threat to the resources in computers that they visit. The environment receiving a mobile agent should decide on which of the local resources it should be allowed to use, based on the identity of the user on whose behalf the agent is acting – their identity must be included in a secure way with the code and data of the mobile agent. In addition, mobile agents can themselves be vulnerable – they may not be able to complete their task if they are refused access to the information they need. The tasks performed by mobile agents can be performed by other means. For example, web crawlers that need to access resources at web servers throughout the Internet work quite successfully by making remote invocations to server processes. For these reasons, the applicability of mobile agents may be limited.

Network computers ◊ In the architecture illustrated in Figure 1.2 applications run on a desktop computer local to the user. The operating systems and application software for

Figure 2.7   Thin clients and compute servers

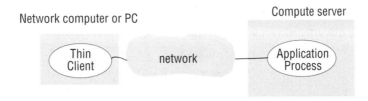

desktop computers typically require much of the active code and data to be located on a local disk. But the management of application files and the maintenance of a local software base requires considerable technical effort of a nature that most users are not qualified to provide.

The network computer is a response to this problem. It downloads its operating system and any application software needed by the user from a remote file server. Applications are run locally but the files are managed by a remote file server. Network applications such as a web browser can also be run. Since all the application data and code is stored by a file server, the users may migrate from one network computer to another. The processor and memory capacities of a network computer can be constrained in order to reduced its cost.

If a disk is included, it holds only a minimum of software. The remainder of the disk is used as *cache storage* holding copies of software and data files that have recently been loaded from servers. The maintenance of the cache requires no manual effort: cached objects are invalidated whenever a new version of the file is written at the relevant server.

Thin clients ◊   The term *thin client* refers to a software layer that supports a window-based user interface on a computer that is local to the user while executing application programs on a remote computer (Figure 2.7). This architecture has the same low management and hardware costs as the network computer scheme, but instead of downloading the code of applications into the user's computer, it runs them on a *compute server* – a powerful computer that has the capacity to run large numbers of applications simultaneously. The compute server will typically be a multiprocessor or cluster computer (see Chapter 6) running a multiprocessor version of an operating system such as UNIX or Windows.

The main drawback of the thin client architecture is in highly interactive graphical activities such as CAD and image processing, where the delays experienced by users are increased by the need to transfer image and vector information between the thin client and the application process, incurring both network and operating system latencies.

Thin client implementations: Thin client systems are simple in concept and their implementation is straightforward in some environments. For example, most variants of UNIX include the X-11 window system which is discussed in the box on the following page.

There are several points in the pipeline of graphical operations required to support a graphical user interface at which the boundary between client and server can be drawn. X-11 draws the boundary at the level of graphical primitives for line and shape drawing and window handling. The Citrix *WinFrame* product [www.citrix.com] is a widely used commercial implementation of the thin client concept that operates in a similar manner. This product provides a thin client process running on a wide variety of platforms and supporting a desktop providing interactive access to applications running on Windows hosts. Other implementations include the Virtual Network Computer (VNC) system developed at AT&T Laboratories in Cambridge, England [Richardson *et al.* 1998]. VNC draws the boundary at the level of operations on screen pixels and maintains the graphical context for users when they move between computers.

Mobile devices and spontaneous interoperation ◊ We have discussed software mobility in the form of mobile agents, which migrate between physical computers. By contrast, mobile devices are *hardware* computing components that move between physical locations and thus networks, carrying software components with them. As Chapter 1 explained, the world is increasingly populated by mobile devices, including laptops, handheld devices such as personal digital assistants (PDAs), mobile phones and digital cameras, and wearable computers such as smart watches. Increasingly many of these devices are capable of wireless networking, with national or greater ranges such as GSM and 3G telecommunications networks, ranges of hundreds of metres such as WiFi (IEEE 802.11), or about ten metres such as Bluetooth.

Device mobility has many implications, with several for client-server systems among them. Both clients and servers may exist on mobile devices – mobile clients being by far the most common case. Consider a bus that moves around on a world tour, exploiting WiFi connectivity when it is available, and lower-bandwidth wide-area telecommunications connectivity elsewhere. The passengers and their families want to update and read a shared web site that contains pictures and postings about the tour. The most obvious way to achieve that would be for all to access a fixed server, with the bus passengers uploading and reading data from their mobile clients. But an alternative would be to run the web server on the bus so that the server itself is mobile. Not only could the server supply the users' pictures and postings but, using an attached GPS

The X-11 window system ◊ The X-11 window system [Scheifler and Gettys 1986] is a process that manages the display and interactive input devices (keyboard, mouse) of the computer on which it runs. X-11 provides an extensive library of procedures (the *X-11 protocol*) for displaying and modifying graphical objects in windows as well as the creation and manipulation of the windows themselves.

The X-11 system is referred to as a *window server* process. The clients of the X-11 server are the application programs that the user is currently interacting with. The client programs communicate with the server by invoking operations in the X-11 protocol; these include operations to draw text and graphical objects in windows. The clients need not be located in the same computer as the server, since the server procedures are always invoked using an RPC mechanism. The X-11 window server therefore has the key properties of a thin client. (X-11 inverts the client-server terminology. The X-11 server derives its name from the graphical display services that it provides to application programs, whereas thin client software is named with reference to its use of application programs running on a compute server.)

(Global Positioning System) receiver, the server could supply a map showing the bus's current location [Kindberg *et al*. 2002a].

Mobility transparency (Section 1.4.7) is often an issue for mobile devices, as it is for mobile agents. In particular, clients of a mobile server such as that on the bus should not need to be aware of movement between networks (even though the families may be interested in the bus's *geographical* location, as shown on the GPS-updated map). Mobile IP, described in Chapter 3, provides a solution whereby the server on the bus retains its Internet (IP) address even though it moves between various networks. Clients can use permanent URLs to the bus's server.

Variable connectivity is another important issue, which would affect both the bus's ability to act as a server and its passengers' ability to access outside services. The bus may be intermittently disconnected from the wireless network as it travels through wireless barriers such as tunnels, or as it becomes disconnected for longer periods in regions where wireless connectivity ceases altogether. And it will experience greatly varying bandwidth as it moves between WiFi and telecommunications connections. Chapter 14 discusses the topic of dealing with disconnections. Chapter 16 discusses adaptation to variable bandwidth.

Finally, mobility leads to *spontaneous interoperation*, a variation on the client-server model in which associations between devices are routinely created and destroyed. In Section 1.2.3 we described a user visiting a host organization, and using her mobile devices in conjunction with the host's devices such as printers. Similarly, the bus passengers could be offered services that are integrated with the physical environments through which the bus travels, such as information about the local attractions. The main challenge applying to such situations is to make interoperation fast and convenient (that is, spontaneous) even though the user is in an environment she may never have visited before. That means enabling the visitor's device to communicate on the host network, and associating the device with suitable local services – a process called *service discovery*. We examine spontaneous interoperation and other aspects of mobility in more depth in Chapter 16. Chapter 16 also covers the strongly related field of ubiquitous computing – which adds emphasis on devices such as sensors embedded in the physical world, and thus *context-aware* services that are dependent on the state of the physical world, such as the map that shows the current position of the bus.

2.2.4   Interfaces and objects

The set of functions available for invocation in a process (whether it is a server or a peer process) is specified by one or more *interface definitions*. Interface definitions are described fully in Chapter 5, but the concept will be familiar to those already conversant with languages such as Modula, C++ or Java. In the basic form of client-server architecture, each server process is seen as a single entity with a fixed interface defining the functions that can be invoked in it.

In object-oriented languages such as C++ and Java, with appropriate additional support, distributed processes can be constructed in a more object-oriented manner. Many objects can be encapsulated in server processes, and references to them are passed to other processes so that their methods can be accessed by remote invocation. This is the approach adopted by CORBA and by Java with its remote method invocation (RMI) mechanism. In this model, the number and the types (in languages that support mobile code such as Java) of objects hosted by each process may vary as system activities require, and in some implementations the locations of objects may also change.

Whether we adopt a static client-server architecture or the more dynamic object-oriented model outlined in the preceding paragraph, the distribution of responsibilities between processes and between computers remains an important aspect of the design. In the traditional architectural model, the responsibilities are statically allocated (a file server, for example, is responsible only for files, not for web pages, their proxies or other types of object). But in the object-oriented model new services, and in some cases new types of object, can be instantiated and immediately made available for invocation.

2.2.5 Design requirements for distributed architectures

The factors motivating the distribution of objects and processes in a distributed system are numerous and their significance is considerable. Sharing was first achieved in the timesharing systems of the 1960s with the use of shared files. The benefits of sharing were quickly recognized and exploited in multi-user operating systems such as UNIX and multi-user database systems such as Oracle to enable processes to share system resources and devices (file storage capacity, printers, audio and video streams) and application processes to share application objects.

The arrival of cheap computing power in the form of microprocessor chips removed the need for the sharing of central processors, and the availability of medium-performance computer networks and the continuing need for the sharing of relatively costly hardware resources such as printers and disk storage led to the development of the distributed systems of the 1970s and 1980s. Today, resource sharing is taken for granted. But effective data sharing on a large scale remains a substantial challenge – with changing data (and most data changes with time), the possibility of concurrent and conflicting updates arises. The control of concurrent updates in shared data is the subject of Chapters 13 and 14.

Performance issues ◊ The challenges arising from the distribution of resources extend well beyond the need for the management of concurrent updates. Performance issues arising from the limited processing and communication capacities of computers and networks are considered under the following subheadings:

Responsiveness: Users of interactive applications require a fast and consistent response to interaction; but client programs often need to access shared resources. When a remote service is involved, the speed at which the response is generated is determined not just by the load and performance of the server and the network but also by delays in all the software components involved – the client and server operating systems' communication and middleware services (remote invocation support, for example) as well as the code of the process that implements the service.

In addition, the transfer of data between processes and the associated switching of control is relatively slow, even when the processes reside in the same computer. To achieve good interactive response times, systems must be composed of relatively few software layers, and the quantities of data transferred between the client and server must be small.

These issues are demonstrated by the performance of web-browsing clients, where the fastest response is achieved when accessing locally cached pages and images because these are held by the client application. Remote text pages are also accessed reasonably quickly because they are small, but graphical images incur longer delays because of the volume of data involved.

Throughput. A traditional measure of performance for computer systems is the throughput – the rate at which computational work is done. We are interested in the ability of a distributed system to perform work for all its users. This is affected by processing speeds at clients and servers and by data transfer rates. Data that is located on a remote server must be transferred from the server process to the client process, passing through several software layers in both computers. The throughput of the intervening software layers is important, as well as that of the network.

Balancing computational loads: One of the purposes of distributed systems is to enable applications and service processes to proceed concurrently without competing for the same resources and to exploit the available computational resources (processor, memory and network capacities). For example, the ability to run applets on client computers removes load from the web server, enabling it to provide a better service. A more significant example is in the use of several computers to host a single service. This is needed, for example, by some heavily loaded web servers (search engines, large commercial sites). This exploits the facility of the DNS domain name lookup service to return one of several host addresses for a single domain name (see Section 9.2.3).

In some cases, load balancing may involve moving partially completed work as the loads on hosts change. This calls for a system that can support the movement of running processes between computers.

Quality of service ◊ Once users are provided with the functionality that they require of a service such as the file service in a distributed system, we can go on to ask about the quality of the service provided. The main non-functional properties of systems that affect the quality of the service experienced by clients and users are *reliability*, *security* and *performance*. *Adaptability* to meet changing system configurations and resource availability has been recognized as a further important aspect of service quality. Birman has long argued for the importance of these quality aspects and his book [Birman 1996] provides some interesting perspectives of their impact on system design.

Reliability and security issues are critical in the design of most computer systems. They are strongly related to two of our fundamental models: the failure model and the security model, introduced in Sections 2.3.2 and 2.3.3.

The performance aspect of quality of service was originally defined in terms of responsiveness and computational throughput, but it has been redefined in terms of ability to meet timeliness guarantees as discussed in the following paragraphs. With either definition, the performance aspect of distributed systems is strongly related to the interaction model defined in Section 2.3.1. All three of these fundamental models are important reference points throughout the book.

Some applications handle *time-critical data* – streams of data that are required to be processed or transferred from one process to another at a fixed rate. For example, a movie service might consist of a client program that is retrieving a film from a video server and presenting it on the user's screen. For a satisfactory result the successive frames of video need to be displayed to the user within some specified time limits.

In fact, the abbreviation QoS has effectively been commandeered to refer to the ability of systems to meet such deadlines. Its achievement depends upon the availability of the necessary computing and network resources at the appropriate times. This implies a requirement for the system to provide guaranteed computing and communication resources that are sufficient to enable applications to complete each task on time (for example, the task of displaying a frame of video).

The networks commonly used today, for example to browse the Web, may have quite good performance characteristics, but when they are heavily loaded their performance deteriorates significantly – in no way can they be said to provide quality of service. QoS applies to operating systems as well as networks. Each critical resource must be reserved by the applications that require QoS and there must be resource managers that provide guarantees. Reservation requests that cannot be met are rejected. These issues will be addressed further in Chapter 17.

Use of caching and replication ◊ The performance issues outlined above often appear to be major obstacles to the successful deployment of distributed systems, but much progress has been made in the design of systems that overcome them by the use of data replication and caching. Section 2.2.2 introduced caches and web proxy servers, without discussing how cached copies of resources can be kept up to date when the resource at a server is updated. A variety of different cache consistency protocols are used to suit different applications for example, Chapter 8 gives the protocols used by two different file server designs. We now outline the web-caching protocol that is part of the HTTP protocol, which is described in Section 4.4.

Web-caching protocol: Both web browsers and proxy servers cache responses to client requests to web servers. Therefore a client request may be satisfied by a response cached by the browser or by a proxy server between it and the web server. The cache consistency protocol can be configured to provide browsers with fresh (reasonably up-to-date) copies of the resources held by the web server. But, to allow for performance, availability and disconnected operation the freshness condition may be relaxed.

A browser or proxy can *validate* a cached response by checking with the original web server to see whether it is still up to date. If it fails the test, the web server returns a fresh response, which is cached instead of the stale response. Browsers and proxies validate cached responses when clients request the corresponding resources. But they need not perform a validation if the cached response is sufficiently fresh. Even though a web server knows when a resource is updated, it does not notify the browsers and proxies with caches – to do that the web server would need to keep a record of interested browsers and proxies for each of its resources. To enable browsers and proxies to determine whether their stored responses are stale, web servers assign approximate expiry times to their resources, for example estimated from the last time they were updated. An expiry time can be misleading, because a web resource may be updated at any time. Whenever a web server replies to a request, the expiry time of the resource and the current time at the server are attached to the response.

Browsers and proxies store the expiry time and server time together with the cached response. This enables a browser or proxy receiving future requests to calculate whether a cached response is likely to be stale. It calculates whether a cached response is stale by comparing its age with the expiry time. The *age* of a response is the sum of the time the response has been cached and the server time. Note that this calculation does not depend on the computer clocks at the web server and the browser or proxy agreeing with one another.

Dependability issues ◊ Dependability is a requirement in most application domains. It is crucial not only in command and control activities, where life and limb may well be at stake, but also in many commercial applications, including the rapidly developing domain of Internet commerce, where the financial safety and soundness of the participants depends upon the dependability of the systems that they operate. In Section 2.1, we defined the dependability of computer systems as *correctness*, *security* and *fault tolerance*. Here we discuss the architectural impact of the needs for security and fault-tolerance, leaving the description of relevant techniques for achieving them to later in the book. The development of techniques for checking or ensuring the correctness of distributed and concurrent programs is the subject of much current and recent research. Although some promising results have been achieved, few if any of them are yet mature enough for deployment in practical applications.

Fault tolerance: Dependable applications should continue to function correctly in the presence of faults in hardware, software and networks. Reliability is achieved through redundancy – the provision of multiple resources so that the system and application software can reconfigure and continue to perform its tasks in the presence of faults. Redundancy is expensive, and there are limits to the extent to which it can be employed; hence there are also limits to the degree of fault tolerance that can be achieved.

At the architectural level, redundancy requires the use of multiple computers at which each component process of the system can run and multiple communication paths through which messages can be transmitted. Data and processes can then be replicated wherever needed to provide the required level of fault tolerance. A common form of redundancy is the provision of several replicas of a data item at different computers – so long as one of the computers is still running, the data may be accessed. Some critical applications such as air traffic control systems require a very high guarantee of fault tolerance of data, which involves a high cost in keeping the multiple replicas up to date. Chapter 15 discusses this matter further.

Other forms of redundancy are used to make communication protocols reliable. For example, messages are retransmitted until an acknowledgement message has been received. The reliability of the protocols underlying RMI is covered in Chapters 4 and 5.

Security: The architectural impact of the requirement for security concerns the need to locate sensitive data and other resources only in computers that can be secured effectively against attack. For example, a hospital database contains patient records with components that are sensitive and should be seen only by certain clinicians, while other components are more widely available. It would not be appropriate to construct a system that loads an entire patient record into a user's desktop computer when it is accessed, because the typical desktop computer does not constitute a secure environment – users can run programs to access or update any part of the data stored in their personal computer. A security model that addresses wider requirements for security is introduced in Section 2.3.3, and Chapter 7 describes the techniques that are available for its achievement.

2.3 Fundamental models

All the above, quite different, models of systems share some fundamental properties. In particular, all of them are composed of processes that communicate with one another by sending messages over a computer network. All of the models share the design requirements given in the previous section, which are concerned primarily with the performance and reliability characteristics of processes and networks and the security of the resources in the system. In this section, we present models based on the fundamental properties that allow us to be more specific about their characteristics and the failures and security risks they might exhibit.

In general, a model contains only the essential ingredients that we need to consider in order to understand and reason about some aspects of a system's behaviour. A system model has to address the questions:

- What are the main entities in the system?

- How do they interact?

- What are the characteristics that affect their individual and collective behaviour?

The purpose of a model is:

- To make explicit all the relevant assumptions about the systems we are modelling.

- To make generalizations concerning what is possible or impossible, given those assumptions. The generalizations may take the form of general-purpose algorithms or desirable properties that are guaranteed. The guarantees are dependent on logical analysis and, where appropriate, mathematical proof.

There is much to be gained by knowing what our designs do, and do not, depend upon. It allows us to decide whether a design will work if we try to implement it in a particular system: we need only ask whether our assumptions hold in that system. Also, by making our assumptions clear and explicit, we can hope to prove system properties using mathematical techniques. These properties will then hold for any system meeting our assumptions. Finally, by abstracting only the essential system entities and characteristics away from details such as hardware, we can clarify our understanding of our systems.

The aspects of distributed systems that we wish to capture in our fundamental models are intended to help us to discuss and reason about:

Interaction: Computation occurs within processes; the processes interact by passing messages, resulting in communication (i.e. information flow) and coordination (synchronization and ordering of activities) between processes. In the analysis and design of distributed systems we are concerned especially with these interactions. The interaction model must reflect the facts that communication takes place with delays that are often of considerable duration, and that the accuracy with which independent processes can be coordinated is limited by these delays and by the difficulty of maintaining the same notion of time across all the computers in a distributed system.

Failure: The correct operation of a distributed system is threatened whenever a fault occurs in any of the computers on which it runs (including software faults) or in the network that connects them. Our model defines and classifies the faults. This provides a basis for the analysis of their potential effects and for the design of systems that are able to tolerate faults of each type while continuing to run correctly.

Security. The modular nature of distributed systems and their openness exposes them to attack by both external and internal agents. Our security model defines and classifies the forms that such attacks may take, providing a basis for the analysis of threats to a system and for the design of systems that are able to resist them.

As aids to discussion and reasoning, the models introduced in this chapter are necessarily simplified, omitting much of the detail of real-world systems. Their relationship to real-world systems, and the solution in that context of the problems that the models help to bring out, is the main subject of this book.

2.3.1   Interaction model

The discussion of system architectures in Section 2.2 indicates that distributed systems are composed of many processes, interacting in complex ways. For example:

- Multiple server processes may cooperate with one another to provide a service; the examples mentioned above were the Domain Name Service, which partitions and replicates its data at servers throughout the Internet; and Sun's Network Information Service, which keeps replicated copies of password files at several servers in a local area network.

- A set of peer processes may cooperate with one another to achieve a common goal: for example, a voice conferencing system that distributes streams of audio data in a similar manner, but with strict real-time constraints.

Most programmers will be familiar with the concept of an *algorithm* – a sequence of steps to be taken in order to perform a desired computation. Simple programs are controlled by algorithms in which the steps are strictly sequential. The behaviour of the program and the state of the program's variables is determined by them. Such a program is executed as a single process. Distributed systems composed of multiple processes such as those outlined above are more complex. Their behaviour and state can be described by a *distributed algorithm* – a definition of the steps to be taken by each of the processes of which the system is composed, *including the transmission of messages between them*. Messages are transmitted between processes to transfer information between them and to coordinate their activity.

The rate at which each process proceeds and the timing of the transmission of messages between them cannot in general be predicted. It is also difficult to describe all the states of a distributed algorithm, because it must deal with the failures of one or more of the processes involved or the failure of message transmissions.

Interacting processes perform all of the activity in a distributed system. Each process has its own state, consisting of the set of data that it can access and update, including the variables in its program. The state belonging to each process is completely private – that is, it cannot be accessed or updated by any other process.

In this section, we discuss two significant factors affecting interacting processes in a distributed system:

- communication performance is often a limiting characteristic;

- it is impossible to maintain a single global notion of time.

Performance of communication channels ◊ The communication channels in our model are realized in a variety of ways in distributed systems, for example by an implementation of streams or by simple message passing over a computer network. Communication over a computer network has the following performance characteristics relating to latency, bandwidth and jitter:

- The delay between the start of a message's transmission from one process and the beginning of its receipt by another is referred to as *latency*. The latency includes:

  - The time taken for the first of a string of bits transmitted through a network to reach its destination. For example, the latency for the transmission of a message through a satellite link is the time for a radio signal to travel to the satellite and back.

  - The delay in accessing the network, which increases significantly when the network is heavily loaded. For example, for Ethernet transmission the sending station waits for the network to be free of traffic.

  - The time taken by the operating system communication services at both the sending and the receiving processes, which varies according to the current load on the operating systems.

- The *bandwidth* of a computer network is the total amount of information that can be transmitted over it in a given time. When a large number of communication channels are using the same network, they have to share the available bandwidth.

- *Jitter* is the variation in the time taken to deliver a series of messages. Jitter is relevant to multimedia data. For example, if consecutive samples of audio data are played with differing time intervals then the sound will be badly distorted.

Computer clocks and timing events ◊ Each computer in a distributed system has its own internal clock, which can be used by local processes to obtain the value of the current time. Therefore two processes running on different computers can associate timestamps with their events. However, even if two processes read their clocks at the same time, their local clocks may supply different time values. This is because computer clocks drift from perfect time and, more importantly, their drift rates differ from one another. The term *clock drift rate* refers to the relative amount that a computer clock differs from a perfect reference clock. Even if the clocks on all the computers in a distributed system are set to the same time initially, their clocks would eventually vary quite significantly unless corrections are applied.

There are several approaches to correcting the times on computer clocks. For example, computers may use radio receivers to get time readings from the Global Positioning System with an accuracy of about 1 microsecond. But GPS receivers do not operate inside buildings, nor can the cost be justified for every computer. Instead, a computer that has an accurate time source such as GPS can send timing messages to other computers in the network. The resulting agreement between the times on the local clocks is, of course, affected by variable message delays. For a more detailed discussion of clock drift and clock synchronization, see Chapter 12.

Two variants of the interaction model ◊ In a distributed system it is hard to set time limits on the time taken for process execution, message delivery or clock drift. Two opposing extreme positions provide a pair of simple models: the first has a strong assumption of time and the second makes no assumptions about time.

Synchronous distributed systems: Hadzilacos and Toueg [1994] define a synchronous distributed system to be one in which the following bounds are defined:

- the time to execute each step of a process has known lower and upper bounds;

- each message transmitted over a channel is received within a known bounded time;

- each process has a local clock whose drift rate from real time has a known bound.

It is possible to suggest likely upper and lower bounds for process execution time, message delay and clock drift rates in a distributed system. But it is difficult to arrive at realistic values and to provide guarantees of the chosen values. Unless the values of the bounds can be guaranteed, any design based on the chosen values will not be reliable. However, modelling an algorithm as a synchronous system may be useful for giving some idea of how it will behave in a real distributed system. In a synchronous system, it is possible to use timeouts, for example to detect the failure of a process, as shown in the section on the failure model.

Synchronous distributed systems can be built. What is required is for the processes to perform tasks with known resource requirements for which they can be guaranteed sufficient processor cycles and network capacity; and for processes to be supplied with clocks with bounded drift rates.

Asynchronous distributed systems: Many distributed systems, for example the Internet, are very useful without being able to qualify as synchronous systems. Therefore we need an alternative model: an asynchronous distributed system is one in which there are no bounds on:

- process execution speeds – for example, one process step may take only a picosecond and another a century; all that can be said is that each step may take an arbitrarily long time;

- message transmission delays – for example, one message from process A to process B may be delivered in negligible time and another may take several years. In other words, a message may be received after an arbitrarily long time;

- clock drift rates – again, the drift rate of a clock is arbitrary.

The asynchronous model allows no assumptions about the time intervals involved in any execution. This exactly models the Internet, in which there is no intrinsic bound on server or network load and therefore on how long it takes, for example, to transfer a file using ftp. Sometimes an email message can take days to arrive. The box on the next page illustrates the difficulty of reaching an agreement in an asynchronous distributed system.

But some design problems can be solved even with these assumptions. For example, although the Web cannot always provide a particular response within a reasonable time limit, browsers have been designed to allow users to do other things while they are waiting. Any solution that is valid for an asynchronous distributed system is also valid for a synchronous one.

Actual distributed systems are very often asynchronous because of the need for processes to share the processors and for communication channels to share the network. For example, if too many processes of unknown character are sharing a processor, then the resulting performance of any one of them cannot be guaranteed. But there are many design problems that cannot be solved for an asynchronous system that can be solved when some aspects of time are used. The need for each element of a multimedia data stream to be delivered before a deadline is such a problem. For problems such as these a synchronous model is required. The box below illustrates the impossibility of synchronizing clocks in an asynchronous system.

Event ordering ◊   In many cases, we are interested in knowing whether an event (sending or receiving a message) at one process occurred before, after or concurrently with another event at another process. The execution of a system can be described in terms of events and their ordering despite the lack of accurate clocks.

For example, consider the following set of exchanges between a group of email users X, Y, Z and A on a mailing list:

1. user X sends a message with the subject *Meeting*;

2. users Y and Z reply by sending a message with the subject *Re: Meeting*.

In real time, X's message was sent first, Y reads it and replies; Z reads both X's message and Y's reply and then sends another reply, which references both X's and Y's

Agreement in Pepperland ◊ Two divisions of the Pepperland army, 'Apple' and 'Orange', are encamped at the top of two nearby hills. Further along the valley below are the invading Blue Meanies. The Pepperland divisions are safe as long as they remain in their encampments, and they can send out messengers reliably through the valley to communicate. The Pepperland divisions need to agree on which of them will lead the charge against the Blue Meanies, and when the charge will take place. Even in an asynchronous Pepperland, it is possible to agree on who will lead the charge. For example, each division sends the number of its remaining members, and the one with most will lead (if a tie, division Apple wins over Orange). But when should they charge? Unfortunately, in asynchronous Pepperland, the messengers are very variable in their speed. If, say, Apple sends a messenger with the message 'Charge!', Orange might not receive the message for, say, three hours; or it may have taken, say, five minutes. In a synchronous Pepperland, there is still a coordination problem, but the divisions know some useful constraints: every message takes at least *min* minutes and at most *max* minutes to arrive. If the division that will lead the charge sends a message 'Charge!', it waits for *min* minutes; then it charges. The other division waits for 1 minute after receipt of the message, then charges. Its charge is guaranteed to be after the leading division's, but no more than ($max - min + 1$) minutes after it.

Figure 2.8   Real-time ordering of events

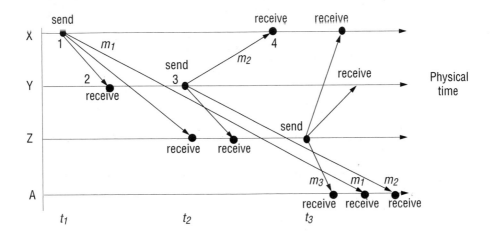

messages. But due to the independent delays in message delivery, the messages may be delivered as shown in Figure 2.8, and some users may view these two messages in the wrong order, for example, user A might see:

		Inbox:
Item	*From*	*Subject*
23	Z	Re: Meeting
24	X	Meeting
25	Y	Re: Meeting

If the clocks on X's, Y's and Z's computers could be synchronized, then each message could carry the time on the local computer's clock when it was sent. For example, messages m_1, m_2 and m_3 would carry times t_1, t_2 and t_3 where $t_1 < t_2 < t_3$. The messages received will be displayed to users according to their time ordering. If the clocks are roughly synchronized then these timestamps, will often be in the correct order.

Since clocks cannot be synchronized perfectly across a distributed system, Lamport [1978] proposed a model of *logical time* that can be used to provide an ordering among the events at processes running in different computers in a distributed system. Logical time allows the order in which the messages are presented to be inferred without recourse to clocks. It is presented in detail in Chapter 11, but we suggest here how some aspects of logical ordering can be applied to our email ordering problem.

Logically, we know that a message is received after it was sent, therefore we can state a logical ordering for pairs of events shown in Figure 2.8, for example, considering only the events concerning X and Y:

X sends m_1 before Y receives m_1;   Y sends m_2 before X receives m_2.

We also know that replies are sent after receiving messages, therefore we have the following logical ordering for Y:

Y receives m_1 before sending m_2.

Logical time takes this idea further by assigning a number to each event corresponding to its logical ordering, so that later events have higher numbers than earlier ones. For example, Figure 2.8 shows the numbers 1 to 4 on the events at X and Y.

2.3.2   Failure model

In a distributed system both processes and communication channels may fail – that is, they may depart from what is considered to be correct or desirable behaviour. The failure model defines the ways in which failure may occur in order to provide an understanding of the effects of failures. Hadzilacos and Toueg [1994] provide a taxonomy that distinguishes between the failures of processes and communication channels. These are presented under the headings omission failures, arbitrary failures and timing failures.

The failure model will be used throughout the book. For example:

- In Chapter 4, we present the Java interfaces to datagram and stream communication, which provide different degrees of reliability.

- Chapter 4 presents the request-reply protocol, which supports RMI. Its failure characteristics depend on the failure characteristics of both processes and communication channels. The protocol can be built from either datagram or stream communication. The choice may be decided according to a consideration of simplicity of implementation, performance and reliability.

- Chapter 14 presents the two-phase commit protocol for transactions. It is designed to complete in the face of well-defined failures of processes and communication channels.

Omission failures ◊ The faults classified as *omission failures* refer to cases when a process or communication channel fails to perform actions that it is supposed to do.

Process omission failures: The chief omission failure of a process is to crash. When we say that a process has crashed we mean that it has halted and will not execute any further steps of its program ever. The design of services that can survive in the presence of faults can be simplified if it can be assumed that the services on which it depends crash cleanly – that is, the processes either function correctly or else stop. Other processes may be able to detect such a crash by the fact that the process repeatedly fails to respond to invocation messages. However, this method of crash detection relies on the use of *timeouts* – that is, a method in which one process allows a fixed period of time for something to occur. In an asynchronous system a timeout can indicate only that a process is not responding – it may have crashed or may be slow, or the messages may not have arrived.

A process crash is called *fail-stop* if other processes can detect certainly that the process has crashed. Fail-stop behaviour can be produced in a synchronous system if the processes use timeouts to detect when other processes fail to respond and messages are guaranteed to be delivered. For example, if processes p and q are programmed for q to reply to a message from p, and if process p has received no reply from process q in a maximum time measured on p's local clock, then process p may conclude that process q has failed. The box below illustrates the difficulty of detecting failures in an asynchronous system or of reaching agreement in the presence of failures.

Communication omission failures: Consider the communication primitives *send* and *receive*. A process p performs a *send* by inserting the message m in its outgoing message buffer. The communication channel transports m to q's incoming message buffer. Process q performs a *receive* by taking m from its incoming message buffer and delivering it (see Figure 2.9). The outgoing and incoming message buffers are typically provided by the operating system.

The communication channel produces an omission failure if it does not transport a message from p's outgoing message buffer to q's incoming message buffer. This is known as 'dropping messages' and is generally caused by lack of buffer space at the receiver or at an intervening gateway, or by a network transmission error, detected by a checksum carried with the message data. Hadzilacos and Toueg [1994] refer to the loss

---

Failure detection ◊   In the case of the Pepperland divisions encamped at the tops of hills (see page 51), suppose that the Blue Meanies are after all sufficient in strength to attack and defeat either division while encamped – that is, that either can fail. Suppose further that, while undefeated, the divisions regularly send messengers to report their status. In an asynchronous system, neither division can distinguish whether the other has been defeated or if the time for the messengers to cross the intervening valley is just very long. In a synchronous Pepperland, a division can tell for sure if the other has been defeated, by the absence of a regular messenger. However, the other division may have been defeated just after it sent the latest messenger.

Impossibility of reaching agreement in the presence of failures ◊ We have been assuming that the Pepperland messengers always manage to cross the valley eventually; but now suppose that the Blue Meanies can capture any messenger and prevent her from arriving. (We shall assume it is impossible for the Blue Meanies to brainwash the messengers to give the wrong message – the Meanies are not aware of their treacherous Byzantine precursors.) Can the Apple and Orange divisions send messages so that they both consistently decide to charge at the Meanies or both decide to surrender? Unfortunately, as the Pepperland theoretician Ringo the Great proved, in these circumstances the divisions cannot guarantee to decide consistently what to do. To see this, assume to the contrary that the divisions run a Pepperland protocol that achieves agreement. Each proposes 'Charge!' or 'Surrender!' and the protocol results in them both agreeing on one or the other course of action. Now consider the last message sent in any run of the protocol. The messenger that carries it could be captured by the Blue Meanies. So the end result must be the same, whether the message arrives or not. We can dispense with it. Now we can apply the same argument to the final message that remains. But this argument applies again to that message and will continue to apply, so we shall end up with no messages sent at all! This shows that no protocol that guarantees agreement between the Pepperland divisions can exist if messengers can be captured.

Figure 2.9   Processes and channels

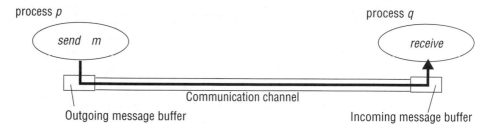

of messages between the sending process and the outgoing message buffer as *send-omission failures*; loss of messages between the incoming message buffer and the receiving process as *receive-omission failures*; and loss of messages in between as channel omission failures. The omission failures are classified together with arbitrary failures in Figure 2.10.

Failures can be categorized according to their severity. All of the failures we have described so far are *benign* failures. Most failures in distributed systems are benign. Benign failures include failures of omission as well as timing failures and performance failures.

Arbitrary failures ◊ The term *arbitrary* or Byzantine failure is used to describe the worst possible failure semantics, in which any type of error may occur. For example, a process may set wrong values in its data items, or it may return a wrong value in response to an invocation.

An arbitrary failure of a process is one in which it arbitrarily omits intended processing steps or takes unintended processing steps. Therefore arbitrary failures in processes cannot be detected by seeing whether the process responds to invocations, because it might arbitrarily omit to reply.

Communication channels can suffer from arbitrary failures; for example, message contents may be corrupted or non-existent messages may be delivered or real messages may be delivered more than once. Arbitrary failures of communication channels are rare because the communication software is able to recognize them and reject the faulty messages. For example, checksums are used to detect corrupted messages, and message sequence numbers can be used to detect non-existent and duplicated messages.

Timing failures ◊ Timing failures are applicable in synchronous distributed systems where time limits are set on process execution time, message delivery time and clock drift rate. Timing failures are listed in Figure 2.11. Any one of these failures may result in responses being unavailable to clients within a specified time interval.

In an asynchronous distributed system, an overloaded server may respond too slowly, but we cannot say that it has a timing failure since no guarantee has been offered.

Real-time operating systems are designed with a view to providing timing guarantees, but they are more complex to design and may require redundant hardware. Most general-purpose operating systems such as UNIX do not have to meet real-time constraints.

Timing is particularly relevant to multimedia computers with audio and video channels. Video information can require a very large amount of data to be transferred.

Figure 2.10   Omission and arbitrary failures

Class of failure	Affects	Description
Fail-stop	Process	Process halts and remains halted. Other processes may detect this state.
Crash	Process	Process halts and remains halted. Other processes may not be able to detect this state.
Omission	Channel	A message inserted in an outgoing message buffer never arrives at the other end's incoming message buffer.
Send-omission	Process	A process completes a *send*, but the message is not put in its outgoing message buffer.
Receive-omission	Process	A message is put in a process's incoming message buffer, but that process does not receive it.
Arbitrary (Byzantine)	Process or channel	Process/channel exhibits arbitrary behaviour: it may send/transmit arbitrary messages at arbitrary times, commit omissions; a process may stop or take an incorrect step.

To deliver such information without timing failures can make very special demands on both the operating system and the communication system.

Masking failures ◊ Each component in a distributed system is generally constructed from a collection of other components. It is possible to construct reliable services from components that exhibit failures. For example, multiple servers that hold replicas of data can continue to provide a service when one of them crashes. A knowledge of the failure characteristics of a component can enable a new service to be designed to mask the failure of the components on which it depends. A service *masks* a failure, either by hiding it altogether or by converting it into a more acceptable type of failure. For an example of the latter, checksums are used to mask corrupted messages – effectively converting an arbitrary failure into an omission failure. We shall see in Chapters 3 and 4 that omission failures can be hidden by using a protocol that retransmits messages that do not arrive at their destination. Chapter 15 presents masking by means of replication. Even process crashes may be masked – by replacing the process and restoring its memory from information stored on disk by its predecessor.

Reliability of one-to-one communication ◊ Although a basic communication channel can exhibit the omission failures described above, it is possible to use it to build a communication service that masks some of those failures.

The term *reliable communication* is defined in terms of validity and integrity as follows:

validity: any message in the outgoing message buffer is eventually delivered to the incoming message buffer;

integrity: the message received is identical to one sent, and no messages are delivered twice.

Figure 2.11   Timing failures

Class of Failure	Affects	Description
Clock	Process	Process's local clock exceeds the bounds on its rate of drift from real time.
Performance	Process	Process exceeds the bounds on the interval between two steps.
Performance	Channel	A message's transmission takes longer than the stated bound.

The threats to integrity come from two independent sources:

- Any protocol that retransmits messages but does not reject a message that arrives twice. Protocols can attach sequence numbers to messages so as to detect those that are delivered twice.

- Malicious users that may inject spurious messages, replay old messages or tamper with messages. Security measures can be taken to maintain the integrity property in the face of such attacks.

2.3.3   Security model

In Section 2.2 we identified the sharing of resources as a motivating factor for distributed systems and we described their system architecture in terms of processes encapsulating objects and providing access to them through interactions with other processes. That architectural model provides the basis for our security model:

> the security of a distributed system can be achieved by securing the processes and the channels used for their interactions and by protecting the objects that they encapsulate against unauthorized access.

Protection is described in terms of objects, although the concepts apply equally well to resources of all types.

Protecting objects ◊   Figure 2.12 shows a server that manages a collection of objects on behalf of some users. The users can run client programs that send invocations to the server to perform operations on the objects. The server carries out the operation specified in each invocation and sends the result to the client.

Objects are intended to be used in different ways by different users. For example, some objects may hold a user's private data, such as their mailbox, and other objects may hold shared data such as web pages. To support this, *access rights* specify who is allowed to perform the operations of an object – for example, who is allowed to read or to write its state.

Thus we must include users in our model as the beneficiaries of access rights. We do so by associating with each invocation and each result the authority on which it is issued. Such an authority is called a *principal*. A principal may be a user or a process. In our illustration, the invocation comes from a user and the result from a server.

Figure 2.12   Objects and principals

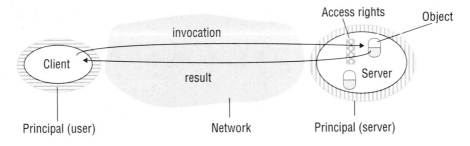

The server is responsible for verifying the identity of the principal behind each invocation and checking that they have sufficient access rights to perform the requested operation on the particular object invoked, rejecting those that do not. The client may check the identity of the principal behind the server to ensure that the result comes from the required server.

Securing processes and their interactions ◊ Processes interact by sending messages. The messages are exposed to attack because the network and the communication service that they use is open, to enable any pair of processes to interact. Servers and peer processes expose their interfaces, enabling invocations to be sent to them by any other process.

Distributed systems are often deployed and used in tasks that are likely to be subject to external attacks by hostile users. This is especially true for applications that handle financial transactions, confidential or classified information or any other information whose secrecy or integrity is crucial. Integrity is threatened by security violations as well as communication failures. So we know that there are likely to be threats to the processes of which such applications are composed and to the messages travelling between the processes. But how can we analyse these threats in order to identify and defeat them? The following discussion introduces a model for the analysis of security threats.

The enemy ◊ To model security threats, we postulate an enemy (sometimes also known as the adversary) that is capable of sending any message to any process and reading or copying any message between a pair of processes, as shown in Figure 2.13. Such attacks can be made simply by using a computer connected to a network to run a program that reads network messages addressed to other computers on the network, or a program that generates messages that make false requests to services and purporting to come from authorized users. The attack may come from a computer that is legitimately connected to the network or from one that is connected in an unauthorized manner.

The threats from a potential enemy are discussed under the headings *threats to processes*, *threats to communication channels* and *denial of service*.

Threats to processes: A process that is designed to handle incoming requests may receive a message from any other process in the distributed system, and it cannot necessarily determine the identity of the sender. Communication protocols such as IP do include the address of the source computer in each message, but it is not difficult for an enemy to generate a message with a forged source address. This lack of reliable

Figure 2.13 The enemy

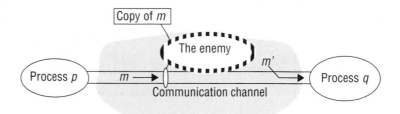

knowledge of the source of a message is a threat to the correct functioning of both servers and clients, as explained below:

Servers: Since a server can receive invocations from many different clients, it cannot necessarily determine the identity of the principal behind any particular invocation. Even if a server requires the inclusion of the principal's identity in each invocation, an enemy might generate an invocation with a false identity. Without reliable knowledge of the sender's identity, a server cannot tell whether to perform the operation or to reject it. For example, a mail server would not know whether the user behind an invocation that requests a mail item from a particular mailbox is allowed to do so or whether it was a request from an enemy.

Clients: When a client receives the result of an invocation from a server, it cannot necessarily tell whether the source of the result message is from the intended server or from an enemy, perhaps 'spoofing' the mail server. Thus the client could receive a result that was unrelated to the original invocation, such as a false mail item (one that is not in the user's mailbox).

Threats to communication channels: An enemy can copy, alter or inject messages as they travel across the network and its intervening gateways. Such attacks present a threat to the privacy and integrity of information as it travels over the network and to the integrity of the system. For example, a result message containing a user's mail item might be revealed to another user or it might be altered to say something quite different.

Another form of attack is the attempt to save copies of messages and to replay them at a later time, making it possible to reuse the same message over and over again. For example, someone could benefit by resending an invocation message requesting a transfer of a sum of money from one bank account to another.

All these threats can be defeated by the use of *secure channels*, which are described below and are based on cryptography and authentication.

Defeating security threats ◊ Here we introduce the main techniques on which secure systems are based. Chapter 7 discusses the design and implementation of secure distributed systems in some detail.

Cryptography and shared secrets: Suppose that a pair of processes (for example, a particular client and a particular server) share a secret; that is they both know the secret but no other process in the distributed system knows it. Then if a message exchanged by that pair of processes includes information that proves the sender's knowledge of the shared secret, the recipient knows for sure that the sender was the other process in the

Figure 2.14   Secure channels

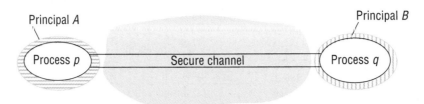

pair. Of course, care must be taken to ensure that the shared secret is not revealed to an enemy.

Cryptography is the science of keeping messages secure, and *encryption* is the process of scrambling a message in such a way as to hide its contents. Modern cryptography is based on encryption algorithms that use secret keys – large numbers that are difficult to guess – to transform data in a manner that can only be reversed with knowledge of the corresponding decryption key.

Authentication: The use of shared secrets and encryption provides the basis for the *authentication* of messages – proving the identities supplied by their senders. The basic authentication technique is to include in a message an encrypted portion that contains enough of the contents of the message to guarantee its authenticity. The authentication portion of a request to a file server to read part of a file, for example, might include a representation of the requesting principal's identity, the identity of the file and the date and time of the request, all encrypted with a secret key shared between the file server and the requesting process. The server would decrypt this and check that it corresponds to the unencrypted details specified in the request.

Secure channels: Encryption and authentication are used to build secure channels as a service layer on top of existing communication services. A secure channel is a communication channel connecting a pair of processes, each of which acts on behalf of a principal, as shown in Figure 2.14. A secure channel has the following properties:

- Each of the processes knows reliably the identity of the principal on whose behalf the other process is executing. Therefore if a client and server communicate via a secure channel, the server knows the identity of the principal behind the invocations and can check their access rights before performing an operation. This enables the server to protect its objects correctly and allows the client to be sure that it is receiving results from a *bona fide* server.

- A secure channel ensures the privacy and integrity (protection against tampering) of the data transmitted across it.

- Each message includes a physical or logical time stamp to prevent messages from being replayed or reordered.

The construction of secure channels is discussed in detail in Chapter 7. Secure channels have become an important practical tool for securing electronic commerce and the protection of communication. Virtual private networks (VPNs, discussed in Chapter 3) and the Secure Sockets Layer (SSL) protocol (discussed in Chapter 7) are instances.

Other possible threats from an enemy ◊ Section 1.4.3 introduced very briefly two security threats – denial of service attacks and the deployment of mobile code. We reiterate these as possible opportunities for the enemy to disrupt the activities of processes:

Denial of service: This is a form of attack in which the enemy interferes with the activities of authorized users by making excessive and pointless invocations on services or message transmissions in a network, resulting in overloading of physical resources (network bandwidth, server processing capacity). Such attacks are usually made with the intention of delaying or preventing actions by other users. For example, the operation of electronic door locks in a building might be disabled by an attack that saturates the computer controlling the electronic locks with invalid requests.

Mobile code: Mobile code raises new and interesting security problems for any process that receives and executes program code from elsewhere, such as the email attachment mentioned in Section 1.4.3. Such code may easily play a Trojan horse role, purporting to fulfil an innocent purpose but in fact including code that accesses or modifies resources that are legitimately available to the host process but not to the originator of the code. The methods by which such attacks might be carried out are many and varied, and the host environment must be very carefully constructed in order to avoid them. Many of these issues have been addressed in Java and other mobile code systems, but the recent history of this topic has included the exposure of some embarrassing weaknesses. This illustrates well the need for rigorous analysis in the design of all secure systems.

The uses of security models ◊ It might be thought that the achievement of security in distributed systems would be a straightforward matter involving the control of access to objects according to predefined access rights and the use of secure channels for communication. Unfortunately, this is not generally the case. The use of security techniques such as encryption and access control incurs substantial processing and management costs. The security model outlined above provides the basis for the analysis and design of secure systems in which these costs are kept to a minimum, but threats to a distributed system arise at many points, and a careful analysis of the threats that might arise from all possible sources in the system's network environment, physical environment and human environment is needed. This analysis involves the construction of a *threat model* listing all the forms of attack to which the system is exposed and an evaluation of the risks and consequences of each. The effectiveness and the cost of the security techniques needed can then be balanced against the threats.

2.4 Summary

Most distributed systems are arranged according to one of a variety of architectural models. The client-server model is prevalent – the Web and other Internet services such as ftp, news and mail as well as web services and the DNS are based on this model, as are filing and other local services. Services such as the DNS that have large numbers of users and manage a great deal of information are based on multiple servers and use data partition and replication to enhance availability and fault tolerance. Caching by clients and proxy servers is widely used to enhance the performance of a service.

In the peer-to-peer model, the processes all play similar roles, in exploiting the resources of large numbers of participating computers to carry out a common task.

The ability to move code from one process to another has resulted in some variants of the client-server model. The most common example of this is the applet whose code is supplied by a web server to be run by a client, providing functionalities not available in the client and improved performance due to being close to the user.

The existence of portable computers, PDAs and other digital devices and their integration into distributed systems allows users to access local and Internet services when they are away from their desktop computer. A characteristic of mobile devices in a distributed system is that they connect and disconnect unpredictably. This leads to variant of the client-server model known as spontaneous interoperation in which the associations between devices are frequently created and destroyed.

We presented models of interaction, failure and security. They identify the common characteristics of the basic components from which distributed systems are constructed. The interaction model is concerned with the performance of processes and communication channels and the absence of a global clock. It identifies a synchronous system as one in which known bounds may be placed on process execution time, message delivery time and clock drift. It identifies an asynchronous system as one in which no bounds may be placed on process execution time, message delivery time and clock drift – which is a description of the behaviour of the Internet.

The failure model classifies the failures of processes and basic communication channels in a distributed system. Masking is a technique by which a more reliable service is built from a less reliable one by masking some of the failures it exhibits. In particular, a reliable communication service can be built from a basic communication channel by masking its failures. For example, its omission failures may be masked by retransmitting lost messages. Integrity is a property of reliable communication – it requires that a message received be identical to one that was sent and that no message be sent twice. Validity is another property – it requires that any message put in the outgoing buffer be delivered eventually to the incoming message buffer.

The security model identifies the possible threats to processes and communication channels in an open distributed system. Some of those threats relate to integrity: malicious users may tamper with messages or replay them. Others threaten their privacy. Another security issue is the authentication of the principal (user or server) on whose behalf a message was sent. Secure channels use cryptographic techniques to ensure the integrity and privacy of messages and to authenticate pairs of communicating principals.

EXERCISES

2.1   Describe and illustrate the client-server architecture of one or more major Internet applications (for example, the Web, email or netnews).   *page 35*

2.2   For the applications discussed in Exercise 2.1 state how the servers cooperate in providing a service.   *page 37*

2.3 How do the applications discussed in Exercise 2.1 involve the partitioning and/or replication (or caching) of data amongst servers? *page 37*

2.4 A search engine is a web server that responds to client requests to search in its stored indexes and (concurrently) runs several web crawler tasks to build and update the indexes. What are the requirements for synchronization between these concurrent activities? *page 35*

2.5 The host computers used in peer-to-peer systems are often simply desktop computers in users' offices or homes. What are the implications of this for the availability and security of any shared data objects that they hold and to what extent can any weaknesses be overcome through the use of replication? *page 35, page 57*

2.6 List the types of local resource that are vulnerable to an attack by an untrusted program that is downloaded from a remote site and run in a local computer. *page 37*

2.7 Give examples of applications where the use of mobile code is beneficial. *page 37*

2.8 What factors affect the responsiveness of an application that accesses shared data managed by a server? Describe remedies that are available and discuss their usefulness. *page 43*

2.9 Distinguish between buffering and caching. *page 45*

2.10 Give some examples of faults in hardware and software that can/cannot be tolerated by the use of redundancy in a distributed system. To what extent does the use of redundancy in the appropriate cases make a system fault-tolerant? *page 46*

2.11 Consider a simple server that carries out client requests without accessing other servers. Explain why it is generally not possible to set a limit on the time taken by such a server to respond to a client request. What would need to be done to make the server able to execute requests within a bounded time? Is this a practical option? *page 48*

2.12 For each of the factors that contribute to the time taken to transmit a message between two processes over a communication channel, state what measures would be needed to set a bound on its contribution to the total time. Why are these measures not provided in current general-purpose distributed systems? *page 49*

2.13 The Network Time Protocol service can be used to synchronize computer clocks. Explain why, even with this service, no guaranteed bound is given for the difference between two clocks. *page 49*

2.14 Consider two communication services for use in asynchronous distributed systems. In service A, messages may be lost, duplicated or delayed and checksums apply only to headers. In service B, messages may be lost, delayed or delivered too fast for the recipient to handle them, but those that are delivered arrive with the correct contents.

Describe the classes of failure exhibited by each service. Classify their failures according to their effect on the properties of validity and integrity. Can service B be described as a reliable communication service? *page 53, page 56*

2.15   Consider a pair of processes X and Y that use the communication service B from Exercise 2.14 to communicate with one another. Suppose that X is a client and Y a server and that an *invocation* consists of a request message from X to Y, followed by Y carrying out the request, followed by a reply message from Y to X. Describe the classes of failure that may be exhibited by an invocation. *page 53*

2.16   Suppose that a basic disk read can sometimes read values that are different from those written. State the type of failure exhibited by a basic disk read. Suggest how this failure may be masked in order to produce a different benign form of failure. Now suggest how to mask the benign failure. *page 56*

2.17   Define the integrity property of reliable communication and list all the possible threats to integrity from users and from system components. What measures can be taken to ensure the integrity property in the face of each of these sources of threats. *pages 56, 59*

2.18   Describe possible occurrences of each of the main types of security threat (threats to processes, threats to communication channels, denial of service) that might occur in the Internet. *page 58*

3

NETWORKING AND INTERNETWORKING

Distributed systems use local area networks, wide area networks and internetworks for communication. The performance, reliability, scalability, mobility and quality of service characteristics of the underlying networks impact the behaviour of distributed systems and hence affect their design. Changes in user requirements have resulted in the emergence of wireless networks and of high-performance networks with quality of service guarantees.

The principles on which computer networks are based include protocol layering, packet switching, routing and data streaming. Internetworking techniques enable heterogeneous networks to be integrated. The Internet is the major example; its protocols are almost universally used in distributed systems. The addressing and routing schemes used in the Internet have withstood the impact of its enormous growth. They are now undergoing revision to accommodate future growth and to meet new application requirements for mobility, security and quality of service.

The design of specific network technologies is illustrated in four case studies: Ethernet, IEEE 802.11 (WiFi) and Bluetooth wireless networking, and Asynchronous Transfer Mode (ATM) networking.

3.1   Introduction

The networks used in distributed systems are built from a variety of *transmission media*, including wire, cable, fibre and wireless channels; *hardware devices,* including routers, switches, bridges, hubs, repeaters and network interfaces; and *software components,* including protocol stacks, communication handlers and drivers. The resulting functionality and performance available to distributed system and application programs is affected by all of these. We shall refer to the collection of hardware and software components that provide the communication facilities for a distributed system as a *communication subsystem*. The computers and other devices that use the network for communication purposes are referred to as *hosts*. The term *node* is used to refer to any computer or switching device attached to a network.

The Internet is a single communication subsystem providing communication between all of the hosts that are connected to it. The Internet is constructed from many *subnets*. A subnet is a unit of routing (delivering data from one part of the Internet to another); it is a collection of nodes that can all be reached on the same physical network. The Internet's infrastructure includes an architecture and hardware and software components that effectively integrate diverse subnets into a single data communication service.

The design of a communication subsystem is strongly influenced by the characteristics of the operating systems used in the computers of which the distributed system is composed as well as the networks that interconnect them. In this chapter, we consider the impact of network technologies on the communication subsystem; operating system issues are discussed in Chapter 6.

This chapter is intended to provide an introductory overview of computer networking with reference to the communication requirements of distributed systems. Readers who are not familiar with computer networking should regard it as an underpinning for the remainder of the book, while those who are will find that this chapter offers an extended summary of those aspects of computer networking that are particularly relevant for distributed systems.

Computer networking was conceived soon after the invention of computers. The theoretical basis for packet switching was introduced in a paper by Leonard Kleinrock [1961]. In 1962, J.C.R. Licklider and W. Clark, who participated in the development of the first timesharing system at MIT in the early 1960s, published a paper discussing the potential for interactive computing and wide-area networking that presaged the Internet in several respects [DEC 1990]. In 1964, Paul Baran produced an outline of a practical design for reliable and effective wide-area networks [Baran 1964]. Further material and links on the history of computer networking and the Internet can be found in the following sources: [www.isoc.org, Comer 2000b, Kurose and Ross 2000].

In the remainder of this section we discuss the communication requirements of distributed systems. We give an overview of network types in Section 3.2 and an introduction to networking principles in Section 3.3. Section 3.4 deals specifically with the Internet. The chapter concludes with detailed case studies on the Ethernet, IEEE 802.11 (WiFi), Bluetooth and ATM networking technologies in Section 3.5.

3.1.1   Networking issues for distributed systems

Early computer networks were designed to meet a few, relatively simple application requirements. Network applications such as file transfer, remote login, electronic mail and newsgroups were supported. The subsequent development of distributed systems with support for distributed application programs accessing share files and other resources set a higher standard of performance to meet the needs of interactive applications.

More recently, following the growth and commercialization of the Internet and the emergence of many new modes of use, more stringent requirements for reliability, scalability, mobility and security and quality of service have emerged. In this section, we define and describe the nature of each of these requirements.

Performance ◊   The network performance parameters that are of primary interest for our purposes are those affecting the speed with which individual messages can be transferred between two interconnected computers. These are the latency and the point-to-point data transfer rate.

Latency is the delay that occurs after a send operation is executed before data starts to arrive at the destination computer. It can be measured as the time required to transfer an empty message. Here we are considering only network latency, which forms a part of the process-to-process latency defined in Section 2.3.1.

Data transfer rate is the speed at which data can be transferred between two computers in the network once transmission has begun, usually quoted in bits per second.

Following from these definitions, the time required for a network to transfer a message containing *length* bits between two computers is:

$$Message\ transmission\ time = latency + length/data\ transfer\ rate$$

The above equation is valid for messages whose length does not exceed a maximum that is determined by the underlying network technology. Longer messages have to be segmented and the transmission time is the sum of the times for the segments.

The transfer rate of a network is determined primarily by its physical characteristics, whereas the latency is determined primarily by software overheads, routing delays and a load-dependent statistical element arising from conflicting demands for access to transmission channels. Many of the messages transferred between processes in distributed systems are small in size; latency is therefore often of equal or greater significance than transfer rate in determining performance.

The *total system bandwidth* of a network is a measure of throughput – the total volume of traffic that can be transferred across the network in a given time. In many local area network technologies, such as Ethernet, the full transmission capacity of the network is used for every transmission and the system bandwidth is the same as the data transfer rate. But in most wide area networks messages can be transferred on several different channels simultaneously, and the total system bandwidth bears no direct relationship to the transfer rate. The performance of networks deteriorates in conditions of overload – when there are too many messages in the network at the same time. The precise effect of overload on the latency, data transfer rate and total system bandwidth of a network depends strongly on the network technology.

Now consider the performance of client-server communication. The time to transmit a short request message and receive a short reply between nodes on a lightly loaded local network (including system overheads) is about half a millisecond. This should be compared with the sub-microsecond time required to invoke an operation on an application-level object in the local memory. Thus, despite advances in network performance the time required to access shared resources on a local network remains about a thousand times greater than to access resources that are resident in local memory. But network latency and bandwidth often outstrip hard disk performance; networked access to a local web server or file server with a large cache of frequently-used files can match or outstrip access to files stored on a local hard disk.

On the Internet, round-trip latencies are in the 50–750 ms range with a mean around 200 ms, so requests transmitted across the Internet are approximately 100 times slower than on fast local networks. The bulk of this time difference derives from switching delays at routers and contention for network circuits.

Section 6.5.1 discusses and compares the performance of local and remote operations in greater detail.

Scalability ◊ Computer networks are an indispensable part of the infrastructure of modern societies. In Figure 1.4 we show the growth in the number of host computers connected to the Internet over a 25-year period. The potential future size of the Internet is commensurate with the population of the planet. It is realistic to expect it to include several billion nodes and hundreds of millions of active hosts.

These numbers indicate the future changes in size and load that the Internet must handle. The network technologies on which it is based were not designed to cope with even the Internet's current scale; but they have performed remarkably well. Some substantial changes to the addressing and routing mechanisms are in progress in order to handle the next phase of the Internet's growth; these will be described in Section 3.4. For simple client-server applications such as the Web, we would expect future traffic to grow at least in proportion to the number of active users. The ability of the Internet infrastructure to cope with this growth will depend upon the economics of use, in particular charges to users and the patterns of communication that actually occur – for example their degree of locality.

Reliability ◊ Our discussion of failure models in Section 2.3.2 describes the impact of communication errors. Many applications are able to recover from communication failures and hence do not require guaranteed error-free communication. The end-to-end argument (Section 2.2.1) further supports the view that the communication subsystem need not provide totally error-free communication; the detection of communication errors and their correction is often best performed by application-level software. The reliability of most physical transmission media is very high. When errors occur they are usually due to failures in the software at the sender or receiver (for example, failure by the receiving computer to accept a packet) or buffer overflow rather than errors in the network.

Security ◊ Chapter 7 sets out the requirements and techniques for achieving security in distributed systems. The first level of defence adopted by most organizations is to protect its networks and the computers attached to them with a *firewall*. A firewall creates a protection boundary between the organization's intranet and the rest of the Internet. The purpose of the firewall is to protect the resources in all of the computers inside the organization from access by external users or processes and to control the use of resources outside the firewall by users inside the organization.

A firewall runs on a gateway – a computer that stand at the network entry point to an organization's intranet. The firewall receives and filters all of the messages travelling into and out of an organization. It is configured according to the organization's security policy to allow certain incoming and outgoing messages to pass through it and to reject all others. We shall return to this topic in Section 3.4.8.

To enable distributed applications to move beyond the restrictions imposed by firewalls there is a need to produce a secure network environment in which a wide range of distributed applications can be deployed, with end-to-end authentication, privacy and security. This finer-grained and more flexible form of security can be achieved through the use of cryptographic techniques. It is usually applied at a level above the communication subsystem and hence is not dealt with here but in Chapter 7. Exceptions include the need to protect network components such as routers against unauthorized interference with their operation and the need for secure links to mobile devices and other external nodes to enable them to participate in a secure intranet – the *virtual private network* (VPN) concept, discussed in Section 3.4.8.

Mobility ◊ Mobile devices such as laptop computers, PDAs and Internet-capable mobile phones are moved frequently between locations and reconnected at convenient network connection points or even used while on the move. Wireless networks provide connectivity to such devices, but the addressing and routing schemes of the Internet were developed before the advent of these mobile devices and are not well-adapted to their need for intermittent connection to many different subnets. The Internet mechanisms have been adapted and extended to support mobility, but the expected future growth in the use of mobile devices will demand further development.

Quality of service ◊ In Chapter 2, we defined quality of service as the ability to meet deadlines when transmitting and processing streams of real-time multimedia data. This imposes major new requirements on computer networks. Applications that transmit multimedia data require guaranteed bandwidth and bounded latencies for the communication channels that they use. Some applications vary their demands dynamically and specify both a minimum acceptable quality of service and a desired optimum. The provision of such guarantees and their maintenance is the subject of Chapter 17.

Multicasting ◊ Most communication in distributed systems is between pairs of processes, but there often is also a need for one-to-many communication. While this can be simulated by *sends* to several destinations, that is more costly than necessary, and may not exhibit the fault-tolerance characteristics required by applications. For these reasons, many network technologies support the simultaneous transmission of messages to several recipients.

3.2 Types of network

Here we introduce the main types of network that are used to support distributed systems: *personal area networks*, *local area networks*, *wide area networks*, *metropolitan area networks* and the wireless variants of them. *Internetworks* such as the Internet are constructed from networks of all these types. Figure 3.1 shows the performance characteristics of the various types of network discussed below.

Some of the names used to refer to types of networks are confusing because they seem to refer to the physical extent (local area, wide area), but they also identify physical transmission technologies and low-level protocols. These are different for local and wide area networks, although some network technologies such as ATM (Asynchronous Transfer Mode) are suitable for both local and wide-area applications and some wireless networks also support local and metropolitan area transmission.

We refer to networks that are composed of many interconnected networks, integrated to provide a single data communication medium, as internetworks. The Internet is the prototypical internetwork; it is composed of millions of local, metropolitan and wide-area networks. We shall describe its implementation in some detail in Section 3.4.

Personal area networks (PANs) ◊ PANs are a sub-category of local networks in which the various digital devices carried by a user are connected by a low-cost, low energy network. Wired PANs are not of much significance because few users wish to be encumbered by a network of wires on their person, but wireless personal area networks (WPANs) are of increasing importance due to the number of personal devices such as mobile phones, PDAs, digital cameras, music players and so on that are now carried by many people. We describe the Bluetooth WPAN in Section 3.5.3.

Local area networks (LANs) ◊ LANs carry messages at relatively high speeds between computers connected by a single communication medium, such as twisted copper wire, coaxial cable or optical fibre. A *segment* is a section of cable that serves a department or a floor of a building and may have many computers attached. No routing of messages is required within a segment, since the medium provides direct connections between all of the computers connected to it. The total system bandwidth is shared between the computers connected to a segment. Larger local networks, such as those that serve a

Figure 3.1   Network performance

	Example	*Range*	*Bandwidth (Mbps)*	*Latency (ms)*
Wired:				
LAN	Ethernet	1–2 kms	10–1000	1–10
WAN	IP routing	worldwide	0.010–600	100–500
MAN	ATM	2–50 kms	1–150	10
Internetwork	Internet	worldwide	0.5–600	100–500
Wireless:				
WPAN	Bluetooth (IEEE 802.15.1)	10–30m	0.5–2	5–20
WLAN	WiFi (IEEE 802.11)	0.15–1.5 km	2–54	5–20
WMAN	WiMAX (IEEE 802.16)	5–50 km	1.5–20	5–20
WWAN	GSM, 3G phone nets	worldwide	0.010–2	100–500

campus or an office building, are composed of many segments interconnected by switches or hubs (see Section 3.3.7). In local area networks, the total system bandwidth is high and latency is low, except when message traffic is very high.

Several local area technologies were developed in the 1970s – Ethernet, token rings and slotted rings. Each provides an effective and high-performance solution, but Ethernet emerged as the dominant technology for wired local area networks. It was originally produced in the early 1970s with a bandwidth of 10 Mbps (million bits per second) and extended to 100 Mbps and 1000 Mbps (1 gigabit per second) versions more recently. We describe the principles of operation of Ethernet networks in Section 3.5.1.

There is a very large installed base of local area networks, serving virtually all working environments that contain more than one or two personal computers or workstations. Their performance is generally adequate for the implementation of distributed systems and applications. Ethernet technology lacks the latency and bandwidth guarantees needed by many multimedia applications. ATM networks were developed to fill this gap, but their cost has inhibited their adoption in local area applications. Instead, high-speed Ethernets have been deployed in a switched mode that overcomes these drawbacks to a significant degree, though not as effectively as ATM.

Wide area networks (WANs) ◊ WANs carry messages at lower speeds between nodes that are often in different organizations and may be separated by large distances. They may be located in different cities, countries or continents. The communication medium is a set of communication circuits linking a set of dedicated computers called *routers*. They manage the communication network and route messages or packets to their destinations. In most networks, the routing operations introduce a delay at each point in the route, so the total latency for the transmission of a message depends on the route that it follows and the traffic loads in the various network segments that it traverses. In current networks these latencies can be as high as 0.1 to 0.5 seconds. The speed of electronic signals in most media is close to the speed of light, and this sets a lower bound on the transmission latency for long-distance networks. For example, the propagation delay for a signal to travel from Europe to Australia via a terrestrial link is approximately 0.13 seconds and signals via a geostationary satellite between any two points on the earth's surface are subject to a delay of approximately 0.20 seconds.

Bandwidths available across the Internet also vary widely. Speeds of up to 600 Mbps are available across some portions of the Internet but speeds of 1–10 Mbps are more typically experienced for bulk transfers of data.

Metropolitan area networks (MANs) ◊ This type of network is based on the high-bandwidth copper and fibre optic cabling recently installed in some towns and cities for the transmission of video, voice and other data over distances of up to 50 kilometres. A variety of technologies have been used to implement the routing of data in MANs, ranging from Ethernet to ATM.

The DSL (digital subscriber line) and cable modem connections now available in many countries are an example. DSL typically uses ATM switches (Section 3.5.4) located in telephone exchanges to route digital data onto twisted pairs of copper wire (using high-frequency signalling on the existing wiring used for telephone connections) to the subscriber's home or office at speeds in the range 0.25–8.0 Mbps. The use of twisted copper wire for DSL subscriber connections limits the range to about 5.5 km from the switch. Cable modem connections use analogue signalling on cable television networks to achieve speeds of 1.5 Mbps over coaxial cable with greater range than DSL.

Wireless local area networks (WLANs) ◊ WLANs are designed for use in place of wired LANs to provide connectivity for mobile devices or simply to remove the need for a wired infrastructure to connect computers within homes and office buildings to each other and the Internet. They are in widespread use in several variants of the IEEE 802.11 standard (WiFi) offering bandwidths of 10–100 Mbps over ranges up to 1.5 kilometres. Section 3.5.2 gives further information on their method of operation.

Wireless metropolitan area networks (WMANs) ◊ The IEEE 802.16 WiMAX standard is targeted at this class of network. It aims to provide an alternative to wired connections to home and office buildings and to supersede 802.11 WiFi networks in some applications.

Wireless wide area networks (WWANs) ◊ Most mobile phone networks are based on digital wireless network technologies such as the GSM (Global System for Mobile communication) standard, which is used in most countries of the world. Mobile phone networks are designed to operate over wide areas (typically entire countries or continents) through the use of cellular radio connections; their data transmission facilities therefore offer wide-area mobile connections to the Internet for portable devices. The cellular networks mentioned above offer relatively low data rates – 9.6 to 33 kbps, but the next 'third generation' of mobile phone networks is now available with data transmission rates in the range 128–384 kbps for cells of few kilometres radius and up to 2Mbps for smaller cells. Readers interested in digging more deeply than we are able to here into the rapidly-evolving technologies of mobile and wireless networks of all types are referred to Stojmenovic's excellent handbook [2002].

Internetworks ◊ An internetwork is a communication subsystem in which several networks are linked together to provide common data communication facilities that overlay the technologies and protocols of the individual component networks and the methods used for their interconnection.

Internetworks are needed for the development of extensible, open distributed systems. The openness characteristic of distributed systems implies that the networks used in distributed systems should be extensible to very large numbers of computers, whereas individual networks have restricted address spaces and some have performance limitations that are incompatible with their large-scale use. In internetworks, a variety of local and wide area network technologies can be integrated to provide the networking capacity needed by each group of users. Thus internetworks bring many of the benefits of open systems to the provision of communication in distributed systems.

Internetworks are constructed from a variety of component networks. They are interconnected by dedicated switching computers called *routers* and general-purpose computers called *gateways*, and an integrated communication subsystem is produced by a software layer that supports the addressing and transmission of data to computers throughout the internetwork. The result can be thought of as a 'virtual network' constructed by overlaying an internetwork layer on a communication medium that consists of the underlying networks, routers and gateways. The Internet is the major instance of internetworking, and its TCP/IP protocols are an example of the integration layer mentioned above.

Network errors ◊ An additional point of comparison not mentioned in Figure 3.1 is the frequency and types of failure that can be expected in the different types of network. The reliability of the underlying data transmission media is very high in all types except wireless networks, where packets are frequently lost due to external interference. But packets may be lost in all types of network due to processing delays and buffer overflow at switches and at the destination node and this is by far the most common cause of packet loss.

Packets may also be delivered in an order different from that in which they were transmitted. This arises only in networks where separate packets are individually routed – principally wide area networks. Duplicate copies of packets can be delivered; this is usually a consequence of an assumption by the sender that a packet has been lost. The packet is retransmitted and both the original and the retransmitted copy then turn up at the destination.

3.3   Network principles

The basis for all computer networks is the packet-switching technique first developed in the 1960s. This enables data packets addressed to different destinations to share a single communications link, unlike the circuit-switching technology that underlies convention-al telephony. Packets are queued in a buffer and transmitted when the link is available. Communication is asynchronous – messages arrive at their destination after a delay that varies depending upon the time that packets take to travel through the network.

3.3.1   Packet transmission

In most applications of computer networks the requirement is for the transmission of logical units of information or *messages* – sequences of data items of arbitrary length. But before a message is transmitted it is subdivided into *packets*. The simplest form of packet is a sequence of binary data (an array of bits or bytes) of restricted length, together with addressing information sufficient to identify the source and destination computers. Packets of restricted length are used:

- so that each computer in the network can allocate sufficient buffer storage to hold the largest possible incoming packet;

- to avoid the undue delays that would occur in waiting for communication channels to become free if long messages were transmitted without subdivision.

3.3.2   Data streaming

We have already noted in Chapter 2 that multimedia applications rely upon the transmission of streams of audio and video data elements at guaranteed rates and with bounded latencies. Such streams differ substantially from the message-based type of traffic for which packet transmission was designed. The streaming of audio and video requires much higher bandwidths than most other forms of communication in distributed systems.

The transmission of a video stream for display in real time requires a bandwidth of about 1.5 Mbps if the data is compressed or 120 Mbps if uncompressed. In addition, the flow is continuous, as opposed to the intermittent traffic generated by typical client-server interactions. The *play time* of a multimedia element is the time at which it must be displayed (for a video element) or converted to sound (for a sound sample). For example, in a stream of video frames with a frame rate of 24 frames per second, frame N has a play time that is $N/24$ seconds after the stream's start time. Elements that arrive at their destination later than their play time are no longer useful and will be dropped by the receiving process.

The timely delivery of such data streams depends upon the availability of connections with guaranteed quality of service – bandwidth, latency and reliability must all be guaranteed. What is required is the ability to establish a channel from the source to the destination of a multimedia stream, with a predefined route through the network and a reserved set of resources at each node through which it will travel and buffering where appropriate to smooth any irregularities in the flow of data through the channel. Data can then be passed through the channel from sender to receiver at the required rate.

ATM networks (Section 3.5.4) are specifically designed to provide high bandwidths and low latencies and to support quality of service by the reservation of network resources. IPv6, the new network protocol for the Internet outlined in Section 3.4.4, includes features that enable each of the IP packets in a real-time stream to be identified and treated separately from other data at the network level.

Communication subsystems that provide quality of service guarantees require facilities for the pre-allocation of network resources and the enforcement of the allocations. The Resource Reservation Protocol (RSVP) [Zhang *et al.* 1993] enables applications to negotiate the pre-allocation of bandwidth for real-time data streams. The Real Time Transport Protocol (RTP) [Schulzrinne *et al.* 1996] is an application-level data transfer protocol that includes details of the play time and other timing requirements in each packet. The availability of effective implementations of these protocols on the Internet will depend upon substantial changes to the transport and network layers. Chapter 17 discusses the needs of distributed multimedia applications in detail.

3.3.3   Switching schemes

A network consists of a set of nodes connected together by circuits. To transmit information between two arbitrary nodes, a switching system is required. Here we define the four types of switching that are used in computer networking.

Broadcast ◊ Broadcasting is a transmission technique that involves no switching. Everything is transmitted to every node, and it is up to potential receivers to notice transmissions addressed to them. Some LAN technologies, including Ethernet, are based on broadcasting. Wireless networking is necessarily based on broadcasting, but in the absence of fixed circuits the broadcasts are arranged to reach nodes grouped in *cells*.

Circuit switching ◊ At one time telephone networks were the only telecommunication networks. Their operation was simple to understand: when a caller dialled a number, the pair of wires from her phone to the local exchange was connected by an automatic switch at the exchange to the pair of wires connected to the other party's phone. For a long-distance call the process was similar but the connection would be switched through a number of intervening exchanges to its destination. This system is sometimes referred to as the plain old telephone system, or POTS. It is a typical *circuit-switching network*.

Packet switching ◊ The advent of computers and digital technology brought many new possibilities for telecommunication. At the most basic level, it brought processing and storage. These made it possible to construct communication networks in a quite different way. This new type of communication network is called a *store-and-forward network*. Instead of making and breaking connections to build circuits, a store-and-forward network just forwards packets from their source to their destination. There is a computer at each switching node (wherever several circuits need to be interconnected). Each packet arriving at a node is first stored in memory at the node and then processed by a program that transmits it on an outgoing circuit that will transfer the packet to another node that is closer to its ultimate destination.

There is nothing really new in this idea: the postal system is a store-and-forward network for letters with the processing done by humans or machinery at sorting offices. But in a computer network packets can be stored and processed fast enough to give an illusion of instantaneous transmission even though the packet has to be routed through many nodes.

Frame relay ◊ In reality it takes anything from a few tens of microseconds to a few milliseconds to switch a packet in a store-and-forward network through each network node. This switching delay depends on the packet size, hardware speed and the quantity of other traffic, but its lower bound is determined by the network bandwidth, since the entire packet must be received before it can be forwarded to another node. Much of the Internet is based on store-and-forward switching, and as we have already seen, even short Internet packets typically take up to 200 milliseconds to reach their destinations. Delays of this magnitude are too long for real-time applications such as telephony and video conferencing, where delays of less than 50 milliseconds are needed to sustain high-quality conversation.

The *frame relay* switching method brings some of the advantages of circuit switching to packet-switching networks. They overcome the delay problems by switching small packets (called frames) on the fly. The switching nodes (which are usually special-purpose parallel digital processors) route frames based on the examination of their first few bits; frames as a whole are not stored at nodes but pass through them as short streams of bits. ATM networks are a prime example; we describe their operation in Section 3.5.4. High-speed ATM networks can transmit packets across networks consisting of many nodes in a few tens of microseconds.

3.3.4 Protocols

The term *protocol* is used to refer to a well-known set of rules and formats to be used for communication between processes in order to perform a given task. The definition of a protocol has two important parts to it:

- a specification of the sequence of messages that must be exchanged;
- a specification of the format of the data in the messages.

Figure 3.2   Conceptual layering of protocol software

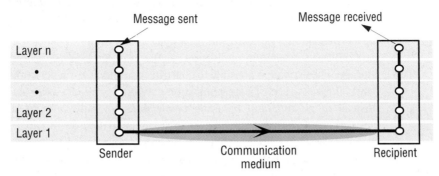

The existence of well-known protocols enables the separate software components of distributed systems to be developed independently and implemented in different programming languages on computers that may have different order codes and data representations.

A protocol is implemented by a pair of software modules located in the sending and receiving computers. For example, a *transport protocol* transmits messages of any length from a sending process to a receiving process. A process wishing to transmit a message to another process issues a call to a transport protocol module, passing it a message in the specified format. The transport software then concerns itself with the transmission of the message to its destination, subdividing it into packets of some specified size and format that can be transmitted to the destination via the *network protocol* – another, lower-level protocol. The corresponding transport protocol module in the receiving computer receives the packet via the network-level protocol module and performs inverse transformations to regenerate the message before passing it to a receiving process.

Protocol layers ◊ Network software is arranged in a hierarchy of layers. Each layer presents an interface to the layers above it that extends the properties of the underlying communication system. A layer is represented by a module in every computer connected to the network. Figure 3.2 illustrates the structure and the flow of data when a message is transmitted using a layered protocol. Each module appears to communicate directly with a module at the same level in another computer in the network, but in reality data is not transmitted directly between the protocol modules at each level. Instead, each layer of network software communicates by local procedure calls with the layers above and below it.

On the sending side, each layer (except the topmost, or *application layer*) accepts items of data in a specified format from the layer above it and applies transformations to encapsulate the data in the format specified for that layer before passing it to the layer below for further processing. Figure 3.3 illustrates this process as it applies to the top four layers of the OSI protocol suite. The figure shows the packet headers that hold most network-related data items, but for clarity it omits the trailers that are present in some types of packet; it also assumes that the application-layer message to be transmitted is shorter than the underlying network's maximum packet size. If not, then it would have to be encapsulated in several network-layer packets. On the receiving side, the converse

Figure 3.3   Encapsulation as it is applied in layered protocols

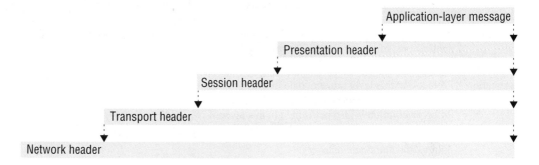

transformations are applied to data items received from the layer below before they are passed to the layer above. The protocol type of the layer above is included in the header of each layer, to enable the protocol stack at the receiver to select the correct software components to unpack the packets.

Thus each layer provides a service to the layer above it and extends the service provided by the layer below it. At the bottom is a *physical layer*. This is implemented by a communication medium (copper or fibre optic cables, satellite communication channels or radio transmission) and by analogue signalling circuits that place signals on the communication medium at the sending node and sense them at the receiving node. At receiving nodes data items are received and passed upwards through the hierarchy of software modules, transformed at each stage until they are in a form that can be passed to the intended recipient process.

Protocol suites ◊ A complete set of protocol layers is referred to as a *protocol suite* or a *protocol stack*, reflecting the layered structure. Figure 3.4 shows a protocol stack that conforms to the seven-layer Reference Model for *open systems interconnection (OSI)* adopted by the International Organization for Standardization (ISO) [ISO 1992]. The

Figure 3.4   Protocol layers in the ISO *Open Systems Interconnection (OSI)* protocol model

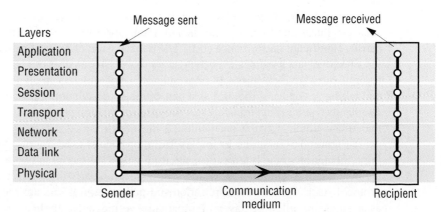

Figure 3.5   OSI protocol summary

Layer	Description	Examples
Application	Protocols that are designed to meet the communication requirements of specific applications, often defining the interface to a service.	HTTP, FTP, SMTP, CORBA IIOP
Presentation	Protocols at this level transmit data in a network representation that is independent of the representations used in individual computers, which may differ. Encryption is also performed in this layer, if required.	TLS security, CORBA Data Rep.
Session	At this level reliability and adaptation are performed, such as detection of failures and automatic recovery.	SIP
Transport	This is the lowest level at which messages (rather than packets) are handled. Messages are addressed to communication ports attached to processes. Protocols in this layer may be connection-oriented or connectionless.	TCP, UDP
Network	Transfers data packets between computers in a specific network. In a WAN or an internetwork this involves the generation of a route passing through routers. In a single LAN no routing is required.	IP, ATM virtual circuits
Data link	Responsible for transmission of packets between nodes that are directly connected by a physical link. In a WAN transmission is between pairs of routers or between routers and hosts. In a LAN it is between any pair of hosts.	Ethernet MAC, ATM cell transfer, PPP
Physical	The circuits and hardware that drive the network. It transmits sequences of binary data by analogue signalling, using amplitude or frequency modulation of electrical signals (on cable circuits), light signals (on fibre optic circuits) or other electromagnetic signals (on radio and microwave circuits).	Ethernet baseband signalling, ISDN

OSI Reference Model was adopted in order to encourage the development of protocol standards that would meet the requirements of open systems.

The purpose of each level in the OSI Reference Model is summarized in Figure 3.5. As its name implies, it is a framework for the definition of protocols and not a definition for a specific suite of protocols. Protocol suites that conform to the OSI model must include at least one specific protocol at each of the seven levels that the model defines.

Protocol layering brings substantial benefits in simplifying and generalizing the software interfaces for access to the communication services of networks, but it also carries significant performance costs. The transmission of an application-level message via a protocol stack with N layers typically involves N transfers of control to the relevant layer of software in the protocol suite, at least one of which is an operating system entry, and taking N copies of the data as a part of the encapsulation mechanism. All of these overheads result in data transfer rates between application processes that are much lower than the available network bandwidth.

Figure 3.5 includes examples from protocols used in the Internet, but the implementation of the Internet does not follow the OSI model in two respects. First, the application, presentation and session layers are not clearly distinguished in the Internet protocol stack. Instead, the application and presentation layers are implemented either as a single middleware layer or separately within each application. Thus CORBA

Figure 3.6   Internetwork layers

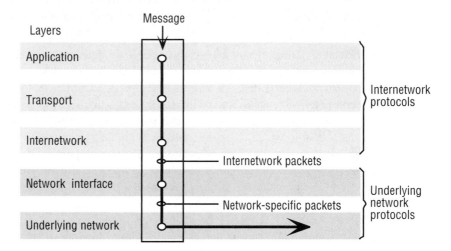

implements inter-object invocations and data representations in a middleware library that is included in each application process (see Chapter 20 for further details on CORBA). Web browsers and other applications that require secure channels employ the Secure Sockets Layer (Chapter 7) as a procedure library in a similar manner.

Second, the session layer is integrated with the transport layer. Internetwork protocol suites include an application layer, a transport layer and an *internetwork layer*. The internetwork layer is a 'virtual' network layer that is responsible for transmitting internetwork packets to a destination computer. An *internetwork packet* is the unit of data transmitted over an internetwork.

Internetwork protocols are overlaid on underlying networks as illustrated in Figure 3.6. The *network interface* layer accepts internetwork packets and converts them into packets suitable for transmission by the network layers of each underlying network.

Packet assembly ◊ The task of dividing messages into packets before transmission and reassembling them at the receiving computer is usually performed in the transport layer.

The network-layer protocol packets consist of a *header* and a *data field*. In most network technologies, the data field is variable in length, with maximum length called the *maximum transfer unit* (MTU). If the length of a message exceeds the MTU of the underlying network layer, it must be fragmented into chunks of the appropriate size, with sequence numbers for use on reassembly, and transmitted in multiple packets. For example, the MTU for Ethernets is 1500 bytes – no more than that quantity of data can be transmitted in a single Ethernet packet.

Although the IP protocol stands in the position of a network layer protocol in the Internet suite of protocols, its MTU is unusually large at 64 kbytes, (8 kbytes is often used in practice because some nodes are unable to handle such large packets). Whichever MTU value is adopted for IP packets, packets larger than the Ethernet MTU can arise and they must be fragmented for transmission over Ethernets.

Ports ◊ The transport layer's task is to provide a network-independent message transport service between pairs of network *ports*. Ports are software-defined destination points at a host computer. They are attached to processes, enabling data transmission to be addressed to a specific process at a destination node. Here we discuss the addressing of ports as they are implemented in the Internet and most other networks. Chapter 4 describes their programming.

Addressing ◊   The transport layer is responsible for delivering messages to destinations with *transport addresses* that are composed of the *network address* of a host computer and a *port number*. A network address is a numeric identifier that uniquely identifies a host computer and enables it to be located by nodes that are responsible for routing data to it. In the Internet every host computer is assigned an IP number, which identifies it and the subnet to which it is connected, enabling data to be routed to it from any other node as described in the following sections. In Ethernets there are no routing nodes; each host is responsible for recognizing and picking up packets addressed to it.

Well-known Internet services such as HTTP or FTP have been allocated *contact port numbers* and these are registered with a central authority (the Internet Assigned Numbers Authority (IANA) [www.iana.org]). To access a service at a given host, a request is sent to the relevant port at the host. Some services, such as FTP (contact port: 21), then allocate a new port (with a private number) and send the number of the new port to the client. The client uses the new port for the remainder of a transaction or a session. Other services, such as HTTP (contact port: 80), transact all of their business through the contact port.

Port numbers below 1023 are defined as *well-known ports* whose use is restricted to privileged processes in most operating systems. The ports between 1024 and 49151 are *registered ports* for which IANA holds service descriptions and the remaining ports up to 65535 are available for private purposes. In practice all of the ports above 1023 can be used for private purposes but computers using them for private purposes cannot simultaneously access the corresponding registered services.

A fixed port number allocation does not provide an adequate basis for the development of distributed systems which often include a multiplicity of servers including dynamically-allocated ones. Solutions to this problem involve the dynamic allocation of ports to services and the provision of binding mechanisms to enable clients to locate services and their ports using symbolic names. Some of these are discussed further in Chapter 5.

Packet delivery ◊   There are two approaches to the delivery of packets by the network layer:

Datagram packet delivery: The term 'datagram' refers to the similarity of this delivery mode to the way in which letters and telegrams are delivered. The essential feature of datagram networks is that the delivery of each packet is a 'one-shot' process; no setup is required and once the packet is delivered the network retains no information about it. In a datagram network a sequence of packets transmitted by a single host to a single destination may follow different routes (if, for example, the network is capable of adaptation to handle failures or to mitigate the effects of localized congestion) and when this occurs they may arrive out of sequence.

Every datagram packet contains the full network address of the source and destination hosts; the latter is an essential parameter for the routing process, as we describe it in the next section. Datagram delivery is the concept on which packet networks were originally based and it can be found in most of the computer networks in use today. The Internet's network layer – IP – the Ethernet and most wired and wireless local network technologies are based on datagram delivery.

Virtual circuit packet delivery: Some network-level services implement packet transmission in a manner that is analogous to a telephone network. A virtual circuit must be set up before packets can pass from a source host A to destination host B. The establishment of a virtual circuit involves the identification of a route from the source to the destination, possibly passing through several intermediate nodes. At each node along the route a table entry is made, indicating which link should be used for the next stage of the route.

Once a virtual circuit has been set up, it can be used to transmit any number of packets. Each network-layer packet contains only a virtual circuit number in place of the source and destination addresses. The addresses are not needed, because packets are routed at intermediate nodes by reference to the virtual circuit number. When a packet reaches its destination the source can be determined from the virtual circuit number.

The analogy with telephone networks should not be taken too literally. In the POTS a telephone call results in the establishment of a physical circuit from the caller to the callee, and the voice links from which it is constructed are reserved for their exclusive use. In virtual circuit packet delivery the circuits are represented only by table entries in routing nodes, and the links along which the packets are routed are used only for the time taken to transmit a packet; they are free for other uses for the rest of the time. A single link may therefore be employed in many separate virtual circuits. The most important virtual circuit network technology in current use is ATM; we have already mentioned (in Section 3.3.3) that it benefits from lower latencies for the transmission of individual packets; this is a direct result of its use of virtual circuits. The requirement for a setup phase does, however, result in a short delay before any packets can be sent to a new destination.

The distinction between datagram and virtual circuit packet delivery in the network layer should not be confused with a similarly-named pair of mechanisms in the transport layer – connectionless and connection-oriented transmission. We shall describe these in Section 3.4.6 in the context of the Internet transport protocols, UDP (connectionless) and TCP (connection-oriented). Here we simply note that each of these modes of transmission can be implemented over either type of network layer.

3.3.5   Routing

Routing is a function that is required in all networks except those LANs, such as the Ethernet, that provide direct connections between all pairs of attached hosts. In large networks, *adaptive routing* is employed: the best route for communication between two points in the network is re-evaluated periodically, taking into account the current traffic in the network and any faults such as broken connections or routers.

The delivery of packets to their destinations in a network such as the one shown in Figure 3.7 is the collective responsibility of the routers located at connection points. Unless the source and destination hosts are on the same LAN, the packet has to be transmitted in a series of hops, passing through router nodes. The determination of

Figure 3.7   Routing in a wide area network

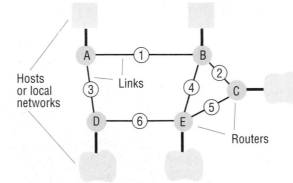

routes for the transmission of packets to their destinations is the responsibility of a *routing algorithm* – implemented by a program in the network layer at each node.

A routing algorithm has two parts:

1. It must make decisions that determine the route taken by each packet as it travels through the network. In circuit-switched network layers such as X.25 and frame-relay networks such as ATM the route is determined whenever a virtual circuit or connection is established. In packet-switched network layers such as IP it is determined separately for each packet, and the algorithm must be particularly simple and efficient if it is not to degrade network performance.

2. It must dynamically update its knowledge of the network based on traffic monitoring and the detection of configuration changes or failures. This activity is less time-critical; slower and more computation-intensive techniques can be used.

Both of these activities are distributed throughout the network. The routing decisions are made on a hop-by-hop basis, using locally held information to determine the next hop to be taken by each incoming packet. The locally held routing information is updated periodically by an algorithm that distributes information about the states of the links (their loads and failure status).

A simple routing algorithm ◊ The algorithm that we describe here is a 'distance vector' algorithm. This will provide a basis for the discussion in Section 3.4.3 of the *link-state* algorithm that has been used since 1979 as the main routing algorithm in the Internet. Routing in networks is an instance of the problem of path finding in graphs. Bellman's shortest path algorithm, published well before computer networks were developed [Bellman 1957], provides the basis for the distance vector method. Bellman's method was converted into a distributed algorithm suitable for implementation in large networks by Ford and Fulkerson [1962], and protocols based on their work are often referred to as 'Bellman–Ford' protocols.

Figure 3.8 shows the routing tables that would be held at each of the routers for the network of Figure 3.7, assuming that the network has no failed links or routers. Each row provides the routing information for packets addressed to a given destination. The *link* field specifies the outgoing link for packets addressed to the destination. The *cost*

Figure 3.8   Routing tables for the network in Figure 3.7

Routings from A		
To	Link	Cost
A	local	0
B	1	1
C	1	2
D	3	1
E	1	2

Routings from B		
To	Link	Cost
A	1	1
B	local	0
C	2	1
D	1	2
E	4	1

Routings from C		
To	Link	Cost
A	2	2
B	2	1
C	local	0
D	5	2
E	5	1

Routings from D		
To	Link	Cost
A	3	1
B	3	2
C	6	2
D	local	0
E	6	1

Routings from E		
To	Link	Cost
A	4	2
B	4	1
C	5	1
D	6	1
E	local	0

field is simply a calculation of the vector distance, or the number of hops to the given destination. For store-and-forward networks with links of similar bandwidth this gives a reasonable estimate of the time for a packet to travel to the destination. The cost information stored in the routing tables is not used during packet-routing actions taken by part 1 of the routing algorithm, but it is required for the routing table construction and maintenance actions in part 2.

The routing tables contain a single entry for each possible destination, showing the next *hop* that a packet must take towards its destination. When a packet arrives at a router the destination address is extracted and looked up in the local routing table. The resulting entry in the routing table identifies the outgoing link that should be used to route the packet onwards towards its destination.

For example, when a packet addressed to C is submitted to the router at A, the router examines the entry for C in its routing table. It shows that the packet should be routed outwards from A on the link labelled 1. The packet arrives at B and the same procedure is followed using the routing table at B, which shows that the onward route to C is via the link labelled 2. When the packet arrives at C the routing table entry shows 'local' instead of a link number. This indicates that the packet should be delivered to a local host.

Now let us consider how the routing tables are built up and how they are maintained when faults occur in the network. That is, how part 2 of the routing algorithm described above is performed. Because each routing table specifies only a single hop for each route, the construction or repair of the routing information can proceed in a distributed fashion. A router exchanges information about the network with its neighbouring nodes by sending a summary of its routing table using a *router*

Figure 3.9   Pseudo-code for RIP routing algorithm

Send: Each *t* seconds or when *Tl* changes, send *Tl* on each non-faulty outgoing link.

Receive. Whenever a routing table *Tr* is received on link *n*:

```
for all rows Rr in Tr {
    if (Rr.link ≠ n) {
        Rr.cost = Rr.cost + 1;
        Rr.link = n;
        if (Rr.destination is not in Tl) add Rr to Tl;   // add new destination to Tl
        else for all rows Rl in Tl {
            if (Rr.destination = Rl.destination and
                (Rr.cost < Rl.cost or Rl.link = n)) Rl = Rr;
            // Rr.cost < Rl.cost : remote node has better route
            // Rl.link = n : remote node is more authoritative
        }
    }
}
```

information protocol (RIP). The RIP actions performed at a router are described informally as follows:

1. *Periodically, and whenever the local routing table changes,* send the table (in a summary form) to all accessible neighbours. That is, send an RIP packet containing a copy of the table on each non-faulty outgoing link.

2. *When a table is received from a neighbouring router,* if the received table shows a route to a new destination, or a better (lower cost) route to an existing destination, then update the local table with the new route. If the table was received on link *n* and it gives a different cost than the local table for a route that begins with link *n*, then replace the cost in the local table with the new cost. This is done because the new table was received from a router that is closer to the relevant destination and is therefore always more authoritative for routes that pass through it.

This algorithm is more precisely described by the pseudo-code program shown in Figure 3.9, where *Tr* is a table received from another router and *Tl* is the local table. Ford and Fulkerson [1962] have shown that the steps described above are sufficient to ensure that the routing tables will converge on the best routes to each destination whenever there is a change in the network. The frequency *t* with which routing tables are propagated, even when no changes have occurred, is designed to ensure that stability is maintained, for example, in the case that some RIP packets are lost. The value for *t* adopted throughout the Internet is 30 seconds.

To deal with faults, each router monitors its links and acts as follows:

When a faulty link n is detected, set *cost* to ∞ for all entries in the local table that refer to the faulty link and perform the *Send* action.

Thus the information that the link is broken is represented by an infinite value for the cost to the relevant destinations. When this information is propagated to neighbouring nodes it will be processed according to the *Receive* action (note $\infty+1 = \infty$) and then propagated further until a node is reached that has a working route to the relevant destinations, if one exists. The node that still has a working route will eventually propagate its table, and the working route will replace the faulty one at all nodes.

The vector-distance algorithm can be improved in various ways: costs (also known as the *metric*) can be based on the actual bandwidths of the links; the algorithm can be modified to increase its speed of convergence and to avoid some undesirable intermediate states, such as loops, that may occur before convergence is achieved. A routing information protocol with these enhancements was the first routing protocol used in the Internet, now known as RIP-1 and described in RFC 1058 [Hedrick 1988]. But the solutions for the problems caused by slow convergence are not totally effective, and this leads to inefficient routing and packet loss while the network is in intermediate states.

Subsequent developments in routing algorithms have been in the direction of increasing the amount of knowledge of the network that is held at each node. The most important family of algorithms of this type are known as *link-state algorithms*. They are based on the distribution and updating of a database at each node that represents all, or a substantial portion, of the network. Each node is then responsible for computing the optimum routes to the destinations shown in its database. This computation can be performed by a variety of algorithms, some of which avoid known problems in the Bellman–Ford algorithm such as slow convergence and undesirable intermediate states. The design of routing algorithms is a substantial topic and our discussion of it here is necessarily limited. We return to it in Section 3.4.3 with a description of the operation of the RIP-1 algorithm, one of the first used for IP routing and still in use in many parts of the Internet. For extensive coverage of routing in the Internet, see Huitema [2000] and for further material on routing algorithms in general see Tanenbaum [2003].

3.3.6 Congestion control

The capacity of a network is limited by the performance of its communication links and switching nodes. When the load at any particular link or node approaches its capacity, queues will build up at hosts trying to send packets and at intermediate nodes holding packets whose onward transmission is blocked by other traffic. If the load continues at the same high level, the queues will continue to grow until they reach the limit of available buffer space.

Once this state is reached at a node, the node has no option but to drop further incoming packets. As we have already noted, the occasional loss of packets at the network level is acceptable and can be remedied by retransmission initiated at higher levels. But if the rate of loss of packets and retransmission reach a substantial level, the effect on the throughput of the network can be devastating. It is easy to see why this is the case: if packets are dropped at intermediate nodes, the network resources that they have already consumed are wasted and the resulting retransmissions will require a similar quantity of resources to reach the same point in the network. As a rule of thumb, when the load on a network exceeds 80% of its capacity, the total throughput tends to drop as a result of packet losses unless usage of heavily loaded links is controlled.

Instead of allowing packets to travel through the network until they reach over-congested nodes, where they will have to be dropped, it would be better to hold them at earlier nodes until the congestion is reduced. This will result in increased delays for packets but will not significantly degrade the total throughput of the network. *Congestion control* is the name given to techniques that are designed to achieve this.

In general, congestion control is achieved by informing nodes along a route that congestion has occurred, and their rate of packet transmission should therefore be reduced. For intermediate nodes, this will result in the buffering of incoming packets for a longer period. For hosts that are sources of the packets, the result may be to queue packets before transmission or to block the application process that is generating them until the network can handle them.

All datagram-based network layers including IP and Ethernets rely on the end-to-end control of traffic. That is, the sending node must reduce the rate at which it transmits packets based only on information that it receives from the receiver. Congestion information may be supplied to the sending node by explicit transmission of special messages (called *choke packets*) requesting a reduction in transmission rate, or by the implementation of a specific transmission control protocol (from which TCP derives its name – Section 3.4.6 explains the mechanism used in TCP) or by observing the occurrence of dropped packets (if the protocol is one in which each packet is acknowledged).

In some virtual circuit-based networks, congestion information can be received and acted on at each node. Although ATM uses virtual circuit delivery, it relies on quality of service management (see Section 3.5.4 and Chapter 17) to ensure that each circuit can carry the required traffic.

3.3.7   Internetworking

There are many network technologies with different network, link and physical layer protocols. Local networks are built from Ethernet and ATM technologies, wide area networks are built over analogue and digital telephone networks of various types, satellite links and wide-area ATM networks. Individual computers and local networks are linked to the Internet or intranets by modems, wireless and DSL connections.

To build an integrated network (an *internetwork*) we must integrate many subnets, each of which is based on one of these network technologies. To make this possible, the following are needed:

1. A unified internetwork addressing scheme that enables packets to be addressed to any host connected to any subnet.

2. A protocol defining the format of internetwork packets and giving rules according to which they are handled.

3. Interconnecting components that route packets to their destinations in terms of internetwork addresses, transmitting the packets using subnets with a variety of network technologies.

For the Internet, (1) is provided by IP addresses, (2) is the IP protocol and (3) is performed by the components called *Internet Routers*. The IP protocol and IP addressing

Figure 3.10   Simplified view of the QMUL Computer Science network (in mid-2000)

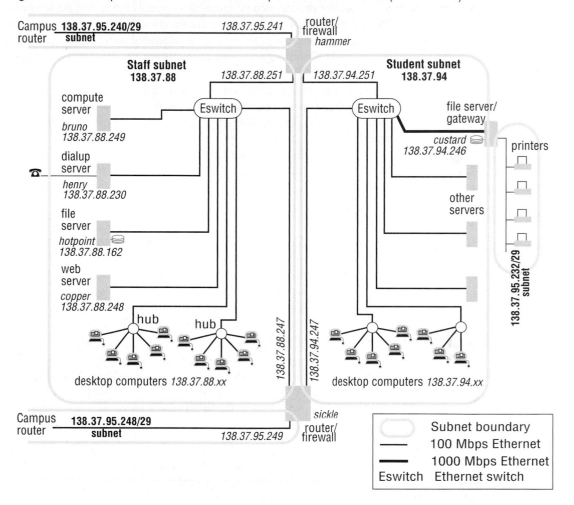

are described in some detail in Section 3.4. Here we shall describe the functions of Internet routers and some other components that are used to link networks together.

Figure 3.10 shows a small part of the intranet located at Queen Mary College at the University of London (QMUL), as it was in mid-2000. Many of the details shown will be explained in later sections. Here we note that the portion shown in the figure comprises several subnets interconnected by routers. There are five subnets; three of which share the IP network 138.37.95 (using the classless interdomain routing scheme described in Section 3.4.3). The numbers in the diagram are IP addresses; their structure will be explained in Section 3.4.1. The routers in the diagram are members of multiple subnets and have an IP address for each subnet, shown against the connecting links.

The routers (host names: *hammer* and *sickle*) are, in fact, general-purpose computers that also fulfil other purposes. One of those purposes is to serve as firewalls; the role of a firewall is closely linked with the routing function, as we shall describe below. The 138.37.95.232/29 subnet is not connected to the rest of the network at the IP level. Only the file server *custard* can access it to provide a printing service on the attached printers via a server process that monitors and controls the use of the printers.

All of the links in Figure 3.10 are Ethernets. The bandwidth of most of them is 100 Mbps, but one is 1000 Mbps because it carries a large volume of traffic between a large number of computers used by students and *custard*, the file server that holds all of their files.

There are two Ethernet switches and several Ethernet hubs in the portion of the network illustrated. Both types of component are transparent to IP packets. An Ethernet hub is simply a means of connecting together several segments of Ethernet cable, all of which form a single Ethernet at the network protocol level. All of the Ethernet packets received by the host are relayed to all of the segments. An Ethernet switch connects several Ethernets, routing the incoming packets only to the Ethernet to which the destination host is connected.

Routers ◊ We have noted that routing is required in all networks except those such as Ethernets and wireless networks, in which all of the hosts are connected by a single transmission medium. Figure 3.7 shows such a network with five routers connected by six links. In an internetwork, the routers may be linked by direct connections, as is shown in Figure 3.7, or they may be interconnected through subnets, as shown for *custard* in Figure 3.10. In both cases, the routers are responsible for forwarding the internetwork packets that arrive on any connection to the correct outgoing connection as explained above. They maintain routing tables for that purpose.

Bridges ◊ Bridges link networks of different types. Some bridges link several networks, and these are referred to as bridge/routers because they also perform routing functions. For example, the campus network at QMW includes a Fibre Distributed Data Interface FDDI backbone (not shown on Figure 3.10), and this is linked to the Ethernet subnets in the figure by bridge/routers.

Hubs ◊ Hubs are simply a convenient means of connecting hosts and extending segments of Ethernet and other broadcast local network technologies. They have a number of sockets (typically 4–64), to each of which a host computer can be connected. They can also be used to overcome the distance limitations on single segments and provide a means of adding additional hosts.

Switches ◊ Switches perform a similar function to routers, but for local networks (normally Ethernets) only. That is, they interconnect several separate Ethernets, routing the incoming packets to the appropriate outgoing network. They perform their task at the level of the Ethernet network protocol. When they start up they have no knowledge of the wider internetwork and build up routing tables by the observation of traffic, supplemented by broadcast requests when they lack information.

The advantage of switches over hubs is that they separate the incoming traffic and transmit it only on the relevant outgoing network, reducing congestion on the other networks to which they are connected.

Tunnelling ◊ Bridges and routers transmit internetwork packets over a variety of underlying networks by translating between their network-layer protocols and an internetwork protocol, but there is one situation in which the underlying network protocol can be hidden from the layers above it without the use of an internetwork protocol. A pair of nodes connected to separate networks of the same type can

Figure 3.11   Tunnelling for IPv6 migration

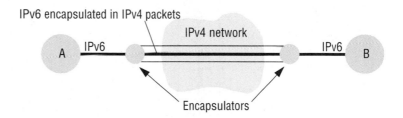

communicate through another type of network, they can do so by constructing a protocol 'tunnel'. A protocol tunnel is a software layer that transmits packets through an alien network environment.

The following analogy explains the reason for the choice of terminology and provides another way to think about tunnelling. A tunnel through a mountain enables a road to transport cars where it would otherwise be impossible. The road is continuous – the tunnel is transparent to the application (cars). The road is the transport mechanism, and the tunnel enables it to work in an alien environment.

Figure 3.11 illustrates the proposed use of tunnelling to support the migration of the Internet to the IPv6 protocol. IPv6 is intended to replace the version of IP currently in use, IPv4, and is incompatible with it. (Both IPv4 and IPv6 are described in Section 3.4.) During the period of transition to IPv6 there will be 'islands' of IPv6 networking in the sea of IPv4. In our illustration A and B are such islands. At the boundaries of islands IPv6 packets are encapsulated in IPv4 and transported over the intervening IPv4 networks in that manner.

For another example, MobileIP (described in Section 3.4.5) transmits IP packets to mobile hosts anywhere in the Internet by constructing a tunnel to them from their home base. The intervening network nodes do not need to be modified to handle the MobileIP protocol. The IP multicast protocol is handled in a similar way, relying on a few routers that support IP multicast routing to determine the routes, but transmitting IP packets through other routers using standard IP addresses. The PPP protocol for the transmission of IP packets over serial links provides yet another example.

3.4   Internet protocols

We describe here the main features of the TCP/IP suite of protocols and discuss their advantages and limitations when used in distributed systems.

The Internet emerged from two decades of research and development work on wide area networking in the USA, commencing in the early 1970s with the ARPANET – the first large-scale computer network development [Leiner *et al.* 1997]. An important part of that research was the development of the TCP/IP protocol suite. TCP stands for Transmission Control Protocol, IP for Internet Protocol. The widespread adoption of the TCP/IP and Internet application protocols in national research networks, and more recently in commercial networks in many countries, has enabled the national networks

Figure 3.12   TCP/IP layers

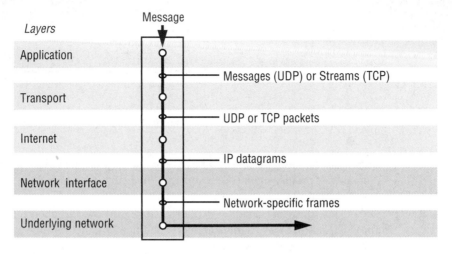

to be integrated into a single internetwork that has grown extremely rapidly to its present size, with more than 60 million hosts. Many application services and application-level protocols (shown in parentheses in the following list) now exist based on TCP/IP, including the Web (HTTP), email (SMTP, POP), netnews (NNTP), file transfer (FTP) and Telnet (telnet). TCP is a transport protocol; it can be used to support applications directly, or additional protocols can be layered on it to provide additional features. For example, HTTP is usually transported by the direct use of TCP, but when end-to-end security is required, the Transport Layer Security (TLS) protocol (described in Section 7.6.3) is layered on top of TCP to produce secure channels and HTTP messages are transmitted via the secure channels.

The Internet protocols were originally developed primarily to support simple wide-area applications such as file transfer and electronic mail, involving communication with relatively high latencies between geographically dispersed computers, but they turned out to be efficient enough to support the requirements of many distributed applications on both wide area and local networks and they are now almost universally used in distributed systems. The resulting standardization of communication protocols has brought immense benefits.

The general illustration of internetwork protocol layers of Figure 3.6 is translated into the specific Internet case in Figure 3.12. There are two transport protocols – TCP (Transport Control Protocol) and UDP (User Datagram Protocol). TCP is a reliable connection-oriented protocol, and UDP is a datagram protocol that does not guarantee reliable transmission. The Internet Protocol (IP) is the underlying 'network' protocol of the Internet virtual network – that is, IP datagrams provide the basic transmission mechanism for the Internet and other TCP/IP networks. We placed the word 'network' in quotation marks in the preceding sentence because it is not the only network layer involved in the implementation of Internet communication. This is because the Internet protocols are usually layered over another network technology, such as the Ethernet, which already provides a network layer that enables the computers attached to the same network to exchange datagrams. Figure 3.13 illustrated the encapsulation of packets that

Figure 3.13   Encapsulation as it occurs when a message is transmitted via TCP over an Ethernet

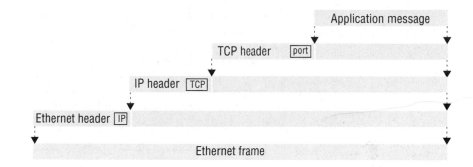

would occur for the transmission of a message via TCP over an underlying Ethernet. The tags in the headers are the protocol type for the layer above, needed for the receiving protocol stack to correctly unpack the packets. In the TCP layer, the receiver's port number serves a similar purpose, enabling the TCP software component at the receiving host to pass the message to a specific application-level process.

The TCP/IP specifications [Postel 1981a; 1981b] do not specify the layers below the Internet datagram layer – IP packets in the Internet layer are transformed into packets for transmission over almost any combination of underlying networks or data links.

For example, IP ran initially over the ARPANET, which consisted of hosts and an early version of routers (called PSEs) connected by long-distance data links. Today it is used over virtually every known network technology, including ATM, local area networks such as Ethernets, and token ring networks. IP is implemented over serial lines and telephone circuits via the PPP protocol [Parker 1992], enabling it to be used for communication with modem connections and other serial links.

The success of TCP/IP is based on their independence of the underlying transmission technology, enabling internetworks to be built up from many heterogeneous networks and data links. Users and application programs perceive a single virtual network supporting TCP and UDP and implementors of TCP and UDP see a single virtual IP network, hiding the diversity of the underlying transmission media. Figure 3.14 illustrates this view.

In the next two sections we describe the IP addressing scheme and the IP protocol. The Domain Name System which converts domain names such as *www.amazon.com, hpl.hp.com, stanford.edu* and *qmw.ac.uk,* with which Internet users are so familiar, into IP addresses, is introduced in Section 3.4.7 and described more fully in Chapter 9.

Figure 3.14   The programmer's conceptual view of a TCP/IP Internet

Application		Application
TCP		UDP
IP		

Figure 3.15   Internet address structure, showing field sizes in bits

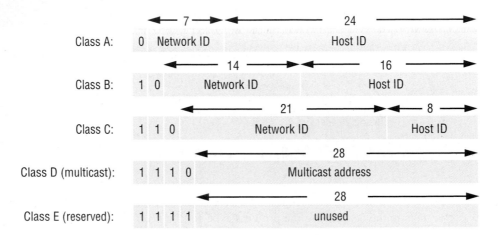

The version of IP in predominant use throughout the Internet is IPv4 (since January 1984), and that is the version that we shall describe in the next two sections. But the rapid growth in the use of the Internet led to the publication of a specification of a new version (IPv6) to overcome the addressing limitations of IPv4 and add features to support some new requirements. We describe IPv6 in Section 3.4.4. Because of the vast amount of software that will be affected, a gradual migration to IPv6 is planned over a period of ten years or more.

3.4.1   IP addressing

Perhaps the most challenging aspect of the design of the Internet protocols was the construction of schemes for naming and addressing hosts and for routing IP packets to their destinations. The scheme used for assigning host addresses to networks and the computers connected to them had to satisfy the following requirements:

- It must be *universal* – any host must be able to send packets to any other host in the Internet.

- It must be efficient in its use of the address space – it is impossible to predict the ultimate size of the Internet and the number of network and host addresses likely to be required. The address space must be carefully partitioned to ensure that addresses will not run out. In 1978–82, when the specifications for the TCP/IP protocols were being developed, provision for 2^{32} or approximately 4 billion addressable hosts (about the same as the population of the world at that time) was considered adequate. This judgement has proved to be short-sighted for two reasons:

  – the rate of growth of the Internet has far outstripped all predictions;

  – the address space has been allocated and used much less efficiently than expected.

Figure 3.16   Decimal representation of Internet addresses

	octet 1	octet 2	octet 3		Range of addresses
	Network ID		Host ID		
Class A:	1 to 127	0 to 255	0 to 255	0 to 255	1.0.0.0 to 127.255.255.255
	Network ID		Host ID		
Class B:	128 to 191	0 to 255	0 to 255	0 to 255	128.0.0.0 to 191.255.255.255
		Network ID		Host ID	
Class C:	192 to 223	0 to 255	0 to 255	1 to 254	192.0.0.0 to 223.255.255.255
		Multicast address			
Class D (multicast):	224 to 239	0 to 255	0 to 255	1 to 254	224.0.0.0 to 239.255.255.255
Class E (reserved):	240 to 255	0 to 255	0 to 255	1 to 254	240.0.0.0 to 255.255.255.255

- The addressing scheme must lend itself to the development of a flexible and efficient routing scheme, but the addresses themselves cannot contain very much of the information needed to route a packet to its destination.

The scheme chosen assigns an IP address to each host in the Internet – a 32-bit numeric identifier containing a network identifier, which uniquely identifies one of the subnetworks in the Internet, and a host identifier, which uniquely identifies the host's connection to that network. It is these addresses that are placed in IP packets and used to route them to their destinations.

The design adopted for Internet address space is shown in Figure 3.15. There are four allocated classes of Internet address – A, B, C and D. Class D is reserved for Internet multicast communication, which is implemented in only some Internet routers and is discussed further in Section 4.5.1. Class E contains a range of unallocated addresses, which are reserved for future requirements.

These 32-bit Internet addresses containing a network identifier and host identifier are usually written as a sequence of four decimal numbers separated by dots. Each decimal number represents one of the four bytes, or *octets* of the IP address. The permissible values for each class of network address are shown in Figure 3.16.

Three classes of address were designed to meet the requirements of different types of organization. The Class A addresses, with a capacity for 2^{24} hosts on each subnet, are reserved for very large networks such as the US NSFNet and other national wide area networks. Class B addresses are allocated to organizations that operate networks likely to contain more than 255 computers, and Class C addresses are allocated to all other network operators.

Internet addresses with host identifiers 0 and all 1s (binary) are used for special purposes. Addresses with host identifier set to 0 are used to refer to 'this host', and a host identifier that is all 1s is used to address a broadcast message to all of the hosts connected to the network specified in the network identifier part of the address.

Figure 3.17   IP packet layout

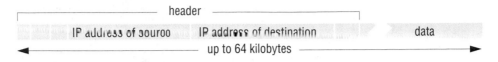

Network identifiers are allocated by the Internet Assigned Numbers Authority (IANA) to organizations with networks connected to the Internet. Host identifiers for the computers on each network connected to the Internet are assigned by the manager of the relevant network.

Since host addresses include a network identifier, any computer that is connected to more than one network must have separate addresses on each, and whenever a computer is moved to a different network, its Internet address must change. These requirements can lead to substantial administrative overheads, for example in the case of portable computers.

In practice, the IP address allocation scheme has not turned out to be very effective. The main difficulty is that network administrators in user organizations cannot easily predict future growth in their need for host addresses and they tend to overestimate, requesting Class B addresses when in doubt. Around 1990 it became evident that based on the rate of allocation at the time, IP addresses were likely to run out around 1996. Three steps were taken. The first was to initiate the development of a new IP protocol and addressing scheme, the result of which was the specification of IPv6.

The second step was to radically modify the way in which IP addresses were allocated. A new address allocation and routing scheme, designed to make more effective use of the IP address space, was introduced, called classless interdomain routing (CIDR). We describe CIDR in Section 3.4.3. The local network illustrated in Figure 3.10 includes several Class C-sized subnets in the range 138.37.88–138.37.95, linked by routers. The routers manage the delivery of IP packets to all of the subnets. They also handle traffic between the subnets and from the subnets to the rest of the world. The figure also illustrates the use of CIDR to subdivide a class B address space to produce several Class C-sized subnets.

The third step was to enable unregistered computers to access the Internet indirectly through routers that implement a Network Address Translation (NAT) scheme. We describe this scheme in Section 3.4.3.

3.4.2   The IP protocol

The IP protocol transmits datagrams from one host to another, if necessary via intermediate routers. The full IP packet format is rather complex, but Figure 3.17 shows the main components. There are several header fields, not shown in the diagram, that are used by the transmission and routing algorithms.

IP provides a delivery service that is described as offering *unreliable* or *best-effort* delivery semantics, because there is no guarantee of delivery. Packets can be lost, duplicated, delayed or delivered out of order, but these errors arise only when the underlying networks fail or buffers at the destination are full. The only checksum in IP is a header checksum, which is inexpensive to calculate and ensures that any corruptions in the addressing and packet management data will be detected. There is no data checksum, which avoids overheads when crossing routers, leaving the higher-level protocols (TCP and UDP) to provide their own checksums – a practical instance of the end-to-end argument (Section 2.2.1).

The IP layer puts IP datagrams into network packets suitable for transmission in the underlying network (which might, for example, be an Ethernet). When an IP datagram is longer than the MTU of the underlying network, it is broken into smaller packets at the source and reassembled at its final destination. Packets can be further broken up to suit the underlying networks encountered during the journey from source to destination. (Each packet has a fragment identifier to enable out-of-order fragments to be collected.)

The IP layer must also insert a 'physical' network address of the message destination to the underlying network. It obtains this from the address resolution module in the Internet Network Interface layer, which is described in the next subsection.

Address resolution ◊ The address resolution module is responsible for converting Internet addresses to network addresses for a specific underlying network (sometimes called physical addresses). For example, if the underlying network is an Ethernet, the Address Resolution module converts 32-bit Internet addresses to 48-bit Ethernet addresses.

This translation is network technology-dependent:

- Some hosts are connected directly to Internet packet switches; IP packets can be routed to them without address translation.

- Some local area networks allow network addresses to be assigned to hosts dynamically, and the addresses can be conveniently chosen to match the host identifier portion of the Internet address – translation is simply a matter of extracting the host identifier from the IP address.

- For Ethernets and some other local networks the network address of each computer is hard-wired into its network interface hardware and bears no direct relation to its Internet address – translation depends upon knowledge of the correspondence between IP addresses and addresses for the hosts on the local network and is done using an address resolution protocol (ARP).

We now outline the implementation of an ARP for Ethernets. It uses dynamic enquiries in order to operate correctly when computers are added to a local network but exploits caching to minimize enquiry messages. Consider first the case in which a host computer connected to an Ethernet uses IP to transmit a message to another computer on the same Ethernet. The IP software module on the sending computer must translate the recipient's Internet address that it finds in the IP packet to an Ethernet address before the packet can be delivered. It invokes the ARP module on the sending computer to do so.

The ARP module on each host maintains a cache of (*IP address, Ethernet address*) pairs that it has previously obtained. If the required IP address is in the cache, then the query is answered immediately. If not, then ARP transmits an Ethernet broadcast packet (an ARP request packet) on the local Ethernet containing the desired IP address. Each of the computers on the local Ethernet receives the ARP request packet and checks the

IP address in it to see whether it matches its own IP address. If it does, an ARP reply packet is sent to the originator of the ARP request containing the sender's Ethernet address; otherwise the ARP request packet is ignored. The originating ARP module adds the new *IP address → Ethernet address* mapping to its local cache of (*IP address*, *Ethernet address*) pairs so that it can respond to similar requests in the future without broadcasting an ARP request. Over a period of time, the ARP cache at each computer will contain an (*IP address*, *Ethernet address*) pair for all of the computers that IP packets are sent to. Thus ARP broadcasts will be needed only when a computer is newly connected to the local Ethernet.

IP spoofing ◊ We have seen that IP packets include a source address – IP address of the sending computer. This, together with a port address encapsulated in the data field (for UDP and TCP packets), is often used by servers to generate a return address. Unfortunately, it is not possible to guarantee that the source address given is in fact the address of the sender. A malicious sender can easily substitute an address that is different from its own. This loophole has been the source of several well-known attacks, including the distributed denial of service attacks of February 2000 [Farrow 2000] mentioned in Chapter 1, Section 1.4.3. The method used was to issue many *ping* service requests to a large number of computers at several sites (ping is a simple service designed to check the availability of a host). These malicious ping requests all contained the IP address of a target computer in their sender address field. The ping responses were therefore all directed to the target, whose input buffers were overwhelmed, preventing any legitimate IP packets getting through. This attack is discussed further in Chapter 7.

3.4.3 IP routing

The IP layer routes packets from their source to their destination. Each router in the Internet implements IP-layer software to provide a routing algorithm.

Backbones ◊ The topological map of the Internet is partitioned conceptually into *autonomous systems* (AS), which are subdivided into *areas*. The intranets of most large organizations such as universities and large companies are regarded as ASs, and they will usually include several areas. In Figure 3.10 the campus intranet is an AS and the portion shown is an area. Every AS in the topological map has a *backbone* area. The collection of routers that connect non-backbone areas to the backbone and the links that interconnect those routers are called the backbone of the network. The links in the backbone are usually of high bandwidth and are replicated for reliability. This hierarchic structure is a conceptual one that is exploited primarily for the management of resources and the maintenance of the components. It does not affect the routing of IP packets.

Routing protocols ◊ RIP-1, the first routing algorithm used in the Internet, is a version of the distance-vector algorithm described in Section 3.3.5. RIP-2 (described in RFC 1388 [Malkin 1993]) was developed from it subsequently to accommodate several additional requirements, including classless interdomain routing, better multicast routing and the need for authentication of RIP packets to prevent attacks on the routers.

As the scale of the Internet has expanded and the processing capacity of routers has increased, there has been a move towards the adoption of algorithms that do not suffer from the slow convergence and potential instability of distance-vector algorithms.

The direction of the move is towards the link-state class of algorithms mentioned in Section 3.3.5 and the algorithm called *open shortest path first* (OSPF). This protocol is based on a path-finding algorithm that is due to Dijkstra [1959] and has been shown to converge more rapidly than the RIP algorithm.

We should note that the adoption of new routing algorithms in IP routers can proceed incrementally. A change in routing algorithm results in a new version of the RIP protocol, and a version number is carried by each RIP packet. The IP protocol does not change when a new RIP protocol is introduced. Any IP router will correctly forward incoming IP packets on a reasonable, if not optimum route, whatever version of RIP they use. But for routers to cooperate in the updating of their routing tables, they must share a similar algorithm. For this purpose the topological areas defined above are used. Within each area a single routing algorithm applies and the routers within an area cooperate in the maintenance of their routing tables. Routers that support only RIP-1 are still commonplace and they coexist with routers that support RIP-2 and OSPF, using backwards compatibility features incorporated in the newer protocols.

In 1993, empirical observations [Floyd and Jacobson 1993] showed that the 30-second frequency with which RIP routers exchange information was producing a periodicity in the performance of IP transmissions. The average latency for IP packet transmissions showed a peak at 30-second intervals. This was traced to the behaviour of routers performing the RIP protocol – on receipt of an RIP packet, routers would delay the onward transmission of any IP packets that they held until the routing table update process was complete for all RIP packets received to date. This tended to cause the routers to perform the RIP actions in lock-step. The correction recommended was for routers to adopt a random value in the range 15–45 seconds for the RIP update period.

Default routes ◊ Up to now, our discussion of routing algorithms has suggested that every router maintains a full routing table showing the route to every destination (subnet or directly connected host) in the Internet. At the current scale of the Internet this is clearly infeasible (the number of destinations is probably already in excess of 1 million and still growing very rapidly).

Two possible solutions to this problem come to mind, and both have been adopted in an effort to alleviate the effects of the Internet's growth. The first solution is to adopt some form of topological grouping of IP addresses. Prior to 1993, nothing could be inferred from an IP address about its location. In 1993, as part of the move to simplify and economize on the allocation of IP addresses that is discussed below under CIDR, the decision was taken that for future allocations, the following regional locations would be applied:

> Addresses 194.0.0.0 to 195.255.255.255 are in Europe
> Addresses 198.0.0.0 to 199.255.255.255 are in North America
> Addresses 200.0.0.0 to 201.255.255.255 are in Central and South America
> Addresses 202.0.0.0 to 203.255.255.255 are in Asia and the Pacific

Because these geographical regions also correspond to well-defined topological regions in the Internet and just a few gateway routers provide access to each region, this enables a substantial simplification of routing tables for those address ranges. For example, a router outside Europe can have a single table entry for the range of addresses 194.0.0.0 to 195.255.255.255 that sends all IP packets with destinations in that range on the same route to the nearest European gateway router. But note that before the date of that decision, IP addresses were allocated largely without regard to topology or geography. Many of those addresses are still in use, and the 1993 decision does nothing to reduce the scale of routing table entries for those addresses.

The second solution to the routing table size explosion is simpler and very effective. It is based on the observation that the accuracy of routing information can be relaxed for most routers as long as some key routers, those closest to the backbone links, have relatively complete routing tables. The relaxation takes the form of a *default* destination entry in routing tables. The default entry specifies a route to be used for all IP packets whose destination is not included in the routing table. To illustrate this, consider Figures 3.7 and 3.8 and suppose that the routing table for node C is altered to show:

Routings from C		
To	*Link*	*Cost*
B	2	1
C	local	0
E	5	1
Default	5	-

Thus node C is ignorant of nodes A and D. It will route all packets addressed to them via link 5 to E. What is the consequence? Packets addressed to D will reach their destination without loss of efficiency in routing, but packets addressed to A will make an extra hop, passing through E and B on the way. In general, the use of default routings trades routing efficiency for table size. But in some cases, especially where a router is on a spur, so that all outward messages must pass through a single point, there is no loss of efficiency. The default routing scheme is heavily used in Internet routing; no single router holds routes to all destinations in the Internet.

Routing on a local subnet ◊ Packets addressed to hosts on the same network as the sender are transmitted to the destination host in a single hop, using the host identifier part of the address to obtain the address of the destination host on the underlying network. The IP layer simply uses ARP to get the network address of the destination and then uses the underlying network to transmit the packets.

If the IP layer in the sending computer discovers that the destination is on a different network, it must send the message to a local router. It uses ARP to get the network address of the gateway or router and then uses the underlying network to transmit the packet to it. Gateways and routers are connected to two or more networks and they have several Internet addresses, one for each network to which they are attached.

Classless interdomain routing (CIDR) ◊ The shortage of IP addresses referred to in Section 3.4.1 led to the introduction in 1996 of this scheme for allocating addresses and managing the entries in routing tables. The main problem was a scarcity of Class B addresses – those for subnets with more than 255 hosts connected. Plenty of Class C addresses were available. The CIDR solution for this problem is to allocate a batch of contiguous class C addresses to a subnet requiring more than 255 addresses. The CIDR scheme also makes it possible to subdivide a Class B address space for allocation to multiple subnets.

Batching Class C addresses sounds like a straightforward step, but unless it is accompanied by a change in routing table format, it has a substantial impact on the size of routing tables and hence the efficiency of the algorithms that manage them. The change adopted was to add a *mask* field to the routing tables. The mask is a bit pattern that is used to select the portion of an IP address that is compared with the routing table entry. This effectively enables the host/subnet address to be any portion of the IP address, providing more flexibility than the classes A, B and C. Hence the name *classless* interdomain routing. Once again, these changes to routers are made on an incremental basis, so some routers perform CIDR and others use the old class-based algorithms.

This works because the newly allocated ranges of Class C addresses are assigned modulo 256, so each range represents an integral number of Class C-sized subnet addresses. On the other hand, some subnets also make use of CIDR to subdivide the range of addresses in a single network, of Class A, B, or C. If a collection of subnets is connected to the rest of the world entirely by CIDR routers, then the ranges of IP addresses used within the collection can be allocated to individual subnets in chunks determined by a binary mask of any size.

For example, a Class C address space can be subdivided into 32 groups of 8. Figure 3.10 contains an example of the use of the CIDR mechanism to split the 138.37.95 Class C-sized subnet into several groups of eight host addresses that are routed differently. The separate groups are denoted by notations 138.37.95.232/29, 138.37.95.248/29 and so on. The /29 portion of these addresses denotes an attached 32-bit binary mask with 29 leading 1s and three trailing 0s.

Unregistered addresses and Network Address Translation (NAT) ◊   Not all of the computers and devices that access the Internet need to be assigned globally-unique IP addresses. Computers that are attached to a local network and access to the Internet through a NAT-enabled router can rely upon the router to redirect incoming UDP and TCP packets for them. Figure 3.18 illustrates a typical home network with computers and other network devices linked to the Internet through a NAT-enabled router. The network includes Internet-enabled computers that are connected to the router by a wired Ethernet connection as well as others that are connected through a WiFi access point. For completeness some Bluetooth-enabled devices are shown but these are not connected to the router and hence cannot access the Internet directly. The home network has been allocated a single registered IP address (83.215.152.95) by its Internet service provider. The approach described here is suitable for any organization wishing to connect computers without registered IP addresses to the Internet.

All of the Internet-enabled devices on the home network have been assigned unregistered IP addresses on the 192.168.1.x Class C subnet. Most of the internal computers and devices are allocated individual IP addresses dynamically by a Dynamic Host Configuration Protocol (DHCP) service running on the router. In our illustration the numbers above 192.168.1.100 are used by the DHCP service and the nodes with lower numbers (such as PC 1) have been allocated numbers manually for a reason explained later in this subsection. Although all of these addresses are completely hidden from the rest of the Internet by the NAT router, it it is conventional to use a range of

Figure 3.18   A typical NAT-based home network

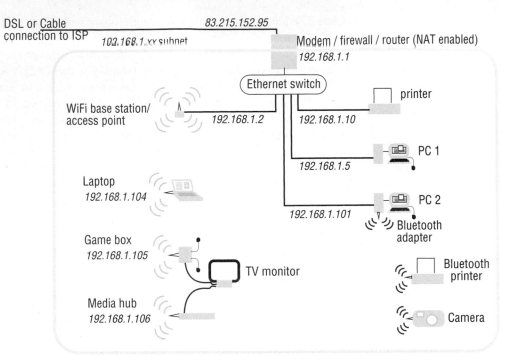

DSL or Cable
connection to ISP
83.215.152.95
192.168.1.xx subnet

Modem / firewall / router (NAT enabled)
192.168.1.1

Ethernet switch

WiFi base station/
access point
192.168.1.2

printer
192.168.1.10

192.168.1.5   PC 1

Laptop
192.168.1.104

192.168.1.101   PC 2

Bluetooth
adapter

Game box
192.168.1.105

TV monitor

Bluetooth
printer

Media hub
192.168.1.106

Camera

addresses from one of three blocks of addresses (10.z.y.x, 172.16.y.x or 192.168.y.x) that IANA has reserved for private internets.

NAT is described in RFC 1631 [Egevang and Francis 1994] and extended in RFC 2663 [Srisuresh and Holdrege 1999]. NAT-enabled routers maintain an address translation table and exploit the source and destination port number fields in the UDP and TCP packets to assign each incoming reply message to the internal computer that sent the corresponding request message. Note that the source port given in a request message is always used as the destination port in the corresponding reply message.

The most commonly used variant of NAT addressing works as follows:

– When a computer on the internal network sends a UDP or TCP packet to a computer outside it, the router receives the packet and saves the source IP address and port number to an available slot in its address translation table.

– The router replaces the source address in the packet with the router's IP address and the source port with a *virtual port number* that indexes the table slot containing the sending computer's address information.

– The packet with modified source address and port number is then forwarded towards its destination by the router. The address translation table now holds a mapping from virtual port numbers to real internal IP addresses and port numbers for all packets sent recently by computers on the internal network.

- When the router receives a UDP or TCP packet from an external computer it uses the destination port number in the packet to access a slot in the address translation table. It replaces the destination address and destination port in the received packet with those stored in the slot and forwards the modified packet to the internal computer identified by the destination address.

The router will retain a port mapping and reuse it as long as it appears to be in use. A timer is reset each time the router accesses an entry in the table. If the entry is not accessed again before the timer expires, the entry is removed from the table.

The scheme described above deals satisfactorily with the commonest modes of communication for non-registered computers, in which they act as clients to external services such as web servers. But it does not enable them to act as servers to handle incoming requests. To deal with that case, NAT routers can be configured manually to forward all of the incoming requests on a given port to one particular internal computers. Computers that act as servers must retain the same internal IP address and this is achieved by allocating their addresses manually (as was done for PC 1). This solution to the problem of providing external access to services is satisfactory as long as there is no requirement for more than one internal computer to offer a service on any given port.

NAT was introduced as a short-term solution to the problem of IP address allocation for personal and home computers. Its has enabled the expansion of Internet use to proceed far further than was originally anticipated, but it does impose some limitations, of which the last point is an example. IPv6 must be seen as the next step, enabling full Internet participation for all computers and portable devices.

3.4.4   IP version 6

A more permanent solution to the addressing limitations of IPv4 was also pursued, and this led to the development and adoption of a new version of the IP protocol with substantially larger addresses. The IETF noticed the potential problems arising from the 32-bit addresses of IPv4 as early as 1990 and initiated a project to develop a new version of the IP protocol. IPv6 was adopted by the IETF in 1994 and a strategy for migration to it was recommended.

Figure 3.19 shows the layout of IPv6 headers. We do not propose to cover their construction in detail here. Readers are referred to Tanenbaum [2003] or Stallings [1998a] for tutorial material on IPv6 and to Huitema [1998] for a blow-by-blow account of the IPv6 design process and implementation plans. Here we will outline the main advances that IPv6 embodies.

Address space: IPv6 addresses are 128 bits (16 bytes) long. This provides for a truly astronomical number of addressable entities: 2^{128}, or approximately 3×10^{38}. Tanenbaum calculates that this is sufficient to provide 7×10^{23} IP addresses per square metre across the entire surface of the Earth. More conservatively, Huitema made a calculation assuming that IP addresses are allocated as inefficiently as telephone numbers and he came up with a figure of 1000 IP addresses per square metre of the Earth's surface (land and water).

The IPv6 address space is partitioned. We cannot detail the partitioning here, but even the minor partitions (one of which will hold the entire range of IPv4 addresses, mapped one-to-one) are far larger than the total IPv4 space. Many

Figure 3.19   IPv6 header layout

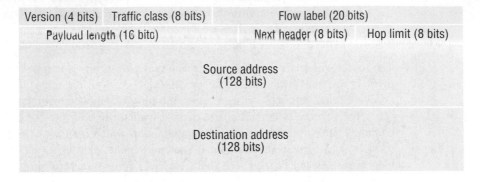

partitions (representing 72% of the total) are reserved for purposes as yet undefined. Two large partitions (each comprising 1/8th of the address space) are allocated for general purposes and will be assigned to normal network nodes. One of them is intended to be organized according to the geographic locations of the addressed nodes and the other according to their organizational locations. This allows two alternative strategies for aggregating addresses for routing purposes – it remains to be seen which will prove more effective or popular.

Routing speed: The complexity of the basic IPv6 header and the processing required at each node are reduced. No checksum is applied to the packet content (payload), and no fragmentation can occur once a packet has begun its journey. The former is considered acceptable because errors can be detected at higher levels (TCP does include a content checksum), and the latter is achieved by supporting a mechanism for determining the smallest MTU before a packet is transmitted.

Real-time and other special services: The *traffic class* and *flow label* fields are concerned with this. Multimedia streams and other sequences of real-time data elements can transmitted as part of an identified flow. The first six bits of the *traffic class* field can be used with the *flow label* or independently to enable specific packets to be handled more rapidly or with higher reliability that others. Traffic class values 0 through 8 are for transmissions that can be slowed without disastrous effects on the application. Other values are reserved for packets whose delivery is time-dependent. Such packets must either be delivered promptly or dropped – late delivery is of no value.

Flow labels enable resources to be reserved in order to meet the timing requirements of specific real-time data streams, such as live audio and video transmissions. Chapter 17 discusses these requirements and methods for the allocation of resources for them. Of course, the routers and transmission links in the Internet have limited resources and the concept of reserving them for specific users and applications has not previously been considered. The use of these facilities of IPv6 will depend upon major enhancements to the infrastructure and the development of suitable methods for charging and arbitrating the allocation of resources.

Future evolution: The key to the provision for future evolution is the *next header* field. If non-zero, it defines the type of an extension header that is included in the packet. There are currently extension header types that provide additional data for special services of the following types: information for routers, route definition, fragment handling, authentication, encryption information and destination handling information. Each extension header type has a specific size and a defined format. Further extension header types will be defined as new service requirements arise. An extension header, if present, follows the basic header and precedes the payload and includes a *next header* field, enabling multiple extension headers to be employed.

Multicast and anycast: Both IPv4 and IPv6 include support for the transmission of IP packets to multiple hosts using a single address (one that is in the range reserved for the purpose). The IP routers are then responsible for routing the packet to all of the hosts that have subscribed to the group identified by the relevant address. Further details on IP multicast communication can be found in Section 4.5.1. In addition, IPv6 supports a new mode of transmission called *anycast*. This service delivers a packet to at least one of the hosts that subscribes to the relevant address.

Security: Up to now, Internet applications that require authenticated or private data transmission have relied on the use of cryptographic techniques in the application layer. The end-to-end argument supports the view that this is the right place for it. If security is implemented at the IP level then users and application developers depend upon the correctness of the code that implements it in each router along the way, and they must trust the routers and other intermediate nodes to handle cryptographic keys.

The advantage of implementing security at the IP level is that it can be applied without the need for security-aware implementations of application programs. For example, system managers can implement it in a firewall and apply it uniformly to all external communication without incurring the cost of encryption for internal communication. Routers may also exploit an IP-level security mechanism to secure the routing table update messages that they exchange between themselves.

Security in IPv6 is implemented through the *authentication* and *encrypted security payload* extension header types. These implement features equivalent to the secure channel concept introduced in Section 2.3.3. The payload is encrypted and/or digitally signed as required. Similar security features are also available in IPv4 using IP tunnelling between routers or hosts that implement the IPSec specification (see RFC 2411 [Thayer 1998]).

Migration from IPv4 ◊ The consequences for the existing Internet infrastructure of a change in its basic protocol are profound. IP is processed in the TCP/IP protocol stack at every host and the software of every router. IP addresses are handled in many application and utility programs. All of these require upgrading to support the new version of IP. But the change is made inevitable by the forthcoming exhaustion of the address space provided by IPv4, and the IETF working group responsible for IPv6 defined a migration strategy – essentially it involves the implementation of 'islands' of IPv6 routers and hosts communicating with other IPv6 islands via tunnels and gradually merging into larger islands.

As we have noted, IPv6 routers and hosts should have no difficulty in handling mixed traffic, since the IPv4 address space is embedded in the IPv6 space. All of the major operating systems (Windows XP, Mac OS X, Linux and other Unix variants) already include implementations of UDP and TCP sockets (as described in Chapter 4) over IPv6, enabling applications to be migrated with a simple upgrade.

The theory of this strategy is technically sound, but implementation progress has been very slow, perhaps because CIDR and NAT have relieved the pressure to a greater extent than anticipated. This has begun to change in the mobile phone and portable device markets. All of these devices are likely to be Internet-enabled in the near future and they cannot easily be hidden behind NAT routers. For example, it is projected that more than a billion IP devices will be deployed in India and China by 2014. Only IPv6 can address needs such as that.

3.4.5 MobileIP

Mobile computers such as laptops and palmtops are connected to the Internet at different locations as they migrate. In its owner's office a laptop may be connected to a local Ethernet, connected to the Internet through a router, it may be connected via a mobile phone while it is in transit by car or train, then it may be attached to an Ethernet at another site. The user will wish to access services such as email and the Web at any of these locations.

Simple access to services does not require a mobile computer to retain a single address, and it may acquire a new IP address at each site; that is the purpose of the Dynamic Host Configuration Protocol (DHCP), which enables a newly connected computer to dynamically acquire an IP address in the address range of the local subnet and discover the addresses of local resources such as a DNS server from a local DHCP server. It will also need to discover what local services (such as printing, mail delivery and so on) are available at each site that it visits. Discovery services are a type of naming service that assist with this; they are described in Chapter 16 (Section 16.2).

There may be files or other resources on the laptop to which others require access, or the laptop may be running a distributed application such as a share-monitoring service that receives notifications of specified events such as stocks that the user holds passing a preset threshold. If a mobile computer is to remain accessible to clients and resource-sharing applications when it moves between local networks and wireless networks, it must retain a single IP number, but IP routing is subnet-based. Subnets are at fixed locations, and the correct routing of packets to them depends upon their position on the network.

MobileIP is a solution for the latter problem. The solution is implemented transparently, so IP communication continues normally when a mobile host computer moves between subnets at different locations. It is based upon the permanent allocation of a normal IP address to each mobile host on a subnet in its 'home' domain.

When the mobile host is connected at its home base, packets are routed to it in the normal way. When it is connected to the Internet elsewhere, two agent processes take responsibility for rerouting. The agents are a *home agent* (HA) and a *foreign agent* (FA). These processes run on convenient fixed computers at the home site and at the current location of the mobile host.

The HA is responsible for holding up-to-date knowledge of the mobile host's current location (the IP address by which it can be reached). It does this with the assistance of the mobile host itself. When a mobile host leaves its home site, it should

Figure 3.20   The MobileIP routing mechanism

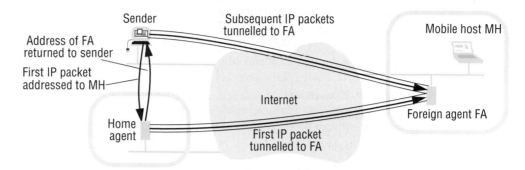

inform the HA, and the HA notes the mobile host's absence. During the absence it will behave as a proxy; in order to do so, it tells the local routers to cancel any cached records relating to the mobile host's IP address. While it is acting as a proxy, the HA responds to ARP requests concerning the mobile host's IP address, giving its own local network address as the network address of the mobile host.

When the mobile host arrives at a new site, it informs the FA at that site. The FA allocates a 'care-of address' to it – a new, temporary IP address on the local subnet. The FA then contacts the HA giving it the mobile host's home IP address and the care-of address that has been allocated to it.

Figure 3.20 illustrates the MobileIP routing mechanism. When an IP packet addressed to the mobile host's home address is received at the home network, it is routed to the HA. The HA then encapsulates the IP packet in a MobileIP packet and sends it to the FA. The FA unpacks the original IP packet and delivers it to the mobile host via the local network to which it is currently attached. Note that the method by which the HA and the FA reroute the original packet to its intended recipient is an instance of the tunnelling technique described in Section 3.3.7.

The HA also sends the care-of address of the mobile host to the original sender. If the sender is MobileIP-enabled, it will note the new address and use it for subsequent communication with the mobile host, avoiding the overheads of rerouting via the HA. If it is not, then it will ignore the change of address and subsequent communication continues to be rerouted via the HA.

The MobileIP solution is effective, but hardly efficient. A solution that treats mobile hosts as first-class citizens would be preferable, allowing them to wander without giving prior notice and routing packets to them without any tunnelling or re-routing. We should note that this apparently difficult feat is exactly what is achieved by the cellular phone network – mobile phones do not change their number as they move between cells, or even between countries. Instead, they simply notify the local cellular phone base station of their presence from time to time.

3.4.6   TCP and UDP

TCP and UDP provide the communication capabilities of the Internet in a form that is useful for application programs. Application developers might wish for other types of transport service, for example to provide real-time guarantees or security, but such services would generally require more support in the network layer than IPv4 provides. TCP and UDP can be viewed as a faithful reflection at the application programming level of the communication facilities that IPv4 has to offer. IPv6 is another story; it will certainly continue to support TCP and UDP, but it includes capabilities that cannot be conveniently accessed through TCP and UDP. It may be useful to introduce additional types of transport service to exploit them, once the deployment of IPv6 is sufficiently wide to justify their development.

Chapter 4 describes the characteristics of both TCP and UDP from the point of view of distributed program developers. Here we shall be quite brief, describing only the functionality that they add to IP.

Use of ports ◊ The first characteristic to note is that, whereas IP supports communication between pairs of computers (identified by their IP addresses), TCP and UDP, as transport protocols, must provide process-to-process communication. This is accomplished by the use of ports. *Port numbers* are used for addressing messages to processes within a particular computer and are valid only within that computer. A port number is a 16-bit integer. Once an IP packet has been delivered to the destination host, the TCP- or UDP-layer software dispatches it to a process via a specific port at that host.

UDP features ◊ UDP is almost a transport-level replica of IP. A UDP datagram is encapsulated inside an IP packet. It has a short header that includes the source and destination port numbers (the corresponding host addresses are present in the IP header), a length field and a checksum. UDP offers no guarantee of delivery. We have already noted that IP packets may be dropped because of congestion or network error. UDP adds no additional reliability mechanisms except the checksum, which is optional. If the checksum field is non-zero the receiving host computes a check value from the packet contents and compares it with the received checksum; packets for which they do not match are dropped.

Thus UDP provides a means of transmitting messages of up to 64 kbytes in size (the maximum packet permitted by IP) between pairs of processes (or from one process to several in the case of datagrams addressed to IP multicast addresses), with minimal additional costs or transmission delays above those due to IP transmission. It incurs no setup costs and it requires no administrative acknowledgement messages. But its use is restricted to those applications and services that do not require reliable delivery of single or multiple messages.

TCP features ◊ TCP provides a much more sophisticated transport service. It provides reliable delivery of arbitrarily long sequences of bytes via stream-based programming abstraction. The reliability guarantee entails the delivery to the receiving process of all of the data presented to the TCP software by the sending process, in the same order. TCP is connection-oriented. Before any data is transferred, the sending and receiving process must cooperate in the establishment of a bi-directional communication channel. The connection is simply an end-to-end agreement to perform reliable data transmission; intermediate nodes such as routers have no knowledge of TCP connections, and the IP packets that transfer the data in a TCP transmission do not necessarily all follow the same route.

The TCP layer includes additional mechanisms (implemented over IP) to meet the reliability guarantees. These are:

Sequencing: A TCP sending process divides the stream into a sequence of data segments and transmits them as IP packets. A sequence number is attached to each TCP segment. It gives the byte number within the stream for the first byte of the segment. The receiver uses the sequence numbers to order the received segments before placing them in the input stream at the receiving process. No segment can be placed in the input stream until all lower-numbered segments have been received and placed in the stream, so segments that arrive out of order must be held in a buffer until their predecessors arrive.

Flow control: The sender takes care not to overwhelm the receiver or the intervening nodes. This is achieved by a system of segment acknowledgements. Whenever a receiver successfully receives a segment it records its sequence number. From time to time the receiver sends an acknowledgement to the sender giving the sequence number of the highest-numbered segment in its input stream together with a *window size*. If there is a reverse flow of data, acknowledgements are carried in the normal data segments, otherwise they travel in acknowledgment segments. The window size field in the acknowledgement segment specifies the quantity of data that the sender is permitted to send before the next acknowledgement.

When a TCP connection is used for communication with a remote interactive program, data may be produced in small quantities but in a very bursty manner. For example, keyboard input may result in only a few characters per second, but the characters should be sent sufficiently quickly for the user to see the results of their typing. This is dealt with by setting a timeout T on local buffering – typically 0.5 seconds. With this simple scheme, a segment is sent to the receiver whenever data has been waiting in the output buffer for T seconds or the contents of the buffer reaches the MTU limit. This buffering scheme cannot add more than T seconds to the interactive delay. Nagle has described another algorithm that produces less traffic and is more effective for some interactive applications [Nagle 1984]. Nagle's algorithm is used in many TCP implementations. Most TCP implementations are configurable, allowing applications to change the value of T or to select one of several buffering algorithms.

Because of the unreliability of wireless networks and the resulting frequent loss of packets, these flow-control mechanisms are not particularly relevant for wireless communication. This is one of the reasons for the adoption of a different transport mechanism in the WAP family of protocols for wide-area mobile communication. But the implementation of TCP for wireless networks is also important, and modifications to the TCP mechanism have been proposed for this purpose [Balakrishnan *et al.* 1995, 1996]. The idea is to implement a TCP support component at the wireless base station (the gateway between wired and wireless networks). The support component snoops on TCP segments to and from the wireless network, retransmitting any outbound segments that are not acknowledged rapidly by the mobile receiver and requesting retransmissions of inbound segments when gaps in the sequence numbers are noticed.

Retransmission: The sender records the sequence numbers of the segments that it sends. When it receives an acknowledgement it notes that the segments were successfully received and it may then delete them from its outgoing buffers. If any segment is not acknowledged within a specified timeout, the sender retransmits it.

Buffering: The incoming buffer at the receiver is used to balance the flow between the sender and the receiver. If the receiving process issues *receive* operations more slowly than the sender issues *send* operations, the quantity of data in the buffer will grow. Usually it is extracted from the buffer before it becomes full, but ultimately the buffer may overflow and when that happens incoming segments are simply dropped without recording their arrival. Their arrival is therefore not acknowledged and the sender is obliged to retransmit them.

Checksum: Each segment carries a checksum covering the header and the data in the segment. If a received segment does not match its checksum the segment is dropped.

3.4.7 Domain names

The design and implementation of the Domain Name System (DNS) is described in detail in Chapter 9; we give a brief overview here to complete our discussion of the Internet protocols. The Internet supports a scheme for the use of symbolic names for hosts and networks, such as *binkley.cs.mcgill.ca* or *essex.ac.uk*. The named entities are organized into a naming hierarchy. The named entities are called *domains* and the symbolic names are called *domain names*. Domains are organized in a hierarchy that is intended to reflect their organizational structure. The naming hierarchy is entirely independent of the physical layout of the networks that constitute the Internet. Domain names are convenient for human users, but they must be translated to Internet (IP) addresses before they can be used as communication identifiers. This is the responsibility of a specific service, the DNS. Application programs pass requests to the DNS to convert the domain names that users specify into Internet addresses.

DNS is implemented as a server process that can be run on host computers anywhere in the Internet. There are at least two DNS servers in each domain and often more. The servers in each domain hold a partial map of the domain name tree below their domain. They must hold at least the portion consisting of all of the domain and host names within their domain, but they often contain a larger portion of the tree. DNS servers handle requests for the translation of domain names outside their portion of the tree by issuing requests to DNS servers in the relevant domains, proceeding recursively from right to left resolving the name in segments. The resulting translation is then cached at the server handling the original request so that future requests for the resolution of names referring to the same domain will be resolved without reference to other servers. The DNS would not be workable without the extensive use of caching, since the 'root' name servers would be consulted in almost every case, creating a service access bottleneck.

3.4.8 Firewalls

Almost all organizations need Internet connectivity in order to provide services to their customers and other external users and to enable their internal users to access information and services. The computers in most organizations are quite diverse, running a variety of operating systems and application software. The security of their software is even more varied; some of it may include state-of-the-art security, but much of it will have little or no capability to ensure that incoming communication can be

Figure 3.21   Firewall configurations

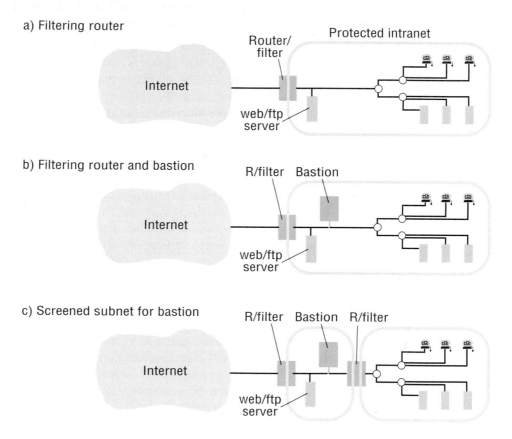

a) Filtering router

Router/filter

Protected intranet

Internet

web/ftp server

b) Filtering router and bastion

R/filter   Bastion

Internet

web/ftp server

c) Screened subnet for bastion

R/filter   Bastion   R/filter

Internet

web/ftp server

trusted and outgoing communication is private when required. In summary, in an intranet with many computers and a wide range of software it is inevitable that some parts of the system will have weaknesses that expose it to security attacks. Forms of attack are detailed further in Chapter 7.

The purpose of a firewall is to monitor and control all communication into and out of an intranet. A firewall is implemented by a set of processes that act as a gateway to an intranet (Figure 3.21(a)), applying a security policy determined by the organization.

The aims of a firewall security policy may include any or all of the following:

Service control: To determine which services on internal hosts are accessible for external access and to reject all other incoming service requests. Outgoing service requests and the responses to them may also be controlled. These filtering actions can be based on the contents of IP packets and the TCP and UDP requests that they contain. For example, incoming HTTP requests may be rejected unless they are directed to an official web server host.

Behaviour control: To prevent behaviour that infringes the organization's policies, is anti-social or has no discernible legitimate purpose and is hence suspected of forming part of an attack. Some of these filtering actions may be applicable at the IP or TCP level, but others may require interpretation of messages at a higher level. For example, filtering of email 'spam' attacks may require examination of the sender's email address in message headers or even the message contents.

User control: The organization may wish to discriminate between its users, allowing some access to external services but inhibiting others from doing so. An example of user control that is perhaps more socially acceptable than some is to prevent the acknowledging of software except to users who are members of the system administration team, in order to prevent virus infection or to maintain software standards. This particular example would in fact be difficult to implement without inhibiting the use of the Web by ordinary users.

Another instance of user control is the management of dial-up and other connections provided for off-site users. If the firewall is also the host for modem connections, it can authenticate the user at connection time and can require the use of a secure channel for all communication (to prevent eavesdropping, masquerading and other attacks on the external connection). That is the purpose of the Virtual Private Network technology described in the next subsection.

The policy has to be expressed in terms of filtering operations that are performed by filtering processes operating at several different levels:

IP packet filtering: This is a filter process examining individual IP packets. It may make decisions based on the destination and source addresses. It may also examine the *service type* field of IP packets and interpret the contents of the packets based on the type. For example, it may filter TCP packets based on the port number to which they are addressed, and since services are generally located at well-known ports, this enables packets to be filtered based on the service requested. For example, many sites prohibit the use of NFS servers by external clients.

For performance reasons, IP filtering is usually performed by a process within the operating system kernel of a router. If multiple firewalls are used, the first may mark certain packets for more exhaustive examination by a later firewall, allowing 'clean' packets to proceed. It is possible to filter based on sequences of IP packets, for example to prevent access to an FTP server before a login has been performed.

TCP gateway: A TCP gateway process checks all TCP connection requests and segment transmissions. When a TCP gateway process is installed, the setting-up of TCP connections can be controlled and TCP segments can be checked for correctness (some denial of service attacks use malformed TCP segments to disrupt client operating systems). When desired, they can be routed through an application-level gateway for content checking.

Application-level gateway: An application-level gateway process acts as a *proxy* for an application process. For example, a policy may be desired that allows certain internal users to make Telnet connections to certain external hosts. When a user runs a Telnet program on his local computer, it attempts to establish a TCP connection with a remote host. The request is intercepted by the TCP gateway. The TCP gateway starts a *Telnet proxy* process and the original TCP connection is routed to it. If the proxy approves the Telnet operation (the user is authorized to use the requested host) it establishes another connection to the requested host and then it relays all of the TCP packets in both directions. A similar proxy process would run on behalf of each Telnet client, and similar proxies might be employed for FTP and other services.

A firewall is usually composed of several processes working at different protocol levels. It is common to employ more than one computer in firewall duties for performance and fault-tolerance reasons. In all of the configurations described below and illustrated in Figure 3.21 we show a public web and FTP server without protection. It holds only published information that requires no protection against public access, and its server software ensures that only authorized internal users can update it.

IP packet filtering is normally done by a router – a computer with at least two network addresses on separate IP networks – that runs an RIP process, an IP packet-filtering process and as few other processes as possible. The router/filter must run only trusted software in a manner that enables its enforcement of filtering policies to be guaranteed. This involves ensuring that no Trojan horse processes can run on it and that the filtering and routing software have not been modified or tampered with. Figure 3.21(a) shows a simple firewall configuration that relies only on IP filtering and employs a single router for that purpose. The network configuration in Figure 3.10 includes two router/filters acting as firewalls of this type. In this configuration, there are two router/filters for performance and reliability reasons. They both obey the same filtering policy and the second does not increase the security of the system.

When TCP and application-level gateway processes are required, these usually run on a separate computer, which is known as a *bastion*. (The term originates from the construction of fortified castles; it is a protruding watchtower from which the castle may be defended or defenders may negotiate with those desiring entry.) A bastion computer is a host that is located inside the intranet protected by an IP router/filter and runs the TCP and application-level gateways (Figure 3.21(b)). Like the router/filter, the bastion must run only trusted software. In a well-secured intranet, proxies must be used for access to all services outside. Readers may be familiar with the use of proxies for web access. These are an instance of the use of firewall proxies; they are often constructed in a manner that integrates a web cache server (described in Chapter 2). This and other proxies are likely to require substantial processing and storage resources.

Security can be enhanced by employing two router/filters in series, with the bastion and any public servers located on a separate subnet linking the router/filters (Figure 3.21(c)). This configuration has several security advantages:

- If the bastion policy is strict, the IP addresses of hosts in the intranet need not even be published to the outside world, and the addresses in the outside world need not be known to internal computers, since all external communication passes through proxy processes in the bastion, which does have access to both.

- If the first router/filter is penetrated or compromised, the second, which is invisible from outside the intranet and hence less vulnerable, remains to pick up and reject unacceptable IP packets.

Virtual private networks ◊ Virtual private networks (VPNs) extend the firewall protection boundary beyond the local intranet by the use of cryptographically protected secure channels at the IP level. In Section 3.4.4, we outlined the IP security extensions available in IPv6 and IPv4 with IPSec tunnelling [Thayer 1998]. These are the basis for the implementation of VPNs. They may be used for individual external users or to implement secure connections between intranets located at different sites using public Internet links.

For example, a member of staff may need to connect to the organization's intranet via an Internet service provider. Once connected, they should have the same capabilities as a user inside the firewall. This can be achieved if their local host implements IP security. The local host holds one or more cryptographic keys that it shares with the firewall, and these are used to establish a secure channel at connection time. Secure channel mechanisms are described in detail in Chapter 7.

3.5 Case studies: Ethernet, WiFi, Bluetooth and ATM

Up to this point we have discussed the principles involved in the construction of computer networks and we have described IP, the 'virtual network layer' of the Internet. To complete the chapter, we describe the principles and implementations of three actual networks in this section.

In the early 1980s, the US Institute of Electrical and Electronic Engineers (IEEE) established a committee to specify a series of standards for local area networks (the 802 Committee [IEEE 1990]), and its subcommittees have produced a series of specifications that have become the key standards for LANs. In most cases, the standards are based on pre-existing industry standards that had emerged from research done in the 1970s. The relevant subcommittees and the standards that they have been published to date are shown in Figure 3.22.

They differ in performance, efficiency, reliability and cost, but they all provide relatively high-bandwidth networking capabilities over short and medium distances. The IEEE 802.3 Ethernet standard has largely won the battle for the wired LAN marketplace, and we describe it in Section 3.5.1 as our representative wired LAN technology. Although Ethernet implementations are available for several bandwidths, the principles of operation are identical in all of them.

The IEEE 802.5 Token Ring standard was a significant competitor for much of the 1990s, offering advantages over Ethernet in efficiency and its support for bandwidth guarantees, but it has now disappeared from the marketplace. Readers interested in a brief description of this interesting LAN technology can find one at www.cdk4.net/networking. The widespread use of Ethernet switches (as opposed to

Figure 3.22   IEEE 802 network standards

IEEE No.	Name	Title	Reference
802.3	Ethernet	CSMA/CD Networks (Ethernet)	[IEEE 1985a]
802.4		Token Bus Networks	[IEEE 1985b]
802.5		Token Ring Networks	[IEEE 1985c]
802.6		Metropolitan Area Networks	[IEEE 1994]
802.11	WiFi	Wireless Local Area Networks	[IEEE 1999]
802.15.1	Bluetooth	Wireless Personal Area Networks	[IEEE 2002]
802.15.4	ZigBee	Wireless Sensor Networks	[IEEE 2003]
802.16	WiMAX	Wireless Metropolitan Area Networks	[IEEE 2004a]

hubs) has enabled Ethernets to be configured in a manner that offers bandwidth and latency guarantees (as discussed further in Section 3.5.1, subsection *Ethernet for real-time and quality-of-service critical applications*) and this is one reason for its displacement of token ring technology.

The IEEE 802.4 Token Bus standard was developed for industrial applications with real-time requirements and is employed in that domain. The IEEE 802.6 Metropolitan Area standard covers distances up to 50 km and is intended for use in networks that span towns and cities.

The IEEE 802.11 Wireless LAN standard emerged somewhat later but holds a major position in the marketplace with products from many vendors under the commercial name WiFi, and is installed in a large proportion of mobile and handheld computing devices. The IEEE 802.11 standard is designed to support communication at speeds up to 54 Mbps over distances of up to 150 m between devices equipped with simple wireless transmitter/receivers. We describe its principles of operation in Section 3.5.2. Further details on IEEE 802.11 networks can be found in Crow *et al.* [1997] and Kurose and Ross [2000].

The IEEE 802.15.1 Wireless personal area network standard (Bluetooth) was based on a technology first developed in 1999 by the Ericsson company to transport low-bandwidth digital voice and data between devices such as PDAs, mobile phones and headsets and was subsequently standardized in 2002 as IEEE 802.15.1. Section 3.5.3 contains a description of Bluetooth.

IEEE 802.15.4 (ZigBee) is another WPAN standard aimed at providing data communication for very low-bandwidth low-energy devices in the home such as remote controls, burglar alarm and heating system sensors and ubiquitous devices such as active badges and tag readers. Such networks are termed *wireless sensor networks* and their applications and communication characteristics are discussed in Chapter 16.

The IEEE 802.16 Wireless MAN standard (commercial name: WiMAX) was ratified in 2004 and 2005. The IEEE 802.16 standard is designed as an alternative to cable and DSL links for the 'last mile' connection to homes and offices. A variant of the standard is intended to supersede 802.11 WiFi networks as the main connection technology for laptop computers and mobile devices in outdoor and indoor public areas.

The ATM technology emerged from major research and standardization efforts in the telecommunications and computer industries in the late 1980s and early 1990s [CCITT 1990]. Its purpose is to provide a high-bandwidth wide-area digital networking technology suitable for telephone, data and multimedia (high-quality audio and video) applications. Although the uptake has been slower than expected, ATM is now the dominant technology for very high-speed wide-area networking. It was also seen in some quarters as a replacement for Ethernet in LAN applications, but it has been less successful in that marketplace due to competition from 100 Mbps and 1000 Mbps Ethernets which are available at much lower cost. We outline the principles of operation of ATM in Section 3.5.4. Further details on ATM and on other high-speed network technologies can be found in Tanenbaum [2003] and Stallings [1998a].

3.5.1   Ethernet

The Ethernet was developed at the Xerox Palo Alto Research Center in 1973 [Metcalfe and Boggs 1976; Shoch *et al.* 1982; 1985] as part of the programme of research carried out there on personal workstations and distributed systems. The pilot Ethernet was the first high-speed local network, demonstrating the feasibility and usefulness of high-speed local networks linking computers on a single site, allowing them to communicate at high transmission speeds with low error rates and without switching delays. The original prototype Ethernet ran at 3 Mbps. Ethernet systems are now available with bandwidths ranging from 10 Mbps to 1000 Mbps.

We shall describe the principles of operation of the 10 Mbps Ethernet specified in IEEE Standard 802.3 [IEEE 1985a]. This was the first widely deployed local area network technology. The 100 Mbps variant is now more commonly used; its principles of operation are identical. We conclude this section with a list of the more important variants of Ethernet transmission technology and bandwidth that are available. For comprehensive descriptions of the Ethernet in all its variations, see Spurgeon [2000].

A single Ethernet is a simple or branching bus-like connection line using a transmission medium consisting of one or more continuous segments of cable linked by hubs or repeaters. Hubs and repeaters are simple devices that link pieces of wire, enabling the same signals to pass through all of them. Several Ethernets can be linked at the Ethernet network protocol level by Ethernet switches or bridges. Switches and bridges operate at the level of Ethernet frames, forwarding them to adjacent Ethernets when their destination is there. Linked Ethernets appear as a single network to higher protocol layers, such as IP (see Figure 3.10, where the IP subnets 138.37.88 and 138.37.94 are each composed of several Ethernets linked by components marked *Eswitch*). In particular, the ARP protocol (Section 3.4.2) is able to resolve IP addresses to Ethernet addresses across linked sets of Ethernets; each ARP request is broadcast on all of the linked networks in a subnet.

The method of operation of Ethernets is defined by the phrase 'carrier sensing, multiple access with collision detection' (abbreviated: CSMA/CD) and they belong to the class of *contention bus* networks. Contention buses use a single transmission medium to link all of the hosts. The protocol that manages access to the medium is called a *medium access control* (MAC) protocol. Because a single link connects all hosts, the MAC protocol combines the functions of a data link layer protocol (responsible for the transmission of packets on communication links) and a network protocol (responsible for delivery of packets to hosts) in a single protocol layer.

Packet broadcasting ◊ The method of communication in CSMA/CD networks is by broadcasting packets of data on the transmission medium. All stations are continuously 'listening' to the medium for packets that are addressed to them. Any station wishing to transmit a message broadcasts one or more packets (called *frames* in the Ethernet specification) on the medium. Each packet contains the address of the destination station, the address of the sending station and a variable-length sequence of bits representing the message to be transmitted. Data transmission proceeds at 10 Mbps (or at the higher speeds specified for 100 and 1000 Mbps Ethernets) and packets vary in length between 64 and 1518 bytes, so the time to transmit a packet on a 10 Mbps Ethernet is 50–1200 microseconds, depending on its length. The MTU is specified as 1518 bytes in the IEEE standard, although there is no technical reason for any particular fixed limit except the need to limit delays caused by contention.

The address of the destination station normally refers to a single network interface. Controller hardware at each station receives a copy of every packet. It compares the destination address in each packet with a wired-in local address, ignoring packets addressed to other stations and passing those with a matching address to the local host. The destination address may also specify a broadcast or a multicast address. Ordinary addresses are distinguished from broadcast and multicast addresses by their higher-order bit (0 and 1, respectively). An address consisting of all 1s is reserved for use as a broadcast address and is used when a message is to be received by all of the stations on the network. This is used, for example, to implement the ARP IP address resolution protocol. Any station that receives a packet with a broadcast address will pass it on to its local host. A multicast address specifies a limited form of broadcast that is received by a group of stations whose network interfaces have been configured to receive packets with that multicast address. Not all implementations of Ethernet network interfaces can recognize multicast addresses.

The Ethernet network protocol (providing for the transmission of Ethernet packets between pairs of hosts) is implemented in the Ethernet hardware interface; protocol software is required for the transport layer and those above it.

Ethernet packet layout ◊   The packets (or more correctly, frames) transmitted by stations on the Ethernet have the following layout:

bytes: 7	1	6	6	2	$46 \leq length \leq 1500$	4
Preamble	S	Destination address	Source address	Length of data	Data for transmission	Checksum

Apart from the destination and source addresses already mentioned, frames include a fixed 8-byte prefix, a length field, a data field and a checksum. The prefix is used for hardware timing purposes and consists of a preamble of seven bytes, each containing the bit pattern 10101010 followed by a single-byte start frame delimiter (S in the diagram) with the pattern 10101011.

Despite the fact that the specification does not allow more than 1024 stations on a single Ethernet, addresses occupy six bytes, providing 2^{48} different addresses. This enables every Ethernet hardware interface to be given a unique address by its manufacturer, ensuring that all of the stations in any interconnected set of Ethernets will have unique addresses. The US Institute of Electrical and Electronic Engineers (IEEE) acts as an allocation authority for Ethernet addresses, allocating separate ranges of 48-bit addresses to the manufacturers of Ethernet hardware interfaces. These are referred to as MAC addresses, since they are used by the medium access control layer. In fact, MAC addresses allocated in this fashion have also been adopted as unique addresses for use other network types in the IEEE 802 family including 802.11 (WiFi) and 802.15.1 (Bluetooth).

The data field contains all or part (if the message length exceeds 1500 bytes) of the message that is being transmitted. The lower bound of 46 bytes on the data field ensures a minimum packet length of 64 bytes, which is necessary in order to guarantee that collisions will be detected by all stations on the network, as explained below.

The frame check sequence is a checksum generated and inserted by the sender and used to validate packets by the receiver. Packets with incorrect checksums are simply dropped by the datalink layer in the receiving station. This is another example of the application of the end-to-end argument: to guarantee the transmission of a message, a transport layer protocol such as TCP, which acknowledges receipt of each packet and retransmits any unacknowledged packets, must be used. The incidence of data corruption in local networks is so small that the use of this method of recovery when guaranteed delivery is required is entirely satisfactory and it enables a less costly transport protocol such as UDP to be employed when there is no need for delivery guarantees.

Packet collisions ◊ Even in the relatively short time that it takes to transmit packets there is a finite probability that two stations on the network will attempt to transmit messages simultaneously. If a station attempts to transmit a packet without checking whether the medium is in use by other stations, a collision may occur.

The Ethernet has three mechanisms to deal with this possibility. The first is called *carrier sensing*; the interface hardware in each station listens for the presence of a signal (known as the *carrier* by analogy with radio broadcasting) in the medium. When a station wishes to transmit a packet, it waits until no signal is present in the medium and then begins to transmit.

Unfortunately, carrier sensing does not prevent all collisions. The possibility of collision remains due to the finite time τ for a signal inserted at a point in the medium (travelling at electronic speed: approximately 2×10^8 metres per second) to reach all other points. Consider two stations A and B that are ready to transmit packets at almost the same time. If A begins to transmit first, B can check and find no signal in the medium at any time $t < \tau$ after A has begun to transmit. B then begins to transmit, *interfering* with A's transmission. Both A's packet and B's packet will be damaged by the interference.

The technique used to recover from such interference is called *collision detection*. Whenever a station is transmitting a packet through its hardware output port, it also listens on its input port and the two signals are compared. If they differ, then a collision has occurred. When this happens the station stops transmitting and produces a *jamming signal* to ensure that all stations recognize the collision. As we have already noted, a minimum packet length is necessary to ensure that collisions are always detected. If two stations transmit approximately simultaneously from opposite ends of the network, they will not become aware of the collision for 2τ seconds (because the first sender must be still transmitting when it receives the second signal). If the packets that they transmit take less than τ to be broadcast, the collision will not be noticed, since each sending station would not see the other packet until after it has finished transmitting its own, whereas stations at intermediate points would receive both packets simultaneously, resulting in data corruption.

After the jamming signal, all transmitting and listening stations cancel the current packet. The transmitting stations then have to try to transmit their packets again. A further difficulty now arises. If the stations involved in the collision all attempt to retransmit their packets immediately after the jamming signal, another collision will probably occur. To avoid this, a technique known as *back-off* is used. Each of the stations involved in a collision chooses to wait a time $n\tau$ before retransmitting. The value of n is a random integer chosen separately at each station and bounded by a constant L defined in the network software. If a further collision occurs, the value of L is doubled and the process is repeated if necessary for up to ten attempts.

Finally, the interface hardware at the receiving station computes the check sequence and compares it with the checksum transmitted in the packet. Using all of these techniques, the stations connected to the Ethernet are able to manage the use of the medium without any centralized control or synchronization.

Ethernet efficiency ◊ The efficiency of an Ethernet is the ratio of the number of packets transmitted successfully as a proportion of the theoretical maximum number that could be transmitted without collisions. It is affected by the value of τ, since the interval of 2τ seconds after a packet transmission starts is the 'window of opportunity' for collisions – no collision can occur later than 2τ seconds after a packet starts to be transmitted. It is also affected by the number of stations on the network and their level of activity.

For a 1 km cable the value of τ is less than 5 microseconds and the probability of collisions is small enough to ensure a high efficiency. The Ethernet can achieve a channel utilization of between 80 and 95%, although the delays due to contention become noticeable when 50% utilization is exceeded. Because the loading is variable, it is impossible to *guarantee* the delivery of a given message within any fixed time, since the network might be fully loaded when the message is ready for transmission. But the *probability* of transferring the message with a given delay is as good as, or better than, other network technologies.

Empirical measurements of the performance of an Ethernet at Xerox PARC and reported by Shoch and Hupp [1980] confirm this analysis. In practice, the load on Ethernets used in distributed systems varies quite widely. Many networks are used primarily for asynchronous client-server interactions, and these operate for most of the time with no stations waiting to transmit and a channel utilization close to 1. Networks that support bulk data access for large numbers of users experience more load, and those that carry multimedia streams are liable to be overwhelmed if more that a few streams are transmitted concurrently.

Physical implementations ◊ The description above defines the MAC-layer protocol for all Ethernets. Widespread adoption across a large marketplace has resulted in the availability of very low-cost controller hardware to perform the algorithms required for its implementation, and this is included as a standard part of many desktop and consumer computers.

A wide range of physical Ethernet implementations have been based on it to offer a variety of performance and cost trade-offs and to exploit increased hardware performance. The variations result from the use of different transmission media – coaxial cable, twisted copper wire (similar to telephone wiring) and optical fibre – with differing limits on transmission range and from the use of higher signalling speeds, resulting in greater system bandwidth and generally shorter transmission ranges. The IEEE has adopted a number of standards for physical-layer implementations, and a naming scheme is used to distinguish them. Names such as 10Base5 and 100BaseT are used. They have the following form:

$<R><B><L>$ Where: R = data rate in Mbps
B = medium signalling type (baseband or broadband)
L = maximum segment length in metres/100 or T (twisted pair cable hierarchy)

We tabulate the bandwidth and maximum range of various currently available standard configurations and cable types in Figure 3.23. Configurations ending with the T designation are implemented with UTP cabling – unshielded twisted wires (telephone

Figure 3.23   Ethernet ranges and speeds

	10Base5	10BaseT	100BaseT	1000BaseT
Data rate	10 Mbps	10 Mbps	100 Mbps	1000 Mbps
Max. segment lengths:				
Twisted wire (UTP)	100 m	100 m	100 m	25 m
Coaxial cable (STP)	500 m	500 m	500 m	25 m
Multi-mode fibre	2000 m	2000 m	500 m	500 m
Mono-mode fibre	25000 m	25000 m	20000 m	2000 m

wiring), and this is organized as a hierarchy of hubs with computers as the leaves of the tree. In that case, the segment lengths given in our table are twice the maximum permissible distance from a computer to a hub.

Ethernet for real-time and quality-of-service critical applications ◊ It is often argued that the Ethernet MAC protocol is inherently unsuitable for real-time or quality-of-service critical applications because of its lack of a guaranteed delivery delay. But it should be noted that most Ethernet installations are now based on the use of MAC-level switches as illustrated in Figure 3.10 and described in Section 3.3.7 (rather than hubs or cables with a tap for each connection, as was formerly the case). The use of switches throughout results in a separate segment for each host with no packets transmitted on it other than those addressed to that host. Hence if traffic to the host is from a single source there is no contention for the medium – efficiency is 100% and latency is constant. The possibility of contention arises only at the switches and these can be, and often are, designed to handle several packets concurrently. Hence a lightly-loaded switched Ethernet installation approximates to 100% efficiency with a constant low latency and they are therefore often successfully used in these critical application areas.

A further step towards real-time support for Ethernet-style MAC protocols is described in [Rether, Pradhan and Chiueh 1998] and a similar scheme is implemented in an open-source Linux extension [RTnet]. These software approaches address the contention problem by implementing an application-level cooperative protocol to reserve timeslots for the use of the medium. It depends upon cooperation of all the hosts connected to a segment.

3.5.2   IEEE 802.11 (WiFi) wireless LAN

In this section, we summarize the special characteristics of wireless networking that must be addressed by a wireless LAN technology and explain how IEEE 802.11 addresses them. The IEEE 802.11 standard extends the carrier-sensing multiple access (CSMA) principle employed by Ethernet (IEEE 802.3) technology to suit the characteristics of wireless communication. The 802.11 standard is intended to support communication between computers located within about 150 metres of each other at speeds up to 54 Mbps.

Figure 3.24 illustrates a portion of an intranet including a wireless LAN. Several mobile wireless devices communicate with the rest of the intranet through a base station

Figure 3.24   Wireless LAN configuration

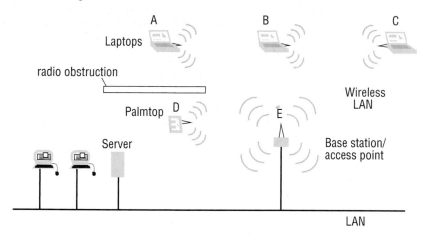

that is an *access point* to the wired LAN. A wireless network that connects to the world through an access point to a conventional LAN is known as an *infrastructure network.*

An alternative configuration for wireless networking is known as an *ad hoc network. Ad hoc* networks do not include an access point or base station. They are built 'on the fly' as a result of the mutual detection of two or more mobile devices with wireless interfaces in the same vicinity. An *ad hoc* network might occur, for example, when two or more laptop users in a room initiate a connection to any available station. They might then share files by launching a file server process on one of the machines.

At the physical level IEEE 802.11 networks use radio frequency signals (in the licence-free 2.4 GHz and 5 GHz bands) or infra-red signalling as the transmission medium. The radio version of the standard has received the most commercial attention and we shall describe that. The IEEE 802.11b standard was the first variant to see widespread use. It operates in the 2.4 GHz band and supports data communication at up to 11 Mbps. It has been installed from 1999 onwards with base stations in many offices, homes and public places, enabling laptop computers and PDAs to access local networked devices or the Internet. IEEE 802.11g is a more recent enhancement of 802.11b that uses the same 2.4 GHz band but a different signalling technique to achieve speeds up to 54 Mbps. Finally, the 802.11a variant works in the 5 GHz band and delivers a more certain 54 Mbps of bandwidth over a somewhat shorter range. All variants use various frequency-selection and frequency-hopping techniques to avoid external interference and mutual interference between independent wireless LANs, which we shall not detail here. We focus instead on the changes to the CSMA/CD mechanism that are needed in the MAC layer for all versions of 802.11 to enable broadcast data transmission to be used with radio transmission.

Like Ethernet, the 802.11 MAC protocol offers equal opportunities to all stations to use the transmission channel, and any station may transmit directly to any other. A MAC protocol controls the use of the channel by the various stations. As for the Ethernet, the MAC layer also performs the functions of both a datalink layer and a network layer, delivering data packets to the hosts on a network.

Several problems arise from the use of radio waves rather than wires as the transmission medium. These problems stem from the fact that the carrier-sensing and collision-detection mechanisms employed in Ethernets are effective only when the strength of signals is approximately the same throughout a network.

We recall that the purpose of carrier sensing is to determine whether the medium is free at all points between the sending and receiving stations and that of collision detection is to determine whether the medium in the vicinity of the receiver is free from interference during the transmission. Because signal strength is not uniform throughout the space in which wireless LANs operate, carrier detection and collision detection may fail in the following ways:

Hidden stations: Carrier sensing may fail to detect that another station on the network is transmitting. This is illustrated in Figure 3.24. If palmtop D is transmitting to the base station E, laptop A may not be able to sense D's signal because of a radio obstruction shown. A might then start transmitting, causing a collision at E unless steps are taken to prevent this.

Fading: Due to the inverse square law of electromagnetic wave propagation, the strength of radio signals diminishes rapidly with the distance from the transmitter. Stations within a wireless LAN may be out of range of other stations in the same LAN. Thus in Figure 3.24, laptop A may not be able to detect a transmission by C, although each of them can transmit successfully to B or E. Fading defeats both carrier sensing and collision detection.

Collision masking: Unfortunately, the 'listening' technique used in the Ethernet to detect collisions is not very effective in radio networks. Because of the inverse square law referred to above, the locally generated signal will always be much stronger than any signal originating elsewhere, effectively drowning out the remote transmission. So laptops A and C might both transmit simultaneously to E. Neither would detect that collision, but E would receive only a garbled transmission.

Despite its fallibility, carrier sensing is not dispensed with in IEEE 802.11 networks; it is augmented by the addition of a *slot reservation* mechanism to the MAC protocol. The resulting scheme is called *carrier sensing multiple access with collision avoidance* (CSMA/CA).

When a station is ready to transmit it senses the medium. If it detects no carrier signal it may assume that one of the following conditions is true:

1. the medium is available;

2. an out-of-range station is in the process of requesting a slot;

3. an out-of-range station is using a slot that it had previously reserved.

The slot-reservation protocol involves the exchange of a pair of short messages (frames) between the intending sender and the receiver. The first is a *request to send* (RTS) frame from the sender to the receiver. The RTS message specifies a duration for the slot requested. The receiver replies with a *clear to send* (CTS) frame, repeating the duration of the slot. The effect of this exchange is as follows:

• Stations within range of the sender will pick up the RTS frame and take note of the duration.

- Stations within range of the receiver will pick up the CTS frame and take note of the duration.

As a result, all of the stations within range of both the sender and the receiver will refrain from transmitting for the duration of the requested slot, leaving the channel free for the sender to transmit a data frame of the appropriate length. Finally, successful receipt of the data frame is acknowledged by the receiver to help deal with the problem of external interference with the channel. The slot-reservation feature of the MAC protocol helps to avoid collisions in these ways:

- The CTS frames help to avoid the hidden station and fading problems.

- The RTS and CTS frames are short, so the risk of collisions with them are low. If one is detected, or an RTS does not result in a CTS, a random back-off period is used, as in the Ethernet.

- When the RTS and CTS frames have been correctly exchanged, there should be no collisions involving the subsequent data and acknowledgement frames unless intermittent fading prevented a third party from receiving either of them.

Security ◊ The privacy and integrity of communication is an obvious concern for wireless networks. Any station that is within range and equipped with a receiver/transmitter might seek to join a network, or failing that, it might eavesdrop on transmissions between other stations. The first attempt to address the security issues for 802.11 is entitled WEP (Wired Equivalent Privacy). Unfortunately, WEP is anything but what its name implies. Its security design was flawed in several ways that enabled it to be broken fairly easily. We describe its weaknesses and summarize the current status concerning the required improvements in Section 7.6.4.

3.5.3   IEEE 802.15.1 Bluetooth wireless PAN

Bluetooth is a wireless personal area network technology that emerged from the need to link mobile phones to PDAs, laptop computers and other personal devices without wires. A special interest group (SIG) of mobile phone and computer manufacturers led by L.M. Ericsson developed a specification for a wireless personal area network (WPAN) for the transmission of digital voice streams as well as data [Haartsen *et al.* 1998]. Version 1.0 of the Bluetooth standard was published in 1999, borrowing its name from a Viking king. The IEEE 802.15 Working Group then adopted it as standard 802.15.1 and published a specification for the physical and data link layers [IEEE 2002].

Bluetooth networks differ substantially from IEEE 802.11 (WiFi), the only other widely-adopted wireless networking standard, in ways that reflect the different application requirements of WPANs and the different cost and energy consumption targets for which they are designed. Bluetooth aims to support very small, low cost devices such as ear-mounted wireless headsets receiving digital audio streams from a mobile phone as well as interconnections between computers, phones, PDAs and other mobile devices. The cost target was to add only five dollars to the cost of a handheld device and the energy target to utilize only a small fraction of the total battery power used by a phone or PDA and to operate for several hours even with lightweight batteries used in wearable devices such as headsets.

The intended applications require less bandwidth and a shorter transmission range than typical wireless LAN applications. This is fortunate because Bluetooth operates in the same crowded 2.4 GHz licence-free frequency band as WiFi networks, cordless phones and many emergency service communication systems. Transmission is at low energy, hopping at a rate of 1600 times per second between 79 1-MHz sub-bands of the permitted frequency band to minimize the effects of interference. The output power of normal Bluetooth devices is 1 milliwatt giving a coverage of only 10 metres; 100 milliwatt devices with a range of up to 100 metres are permitted for applications such as home networks. Energy efficiency is further improved by the inclusion of an *adaptive range* facility which adjusts the transmitted power to a lower level when partner devices are nearby (as determined by the strength of the signals initially received).

Bluetooth nodes associate dynamically in pairs with no prior knowledge required. The protocol for association is described below. After a successful association the initiating node has the role of *master* and the other *slave*. A *Piconet* is a dynamically-associated network composed of one master and up to seven active slaves. The master controls the use of the communication channel, allocating timeslots to each slave. A node that is in more than one Piconet can act as bridge enabling the masters to communicate – multiple Piconets linked in this fashion are termed a *Scatternet*. Most types of device have the capacity to act as either master or slave.

All Bluetooth nodes are also equipped with a globally unique 48-bit MAC address (see Section 3.5.1) although it is only the master's MAC address that is used in the protocol. When a slave becomes active in a Piconet, it is assigned a temporary local address in the range 1 to 7 to reduce the length of packet headers. In addition to the seven active slaves a Piconet may contain up to 255 *parked* nodes in low power mode awaiting an activation signal from the master.

Association protocol ◊ To conserve energy, devices remain in sleep or *standby* mode before any associations are made or when no recent communication has ocurred. In standby mode they wake to listen for activation messages at intervals ranging from 0.64 to 2.56 seconds. To associate with a known nearby node (parked), the initiating node transmits a train of 16 *page* packets, on 16 frequency sub-bands, which may have to be repeated several times. To contact any unknown node within range the initiator must first broadcast a train of *inquiry* messages. These transmission trains can occupy up to about 5 seconds in the worst case, leading to a maximum association time of 7–10 seconds.

Association is followed by an optional authentication exchange based on user-supplied or previously-received authentication tokens, to ensure that the association is with the intended node and not an imposter. A slave then remains synchronized to the master by observing regularly-tranmitted packets from the master, even when they are not addressed to the slave. A slave that is inactive can be placed in parked mode by the master, freeing its slot in the Piconet for use by another node.

The requirement to support synchronous communication channels with adequate quality of service for the transmission of two-way real-time audio (e.g. between a phone and its owner's wireless headset) as well as asynchronous communication for data exchange dictated a network architecture very different from the best-efforts multiple-access design of Ethernet and WiFi networks. Synchronous communication is achieved by the use of a simple two-way communication protocol between a master and one of

Figure 3.25   Bluetooth frame structure

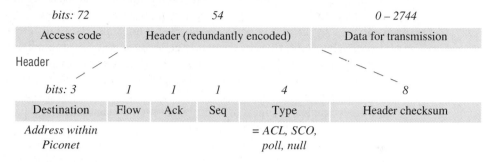

SCO packets (e.g. for voice data) have a 240-bit payload containing 80 bits of data triplicated, filling exactly one timeslot.

its slaves, termed a *synchronous connection oriented (SCO)* link on which master and slave must send alternating synchronized packets. Asynchronous communication is achieved by an an *asynchronous connection-less (ACL)* link on which the master sends asynchronous poll packets to its slaves periodically and the slaves transmit only after receiving a poll.

All variants of the Bluetooth protocol use frames that fit within the structure shown in Figure 3.25. Once a Piconet has been established, the *Access code* consists of a fixed preamble to synchronize the sender and receiver and identify the start of a slot, followed by a code derived from the master's MAC address that uniquely identifies the Piconet. The latter ensures that frames are correctly routed in situations where there are multiple overlapping Piconets. Because the medium is likely to be noisy and real-time communication cannot rely on re-transmission, each bit in the header is transmitted in triplicate to provide redundancy for both the information and the checksum parts.

The address field is just three bits to allow addressing to any of the seven currently active slaves. A zero address from the master indicates a broadcast. There are single-bit fields for flow control, acknowledgement and sequence numbering. The flow control bit is used by a slave to indicate to the master that its buffers are full; the master should await frame with a non-zero acknowledgement bit from the slave. The sequence number bit is inverted on each new frame sent to the same node; this enables duplicate (i.e. re-transmitted) frames to be detected.

SCO links are used in time-critical applications such as the transmission of a two-way voice conversation. Packets must be short to keep the latency low and there is little purpose in reporting or retransmitting corrupted packets in such applications since the retransmitted data would arrive too late to be useful. So the SCO protocol uses a simple, highly redundant protocol in which 80 bits of voice data are normally transmitted in triplicate to produce a 240-bit payload. Any two matching 80-bit replicas are taken as valid.

On the other hand, ACL links are used for data transfer applications such as address book synchronization between a computer and a phone with a larger payload.

The payload is not replicated but may contain an internal checksum that is checked at application level and in the case of failure retransmission can be requested.

Data is transmitted in packets occupying timeslots of 625 microseconds clocked and allocated by the master node. Each packet is transmitted on a different frequency in a hopping sequence defined by the master node. Because these slots are not large enough to allow a substantial payload, frames may be extended to occupy one, three or five slots. These characteristics and the underlying physical transmission method result in a maximum total throughput of 1 Mbps for a Piconet, accommodating up to three synchronous duplex channels of 64 Kpbs between a master and its slaves or a channel for asynchronous data transfer at rates up to 723 Kbps. These throughputs are calculated for the most redundant version of the SCO protocol, as described above. Other protocol variants are defined that trade-off the robustness and simplicity (and therefore low computational cost) of triplicated data for higher throughput.

Unlike most network standards, Bluetooth includes specifications (called *profiles*) for several application-level protocols, some of which are very specific to particular applications. The purpose of these profiles is to increase the likelihood that devices manufactured by different vendors will interwork. Thirteen application profiles are covered: generic access, service discovery, serial port, generic object exchange, LAN access, dial-up networking, fax, cordless telephony, intercom, headset, object push, file transfer and synchronization. Others are in preparation, including ambitous attempts to transmit high-quality music and even video over Bluetooth.

Bluetooth occupies a special niche in the range of wireless local networks. It achieves its ambitious design goal of supporting synchronous real-time audio communication with satisfactory quality of service (see Chapter 17 for further discussion of quality of service issues) as well as asynchronous data transfer using very low cost, compact and portable hardware, low power and very limited bandwidth.

Its principal limitation is the time taken (up to 10 seconds) for association of new devices. This impedes its use for certain applications, especially where devices are moving relative to each other, preventing its use, for example, to pay road tolls or to transmit promotional information to mobile phone users as they pass a store. A useful further reference on Bluetooth networking is the book by Bray and Sturman [2002].

Version 2.0 of the Bluetooth standard, with data throughputs up to 3 mbps – sufficient to carry CD-quality audio – was in the process of approval at the time of writing and improvements including a faster association mechanism and larger Piconet addresses were under development.

3.5.4   Asynchronous Transfer Mode networks

ATM has been designed to carry a wide variety of data including multimedia data such as voice and video. It is a fast packet-switching network based on a method of packet routing known as *cell relay*, which can operate much faster than conventional packet switching. It achieves its speed by avoiding flow control and error checking at the intermediate nodes in a transmission. The transmission links and nodes must therefore have a low likelihood of corrupting data. Another factor affecting the performance is the small, fixed-length units of data transmitted, which reduces buffer size and complexity and queuing delay at intermediate nodes. ATM operates in a connected mode, but a connection can only be set up if sufficient resources are available. Once a connection is

Figure 3.26   ATM protocol layers

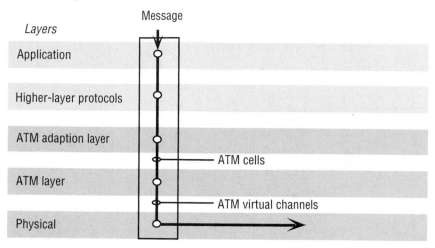

established, its quality (that is, its bandwidth and latency characteristics) can be guaranteed.

ATM is a data-switching technology that can be implemented over existing digital telephony networks, which were hitherto synchronous. When ATM is layered over a network of high-speed synchronous digital links such as those specified for the SONET Synchronous Optical Network [Omidyar and Aldridge 1993], it produces a much more flexible high-speed digital packet network with many virtual connections. Each ATM virtual connection provides bandwidth and latency guarantees. The resulting virtual circuits can be used to support a wide range of services with varying speeds. These include voice (32 kbps), fax, distributed systems services, video and high-definition television (100–150 Mbps). The ATM [CCITT 1990] standard recommends the provision of virtual circuits with data transfer rates of up to 155 Mbps or 622 Mbps.

ATM networks can also be implemented in *native mode* directly over optical fibre, copper and other transmission media, allowing bandwidths of up to several gigabits per second with current fibre technology. This is the mode in which it is employed on local and metropolitan area networks.

The ATM service is structured in three layers, represented by the darker panels in Figure 3.26. The *ATM adaptation layer* is an end-to-end layer implemented only at the sending and receiving hosts. It is intended to support existing higher-level protocols such as TCP/IP and X25 over the ATM layer. Different versions of the adaptation layer can provide a variety of different adaptation functions to suit the requirements of different higher-level protocols. It will include some common functions such as packet assembly and disassembly for use in building specific higher-level protocols.

The *ATM layer* provides a connection-oriented service that transmits fixed length packets called *cells*. A connection consists of a sequence of virtual channels within virtual paths. A *virtual channel* (VC) is a logical unidirectional association between two endpoints of a link in the physical path from source to destination. A *virtual path* (VP) is a bundle of virtual channels that are associated with a physical path between two switching nodes. Virtual paths are intended to be used to support semi-permanent

Figure 3.27   ATM cell layout

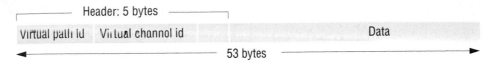

connections between pairs of end-points. Virtual channels are allocated dynamically when connections are set up.

The nodes in an ATM network can play three distinct roles:

- *hosts*, that send and receive messages;
- *VP switches*, that hold tables showing the correspondence between incoming and outgoing virtual paths;
- *VP/VC switches*, that hold similar tables for both virtual paths and virtual channels.

An ATM cell has a 5-byte header and a 48-byte data field (Figure 3.27). The full data field is always sent, even when it is only partially filled with data. The header contains an identifier for a virtual channel and an identifier for a virtual path, which together provide the information required to route the cell across the network. The virtual path identifier refers to a particular virtual path on the physical link on which the cell is transmitted. The virtual channel identifier refers to one specific virtual channel inside the virtual path. Other header fields are used to indicate the type of cell, its cell loss priority and the cell boundary.

When a cell arrives at a VP switch, the virtual path identifier in the header is looked up in its routing table to work out the corresponding virtual path identifier for the

Figure 3.28   Switching virtual paths in an ATM network

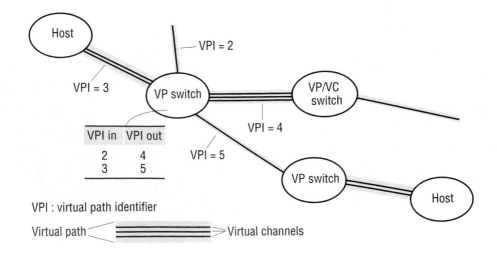

outgoing physical path; see Figure 3.28. It puts the new virtual path identifier in the header and then transmits the cell on the outgoing physical path. A VP/VC switch can perform similar routing based on both VP and VC identifiers.

Note that the VP and VC identifiers are defined locally. This scheme has the advantage that there is no need for global network-wide identifiers, which would need to be very large numbers. A global addressing scheme would introduce administrative overheads and would require cell headers and the tables in switches to hold more information.

ATM provides a service with low latency – the switching delay is about 25 microseconds per switch, giving, for example, a latency of 250 microseconds when a message passes through ten switches. This compares well with our estimated performance requirements for distributed systems (Section 3.2), suggesting that an ATM network will support interprocess communication and client-server interactions with a performance similar to, or better than, that now available from local area networks. Very high-bandwidth channels with guaranteed quality of service, suitable for transmitting streams of multimedia data at speeds up to 600 Mbps, will also be available. Gigabits per second are attainable in pure ATM networks.

3.6 Summary

We have focused on the networking concepts and techniques that are needed as a basis for distributed systems and have approached them from the point of view of a distributed system designer. Packet networks and layered protocols provide the basis for communication in distributed systems. Local area networks are based on packet broadcasting on a shared medium; Ethernet is the dominant technology. Wide area networks are based on packet switching to route packets to their destinations through a connected network. Routing is a key mechanism and a variety of routing algorithms are used, of which the distance-vector method is the most basic but effective. Congestion control is needed to prevent overflow of buffers at the receiver and at intermediate nodes.

Internetworks are constructed by layering a 'virtual' internetwork protocol over collections of networks linked together by routers. The Internet TCP/IP protocols enable computers in the Internet to communicate with one another in a uniform manner, irrespective of whether they are on the same local area network or in different countries. The Internet standards include many application-level protocols that are suitable for use in wide area distributed applications. IPv6 has the much larger address space needed for the future evolution of the Internet and provision for new application requirements such as quality of service and security.

Mobile users are supported by MobileIP for wide-area roaming and by wireless LANs based on IEEE 802 standards for local connectivity. ATM offers very high-bandwidth asynchronous communication based on virtual circuits with guaranteed quality of service.

EXERCISES

3.1 A client sends a 200 byte request message to a service, which produces a response containing 5000 bytes. Estimate the total time to complete the request in each of the following cases, with the performance assumptions listed below:

i) Using connectionless (datagram) communication (for example, UDP);

ii) Using connection-oriented communication (for example, TCP);

iii) The server process is in the same machine as the client.

[Latency per packet (local or remote,
incurred on both send and receive):   5 ms
Connection setup time (TCP only):   5 ms
Data transfer rate: 10 Mbps
MTU: 1000 bytes
Server request processing time: 2 ms
Assume that the network is lightly loaded.]

pages 66, 105

3.2 The Internet is far too large for any router to hold routing information for all destinations. How does the Internet routing scheme deal with this issue? *pages 81, 97*

3.3 What is the task of an Ethernet switch? What tables does it maintain?   *pages 88, 113*

3.4 Make a table similar to Figure 3.5 describing the work done by the software in each protocol layer when Internet applications and the TCP/IP suite are implemented over an Ethernet.   *pages 77, 105, 113*

3.5 How has the end-to-end argument [Saltzer *et al.* 1984] been applied to the design of the Internet? Consider how the use of a virtual circuit network protocol in place of IP would impact the feasibility of the World Wide Web.   *pages 39, 79, 89,* [www.reed.com]

3.6 Can we be sure that no two computers in the Internet have the same IP addresses?

page 92

3.7 Compare connectionless (UDP) and connection-oriented (TCP) communication for the implementation of each of the following application-level or presentation-level protocols:

i)   virtual terminal access (for example, Telnet);

ii)   file transfer (for example, FTP);

iii) user location (for example, rwho, finger);

iv)   information browsing (for example, HTTP);

v)   remote procedure call.

page 105

3.8 Explain how it is possible for a sequence of packets transmitted through a wide area network to arrive at their destination in an order that differs from that in which they were sent. Why can't this happen in a local network? Can it happen in an ATM network?

pages 80, 114, 124

3.9   A specific problem that must be solved in remote terminal access protocols such as Telnet is the need to transmit exceptional events such as 'kill signals' from the 'terminal' to the host in advance of previously-transmitted data. Kill signals should reach their destination ahead of any other ongoing transmissions. Discuss the solution of this problem with connection-oriented and connectionless protocols.   *page 105*

3.10   What are the disadvantages of using network-level broadcasting to locate resources:

  i)   in a single Ethernet?

  ii)   in an intranet?

  To what extent is Ethernet multicast an improvement on broadcasting?   *page 113*

3.11   Suggest a scheme that improves on MobileIP for providing access to a web server on a mobile device which is sometimes connected to the Internet by mobile phone and at other times has a wired connection to the Internet at one of several locations.

  page 104

3.12   Show the sequence of changes to the routing tables in Figure 3.8 that would occur (according to the RIP algorithm given in Figure 3.9) after the link labelled 3 in Figure 3.7 is broken.   *pages 81–85*

3.13   Use the diagram in Figure 3.13 as a basis for an illustration showing the segmentation and encapsulation of an HTTP request to a server and the resulting reply. Assume that request is a short HTTP message, but the reply includes at least 2000 bytes of HTML.

  page 76, 91

3.14   Consider the use of TCP in a Telnet remote terminal client. How should the keyboard input be buffered at the client? Investigate Nagle's and Clark's algorithms [Nagle 1984, Clark 1982] for flow control and compare them with the simple algorithm described on page 103 when TCP is used by (a) a web server, (b) a Telnet application, (c) a remote graphical application with continuous mouse input.   *pages 85, 107*

3.15   Construct a network diagram similar to Figure 3.10 for the local network at your institution or company.   *page 87*

3.16   Describe how you would configure a firewall to protect the local network at your institution or company. What incoming and outgoing requests should it intercept?

  page 108

3.17   How does a newly-installed personal computer connected to an Ethernet discover the IP addresses of local servers? How does it translate them to Ethernet addresses?   *page 94*

3.18   Can firewalls prevent denial of service attacks such as the one described on page 96? What other methods are available to deal with such attacks?   *page 96, 108*

4

INTERPROCESS COMMUNICATION

This chapter is concerned with the characteristics of protocols for communication between processes in a distributed system, both in its own right and as support for communication between distributed objects.

The Java API for interprocess communication in the Internet provides both datagram and stream communication. These are presented, together with a discussion of their failure models. They provide alternative building blocks for communication protocols.

We discuss protocols for the representation of collections of data objects in messages and of references to remote objects.

We discuss the construction of protocols to support the two communication patterns that are most commonly used in distributed programs:

- client-server communication – in which request and reply messages provide the basis for remote method invocation or remote procedure call;

- group communication – in which the same message is sent to several processes.

Interprocess communication in UNIX is dealt with as a case study.

Figure 4.1   Middleware layers

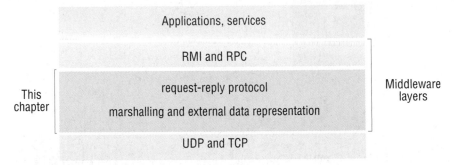

4.1   Introduction

This chapter and the next are concerned with middleware. This one is concerned with the design of the components shown in the darker blue layer in Figure 4.1. The layer above is discussed in Chapter 5; it is concerned with integrating communication into a programming language paradigm, for example by providing remote method invocation (RMI) or remote procedure calling (RPC). *Remote method invocation* allows an object to invoke a method in an object in a remote process. Examples of systems for remote invocation are CORBA and Java RMI. In a similar way, a *remote procedure call* allows a client to call a procedure in a remote server.

Chapter 3 discusses the Internet transport-level protocols UDP and TCP without saying how middleware and application programs could use these protocols. The next section of this chapter introduces the characteristics of interprocess communication and then discusses UDP and TCP from a programmer's point of view, presenting the Java interface to each of these two protocols, together with a discussion of their failure models. The last section of this chapter presents the UNIX socket interface to UDP and TCP as a case study.

The application program interface to UDP provides a *message passing* abstraction – the simplest form of interprocess communication. This enables a sending process to transmit a single message to a receiving process. The independent packets containing these messages are called *datagrams*. In the Java and UNIX APIs, the sender specifies the destination using a socket – an indirect reference to a particular port used by the destination process at a destination computer.

The application program interface to TCP provides the abstraction of a two-way *stream* between pairs of processes. The information communicated consists of a stream of data items with no message boundaries. Streams provide a building block for producer–consumer communication [Bacon 2002]. A producer and a consumer form a pair of processes in which the role of the first is to produce data items and the role of the second is to consume them. The data items sent by the producer to the consumer are queued on arrival until the consumer is ready to receive them. The consumer must wait when no data items are available. The producer must wait if the storage used to hold the queued data items is exhausted.

The third section of this chapter is concerned with how the objects and data structures used in application programs can be translated into a form suitable for sending in messages over the network, taking into account the fact that different computers may use different representations for simple data items. It also discusses a suitable representation for object references in a distributed system.

The fourth and fifth sections of this chapter deal with the design of suitable protocols to support client-server and group communication. Request-reply protocols are designed to support client-server communication in the form of either RMI or RPC. Group multicast protocols are designed to support group communication. Group multicast is a form of interprocess communication in which one process in a group of processes transmits the same message to all members of the group.

Message-passing operations can be used to construct protocols to support particular process roles and communication patterns, for example remote method invocations. By examining the roles and communication patterns, it is possible to design suitable communication protocols based on the actual exchanges and avoid redundancy. In particular, these specialized protocols should not include redundant acknowledgements. For example, in a request-reply communication, it is generally considered redundant to acknowledge the request message, because the reply message serves as an acknowledgement. If a more specialized protocol requires sender acknowledgement or any other particular characteristics, these are supplied with the specialized operations. The idea is to add specialized functions only where they are needed, with a view to achieving protocols that use a minimum of message exchanges.

4.2   The API for the Internet protocols

In this section, we discuss the general characteristics of interprocess communication and then discuss the Internet protocols as an example, explaining how programmers can use them, either by means of UDP messages or through TCP streams.

Section 4.2.1 revisits the message communication operations *send* and *receive* introduced in Section 2.3.2 with a discussion of how they synchronize with one another and how message destinations are specified in a distributed system. Section 4.2.2 introduces *sockets*, which are used in the application programming interface to UDP and TCP. Section 4.2.3 discusses UDP and its API in Java. Section 4.2.4 discusses TCP and its API in Java. The APIs for Java are object-oriented but are similar to the ones designed originally in the Berkeley BSD 4.x UNIX operating system and discussed in Section 4.6. Readers studying the programming examples in this section should consult the on-line Java documentation or Flanagan [2002] for the full specification of the classes discussed, which are in the package *java.net*.

4.2.1   The characteristics of interprocess communication

Message passing between a pair of processes can be supported by two message communication operations: *send* and *receive*, defined in terms of destinations and messages. In order for one process to communicate with another, one process sends a message (a sequence of bytes) to a destination and another process at the destination receives the message. This activity involves the communication of data from the sending process to the receiving process and may involve the synchronization of the two processes. Section 4.2.3 gives definitions for the *send* and *receive* operations in the Java API for the Internet protocols.

Synchronous and asynchronous communication ◊ A queue is associated with each message destination. Sending processes cause messages to be added to remote queues and receiving processes remove messages from local queues. Communication between the sending and receiving process may be either synchronous or asynchronous. In the *synchronous* form of communication, the sending and receiving processes synchronize at every message. In this case, both *send* and *receive* are *blocking* operations. Whenever a *send* is issued the sending process (or thread) is blocked until the corresponding *receive* is issued. Whenever a *receive* is issued the process (or thread) blocks until a message arrives.

In the *asynchronous* form of communication, the use of the *send* operation is *non-blocking* in that the sending process is allowed to proceed as soon as the message has been copied to a local buffer, and the transmission of the message proceeds in parallel with the sending process. The *receive* operation can have blocking and non-blocking variants. In the non-blocking variant, the receiving process proceeds with its program after issuing a *receive* operation, which provides a buffer to be filled in the background, but it must separately receive notification that its buffer has been filled, by polling or interrupt.

In a system environment such as Java, which supports multiple threads in a single process, the blocking *receive* has no disadvantages, for it can be issued by one thread while other threads in the process remain active, and the simplicity of synchronizing the receiving threads with the incoming message is a substantial advantage. Non-blocking communication appears to be more efficient, but it involves extra complexity in the receiving process associated with the need to acquire the incoming message out of its flow of control. For these reasons, today's systems do not generally provide the non-blocking form of *receive*.

Message destinations ◊ Chapter 3 explains that in the Internet protocols, messages are sent to (*Internet address*, *local port*) pairs. A local port is a message destination within a computer, specified as an integer. A port has exactly one receiver (multicast ports are an exception, see Section 4.5.1) but can have many senders. Processes may use multiple ports from which to receive messages. Any process that knows the number of a port can send a message to it. Servers generally publicize their port numbers for use by clients.

If the client uses a fixed Internet address to refer to a service, then that service must always run on the same computer for its address to remain valid. This can be avoided by using one of the following approaches to providing location transparency:

- Client programs refer to services by name and use a name server or binder (see Section 5.2.5) to translate their names into server locations at run time. This allows services to be relocated but not to migrate – to be moved while the system is running.

- The operating system, for example Mach (www.cdk4.net/oss), provides location-independent identifiers for message destinations, mapping them onto a lower-level address in order to deliver messages to ports, allowing service migration and relocation.

An alternative to ports is that messages should be addressed to processes, which was the case in the V system [Cheriton 1984]. However, ports have the advantage that they

Figure 4.2   Sockets and ports

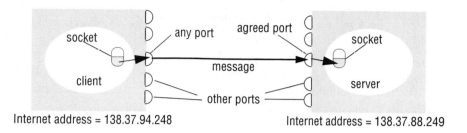

Internet address = 138.37.94.248   Internet address = 138.37.88.249

provide several alternative points of entry to a receiving process. In some applications, it is very useful to be able to deliver the same message to the members of a set of processes. Therefore, some IPC systems provide the ability to send messages to groups of destinations – either processes or ports. For example, Chorus [Rozier *et al.* 1990] provided groups of ports.

Reliability ◊ Chapter 2 defines reliable communication in terms of validity and integrity. As far as the validity property is concerned, a point-to-point message service can be described as reliable if messages are guaranteed to be delivered despite a 'reasonable' number of packets being dropped or lost. In contrast, a point-to-point message service can be described as unreliable if messages are not guaranteed to be delivered in the face of even a single packet dropped or lost. For integrity, messages must arrive uncorrupted and without duplication.

Ordering ◊ Some applications require that messages be delivered in *sender order* – that is, the order in which they were transmitted by the sender. The delivery of messages out of sender order is regarded as a failure by such applications.

4.2.2   Sockets

Both forms of communication (UDP and TCP) use the *socket* abstraction, which provides an endpoint for communication between processes. Sockets originate from BSD UNIX but are also present in most versions of UNIX, including Linux as well as Windows and the Macintosh OS. Interprocess communication consists of transmitting a message between a socket in one process and a socket in another process, as illustrated in Figure 4.2. For a process to receive messages, its socket must be bound to a local port and one of the Internet addresses of the computer on which it runs. Messages sent to a particular Internet address and port number can be received only by a process whose socket is associated with that Internet address and port number. Processes may use the same socket for sending and receiving messages. Each computer has a large number (2^{16}) of possible port numbers for use by local processes for receiving messages. Any process may make use of multiple ports to receive messages, but a process cannot share ports with other processes on the same computer. Processes using IP multicast are an exception in that they do share ports – see Section 4.5.1. However, any number of processes may send messages to the same port. Each socket is associated with a particular protocol – either UDP or TCP.

Java API for Internet addresses ◊ As the IP packets underlying UDP and TCP are sent to Internet addresses, Java provides a class, *InetAddress*, that represents Internet addresses. Users of this class refer to computers by Domain Name Service (DNS) hostnames (see Section 3.4.7). For example, instances of *InetAddress* that contain Internet addresses can be created by calling a static method of *InetAddress,* giving a DNS hostname as argument. The method uses the DNS to get the corresponding Internet address. For example, to get an object representing the Internet address of the host whose DNS name is *bruno.dcs.qmul.ac.uk*, use:

> *InetAddress aComputer = InetAddress.getByName("bruno.dcs.qmul.ac.uk");*

This method can throw an *UnknownHostException*. Note that the user of the class does not need to state the explicit value of an Internet address. In fact, the class encapsulates the details of the representation of Internet addresses. Thus the interface for this class is not dependent on the number of bytes needed to represent Internet address – 4 bytes in IPv4 and 16 bytes in IPv6.

4.2.3 UDP datagram communication

A datagram sent by UDP is transmitted from a sending process to a receiving process without acknowledgement or retries. If a failure occurs, the message may not arrive. A datagram is transmitted between processes when one process *sends* it and another *receives* it. To send or receive messages a process must first create a socket bound to an Internet address of the local host and a local port. A server will bind its socket to a *server port* – one that it makes known to clients so that they can send messages to it. A client binds its socket to any free local port. The *receive* method returns the Internet address and port of the sender, in addition to the message, allowing the recipient to send a reply.

The following paragraphs discuss some issues relating to datagram communication:

Message size: The receiving process needs to specify an array of bytes of a particular size in which to receive a message. If the message is too big for the array, it is truncated on arrival. The underlying IP protocol allows packet lengths of up to 2^{16} bytes, which includes the headers as well as the message. However, most environments impose a size restriction of 8 kilobytes. Any application requiring messages larger than the maximum must fragment them into chunks of that size. Generally, an application, for example DNS, will decide on a size that is not excessively large but is adequate for its intended use.

Blocking: Sockets normally provide non-blocking *sends* and blocking *receives* for datagram communication (a non-blocking *receive* is an option in some implementations). The *send* operation returns when it has handed the message to the underlying UDP and IP protocols, which are responsible for transmitting it to its destination. On arrival, the message is placed in a queue for the socket that is bound to the destination port. The message can be collected from the queue by an outstanding or future invocation of *receive* on that socket. Messages are discarded at the destination if no process already has a socket bound to the destination port.

The method *receive* blocks until a datagram is received, unless a timeout has been set on the socket. If the process that invokes the *receive* method has other work to do while waiting for the message, it should arrange to use a separate thread.

Threads are discussed in Chapter 6. For example, when a server receives a message from a client, the message may specify work to do, in which case the server will use separate threads to do the work and to wait for messages from other clients.

Timeouts: The *receive* that blocks for ever is suitable for use by a server that is waiting to receive requests from its clients. But in some programs, it is not appropriate that a process that has used a *receive* operation should wait indefinitely in situations where the potential sending process has crashed or the expected message has been lost. To allow for such requirements, timeouts can be set on sockets. Choosing an appropriate timeout interval is difficult, but it should be fairly large in comparison with the time required to transmit a message.

Receive from any: The *receive* method does not specify an origin for messages. Instead, an invocation of *receive* gets a message addressed to its socket from any origin. The *receive* method returns the Internet address and local port of the sender, allowing the recipient to check where it came from. It is possible to connect a datagram socket to a particular remote port and Internet address, in which case the socket is only able to send messages to and receive messages from that address.

Failure model ◊ Chapter 2 presents a failure model for communication channels and defines reliable communication in terms of two properties: integrity and validity. The integrity property requires that messages should not be corrupted or duplicated. The use of a checksum ensures that there is a negligible probability that any message received is corrupted. The failure model can be used to provide a failure model for UDP datagrams, which suffer from the following failures:

Omission failures: Messages may be dropped occasionally, either because of a checksum error or because no buffer space is available at the source or destination. To simplify the discussion, we regard send-omission and receive-omission failures (see Figure 2.11) as omission failures in the communication channel.

Ordering: Messages can sometimes be delivered out of sender order.

Applications using UDP datagrams are left to provide their own checks to achieve the quality of reliable communication they require. A reliable delivery service may be constructed from one that suffers from omission failures by the use of acknowledgements. Section 4.4 discusses how reliable request-reply protocols for client-server communication may be built over UDP.

Use of UDP ◊ For some applications, it is acceptable to use a service that is liable to occasional omission failures. For example, the Domain Naming Service, which looks up DNS names in the Internet, is implemented over UDP. Voice Over IP (VOIP) also runs over UDP. UDP datagrams are sometimes an attractive choice because they do not suffer from the overheads associated with guaranteed message delivery. There are three main sources of overhead:

1. the need to store state information at source and destination;
2. the transmission of extra messages; and
3. latency for the sender.

The reasons for these overheads are discussed in Section 4.2.4.

Figure 4.3   UDP client sends a message to the server and gets a reply

```
import java.net.*;
import java.io.*;
public class UDPClient{
    public static void main(String args[]){
        // args give message contents and server hostname
        DatagramSocket aSocket = null;
        try {
            aSocket = new DatagramSocket();
            byte [] m = args[0].getBytes();
            InetAddress aHost = InetAddress.getByName(args[1]);
            int serverPort = 6789;
            DatagramPacket request =
                new DatagramPacket(m, m.length(), aHost, serverPort);
            aSocket.send(request);
            byte[] buffer = new byte[1000];
            DatagramPacket reply = new DatagramPacket(buffer, buffer.length);
            aSocket.receive(reply);
            System.out.println("Reply: " + new String(reply.getData()));
        } catch (SocketException e){System.out.println("Socket: " + e.getMessage());
        } catch (IOException e){System.out.println("IO: " + e.getMessage());
        } finally { if(aSocket != null) aSocket.close();}
    }
}
```

Java API for UDP datagrams ◊   The Java API provides datagram communication by means of two classes: *DatagramPacket* and *DatagramSocket*.

DatagramPacket: This class provides a constructor that makes an instance out of an array of bytes comprising a message, the length of the message and the Internet address and local port number of the destination socket, as follows:

Datagram packet

array of bytes containing message	length of message	Internet address	port number

Instances of *DatagramPacket* may be transmitted between processes when one process *sends* it and another *receives* it.

This class provides another constructor for use when receiving a message. Its arguments specify an array of bytes in which to receive the message and the length of the array. A received message is put in the *DatagramPacket* together with its length and the Internet address and port of the sending socket. The message can be retrieved from the *DatagramPacket* by means of the method *getData*. The methods *getPort* and *getAddress* access the port and Internet address.

DatagramSocket: This class supports sockets for sending and receiving UDP datagrams. It provides a constructor that takes a port number as argument, for use by

Figure 4.4   UDP server repeatedly receives a request and sends it back to the client

```
import java.net.*;
import java.io.*;
public class UDPServer{
    public static void main(String args[]){
        DatagramSocket aSocket = null;
        try{
            aSocket = new DatagramSocket(6789);
            byte[] buffer = new byte[1000];
            while(true){
                DatagramPacket request = new DatagramPacket(buffer, buffer.length);
                aSocket.receive(request);
                DatagramPacket reply = new DatagramPacket(request.getData(),
                        request.getLength(), request.getAddress(), request.getPort());
                aSocket.send(reply);
            }
        } catch (SocketException e){System.out.println("Socket: " + e.getMessage());
        } catch (IOException e) {System.out.println("IO: " + e.getMessage());
        } finally {if (aSocket != null) aSocket.close();}
    }
}
```

processes that need to use a particular port. It also provides a no-argument constructor that allows the system to choose a free local port. These constructors can throw a *SocketException* if the port is already in use or if a reserved port (a number below 1024) is specified when running over UNIX.

The class *DatagramSocket* provides methods that include the following:

send and *receive*: These methods are for transmitting datagrams between a pair of sockets. The argument of *send* is an instance of *DatagramPacket* containing a message and its destination. The argument of *receive* is an empty *DatagramPacket* in which to put the message, its length and origin. The methods *send* and *receive* can throw *IOExceptions*.

setSoTimeout: This method allows a timeout to be set. With a timeout set, the *receive* method will block for the time specified and then throw an *InterruptedIOException*.

connect: This method is used for connecting it to a particular remote port and Internet address, in which case the socket is only able to send messages to and receive messages from that address.

Figure 4.3 shows the program for a client that creates a socket, sends a message to a server at port 6789 and then waits to receive a reply. The arguments of the *main* method supply a message and the DNS hostname of the server. The message is converted to an array of bytes, and the DNS hostname is converted to an Internet address. Figure 4.4 shows the program for the corresponding server, which creates a socket bound to its server port (6789) then repeatedly waits to receive a request message from a client, to which it replies by sending back the same message.

4.2.4   TCP stream communication

The API to the TCP protocol, which originates from BSD 4.x UNIX, provides the abstraction of a stream of bytes to which data may be written and from which data may be read. The following characteristics of the network are hidden by the stream abstraction:

Message sizes: The application can choose how much data it writes to a stream or reads from it. It may deal in very small or very large sets of data. The underlying implementation of a TCP stream decides how much data to collect before transmitting it as one or more IP packets. On arrival, the data is handed to the application as requested. Applications can, if necessary, force data to be sent immediately.

Lost messages: The TCP protocol uses an acknowledgement scheme. As an example of a simple scheme (which is not used in TCP), the sending end keeps a record of each IP packet sent and the receiving end acknowledges all the arrivals. If the sender does not receive an acknowledgement within a timeout, it retransmits the message. The more sophisticated sliding window scheme [Comer 2000a] cuts down on the number of acknowledgement messages required.

Flow control: The TCP protocol attempts to match the speeds of the processes that read from and write to a stream. If the writer is too fast for the reader, then it is blocked until the reader has consumed sufficient data.

Message duplication and ordering: Message identifiers are associated with each IP packet, which enables the recipient to detect and reject duplicates, or to reorder messages that do not arrive in sender order.

Message destinations: A pair of communicating processes establish a connection before they can communicate over a stream. Once a connection is established, the processes simply read from and write to the stream without needing to use Internet addresses and ports. Establishing a connection involves a *connect* request from client to server followed by an *accept* request from server to client before any communication can take place. This could be a considerable overhead for a single client-server request and reply.

The API for stream communication assumes that when a pair of processes are establishing a connection, one of them plays the client role and the other plays the server role, but thereafter they could be peers. The client role involves creating a stream socket bound to any port and then making a *connect* request asking for a connection to a server at its server port. The server role involves creating a listening socket bound to a server port and waiting for clients to request connections. The listening socket maintains a queue of incoming connection requests. In the socket model, when the server *accept*s a connection, a new stream socket is created for the server to communicate with a client, meanwhile retaining its socket at the server port for listening for *connect* requests from other clients. Further details of the *connect* and *accept* operations are described in the UNIX case study at the end of this chapter.

The pair of sockets in client and server are connected by a pair of streams, one in each direction. Thus each socket has an input stream and an output stream. One of the pair of processes can send information to the other by writing to its output stream, and the other process obtains the information by reading from its input stream.

When an application *closes* a socket, this indicates that it will not write any more data to its output stream. Any data in the output buffer is sent to the other end of the stream and put in the queue at the destination socket with an indication that the stream is broken. The process at the destination can read the data in the queue, but any further reads after the queue is empty will result in an indication of end of stream. When a process exits or fails, all of its sockets are eventually closed and any process attempting to communicate with it will discover that its connection has been broken.

The following paragraphs address some outstanding issues related to stream communication:

Matching of data items: Two communicating processes need to agree as to the contents of the data transmitted over a stream. For example, if one process writes an *int* followed by a *double* to a stream, then the reader at the other end must read an *int* followed by a *double*. When a pair of processes do not cooperate correctly in their use of a stream, the reading process may experience errors when interpreting the data or may block due to insufficient data in the stream.

Blocking: The data written to a stream is kept in a queue at the destination socket. When a process attempts to read data from an input channel, it will get data from the queue or it will block until data becomes available. The process that writes data to a stream may be blocked by the TCP flow control mechanism if the socket at the other end is queuing as much data as the protocol allows.

Threads: When a server accepts a connection, it generally creates a new thread in which to communicate with the new client. The advantage of using a separate thread for each client is that the server can block when waiting for input without delaying other clients. In an environment in which threads are not provided, an alternative is to test whether input is available from a stream before attempting to read it; for example, in a UNIX environment the *select* system call may be used for this purpose.

Failure model ◊ To satisfy the integrity property of reliable communication, TCP streams use checksums to detect and reject corrupt packets and sequence numbers to detect and reject duplicate packets. For the sake of the validity property, TCP streams use timeouts and retransmissions to deal with lost packets. Therefore, messages are guaranteed to be delivered even when some of the underlying packets are lost.

But if the packet loss over a connection passes some limit or the network connecting a pair of communicating processes is severed or becomes severely congested, the TCP software responsible for sending messages will receive no acknowledgements and after a time will declare the connection to be broken. Thus TCP does not provide reliable communication, because it does not guarantee to deliver messages in the face of all possible difficulties.

When a connection is broken, a process using it will be notified if it attempts to read or write. This has the following effects:

- the processes using the connection cannot distinguish between network failure and failure of the process at the other end of the connection;

- the communicating processes cannot tell whether the messages they sent recently have been received or not.

Figure 4.5   TCP client makes connection to server, sends request and receives reply

```java
import java.net.*;
import java.io.*;
public class TCPClient {
    public static void main (String args[]) {
        // arguments supply message and hostname of destination
        Socket s = null;
        try{
            int serverPort = 7896;
            s = new Socket(args[1], serverPort);
            DataInputStream in = new DataInputStream( s.getInputStream());
            DataOutputStream out =
                new DataOutputStream( s.getOutputStream());
            out.writeUTF(args[0]);        // UTF is a string encoding see Sn 4.3
            String data = in.readUTF();
            System.out.println("Received: "+ data) ;
        }catch (UnknownHostException e){
            System.out.println("Sock:"+e.getMessage());
        } catch (EOFException e){System.out.println("EOF:"+e.getMessage());
        } catch (IOException e){System.out.println("IO:"+e.getMessage());
        } finally {if(s!=null) try {s.close();}catch (IOException e){/*close failed*/}}
    }
}
```

Use of TCP ◊ Many frequently used services run over TCP connections, with reserved port numbers. These include the following:

HTTP: The hypertext transfer protocol is used for communication between web browsers and web servers; it is discussed later in this chapter.

FTP: The file transfer protocol allows directories on a remote computer to be browsed and files to be transferred from one computer to another over a connection.

Telnet: telnet provides access by means of a terminal session to a remote computer.

SMTP: The simple mail transfer protocol is used to send mail between computers.

Java API for TCP streams ◊ The Java interface to TCP streams is provided in the classes *ServerSocket* and *Socket*.

ServerSocket: This class is intended for use by a server to create a socket at a server port for listening for *connect* requests from clients. Its *accept* method gets a *connect* request from the queue, or if the queue is empty, it blocks until one arrives. The result of executing *accept* is an instance of *Socket* – a socket for giving access to streams for communicating with the client.

Socket: This class is for use by a pair of processes with a connection. The client uses a constructor to create a socket, specifying the DNS hostname and port of a server. This constructor not only creates a socket associated with a local port but also

Figure 4.6   TCP server makes a connection for each client and then echoes the client's request

```
import java.net.*;
import java.io.*;
public class TCPServer {
    public static void main (String args[]) {
        try{
            int serverPort = 7896;
            ServerSocket listenSocket = new ServerSocket(serverPort);
            while(true) {
                Socket clientSocket = listenSocket.accept();
                Connection c = new Connection(clientSocket);
            }
        } catch(IOException e) {System.out.println("Listen :"+e.getMessage());}
    }
}
class Connection extends Thread {
    DataInputStream in;
    DataOutputStream out;
    Socket clientSocket;
    public Connection (Socket aClientSocket) {
        try {
            clientSocket = aClientSocket;
            in = new DataInputStream( clientSocket.getInputStream());
            out =new DataOutputStream( clientSocket.getOutputStream());
            this.start();
        } catch(IOException e) {System.out.println("Connection:"+e.getMessage());}
    }
    public void run(){
        try {                      // an echo server
            String data = in.readUTF();
            out.writeUTF(data);
        } catch(EOFException e) {System.out.println("EOF:"+e.getMessage());
        } catch(IOException e) {System.out.println("IO:"+e.getMessage());
        } finally { try {clientSocket.close();}catch (IOException e){/*close failed*/}}
    }
}
```

connects it to the specified remote computer and port number. It can throw an *UnknownHostException* if the hostname is wrong or an *IOException* if an IO error occurs.

The *Socket* class provides methods *getInputStream* and *getOutputStream* for accessing the two streams associated with a socket. The return types of these methods are *InputStream* and *OutputStream*, respectively – abstract classes that define methods for reading and writing bytes. The return values can be used as the arguments of constructors for suitable input and output streams. Our example uses *DataInputStream* and *DataOutputStream*, which allow binary representations of primitive data types to be read and written in a machine-independent manner.

Figure 4.5 shows a client program in which the arguments of the *main* method supply a message and the DNS hostname of the server. The client creates a socket bound to the hostname and server port 7896. It makes a *DataInputStream* and a *DataOutputStream* from the socket's input and output streams then writes the message to its output stream and waits to read a reply from its input stream. The server program in Figure 4.6 opens a server socket on its server port (7896) and listens for *connect* requests. When one arrives, it makes a new thread in which to communicate with the client. The new thread creates a *DataInputStream* and a *DataOutputStream* from its socket's input and output streams and then waits to read a message and write it back.

As our message consists of a string, the client and server processes use the method *writeUTF* of *DataOutputStream* to write it to the output stream and the method *readUTF* of *DataInputStream* to read it from the input stream. UTF-8 is an encoding that represents strings in a particular format, which is described in Section 4.3.

When a process has closed its socket, it will no longer be able to use its input and output streams. The process to which it has sent data can read the data in its queue, but any further reads after the queue is empty will result in an *EOFException*. Attempts to use a closed socket or to write to a broken stream result in an *IOException*.

4.3   External data representation and marshalling

The information stored in running programs is represented as data structures – for example by sets of interconnected objects – whereas the information in messages consists of sequences of bytes. Irrespective of the form of communication used, the data structures must be flattened (converted to a sequence of bytes) before transmission and rebuilt on arrival. The individual primitive data items transmitted in messages can be data values of many different types, and not all computers store primitive values such as integers in the same order. The representation of floating-point numbers also differs between architectures. There are two variants for the ordering of integers: the so-called *big-endian* order, in which the most significant byte comes first; and *little-endian* order, in which it comes last. Another issue is the set of codes used to represent characters: for example, the majority of applications on systems such as UNIX use ASCII character coding, taking one byte per character, whereas the Unicode standard allows for the representation of texts in many different languages and takes two bytes per character.

One of the following methods can be used to enable any two computers to exchange binary data values:

- The values are converted to an agreed external format before transmission and converted to the local form on receipt; if the two computers are known to be the same type, the conversion to external format can be omitted.

- The values are transmitted in the sender's format, together with an indication of the format used, and the recipient converts the values if necessary.

Note, however, that bytes themselves are never altered during transmission. To support RMI or RPC, any data type that can be passed as an argument or returned as a result must be able to be flattened and the individual primitive data values represented in an agreed format. An agreed standard for the representation of data structures and primitive values is called an *external data representation*.

Marshalling is the process of taking a collection of data items and assembling them into a form suitable for transmission in a message. *Unmarshalling* is the process of disassembling them on arrival to produce an equivalent collection of data items at the destination. Thus marshalling consists of the translation of structured data items and primitive values into an external data representation. Similarly, unmarshalling consists of the generation of primitive values from their external data representation and the rebuilding of the data structures.

Three alternative approaches to external data representation and marshalling are discussed:

- CORBA's common data representation, which is concerned with an external representation for the structured and primitive types that can be passed as arguments and results of remote method invocations in CORBA. It can be used by a variety of programming languages (see Chapter 20).

- Java's object serialization, which is concerned with the flattening and external data representation of any single object or tree of objects that may need to be transmitted in a message or stored on a disk. It is for use only by Java.

- XML or Extensible Markup Language, which defines a textual fomat for representing structured data. It was originally intended for documents containing textual self-describing structured data, for example documents accessible on the web. But it is now also used to represent the data sent in messages exchanged by clients and servers in web services – see Chapter 19.

In the first two cases, the marshalling and unmarshalling activities are intended to be carried out by a middleware layer without any involvement on the part of the application programmer. Even in the case of XML, which is textual and therefore more accessible to hand encoding, software for marshalling and unmarshalling is available for all commonly used platforms and programming environments. Because marshalling requires the consideration of all the finest details of the representation of the primitive components of composite objects, the process is likely to be error-prone if carried out by hand. Compactness is another issue that can be addressed in the design of automatically generated marshalling procedures.

In the first two approaches, the primitive data types are marshalled into a binary form. In the third approach (XML), the primitive data types are represented textually. The textual representation of a data value will generally be longer than the equivalent binary representation. The HTTP protocol, which is described in Section 4.4, is another example of the textual approach.

Another issue with regard to the design of marshalling methods is whether the marshalled data should include information concerning the type of its contents. For example, CORBA's representation includes just the values of the objects transmitted – nothing about their types. On the other hand, both Java serialization and XML do include type information, but in different ways. Java puts all of the required type information into the serialized form. But XML documents may refer to externally defined sets of names (with types) called *namespaces*.

Although we are interested in the use of an external data representation for the arguments and results of RMIs and RPCs, it does have a more general use for representing data structures, objects or structured documents in a form suitable for transmission in messages or storing in files.

4.3.1 CORBA's Common Data Representation (CDR)

CORBA CDR is the external data representation defined with CORBA 2.0 [OMG 2004a]. CDR can represent all of the data types that can be used as arguments and return values in remote invocations in CORBA. These consist of 15 primitive types, which include *short* (16-bit), *long* (32-bit), *unsigned short*, *unsigned long*, *float* (32-bit), *double* (64-bit), *char*, *boolean* (TRUE, FALSE), *octet* (8-bit), and *any* (which can represent any basic or constructed type); together with a range of composite types, which are described in Figure 4.7. Each argument or result in a remote invocation is represented by a sequence of bytes in the invocation or result message.

Primitive types: CDR defines a representation for both big-endian and little-endian orderings. Values are transmitted in the sender's ordering, which is specified in each message. The recipient translates if it requires a different ordering. For example, a 16-bit *short* occupies two bytes in the message and for big-endian ordering, the most significant bits occupy the first byte and the least significant bits occupy the second byte. Each primitive value is placed at an index in the sequence of bytes according to its size. Suppose that the sequence of bytes is indexed from zero upwards. Then a primitive value of size n bytes (where $n = 1, 2, 4$ or 8) is appended to the sequence at an index that is a multiple of n in the stream of bytes. Floating-point values follow the IEEE standard – in which the sign, exponent and fractional part are in bytes 0–n for big-endian ordering and the other way round for little-endian. Characters are represented by a code set agreed between client and server.

Figure 4.7 CORBA CDR for constructed types

Type	Representation
sequence	length (unsigned long) followed by elements in order
string	length (unsigned long) followed by characters in order (can also can have wide characters)
array	array elements in order (no length specified because it is fixed)
struct	in the order of declaration of the components
enumerated	unsigned long (the values are specified by the order declared)
union	type tag followed by the selected member

Figure 4.8   CORBA CDR message

index in sequence of bytes	← 4 bytes →	notes on representation
0–3	5	*length of string*
4–7	"Smit"	*'Smith'*
8–11	"h___"	
12–15	6	*length of string*
16–19	"Lond"	*'London'*
20–23	"on__"	
24–27	1934	*unsigned long*

The flattened form represents a *Person* struct with value: {'Smith', 'London', 1934}

Constructed types: The primitive values that comprise each constructed type are added to a sequence of bytes in a particular order, as shown in Figure 4.7.

Figure 4.8 shows a message in CORBA CDR that contains the three fields of a *struct* whose respective types are *string*, *string* and *unsigned long*. The figure shows the sequence of bytes with four bytes in each row. The representation of each string consists of an *unsigned long* representing its length followed by the characters in the string. For simplicity, we assume that each character occupies just one byte. Variable length data is padded with zeros so that it has a standard form, enabling marshalled data or its checksum to be compared. Note that each *unsigned long*, which occupies four bytes, starts at an index that is a multiple of four. The figure does not distinguish between the big- and little-endian ordering. Although the example in Figure 4.8 is simple, CORBA CDR can represent any data structure that can be composed from the primitive and constructed types, but without using pointers.

Another example of an external data representation is the Sun XDR standard, which is specified in RFC 1832 [Srinivasan 1995b] and described in www.cdk4.net/ipc. It was developed by Sun for use in the messages exchanged between clients and servers in Sun NFS (see Chapter 8).

The type of a data item is not given with the data representation in the message in either the CORBA CDR or the Sun XDR standard. This is because it is assumed that the sender and recipient have common knowledge of the order and types of the data items in a message. In particular for RMI or RPC, each method invocation passes arguments of particular types, and the result is a value of a particular type.

Marshalling in CORBA ◊ Marshalling operations can be generated automatically from the specification of the types of data items to be transmitted in a message. The types of the data structures and the types of the basic data items are described in CORBA IDL (see Section 20.2.3), which provides a notation for describing the types of the arguments and results of RMI methods. For example, we might use CORBA IDL to describe the data structure in the message in Figure 4.8 as follows:

```
struct Person{
    string name;
    string place;
    unsigned long year;
};
```

The CORBA interface compiler (see Chapter 5) generates appropriate marshalling and unmarshalling operations for the arguments and results of remote methods from the definitions of the types of their parameters and results.

4.3.2   Java object serialization

In Java RMI, both objects and primitive data values may be passed as arguments and results of method invocations. An object is an instance of a Java class. For example, the Java class equivalent to the *Person struct* defined in CORBA IDL might be:

```
public class Person implements Serializable {
    private String name;
    private String place;
    private int year;
    public Person(String aName, String aPlace, int aYear) {
        name = aName;
        place = aPlace;
        year = aYear;
    }
    // followed by methods for accessing the instance variables
}
```

The above class states that it implements the *Serializable* interface, which has no methods. Stating that a class implements the *Serializable* interface (which is provided in the *java.io* package) has the effect of allowing its instances to be serialized.

In Java, the term *serialization* refers to the activity of flattening an object or a connected set of objects into a serial form that is suitable for storing on disk or transmitting in a message, for example, as an argument or result of an RMI. Deserialization consists of restoring the state of an object or a set of objects from their serialized form. It is assumed that the process that does the deserialization has no prior knowledge of the types of the objects in the serialized form. Therefore, some information about the class of each object is included in the serialized form. This information enables the recipient to load the appropriate class when an object is deserialized.

The information about a class consists of the name of the class and a version number. The version number is intended to change when major changes are made to the class. It can be set by the programmer or calculated automatically as a hash of the name of the class, its instance variables, methods and interfaces. The process that deserializes an object can check that it has the correct version of the class.

Java objects can contain references to other objects. When an object is serialized, all the objects that it references are serialized together with it to ensure that when the object is reconstructed, all of its references can be fulfilled at the destination. References are serialized as *handles* – in this case, the handle is a reference to an object within the serialized form, for example the next number in a sequence of positive integers. The serialization procedure must ensure that there is a 1–1 correspondence between object references and handles. It must also ensure that each object is written once only – on the second or subsequent occurrence of an object, the handle is written instead of the object.

To serialize an object, its class information is written out, followed by the types and names of its instance variables. If the instance variables belong to new classes, then their class information must also be written out, followed by the types and names of their instance variables. This recursive procedure continues until the class information and types and names of instance variables of all of the necessary classes have been written out. Each class is given a handle, and no class is written more than once to the stream of bytes – the handles being written instead where necessary.

The contents of the instance variables that are primitive types, such as integers, chars, booleans, bytes and longs, are written in a portable binary format using methods of the *ObjectOutputStream* class. Strings and characters are written by its method called *writeUTF* using Universal Transfer Format (UTF-8), which enables ASCII characters to be represented unchanged (in one byte), whereas Unicode characters are represented by multiple bytes. Strings are preceded by the number of bytes they occupy in the stream.

As an example, consider the serialization of the following object:

Person p = new Person("Smith", "London", 1934);

The serialized form is illustrated in Figure 4.9, which omits the values of the handles and of the type markers that indicate the objects, classes, strings and other objects in the full serialized form. The first instance variable (1934) is an integer that has a fixed length; the second and third instance variables are strings and are preceded by their lengths.

To make use of Java serialization, for example to serialize the *Person* object, create an instance of the class *ObjectOutputStream* and invoke its *writeObject* method, passing the *Person* object as argument. To deserialize an object from a stream of data, open an *ObjectInputStream* on the stream and use its *readObject* method to reconstruct the original object. The use of this pair of classes is similar to the use of *DataOutputStream* and *DataInputStream* illustrated in Figures 4.5 and 4.6.

Serialization and deserialization of the arguments and results of remote invocations are generally carried out automatically by the middeware, without any participation by the application programmer. If necessary, programmers with special requirements may write their own version of the methods that read and write objects. To find out how to do this and to get further information about serialization in Java, read the tutorial on object serialization [java.sun.com II]. Another way in which a programmer may modify the effects of serialization is by declaring variables that should not be serialized as *transient*. Examples of things that should not be serialized are references to local resources such as files and sockets.

The use of reflection ◊ The Java language supports *reflection* – the ability to enquire about the properties of a class, such as the names and types of its instance variables and methods. It also enables classes to be created from their names, and a constructor with given argument types to be created for a given class. Reflection makes it possible to do serialization and deserialization in a completely generic manner. This means that there is no need to generate special marshalling functions for each type of object as described above for CORBA. To find out more about reflection, see Flanagan [2002].

Figure 4.9   Indication of Java serialized form

	Serialized values			Explanation
Person	8-byte version number		h0	*class name, version number*
3	int year	java.lang.String name	java.lang.String place	*number, type and name of instance variables*
1934	5 Smith	6 London	h1	*values of instance variables*

The true serialized form contains additional type markers; h0 and h1 are handles

Java object serialization uses reflection to find out the class name of the object to be serialized and the names, types and values of its instance variables. That is all that is needed for the serialized form.

For deserialization, the class name in the serialized form is used to create a class. This is then used to create a new constructor with argument types corresponding to those specified in the serialized form. Finally, the new constructor is used to create a new object with instance variables whose values are read from the serialized form.

4.3.3   Extensible markup language (XML)

XML is a markup language that was defined by the World Wide Web Consortium (W3C) for general use on the web. In general, the term *markup language* refers to a textual encoding that represents both a text and details as to its structure or its appearance. Both XML and HTML were derived from SGML (Standardized Generalized Markup Language) [ISO 8879], a very complex markup language. HTML (see Section 1.3.1) was designed for defining the appearance of web pages. XML was designed for writing structured documents for the web.

XML data items are tagged with 'markup' strings. The tags are used to describe the logical structure of the data and to associate attribute-value pairs with logical structures. That is, in XML, the tags relate to the structure of the text that they enclose, in contrast to HTML in which the tags specify how a browser could display the text. For a specification of XML, see the pages on XML provided by W3C at [www.w3.org VI].

XML is used to enable clients to communicate with web services and for defining the interfaces and other properties of web services. However, XML is also used in many other ways. It is used in archiving and retrieval systems – although an XML archive may be larger than a binary one, it has the advantage of being readable on any computer. Other examples of the use of XML include the specification of user interfaces and the encoding of configuration files in operating systems.

XML is *extensible* in the sense that users can define their own tags, in contrast to HTML which uses a fixed set of tags. However, if an XML document is intended to be used by more than one application, then the names of the tags must be agreed between them. For example, clients usually use SOAP messages to communicate with web services. SOAP (see Section 19.2.1) is an XML format whose tags are published for use by web services and their clients.

Figure 4.10   XML definition of the *Person* structure

```
<person id="123456789">
        <name>Smith</name>
        <place>London</place>
        <year>1934</year>
        <!-- a comment -->
</person >
```

Some external data representations (such as CORBA CDR) do not need to be self-describing, because it is assumed that the client and server exchanging a message have prior knowledge of the order and the types of the information it contains. However, XML was intended to be used by multiple applications for different purposes. The provision of tags, together with the use of namespaces to define the meaning of the tags has made this possible. In addition, the use of tags enables applications to select just those parts of a document it needs to process: it will not be affected by the addition of information relevant to other applications.

XML documents, being textual, can be read by humans. In practice, most XML documents are generated and read by XML processing software, but the ability to read XML can be useful when things go wrong. In addition, the use of text makes XML independent of any particular platform. The use of a textual, rather than a binary representation, together with the use of tags makes the messages much larger, which causes them to require longer processing and transmission times, as well as more space to store. A comparison of the efficiency of messages using the SOAP XML format and CORBA CDR is given in Section 19.2.4. However, files and messages can be compressed – HTTP version 1.1 allows data to be compressed, which saves bandwidth during transmission.

XML elements and attributes ◊ Figure 4.10 shows the XML definition of the *Person* structure which was used to illustrate marshalling in CORBA CDR and Java. It shows that XML consists of tags and character data. The character data, for example, *Smith* or *1934*, is the actual data. As in HTML, the structure of an XML document is defined by pairs of tags enclosed in angle brackets. In the above example, *<name>* and *<place>* are both tags. As in HTML, layout can generally be used to improve readability. Comments in XML are denoted in the same way as those in HTML.

Elements: An element in XML consists of a portion of character data surrounded by matching start and end tags. For example, one of the elements in Figure 4.10 consists of the data *Smith* contained within the *<name>* ... *</name>* tag pair. Note that the element with the *<name>* tag is enclosed in the element with the *<person id="123456789">* ... *</person >* tag pair. The ability of an element to enclose another element allows hierarchic data to be represented – a very important aspect of XML. An empty tag has no content and is terminated with /> instead of >. For example, the empty tag *<european/>* could be included within the *<person>* ...*</person>* tag.

Attributes: A start tag may optionally include pairs of associated attribute names and values such as *id="123456789"* as shown above. The syntax is the same as for HTML, in which an attribute name is followed by an equal sign and an attribute value in quotes. Multiple attribute values are separated by spaces.

It is a matter of choice as to which items are represented as elements and which ones as attributes. An element is generally a container for data, whereas an attribute is used for labelling that data. In our example, *123456789* might be an identifier used by the application, whereas *name*, *place* and *year* might be displayed. Also, if data contains substructures or several lines, it must be defined as an element. Attributes are for simple values.

Names: The names of tags and attributes in XML generally start with a letter, but can also start with an underline or a colon. The names continue with letters, digits, hyphens, underscores, colons or full stops. Letters are case-sensitive. Names that start with *xml* are reserved.

Binary data: All of the information in XML elements must be expressed as character data. But the question is: how do we represent encrypted elements or secure hashes? – both of which we shall see are used in XML security in Section 19.5. The answer is that they can be represented in *base64* notation [Freed and Borenstein 1996], which uses only the alphanumeric characters together with +, / and = which has a special meaning.

Parsing and well-formed documents ◊ An XML document must be well formed – that is, it must conform to rules about its structure. A basic rule is that every start tag has a matching end tag. Another basic rule is that all tags are correctly nested, for example <x>..<y>..</y>..</x> is correct, whereas <x>..<y>....</x>.. </y> is not. Finally, every XML document must have a single root element that encloses all the other elements. These rules make it very simple to implement parsers for XML documents. When a parser reads an XML document that is not well formed it will report a fatal error.

CDATA: XML parsers normally parse the contents of elements because they may contain further nested structures. But if text needs to contain an angle bracket or a quote, it may be represented in a special way, for example, *&lt* represents the opening angle bracket. However, if a section should not be parsed, for any reason, for example, if it contains special characters, it can be denoted as *CDATA*. For example, if a place name is to include an apostrophe, then it could be specified in either of the two following ways:

> *<place> King&apos Cross </place >*
> *<place> <![CDATA [King's Cross]]></place >*

XML Prolog: Every XML document must have a *prolog* as its first line. The prolog must at least specify the version of XML in use (which is currently 1.0). For example:

> *<?XML version = "1.0" encoding = "UTF-8" standalone = "yes"?>*

A third attribute may be used to state whether the document stands alone or is dependent on external definitions.

> *Encodings:* The prolog may also specify the encoding (UTF-8 is the default and was explained in Section 4.3.2). The term *encoding* refers to the set of codes used to represent characters – ASCII being the best known example. Note that in the XML prolog, ASCII is specified as *us-ascii*. Other possible encodings include ISO-8859-1 (or Latin-1), an eight-bit encoding whose first 128 values are ASCII, the rest are used to represent the characters in western european languages. Other eight-bit encodings are available for representing other alphabets, for example, greek or cyrillic.

Figure 4.11   Illustration of the use of a namespace in the *Person* structure

> *<person pers:id="123456789" xmlns:pers = "http://www.cdk4.net/person">*
> *   <pers:name> Smith </pers:name>*
> *   <pers:place> London </pers:place >*
> *   <pers:year> 1934 </pers:year>*
> *</person>*

XML namespaces ◊ Traditionally, namespaces provide a means for scoping names. An XML namespace is a set of names for a collection of element types and attributes, that is referenced by a URL. An XML namespace may be used by any other XML document by referring to its URL.

Any element that makes use of an XML namespace can specify that namespace as an attribute called *xmlns*, whose value is a URL referring to the file containing the namespace definitions. For example:

> *xmlns:pers = "http://www.cdk4.net/person"*

The name after *xmlns,* in this case *pers* can be used as a prefix to refer to the elements in a particular namespace, as shown in Figure 4.11. The *pers* prefix is bound to *http://www.cdk4.net/person* for the *person* element. A namespace applies within the context of the enclosing pair of start and end tags unless overridden by an enclosed namespace declaration. An XML document may be defined in terms of several different namespaces, each of which would be referenced by a unique prefix.

The namespace convention allows an application to make use of multiple sets of external definitions in different namespaces without the risk of name clashes.

XML schemas ◊ An XML schema [www.w3.org VIII] defines the elements and attributes that can appear in a document, how the elements are nested and the order and number of elements, whether an element is empty or can include text. For each element, it defines the type and default value. Figure 4.12 gives an example of a schema that

Figure 4.12   An XML schema for the *Person* structure

> *<xsd:schema xmlns:xsd = URL of XML schema definitions >*
> *   <xsd:element name= "person" type ="personType" />*
> *   <xsd:complexType name="personType">*
> *   <xsd:sequence>*
> *   <xsd:element name = "name" type="xs:string"/>*
> *   <xsd:element name = "place" type="xs:string"/>*
> *   <xsd:element name = "year" type="xs:positiveInteger"/>*
> *   </xsd:sequence>*
> *   <xsd:attribute name= "id"   type = "xs:positiveInteger"/>*
> *   </xsd:complexType>*
> *</xsd:schema>*

defines the data types and structure of the XML definition of the *person* structure in Figure 4.10.

The intention is that a single schema definition may be shared by many different documents. An XML document that is defined to conform to a particular schema may also be validated by means of that schema. For example, the sender of a SOAP message may use an XML schema to encode it and the recipient will use the same XML schema to validate and decode it.

Document type definitions: Document type definitions (or DTDs) [www.w3.org VI] were provided as a part of the XML 1.0 specification, for defining the structure of XML documents and are still widely used for that purpose. The syntax of DTDs is different from the rest of XML and it is quite limited in what it can specify, for example, it cannot describe data types and its definitions are global, preventing element names from being duplicated. DTDs are not used for defining web services although they may still be used to define documents that are transmitted by web services.

APIs for accessing XML ◊ XML parsers and generators are available for most commonly used programming languages. For example, there is Java software for writing out Java objects as XML (marshalling) and for creating Java objects from such structures (unmarshalling). Similar software is available in Python for Python data types and objects.

4.3.4   Remote object references

This section applies only to languages such as Java and CORBA that support the distributed object model. It is not relevant to XML.

When a client invokes a method in a remote object, an invocation message is sent to the server process that hosts the remote object. This message needs to specify which particular object is to have its method invoked. A *remote object reference* is an identifier for a remote object that is valid throughout a distributed system. A remote object reference is passed in the invocation message to specify which object is to be invoked. Chapter 5 explains that remote object references are also passed as arguments and returned as results of remote method invocations, that each remote object has a single remote object reference and that remote object references can be compared to see whether they refer to the same remote object. We now discuss the external representation of remote object references.

Remote object references must be generated in a manner that ensures uniqueness over space and time. In general, there may be many processes hosting remote objects, so remote object references must be unique among all of the processes in the various computers in a distributed system. Even after the remote object associated with a given

Figure 4.13   Representation of a remote object reference

32 bits	*32 bits*	*32 bits*	*32 bits*	
Internet address	port number	time	object number	interface of remote object

remote object reference is deleted, it is important that the remote object reference is not reused, because its potential invokers may retain obsolete remote object references. Any attempt to invoke a deleted object should produce an error rather than allow access to a different object.

There are several ways to ensure that a remote object reference is unique. One way is to construct a remote object reference by concatenating the Internet address of its computer and the port number of the process that created it with the time of its creation and a local object number. The local object number is incremented each time an object is created in that process.

The port number and time together produce a unique process identifier on that computer. With this approach, remote object references might be represented with a format such as that shown in Figure 4.13. In the simplest implementations of RMI, remote objects live only in the process that created them and survive only as long as that process continues to run. In such cases, the remote object reference can be used as an address of the remote object. In other words, invocation messages are sent to the Internet address in the remote reference and to the process on that computer using the given port number.

To allow remote objects to be relocated in a different process on a different computer, the remote object reference should not be used as the address of the remote object. Section 20.2.4 discusses a form of remote object reference that allows objects to be activated in different servers throughout its lifetime.

The peer-to-peer overlay systems described in Chapter 10 use a form of remote object reference that is completely independent of location. Messages are routed to resources by means of a distributed routing algorithm.

The last field of the remote object reference shown in Figure 4.13 contains some information about the interface of the remote object, for example, the interface name. This information is relevant to any process that receives a remote object reference as an argument or result of a remote invocation, because it needs to know about the methods offered by the remote object. This point is explained again in Section 5.2.5.

4.4   Client-server communication

This form of communication is designed to support the roles and message exchanges in typical client-server interactions. In the normal case, request-reply communication is synchronous because the client process blocks until the reply arrives from the server. It can also be reliable because the reply from the server is effectively an acknowledgement to the client. Asynchronous request-reply communication is an alternative that may be useful in situations where clients can afford to retrieve replies later – see Section 6.5.2.

The client-server exchanges are described in the following paragraphs in terms of the *send* and *receive* operations in the Java API for UDP datagrams, although many current implementations use TCP streams. A protocol built over datagrams avoids unnecessary overheads associated with the TCP stream protocol. In particular:

- acknowledgements are redundant, since requests are followed by replies;

Figure 4.14   Request-reply communication

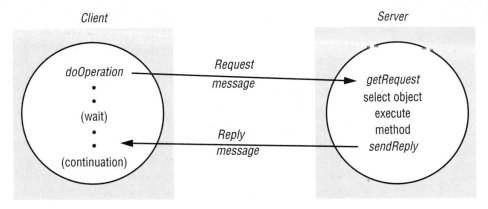

- establishing a connection involves two extra pairs of messages in addition to the pair required for a request and a reply;

- flow control is redundant for the majority of invocations, which pass only small arguments and results.

The request-reply protocol ◊ The following protocol is based on a trio of communication primitives: *doOperation*, *getRequest* and *sendReply*, as shown in Figure 4.14. Most RMI and RPC systems are supported by a similar protocol. The one we describe here is tailored for supporting RMI in that it passes a remote object reference for the object whose method is to be invoked in the request message.

This specially designed request-reply protocol matches requests to replies. It may be designed to provide certain delivery guarantees. If UDP datagrams are used, the delivery guarantees must be provided by the request-reply protocol, which may use the server reply message as an acknowledgement of the client request message. Figure 4.15 outlines the three communication primitives.

The *doOperation* method is used by clients to invoke remote operations. Its arguments specify the remote object and which method to invoke, together with additional information (arguments) required by the method. Its result is an RMI reply. It is assumed that the client calling *doOperation* marshals the arguments into an array of bytes and unmarshals the results from the array of bytes that is returned. The first argument of *doOperation* is an instance of the class *RemoteObjectRef*, which represents references for remote objects, for example, as shown in Figure 4.13. This class provides methods for getting the Internet address and port of the server of the remote object. The *doOperation* method sends a request message to the server whose Internet address and port are specified in the remote object reference given as argument. After sending the request message, *doOperation* invokes *receive* to get a reply message, from which it extracts the result and returns it to the caller. The caller of *doOperation* is blocked until the remote object in the server performs the requested operation and transmits a reply message to the client process.

GetRequest is used by a server process to acquire service requests as shown in Figure 4.14. When the server has invoked the method in the specified object it then uses

Figure 4.15   Operations of the request-reply protocol

public byte[] doOperation (RemoteObjectRef o, int methodId, byte[] arguments)
    sends a request message to the remote object and returns the reply.
    The arguments specify the remote object, the method to be invoked and the
    arguments of that method.

public byte[] getRequest ();
    acquires a client request via the server port.

public void sendReply (byte[] reply, InetAddress clientHost, int clientPort);
    sends the reply message *reply* to the client at its Internet address and port.

---

sendReply to send the reply message to the client. When the reply message is received
by the client the original *doOperation* is unblocked and execution of the client program
continues.

        The information to be transmitted in a request message or a reply message is
shown in Figure 4.16. The first field indicates whether the message is a *Request* or a
Reply message. The second field *requestId* contains a message identifier. A
doOperation in the client generates a *requestId* for each request message, and the server
copies them into the corresponding reply messages. This enables *doOperation* to check
that a reply message is the result of the current request, not from a delayed earlier call.
The third field is a remote object reference marshalled in the form shown in Figure 4.13.
The fourth field is an identifier for the method to be invoked, for example, the methods
in an interface might be numbered 1, 2, 3, ... ; if client and server use a common language
that supports reflection, then a representation of the method itself may be put in this field
– in Java an instance of *Method* may be put in this field.

Message identifiers ◊ Any scheme that involves the management of messages to
provide additional properties such as reliable message delivery or request-reply
communication requires that each message have a unique message identifier by which
it may be referenced. A message identifier consists of two parts:

    1. a *requestId*, which is taken from an increasing sequence of integers by the sending
       process; and

    2. an identifier for the sender process, for example its port and Internet address.

Figure 4.16   Request-reply message structure

messageType	*int (0=Request, 1= Reply)*
requestId	*int*
objectReference	*RemoteObjectRef*
methodId	*int or Method*
arguments	*// array of bytes*

The first part makes the identifier unique to the sender, and the second part makes it unique in the distributed system. (The second part can be obtained independently, for example if UDP is in use, from the message received.)

When the value of the *requestId* reaches the maximum value for an unsigned integer (for example, $2^{32} - 1$) it is reset to zero. The only restriction here is that the lifetime of a message identifier should be much less than the time taken to exhaust the values in the sequence of integers.

Failure model of the request-reply protocol ◊ If the three primitives *doOperation*, *getRequest* and *sendReply* are implemented over UDP datagrams, then they suffer from the same communication failures. That is:

- they suffer from omission failures;

- messages are not guaranteed to be delivered in sender order.

In addition, the protocol can suffer from the failure of processes (see Section 2.3.2). We assume that processes have crash failures. That is, when they halt, they remain halted – they do not produce byzantine behaviour.

To allow for occasions when a server has failed or a request or reply message is dropped, *doOperation* uses a timeout when it is waiting to get the server's reply message. The action taken when a timeout occurs depends upon the delivery guarantees to be offered.

Timeouts ◊ There are various options as to what *doOperation* can do after a timeout. The simplest option is to return immediately from *doOperation* with an indication to the client that the *doOperation* has failed. This is not the usual approach – the timeout may have been due to the request or reply message getting lost – and in the latter case, the operation will have been performed. To compensate for the possibility of lost messages, *doOperation* sends the request message repeatedly until either it gets a reply or else it is reasonably sure that the delay is due to lack of response from the server rather than to lost messages. Eventually, when *doOperation* returns it will indicate to the client by an exception that no result was received.

Discarding duplicate request messages ◊ In cases when the request message is retransmitted, the server may receive it more than once. For example, the server may receive the first request message but take longer than the client's timeout to execute the command and return the reply. This can lead to the server executing an operation more than once for the same request. To avoid this, the protocol is designed to recognize successive messages (from the same client) with the same request identifier and to filter out duplicates. If the server has not yet sent the reply, it need take no special action – it will transmit the reply when it has finished executing the operation.

Lost reply messages ◊ If the server has already sent the reply when it receives a duplicate request it will need to execute the operation again to obtain the result, unless it has stored the result of the original execution. Some servers can execute their operations more than once and obtain the same results each time. An *idempotent operation* is an operation that can be performed repeatedly with the same effect as if it had been performed exactly once. For example, an operation to add an element to a set is an idempotent operation because it will always have the same effect on the set each time it is performed, whereas an operation to append an item to a sequence is not an

Figure 4.17   RPC exchange protocols

Name	Messages sent by		
	Client	*Server*	*Client*
R	*Request*		
RR	*Request*	*Reply*	
RRA	*Request*	*Reply*	*Acknowledge reply*

idempotent operation, because it extends the sequence each time it is performed. A server whose operations are all idempotent need not take special measures to avoid executing its operations more than once.

History ◊ For servers that require retransmission of replies without re-execution of operations, a history may be used. The term 'history' is used to refer to a structure that contains a record of (reply) messages that have been transmitted. An entry in a history contains a request identifier, a message and an identifier of the client to which it was sent. Its purpose is to allow the server to retransmit reply messages when client processes request them. A problem associated with the use of a history is its memory cost. A history will become very large unless the server can tell when the messages will no longer be needed for retransmission.

As clients can make only one request at a time, the server can interpret each request as an acknowledgement of its previous reply. Therefore the history need contain only the last reply message sent to each client. However, the volume of reply messages in a server's history may be a problem when it has a large number of clients. In particular, when a client process terminates, it does not acknowledge the last reply it has received – messages in the history are therefore normally discarded after a limited period of time.

RPC exchange protocols ◊ Three protocols, which produce differing behaviours in the presence of communication failures, are used for implementing various types of RPC. They were originally identified by Spector [1982]:

- the *request (R)* protocol;
- the *request-reply (RR)* protocol;
- the *request-reply-acknowledge reply (RRA)* protocol.

The messages passed in these protocols are summarized in Figure 4.17. In the R protocol, a single *Request* message is sent by the client to the server. The R protocol may be used when there is no value to be returned from the remote method and the client requires no confirmation that the method has been executed. The client may proceed immediately after the request message is sent as there is no need to wait for a reply message. This protocol is implemented over UDP datagrams and therefore suffers from the same communication failures.

The RR protocol is useful for most client-server exchanges because it is based on the request-reply protocol. Special acknowledgement messages are not required, because a server's reply message is regarded as an acknowledgement of the client's request message. Similarly, a subsequent call from a client may be regarded as an acknowledgement of a server's reply message. As we have seen above, communication failures due to UDP datagrams may be masked by the retransmission of requests with duplicate filtering and the saving of replies in a history for retransmission.

The RRA protocol is based on the exchange of three messages: request-reply-acknowledge reply. The *acknowledge reply* message contains the *requestId* from the reply message being acknowledged. This will enable the server to discard entries from its history. The arrival of a *requestId* in an acknowledgement message will be interpreted as acknowledging the receipt of all reply messages with lower *requestId*s, so the loss of an acknowledgement message is harmless. Although the exchange involves an additional message, it need not block the client, as the acknowledgement may be transmitted after the reply has been given to the client, but it does use processing and network resources. Exercise 4.23 suggests an optimization to the RRA protocol.

Use of TCP streams to implement the request-reply protocol ◊ The section on datagrams mentioned that it is often difficult to decide on an appropriate size for the buffer in which to receive datagrams. In the request-reply protocol, this applies to the buffers used by the server to receive request messages and by the client to receive replies. The limited length of datagrams (usually 8 kilobytes) may not be regarded as adequate for use in transparent RMI systems, since the arguments or results of procedures may be of any size.

The desire to avoid implementing multi-packet protocols is one of the reasons for choosing to implement request-reply protocols over TCP streams, allowing arguments and results of any size to be transmitted. In particular, Java object serialization is a stream protocol that allows arguments and results to be sent over streams between client and server, making it possible for collections of objects of any size to be transmitted reliably. If the TCP protocol is used, it ensures that request and reply messages are delivered reliably, so there is no need for the request-reply protocol to deal with retransmission of messages and filtering of duplicates or with histories. In addition the flow-control mechanism allows large arguments and results to be passed without taking special measures to avoid overwhelming the recipient. Thus, the TCP protocol is chosen for request-reply protocols because it can simplify their implementation. If successive requests and replies between the same client-server pair are sent over the same stream, the connection overhead need not apply to every remote invocation. Also the overhead due to TCP acknowledgement messages is reduced when a reply message follows soon after a request message.

Sometimes, the application does not require all of the facilities offered by TCP, and a more efficient, specially tailored protocol can be implemented over UDP. For example, as we mentioned earlier Sun NFS does not require messages of unlimited size, since it transmits fixed-size file blocks between client and server. In addition to that, its operations are designed to be idempotent, so that it does not matter if operations are executed more than once in order to retransmit lost reply messages, making it unnecessary to maintain a history.

HTTP: an example of a request-reply protocol ◊ Chapter 1 introduced the Hypertext Transfer Protocol (HTTP) used by web browser clients to make requests to web servers and to receive replies from them. To recap, web servers manage resources implemented in different ways:

- as data, for example the text of an HTML page, an image or the class of an applet;

- as a program, for example, *cgi* programs and servlets (see [java.sun.com III]) that can be run on the web server.

Client requests specify a URL that includes the DNS hostname of a web server and an optional port number on the web server as well as the identifier of a resource on that server.

HTTP is a protocol that specifies the messages involved in a request-reply exchange, the methods, arguments and results and the rules for representing (marshalling) them in the messages. It supports a fixed set of methods (*GET, PUT, POST, etcetera*) that are applicable to all of its resources. It is unlike the above protocols, where each object has its own methods. In addition to invoking methods on web resources, the protocol allows for content negotiation and password-style authentication.

Content negotiation: Clients' requests can include information as to what data representation they can accept (for example, language or media type), enabling the server to choose the representation that is the most appropriate for the user.

Authentication: Credentials and challenges are used to support password-style authentication. On the first attempt to access a password-protected area, the server reply contains a challenge applicable to the resource. Chapter 7 explains challenges. When a client receives a challenge, it gets the user to type a name and password and submits the associated credentials with subsequent requests. HTTP is implemented over TCP. In the original version of the protocol, each client-server interaction consists of the following steps:

- the client requests and the server accepts a connection at the default server port or at a port specified in the URL;

- the client sends a request message to the server;

- the server sends a reply message to the client;

- the connection is closed.

However, the need to establish and close a connection for every request-reply exchange is expensive, both in overloading the server and in sending too many messages over the network. Bearing in mind that browsers generally make multiple requests to the same server, a later version of the protocol (HTTP 1.1, see RFC 2616 [Fielding *et al.* 1999]) uses *persistent connections* – connections that remain open over a series of request-reply exchanges between client and server. A persistent connection can be closed by client or server at any time by sending an indication to the other participant. Servers will close a persistent connection when it has been idle for a period of time. It is possible that a client may receive a message from the server saying that the connection is closed while it is in the middle of sending another request or requests. In such cases, the browser will resend the requests without user involvement, provided that the operations involved are idempotent. For example, the method GET described below is idempotent. Where non-idempotent operations are involved, the browser should consult the user as to what to do next.

Figure 4.18   HTTP *request* message

method	*URL or pathname*	*HTTP version*	*headers*	*message body*
GET	http://www.dcs.qmul.ac.uk/index.html	HTTP/ 1.1		

Requests and replies are marshalled into messages as ASCII text strings, but resources can be represented as byte sequences and may be compressed. The use of text in the external data representation has simplified the use of HTTP for application programmers who work directly with the protocol. In this context, a textual representation does not add much to the length of the messages.

Resources implemented as data are supplied as MIME-like structures in arguments and results. Multipurpose Internet Mail Extensions (MIME) is a standard for sending multipart data containing, for example, text, images and sound in email messages, specified in RFC 2045 [Freed and Borenstein 1996]. Data is prefixed with its *Mime type* so that the recipient will know how to handle it. A *Mime type* specifies a type and a subtype, for example *text/plain*, *text/html*, *image/gif*, *image/jpeg*. Clients can also specify the Mime types that they are willing to accept.

HTTP methods ◊ Each client request specifies the name of a method to be applied to a resource at the server and the URL of that resource. The reply reports on the status of the request. Requests and replies may also contain resource data, the contents of a form or the output of a program resource run on the web server. The methods include the following:

GET: requests the resource whose URL is given as argument. If the URL refers to data, then the web server replies by returning the data identified by that URL. If the URL refers to a program, then the web server runs the program and returns its output to the client. Arguments may be added to the URL; for example, GET can be used to send the contents of a form to a *cgi* program as an argument. The *GET* operation can be made conditional on the date a resource was last modified. *GET* can also be configured to obtain parts of the data.

HEAD: this request is identical to *GET*, but it does not return any data. However, it does return all the information about the data, such as the time of last modification, its type or its size.

POST: specifies the URL of a resource (for example a program) that can deal with the data supplied with the request. The processing carried out on the data depends on the function of the program specified in the URL. This method is designed to deal with:

- providing a block of data (for example, a form) to a data-handling process such as a servlet or a *cgi* program;

- posting a message to a bulletin board, mailing list or newsgroup;

- extending a database with an append operation.

Figure 4.19   HTTP *reply* message

HTTP version	*status code*	*reason*	*headers*	*message body*
HTTP/1.1	200	OK		resource data

PUT: requests that the data supplied in the request is stored with the given URL as its identifier, either as a modification of an existing resource or as a new resource.

DELETE: the server deletes the resource identified by the given URL. Servers may not always allow this operation, in which case the reply indicates failure.

OPTIONS: the server supplies the client with a list of methods it allows to be applied to the given URL (e.g. *GET*, *HEAD*, *PUT*) and its special requirements.

TRACE: the server sends back the request message. Used for diagnostic purposes.

The requests described above may be intercepted by a proxy server (see Section 2.2.3). The responses to *GET* and *HEAD* may be cached by proxy servers.

Message contents ◊ The *Request* message specifies the name of a method, the URL of a resource, the protocol version, some headers and an optional message body. Figure 4.18 shows the contents of an HTTP *Request* message whose method is GET. When the URL specifies a data resource, the GET method does not have a message body.

Requests to proxies need the absolute URL, as shown in Figure 4.18. Requests to origin servers (the origin server is where the resource resides) specify a pathname and give the DNS name of the origin server in a *Host* header field. For example,

GET /index.html   HTTP/1.1
Host: www.dcs.qmul.ac.uk

In general, the header fields contain request modifiers and client information, such as conditions on the latest date of modification of the resource or acceptable content type (for example, HTML text, audio or JPEG images). An authorization field can be used to provide the client's credentials in the form of a certificate specifying their rights to access a resource.

A *Reply* message specifies the protocol version, a status code and 'reason', some headers and an optional message body, as shown in Figure 4.19. The *status code* and *reason* provide a report on the success or otherwise in carrying out the request: the former is a three-digit integer for interpretation by a program, and the latter is a textual phrase that can be understood by a person. The header fields are used to pass additional information about the server, or concerning access to the resource. For example, if the request requires authentication, the status of the response indicates this and a header field contains a challenge. Some status returns have quite complex effects. In particular, a 303 status response tells the browser to look under a different URL, which is supplied in a header field in the reply. It is intended for use in a response from a program activated by a POST request when the program needs to redirect the browser to a selected resource.

The message body in request or reply messages contains the data associated with the URL specified in the request. The message body has its own headers specifying information about the data, such as its length, its Mime type, its character set, its content encoding, and the last date it was modified. The Mime type field specifies the type of the data, for example *image/jpeg* or *text/plain*. The content-encoding field specifies the compression algorithm to be used.

4.5   Group communication

The pairwise exchange of messages is not the best model for communication from one process to a group of other processes, as for example when a service is implemented as a number of different processes in different computers, perhaps to provide fault tolerance or to enhance availability. A *multicast operation* is more appropriate – this is an operation that sends a single message from one process to each of the members of a group of processes, usually in such a way that the membership of the group is transparent to the sender. There is a range of possibilities in the desired behaviour of a multicast. The simplest provides no guarantees about message delivery or ordering.

Multicast messages provide a useful infrastructure for constructing distributed systems with the following characteristics:

1. *Fault tolerance based on replicated services*: A replicated service consists of a group of servers. Client requests are multicast to all the members of the group, each of which performs an identical operation. Even when some of the members fail, clients can still be served.

2. *Finding the discovery servers in spontaneous networking*: Section 16.2.1 discusses discovery services for spontaneous networking. Multicast messages can be used by servers and clients to locate available discovery services in order to register their interfaces or to look up the interfaces of other services in the distributed system.

3. *Better performance through replicated data*: Data are replicated to increase the performance of a service – in some cases replicas of the data are placed in users' computers. Each time the data changes, the new value is multicast to the processes managing the replicas.

4. *Propagation of event notifications*: Multicast to a group may be used to notify processes when something happens. For example, a news system might notify interested users when a new message has been posted on a particular newsgroup.

We introduce IP multicast and then review the needs of the above uses of group communication to see which of them can be satisfied by IP multicast. For those that cannot, we propose some further properties for group communication protocols in addition to those provided by IP multicast.

4.5.1   IP multicast – an implementation of group communication

This section discusses IP multicast and presents Java's API to it via the *MulticastSocket* class.

IP multicast ◊   *IP multicast* is built on top of the Internet Protocol, IP. Note that IP packets are addressed to computers – ports belong to the TCP and UDP levels. IP multicast allows the sender to transmit a single IP packet to a set of computers that form a multicast group. The sender is unaware of the identities of the individual recipients and of the size of the group. A *multicast group* is specified by a class D Internet address (see Figure 3.15) – that is, an address whose first 4 bits are 1110 in IPv4.

Being a member of a multicast group allows a computer to receive IP packets sent to the group. The membership of multicast groups is dynamic, allowing computers to join or leave at any time and to join an arbitrary number of groups. It is possible to send datagrams to a multicast group without being a member.

At the application programming level, IP multicast is available only via UDP. An application program performs multicasts by sending UDP datagrams with multicast addresses and ordinary port numbers. It can join a multicast group by making its socket join the group, enabling it to receive messages to the group. At the IP level, a computer belongs to a multicast group when one or more of its processes has sockets that belong to that group. When a multicast message arrives at a computer, copies are forwarded to all of the local sockets that have joined the specified multicast address and are bound to the specified port number. The following details are specific to IPv4:

Multicast routers: IP packets can be multicast both on a local network and on the wider Internet. Local multicasts use the multicast capability of the local network, for example, of an Ethernet. Those that are multicast in the Internet make use of multicast routers, which forward single datagrams to routers on other networks with members, where they are again multicast to local members. To limit the distance of propagation of a multicast datagram, the sender can specify the number of routers it is allowed to pass – called the time to live, or TTL for short. To understand how routers know which other routers have members of a multicast group, see Comer [2000b].

Multicast address allocation: Multicast addresses may be permanent or temporary. Permanent groups exist even when there are no members – their addresses are assigned by the Internet authority from the range 224.0.0.1 to 224.0.0.255. For example, the first address refers to all multicast hosts.

The remainder of the multicast addresses are available for use by temporary groups, which must be created before use and cease to exist when all the members have left. When a temporary group is created, it requires a free multicast address to avoid accidental participation in an existing group. The IP multicast protocol does not address this issue. But when its users only need to communicate locally, they set the TTL to a small value, making it unlikely that they will pick the same address as another group. However, programs using IP multicast throughout the Internet require a solution to the problem. The session directory (*sd*) program can be used to start or join a multicast session [Handley 1998, session directory]. It provides a tool with an interactive interface that allows people to browse advertised multicast sessions and

Figure 4.20   Multicast peer joins a group and sends and receives datagrams

```
import java.net.*;
import java.io.*;
public class MulticastPeer{
    public static void main(String args[]){
        // args give message contents & destination multicast group (e.g. "228.5.6.7")
        MulticastSocket s =null;
        try {
            InetAddress group = InetAddress.getByName(args[1]);
            s = new MulticastSocket(6789);
            s.joinGroup(group);
            byte [] m = args[0].getBytes();
            DatagramPacket messageOut =
                new DatagramPacket(m, m.length, group, 6789);
            s.send(messageOut);
            byte[] buffer = new byte[1000];
            for(int i=0; i< 3; i++) {   // get messages from others in group
                DatagramPacket messageIn =
                    new DatagramPacket(buffer, buffer.length);
                s.receive(messageIn);
                System.out.println("Received:" + new String(messageIn.getData()));
            }
            s.leaveGroup(group);
        } catch (SocketException e){System.out.println("Socket: " + e.getMessage());
        } catch (IOException e){System.out.println("IO: " + e.getMessage());
        } finally { if(s != null) s.close();}
    }
}
```

to advertise their own sessions, specifying the time and duration – it chooses a multicast address for new sessions.

Failure model for multicast datagrams ◊ Datagrams multicast over IP multicast have the same failure characteristics as UDP datagrams – that is, they suffer from omission failures. The effect on a multicast is that messages are not guaranteed to be delivered to any particular group member in the face of even a single omission failure. That is, some but not all of the members of the group may receive it. This can be called *unreliable* multicast, because it does not guarantee that a message will be delivered to any member of a group. Reliable multicast is discussed in Chapter 12.

Java API to IP multicast ◊ The Java API provides a datagram interface to IP multicast through the class *MulticastSocket*, which is a subclass of *DatagramSocket* with the additional capability of being able to join multicast groups. The class *MulticastSocket* provides two alternative constructors, allowing sockets to be created to use either a specified local port (as for example 6789 illustrated in Figure 4.20), or any free local port. A process can join a multicast group with a given multicast address by invoking the *joinGroup* method of its multicast socket. Effectively, the socket joins a multicast group at a given port and it will receive datagrams sent by processes on other computers to that group at that port. A process can leave a specified group by invoking the *leaveGroup* method of its multicast socket.

In the example in Figure 4.20, the arguments to the *main* method specify a message to be multicast and the multicast address of a group (for example, *"228.5.6.7"*). After joining that multicast group the process makes an instance of *DatagramPacket* containing the message and sends it through its multicast socket to the multicast group address at port 6789. After that, it attempts to receive three multicast messages from its peers via its socket, which also belongs to the group on the same port. When several instances of this program are run simultaneously on different computers, all of them join the same group, and each of them should receive its own message and the messages from those that joined after it.

The Java API allows the TTL to be set for a multicast socket by means of the *setTimeToLive* method. The default is 1, allowing the multicast to propagate only on the local network.

An application implemented over IP multicast may use more that one port. For example, the MultiTalk [mbone] application, which allows groups of users to hold text-based conversations, has one port for sending and receiving data and another for exchanging control data.

4.5.2 Reliability and ordering of multicast

The previous section stated the failure model for IP multicast. That is, it suffers from omission failures. For a multicast on a local area network that uses the multicasting capabilities of the network to allow a single datagram to arrive at multiple recipients, any one of those recipients may drop the message because its buffer is full. Also, a datagram sent from one multicast router to another may be lost, thus preventing all recipients beyond that router receiving the message.

Another factor is that any process may fail. If a multicast router fails, the group members beyond that router will not receive the multicast message, although local members may do so.

Ordering is another issue. IP packets sent over an internetwork do not necessarily arrive in the order in which they were sent, with the possible effect that some group members receive datagrams from a single sender in a different order from other group members. In addition, messages sent by two different processes will not necessarily arrive in the same order at all the members of the group.

Some examples of the effects of reliability and ordering ◊ We now consider the effect of the failure semantics of IP multicast on the four examples of the use of replication in the introduction to Section 4.5.

1. *Fault tolerance based on replicated services*: Consider a replicated service that consists of the members of a group of servers that start in the same initial state and always perform the same operations in the same order, so as to remain consistent with one another. This application of multicast requires that either all of the replicas or none of them should receive each request to perform an operation – if one of them misses a request, it will become inconsistent with the others. In most

cases, this service would require that all members receive request messages in the same order as one another.

2. *Finding the discovery servers in spontaneous networking*: Provided that any process that wants to locate the *discovery* servers multicasts requests at periodic intervals for a time after it starts up, an occasional lost request is not an issue when locating a *discovery* server. In fact, Jini uses IP multicast in its protocol for finding the discovery servers. This is described in Section 16.2.1.

3. *Better performance through replicated data*: Consider the case where the replicated data itself, rather than operations on the data, is distributed by means of multicast messages. The effect of lost messages and inconsistent ordering would depend on the method of replication and the importance of all replicas being totally up to date. For example, the replicas of newsgroups are not necessarily consistent with one another at any one time – messages even appear in different orders, but users can cope with this.

4. *Propagation of event notifications*: The particular application determines the qualities required of multicast. For example, the Jini lookup services use IP multicast announce their existence (see Section 16.2.1).

These examples suggest that some applications require a multicast protocol that is more reliable than IP multicast. In particular, there is a need for *reliable multicast* – in which any message transmitted is either received by all members of a group or by none of them. The examples also suggest that some applications have strong requirements for ordering, the strictest of which is called *totally ordered multicast,* in which all of the messages transmitted to a group reach all of the members in the same order.

Chapter 12 will define and show how to implement *reliable* multicast and various useful ordering guarantees, including totally ordered multicast.

4.6   Case study: interprocess communication in UNIX

The IPC primitives in BSD 4.x versions of UNIX are provided as system calls that are implemented as a layer over the Internet TCP and UDP protocols. Message destinations are specified as *socket addresses* – a socket address consists of an Internet address and a local port number.

The interprocess communication operations are based on the socket abstraction described in Section 4.2.2. As described there, messages are queued at the sending socket until the networking protocol has transmitted them, and until an acknowledgement arrives, if the protocol requires one. When messages arrive, they are queued at the receiving socket until the receiving process makes an appropriate system call to receive them.

Any process can create a socket for use in communication with another process. This is done by invoking the *socket* system call, whose arguments specify the communication domain (normally the Internet), the type (datagram or stream) and sometimes a particular protocol. The protocol (for example, TCP or UDP) is usually selected by the system according to whether the communication is datagram or stream.

Figure 4.21   Sockets used for datagrams

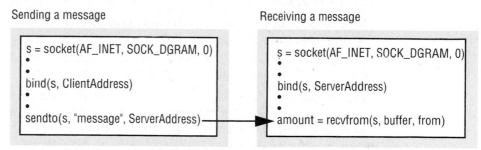

Sending a message

```
s = socket(AF_INET, SOCK_DGRAM, 0)
•
•
bind(s, ClientAddress)
•
•
sendto(s, "message", ServerAddress)
```

Receiving a message

```
s = socket(AF_INET, SOCK_DGRAM, 0)
•
•
bind(s, ServerAddress)
•
•
amount = recvfrom(s, buffer, from)
```

ServerAddress and *ClientAddress* are socket addresses

The socket call returns a descriptor by which the socket may be referenced in subsequent system calls. The socket lasts until it is *closed* or until every process with the descriptor exits. A pair of sockets may be used for communication in both or either direction between processes in the same or different computers.

Before a pair of processes can communicate, the recipient must *bind* its socket descriptor to a socket address. The sender must also bind its socket descriptor to a socket address if it requires a reply. The *bind* system call is used for this purpose; its arguments are a socket descriptor and a reference to a structure containing the socket address to which the socket is to be bound. Once a socket has been bound, its address cannot be changed.

It might seem more reasonable to have one system call for both socket creation and binding a name to a socket, as for example in the Java API. The supposed advantage of having two separate calls is that sockets can be useful without socket addresses.

Socket addresses are public in the sense that they can be used as destinations by any process. After a process has bound its socket to a socket address, the socket may be addressed indirectly by another process referring to the appropriate socket address. Any process, for example a server that plans to receive messages via its socket, must first bind that socket to a socket address and make the socket address known to potential clients.

4.6.1   Datagram communication

In order to send datagrams, a socket pair is identified each time a communication is made. This is achieved by the sending process using its local socket descriptor and the socket address of the receiving socket each time it sends a message.

This is illustrated in Figure 4.21, in which the details of the arguments are simplified.

- Both processes use the *socket* call to create a socket and get a descriptor for it. The first argument of *socket* specifies the communication domain as the Internet domain and the second argument indicates that datagram communication is required. The last argument to the socket call may be used to specify a particular protocol, but setting it to zero causes the system to select a suitable protocol – UDP in this case.

- Both processes then use the *bind* call to bind their sockets to socket addresses. The sending process binds its socket to a socket address referring to any available local port number. The receiving process binds its socket to a socket address that contains its server port and must be made known to the sender.

- The sending process uses the *sendto* call with arguments specifying the socket through which the message is to be sent, the message itself and (a reference to a structure containing) the socket address of the destination. The *sendto* call hands the message to the underlying UDP and IP protocols and returns the actual number of bytes sent. As we have requested datagram service, the message is transmitted to its destination without an acknowledgement. If the message is too long to be sent, there is an error return (and the message is not transmitted).

- The receiving process uses the *recvfrom* call with arguments specifying the local socket on which to receive a message and memory locations in which to store the message and (a reference to a structure containing) the socket address of the sending socket. The *recvfrom* call collects the first message in the queue at the socket, or if the queue is empty it will wait until a message arrives.

Communication occurs only when a *sendto* in one process addresses its message to the socket used by a *recvfrom* in another process. In client-server communication, there is no need for servers to have prior knowledge of clients' socket addresses, because the *recvfrom* operation supplies the sender's address with each message it delivers. The properties of datagram communication in UNIX are the same as those described in Section 4.2.3.

4.6.2 Stream communication

In order to use the stream protocol, two processes must first establish a connection between their pair of sockets. The arrangement is asymmetric because one of the sockets will be listening for a request for a connection and the other will be asking for a connection, as described in Section 4.2.4. Once a pair of sockets has been connected, they may be used for transmitting data in both or either direction. That is, they behave like streams in that any available data is read immediately in the same order as it was written and there is no indication of boundaries of messages. However, there is a bounded queue at the receiving socket and the receiver blocks if the queue is empty; the sender blocks if it is full.

For communication between clients and servers, clients request connections and a listening server accepts them. When a connection is accepted, UNIX automatically creates a new socket and pairs it with the client's socket so that the server may continue listening for other clients' connection requests through the original socket. A connected pair of stream sockets can be used in subsequent stream communication until the connection is closed.

Stream communication is illustrated in Figure 4.22, in which the details of the arguments are simplified. The figure does not show the server closing the socket on which it listens. Normally, a server would first listen and accept a connection and then

Figure 4.22   Sockets used for streams

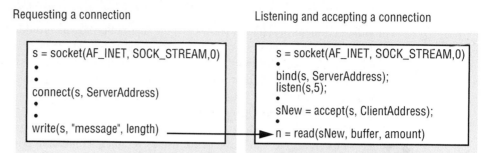

ServerAddress and *ClientAddress* are socket addresses

fork a new process to communicate with the client. Meanwhile, it will continue to listen in the original process.

- The server or listening process first uses the *socket* operation to create a stream socket and the *bind* operation to bind its socket to the server's socket address. The second argument to the *socket* system call is given as SOCK_STREAM, to indicate that stream communication is required. If the third argument is left as zero, the TCP/IP protocol will be selected automatically. It uses the *listen* operation to listen on its socket for client requests for connections. The second argument to the *listen* system call specifies the maximum number of requests for connections that can be queued at this socket.

- The server uses the *accept* system call to accept a connection requested by a client and obtain a new socket for communication with that client. The original socket may still be used to accept further connections with other clients.

- The client process uses the *socket* operation to create a stream socket and then uses the *connect* system call to request a connection via the socket address of the listening process. As the *connect* call automatically binds a socket name to the caller's socket, prior binding is unnecessary.

- After a connection has been established, both processes may then use the *write* and *read* operations on their respective sockets to send and receive sequences of bytes via the connection. The *write* operation is similar to the write operation for files. It specifies a message to be sent to a socket. It hands the message to the underlying TCP/IP protocol and returns the actual number of characters sent. The *read* operation receives some characters in its buffer and returns the number of characters received.

The properties of stream communication in UNIX are the same as those described in Section 4.2.4.

4.7 Summary

The first section of this chapter shows that the Internet protocols provide two alternative building blocks from which protocols may be constructed. There is an interesting trade-off between the two protocols: UDP provides a simple message-passing facility that suffers from omission failures but carries no built-in performance penalties. On the other hand, in good conditions, TCP guarantees message delivery but at the expense of additional messages, and higher latency and storage costs.

The second section shows three alternative styles of marshalling. CORBA and its predecessors choose to marshal data for use by recipients that have prior knowledge of the types of its components. In contrast, when Java serializes data, it includes full information about the types of its contents, allowing the recipient to reconstruct it purely from the content. XML, like Java, includes full type information. Another big difference is that CORBA requires a specification of the types of data items to be marshalled (in IDL) in order to generate the marshalling and unmarshalling methods, whereas Java uses reflection in order to serialize objects and deserialize their serial form. But a variety of different means are used for generating XML, depending on the context. For example, many programming languages, including Java, provide processors for translating between XML and language level objects.

The section on the request-reply protocol shows that an effective special-purpose protocol for distributed systems can be based on UDP datagrams. The reply message forms an acknowledgement for the request message, thus avoiding the overheads of additional acknowledgement messages. The protocol can be made more reliable if necessary. As it stands, there is no guarantee that the sending of a request message will result in a method being executed – for some applications this may suffice. But additional reliability can be added by making use of message identifiers and message retransmissions to ensure that a method does eventually get executed. For services with idempotent operations, this is sufficient. However, other applications require that reply messages be transmitted without re-executing the method in the request. This can be achieved with the help of a history. This illustrates the point that it is a good idea to build protocols to suit different classes of applications rather than to build a single ultra-reliable protocol for general use, because the latter might perform poorly in the normal case, in which faults seldom occur.

Multicast messages are used in communication between the members of a group of processes. IP multicast provides a multicast service for both local area networks and the Internet. This form of multicast has the same failure semantics as UDP datagrams, but in spite of suffering from omission failures it is a useful tool for many applications of multicast. Some other applications have stronger requirements – in particular, that multicast delivery should be atomic; that is, it should have all-or-nothing delivery. Further requirements on multicast are related to the ordering of messages, the strongest of which requires that all members of a group receive all of the messages in the same order.

EXERCISES

4.1   Is it conceivably useful for a port to have several receivers?   *page 134*

4.2   A server creates a port which it uses to receive requests from clients. Discuss the design issues concerning the relationship between the name of this port and the names used by clients.   *page 134*

4.3   The programs in Figure 4.3 and Figure 4.4 are available at www.cdk4.net/ipc. Use them to make a test kit to determine the conditions in which datagrams are sometimes dropped. Hint: the client program should be able to vary the number of messages sent and their size; the server should detect when a message from a particular client is missed.   *page 136*

4.4   Use the program in Figure 4.3 to make a client program that repeatedly reads a line of input from the user, sends it to the server in a UDP datagram message, then receives a message from the server. The client sets a timeout on its socket so that it can inform the user when the server does not reply. Test this client program with the server in Figure 4.4.   *page 136*

4.5   The programs in Figure 4.5 and Figure 4.6 are available at www.cdk4.net/ipc. Modify them so that the client repeatedly takes a line of user's input and writes it to the stream and the server reads repeatedly from the stream, printing out the result of each read. Make a comparison between sending data in UDP datagram messages and over a stream.   *page 140*

4.6   Use the programs developed in Exercise 4.5 to test the effect on the sender when the receiver crashes and vice-versa.   *page 140*

4.7   Sun XDR marshals data by converting it into a standard big-endian form before transmission. Discuss the advantages and disadvantages of this method when compared with CORBA's CDR.   *page 146*

4.8   Sun XDR aligns each primitive value on a four byte boundary, whereas CORBA CDR aligns a primitive value of size n on an n-byte boundary. Discuss the trade-offs in choosing the sizes occupied by primitive values.   *page 146*

4.9   Why is there no explicit data-typing in CORBA CDR?   *page 146*

4.10   Write an algorithm in pseudocode to describe the serialization procedure described in Section 4.3.2. The algorithm should show when handles are defined or substituted for classes and instances. Describe the serialized form that your algorithm would produce when serializing an instance of the following class *Couple*.

```
class Couple implements Serializable{
        private Person one;
        private Person two;
        public Couple(Person a, Person b) {
            one = a;
            two = b;
        }
}
```
   page 148

4.11   Write an algorithm in pseudocode to describe deserialization of the serialized form produced by the algorithm defined in Exercise 4.10. Hint: use reflection to create a class from its name, to create a constructor from its parameter types and to create a new instance of an object from the constructor and the argument values.   *page 148*

4.12   Why can't binary data be represented directly in XML, for example, by representing it as Unicode byte values? XML elements can carry strings represented as *base64*. Discuss the advantages or disadvantages of using this method to represent binary data.
    page 150

4.13   Define a class whose instances represent remote object references. It should contain information similar to that shown in Figure 4.13 and should provide access methods needed by the request-reply protocol. Explain how each of the access methods will be used by that protocol. Give a justification for the type chosen for the instance variable containing information about the interface of the remote object.   *page 154*

4.14   Define a class whose instances represent request and reply messages as illustrated in Figure 4.16. The class should provide a pair of constructors, one for request messages and the other for reply messages, showing how the request identifier is assigned. It should also provide a method to marshal itself into an array of bytes and to unmarshal an array of bytes into an instance.   *page 154*

4.15   Program each of the three operations of the request-reply protocol in Figure 4.15, using UDP communication, but without adding any fault-tolerance measures. You should use the classes you defined in Exercise 4.13 and Exercise 4.14.   *page 156*

4.16   Give an outline of the server implementation showing how the operations *getRequest* and *sendReply* are used by a server that creates a new thread to execute each client request. Indicate how the server will copy the *requestId* from the request message into the reply message and how it will obtain the client IP address and port.   *page 156*

4.17   Define a new version of the *doOperation* method that sets a timeout on waiting for the reply message. After a timeout, it retransmits the request message *n* times. If there is still no reply, it informs the caller.   *page 158*

4.18   Describe a scenario in which a client could receive a reply from an earlier call.
    page 156

4.19   Describe the ways in which the request-reply protocol masks the heterogeneity of operating systems and of computer networks.   *page 156*

4.20   Discuss whether the following operations are *idempotent*:
   •   Pressing a lift (elevator) request button;
   •   Writing data to a file;
   •   Appending data to a file.

   Is it a necessary condition for idempotence that the operation should not be associated with any state?   *page 158*

4.21   Explain the design choices that are relevant to minimizing the amount of reply data held at a server. Compare the storage requirements when the RR and RRA protocols are used.
    page 158

4.22 Assume the RRA protocol is in use. How long should servers retain unacknowledged reply data? Should servers repeatedly send the reply in an attempt to receive an acknowledgement? *page 158*

4.23 Why might the number of messages exchanged in a protocol be more significant to performance than the total amount of data sent? Design a variant of the RRA protocol in which the acknowledgement is piggy-backed on, that is, transmitted in the same message as, the next request where appropriate, and otherwise sent as a separate message. (Hint: use an extra timer in the client.) *page 158*

4.24 IP multicast provides a service that suffers from omission failures. Make a test kit, possibly based on the program in Figure 4.20, to discover the conditions under which a multicast message is sometimes dropped by one of the members of the multicast group. The test kit should be designed to allow for multiple sending processes. *page 165*

4.25 Outline the design of a scheme that uses message retransmissions with IP multicast to overcome the problem of dropped messages. Your scheme should take the following points into account:

i) there may be multiple senders;

ii) generally only a small proportion of messages are dropped;

iii) unlike the request-reply protocol, recipients may not necessarily send a message within any particular time limit.

Assume that messages that are not dropped arrive in sender ordering. *page 167*

4.26 Your solution to Exercise 4.25 should have overcome the problem of dropped messages in IP multicast. In what sense does your solution differ from the definition of reliable multicast? *page 167*

4.27 Devise a scenario in which multicasts sent by different clients are delivered in different orders at two group members. Assume that some form of message retransmissions are in use, but that messages that are not dropped arrive in sender ordering. Suggest how recipients might remedy this situation. *page 167*

4.28 Define the semantics for and design a protocol for a group form of request-reply interaction, for example using IP multicast. *pages 156, 165*

5

DISTRIBUTED OBJECTS AND REMOTE INVOCATION

In this chapter we introduce communication between distributed objects by means of remote method invocation (RMI). Objects that can receive remote method invocations are called remote objects and they implement a remote interface. Due to the possibility of independent failure of invoker and invoked objects, RMIs have different semantics from local calls. They can be made to look very similar to local invocations, but total transparency is not necessarily desirable. The code for marshalling and unmarshalling arguments and sending request and reply messages can be generated automatically by an interface compiler from the definition of the remote interface.

Remote procedure call is to RMI as procedure call is to object invocation. It is described briefly and illustrated by a case study of Sun RPC.

Distributed event-based systems allow objects to subscribe to events occurring at remote objects of interest and in turn to receive notifications when such events occur. Events and notifications provide a way for heterogeneous objects to communicate with one another asynchronously. The Jini distributed event specification is presented as a case study.

The use of RMI is illustrated in a case study of Java RMI.

Chapter 20 contains a case study on CORBA that includes CORBA RMI and the CORBA Event Service.

5.1   Introduction

This chapter is concerned with programming models for distributed applications – that is, those applications that are composed of cooperating programs running in several different processes. Such programs need to be able to invoke operations in other processes, often running in different computers. To achieve this, some familiar programming models have been extended to apply to distributed programs:

- The earliest and perhaps the best-known of these was the extension of the conventional procedure call model to the *remote procedure call* model, which allows client programs to call procedures in server programs running in separate processes and generally in different computers from the client.

- In the 1990s, the object-based programming model was extended to allow objects in different processes to communicate with one another by means of *remote method invocation* (RMI). RMI is an extension of local method invocation that allows an object living in one process to invoke the methods of an object living in another process.

- The event-based programming model allows objects to receive notification of the events at other objects in which they have registered interest. This model has been extended to allow distributed event-based programs to be written.

Note that we use the term 'RMI' to refer to remote method invocation in a generic way – this should not be confused with particular examples of remote method invocation such as Java RMI. A large proportion of current distributed systems software is written in object-oriented languages, and RPC can be understood in relation to RMI. Therefore this chapter concentrates on the RMI and event paradigms, each of which applies to distributed objects. Communication between distributed objects is introduced in Section 5.2, followed by a discussion of the design and implementation of RMI. A Java RMI case study is given in Section 5.5. RPC is discussed in the context of a case study of Sun RPC in Section 5.3; RPC is also used by web services which are discussed Chapter 19. Events and distributed notifications are discussed in Section 5.4. A further case study on CORBA is given in Chapter 20.

Middleware ◊ Software that provides a programming model above the basic building blocks of processes and message passing is called middleware. The middleware layer uses protocols based on messages between processes to provide its higher-level abstractions such as remote invocations and events, as illustrated in Figure 5.1. For example, the remote method invocation abstraction is based on the request-reply protocol discussed in Section 4.4.

An important aspect of middleware is the provision of location transparency and independence from the details of communication protocols, operating systems and computer hardware. Some forms of middleware allow the separate components to be written in different programming languages.

Location transparency: In RPC, the client that calls a procedure cannot tell whether the procedure runs in the same process or in a different process, possibly on a different computer. Nor does the client need to know the location of the server. Similarly, in RMI the object making the invocation cannot tell whether the object it invokes is local or not

Figure 5.1   Middleware layer

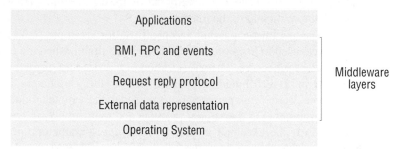

and does not need to know its location. Also in distributed event-based programs, the objects generating events and the objects that receive notifications of those events need not be aware of one anothers' locations.

Communication protocols: The protocols that support the middleware abstractions are independent of the underlying transport protocols. For example, the request-reply protocol can be implemented over either UDP or TCP.

Computer hardware: Three agreed standards for external data representation are described in Section 4.3. These are used when marshalling and unmarshalling messages. They hide the differences due to hardware architectures, such as byte ordering.

Operating systems: The higher-level abstractions provided by the middleware layer are independent of the underlying operating systems.

Use of several programming languages: Some middleware is designed to allow distributed applications to use more than one programming language. In particular, CORBA (see Chapter 20) allows clients written in one language to invoke methods in objects that live in server programs written in another language. This is achieved by using an *interface definition language* or IDL to define interfaces. IDLs are discussed in the next section.

5.1.1   Interfaces

Most modern programming languages provide a means of organizing a program as a set of modules that can communicate with one another. Communication between modules can be by means of procedure calls between modules or by direct access to the variables in another module. In order to control the possible interactions between modules, an explicit *interface* is defined for each module. The interface of a module specifies the procedures and the variables that can be accessed from other modules. Modules are implemented so as to hide all the information about them except that which is available through its interface. So long as its interface remains the same, the implementation may be changed without affecting the users of the module.

Interfaces in distributed systems ◊ In a distributed program, the modules can run in separate processes. It is not possible for a module running in one process to access the variables in a module in another process. Therefore, the interface of a module that is intended for RPC or RMI cannot specify direct access to variables. Note that CORBA

IDL interfaces can specify attributes, which seems to break this rule. However, the attributes are not accessed directly but by means of some getter and setter procedures added automatically to the interface.

The parameter-passing mechanisms, for example, call by value and call by reference, used in local procedure call are not suitable when the caller and procedure are in different processes. The specification of a procedure or method in the interface of a module in a distributed program describes the parameters as *input* or *output* or sometimes both. *Input* parameters are passed to the remote module by sending the values of the arguments in the request message and then supplying them as arguments to the operation to be executed in the server. *Output* parameters are returned in the reply message and are used as the result of the call or to replace the values of the corresponding variables in the calling environment. When a parameter is used for both input and output the value must be transmitted in both the request and reply messages.

Another difference between local and remote modules is that pointers in one process are not valid in another remote one. Therefore, pointers cannot be passed as arguments or returned as results of calls to remote modules.

The next two paragraphs discuss the interfaces used in the original client-server model for RPC and in the distributed object model for RMI:

Service interfaces: In the client-server model, each server provides a set of procedures that are available for use by clients. For example, a file server would provide procedures for reading and writing files. The term *service interface* is used to refer to the specification of the procedures offered by a server, defining the types of the input and output arguments of each of the procedures.

Remote interfaces: In the distributed object model, a *remote interface* specifies the methods of an object that are available for invocation by objects in other processes, defining the types of the input and output arguments of each of them. However, the big difference is that the methods in remote interfaces can pass objects as arguments and results of methods. In addition, references to remote objects may also be passed – these should not be confused with pointers, which refer to specific memory locations. (Section 4.3.4 describes the contents of remote object references.)

Neither service interfaces nor remote interfaces may specify direct access to variables. In the latter case, this prohibits direct access to the instance variables of an object.

Interface definition languages ◊ An RMI mechanism can be integrated with a particular programming language if it includes an adequate notation for defining interfaces, allowing input and output parameters to be mapped onto the language's normal use of parameters. Java RMI is an example in which an RMI mechanism has been added to an object-oriented programming language. This approach is useful when all the parts of a distributed application can be written in the same language. It is also convenient because it allows the programmer to use a single language for local and remote invocation.

However, many existing useful services are written in C++ and other languages. It would be beneficial to allow programs written in a variety of languages, including Java, to access them remotely. *Interface definition languages* (or IDLs) are designed to allow objects implemented in different languages to invoke one another. An IDL provides a notation for defining interfaces in which each of the parameters of a method may be described as for *input* or *output* in addition to having its type specified.

Figure 5.2   CORBA IDL example

```
// In file Person.idl
struct Person {
    string name;
    string place;
    long year;
} ;
interface PersonList {
    readonly attribute string listname;
    void addPerson(in Person p) ;
    void getPerson(in string name, out Person p);
    long number();
};
```

Figure 5.2 shows a simple example of CORBA IDL. The *Person* structure is the same as the one used to illustrate marshalling in Section 4.3.1. The interface named *PersonList* specifies the methods available for RMI in a remote object that implements that interface. For example, the method *addPerson* specifies its argument as *in*, meaning that it is an *input* argument; and the method *getPerson* that retrieves an instance of *Person* by name specifies its second argument as *out*, meaning that it is an *output* argument.

Our case studies include CORBA IDL as an example of an IDL for RMI (in Chapter 20) and Sun XDR as example of an IDL for RPC (in Section 5.3). The web services description language (WSDL) is designed for internet-wide RPC (see Section 19.3).

Other examples include the interface definition language for the RPC system in the OSF's Distributed Computing Environment (DCE) [OSF 1997], which uses C language syntax and is called IDL; and DCOM IDL which is based on DCE IDL [Box 1998] and is used in Microsoft's Distributed Component Object Model.

5.2   Communication between distributed objects

The object-based model for a distributed system extends the model supported by object-oriented programming languages to make it apply to distributed objects. This section addresses communication between distributed objects by means of RMI. The material is presented under the following headings:

The object model: A brief review of the relevant aspects of the object model, suitable for the reader with a basic knowledge of an object-oriented programming language, for example Java or C++.

Distributed objects: A presentation of object-based distributed systems, which argues that the object model is very appropriate for distributed systems.

The distributed object model: A discussion of the extensions to the object model necessary for it to support distributed objects.

Design issues: A set of arguments about the design alternatives:

1. Local invocations are executed exactly once, but what suitable semantics is possible for remote invocations?

2. How can RMI semantics be made similar to those of local method invocation and what differences cannot be eliminated?

Implementation: An explanation as to how a layer of middleware above the request-reply protocol may be designed to support RMI between application-level distributed objects.

Distributed garbage collection: A presentation of an algorithm for distributed garbage collection that is suitable for use with the RMI implementation.

5.2.1   The object model

An object-oriented program, for example in Java or C++, consists of a collection of interacting objects, each of which consists of a set of data and a set of methods. An object communicates with other objects by invoking their methods, generally passing arguments and receiving results. Objects can encapsulate their data and the code of their methods. Some languages, for example Java and C++, allow programmers to define objects whose instance variables can be accessed directly. But for use in a distributed object system, an object's data should be accessible only via its methods.

Object references ◊ Objects can be accessed via object references. For example, in Java, a variable that appears to hold an object actually holds a reference to that object. To invoke a method in an object, the object reference and method name are given, together with any necessary arguments. The object whose method is invoked is sometimes called the *target* and sometimes the *receiver*. Object references are first-class values, meaning that they may, for example, be assigned to variables, passed as arguments and returned as results of methods.

Interfaces ◊ An interface provides a definition of the signatures of a set of methods (that is, the types of their arguments, return values and exceptions) without specifying their implementation. An object will provide a particular interface if its class contains code that implements the methods of that interface. In Java, a class may implement several interfaces, and the methods of an interface may be implemented by any class. An interface also defines types that can be used to declare the type of variables or of the parameters and return values of methods. Note that interfaces do not have constructors.

Actions ◊ Action in an object-oriented program is initiated by an object invoking a method in another object. An invocation can include additional information (arguments) needed to carry out the method. The receiver executes the appropriate method and then returns control to the invoking object, sometimes supplying a result. An invocation of a method can have three effects:

1. the state of the receiver may be changed;

2. a new object may be instantiated, for example, by using a constructor in Java or C++; and

3. further invocations on methods in other objects may take place.

As an invocation can lead to further invocations of methods in other objects, an action is a chain of related method invocations, each of which eventually returns. This explanation does not take account of exceptions.

Exceptions ◊ Programs can encounter many sorts of errors and unexpected conditions of varying seriousness. During the execution of a method, many different problems may be discovered: for example, inconsistent values in the object's variables, or failure in attempts to read or write to files or network sockets. When programmers need to insert tests in their code to deal with all possible unusual or erroneous cases, this detracts from the clarity of the normal case. Exceptions provide a clean way to deal with error conditions without complicating the code. In addition, each method heading explicitly lists as exceptions the error conditions it might encounter, allowing users of the method to deal with them. A block of code may be defined to *throw* an exception whenever particular unexpected conditions or errors arise. This means that control passes to another block of code that *catches* the exception. Control does not return to the place where the exception was thrown.

Garbage collection ◊ It is necessary to provide a means of freeing the space occupied by objects when they are no longer needed. A language, for example Java, that can detect automatically when an object is no longer accessible recovers the space and makes it available for allocation to other objects. This process is called *garbage collection*. When a language (for example C++) does not support garbage collection, the programmer has to cope with the freeing of space allocated to objects. This can be a major source of errors.

5.2.2   Distributed objects

The state of an object consists of the values of its instance variables. In the object-based paradigm the state of a program is partitioned into separate parts, each of which is associated with an object. Since object-based programs are logically partitioned, the physical distribution of objects into different processes or computers in a distributed system is a natural extension.

Distributed object systems may adopt the client-server architecture. In this case, objects are managed by servers and their clients invoke their methods using remote method invocation. In RMI, the client's request to invoke a method of an object is sent in a message to the server managing the object. The invocation is carried out by executing a method of the object at the server and the result is returned to the client in another message. To allow for chains of related invocations, objects in servers are allowed to become clients of objects in other servers.

Distributed objects can assume other architectural models. For example, objects can be replicated in order to obtain the usual benefits of fault tolerance and enhanced

Figure 5.3   Remote and local method invocations

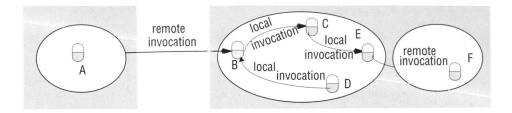

performance, and objects can be migrated with a view to enhancing their performance and availability.

Having client and server objects in different processes enforces encapsulation. That is, the state of an object can be accessed only by the methods of the object, which means that it is not possible for unauthorized methods to act on the state. For example, the possibility of concurrent RMIs from objects in different computers implies that an object may be accessed concurrently. Therefore, the possibility of conflicting accesses arises. However, the fact that the data of an object is accessed only by its own methods allows objects to provide methods for protecting themselves against incorrect accesses. For example, they may use synchronization primitives such as condition variables to protect access to their instance variables.

Another advantage of treating the shared state of a distributed program as a collection of objects is that an object may be accessed via RMI or it may be copied into a local cache and accessed directly provided that the class implementation is available locally.

The fact that objects are accessed only via their methods gives another advantage for heterogeneous systems in that different data formats may be used at different sites – these formats will be unnoticed by clients that use RMI to access the methods of the objects.

5.2.3 The distributed object model

This section discusses extensions to the object model to make it applicable to distributed objects. Each process contains a collection of objects, some of which can receive both local and remote invocations, whereas the other objects can receive only local invocations, as shown in Figure 5.3. Method invocations between objects in different processes, whether in the same computer or not, are known as *remote method invocations*. Method invocations between objects in the same process are local method invocations.

We refer to objects that can receive remote invocations as *remote objects*. In Figure 5.3, the objects B and F are remote objects. All objects can receive local invocations, although they can receive them only from other objects that hold references to them. For example, object C must have a reference to object E so that it can invoke one of its methods. The following two fundamental concepts are at the heart of the distributed object model:

Figure 5.4   A remote object and its remote interface

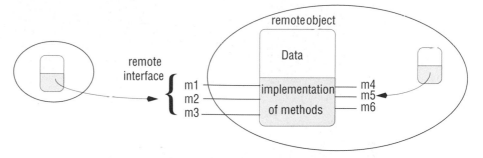

Remote object reference: Other objects can invoke the methods of a remote object if they have access to its *remote object reference*. For example, a remote object reference for B in Figure 5.3 must be available to A.

Remote interface: Every remote object has a *remote interface* that specifies which of its methods can be invoked remotely. For example, the objects B and F must have remote interfaces.

The following paragraphs discuss remote object references, remote interfaces and other aspects of the distributed object model.

Remote object references ◊ The notion of object reference is extended to allow any object that can receive an RMI to have a remote object reference. A remote object reference is an identifier that can be used throughout a distributed system to refer to a particular unique remote object. Its representation, which is generally different from that of local object references, is discussed in the Section 4.3.4. Remote object references are analogous to local ones in that:

1. the remote object to receive a remote method invocation is specified by the invoker as a remote object reference; and

2. remote object references may be passed as arguments and results of remote method invocations.

Remote interfaces ◊ The class of a remote object implements the methods of its remote interface, for example as public instance methods in Java. Objects in other processes can invoke only the methods that belong to its remote interface, as shown in Figure 5.4. Local objects can invoke the methods in the remote interface as well as other methods implemented by a remote object. Note that remote interfaces, like all interfaces, do not have constructors.

The CORBA system provides an interface definition language (IDL), which is used for defining remote interfaces. See Figure 5.2 for an example of a remote interface defined in CORBA IDL. The classes of remote objects and the client programs may be implemented in any language such as C++, Java or Python for which an IDL compiler is available. CORBA clients need not use the same language as the remote object in order to invoke its methods remotely.

In Java RMI, remote interfaces are defined in the same way as any other Java interface. They acquire their ability to be remote interfaces by extending an interface

Figure 5.5   Instantiation of remote objects

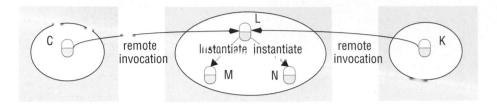

named *Remote*. Both CORBA IDL (Section 20.2.3) and Java support multiple inheritance of interfaces. That is, an interface is allowed to extend one or more other interfaces.

Actions in a distributed object system ◊ As in the non-distributed case, an action is initiated by a method invocation, which may result in further invocations on methods in other objects. But in the distributed case, the objects involved in a chain of related invocations may be located in different processes or different computers. When an invocation crosses the boundary of a process or computer, RMI is used, and the remote reference of the object must be available to the invoker. In Figure 5.3, the object A needs to hold a remote object reference to object B. Remote object references may be obtained as the results of remote method invocations. For example, object A in Figure 5.3 might obtain a remote reference to object F from object B.

When an action leads to the instantiation of a new object, that object will normally live within the process where instantiation is requested, for example, where the constructor was used. If the newly instantiated object has a remote interface, it will be a remote object with a remote object reference.

Distributed applications may provide remote objects with methods for instantiating objects which can be accessed by RMI, thus effectively providing the effect of remote instantiation of objects. For example, suppose that the object L in Figure 5.5 contains a method for creating remote objects, then the remote invocations from C and K could lead to the instantiation of the objects M and N respectively.

Garbage collection in a distributed-object system ◊ If a language, for example Java, supports garbage collection, then any associated RMI system should allow garbage collection of remote objects. Distributed garbage collection is generally achieved by cooperation between the existing local garbage collector and an added module that carries out a form of distributed garbage collection, usually based on reference counting. Section 5.2.6 describes such a scheme in detail. If garbage collection is not available, then remote objects that are no longer required should be deleted.

Exceptions ◊ Any remote invocation may fail for reasons related to the invoked object being in a different process or computer from the invoker. For example, the process containing the remote object may have crashed or may be too busy to reply, or the invocation or result message may be lost. Therefore, remote method invocation should be able to raise exceptions such as timeouts that are due to distribution as well as those raised during the execution of the method invoked. Examples of the latter are an attempt to read beyond the end of a file, or to access a file without the correct permissions.

Figure 5.6   Invocation semantics

Fault tolerance measures			Invocation semantics
Retransmit request message	Duplicate filtering	Re-execute procedure or retransmit reply	
No	Not applicable	Not applicable	*Maybe*
Yes	No	Re-execute procedure	*At-least-once*
Yes	Yes	Retransmit reply	*At-most-once*

CORBA IDL provides a notation for specifying application-level exceptions, and the underlying system generates standard exceptions when errors due to distribution occur. CORBA client programs need to be able to handle exceptions. For example, a C++ client program will use the exception mechanisms in C++.

5.2.4   Design Issues for RMI

The previous section suggested that RMI is a natural extension of local method invocation. In this section, we discuss two design issues that arise in making this extension:

- The choice of invocation semantics – although local invocations are executed exactly once, this cannot always be the case for remote method invocations.
- The level of transparency that is desirable for RMI.

In the remainder of Section 5.2, we refer to the processes that host remote objects as servers and the processes that host their invokers as clients. Servers can also be clients.

RMI invocation semantics ◊ Request-reply protocols were discussed in Section 4.4, where we showed that *doOperation* can be implemented in different ways to provide different delivery guarantees. The main choices are:

Retry request message: whether to retransmit the request message until either a reply is received or the server is assumed to have failed.

Duplicate filtering: when retransmissions are used, whether to filter out duplicate requests at the server.

Retransmission of results: whether to keep a history of result messages to enable lost results to be retransmitted without re-executing the operations at the server.

Combinations of these choices lead to a variety of possible semantics for the reliability of remote invocations as seen by the invoker. Figure 5.6 shows the choices of interest, with corresponding names for the invocation semantics that they produce. Note that for local method invocations, the semantics are *exactly once*, meaning that every method is executed exactly once. The choices of RMI invocation semantics are defined as follows:

Maybe invocation semantics: With *maybe* invocation semantics, the remote method may be executed once or not at all. Maybe semantics arises when none of the fault tolerance measures is applied. This can suffer from the following types of failure:

- omission failures if the invocation or result message is lost;
- crash failures when the server containing the remote object fails.

If the result message has not been received after a timeout and there are no retries, it is uncertain whether the method has been executed. If the invocation message was lost, then the method will not have been executed. On the other hand, the method may have been executed and the result message lost. A crash failure may occur either before or after the method is executed. Moreover, in an asynchronous system, the result of executing the method may arrive after the timeout. *Maybe* semantics is useful only for applications in which occasional failed invocations are acceptable.

At-least-once invocation semantics: With *at-least-once* invocation semantics, the invoker receives either a result, in which case the invoker knows that the method was executed at least once, or an exception informing it that no result was received. *At-least-once* invocation semantics can be achieved by the retransmission of request messages, which masks the omission failures of the invocation or result message. *At-least-once* invocation semantics can suffer from the following types of failure:

- crash failures when the server containing the remote object fails;
- arbitrary failures. In cases when the invocation message is retransmitted, the remote object may receive it and execute the method more than once, possibly causing wrong values to be stored or returned.

Chapter 4 defines an *idempotent operation* as one that can be performed repeatedly with the same effect as if it had been performed exactly once. Non-idempotent operations can have the wrong effect if they are performed more than once. For example, an operation to increase a bank balance by $10 should be performed only once; if it were to be repeated, the balance would grow and grow! If the objects in a server can be designed so that all of the methods in their remote interfaces are idempotent operations, then *at-least-once* call semantics may be acceptable.

At-most-once invocation semantics: With *at-most-once* invocation semantics, the invoker receives either a result, in which case the invoker knows that the method was executed exactly once, or an exception informing it that no result was received, in which case the method will have been executed either once or not at all. *At-most-once* invocation semantics can be achieved by using all of the fault tolerance measures. As in the previous case, the use of retries masks any omission failures of the invocation or result messages. This set of fault tolerance measures prevent arbitrary failures by ensuring that for each RMI a method is never executed more than once. In both Java RMI and CORBA, the invocation semantics is *at-most-once*, but CORBA allows *maybe* semantics to be requested for methods that do not return results. Sun RPC provides at-least-once call semantics.

Transparency ◊ The originators of RPC, Birrell and Nelson [1984], aimed to make remote procedure calls as much like local procedure calls as possible, with no distinction in syntax between a local and a remote procedure call. All the necessary calls to marshalling and message-passing procedures were hidden from the programmer making the call. Although request messages are retransmitted after a timeout, this is transparent to the caller – to make the semantics of remote procedure calls like that of local procedure calls. This notion of transparency has been extended to apply to distributed objects, but it involves hiding not only marshalling and message passing but also the task of locating and contacting a remote object. As an example, Java RMI makes remote method invocations very like local ones by allowing them to use the same syntax.

However, remote invocations are more vulnerable to failure than local ones, since they involve a network, another computer and another process. Whichever of the above invocation semantics is chosen, there is always the chance that no result will be received and in the case of failure, it is impossible to distinguish between failure of the network and of the remote server process. This requires that objects making remote invocations be able to recover from such situations.

The latency of a remote invocation is several orders of magnitude greater than that of a local one. This suggests that programs that make use of remote invocations need to be able to take this factor into account, perhaps by minimizing remote interactions. The designers of Argus [Liskov and Scheifler 1982] suggested that a caller should be able to abort a remote procedure call that is taking too long in such a way that it has no effect on the server. To allow this, the server would need to be able to restore things to how they were before the procedure was called. These issues are discussed in Chapter 13.

Waldo *et al.* [1994] say that the difference between local and remote objects should be expressed at the remote interface, to allow objects to react in a consistent way to possible partial failures. Other systems went further than this by arguing that the syntax of a remote call should be different from that of a local call: in the case of Argus, the language was extended to make remote operations explicit to the programmer.

The choice as to whether remote invocations should be transparent is also available to the designers of IDLs. For example, in CORBA, a remote invocation throws an exception when the client is unable to communicate with a remote object. This requires that the client program handle such exceptions, allowing it to deal with such failures. An IDL can also provide a facility for specifying the call semantics of a method. This can help the designer of the remote object – for example, if at-least-once call semantics is chosen to avoid the overheads of at-most-once, the operations of the object are designed to be idempotent.

The current consensus seems to be that remote invocations should be made transparent in the sense that the syntax of a remote invocation is the same as that of a local invocation, but that the difference between local and remote objects should be expressed in their interfaces. In the case of Java RMI, remote objects can be distinguished by the fact that they implement the *Remote* interface and throw *RemoteExceptions*. Implementors of a remote object whose interface is specified in an IDL are also aware of the difference. The knowledge that an object is intended to be accessed by remote invocation has another implication for its designer: it should be able to keep its state consistent in the presence of concurrent accesses from multiple clients.

Figure 5.7   The role of proxy and skeleton in remote method invocation

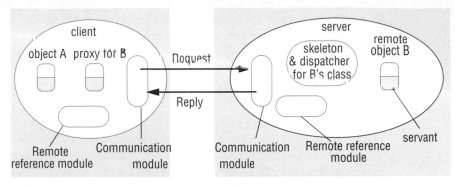

5.2.5   Implementation of RMI

Several separate objects and modules are involved in achieving a remote method invocation. These are shown in Figure 5.7, in which an application-level object A invokes a method in a remote application-level object B for which it holds a remote object reference. This section discusses the roles of each of the components shown in that figure, dealing first with the communication and remote reference modules and then with the RMI software that runs over them.

The remainder of this section deals with the following related topics: the generation of proxies, the binding of names to their remote object references, the activation and passivation of objects and the location of objects from their remote object references.

Communication module ◊   The two cooperating communication modules carry out the request-reply protocol, which transmits *request* and *reply* messages between client and server. The contents of *request* and *reply* messages are shown in Figure 4.16. The communication module uses only the first three items, which specify the message type, its *requestId* and the remote reference of the object to be invoked. The *methodId* and all the marshalling and unmarshalling is the concern of the RMI software discussed below. The communication modules are together responsible for providing a specified invocation semantics, for example at-most-once.

The communication module in the server selects the dispatcher for the class of the object to be invoked, passing on its local reference, which it gets from the remote reference module in return for the remote object identifier in the *request* message. The role of dispatcher is discussed under RMI software below.

Remote reference module ◊   A remote reference module is responsible for translating between local and remote object references and for creating remote object references. To support its responsibilities, the remote reference module in each process has a *remote object table* that records the correspondence between local object references in that process and remote object references (which are system-wide). The table includes:

• An entry for all the remote objects held by the process. For example, in Figure 5.7, the remote object B will be recorded in the table at the server.

- An entry for each local proxy. For example, in Figure 5.7 the proxy for B will be recorded in the table at the client.

The role of a proxy is discussed under RMI software below. The actions of the remote reference module are as follows:

- When a remote object is to be passed as argument or result for the first time, the remote reference module is asked to create a remote object reference, which it adds to its table.

- When a remote object reference arrives in a request or reply message, the remote reference module is asked for the corresponding local object reference, which may refer either to a proxy or to a remote object. In the case that the remote object reference is not in the table, the RMI software creates a new proxy and asks the remote reference module to add it to the table.

This module is called by components of the RMI software when they are marshalling and unmarshalling remote object references. For example, when a request message arrives, the table is used to find out which local object is to be invoked.

Servants ◊ A servant is an instance of a class which provides the body of a remote object. It is the servant that eventually handles the remote requests passed on by the corresponding skeleton. Servants live within a server process. They are created when remote objects are instantiated and remain in use until they are no longer needed; finally being garbage collected or deleted.

The RMI software ◊ This consists of a layer of software between the application-level objects and the communication and remote reference modules. The roles of the middleware objects shown in Figure 5.7 are as follows:

Proxy: The role of a proxy is to make remote method invocation transparent to clients by behaving like a local object to the invoker; but instead of executing an invocation, it forwards it in a message to a remote object. It hides the details of the remote object reference, the marshalling of arguments, unmarshalling of results and sending and receiving of messages from the client. There is one proxy for each remote object for which a process holds a remote object reference. The class of a proxy implements the methods in the remote interface of the remote object it represents. This ensures that remote method invocations are suitable for the type of the remote object. However, the proxy implements them quite differently. Each method of the proxy marshals a reference to the target object, its own *methodId* and its arguments into a *request* message and sends it to the target, awaits the *reply* message, unmarshals it and returns the results to the invoker.

Dispatcher: A server has one dispatcher and skeleton for each class representing a remote object. In our example, the server has a dispatcher and skeleton for the class of remote object B. The dispatcher receives the *request* message from the communication module. It uses the *methodId* to select the appropriate method in the skeleton, passing on the *request* message. The dispatcher and proxy use the same allocation of *methodId*s to the methods of the remote interface.

Skeleton: The class of a remote object has a *skeleton*, which implements the methods in the remote interface. They are implemented quite differently from the methods in the servant that incarnates a remote object. A skeleton method unmarshals the arguments in the *request* message and invokes the corresponding method in the servant. It waits for the invocation to complete and then marshals the result, together with any exceptions, in a *reply* message to the sending proxy's method.

Remote object references are marshalled in the form shown in Figure 4.13, which includes information about the remote interface of the remote object, for example, the the name of the remote interface or the class of the remote object. This information enables the proxy class to be determined so that a new proxy may be created when it is needed. For example, the proxy class name may be generated by appending "*_proxy*" to the name of the remote interface.

Generation of the classes for proxies, dispatchers and skeletons ◊ The classes for the proxy, dispatcher and skeleton used in RMI are generated automatically by an interface compiler. For example, in the Orbix implementation of CORBA, interfaces of remote objects are defined in CORBA IDL, and the interface compiler can be used to generate the classes for proxies, dispatchers and skeletons in C++ or in Java [www.iona.com]. For Java RMI, the set of methods offered by a remote object is defined as a Java interface that is implemented within the class of the remote object. The Java RMI compiler generates the proxy, dispatcher and skeleton classes from the class of the remote object.

Dynamic invocation: an alternative to proxies ◊ The proxy just described is static, in the sense that its class is generated from an interface definition and then compiled into the client code. Sometimes this is not practical: suppose that a client program receives a remote reference to an object whose remote interface was not available at compile time. In this case it needs another way for invoking the remote object: this is called *dynamic invocation*. It gives the client access to a generic representation of a remote invocation like the *DoOperation* method used in Exercise 5.8, which is available as part of the infrastructure for RMI (see Section 4.4). The client will supply the remote object reference, the name of the method and the arguments to *DoOperation* and then wait to receive the results.

Note that although the remote object reference includes information about the interface of the remote object, such as its name, this is not enough – the names of the methods and the types of the arguments are required for making a dynamic invocation. CORBA provides this information via a component called the Interface Repository, which is described in Section 20.2.2.

The dynamic invocation interface is not so convenient to use as a proxy, but is useful in applications where not all the interfaces of the remote objects to be used can be predicted at design time. An example of such an application is the shared whiteboard that we use to illustrate Java RMI (Section 5.5), CORBA (Section 20.2) and web services (Section 19.2.3). To summarize: the shared whiteboard application displays many different types of shapes, such as circles, rectangles and lines, but it should be able to display new shapes that were not predicted when the client was compiled. A client that uses dynamic invocation is able to address this challenge. We shall see in Section 5.5 that the dynamic downloading of classes to clients is an alternative to dynamic invocation. This is available in Java RMI – a single language system.

Dynamic skeletons: It is clear, from the above example, that it can also arise that a server will need to host remote objects whose interfaces were not known at compile time. For example, a client may supply a new type of shape to the shared whiteboard server for it to store. A server with dynamic skeletons would be able to deal with this situation. We defer describing dynamic skeletons until the chapter on CORBA in Section 20.2.2. However, as we shall see in Section 5.2, Java RMI addresses this problem by using a generic dispatcher and the dynamic downloading of classes to the server.

Server and client programs ◊ The server program contains the classes for the dispatchers and skeletons, together with the implementations of the classes of all of the servants that it supports. In addition, the server program contains an *initialization* section (for example, in a *main* method in Java or C++). The *initialization* section is responsible for creating and initializing at least one of the servants to be hosted by the server. Additional servants may be created in response to requests from clients. The *initialization* section may also register some of its servants with a binder (see the next paragraph). Generally, it will register just one servant, which can be used to access the rest.

The client program will contain the classes of the proxies for all of the remote objects that it will invoke. It can use a binder to look up remote object references.

Factory methods: We noted earlier that remote object interfaces cannot include constructors. This means that servants cannot be created by remote invocation on constructors. Servants are created either in the *initialization* section or in methods in a remote interface designed for that purpose. The term *factory method* is sometimes used to refer to a method that creates servants, and a *factory object* is an object with factory methods. Any remote object that needs to be able to create new remote objects on demand for clients must provide methods in its remote interface for this purpose. Such methods are called factory methods, although they are really just normal methods.

The binder ◊ Client programs generally require a means of obtaining a remote object reference for at least one of the remote objects held by a server. For example, in Figure 5.3, object A would require a remote object reference for object B. A *binder* in a distributed system is a separate service that maintains a table containing mappings from textual names to remote object references. It is used by servers to register their remote objects by name and by clients to look them up. Chapter 20 contains a discussion of the CORBA Naming Service. The Java binder, RMIregistry, is discussed briefly in the case study on Java RMI in Section 5.5.

Server threads ◊ Whenever an object executes a remote invocation, that execution may lead to further invocations of methods in other remote objects, which may take some time to return. To avoid the execution of one remote invocation delaying the execution of another, servers generally allocate a separate thread for the execution of each remote invocation. When this is the case, the designer of the implementation of a remote object must allow for the effects on its state of concurrent executions.

Activation of remote objects ◊ Some applications require that information survive for long periods of time. However, it is not practical for the objects representing such information to be kept in running processes for unlimited periods, particularly since they are not necessarily in use all of the time. To avoid the potential waste of resources due to running all of the servers that manage remote objects all of the time, the servers can be started whenever they are needed by clients, as is done for the standard set of TCP services such as FTP, which are started on demand by a service called *Inetd*. Processes that start server processes to host remote objects are called *activators* for the following reasons.

A remote object is described as *active* when it is available for invocation within a running process, whereas it is called *passive* if is not currently active but can be made active. A passive object consists of two parts:

1. the implementation of its methods; and

2. its state in the marshalled form.

Activation consists of creating an active object from the corresponding passive object by creating a new instance of its class and initializing its instance variables from the stored state. Passive objects can be activated on demand, for example when they need to be invoked by other objects.

An *activator* is responsible for:

• Registering passive objects that are available for activation, which involves recording the names of servers against the URLs or file names of the corresponding passive objects.

• Starting named server processes and activating remote objects in them.

• Keeping track of the locations of the servers for remote objects that it has already activated.

Java RMI provides the ability to make some remote objects *activatable* [java.sun.com IX] When an activatable object is invoked, if that object is not currently active, the object is made active from its marshalled state and then passed the invocation. It uses one activator on each server computer.

The CORBA case study describes the implementation repository – a weak form of activator that starts services containing objects in an initial state.

Persistent object stores ◊ An object that is guaranteed to live between activations of processes is called a *persistent object*. Persistent objects are generally managed by persistent object stores which store their state in a marshalled form on disk. Examples include the CORBA persistent state service (see Section 20.3), Java Data Objects [java.sun.com VIII] and Persistent Java [Jordan 1996, java.sun.com IV].

In general, a persistent object store will manage very large numbers of persistent objects, which are stored on disk or in a database until they are needed. They will be activated when their methods are invoked by other objects. Activation is generally designed to be transparent – that is, the invoker should not be able to tell whether an object is already in main memory or has to be activated before its method is invoked. Persistent objects that are no longer needed in main memory can be passivated. In most cases, objects are saved in the persistent object store whenever they reach a consistent state, for the sake of fault tolerance. The persistent object store needs a strategy for deciding when to passivate objects. For example, it may do so in response to a request in the program that activated the objects, for example at the end of a transaction or when the program exits. Persistent object stores generally attempt to optimize passivation by saving only those objects that have been modified since the last time they were saved.

Persistent object stores generally allow collections of related persistent objects to have human-readable names such as pathnames or URLs. In practice, each human-readable name is associated with the root of a connected set of persistent objects.

There are two approaches to deciding whether an object is persistent or not:

- The persistent object store maintains some persistent roots and any object that is reachable from a persistent root is defined to be persistent. This approach is used by Persistent Java, Java Data Objects and by PerDiS [Ferreira *et al.* 2000]. They make use of a garbage collector to dispose of objects that are no longer reachable from the persistent roots.

- The persistent object store provides some classes on which persistence is based – persistent objects belong to their subclasses. For example, in Arjuna [Parrington *et al.* 1995], persistent objects are based on C++ classes that provide transactions and recovery. Unwanted objects must be deleted explicitly.

Some persistent object stores, for example PerDiS and Khazana [Carter *et al.* 1998] allow objects to be activated in multiple caches local to users, instead of in servers. In this case, a cache consistency protocol is required; Chapter 18 discusses a variety of consistency models.

Object location ◊   Section 4.3.4 describes a form of remote object reference that contains the Internet address and port number of the process that created the remote object as a way of guaranteeing uniqueness. This form of remote object reference can also be used as an address for a remote object so long as that object remains in the same process for the rest of its life. But some remote objects will exist in a series of different processes, possibly on different computers, throughout their lifetime. In this case, a remote object reference cannot act as an address. Clients making invocations require both a remote object reference and an address to which to send invocations.

A *location service* helps clients to locate remote objects from their remote object references. It uses a database that maps remote object references to their probable current locations – the locations are probable because an object may have migrated again since it was last heard of. For example, the Clouds system [Dasgupta *et al.* 1991] and the Emerald system [Jul *et al.* 1988] used a cache/broadcast scheme in which a member of a location service on each computer holds a small cache of remote object reference-to-location mappings. If a remote object reference is in the cache, that address is tried for the invocation and will fail if the object has moved. To locate an object that has moved or whose location is not in cache, the system broadcasts a request. This scheme may be enhanced by the use of forward location pointers, which contain hints as to the new location of an object. Another example is the resolution service required for resolving the URN of a resource into its current URL, mentioned in Section 9.1.

5.2.6   Distributed garbage collection

The aim of a distributed garbage collector is to ensure that if a local or remote reference to an object is still held anywhere in a set of distributed objects, then the object itself will continue to exist, but as soon as no object any longer holds a reference to it, the object will be collected and the memory it uses recovered.

We describe the Java distributed garbage collection algorithm, which is similar to the one described by Birrell *et al.* [1995]. It is based on reference counting. Whenever a remote object reference enters a process, a proxy will be created and will stay there for as long as it is needed. The process where the object lives (its server) should be informed of the new proxy at the client. Then later when there is no longer a proxy at the client, the server should be informed. The distributed garbage collector works in cooperation with the local garbage collectors as follows:

- Each server process maintains a set of the names of the processes that hold remote object references for each of its remote objects; for example, *B.holders* is the set of client processes (virtual machines) that have proxies for object B. (In Figure 5.7, this set will include the client process illustrated.) This set can be held in an additional column in the remote object table.

- When a client *C* first receives a remote reference to a particular remote object, *B*, it makes an *addRef(B)* invocation to the server of that remote object and then creates a proxy; the server adds *C* to *B.holders*.

- When a client *C*'s garbage collector notices that a proxy for remote object *B* is no longer reachable, it makes a *removeRef(B)* invocation to the corresponding server and then deletes the proxy; the server removes *C* from *B.holders*.

- When *B.holders* is empty, the server's local garbage collector will reclaim the space occupied by *B* unless there are any local holders.

This algorithm is intended to be carried out by means of pairwise request-reply communication with at-most-once invocation semantics between the remote reference modules in processes – it does not require any global synchronization. Note also that the extra invocations made on behalf of the garbage collection algorithm do not affect every normal RMI; they occur only when proxies are created and deleted.

There is a possibility that one client may make a *removeRef(B)* invocation at about the same time as another client makes an *addRef(B)* invocation. If the *removeRef* arrives first and *B.holders* is empty, the remote object *B* could be deleted before the *addRef* arrives. To avoid this situation, if the set *B.holders* is empty at the time when a remote object reference is transmitted, a temporary entry is added until the *addRef* arrives.

The Java distributed garbage collection algorithm tolerates communication failures by using the following approach. The *addRef* and *removeRef* operations are idempotent. In the case that an *addRef(B)* call returns an exception (meaning that the method was either executed once or not at all), the client will not create a proxy but will make a *removeRef(B)* call. The effect of *removeRef* is correct whether or not the *addRef* succeeded. The case where *removeRef* fails is dealt with by leases, as described in the next paragraph.

The Java distributed garbage collection algorithm can tolerate the failure of client processes. To achieve this, servers *lease* their objects to clients for a limited period of time. The lease period starts when the client makes an *addRef* invocation to the server. It ends either when the time has expired or when the client makes a *removeRef* invocation to the server. The information stored by the server concerning each lease contains the identifier of the client's virtual machine and the period of the lease. Clients are responsible for requesting the server to renew their leases before they expire.

Leases in Jini ◊ The Jini distributed system includes a specification for leases [Arnold *et al.* 1999] that can be used in a variety of situations when one object offers a resource to another object, as for example when remote objects offer references to other objects. Objects that offer such resources are at risk of having to maintain the resources when the users are no longer interested or their programs may have exited. To avoid complicated protocols to discover whether the resource users are still interested, the resources are offered for a limited period of time. The granting of the use of a resource for a period of time is called a *lease*. The object offering the resource will maintain it until the time in the lease expires. The resource users are responsible for requesting their renewal when they expire.

The period of a lease may be negotiated between the grantor and the recipient, although this does not happen with the leases used in Java RMI. An object representing a lease implements the *Lease* interface. It contains information about the period of the lease and methods enabling the lease to be renewed or cancelled. The grantor returns an instance of a *Lease* when it supplies a resource to another object.

5.3 Remote procedure call

A remote procedure call is very similar to a remote method invocation in that a client program calls a procedure in another program running in a server process. Servers may be clients of other servers to allow chains of RPCs. As mentioned in the introduction to this chapter, a server process defines in its *service interface* the procedures that are available for calling remotely. In effect, this sort of service is rather like a single remote object in that it has state and methods. However, it lacks the ability to create new instances of objects and therefore does not support remote object references.

RPC, like RMI, may be implemented to have one of the choices of invocation semantics discussed in Section 5.2.4 – at-least-once or at-most-once are generally chosen. RPC is generally implemented over a request-reply protocol like the one discussed in Section 4.4, which is simplified by the omission of object references from request messages. The contents of request and reply messages are the same as those illustrated for RMI in Figure 4.16, except that the *ObjectReference* field is omitted.

The software that supports RPC is shown in Figure 5.8 as it would be for a procedural language, such as C, which does not support classes or objects. It is relevant for our case study of Sun RPC, which uses the C language. It is also interesting for historical reasons because most of the early RPC systems were C-based.

This software is similar to that shown in Figure 5.7 except that no remote reference modules are required, since procedure call is not concerned with objects and object references. The client that accesses a service includes one *stub procedure* for each procedure in the service interface. The role of a stub procedure is similar to that of a proxy method. It behaves like a local procedure to the client, but instead of executing the call, it marshals the procedure identifier and the arguments into a request message, which it sends via its communication module to the server. When the reply message arrives, it unmarshals the results. The server process contains a dispatcher together with one server stub procedure and one service procedure for each procedure in the service interface. The dispatcher selects one of the server stub procedures according to the

Figure 5.8   Role of client and server stub procedures in RPC in the context of a procedural language

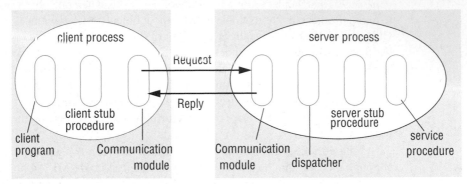

procedure identifier in the request message. A *server stub procedure* is like a skeleton method in that it unmarshals the arguments in the request message, calls the corresponding service procedure and marshals the return values for the reply message. The service procedures implement the procedures in the service interface.

The client and server stub procedures and the dispatcher can be generated by an interface compiler from the interface definition of the service. If the client or server uses an object-based language, such as C++ or Java, the set of client stub procedures for a service may be implemented as a proxy or the set of server stubs procedures as a skeleton.

5.3.1   Case study: Sun RPC

RFC 1831 [Srinivasan 1995a] describes Sun RPC which was designed for client-server communication in the Sun NFS network file system. Sun RPC is sometimes called ONC (Open Network Computing) RPC. It is supplied as a part of the various Sun and other UNIX operating systems and is also available with NFS installations. Implementors have the choice of using remote procedure calls over either UDP or TCP. When Sun RPC is used with UDP, the length of request and reply messages is restricted in length – theoretically to 64 kilobytes, but more often in practice to 8 or 9 kilobytes. It uses at-least-once call semantics. Broadcast RPC is an option.

The Sun RPC system provides an interface language called XDR and an interface compiler called *rpcgen* which is intended for use with the C programming language.

Interface definition language ◊ The Sun XDR language, which was originally designed for specifying external data representations, was extended to become an interface definition language. It may be used to define a service interface for Sun RPC by specifying a set of procedure definitions together with supporting type definitions. The notation is rather primitive in comparison with that used by CORBA IDL or Java. In particular:

- Most languages allow interface names to be specified, but Sun RPC does not – instead of this, a program number and a version number are supplied. The program numbers can be obtained from a central authority to allow every program to have its own unique number. The version number changes when a procedure signature

Figure 5.9   Files interface in Sun XDR

```
const MAX = 1000;
typedef int FileIdentifier;
typedef int FilePointer;
typedef int Length;
struct Data {
    int length;
    char buffer[MAX];
};
struct writeargs {
    FileIdentifier f;
    FilePointer position;
    Data data;
};
struct readargs {
    FileIdentifier f;
    FilePointer position;
    Length length;
};

program FILEREADWRITE {
    version VERSION {
        void WRITE(writeargs)=1;                    1
        Data READ(readargs)=2;                      2
    }=2;
} = 9999;
```

changes. Both program and version number are passed in the request message, so that client and server can check that they are using the same version.

- A procedure definition specifies a procedure signature and a procedure number. The procedure number is used as a procedure identifier in request messages. (It would be possible for the interface compiler to generate procedure identifiers.)

- Only a single input parameter is allowed. Therefore, procedures requiring multiple parameters must include them as components of a single structure.

- The output parameters of a procedure are returned via a single result.

- The procedure signature consists of the result type, the name of the procedure and the type of the input parameter. The type of both the result and the input parameter may specify either a single value or a structure containing several values.

For example, see the XDR definition in Figure 5.9 of an interface with a pair of procedures for writing and reading files. The program number is 9999 and the version number is 2. The *READ* procedure (line 2) takes as input parameter a structure with three components specifying a file identifier, a position in the file and the number of bytes required. Its result is a structure containing the number of bytes returned and the file data. The *WRITE* procedure (line 1) has no result. The *WRITE* and *READ* procedures are given numbers 1 and 2. The number zero is reserved for a null procedure, which is generated automatically and is intended to be used to test whether a server is available.

This interface definition language provides a notation for defining constants, typedefs, structures, enumerated types, unions and programs. Typedefs, structures and enumerated types use the C language syntax. The interface compiler *rpcgen* can be used to generate the following from an interface definition:

- client stub procedures;
- server *main* procedure, dispatcher and server stub procedures;
- XDR marshalling and unmarshalling procedures for use by the dispatcher and client and server stub procedures.

Binding ◊ Sun RPC runs a local binding service called the *port mapper* at a well-known port number on each computer. Each instance of a port mapper records the program number, version number and port number in use by each service running locally. When a server starts up it registers its program number, version number and port number with the local port mapper. When a client starts up, it finds out the server's port by making a remote request to the port mapper at the server's host, specifying the program number and version number.

When a service has multiple instances running on different computers, the instances may use different port numbers for receiving client requests. If a client needs to multicast a request to all the instances of a service that are using different port numbers, it cannot use a direct IP multicast message for this purpose. The solution is that clients make multicast remote procedure calls by multicasting them to all the port mappers, specifying the program and version number. Each port mapper forwards all such calls to the appropriate local service program, if there is one.

Authentication ◊ Sun RPC request and reply messages provide additional fields enabling authentication information to be passed between client and server. The request message contains the credentials of the user running the client program. For example, in the UNIX style of authentication the credentials include the *uid* and *gid* of the user. Access control mechanisms can be built on top of the authentication information which is made available to the server procedures via a second argument. The server program is responsible for enforcing access control by deciding whether to execute each procedure call according to the authentication information. For example, if the server is an NFS file server, it can check whether the user has sufficient rights to carry out a requested file operation.

Several different authentication protocols can be supported. These include:

- none;
- UNIX style as described above;
- a style in which a shared key is established for signing the RPC messages; or
- Kerberos style of authentication (see Chapter 7).

A field in the RPC header indicates which style is being used.

A more generic approach to security is described in RFC 2203 [Eisler *et al*. 1997]. It provides for secrecy and integrity of RPC messages as well as authentication. It allows client and server to negotiate a security context in which either no security is applied or in the case that security is required, message integrity or message privacy or both may be applied.

Client and server programs ◊ Further material on Sun RPC is available at www.cdk4.net/rmi. It includes example client and server programs corresponding to the interface defined in Figure 5.9.

5.4   Events and notifications

The idea behind the use of events is that one object can react to a change occurring in another object. Notifications of events are essentially asynchronous and determined by their receivers. In particular, in interactive applications, the actions that the user performs on objects, for example, by manipulating a button with the mouse or entering text in a text box via the keyboard, are seen as *events* that cause changes in the objects that maintain the state of the application. The objects that are responsible for displaying a view of the current state are *notified* whenever the state changes.

Distributed event-based systems extend the local event model by allowing multiple objects at different locations to be notified of events taking place at an object. They use the *publish-subscribe* paradigm, in which an object that generates events *publishes* the type of events that it will make available for observation by other objects. Objects that want to receive notifications from an object that has published its events *subscribe* to the types of events that are of interest to them. Different event *types* may, for example, refer to the different methods executed by the object of interest. Objects that represent events are called *notifications*. Notifications may be stored, sent in messages, queried and applied in a variety of orders to different things. When a publisher experiences an event, subscribers that expressed an interest in that type of event will receive notifications. Subscribing to a particular type of event is also called *registering interest* in that type of event.

Events and notifications can be used in a wide variety of different applications, for example to communicate a shape added to a drawing, a modification to a document, the fact that a person has entered or left a room, or that a piece of equipment or an electronically tagged book is at a new location. The latter two examples are made possible with the use of active badges or embedded devices (see Section 16.1).

Distributed event-based systems have two main characteristics:

Heterogeneous: When event notifications are used as a means of communication between distributed objects, components in a distributed system that were not designed to interoperate can be made to work together. All that is required is that event-generating objects publish the types of events they offer, and that other objects subscribe to events and provide an interface for receiving notifications. For example, Bates *et al*. [1996] describe how event-based systems can be used to connect heterogeneous components in the Internet. They describe a system in which applications can be made aware of users' locations and activities, such as using

Figure 5.10   Dealing room system

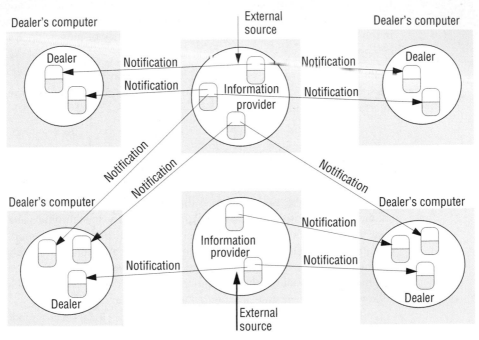

computers, printers or electronically tagged books. They envisage its future use in the context of a home network with commands such as: 'if the children come home, turn on the central heating'.

Asynchronous: Notifications are sent asynchronously by event-generating objects to all the objects that have subscribed to them to prevent publishers needing to synchronize with subscribers – publishers and subscribers need to be decoupled. Mushroom [Kindberg *et al.* 1996] is a distributed event-based system designed to support collaborative work, in which the user interface displays objects representing users and information objects such as documents and notepads within shared workspaces called *network places*. The state of each place is replicated at the computers of users currently in that place. Events are used to describe changes to objects and to a user's focus of interest. For example, an event could specify that a particular user has entered or left a place or has performed a particular action on an object. Each replica of any object to which particular types of events are relevant subscribes to them and receives notifications when they occur. But subscribers are decoupled from objects experiencing events, because different users are active at different times.

A situation in which events can be useful is illustrated in the following dealing room example.

Simple dealing room system ◊ Consider a simple dealing room system whose task is to allow dealers using computers to see the latest information about the market prices of the stocks they deal in. The market price for a single named stock is represented by an object with several instance variables. The information arrives in the dealing room from several different external sources in the form of updates to some or all of the instance variables of the objects representing the stocks and is collected by processes we call information providers. Dealers are typically interested only in their specialist stocks. A dealing room system could be modelled by processes with two different tasks:

- An information provider process continuously receives new trading information from a single external source and applies it to the appropriate stock objects. Each of the updates to a stock object is regarded as an event. The stock object experiencing such events notifies all of the dealers who have subscribed to the corresponding stock. There will be a separate information provider process for each external source.

- A dealer process creates an object to represent each named stock that the user asks to have displayed. This local object subscribes to the object representing that stock at the relevant information provider. It then receives all the information sent to it in notifications and displays it to the user.

The communication of notifications is shown in Figure 5.10.

Event types ◊ An event source can generate events of one or more different *types*. Each event has *attributes* that specify information about that event, such as the name or identifier of the object that generated it, the operation, its parameters and the time (or a sequence number). Types and attributes are used both in subscribing to events and in notifications. When subscribing to an event, the type of event is specified, sometimes modified with a criterion as to the values of the attributes. Whenever an event of that type occurs that matches the attributes, the interested parties will be notified. In the dealing room example, there is one type of event (the arrival of an update to a stock), and the attributes might specify the name of a stock, its current price, and latest rise or fall. Dealers may for example specify that they are interested in all the events relating to a stock with a particular name.

We present an architecture that specifies the roles of the participants in distributed event notification in Section 5.4.1. This architecture addresses the heterogeneous and asynchronous characteristics of event notification. This is followed by a case study of the Jini event service in Section 5.4.2. Section 16.3.1 in the chapter on mobile and ubiquitous computing discusses the use of event services for the communication of data between components in volatile systems. Section 20.3.2 in the CORBA case study presents the CORBA Event Service.

Figure 5.11   Architecture for distributed event notification

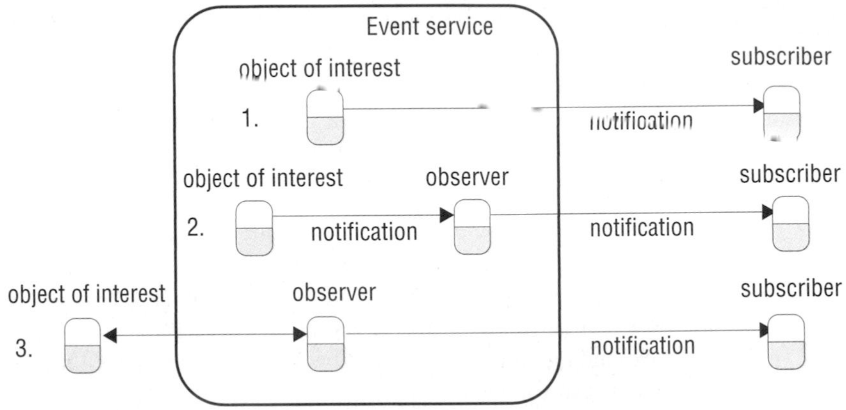

5.4.1   The participants in distributed event notification

Figure 5.11 shows an architecture that specifies the roles played by the objects that participate in distributed event-based systems. Our description is derived from the paper on events and notifications in the Internet by Rosenblum and Wolf [1997]. The architecture is designed to decouple the publishers from the subscribers, allowing publishers to be developed independently of their subscribers, and as far as possible limiting the work imposed on publishers by subscribers. The main component is an event service that maintains a database of published events and of subscribers' interests. Events at an object of interest are published at the event service. Subscribers inform the event service about the types of events they are interested in. When an event occurs at an object of interest a notification is sent to the subscribers to that type of event.

The roles of the participating objects are as follows:

The object of interest: This is an object that experiences changes of state, as a result of its operations being invoked. Its changes of state might be of interest to other objects. This description allows for events such as a person wearing an active badge entering a room, in which case the room is the object of interest and the operation consists of adding information about the new person to its record of who is in the room. The object of interest is considered as part of the event service if it transmits notifications.

Event: An event occurs at an object of interest as the result of the completion of a method execution.

Notification: A notification is an object that contains information about an event. Typically, it contains the type of the event and its attributes, which generally include the identity of the object of interest, the method invoked, and the time of occurrence or a sequence number.

Subscriber: A subscriber is an object that has subscribed to some type of events in another object. It receives notifications about such events.

Observer objects: The main purpose of an observer is to decouple an object of interest from its subscribers. An object of interest can have many different subscribers with different interests. For example, the subscribers may differ as to the type of events they are interested in, or those sharing the same requirements as to type may differ in the attribute values that are of interest. It could over-complicate the object of interest if it had to perform all of the logic for distinguishing between the needs of its subscribers. One or more observers can be interposed between an object of interest and subscribers. The roles for observers are discussed in more detail in a subsequent paragraph.

Publisher: This is an object that declares that it will generate notifications of particular types of event. A publisher may be an object of interest or an observer.

Figure 5.11 shows three cases:

1. An object of interest inside the event service without an observer. It sends notifications directly to the subscribers.

2. An object of interest inside the event service with an observer. The object of interest sends notifications via the observer to the subscribers.

3. An object of interest outside the event service. In this case, an observer queries the object of interest in order to discover when events occur. The observer sends notifications to the subscribers.

Delivery semantics ◊ A variety of different delivery guarantees can be provided for notifications – the one that is chosen should depend on the requirements of applications. For example, if IP multicast is used to send notifications to a group of receivers, the failure model will relate to the one described for IP multicast in Section 4.5.1 and will not guarantee that any particular recipient will receive a particular notification message. This is adequate for some applications, for example, to deliver the latest state of a player in an Internet game, because the next update is likely to get through.

However, other applications have stronger requirements. Consider the dealing room application: to be fair to the dealers interested in a particular stock, we require that all the dealers for the same stock receive the same information. This implies that a reliable multicast protocol should be used.

In the Mushroom system mentioned above, notifications about the change of object state are delivered reliably to a server, whose responsibility it is to maintain up-to-date copies of objects. However, notifications may also be sent to object replicas in users' computers by means of unreliable multicast; in the case that the latter lose notifications, they can retrieve an object state from the server. When the application requires it, notifications may be ordered and sent reliably to object replicas.

Some applications have real-time requirements.These include events in a nuclear power station or a hospital patient monitor. It is possible to design multicast protocols that provide real-time guarantees as well as reliability and ordering in a system that satisfies the properties of a synchronous distributed system.

Roles for observers ◊ Although notifications could be sent directly from the object of interest to the recipient, the task of processing notifications can be divided among observer processes playing a variety of different roles. We describe some examples:

Forwarding: A forwarding observer may carry out all the work of sending notifications to subscribers on behalf of one or more objects of interest. All an object of interest need do is to send a notification to the forwarding observer, leaving it to continue with its normal task. To use a forwarding observer, an object of interest passes on the information about its subscribers' interests to that forwarding observer.

Filtering of notifications: Filters may be applied by an observer so as to reduce the number of notifications received according to some predicate on the contents of each notification. For example, an event might relate to withdrawals from a bank account, but the recipient is interested only in those greater than $100.

Patterns of events: When an object subscribes to events at an object of interest, they can specify patterns of events that they are interested in. A pattern specifies a relationship between several events. For example, a subscriber may be interested when there are three withdrawals from a bank account without an intervening deposit. A similar requirement is to correlate events at a variety of objects of interest; for example, notifying the subscriber only when a certain number of them have generated events.

Notification mailboxes: In some cases, notifications need to be delayed until a potential subscriber is ready to receive them. For example, if the subscriber has faulty connections or when an object has been passivated and is activated again. An observer may take on the role of a notification mailbox, which is to receive notifications on behalf of a subscriber, only passing them on (in a single batch) when the subscriber is ready to receive them. The subscriber should be able to turn delivery on and off as required. The subscriber sets up a notification mailbox when it registers with an object of interest by specifying the notification mailbox as the place to send notifications.

5.4.2   Case study: Jini distributed event specification

The Jini distributed event specification described by Arnold *et al.* [1999] allows a potential subscriber in one Java Virtual Machine (JVM) to subscribe to and receive notifications of events in an object of interest in another JVM, usually on another computer. A chain of observers may be inserted between the object of interest and the subscriber. The main objects involved in the Jini distributed event specification are:

Event generators: An event generator is an object that allows other objects to subscribe to its events and generates notifications.

Remote event listeners: A remote event listener is an object that can receive notifications.

Remote events: A remote event is an object that is passed by value to remote event listeners. A remote event is the equivalent of what we called a notification.

Third-party agents: Third-party agents may be interposed between an object of interest and a subscriber. They are the equivalent of our observers.

An object subscribes to events by informing the event generator about the type of event and specifying a remote event listener as the target for notifications.

Java RMI is used to send notifications from the event generator to the subscriber, possibly via one or more first third-party agents. The designers state that event listeners should reply to notification calls as soon as possible to avoid delaying event generators. They can process a notification after the return. Java RMI is also used to subscribe to events. Jini events are provided by means of the following interfaces and classes:

RemoteEventListener: This interface provides a method called *notify*. Subscribers and third-party agents implement the *RemoteEventListener* interface so that they can receive notifications when the *notify* method is invoked. An instance of the *RemoteEvent* class represents a notification and is passed as argument to the *notify* method.

RemoteEvent: This class has instance variables that hold:

- a reference to the event generator in which the event occurred;

- an event identifier, which specifies the type of event at that event generator;

- a sequence number, which applies to events of that type. The sequence number should increase as events occur over time. It can be used to enable recipients to order events of a particular type from a given source or to avoid applying the same event twice;

- a marshalled object. This is supplied when the recipient subscribes to that type of event and may be used by a recipient for any purpose. It generally holds any information needed by the recipient to identify the event and react to its occurrence. For example, it could include a closure that is to be run when it is notified.

EventGenerator: This interface provides a method called *register*. Event generators implement the *EventGenerator* interface, whose *register* method is used to subscribe to events at the event generator. The arguments of *register* specify:

- an event identifier, which specifies the type of event;

- a marshalled object to be handed back with each notification;

- a remote reference to an event listener object – the place to send notifications;

- a requested leasing period. The lease period specifies the duration of lease required by the subscriber, but the actual lease granted is returned with the results of *register*. Time limits on subscriptions avoid the problem of event generators holding stale event subscriptions. Subscriptions can be renewed whenever the time limit in the lease expires.

The Jini specification says that the *EventGenerator* interface is just an example of the kind of interface that might be used by subscribers to register interest in events at an object of interest. Some applications may require a different interface.

Third-party agents ◊ The third-party agents that are interposed between an event generator and a subscriber may play a variety of useful roles, including all of those described above.

In the simplest case, a subscriber registers interest in a particular type of event at an event generator and specifies itself as the remote event listener. This corresponds to case 1 illustrated in Figure 5.11.

Third-party agents can be set up by an event generator or by a subscriber.

An event generator can interpose one or more third-party agents between itself and a subscriber. For example, the event generators on each computer could make use of a shared third-party agent that is responsible for reliable delivery of notifications.

A subscriber can build a chain of third-party agents in order to produce whatever delivery policy it requires. It then registers interest with an event generator, specifying the first in the chain of third-party agents as the place to send notifications. For example, a subscriber may arrange for its notifications to be stored by a third-party agent until such time as it is ready to receive them. The third-party agent can take responsibility for renewing leases.

5.5 Case study: Java RMI

Java RMI extends the Java object model to provide support for distributed objects in the Java language. In particular, it allows objects to invoke methods on remote objects using the same syntax as for local invocations. In addition, type checking applies equally to remote invocations as to local ones. However, an object making a remote invocation is aware that its target is remote because it must handle *RemoteException*s; and the implementor of a remote object is aware that it is remote because it must implement the *Remote* interface. Although the distributed object model is integrated into Java in a natural way, the semantics of parameter passing differ because invoker and target are remote from one another.

The programming of distributed applications in Java RMI should be relatively simple because it is a single-language system – remote interfaces are defined in the Java language. If a multiple-language system such as CORBA is used, the programmer needs to learn an IDL and to understand how it maps onto the implementation language. However, even in a single-language system, the programmer of a remote object must consider its behaviour in a concurrent environment.

In the remainder of this introduction, we give an example of a remote interface, then discuss the parameter-passing semantics with reference to the example. Finally, we discuss the downloading of classes and the binder. The second section of this case study discusses how to build client and server programs for the example interface. The third section is concerned with the design and implementation of Java RMI. For full details of Java RMI, see the tutorial on remote invocation [java.sun.com I].

In this case study and the CORBA case study in Chapter 20 as well as in the discussion of web services in Chapter 19, we use a *shared whiteboard* as an example. This is a distributed program that allows a group of users to share a common view of a drawing surface containing graphical objects, such as rectangles, lines and circles, each of which has been drawn by one of the users. The server maintains the current state of a drawing by providing an operation for clients to inform it about the latest shape their users have drawn and keeping a record of all the shapes it has received. The server also provides operations allowing clients to retrieve the latest shapes drawn by other users by polling the server. The server has a version number (an integer) that it increments each time a new shape arrives and attaches to the new shape. The server provides operations

Figure 5.12   Java Remote interfaces *Shape* and *ShapeList*

```
import java.rmi.*;
import java.util.Vector;
public interface Shape extends Remote {
    int getVersion() throws RemoteException;
    GraphicalObject  getAllState() throws RemoteException;         1
}
public interface ShapeList extends Remote {
    Shape newShape(GraphicalObject g) throws RemoteException;      2
    Vector allShapes() throws RemoteException;
    int getVersion() throws RemoteException;
}
```

allowing clients to enquire about its version number and the version number of each shape, so that they may avoid fetching shapes that they already have.

Remote interfaces in Java RMI ◊ Remote interfaces are defined by extending an interface called *Remote* provided in the *java.rmi* package. The methods must throw *RemoteException*, but application-specific exceptions may also be thrown. Figure 5.12 shows an example of two remote interfaces called *Shape* and *ShapeList*. In this example, *GraphicalObject* is a class that holds the state of a graphical object, for example, its type, its position, enclosing rectangle, line colour and fill colour, and provides operations for accessing and updating its state. *GraphicalObject* must implement the *Serializable* interface. Consider the interface *Shape* first: the *getVersion* method returns an integer, whereas the *getAllState* method returns an instance of the class *GraphicalObject*. Now consider the interface *ShapeList*: its *newShape* method passes an instance of *GraphicalObject* as argument but returns an object with a remote interface (that is, a remote object) as its result. An important point to note is that both ordinary objects and remote objects can appear as arguments and results in a remote interface. The latter are always denoted by the name of their remote interface. In the next paragraph, we discuss how ordinary objects and remote objects are passed as arguments and results.

Parameter and result passing ◊ In Java RMI, the parameters of a method are assumed to be *input* parameters and the result of a method is a single *output* parameter. Section 4.3.2 describes Java serialization, which is used for marshalling arguments and results in Java RMI. Any object that is serializable – that is, that implements the *Serializable* interface – can be passed as an argument or result in Java RMI. All primitive types and remote objects are serializable. Classes for arguments and result values are downloaded to the recipient by the RMI system where necessary.

Passing remote objects: When the type of a parameter or result value is defined as a remote interface, the corresponding argument or result is always passed as a remote object reference. For example, in Figure 5.12, line 2, the return value of the method *newShape* is defined as *Shape* – a remote interface. When a remote object reference is received, it can be used to make RMI calls on the remote object to which it refers.

Passing non-remote objects: All serializable non-remote objects are copied and passed by value. For example, in Figure 5.12 (lines 2 and 1) the argument of *newShape* and the return value of *getAllState* are both of type *GraphicalObject*, which is serializable and is passed by value. When an object is passed by value, a new object is created in the receiver's process. The methods of this new object can be invoked locally, possibly causing its state to differ from the state of the original object in the sender's process.

Thus, in our example, the client uses the method *newShape* to pass an instance of *GraphicalObject* to the server; the server makes a remote object of type *Shape* containing the state of the *GraphicalObject* and returns a remote object reference to it. The arguments and return values in a remote invocation are serialized to a stream using the method described in Section 4.3.2, with the following modifications:

1. Whenever an object that implements the *Remote* interface is serialized, it is replaced by its remote object reference, which contains the name of its (the remote object's) class.

2. When any object is serialized, its class information is annotated with the location of the class (as a URL), enabling the class to be downloaded by the receiver.

Downloading of classes ◊ Java is designed to allow classes to be downloaded from one virtual machine to another. This is particularly relevant to distributed objects that communicate by means of remote invocation. We have seen that non-remote objects are passed by value and remote objects are passed by reference as arguments and results of RMIs. If the recipient does not already possess the class of an object passed by value, its code is downloaded automatically. Similarly, if the recipient of a remote object reference does not already possess the class for a proxy, its code is downloaded automatically. This has two advantages:

1. There is no need for every user to keep the same set of classes in their working environment.

2. Both client and server programs can make transparent use of instances of new classes whenever they are added.

As an example, consider the whiteboard program and suppose that its initial implementation of *GraphicalObject* does not allow for text. Then a client with a textual object can implement a subclass of *GraphicalObject* that deals with text and pass an instance to the server as an argument of the *newShape* method. After that, other clients may retrieve the instance using the *getAllState* method. The code of the new class will be downloaded automatically from the first client to the server and then to other clients as needed.

RMIregistry ◊ The RMIregistry is the binder for Java RMI. An instance of RMIregistry must run on every server computer that hosts remote objects. It maintains a table mapping textual, URL-style names to references to remote objects hosted on that computer. It is accessed by methods of the *Naming* class, whose methods take as argument a URL-formatted string of the form:

//computerName:port/objectName

Figure 5.13   The *Naming* class of Java RMIregistry

---

void rebind (String name, Remote obj)
>   This method is used by a server to register the identifier of a remote object by name, as shown in Figure 5.14, line 3.

void bind (String name, Remote obj)
>   This method can alternatively be used by a server to register a remote object by name, but if the name is already bound to a remote object reference an exception is thrown.

void unbind (String name, Remote obj)
>   This method removes a binding.

Remote lookup(String name)
>   This method is used by clients to look up a remote object by name, as shown in Figure 5.16 line 1. A remote object reference is returned.

String [] list()
>   This method returns an array of *Strings* containing the names bound in the registry.

---

where *computerName* and *port* refer to the location of the RMIregistry. If they are omitted, the local computer and default port are assumed. Its interface offers the methods shown in Figure 5.13, in which the exceptions are not listed – all of the methods can throw *RemoteException*. This service is not a system-wide binding service. Clients must direct their *lookup* enquiries to particular hosts.

5.5.1   Building client and server programs

This section outlines the steps necessary to produce client and server programs that use the *Remote* interfaces *Shape* and *ShapeList* shown in Figure 5.12. The server program is a simplified version of a whiteboard server that implements the two interfaces *Shape* and *ShapeList*. We describe a simple polling client program and then introduce the callback technique that can be used to avoid the need to poll the server. Complete versions of the classes illustrated in this section are available at www.cdk4.net/rmi.

Server program ◊   The server is a whiteboard server: it represents each shape as a remote object instantiated by a servant that implements the *Shape* interface and holds the state of a graphical object as well as its version number; it represents its collection of shapes by another servant that implements the *ShapeList* interface and holds a collection of shapes in a *Vector*.

The server consists of a *main* method and a servant class to implement each of its remote interfaces. The *main* method of the server creates an instance of *ShapeListServant* and binds it to a name in the RMIregistry, as shown in Figure 5.14 (lines 1 and 2). Note that the value bound to the name is a remote object reference, and its type is the type of its remote interface – *ShapeList*. The two servant classes are *ShapeListServant*, which implements the *ShapeList* interface, and *ShapeServant*, which implements the *Shape* interface. Figure 5.15 gives an outline of the class *ShapeListServant*. Note that *ShapeListServant* (line 1), like many servant classes,

Figure 5.14   Java class *ShapeListServer* with *main* method

```
import java.rmi.*;
public class ShapeListServer{
    public static void main(String args[]){
        System.setSecurityManager(new RMISecurityManager());
        try{
            ShapeList aShapeList = new ShapeListServant();              1
            Naming.rebind("Shape List", aShapeList );                   2
            System.out.println("ShapeList server ready");
        }catch(Exception e) {
            System.out.println("ShapeList server main " + e.getMessage());}
    }
}
```

Figure 5.15   Java class *ShapeListServant* implements interface *ShapeList*

```
import java.rmi.*;
import java.rmi.server.UnicastRemoteObject;
import java.util.Vector;

public class ShapeListServant extends UnicastRemoteObject implements ShapeList {
    private Vector theList;              // contains the list of Shapes     1
    private int version;
    public ShapeListServant()throws RemoteException{...}

    public Shape newShape(GraphicalObject g) throws RemoteException {      2
        version++;
        Shape s = new ShapeServant( g, version);                          3
        theList.addElement(s);
        return s;
    }
    public  Vector allShapes()throws RemoteException{...}
    public int getVersion() throws RemoteException { ... }
}
```

extends a class named *UnicastRemoteObject*, which provides remote objects that live
only as long as the process in which they are created. (An activatable object would
extend a class named *Activatable*.)

The implementations of the methods of the remote interface in a servant class is
completely straightforward because they can be done without any concern for the details
of communication. Consider the method of *newShape* in Figure 5.15 (line 2), which
could be called a factory method because it allows the client to request the creation of a
servant. It uses the constructor of *ShapeServant*, which creates a new servant containing
the *GraphicalObject* and version number passed as arguments. The type of the return

Figure 5.16   Java client of *ShapeList*

```
import java.rmi.*;
import java.rmi.server.*;
import java.util.Vector;

public class ShapeListClient{
    public static void main(String args[]){
        System.setSecurityManager(new RMISecurityManager());
        ShapeList aShapeList = null;
        try{
            aShapeList  = (ShapeList) Naming.lookup("//bruno.ShapeList");    1
            Vector sList = aShapeList.allShapes();                          2
        } catch(RemoteException e) {System.out.println(e.getMessage());
        }catch(Exception e) {System.out.println("Client: " + e.getMessage());}
    }
}
```

value of *newShape* is *Shape* – the interface implemented by the new servant. Before returning, the method *newShape* adds the new shape to its vector that contains the list of shapes (line 3).

The *main* method of a server needs to create a security manager to enable Java security to apply the protection appropriate for an RMI server. A default security manager called *RMISecurityManager* is provided. It protects the local resources to ensure that the classes that are loaded from remote sites cannot have any effect on resources such as files, but it differs in allowing the program to provide its own class loader and to use reflection. If an RMI server sets no security manager, proxies and classes can only be loaded from the local classpath, in order to protect the program from code that is downloaded as a result of remote method invocations.

Client program ◊ A simplified client for the *ShapeList* server is illustrated in Figure 5.16. Any client program needs to get started by using a binder to look up a remote object reference. Our client sets a security manager and then looks up a remote object reference for the remote object using the *lookup* operation of the RMIregistry (line 1). Having obtained an initial remote object reference, the client continues by sending RMIs to that remote object or to others discovered during its execution according to the needs of its application. In our example, the client invokes the method *allShapes* in the remote object (line 2) and receives a vector of remote object references to all of the shapes currently stored in the server. If the client was implementing a whiteboard display, it would use the server's *getAllState* method in the *Shape* interface to retrieve each of the graphical objects in the vector and display them in a window. Each time the user finishes drawing a graphical object, it will invoke the method *newShape* in the server, passing on the new graphical object as argument. The client will keep a record of the latest version number at the server, and from time to time it will invoke *getVersion* at the server to find out whether any new shapes have been added by other users. If so, it will retrieve and display them.

Callbacks ◊ The general idea behind callbacks is that instead of clients polling the server to find out whether some event has occurred, the server should inform its clients whenever that event does occur. The term *callback* is used to refer to a server's action of notifying clients about an event. Callbacks can be implemented in RMI as follows:

- The client creates a remote object that implements an interface that contains a method for the server to call. We refer to this as a callback object.

- The server provides an operation allowing interested clients to inform it of the remote object references of their callback objects. It records these in a list.

- Whenever an event of interest occurs, the server calls the interested clients. For example, the whiteboard server would call its clients whenever a graphical object is added.

The use of callbacks avoids the need for a client to poll the objects of interest in the server and its attendant disadvantages:

- The performance of the server may be degraded by the constant polling.

- Clients cannot notify users of updates in a timely manner.

However, callbacks have problems of their own: first the server needs to have up-to-date lists of the clients' callback objects. But clients may not always inform the server before they exit, leaving the server with incorrect lists. The *leasing* technique discussed in Section 5.2.6 can be used to overcome this problem. The second problem associated with callbacks is that the server needs to make a series of synchronous RMIs to the callback objects in the list. See Section 5.4.1 and Exercise 5.18 for some ideas about solving the second problem.

We illustrate the use of callbacks in the context of the whiteboard application. The *WhiteboardCallback* interface could be defined as follows:

```
public interface WhiteboardCallback implements Remote {
    void callback(int version) throws RemoteException;
};
```

This interface is implemented as a remote object by the client, enabling the server to send the client a version number whenever a new object is added. But before the server can do this, the client needs to inform the server about its callback object. To make this possible, the *ShapeList* interface requires additional methods such as *register* and *deregister*, defined as follows:

```
int register(WhiteboardCallback callback) throws RemoteException;
void deregister(int callbackId) throws RemoteException;
```

After the client has obtained a reference to the remote object with the *ShapeList* interface (for example, in Figure 5.16, line 1) and created an instance of its callback object, it uses the *register* method of *ShapeList* to inform the server that it is interested in receiving callbacks. The *register* method returns an integer (the *callbackId*) referring to the registration. When the client is finished it should call *deregister* to inform the server it no longer requires callbacks. The server is responsible for keeping a list of interested clients and notifying all of them each time its version number increases.

Figure 5.17   Classes supporting Java RMI

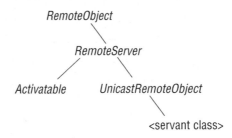

5.5.2   Design and implementation of Java RMI

The original Java RMI system used all of the components shown in Figure 5.7. But in Java 1.2, the reflection facilities were used to make a generic dispatcher and to avoid the need for skeletons. The client proxies are generated by a compiler called *rmic* from the compiled server classes – not from the definitions of the remote interfaces.

Use of reflection ◊ Reflection is used to pass information in request messages about the method to be invoked. This is achieved with the help of the class *Method* in the reflection package. Each instance of *Method* represents the characteristics of a particular method, including its class, the types of its arguments, return value and exceptions. The most interesting feature of this class is that an instance of *Method* can be invoked on an object of a suitable class by means of its *invoke* method. The invoke method requires two arguments: the first specifies the object to receive the invocation and the second is an array of *Object* containing the arguments. The result is returned as type *Object*.

To return to the use of the *Method* class in RMI: the proxy has to marshal information about a method and its arguments into the *request* message. For the method it marshals an object of class *Method*. It puts the arguments into an array of *Object*s and then marshals that array. The dispatcher unmarshals the *Method* object and its arguments in the array of *Object*s from the *request* message. As usual, the remote object reference of the target will have been unmarshalled and the corresponding local object reference obtained from the remote reference module. The dispatcher then calls the *Method* object's *invoke* method, supplying the target and the array of argument values. When the method has been executed, the dispatcher marshals the result or any exceptions into the *reply* message.

Thus the dispatcher is generic – that is, the same dispatcher can be used for all classes of remote object, and no skeletons are required.

Java classes supporting RMI ◊ Figure 5.17 shows the inheritance structure of the classes supporting Java RMI servers. The only class that the programmer need be aware of is *UnicastRemoteObject,* which every simple servant class needs to extend. The class *UnicastRemoteObject* extends an abstract class called *RemoteServer*, which provides abstract versions of the methods required by remote servers. *UnicastRemoteObject* was the first example of *RemoteServer* to be provided. Another called *Activatable* is available for providing activatable objects. Further alternatives might provide for replicated objects. The class *RemoteServer* is a subclass of *RemoteObject* that has an instance variable holding the remote object reference and provides the following methods:

equals this method compares remote object references;

toString this method gives the contents of the remote object reference as a *String*;

readObject, writeObject: these methods deserialize/serialize remote objects.

In addition, the *instanceOf* operator can be used to test remote objects.

5.6 Summary

This chapter has discussed two paradigms for distributed programming – remote method invocation and event-based systems. Both of these paradigms regard distributed objects as independent entities that can communicate with one another. In the first case, a method in the remote interface of a particular object is invoked synchronously – with the invoker waiting for a reply. In the second case, notifications are sent asynchronously to multiple subscribers whenever a published event occurs at an object of interest.

The distributed object model is an extension of the local object model used in object-based programming languages. Encapsulated objects form useful components in a distributed system, since encapsulation makes them entirely responsible for managing their own state, and local invocation of methods can be extended to remote invocation. Each object in a distributed system has a remote object reference (a globally unique identifier) and a remote interface that specifies which of its operations can be invoked remotely.

Local method invocations provide exactly-once semantics, whereas remote method invocations cannot guarantee the same because the two participating objects are in different computers, which can fail independently and are linked by a network, which might also fail. The best that can be managed is at-most-once call semantics. Due to their different failure and performance characteristics and to the possibility of concurrent access to remote objects, it is not necessarily a good idea to make remote invocation appear to be exactly the same as local invocation.

Middleware implementations of RMI provide components (including proxies, skeletons and dispatchers) that hide the details of marshalling, message passing and locating remote objects from client and server programmers. These components can be generated by an interface compiler. Java RMI extends local invocation to remote invocation using the same syntax, but remote interfaces must be specified by extending an interface called *Remote* and making each method throw a *RemoteException*. This ensures that programmers know when they make remote invocations or implement remote objects, enabling them to handle errors or to design objects suitable for concurrent access.

Distributed event-based systems can be used to allow distributed collections of heterogeneous objects to communicate with one another. Unlike RMI, objects do not need to have remote interfaces to receive messages – all they need to do is to implement an interface for receiving notifications and to subscribe to events. Objects that generate events need to send asynchronous notifications. The simplicity of interfaces should make the addition of events to existing objects quite straightforward. The additional work of processing events, for example, filtering and looking for patterns, can be carried out by observers – third-party objects added to the system for that purpose.

EXERCISES

5.1 The *Election* interface provides two remote methods:

vote: with two parameters through which the client supplies the name of a candidate (a string) and the 'voter's number' (an integer used to ensure each user votes once only). The voter's numbers are allocated sparsely from the range of integers to make them hard to guess.

result: with two parameters through which the server supplies the client with the name of a candidate and the number of votes for that candidate.

Which of the parameters of these two procedures are *input* and which are *output* parameters? *page 179*

5.2 Discuss the invocation semantics that can be achieved when the request-reply protocol is implemented over a TCP/IP connection, which guarantees that data is delivered in the order sent, without loss or duplication. Take into account all of the conditions causing a connection to be broken. *Section 4.2.4 and page 187*

5.3 Define the interface to the *Election* service in CORBA IDL and Java RMI. Note that CORBA IDL provides the type *long* for 32 bit integers. Compare the methods in the two languages for specifying *input* and *output* arguments. *Figure 5.2, Figure 5.12*

5.4 The *Election* service must ensure that a vote is recorded whenever any user thinks they have cast a vote.

Discuss the effect of maybe call semantics on the *Election* service.

Would at-least-once call semantics be acceptable for the *Election* service or would you recommend at-most-once call semantics? *page 188*

5.5 A request-reply protocol is implemented over a communication service with omission failures to provide at-least-once RMI invocation semantics. In the first case the implementor assumes an asynchronous distributed system. In the second case the implementor assumes that the maximum time for the communication and the execution of a remote method is *T*. In what way does the latter assumption simplify the implementation? *page 187*

5.6 Outline an implementation for the *Election* service that ensures that its records remain consistent when it is accessed concurrently by multiple clients. *page 189*

5.7 The *Election* service must ensure that all votes are safely stored even when the server process crashes. Explain how this can be achieved with reference to the implementation outline in your answer to Exercise 5.6. *pages 193–194*

5.8 Show how to use Java reflection to construct the client proxy class for the *Election* interface. Give the details of the implementation of one of the methods in this class, which should call the method *doOperation* with the following signature:

byte [] doOperation (RemoteObjectRef o, Method m, byte[] arguments);

Hint: an instance variable of the proxy class should hold a remote object reference (see Exercise 4.12). *Figure 4.15, page 215*

5.9   Show how to generate a client proxy class using a language such as C++ that does not support reflection, for example from the CORBA interface definition given in your answer to Exercise 5.3. Give the details of the implementation of one of the methods in this class, which should call the method *doOperation* defined in Figure 4.15.

page 192

5.10   Explain how to use Java reflection to construct a generic dispatcher. Give Java code for a dispatcher whose signature is:

public void dispatch(Object target, Method aMethod, byte[] args)

The arguments supply the target object, the method to be invoked and the arguments for that method in an array of bytes.   *page 215*

5.11   Exercise 5.8 required the client to convert *Object* arguments into an array of bytes before invoking *doOperation* and Exercise 5.10 required the dispatcher to convert an array of bytes into an array of *Object*s before invoking the method. Discuss the implementation of a new version of *doOperation* with the following signature:

Object [] doOperation (RemoteObjectRef o, Method m, Object[] arguments);

which uses the *ObjectOutputStream* and *ObjectInputStream* classes to stream the request and reply messages between client and server over a TCP connection. How would these changes affect the design of the dispatcher?   *Section 4.3.2 and page 215*

5.12   A client makes remote procedure calls to a server. The client takes 5 milliseconds to compute the arguments for each request, and the server takes 10 milliseconds to process each request. The local operating system processing time for each send or receive operation is 0.5 milliseconds, and the network time to transmit each request or reply message is 3 milliseconds. Marshalling or unmarshalling takes 0.5 milliseconds per message.

Calculate the time taken by the client to generate and return from two requests:

(i)   if it is single-threaded, and

(ii)   if it has two threads that can make requests concurrently on a single processor.

You can ignore context-switching times. Is there a need for asynchronous RPC if client and server processes are threaded?   *page 193*

5.13   Design a remote object table that can support distributed garbage collection as well as translating between local and remote object references. Give an example involving several remote objects and proxies at various sites to illustrate the use of the table. Show the changes in the table when an invocation causes a new proxy to be created. Then show the changes in the table when one of the proxies becomes unreachable.   *page 195*

5.14   A simpler version of the distributed garbage collection algorithm described in Section 5.2.6 just invokes *addRef* at the site where a remote object lives whenever a proxy is created and *removeRef* whenever a proxy is deleted. Outline all the possible effects of communication and process failures on the algorithm. Suggest how to overcome each of these effects, but without using leases.   *page 195*

5.15 Discuss how to use events and notifications as described in the Jini distributed event specification in the context of the shared whiteboard application. The *RemoteEvent* class is defined as follows in Arnold *et al.* [1999].

```
public class RemoteEvent extends java.util.EventObject {
    public RemoteEvent(Object source, long eventID,
        long seqNum, MarshalledObject handback)
    public Object getSource () {...}
    public long getID() {...}
    public long getSequenceNumber() {...}
    public MarshalledObject getRegistrationObject() {...}
}
```

The first argument of the constructor is a remote object. Notifications inform listeners that an event has occurred but the listeners are responsible for obtaining further details.
page 206, 208

5.16 Suggest a design for a notification mailbox service which is intended to store notifications on behalf of multiple subscribers, allowing subscribers to specify when they require notifications to be delivered. Explain how subscribers that are not always active can make use of the service you describe. How will the service deal with subscribers that crash while they have delivery turned on? *page 206*

5.17 Explain how a forwarding observer may be used to enhance the reliability and performance of objects of interest in an event service. *page 205*

5.18 Suggest ways in which observers can be used to improve the reliability or performance of your solution to Exercise 5.15. *page 205*

6

OPERATING SYSTEM SUPPORT

This chapter describes how middleware is supported by the operating system facilities at the nodes of a distributed system. The operating system facilitates the encapsulation and protection of resources inside servers; and it supports the invocation mechanisms required to access these resources, including communication and scheduling.

An important theme of the chapter is the role of the system kernel. The chapter aims to give the reader an understanding of the advantages and disadvantages of splitting functionality between protection domains – in particular, of splitting functionality between kernel and user-level code. The trade-offs between kernel-level facilities and user-level facilities are discussed, including the tension between efficiency and robustness.

The chapter examines the design and implementation of multi-threaded processing and communication facilities. It goes on to explore the main kernel architectures that have been devised.

6.1   Introduction

Chapter 2 introduced the chief software layers in a distributed system. We have learned that an important aspect of distributed systems is resource sharing. Client applications invoke operations on resources that are often on another node or at least in another process. Applications (in the form of clients) and services (in the form of resource managers) use the middleware layer for their interactions. Middleware provides remote invocations between objects or processes at the nodes of a distributed system. Chapter 5 has explained the main types of remote invocation found in middleware, such as Java RMI and CORBA. In this chapter we shall continue to focus on remote invocations, without real-time guarantees. (Chapter 17 examines support for multimedia communication, which is real-time and stream-oriented.)

Below the middleware layer is the operating system (OS) layer, which is the subject of this chapter. We shall be examining the relationship between the two, and in particular how well the requirements of middleware can be met by the operating system. Those requirements include efficient and robust access to physical resources, and the flexibility to implement a variety of resource-management policies.

The task of any operating system is to provide problem-oriented abstractions of the underlying physical resources – the processors, memory, communications, and storage media. An operating system such as UNIX (and its variants such as Linux) or Windows (and its variants such as XP) provides the programmer with, for example, files rather than disk blocks, and with sockets rather than raw network access. It takes over the physical resources on a single node and manages them to present these resource abstractions through the system-call interface.

Before we begin our detailed coverage of the operating system's middleware support role, it is useful to gain some historical perspective by examining two operating system concepts that have come about during the development of distributed systems: network operating systems and distributed operating systems. Definitions vary, but the concepts behind them are something like the following.

Both UNIX and Windows are examples of *network operating systems*. They have a networking capability built into them and so can be used to access remote resources. Access is network-transparent for some – not all – types of resource. For example, through a distributed file system such as NFS, users have network-transparent access to files. That is, many of the files that users access are stored remotely, on a server, and this is largely transparent to their applications.

But the defining characteristic is that the nodes running a network operating system retain autonomy in managing their own processing resources. In other words, there are multiple system images, one per node. With a network operating system, a user can remotely log in to another computer, using *rlogin* or *telnet*, and run processes there. However, unlike the operating system's control of the processes running at its own node, it does not schedule processes across the nodes.

By contrast, one could envisage an operating system in which users are never concerned with where their programs run, or the location of any resources. There is a *single system image*. The operating system has control over all the nodes in the system, and it transparently locates new processes at whatever node suits its scheduling policies.

For example, it could create a new process at the least loaded node in the system, to prevent individual nodes becoming unfairly overloaded.

An operating system that produces a single system image like this for all the resources in a distributed system is called a *distributed operating system* [Tanenbaum and van Renesse 1985].

Middleware and network operating systems ◊ In fact, there are no distributed operating systems in general use, only network operating systems such as UNIX, Mac OS and Windows. This is likely to remain the case, for two main reasons. The first is that users have much invested in their application software, which often meets their current problem-solving needs; they will not adopt a new operating system that will not run their applications, whatever efficiency advantages it offers. Attempts have been made to emulate UNIX and other operating system kernels on top of new kernels, but the emulations' performance has not been satisfactory. Anyway, keeping emulations of all the major operating systems up to date as they evolve would be a huge undertaking.

The second reason against the adoption of distributed operating systems is that users tend to prefer to have a degree of autonomy for their machines, even in a closely knit organization. This is particularly so because of performance [Douglis and Ousterhout 1991]. For example, Jones needs good interactive responsiveness while she writes her documents and would resent it if Smith's programs were slowing her down.

The combination of middleware and network operating systems provides an acceptable balance between the requirement for autonomy, on the one hand, and network-transparent resource access on the other. The network operating system enables users to run their favourite word processor and other standalone applications. Middleware enables them to take advantage of services that become available in their distributed system.

The next section explains the function of the operating system layer. Section 6.3 examines low-level mechanisms for resource protection, which we need to understand in order to appreciate the relationship between processes and threads, and the role of the kernel itself. Section 6.4 goes on to examine the process, address space and thread abstractions. Here the main topics are concurrency, local resource management and protection, and scheduling. Section 6.5 then covers communication as part of invocation mechanisms. Section 6.6 discusses the different types of operating system architecture, including the so-called monolithic and microkernel designs. The reader can find case studies of the Mach kernel and the Amoeba, Chorus and Clouds operating systems at www.cdk4.net/oss.

6.2   The operating system layer

Users will only be satisfied if their middleware–OS combination has good performance. Middleware runs on a variety of OS–hardware combinations (platforms) at the nodes of a distributed system. The OS running at a node – a kernel and associated user-level services, e.g. libraries – provides its own flavour of abstractions of local hardware resources for processing, storage and communication. Middleware utilizes a combination of these local resources to implement its mechanisms for remote invocations between objects or processes at the nodes.

Figure 6.1   System layers

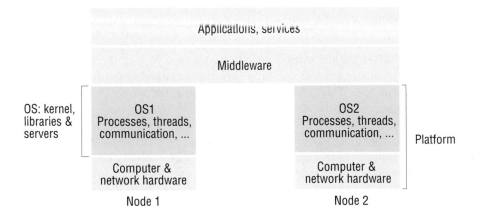

Figure 6.1 shows how the operating system layer at each of two nodes supports a common middleware layer in providing a distributed infrastructure for applications and services.

Our goal in this chapter is to examine the impact of particular OS mechanisms on middleware's ability to deliver distributed resource sharing to users. Kernels and the client and server processes that execute upon them are the chief architectural components that concern us. Kernels and server processes are the components that manage resources and present clients with an interface to the resources. As such, we require at least the following of them:

Encapsulation: They should provide a useful service interface to their resources – that is, a set of operations that meet their clients' needs. Details such as management of memory and devices used to implement resources should be hidden from clients.

Protection: Resources require protection from illegitimate accesses – for example, files are protected from being read by users without read permissions, and device registers are protected from application processes.

Concurrent processing: Clients may share resources and access them concurrently. Resource managers are responsible for achieving concurrency transparency.

Clients access resources by making, for example, remote method invocations to a server object, or system calls to a kernel. We call a means of accessing an encapsulated resource an *invocation mechanism*, however it is implemented. A combination of libraries, kernels and servers may be called upon to perform the following invocation-related tasks:

Communication: Operation parameters and results have to be passed to and from resource managers, over a network or within a computer.

Scheduling: When an operation is invoked, its processing must be scheduled within the kernel or server.

Figure 6.2   Core OS functionality

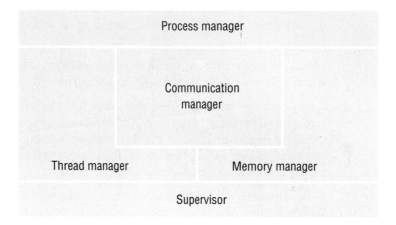

Figure 6.2 shows the core OS functionality that we shall be concerned with: process and thread management, memory management, and communication between processes on the same computer (horizontal divisions in the figure denote dependencies). The kernel supplies much of this functionality – all of it in the case of some operating systems.

OS software is designed to be portable between computer architectures where possible. This means that the majority of it is coded in a high-level language such as C, C++ or Modula-3, and that its facilities are layered so that machine-dependent components are reduced to a minimal bottom layer. Some kernels can execute on shared-memory multiprocessors, which are described in the box below.

Shared-memory multiprocessors ◊ Shared-memory multiprocessor computers are equipped with several processors that share one or more modules of memory (RAM). The processors may also have their own private memory. Multiprocessor computers can be constructed in a variety of forms [Stone 1993]. The simplest and least expensive multiprocessors are constructed by incorporating a circuit board holding a few (2–8) processors in a personal computer.

In the common *symmetric processing architecture*, each processor executes the same kernel and the kernels play largely equivalent roles in managing the hardware resources. The kernels share key data structures such as the queue of runnable threads, but some of their working data is private. Each processor can execute a thread simultaneously, accessing data in the shared memory, which may be private (hardware-protected) or shared with other threads.

Multiprocessors can be used for many high-performance computing tasks. In distributed systems, they are particularly useful for the implementation of high-performance servers because the server can run a single program with several threads that handle several requests from clients simultaneously – for example, providing access to a shared database (see Section 6.4)

The core OS components are the following:

Process manager: Handles the creation of and operations upon processes. A process is a unit of resource management, including an address space and one or more threads.

Thread manager: Thread creation, synchronization and scheduling. Threads are schedulable activities attached to processes and are fully described in Section 6.4.

Communication manager: Communication between threads attached to different processes on the same computer. Some kernels also support communication between threads in remote processes. Other kernels have no notion of other computers built into them, and an additional service is required for external communication. Section 6.5 discusses the communication design.

Memory manager: Management of physical and virtual memory. Section 6.4 and Section 6.5 describe the utilization of memory management techniques for efficient data copying and sharing.

Supervisor: Dispatching of interrupts, system call traps and other exceptions; control of memory management unit and hardware caches; processor and floating point unit register manipulations. This is known as the Hardware Abstraction Layer in Windows. The reader is referred to Bacon [2002] and Tanenbaum [2001] for a fuller description of the computer-dependent aspects of the kernel.

6.3   Protection

We said above that resources require protection from illegitimate accesses. Note that the threat to a system's integrity does not come only from maliciously contrived code. Benign code that contains a bug or which has unanticipated behaviour may cause part of the rest of the system to behave incorrectly.

To understand what we mean by an 'illegitimate access' to a resource, consider a file. Let us suppose, for the sake of explanation, that open files have only two operations, *read* and *write*. Protecting the file consists of two sub-problems. The first is to ensure that each of the file's two operations can be performed only by clients with the right to perform it. For example, Smith, who owns the file, has *read* and *write* rights to it. Jones may only perform the *read* operation. An illegitimate access here would be if Jones somehow managed to perform a *write* operation on the file. A complete solution to this resource-protection sub-problem in a distributed system requires cryptographic techniques, and we defer it to Chapter 7.

The other type of illegitimate access, which we shall address here, is where a misbehaving client sidesteps the operations that a resource exports. In our example, this would be if Smith or Jones somehow managed to execute an operation that was neither *read* nor *write*. Suppose, for example, that Smith managed to access the file pointer variable directly. She could then construct a *setFilePointerRandomly* operation, which sets the file pointer to a random number. Of course, this is a meaningless operation that would upset normal use of the file and that files would never be designed to export.

We can protect resources from illegitimate invocations such as *setFilePointerRandomly*. One way is to use a type-safe programming language, such as Java or Modula-3. A type-safe language is such that no module may access a target module unless it has a reference to it – it cannot make up a pointer to it, as would be possible in C or C++. And it may only use its reference to the target module to perform the invocations (method calls or procedure calls) that the programmer of the target made available to it. It may not, in other words, arbitrarily change the target's variables. By contrast, in C++ the programmer may cast a pointer however she likes, and thus perform non-type-safe invocations.

We can also employ hardware support to protect modules from one another at the level of individual invocations, regardless of the language in which they are written. To operate this scheme on a general-purpose computer, we require a kernel.

Kernels and protection ◊ The kernel is a program that is distinguished by the facts that it it always runs and its code is executed with complete access privileges for the physical resources on its host computer. In particular, it can control the memory management unit and set the processor registers so that no other code may access the machine's physical resources except in acceptable ways.

Most processors have a hardware mode register whose setting determines whether privileged instructions can be executed, such as those used to determine which protection tables are currently employed by the memory management unit. A kernel process executes with the processor in *supervisor* (privileged) mode; the kernel arranges that other processes execute in *user* (unprivileged) mode.

The kernel also sets up *address spaces* to protect itself and other processes from the accesses of an aberrant process, and to provide processes with their required virtual memory layout. An address space is a collection of ranges of virtual memory locations, in each of which a specified combination of memory access rights applies, such as read-only or read-write. A process cannot access memory outside its address space. The terms *user process* or *user-level process* are normally used to describe one that executes in user mode and has a user-level address space (that is, one with restricted memory access rights compared with the kernel's address space).

When a process executes application code it executes in a distinct user-level address space for that application; when the same process executes kernel code it executes in the kernel's address space. The process can safely transfer from a user-level address space to the kernel's address space via an exception such as an interrupt or a *system call trap* – the invocation mechanism for resources managed by the kernel. A system call trap is implemented by a machine-level *TRAP* instruction, which puts the processor into supervisor mode and switches to the kernel address space. When the *TRAP* instruction is executed, as with any type of exception, the hardware forces the processor to execute a kernel-supplied handler function, in order that no process may gain illicit control of the hardware.

Programs pay a price for protection. Switching between address spaces may take many processor cycles, and a system call trap is a more expensive operation than a simple procedure or method call. We shall now see how these penalties factor into invocation costs.

6.4   Processes and threads

The traditional operating system notion of a process that executes a single activity was found in the 1980s to be unequal to the requirements of distributed systems – and also to those of more sophisticated single-computer applications that require internal concurrency. The problem, as we shall show, is that the traditional process makes sharing between related activities awkward and expensive.

The solution reached was to enhance the notion of process so that it could be associated with multiple activities. Nowadays, a process consists of an execution environment together with one or more threads. A *thread* is the operating system abstraction of an activity (the term derives from the phrase 'thread of execution'). An *execution environment* is the unit of resource management: a collection of local kernel-managed resources to which its threads have access. An execution environment primarily consists of:

- an address space;

- thread synchronization and communication resources such as semaphores and communication interfaces (for example sockets);

- higher-level resources such as open files and windows.

Execution environments are normally expensive to create and manage, but several threads can share them – that is, they can share all resources accessible within them. In other words, an execution environment represents the protection domain in which its threads execute.

Threads can be created and destroyed dynamically as needed. The central aim of having multiple threads of execution is to maximize the degree of concurrent execution between operations, thus enabling the overlap of computation with input and output, and enabling concurrent processing on multiprocessors. This can be particularly helpful within servers, where concurrent processing of clients' requests can reduce the tendency for servers to become bottlenecks. For example, one thread can process a client's request while a second thread servicing another request waits for a disk access to complete.

An execution environment provides protection from threads outside it, so that the data and other resources contained in it are by default inaccessible to threads residing in other execution environments. But certain kernels allow the controlled sharing of resources such as physical memory between execution environments residing at the same computer.

As many older operating systems allow only one thread per process, we shall sometimes use the term *multi-threaded process* for emphasis. Confusingly, in some programming models and operating system designs the term 'process' means what we have called a thread. The reader may encounter in the literature the terms *heavyweight process*, where an execution environment is taken to be included, and *lightweight process*, where it is not. See the box opposite for an analogy describing threads and execution environments.

Figure 6.3   Address space

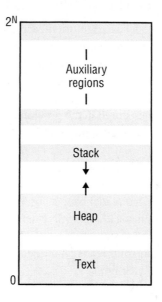

6.4.1 Address spaces

An address space, introduced in the previous section, is a unit of management of a process's virtual memory. It is large (typically up to 2^{32} bytes, and sometimes up to 2^{64} bytes) and consists of one or more *regions*, separated by inaccessible areas of virtual memory. A region (Figure 6.3) is an area of contiguous virtual memory that is accessible by the threads of the owning process. Regions do not overlap. Note that we distinguish between the regions and their contents. Each region is specified by the following properties:

- its extent (lowest virtual address and size);

An analogy for threads and processes ◊ The following memorable, if slightly unsavoury, way to think of the concepts of threads and execution environments was seen on the *comp.os.mach* USENET group and is due to Chris Lloyd. An execution environment consists of a stoppered jar and the air and food within it. Initially, there is one fly – a thread – in the jar. This fly can produce other flies and kill them, as can its progeny. Any fly can consume any resource (air or food) in the jar. Flies can be programmed to queue up in an orderly manner to consume resources. If they lack this discipline, they might bump into one another within the jar – that is, collide and produce unpredictable results when attempting to consume the same resources in an unconstrained manner. Flies can communicate with (send messages to) flies in other jars, but none may escape from the jar, and no fly from outside may enter it. In this view, a standard UNIX process is a single jar with a single sterile fly within it.

- read/write/execute permissions for the process's threads;

- whether it can be grown upwards or downwards.

Note that this model is page-oriented rather than segment-oriented. Regions, unlike segments, would eventually overlap if they were extended in size. Gaps are left between regions to allow for growth. This representation of an address space as a sparse set of disjoint regions is a generalization of the UNIX address space, which has three regions: a fixed, unmodifiable text region containing program code; a heap, part of which is initialized by values stored in the program's binary file, and which is extensible towards higher virtual addresses; and a stack, which is extensible towards lower virtual addresses.

The provision of an indefinite number of regions is motivated by several factors. One of these is the need to support a separate stack for each thread. Allocating a separate stack region to each thread makes it possible to detect attempts to exceed the stack limits and to control each stack's growth. Unallocated virtual memory lies beyond each stack region, and attempts to access this will cause an exception (a page fault). The alternative is to allocate stacks for threads on the heap, but then it is difficult to detect when a thread has exceeded its stack limit.

Another motivation is to enable files in general – and not just the text and data sections of binary files – to be mapped into the address space. A *mapped file* is one that is accessed as an array of bytes in memory. The virtual memory system ensures that accesses made in memory are reflected in the underlying file storage. Section CDK3-18.6 (in www.cdk4.net/oss/mach) describes how the Mach kernel extends the abstraction of virtual memory so that regions can correspond to arbitrary 'memory objects' – not just to files.

The need to share memory between processes, or between processes and the kernel, is another factor leading to extra regions in the address space. A *shared memory region* (or *shared region* for short) is one that is backed by the same physical memory as one or more regions belonging to other address spaces. Processes therefore access identical memory contents in the regions that are shared, while their non-shared regions remain protected. The uses of shared regions include the following:

Libraries: Library code can be very large and would waste considerable memory if it was loaded separately into every process that used it. Instead, a single copy of the library code can be shared by being mapped as a region in the address spaces of processes that require it.

Kernel: Often the kernel code and data are mapped into every address space at the same location. When a process makes a system call or an exception occurs, there is no need to switch to a new set of address mappings.

Data sharing and communication: Two processes, or a process and the kernel, might need to share data in order to cooperate on some task. It can be considerably more efficient for the data to be shared by being mapped as regions in both address spaces than by being passed in messages between them. The use of region sharing for communication is described in Section 6.5.

6.4.2 Creation of a new process

The creation of a new process has traditionally been an indivisible operation provided by the operating system. For example, the UNIX *fork* system call creates a process with an execution environment copied from the caller (except for the return value from *fork*). The UNIX *exec* system call transforms the calling process into one executing the code of a named program.

For a distributed system, the design of the process creation mechanism has to take account of the utilization of multiple computers; consequently, the process support infrastructure is divided into separate system services.

The creation of a new process can be separated into two independent aspects:

- The choice of a target host. For example, the host may be chosen from among the nodes in a cluster of computers acting as a compute server (see box below).

- The creation of an execution environment (and an initial thread within it).

Choice of process host ◊ The choice of node at which the new process will reside – the process allocation decision – is a matter of policy. In general, process allocation policies range from always running new processes at their originator's workstation to sharing the processing load between a set of computers. Eager *et al.* [1986] distinguish the following policy categories for load sharing.

The *transfer policy* determines whether to situate a new process locally or remotely. This may depend, for example, on whether the local node is lightly or heavily loaded.

The *location policy* determines which node should host a new process selected for transfer. This decision may depend on the relative loads of nodes, on their machine architectures and on any specialized resources they may possess. The V system [Cheriton 1984] and Sprite [Douglis and Ousterhout 1991] both provide commands for users to execute a program at a currently idle workstation (there are often many of these at any given time) chosen by the operating system. In the Amoeba system [Tanenbaum *et al.* 1990], the *run server* chooses a host for each process from a shared pool of processors. In all cases, the choice of target host is transparent to the programmer and the user. Those programming for explicit parallelism or fault tolerance, however, may require a means of specifying process location.

Process location policies may be *static* or *adaptive*. The former operate without regard to the current state of the system, although they are designed according to the system's expected long-term characteristics. They are based on a mathematical analysis

Clusters ◊ A cluster is a set of off-the-shelf computers (sometimes thousands of them) interconnected by a high-speed communication network such as a switched gigabit/second Ethernet. The individual computers may be standard PCs or workstations, or rack-mounted PC processor boards; they may be uniprocessors or multiprocessors. One application of clusters is the provision of highly available and scalable services – such as search engines provided for users throughout the Internet – by the replication or partitioning of processing and server state across the cluster's processors [Fox *et al.* 1997]. Clusters are also used to run parallel programs [Anderson *et al.* 1995, now.cs.berkeley.edu, TFCC].

aimed at optimizing a parameter such as the overall process throughput. They may be deterministic ('node A should always transfer processes to node B') or probabilistic ('node A should transfer processes to any of nodes B–E at random'). Adaptive policies, on the other hand, apply heuristics to make their allocation decisions, based on unpredictable runtime factors such as a measure of the load on each node.

Load-sharing systems may be centralized, hierarchical or decentralized. In the first case there is one *load manager* component, and in the second there are several, organized in a tree structure. Load managers collect information about the nodes and use it to allocate new processes to nodes. In hierarchical systems, managers make process allocation decisions as far down the tree as possible, but managers may transfer processes to one another, via a common ancestor, under certain load conditions. In a decentralized load-sharing system, nodes exchange information with one another directly to make allocation decisions. The Spawn system [Waldspurger *et al.* 1992], for example, considers nodes to be 'buyers' and 'sellers' of computational resources and arranges them in a (decentralized) 'market economy'.

In *sender-initiated* load-sharing algorithms, the node that requires a new process to be created is responsible for initiating the transfer decision. It typically initiates a transfer when its own load crosses a threshold. By contrast, in *receiver-initiated* algorithms, a node whose load is below a given threshold advertises its existence to other nodes so that relatively loaded nodes will transfer work to it.

Migratory load-sharing systems can shift load at any time, not just when a new process is created. They use a mechanism called *process migration*: the transfer of an executing process from one node to another. Milojicic *et al.* [1999] provide a collection of papers on process migration and other types of mobility. While several process migration mechanisms have been constructed, they have not been widely deployed. This is largely because of their expense, and the tremendous difficulty of extracting the state of a process that lies within the kernel, in order to move it to another node.

Eager *et al.* [1986] studied three approaches to load sharing and concluded that simplicity is an important property of any load-sharing scheme. This is because relatively high overheads – for example, state-collection overheads – can outweigh the advantages of more complex schemes.

Creation of a new execution environment ◊ Once the host computer has been selected, a new process requires an execution environment consisting of an address space with initialized contents (and perhaps other resources such as default open files).

There are two approaches to defining and initializing the address space of a newly created process. The first approach is used where the address space is of statically defined format. For example, it could contain just a program text region, heap region and stack region. In this case, the address space regions are created from a list specifying their extent. Address space regions are initialized from an executable file or filled with zeroes as appropriate.

Alternatively, the address space can be defined with respect to an existing execution environment. In the case of UNIX *fork* semantics, for example, the newly created child process physically shares the parent's text region, and has heap and stack regions that are copies of the parent's in extent (as well as in initial contents). This scheme has been generalized so that each region of the parent process may be inherited by (or omitted from) the child process. An inherited region may either be shared with or

Figure 6.4 Copy-on-write

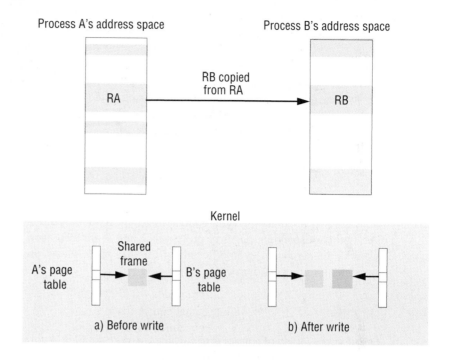

logically copied from the parent's region. When parent and child share a region, the page frames (units of physical memory corresponding to virtual memory pages) belonging to the parent's region are mapped simultaneously into the corresponding child region.

Mach [Accetta *et al.* 1986] and Chorus [Rozier *et al.* 1988, 1990], for example, apply an optimization called *copy-on-write* when an inherited region is copied from the parent. The region is copied, but no physical copying takes place by default. The page frames that make up the inherited region are shared between the two address spaces. A page in the region is only physically copied when one or other process attempts to modify it.

Copy-on-write is a general technique – for example, it is also used in copying large messages, so we take some time to explain its operation here. Let us follow through an example of regions *RA* and *RB*, whose memory is shared copy-on-write between two processes, *A* and *B* (Figure 6.4). For the sake of definiteness, let us assume that process *A* set region *RA* to be copy-inherited by its child, process *B*, and that the region *RB* was thus created in process *B*.

We assume, for the sake of simplicity, that the pages belonging to region A are resident in memory. Initially, all page frames associated with the regions are shared between the two processes' page tables. The pages are initially write-protected at the hardware level, even though they may belong to regions that are logically writable. If a thread in either process attempts to modify the data, a hardware exception called a *page fault* is taken. Let us say that process *B* attempted the write. The page fault handler allocates a new frame for process *B* and copies the original frame's data into it byte for byte. The old frame number is replaced by the new frame number in one process's page

Figure 6.5   Client and server with threads

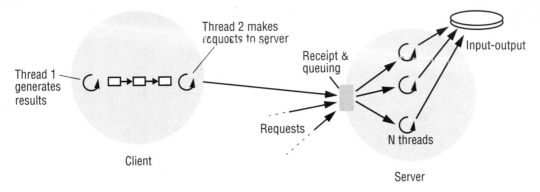

table – it does not matter which – and the old frame number is left in the other page table. The two corresponding pages in processes *A* and *B* are then each made writable once more at the hardware level. After all of this has taken place, process *B*'s modifying instruction is allowed to proceed.

6.4.3   Threads

The next key aspect of a process to consider in more detail is its threads. This subsection examines the advantages of enabling client and server processes to possess more than one thread. It then discusses programming with threads, using Java threads as a case study, and ends with alternative designs for implementing threads.

Consider the server shown in Figure 6.5 (we shall turn to the client shortly). The server has a pool of one or more threads, each of which repeatedly removes a request from a queue of received requests and processes it. We shall not concern ourselves for the moment with how the requests are received and queued up for the threads. Also, for the sake of simplicity, we assume that each thread applies the same procedure to process the requests. Let us assume that each request takes, on average, 2 milliseconds of processing and 8 milliseconds of I/O (input/output) delay when the server reads from a disk (there is no caching). Let us further assume for the moment that the server executes at a single-processor computer.

Consider the *maximum* server throughput, measured in client requests handled per second, for different numbers of threads. If a single thread has to perform all processing, then the turnaround time for handling any request is on average 2 + 8 = 10 milliseconds, so this server can handle 100 client requests per second. Any new request messages that arrive while the server is handling a request are queued at the server port.

Now consider what happens if the server pool contains two threads. We assume that threads are independently schedulable – that is, one thread can be scheduled when another becomes blocked for I/O. Then thread number two can process a second request, while thread number one is blocked, and *vice versa*. This increases the server throughput. Unfortunately, in our example, the threads may become blocked behind the single disk drive. If all disk requests are serialized and take 8 milliseconds each, then the maximum throughput is 1000/8 = 125 requests per second.

Suppose, now, that disk block caching is introduced. The server keeps the data that it reads in buffers in its address space; a server thread that is asked to retrieve data first examines the shared cache and avoids accessing the disk if it finds it there. If a 75% hit rate is achieved, the mean I/O time per request reduces to $(0.75 \times 0 + 0.25 \times 8) = 2$ milliseconds, and the maximum theoretical throughput increases to 500 requests per second. But if the average *processor* time for a request has been increased to 2.5 milliseconds per request as a result of caching (it takes time to search for cached data on every operation) then this figure cannot be reached. The server, limited by the processor, can now handle at most $1000/2.5 = 400$ requests per second.

The throughput can be increased by using a shared memory multiprocessor to ease the processor bottleneck. A multi-threaded process maps naturally onto a shared memory multiprocessor. The shared execution environment can be implemented in shared memory, and the multiple threads can be scheduled to run on the multiple processors. Consider now the case in which our example server executes at a multiprocessor with two processors. Given that threads can be independently scheduled to the different processors, then up to two threads can process requests in parallel. The reader should check that two threads can process 444 requests per second and three or more threads, bounded by the I/O time, can process 500 requests per second.

Architectures for multi-threaded servers ◊ We have described how multi-threading enables servers to maximize their throughput, measured as the number of requests processed per second. To describe the various ways of mapping requests to threads within a server we summarize the account by Schmidt [1998], who describes the threading architectures of various implementations of the CORBA Object Request Broker (ORB). ORBs process requests that arrive over a set of connected sockets. Their threading architectures are relevant to many types of server, regardless of whether CORBA is used.

Figure 6.5 shows one of the possible threading architectures, the *worker pool architecture*. In its simplest form, the server creates a fixed pool of 'worker' threads to process the requests when it starts up. The module marked 'receipt and queuing' in Figure 6.5 is typically implemented by an 'I/O' thread, which receives requests from a collection of sockets or ports and places them on a shared request queue for retrieval by the workers.

There is sometimes a requirement to treat the requests with varying priorities. For example, a corporate web server could prioritize request processing according to the class of customer from which the request derives [Bhatti and Friedrich 1999]. We may handle varying request priorities by introducing multiple queues into the worker pool architecture, so that the worker threads scan the queues in the order of decreasing priority. A disadvantage of this architecture is its inflexibility: as we saw with our worked-out example, the number of worker threads in the pool may be too few to deal adequately with the current rate of request arrival. Another disadvantage is the high level of switching between the I/O and worker threads as they manipulate the shared queue.

In the *thread-per-request architecture* (Figure 6.6a) the I/O thread spawns a new worker thread for each request, and that worker destroys itself when it has processed the request against its designated remote object. This architecture has the advantage that the threads do not contend for a shared queue, and throughput is potentially maximized

Figure 6.6   Alternative server threading architectures (see also Figure 6.5)

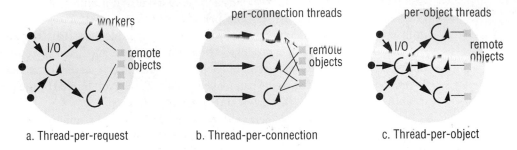

a. Thread-per-request   b. Thread-per-connection   c. Thread-per-object

because the I/O thread can create as many workers as there are outstanding requests. Its disadvantage is the overhead of the thread creation and destruction operations.

The *thread-per-connection architecture* (Figure 6.6b) associates a thread with each connection. The server creates a new worker thread when a client makes a connection and destroys the thread when the client closes the connection. In between, the client may make many requests over the connection, targeted at one or more remote objects. The *thread-per-object architecture* (Figure 6.6c) associates a thread with each remote object. An I/O thread receives requests and queues them for the workers, but this time there is a per-object queue.

In each of these last two architectures the server benefits from lowered thread-management overheads compared with the thread-per-request architecture. Their disadvantage is that clients may be delayed while a worker thread has several outstanding requests but another thread has no work to perform.

Schmidt [1998] describes variations on these architectures as well as hybrids of them, and discusses their advantages and disadvantages in more detail. Section 6.5 describes a different threading model in the context of invocations within a single machine, in which client threads enter the server's address space.

Threads within clients ◊ Threads can be useful for clients as well as servers. Figure 6.5 also shows a client process with two threads. The first thread generates results to be passed to a server by remote method invocation, but does not require a reply. Remote method invocations typically block the caller, even when there is strictly no need to wait. This client process can incorporate a second thread, which performs the remote method invocations and blocks while the first thread is able to continue computing further results. The first thread places its results in buffers, which are emptied by the second thread. It is only blocked when all the buffers are full.

The case for multi-threaded clients is also evident in the example of web browsers. Users experience substantial delays while pages are fetched; it is essential, therefore, for browsers to handle multiple concurrent requests for web pages.

Threads versus multiple processes ◊ We can see from the above examples the utility of threads, which allow computation to be overlapped with I/O and, in the case of a multiprocessor, with other computation. The reader may have noted, however, that the same overlap could be achieved through the use of multiple single-threaded processes. Why, then, should the multi-threaded process model be preferred? The answer is twofold: threads are cheaper to create and manage than processes, and, resource sharing

Figure 6.7   State associated with execution environments and threads

Execution environment	Thread
Address space tables	Saved processor registers
Communication interfaces, open files	Priority and execution state (such as *BLOCKED*)
Semaphores, other synchronization objects	Software interrupt handling information
List of thread identifiers	Execution environment identifier
Pages of address space resident in memory; hardware cache entries	

can be achieved more efficiently between threads than between processes because threads share an execution environment.

Figure 6.7 shows some of the main state components that must be maintained for execution environments and threads, respectively. An execution environment has an address space, communication interfaces such as sockets, higher-level resources such as open files, and thread synchronization objects such as semaphores; it also lists the threads associated with it. A thread has a scheduling priority, an execution state (such as *BLOCKED* or *RUNNABLE*), saved processor register values when the thread is *BLOCKED*, and state concerning the thread's *software interrupt* handling. A *software interrupt* is an event that causes a thread to be interrupted (similar to the case of a hardware interrupt). If the thread has assigned a handler procedure, control is transferred to it. UNIX signals are examples of software interrupts.

The figure shows that an execution environment and the threads belonging to it are both associated with pages belonging to the address space held in main memory, and data and instructions held in hardware caches.

We can summarize a comparison of processes and threads as follows:

- Creating a new thread within an existing process is cheaper than creating a process.

- More importantly, switching to a different thread within the same process is cheaper than switching between threads belonging to different processes.

- Threads within a process may share data and other resources conveniently and efficiently compared with separate processes.

- But, by the same token, threads within a process are not protected from one another.

Consider the cost of creating a new thread in an existing execution environment. The main tasks are to allocate a region for its stack and to provide initial values of the processor registers and the thread's execution state (it may initially be *SUSPENDED* or *RUNNABLE*) and priority. Since the execution environment exists, only an identifier for this has to be placed in the thread's descriptor record (which contains data necessary to manage the thread's execution).

The overheads associated with creating a process are in general considerably greater than those of creating a new thread. A new execution environment must first be created, including address space tables. Anderson *et al.* [1991] quote a figure of about 11 milliseconds to create a new UNIX process, and about 1 millisecond to create a thread on the same CVAX processor architecture running the Topaz kernel; in each case the time measured includes the new entity simply calling a null procedure and then exiting. These figures are given as a rough guide only.

When the new entity performs some useful work rather than calling a null procedure, there are also long-term costs, which are liable to be greater for a new process than for a new thread within an existing process. In a kernel supporting virtual memory, the new process will incur page faults as data and instructions are referenced for the first time; hardware caches will initially contain no data values for the new process, and it must acquire cache entries as it executes. In the case of thread creation, on the other hand, these long-term overheads may also occur, but they are liable to be less. When the thread accesses code and data that have recently been accessed by other threads within the process, it automatically takes advantage of any hardware or main memory caching that has taken place.

The second performance advantage of threads concerns *switching* between threads – that is, running one thread instead of another at a given processor. This cost is the most important, because it may be incurred many times in the lifetime of a thread. Switching between threads sharing the same execution environment is considerably cheaper than switching between threads belonging to different processes. The overheads associated with thread switching are scheduling (choosing the next thread to run) and context switching.

A processor context comprises the values of the processor registers such as the program counter, and the current hardware protection domain: the address space and the processor protection mode (supervisor or user). A *context switch* is the transition between contexts that takes place when switching between threads, or when a single thread makes a system call or takes another type of exception. It involves the following:

- The saving of the processor's original register state, and the loading of the new state.

- In some cases, a transfer to a new protection domain – this is known as a *domain transition*.

Switching between threads sharing the same execution environment entirely at user-level involves no domain transition and is relatively cheap. Switching to the kernel, or to another thread belonging to the same execution environment via the kernel, involves a domain transition. The cost is therefore greater but, if the kernel is mapped into the process's address space, it is still relatively low. When switching between threads belonging to different execution environments, however, there are greater overheads. The box opposite explains the expensive implications of hardware caching for these domain transitions. Longer-term costs of having to acquire hardware cache entries and main memory pages are more liable to apply when such a domain transition occurs. Figures quoted by Anderson *et al.* [1991] are 1.8 milliseconds to switch between UNIX processes and 0.4 milliseconds for the Topaz kernel to switch between threads belonging to the same execution environment. Even lower costs (0.04 milliseconds) are achieved if threads are switched at user level. These figures are given as a rough guide only; they do not measure the longer-term caching costs.

In the example above of the client process with two threads, the first thread generates data and passes it to the second thread, which makes a remote method invocation or remote procedure call. Since the threads share an address space, there is no need to use message passing to pass the data. Both threads may access the data via a common variable. Herein lies both the advantage and the danger of using multi-threaded processes. The convenience and efficiency of access to shared data is an advantage. This is particularly so for servers, as the example of caching file data given above showed. However, threads that share an address space and that are not written in a type-safe language are not protected from one another. An errant thread can arbitrarily alter data used by another thread, causing a fault. If protection is required, then either a type-safe language should be used or it may be preferable to use multiple processes instead of multiple threads.

Threads programming ◊ Threads programming is concurrent programming, as traditionally studied in, for example, the field of operating systems. This section refers to the following concurrent programming concepts, which are explained fully by Bacon [2002]: *race condition*, *critical section* (Bacon calls this a *critical region*), *monitor*, *condition variable*, *semaphore*.

Much threads programming is done in a conventional language such as C, which has been augmented with a threads library. The C Threads package developed for the Mach operating system is an example of this. More recently, the POSIX Threads standard IEEE 1003.1c-1995, known as *pthreads*, has been widely adopted. Boykin *et al.* [1993] describe both C Threads and pthreads in the context of Mach.

Some languages provide direct support for threads, including Ada95 [Burns and Wellings 1998], Modula-3 [Harbison 1992] and, more recently, Java [Oaks and Wong 1999]. We shall give an overview of Java threads here.

As in any threads implementation, Java provides methods for creating threads, destroying them and synchronizing them. The Java *Thread* class includes the constructor and management methods listed in Figure 6.8. The *Thread* and *Object* synchronization methods are in Figure 6.9.

The aliasing problem ◊ Memory management units usually include a hardware cache to speed up the translation between virtual and physical addresses, called a *translation lookaside buffer* (TLB). TLBs, and also virtually addressed data and instruction caches, suffer in general from the so-called *aliasing problem*. The same virtual address can be valid in two different address spaces, but in general it is supposed to refer to different physical data in the two spaces. Unless their entries are tagged with a context identifier, TLBs and virtually addressed caches are unaware of this and so might contain incorrect data. Therefore the TLB and cache contents have to be flushed on a switch to a different address space. Physically addressed caches do not suffer from the aliasing problem; but using virtual addresses for cache lookups is a common practice, largely because it allows the lookups to be overlapped with address translation.

Figure 6.8   Java thread constructor and management methods

Thread(ThreadGroup group, Runnable target, String name)
  Creates a new thread in the *SUSPENDED* state, which will belong to *group* and be
  identified as *name*; the thread will execute the *run()* method of *target*.

setPriority(int newPriority), getPriority()
  Set and return the thread's priority.

run()
  A thread executes the *run()* method of its target object, if it has one, and otherwise its
  own *run()* method (*Thread* implements *Runnable*).

start()
  Change the state of the thread from *SUSPENDED* to *RUNNABLE*.

sleep(int millisecs)
  Cause the thread to enter the *SUSPENDED* state for the specified time.

yield()
  Enter the *READY* state and invoke the scheduler.

destroy()
  Destroy the thread.

Thread lifetimes ◊   A new thread is created on the same Java virtual machine (JVM) as
its creator, in the *SUSPENDED* state. After it is made *RUNNABLE* with the *start*()
method, it executes the *run*() method of an object designated in its constructor. The JVM
and the threads on top of it all execute in a process on top of the underlying operating
system. Threads can be assigned a priority, so that a Java implementations that supports
priorities will run a particular thread in preference to any thread with lower priority. A
thread ends its life when it returns from the *run*() method, or when its *destroy*() method
is called.

Programs can manage threads in groups. Every thread belongs to one group,
which it is assigned at the time of its creation. Thread groups are useful when several
applications coexist on the same JVM. One example of their use is security: by default,
a thread in one group cannot perform management operations on a thread in another
group. So, for example, an application thread cannot mischievously interrupt a system
windowing (AWT) thread.

Thread groups also facilitate control of the relative priorities of threads (on Java
implementations that support priorities). This is useful for browsers running applets, and
for web servers running programs called *servlets* [Hunter and Crawford 1998], which
create dynamic web pages. An unprivileged thread within an applet or servlet can only
create a new thread that belongs to its own group, or to a descendant group created
within it (the exact restrictions depend upon the SecurityManager in place). Browsers
and servers can assign threads belonging to different applets or servlets to different
groups and set the maximum priority of each group as a whole (including descendant

Figure 6.9   Java thread synchronization calls

---

thread.join(int millisecs)
   Blocks the calling thread for up to the specified time until *thread* has terminated.

thread.interrupt()
   Interrupts *thread*: causes it to return from a blocking method call such as *sleep()*.

object.wait(long millisecs, int nanosecs)
   Blocks the calling thread until a call made to *notify()* or *notifyAll()* on *object* wakes the thread, or the thread is interrupted, or the specified time has elapsed.

object.notify(), object.notifyAll()
   Wakes, respectively, one or all of any threads that have called *wait()* on *object*.

---

groups). There is no way for an applet or servlet thread to override the group priorities set by the manager threads, since they cannot be overridden by calls to *setPriority()*.

Thread synchronization ◊ Programming a multi-threaded process requires great care. The main difficult issues are the sharing of objects and the techniques used for thread coordination and cooperation. Each thread's local variables in methods are private to it – threads have private stacks. However, threads are not given private copies of static (class) variables or object instance variables.

Consider, for example, the shared queues that we described above in this section, which I/O threads and worker threads use to transfer requests in some server threading architectures. Race conditions can in principle arise when threads manipulate data structures such as queues concurrently. The queued requests can be lost or duplicated unless the threads' pointer manipulations are carefully coordinated.

Java provides the *synchronized* keyword for programmers to designate the well-known monitor construct for thread coordination. Programmers designate either entire methods or arbitrary blocks of code as belonging to a monitor associated with an individual object. The monitor's guarantee is that at most one thread can execute within it at any time. We could serialize the actions of the I/O and worker threads in our example by designating *addTo()* and *removeFrom()* methods in the *Queue* class as *synchronized* methods. All accesses to variables within those methods are thus carried out in mutual exclusion with respect to invocations of these methods.

Java allows threads to be blocked and woken up via arbitrary objects that act as condition variables. A thread that needs to block awaiting a certain condition calls an object's *wait()* method. All objects implement this method, since it belongs to Java's root *Object* class. Another thread calls *notify()* to unblock at most one thread or *notifyAll()* to unblock all threads waiting on that object. Both notification methods also belong to the *Object* class.

As an example, when a worker thread discovers that there are no requests to process, it calls *wait()* on the instance of *Queue*. When the I/O thread subsequently adds a request to the queue, it calls the queue's *notify()* method to wake up the worker.

The Java synchronization methods are given in Figure 6.9. In addition to the synchronization primitives that we have mentioned, the *join()* method blocks the caller until the target thread's termination. The *interrupt*() method is useful for prematurely waking a waiting thread. All the standard synchronization primitives, such as semaphores, can be implemented in Java. But care is required, since Java's monitor guarantees apply only to an object's *synchronized* code; a class may have a mixture of *synchronized* and non-*synchronized* methods. Note also that the monitor implemented by a Java object has only one implicit condition variable, whereas in general a monitor may have several condition variables.

Thread scheduling ◊ An important distinction is between preemptive and non-preemptive scheduling of threads. In *preemptive scheduling*, a thread may be suspended at any point to make way for another thread, even when the preempted thread would otherwise continue running. In *non-preemptive scheduling* (sometimes called *coroutine scheduling*), a thread runs until it makes a call to the threading system (for example, a system call), when the system may de-schedule it and schedule another thread to run.

The advantage of non-preemptive scheduling is that any section of code that does not contain a call to the threading system is automatically a critical section. Race conditions are thus conveniently avoided. On the other hand, non-preemptively scheduled threads cannot take advantage of a multiprocessor, since they run exclusively. Care must be taken over long-running sections of code that do not contain calls to the threading system. The programmer may need to insert special *yield*() calls, whose sole function is to enable other threads to be scheduled and make progress. Non-preemptively scheduled threads are also unsuited to real-time applications, in which events are associated with absolute times by which they must be processed.

Java does not, by default, support real-time processing, although real-time implementations exist [www.rtj.org]. For example, multimedia applications that process data such as voice and video have real-time requirements for both communication and processing (for example, filtering and compression) [Govindan and Anderson 1991]. Chapter 17 will examine real-time thread-scheduling requirements. Process control is another example of a real-time domain. In general, each real-time domain has its own thread scheduling requirements. It is therefore sometimes desirable for applications to implement their own scheduling policies. To consider this, we turn now to the implementation of threads.

Threads implementation ◊ Many kernels provide native support for multi-threaded processes, including Windows, Linux, Solaris, Mach and Chorus. These kernels provide thread creation and management system calls, and they schedule individual threads. Some other kernels have only a single-threaded process abstraction. Multi-threaded processes must then be implemented in a library of procedures linked to application programs. In such cases, the kernel has no knowledge of these user-level threads and therefore cannot schedule them independently. A threads runtime library organizes the scheduling of threads. A thread would block the process, and therefore all threads within it if it made a blocking system call, so the asynchronous (non-blocking) I/O facilities of the underlying kernel are exploited. Similarly, the implementation can utilize the kernel-provided timers and software interrupt facilities to timeslice between threads.

When no kernel support for multi-threaded processes is provided, a user-level threads implementation suffers from the following problems:

• The threads within a process cannot take advantage of a multiprocessor.

- A thread that takes a page fault blocks the entire process and all threads within it.

- Threads within different processes cannot be scheduled according to a single scheme of relative prioritization.

User-level threads implementations, on the other hand, have significant advantages over kernel-level implementations:

- Certain thread operations are significantly less costly. For example, switching between threads belonging to the same process does not necessarily involve a system call – that is, a relatively expensive trap to the kernel.

- Given that the thread-scheduling module is implemented outside the kernel, it can be customized or changed to suit particular application requirements. Variations in scheduling requirements occur largely because of application-specific considerations such as the real-time nature of multimedia processing.

- Many more user-level threads can be supported than could reasonably be provided by default by a kernel.

It is possible to combine the advantages of user-level and kernel-level threads implementations. One approach, applied, for example, to the Mach kernel [Black 1990], is to enable user-level code to provide scheduling hints to the kernel's thread scheduler. Another, adopted in the Solaris 2 operating system, is a form of hierarchical scheduling. Each process creates one or more kernel-level threads, known in Solaris as 'lightweight processes'. User-level threads are also supported. A user-level scheduler assigns each user-level thread to a kernel-level thread. This scheme can take advantage of multiprocessors, and also benefit because some thread-creation and thread-switching operations take place at user level. The scheme's disadvantage is that it still lacks flexibility: if a thread blocks in the kernel, then all user-level threads assigned to it are also prevented from running, regardless of whether they are eligible to run.

Several research projects have developed hierarchical scheduling further in order to provide greater efficiency and flexibility. These include work on so-called scheduler activations [Anderson *et al.* 1991], in the multimedia work of Govindan and Anderson [1991], the Psyche multiprocessor operating system [Marsh *et al.* 1991], the Nemesis kernel [Leslie *et al.* 1996] and in the SPIN kernel [Bershad *et al.* 1995]. The insight driving these designs is that what a user-level scheduler requires from the kernel is not just a set of kernel-supported threads onto which it can map user-level threads. The user-level scheduler also requires the kernel to notify it of the *events* that are relevant to its scheduling decisions. We describe the scheduler activations design in order to make this clear.

The FastThreads package of Anderson *et al.* [1991] is an implementation of a hierarchic, event-based scheduling system. They consider the main system components to be a kernel running on a computer with one or more processors, and a set of application programs running on it. Each application process contains a user-level scheduler, which manages the threads inside the process. The kernel is responsible for allocating *virtual processors* to processes. The number of virtual processors assigned to a process depends on such factors as the applications' requirements, their relative priorities and the total demand on the processors. Figure 6.10a shows an example of a three-processor machine, on which the kernel allocates one virtual processor to process

Figure 6.10   Scheduler activations

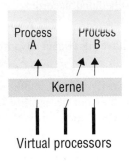

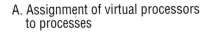

A. Assignment of virtual processors
   to processes

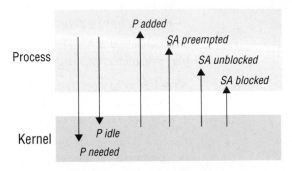

B. Events between user-level scheduler & kernel
   Key: P = processor; SA = scheduler activation

A, running a relatively low-priority job, and two virtual processors to process *B*. They are *virtual* processors because the kernel can allocate different physical processors to each process as time goes by, while keeping its guarantee of how many processors it has allocated.

The number of virtual processors assigned to a process can also vary. Processes can give back a virtual processor that they no longer need; they can also request extra virtual processors. For example, if process *A* has requested an extra virtual processor and *B* terminates, then the kernel can assign one to *A*.

Figure 6.10b shows that a process notifies the kernel when either of two types of event occurs: when a virtual processor is 'idle' and no longer needed, or when an extra virtual processor is required.

Figure 6.10b also shows that the kernel notifies the process when any of four types of event occurs. A *scheduler activation* (SA) is a call from the kernel to a process, which notifies the process's scheduler of an event. Entering a body of code from a lower layer (the kernel) in this way is sometimes called an *upcall*. The kernel creates an SA by loading a physical processor's registers with a context that causes it to commence execution of code in the process, at a procedure address designated by the user-level scheduler. An SA is thus also a unit of allocation of a timeslice on a virtual processor. The user-level scheduler has the task of assigning its *READY* threads to the set of SAs currently executing within it. The number of those SAs is at most the number of virtual processors that the kernel has assigned to the process.

The four types of event that the kernel notifies to the user-level scheduler (which we shall refer to simply as 'the scheduler') are as follows:

Virtual processor allocated: the kernel has assigned a new virtual processor to the process, and this is the first timeslice upon it; the scheduler can load the SA with the context of a *READY* thread, which can thus recommence execution.

SA blocked: an SA has blocked in the kernel, and the kernel is using a fresh SA to notify the scheduler; the scheduler sets the state of the corresponding thread to *BLOCKED* and can allocate a *READY* thread to the notifying SA.

SA unblocked: an SA that was blocked in the kernel has become unblocked and is ready to execute at user level again; the scheduler can now return the corresponding thread to the *READY* list. In order to create the notifying SA, the kernel either allocates a new virtual processor to the process or it has to preempt another SA in the same process. In the latter case, it also communicates the preemption event to the scheduler, which can re-evaluate its allocation of threads to SAs.

SA preempted: the kernel has taken away the specified SA from the process (although it may do this to allocate a processor to a fresh SA in the same process); the scheduler places the preempted thread in the *READY* list and re-evaluates the thread allocation.

This hierarchical scheduling scheme is flexible because the process's user-level scheduler can allocate threads to SAs in accordance with whatever policies can be built on top of the low-level events. The kernel always behaves the same way. It has no influence on the user-level scheduler's behaviour, but it assists the scheduler through its event notifications and by providing the register state of blocked and preempted threads. The scheme is potentially efficient because no user-level thread need stay in the *READY* state if there is a virtual processor on which to run it.

6.5   Communication and invocation

Here we concentrate on communication as part of the implementation of what we have called an invocation – a construct, such as a remote method invocation, remote procedure call or event notification, whose purpose is to bring about an operation on a resource in a different address space.

We shall cover operating system design issues and concepts by asking the following questions about the OS:

- What communication primitives does it supply?

- Which protocols does it support and how open is the communication implementation?

- What steps are taken to make communication as efficient as possible?

- What support is provided for high-latency and disconnected operation?

Communication primitives ◊ Some kernels designed for distributed systems have provided communication primitives tailored to the types of invocation that Chapter 5 described. Amoeba [Tanenbaum *et al.* 1990], for example, provides *doOperation*, *getRequest* and *sendReply* as primitives. Amoeba, the V system and Chorus provide group communication primitives. Placing relatively high-level communication functionality in the kernel has the advantage of efficiency. If, for example, middleware provides RMI over UNIX's connected (TCP) sockets, then a client must make two communication system calls (socket *write* and *read*) for each remote invocation. Over Amoeba, it would require only a single call to *doOperation*. The savings in system call overhead are liable to be even greater with group communication.

In practice, middleware, and not the kernel, provides most high-level communication facilities found in systems today, including RPC/RMI, event notification and group communication. Developing such complex software as user-level code is much simpler than developing it for the kernel. Developers typically implement middleware over sockets giving access to Internet standard protocols – often connected sockets using TCP but sometimes unconnected UDP sockets. The principal reasons for using sockets are portability and interoperability: middleware is required to operate over as many widely used operating systems as possible, and all common operating systems such as UNIX and the Windows family provide similar socket APIs giving access to TCP and UDP protocols.

Despite the widespread use of TCP and UDP sockets provided by common kernels, research continues to be carried out into lower-cost communication primitives in experimental kernels. We examine performance issues further in Section 6.5.1.

Protocols and openness ◊ One of the main requirements of the operating system is to provide standard protocols that enable interworking between middleware implementations on different platforms. Several research kernels in the 1980s incorporated their own network protocols tuned to RPC interactions – notably Amoeba RPC [van Renesse et al. 1989], VMTP [Cheriton 1986] and Sprite RPC [Ousterhout et al. 1988]. However, these protocols were not widely used beyond their native research environments. By contrast, the designers of the Mach 3.0 and Chorus kernels (as well as L4 [Härtig et al. 1997]) decided to leave the choice of networking protocols entirely open. These kernels provide message passing between local processes only, and leave network protocol processing to a server that runs on top of the kernel.

Given the everyday requirement for access to the Internet, compatibility at the level of TCP and UDP is required of operating systems for all but the smallest of networked devices. And the operating system is still required to enable middleware to take advantage of novel low-level protocols. For example, users want to benefit from wireless technologies such as infrared and radio frequency (RF) transmission, preferably without having to upgrade their applications. This requires that corresponding protocols, such as IrDA for infrared networking and BlueTooth or HomeRF for RF networking can be integrated.

Protocols are normally arranged in a *stack* of layers (see Chapter 3). Many operating systems allow new layers to be integrated statically, by including a layer such as IrDA as a permanently installed protocol 'driver'. By contrast, *dynamic protocol composition* is a technique whereby a protocol stack can be composed on the fly to meet the requirements of a particular application, and to utilize whichever physical layers are available given the platform's current connectivity. For example, a web browser running on a notebook computer should be able to take advantage of a wide-area wireless link while the user is on the road, and then a faster Ethernet connection when the user is back in the office.

Another example of dynamic protocol composition is use of a customized request-reply protocol over a wireless networking layer, to reduce round-trip latencies. Standard TCP implementations have been found to work poorly over wireless networking media [Balakrishnan et al. 1996], which tend to exhibit higher rates of packet loss than wired media. In principle, a request-response protocol such as HTTP could be engineered to work more efficiently between wirelessly connected nodes by using the wireless transport layer directly, rather than using an intermediate TCP layer.

Support for protocol composition appeared in the design of the UNIX Streams facility [Ritchie 1984]. More recently, Horus [van Renesse *et al.* 1995] and the x-kernel [Hutchinson and Peterson 1991] both have provision for dynamic protocol composition.

6.5.1   Invocation performance

Invocation performance is a critical factor in distributed system design. The more designers separate functionality between address spaces, the more remote invocations are required. Clients and servers may make many millions of invocation-related operations in their lifetimes, so that small fractions of milliseconds count in invocation costs. Network technologies continue to improve, but invocation times have not decreased in proportion with increases in network bandwidth. This section will explain how software overheads often predominate over network overheads in invocation times – at least, for the case of a LAN or intranet. This is in contrast to a remote invocation over the Internet – for example, fetching a web resource. On the Internet, network latencies are highly variable but high on average, bandwidth is often low, and server load often predominates over per-request processing costs.

RPC and RMI implementations have been the subject of study because of the widespread acceptance of these mechanisms for general-purpose client-server processing. Much of the research has been carried out into invocations over the network, and particularly into how invocation mechanisms can take advantage of high-performance networks [Hutchinson *et al.* 1989, van Renesse *et al.* 1989, Schroeder and Burrows 1990, Johnson and Zwaenepoel 1993, von Eicken *et al.* 1995, Gokhale and Schmidt 1996]. There is also, as we shall show, an important special case of RPCs between processes hosted by the same computer [Bershad *et al.* 1990, Bershad *et al.* 1991].

Invocation costs ◊ Calling a conventional procedure or invoking a conventional method, making a system call, sending a message, remote procedure calling and remote method invocation are all examples of invocation mechanisms. Each mechanism causes code to be executed out of scope of the calling procedure or object. Each involves, in general, the communication of arguments to this code and the return of data values to the caller. Invocation mechanisms can be either synchronous, as for example in the case of conventional and remote procedure calls, or they can be asynchronous.

The important performance-related distinctions between invocation mechanisms, apart from whether or not they are synchronous, are whether they involve a domain transition (that is, whether they cross an address space), whether they involve communication across a network, and whether they involve thread scheduling and switching. Figure 6.11 shows the particular cases of a system call, a remote invocation between processes hosted by the same computer, and a remote invocation between processes at different nodes in the distributed system.

Invocation over the network ◊ A *null RPC* (similarly, a *null RMI*) is defined as an RPC without parameters that executes a null procedure, and returns no values. Its execution involves an exchange of messages carrying some system data but no user data. The time for a null RPC between user processes on two 500MHz PCs across a 100

Figure 6.11   Invocations between address spaces

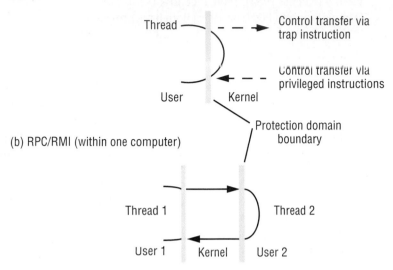

(a) System call

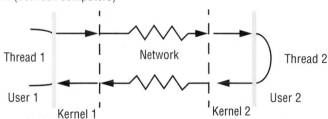

(b) RPC/RMI (within one computer)

(c) RPC/RMI (between computers)

megabits/second LAN is in the order of tenths of a millisecond. By comparison, a null conventional procedure call takes a small fraction of a microsecond. In the order of 100 bytes in total are passed across the network for a null RPC. With a raw bandwidth of 100 megabits/second, the total network transfer time for this amount of data is about 0.01 milliseconds. Clearly, much of the observed *delay* – the total RPC call time experienced by a client – has to be accounted for by the actions of the operating system kernel and user-level RPC runtime code.

Null invocation (RPC, RMI) costs are important because they measure a fixed overhead, the *latency*. Invocation costs increase with the sizes of arguments and results, but in many cases the latency is significant compared with the remainder of the delay.

Consider an RPC that fetches a specified amount of data from a server. It has one integer request argument, specifying the size of data required. It has two reply arguments, an integer specifying success or failure (the client might have given an invalid size), and, when the call is successful, an array of bytes from the server.

Figure 6.12   RPC delay against parameter size

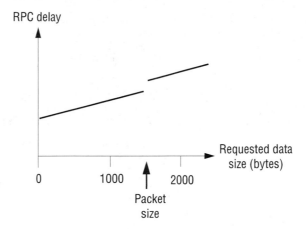

Figure 6.12 shows, schematically, client delay against requested data size. The delay is roughly proportional to the size until the size reaches a threshold at about network packet size. Beyond that threshold, at least one extra packet has to be sent, to carry the extra data. Depending on the protocol, a further packet might be used to acknowledge this extra packet. Jumps in the graph occur each time the number of packets increases.

Delay is not the only figure of interest for an RPC implementation: RPC bandwidth (or *throughput*) is also of concern when data has to be transferred in bulk. This is the rate of data transfer between computers in a single RPC. If we examine Figure 6.12, we can see that the bandwidth is relatively low for small amounts of data, when the fixed processing overheads predominate. As the amount of data is increased, the bandwidth rises as those overheads become less significant. Gokhale and Schmidt [1996] quote a throughput of about 80 megabits/second when transferring 64 kilobytes in an RPC between workstations over an ATM network with a nominal bandwidth of 155 megabits/second. At about 0.8 milliseconds to transfer 64 kilobytes, this is in the same order of magnitude as the time quoted above for a null RPC over a 100 megabits/second Ethernet.

Recall that the steps in an RPC are as follows (RMI involves similar steps):

- a client stub marshals the call arguments into a message, sends the request message and receives and unmarshals the reply;

- at the server, a worker thread receives the incoming request, or an I/O thread receives the request and passes it to a worker thread; in either case, the worker calls the appropriate server stub;

- the server stub unmarshals the request message, calls the designated procedure, and marshals and sends the reply.

The following are the main components accounting for remote invocation delay, besides network transmission times:

Marshalling: Marshalling and unmarshalling, which involve copying and converting data, become a significant overhead as the amount of data grows.

Data copying: Potentially, even after marshalling, message data is copied several times in the course of an RPC:

1. across the user–kernel boundary, between the client or server address space and kernel buffers;

2. across each protocol layer (for example, RPC/UDP/IP/Ethernet);

3. between the network interface and kernel buffers.

Transfers between the network interface and main memory are usually handled by direct memory access (DMA). The processor handles the other copies.

Packet initialization: This involves initializing protocol headers and trailers, including checksums. The cost is therefore proportional, in part, to the amount of data sent.

Thread scheduling and context switching: These may occur as follows:

1. several system calls (that is, context switches) are made during an RPC, as stubs invoke the kernel's communication operations;

2. one or more server threads is scheduled;

3. if the operating system employs a separate network manager process, then each *Send* involves a context switch to one of its threads.

Waiting for acknowledgements: The choice of RPC protocol may influence delay, particularly when large amounts of data are sent.

Careful design of the operating system can help reduce some of these costs. The case study of the Firefly RPC design available at www.cdk3.net/oss shows some of these in detail, as well as techniques that are applicable within the middleware implementation. We have already shown how appropriate operating system support for threads can help reduce multi-threading overheads. The operating system can also have an impact in reducing memory-copying overheads through memory-sharing facilities.

Memory sharing ◊ Shared regions (introduced in Section 6.4) may be used for rapid communication between a user process and the kernel, or between user processes. Data is communicated by writing to and reading from the shared region. Data is thus passed efficiently, without copying them to and from the kernel's address space. But system calls and software interrupts may be required for synchronization – such as when the user process has written data that should be transmitted, or when the kernel has written data for the user process to consume. Of course, a shared region is only justified if it is used sufficiently to offset the initial cost of setting it up.

Even with shared regions, the kernel still has to copy data from the buffers to the network interface. The U-Net architecture [von Eicken *et al.* 1995] even allows user-level code to have direct access to the network interface itself, so that user-level code can transfer the data to the network without any copying.

Choice of protocol ◊ The delay that a client experiences during request-reply interactions over TCP is not necessarily worse than for UDP and it is sometimes better, particularly for large messages. However, care is required when implementing request-reply interactions on top of a protocol such as TCP, which was not specifically designed for this purpose. In particular, TCP's buffering behaviour can hinder good performance, and its connection overheads put it at a disadvantage compared with UDP, unless enough messages are made over a single connection to render the overhead per request negligible.

The connection overheads of TCP are particularly evident in web invocations, since HTTP 1.0 makes a separate TCP connection for every invocation. Client browsers are delayed while the connection is made. Furthermore, TCP's slow-start algorithm has the effect of delaying the transfer of HTTP data unnecessarily in many cases. The slow-start algorithm operates pessimistically in the face of possible network congestion by allowing only a small window of data to be sent at first, before an acknowledgement is received. Nielson *et al.* [1997] discuss how HTTP 1.1 makes use of so-called *persistent connections*, which last over the course of several invocations. The initial connection costs are thus amortized, as long as several invocations are made to the same web server. This is likely, as users often fetch several pages from the same site, each containing several images.

Nielson *et al.* also found that overriding the operating system's default buffering behaviour could have a significant impact on the invocation delay. It is often beneficial to collect several small messages and then send them together, rather than sending them in separate packets, because of the per-packet latency that we described above. For this reason, the OS does not necessarily dispatch data over the network immediately after the corresponding socket *write*() call. The default OS behaviour is to wait until its buffer is full or to use a timeout as the criterion for dispatching the data over the network, in the hope that more data will arrive.

Nielson *et al.* found that in the case of HTTP 1.1 the default operating system buffering behaviour could cause significant unnecessary delays because of the timeouts. To remove these delays they altered the kernel's TCP settings, and they forced network dispatch on HTTP request boundaries. This is a good example of how an operating system can help or hinder middleware because of the policies it implements.

Invocation within a computer ◊ Bershad *et al.* [1990] report a study which showed that, in the installation examined, most cross-address-space invocation took place within a computer and not, as might be expected in a client-server installation, between computers. The trend towards placing service functionality inside user-level servers means that more and more invocations will be to a local process. This is especially so as caching is pursued aggressively, when the data needed by a client is liable to be held in a local server. The cost of an RPC within a computer is growing in importance as a system performance parameter. These considerations suggest that this local case should be optimized.

Figure 6.11 suggests that a cross-address-space invocation is implemented within a computer exactly as it is between computers, except that the underlying message passing happens to be local. Indeed, this has often been the model implemented. Bershad *et al.* [1990] developed a more efficient invocation mechanism for the case of two processes on the same machine called *lightweight RPC* (*LRPC*). The LRPC design is based on optimizations concerning data copying and thread scheduling.

Figure 6.13   A lightweight remote procedure call

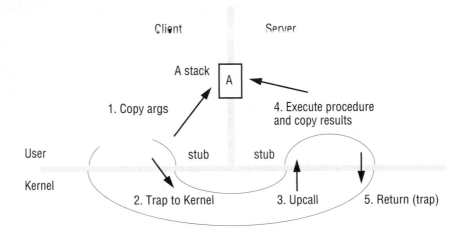

First, they noted that it would be more efficient to use shared memory regions for client-server communication, with a different (private) region between the server and each of its local clients. Such a region contains one or more *A* (for argument) *stacks* (see Figure 6.13). Instead of RPC parameters being copied between the kernel and user address spaces involved, client and server are able to pass arguments and return values directly via an A stack. The same stack is used by the client and server stubs. In LRPC, arguments are copied once: when they are marshalled onto the A stack. In an equivalent RPC, they are copied four times: from the client stub's stack onto a message; from the message to a kernel buffer; from the kernel buffer to a server message; from the message to the server stub's stack. There may be several A stacks in a shared region, because several threads in the same client may call the server at the same time.

Bershad *et al.* also considered the cost of thread scheduling. Compare the model of system call and remote procedure calls in Figure 6.11. When a system call occurs, most kernels do not schedule a new thread to handle the call but instead perform a context switch on the calling thread so that it handles the system call. In an RPC, a remote procedure may exist in a different computer from the client thread, so a different thread must be scheduled to execute it. In the local case, however, it may be more efficient for the client thread – which would otherwise be *BLOCKED* – to call the invoked procedure in the server's address space.

A server must be programmed differently in this case to the way we have described servers before. Instead of setting up one or more threads, which then listen on ports for invocation requests, the server exports a set of procedures that it is prepared to have called. Threads in local processes may enter the server's execution environment as long as they start by calling one of the server's exported procedures. A client needing to invoke a server's operations must first bind to the server interface (not shown in the figure). It does this via the kernel, which notifies the server; when the server has responded to the kernel with a list of allowed procedure addresses, the kernel replies to the client with a capability for invoking the server's operations.

An invocation is shown in Figure 6.13. A client thread enters the server's execution environment by first trapping to the kernel and presenting it with a capability. The kernel checks this and only allows a context switch to a valid server procedure; if it is valid, the kernel switches the thread's context to call the procedure in the server's execution environment. When the procedure in the server returns, the thread returns to the kernel, which switches the thread back to the client execution environment. Note that clients and servers employ stub procedures to hide the details just described from application writers.

Discussion of LRPC ◊ There is little doubt that LRPC is more efficient than RPC for the local case, as long as enough invocations take place to offset the memory management costs. Bershad *et al.* record LRPC delays a factor of three smaller than those of RPC executed locally.

Location transparency is not sacrificed in Bershad's implementation. A client stub examines a bit set at bind time that records whether the server is local or remote, and proceeds to use LRPC or RPC, respectively. The application is unaware of which is used. However, migration transparency might be hard to achieve when a resource is transferred from a local server to a remote server, or *vice versa*, because of the need to change invocation mechanisms.

In later work, Bershad *et al.* [1991] describe several performance improvements, which are addressed particularly to multiprocessor operation. The improvements largely concern avoiding traps to the kernel and scheduling processors in such a way as to avoid unnecessary domain transitions. For example, if a processor is idling in the server's memory management context at the time a client thread attempts to invoke a server procedure, then the thread should be transferred to that processor. This avoids a domain transition; at the same time, the client's processor may be reused by another thread in the client. These enhancements involve an implementation of two-level (user and kernel) thread scheduling, as described in Section 6.4.

6.5.2 Asynchronous operation

We have discussed how the operating system can help the middleware layer to provide efficient remote invocation mechanisms. But we also observed that in the Internet environment the effects of high latencies, low bandwidths and high server loads may outweigh any benefits that the OS can provide. We can add to this the phenomena of network disconnection and reconnection, which can be regarded as causing extremely high-latency communication. Users' mobile computers are not connected to the network all the time. Even if they have wide-area wireless access (for example, using GSM), they may be peremptorily disconnected when, for example, their train enters a tunnel.

A common technique to defeat high latencies is asynchronous operation, which arises in two programming models: concurrent invocations and asynchronous invocations. These models are largely in the domain of middleware rather than operating system kernel design, but it is useful to consider them here, while we are examining the topic of invocation performance.

Making invocations concurrently ◊ In the first model, the middleware provides only blocking invocations, but the application spawns multiple threads to perform blocking invocations concurrently.

Figure 6.14   Times for serialized and concurrent invocations

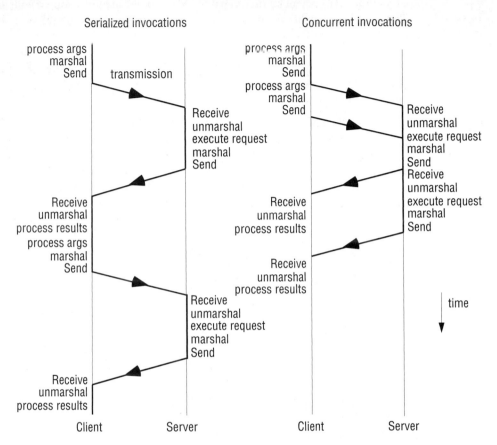

A good example of such an application is a web browser. A web page typically contains several images. The browser has to fetch each of these images in a separate HTTP *GET* request (since standard HTTP 1.0 web servers only support requests for single resources). The browser does not need to obtain the images in a particular sequence, so it makes concurrent requests – typically up to about four at a time. That way, the time taken to complete all the image requests is typically lower than the delay of making the requests serially. Not only is the total communication delay less, in general, but the browser can overlap computation such as image rendering with communication.

Figure 6.14 shows the potential benefits of interleaving invocations (such as HTTP requests) between a client and a single server on a single-processor machine. In the serialized case, the client marshals the arguments, calls the *Send* operation and then waits until the reply from the server arrives – whereupon it *Receives*, unmarshals and then processes the results. After this it can make the second invocation.

In the concurrent case, the first client thread marshals the arguments and calls the *Send* operation. The second thread then immediately makes the second invocation. Each thread waits to receive its results. The total time taken is liable to be lower than the serialized case, as the figure shows. Similar benefits apply if the client threads make concurrent requests to several servers; and if the client executes on a multiprocessor then even greater throughput is potentially possible, since the two threads' processing can also be overlapped.

Returning to the particular case of HTTP, the study by Nielson *et al.* [1997] that we referred to above also measured the effects of concurrently interleaved HTTP 1.1 invocations (which they call *pipelining*) over persistent connections. They found that pipelining reduced network traffic and could lead to performance benefits for clients, as long as the operating system provides a suitable interface for flushing buffers, to override the default TCP behaviour.

Asynchronous invocations ◊ An *asynchronous invocation* is one that is performed asynchronously with respect to the caller. That is, it is made with a non-blocking call, which returns as soon as the invocation request message has been created and is ready for dispatch.

Sometimes the client does not require any response (except perhaps an indication of failure if the target host could not be reached). For example, CORBA *oneway* invocations have *maybe* semantics. Otherwise, the client uses a separate call to collect the results of the invocation. For example, the Mercury communication system [Liskov and Shrira 1988] supports asynchronous invocations. An asynchronous operation returns an object called a *promise*. Eventually, when the invocation succeeds or is deemed to have failed, the Mercury system places the status and any return values in the promise. The caller uses the *claim* operation to obtain the results from the promise. The claim operation blocks until the promise is ready, whereupon it returns the results or exceptions from the call. The *ready* operation is available for testing a promise without blocking – it returns *true* or *false* according to whether the promise is ready or blocked.

Persistent asynchronous invocations ◊ Traditional asynchronous invocation mechanisms such as Mercury invocations and CORBA *oneway* invocations are implemented upon TCP streams and fail if a stream breaks – that is, if the network link is down or the target host crashes.

But a more developed form of the asynchronous invocation model, which we shall call *persistent asynchronous invocation*, is becoming increasingly relevant because of disconnected operation. This model is similar to Mercury in terms of the programming operations it provides, but the difference is in its failure semantics. A conventional invocation mechanism (synchronous or asynchronous) is designed to fail after a given number of timeouts have occurred. But these short-term timeouts are often not appropriate where disconnections or very high latencies occur.

A system for persistent asynchronous invocation tries indefinitely to perform the invocation, until it is known to have succeeded or failed, or until the application cancels the invocation. An example is QRPC (Queued RPC) in the Rover toolkit for mobile information access [Joseph *et al.* 1997].

As its name suggests, QRPC queues outgoing invocation requests in a stable log while there is no network connection and schedules their dispatch over the network to servers when there is a connection. Similarly, it queues invocation results from servers in what we can consider to be the client's invocation 'mailbox' until the client reconnects and collects them. Requests and results may be compressed when they are queued, before their transmission over a low-bandwidth network.

QRPC can take advantage of different communication links for sending an invocation request and receiving the reply. For example, a request could be dispatched over a GSM link while the user is on the road, and then the response delivered over an Ethernet link when the user connects her device to the corporate intranet. In principle, the invocation system can even store the invocation results near to the user's next expected point of connection.

The client's network scheduler operates according to various criteria and does not necessarily dispatch invocations in FIFO order. Applications can assign priorities to individual invocations. When a connection becomes available, QRPC evaluates its bandwidth and the expense of using it. It dispatches high-priority invocation requests first, and may not dispatch all of them if the link is slow and expensive (such as a wide-area wireless connection) – assuming that a faster, cheaper link such as an Ethernet will become available eventually. Similarly, QRPC takes priority into account when fetching invocation results from the mailbox over a low-bandwidth link.

Programming with an asynchronous invocation system (persistent or otherwise) raises the issue of how users can continue using the applications on their client device while the results of invocations are still not known. For example, the user may wonder whether they have succeeded in updating a paragraph to a shared document, or has someone else perhaps made a conflicting update, such as deleting the paragraph? Chapter 15 examines this issue.

6.6 Operating system architecture

In this section, we examine the architecture of a kernel suitable for a distributed system. We adopt a first-principles approach of starting with the requirement of openness and examining the major kernel architectures that have been proposed, with this in mind.

An open distributed system should make it possible to:

- Run only that system software at each computer that is necessary for it to carry out its particular role in the system architecture; system software requirements can vary between, for example, personal digital assistants and dedicated server computers. Loading redundant modules wastes memory resources.

- Allow the software (and the computer) implementing any particular service to be changed independently of other facilities.

- Allow for alternatives of the same service to be provided, when this is required to suit different users or applications.

- Introduce new services without harming the integrity of existing ones.

The separation of fixed resource management *mechanisms* from resource management *policies*, which vary from application to application and service to service, has been a guiding principle in operating system design for a long time [Wulf *et al.* 1974]. For example, we said that an ideal scheduling system would provide mechanisms that enable

Figure 6.15   Monolithic kernel and microkernel

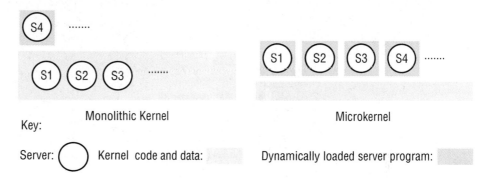

a multimedia application such as videoconferencing to meet its real-time demands while coexisting with a non-real-time application such as web browsing.

Ideally, the kernel would provide only the most basic mechanisms upon which the general resource management tasks at a node are carried out. Server modules would be dynamically loaded as required, to implement the required resource management policies for the currently running applications.

Monolithic kernels and microkernels ◊ There are two key examples of kernel design: the so-called *monolithic* and *microkernel* approaches. Where these designs differ primarily is in the decision as to what functionality belongs in the kernel and what is to be left to server processes that can be dynamically loaded to run on top of it. Although microkernels have not been deployed widely, it is instructive to understand their advantages and disadvantages compared to the typical kernels found today.

The UNIX operating system kernel has been called *monolithic* (see definition in the box below). This term is meant to suggest the facts that it is *massive*: it performs all basic operating system functions and takes up in the order of megabytes of code and data, and that it is *undifferentiated*: it is coded in a non-modular way. The result is that to a large extent it is *intractable*: altering any individual software component to adapt it to changing requirements is difficult. Another example of a monolithic kernel is that of the Sprite network operating system [Ousterhout *et al.* 1988]. A monolithic kernel can contain some server processes that execute within its address space, including file servers and some networking. The code that these processes execute is part of the standard kernel configuration (see Figure 6.15).

By contrast, in the case of a microkernel design the kernel provides only the most basic abstractions, principally address spaces, threads and *local* interprocess communication; *all* other system services are provided by servers that are dynamically

Monolithic ◊ The Chambers 20th Century Dictionary gives the following definition of *monolith* and *monolithic*. **monolith**, *n.* a pillar, or column, of a single stone: anything resembling a monolith in uniformity, massiveness or intractability. – *adj.* monolithic pertaining to or resembling a monolith: of a state, an organization, etc., massive, and undifferentiated throughout: intractable for this reason.

Figure 6.16   The role of the microkernel

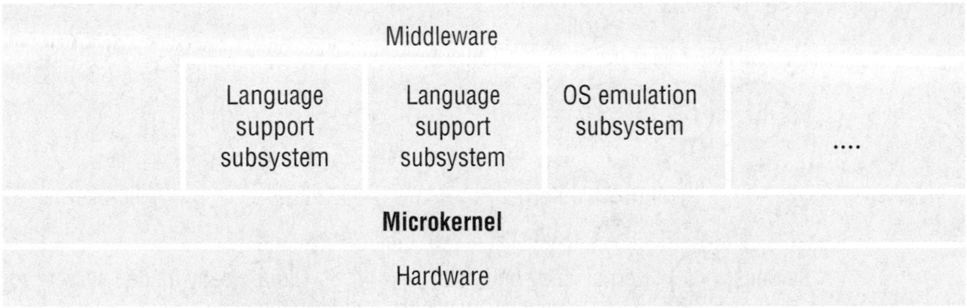

The microkernel supports middleware via subsystems

loaded at precisely those computers in the distributed system that require them (Figure 6.15). Clients access these system services using the kernel's message-based invocation mechanisms.

We said above that users are liable to reject operating systems that do not run their applications. But in addition to extensibility, microkernel designers have another goal: the binary emulation of standard operating systems such as UNIX [Armand *et al.* 1989, Golub *et al.* 1990, Härtig *et al.* 1997].

The place of the microkernel – in its most general form – in the overall distributed system design is shown in Figure 6.16. The microkernel appears as a layer between the hardware layer and a layer consisting of major system components called *subsystems*. If performance is the main goal, rather than portability, then middleware may use the facilities of the microkernel directly. Otherwise, it uses a language runtime support subsystem, or a higher-level operating system interface provided by an operating system emulation subsystem. Each of these, in turn, is implemented by a combination of library procedures linked into applications, and a set of servers running on top of the microkernel.

There can be more than one system call interface – more than one 'operating system' – presented to the programmer on the same underlying platform. An example is the implementation of UNIX and OS/2 on top of the Mach distributed operating system kernel. Note that operating system emulation is different from machine *virtualization* (see box on the next page).

Comparison ◊ The chief advantages of a microkernel-based operating system are its extensibility and its ability to enforce modularity behind memory protection boundaries. In addition, a relatively small kernel is more likely to be free of bugs than one that is larger and more complex.

The advantage of a monolithic design is the relative efficiency with which operations can be invoked. System calls may be more expensive than conventional procedures but, even using the techniques we examined in the previous section, an invocation to a separate user-level address space on the same node is more costly still.

The lack of structure in monolithic designs can be avoided by the use of software engineering techniques such as layering (used in MULTICS [Organick 1972]), or object-oriented design, used for example in Choices [Campbell *et al.* 1993]. Windows employs a combination of both [Custer 1998]. But Windows remains 'massive', and the majority of its functionality is not designed to be routinely replaceable. Even a modularized large kernel can be hard to maintain, and it provides limited support for an open distributed system. As long as modules are executed within the same address space, using a language such as C or C++ that compiles to efficient code but permits arbitrary data accesses, it is possible for strict modularity to be broken by programmers seeking efficient implementations, and for a bug in one module to corrupt the data in another.

Some hybrid approaches ◊ Two of the original microkernels, Mach [Acetta *et al.* 1986] and Chorus [Rozier *et al.* 1990], began their developmental life running servers only as user processes. Modularity is then hardware-enforced through address spaces. Where servers require direct access to hardware, special system calls can be provided for these privileged processes, which map device registers and buffers into their address spaces. The kernel turns interrupts into messages, which enables user-level servers to handle interrupts.

Because of performance problems, the Chorus and Mach microkernel designs eventually changed to allow servers to be loaded dynamically either into the kernel address space or into a user-level address space. In each case, clients interact with servers using the same interprocess communication calls. A developer can thus debug a server at user level and then, when the development is deemed complete, allow the server to run inside the kernel's address space in order to optimize system performance. But such a server then threatens the integrity of the system, should it turn out still to contain bugs.

The SPIN operating system [Bershad *et al.* 1995] design finesses the problem of trading off efficiency for protection by employing language facilities for protection. The kernel and all dynamically loaded modules grafted onto the kernel execute within a single address space. But all are written in a type-safe language (Modula-3), so they can be mutually protected. Protection domains within the kernel address space are established using protected name spaces. No module grafted onto the kernel may access a resource unless it has been handed a reference for it; and Modula-3 enforces the rule that a reference can only be used to perform operations allowed by the programmer.

Virtualization ◊ *Virtualization* is where a single machine's hardware is allocated between multiple virtual machines (virtual hardware images), each running a separate operating system instance. Virtualization began with the IBM 370 architecture, whose VM operating system can present several complete virtual machines to different programs running at the same computer. More recently, projects such as Xen [Barham *et al.* 2003] have developed *virtual machine monitors* for commodity PCs. A virtual machine monitor is a software layer between the hardware and commodity operating systems such as Linux or Windows. It enables a single PC to run any combination of unmodified instances of those operating systems at the same time, and isolates and protects them from one another. Commercial implementations such as VMWare are available for PCs and for the nodes of clusters, enabling work to be flexibly allocated to them.

In an attempt to minimize the dependencies between system modules, the SPIN designers chose an event-based model as a mechanism for interaction between modules grafted into the kernel's address space (see Section 5.4 for a discussion of event-based programming). The system defines a set of core events, such as network packet arrival, timer interrupts, page fault occurrences and thread state changes. System components operate by registering themselves as handlers for the events that affect them. For example, a scheduler would register itself to handle events similar to those we studied in the scheduler activations system in Section 6.4.

Operating systems such as Nemesis [Leslie *et al.* 1996] exploit the fact that, even at the hardware level, an address space is not necessarily also a single protection domain. The kernel co-exists in a single address space with all dynamically loaded system modules and all applications. When it loads an application, the kernel places the application's code and data in regions chosen from those that are available at runtime. The advent of processors with 64-bit addressing has made single-address space operating systems particularly attractive, since they support very large address spaces that can accommodate many applications.

The kernel of a single-address-space operating system sets the protection attributes on individual regions within the address space to restrict access by user-level code. User-level code still runs with the processor in a particular protection context (determined by settings in the processor and memory management unit), which gives it full access to its own regions and only selectively shared access to others. The saving of a single address space, compared with using multiple address spaces, is that the kernel need never flush any caches when it implements a domain transition.

Some more recent kernel designs, such as L4 [Härtig *et al.* 1997] and the Exokernel [Kaashoek *et al.* 1997], take the approach that what we have described as 'microkernels' still contain too much policy as opposed to mechanism. L4 is a 'second-generation' microkernel design that forces dynamically loaded system modules to execute in user-level address spaces, but it optimizes interprocess communication to offset the costs of doing so. It offloads much of the kernel's complexity by delegating the management of address spaces to user-level servers. The Exokernel takes a quite different approach, of employing user-level libraries instead of user-level servers to supply functional extensions. It provides protected allocation of extremely low-level resources such as disk blocks, and it expects all other resource management functionality – even a file system – to be linked into applications as libraries.

In the words of one microkernel designer [Liedtke 1996], 'the microkernel story is full of good ideas and blind alleys.' The jury is still out on how to design an operating system architecture that is sufficiently extensible but that performs well relative to monolithic designs.

6.7 Summary

This chapter has described how the operating system supports the middleware layer in providing invocations upon shared resources. The operating system provides a collection of mechanisms upon which varying resource management policies can be implemented – to meet local requirements, and to take advantage of technological improvements. It allows servers to encapsulate and protect resources, while allowing clients to share them concurrently. It provides mechanisms necessary for clients to invoke operations upon resources.

A process consists of an execution environment and threads: an execution environment consists of an address space, communication interfaces and other local resources such as semaphores; a thread is an activity abstraction that executes within an execution environment. Address spaces need to be large and sparse in order to support sharing and mapped access to objects such as files. New address spaces may be created with their regions inherited from parent processes. An important technique for copying regions is copy-on-write.

Processes can have multiple threads, which share the execution environment. Multi-threaded processes allow us to achieve relatively cheap concurrency, and to take advantage of multiprocessors for parallelism. They are useful for both clients and servers. Recent threads implementations allow for two-tier scheduling: the kernel provides access to multiple processors, while user-level code handles the details of scheduling policy.

The operating system provides basic message-passing primitives and mechanisms for communication via shared memory. Most kernels include network communication as a basic facility; others provide only local communication and leave network communication to servers, which may implement a range of communication protocols. This is a trade-off of performance against flexibility.

We discussed remote invocations and accounted for the difference between overheads due directly to network hardware and overheads that are due to the execution of operating system code. We found the proportion of the total time due to software to be relatively large for a null invocation but to decrease as a proportion of the total with the size of the invocation arguments. The chief overheads involved in an invocation that are candidates for optimization are marshalling, data copying, packet initialization, thread scheduling and context switching, and the flow control protocol used. Invocation between address spaces within a computer is an important special case, and we described the thread-management and parameter-passing techniques used in lightweight RPC.

There are two main approaches to kernel architecture: monolithic kernels and microkernels. The main difference between them lies in where the line is drawn between resource management by the kernel and resource management performed by dynamically loaded (and usually user-level) servers. A microkernel must support at least a notion of process and interprocess communication. It supports operating system emulation subsystems as well as language support and other subsystems, such as those for real-time processing.

EXERCISES

6.1   Discuss each of the tasks of encapsulation, concurrent processing, protection, name resolution, communication of parameters and results, and scheduling in the case of the UNIX file service (or that of another kernel that is familiar to you).   *page 224*

6.2   Why are some system interfaces implemented by dedicated system calls (to the kernel), and others on top of message-based system calls?   *page 224*

6.3   Smith decides that every thread in his processes ought to have its own *protected* stack – all other regions in a process would be fully shared. Does this make sense?   *page 228*

6.4   Should signal (software interrupt) handlers belong to a process or to a thread?

page 228

6.5   Discuss the issue of naming applied to shared memory regions.   *page 230*

6.6   Suggest a scheme for balancing the load on a set of computers. You should discuss:

   i)   what user or system requirements are met by such a scheme;

   ii)   to what categories of applications it is suited;

   iii) how to measure load and with what accuracy; and

   iv)   how to monitor load and choose the location for a new process. Assume that processes may not be migrated.

How would your design be affected if processes could be migrated between computers? Would you expect process migration to have a significant cost?   *page 231*

6.7   Explain the advantage of copy-on-write region copying for UNIX, where a call to *fork* is typically followed by a call to *exec*. What should happen if a region that has been copied using copy-on-write is itself copied?   *page 233*

6.8   A file server uses caching, and achieves a hit rate of 80%. File operations in the server cost 5 ms of CPU time when the server finds the requested block in the cache, and take an additional 15 ms of disk I/O time otherwise. Explaining any assumptions you make, estimate the server's throughput capacity (average requests/sec) if it is:

   i)   single-threaded;

   ii)   two-threaded, running on a single processor;

   iii) two-threaded, running on a two-processor computer.   *page 234*

6.9   Compare the worker pool multi-threading architecture with the thread-per-request architecture.   *page 235*

6.10   What thread operations are the most significant in cost?   *page 237*

6.11   A spin lock (see Bacon [2002]) is a boolean variable accessed via an atomic *test-and-set* instruction, which is used to obtain mutual exclusion. Would you use a spin lock to obtain mutual exclusion between threads on a single-processor computer?   *page 241*

6.12   Explain what the kernel must provide for a user-level implementation of threads, such as Java on UNIX.   *page 242*

6.13   Do page faults present a problem for user-level threads implementations?   *page 242*

6.14   Explain the factors that motivate the hybrid scheduling approach of the 'scheduler activations' design (instead of pure user-level or kernel-level scheduling).   *page 243*

6.15 Why should a threads package be interested in the events of a thread's becoming blocked or unblocked? Why should it be interested in the event of a virtual processor's impending preemption? (Hint: other virtual processors may continue to be allocated.)

page 244

6.16 Network transmission time accounts for 20% of a null RPC and 80% of an RPC that transmits 1024 user bytes (less than the size of a network packet). By what percentage will the times for these two operations improve if the network is upgraded from 10 megabits/second to 100 megabits/second?

page 247

6.17 A 'null' RMI that takes no parameters, calls an empty procedure and returns no values delays the caller for 2.0 milliseconds. Explain what contributes to this time.

In the same RMI system, each 1K of user data adds an extra 1.5 milliseconds. A client wishes to fetch 32K of data from a file server. Should it use one 32K RMI or 32 1K RMIs?

page 247

6.18 Which factors identified in the cost of a remote invocation also feature in message passing?

page 249

6.19 Explain how a shared region could be used for a process to read data written by the kernel. Include in your explanation what would be necessary for synchronization.

page 250

6.20 i) Can a server invoked by lightweight procedure calls control the degree of concurrency within it?

ii) Explain why and how a client is prevented from calling arbitrary code within a server under lightweight RPC.

iii) Does LRPC expose clients and servers to greater risks of mutual interference than conventional RPC (given the sharing of memory)?

page 251

6.21 A client makes RMIs to a server. The client takes 5 ms to compute the arguments for each request, and the server takes 10ms to process each request. The local OS processing time for each *send* or *receive* operation is 0.5 ms, and the network time to transmit each request or reply message is 3 ms. Marshalling or unmarshalling takes 0.5 ms per message.

Estimate the time taken by the client to generate and return from 2 requests (i) if it is single-threaded, and (ii) if it has two threads which can make requests concurrently on a single processor. Is there a need for asynchronous RMI if processes are multi-threaded?

page 253

6.22 Explain what is security policy and what are the corresponding mechanisms in the case of a multi-user operating system such as UNIX.

page 256

6.23 Explain the program linkage requirements that must be met if a server is to be dynamically loaded into the kernel's address space, and how these differ from the case of executing a server at user level.

page 257

6.24 How could an interrupt be communicated to a user-level server?

page 259

6.25   On a certain computer we estimate that, regardless of the OS it runs, thread scheduling costs about 50 μs, a null procedure call 1 ms, a context switch to the kernel 20 μs and a domain transition 40 μs. For each of Mach and SPIN, estimate the cost to a client of calling a dynamically loaded null procedure.   *page 259*

7

SECURITY

There is a pervasive need for measures to guarantee the privacy, integrity and availability of resources in distributed systems. Security attacks take the forms of eavesdropping, masquerading, tampering and denial of service. Designers of secure distributed systems must cope with exposed service interfaces and insecure networks in an environment where attackers are likely to have knowledge of the algorithms used and to deploy computing resources.

Cryptography provides the basis for the authentication of messages as well as their secrecy and integrity; carefully designed security protocols are required to exploit it. The selection of cryptographic algorithms and the management of keys are critical to the effectiveness, performance and usability of security mechanisms. Public-key cryptography makes it easy to distribute cryptographic keys but its performance is inadequate for the encryption of bulk data. Secret-key cryptography is more suitable for bulk encryption tasks. Hybrid protocols such as TLS (Transport Layer Security) establish a secure channel using public-key cryptography and then use it to exchange secret keys for use in subsequent data exchanges.

Digital information can be signed, producing digital certificates. Certificates enable trust to be established among users and organizations.

7.1   Introduction

In Section 2.3.3 we introduced a simple model for examining the security requirements in distributed systems. We concluded that the need for security mechanisms in distributed systems arises from the desire to share resources. (Resources that are not shared can generally be protected by isolating them from external access.) If we regard shared resources as objects, then the requirement is to protect any processes that encapsulate shared objects and any communication channels that are used to interact with them against all conceivable forms of attack. The model introduced in Section 2.3.3 provides a good starting point for the identification of security requirements. It can be summarized as follows:

- Processes encapsulate resources (both programming language-level objects and system-defined resources) and allow clients to access them through interfaces. Principals (users or other processes) are authorized to operate on resources. Resources must be protected against unauthorized access (Figure 2.13).

- Processes interact through a network that is shared by many users. Enemies (attackers) can access the network. They can copy or attempt to read any message transmitted through the network and they can inject arbitrary messages, addressed to any destination and purporting to come from any source, into the network (Figure 2.14).

The need to protect the integrity and privacy of information and other resources belonging to individuals and organizations is pervasive in both the physical and the digital world. It arises from the desire to share resources. In the physical world, organizations adopt *security policies* that provide for the sharing of resources within specified limits. For example, a company may permit entry to its buildings for its employees and for accredited visitors. A security policy for documents may specify groups of employees who can access classes of documents or it may be defined for individual documents and users.

Security policies are enforced with the help of *security mechanisms*. For example, access to a building may be controlled by a reception clerk, who issues badges to accredited visitors, and enforced by a security guard or by electronic door locks. Access to paper documents is usually controlled by concealment and restricted distribution. In the electronic world, the distinction between security policies and mechanisms is equally important; without it, it would be difficult to determine whether a particular system was secure. Security policies are independent of the technology used, just as the provision of a lock on a door does not ensure the security of a building unless there is a policy for its use (for example, that the door will be locked whenever nobody is guarding the entrance). The security mechanisms that we shall describe do not in themselves ensure the security of a system. In Section 7.1.2, we outline the requirements for security in various simple electronic commerce scenarios, illustrating the need for policies in that context.

The provision of mechanisms for the protection of data and other resources in distributed systems while allowing interactions between computers implied by security policies is the concern of this chapter. The mechanisms that we shall describe are designed to enforce security policies against the most determined attacks.

The role of cryptography ◊ Digital cryptography provides the basis for most computer security mechanisms, but it is important to note that computer security and cryptography are distinct subjects. Cryptography is the art of encoding information in a format that only the intended recipients can access. Cryptography can also be employed to provide a proof of the authenticity of information, in a manner analogous to the use of signatures in conventional transactions.

Cryptography has a long and fascinating history. The military need for secure communication and the corresponding need of an enemy to intercept and decrypt it led to the investment of much intellectual effort by some of the best mathematical brains of their time. Readers interested in exploring this history will find absorbing reading in books on the topic by David Kahn [Kahn 1967, 1983, 1991] and Simon Singh [Singh 1999]. Whitfield Diffie, one of the inventors of public-key cryptography, has written with first-hand knowledge on the recent history and politics of cryptography [Diffie 1988, Diffie and Landau 1998].

But it is only in recent times that cryptography has emerged from the wraps previously placed on it by the political and military establishments that used to control its development and use. It is now the subject of open research by a large and active community, with the results published in many books, journals and conferences. The publication of Schneier's book *Applied Cryptography* [Schneier 1996] was a milestone in the opening up of knowledge in the field. It was the first book to publish many important algorithms with source code – a courageous step, because when the first edition appeared in 1994 the legal status of such publication was unclear. Schneier's book remains the definitive reference on most aspects of modern cryptography. A more recent book co-authored by Schneier [Ferguson and Schneier 2003] provides an excellent introduction to computer cryptography including a discursive overview of virtually all the important algorithms and techniques in current use, including several published since Schneier's earlier book. In addition, Menezes *et al.* [1997] provide a good practical handbook with a strong theoretical basis and the Network Security Library [www.secinf.net] is an excellent online source of practical knowledge and experience.

Ross Anderson's *Security Engineering* [Anderson 2001] is also outstanding. It is replete with object-lessons on the design of secure systems, drawn from real-world situations and system security failures.

The new openness is largely a result of the tremendous growth of interest in non-military applications of cryptography and the security requirements of distributed computer systems. This resulted in the existence for the first time of a self-sustaining community of cryptographic researchers outside the military domain.

Ironically, the opening of cryptography to public access and use has resulted in a great improvement in cryptographic techniques, both in their strength to withstand attacks by enemies and in the convenience with which they can be deployed. Public-key cryptography is one of the fruits of this openness. As another example, we note that the DES encryption algorithm which was adopted and used by the US military and government agencies was initially a military secret. Its eventual publication and successful efforts to crack it resulted in the development of much stronger secret-key encryption algorithms.

Another useful spin-off has been the development of a common terminology and approach. An example of the latter is the adoption of a set of familiar names for

Figure 7.1   Familiar names for the protagonists in security protocols

Alice	First participant
Bob	Second participant
Carol	Participant in three- and four-party protocols
Dave	Participant in four-party protocols
Eve	Eavesdropper
Mallory	Malicious attacker
Sara	A server

protagonists (principals) involved in the transactions that are to be secured. The use of familiar names for principals and attackers helps to clarify and bring to life descriptions of security protocols and potential attacks on them, which is an important step towards identifying their weaknesses. The names shown in Figure 7.1 are used extensively in the security literature and we shall use them freely here. We have not been able to discover their origins; the earliest occurrence of which we are aware is in the original RSA public-key cryptography paper [Rivest *et al.* 1978]. An amusing commentary on their use can be found in Gordon [1984].

7.1.1   Threats and attacks

Some threats are obvious – for example, in most types of local network it is easy to construct and run a program on a connected computer that obtains copies of the messages transmitted between other computers. Other threats are more subtle – if clients fail to authenticate servers, a program might install itself in place of an authentic file server and thereby obtain copies of confidential information that clients unwittingly send to it for storage.

In addition to the danger of loss or damage to information or resources through direct violations, fraudulent claims may be made against the owner of a system that is not demonstrably secure. To avoid such claims, the owner must be in a position to disprove the claim by showing that the system is secure against such violations or by producing a log of all of the transactions for the period in question. A common instance is the 'phantom withdrawal' problem in automatic cash dispensers (teller machines). The best answer that a bank can supply to such a claim is to provide a record of the transaction that is digitally signed by the account holder in a manner that cannot be forged by a third party.

The main goal of security is to restrict access to information and resources to just those principals that are authorized to have access. Security threats fall into three broad classes:

Leakage – the acquisition of information by unauthorized recipients;

Tampering – the unauthorized alteration of information;

Vandalism – interference with the proper operation of a system without gain to the perpetrator.

Attacks on distributed systems depend upon obtaining access to existing communication channels or establishing new channels that masquerade as authorized connections. (We use the term *channel* to refer to any communication mechanism between processes.) Methods of attack can be further classified according to the way in which a channel is misused:

Eavesdropping – obtaining copies of messages without authority.

Masquerading – sending or receiving messages using the identity of another principal without their authority.

Message tampering – intercepting messages and altering their contents before passing them on to the intended recipient. The *man-in-the-middle attack* is a form of message tampering in which an attacker intercepts the very first message in an exchange of encryption keys to establish a secure channel. The attacker substitutes compromised keys that enable him to decrypt subsequent messages before re-encrypting them in the correct keys and passing them on.

Replaying – storing intercepted messages and sending them at a later date. This attack may be effective even with authenticated and encrypted messages.

Denial of service – flooding a channel or other resource with messages in order to deny access for others.

These are the dangers in theory, but how are attacks carried out in practice? Successful attacks depend upon the discovery of loopholes in the security of systems. Unfortunately, these are all too common in today's systems, and they are not necessarily particularly obscure. Cheswick and Bellovin [1994] identify forty-two weaknesses that they regard as posing serious risks in widely used Internet systems and components. They range from password guessing to attacks on the programs that perform the network time protocol or handle mail transmission. Some of these have led to successful and well-publicized attacks [Stoll 1989, Spafford 1989], and many of them have been exploited for mischievous or criminal purposes.

When the Internet and the systems that are connected to it were designed, security was not a priority. The designers probably had no conception of the scale to which the Internet would grow, and the basic design of systems such as UNIX predates the advent of computer networks. As we shall see, the incorporation of security measures needs to be carefully thought out at the basic design stage, and the material in this chapter is intended to provide the basis for such thinking.

We have focused on the threats to distributed systems that arise from the exposure of their communication channels and their interfaces. For many systems, these are the only threats that need to be considered (other than those that arise from human error – security mechanisms cannot guard against a badly chosen password or one that is carelessly disclosed). But for systems that include mobile programs and systems whose security is particularly sensitive to information leakage, there are further threats.

Threats from mobile code ◊ Several recently developed programming languages have been designed to enable programs to be loaded into a process from a remote server and then executed locally. In that case, the internal interfaces and objects within an executing process may be exposed to attack by mobile code.

Java is the most widely used language of this type, and the designers paid considerable attention to the design and construction of the language and the mechanisms for remote loading in an effort to restrict the exposure (the *sandbox* model of protection against mobile code).

The Java Virtual Machine (JVM) is designed with mobile code in view. It gives each application its own environment in which to run. Each environment has a security manager that determines which resources are available to the application. For example, the security manager might stop an application reading and writing files or give it limited access to network connections. Once a security manager has been set, it cannot be replaced. When a user runs a program such as a browser that downloads mobile code to be run locally on their behalf, they have no very good reason to trust the code to behave in a responsible manner. In fact, there is a danger of downloading and running malicious code that removes files or accesses private information. To protect users against untrusted code, most browsers specify that applets cannot access local files, printers or network sockets. Some applications of mobile code are able to assume various levels of trust in downloaded code. In this case, the security managers are configured to provide more access to local resources.

The JVM takes two further measures to protect the local environment:

1. the downloaded classes are stored separately from the local classes, preventing them from replacing local classes with spurious versions;

2. the bytecodes are checked for validity. Valid Java bytecode is composed of Java virtual machine instructions from a specified set. The instructions are also checked to ensure that they will not produce certain errors when the program runs, such as accessing illegal memory addresses.

The security of Java has been the subject of much subsequent investigation, in the course of which it became clear that the original mechanisms adopted were not free of loopholes [McGraw and Felden 1999]. The identified loopholes were corrected and the Java protection system was refined to allow mobile code to access local resources when authorized to do so [java.sun.com V].

Despite the inclusion of type-checking and code-validation mechanisms, the security mechanisms incorporated into mobile code systems do not yet produce the same level of confidence in their effectiveness as those used to protect communication channels and interfaces. This is because the construction of an environment for execution of programs offers many opportunities for error, and it is difficult to be confident that all have been avoided. Volpano and Smith [1999] have pointed out that an alternative approach, based on proofs that the behaviour of mobile code is sound, might offer a better solution.

Information leakage ◊ If the transmission of a message between two processes can be observed, some information can be gleaned from its mere existence – for example, a flood of messages to a dealer in a particular stock might indicate a high level of trading in that stock. There are many more subtle forms of information leakage, some malicious and others arising from inadvertent error. The potential for leakage arises whenever the results of a computation can be observed. Work was done on the prevention of this type of security threat in the 1970s [Denning and Denning 1977]. The approach taken is to assign security levels to information and channels and to analyse the flow of information into channels with the aim of ensuring that high-level information cannot flow into lower-level channels. A method for the secure control of information flows was first described by Bell and LaPadula [1975]. The extension of this approach to distributed systems with mutual distrust between components is the subject of recent research [Myers and Liskov 1997].

7.1.2 Securing electronic transactions

Many uses of the Internet in industry, commerce and elsewhere involve transactions that depend crucially on security. For example:

Email: Although email systems did not originally include support for security, there are many uses of email in which the contents of messages must be kept secret (for example, when sending a credit card number) or the contents and sender of a message must be authenticated (for example when submitting an auction bid by email). Cryptographic security based on the techniques described in this chapter is now included in many mail clients.

Purchase of goods and services: Such transactions are now commonplace. Buyers select goods and pay for them using the Web and they are delivered to them through an appropriate delivery mechanism. Software and other digital products (such as recordings and videos) can be delivered by downloading through the Internet. Tangible goods such as books, CDs and almost every other type of product are also sold by Internet vendors; these are supplied via a delivery service.

Banking transactions: Electronic banks now offer users virtually all of the facilities provided by conventional banks. They can check their balances and statements, transfer money between accounts, set up regular automatic payments and so on.

Micro-transactions: The Internet lends itself to the supply of small quantities of information and other services to many customers. For example, most web pages are not currently charged for, but the development of the Web as a high-quality publishing medium surely depends upon the extent to which information suppliers can obtain payments from consumers of the information. The use of the Internet for voice and videoconferencing provides another example of a service that is likely to be supplied only when it is paid for by end-users. The price for such services may amount to only a fraction of a cent, and the payment overheads must be correspondingly low. In general, schemes based on the involvement of a bank or credit card server for each transaction cannot achieve this.

Transactions such as these can be safely performed only when they are protected by appropriate security policies and mechanisms. A purchaser must be protected against the disclosure of credit codes (card numbers) during transmission and against a fraudulent vendor who obtains payment with no intention of supplying the goods. Vendors must obtain payment before releasing the goods and for downloadable products they must ensure that only the customer obtains the data in a usable form. The required protection must be achieved at a cost that is reasonable in comparison with the value of the transaction.

Sensible security policies for Internet vendors and buyers lead to the following requirements for securing web purchases:

1. Authenticate the vendor to the buyer, so that the buyer can be confident that they are in contact with a server operated by the vendor that they intended to deal with.

2. Keep the buyer's credit card number and other payment details from falling into the hands of any third party and ensure that they are transmitted unaltered from the buyer to the vendor.

3. If the goods are in a form suitable for downloading, ensure that their content is delivered to the buyer without alteration and without disclosure to third parties.

The identity of the buyer is not normally required by the vendor (except for the purpose of delivering the goods in the case that they are not downloaded). The vendor will wish to check that the buyer has sufficient funds to pay for the purchase, but this is usually done by demanding payment from the buyer's bank before delivering the goods.

The security needs of banking transactions using an open network are similar to those for purchase transactions, with the buyer as account holder and the bank as the vendor, but here there certainly *is* the need to:

4. Authenticate the identity of the account holder to the bank before giving them access to their account.

Note that in this situation, it is important for the bank to ensure that the account holder cannot deny that they participated in a transaction. *Non-repudiation* is the name given to this requirement.

In addition to the above requirements, which are dictated by security policies, there are some system requirements. These arise from the very large scale of the Internet, which makes it impractical to require buyers to enter into special relationships with vendors (by registering encryption keys for later use, etc.). It should be possible for a buyer to complete a secure transaction with a vendor even if there has been no previous contact between buyer and vendor and without the involvement of a third party. Techniques such as the use of 'cookies' – records of previous transactions stored on the user's client host – have obvious security weaknesses; desktop and mobile hosts are often located in insecure physical environments.

Because of the importance of security for Internet commerce and the rapid growth in Internet commerce, we have chosen to illustrate the use of cryptographic security techniques by describing in Section 7.6 the *de facto* standard security protocol used in most electronic commerce – Transport Layer Security (TLS). A description of Millicent, a protocol specifically designed for micro-transactions can be found at www.cdk4.net/security.

Internet commerce is an important application of security techniques, but it is certainly not the only one. It is needed wherever computers are used by individuals or organizations to store and communicate important information. The use of encrypted email for private communication between individuals is a case in point that has been the subject of considerable political discussion. We refer to this debate in Section 7.5.2.

7.1.3   Designing secure systems

Immense strides have been made in recent years in the development of cryptographic techniques and their application, yet the design of secure systems remains an inherently difficult task. At the heart of this dilemma is the fact that the designer's aim is to exclude *all* possible attacks and loopholes. The situation is analogous to that of the programmer whose aim must be to exclude all bugs from his program. In neither case is there a concrete method to ensure the goals during the design. One designs to the best available standards and applies informal analysis and checks. Once a design is complete, formal validation is an option. Work on the formal validation of security protocols has produced some important results [Lampson *et al.* 1992, Schneider 1996, Abadi and Gordon 1999]. A description of one of the first steps in this direction, the BAN logic of authentication [Burrows *et al.* 1990] and its application can be found at www.cdk4.net/security.

Security is about avoiding disasters and minimizing mishaps. When designing for security it is necessary to assume the worst. The box on page 274 shows a set of useful assumptions and design guidelines. These assumptions underly the thinking behind the techniques that we shall describe in this chapter.

To demonstrate the validity of the security mechanisms employed in a system, the system's designers must first construct a list of threats – methods by which the security policies might be violated – and show that each of them is prevented by the mechanisms employed. This demonstration may take the form of informal argument, or better, it can take the form of a logical proof.

No list of threats is likely to be exhaustive, so auditing methods must also be used in security-sensitive applications to detect violations. These are straightforward to implement if a secure log of security-sensitive system actions is always recorded with details of the users performing the actions and their authority.

A security log will contain a sequence of timestamped records of users' actions. At a minimum the records will include the identity of a principal, the operation performed (e.g. delete file, update accounting record), the identity of the object operated on and a timestamp. Where particular violations are suspected, the records may be extended to include physical resource utilization (network bandwidth, peripherals), or the logging process may be targeted at operations on particular objects. Subsequent analysis may be statistical or search-based. Even when no violations are suspected, the statistics may be compared over time to help to discover any unusual trends or events.

The design of secure systems is an exercise in balancing costs against the threats. The range of techniques that can be deployed for protecting processes and securing interprocess communication is strong enough to withstand almost any attack, but their use incurs costs and inconvenience:

- a cost (in computational effort and in network usage) is incurred for their use. The costs must be balanced against the threats;

- inappropriately specified security measures may exclude legitimate users from performing necessary actions.

Such trade-offs are difficult to identify without compromising security and may seem to conflict with the advice in the first paragraph of this subsection, but the strength of security techniques can be quantified and selected based on the estimated cost of attacking them. The relatively low-cost techniques employed in the Millicent protocol for small commercial transactions described at www.cdk4.net/security provide an example.

As an illustration of the difficulties and mishaps that can arise in the design of secure systems, we review difficulties that arose with the security design incorporated in the IEEE 802.11 WiFi networking standard in Section 7.6.4.

7.2   Overview of security techniques

The purpose of this section is to introduce the reader to some of the more important techniques and mechanisms for securing distributed systems and applications. Here we describe them informally, reserving more rigorous descriptions for Sections 7.3 and 7.4. We shall use the familiar names for principals introduced in Figure 7.1 and the notations for encrypted and signed items shown in Figure 7.2.

Worst-case assumptions and design guidelines

Interfaces are exposed: Distributed systems are composed of processes that offer services or share information. Their communication interfaces are necessarily open (to allow new clients to access them) – an attacker can send a message to any interface.

Networks are insecure: For example, message sources can be falsified – messages can be made to look as though they came from Alice when they were actually sent by Mallory. Host addresses can be 'spoofed' – Mallory can connect to the network with the same address as Alice and receive copies of messages intended for her.

Limit the lifetime and scope of each secret: When a secret key is first generated we can be confident that it has not been compromised. The longer we use it and the more widely it is known, the greater the risk. The use of secrets such as passwords and shared secret keys should be time-limited, and sharing should be restricted.

Algorithms and program code are available to attackers: The bigger and the more widely distributed a secret is, the greater the risk of its disclosure. Secret encryption algorithms are totally inadequate for today's large-scale network environments. Best practice is to publish the algorithms used for encryption and authentication, relying only on the secrecy of cryptographic keys. This helps to ensure that the algorithms are strong by throwing them open to scrutiny by third parties.

Attackers may have access to large resources: The cost of computing power is rapidly decreasing. We should assume that attackers will have access to the largest and most powerful computers projected in the lifetime of a system, then add a few orders of magnitude to allow for unexpected developments.

Minimize the trusted base: The portions of a system that are responsible for the implementation of its security, *and all the hardware and software components upon which they rely,* have to be trusted – this is often referred to as the *trusted computing base.* Any defect or programming error in this trusted base can produce security weaknesses, so we should aim to minimize its size. For example, application programs should not be trusted to protect data from their users.

Figure 7.2   Cryptography notations

K_A	Alice's secret key
K_B	Bob's secret key
K_{AB}	Secret key shared between Alice and Bob
K_{Apriv}	Alice's private key (known only to Alice)
K_{Apub}	Alice's public key (published by Alice for all to read)
$\{M\}_K$	Message M encrypted with key K
$[M]_K$	Message M signed with key K

7.2.1 Cryptography

Encryption is the process of encoding a message in such a way as to hide its contents. Modern cryptography includes several secure algorithms for encrypting and decrypting messages. They are all based on the use of secrets called *keys*. A cryptographic key is a parameter used in an encryption algorithm in such a way that the encryption cannot be reversed without a knowledge of the key.

There are two main classes of encryption algorithm in general use. The first uses *shared secret keys* – the sender and the recipient must share a knowledge of the key and it must not be revealed to anyone else. The second class of encryption algorithms uses *public/private key pairs* – the sender of a message uses a *public key* – one that has already been published by the recipient – to encrypt the message. The recipient uses a corresponding *private key* to decrypt the message. Although many principals may examine the public key, only the recipient can decrypt the message, because he has the private key.

Both classes of encryption algorithm are extremely useful and are used widely in the construction of secure distributed systems. Public-key encryption algorithms typically require 100 to 1000 times as much processing power as secret-key algorithms, but there are situations where their convenience outweighs this disadvantage.

7.2.2 Uses of cryptography

Cryptography plays three major roles in the implementation of secure systems. We introduce them here in outline by means of some simple scenarios. In later sections of this chapter, we describe these and other protocols in greater detail, addressing some unresolved problems that are merely highlighted here.

In all of our scenarios below, we can assume that Alice, Bob and any other participants have already agreed about the encryption algorithms that they wish to use and they have implementations of them. We also assume that any secret keys or private keys that they hold can be stored securely to prevent attackers obtaining them.

Secrecy and integrity ◊ Cryptography is used to maintain the secrecy and integrity of information whenever it is exposed to potential attacks, for example during transmission across networks that are vulnerable to eavesdropping and message tampering. This use of cryptography corresponds to its traditional role in military and intelligence activities.

It exploits the fact that a message that is encrypted with a particular encryption key can only be decrypted by a recipient who knows the corresponding decryption key. Thus it maintains the secrecy of the encrypted message as long as the decryption key is not *compromised* (disclosed to non-participants in the communication) and provided that the encryption algorithm is strong enough to defeat any possible attempts to crack it. Encryption also maintains the integrity of the encrypted information, provided that some redundant information such as a checksum is included and checked.

Scenario 1. Secret communication with a shared secret key: Alice wishes to send some information secretly to Bob. Alice and Bob share a secret key K_{AB}.

1. Alice uses K_{AB} and an agreed encryption function $E(K_{AB}, M)$ to encrypt and send any number of messages $\{M_i\}_{K_{AB}}$ to Bob. (Alice can go on using K_{AB} as long as it is safe to assume that K_{AB} has not been compromised.)

2. Bob reads the encrypted messages using the corresponding decryption function $D(K_{AB}, M)$.

Bob can now read the original message M. If the message makes sense when it is decrypted by Bob, or better, if it includes some value agreed between Alice and Bob, such as a checksum of the message, then Bob knows that the message is from Alice and that it hasn't been tampered with. But there are still some problems:

Problem 1: How can Alice send a shared key K_{AB} to Bob securely?

Problem 2: How does Bob know that any $\{M_i\}$ isn't a copy of an earlier encrypted message from Alice that was captured by Mallory and replayed later? Mallory needn't have the key K_{AB} to carry out this attack – he can simply copy the bit pattern that represents the message and send it to Bob later. For example, if the message is a request to pay some money to someone, Mallory might trick Bob into paying twice.

We shall show how these problems can be resolved later in this chapter.

Authentication ◊ Cryptography is used in support of mechanisms for authenticating communication between pairs of principals. A principal who decrypts a message successfully using a particular key can assume that the message is authentic if it contains a correct checksum or (if the block-chaining mode of encryption, described in Section 7.3, is used) some other expected value. They can infer that the sender of the message possessed the corresponding encryption key and hence deduce the identity of the sender if the key is known only to two parties. Thus if keys are held in private, a successful decryption authenticates the decrypted message as coming from a particular sender.

Scenario 2. Authenticated communication with a server: Alice wishes to access files held by Bob, a file server on the local network of the organization where she works. Sara is an authentication server that is securely managed. Sara issues users with passwords and holds current secret keys for all of the principals in the system it serves (generated by applying some transformation to the user's password). For example, it knows Alice's key K_A and Bob's K_B. In our scenario we refer to a *ticket*. A ticket is an encrypted item issued by an authentication server, containing the identity of the principal to whom it is issued and a shared key that has been generated for the current communication session.

1. Alice sends an (unencrypted) message to Sara stating her identity and requesting a ticket for access to Bob.

2. Sara sends a response to Alice encrypted in K_A consisting of a ticket (to be sent to Bob with each request for file access) encrypted in K_B and a new secret key K_{AB} for use when communicating with Bob. So the response that Alice receives looks like this: $\{\{Ticket\}_{K_B}, K_{AB}\}_{K_A}$.

3. Alice decrypts the response using K_A (which she generates from her password using the same transformation; the password is not transmitted over the network and once it has been used, it is deleted from local storage to avoid compromising it). If Alice has the correct password-derived key K_A, she obtains a valid ticket for using Bob's service and a new encryption key for use in communicating with Bob. Alice can't decrypt or tamper with the ticket, because it is encrypted in K_B. If the recipient isn't Alice then they won't know Alice's password, so they won't be able to decrypt the message.

4. Alice sends the ticket to Bob together with her identity and a request R to access a file: $\{Ticket\}_{K_B}, Alice, R$.

5. The ticket, originally created by Sara, is actually: $\{K_{AB}, Alice\}_{K_B}$. Bob decrypts the ticket using his key K_B. So Bob gets the authentic identity of Alice (based on the knowledge shared between Alice and Sara of Alice's password) and a new shared secret key K_{AB} for use when interacting with Alice. (This is called a *session key* because it can safely be used by Alice and Bob for a sequence of interactions.)

This scenario is a simplified version of the authentication protocol originally developed by Roger Needham and Michael Schroeder [1978] and subsequently used in the Kerberos system developed and used at MIT [Steiner *et al.* 1988], which is described in Section 7.6.2. In our simplified description of their protocol above there is no protection against the replay of old authentication messages. This and some other weaknesses are dealt with in our description of the full Needham–Schroeder protocol, described in Section 7.6.1.

The authentication protocol we have described depends upon prior knowledge by the authentication server Sara of Alice's and Bob's keys K_A and K_B. This is feasible in a single organization where Sara runs on a physically secure computer and is managed by a trusted principal who generates initial values of the keys and transmits them to users by a separate secure channel. But it isn't appropriate for electronic commerce or other wide-area applications, where the use of a separate channel is extremely inconvenient and the requirement for a trusted third party is unrealistic. Public-key cryptography rescues us from this dilemma.

The usefulness of challenges: An important aspect of Needham and Schroeder's 1978 breakthrough was the realization that a user's password does not have to be submitted to an authentication service (and hence exposed in the network) each time it is authenticated. Instead, they introduced the concept of a cryptographic *challenge*. This can be seen in step 2 of our scenario above, where the server, Sara issues a ticket to Alice *encrypted in Alice's secret key*, K_A. This constitutes a challenge because Alice cannot make use of the ticket unless she can decrypt it, and she can only decrypt it if she can determine K_A, which is derived from Alice's password. An imposter claiming to be Alice would be defeated at this point.

Scenario 3. Authenticated communication with public keys: Assuming that Bob has generated a public/private key pair, the following dialogue enables Bob and Alice to establish a shared secret key K_{AB}:

1. Alice accesses a key distribution service to obtain *public-key certificate* giving Bob's public key. It's called a certificate because it is signed by a trusted authority – a person or organization that is widely known to be reliable. After checking the signature, she reads Bob's public key K_{Bpub} from the certificate. (We discuss the construction and use of public-key certificates in Section 7.2.3.)

2. Alice creates a new shared key K_{AB} and encrypts it using K_{Bpub} with a public-key algorithm. She sends the result to Bob, along with a name that uniquely identifies a public/private key pair (since Bob may have several of them). So Alice sends *keyname*, $\{K_{AB}\}_{K_{Bpub}}$ to Bob.

3. Bob selects the corresponding private key K_{Bpriv} from his private key store and uses it to decrypt K_{AB}. Note that Alice's message to Bob might have been corrupted or tampered with in transit. The consequence would simply be that Bob and Alice don't share the same key K_{AB}. If this is a problem, it can be circumvented by adding an agreed value or string to the message, such as Bob's and Alice's names or email addresses, which Bob can check after decrypting.

The above scenario illustrates the use of public-key cryptography to distribute a shared secret key. This technique is known as a *hybrid cryptographic protocol* and is very widely used, since it exploits useful features of both public-key and secret-key encryption algorithms.

> *Problem*:   This key exchange is vulnerable to man-in-the-middle attacks. Mallory may intercept Alice's initial request to the key distribution service for Bob's public-key certificate and send a response containing his own public key. He can then intercept all the subsequent messages. In our description above, we guard against this attack by requiring Bob's certificate to be signed by a well-known authority. To protect against this attack, Alice must ensure that Bob's public-key certificate is signed with a public key (as described below) that she has received in a totally secure manner.

Digital signatures ◊   Cryptography is used to implement a mechanism known as a *digital signature*. This emulates the role of conventional signatures, verifying to a third party that a message or a document is an unaltered copy of one produced by the signer.

Digital signature techniques are based upon an irreversible binding to the message or document of a secret known only to the signer. This can be achieved by encrypting the message – or better, a compressed form of the message called a *digest*, using a key that is known only to the signer. A digest is a fixed-length value computed by applying a *secure digest function*. A secure digest function is similar to a checksum function, but it is very unlikely to produce a similar digest value for two different messages. The resulting encrypted digest acts as a signature that accompanies the message. Public-key cryptography is generally used for this: the originator generates a signature with their private key; the signature can be decrypted by any recipient using the corresponding public key. There is an additional requirement: the verifier should be sure that the public

Figure 7.3   Alice's bank account certificate

1. *Certificate type*:	Account number
2. *Name*:	Alice
3. *Account*:	6262626
4. *Certifying authority*:	Bob's Bank
5. *Signature*:	$\{Digest(field\ 2 + field\ 3)\}_{K_{Bpriv}}$

key really is that of the principal claiming to be the signer – this is dealt with by the use of public-key certificates, described in Section 7.2.3.

Scenario 4. Digital signatures with a secure digest function: Alice wants to sign a document M so that any subsequent recipient can verify that she is the originator of it. Thus when Bob later accesses the signed document after receiving it by any route and from any source (for example, it could be sent in a message or it could be retrieved from a database) he can verify that Alice is the originator.

1. Alice computes a fixed-length digest of the document $Digest(M)$.

2. Alice encrypts the digest in her private key, appends it to M and makes the result $M, \{Digest(M)\}_{K_{Apriv}}$ available to the intended users.

3. Bob obtains the signed document, extracts M and computes $Digest(M)$.

4. Bob decrypts $\{Digest(M)\}_{K_{Apriv}}$ using Alice's public key K_{Apub} and compares the result with his calculated $Digest(M)$. If they match, the signature is valid.

7.2.3   Certificates

A digital certificate is a document containing a statement (usually short) signed by a principal. We illustrate the concept with a scenario.

Scenario 5. The use of certificates: Bob is a bank. When his customers establish contact with him they need to be sure that they are talking to Bob the bank, even if they have never contacted him before. Bob needs to authenticate his customers before he gives them access to their accounts.

For example, Alice might find it useful to obtain a certificate from her bank stating her bank account number (Figure 7.3). Alice could use this certificate when shopping to certify that she has an account with Bob's Bank. The certificate is signed in Bob's private key K_{Bpriv}. A vendor Carol can accept such a certificate for charging items to Alice's account provided she can validate the signature in field 5. To do so, Carol needs to have Bob's public key and she needs to be sure that it is authentic to guard against the possibility that Alice might sign a false certificate associating her name with someone else's account. To carry out this attack, Alice would simply generate a new key pair $K_{B'pub}, K_{B'priv}$ and use them to generate a forged certificate purporting to come from Bob's bank.

What Carol needs is a certificate stating Bob's public key, signed by a well-known and trusted authority. Let us assume that Fred represents the Bankers Federation, one of

Figure 7.4   Public-key certificate for Bob's Bank

1. *Certificate type*:	Public key
2. *Name*:	Bob's Bank
3. *Public key*:	K_{Bpub}
4. *Certifying authority*:	Fred – The Bankers Federation
5. *Signature*:	$\{Digest(field\ 2 + field\ 3)\}_{K_{Fpriv}}$

whose roles is to certify the public keys of banks. Then Fred would issue a *public-key certificate* for Bob (Figure 7.4).

Of course, this certificate depends upon the authenticity of Fred's public key K_{Fpub}, so we have a recursive problem of authenticity – Carol can only rely on this certificate if she can be sure she knows Fred's authentic public key K_{Fpub}. We can break this recursion by ensuring that Carol obtains K_{Fpub} by some means in which she can have confidence – she might be handed it by a representative of Fred or she might receive a signed copy of it from someone she knows and trusts who says they got it directly from Fred. Our example illustrates a certification chain – one with two links in this case.

We have already alluded to one of the problems arising with certificates – the difficulty of choosing a trusted authority from which a chain of authentications can start. Trust is seldom absolute, so the choice of an authority must depend upon the purpose to which the certificate is to be put. Other problems arise over the risk of private keys being compromised (disclosed) and the permissible length of a certification chain – the longer the chain, the greater the risk of a weak link.

Provided that care is taken to address these issues, chains of certificates are an important cornerstone for electronic commerce and other kinds of real-world transaction. They help to address the problem of scale: there are six billion people in the world, so how can we construct an electronic environment in which we can establish the credentials of any of them?

Certificates can be used to establish the authenticity of many types of statement. For example, the members of a group or association might wish to maintain am email list that is open only to members of the group. A good way to do this would be for the membership manager (Bob) to issue a membership certificate $(S,Bob,\{Digest(S)\}_{K_{Bpriv}})$ to each member, where S is a statement of the form *Alice is a member of the Friendly Society* and K_{Bpriv} is Bob's private key. A member applying to join the Friendly Society email list would have to supply a copy of this certificate to the list management system, which checks the certificate before allowing Alice to join the list.

To make certificates useful, two things are needed:

- a standard format and representation for them so that certificate issuers and certificate users can successfully construct and interpret them;

- agreement on the manner in which chains of certificates are constructed, and in particular the notion of a trusted authority.

We shall return to these requirements in Section 7.4.4.

There is sometimes a need to revoke a certificate – for example, Alice might discontinue her membership of the Friendly Society, but she and others would probably continue to hold stored copies of her membership certificate. It would be expensive or impossible to track down and delete all such certificates, and it is not easy to invalidate a certificate – it would be necessary to notify all possible recipients of a revoked certificate. The usual solution to this problem is to include an expiry date in the certificate. Anyone receiving an expired certificate should reject it, and the subject of the certificate must request its renewal. If a more rapid revocation is required, then one of the more cumbersome mechanisms mentioned above must be resorted to.

7.2.4   Access control

Here we outline the concepts on which the control of access to resources is based in distributed systems and the techniques by which it is implemented. The conceptual basis for protection and access control was very clearly set out in a classic paper by Lampson [1971], and details of non-distributed implementations can be found in many books on operating systems [Stallings 1998b].

Historically, the protection of resources in distributed systems has been largely service-specific. Servers receive request messages of the form *<op, principal, resource>*, where *op* is the requested operation, *principal* is an identity or a set of credentials for the principal making the request and *resource* identifies the resource to which the operation is to be applied. The server must first authenticate the request message and the principal's credentials and then apply access control, refusing any request for which the requesting principal does not have the necessary access rights to perform the requested operation on the specified resource.

In object-oriented distributed systems there may be many types of object to which access control must be applied, and the decisions are often application-specific. For example, Alice may be allowed only one cash withdrawal from her bank account per day, while Bob is allowed three. Access control decisions are usually left to the application-level code, but generic support is provided for much of the machinery that supports the decisions. This includes the authentication of principals, the signing and authentication of requests, and the management of credentials and access rights data.

Protection domains ◊ A protection domain is an execution environment shared by a collection of processes: it contains a set of *<resource, rights>* pairs, listing the resources that can be accessed by all processes executing within the domain and specifying the operations permitted on each resource. A protection domain is usually associated with a given principal – when a user logs in, her identity is authenticated and a protection domain is created for the processes that she will run. Conceptually, the domain includes all of the access rights that the principal possesses, including any rights that she acquires through membership of various groups. For example, in UNIX, the protection domain of a process is determined by the user and group identifiers attached to the process at login time. Rights are specified in terms of allowed operations. For example, a file might be readable and writable by one process and only readable by another.

A protection domain is only an abstraction. Two alternative implementations are commonly used in distributed systems. These are *capabilities* and *access control lists*.

Capabilities: A set of capabilities is held by each process according to the domain in which it is located. A capability is a binary value that act as an access key allowing the holder access to certain operations on a specified resource. For use in distributed systems, where capabilities must be unforgeable, they take a form such as:

Resource identifier	A unique Identifier for the target resource
Operations	A list of the operations permitted on the resource
Authentication code	A digital signature making the capability unforgeable

Services only supply capabilities to clients when they have authenticated them as belonging to the claimed protection domain. The list of operations in the capability is a subset of the operations defined for the target resource and is often encoded as a bit map. Different capabilities are used for different combinations of access rights to the same resource.

When capabilities are used, client requests are of the form *<op, userid, capability>*. That is, they include a capability for the resource to be accessed instead of a simple identifier, giving the server immediate proof that the client is authorized to access the resource identified by the capability with the operations specified by the capability. An access control check on a request that is accompanied by a capability involves only the validation of the capability and a check that the requested operation is in the set permitted by the capability. This feature is the major advantage of capabilities – they constitute a self-contained access key, just as a physical key to a door lock is an access key to the building that the lock protects.

Capabilities share two drawbacks of keys to a physical lock:

Key theft: Anyone who holds the key to a building can use it to gain access, whether or not they are an authorized holder of the key – they may have stolen the key or obtained it in some fraudulent manner.

The revocation problem: The entitlement to hold a key changes with time. For example, the holder may cease to be an employee of the owner of the building, but they might retain the key, or a copy of it, and use it in an unauthorized manner.

The only available solutions to these problems for physical keys are (1) to put the illicit key holder in jail – not always feasible on a timescale that will prevent them doing damage, or (2) to change the lock and reissue keys to all key holders – a clumsy and expensive operation.

The analogous problems for capabilities are clear:

• Capabilities may, through carelessness or as a result of an eavesdropping attack, fall into the hands of principals other than those to whom they were issued. If this happens, servers are powerless to prevent them being used illicitly.

• It is difficult to cancel capabilities. The status of the holder may change and their access rights should change accordingly, but they can still use the capability.

Solutions to both of these problems, based on the inclusion of information identifying the holder and on timeouts plus lists of revoked capabilities, respectively, have been proposed and developed [Gong 1989, Hayton *et al.* 1998]. Although they add complexity to an otherwise simple concept, capabilities remain an important technique, for example, they can be used in conjunction with access control lists to optimize access control on repeated access to the same resource and they provide the neatest mechanism for the implementation of delegation (see Section 7.2.5).

It is interesting to note the similarity between capabilities and certificates. Consider Alice's certificate of ownership of her bank account introduced in Section 7.2.3. It differs from capabilities as described here only in that there is no list of permitted operations and that the issuer is identified. Certificates and capabilities may be interchangeable concepts in some circumstances. Alice's certificate might be regarded as an access key to perform all the operations on Alice's bank account permitted to account holders, provided that the requester can be proven to be Alice.

Access control lists: A list is stored with each resource, with an entry of the form *<domain, operations>* for each domain that has access to the resource and giving the operations permitted to the domain. A domain may be specified by an identifier for a principal or it may be an expression that can be used to determine a principal's membership of the domain. For example, *the owner of this file* is an expression that can be evaluated by comparing the requesting principal's identity with the owner's identity stored with a file.

This is the scheme adopted in most file systems, including UNIX and Windows NT, where a set of access permission bits is associated with each file, and the domains to which the permissions are granted are defined by reference to the ownership information stored with each file.

Requests to servers are of the form *<op, principal, resource>*. For each request, the server authenticates the principal and checks to see that the requested operation is included in the principal's entry in the access control list of the relevant resource.

Implementation ◊ Digital signatures, credentials and public-key certificates provide the cryptographic basis for secure access control. Secure channels offer performance benefits, enabling multiple requests to be handled without a need for repeated checking of principals and credentials [Wobber *et al.* 1994].

Both CORBA and Java offer Security APIs. Support for access control is one of their major purposes. Java provides support for distributed objects to manage their own access control with Principal, Signer and ACL classes and default methods for authentication and support for certificates, signature validation and access control checks. Secret-key and public-key cryptography are also supported. Farley [1998] provides a good introduction to these features of Java. The protection of Java programs that include mobile code is based upon the protection domain concept – local code and downloaded code are provided with different protection domains in which to execute. There can be a protection domain for each download source, with access rights for different sets of local resources depending upon the level of trust that is placed in the downloaded code.

Corba offers a Security Service specification [Blakley 1999, OMG 2002b] with a model for ORBs to provide secure communication, authentication, access control with credentials, ACLs and auditing; these are described further in Section 17.3.4.

7.2.5 Credentials

Credentials are a set of evidence provided by a principal when requesting access to a resource. In the simplest case, a certificate from a relevant authority stating the principal's identity is sufficient, and this would be used to check the principal's permissions in an access control list (see Section 7.2.4). This is often all that is required or provided, but the concept can be generalized to deal with many more subtle requirements.

It is not convenient to require users to interact with the system and authenticate themselves each time their authority is required to perform an operation on a protected resource. Instead, the notion that a credential *speaks for* a principal is introduced. Thus a user's public-key certificate speaks for that user – any process receiving a request authenticated with the user's private key can assume that the request was issued by that user.

The *speaks for* idea can be carried much further. For example, in a cooperative task, it might be required that certain sensitive actions should only be performed with the authority of two members of the team; in that case, the principal requesting the action would submit its own identifying credential and a backing credential from another member of the team, together with an indication that they are to be taken together when checking the credentials.

Similarly, to vote in an election, a vote request would be accompanied by an elector certificate as well as an identifying certificate. A delegation certificate allows a principal to act on behalf of another, and so on. In general, an access control check involves the evaluation of a logical formula combining the certificates supplied. Lampson *et al.* [1992] have developed a comprehensive logic of authentication for use in evaluating the *speaks for* authority carried by a set of credentials. Wobber *et al.* [1994] describe a system that supports this very general approach. Further work on useful forms of credential for use in real-world cooperative tasks can be found in [Rowley 1998].

Role-based credentials seem particularly useful in the design of practical access control schemes [Sandhu *et al.* 1996]. Sets of role-based credentials are defined for organizations or for cooperative tasks, and application-level access rights are constructed with reference to them. Roles can then be assigned to specific principals by the generation of a role certificate associating a principal with a named role in a specific task or organization [Coulouris *et al.* 1998].

Delegation ◊ A particularly useful form of credential is one that entitles a principal, or a process acting for a principal, to perform an action with the authority of another principal. A need for delegation can arise in any situation where a service needs to access a protected resource in order to complete an action on behalf of its client. Consider the example of a print server that accepts requests to print files. It would be wasteful of resources to copy the file, so the name of the file is passed to the print server and it is accessed by the print server on behalf of the user making the request. If the file is read-protected, this does not work unless the print server can acquire temporary rights to read the file. Delegation is a mechanism designed to solve problems such as this.

Delegation can be achieved using a delegation certificate or a capability. The certificate is signed by the requesting principal and it authorizes another principal (the print server in our example) to access a named resource (the file to be printed). In systems that support them, capabilities can achieve the same result without the need to identify the principals – a capability to access a resource can be passed in a request to a server. The capability is an unforgeable, encoded set of rights to access the resource.

When rights are delegated, it is common to restrict them to a subset of the rights held by the issuing principal, so that the delegated principal cannot misuse them. In our example, the certificate could be time-limited to reduce the risk that the print server's code is subsequently compromised and the file disclosed to third parties. The CORBA Security Service includes a mechanism for the delegation of rights based on certificates, with support for the restriction of the rights carried.

7.2.6   Firewalls

Firewalls were introduced and described in Section 3.4.8. They protect intranets, performing filtering actions on incoming and outgoing communications. Here we discuss their advantages and drawbacks as security mechanisms.

In an ideal world, communication would always be between mutually trusting processes and secure channels would always be used. There are many reasons why this ideal is not attainable, some fixable, but others inherent in the open nature of distributed systems or resulting from the errors that are present in most software. The ease with which request messages can be sent to any server, anywhere, and the fact that many servers are not designed to withstand malicious attacks from hackers or accidental errors, makes it easy for information that is intended to be confidential to leak out of the owning organization's servers. Undesirable items can also penetrate an organization's network, allowing worm programs and viruses to enter its computers. See [web.mit.edu II] for a further critique of firewalls.

Firewalls produce a local communication environment in which all external communication is intercepted. Messages are forwarded to the intended local recipient only for communications that are explicitly authorized.

Access to internal networks may be controlled by firewalls, but access to public services on the Internet is unrestricted because their purpose is to offer services to a wide range of users. The use of firewalls offers no protection against attacks from inside an organization, and it is crude in its control of external access. There is a need for finer-grained security mechanisms, enabling individual users to share information with selected others without compromising privacy and integrity. Abadi *et al.* [1998] describe an approach to the provision of access to private web data for external users based on a *web tunnel* mechanism that can be integrated with a firewall. It offers access for trusted and authenticated users to internal web servers via a secure proxy based on the HTTPS (HTTP over TLS) protocol.

Firewalls are not particularly effective against denial-of-service attacks such as the one based on IP spoofing that was outlined in Section 3.4.2. The problem is that the flood of messages generated by such attacks overwhelms any single point of defence such as a firewall. Any remedy for incoming floods of messages must be applied well upstream of the target. Remedies based on the use of quality-of-service mechanisms to restrict the flow of messages from the network to a level that the target can handle seem the most promising.

7.3   Cryptographic algorithms

A message is encrypted by the sender applying some rule to transform the *plaintext* message (any sequence of bits) to a *ciphertext* (a different sequence of bits). The recipient must know the inverse rule in order to transform the ciphertext into the original plaintext. Other principals are unable to decipher the message unless they know the inverse rule. The encryption transformation is defined with two parts, a *function E* and a *key K*. The resulting encrypted message is written $\{M\}_K$.

$$E(K, M) = \{M\}_K$$

The encryption function E defines an algorithm that transforms data items in plaintext into encrypted data items by combining them with the key and transposing them in a manner that is heavily dependent on the value of the key. We can think of an encryption algorithm as the specification of a large family of functions from which a particular member is selected by any given key. Decryption is carried out using an inverse function D, which also takes a key as a parameter. For secret-key encryption, the key used for decryption is the same as that used for encryption:

$$D(K, E(K, M)) = M$$

Because of its symmetrical use of keys, secret-key cryptography is often referred to as *symmetric cryptography*, whereas public-key cryptography is referred to as *asymmetric* because the keys used for encryption and decryption are different, as we shall see below. In the next section, we shall describe several widely used encryption functions of both types.

Symmetric algorithms ◊ If we remove the key parameter from consideration by defining $F_K([M]) = E(K, M)$ then it is a property of strong encryption functions that $F_K([M])$ is relatively easy to compute, whereas the inverse, $F_K^{-1}([M])$ is so hard to compute that it is not feasible. Such functions are known as one-way functions. The effectiveness of any method for encrypting information depends upon the use of an encryption function F_K that has this one-way property. It is this that protects against attacks designed to discover M given $\{M\}_K$.

For well-designed symmetric algorithms such as those described in the next section, their strength against attempts to discover K given a plaintext M and the corresponding ciphertext $\{M\}_K$ depends on the size of K. This is because the most effective general form of attack is the crudest, known as a *brute-force attack*. The brute-force approach is to run through all possible values of K, computing $E(K, M)$ until the result matches the value of $\{M\}_K$ that is already known. If K has N bits then such an attack requires 2^{N-1} iterations on average, and a maximum of 2^N iterations, to find K. Hence the time to crack K is exponential in the number of bits in K.

Asymmetric algorithms ◊ When a public/private key pair is used, one-way functions are exploited in another way. The feasibility of a public-key scheme was first proposed by Diffie and Hellman [1976] as a cryptographic method that eliminates the need for trust between the communicating parties. The basis for all public-key schemes is the existence of *trap-door functions*. A trap-door function is a one-way function with a secret exit – it is easy to compute in one direction but infeasible to compute its inverse

Figure 7.5   Cipher block chaining

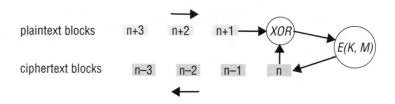

unless a secret is known. It was the possibility of finding such functions and using them in practical cryptography that Diffie and Hellman first suggested. Since then, several practical public-key schemes have been proposed and developed. They all depend upon the use of functions of large numbers as trap-door functions.

The pair of keys needed for asymmetric algorithms is derived from a common root. For the RSA algorithm, described in Section 7.3.2, the root is an arbitrarily chosen pair of very large prime numbers. The derivation of the pair of keys from the root is a one-way function. In the case of the RSA algorithm, the large primes are multiplied together – a computation that takes only a few seconds, even for the very large primes used. The resulting product, N, is of course much larger than the multiplicands. This use of multiplication is a one-way function in the sense that it is computationally infeasible to derive the original multiplicands from the product – that is, to factorize the product.

One of the pair of keys is used for encryption. For RSA, the encryption function obscures the plaintext by treating each block of bits as a binary number and raising it to the power of the key, modulo N. The resulting number is the corresponding ciphertext block.

The size of N and at least one of the pair of keys is much larger than the safe key size for symmetric keys to ensure that N is not factorizable. For this reason, the potential for brute-force attacks on RSA is small; its resistance to attacks depends on the infeasibility of factorizing N. We shall discuss safe sizes for N in Section 7.3.2.

Block ciphers ◊ Most encryption algorithms operate on fixed-size blocks of data; 64 bits is a popular size for the blocks. A message is subdivided into blocks, the last block is padded to the standard length if necessary and each block is encrypted independently. The first block is available for transmission as soon as it has been encrypted.

For a simple block cipher, the value of each block of ciphertext does not depend upon the preceding blocks. This constitutes a weakness, since an attacker can recognize repeated patterns and infer their relationship to the plaintext. Nor is the integrity of messages guaranteed unless a checksum or secure digest mechanism is used. Most block cipher algorithms employ cipher block chaining (CBC) to overcome these weaknesses.

Cipher block chaining: In cipher block chaining mode, each plaintext block is combined with the preceding ciphertext block using the exclusive-or operation (XOR) before it is encrypted (Figure 7.5). On decryption, the block is decrypted and then the preceding encrypted block (which should have been stored for this purpose) is XOR-ed with it to obtain the new plaintext block. This works because the XOR operation is its own inverse – two applications of it produce the original value.

Figure 7.6   Stream cipher

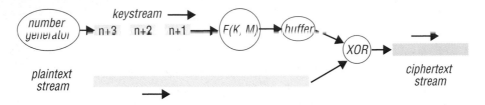

CBC is intended to prevent identical portions of plaintext encrypting to identical pieces of cipher text. But there is a weakness at the start of each sequence of blocks – if we open encrypted connections to two destinations and send the same message, the encrypted sequences of blocks will be the same, and an eavesdropper might gain some useful information from this. To prevent this, we need to insert a different piece of plaintext in front of each message. Such a text is called an *initialization vector*. A timestamp makes a good initialization vector, forcing each message to start with a different plaintext block. This, combined with CBC operation, will result in different ciphertexts, even for two identical plaintexts.

The use of CBC mode is restricted to the encryption of data that is transferred across a reliable connection. Decryption will fail if any blocks of ciphertext are lost, since the decryption process will be unable to decrypt any further blocks. It is therefore unsuitable for use in applications such as those described in Chapter15, in which some data loss can be tolerated. A stream cipher should be used in such circumstances.

Stream ciphers ◊ For some applications, such as the encryption of telephone conversations, encryption in blocks is inappropriate because the data streams are produced in real time in small chunks. Data samples can be as small as 8 bits or even a single bit, and it would be wasteful to pad each of these to 64 bits before encrypting and transmitting them. Stream ciphers are encryption algorithms that can perform encryption incrementally, converting plaintext to ciphertext one bit at a time.

This sounds difficult to achieve, but in fact it is very simple to convert a block cipher algorithm for use as a stream cipher. The trick is to construct a *keystream generator*. A keystream is an arbitrary-length sequence of bits that can be used to obscure the contents of a data stream by XOR-ing the keystream with the data stream (Figure 7.6). If the keystream is secure, then so is the resulting encrypted data stream.

The idea is analogous to a technique used in the intelligence community to foil eavesdroppers where 'white noise' is played to hide the conversation in a room while still recording the conversation. If the noisy room sound and the white noise are recorded separately, the conversation can be played back without noise by subtracting the white noise recording from the noisy room recording.

A keystream generator can be constructed by iterating a mathematical function over a range of input values to produce a continuous stream of output values. The output values are then concatenated to make plaintext blocks, and the blocks are encrypted using a key shared by the sender and the receiver. The keystream can be further disguised by applying CBC. The resulting encrypted blocks are used as the keystream. An iteration of almost any function that delivers a range of different non-integer values will do for the source material, but a random number generator is generally used with a starting value for the iteration agreed between the sender and receiver. To maintain quality of service for the data stream, the keystream blocks should be produced a little ahead of the time at which they will be used, and the process that produces them should not demand so much processing effort that the data stream is delayed.

Thus in principle, real-time data streams can be encrypted just as securely as batched data, provided that sufficient processing power is available to encrypt the keystream in real time. Of course, some devices that could benefit from real-time encryption, such as mobile phones, are not equipped with very powerful processors and in that case it may be necessary to reduce the security of the keystream algorithm.

Design of cryptographic algorithms ◊ There are many well-designed cryptographic algorithms such that $E(K, M) = \{M\}_K$ conceals the value of M and makes it practically impossible to retrieve K more quickly than by brute force. All encryption algorithms rely on the information-preserving manipulations of M using principles based on information theory [Shannon 1949]. Schneier [1996] describes Shannon's principles of *confusion* and *diffusion* to conceal the content of a ciphertext block M, combining it with a key K of sufficient size to render it proof against brute-force attacks.

Confusion: Non-destructive operations such as XOR and circular shifting are used to combine each block of plaintext with the key, producing a new bit pattern that obscures the relationship between the blocks in M and $\{M\}_K$. If the blocks are larger than a few characters this will defeat analysis based on a knowledge of character frequencies. (The WWII German Enigma machine used chained single-letter blocks, and this could be defeated by statistical analysis.)

Diffusion: There is usually repetition and redundancy in the plaintext. Diffusion dissipates the regular patterns that result by transposing portions of each plaintext block. If CBC is used, the redundancy is also distributed throughout a longer text. Stream ciphers cannot use diffusion since there are no blocks.

In the next two sections, we describe the design of several important practical algorithms. All of them have been designed in the light of the above principles and have been subject to rigorous analysis and are considered to be secure against all known attacks with a considerable margin of safety. With the exception of the TEA algorithm, which is described for illustrative purposes, the algorithms describe here are among those most widely used in applications where strong security is required. In some of them there remain some minor weaknesses or areas of concern; space does not allow us to describe all of those concerns here, and the reader is referred to Schneier [1996] for further information. We summarize and compare the security and performance of the algorithms in Section 7.5.1.

Readers who do not require an understanding of the operation of cryptographic algorithms may omit Sections 7.3.1 and 7.3.2.

7.3.1   Secret-key (symmetric) algorithms

Many cryptographic algorithms have been developed and published in recent years. Schneier [1996] describes more than 25 symmetric algorithms, many of which he identifies as secure against known attacks. Here we have room to describe only three of them. We have chosen the first, TEA, for the simplicity of its design and implementation

Figure 7.7   TEA encryption function

```
void encrypt(unsigned long k[], unsigned long text[]) {
    unsigned long y = text[0], z = text[1];                              1
    unsigned long delta = 0x9e3779b9, sum = 0; int n;                   2
    for (n= 0; n < 32; n++) {                                           3
        sum += delta;                                                   4
        y += ((z << 4) + k[0]) ^ (z+sum) ^ ((z >> 5) + k[1]);          5
        z += ((y << 4) + k[2]) ^ (y+sum) ^ ((y >> 5) + k[3]);          6
    }
    text[0] = y;  text[1] = z;                                          7
}
```

and we use it to give a concrete illustration of the nature of such algorithms. We go on to discuss the DES and IDEA algorithms in less detail. DES was a US national standard for many years, but it is now largely of historical interest because its 56-bit keys are too small to resist brute-force attack with modern hardware. IDEA uses a 128-bit key and is one of the most effective symmetric block encryption algorithm and a good all-round choice for bulk encryption.

In 1997, the US National Institute for Standards and Technology (NIST) issued an invitation for proposals for an algorithm to replace DES as a new U.S. Advanced Encryption Standard (AES). In October 2000 the winner was selected from twenty-one algorithms submitted by cryptographers from eleven countries. The winning Rijndael algorithm was chosen for its combination of strength and efficiency. Further information on it is given below.

TEA ◊ The design principles for symmetric algorithms outlined above are illustrated well in the Tiny Encryption Algorithm developed at Cambridge University [Wheeler and Needham 1994]. The encryption function, programmed in C, is given in its entirety in Figure 7.7.

The TEA algorithm uses rounds of integer addition, XOR (the ^ operator) and bitwise logical shifts (<< and >>) to achieve diffusion and confusion of the bit patterns in the plaintext. The plaintext is a 64-bit block represented as two 32-bit integers in the vector *text[]*. The key is 128 bits long, represented as four 32-bit integers.

On each of the 32 rounds, the two halves of the text are repeatedly combined with shifted portions of the key and each other in lines 5 and 6. The use of XOR and shifted portions of the text provides confusion, and the shifting and swapping of the two portions of the text provides diffusion. The non-repeating constant *delta* is combined with each portion of the text on each cycle to obscure the key in case it might be revealed by a section of text that does not vary. The decryption function is the inverse of that for encryption and is given in Figure 7.8.

This short program provides secure and reasonably fast secret-key encryption. It is somewhat faster than the DES algorithm, and the conciseness of the program lends itself to optimization and hardware implementation. The 128-bit key is secure against brute-force attacks. Studies by its authors and others have revealed only two very minor weaknesses, which they addressed in a subsequent note [Wheeler and Needham 1997].

Figure 7.8   TEA decryption function

```
void decrypt(unsigned long k[], unsigned long text[]) {
    unsigned long y = text[0], z = text[1];
    unsigned long delta = 0x9e3779b9, sum = delta << 5;  int n;

    for (n= 0; n < 32; n++) {
        z -= ((y << 4) + k[2]) ^ (y + sum) ^ ((y >> 5) + k[3]);
        y -= ((z << 4) + k[0]) ^ (z + sum) ^ ((z >> 5) + k[1]);
        sum -= delta;
    }
    text[0] = y; text[1] = z;
}
```

To illustrate its use, Figure 7.9 shows a simple procedure that uses TEA to encrypt or decrypt between a pair of previously opened files (using the C *stdio* library).

DES ◊ The Data Encryption Standard (DES) [National Bureau of Standards 1977] was developed by IBM and subsequently adopted as a US national standard for government and business applications. In this standard, the encryption function maps a 64-bit plaintext input into a 64-bit encrypted output using a 56-bit key. The algorithm has 16 key-dependent stages known as *rounds*, in which the data to be encrypted is bit-rotated by a number of bits determined by the key and three key-independent transpositions. The algorithm was time-consuming to perform in software on the computers of the 1970s and 1980s, but it was implemented in fast VLSI hardware and can easily be incorporated into network interface and other communication chips.

Figure 7.9   TEA in use

```
void tea(char mode, FILE *infile, FILE *outfile, unsigned long k[]) {
/* mode is 'e' for encrypt, 'd' for decrypt, k[] is the key.*/
    char ch, Text[8]; int i;

    while(!feof(infile)) {
        i = fread(Text, 1, 8, infile);          /* read 8 bytes from infile into Text */
        if (i <= 0) break;
        while (i < 8) { Text[i++] = ' ';}        /* pad last block with spaces */
        switch (mode) {
        case 'e':
            encrypt(k, (unsigned long*) Text); break;
        case 'd':
            decrypt(k, (unsigned long*) Text); break;
        }
        fwrite(Text, 1, 8, outfile);            /* write 8 bytes from Text to outfile */
    }
}
```

In June 1997, it was successfully cracked in a widely publicized brute-force attack. The attack was performed in the context of a competition to demonstrate the lack of security of encryption with keys shorter than 128 bits [www.rsasecurity.com I]. A consortium of Internet users ran a client application program on a number of computers (PCs and other workstations) that grew from 1000 to 14,000 [Curtin and Dolske 1998].

The client program was aimed at cracking the particular key used in a known plaintext/ciphertext sample and then using it to decrypt a secret challenge message. The clients interacted with a single server, which coordinated their work, issuing each client with ranges of key values to check and receiving progress reports from them. The typical client computer ran the client program only as a background activity and had a performance approximately equal to a 200 MHz Pentium processor. The key was cracked in about twelve weeks, after approximately 25% of the possible 2^{56} or 6×10^{16} values had been checked. In 1998 a machine was developed by the Electronic Frontier Foundation [EFF 1998] that can successfully crack DES keys in around three days.

Although it is still used in many commercial and other applications, DES in its basic form should be considered obsolete for the protection of all but low-value information. A solution that is frequently used is known as *triple-DES* (or *3DES*) [ANSI 1985, Schneier 1996]. This involves applying DES three times with two keys K_1 and K_2:

$$E_{3DES}(K_1, K_2, M) = E_{DES}(K_1, D_{DES}(K_2, E_{DES}(K_1, M)))$$

This gives a strength against brute-force attacks equivalent to a key length of 112 bits, providing adequate strength for the foreseeable future, but it has the drawback of poor performance resulting from the triple application of an algorithm that is already slow by modern standards.

IDEA ◊ The International Data Encryption Algorithm was developed in the early 1990s [Lai and Massey 1990, Lai 1992] as a successor to DES. Like TEA, it uses a 128-bit key to encrypt 64-bit blocks. Its algorithm is based on the algebra of groups and has eight rounds of XOR, addition modulo 2^{16} and multiplication. For both DES and IDEA, the same function is used for encryption and decryption: a useful property for algorithms that are to be implemented in hardware.

The strength of IDEA has been extensively analysed, and no significant weaknesses have been found. It performs encryption and decryption at approximately three times the speed of DES.

RC4 ◊ RC4 is a stream cipher developed by Ronald Rivest [Rivest 1992a]. Keys can be of any length up to 256 bytes. RC4 is easy to implement [Schneier 1996, pp. 397–8] and performs encryption and decryption about ten times as fast as DES. It was therefore widely adopted in products including IEEE 802.11 WiFi networks, but a weakness was subsequently discovered by Fluhrer *et al.* [2001] that enabled attackers to crack some keys and this led to a redesign of 802.11 security (see Section 7.6.4 for further details).

AES ◊ The Rijndael algorithm selected to become the Advanced Encryption Standard algorithm by the U.S. NIST was developed by Joan Daemen and Vincent Rijmen [Daemen and Rijmen 2000, 2002]. The cipher has a variable block length and key length with specifications for keys with a length of 128, 192, or 256 bits to encrypt blocks with a length of 128, 192 or 256 bits. Both block length and key length can be extended by multiples of 32 bits. The number of rounds in the algorithm varies from 9 to 13 depending on the key and block sizes. Rijndael can be implemented efficiently on a wide range of processors and in hardware.

7.3.2   Public-key (asymmetric) algorithms

Only a few practical public-key schemes have been developed to date. They depend upon the use of trap-door functions of large numbers to produce the keys. The keys K_e and K_d are a pair of very large numbers, and the encryption function performs an operation, such as exponentiation on M, using one of them. Decryption is a similar function using the other key. If the exponentiation uses modular arithmetic, it can be shown that the result is the same as the original value of M; that is:

$$D(K_d, E(K_e, M)) = M$$

A principal wishing to participate in secure communication with others makes a pair of keys K_e and K_d and keeps the decryption key K_d a secret. The encryption key K_e can be made known publicly for use by anyone who wants to communicate. The encryption key K_e can be seen as a part of the one-way encryption function E, and the decryption key K_d is the piece of secret knowledge that enables principal p to reverse the encryption. Any holder of K_e (which is widely available) can encrypt messages $\{M\}_{K_e}$, but only the principal who has the secret K_d can operate the trap-door.

The use of functions of large numbers leads to large processing costs in computing the functions E and D. We shall see later that this is a problem that has to be addressed by the use of public keys only in the initial stages of secure communication sessions. The RSA algorithm is certainly the most widely known public-key algorithm and we describe it in some detail here. Another class of algorithms is based on functions derived from the behaviour of elliptic curves in a plane. These algorithms offer the possibility of less costly encryption and decryption functions with the same level of security, but their practical application is less advanced and we shall deal with them only briefly.

RSA ◊ The Rivest, Shamir and Adelman (RSA) design for a public-key cipher [Rivest *et al.* 1978] is based on the use of the product of two very large prime numbers (greater than 10^{100}), relying on the fact that the determination of the prime factors of such large numbers is so computationally difficult as to be effectively impossible to compute.

Despite extensive investigations no flaws have been found in it, and it is now very widely used. An outline of the method follows. To find a key pair e, d:

1. Choose two large prime numbers, P and Q (each greater than 10^{100}), and form
   $N = P \times Q$
   $Z = (P{-}1) \times (Q{-}1)$

2. For d choose any number that is relatively prime with Z (that is, such that d has no common factors with Z).

We illustrate the computations involved using small integer values for P and Q:
   $P = 13, Q = 17 \rightarrow N = 221, Z = 192$
   $d = 5$

3. To find e solve the equation:

$e \times d = 1\ mod\ Z$

That is, $e \times d$ is the smallest element divisible by d in the series $Z+1$, $2Z+1$, $3Z+1$, ...

> $e \times d = 1\ mod\ 192\ = 1, 193, 385, ...$
> 385 is divisible by d
> $e = 385/5 = 77$

To encrypt text using the RSA method, the plaintext is divided into equal blocks of length k bits where $2^k < N$ (that is, such that the numerical value of a block is always less than N; in practical applications, k is usually in the range 512 to 1024).

> $k = 7$, since $2^7 = 128$

The function for encrypting a single block of plaintext M is:

$E'(e,N,M) = M^e\ mod\ N$

> for a message M, the ciphertext is $M^{77}\ mod\ 221$

The function for decrypting a block of encrypted text c to produce the original plaintext block is:

$D'(d,N,c) = c^d\ mod\ N$

Rivest, Shamir and Adelman proved that E' and D' are mutual inverses (that is, $E'(D'(x)) = D'(E'(x)) = x$) for all values of P in the range $0 \le P \le N$.

The two parameters e,N can be regarded as a key for the encryption function, and similarly d,N represent a key for the decryption function. So we can write $K_e = <e,N>$ and $K_d = <d,N>$, and we get the encryption functions $E(K_e, M) = \{M\}_K$ (the notation here indicating that the encrypted message can be decrypted only by the holder of the *private* key K_d) and $D(K_d, \{M\}_K) = M$.

It is worth noting one potential weakness of all public-key algorithms – because the public key is available to attackers, they can easily generate encrypted messages. Thus they can attempt to decrypt an unknown message by exhaustively encrypting arbitrary bit sequences until a match with the target message is achieved. This attack, which is known as a *chosen plaintext attack*, is defeated by ensuring that all messages are longer than the key length, so that this form of brute-force attack is less feasible than a direct attack on the key.

An intending recipient of secret information must publish or otherwise distribute the pair $<e,N>$ while keeping d secret. The publication of $<e,N>$ does not compromise the secrecy of d, because any attempt to determine d requires knowledge of the original prime numbers P and Q, and these can only be obtained by the factorization of N. Factoring of large numbers (we recall that P and Q were chosen to be $> 10^{100}$, so $N > 10^{200}$) is extremely time-consuming, even on very high-performance computers. In 1978, Rivest *et al.* concluded that factoring a number as large as 10^{200} would take more than four billion years with the best known algorithm on a computer that performs one million instructions per second. A similar calculation for today's computers would reduce this time to around a million years,

The RSA Corporation has issued a series of challenges to factor numbers of more than 100 decimal digits [www.rsasecurity.com II]. At the time of writing, numbers of up to 174 decimal digits (576 binary digits) have been successfully factored, so the use of the RSA algorithm with 512-bit keys is clearly unacceptably weak for many purposes. The RSA Corporation (holders of the patents in the RSA algorithm) recommends a key length of at least 768 bits, or about 230 decimal digits, for long-term (~ 20 years) security. Keys as large as 2048 bits are used in some applications.

The above strength calculations assume that the currently known factoring algorithms are the best available. RSA and other forms of asymmetric cryptography that use prime number multiplication as their one-way function would be vulnerable if and when a faster factorization algorithm is discovered.

Elliptic curve algorithms ◊ A method for generating public/private key pairs based on the properties of elliptic curves has been developed and tested. Full details can be found in the book by Menezes devoted to the subject [Menezes 1993]. The keys are derived from a different branch of mathematics, and unlike RSA their security does not depend upon the difficulty of factoring large numbers. Shorter keys are secure, and the processing requirements for encryption and decryption are lower than those for RSA. Elliptic curve encryption algorithms are likely to be adopted more widely in the future, especially in systems such as those incorporating mobile devices, which have limited processing resources. The relevant mathematics involves some quite complex properties of elliptic curves and is beyond the scope of this book.

7.3.3 Hybrid cryptographic protocols

Public-key cryptography is convenient for electronic commerce because there is no need for a secure key-distribution mechanism. (There is a need to authenticate public keys but this is much less onerous, requiring only a public-key certificate to be sent with the key.) But the processing costs of public-key cryptography are too high for the encryption of even the medium-sized messages normally encountered in electronic commerce. The solution adopted in most large-scale distributed systems is to use a hybrid encryption scheme in which public-key cryptography is used to authenticate the parties and to encrypt an exchange of secret keys, which are used for all subsequent communication. We describe the implementation of a hybrid protocol in the TLS case study in Section 7.6.3.

7.4 Digital signatures

Strong digital signatures are an essential requirement for secure systems. They are needed in order to certify certain pieces of information, for example to provide trustworthy statements binding users' identities to their public keys or binding some access rights or roles to users' identities.

The need for signatures in many kinds of business and personal transaction is beyond dispute. Handwritten signatures have been used as a means of verifying documents for as long as documents have existed. Handwritten signatures are used to meet the needs of document recipients to verify that the document is:

Authentic: It convinces the recipient that the signer deliberately signed the document and it has not been altered by anyone else.

Unforgeable: It provides proof that the signer, and no one else, deliberately signed the document. The signature cannot be copied and placed on another document.

Non-repudiable: The signer cannot credibly deny that the document was signed by them.

In reality, none of these desirable properties of signing is entirely achieved by conventional signatures – forgeries and copies are hard to detect, documents can be altered after signing and signers are sometimes deceived into signing a document involuntarily or unwittingly – but we are willing to live with their imperfection because of the difficulty of cheating and the risk of detection. Like handwritten signatures, digital signatures depend upon the binding of a unique and secret attribute of the signer to a document. In the case of handwritten signatures, the secret is the handwriting pattern of the signer.

The properties of digital documents held in stored files or messages are completely different from those of paper documents. Digital documents are trivially easy to generate, copy and alter. Simply appending the identity of the originator, whether as a text string, a photograph or a handwritten image, has no value for verification purposes.

What is needed is a means to irrevocably bind a signer's identity to the entire sequence of bits representing a document. This should meet the first requirement above, for authenticity. As with handwritten signatures, the date of a document cannot be guaranteed by a signature. The recipient of a signed document knows only that the document was signed before they received it.

Regarding non-repudiation, there is a problem that does not arise with handwritten signatures. What if the signer deliberately reveals their private key and subsequently denies having signed, saying that there are others who could have done so, since the key was not private? Some protocols have been developed to address this problem under the heading of *undeniable digital signatures* [Schneier 1996], but they add considerably to the complexity.

A document with a digital signature can be considerably more resistant to forgery than a handwritten one. But the word 'original' has little meaning with reference to digital documents. As we shall see in our discussion of the needs of electronic commerce, digital signatures alone cannot for example prevent double-spending of electronic cash – other measures are needed to prevent that. We shall now describe two techniques for signing documents digitally, binding a principal's identity to the document. Both depend upon the use of cryptography.

Digital signing ◊ An electronic document or message M can be signed by a principal A by encrypting a copy of M with a key K_A and attaching it to a plaintext copy of M and A's identifier. The signed document then consists of: $M, A, [M]_{K_A}$. The signature can be

Figure 7.10   Digital signatures with public keys

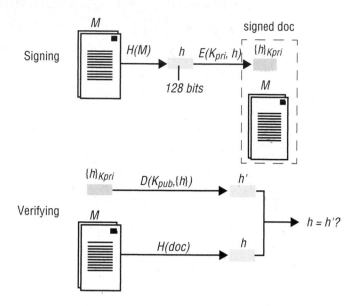

verified by a principal that subsequently receives the document to check that it was originated by *A* and that its contents, *M*, have not subsequently been altered.

If a secret key is used to encrypt the document, only principals that share the secret can verify the signature. But if public-key cryptography is used, then the signer uses her private key and anyone who has the corresponding public key can verify the signature. This is a better analogue for conventional signatures and meets a wider range of user needs. The verification of signatures proceeds differently depending on whether secret-key or public-key cryptography is used to produce the signature. We describe the two cases in Sections 7.4.1 and 7.4.2.

Digest functions ◊ Digest functions are also called *secure hash functions* and denoted *H(M)*. They must be carefully designed to ensure that *H(M)* is different from *H(M′)* for all likely pairs of messages *M* and *M′*. If there are any pairs of different messages *M* and *M′* such that *H(M) = H(M′)*, then a duplicitous principal could send a signed copy of *M*, but when confronted with it claim that *M′* was originally sent, and that it must have been altered in transit. We discuss some secure hash functions in Section 7.4.3.

7.4.1   Digital signatures with public keys

Public-key cryptography is particularly well adapted for the generation of digital signatures because it is relatively simple and does not require any communication between the recipient of a signed document and the signer or any third party.

The method for A to sign a message *M* and B to verify it is as follows (and is illustrated graphically in Figure 7.10):

1. A generates a key pair K_{pub} and K_{priv} and publishes the public key K_{pub} by placing it in a well-known location.

2. A computes the digest of M, $H(M)$ using an agreed secure hash function H and encrypts it using the private key K_{priv} to produce the signature $S = \{H(M)\}_{K_{priv}}$.

3. A sends the signed message $[M]_K = M,S$ to B.

4. B decrypts S using K_{pub} and computes the digest of M, $H(M)$. If they match, the signature is valid.

The RSA algorithm is quite suitable for use in constructing digital signatures. Note that the *private* key of the signer is used to encrypt the signature, in contrast to the use of the recipient's *public* key for encryption when the aim is to transmit information in secrecy. The explanation for this difference is straightforward – a signature must be created using a secret known only to the signer and it should be accessible to all for verification.

7.4.2   Digital signatures with secret keys – MACs

There is no technical reason why a secret-key encryption algorithm should not be used to encrypt a digital signature, but in order to verify such signatures the key must be disclosed, and this causes some problems:

- The signer must arrange for the verifier to receive the secret key used for signing securely.

- It may be necessary to verify a signature in several contexts and at different times – at the time of signing the signer may not know the identities of the verifiers. To resolve this, verification could be delegated to a trusted third party who holds secret keys for all signers, but this adds complexity to the security model and requires secure communication with the trusted third party.

- The disclosure of a secret key used for signing is undesirable because it weakens the security of signatures made with that key – a signature could be forged by a holder of the key who is not the owner of it.

For all these reasons, the public-key method for generating and verifying signatures offers the most convenient solution in most situations.

An exception arises when a secure channel is used to transmit unencrypted messages but there is a need to verify the authenticity of the messages. Since a secure channel provides secure communication between a pair of processes, a shared secret key can be established using the hybrid method outlined in Section 7.3.3 and used to produce low-cost signatures. These signatures are called *message authentication codes (MAC)* to reflect their more limited purpose – they authenticate communication between pairs of principals based on a shared secret.

A low-cost signing technique based on shared secret keys that has adequate security for many purposes is illustrated in Figure 7.11 and outlined below. The method depends upon the existence of a secure channel through which the shared key can be distributed:

1. A generates a random key K for signing and distributes it using secure channels to one or more principals who will need to authenticate messages received from A. The principals are *trusted* not to disclose the shared key.

Figure 7.11   Low-cost signatures with a shared secret key

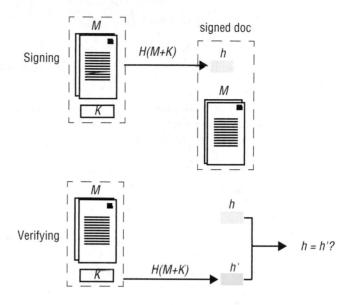

2. For any document M that A wishes to sign, A concatenates M with K, computes the digest of the result: $h = H(M + K)$ and sends the signed document $[M]_K = M, h$ to anyone wishing to verify the signature. (The digest h is a MAC). K will not be compromised by the disclosure of h, since the hash function has totally obscured its value.

3. The receiver, B, concatenates the secret key K with the received document M and computes the digest $h' = H(M + K)$. The signature is verified if $h = h'$.

Although this method suffers from the disadvantages listed above, it has a performance advantage because it involves no encryption. (Secure hashing is typically about 3–10 times faster than symmetric encryption, see Section 7.5.1.) The TLS secure channel protocol described in Section 7.6.3 supports the use of a wide variety of MACs, including the scheme described here. The method is also used in the Millicent electronic cash protocol described at www.cdk4.net/security, where it is important to keep the processing cost low for low-value transactions.

7.4.3   Secure digest functions

There are many ways to produce a fixed-length bit pattern that characterizes an arbitrary-length message or document. Perhaps the simplest is to use the XOR operation iteratively to combine fixed-length pieces of the source document. Such a function is often used in communication protocols to produce a short fixed-length hash to characterize a message for error-detection purposes, but it is inadequate as the basis for a digital signature scheme. A secure digest function $h = H(M)$ should have the following properties:

1. Given M, it is easy to compute h.

2. Given h, it is hard to compute M.

3. Given M, it is hard to find another message M', such that $H(M) = H(M')$.

Such functions are also called *one-way hash functions*. The reason for this name is self-evident based on the first two properties. Property 3 demands an additional feature: even though we know that the result of a hash function cannot be unique (because the digest is an information-reducing transformation), we need to be sure that an attacker, given a message M that produces a hash h, cannot discover another message M' that also produces h. If an attacker *could* do this, then they could forge a signed document M' without knowledge of the signing key by copying the signature from the signed document M and appending it to M'.

Admittedly, the set of messages that hash to the same value is restricted and the attacker would have difficulty in producing a meaningful forgery, but with patience it could be done, so it must be guarded against. The feasibility of doing so is considerably enhanced in the case of a so-called *birthday attack*:

1. Alice prepares two versions M and M' of a contract for Bob. M is favourable to Bob and M' is not.

2. Alice makes several subtly different versions of both M and M' that are visually indistinguishable from each other by methods such as adding spaces at the ends of lines. She compares the hashes of all the Ms with all the M's. If she finds two that are the same, she can proceed to the next step; if not, she goes on producing visually indistinguishable versions of the two documents until she gets a match.

3. When she has a pair of documents M and M' that hash to the same value, she gives the favourable document M to Bob for him to sign with a digital signature using his private key. When he returns it, she substitutes the matching unfavourable version M', retaining the signature from M.

If our hash values are 64 bits long, we require only 2^{32} versions of M and M' on average. This is too small for comfort. We need to make our hash values at least 128 bits long to guard against this attack.

The attack relies on a statistical paradox known as the *birthday paradox* – the probability of finding a matching pair in a given set is far greater than for finding a match for a given individual. Stallings [1999] gives the statistical derivation for the probability that there will be two people with the same birthday in a set of n people. The result is that for a set of only 23 people the chances are even, whereas we require a set of 253 people for an even chance that there will be one with a birthday on a given day.

To satisfy the properties listed above, a secure digest function needs to be carefully designed. The bit-level operations used and their sequencing are similar to those found in symmetric cryptography, but in this case the operations need not be information-preserving, since the function is definitely not intended to be reversible. So a secure digest function can make use of the full range of arithmetic and bit-wise logical operations. The length of the source text is usually included in the digested data.

Figure 7.12   X509 Certificate format

Subject	Distinguished Name, Public Key
Issuer	Distinguished Name, Signature
Period of validity	Not Before Date, Not After Date
Administrative information	Version, Serial Number
Extended Information	

Two widely used digest functions for practical applications are the MD5 algorithm (so called because it is the fifth in a sequence of message digest algorithms developed by Ron Rivest) and the SHA-1 (Secure Hash Algorithm) adopted for standardization by the US National Institute for Standards and Technology (NIST). Both have been carefully tested and analysed and can be considered adequately secure for the foreseeable future, while their implementations are reasonably efficient. We describe them briefly here. Schneier [1996] and Mitchell *et al.* [1992] survey digital signature techniques and message digest functions in depth.

MD5 ◊ The MD5 algorithm [Rivest 1992] uses four rounds, each applying one of four non-linear functions to each of sixteen 32-bit segments of a 512-bit block of source text. The result is a 128-bit digest. MD5 is one of the most efficient algorithms currently available.

SHA-1 ◊ SHA-1 [NIST 2002] is an algorithm that produces a 160-bit digest. It is based on Rivest's MD4 algorithm (which is similar to MD5) with some additional operations. It is substantially slower than MD5, but the 160-bit digest does offer greater security against brute-force and birthday-style attacks. SHA algorithms that deliver longer digests (224, 256 and 512 bits) are also included in the standard [NIST 2002]. Of course, their additional length implies additional costs for the generation, storage and communication of digital signatures and MACs, but following the publication of attacks on SHA-1's predecessors which suggest that SHA-1 is vulnerable [Randall and Szydlo 2004] NIST announced that is to be superseded by the longer SHA digest versions in US government software by 2010 [NIST 2004].

Using an encryption algorithm to make a digest ◊ It is possible to use a symmetric encryption algorithm such as those detailed in Section 7.3.1 to produce a secure digest. In this case, the key should be published so that the digest algorithm can be applied by anyone wishing to verify a digital signature. The encryption algorithm is used in CBC mode, and the digest is the result of combining the penultimate CBC value with the final encrypted block.

7.4.4   Certificate standards and certificate authorities

X.509 is the most widely used standard format for certificates [CCITT 1988b]. Although the X.509 certificate format is a part of the X.500 standard for the construction of global directories of names and attributes [CCITT 1988a], it is commonly used in cryptographic work as a format definition for free-standing certificates. We describe the X.500 naming standard in Chapter 9.

The structure and content of an X.509 certificate is illustrated in Figure 7.12. As can be seen, it binds a public key to a named entity called a *subject*. The binding is in the signature, which is issued by another named entity called the *issuer*. The certificate has a *period of validity,* which is defined by a pair of dates. The <Distinguished Name> entries are intended to be the name of a person, organization or other entity together with sufficient contextual information to render it unique. In a full X.500 implementation this contextual information would be drawn from a directory hierarchy in which the named entity appears, but in the absence of global X.500 implementations it can only be a descriptive string.

This format is included in the TLS protocol for electronic commerce and is widely used in practice to authenticate the public keys of services and their clients. Certain well-known companies and organizations have established themselves to act as *certificate authorities* (for example Verisign [www.verisign.com], CREN [www.cren.net]), and other companies and individuals can obtain X.509 public-key certificates from them by submitting satisfactory evidence of their identity. This leads to a two-step verification procedure for any X.509 certificate:

1. Obtain the public-key certificate of the issuer (a certification authority) from a reliable source.

2. Validate the signature.

The SPKI approach ◊ The X.509 approach is based on the global uniqueness of distinguished names. It has been pointed out that this is an impractical goal that does not reflect the reality of current legal and commercial practice [Ellison 1996] in which the identity of individuals is not assumed to be unique but is made unique by reference to other people and organizations. This can be seen in the use of a driving licence or a letter from a bank to authenticate an individual's name and address (a name alone is unlikely to be unique among the world's population). This leads to longer verification chains, because there are many possible issuers of public-key certificates, and their signatures must be validated through a chain of verification that leads back to someone known and trusted by the principal performing the verification. But the resulting verification is likely to be more convincing, and many of the steps in such a chain can be cached to shorten the process on future occasions.

The arguments above are the basis for the recently developed Simple Public-key Infrastructure (SPKI) proposals (see RFC 2693 [Ellison *et al.* 1999]). This is a scheme for the creation and management of sets of public certificates. It enables chains of certificates to be processed using logical inference to produce derived certificates. For example, 'Bob believes that Alice's public key is K_{Apub}' and 'Carol trusts Bob on Alice's keys' implies 'Carol believes that Alice's public key is K_{Apub}'.

7.5 Cryptography pragmatics

In Section 7.5.1, we compare the performance of the encryption and secure hash algorithms described or mentioned above. We consider encryption algorithms alongside secure hash functions because encryption can also be used as a method for digital signing.

Figure 7.13   Performance of symmetric encryption and secure digest algorithms

	Key size/hash size (bits)	PRB optimized 90 Mhz Pentium 1 (Mbytes/s)	Crypto++ 2.1 GHz Pentium 4 (Mbytes/s)
TEA	128	–	23.801
DES	56	2.113	21.340
Triple-DES	112	0.775	9.848
IDEA	128	1.219	18.963
AES	128	–	61.010
AES	192	–	53.145
AES	256	–	48.229
MD5	128	17.025	216.674
SHA-1	160	–	67.977

In Section 7.5.2, we discuss some non-technical issues surrounding the use of cryptography. There is not space to do justice to the vast amount of political discussion that has taken place on this subject since strong cryptographic algorithms first appeared in the public domain, nor have the debates yet reached many definitive conclusions. Our aim is merely to give the reader some awareness of this ongoing debate.

7.5.1   Performance of cryptographic algorithms

Figure 7.13 and the speed of the symmetric encryption algorithms and the secure digest functions that we have discussed in this chapter. Where available, we give two speed measurcments. In the column labelled *PRB optimized* we give figures based on those published by Preneel *et al.* [Preneel *et al.* 1998]. The figures in the column labelled *Crypto++* were obtained much more recently by the authors of the Crypto++ open-source library of cryptographic schemes [www.cryptopp.com]. The column headings indicate the speed of the hardware used for these benchmarks. The Preneel implementations were hand-optimized assembler programs whereas the Crypto++ ones were C++ programs generated with an optimizing compiler.

The key lengths give an indication of computational cost of a brute force attack on the key; the true strength of cryptographic algorithms is much more difficult to evaluate and rests on reasoning about the success of the algorithm in obscuring the plain text. Preneel *et al.* [1998] provide a useful discussion on the strength and performance of the main symmetric algorithms.

What do these performance figures signify for real applications of cryptography, such as their use in the TLS scheme for secure web interactions (the *https* protocol, described in Section 7.6.3)? Web pages are seldom larger than 100 kilobytes, so the contents of a page can be encrypted using any of the symmetric algorithms in a few milliseconds even with a processor that is quite slow by today's standards. RSA is used primarily for digital signatures and that step can also be performed in a few milliseconds. Thus the impact of algorithm performance on the perceived speed of the *https* application is minimal.

Asymmetric algorithms such as RSA are seldom used for data encryption, but their performance for signing is of interest. The Crypto++ library pages indicate that with the hardware mentioned in the last column of Figure 7.13 it takes about 4.75 ms using RSA with a 1024-bit key to sign a secure hash (presumably using 160-bit SHA-1) and about 0.18 ms to verify the signature.

7.5.2 Applications of cryptography and political obstacles

The algorithms described above all emerged during the 1980s and 90s, when computer networks were beginning to be used for commercial purposes and it was becoming evident that their lack of security was a major problem. As we mentioned in the introduction to this chapter, the emergence of cryptographic software was strongly resisted by the US government. The resistance had two sources, the US National Security Agency (NSA) which was thought to have a policy to restrict the strength of cryptography available to other nations to a level at which the NSA could decrypt any secret communication for military intelligence purposes, and the US Federal Bureau of Investigation (FBI) which aimed to ensure that its agents could have privileged access to the cryptographic keys used by all private organizations and individuals in the US for law enforcement purposes.

Cryptographic software was classified as a munition in the United States and was subject to stringent export restrictions. Other countries, especially allies of the USA, applied similar, or in some cases even more stringent restrictions. The problem was compounded by the general ignorance among politicians and the general public as to what cryptographic software was and its potential non-military applications. US software companies protested that the restrictions were inhibiting the export of software such as browsers, and the export restrictions were eventually formulated in a form that allowed the export of code using keys of no more than 40 bits – hardly strong cryptography!

The export restrictions may have hindered the growth of electronic commerce, but they were not particularly effective in preventing the spread of cryptographic expertise nor in keeping cryptographic software out of the hands of users in other countries, since many programmers inside and outside the USA were eager and able to implement and distribute cryptographic code. The current position is that software that implements most of the major cryptographic algorithms has been available worldwide for several years, in print [Schneier 1996] and online, in commercial and freeware versions [www.rsasecurity.com, cryptography.org, privacy.nb.ca, www.openssl.org].

An example is the program called PGP (Pretty Good Privacy) [Garfinkel 1994, Zimmermann 1995], originally developed by Philip Zimmermann and carried forward by him and others. This is part of a technical and political campaign to ensure that the availability of cryptographic methods is not controlled by the US government. PGP has been developed and distributed with the aim of enabling all computer users to enjoy the level of privacy and integrity afforded by the use of public-key cryptography in their communications. PGP generates and manages public and secret keys on behalf of a user. It uses RSA public-key encryption for authentication and to transmit secret keys to the intended communication partner and it uses the IDEA or 3DES secret-key encryption algorithms to encrypt mail messages and other documents. (At the time PGP was first developed, use of the DES algorithm was controlled by the US government.) PGP is widely available in both free and commercial versions. It is distributed via separate distribution sites for North American users [www.pgp.com] and those in other parts of the world [International PGP] to circumvent (perfectly legally) the US export regulations.

The US government eventually recognized the futility of the NSA's position and the harm that it was causing to the US computer industry (which was unable to market secure versions of web browsers, distributed operating systems and many other products worldwide). In January 2000 the US government introduced a new policy [www.bxa.doc.gov] intended to allow US software vendors to export software that incorporates strong encryption. The regulations current in 2004 allowed export of software products incorporating up to 64-bit encryption keys and up to 1024-bit public keys used for signing and key exchange. They require a government 'review' of exported software with larger keys. Of course, the US does not have a monopoly on the production or the publication of cryptographic software; open-source implementations are available for all the well-known algorithms [www.cryptopp.com]. The effect of the regulations is simply to hamper the marketing of some US-produced commercial software products.

Other political initiatives have aimed to maintain control over the use of cryptography by introducing legislation insisting on the inclusion of loopholes or trapdoors available only to government law-enforcement and security agencies. Such proposals spring from the perception that secret communication channels can be very useful to criminals of all sorts. Before the advent of digital cryptography, governments always had the means to intercept and analyse communications between members of the public. Strong digital cryptography radically alters that situation. But these proposals to legislate to prevent the use of strong, uncompromized cryptography have been strongly resisted by citizens and civil liberties bodies, who are concerned about their impact on citizens' privacy rights. So far, none of these legislative proposals has been adopted, but political efforts are continuing and the eventual introduction of a legal framework for the use of cryptography may be inevitable.

7.6 Case studies: Needham–Schroeder, Kerberos, TLS, 802.11 WiFi

The authentication protocols originally published by Needham and Schroeder [1978] are at the heart of many security techniques. We give them in detail in Section 7.6.1. One of the most important applications of their secret-key authentication protocol is the Kerberos system [Neuman and Ts'o 1994], which is the subject of our second case study (Section 7.6.2). Kerberos was designed to provide authentication between clients and servers in networks that form a single management domain (intranets).

Our third case study (Section 7.6.3) deals with the Transport Layer Security (TLS) protocol. This was designed specifically to meet the need for secure electronic transactions. It is now supported by most web browsers and servers and is employed in most of the commercial transactions that take place via the Web.

Our final case study (Section 7.6.4) illustrates the difficulty of engineering secure systems. The IEEE 802.11 WiFi standard was published in 1999 with a security specification included. But subsequent analysis and attacks have shown the specification to be severely inadequate. We identify the weaknesses and relate them to the cryptographic principles covered in this chapter.

7.6.1   The Needham–Schroeder authentication protocol

The protocols described here were developed in response for the need for a secure means to manage keys (and passwords) in a network. At the time the work was published [Needham and Schroeder 1978], network file services were just emerging and there was an urgent need for better ways to manage security in local networks.

In networks that are integrated for management purposes, this need can be met by a secure key service that issues session keys in the form of challenges (see Section 7.2.2). That is the purpose of the secret-key protocol developed by Needham and Schroeder. In the same paper, Needham and Schroeder also set out a protocol based on the use of public keys for authentication and key distribution that does not depend upon the existence of secure key servers and is hence more suitable for use in networks with many independent management domains, such as the Internet. We do not describe the public-key version here, but the TLS protocol described in Section 7.6.3 is a variation of it.

Needham and Schroeder proposed a solution to authentication and key distribution based on an *authentication server* that supplies secret keys to clients. The job of the authentication server is to provide a secure way for pairs of processes to obtain shared keys. To do this, it must communicate with its clients using encrypted messages.

Needham and Schroeder with secret keys ◊   In their model, a process acting on behalf of a principal A that wishes to initiate secure communication with another process acting on behalf of a principal B can obtain a key for the purpose. The protocol is described for two arbitrary processes A and B, but in client-server systems, A is likely to be a client initiating a sequence of requests to some server B. The key is supplied to A in two forms, one that A can use to encrypt the messages that it sends to B and one that it can transmit securely to B. (The latter is encrypted in a key that is known to B but not to A, so that B can decrypt it and the key is not compromised during transmission.)

The authentication server S maintains a table containing a name and a secret key for each principal known to the system. The secret key is used only to authenticate client processes to the authentication server and to transmit messages securely between client processes and the authentication server. It is never disclosed to third parties and it is transmitted across the network at most once, when it is generated. (Ideally, a key should always be transmitted by some other means, such as on paper or in a verbal message, avoiding any exposure on the network.) A secret key is the equivalent of the password used to authenticate users in centralized systems. For human principals, the name held by the authentication service is their 'user name' and the secret key is their password. Both are supplied by the user on request to client processes acting on the user's behalf.

The protocol is based on the generation and transmission of tickets by the authentication server. A ticket is an encrypted message containing a secret key for use in communication between A and B. We tabulate the messages in the Needham and Schroeder secret-key protocol in Figure 7.14. The authentication server is S.

N_A and N_B are *nonces*. A nonce is an integer value that is added to a message to demonstrate its freshness. Nonces are used only once and are generated on demand. For

Figure 7.14   The Needham–Schroeder secret-key authentication protocol

Header	Message	Notes
1. A $\rightarrow$ S:	A, B, N_A	A requests S to supply a key for communication with B.
2. S $\rightarrow$ A:	$\{N_A, B, K_{AB}, \{K_{AB}, A\}_{K_B}\}_{K_A}$	S returns a message encrypted in A's secret key, containing a newly generated key K_{AB}, and a 'ticket' encrypted in B's secret key. The nonce N_A demonstrates that the message was sent in response to the preceding one. A believes that S sent the message because only S knows A's secret key.
3. A $\rightarrow$ B:	$\{K_{AB}, A\}_{K_B}$	A sends the 'ticket' to B.
4. B $\rightarrow$ A:	$\{N_B\}_{K_{AB}}$	B decrypts the ticket and uses the new key K_{AB} to encrypt another nonce N_B.
5. A $\rightarrow$ B:	$\{N_B - 1\}_{K_{AB}}$	A demonstrates to B that it was the sender of the previous message by returning an agreed transformation of N_B.

example, the nonces may be generated as a sequence of integer values or by reading the clock at the sending machine.

If the protocol is successfully completed, both A and B can be sure that any message encrypted in K_{AB} that they receive comes from the other, and that any message encrypted in K_{AB} that they send can be understood only by the other or by S (and S is assumed to be trustworthy). This is so because the only messages that have been sent containing K_{AB} were encrypted in A's secret key or B's secret key.

There is a weakness in this protocol in that B has no reason to believe that message 3 is fresh. An intruder who manages to obtain the key K_{AB} and make a copy of the ticket and authenticator $\{K_{AB}, A\}_{K_B}$ (both of which might have been left in an exposed storage location by a careless or a failed client program running under A's authority), can use them to initiate a subsequent exchange with B, impersonating A. For this attack to occur an old value of K_{AB} has to be compromised; in today's terminology, Needham and Schroeder did not include this possibility on their threat list, and the consensus of opinion is that one should do so. The weakness can be remedied by adding a nonce or timestamp to message 3, so that it becomes: $\{K_{AB}, A,t\}_{K_{Bpub}}$. B decrypts this message and checks that t is recent. This is the solution adopted in Kerberos.

7.6.2   Kerberos

Kerberos was developed at MIT in the 1980s [Steiner *et al.* 1988] to provide a range of authentication and security facilities for use in the campus computing network at MIT and other intranets. It has undergone several revisions and enhancements in the light of experience and feedback from user organizations. Kerberos version 5 [Neuman and Ts'o 1994], which we describe here, is on the Internet standards track (see RFC 1510 [Kohl and Neuman 1993]) and is now used by many companies and universities. Source code

Figure 7.15   System architecture of Kerberos

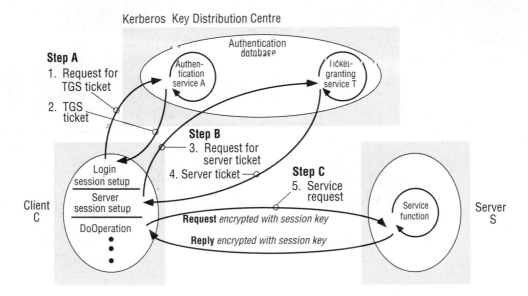

for an implementation of Kerberos is available from MIT [web.mit.edu I]; it is included in the OSF Distributed Computing Environment (DCE) [OSF 1997] and in the Microsoft Windows 2000 operating system as the default authentication service [www.microsoft.com II]. An extension has been proposed to incorporate the use of public-key certificates for the initial authentication of principals (Step A in Figure 7.15) [Neuman *et al.* 1999].

Figure 7.15 shows the process architecture. Kerberos deals with three kinds of security object:

Ticket: A token issued to a client by the Kerberos ticket-granting service for presentation to a particular server, verifying that the sender has recently been authenticated by Kerberos. Tickets include an expiry time and a newly generated session key for use by the client and the server.

Authentication: A token constructed by a client and sent to a server to prove the identity of the user and the currency of any communication with a server. An authenticator can be used only once. It contains the client's name and a timestamp and is encrypted in the appropriate session key.

Session key: A secret key randomly generated by Kerberos and issued to a client for use when communicating with a particular server. Encryption is not mandatory for all communication with servers; the session key is used for encrypting communication with those servers that demand it and for encrypting all authenticators (see above).

Client processes must possess a ticket and a session key for each server that they use. It would be impractical to supply a new ticket and key for each client-server interaction, so most tickets are granted to clients with a lifetime of several hours so that they can be used for interaction with a particular a server until they expire.

A Kerberos server is known as a Key Distribution Centre (KDC). Each KDC offers an Authentication Service (AS) and a Ticket-Granting Service (TGS). On login, users are authenticated by the AS, using a network-secure variation of the password method, and the client process acting on behalf of the user is supplied with a *ticket-granting ticket* and a session key for communicating with the TGS. Subsequently, the original client process and its descendants can use the ticket-granting ticket to obtain tickets and session keys for specific services from the TGS.

The Needham and Schroeder protocol is followed quite closely in Kerberos, with time values (integers representing a date and time) used as nonces. This serves two purposes:

- to guard against replay of old messages intercepted in the network or the reuse of old tickets found lying in the memory of machines from which the authorized user has logged out (nonces were used to achieve this purpose in Needham and Schroeder);

- to apply a lifetime to tickets, enabling the system to revoke users' rights when, for example, they cease to be authorized users of the system.

Below we describe the Kerberos protocols in detail, using the notation defined at the bottom of the page. First, we describe the protocol by which the client obtains a ticket and a session key for access to the TGS.

A Kerberos ticket has a fixed period of validity starting at time t_1 and ending at time t_2. A ticket for a client C to access a server S takes the form:

$$\{C, S, t_1, t_2, K_{CS}\}_{K_S}, \text{ which we shall denote as } \{ticket(C, S)\}_{K_S}$$

The client's name is included in the ticket to avoid possible use by impostors, as we shall see later. The step and message numbers in Figure 7.15 correspond to those in tabulated description Λ. Note that message 1 is not encrypted and does not include C's password. It contains a nonce that is used to check the validity of the reply.

Message 2 is sometimes called a 'challenge' because it presents the requester with information that is only useful if it knows C's secret key, K_C. An impostor who attempts to impersonate C by sending message 1 can get no further, since they cannot decrypt message 2. For principals that are users, K_C is a scrambled version of the user's password. The client process will prompt the user to type their password and will attempt to decrypt message 2 with it. If the user gives the right password, the client process obtains the session key K_{CT} and a valid ticket for the ticket-granting service; if not, it obtains gibberish. Servers have secret keys of their own, known only to the relevant server process and to the authentication server.

When a valid ticket has been obtained from the authentication service, the client C can use it to communicate with the ticket-granting service to obtain tickets for other

Notation:			
A	Name of Kerberos authentication service.	n	A nonce.
T	Name of Kerberos ticket-granting service.	t	A timestamp.
C	Name of client.	t_1	Starting time for validity of ticket.
		t_2	Ending time for validity of ticket.

A.	Obtain Kerberos session key and TGS ticket, once per login session	
Header	**Message**	**Notes**
1. C → A: Request for TGS ticket	C, T, n	Client C requests the Kerberos authentication server A to supply a ticket for communication with the ticket-granting service T.
2. A → C: TGS session key and ticket	$\{K_{CT}, n\}_{K_C}$, $\{ticket(C,T)\}_{K_T}$ containing C, T, t_1, t_2, K_{CT}	A returns a message containing a ticket encrypted in its secret key and a session key for C to use with T. The inclusion of the nonce n encrypted in K_C shows that the message comes from the recipient of message 1, who must know K_C.

servers any number of times until the ticket expires. Thus to obtain a ticket for any server S, C constructs an authenticator encrypted in K_{CT} of the form:

$\{C, t\}_{K_{CT}}$, which we shall denote as $\{auth(C)\}_{K_{CT}}$ and sends a request to T:

B.	Obtain ticket for a server S, once per client-server session	
3. C → T: Request ticket for service S	$\{auth(C)\}_{K_{CT}}$, $\{ticket(C,T)\}_{K_T}$, S, n	C requests the ticket-granting server T to supply a ticket for communication with another server S.
4. T → C: Service ticket	$\{K_{CS}, n\}_{K_{CT}}$, $\{ticket(C,S)\}_{K_S}$	T checks the ticket. If it is valid T generates a new random session key K_{CS} and returns it with a ticket for S (encrypted in the server's secret key K_S).

C is then ready to issue request messages to the server, S:

C.	Issue a server request with a ticket	
5. C → S: Service request	$\{auth(C)\}_{K_{CS}}$, $\{ticket(C,S)\}_{K_S}$, request, n	C sends the ticket to S with a newly generated authenticator for C and a request. The request would be encrypted in K_{CS} if secrecy of the data is required.

For the client to be sure of the server's authenticity, S should return the nonce n to C. (To reduce the number of messages required, this could be included in the messages that contain the server's reply to the request):

D.	Authenticate server (optional)	
6. S → C: Server authentication	$\{n\}_{K_{CS}}$	(Optional): S sends the nonce to C, encrypted in K_{CS}.

Application of Kerberos ◊ Kerberos was developed for use in Project Athena at MIT – a campus-wide networked computing facility for undergraduate education with many workstations and servers providing a service to more than 5000 users. The environment is such that neither the trustworthiness of clients nor the security of the network and the machines that offer network services can be assumed – for example, workstations are not protected against the installation of user-developed system software, and server machines (other than the Kerberos server) are not necessarily secured against physical interference with their software configuration.

Kerberos provides virtually all of the security in the Athena system. It is used to authenticate users and other principals. Most of the servers running on the network have been extended to require a ticket from each client at the start of every client-server interaction. These include file storage (NFS and Andrew File System), electronic mail, remote login and printing. Users' passwords are known only to the user and to the Kerberos authentication service. Services have secret keys that are known only to Kerberos and the servers that provide the service.

We will describe the way in which Kerberos is applied to the authentication of users on login. Its use to secure the NFS file service is described in Chapter 8.

Login with Kerberos ◊ When a user logs in to a workstation, the login program sends the user's name to the Kerberos authentication service. If the user is known to the authentication service it replies with a session key and a nonce encrypted in the user's password and a ticket for the TGS. The login program then attempts to decrypt the session key and the nonce using the password that the user typed in response to the password prompt. If the password is correct, the login program obtains the session key and the nonce. It checks the nonce and stores the session key with the ticket for subsequent use when communicating with the TGS. At this point, the login program can erase the user's password from its memory, since the ticket now serves to authenticate the user. A login session is then started for the user on the workstation. Note that the user's password is never exposed to eavesdropping on the network – it is retained in the workstation and is erased from memory soon after it is entered.

Accessing servers with Kerberos ◊ Whenever a program running on a workstation needs to access a new service, it requests a ticket for the service from the ticket-granting service. For example, when a UNIX user wishes to log in to a remote computer, the *rlogin* command program on the user's workstation obtains a ticket from the Kerberos ticket-granting service for access to the *rlogind* network service. The *rlogin* command program sends the ticket, together with a new authenticator, in a request to the *rlogind* process on the computer where the user wishes to log in. The *rlogind* program decrypts the ticket with the *rlogin* service's secret key and checks the validity of the ticket (that is, that the ticket's lifetime has not expired). Server machines must take care to store their secret keys in storage that is inaccessible to intruders.

The *rlogind* program then uses the session key included in the ticket to decrypt the authenticator and checks that the authenticator is fresh (authenticators can be used only once). Once the *rlogind* program is satisfied that the ticket and authenticator are valid, there is no need for it to check the user's name and password, because the user's identity is known to the *rlogind* program and a login session is established for that user on the remote machine.

Implementation of Kerberos ◊ Kerberos is implemented as a server that runs on a secure machine. A set of libraries is provided for use by client applications and services. The DES encryption algorithm is used, but this is implemented as a separate module that can be easily replaced.

The Kerberos service is scalable — the world is divided into separate domains of authentication authority, called *realms*, each with its own Kerberos server. Most principals are registered in just one realm, but the Kerberos ticket-granting servers are registered in all of the realms. Principals can authenticate themselves to servers in other realms through their local ticket-granting server.

Within a single realm, there can be several authentication servers, all of which have copies of the same authentication database. The authentication database is replicated by a simple master–slave technique. Updates are applied to the master copy by a single Kerberos Database Management service (KDBM) that runs only on the master machine. The KDBM handles requests from users to change their passwords and requests from system administrators to add or delete principals and to change their passwords.

To make this scheme transparent to users, the lifetime of TGS tickets ought to be as long as the longest possible login session, since the use of an expired ticket will result in the rejection of service requests, and the only remedy is for the user to re-authenticate the login session and then request new server tickets for all of the services in use. In practice, ticket lifetimes in the region of 12 hours are used.

Critiques of Kerberos ◊ The protocol for Kerberos version 5 described above contains several improvements designed to deal with criticisms of earlier versions [Bellovin and Merritt 1990, Burrows *et al.* 1990]. The most important criticism of Version 4 was that the nonces used in authenticators are implemented as timestamps, and protection against the replay of authenticators depends upon at least loose synchronization of clients' and servers' clocks. Furthermore, if a synchronization protocol is used to bring client and server clocks into loose synchrony, the synchronization protocol must itself be secure against security attacks. See Chapter 11 for information on clock synchronization protocols.

The protocol definition for version 5 allows the nonces in authenticators to be implemented as timestamps or as sequence numbers. In both cases, it requires that they be unique, and that servers hold a list of recently received nonces from each client to check that they are not replayed. This is an inconvenient implementation requirement and is difficult for servers to guarantee in case of failures. Kehne *et al.* [1992] have published a proposed improvement to the Kerberos protocol that does not rely on synchronized clocks.

The security of Kerberos depends on limited session lifetimes – the period of validity of TGS tickets is generally limited to a few hours; the period must be chosen to be long enough to avoid inconvenient interruptions of service but short enough to ensure that users who have been de-registered or downgraded do not continue to use the resources for more than a short period. This might cause difficulties in some commercial environments, because the consequent requirement for the user to supply a new set of authentication details at an arbitrary point in the interaction might intrude on the application.

7.6.3   Securing electronic transactions with secure sockets

The Secure Sockets Layer (SSL) protocol was originally developed by the Netscape Corporation [Netscape 1996] and proposed as a standard specifically to meet the needs described below. An extended version of SSL has been adopted as an Internet standard under the name Transport Layer Security (TLS) protocol, described in RFC 2246 [Dierks and Allen 1999]. TLS is supported by most browsers and is widely used in Internet commerce. Its main features are:

Negotiable encryption and authentication algorithms ◊ In an open network we should not assume that all parties use the same client software or that all client and server software includes a particular encryption algorithm. In fact, the laws of some countries attempt to restrict the use of certain encryption algorithms to those countries alone. TLS has been designed so that the algorithms used for encryption and authentication are negotiated between the processes at the two ends of the connection during the initial handshake. It may turn out that they do not have sufficient algorithms in common and in that case the connection attempt will fail.

Bootstrapped secure communication ◊ To meet the need for secure communication without previous negotiation or help from third parties, the secure channel is established using a protocol similar to the hybrid scheme described earlier. Unencrypted communication is used for the initial exchanges, then public-key cryptography and finally switching to secret-key cryptography once a shared secret key has been established. Each switch is optional and preceded by a negotiation.

Thus the secure channel is fully configurable, allowing communication in each direction to be encrypted and authenticated but not requiring it, so that computing resources need not be consumed in performing unnecessary encryption.

The details of the TLS protocol are published and standardized, and several software libraries and toolkits are available to support it [Hirsch 1997, www.openssl.org], some of them in the public domain. It has been incorporated in a wide range of application software, and its security has been verified by independent review.

TLS consists of two layers (Figure 7.16) an TLS Record Protocol layer, which implements a secure channel, encrypting and authenticating messages transmitted through any connection-oriented protocol; and a handshake layer, containing the TLS handshake protocol and two other related protocols that establish and maintain an TLS session (that is, a secure channel) between a client and a server. Both are usually implemented by software libraries at the application level in the client and the server. The TLS record protocol is a session-level layer; it can be used to transport application-level data transparently between a pair of processes while guaranteeing its secrecy, integrity and authenticity. These are exactly the properties we specified for secure channels in our security model (Section 2.3.3), but in TLS there are options for the communicating partners to choose whether or not to deploy decryption and authentication of messages in each direction. Each secure session is given an identifier, and each partner can store session identifiers in a cache for subsequent reuse, avoiding the overhead of establishing a new session when another secure session with the same partner is required.

Figure 7.16   TLS protocol stack

(Figures 7.16 to 7.19 are based on diagrams in Hirsch [1997] and are used with Frederick Hirsch's permission)

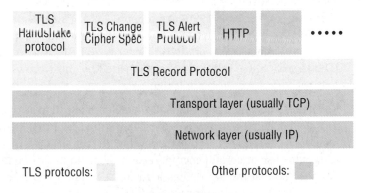

TLS protocols: Other protocols:

TLS is widely used to add a secure communication layer below existing application-level protocols. It is probably most widely used to secure HTTP interactions for use in Internet commerce and other security-sensitive applications. It is implemented by virtually all web browsers and web servers: the use of the protocol prefix *https:* in URLs initiates the establishment of an TLS secure channel between a browser and a web server. It has also been widely deployed to provide secure implementations of Telnet, FTP and many other application protocols. TLS is the *de facto* standard for use in applications requiring secure channels, and there is a wide choice of available implementations, both commercial and public-domain, with APIs for CORBA and Java.

The TLS handshake protocol is illustrated in Figure 7.17. The handshake is performed over an existing connection. It begins in the clear and it establishes an TLS session by exchanging the agreed options and parameters needed to perform encryption and authentication. The handshake sequence varies depending on whether client and server authentication are required. The handshake protocol may also be invoked at a later time to change the specification of a secure channel, for example, communication may begin with message authentication using message authentication codes only. At a later point, encryption may be added. This is achieved by performing the handshake protocol again to negotiate a new cipher specification using the existing channel.

The TLS initial handshake is potentially vulnerable to man-in-the-middle attacks as described in Section 7.2.2, Scenario 3. To protect against them, the public key used to verify the first certificate received may be delivered by a separate channel – for example, browsers and other Internet software delivered on a CD-ROM may include a set of public keys for some well-known certificate authorities. Another defence for the clients of well-known services is based on the inclusion of the service's domain name in its public key certificates – clients should only deal with the service at the IP address corresponding to that domain name.

TLS supports a variety of options for the cryptographic functions to be used. These are collectively known as a *cipher suite*. A cipher suite includes a single choice for each of the features shown in Figure 7.18.

A variety of popular cipher suites are preloaded, with standard identifiers in the client and the server. During the handshake, the server offers the client a list of the cipher suite identifiers that it has available, and the client responds by selecting one of them (or

Figure 7.17   TLS handshake protocol

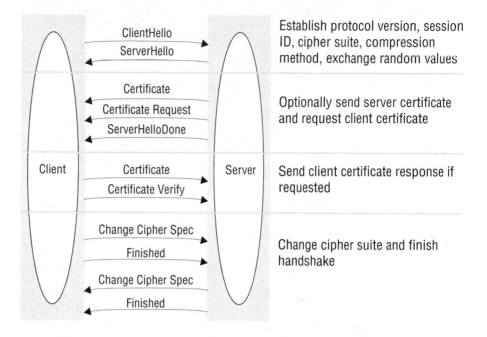

giving an error indication if it has none that match). At this stage they also agree on an (optional) compression method and a random start value for CBC block encryption functions (see Section 7.3).

Next, the partners optionally authenticate each other by exchanging signed public-key certificates in X.509 format. These certificates may be obtained from a public-key authority or they may simply be generated temporarily for the purpose. In any case, at least one public key must be available for use in the next stage of the handshake.

One partner then generates a *pre-master secret* and sends it to the other partner encrypted with the public key. A pre-master secret is a large random value that is used by both partners to generate the two session keys (called *write* keys) for encrypting data in each direction and the message authentication secrets to be used for message authentication. When all this has been done, a secure session begins. This is triggered

Figure 7.18   TLS handshake configuration options

Component	*Description*	*Example*
Key exchange method	the method to be used for exchange of a session key	RSA with public-key certificates
Cipher for data transfer	the block or stream cipher to be used for data	IDEA
Message digest function	for creating message authentication codes (MACs)	SHA-1

Figure 7.19   TLS record protocol

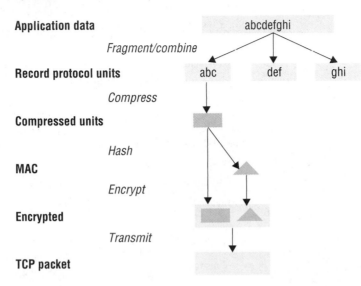

by the *ChangeCipherSpec* messages exchanged between the partners. These are followed by *Finished* messages. Once the *Finished* messages have been exchanged, all further communication is encrypted and signed according to the chosen cipher suite with the agreed keys.

Figure 7.19 shows the operation of the record protocol. A message for transmission is first fragmented into blocks of a manageable size, then the blocks are optionally compressed. Compression is not strictly a feature of secure communication, but it is provided here because a compression algorithm can usefully share some of the work of processing the bulk data with the encryption and digital signature algorithms. In other words, a pipeline of data transformations can be set up within the TLS record layer that will perform all of the transformations required more efficiently than could be done independently.

The encryption and message authentication (MAC) transformations deploy the algorithms specified in the agreed cipher suite exactly as described in Sections 7.3.1 and 7.4.2. Finally, the signed and encrypted block is transmitted to the partner through the associated TCP connection, where the transformations are reversed to produce the original data block.

Summary ◊ TLS provides a practical implementation of a hybrid encryption scheme with authentication and key exchange based on public keys. Because the ciphers are negotiated in the handshake, it does not depend upon the availability of any particular algorithms. Nor does it depend upon any secure services at the time of session establishment. The only requirement is that the public-key certificates are issued by an authority recognized by both parties.

Because the SSL basis for TLS and its reference implementation were published [Netscape 1996], it was the subject of review and debate. Some amendments were made to the early designs, and it was widely endorsed as a valuable standard. TLS is now integrated in most web browsers and web servers and is used in other applications such as secure Telnet and FTP. Commercial and public-domain [www.rsasecurity.com, Hirsch 1997, www.openssl.org] implementations are widely available in the form of libraries and browser plugins.

7.6.4   Weaknesses in the IEEE 802.11 WiFi security design

The IEEE 802.11 standard for wireless LANs described in Section 3.5.2 was first released in 1999 [IEEE 1999]. It was implemented in base stations, laptops and portable devices from a similar date and widely used for mobile communication. Unfortunately, the security design in the standard was subsequently found to be severely inadequate in several respects. We shall outline that initial design and its weaknesses as a case-study in the difficulties of security design already referred to in Section 7.1.3.

It was recognized that wireless networks are by their nature more exposed to attack than wired networks because the network and the transmitted data are available for eavesdropping and masquerading by any device equipped with a transmitter/receiver within range. The initial 802.11 design therefore aimed to provide access control for WiFi networks and privacy and integrity for the data transmitted on them through a security specification entitled Wired Equivalent Privacy (WEP) which embodies the following measures, all of which are optionally activated by a network administrator:

Access control by a challenge-response protocol (*cf.* Kerberos, Section 7.6.2), in which a joining node is challenged by the base station to demonstrate that it has the correct shared key. A single key *K* is assigned by a network administrator and shared between the base station and all authorized devices.

Privacy and integrity using an optional encryption mechanism based on the RC4 stream cipher. The same key *K* used for access control is also used in encryption. There are key length options of 40, 64 or 128 bits. An encrypted checksum is included in each packet to protect its integrity.

The following deficiencies and design weaknesses were discovered soon after the standard was deployed:

The sharing of a single key by all users of a network renders the design weak in practice, since:

- the key is liable to be transmitted to new users on unprotected channels.

- a single careless or malicious user (such as a disgruntled former employee) who has gained access to the key can compromise the security of the entire network and this can go undiscovered.

Solution: A public-key based protocol for negotiating individual keys, as is done in TLS/SSL (see Section 7.6.3).

Base stations are never authenticated, so an attacker who knows the current shared key could introduce a spoof base station and eavesdrop, insert or tamper with any traffic.

Solution: Base stations should supply a certificate that can be authenticated by the use of a public key obtained from a third party.

Figure 7.20   Use of RC4 stream cipher in IEEE 802.11 WEP

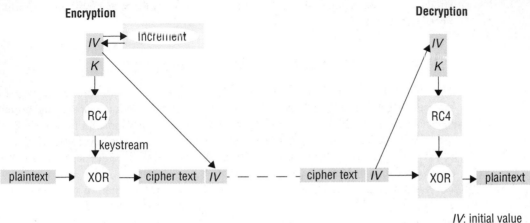

IV: initial value
K: shared key

Inappropriate use of a stream cipher rather than a block cipher (see descriptions of block and stream ciphers in Section 7.3). Figure 7.20 shows the process of encryption and decyption in 802.11 WEP security. Each packet is encrypted by XOR-ing its content with a key stream produced by the RC4 algorithm. The receiving station uses RC4 to generate the same key stream and decrypt the packet with another XOR. To avoid key stream synchronization errors when packets are lost or corrupted, RC4 is restarted with a start value consisting of a 24-bit *initial value* concatenated with the globally shared key. The initial value is updated and included (in clear) in each packet transmitted. The shared key cannot easily be changed in normal use, so the starting value has only $s = 2^{24}$ (or about 10^7) different states, resulting in the repetition of the start value and hence the keystream, after 10^7 packets are sent. In practice this can occur within a few hours, and even shorter repetition cycles can arise if packets are lost. An attacker receiving the encrypted packets can always detect repetitions since the initial value is sent in clear.

The RC4 specification explicitly warns against keystream repetition. This is because an attacker who receives an encrypted packet C_i and knows the plain text P_i (for example, by guessing that it is a standard enquiry to a server) can calculate the keystream K_i used to encrypt the packet. But the same value of K_i will recur after s packets are transmitted and the attacker can use it to decrypt the newly-transmitted packet. The attacker may eventually succeed in decrypting a high proportion of packets in this manner by guessing plaintext packets correctly. This weakness was first pointed out by Borisov *et al.* [2001] and led to a major reappraisal of WEP security and its replacement in later versions of 802.11.

Solution: Negotiate a new key after a time less than the worst case for repetition. An explicit termination code would be needed, as is the case in TLS.

Key lengths of 40 bits and 64 bits were included in the standard to enable products to be shipped abroad by US suppliers at a time when the US government regulations referred to in Section 7.5.2 restricted key lengths for exported devices to 40 bits (and subsequently 64 bits). But 40-bit keys are so easily cracked by brute force that they offer very little security and even 64-bit keys are potentially crackable with a determined attack.

Solution: Use 128-bit keys only. This has been adopted in many recent WiFi products.

The RC4 stream cipher was shown, after publication of the 802.11 standard, to have weaknesses that enabled the key to be discovered after observation of a substantial quantity of traffic even without repetition of the keystream [Fluhrer *et al.* 2001]. This weakness was demonstrated in practice. It rendered the WEP scheme insecure even with 128-bit keys and led some companies to ban the use of WiFi networks by their employees.

Solution: Provision for the negotiation of cipher specifications as is done in TLS, giving a choice of encryption algorithms. RC4 is hard-wired into the WEP standard, with no provision for the negotiation of encryption algorithms.

Users often didn't deploy the protection offered by the WEP scheme, probably because they didn't realize just how exposed their data was. This was not a weakness in the design of the standard but in the marketing of products based on it. Most were designed to start up with security disabled and their documentation of the security risks was often weak.

Solution: Better default settings and documentation. But users were concerned to obtain optimum performance, and communication was perceptibly slower with encryption enabled using the hardware available at the time. Attempts to avoid the use of WEP encryption led to the addition to base stations of features for the suppression of the identifying packets normally broadcast by base stations and the rejection of packets not sent from an authorized MAC address (see Section 3.5.1). Neither of these offered much security, since a network can be discovered by intercepting ('sniffing') packets in transmission and MAC addresses can be spoofed by operating system modifications.

IEEE 802.11i is an updated 802.11 security standard released in 2004 that addresses all of the above weaknesses, with options for mutual authentication, dynamically negotiated pair-wise keys and the use of AES encryption [IEEE 2004b, Edney and Arbaugh 2003].

7.7   Summary

Threats to the security of distributed systems are pervasive. It is essential to protect the communication channels and the interfaces of any system that handles information that could be the subject of attacks. Personal mail, electronic commerce and other financial transactions are all examples of such information. Security protocols are carefully designed to guard against loopholes. The design of secure systems starts from a list of threats and a set of 'worst case' assumptions.

Security mechanisms are based on public-key and secret-key cryptography. Cryptographic algorithms scramble messages in a manner that cannot be reversed without knowledge of the decryption key. Secret-key cryptography is symmetric – the same key serves for both encryption and decryption. If two parties share a secret key, they can exchange encrypted information without risk of eavesdropping or tampering and with guarantees of authenticity.

Public-key cryptography is asymmetric – separate keys are used for encryption and decryption, and knowledge of one does not reveal the other. One key is made public, enabling anyone to send secure messages to the holder of the corresponding private key and allowing the holder of the private key to sign messages and certificates. Certificates can act as credentials for the use of protected resources.

Resources are protected by access control mechanisms. Access control schemes assign rights to principals (that is, the holders of credentials) to perform operations on distributed objects and collections of objects. Rights may be held in access control lists (ACLs) associated with collections of objects or they may be held by principals in the form of capabilities – unforgeable keys for access to collections of resources. Capabilities are convenient for the delegation of access rights but are hard to revoke. Changes to ACLs take effect immediately, revoking the previous access rights, but they are more complex and costly to manage than capabilities.

Until recently, the DES encryption algorithm was the most widely used symmetric encryption scheme, but its 56-bit keys are no longer safe against brute-force attacks. The triple version of DES gives 112-bit key strength, which is safe, but other modern algorithms such as IDEA and AES are much faster and provide greater strength.

RSA is the most widely used asymmetric encryption scheme. For safety against factoring attacks, it should be used with 768-bit keys or greater. Public-key (asymmetric) algorithms are out-performed by secret-key (symmetric) algorithms by several orders of magnitude, so they are generally used only in hybrid protocols such as TLS, for the establishment of secure channels that use shared keys for subsequent exchanges.

The Needham–Schroeder authentication protocol was the first general-purpose, practical security protocol, and it still provides the basis for many practical systems. Kerberos is a well-designed scheme for the authentication of users and the protection of services within a single organization. Kerberos is based on Needham–Schroeder and symmetric cryptography. TLS is the security protocol designed for, and used widely in electronic commerce. It is a flexible protocol for the establishment and use of secure channels based on both symmetric and asymmetric cryptography. The weaknesses of IEEE 802.11 WiFi security provide an object lesson in the difficulties of security design.

EXERCISES

7.1   Describe some of the physical security policies in your organization. Express them in terms that could be implemented in a computerized door locking system.   *page 266*

7.2   Describe some of the ways in which conventional email is vulnerable to eavesdropping, masquerading, tampering, replay, denial of service. Suggest methods by which email could be protected against each of these forms of attack.   *page 268*

7.3   Initial exchanges of public keys are vulnerable to the man-in-the-middle attack. Describe as many defences against it as you can. *pages 275, 313*

7.4   PGP is often used to secure email communication. Describe the steps that a pair of users using PGP must take before they can exchange email messages with privacy and authenticity guarantees. What scope is there to make the preliminary key negotiation invisible to users? (The PGP negotiation is an instance of the hybrid scheme.)

pages 295, 304

7.5   How would email be sent to a large list of recipients using PGP or a similar scheme? Suggest a scheme that is simpler and faster when the list is used frequently.

page 304, Section 4.5

7.6   The implementation of the TEA symmetric encryption algorithm given in Figures 7.7–7.9 is not portable between all machine architectures. Explain why. How could a message encrypted using the TEA implementation be transmitted to decrypt it correctly on all other architectures? *page 290*

7.7   Modify the TEA application program in Figure 7.10 to use cipher block chaining (CBC). *pages 287, 290*

7.8   Construct a stream cipher application based on the program in Figure 7.9.

pages 288, 290

7.9   Estimate the time required to crack a 56-bit DES key by a brute-force attack using a 2000 MIPS (million instruction per second) computer, assuming that the inner loop for a brute-force attack program involves around 10 instructions per key value, plus the time to encrypt an 8-byte plaintext (see Figure 7.13). Perform the same calculation for a 128-bit IDEA key. Extrapolate your calculations to obtain the cracking time for a 200,000 MIPS parallel processor (or an Internet consortium with similar processing power).

page 291

7.10   In the Needham and Shroeder authentication protocol with secret keys, explain why the following version of message 5 is not secure:

$$A \rightarrow B: \quad \{N_B\}_{K_{AB}}$$

page 306

7.11   Review the solutions proposed in the discussion of the 802.11 Wireless Equivalent Privacy protocol design, outlining ways in which each solution could be implemented and mentioning any drawbacks or inconveniences. (5 answers) *page 317*

DISTRIBUTED FILE SYSTEMS

A distributed file system enables programs to store and access remote files exactly as they do local ones, allowing users to access files from any computer on a network. The performance and reliability experienced for access to files stored at a server should be comparable to files stored on local disks.

In this chapter we define a simple architecture for file systems and describe two basic distributed file service implementations with contrasting designs that have been in widespread use for two decades:

- Sun Network File System, NFS
- the Andrew File System, AFS

Each emulates the UNIX file system interface with differing degrees of scalability, fault tolerance and deviation from the strict UNIX one-copy file update semantics.

Several related file systems that exploit new modes of data organization on disk or across multiple servers to achieve high-performance, fault-tolerant and scalable file systems are also reviewed. Other types of distributed storage system are described elsewhere in the book. These include peer-to-peer storage systems (Chapter 10), replicated file systems (Chapter 15) and multimedia data servers (Chapter 17).

8.1   Introduction

In Chapters 1 and 2, we identified the sharing of resources as a key goal for distributed systems. The sharing of stored information is perhaps the most important aspect of distributed resource sharing. Mechanisms for data sharing take many forms and are described in several parts of this book. Web servers provide a restricted form of data sharing in which files stored locally to the server are available to clients throughout the Internet, but the data accessed through web servers is managed and updated in file systems at the server or distributed on a local network. The design of large-scale wide-area read-write file storage systems poses problems of load balancing, reliability, availability and security whose resolution is the goal of the peer-to-peer file storage systems described in Chapter 10. Chapter 15 focuses on replicated storage systems that are suitable for applications requiring reliable access to data stored on systems where the availability of individual hosts cannot be guaranteed. In Chapter 17 we describe a media server that is designed to serve stream of video data to large numbers of users in real time.

The requirements for sharing within local networks and intranets lead to a need for a different type of service – one that supports the persistent storage of data and programs of all types on behalf of clients and the consistent distribution of up-to-date data. The purpose of this chapter is to describe the architecture and implementation of these *basic* distributed file systems. We use the word 'basic' here to denote distributed file systems whose primary purpose is to emulate the functionality of a non-distributed file system for client programs running on multiple remote computers. They do not maintain multiple persistent replicas of files, nor do they support the bandwidth and timing guarantees required for multimedia data streaming – those requirements are addressed in later chapters. Basic distributed file systems provide an essential underpinning for organizational computing based on intranets.

File systems were originally developed for centralized computer systems and desktop computers as an operating system facility providing a convenient programming interface to disk storage. They subsequently acquired features such as access control and file-locking mechanisms that made them useful for the sharing of data and programs. Distributed file systems support the sharing of information in the form of files and hardware resources in the form of persistent storage throughout an intranet. A well-designed file service provides access to files stored at a server with performance and reliability similar to, and in some cases better than, files stored on local disks. Their design is adapted to the performance and reliability characteristics of local networks and hence they are most effective in providing shared persistent storage for use in intranets. The first file servers were developed by researchers in the 1970s [Birrell and Needham 1980, Mitchell and Dion 1982, Leach *et al.* 1983], and Sun's Network File System became available in the early 1980s [Sandberg *et al.* 1985, Callaghan 1999].

A file service enables programs to store and access remote files exactly as they do local ones, allowing users to access their files from any computer in an intranet. The concentration of persistent storage at a few servers reduces the need for local disk storage and (more importantly) enables economies to be made in the management and archiving of the persistent data owned by an organization. Other services, such as the name service, the user authentication service and the print service, can be more easily

Figure 8.1   Storage systems and their properties

	Sharing	Persis-tence	Distributed cache/replicas	Consistency maintenance	Example
Main memory	✗	✗	✗	1	RAM
File system	✗	✓	✗	1	UNIX file system
Distributed file system	✓	✓	✓	✓	Sun NFS
Web	✓	✓	✓	✗	Web server
Distributed shared memory	✓	✗	✓	✓	Ivy (DSM, Ch. 18)
Remote objects (RMI/ORB)	✓	✗	✗	1	CORBA
Persistent object store	✓	✓	✗	1	CORBA Persistent State Service
Peer-to-peer storage system	✓	✓	✓	2	OceanStore (Ch. 10)

Types of consistency:
   1: strict one-copy. ✓: slightly weaker guarantees. 2: considerably weaker guarantees.

implemented when they can call upon the file service to meet their needs for persistent storage. Web servers are reliant on filing systems for the storage of the web pages that they serve. In organizations that operate web servers for external and internal access via an intranet, the web servers often store and access the material from a local distributed file system.

With the advent of distributed object-oriented programming, a need arose for the persistent storage and distribution of shared objects. One way to achieve this is to serialize objects (in the manner described in Section 4.3.2) and to store and retrieve the serialized objects using files. But this method for achieving persistence and distribution becomes impractical for rapidly changing objects, and several more direct approaches have therefore been developed. Java remote object invocation and CORBA ORBs provide access to remote, shared objects, but neither of these ensures the persistence of the objects, nor are the distributed objects replicated.

Figure 8.1 provides an overview of types of storage system. In addition to those already mentioned, the table includes distributed shared memory (DSM) systems and persistent object stores. DSM is described in detail in Chapter 18. It provides an emulation of a shared memory by the replication of memory pages or segments at each host. It does not necessarily provide automatic persistence. Persistent object stores were introduced in Chapter 5. They aim to provide persistence for distributed shared objects. Examples include the CORBA Persistent State Service (see Chapter 20) and persistent extensions to Java [Jordan 1996, java.sun.com VIII]. Some research projects have developed in platforms that support the automatic replication and persistent storage of objects (for example, PerDiS [Ferreira *et al.* 2000] and Khazana [Carter *et al.* 1998]). Peer-to-peer storage systems offer scalability to support client loads much larger than the systems described in this chaper, but they incur high performance costs in providing secure access control and consistency between updatable replicas.

Figure 8.2   File system modules

Directory module:	relates file names to file IDs
File module:	relates file IDs to particular files
Access control module:	checks permission for operation requested
File access module:	reads or writes file data or attributes
Block module:	accesses and allocates disk blocks
Device module:	disk I/O and buffering

The *consistency* column indicates whether mechanisms exist for the maintenance of consistency between multiple copies of data when updates occur. Virtually all storage systems rely on the use of caching to optimize the performance of programs. Caching was first applied to main memory and non-distributed file systems, and for those the consistency is strict (denoted by a '1', for one-copy consistency in Figure 8.1) – programs cannot observe any discrepancies between cached copies and stored data after an update. When distributed replicas are used, strict consistency is more difficult to achieve. Distributed file systems such as Sun NFS and the Andrew File System cache copies of portions of files at client computers, and they adopt specific consistency mechanisms to maintain an approximation to strict consistency. This is indicated by a tick (✔) in the consistency column of Figure 8.1 – we discuss these mechanisms and the degree to which they deviate from strict consistency in Sections 8.3 and 8.4.

The Web uses caching extensively both at client computers and at proxy servers maintained by user organizations. The consistency between the copies stored at web proxies and client caches and the original server is only maintained by explicit user actions. Clients are not notified when a page stored at the original server is updated; they must perform explicit checks to keep their local copies up to date. This serves the purposes of web browsing adequately, but it does not support the development of cooperative applications such as a shared distributed whiteboard. The consistency mechanisms used in DSM systems are discussed in detail in Chapter 18. Persistent object systems vary considerably in their approach to the use of caching and consistency. The CORBA and Persistent Java schemes maintain single copies of persistent objects, and remote invocation is required to access them, so the only consistency issue is between the persistent copy of an object on disk and the active copy in memory, which is not visible to remote clients. The PerDiS and Khazana projects that we have mentioned above maintain cached replicas of objects and employ quite elaborate consistency mechanisms to produce forms of consistency similar to those found in DSM systems.

Having introduced some wider issues relating to storage and distribution of persistent and non-persistent data, we now return to the main topic of this chapter – the design of basic distributed file systems. We describe some relevant characteristics of (non-distributed) file systems in Section 8.1.1 and the requirements for distributed file systems in Section 8.1.2. Section 8.1.3 introduces the case studies that will be used throughout the chapter. In Section 8.2, we define an abstract model for a basic

Figure 8.3   File attribute record structure

File length
Creation timestamp
Read timestamp
Write timestamp
Attribute timestamp
Reference count
Owner
File type
Access control list

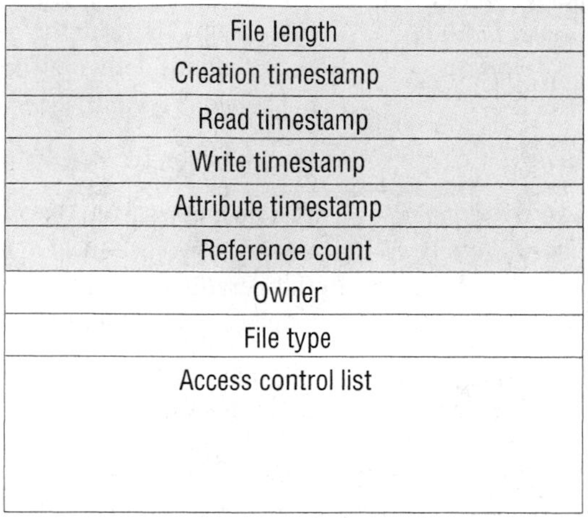

distributed file service, including a set of programming interfaces. The Sun NFS system is described in Section 8.3; it shares many of the features of the abstract model. In Section 8.4, we describe the Andrew File System – a widely used system that employs substantially different caching and consistency mechanisms. Section 8.5 reviews some recent developments in the design of file services.

The systems described in this chapter do not cover the full spectrum of distributed file and data management systems. Several systems with more advanced characteristics will be described later in the book. Chapter 15 includes a description of Coda, a distributed file system that maintains persistent replicas of files for reliability, availability and disconnected working. Bayou, a distributed data management system which provides a weakly consistent form of replication for high availability is also covered in Chapter 15. Chapter 17 covers the Tiger video file server, which is designed to provide timely delivery of streams of data to large numbers of clients.

8.1.1   Characteristics of file systems

File systems are responsible for the organization, storage, retrieval, naming, sharing and protection of files. They provide a programming interface that characterizes the file abstraction, freeing programmers from concern with the details of storage allocation and layout. Files are stored on disks or other non-volatile storage media.

Files contain both *data* and *attributes*. The data consist of a sequence of data items (typically 8-bit bytes), accessible by operations to read and write any portion of the sequence. The attributes are held as a single record containing information such as the length of the file, timestamps, file type, owner's identity and access-control lists. A typical attribute record structure is illustrated in Figure 8.3. The shaded attributes are managed by the file system and are not normally updatable by user programs.

File systems are designed to store and manage large numbers of files, with facilities for creating, naming and deleting files. The naming of files is supported by the

Figure 8.4   UNIX file system operations

filedes = open(name, mode)	Opens an existing file with the given *name*.
filedes = creat(name, mode)	Creates a new file with the given *name*. Both operations deliver a file descriptor referencing the open file. The *mode* is *read*, *write* or both.
status = close(filedes)	Closes the open file *filedes*.
count = read(filedes, buffer, n)	Transfers *n* bytes from the file referenced by *filedes* to *buffer*.
count = write(filedes, buffer, n)	Transfers *n* bytes to the file referenced by *filedes* from *buffer*. Both operations deliver the number of bytes actually transferred and advance the read-write pointer.
pos = lseek(filedes, offset, whence)	Moves the read-write pointer to offset (relative or absolute, depending on *whence*).
status = unlink(name)	Removes the file *name* from the directory structure. If the file has no other names, it is deleted.
status = link(name1, name2)	Adds a new name (*name2*) for a file (*name1*).
status = stat(name, buffer)	Gets the file attributes for file *name* into *buffer*.

use of directories. A *directory* is a file, often of a special type, that provides a mapping from text names to internal file identifiers. Directories may include the names of other directories, leading to the familiar hierarchic file-naming scheme and the multi-part *pathnames* for files used in UNIX and other operating systems. File systems also take responsibility for the control of access to files, restricting access to files according to users' authorizations and the type of access requested (reading, updating, executing and so on).

The term *metadata* is often used to refer to all of the extra information stored by a file system that is needed for the management of files. It includes file attributes, directories and all other persistent information used by the file system.

Figure 8.2 shows a typical layered module structure for the implementation of a non-distributed file system in a conventional operating system. Each layer depends only on the layers below it. The implementation of a distributed file service requires all of the components shown there, with additional components to deal with client-server communication and with the distributed naming and location of files.

File system operations ◊ Figure 8.4 summarizes the main operations on files that are available to applications in UNIX systems. These are the system calls implemented by the kernel; application programmers usually access them through library procedures such as the C Standard Input–Output Library or Java file classes. We give the primitives here as an indication of the operations that file services are expected to support and for comparison with the file service interfaces that we shall introduce below.

The UNIX operations are based on a programming model in which some file state information is stored by the file system for each running program. This consists of a list of currently open files with a read-write pointer for each, giving the position within the file at which the next read or write operation will be applied.

The file system is responsible for applying access control for files. In local file systems such as UNIX, it does so when each file is opened, checking the rights allowed for the user's identity in the access control list against the *mode* of access requested in the *open* system call. If the rights match the mode, the file is opened and the *mode* is recorded in the open file state information.

8.1.2   Distributed file system requirements

Many of the requirements and potential pitfalls in the design of distributed services were first observed in the early development of distributed file systems. Initially, they offered access transparency and location transparency; performance, scalability, concurrency control, fault tolerance and security requirements emerged and were met in subsequent phases of development. We discuss these and related requirements in the following subsections.

Transparency ◊ The file service is usually the most heavily loaded service in an intranet, so its functionality and performance are critical. The design of the file service should support many of the transparency requirements for distributed systems identified in Section 1.4.7. The design must balance the flexibility and scalability that derive from transparency against software complexity and performance. The following forms of transparency are partially or wholly addressed by current file services:

Access transparency: Client programs should be unaware of the distribution of files. A single set of operations is provided for access to local and remote files. Programs written to operate on local files are able to access remote files without modification.

Location transparency: Client programs should see a uniform file name space. Files or groups of files may be relocated without changing their pathnames, and user programs see the same name space wherever they are executed.

Mobility transparency: Neither client programs nor system administration tables in client nodes need to be changed when files are moved. This allows file mobility – files or, more commonly, sets or volumes of files may be moved, either by system administrators or automatically.

Performance transparency: Client programs should continue to perform satisfactorily while the load on the service varies within a specified range.

Scaling transparency: The service can be expanded by incremental growth to deal with a wide range of loads and network sizes.

Concurrent file updates ◊ Changes to a file by one client should not interfere with the operation of other clients simultaneously accessing or changing the same file. This is the well-known issue of concurrency control, discussed in detail in Chapter 13. The need for concurrency control for access to shared data in many applications is widely accepted and techniques are known for its implementation, but they are costly. Most current file services follow modern UNIX standards in providing advisory or mandatory file- or record-level locking.

File replication ◊ In a file service that supports replication, a file may be represented by several copies of its contents at different locations. This has two benefits – it enables multiple servers to share the load of providing a service to clients accessing the same set of files, enhancing the scalability of the service, and it enhances fault tolerance by enabling clients to locate another server that holds a copy of the file when one has failed. Few file services support replication fully, but most support the caching of files or portions of files locally, a limited form of replication. The replication of data is discussed in Chapter 15, which includes a description of the Coda replicated file service.

Hardware and operating system heterogeneity ◊ The service interfaces should be defined so that client and server software can be implemented for different operating systems and computers. This requirement is an important aspect of openness.

Fault tolerance ◊ The central role of the file service in distributed systems makes it essential that the service continue to operate in the face of client and server failures. Fortunately, a moderately fault-tolerant design is straightforward for simple servers. To cope with transient communication failures, the design can be based on at-most-once invocation semantics (see Section 5.2.4). Or it can use the simpler at-least-once semantics with a server protocol designed in terms of *idempotent* operations, ensuring that duplicated requests do not result in invalid updates to files. The servers can be *stateless*, so that they can be restarted and the service restored after a failure without any need to recover previous state. Tolerance of disconnection or server failures requires file replication, which is more difficult to achieve and will be discussed in Chapter 15.

Consistency ◊ Conventional file systems such as that provided in UNIX offer *one-copy update semantics*. This refers to a model for concurrent access to files in which the file contents seen by all of the processes accessing or updating a given file are those that they would see if only a single copy of the file contents existed. When files are replicated or cached at different sites, there is an inevitable delay in the propagation of modifications made at one site to all of the other sites that hold copies, and this may result in some deviation from one-copy semantics.

Security ◊ Virtually all file systems provide access control mechanisms based on the use of access control lists. In distributed file systems, there is a need to authenticate client requests so that access control at the server is based on correct user identities and to protect the contents of request and reply messages with digital signatures and (optionally) encryption of secret data. We shall discuss the impact of these requirements in our case study descriptions.

Efficiency ◊ A distributed file service should offer facilities that are of at least the same power and generality as those found in conventional file systems and should achieve a comparable level of performance. Birrell and Needham [1980] expressed their design aims for the Cambridge File Server (CFS) in these terms:

> We would wish to have a simple, low-level, file server in order to share an expensive resource, namely a disk, whilst leaving us free to design the filing system most appropriate to a particular client, but we would wish also to have available a high-level system shared between clients.

The changed economics of disk storage have reduced the significance of their first goal, but their perception of the need for a range of services addressing the requirements of clients with different goals remains and can best be addressed by a modular architecture of the type outlined above.

The techniques used for the implementation of file services are an important part of the design of distributed systems. A distributed file system should provide a service that is comparable with, or better than, local file systems in performance and reliability. It must be convenient to administer, providing operations and tools that enable system administrators to install and operate the system conveniently.

8.1.3 Case studies

We have constructed an abstract model for a file service to act as an introductory example, separating implementation concerns and providing a simplified model. We describe the Sun Network File System in some detail, drawing on our simpler abstract model to clarify its architecture. The Andrew File System is then described, providing a view of a distributed file system that takes a different approach to scalability and consistency maintenance.

File service architecture ◊ This is an abstract architectural model that underpins both NFS and AFS. It is based upon a division of responsibilities between three modules – a client module which emulates a conventional file system interface for application programs and server modules, which perform operations for clients on directories and on files. The architecture is designed to enable a *stateless* implementation of the server module.

SUN NFS ◊ Sun Microsystem's *Network File System* (*NFS*) has been widely adopted in industry and in academic environments since its introduction in 1985. The design and development of NFS were undertaken by staff at Sun Microsystems in 1984 [Sandberg *et al.* 1985; Sandberg 1987, Callaghan 1999]. Although several distributed file services had already been developed and used in universities and research laboratories, NFS was the first file service that was designed as a product. The design and implementation of NFS have achieved success both technically and commercially.

To encourage its adoption as a standard, the definitions of the key interfaces were placed in the public domain [Sun 1989], enabling other vendors to produce implementations, and the source code for a reference implementation was made available to other computer vendors under licence. It is now supported by many vendors, and the NFS protocol (version 3) is an Internet standard, defined in RFC 1813 [Callaghan *et al.* 1995]. Callaghan's book on NFS [Callaghan 1999] is an excellent source on the design and development of NFS and related topics.

NFS provides transparent access to remote files for client programs running on UNIX and other systems. The client-server relationship is symmetrical: each computer in an NFS network can act as both a client and a server, and the files at every machine can be made available for remote access by other machines. Any computer can be a server, exporting some of its files, and a client, accessing files on other machines. But it is common practice to configure larger installations with some machines as dedicated servers and others as workstations.

An important goal of NFS is to achieve a high level of support for hardware and operating system heterogeneity. The design is operating-system independent: client and server implementations exist for almost all operating systems and platforms, including

Figure 8.5   File service architecture

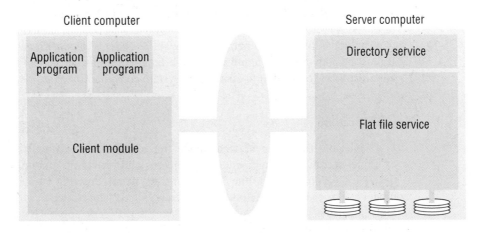

all versions of Windows, Mac OS, Linux and every other version of UNIX. Implementations of NFS on high-performance multiprocessor hosts have been developed by several vendors, and these are widely used to meet storage requirements in intranets with many concurrent users.

Andrew File System ◊ Andrew is a distributed computing environment developed at Carnegie Mellon University (CMU) for use as a campus computing and information system [Morris *et al.* 1986]. The design of the Andrew File System (henceforth abbreviated AFS) reflects an intention to support information sharing on a large scale by minimizing client-server communication. This was achieved by transferring whole files between server and client computers and caching them at clients until the server receives a more up-to-date version. We shall describe AFS-2, the first 'production' implementation, following the descriptions by Satyanarayanan [1989a; 1989b]. More recent descriptions can be found in Campbell [1997] and [Linux AFS].

AFS was initially implemented on a network of workstations and servers running BSD UNIX and the Mach operating system at CMU and was subsequently made available in commercial and public-domain versions. A public-domain implementation of AFS is available in the Linux operating system [Linux AFS]. AFS was adopted as the basis for the DCE/DFS file system in the Open Software Foundation's Distributed Computing Environment (DCE) [www.opengroup.org]. The design of DCE/DFS went beyond AFS in several important respects, which we outline in Section 8.5.

8.2   File service architecture

An architecture that offers a clear separation of the main concerns in providing access to files is obtained by structuring the file service as three components – a *flat file service*, a *directory service* and a *client module*. The relevant modules and their relationships are shown in Figure 8.5. The flat file service and the directory service each export an interface for use by client programs, and their RPC interfaces, taken together, provide a comprehensive set of operations for access to files. The client module provides a single programming interface with operations on files similar to those found in conventional file systems. The design is *open* in the sense that different client modules can be used to implement different programming interfaces, simulating the file operations of a variety of different operating systems and optimizing the performance for different client and server hardware configurations.

The division of responsibilities between the modules can be defined as follows:

Flat file service ◊   The flat file service is concerned with implementing operations on the contents of files. *Unique file identifiers* (UFIDs) are used to refer to files in all requests for flat file service operations. The division of responsibilities between the file service and the directory service is based upon the use of UFIDs. UFIDs are long sequences of bits chosen so that each file has a UFID that is unique among all of the files in a distributed system. When the flat file service receives a request to create a file, it generates a new UFID for it and returns the UFID to the requester.

Directory service ◊   The directory service provides a mapping between *text names* for files and their UFIDs. Clients may obtain the UFID of a file by quoting its text name to the directory service. The directory service provides the functions needed to generate directories, to add new file names to directories and to obtain UFIDs from directories. It is a client of the flat file service; its directory files are stored in files of the flat file service. When a hierarchic file-naming scheme is adopted, as in UNIX, directories hold references to other directories.

Client module ◊   A client module runs in each client computer, integrating and extending the operations of the flat file service and the directory service under a single application programming interface that is available to user-level programs in client computers. For example, in UNIX hosts, a client module would be provided that emulates the full set of UNIX file operations, interpreting UNIX multi-part file names by iterative requests to the directory service. The client module also holds information about the network locations of the flat file server and directory server processes. Finally, the client module can play an important role in achieving satisfactory performance through the implementation of a cache of recently used file blocks at the client.

Flat file service interface ◊   Figure 8.6 contains a definition of the interface to a flat file service. This is the RPC interface used by client modules. It is not normally used directly by user-level programs. A *FileId* is invalid if the file that it refers to is not present in the server processing the request or if its access permissions are inappropriate for the operation requested. All of the procedures in the interface except *Create* throw exceptions if the *FileId* argument contains an invalid UFID or the user doesn't have sufficient access rights. These exceptions are omitted from the definition for clarity.

The most important operations are those for reading and writing. Both the *Read* and the *Write* operation require a parameter *i* specifying a position in the file. The *Read* operation copies the sequence of *n* data items beginning at item *i* from the specified file into *Data*, which is then returned to the client. The *Write* operation copies the sequence of data items in *Data* into the specified file beginning at item *i*, replacing the previous contents of the file at the corresponding position and extending the file if necessary.

Create creates a new, empty file and returns the UFID that is generated. *Delete* removes the specified file.

Figure 8.6   Flat file service operations

Read(FileId, i, n) → Data — throws *BadPosition*	If $1 \leq i \leq Length(File)$: Reads a sequence of up to *n* items from a file starting at item *i* and returns it in *Data*.
Write(FileId, i, Data) — throws *BadPosition*	If $1 \leq i \leq Length(File)+1$; Writes a sequence of *Data* to a file, starting at item *i*, extending the file if necessary.
Create() → FileId	Creates a new file of length 0 and delivers a UFID for it.
Delete(FileId)	Removes the file from the file store.
GetAttributes(FileId) → Attr	Returns the file attributes for the file.
SetAttributes(FileId, Attr)	Sets the file attributes (only those attributes that are not shaded in Figure 8.3).

GetAttributes and *SetAttributes* enable clients to access the attribute record. *GetAttributes* is normally available to any client that is allowed to read the file. Access to the *SetAttributes* operation would normally be restricted to the directory service that provides access to the file. The values of the length and timestamp portions of the attribute record are not affected by *SetAttributes*; they are maintained separately by the flat file service itself.

Comparison with UNIX: Our interface and the UNIX file system primitives are functionally equivalent. It is a simple matter to construct a client module that emulates the UNIX system calls in terms of our flat file service and the directory service operations described in the next section.

In comparison with the UNIX interface, our flat file service has no *open* and *close* operations – files can be accessed immediately by quoting the appropriate UFID. The *Read* and *Write* requests in our interface include a parameter specifying a starting point within the file for each transfer, whereas the equivalent UNIX operations do not. In UNIX, each *read* or *write* operation starts at the current position of the read-write pointer, and the read-write pointer is advanced by the number of bytes transferred after each *read* or *write*. A *seek* operation is provided to enable the read-write pointer to be explicitly repositioned.

The interface to our flat file service differs from the UNIX file system interface mainly for reasons of fault tolerance:

Repeatable operations: With the exception of *Create*, the operations are *idempotent*, allowing the use of at-least-once RPC semantics – clients may repeat calls to which they receive no reply. Repeated execution of *Create* produces a different new file for each call.

Stateless servers: The interface is suitable for implementation by *stateless* servers. Stateless servers can be restarted after a failure and resume operation without any need for clients or the server to restore any state.

The UNIX file operations are neither idempotent nor consistent with the requirement for a stateless implementation. A read-write pointer is generated by the UNIX file system whenever a file is opened, and it is retained, together with the results of access control checks, until the file is closed. The UNIX *read* and *write* operations are not idempotent; if an operation is accidentally repeated, the automatic advance of the read-write pointer results in access to a different portion of the file in the repeated operation. The read-write pointer is a hidden, client-related state variable. To mimic it in a file server, *open* and *close* operations would be needed, and the read-write pointer's value would have to be retained by the server as long as the relevant file is open. By eliminating the read-write pointer, we have eliminated most of the need for the file server to retain state information on behalf of specific clients.

Access control ◊ In the UNIX file system, the user's access rights are checked against the access *mode* (read or write) requested in the *open* call (Figure 8.4 shows the UNIX file system API) and the file is opened only if the user has the necessary rights. The user identity (UID) used in the access rights check is the result of the user's earlier authenticated login and cannot be tampered with in non-distributed implementations. The resulting access rights are retained until the file is closed, and no further checks are required when subsequent operations on the same file are requested.

In distributed implementations, access rights checks have to be performed at the server because the server RPC interface is an otherwise unprotected point of access to files. A user identity has to be passed with requests, and the server is vulnerable to forged identities. Furthermore, if the results of an access rights check were retained at the server and used for future accesses, the server would no longer be stateless. Two alternative approaches to the latter problem can be adopted:

- An access check is made whenever a file name is converted to a UFID, and the results are encoded in the form of a capability (see Section 7.2.4), which is returned to the client for submission with subsequent requests.

- A user identity is submitted with every client request, and access checks are performed by the server for every file operation.

Both methods enable stateless server implementation, and both have been used in distributed file systems. The second is more common; it is used in both NFS and AFS. Neither of these approaches overcomes the security problem concerning forged user identities. We have seen in Chapter 7 that this can be addressed by the use of digital signatures. Kerberos is an effective authentication scheme that has been applied to both NFS and AFS.

In our abstract model, we make no assumption about the method by which access control is implemented. The user identity is passed as an implicit parameter and can be used whenever it is needed.

Directory service interface ◊ Figure 8.7 contains a definition of the RPC interface to a directory service. The primary purpose of the directory service is to provide a service for translating text names to UFIDs. In order to do so, it maintains directory files containing the mappings between text names for files and UFIDs. Each directory is stored as a conventional file with a UFID, so the directory service is a client of the file service.

We define only operations on individual directories. For each operation, a UFID for the file containing the directory is required (in the *Dir* parameter). The *Lookup* operation in the basic directory service performs a single *Name* → *UFID* translation. It

Figure 8.7   Directory service operations

Lookup(Dir, Name) → *FileId* — throws *NotFound*	Locates the text name in the directory and returns the relevant UFID. If *Name* is not in the directory, throws an exception.
AddName(Dir, Name, FileId) — throws *NameDuplicate*	If *Name* is not in the directory, adds *(Name, File)* to the directory and updates the file's attribute record. If *Name* is already in the directory: throws an exception.
UnName(Dir, Name) — throws *NotFound*	If *Name* is in the directory: the entry containing *Name* is removed from the directory. If *Name* is not in the directory: throws an exception.
GetNames(Dir, Pattern) → *NameSeq*	Returns all the text names in the directory that match the regular expression *Pattern*.

is a building block for use in other services or in the client module to perform more complex translations, such as the hierarchic name interpretation found in UNIX. As before, exceptions caused by inadequate access rights are omitted from the definitions.

There are two operations for altering directories: *AddName* and *UnName*. *AddName* adds an entry to a directory and increments the reference count field in the file's attribute record.

UnName removes an entry from a directory and decrements the reference count. If this causes the reference count to reach zero, the file is removed. *GetNames* is provided to enable clients to examine the contents of directories and to implement pattern-matching operations on file names such as those found in the UNIX shell. It returns all or a subset of the names stored in a given directory. The names are selected by pattern matching against a regular expression supplied by the client.

The provision of pattern matching in the *GetNames* operation enables users to determine the names of one or more files by giving an incomplete specification of the characters in the names. A regular expression is a specification for a class of strings in the form of an expression containing a combination of literal sub-strings and symbols denoting variable characters or repeated occurrences of characters or sub-strings.

Hierarchic file system ◊ A hierarchic file system such as the one that UNIX provides consists of a number of directories arranged in a tree structure. Each directory holds the names of the files and other directories that are accessible from it. Any file or directory can be referenced using a *pathname* – a multi-part name that represents a path through the tree. The root has a distinguished name, and each file or directory has a name in a directory. The UNIX file-naming scheme is not a strict hierarchy – files can have several names, and they can be in the same or different directories. This is implemented by a *link* operation, which adds a new name for a file to a specified directory.

A UNIX-like file-naming system can be implemented by the client module using the flat file and directory services that we have defined. A tree-structured network of directories is constructed with files at the leaves and directories at the other nodes of the tree. The root of the tree is a directory with a 'well-known' UFID. Multiple names for files can be supported using the *AddName* operation and the reference count field in the attribute record.

A function can be provided in the client module that gets the UFID of a file given its pathname. The function interprets the pathname starting from the root, using *Lookup* to obtain the UFID of each directory in the path.

In a hierarchic directory service, the file attributes associated with files should include a type field that distinguishes between ordinary files and directories. This is used when following a path to ensure that each part of the name, except the last, refers to a directory.

File groups ◊ A *file group* is a collection of files located on a given server. A server may hold several file groups, and groups can be moved between servers, but a file cannot change the group to which it belongs. A similar construct (called a *filesystem*) is used in UNIX and in most other operating systems. File groups were originally introduced to support facilities for moving collections of files stored on removable media between computers. In a distributed file service, file groups support the allocation of files to file servers in larger logical units and enable the service to be implemented with files stored on several servers. In a distributed file system that supports file groups, the representation of UFIDs includes a file group identifier component, enabling the client module in each client computer to take responsibility for dispatching requests to the server that holds the relevant file group.

File group identifiers must be unique throughout a distributed system. Since file groups can be moved, and distributed systems that are initially separate can be merged to form a single system, the only way to ensure that file group identifiers will always be distinct in a given system is to generate them with an algorithm that ensures global uniqueness. For example, whenever a new file group is created, a unique identifier can be generated by concatenating the 32 bit IP address of the host creating the new group with a 16-bit integer derived from the date, producing a unique 48-bit integer:

32 bits   *16 bits*

file group identifier: | IP address | date |

Note that the IP address *cannot* be used for the purpose of locating the file group, since it may be moved to another server. Instead, a mapping between group identifiers and servers should be maintained by the file service.

8.3   Case study: Sun Network File System

Figure 8.8 shows the architecture of Sun NFS. It follows the abstract model defined in the preceding section. All implementations of NFS support the NFS protocol – a set of remote procedure calls that provide the means for clients to perform operations on a remote file store. The NFS protocol is operating-system-independent but was originally developed for use in networks of UNIX systems, and we shall describe the UNIX implementation the NFS protocol (version 3).

Figure 8.8   NFS architecture

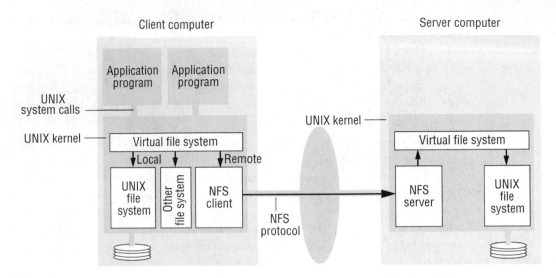

The *NFS server* module resides in the kernel on each computer that acts as an NFS server. Requests referring to files in a remote file system are translated by the client module to NFS protocol operations and then passed to the NFS server module at the computer holding the relevant file system.

The NFS client and server modules communicate using remote procedure calling. Sun's RPC system, described in Section 5.3.1, was developed for use in NFS. It can be configured to use either UDP or TCP, and the NFS protocol is compatible with both. A port mapper service is included to enable clients to bind to services in a given host by name. The RPC interface to the NFS server is open: any process can send requests to an NFS server; if the requests are valid and they include valid user credentials, they will be acted upon. The submission of signed user credentials can be required as an optional security feature, as can the encryption of data for privacy and integrity.

Virtual file system ◊   Figure 8.8 makes it clear that NFS provides access transparency: user programs can issue file operations for local or remote files without distinction. Other distributed file systems may be present that support UNIX system calls, and if so, they could be integrated in the same way.

The integration is achieved by a virtual file system (VFS) module, which has been added to the UNIX kernel to distinguish between local and remote files and to translate between the UNIX-independent file identifiers used by NFS and the internal file identifiers normally used in UNIX and other file systems. In addition, VFS keeps track of the filesystems that are currently available both locally and remotely, and it passes each request to the appropriate local system module (the UNIX file system, the NFS client module or the service module for another file system).

The file identifiers used in NFS are called *file handles*. A file handle is opaque to clients and contains whatever information the server needs to distinguish an individual file. In UNIX implementations of NFS, the file handle is derived from the file's *i-node number* by adding two extra fields as follows (the i-node number of a UNIX file is a number that serves to identify and locate the file within the file system in which the file is stored):

File handle:	Filesystem identifier	i-node number of file	i-node generation number

NFS adopts the UNIX mountable filesystem as the unit of file grouping defined in the preceding section. (Terminology note: the single word *filesystem* refers to the set of files held in a storage device or partition, whereas the words *file system* refer to a software component that provides access to files.) The *filesystem identifier* field is a unique number that is allocated to each filesystem when it is created (and in the UNIX implementation is stored in the superblock of the file system). The *i-node generation number* is needed because in the conventional UNIX file system i-node numbers are reused after a file is removed. In the VFS extensions to the UNIX file system, a generation number is stored with each file and is incremented each time the i-node number is reused (for example, in a UNIX *creat* system call). The client obtains the first file handle for a remote file system when it mounts it. File handles are passed from server to client in the results of *lookup*, *create* and *mkdir* operations (see Figure 8.9) and from client to server in the argument lists of all server operations.

The virtual file system layer has one VFS structure for each mounted file system and one *v-node* per open file. A VFS structure relates a remote file system to the local directory on which it is mounted. The v-node contains an indicator to show whether a file is local or remote. If the file is local, the v-node contains a reference to the index of the local file (an i-node in a UNIX implementation). If the file is remote, it contains the file handle of the remote file.

Client integration ◊ The NFS client module plays the role described for the client module in our architectural model, supplying an interface suitable for use by conventional application programs. But unlike our model client module, it emulates the semantics of the standard UNIX file system primitives precisely and is integrated with the UNIX kernel. It is integrated with the kernel and not supplied as a library for loading into client processes so that:

- user programs can access files via UNIX system calls without recompilation or reloading;

- a single client module serves all of the user-level processes, with a shared cache of recently used blocks (described below);

- the encryption key used to authenticate user IDs passed to the server (see below) can be retained in the kernel, preventing impersonation by user-level clients.

The NFS client module cooperates with the virtual file system in each client machine. It operates in a similar manner to the conventional UNIX file system, transferring blocks of files to and from the server and caching the blocks in the local memory whenever possible. It shares the same buffer cache that is used by the local input–output system. But since several clients in different host machines may simultaneously access the same remote file, a new and significant cache consistency problem arises.

Figure 8.9   NFS server operations (NFS Version 3 protocol, simplified)

lookup(dirfh, name) → *fh, attr*	Returns file handle and attributes for the file *name* in the directory *dirfh*.
create(dirfh, name, attr) → *newfh, attr*	Creates a new file *name* in directory *dirfh* with attributes *attr* and returns the new file handle and attributes.
remove(dirfh, name) → *status*	Removes file *name* from directory *dirfh*.
getattr(fh) → *attr*	Returns file attributes of file *fh*. (Similar to the UNIX *stat* system call.)
setattr(fh, attr) → *attr*	Sets the attributes (mode, user ID, group ID, size, access time and modify time of a file). Setting the size to 0 truncates the file.
read(fh, offset, count) → *attr, data*	Returns up to *count* bytes of data from a file starting at *offset*. Also returns the latest attributes of the file.
write(fh, offset, count, data) → *attr*	Writes *count* bytes of data to a file starting at *offset*. Returns the attributes of the file after the write has taken place.
rename(dirfh, name, todirfh, toname) → *status*	Changes the name of file *name* in directory *dirfh* to *toname* in directory to *dirfh*.
link(newdirfh, newname, fh) → *status*	Creates an entry *newname* in the directory *newdirfh* which refers to the file *or* directory *fh*.
symlink(newdirfh, newname, string) → *status*	Creates an entry *newname* in the directory *newdirfh* of type *symbolic link* with the value *string*. The server does not interpret the *string* but makes a symbolic link file to hold it.
readlink(fh) → *string*	Returns the string that is associated with the symbolic link file identified by *fh*.
mkdir(dirfh, name, attr) → *newfh, attr*	Creates a new directory *name* with attributes *attr* and returns the new file handle and attributes.
rmdir(dirfh, name) → *status*	Removes the empty directory *name* from the parent directory *dirfh*. Fails if the directory is not empty.
readdir(dirfh, cookie, count) → *entries*	Returns up to *count* bytes of directory entries from the directory *dirfh*. Each entry contains a file name, a file handle, and an opaque pointer to the next directory entry, called a *cookie*. The *cookie* is used in subsequent *readdir* calls to start reading from the following entry. If the value of *cookie* is 0, reads from the first entry in the directory.
statfs(fh) → *fsstats*	Returns file system information (such as block size, number of free blocks and so on) for the file system containing a file *fh*.

Access control and authentication ◊ Unlike the conventional UNIX file system, the NFS server is stateless and does not keep files open on behalf of its clients. So the server must check the user's identity against the file's access permission attributes afresh on each request, to see whether the user is permitted to access the file in the manner requested. The Sun RPC protocol requires clients to send user authentication information (for example, the conventional UNIX 16-bit user ID and group ID) with each request and this is checked against the access permission in the file attributes. These additional parameters are not shown in our overview of the NFS protocol in Figure 8.9; they are supplied automatically by the RPC system.

In its simplest form, there is a security loophole in this access-control mechanism. An NFS server provides a conventional RPC interface at a well-known port on each host and any process can behave as a client, sending requests to the server to access or update a file. The client can modify the RPC calls to include the user ID of any user, impersonating the user without their knowledge or permission. This security loophole has been closed by the use of an option in the RPC protocol for the DES encryption of the user's authentication information. More recently, Kerberos has been integrated with Sun NFS to provide a stronger and more comprehensive solution to the problems of user authentication and security, and we describe this below.

NFS server interface ◊ A simplified representation of the RPC interface provided by NFS Version 3 servers (defined in RFC 1813 [Callaghan *et al.* 1995]) is shown in Figure 8.9. The NFS file access operations *read*, *write*, *getattr* and *setattr* are almost identical to the *Read*, *Write*, *GetAttributes* and *SetAttributes* operations defined for our flat file service model (Figure 8.6). The *lookup* operation and most of the other directory operations defined in Figure 8.9 are similar to those in our directory service model (Figure 8.7).

The file and directory operations are integrated in a single service; the creation and insertion of file names in directories is performed by a single *create* operation, which takes the text name of the new file and the file handle for the target directory as arguments. The other NFS operations on directories are *create*, *remove*, *rename*, *link*, *symlink*, *readlink*, *mkdir*, *rmdir*, *readdir* and *statfs*. They resemble their UNIX counterparts with the exception of *readdir*. which provides a representation-independent method for reading the contents of directories, and *statfs*, which gives the status information on remote file systems.

Mount service ◊ The mounting of sub-trees of remote filesystems by clients is supported by a separate *mount service* process that runs at user level on each NFS server computer. On each server, there is a file with a well-known name (*/etc/exports*) containing the names of local filesystems that are available for remote mounting. An access list is associated with each filesystem name indicating which hosts are permitted to mount the filesystem.

Clients use a modified version of the UNIX *mount* command to request mounting of a remote filesystem, specifying the remote host name, pathname of a directory in the remote filesystem and the local name with which it is to be mounted. The remote directory may be any sub-tree of the required remote file system, enabling clients to mount any part of the remote filesystem. The modified *mount* command communicates with the mount service process on the remote host using a *mount protocol*. This is an RPC protocol and includes an operation that takes a directory pathname and returns the file handle of the specified directory if the client has access permission for the relevant filesystem. The location (IP address and port number) of the server and the file handle for the remote directory are passed on to the VFS layer and the NFS client.

Figure 8.10 illustrates a *Client* with two remotely mounted file stores. The nodes *people* and *users* in filesystems at *Server 1* and *Server 2* are mounted over nodes *students* and *staff* in *Client*'s local file store. The meaning of this is that programs running at

Figure 8.10   Local and remote file systems accessible on an NFS client

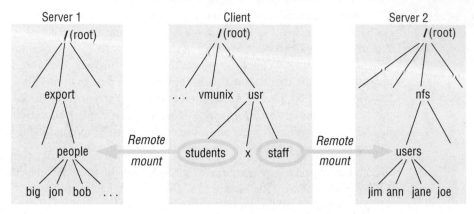

Note: The file system mounted at */usr/students* in the client is actually the sub-tree located at */export/people* in Server 1; the file system mounted at */usr/staff* in the client is actually the sub-tree located at */nfs/users* in Server 2.

Client can access files at *Server 1* and *Server 2* by using pathnames such as /usr/students/jon and /usr/staff/ann.

Remote filesystems may be *hard-mounted* or *soft-mounted* in a client computer. When a user-level process accesses a file in a filesystem that is hard-mounted, the process is suspended until the request can be completed and if the remote host is unavailable for any reason the NFS client module continues to retry the request until it is satisfied. Thus in the case of a server failure, user-level processes are suspended until the server restarts and then they continue just as though there had been no failure. But if the relevant filesystem is soft-mounted, the NFS client module returns a failure indication to user-level processes after a small number of retries. Properly-constructed programs will then detect the failure and take appropriate recovery or reporting actions. But many UNIX utilities and applications do not test for the failure of file access operations, and these behave in unpredictable ways in the case of failure of a soft-mounted filesystem. For this reason, many installations use hard mounting exclusively, with the consequence that programs are unable to recover gracefully when an NFS server is unavailable for a significant period.

Path name translation ◊ UNIX file systems translate multi-part file *pathnames* to i-node references in a step-by-step process whenever the *open*, *creat* or *stat* system calls are used. In NFS, pathnames cannot be translated at a server, because the name may cross a 'mount point' at the client – directories holding different parts of a multi-part name may reside in filesystems at different servers. So pathnames are parsed, and their translation is performed in an iterative manner by the client. Each part of a name that refers to a remote-mounted directory is translated to a file handle using a separate *lookup* request to the remote server.

The *lookup* operation looks for a single part of a pathname in a given directory and returns the corresponding file handle and file attributes. The file handle returned in the previous step is used as a parameter in the next *lookup* step. Since file handles are opaque to NFS client code, the virtual file system is responsible for resolving file handles to a local or a remote directory and performing the necessary indirection when it references a local mount point. Caching of the results of each step in pathname translations alleviates the apparent inefficiency of this process, taking advantage of locality of reference to files and directories; users and programs typically access files in only one or a small number of directories.

Automounter ◊ The automounter was added to the UNIX implementation of NFS in order to mount a remote directory dynamically whenever an 'empty' mount point is referenced by a client. The original implementation of the automounter ran as a user-level UNIX process in each client computer. Later versions (called *autofs*), were implemented in the kernel for Solaris and Linux. We describe the original version here.

The automounter maintains a table of mount points (pathnames) with a reference to one or more NFS servers listed against each. It behaves like a local NFS server at the client machine. When the NFS client module attempts to resolve a pathname that includes one of these mount points, it passes a *lookup*() request to the local automounter which locates the required filesystem in its table and sends a 'probe' request to each server listed. The filesystem on the first server to respond is then mounted at the client using the normal mount service. The mounted filesystem is linked to the mount point using a symbolic link, so that accesses to it will not result in further requests to the automounter. File access then proceeds in the normal way without further reference to the automounter unless there are no references to the symbolic link for several minutes. In the latter case, the automounter unmounts the remote filesystem.

The later kernel implementations replaced the symbolic links with real mounts, avoiding some problems that arose with applications that cached the temporary pathnames used in user-level automounters [Callaghan 1999].

A simple form of read-only replication can be achieved by listing several servers containing identical copies of a filesystem or file sub-tree against a name in the automounter table. This is useful for heavily used file systems that change infrequently, such as UNIX system binaries. For example, copies of the */usr/lib* directory and its sub-tree might be held on more than one server. On the first occasion that a file in */usr/lib* is opened at a client, all of the servers will be sent probe messages, and the first to respond will be mounted at the client. This provides a limited degree of fault tolerance and load balancing, since the first server to respond will be one that has not failed and is likely to be one that is not heavily occupied with servicing other requests.

Server caching ◊ Caching in both the client and the server computer are indispensable features of NFS implementations in order to achieve adequate performance.

In conventional UNIX systems, file pages, directories and file attributes that have been read from disk are retained in a main memory *buffer cache* until the buffer space is required for other pages. If a process then issues a read or a write request for a page that is already in the cache, it can be satisfied without another disk access. *Read-ahead* anticipates read accesses and fetches the pages following those that have most recently been read, and *delayed-write* optimizes writes: when a page has been altered (by a write request), its new contents are written to disk only when the buffer page is required for another page. To guard against loss of data in a system crash, the UNIX *sync* operation flushes altered pages to disk every 30 seconds. These caching techniques work in a conventional UNIX environment because all read and write requests issued by user-level processes pass through a single cache that is implemented in the UNIX kernel space. The cache is always kept up to date, and file accesses cannot bypass the cache.

NFS servers use the cache at the server machine just as it is used for other file accesses. The use of the server's cache to hold recently read disk blocks does not raise any consistency problems, but when a server performs write operations, extra measures are needed to ensure that clients can be confident that the results of write operations are persistent, even when server crashes occur. In version 3 of the NFS protocol, the *write* operation offers two options for this (not shown in Figure 8.9):

1. Data in *write* operations received from clients is stored in the memory cache at the server *and* written to disk before a reply is sent to the client. This is called *write-through* caching. The client can be sure that the data is stored persistently as soon as the reply has been received.

2. Data in *write* operations is stored only in the memory cache. It will be written to disk when a *commit* operation is received for the relevant file. The client can be sure that the data is persistently stored only when a reply to a *commit* operation for the relevant file has been received. Standard NFS clients use this mode of operation, issuing a *commit* whenever a file that was open for writing is closed.

Commit is an additional operation provided in version 3 of the NFS protocol; it was added to overcome a performance bottleneck caused by the write-through mode of operation in servers that receive large numbers of *write* operations.

The requirement for write-through in distributed file systems is an instance of the independent failure modes discussed in Chapter 1 – clients continue to operate when a server fails, and application programs may take actions on the assumption that the results of previous writes are committed to disk storage. This is unlikely to occur in the case of local file updates, because the failure of a local file system is almost certain to result in the failure of all the application processes running on the same computer.

Client caching ◊ The NFS client module caches the results of *read*, *write*, *getattr*, *lookup* and *readdir* operations in order to reduce the number of requests transmitted to servers. Client caching introduces the potential for different versions of files or portions of files to exist in different client nodes, because writes by a client do not result in the immediate updating of cached copies of the same file in other clients. Instead, clients are responsible for polling the server to check the currency of the cached data that they hold.

A timestamp-based method is used to validate cached blocks before they are used. Each data or metadata item in the cache is tagged with two timestamps:

Tc is the time when the cache entry was last validated.
Tm is the time when the block was last modified at the server.

A cache entry is valid at time T if $T - Tc$ is less than a freshness interval t, or if the value for Tm recorded at the client matches the value of Tm at the server (that is, the data has not been modified at the server since the cache entry was made). Formally, the validity condition is:

$$(T - Tc < t) \vee (Tm_{client} = Tm_{server})$$

The selection of a value for t is a compromise between consistency and efficiency. A very short freshness interval will result in a close approximation to one-copy consistency, at the cost of a relatively heavy load of calls to the server to check the value of Tm_{server}. In Sun Solaris clients, t is set adaptively for individual files to a value in the range 3 to 30 seconds depending on the frequency of updates to the file. For directories the range is 30 to 60 seconds, reflecting the lower risk of concurrent updates.

There is one value of Tm_{server} for all the data blocks in a file and another for the file attributes. Since NFS clients cannot determine whether a file is being shared or not, the validation procedure must be used for all file accesses. A validity check is performed whenever a cache entry is used. The first half of the validity condition can be evaluated without access to the server. If it is true, then the second half need not be evaluated; if it is false, the current value of Tm_{server} is obtained (by means of a *getattr* call to the server) and compared with the local value Tm_{client}. If they are the same, then the cache entry is taken to be valid and the value of T_c for that cache entry is updated to the current time. If they differ, then the cached data has been updated at the server and the cache entry is invalidated, resulting in a request to the server for the relevant data.

Several measures are used to reduce the traffic of *getattr* calls to the server:

- Whenever a new value of Tm_{server} is received at a client, it is applied to all cache entries derived from the relevant file.

- The current attribute values are sent 'piggybacked' with the results of every operation on a file, and if the value of Tm_{server} has changed the client uses it to update the cache entries relating to the file.

- The adaptive algorithm for setting freshness interval t outlined above reduces the traffic considerably for most files.

The validation procedure does not guarantee the same level of consistency of files that is provided in conventional UNIX systems, since recent updates are not always visible to clients sharing a file; there are two sources of time lag, the delay after write before the updated data leaves the cache in the updating client's kernel and the 3-second 'window' for cache validation. Fortunately, most UNIX applications do not depend critically upon the synchronization of file updates, and few difficulties have been reported from this source.

Writes are handled differently. When a cached page is modified it is marked as dirty and is scheduled to be flushed to the server asynchronously. Modified pages are flushed when the file is closed or a *sync* occurs at the client, and they are flushed more frequently if bio-daemons are in use (see below). This does not provide the same persistence guarantee as the server cache, but it emulates the behaviour for local writes.

To implement read-ahead and delayed-write, the NFS client needs to perform some reads and writes asynchronously. This is achieved in UNIX implementations of NFS by the inclusion of one or more *bio–daemon* processes at each client. (*Bio* stands for block input-output; the term *daemon* is often used to refer to user-level processes that perform system tasks.) The role of the bio-daemons is to perform read-ahead and delayed-write operations. A bio-daemon is notified after each read request, and it requests the transfer of the following file block from the server to the client cache. In the case of writing, the bio-daemon will send a block to the server whenever a block has been filled by a client operation. Directory blocks are sent whenever a modification has occurred.

Bio-daemon processes improve performance, ensuring that the client module does not block waiting for *read*s to return or *write*s to commit at the server. They are not a logical requirement, since in the absence of read-ahead, a *read* operation in a user process will trigger a synchronous request to the relevant server, and the results of *write*s in user processes will be transferred to the server when the relevant file is closed or when the virtual file system at the client performs a *sync* operation.

Other optimizations ◊ The Sun file system is based on the UNIX BSD Fast File System which uses 8-kbyte disk blocks, resulting in fewer file system calls for sequential file access than previous UNIX systems. The UDP packets used for the implementation of Sun RPC are extended to 9 kilobytes, enabling an RPC call containing an entire block as an argument to be transferred in a single packet and minimizing the effect of network latency when reading files sequentially. In NFS version 3, there is no limit on the maximum size of file blocks that can be handled in *read* and *write* operations; clients and servers can negotiate sizes larger than 8 kbytes if both are able to handle them.

As mentioned above, the file status information cached at clients must be updated at least every three seconds for active files. To reduce the consequential server load resulting from *getattr* requests, all operations that refer to files or directories are taken as implicit *getattr* requests, and the current attribute values are 'piggybacked' along with the other results of the operation.

Securing NFS with Kerberos ◊ In Section 7.6.2 we described the Kerberos authentication system developed at MIT, which has become an industry standard for securing intranet servers against unauthorized access and imposter attacks. The security of NFS implementations has been strengthened by the use of the Kerberos scheme to authenticate clients. In this subsection, we describe the 'Kerberization' of NFS as it was carried out by the designers of Kerberos.

In the original standard implementation of NFS, the user's identity is included in each request in the form of an unencrypted numeric identifier. (The identifier can be encrypted in later versions of NFS.) NFS does not take any further steps to check the authenticity of the identifier supplied. This implies a high degree of trust in the integrity of the client computer and its software by NFS, whereas the aim of Kerberos and other authentication-based security systems is to reduce to a minimum the range of components in which trust is assumed. Essentially, when NFS is used in a 'Kerberized' environment it should accept requests only from clients whose identity can be shown to have been authenticated by Kerberos.

One obvious solution considered by the Kerberos developers was to change the nature of the credentials required by NFS to be a full-blown Kerberos ticket and authenticator. But because NFS is implemented as a stateless server, each individual file access request is handled on its face value and the authentication data would have be included in each request. This was considered unacceptably expensive in time required to perform the necessary encryptions and would have entailed adding the Kerberos client library to the kernel of all workstations.

Instead, a hybrid approach was adopted in which the NFS mount server is supplied with full Kerberos authentication data for the user when their home and root filesystems are mounted. The results of this authentication, including the user's conventional numerical identifier and the address of the client computer, is retained by the server with the mount information for each filesystem. (Although the NFS server does not retain state relating to individual client processes, it does retain the current mounts at each client computer.)

On each file access request, the NFS server checks the user identifier and the sender's address and grants access only if they match those stored at the server for the relevant client at mount time. This hybrid approach involves only minimal additional cost and is safe against most forms of attack, provided that only one user at a time can log in to each client computer. At MIT, the system is configured so that this is the case. Recent NFS implementations include Kerberos authentication as one of several options for authentication, and sites that also run Kerberos servers are advised to use this option.

Performance ◊ Early performance figures reported by Sandberg [1987] showed that the use of NFS did not normally impose a performance penalty in comparison with access to files stored on local disks. He identified two remaining problem areas:

- frequent use of the *getattr* call in order to fetch timestamps from servers for cache validation;

- relatively poor performance of the *write* operation because write-through was used at the server.

He noted that writes are relatively infrequent in typical UNIX workloads (about 5% of all calls to the server), and the cost of write-through is therefore tolerable except when large files are written to the server. The version of NFS that he tested did not include the *commit* mechanism outlined above, and this has resulted in a substantial improvement in write performance in current versions. His results also show that the *lookup* operation accounts for almost 50% of server calls. This is a consequence of the step-by-step pathname translation method necessitated by UNIX's file-naming semantics.

Measurements are taken regularly by Sun and other NFS implementors using an updated version of an exhaustive set of benchmark programs known as LADDIS [Keith and Wittle 1993]. Current and past results are available at [www.spec.org]. Performance is summarized there for NFS server implementations from many vendors and different hardware configurations. Single-CPU implementations based on PC hardware but with dedicated operating systems achieve throughputs in excess of 12,000 server operations per second and large multi-processor configurations with many disks and controllers have achieved throughputs of up to 300,000 server operations per second. These figures indicate that NFS offers a very effective solution to distributed storage needs in intranets of most sizes and types of use, ranging for example from a traditional UNIX load of development by several hundred software engineers to a battery of web servers serving material from an NFS server.

NFS summary ◊ Sun NFS closely follows our abstract model. The resulting design provides good location and access transparency if the NFS mount service is used properly to produce similar name spaces at all clients. NFS supports heterogeneous hardware and operating systems. The NFS server implementation is stateless, enabling clients and servers to resume execution after a failure without the need for any recovery procedures. Migration of files or filesystems is not supported, except at the level of manual intervention to reconfigure mount directives after the movement of a filesystem to a new location.

The performance of NFS is much enhanced by the caching of file blocks at each client computer. This is important for the achievement of satisfactory performance but results in some deviation from strict UNIX one-copy file update semantics.

The other design goals of NFS and the extent to which they have been achieved are discussed below.

Access transparency: The NFS client module provides an application programming interface to local processes that is identical to the local operating system's interface. Thus in a UNIX client, accesses to remote files are performed using the normal UNIX system calls. No modifications to existing programs are required to enable them to operate correctly with remote files.

Location transparency: Each client establishes a file name space by adding mounted directories in remote filesystems to its local name space. File systems have to be *exported* by the node that holds them and *remote-mounted* by a client before they can be accessed by processes running in the client (see Figure 8.10). The point in a client's name hierarchy at which a remote-mounted file system appears is determined by the client; thus NFS does not enforce a single network-wide file name space – each client sees a set of remote filesystems that is determined locally, and remote files may have different pathnames on different clients, but a uniform name space can be established with appropriate configuration tables in each client, achieving the goal of location transparency.

Mobility transparency: Filesystems (in the UNIX sense, that is, sub-trees of files) may be moved between servers, but the remote mount tables in each client must then be updated separately to enable the clients to access the filesystem in its new location, so migration transparency is not fully achieved by NFS.

Scalability: The published performance figures show that NFS servers can be built to handle very large real-world loads in an efficient and cost-effective manner. The performance of a single server can be increased by the addition of processors, disks and controllers. When the limits of that process are reached, additional servers must be installed and the filesystems must be reallocated between them. The effectiveness of that strategy is limited by the existence of 'hot spot' files – single files that are accessed so frequently that the server reaches a performance limit. When loads exceed the maximum performance available with that strategy, a distributed file system that supports replication of updatable files (such as Coda, described in Chapter 15), or one such as AFS that reduces the protocol traffic by the caching of whole files, may offer a better solution. We discuss other approaches to scalability in Section 8.5.

File replication: Read-only file stores can be replicated on several NFS servers, but NFS does not support file replication with updates. The Sun Network Information Service (NIS) is a separate service available for use with NFS that supports the replication of simple databases organized as key-value pairs (for example, the UNIX system files */etc/passwd* and */etc/hosts*). It manages the distribution of updates and accesses to the replicated files based on a simple master–slave replication model (also known as the *primary copy* model, discussed further in Chapter 15) with provision for the replication of part or all of the database at each site. NIS provides a shared repository for system information that changes infrequently and does not require updates to occur simultaneously at all sites.

Hardware and operating system heterogeneity: NFS has been implemented for almost every known operating system and hardware platform and is supported by a variety of filing systems.

Fault tolerance: The stateless and idempotent nature of the NFS file access protocol ensures that the failure modes observed by clients when accessing remote files are similar to those for local file access. When a server fails, the service that it provides is suspended until the server is restarted, but once it has been restarted, user-level client processes proceed from the point at which the service was interrupted, unaware of the failure (except in the case of access to *soft-mounted* remote file systems). In practice, hard mounting is used in most instances, and this tends to impede application programs handling server failures gracefully.

The failure of a client computer or a user-level process in a client has no effect on any server that it may be using, since servers hold no state on behalf of their clients.

Consistency: We have described the update behaviour in some detail. It provides a close approximation to one-copy semantics and meets the needs of the vast majority of applications, but the use of file sharing via NFS for communication or close coordination between processes on different computers cannot be recommended.

Security: The need for security in NFS emerged with the connection of most intranets to the Internet. The integration of Kerberos with NFS was a major step forward. Other recent developments include the option to use a secure RPC implementation (RPCSEC_GSS, documented in RFC 2203 [Eisler *et al.* 1997]) for authentication and the privacy and security of the data transmitted with read and write operations. Installations that have not deployed these mechanisms abound, and they are insecure.

Efficiency: The measured performance of several implementations of NFS and its widespread adoption for use in situations that generate very heavy loads are clear indications of the efficiency with which the NFS protocol can be implemented.

8.4   Case study: The Andrew File System

Like NFS, AFS provides transparent access to remote shared files for UNIX programs running on workstations. Access to AFS files is via the normal UNIX file primitives, enabling existing UNIX programs to access AFS files without modification or recompilation. AFS is compatible with NFS. AFS servers hold 'local' UNIX files, but the filing system in the servers is NFS-based, so files are referenced by NFS-style file handles rather than i-node numbers, and the files may be remotely accessed via NFS.

AFS differs markedly from NFS in its design and implementation. The differences are primarily attributable to the identification of scalability as the most important design goal. AFS is designed to perform well with larger numbers of active users than other distributed file systems. The key strategy for achieving scalability is the caching of whole files in client nodes. AFS has two unusual design characteristics:

Whole-file serving: The entire contents of directories and files are transmitted to client computers by AFS servers (in AFS-3, files larger than 64 kbytes are transferred in 64-kbyte chunks).

Whole-file caching: Once a copy of a file or a chunk has been transferred to a client computer it is stored in a cache on the local disk. The cache contains several hundred of the files most recently used on that computer. The cache is permanent, surviving reboots of the client computer. Local copies of files are used to satisfy clients' *open* requests in preference to remote copies whenever possible.

Scenario ◊ Here is a simple scenario illustrating the operation of AFS:

- When a user process in a client computer issues an *open* system call for a file in the shared file space and there is not a current copy of the file in the local cache, the server holding the file is located and is sent a request for a copy of the file.

- The copy is stored in the local UNIX file system in the client computer; the copy is then *open*ed and the resulting UNIX file descriptor is returned to the client.

- Subsequent *read*, *write* and other operations on the file by processes in the client computer are applied to the local copy.

- When the process in the client issues a *close* system call, if the local copy has been updated its contents are sent back to the server. The server updates the file contents and the timestamps on the file. The copy on the client's local disk is retained in case it is needed again by a user-level process on the same workstation.

We shall discuss the observed performance of AFS below, but we can make some general observations and predictions here based on the design characteristics described above:

- For shared files that are infrequently updated (such as those containing the code of UNIX commands and libraries) and for files that are normally accessed by only a single user (such as most of the files in a user's home directory and its sub-tree), locally cached copies are likely to remain valid for long periods – in the first case because they are not updated and in the second because if they are updated, the updated copy will be in the cache on the owner's workstation. These classes of file account for the overwhelming majority of file accesses.

- The local cache can be allocated a substantial proportion of the disk space on each workstation, say 100 megabytes. This is normally sufficient for the establishment of a working set of the files used by one user. The provision of sufficient cache storage for the establishment of a working set ensures that files in regular use on a given workstation are normally retained in the cache until they are needed again.

- The design strategy is based on some assumptions about average and maximum file size and locality of reference to files in UNIX systems. These assumptions are derived from observations of typical UNIX workloads in academic and other environments [Satyanarayanan 1981; Ousterhout *et al.* 1985; Floyd 1986]. The most important observations are:

- Files are small; most are less than 10 kilobytes in size.

- Read operations on files are much more common than writes (about six times more common).

- Sequential access is common, and random access is rare.

- Most files are read and written by only one user. When a file is shared, it is usually only one user who modifies it.

- Files are referenced in bursts. If a file has been referenced recently, there is a high probability that it will referenced again in the near future.

These observations were used to guide the design and optimization of AFS, *not* to restrict the functionality seen by users.

- AFS works best with the classes of file identified in the first point above. There is one important type of file that does not fit into any of these classes – databases are typically shared by many users and are often updated quite frequently. The designers of AFS have explicitly excluded the provision of storage facilities for databases from their design goals, stating that the constraints imposed by different naming structures (that is, content-based access) and the need for fine-grained data access, concurrency control and atomicity of updates make it difficult to design a distributed database system that is also a distributed file system. They argue that the provision of facilities for distributed databases should be addressed separately [Satyanarayanan 1989a].

8.4.1   Implementation

The above scenario illustrates AFS's operation but leaves many questions about its implementation unanswered. Among the most important are:

- How does AFS gain control when an *open* or *close* system call referring to a file in the shared file space is issued by a client?

- How is the server holding the required file located?

- What space is allocated for cached files in workstations?

- How does AFS ensure that the cached copies of files are up to date when files may be updated by several clients?

We answer these questions below.

AFS is implemented as two software components that exist as UNIX processes called *Vice* and *Venus*. Figure 8.11 shows the distribution of Vice and Venus processes. Vice is the name given to the server software that runs as a user-level UNIX process in each server computer, and Venus is a user-level process that runs in each client computer and corresponds to the client module in our abstract model.

The files available to user processes running on workstations are either *local* or *shared*. Local files are handled as normal UNIX files. They are stored on a workstation's disk and are available only to local user processes. Shared files are stored on servers, and copies of them are cached on the local disks of workstations. The name space seen by user processes is illustrated in Figure 8.12. It is a conventional UNIX directory

Figure 8.11   Distribution of processes in the Andrew File System

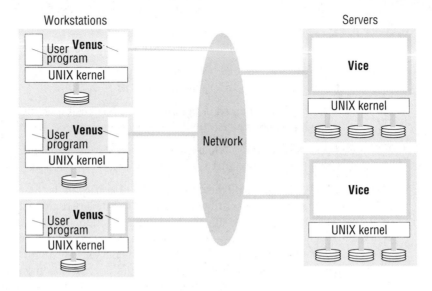

Figure 8.12   File name space seen by clients of AFS

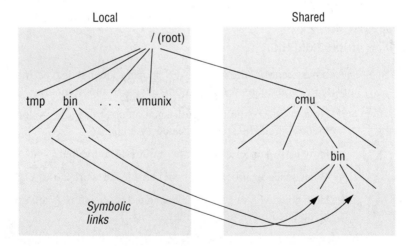

hierarchy, with a specific sub-tree (called *cmu*) containing all of the shared files. This splitting of the file name space into local and shared files leads to some loss of location transparency, but this is hardly noticeable to users other than system administrators. Local files are used only for temporary files (*/tmp*) and processes that are essential for workstation start-up. Other standard UNIX files (such as those normally found in */bin*, */lib*, and so on) are implemented as symbolic links from local directories to files held in the shared space. Users' directories are in the shared space, enabling users to access their files from any workstation.

Figure 8.13   System call interception in AFS

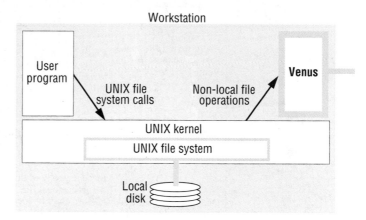

The UNIX kernel in each workstation and server is a modified version of BSD UNIX. The modifications are designed to intercept *open*, *close* and some other file system calls when they refer to files in the shared name space and pass them to the Venus process in the client computer (illustrated in Figure 8.13). One other kernel modification is included for performance reasons, and this is described later.

One of the file partitions on the local disk of each workstation is used as a cache, holding the cached copies of files from the shared space. Venus manages the cache, removing the least recently used files when a new file is acquired from a server to make the required space if the partition is full. The workstation cache is usually large enough to accommodate several hundred average-sized files, rendering the workstation largely independent of the Vice servers once a working set of the current user's files and frequently used system files has been cached.

AFS resembles the abstract file service model described in Section 8.2 in these respects:

- A flat file service is implemented by the Vice servers, and the hierarchic directory structure required by UNIX user programs is implemented by the set of Venus processes in the workstations.

- Each file and directory in the shared file space is identified by a unique, 96-bit file identifier (*fid*) similar to a UFID. The Venus processes translate the pathnames issued by clients to *fid*s.

Files are grouped into *volumes* for ease of location and movement. Volumes are generally smaller than the UNIX filesystems, which are the unit of file grouping in NFS. For example, each user's personal files are generally located in a separate volume. Other volumes are allocated for system binaries, documentation and library code.

The representation of *fid*s includes the volume number for the volume containing the file (*cf.* the *file group identifier* in UFIDs), an NFS file handle identifying the file

Figure 8.14   Implementation of file system calls in AFS

User process	UNIX kernel	Venus	Net	Vice
open(FileName, mode)	If FileName refers to a file in shared file space, pass the request to Venus.	Check list of files in local cache. If not present or there is no valid callback promise, send a request for the file to the Vice server that is custodian of the volume containing the file.		Transfer a copy of the file and a callback promise to the workstation. Log the callback promise.
	Open the local file and return the file descriptor to the application.	Place the copy of the file in the local file system, enter its local name in the local cache list and return the local name to UNIX.		
read(FileDescriptor, Buffer, length)	Perform a normal UNIX read operation on the local copy.			
write(FileDescriptor, Buffer, length)	Perform a normal UNIX write operation on the local copy.			
close(FileDescriptor)	Close the local copy and notify Venus that the file has been closed.	If the local copy has been changed, send a copy to the Vice server that is the custodian of the file.		Replace the file contents and send a callback to all other clients holding callback promises on the file.

within the volume (cf. the *file number* in UFIDs) and a *uniquifier* to ensure that file identifiers are not reused:

32 bits	32 bits	32 bits
Volume number	File handle	Uniquifier

User programs use conventional UNIX pathnames to refer to files, but AFS uses *fid*s in the communication between the Venus and Vice processes. The Vice servers accept requests only in terms of *fid*s. Venus translates the pathnames supplied by clients into *fid*s using a step-by-step lookup to obtain the information from the file directories held in the Vice servers.

Figure 8.14 describes the actions taken by Vice, Venus and the UNIX kernel when a user process issues each of the system calls mentioned in our outline scenario above. The *callback promise* mentioned here is a mechanism for ensuring that cached copies of files are updated when another client closes the same file after updating it. This mechanism is discussed in the next section.

8.4.2   Cache consistency

When Vice supplies a copy of a file to a Venus process it also provides a *callback promise* – a token issued by the Vice server that is the custodian of the file, guaranteeing that it will notify the Venus process when any other client modifies the file. Callback promises are stored with the cached files on the workstation disks and have two states: *valid* or *cancelled*. When a server performs a request to update a file it notifies all of the Venus processes to which it has issued callback promises by sending a *callback* to each – a callback is a remote procedure call from a server to a Venus process. When the Venus process receives a callback, it sets the *callback promise* token for the relevant file to *cancelled*.

Whenever Venus handles an *open* on behalf of a client, it checks the cache. If the required file is found in the cache, then its token is checked. If its value is *cancelled*, then a fresh copy of the file must be fetched from the Vice server, but if the token is *valid*, then the cached copy can be opened and used without reference to Vice.

When a workstation is restarted after a failure or a shutdown, Venus aims to retain as many as possible of the cached files on the local disk, but it cannot assume that the callback promise tokens are correct, since some callbacks may have been missed. Before the first use of each cached file or directory after a restart, Venus therefore generates a cache validation request containing the file modification timestamp to the server that is the custodian of the file. If the timestamp is current, the server responds with *valid* and the token is reinstated. If the timestamp shows that the file is out of date, then the server responds with *cancelled* and the token is set to *cancelled*. Callbacks must be renewed before an *open* if a time T (typically of the order of a few minutes) has elapsed since the file was cached without communication from the server. This is to deal with possible communication failures, which can result in the loss of callback messages.

This callback-based mechanism for maintaining cache consistency was adopted as offering the most scalable approach, following the evaluation in the prototype (AFS-1) of a timestamp-based mechanism similar to that used in NFS. In AFS-1, a Venus process holding a cached copy of a file interrogates the Vice process on each *open* to determine whether the timestamp on the local copy agrees with that on the server. The callback-based approach is more scalable because it results in communication between client and server and activity in the server only when the file has been updated, whereas the timestamp approach results in a client-server interaction on each *open*, even when there is a valid local copy. Since the majority of files are not accessed concurrently, and *read* operations predominate over *write* in most applications, the *callback* mechanism results in a dramatic reduction in the number of client-server interactions.

The callback mechanism used in AFS-2 and later versions of AFS requires Vice servers to maintain some state on behalf of their Venus clients, unlike AFS-1, NFS and our file service model. The client-dependent state required consists of a list of the Venus processes to which callback promises have been issued for each file. These callback lists must be retained over server failures – they are held on the server disks and are updated using atomic operations.

Figure 8.15 shows the RPC calls provided by AFS servers for operations on files (that is, the interface provided by AFS servers to Venus processes).

Update semantics ◊   The goal of this cache consistency mechanism is to achieve the best approximation to one-copy file semantics that is practicable without serious

Figure 8.15   The main components of the Vice service interface

Fetch(fid) → *attr, data*	Returns the attributes (status) and, optionally, the contents of file identified by the *fid* and records a callback promise on it.
Store(fid, attr, data)	Updates the attributes and (optionally) the contents of a specified file.
Create() → *fid*	Creates a new file and records a callback promise on it.
Remove(fid)	Deletes the specified file.
SetLock(fid, mode)	Sets a lock on the specified file or directory. The mode of the lock may be shared or exclusive. Locks that are not removed expire after 30 minutes.
ReleaseLock(fid)	Unlocks the specified file or directory.
RemoveCallback(fid)	Informs server that a Venus process has flushed a file from its cache.
BreakCallback(fid)	This call is made by a Vice server to a Venus process. It cancels the callback promise on the relevant file.

Note: Directory and administrative operations (*Rename, Link, Makedir, Removedir, GetTime, CheckToken* and so on) are not shown.

performance degradation. A strict implementation of one-copy semantics for UNIX file access primitives would require that the results of each *write* to a file be distributed to all sites holding the file in their cache before any further accesses can occur. This is not practicable in large-scale systems; instead, the callback promise mechanism maintains a well-defined approximation to one-copy semantics.

For AFS-1, the update semantics can be formally stated in very simple terms. For a client C operating on a file F whose custodian is a server S, the following guarantees of currency for the copies of F are maintained:

after a successful *open*:	*latest(F, S)*
after a failed *open*:	*failure(S)*
after a successful *close*:	*updated(F, S)*
after a failed *close*:	*failure(S)*

Where *latest(F, S)* denotes a guarantee that the current value of F at C is the same as the value at S, *failure(S)* denotes that the *open* or *close* operation has not been performed at S (and the failure can be detected by C), and *updated(F, S)* denotes that C's value of F has been successfully propagated to S.

For AFS-2, the currency guarantee for *open* is slightly weaker, and the corresponding formal statement of the guarantee is more complex. This is because a client may open an old copy of a file after it has been updated by another client. This occurs if a *callback* message is lost, for example as a result of a network failure. But there is a maximum time T for which a client can remain unaware of a newer version of a file. Hence we have the following guarantee:

after a successful *open*: $latest(F, S, 0)$
                            or $(lostCallback(S, T)$ and $inCache(F)$ and
                            $latest(F, S, T))$

Where $latest(F, S, T)$ denotes that the copy of F seen by the client is no more than T seconds out of date, $lostCallback(S, T)$ denotes that a callback message from S to C has been lost at some time during the last T seconds, and $inCache(F)$ that the file F was in the cache at C before the open operation was attempted. The above formal statement expresses the fact that either the cached copy of F at C after an *open* operation is either the most recent version in the system or a callback message has been lost (due to a communication failure) and the version that was already in the cache has been used; the cached version will be no more than T seconds out of date. (T is a system constant representing the interval at which callback promises must be renewed. At most installations, the value of T is set to about 10 minutes.)

In line with its goal – to provide a large-scale, UNIX-compatible distributed file service – AFS does not provide any further mechanism for the control of concurrent updates. The cache consistency algorithm described above comes into action only on *open* and *close* operations. Once a file has been opened, the client may access and update the local copy in any way it chooses without the knowledge of any processes on other workstations. When the file is closed, a copy is returned to the server, replacing the current version.

If clients in different workstations *open*, *write* and *close* the same file concurrently, all but the update resulting from the last *close* will be silently lost (no error report is given). Clients must implement concurrency control independently if they require it. On the other hand, when two client processes in the same workstation open a file, they share the same cached copy and updates are performed in the normal UNIX fashion – block by block.

Although the update semantics differ depending on the locations of the concurrent processes accessing a file and are not precisely the same as those provided by the standard UNIX file system, they are sufficiently close for the vast majority of existing UNIX programs to operate correctly.

8.4.3   Other aspects

UNIX kernel modifications ◊ We have noted that the Vice server is a user-level process running in the server computer and the server host is dedicated to the provision of an AFS service. The UNIX kernel in AFS hosts is altered so that Vice can perform file operations in terms of file handles instead of the conventional UNIX file descriptors. This is the only kernel modification required by AFS and is necessary if Vice is not to maintain any client state (such as file descriptors).

Location database ◊ Each server contains a copy of a fully replicated location database giving a mapping of volume names to servers. Temporary inaccuracies in this database may occur when a volume is moved, but they are harmless because forwarding information is left behind in the server from which the volume is moved.

Threads ◊ The implementations of Vice and Venus make use of a non-pre-emptive threads package to enable requests to be processed concurrently at both the client (where several user processes may have file access requests in progress concurrently) and at the server. In the client, the tables describing the contents of the cache and the volume database are held in memory that is shared between the Venus threads.

Read-only replicas ◊ Volumes containing files that are frequently read but rarely modified, such as the UNIX /bin and /usr/bin directories of system commands and /man directory of manual pages, can be replicated as read-only volumes at several servers. When this is done, there is only one read-write replica and all updates are directed to it. The propagation of the changes to the read-only replicas is performed after the update by an explicit operational procedure. Entries in the location database for volumes that are replicated in this way are one-to-many, and the server for each client request is selected on the bases of server loads and accessibility.

Bulk transfers ◊ AFS transfers files between clients and servers in 64-kilobyte chunks. The use of such a large packet size is an important aid to performance, minimizing the effect of network latency. Thus the design of AFS enables the use of the network to be optimized.

Partial file caching ◊ The need to transfer the entire contents of files to clients even when the application requirement is to read only a small portion of the file is an obvious source of inefficiency. Versions 3 of AFS removed this requirement, allowing file data to be transferred and cached in 64-kbyte blocks while still retaining the consistency semantics and other features of the AFS protocol.

Performance ◊ The primary goal of AFS is scalability, so its performance with large numbers of users is of particular interest. Howard *et al.* [1988] give details of extensive comparative performance measurements, which were undertaken using a specially developed *AFS benchmark* that has subsequently been widely used for the evaluation of distributed file systems. Not surprisingly, whole-file caching and the callback protocol led to dramatically reduced loads on the servers. Satyanarayanan [1989a] states that a server load of 40% was measured with eighteen client nodes running a standard benchmark, against a load of 100% for NFS running the same benchmark. Satyanarayanan attributes much of the performance advantage of AFS to the reduction in server load deriving from the use of callbacks to notify clients of updates to files, compared with the timeout mechanism used in NFS for checking the validity of pages cached at clients.

Wide-area support: ◊ Version 3 of AFS supports multiple administrative cells, each with its own servers, clients, system administrators and users. Each cell is a completely autonomous environment, but a federation of cells can cooperate in presenting users with a uniform, seamless file name space. The resulting system was widely deployed by the Transarc Corporation, and a detailed survey of the resulting performance usage patterns was published [Spasojevic and Satyanarayanan 1996]. The system was installed on over 1000 servers at over 150 sites. The survey showed cache hit ratios in the range 96 –98% for accesses to a sample of 32,000 file volumes holding 200 Gbytes of data.

8.5   Enhancements and further developments

Several advances have been made in the design of distributed file systems since the emergence of NFS and AFS. In this section, we describe advances that enhance the performance, availability and scalability of conventional distributed file systems. More radical advances are described elsewhere in the book, including the maintenance of consistency in replicated read-write filesystems to support disconnected operation and high availability in the Bayou and Coda systems (Sections 14.4.2 and 14.4.3) and a highly scalable architecture for the delivery of streams of real-time data with quality guarantees in the Tiger video file server (Section 17.6).

NFS enhancements ◊ Several research projects have addressed the question of one-copy update semantics by extending the NFS protocol to include *open* and *close* operations and adding a callback mechanism to enable the server to notify clients of the need to invalidate cache entries. We describe two such efforts here; their results seem to indicate that these enhancements can be accommodated without undue complexity or extra communication costs.

Some recent efforts by Sun and other NFS developers have been directed at making NFS servers more accessible and useful in wide-area networks. While the HTTP protocol supported by web servers offers an effective and highly scalable method for making whole files available to clients throughout the Internet, it is less useful to application programs that require access to portions of large files or those that update portions of files. The WebNFS development (described below) makes it possible for application programs to become clients of NFS servers anywhere in the Internet (using the NFS protocol directly instead of indirectly through a kernel module). This, together with appropriate libraries for Java and other network programming languages, should offer the possibility of implementing Internet applications that share data directly, such as multi-user games or clients of large dynamic databases.

Achieving one-copy update semantics: The stateless server architecture of NFS brought great advantages in robustness and ease of implementation for NFS, but it precluded the achievement of precise one-copy update semantics (the effects of concurrent writes by different clients to the same file are not guaranteed to be the same as they would be in a single UNIX system when multiple processes write to a local file). It also prevents the use of callbacks notifying clients of changes to files, and this results in frequent *getattr* requests from clients to check for file modification.

Two research systems have been developed that address these drawbacks. Spritely NFS [Srinivasan and Mogul 1989, Mogul 1994] is a development of the file system developed for the Sprite distributed operating system at Berkeley [Nelson *et al.* 1988]. Spritely NFS is an implementation of the NFS protocol with the addition of *open* and *close* calls. Clients' modules must send an *open* operation whenever a local user-level process opens a file that is on the server. The parameters of the Sprite *open* operation specify a mode (read, write or both) and include counts of the number of local processes that currently have the file open for reading and for writing. Similarly, when a local process closes a remote file a *close* operation is sent to the server with updated counts of readers and writers. The server records these numbers in an *open files table* with the IP address and port number of the client.

When the server receives an *open*, it checks the *open files table* for other clients that have the same file open and sends callback messages to those clients instructing them to modify their caching strategy. If the *open* specifies write mode, then it will fail if any other client has the file open for writing. Other clients that have the file open for reading will be instructed to invalidate any locally cached portions of the file.

For *open* operations that specify read mode, the server sends a callback message to any client that is writing, instructing it to stop caching (i.e. to use a strictly write-through mode of operation), and it instructs all clients that are reading to cease caching the file (so that all local read calls result in a request to the server).

These measures result in a file service that maintains the UNIX one-copy update semantics at the expense of carrying some client-related state at the server. They also enable some efficiency gains in the handling of cached writes. If the client-related state is held in volatile memory at the server, it is vulnerable to server crashes. Spritely NFS implements a recovery protocol that interrogates a list of clients that have recently opened files on the server to recover the full *open files table*. The list of clients is stored on disk and is updated relatively infrequently and is 'pessimistic' – it may safely include more clients than those that had files open at the time of a crash. Failed clients may also result in excess entries in the *open files table*, but they will be removed when the client restarts.

When Spritely NFS was evaluated against NFS version 2, it showed a modest performance improvement. This was due to the improved caching of writes. Changes in NFS version 3 would probably result in at least as great an improvement, but the results of the Spritely NFS project certainly indicate that it is possible to achieve one-copy update semantics without substantial loss of performance, albeit at the expense of some extra implementation complexity in the client and server modules and the need for a recovery mechanism to restore the state after a server crash.

NQNFS: The NQNFS (Not Quite NFS) project [Macklem 1994] had similar aims to Spritely NFS – to add more precise cache consistency to the NFS protocol and to improve performance through better use of caching. An NQNFS server maintains similar client-related state concerning open files, but it uses leases (Section 5.2.6) to aid recovery after a server crash. The server sets an upper bound on the time for which a client may hold a lease on an open file. If the client wishes to continue beyond that time, it must renew the lease. Callbacks are used in a similar manner to Spritely NFS to request clients to flush their caches when a write request occurs, but if the clients don't reply, the server simply waits until their leases expire before responding to the new write request.

WebNFS: The advent of the Web and Java applets led to the recognition by the NFS development team and others that some Internet applications could benefit from direct access to NFS servers without many of the overheads associated with the emulation of UNIX file operations included in standard NFS clients.

The aim of WebNFS (described in RFCs 2055 and 2056 [Callaghan 1996a, 1996b]) is to enable web browsers, Java programs and other applications to interact with an NFS server directly to access files that are 'published' using a *public file handle* to access files relative to a public root directory. This mode of use bypasses the *mount* service and the port mapper service (described in Chapter 5). WebNFS clients interact with an NFS server at a well-known port number (2049). To access files by pathname, they issue *lookup* requests using a public file handle. The public file handle has a well-known value that is interpreted specially by the virtual file system at the server. Because of the high latency of wide-area networks, a *multicomponent* variant of the *lookup* operation is used to look up a multi-part pathname in a single request.

Thus WebNFS enables clients to be written that access portions of files stored in NFS servers at remote sites with minimal setup overheads. There is provision for access control and authentication, but in many cases the client will require only read access to public files and in that case the authentication option can be turned off. To read a portion of a single file located on an NFS server that supports WebNFS requires the establishment of a TCP connection and two RPC calls – a multicomponent *lookup* and a *read* operation. The size of the block of data read is not limited by the NFS protocol.

For example, a weather service might publish a file on its NFS server containing a large database of frequently updated weather data with a URL such as:

nfs://data.weather.gov/weatherdata/global.data

An interactive WeatherMap client, which displays weather maps, could be constructed in Java or any other language that supports a WebNFS procedure library. The client reads only those portions of the /weatherdata/global.data file that are needed to construct the particular maps requested by a user, whereas a similar application that used HTTP to access a weather data server would either have to transfer the entire database to the client or would require the support of a special-purpose server program to supply it with the data it requires.

NFS version 4: A new version of the NFS protocol was under development at the time of publication of this book. The goals of NFS version 4 are described in RFC 2624 [Shepler 1999] and in Brent Callaghan's book [Callaghan 1999]. Like WebNFS, it aims to make it practical to use NFS in wide-area networks and Internet applications. It will include the features of WebNFS, but the introduction of a new protocol also offers an opportunity to make more radical enhancements. (WebNFS was restricted to changes to the server that did not involve that addition of new operations to the protocol.)

The working group developing NFS version 4 intends to exploit results that have emerged from research in file server design over the past decade, such as the use of callbacks or leases to maintain consistency. NFS version 4 will support on-the-fly recovery from server faults by allowing file systems to be moved to new servers transparently. Scalability will be improved by using proxy servers in a manner analogous to their use in the Web.

AFS enhancements ◊ We have mentioned that DCE/DFS, the distributed file system included in the Open Software Foundation's Distributed Computing Environment [www.opengroup.org], was based on the Andrew File System. The design of DCE/DFS goes beyond AFS, particularly in its approach to cache consistency. In AFS, callbacks are generated only when the server receives a *close* operation for a file that has been updated. DFS adopted a similar strategy to Spritely NFS and NQNFS to generating callbacks as soon as a file is updated. In order to update a file, a client must obtain a *write* token from the server, specifying a range of bytes in the file that the client is permitted to update. When a *write* token is requested, clients holding copies of the same file for reading receive revocation callbacks. Tokens of other types are used to achieve consistency for cached file attributes and other metadata. All tokens have an associated lifetime, and clients must renew them after their lifetime has expired.

Improvements in storage organization ◊ There has been considerable progress in the organization of file data stored on disks. The impetus for much of this work arose from the increased loads and greater reliability that distributed file systems need to support, and they have resulted in file systems with substantially improved performance. The principal results of this work are:

Redundant Arrays of Inexpensive Disks (RAID): This is a mode of storage [Patterson *et al.* 1988, Chen *et al.* 1994] in which data blocks are segmented into fixed-size chunks and stored in 'stripes' across several disks, along with redundant error-correcting codes that enable the data blocks to be reconstructed completely and operation to continue normally in case of disk failures. RAID also produces considerably better performance than a single disk, because the stripes that make up a block are read and written concurrently.

Log-structured file storage (LFS): Like Spritely NFS, this technique originated in the Sprite distributed operating system project at Berkeley [Rosenblum and Ousterhout 1992]. The authors observed that as larger amounts of main memory became available for caching in file servers, an increased level of cache hits resulted in excellent read performance, but write performance remained mediocre. This arose from the high latencies associated with writing individual data blocks to disk and associated updates to metadata blocks (that is, the blocks known as *i-nodes* that hold file attributes and a vector of pointers to the blocks in a file).

The LFS solution is to accumulate a set of writes in memory and then commit them to disk in large, contiguous, fixed-sized segments. These are called *log segments* because the data and metadata blocks are stored strictly in the order in which they were updated. A log segment is 1 Mbyte or larger in size and is stored in a single disk track, removing the disk head latencies associated with writing individual blocks. Fresh copies of updated data and metadata blocks are always written, requiring the maintenance of a dynamic map (in memory with a persistent backup) pointing to the i-node blocks. Garbage collection of stale blocks is also required, with compaction of 'live' blocks to leave contiguous areas of storage free for the storage of log segments. The latter is a fairly complex process; it is carried out as a background activity by a component called the *cleaner*. Some sophisticated cleaner algorithms were developed for it based on the results of simulations.

Despite these extra costs, the overall performance gain is outstanding; Rosenblum and Ousterhout measured a write throughput as high as 70% of the available disk bandwidth, compared with less than 10% for a conventional UNIX file system. The log structure also simplifies recovery after server crashes. The Zebra file system [Hartman and Ousterhout 1995], developed as a follow-on to the original LFS work, combines log-structured writes with a distributed RAID approach – the log segments are subdivided into sections with error-correcting data and written to disks on separate network nodes. Performance four to five times that of NFS is claimed for writing large files, with smaller gains for short files.

New design approaches ◊ The availability of high-performance switched networks (such as ATM and switched high-speed Ethernet) have prompted several efforts to provide persistent storage systems that distribute file data in a highly scalable and fault-tolerant manner among many nodes on an intranet, separating the responsibilities for the reading and writing of data from the responsibilities for managing the metadata and servicing client requests. In the following, we outline two such developments.

These approaches scale better than the more centralized servers that we have described in the preceding sections. They generally demand a high level of trust among the computers that cooperate to provide the service, because they include a fairly low-level protocol for communication with the nodes holding data (somewhat analogous to a 'virtual disk' API). Hence their scope is likely to be limited to a single local network.

xFS: A group at the University of California, Berkeley, proposed a serverless network file system architecture and developed a prototype implementation, xFS [Anderson *et al.* 1996]. Their approach was motivated by three factors:

1. the opportunity provided by fast switched LANs for multiple file servers in a local network to transfer bulk data to clients concurrently;

2. increased demand for access to shared data;

3. the fundamental limitations of systems based on central file servers.

Concerning (3), they refer to the fact that the construction of high-performance NFS servers requires relatively costly hardware with multiple CPUs, disks and network controllers, and that there are limits to the process of partitioning the file space – placing shared files in separate filesystems mounted on different servers. They also point to the fact that a central server represents a single point of failure.

xFS is 'serverless' in the sense that it distributes file server processing responsibilities across a set of available computers in a local network at the granularity of individual files. Storage responsibilities are distributed independently of management and other service responsibilities: xFS implements a software RAID storage system, striping file data across disks on multiple computers (in this regard it is a precursor to the Tiger Video File System described in Chapter 17) together with a log-structuring technique in a manner similar to the Zebra file system.

Responsibility for the management of each file can be allocated to any of the computers supporting the xFS service. This is achieved through a metadata structure called the *manager map,* which is replicated at all clients and servers. File identifiers include a field that acts as an index into the manager map, and each entry in the map identifies the computer that is currently responsible for managing the corresponding file. Several other metadata structures, similar to those found in other log-structured and RAID storage systems, are used for the management of the log-structured file storage and the striped disk storage.

A preliminary prototype of xFS was constructed and its performance evaluated. The prototype was incomplete at the time the evaluation was carried out – the implementation of crash recovery was unfinished and the log-structured storage scheme lacked a cleaner component to recover space occupied by stale logs and compact files.

The performance evaluations carried out with this preliminary prototype used 32 single-processor and dual-processor Sun SPARCStations connected to a high-speed network. The evaluations compared the xFS file service running on up to 32 workstations with NFS and with AFS, each running on a single dual-processor Sun SPARCStation. The read and write bandwidths achieved with xFS with 32 servers exceeded those of NFS and AFS with a single dual-processor server by approximately a factor of ten. The difference in performance was much less marked when xFS was compared with NFS and AFS using the standard AFS benchmark. But overall, the results indicate that the highly distributed processing and storage architecture of xFS offers a promising direction for achieving better scalability in distributed file systems.

Frangipani: Frangipani is a highly scalable distributed file system developed and deployed at the Digital Systems Research Center (now Compaq Systems Research Center) [Thekkath *et al.* 1997]. Its goals are very similar to those of xFS, and like xFS, it approaches them with a design that separates persistent storage responsibilities from other file service actions. But Frangipani's service is structured as two totally independent layers. The lower layer is provided by the Petal distributed virtual disk system [Lee and Thekkath 1996].

Petal provides a distributed virtual disk abstraction across many disks located on multiple servers on a switched local network. The virtual disk abstraction tolerates most hardware and software failures with the aid of replicas of the stored data and autonomously balances the load on servers by relocating data. Petal virtual disks are accessed through a UNIX disk driver using standard block input-output operations, so they can be used to support most file systems. Petal adds between 10 and 100% to the latency of disk accesses, but the caching strategy results in read and write throughputs at least as good as the underlying disk drives.

Frangipani server modules run within the operating system kernel. As in xFS, the responsibility for managing files and associated tasks (including the provision of a file-locking service for clients) is assigned to hosts dynamically, and all machines see a unified file name space with coherent access (with approximately single-copy semantics) to shared updatable files. Data is stored in a log-structured and striped format in the Petal virtual disk store. The use of Petal relieves Frangipani of the need to manage physical disk space, resulting in a much simpler distributed file system implementation. Frangipani can emulate the service interfaces of several existing file services, including NFS and DCE/DFS. Frangipani's performance is at least as good as the Digital implementation of the UNIX file system.

8.6 Summary

The key design issues for distributed file systems are:

- the effective use of client caching to achieve performance equal to or better than that of local file systems;

- the maintenance of consistency between multiple cached client copies of files when they are updated;

- recovery after client or server failure;

- high throughput for reading and writing files of all sizes;

- scalability.

Distributed file systems are very heavily employed in organizational computing, and their performance has been the subject of much tuning. NFS has a simple stateless protocol, but it has maintained its early position as the dominant distributed file system technology with the help of some relatively minor enhancements to the protocol, tuned implementations and high-performance hardware support.

AFS demonstrated the feasibility of a relatively simple architecture using server state to reduce the cost of maintaining coherent client caches. AFS outperforms NFS in many situations. Recent advances have employed data striping across multiple disks and log-structured writing to further improve performance and scalability.

Current state-of-the-art distributed file systems are highly scalable, provide good performance across both local- and wide-area networks, maintain one-copy file update semantics, and tolerate and recover from failures. Future requirements include support for mobile users with disconnected operation, and automatic reintegration and quality-of-service guarantees to meet the need for the persistent storage and delivery of streams of multimedia and other time-dependent data. Solutions to these requirements are discussed in Chapters 15 and 17.

EXERCISES

8.1   Why is there no *open* or *close* operation in our interface to the flat file service or the directory service. What are the differences between our directory service *Lookup* operation and the UNIX *open*?   *pages 334–336*

8.2   Outline methods by which a client module could emulate the UNIX file system interface using our model file service.   *pages 334–336*

8.3   Write a procedure *PathLookup(Pathname, Dir)* → *UFID* that implements *Lookup* for UNIX-like pathnames based on our model directory service.   *pages 334–336*

8.4   Why should UFIDs be unique across all possible file systems? How is uniqueness for UFIDs ensured?   *page 337*

8.5   To what extent does Sun NFS deviate from one-copy file update semantics? Construct a scenario in which two user-level processes sharing a file would operate correctly in a single UNIX host but would observe inconsistencies when running in different hosts.

page 344

8.6   Sun NFS aims to support heterogeneous distributed systems by the provision of an operating system-independent file service. What are the key decisions that the implementer of an NFS server for an operating system other than UNIX would have to take? What constraints should an underlying filing system obey to be suitable for the implementation of NFS servers?   *page 338*

8.7   What data must the NFS client module hold on behalf of each user-level process?

pages 338–339

8.8   Outline client module implementations for the UNIX *open()* and *read()* system calls, using the NFS RPC calls of Figure 8.9, (i) without, and (ii) with a client cache.

pages 340, 344

8.9   Explain why the RPC interface to early implementations of NFS is potentially insecure. The security loophole has been closed in NFS 3 by the use of encryption. How is the encryption key kept secret? Is the security of the key adequate?   *pages 340, 346*

8.10   After the timeout of an RPC call to access a file on a hard-mounted file system the NFS client module does not return control to the user-level process that originated the call. Why?   *page 341*

8.11   How does the NFS Automounter help to improve the performance and scalability of NFS?   *page 343*

8.12   How many lookup calls are needed to resolve a 5-part pathname (for example, /usr/users/jim/code/xyz.c) for a file that is stored on an NFS server? What is the reason for performing the translation step-by-step?   *page 342*

8.13   What condition must be fulfilled by the configuration of the mount tables at the client computers for access transparency to be achieved in an NFS-based filing system?
          page 342

8.14   How does AFS gain control when an open or close system call referring to a file in the shared file space is issued by a client?   *page 351*

8.15   Compare the update semantics of UNIX when accessing local files with those of NFS and AFS. Under what circumstances might clients become aware of the differences?
          pages 344, 355

8.16   How does AFS deal with the risk that callback messages may be lost?   *page 355*

8.17   Which features of the AFS design make it more scalable than NFS? What are the limits on its scalability, assuming that servers can be added as required? Which recent developments offer greater scalability?   *pages 347, 358, 362*

9

NAME SERVICES

This chapter introduces the name service as a distinct service that is used by client processes to obtain attributes such as the addresses of resources or objects when given their names. The entities named can be of many types, and they may be managed by different services. For example, name services are often used to hold the addresses and other details of users, computers, network domains, services and remote objects. As well as name services, we describe directory services, which look up services when given some of their attributes.

Basic design issues for name services, such as the structure and management of the space of names recognized by the service and the operations that the name service supports, are outlined and illustrated in the context of the Internet Domain Name Service.

We also examine how name services are implemented, covering such aspects as navigation through a collection of name servers when resolving a name, caching naming data, and replicating naming data to increase performance and availability.

Two further case studies are included: the Global Name Service, and the X.500 Directory Service including LDAP.

9.1   Introduction

In a distributed system, names are used to refer to a wide variety of resources such as computers, services, remote objects and files, as well as to users. Naming is an issue that is easily overlooked but is nonetheless fundamental in distributed system design. Names facilitate communication and resource sharing. A name is needed to request a computer system to act upon a specific resource chosen out of many; for example, a name in the form of a URL is needed to access a specific web page. Processes cannot share particular resources managed by a computer system unless they can name them consistently. Users cannot communicate with one another via a distributed system unless they can name one another, for example, with email addresses.

Names are not the only useful means of identification: descriptive attributes are another. Sometimes clients do not know the name of the particular entity that they seek, but they do have some information that describes it. Or the client requires a service (rather than a particular entity that implements it) and knows some of the characteristics that the required service must have.

This chapter introduces name services, which provide clients with data about named objects in distributed systems; and the related concept of directory services, which provide data about objects that satisfy a given description. We describe approaches to be taken in the design and implementation of these services, using the Domain Name Service (DNS), GNS and X500 as case studies. We begin by examining the fundamental concepts of names and attributes.

9.1.1   Names, addresses and other attributes

Any process that requires access to a specific resource must possess a name or an identifier for it. Examples of human-readable names are file names such as */etc/passwd*, URLs such as *http://www.cdk4.net/* and Internet domain names, such as *www.cdk4.net*. The term *identifier* is sometimes used to refer to names that are interpreted only by programs. Remote object references and NFS file handles are examples of identifiers. Identifiers are chosen for the efficiency with which they can be looked up and stored by software.

Needham [1993] makes the distinction between a *pure* name and other names. Pure names are simply uninterpreted bit patterns. Non-pure names contain information about the object that they name; in particular, they may contain information about the location of the object. Pure names always have to be looked up before they can be any use. At the other extreme from a pure name is an object's *address*: a value that identifies the location of the object rather than the object itself. Addresses are efficient for accessing objects, but objects can sometimes be relocated, so addresses are inadequate as a means of identification. For example, users' email addresses usually have to change when they move between organizations or Internet service providers; they are not enough in themselves to refer to a specific individual over time.

We say that a name is *resolved* when it is translated into data about the named resource or object, often in order to invoke an action upon it. The association between a name and an object is called a *binding*. In general, names are bound to *attributes* of the named objects, rather than the implementation of the objects themselves. An attribute is

Figure 9.1   Composed naming domains used to access a resource from a URL

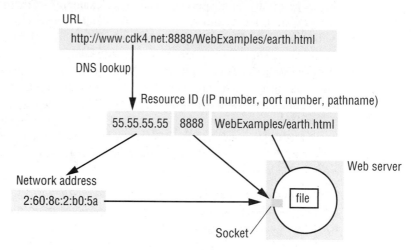

the value of a property associated with an object. A key attribute of an entity that is usually relevant in a distributed system is its address. For example:

- DNS maps domain names to the attributes of a host computer: its IP address, the type of entry (e.g. a reference to a mail server or another host) and, for example, the length of time the host's entry will remain valid.

- The X500 directory service can be used to map a person's name onto attributes including their email address and telephone number.

- The CORBA Naming Service and Trading Service are presented in Chapter 20. The naming service maps the name of a remote object onto its remote object reference, whereas the trading service maps the name of a remote object onto its remote object reference, together with an arbitrary number of attributes describing the object in terms understandable by human users.

Note that an 'address' can often be considered just another name that must be looked up, or it may contain such a name. An IP address must be looked up to obtain a network address such as an Ethernet address. Similarly, web browsers and email clients make use of DNS to interpret the domain names in URLs and email addresses. Figure 9.1 shows the domain name portion of a URL resolved first via the DNS into an IP address and then via ARP to an Ethernet address for the web server. The last part of the URL is resolved by the file system on the web server to locate the relevant file.

Names and services ◊ Many of the names used in a distributed system are specific to some particular service. A client uses such a name when requesting a service to perform an operation upon a named object or resource that it manages. For example, a file name is given to the file service when requesting that the file be deleted; a process identifier is presented to the process management service when requesting that it be sent a signal. These names are used only in the context of the service that manages the objects named, except when clients communicate about shared objects.

Names are also needed to refer to entities in a distributed system that are beyond the scope of any single service. The major examples of these entities are users (with proper names, login names, user identifiers and electronic mail addresses), computers (with names – *host names* – such as *bruno, bronwyn*) and services themselves (such as *file service, printer service*). In object-based middleware, names refer to remote objects that provide services or applications. Note that all of these names must be readable by and meaningful to humans, since users and system administrators need to refer to the major components and configuration of distributed systems; programmers need to refer to services in programs; and users need to communicate with each other via the distributed system and discuss what services are available in different parts of it. Given the connectivity provided by the Internet, these naming requirements are potentially world-wide in scope.

Uniform Resource Identifiers ◊ *Uniform Resource Identifiers* (URIs) [Berners Lee *et al.* 2005] came about from the need to identify resources on the Web, and other Internet resources such as electronic mailboxes. An important goal was to identify resources in a coherent way, so that they could all be processed by common software such as browsers. URIs are 'uniform' in that their syntax incorporates that of indefinitely many individual types of resource identifiers (that is, URI *schemes*), and there are procedures for managing the global namespace of schemes. The advantage of uniformity is that it eases the process of introducing new types of identifier, as well as using existing types of identifier in new contexts, without disrupting existing usage.

For example, if someone was to invent a new type of 'widget' URI, then URIs beginning *widget:* would have to obey the global URI syntax, as well as any local rules defined for the widget identifier scheme. These URIs would identify *widget* resources in a well-defined way. But even existing software that did not access *widget* resources could still process *widget* URIs – for example, by managing directories containing them. Turning to an example of incorporating existing identifiers, that has been done for telephone numbers by prefixing the scheme name *tel* and standardizing the representation of telephone numbers, as in *tel:+1-816-555-1212*. These *tel* URIs are intended for uses such as web links that cause telephone calls to be made when invoked.

Uniform Resource Locators: Some URIs provide information to locate a resource (such as a DNS host name and a pathname on that machine), while some are used as pure resource names. The familiar term *Uniform Resource Locator* (URL) is reserved for identifiers that are resource locators, including 'http' URLs introduced in Section 1.3, such as *http://www.cdk4.net/*. which identifies the web page at the given path ('/') on the host *www.cdk4.net*. Another example is 'mailto' URLs, such as *mailto:fred@flintstone.org*, which identifies the mailbox at the given address.

URLs are efficient identifiers for accessing resources. But they suffer from the disadvantage that if a resource is deleted or if it moves, say from one web site to another, then there may be dangling links to the resource containing the old URL. If a user clicks on a dangling link to a web resource, then the web server will either respond that the resource is not found or – worse, perhaps – supply a different resource that now occupies the same location.

Uniform Resource Names: *Uniform Resource Names* (URNs) are URIs that are used as pure resource names rather than locators. For example, the URI:

mid:0E4FC272-5C02-11D9-B115-000A95B55BC8@hpl.hp.com

is a URN that identifies the email message containing it in its 'Message-Id' field. The URI serves to distinguish that message from any other email message. But it does not of itself provide the message's address in any store, and a lookup operation is needed to find it.

A special sub-tree of URIs beginning with *urn:* has been reserved for URNs – although, as the *mid:* example shows, not all URNs are *urn:* URIs. The latter *urn* prefixed URIs are all of the form *urn:nameSpace:nameSpace-specificName*. For example, urn:ISBN:0-201-62433-8 identifies books that bear the name 0-201-62433-8 in the standard ISBN naming scheme. For another example, the (invented) name *urn:doi:10.555/music-pop-1234* refers to the publication called *music-pop-1234* in the naming scheme of the publisher known as *10.555* in the Digital Object Identifier (DOI) scheme [www.doi.org].

There are *resolution services* (name services, in the terminology of this chapter) such as the Handle System for resolving URNs such as DOIs [www.handle.net] to resource attributes, but none is in widespread use. Indeed, there continues to be debate in the Web and Internet research communities about the extent to which a separate category of URNs is needed. One school of thought is that 'cool URLs do not change' – in other words, that everyone should assign URLs to resources with guarantees about their continuity of reference. Against that point of view is the observation that not everyone is in a position to make such guarantees, which requires the wherewithal to maintain control of a domain name and administer resources carefully.

9.2 Name services and the Domain Name System

A *name service* stores a collection of one or more naming *contexts* – sets of bindings between textual names and attributes for objects such as users, computers, services and remote objects. The major operation that a name service supports is to resolve a name – that is, to look up attributes from a given name. We describe the implementation of name resolution in Section 9.2.2. Operations are also required for creating new bindings, deleting bindings and listing bound names and adding and deleting contexts.

Name management is separated from other services largely because of the openness of distributed systems, which brings the following motivations:

Unification: It is often convenient for resources managed by different services to use the same naming scheme. URIs are a good example of this.

Integration: It is not always possible to predict the scope of sharing in a distributed system. It may become necessary to share and therefore name resources that were created in different administrative domains. Without a common name service, the administrative domains may use entirely different naming conventions.

General name service requirements ◊ Name services were originally quite simple, since they were designed only to meet the need to bind names to addresses in a single management domain, corresponding to a single LAN or WAN. The interconnection of networks and the increased scale of distributed systems have produced a much larger name-mapping problem.

Grapevine [Birrell *et al.* 1982] was one of the earliest extensible, multi-domain name services. It was explicitly designed to be scalable over at least two orders of magnitude in the number of names and the load of requests that it could handle.

The Global Name Service, developed at the Digital Equipment Corporation Systems Research Center [Lampson 1986], is a descendant of Grapevine with more ambitious goals, including:

To handle an essentially arbitrary number of names and to serve an arbitrary number of administrative organizations: For example, the system should be capable, among other things, of handling the electronic mail addresses of all of the computer users in the world.

A long lifetime: Many changes will occur in the organization of the set of names and in the components that implement the service during its lifetime.

High availability: Most other systems depend upon the name service; they can't work when it is broken.

Fault isolation: So that local failures do not cause the entire service to fail.

Tolerance of mistrust: A large open system cannot have any component that is trusted by all of the clients in the system.

Two examples of name services that have concentrated on the goal of scalability to large numbers of objects such as users email addresses or documents are the Globe name service [van Steen *et al.* 1998] and the Handle System [www.handle.net]. The Internet Domain Name System (DNS), introduced in Chapter 3, names objects (in practice, computers) across the Internet. To provide satisfactory service, it relies heavily upon replication and caching of naming data. The design of DNS and other name services makes the assumption that cache consistency need not be so strictly maintained as in the case of cached copies of files, because updates are less frequent and the use of an out-of-date copy of a name translation can generally be detected by client software.

In this section, we discuss the main design issues for name services, giving examples from DNS. We follow this with a detailed case study of DNS.

9.2.1 Name spaces

A *name space* is the collection of all valid names recognized by a particular service. For a name to be valid means that the service will attempt to look it up, even though that name may prove not to correspond to any object – to be *unbound*. Name spaces require a syntactic definition. For example, the name 'Two' could not possibly be the name of a UNIX process, whereas the integer '2' might be. Similarly, the name '...' is not acceptable as the DNS name of a computer.

Names may have an internal structure that represents their position in a hierarchic name space, as in the UNIX file system, or in an organizational hierarchy, as is the case for Internet domain names; or they may be chosen from a flat set of numeric or symbolic identifiers. The most important advantage of hierarchic name spaces is that each part of a name is resolved relative to a separate context, and the same name may be used with different meanings in different contexts. In the case of file systems, each directory represents a context. Thus */etc/passwd* is a hierarchic name with two components. The first, 'etc', is resolved relative to the context '/' or root, and the second part, 'passwd', is relative to the context '/etc'. The name */oldetc/passwd* can have a different meaning because its second component is resolved in a different context. Similarly, the same name */etc/passwd* may resolve to different files in the contexts of two different computers.

Hierarchic name spaces are potentially infinite, so they enable a system to grow indefinitely. Flat name spaces are usually finite; their size is determined by fixing a maximum permissible length on names. If no limit is set on the length of the names in a flat name space, then it also is potentially infinite. Another potential advantage of a hierarchic name space is that different contexts can be managed by different people.

The structure of 'http' URLs was introduced in Chapter 1. The URL name space includes *relative names* such as *../images/figure1.jpg*. In this URL scheme, the server's host name and the server directory to which this pathname is referred are taken by a browser to be the same as those of the document in which it is embedded.

DNS names are called *domain names* – they are strings similar to absolute UNIX file names. Some examples of these are *www.cdk4.net* (a computer), *net*, *com* and *ac.uk* (the latter three are domains).

The DNS name space has a hierarchic structure: a domain name consists of one or more strings called *name components* or *labels*, separated by the delimiter '.'. There is no delimiter at the beginning or end of a domain name, although the root of the DNS name space is sometimes referred to as '.' for administrative purposes. The name components are non-null printable strings that do not contain '.'. In general, a *prefix* of a name is an initial section of the name that contains only zero or more entire components. For example, in DNS *www* and *www.cdk4* are both prefixes of *www.cdk4.net*. DNS names are not case-sensitive, so *www.cdk4.net* and *WWW.CDK4.NET* have the same meaning.

DNS servers do not recognize relative names: all names are referred to the global root. However, in practical implementations, client software keeps a list of domain names that are appended automatically to any single-component name before resolution. For example, the name *www* presented in the domain *cdk4.net* probably refers to *www.cdk4.net*; client software will append the default domain *cdk4.net* and attempt to resolve this name. If this fails, then further default domain names may be appended; finally, the (absolute) name *www* is presented to the root for resolution (an operation which will of course fail in this case). Names with more than one component, however, are normally presented intact to the DNS – as absolute names.

Aliases ◊ Unfortunately, names with more than one or two components are awkward to type and remember. In general, an *alias* is similar to a UNIX-style symbolic link, allowing a convenient name to be substituted for a more complicated one. The DNS allows aliases in which one domain name is defined to stand for another. The reason for having aliases is to provide for transparency. For example, aliases are generally used to specify the names of machines that run a web server or an FTP server. The name *www.example.net* might be an alias for a computer called *fred.example.net*. This has the advantage that clients can refer to the web server by a generic name that does not refer to a particular machine, and if the web server is moved to another computer, all that needs to be done is to update the alias in the DNS database.

Naming domains ◊ A *naming domain* is a name space for which there exists a single overall administrative authority for assigning names within it. This authority is in overall control of which names may be bound within the domain, but it is free to delegate this task.

Domains in DNS are collections of domain names; syntactically, a domain's name is the common suffix of the domain names within it, but otherwise it cannot be distinguished from, for example, a computer name. For example, *net* is a domain that contains *cdk4.net*. Note that the term 'domain name' is potentially confusing, since only some domain names identify domains (others identify computers).

The administration of domains may be devolved to sub-domains. The domain *dcs.qmul.ac.uk* – the Department of Computer Science at Queen Mary College (University of London) in the UK – can contain any name the department wishes. But the domain name *dcs.qmul.ac.uk* itself had to be agreed with the college authorities, who manage the domain *qmul.ac.uk*. Similarly, *qmul.ac.uk* had to be agreed with the registered authority for *ac.uk*, and so on.

Responsibility for a naming domain normally goes hand in hand with responsibility for managing and keeping up to date the corresponding part of the database stored in an authoritative name server and used by the name service. Naming data belonging to different naming domains are in general stored by distinct name servers managed by the corresponding authorities.

Combining and customizing name spaces ◊ DNS provides a global and homogeneous name space in which a given name refers to the same entity, no matter which process on which computer looks up the name. By contrast, some name services allow distinct name spaces – sometimes heterogeneous name spaces – to be embedded into them; and some name services allow the name space to be customized to suit the needs of individual groups, users or even processes.

Merging: The practice of mounting file systems in UNIX and NFS (see Section 8.3) provides an example in which a part of one name space is conveniently embedded in another. But consider how to merge the *entire* UNIX file systems of two (or more) computers called *red* and *blue*. Each computer has its own root, with overlapping file names. For example, */etc/passwd* refers to one file on *red* and a different file on *blue*. The obvious way to merge the file systems is to replace each computer's root by a 'super root' and mount each computer's file system in this super root, say as */red* and */blue*. Users and programs can then refer to */red/etc/passwd* and */blue/etc/passwd*. But the new naming convention by itself would cause programs on the two computers that still use the old name */etc/passwd* to malfunction. A solution is to leave the old root contents on each computer and embed the mounted file systems */red* and */blue* of both computers (assuming that this does not produce name clashes with the old root contents).

The moral is that we can always merge name spaces by creating a higher-level root context, but this may raise a problem of backwards compatibility. Fixing the compatibility problem, in turn, leaves us with hybrid name spaces and the inconvenience of having to translate old names between the users of the two computers.

Heterogeneity: The Distributed Computing Environment (DCE) name space [OSF 1997] allows heterogeneous name spaces to be embedded within it. DCE names may contain *junctions*, which are similar to mount points in NFS and UNIX (see Section 8.3), except that they allow heterogeneous name spaces to be mounted. For example, consider the full DCE name */.../dcs.qmul.ac.uk/principals/Jean.Dollimore*. The first part of this name */.../dcs.qmul.ac.uk* denotes a context called a *cell*. The next component is a junction. For example, the junction *principals* is a context containing security principals in which the final component *Jean.Dollimore* may be looked up. Similarly, in */.../dcs.qmul.ac.uk/files/pub/reports/TR2000-99*, the junction *files* is a context corresponding to a file system directory, in which the final component *pub/reports/TR2000-99* is looked up. The two junctions *principals* and *files* are the roots of heterogeneous name spaces, implemented by heterogeneous name services.

Customization: We saw in the example of embedding NFS-mounted file systems above that sometimes users prefer to construct their name spaces independently rather than sharing a single name space. File system mounting enables users to import files that are stored on servers and shared, while the other names continue to refer to local, unshared files and can be administered autonomously. But even the same files accessed from two different computers may be mounted at different points and thus have different names. By not sharing the entire name space, users must translate names between computers.

Another example of a motive for customization is where the same name is made to refer to different files on different computers. For example, the same name */bin/netscape* could in principle be bound to a program in x86 binary format on a Pentium-based computer and to a PowerPC binary on a Mac OS X computer. This mapping of the same names to different files makes it possible to write scripts involving those names that execute correctly on all machine configurations.

The Spring naming service [Radia *et al.* 1993] provides the ability to construct name spaces dynamically and to share individual naming contexts selectively. Unlike the examples just given, even two different processes on the same computer can have different naming contexts. Spring naming contexts are first-class objects that can be shared around a distributed system. For example, suppose a user on computer *red* wishes to run a program on *blue* that issues file pathnames such as */etc/passwd*, but these names are to resolve to the files on *red*'s file system, not *blue*'s. This can be achieved in Spring by passing a reference to *red*'s local naming context to *blue* and using it as the program's naming context. Plan 9 [Pike *et al.* 1993] also allows processes to have their own file system name space. A novel feature of Plan 9 (but which can also be implemented in Spring) is that physical directories can be ordered and merged into a single logical directory. The effect is that a name looked up in the single logical directory is looked up in the succession of physical directories until there is a match, when the attributes are returned. This eliminates the need to supply lists of paths when looking for program or library files.

9.2.2 Name resolution

In general, resolution is an iterative process whereby a name is repeatedly presented to naming contexts. A naming context either maps a given name onto a set of primitive attributes (such as those of a user) directly, or it maps it onto a further naming context and a derived name to be presented to that context. To resolve a name, it is first presented to some initial naming context; resolution iterates as long as further contexts and derived names are output. We illustrated this at the start of Section 9.2.1 with the example of */etc/passwd*, in which 'etc' is presented to the context /, and then 'passwd' is presented to the context */etc*.

Another example of the iterative nature of resolution is the use of aliases. For example, whenever a DNS server is asked to resolve an alias such as *www.dcs.qmul.ac.uk*, the server first resolves the alias to another domain name (in this case *apricot.dcs.qmul.ac.uk*), which must be further resolved to produce an IP address.

In general, the use of aliases makes it possible for cycles to be present in the name space, in which case resolution may never terminate. Two solutions are, first, to abandon a resolution process if it passes a threshold number of resolutions; and, second, to leave administrators to veto any aliases that would introduce cycles.

Name servers and navigation ◊ Any name service, such as DNS, that stores a very large database and is used by a large population will not store all of its naming information on a single server computer. Such a server would be a bottleneck and a critical point of failure. Any heavily used name services should use replication to achieve high availability. We shall see that DNS specifies that each subset of its database is replicated in at least two failure-independent servers.

We mentioned above that the data belonging to a naming domain is usually stored by a local name server managed by the authority responsible for that domain. Although, in some cases, a name server may store data for more than one domain, it is generally true to say that data is partitioned into servers according to its domain. We shall see that in DNS, most of the entries are for local computers. But there are also name servers for the higher domains, such as *yahoo.com* and *ac.uk*, and for the root.

The partitioning of data implies that the local name server cannot answer all enquiries without the help of other name servers. For example, a name server in the *dcs.qmul.ac.uk* domain would not be able to supply the IP address of a computer in the domain *cs.purdue.edu* unless it was cached – certainly not the first time it is asked.

The process of locating naming data from among more than one name server in order to resolve a name is called *navigation*. The client name resolution software carries out navigation on behalf of the client. It communicates with name servers as necessary to resolve a name. It may be provided as library code and linked into clients, as for example in the BIND implementation for DNS (see Section 9.2.3) or in Grapevine [Birrell *et al.* 1982]. The alternative, used with X500, is to provide name resolution in a separate process that is shared by all of the client processes on that computer.

DNS supports the model known as *iterative navigation* (see Figure 9.2). To resolve a name, a client presents the name to the local name server, which attempts to resolve it. If the local name server has the name, it returns the result immediately. If it does not, it will suggest another server that will be able to help. Resolution proceeds at the new server, with further navigation as necessary until the name is located or is discovered to be unbound.

As DNS is designed to hold entries for millions of domains and is accessed by vast numbers of clients, it would not be feasible to have all queries starting at a root server, even if it were to be replicated heavily. The DNS database is partitioned between servers in such a way as to allow many queries to be satisfied locally and others to be satisfied

Figure 9.2   Iterative navigation

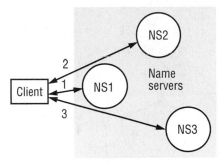

A client iteratively contacts name servers NS1–NS3 in order to resolve a name

without needing to resolve each part of the name separately. The scheme for resolving names in DNS will be described in more detail in Section 9.2.3.

NFS also employs iterative navigation in the resolution of a file name, on a component-by-component basis (see Chapter 8). This is because the file service may encounter a symbolic link when resolving a name. A symbolic link must be interpreted in the client's file system name space because it may point to a file in a directory stored at another server. The client computer must determine which server this is, because only the client knows its mount points.

In *multicast navigation*, a client multicasts the name to be resolved and the required object type to the group of name servers. Only the server that holds the named attributes responds to the request. Unfortunately, however, if the name proves to be unbound, then the request is greeted with silence. Cheriton and Mann [1989] describe a multicast-based navigation scheme in which a separate server is included in the group to respond when the required name is unbound.

Another alternative to the iterative navigation model is one in which a name server coordinates the resolution of the name and passes the result back to the user agent. Ma [1992] distinguishes *non-recursive* and *recursive server-controlled navigation* (Figure 9.3). Under non-recursive server-controlled navigation, any name server may be chosen by the client. This server communicates by multicast or iteratively with its peers in the style described above, as though it were a client. Under recursive server-controlled navigation, the client once more contacts a single server. If this server does not store the name, the server contacts a peer storing a (larger) prefix of the name, which in turn attempts to resolve it. This procedure continues recursively until the name is resolved.

If a name service spans distinct administrative domains, then clients executing in one administrative domain may be prohibited from accessing name servers belonging to another such domain. Moreover, even name servers may be prohibited from discovering the disposition of naming data across name servers in another administrative domain. Then, both client-controlled and non-recursive server-controlled navigation are inappropriate, and recursive server-controlled navigation must be used. Authorized name servers request name service data from designated name servers managed by

Figure 9.3   Non-recursive and recursive server-controlled navigation

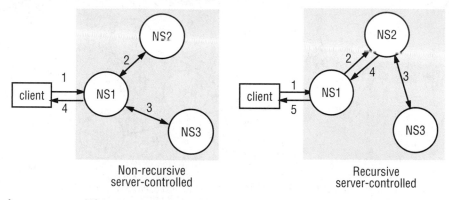

Non-recursive
server-controlled

Recursive
server-controlled

A name server NS1 communicates with other name servers on behalf of a client

different administrations, which return the attributes without revealing where the different parts of the naming database are stored.

Caching ◊ In DNS and other name services, client name resolution software and servers maintain a cache of the results of previous name resolutions. When a client requests a name lookup, the name resolution software consults its cache. If it holds a recent result from a previous lookup for the name, it returns it to the client; otherwise, it sets about finding it from a server. That server, in turn, may return data cached from other servers.

Caching is a key to a name service's performance and assists in maintaining the availability of both the name service and other services despite name server crashes. Its role in enhancing response times by saving communication with name servers is clear. Caching can be used to eliminate high-level name servers – the root server, in particular – from the navigation path, allowing resolution to proceed despite some server failures.

Caching by client name resolvers is widely applied in name services and is particularly successful because naming data are changed relatively rarely. For example, information such as computer or service addresses are liable to remain unchanged for months or years. However, the possibility exists of a name service returning out-of-date attributes, for example, an out-of-date address, during resolution.

9.2.3 The Domain Name System

The Domain Name System is a name service design whose main naming database is used across the Internet. It was devised principally by Mockapetris [1987] in RFC 1034 to replace the original Internet naming scheme, in which all host names and addresses were held in a single central master file and downloaded by FTP to all computers that required them [Harrenstien *et al.* 1985]. This original scheme was soon seen to suffer from three major shortcomings:

- It did not scale to large numbers of computers.

- Local organizations wished to administer their own naming systems.

- A general name service was needed – not one that serves only for looking up computer addresses.

The objects named by the DNS are primarily computers – for which mainly IP addresses are stored as attributes – and what we have referred to in this chapter as naming domains are called simply *domains* in the DNS. In principle, however, any type of object can be named, and its architecture gives scope for a variety of implementations. Organizations and departments within them can manage their own naming data. Millions of names are bound by the Internet DNS, and lookups are made against it from around the world. Any name can be resolved by any client. This is achieved by hierarchical partitioning of the name database, by replication of the naming data, and by caching.

Domain names   ◊ The DNS is designed for use in multiple implementations, each of which may have its own name space. In practice, however, only one is in widespread use, and that is the one used for naming across the Internet. The Internet DNS name space is partitioned both organizationally and according to geography. The names are written with the highest-level domain on the right. The original top-level organizational domains (also called *generic domains*) in use across the Internet were:

com	–	Commercial organizations
edu	–	Universities and other educational institutions
gov	–	US governmental agencies
mil	–	US military organizations
net	–	Major network support centres
org	–	Organizations not mentioned above
int	–	International organizations

New top-level domains were added in the early 2000s. A full list of current generic domain names is available from the Internet Assigned Numbers Authority at [www.iana.org].

In addition, every country has its own domains:

us	–	United States
uk	–	United Kingdom
fr	–	France
...	–	...

Countries, particularly those other than the USA, use their own domain to distinguish their organizations. The UK, for example, has domains *co.uk* and *ac.uk*, which correspond to *com* and *edu* respectively (*ac* stands for 'academic community'). Note that, despite its geographic-sounding suffix *uk*, a domain such as *doit.co.uk* could have data located in the Spanish office of Doit Ltd, a British company. In other words, even geographic-sounding domain names are conventional and are completely independent of their physical locations.

DNS queries ◊ The Internet DNS is primarily used for simple host name resolution and for looking up electronic mail hosts, as follows:

Host name resolution: In general, applications use the DNS to resolve host names into IP addresses. For example, when a web browser is given a URL containing the domain name *www.dcs.qmul.ac.uk*, it makes a DNS enquiry and obtains the corresponding IP address. As was pointed out in Chapter 4, browsers use HTTP to communicate with web servers at an IP address with a reserved port number. The services FTP and SMTP work in a similar way; for example, an FTP program may be given the domain name *ftp.dcs.qmul.ac.uk* and can make a DNS enquiry to get its IP address and then use TCP to communicate with it at the reserved port number. The names *www*, *ftp* and *smtp* may be aliases for the domain names of the actual computers on which those services run. For an example without aliases, consider the case when a user gets a *telnet* program to contact a host whose domain name is *jeans-pc.dcs.qmul.ac.uk*; *telnet* makes a DNS enquiry to get the corresponding IP address and uses the default port number.

Mail host location: Electronic mail software uses the DNS to resolve domain names into the IP addresses of mail hosts – computers that will accept mail for those domains. For example, when the address *tom@dcs.rnx.ac.uk* is to be resolved, the DNS is queried with the address *dcs.rnx.ac.uk* and the type designation 'mail'. It returns a list of domain names of hosts that can accept mail for *dcs.rnx.ac.uk*, if such exist (and, optionally, the corresponding IP addresses). The DNS may return more than one domain name so that the mail software can try alternatives if the main mail host is unreachable for some reason. The DNS returns an integer preference value for each mail host, indicating the order in which the mail hosts should be tried.

Some other types of query that are implemented in some installations but are considerably less used than those just given are:

Reverse resolution: Some software requires a domain name to be returned given an IP address. This is just the reverse of the normal host name query, but the name server receiving the query replies only if the IP address is in its own domain.

Host information: The DNS can store the machine architecture type and operating system against the domain names of hosts. It has been suggested that this option should not be implemented, because it provides useful information for those attempting to gain unauthorized access to computers.

Well-known services: A list of the services run by a computer (for example, telnet, FTP) and the protocol used to obtain them (that is, UDP or TCP on the Internet) can be returned, given the computer's domain name, provided that the name server supports this information.

In principle, the DNS can be used to store arbitrary attributes. A query is specified by a domain name, class and type. For domain names in the Internet, the class is IN. The type of query specifies whether an IP address, a mail host, a name server or some other type of information is required. A special domain, in-addr.arpa, exists to hold IP addresses for reverse lookups. The class attribute is used to distinguish, for example, the Internet naming database from other, experimental, DNS naming databases. A set of types is defined for a given database; those for the Internet database are given in Figure 9.5.

DNS name servers ◊ The problems of scale are treated by a combination of partitioning the naming database and replicating and caching parts of it close to the points of need. The DNS database is distributed across a logical network of servers. Each server holds part of the naming database – primarily data for the local domain. Most queries concern computers in the local domain and are satisfied by servers within that domain. However, each server records the domain names and addresses of other name servers, so that queries pertaining to objects outside the domain can be satisfied.

The DNS naming data are divided into *zones*. A zone contains the following data:

- Attribute data for names in a domain, less any sub-domains administered by lower-level authorities. For example, a zone could contain data for Queen Mary College, University of London – *qmul.ac.uk* – less the data held by departments, for example the Department of Computer Science – *dcs.qmul.ac.uk*.

- The names and addresses of at least two name servers that provide *authoritative* data for the zone. These are versions of zone data that can be relied upon as being reasonably up to date.

- The names of name servers that hold authoritative data for delegated sub-domains; and 'glue' data giving the IP addresses of these servers.

- Zone management parameters, such as those governing the caching and replication of zone data.

A server may hold authoritative data for zero or more zones. In order that naming data are available even when a single server fails, the DNS architecture specifies that each zone must be replicated authoritatively in at least two servers.

System administrators enter the data for a zone into a master file, which is the source of authoritative data for the zone. There are two types of server that are considered to provide authoritative data. A *primary* or *master server* reads zone data directly from a local master file. *Secondary servers* download zone data from a primary server. They communicate periodically with the primary server to check whether their stored version matches that held by the primary server. If a secondary's copy is out of date, the primary sends it the latest version. The frequency of the secondary's check is set by administrators as a zone parameter, and its value is typically once or twice a day.

Any server is free to cache data from other servers to avoid having to contact them when name resolution requires the same data again; it does this on the proviso that clients are told that such data is non-authoritative as supplied. Each entry in a zone has a time-to-live value. When a non-authoritative server caches data from an authoritative server, it notes the time to live. It will only provide its cached data to clients for up to this time; when queried after the time period has expired, it recontacts the authoritative server to check its data. This is a useful feature that minimizes the amount of network traffic while retaining flexibility for system administrators. When attributes are expected to change rarely, they can be given a correspondingly large time to live. If an administrator knows that attributes are likely to change soon, then he or she can reduce the time to live accordingly.

Figure 9.4 shows the arrangement of some of the DNS database as it stood in the year 2001. Note that, in practice, root servers such as *a.root-servers.net* hold entries for several levels of domain, as well as entries for first-level domain names. This is to reduce the number of navigation steps when domain names are resolved. Root name

Figure 9.4   DNS name servers (as in the year 2001)

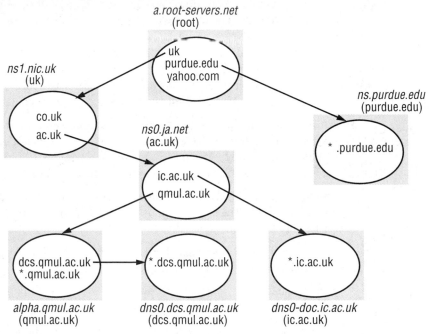

Note: Name server names are in italics, and the corresponding domains are in parentheses. Arrows denote name server entries

servers hold authoritative entries for the name servers for the top-level domains. They are also authoritative name servers for the generic top-level domains such as *com* and *edu*. However, the root name servers are not name servers for the country domains. For example, the *uk* domain has a collection of name servers, one of which is called *ns1.nic.net*. These name servers know the name servers for the second-level domains in the United Kingdom such as *ac.uk* and *co.uk*. The name servers for the domain *ac.uk* know the name servers for all of the university domains in the country, such as *qmul.ac.uk* or *ic.ac.uk*. In some cases, a university domain delegates some of its responsibilities to a sub-domain such as *dcs.qmul.ac.uk*.

The root domain information is replicated by a primary server to a collection of secondary servers as described above. In spite of this, some root servers need to serve about 1000 queries per second, according to Liu and Albitz [1998]. All DNS servers store the addresses of one or more root name servers, which do not change very often. They also usually store the address of an authoritative server for the parent domain. A query involving a three-component domain name such as *www.berkeley.edu* can be satisfied using at worst two navigation steps: one to a root server that stores an appropriate name server entry, and a second to the server whose name is returned.

Referring to Figure 9.4, the domain name *jeans-pc.dcs.qmul.ac.uk* can be looked up from within *dcs.qmul.ac.uk* using the local server *dns0.dcs.qmul.ac.uk*. This server does not store an entry for the web server *www.ic.ac.uk*, but it does keep a cached entry

Figure 9.5   DNS resource records

Record type	Meaning	Main contents
A	A computer address	IP number
NS	An authoritative name server	Domain name for server
CNAME	The canonical name for an alias	Domain name for alias
SOA	Marks the start of data for a zone	Parameters governing the zone
WKS	A well-known service description	List of service names and protocols
PTR	Domain name pointer (reverse lookups)	Domain name
HINFO	Host information	Machine architecture and operating system
MX	Mail exchange	List of *<preference, host>* pairs
TXT	Text string	Arbitrary text

for *ic.ac.uk* (which it obtained from the authorized server *ns0.ja.net*). The server *dns0-doc.ic.ac.uk* can be contacted to resolve the full name.

Navigation and query processing ◊ A DNS client is called a *resolver*. It is normally implemented as library software. It accepts queries, formats them into messages expected under the DNS protocol and communicates with one or more name servers in order to satisfy the queries. A simple request-reply protocol is used, typically using UDP packets on the Internet (DNS servers use a well-known port number). The resolver times out and resends its query if necessary. The resolver can be configured to contact a list of initial name servers in order of preference in case one or more are unavailable.

The DNS architecture allows for recursive navigation as well as iterative navigation. The resolver specifies which type of navigation is required when contacting a name server. However, name servers are not bound to implement recursive navigation. As was pointed out above, recursive navigation may tie up server threads, meaning that other requests might be delayed.

In order to save network communication, the DNS protocol allows multiple queries to be packed into the same request message, and for name servers correspondingly to send multiple replies in their response messages.

Resource records ◊ Zone data are stored by name servers in files in one of several fixed types of resource record. For the Internet database, these include the types given in Figure 9.5. Each record refers to a domain name, which is not shown. The entries in the table refer to items already mentioned, except that *TXT* entries are included to allow arbitrary other information to be stored against domain names. The tables below are based on data in place in 2001.

The data for a zone starts with an *SOA*-type record, which contains the zone parameters that specify, for example, the version number and how often secondaries should refresh their copies. This is followed by a list of records of type *NS* specifying the name servers for the domain and a list of records of type *MX* giving preferences and domain names of mail hosts. For example, part of the database for the domain *dcs.qmul.ac.uk* is shown in Figure 9.6, where the time to live *1D* means 1 day.

Figure 9.6   DNS zone data records

domain name	time to live	class	type	value
	1D	IN	NS	dns0
	1D	IN	NS	dns1
	1D	IN	NS	cancer.ucs.ed.ac.uk
	1D	IN	MX	1 mail1.qmul.ac.uk
	1D	IN	MX	2 mail2.qmul.ac.uk

Further records of type *A* later in the database give the IP addresses for the two name servers *dns0* and *dns1*. The IP addresses of the mail hosts and the third name server are given in the databases corresponding to their domains.

The majority of the remainder of the records in a lower-level zone like *dcs.qmul.ac.uk* will be of type *A* and map the domain name of a computer onto its IP address. They may contain some aliases for the well-known services, for example:

domain name	time to live	class	type	value
www	1D	IN	CNAME	apricot
apricot	1D	IN	A	138.37.88.248

If the domain has any sub-domains, there will be further records of type *NS* specifying their name servers, which will also have individual *A* entries. For example, the database for *qmul.ac.uk* contains the following records for the name servers in its sub-domain *dcs.qmul.ac.uk*:

domain name	time to live	class	type	value
dcs	1D	IN	NS	dns0.dcs
dns0.dcs	1D	IN	A	138.37.88.249
dcs	1D	IN	NS	dns1.dcs
dns1.dcs	1D	IN	A	138.37.94.248
dcs	1D	IN	NS	cancer.ucs.ed.ac.uk

Load sharing by name servers: At some sites, heavily used services such as the Web and FTP are supported by a group of computers on the same network. In this case, the same domain name is used for each member of the group. When a domain name is shared by several computers, there is one record for each computer in the group, giving its IP address. The name server responds to queries regarding multiple records with the same name by returning the IP addresses according to a round robin schedule. Successive clients are given access to different servers so that the servers can share the workload. Caching has a potential for spoiling this scheme, for once a non-authoritative name server or a client has the server's address in its cache it will continue to use it. To counteract this effect, the records are given a short time to live.

The BIND implementation of the DNS ◊ The Berkeley Internet Name Domain (BIND) is an implementation of the DNS for computers running UNIX. Client programs link in library software as the resolver. DNS name server computers run the named daemon.

BIND allows for three categories of name server: primary servers, secondary servers and caching-only servers; the named program implements just one of these types according to the contents of a configuration file. The first two categories are as described above. Caching-only servers read in from a configuration file sufficient names and addresses of authoritative servers to resolve any name. Thereafter, they only store this data and data that they learn by resolving names for clients.

A typical organization has one primary server, with one or more secondary servers that provide name serving on different local area networks at the site. Additionally, individual computers often run their own caching-only server, to reduce network traffic and speed up response times still further.

Discussion of the DNS ◊ The DNS Internet implementation achieves relatively short average response times for lookups, considering the amount of naming data and the scale of the networks involved. We have seen that it achieves this by a combination of partitioning, replicating and caching naming data. The objects named are primarily computers, name servers and mail hosts. Computer (host) name to IP address mappings change relatively rarely, as do the identities of name servers and mail hosts, so caching and replication occur in a relatively clement environment.

The DNS allows naming data to become inconsistent. That is, if naming data is changed, then other servers may provide clients with stale data for periods in the order of days. None of the replication techniques explored in Chapter 15 is applied. However, inconsistency is of no consequence until such time as a client attempts to use stale data. The DNS does not address itself to how staleness of addresses is detected.

Apart from computers, the DNS also names one particular type of service: the mail service, on a per-domain basis. DNS assumes there to be only one mail service per addressed domain, so users do not have to include the name of this service explicitly in names. Electronic mail applications transparently select this service by using the appropriate type of query when contacting DNS servers.

In summary, the DNS stores a limited variety of naming data, but this is sufficient in so far as applications such as electronic mail impose their own naming schemes on top of domain names. It might be argued that the DNS database represents the lowest common denominator of what would be considered useful by the many user communities on the Internet. The DNS was not designed to be the only name service in the Internet; it coexists with local name and directory services that store data most pertinent to local needs (such as Sun's Network Information Service, which stores encoded passwords, for example, or Microsoft's Active Directory Service [www.microsoft.com I], which stores detailed information about all the resources within a domain).

What remains as a potential problem for the DNS design is its rigidity with respect to changes in the structure of the name space, and the lack of ability to customize the name space to suit local needs. These aspects of naming design are taken up by the case study of the global name service in Section 9.4. Before that, we consider directory services.

9.3   Directory services

We have described how name services store collections of <*name, attribute*> pairs, and how the attributes are looked up from a name. It is natural to consider the dual of this arrangement, in which *attributes* are used as values to be looked up. In these services, textual names can be considered to be just another attribute. Sometimes users wish to find a particular person or resource, but they do not know its name, only some of its other attributes. For example, a user may ask: 'What is the name of the user with telephone number 020-555 9980?' Sometimes users require a service, but they are not concerned with what system entity supplies that service, as long as the service is conveniently accessible. For example, a user might ask 'Which computers in this building are Macintoshes running the Mac OS X operating system?' or 'where can I print a high-resolution colour image?'

A service that stores collections of bindings between names and attributes and that looks up entries that match attribute-based specifications is called a *directory service*. Examples are Microsoft's Active Directory Services, X.500 and its cousin LDAP (described in Section 9.5), Univers [Bowman *et al.* 1990] and Profile [Peterson 1988]. Directory services are sometimes called *yellow pages services*, and conventional name services are correspondingly called *white pages services*, in an obvious analogy with the different types of telephone directory. Directory services are also sometimes known as *attribute-based name services*.

A directory service returns the sets of attributes of any objects found to match some specified attributes. So, for example, the request 'TelephoneNumber = 020-555 9980' might return {'Name = John Smith', 'TelephoneNumber = 020-555 9980', 'emailAddress = john@dcs.gormenghast.ac.uk', ...}. The client may specify that only a subset of the attributes is of interest – for example, just the email addresses of matching objects. X.500 and some other directory services also allow objects to be looked up by conventional hierarchic textual names. The Universal Directory and Discovery Service (UDDI), which is presented in Section 19.4 provides both white pages and yellow pages services to provide information about organizations and the web services they provide.

UDDI aside, the term *discovery service* normally denotes the special case of a directory service for services provided by devices in a spontaneous networking environment. As Section 2.2.3 described, devices in spontaneous networks are liable to connect and disconnect unpredictably. One core difference between a discovery service and other directory services is that the address of a directory service is normally well known and pre-configured in clients, whereas a device entering a spontaneous networking environment has to resort to multicast navigation, at least the first time it accesses the local discovery service. Section 16.2 describes discovery services in detail.

Attributes are clearly more powerful than names as designators of objects: programs can be written to select objects according to precise attribute specifications where names might not be known. Another advantage of attributes is that they do not expose the structure of organizations to the outside world, as do organizationally partitioned names. However, the relative simplicity of use of textual names makes them unlikely to be replaced by attribute-based naming in many applications.

9.4   Case study of the Global Name Service

A Global Name Service (GNS) was designed and implemented by Lampson and colleagues at the DEC Systems Research Center [Lampson 1986] to provide facilities for resource location, mail addressing and authentication. The design goals of GNS have already been listed at the end of Section 9.1; they reflect the fact that a name service for use in an internetwork must support a naming database that may extend to include the names of millions of computers and (eventually) email addresses for billions of users. The designers of GNS also recognized that the naming database is likely to have a long lifetime, that it must continue to operate effectively while it grows from small to large scale and while the network on which it is based evolves. The structure of the name space may change during that time to reflect changes in organizational structures. The service should accommodate changes in the names of the individuals, organizations and groups that it holds; and changes in the naming structure such as those that occur when one company is taken over by another. In this description, we shall focus on those features of the design that enable it to accommodate such changes.

The potentially large naming database and the scale of the distributed environment in which GNS is intended to operate make the use of caching essential and render it extremely difficult to maintain complete consistency between all copies of a database entry. The cache consistency strategy adopted relies on the assumption that updates to the database will be infrequent and that slow dissemination of updates is acceptable, since clients can detect and recover from the use of out-of-date naming data.

GNS manages a naming database that is composed of a tree of directories holding names and values. Directories are named by multi-part pathnames referred to a root, or relative to a working directory, much like filenames in a UNIX file system. Each directory is also assigned an integer, which serves as a unique *directory identifier* (DI). In this section, we use names in italics when referring to the DI of a directory, so that *EC* is the identifier of the EC directory. A directory contains a list of names and references. The values stored at the leaves of the directory tree are organized into *value trees*, so that the attributes associated with names can be structured values.

Names in GNS have two parts: *<directory name, value name>*. The first part identifies a directory; the second refers to a value tree, or some portion of a value tree. For example, see Figure 9.7, in which the DIs are illustrated as small integers although they are actually chosen from a range of integers to ensure uniqueness. The attributes of a user Peter.Smith in the directory QMUL would be stored in the value tree named *<EC/UK/AC/QMUL, Peter.Smith>*. The value tree includes a password, which can be referenced as *<EC/UK/AC/QMUL, Peter.Smith/password>*, and several mail addresses, each of which would be listed in the value tree as a single node with the name *<EC/UK/AC/QMUL, Peter.Smith/mailboxes>*.

The directory tree is partitioned and stored in many servers, with each partition replicated in several servers. The consistency of the tree is maintained in the face of two or more concurrent updates – for example, two users may simultaneously attempt to create entries with the same name, and only one should succeed. Replicated directories present a second consistency problem; this is addressed by an asynchronous update distribution algorithm that ensures eventual consistency, but with no guarantee that all

Figure 9.7   GNS directory tree and value tree for user Peter.Smith

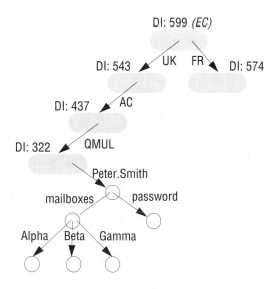

copies are always current. This level of consistency is considered satisfactory for the purpose.

Accommodating change ◊ We now turn to the aspects of the design that are concerned with accommodating growth and change in the structure of the naming database. At the level of clients and administrators, growth is accommodated through extension of the directory tree in the usual manner. But we may wish to integrate the naming trees of two previously separate GNS services. For example, how could we integrate the database rooted at the *EC* directory shown in Figure 9.7 with another database for *NORTH AMERICA*? Figure 9.8 shows a new root *WORLD* introduced above the existing roots of the two trees to be merged. This is a straightforward technique, but how does it affect clients that continue to use names that are referred to what was 'the root' before integration took place? For example, </UK/AC/QMUL, Peter.Smith> is a name used by clients before integration. It is an absolute name (since it begins with the symbol for the

Figure 9.8   Merging trees under a new root

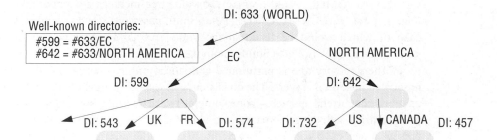

Figure 9.9   Restructuring the directory

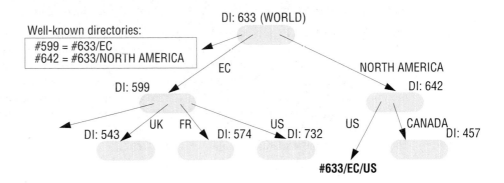

root '/'), but the root it refers to is *EC*, not *WORLD*. *EC* and *NORTH AMERICA* are *working roots* – initial contexts against which names beginning with the root '/' are to be looked up.

The existence of unique directory identifiers can be used to solve this problem. The working root for each program must be identified as part of its execution environment (much as is done for a program's working directory). When a client in the European Community uses a name of the form </UK/AC/QMUL, Peter.Smith>, its local user agent, which is aware of the working root, prefixes the directory identifier EC (#599), thus producing the name <#599/UK/AC/QMUL, Peter.Smith>. The user agent passes this derived name in the lookup request to a GNS server. The user agent may deal similarly with relative names referred to working directories. Clients that are aware of the new configuration may also supply absolute names to the GNS server, which are referred to the conceptual super-root directory containing all directory identifiers, for example, <*WORLD*/EC/UK/AC/QMUL, Peter.Smith>, but the design cannot assume that all clients will be updated to take account of such a change.

The technique described above solves the logical problem, allowing users and client programs to continue to use names that are defined relative to an old root, even when a new real root is inserted, but it leaves an implementation problem: in a distributed naming database that may contain millions of directories, how can the GNS service locate a directory given only its identifier, such as #599? The solution adopted by GNS is to list those directories that are used as working roots, such as EC, in a table of 'well-known directories' held in the current real root directory of the naming database. Whenever the real root of the naming database changes, as it does in Figure 9.8, all GNS servers are informed of the new location of the real root. They can then interpret names of the form WORLD/EC/UK/AC/QMUL (referred to the real root) in the usual way, and they can interpret names of the form #599/UK/AC/QMUL by using the table of 'well-known directories' to translate them to full pathnames beginning at the real root.

GNS also supports the restructuring of the database to accommodate organizational change. Suppose that the United States becomes part of the European Community(!). Figure 9.9 shows the new directory tree. But if the US sub-tree is simply moved to the EC directory, names beginning *WORLD*/NORTH AMERICA/US will no longer work. The solution adopted by GNS is to insert a 'symbolic link' in place of the original US entry (shown in bold in Figure 9.9). The GNS directory lookup procedure interprets the link as a redirection to the US directory in its new location.

Discussion of GNS ◊ GNS is descended from Grapevine [Birrell *et al* 1982] and Clearinghouse [Oppen and Dalal 1983], two successful naming systems developed primarily for the purposes of mail delivery by the Xerox Corporation. GNS successfully addresses needs for scalability and reconfigurability, but the solution adopted for merging and moving directory trees results in a requirement for a database (the table of well-known directories) that must be replicated at every node. In a large-scale network, reconfigurations may occur at any level, and this table could grow to a large size, conflicting with the scalability goal.

9.5   Case study of the X.500 Directory Service

X.500 is a directory service in the sense defined in Section 9.3. It can be used in the same way as a conventional name service, but it is primarily used to satisfy descriptive queries, designed to discover the names and attributes of other users or system resources. Users may have a variety of requirements for searching and browsing in a directory of network users, organizations and system resources to obtain information about the entities that the directory contains. The uses for such a service are likely to be quite diverse. They range from enquiries that are directly analogous to the use of telephone directories, such as a simple 'white pages' access to obtain a user's electronic mail address or a 'yellow pages' query aimed, for example, at obtaining the names and telephone numbers of garages specializing in the repair of a particular make of car, to the use of the directory to access personal details such as job roles, dietary habits or even photographic images of the individuals.

Such queries may originate from users, such as 'yellow pages' uses exemplified by the enquiry about garages mentioned above, or from processes, when they may be used to identify services to meet a functional requirement.

Individuals and organizations can use a directory service to make available a wide range of information about themselves and the resources that they wish to offer for use in the network. Users can search the directory for specific information with only partial knowledge of its name, structure or content.

The ITU and ISO standards organizations have defined the *X.500 Directory Service* [ITU/ISO 1997] as a network service intended to meet these requirements. The standard refers to it as a service for access to information about 'real-world entities', but it is also likely to be used for access to information about hardware and software services and devices. X.500 is specified as an application level service in the Open Systems Interconnection (OSI) set of standards, but its design does not depend to any significant extent on the other OSI standards, and it can be viewed as a design for a general-purpose directory service. We shall outline the design of the X.500 directory service and its implementation here. Readers interested in a more detailed description of X.500 and methods for its implementation are advised to study Rose's book on the subject [Rose 1992]. X.500 is also the basis for LDAP (discussed below); and it is used in the DCE directory service [OSF 1997].

Figure 9.10   X.500 service architecture

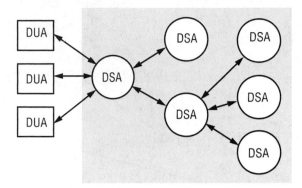

The data stored in X.500 servers is organized in a tree structure with named nodes as in the case of the other name servers discussed in this chapter, but in X.500 a wide range of attributes are stored at each node in the tree, and access is not just by name but also by searching for entries with any required combination of attributes.

The X.500 name tree is called the *Directory Information Tree* (DIT), and the entire directory structure including the data associated with the nodes is called the *Directory Information Base* (DIB). There is intended to be a single integrated DIB containing information provided by organizations throughout the world, with portions of the DIB located in individual X.500 servers. Typically, a medium-sized or large organization would provide at least one server. Clients access the directory by establishing a connection to a server and issuing access requests. Clients can contact any server with an enquiry. If the data required are not in the segment of the DIB held by the contacted server, it will either invoke other servers to resolve the query or redirect the client to another server.

In the terminology of the X.500 standard, servers are *Directory Service Agents* (DSAs), and their clients are termed *Directory User Agents* (DUAs). Figure 9.10 shows the software architecture and one of the several possible navigation models, with each DUA client process interacting with a single DSA process, which accesses other DSAs as necessary to satisfy requests.

Each entry in the DIB consists of a name and a set of attributes. As in other name servers, the full name of an entry corresponds to a path through the DIT from the root of the tree to the entry. In addition to full or *absolute* names, a DUA can establish a context, which includes a base node, and then use shorter relative names that give the path from the base node to the named entry.

Figure 9.11 shows the portion of the Directory Information Tree that includes the University of Gormenghast, Great Britain, and Figure 9.12 is one of the associated DIB entries. The data structure for the entries in the DIB and the DIT is very flexible. A DIB entry consists of a set of attributes, where an attribute has a *type* and one or more *values*. The type of each attribute is denoted by a type name (for example, *countryName*, *organizationName*, *commonName*, *telephoneNumber*, *mailbox*, *objectClass*). New attribute types can be defined if they are required. For each distinct type name there is a

Figure 9.11   Part of the X.500 Directory Information Tree

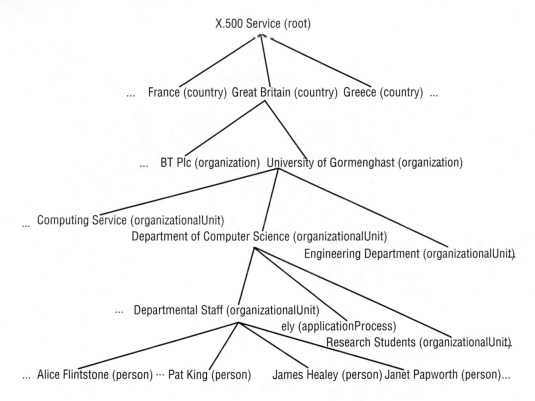

corresponding type definition, which includes a type description and a syntax definition in the ASN.1 Notation (a standard notation for syntax definitions) defining representations for all permissible values of the type.

DIB entries are classified in a manner similar to the object class structures found in object-oriented programming languages. Each entry includes an *objectClass* attribute, which determines the class (or classes) of the object to which an entry refers. *Organization*, *organizationalPerson* and *document* are all examples of *objectClass* values. Further classes can be defined as they are required. The definition of a class determines which attributes are mandatory and which are optional for entries of the given class. The definitions of classes are organized in an inheritance hierarchy in which all classes except one (called *topClass*) must contain an *objectClass* attribute, and the value of the *objectClass* attribute must be the name of one or more classes. If there are several *objectClass* values, the object inherits the mandatory and optional attributes of each of the classes.

The name of a DIB entry (the name that determines its position in the DIT) is determined by selecting one or more of its attributes as *distinguished attributes*. The attributes selected for this purpose are referred to as the entry's *Distinguished Name* (DN).

Now we can consider the methods by which the directory is accessed. There are two main types of access request:

Figure 9.12   An X.500 DIB Entry

info
Alice Flintstone, Departmental Staff, Department of Computer Science, University of Gormenghast, GB

commonName	*uid*
Alice.L.Flintstone	alf
Alice.Flintstone	*mail*
Alice Flintstone	
A. Flintstone	alf@dcs.gormenghast.ac.uk
surname	Alice.Flintstone@dcs.gormenghast.ac.uk
Flintstone	*roomNumber*
telephoneNumber	Z42
+44 986 33 4604	*userClass*
	Research Fellow

read: An absolute or relative name (a *domain name* in X.500 terminology) for an entry is given, together with a list of attributes to be read (or an indication that all attributes are required). The DSA locates the named entry by navigating in the DIT, passing requests to other DSA servers where it does not hold relevant parts of the tree. It retrieves the required attributes and returns them to the client.

search: This is an attribute-based access request. A base name and a filter expression are supplied as arguments. The base name specifies the node in the DIT from which the search is to commence; the filter expression is a boolean expression that is to be evaluated for every node below the base node. The filter specifies a search criterion: a logical combination of tests on the values of any of the attributes in an entry. The *search* command returns a list of names (Domain Names) for all of the entries below the base node for which the filter evaluates to *TRUE*.

For example, a filter might be constructed and applied to find the *commonNames* of members of staff who occupy room Z42 in the Department of Computer Science at the University of Gormenghast (Figure 9.12). A read request could then be used to obtain any or all of the attributes of those DIB entries.

Searching can be quite costly when it is applied to large portions of the directory tree (which may reside in several servers). Additional arguments can be supplied to *search* to restrict the scope of its search, the time for which a search is allowed to continue and the size of the list of entries that is returned.

Administration and updating of the DIB ◊ The DSA interface includes operations for adding, deleting and modifying entries. Access control is provided for both queries and updating operations, so access to parts of the DIT may be restricted to certain users or classes of user.

The DIB is partitioned, with the expectation that each organization will provide at least one server holding the details of the entities in that organization. Portions of the DIB may be replicated in several servers.

As a standard (or a 'recommendation' in CCITT terminology), X.500 does not address implementation issues. However, it is quite clear that any implementation involving multiple servers in a wide area network must rely on extensive use of replication and caching techniques to avoid too much redirection of queries.

One implementation, described in Rose [1992], is a system developed at University College, London, known as QUIPU [Kille 1991]. In this implementation, both caching and replication are performed at the level of individual DIB entries, and at the level of collections of entries descended from the same node. It is assumed that values may become inconsistent after an update, and the time interval in which the consistency is restored may be several minutes. This form of update dissemination is generally considered acceptable for directory service applications.

Lightweight directory access protocol ◊ The standard interface to X.500 uses a protocol that involves the upper layers of the ISO protocol stack. A group at the University of Michigan proposed a more lightweight approach called the *Lightweight Directory Access Protocol* (*LDAP*), in which a DUA accesses X.500 directory services directly over TCP/IP. This is described in RFC 2251 [Wahl *et al.* 1997]. LDAP simplifies the interface to X.500 in other ways, for example, it provides a relatively simple API and it replaces ASN.1 encoding with textual encoding.

Although the LDAP specification is based on X.500, LDAP does not require it. An implementation may use any other directory server that obeys the simpler LDAP specification – as opposed to the X.500 specification. For example, Microsoft's Active Directory Service provides an LDAP interface. LDAP has been widely adopted, particularly for intranet directory services. It provides secure access to directory data through authentication.

9.6 Summary

This chapter has described the design and implementation of name services in distributed systems. Name services store the attributes of objects in a distributed system – in particular, their addresses – and return these attributes when a textual name is supplied to be looked up.

The main requirements for the name service are an ability to handle an arbitrary number of names; a long lifetime; high availability; the isolation of faults; and the tolerance of mistrust.

The main design issues are, first, the structure of the name space – the syntactic rules governing names. A related issue is the resolution model: the rules by which a multi component name is resolved to a set of attributes. The set of bound names must be managed. Most designs consider the name space to be divided into domains – discrete sections of the name space, each of which is associated with a single authority controlling the binding of names within it.

The implementation of the name service may span different organizations and user communities. The collection of bindings between names and attributes, in other words, is stored at multiple name servers, each of which stores at least part of the set of names within a naming domain. The question of navigation therefore arises – of the procedure by which a name is resolved when the necessary information is stored at several sites. The types of navigation that are supported are iterative, multicast, recursive server-controlled and non-recursive server-controlled.

Another important aspect of the implementation of a name service is the use of replication and caching. Both of these assist in making the service highly available, and both also reduce the time taken to resolve a name.

The chapter has considered two main cases of name service designs and implementations. The Domain Name System is widely used for naming computers and addressing electronic mail across the Internet; it achieves good response times through replication and caching. The Global Name Service is a design that has tackled the issue of reconfiguring the name space as organizational changes occur.

The chapter also considers directory services, which provide data about matching objects and services when clients supply attribute-based descriptions. X.500 is a model for directory services that might range in scope from individual organisations to global directories. It has been taken up more widely for use in intranets since the arrival of the LDAP software.

EXERCISES

9.1   Describe the names (including identifiers) and attributes used in a distributed file service such as NFS (see Chapter 8).   *page 368*

9.2   Discuss the problems raised by the use of aliases in a name service, and indicate how, if at all, these may be overcome.   *page 373*

9.3   Explain why iterative navigation is necessary in a name service in which different name spaces are partially integrated, such as the file naming scheme provided by NFS.
                                                                                     page 376

9.4   Describe the problem of unbound names in multicast navigation. What is implied by the installation of a server for responding to lookups of unbound names?   *page 377*

9.5   How does caching help a name service's availability?   *page 378*

9.6   Discuss the absence of a syntactic distinction (such as use of a final '.') between absolute and relative names in DNS.   *page 379*

9.7   Investigate your local configuration of DNS domains and servers. You may find a program such as *nslookup* installed on UNIX systems, which enables you to carry out individual name server queries.   *page 381*

9.8   Why do DNS root servers hold entries for two-level names such as *yahoo.com* and *purdue.edu*, rather than one-level names such as *edu* and *com*?   *page 381*

9.9   Which other name server addresses do DNS name servers hold by default, and why?
                                                                                     page 381

9.10   Why might a DNS client choose recursive navigation rather than iterative navigation? What is the relevance of the recursive navigation option to concurrency within a name server?   *page 383*

9.11   When might a DNS server provide multiple answers to a single name lookup, and why?
page 383

9.12   GNS does not guarantee that all copies of entries in the naming database are up-to-date. How are clients of GNS likely to become aware that they have been given an out-of-date entry? Under what circumstances might it be harmful?   *page 387*

9.13   Discuss the potential advantages and drawbacks in the use of a X.500 directory service in place of DNS and the Internet mail delivery programs. Sketch the design of a mail delivery system for an internetwork in which all mail users and mail hosts are registered in an X.500 database.   *page 390*

9.14   What security issues are liable to be relevant to a directory service such as X500 operating within an organization such as a university?   *page 390*

10

PEER-TO-PEER SYSTEMS

Peer-to-peer systems represent a paradigm for the construction of distributed systems and applications in which data and computational resources are contributed by many hosts on the Internet, all of which participate in the provision of a uniform service. Their emergence is a consequence of the very rapid growth of the Internet, embracing many millions of computers and similar numbers of users requiring access to shared resources.

A key problem for peer-to-peer systems is the placement of data objects across many hosts and subsequent provision for access to them in a manner that balances the workload and ensures availability without adding undue overheads. We describe several recently-developed systems and applications that are designed to achieve this.

Peer-to-peer middleware systems are emerging that have the capacity to share computing resources, storage and data present in computers 'at the edges of the Internet' on a global scale. They exploit existing naming, routing, data replication and security techniques in new ways to build a reliable resource sharing layer over an unreliable and untrusted collection of computers and networks.

Peer-to-peer applications have been used to provide file sharing, web caching, information distribution and other services exploiting the resources of tens of thousands of machines across the Internet. They are at their most effective when used to store very large collections of immutable data. Their design diminishes their effectiveness for applications that store and update mutable data objects.

10.1 Introduction

The demand for services in the Internet can be expected to grow to a scale that is limited only by the size of the world's population. The goal of peer-to-peer systems is to enable the sharing of data and resources on a very large scale by eliminating any requirement for separately-managed servers and their associated infrastructure.

The scope for expanding popular services by adding to the number of the computers hosting them is limited when all the hosts must be owned and managed by the service provider. Administration and fault recovery costs tend to dominate. The network bandwidth that can be provided to a single server site over available physical links is also a major constraint. System-level services such as Sun NFS (Section 8.3), the Andrew File System (Section 8.4) or video servers (Section 17.6) and application-level services such as Google, Amazon or eBay all exhibit this problem to varying degrees.

Peer-to-peer systems aim to support useful distributed services and applications using data and computing resources available in the personal computers and workstations that are present on the Internet and other networks in ever-increasing numbers. This is increasingly attractive as the performance difference between desktop and server machines narrows and broadband network connections proliferate.

But there is another, broader aim: one author [Shirky 2000] has defined peer-to-peer applications as 'applications that exploit resources available at the edges of the Internet – storage, cycles, content, human presence'. Each type of resource sharing mentioned in that definition is already represented by distributed applications available for most types of personal computer. The purpose of this chapter is to describe some general techniques that simplify the construction of peer-to-peer applications and enhance their scalability, reliability and security.

Traditional client-server systems manage and provide access to resources such as files, web pages or other information objects located on a single server computer or a small cluster of tightly-coupled servers. With such centralized designs, few decisions are required about the placement of the resources or the management of server hardware resources, but the scale of the service is limited by the server hardware capacity and network connectivity. Peer-to-peer systems provide access to information resources located on computers throughout a network (whether it be the Internet or a corporate network). Algorithms for the placement and subsequent retrieval of information objects are a key aspect of the system design. Their design aims to deliver a service that is fully decentralized and self-organizing, dynamically balancing the storage and processing loads between all the participating computers as computers join and leave the service.

Peer-to-peer systems share these characteristics:

- Their design ensures that each user contributes resources to the system.

- Although they may differ in the resources that they contribute, all the nodes in a peer-to-peer system have the same functional capabilities and responsibilities.

- Their correct operation does not depend on the existence of any centrally-administered systems.

- They can be designed to offer a limited degree of anonymity to the providers and users of resources.

- A key issue for the their efficient operation is the choice of an algorithm for the placement of data across many hosts and subsequent access to it in a manner that balances the workload and ensures availability without adding undue overheads.

Computers and network connections owned and managed by a multitude of different users and organizations are necessarily volatile resources; their owners do not guarantee to keep them switched on, connected and fault-free. So the availability of the processes and computers participating in peer-to-peer systems is unpredictable. Peer-to-peer services therefore cannot rely on guaranteed access to individual resources, although they can be designed to make the probability of failure to access a copy of a replicated object arbitrarily small. It is worth noting that this weakness of peer-to-peer systems can be turned into a strength if the replication of resources that it calls for is exploited to achieve a degree of resistance to tampering by malicious nodes (i.e. through Byzantine fault tolerance techniques, see Chapter 15).

Several early Internet-based services including DNS (Section 9.2.3) and Netnews/Usenet [Kantor and Lapsley 1986] adopted a multi-server scalable and fault-tolerant architecture. The Xerox Grapevine name registration and mail delivery service [Birrell *et al.* 1982, Schroeder *et al.* 1984] provides an interesting early example of a scalable, fault-tolerant distributed service. Lamport's part-time parliament algorithm for distributed consensus [Lamport 1989], the Bayou replicated storage system (see Section 14.4.2) and the classless inter-domain IP routing algorithm (see Section 3.4.3) are all examples of distributed algorithms for the placement or location of information and can be considered as antecedents of peer-to-peer systems.

But the potential for the deployment of peer-to-peer services using resources at the edges of the Internet emerged only when a significant number of users had acquired always-on, broadband connections to the network, making their desktop computers suitable platforms for resource sharing. This occurred first in the United States around 1999. By mid-2004 the worldwide number of broadband Internet connections had comfortably exceeded 100 million [Internet World Stats 2004].

Three generations of peer-to-peer system and application development can be identified. The first generation was launched by the Napster music exchange service [OpenNap 2001], which we describe in the next section. A second generation of file-sharing applications offering greater scalability, anonymity and fault tolerance quickly followed including Freenet [Clarke *et al.* 2000, Freenet 2004], Gnutella, Kazaa [Leibowitz *et al.* 2003] and BitTorrent [Cohen 2003].

Peer-to-peer middleware ◊ The third generation is characterized by the emergence of middleware layers for the application-independent management of distributed resources on a global scale. Several research teams have now completed the development, evaluation and refinement of peer-to-peer middleware platforms and demonstrated or deployed them in a range of application services. The best-known and most fully-developed examples include Pastry [Rowstron and Druschel 2001], Tapestry [Zhao *et al.* 2004], CAN [Ratnasamy *et al.* 2001], Chord [Stoica *et al.* 2001] and Kademlia [Maymounkov and Mazieres 2002].

Figure 10.1   Distinctions between IP and overlay routing for peer-to-peer applications

	IP	*Application-level routing overlay*
Scale	IPv4 is limited to 2^{32} addressable nodes. The IPv6 name space is much more generous (2^{128}), but addresses in both versions are hierarchically structured and much of the space is pre-allocated according to administrative requirements.	Peer-to-peer systems can address more objects. The GUID name space is very large and flat ($>2^{128}$), allowing it to be much more fully occupied.
Load balancing	Loads on routers are determined by network topology and associated traffic patterns.	Object locations can be randomized and hence traffic patterns are divorced from the network topology.
Network dynamics (addition/deletion of objects/nodes)	IP routing tables are updated asynchronously on a best-efforts basis with time constants on the order of 1 hour.	Routing tables can be updated synchronously or asynchronously with fractions of a second delays.
Fault tolerance	Redundancy is designed into the IP network by its managers, ensuring tolerance of a single router or network connectivity failure. n-fold replication is costly.	Routes and object references can be replicated n-fold, ensuring tolerance of n failures of nodes or connections.
Target identification	Each IP address maps to exactly one target node.	Messages can be routed to the nearest replica of a target object.
Security and anonymity	Addressing is only secure when all nodes are trusted. Anonymity for the owners of addresses is not achievable.	Security can be achieved even in environments with limited trust. A limited degree of anonymity can be provided.

These platforms are designed to place resources (data objects, files) on a set of computers that are widely distributed throughout the Internet and to route messages to them on behalf of clients, relieving clients of decisions about placing resources and holding information about the whereabouts of the resources they require. Unlike the second-generation systems, they provide guarantees of delivery for requests in a bounded number of network hops. They place replicas of resources on available host computers in a structured manner, taking account of their volatile availability, their variable trustworthiness and requirements for load balancing and locality of information storage and use.

Resources are identified by globally unique identifiers (GUIDs) and these are usually derived as a secure hash (described in Section 7.4.3) from some or all of the resource's state. The use of a secure hash makes a resource 'self certifying' – clients receiving a resource can check the validity of the hash. This protects it against tampering by untrusted nodes on which it may be stored. But this technique requires that the states of resources are immutable, since a change to the state would result in a different hash value. Hence peer-to-peer storage systems are inherently best suited to the storage of immutable objects (such as music or video files). Their use for objects with changing values is more challenging but can be addressed by the addition of trusted servers to manage a sequence of versions and identify the current version (as is done e.g. in OceanStore and Ivy, described in Sections 10.6.2 and 10.6.3).

The use of peer-to-peer systems for applications that demand a high level of availability for the objects stored requires careful application design to avoid situations in which all of the replicas of an object are simultaneously unavailable. There is a risk of this for objects stored on computers with the same ownership, geographic location, administration, network connectivity, country or jurisdiction. The use of randomly-distributed GUIDs assists by distributing the object replicas to randomly-located nodes in the underlying network. If the underlying network spans many organizations across the globe then the risk of simultaneous unavailability is much reduced.

Overlay routing versus IP routing ◊ At first sight, routing overlays share many character-istics with the IP packet routing infrastructure that constitutes the primary communica-tion mechanism of the Internet (see Section 3.4.3). It is therefore legitimate to ask why an additional application-level routing mechanism is required in peer-to-peer systems. The answer lies in several distinctions that are identified in the table of Figure 10.1. It may be argued that some of these distinctions arise from the 'legacy' nature of IP as the Internet's primary protocol, but the legacy's impact is probably too strong for it to be overcome in order to re-design IP to support peer-to-peer applications more directly.

Distributed computation ◊ The exploitation of spare computing power on end-user computers has long been a subject of interest and experiment. Work with the first personal computers at Xerox PARC [Shoch and Hupp 1982] showed the feasibility of performing loosely-coupled compute-intensive tasks by running background processes on ~100 personal computers linked by a local network. More recently, much larger numbers of computers have been put to use to perform several scientific calculations that require almost unlimited quantities of computing power.

The most widely known effort of this type is the *SETI@home* project [Anderson *et al*. 2002] which is part of a wider project to Search for Extra-Terrestrial Intelligence. SETI@home partitions a stream of digitized radio telescope data into 107-second work units, each of about 350KB and distributes them to client computers whose computing power is contributed by volunteers. Each work unit is distributed redundantly to 3-4 personal computers to guard against erroneous or malicious nodes and examined for significant signal patterns. The distribution of work units and the coordination of results is handled by a single server that is responsible for communication with all of the clients. Anderson *et al*. [2002] reported that 3.91 million personal computers had participated in the SETI@home project by August 2002, resulting in the processing of 221 million work units representing an average 27.36 teraflops of computational power during the 12 months to July 2002. The work completed to that date represented the largest single computation on record.

The SETI computation is unusual in that it does not involve any communication or coordination between computers while they are processing the work units and the results are communicated to a central server in a single short message that may be delivered whenever the client and server are available. Some other scientific tasks of this nature have been identified, including the search for large prime numbers and attempts at brute-force decryption. But the unleashing of the computational power in the Internet

Figure 10.2   Napster: peer-to-peer file sharing with a centralized, replicated index

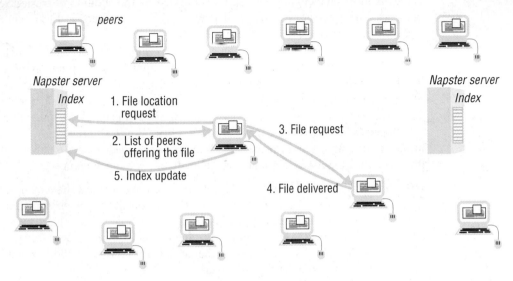

for a broader range of tasks will depend upon the development of a distributed platform that support data sharing and the coordination of computation between participating computers on a large scale. That is the goal of the Grid project, discussed in Chapter 19.

In this chapter we focus on algorithms and systems developed to date for the sharing of data in peer-to-peer networks. In Section 10.2 we summarize Napster's design and review the lessons learned from it. In Section 10.3 we describe the general requirements for peer-to-peer middleware layers. The following sections cover the design and application of peer-to-peer middleware platforms, starting with an abstract specification in Section 10.4, followed by detailed descriptions of two fully-developed examples in Section 10.5 and some applications of them in Section 10.6.

10.2 Napster and its legacy

The first application in which a demand for a globally-scalable information storage and retrieval service emerged was the downloading of digital music files. Both the need and the feasibility of a peer-to-peer solution were first demonstrated by the Napster file sharing system [OpenNap 2001] which provided a means for users to share files. Napster became very popular for music exchange soon after its launch in 1999. At its peak, several million users were registered and thousands were swapping music files simultaneously.

Napster's architecture included centralized indexes but users supplied the files, which were stored and accessed on their personal computers. Napster's method of operation is illustrated by the sequence of steps shown in Figure 10.2. Note that in step 5 clients are expected to add their own music files to the pool of shared resources by transmitting a link to the Napster indexing service for each available file. Thus the motivation for Napster and the key to its success was to make a large, widely-distributed set of files available to users throughout the Internet, fulfilling Shirky's dictum by providing access to 'shared resources at the edges of the Internet'.

Napster was shut down as a result of legal proceedings that were instituted against the operators of the Napster service by the owners of the copyright in some of the material (i.e. digitally encoded music) that was made available on it. (See the box: *Peer-to-peer systems and copyright ownership issues*.)

Anonymity for the receivers and the providers of shared data and other resources is a concern for the designers of peer-to-peer systems. In systems with many nodes, the routing of requests and results can be made sufficiently tortuous to conceal their source and the contents of files can be distributed across multiple nodes, spreading the responsibility for making them available. Mechanisms for anonymous communication that are resistant to most forms of traffic analysis are available [Goldschlag *et al.* 1999]. If files are also encrypted before they are placed on servers, the owners of the servers can plausibly deny any knowledge of the contents. But these anonymity techniques add to the cost of resource-sharing and recent work has shown that the anonymity available is weak against some attacks [Wright *et al.* 2002].

The Freenet [Clarke *et al.* 2000] and FreeHaven [Dingledine *et al.* 2000] projects are focused on providing Internet-wide file services that offer anonymity for the providers and users of files. Ross Anderson has proposed the Eternity Service

Peer-to-peer systems and copyright ownership issues

The developers of Napster argued that they were not liable for the infringement of the copyright owners' rights because they were not participating in the copying process; which was performed entirely between users' machines. Their argument failed because the index servers were deemed an essential part of the process. Since the index servers were located at well-known addresses, their operators were unable to remain anonymous and so could be targeted in lawsuits.

A more fully distributed file sharing service might have achieved a better separation of legal responsibilities, spreading the responsibility across all of Napsters' users and thus making the pursuit of legal remedies very difficult, if not impossible. Whatever view one takes about the legitimacy of file copying for the purpose of sharing copyright-protected material, there are legitimate social and political justifications for the anonymity of clients and servers in some application contexts. The most persuasive justification arises when anonymity is used to overcome censorship and maintain freedom of expression for individuals in oppressive societies or organizations.

It is known that email and web sites have played a significant role in achieving public awareness at times of political crisis in such societies; their role could be strengthened if the authors could be protected by anonymity. 'Whistle-blowing' is a related case: a 'whistle-blower' is an employee who publicizes or reports their employer's wrongdoings to authorities without revealing their own identity for fear of sanctions or dismissal. In some circumstances it is reasonable for such an action to be protected by anonymity.

[Anderson 1996], a storage service that provides long-term guarantees of data availability through resistance to all sorts of accidental data loss and denial of service attacks. He bases the need for such a service on the observation that whereas publication is a permanent state for printed information – it is virtually impossible to delete once it has been published and distributed to a few thousand libraries in diverse organizations and jurisdictions around the world – electronic publications cannot easily achieve the same level of resistance to censorship or suppression. Anderson covers the technical and economic requirements to ensure the integrity of the store and also points out that anonymity is often an essential requirement for the persistence of information, since it provides the best defence against legal challenges, or illegal actions such as bribes or attacks on the originators, owners or keepers of the data.

Lessons learned from Napster ◊ Napster demonstrated the feasibility of building a useful large-scale service which depends almost wholly on data and computers owned by ordinary Internet users. To avoid swamping the computing resources of individual users (for example the first user to offer a chart-topping song) and their network connections, Napster took account of network locality – the number of hops between the client and the server – when allocating a server to a client requesting a song. This simple load distribution mechanism enabled the service to scale to meet the needs of large numbers of users.

Limitations: Napster used a (replicated) unified index of all available music files. For the application in question, the requirement for consistency between the replicas was not strong, so this did not hamper performance, but for many applications it would constitute a limitation. Unless the access path to the data objects is distributed, object discovery and addressing is likely to become a bottleneck.

Napster took advantage of the special characteristics of the application for which it was designed in other ways:

• Music files are never updated, avoiding any need to make all the replicas of files consistent after updates.

• No guarantees are required concerning the availability of individual files – if a music file is temporarily unavailable, it can be downloaded later. This reduces the requirement for dependability of individual computers and their connections to the Internet.

10.3 Peer-to-peer middleware

A key problem in the design of peer-to-peer applications is to provide a mechanism to enable clients to access data resources quickly and dependably wherever they are located throughout the network. Napster maintained a unified index of available files for this purpose giving the network addresses of their hosts. Second-generation peer-to-peer file storage systems such as Gnutella and Freenet employ partitioned and distributed indexes, but the algorithms used are specific to each system.

This location problem existed in several services that predate the peer-to-peer paradigm. For example, Sun NFS addresses this need with the aid of a virtual file system abstraction layer at each client which accepts requests to access files stored on multiple servers in terms of virtual file references (i.e. v-nodes, see Section 8.3). This solution relies on a substantial amount of preconfiguration at each client and manual intervention when file distribution patterns or server provision changes. It is clearly not scalable beyond a service managed by a single organization. AFS (Section 8.4) has similar properties.

Peer-to-peer middleware systems are designed specifically to meet the need for the automatic placement and subsequent location of the distributed objects managed by peer-to-peer systems and applications.

Functional requirements ◊ The function of peer-to-peer middleware is to simplify the construction of services that are implemented across many hosts in a widely distributed network. To achieve this it must enable clients to locate and communicate with any individual resource made available to a service, even though the resources are widely distributed amongst the hosts. Other important requirements include the ability to add new resources and to remove them at will and to add hosts to the service and remove them. Like other middleware, peer-to-peer middleware should offer a simple programming interface to application programmers that is independent of the types of distributed resource that the application manipulates.

Non-functional requirements ◊ To perform effectively, peer-to-peer middleware must also address the following non-functional requirements [cf. Kubiatowicz 2003]:

Global scalability: One of the aims of peer-to-peer applications is to exploit the hardware resources of very large numbers of hosts connected to the Internet. Peer-to-peer middleware must therefore be designed to support applications that access millions of objects on tens of thousands or hundreds of thousands of hosts.

Load balancing: The performance of any system designed to exploit a large number of computers depends upon the balanced distribution of workload across them. For the systems we are considering, this will be achieved by a random placement of resources together with the use of replicas of heavily-used resources.

Optimization for local interactions between neighbouring peers: The 'network distance' between nodes that interact has a substantial impact on the latency of individual interactions, such as client requests for access to resources. Network traffic loadings are also impacted by it. The middleware should aim to place resources close to the nodes that access them the most.

Accommodating to highly dynamic host availability: Most peer-to-peer systems are constructed from host computers that are free to join or leave the system at any time. The hosts and network segments used in peer-to-peer systems are not owned or managed by any single authority; neither their reliability nor their continuous participation in the provision of a service is guaranteed. A major challenge for peer-to-peer systems is to provide a dependable service despite these facts. As hosts join the system, they must be integrated into the system and the load must be re-distributed to exploit their new resources. When they leave the system voluntarily or involuntarily, the system must detect their departure and redistribute their load and resources.

Studies of peer-to-peer applications and systems such as Gnutella and Overnet have shown a considerable turnover of participating hosts [Saroiu et al. 2002,

Baghwan *et al.* 2003]. For the Overnet peer-to-peer file sharing system, with 85,000 active hosts throughout the Internet, Baghwan *et al.* measured an average session length of 135 minutes (and a median of 79 minutes) for a random sample of 1,468 hosts over a 7 day period, with 260 to 650 of the 1,468 hosts available to the service at any time. (A session represents a period during which a host is available before it is voluntarily or unavoidably disconnected.)

On the other hand, Microsoft researchers measured a session length of 37.7 hours for a random sample of 20,000 machines connected to the Microsoft corporate network, with between 14,700 and 15,600 of the machines available for service at any given time [Castro *et al.* 2003]. These measurements are based on a feasibility study for the Farsite peer-to-peer file system [Bolosky *et al.* 2000]. The huge variance amongst the figures obtained in these studies is mainly attributable to the differences in behaviour and network environment between individual Internet users and the users in a corporate network such as Microsoft's.

Security of data in an environment with heterogeneous trust: In global-scale systems with participating hosts of diverse ownership, trust must be built up by the use of authentication and encryption mechanisms to ensure the integrity and privacy of information.

Anonymity, deniability and resistance to censorship: We have noted (in the box on page 403) that anonymity for the holders and recipients of data is a legitimate concern in many situations demanding resistance to censorship. A related requirement is that the hosts that hold data should be able plausibly to deny responsibility for holding or supplying it. The use of large numbers of hosts in peer-to-peer systems can be helpful in achieving these properties.

The design of a middleware layer to support global-scale peer-to-peer systems is therefore a difficult problem. The requirements for scalability and availability make it infeasible to maintain a database at all client nodes giving the locations of all the resources (objects) of interest.

Knowledge of the locations of objects must be partitioned and distributed throughout the network. Each node is made responsible for maintaining detailed knowledge of the locations of nodes and objects in a portion of the name space as well as a general knowledge of the topology of the entire name space (Figure 10.3). A high degree of replication of this knowledge is necessary to ensure dependability in the face of the volatile availability of hosts and intermittent network connectivity. In the systems we shall describe below replication factors as high as 16 are typically used.

10.4 Routing overlays

The development of middleware that meets the above requirements is an active research topic and several significant middleware systems have already emerged. In this chapter we describe two of them in detail.

A distributed algorithm known as a *routing overlay* takes responsibility for locating nodes and objects. The name denotes the fact that the middleware takes the

Figure 10.3   Distribution of information in a routing overlay

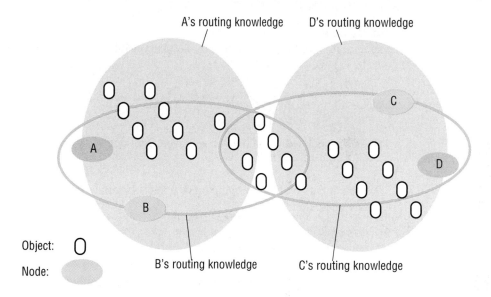

form of a layer that is responsible for routing requests from any client to a host that holds the object to which the request is addressed. The objects of interest may be placed and subsequently relocated to any node in the network without client involvement. It is termed an overlay since it implements a routing mechanism in the application layer that is quite separate from any other routing mechanisms deployed at the network level such as IP routing. This approach to the management and location of replicated objects was first analyzed and shown to be effective for networks involving sufficiently many nodes in a ground-breaking paper by Plaxton *et al.* [1997].

The routing overlay ensures that any node can access any object by routing each request through a sequence of nodes, exploiting knowledge at each of them to locate the destination object. Peer-to-peer systems usually store multiple replicas of objects to ensure availability. In that case, the routing overlay maintains knowledge of the location of all the available replicas and delivers requests to the nearest 'live' node (i.e. one that has not failed) that has a copy of the relevant object.

The GUIDs used to identify nodes and objects are an example of the 'pure' names referred to in Section 9.1.1, also known as *opaque identifiers,* since they reveal nothing about the locations of the objects to which they refer.

The main task of a routing overlay is the following:

1. A client wishing to invoke an operation on an object submits a request including the object's GUID to the routing overlay, which routes the request to a node at which a replica of the object resides.

The routing overlay must also perform some other tasks:

2. A node wishing to make a new object available to a peer-to-peer service computes a GUID for the object and announces it to the routing overlay, which then ensures that the object is reachable by all other clients.

Figure 10.4   Basic programming interface for a distributed hash table (DHT) as implemented by the PAST API over Pastry

put(GUID, data)
> The *data* is stored in replicas at all nodes responsible for the object identified by *GUID*.

remove(GUID)
> Deletes all references to *GUID* and the associated data.

value = get(GUID)
> The data associated with *GUID* is retrieved from one of the nodes responsible it.

---

3. When clients request the removal of objects from the service the routing overlay must make them unavailable.

4. Nodes (i.e. computers) may join and leave the service. When a node joins the service, the routing overlay arranges for it to assume some of the responsibilities of other nodes. When a node leaves (either voluntarily or as a result of a system or network fault), its responsibilities are distributed amongst the other nodes.

An object's GUID is computed from all or part of the state of the object using a function that delivers a value that is with very high probability, unique. Uniqueness is verified by searching for another object with the same GUID. A hash function (such as SHA-1, see Section 7.4) is used to generate the GUID from the object's value. Because these randomly distributed identifiers are used to determine the placement of objects and to retrieve them, overlay routing systems are sometimes described as *distributed hash tables (DHT)* and this is reflected by the simplest form of API used to access them, as shown in Figure 10.4. With this API the *put()* operation is used to submit a data item to be stored together with its GUID. The DHT layer takes responsibility for choosing a location for it, storing it (with replicas to ensure availability) and providing access to it via the *get()* operation.

A slightly more flexible form of API is provided by a *distributed object location and routing (DOLR)* layer as shown in Figure 10.5. With this interface objects can be stored anywhere and the DOLR layer is responsible for maintaining a mapping between object identifiers (GUIDs) and the addresses of the nodes at which replicas of the objects are located. Objects may be replicated and stored with the same GUID at different hosts and the routing overlay takes responsibility for routing requests to the nearest available replica.

With the DHT model, a data item with GUID X is stored at the node whose GUID is numerically closest to X and at the r hosts with GUIDs numerically closest to it, where r is a replication factor chosen to ensure a very high probability of availability. With the DOLR model, locations for the replicas of data objects are decided outside the routing layer and the host address of each replica is notified to the DOLR using the *publish()* operation.

The interfaces in Figures 10.4 and 10.5 are based on a set of abstract representations proposed by Dabek *et al.* [2003] to show that most peer-to-peer routing overlay implementations developed to date provide very similar functionality.

Figure 10.5   Basic programming interface for distributed object location and routing (DOLR) as implemented by Tapestry

publish(GUID)
> *GUID* can be computed from the object (or some part of it, e.g. its name). This function makes the node performing a *publish* operation the host for the object corresponding to *GUID*.

unpublish(GUID)
> Makes the object corresponding to *GUID* inaccessible.

sendToObj(msg, GUID, [n])
> Following the object-oriented paradigm, an invocation message is sent to an object in order to access it. This might be a request to open a TCP connection for data transfer or to return a message containing all or part of the object's state. The final optional parameter *[n]*, if present, requests the delivery of the same message to *n* replicas of the object.

Work on the design of routing overlay systems began in 2000 and remains an active research area. Several have now been successfully developed and evaluated. Evaluations of these prototypes have demonstrated that their performance and dependability are adequate for use in many production environments. In the next section we shall describe two of these in detail: Pastry, which implements a distributed hash table API similar to the one presented in Figure 10.4, and Tapestry, which implements an API similar to that shown in Figure 10.5. Both Pastry and Tapestry employ a routing mechanism known as *prefix routing* to determine routes for the delivery of messages based on the values of the GUIDs to which they are addressed. Prefix routing narrows the search for the next node along the route by applying a binary mask that selects an increasing number of hexadecimal digits from the destination GUID after each hop. (This technique is also employed in Classless Interdomain Routing for IP packets, outlined in Section 3.4.3.)

Other routing schemes have been developed that exploit different measures of distance to narrow the search for the next hop destination. Chord [Stoica *et al.* 2001] bases the choice on numerical difference between the GUIDs of the selected node and the destination node. CAN [Ratnasamy *et al.* 2001] uses distance in a *d*-dimensional hyperspace into which nodes are placed. Kademlia [Maymounkov and Mazieres 2002] uses the XOR of pairs of GUIDs as a metric for distance between the nodes. Because XOR is symmetric, Kademlia can maintain participants' routing tables very simply since they always receive requests from the same nodes contained in their routing tables.

GUIDs are not human-readable, so client applications must obtain the GUIDs for resources of interest through some form of indexing service using human-readable names or search requests. Ideally, these indexes are also stored in a peer-to-peer manner to overcome the weaknesses of centralized indexes evidenced by Napster. But in simple cases, such as music or publications available for peer-to-peer download, they can simply be indexed on web pages (*cf.* BitTorrent [Cohen 2003]). In BitTorrent a web index search leads to a stub file containing details of the desired resource including its

GUID and the URL of a *tracker* – a host that holds an up-to-date list of network addresses for providers willing to supply the file.

The foregoing description of routing overlays will probably have raised questions in the reader's mind about their performance and reliability. Answers to these questions will emerge from the descriptions of practical routing overlay systems in the next section.

10.5 Overlay case studies: Pastry, Tapestry

The prefix routing approach is adopted by both Pastry and Tapestry. Pastry has a straightforward but effective design which makes it a good first example for us to study in detail. Pastry is the message routing infrastructure deployed in several applications including PAST [Druschel and Rowstron 2001] an archival (immutable) file storage system implemented as a distributed hash table with the API in Figure 10.4 and Squirrel, a peer-to-peer web caching service described in Section 10.6.1.

Tapestry is the basis for the OceanStore storage system which we describe in Section 10.6.2. It has a more complex architecture than Pastry because it aims to support a wider range of locality approaches. We describe this in Section 10.5.2 by comparison with Pastry.

10.5.1 Pastry

Pastry [Rowstron and Druschel 2001, Castro *et al.* 2002, FreePastry project 2004] is a routing overlay with the characteristics that we have outlined in Section 10.4. All the nodes and objects that can be accessed through Pastry are assigned 128-bit GUIDs. For nodes, these are computed by applying a secure hash function (such as SHA-1, see Section 7.4.1) to the public key with which each node is provided. For objects such as files the GUID is computed by applying a secure hash function to the object's name or to some part of the object's stored state. The resulting GUID has the usual properties of secure hash values – that is, they are randomly distributed in the range 0 to 2^{128}-1. They provide no clues as to the value from which they were computed and clashes between GUIDs for different nodes or objects are extremely unlikely. (In this unlikely event, Pastry detects it and takes remedial action.)

In a network with N participating nodes, the Pastry routing algorithm will correctly route a message addressed to any GUID in $O(log\ N)$ steps. If the GUID identifies a node that is currently active, the message is delivered to that node; otherwise the message is delivered to the active node whose GUID is numerically closest to it. Active nodes take responsibility for processing requests addressed to all objects in their numerical neighbourhood.

Routing steps involve the use of an underlying transport protocol (normally UDP) to transfer the message to a Pastry node that is 'closer' to its destination. But note that the closeness referred to here is in an entirely artificial space – the space of GUIDs. The real transport of a message across the Internet between two Pastry nodes may require a substantial number of IP hops. To minimize the risk of unnecessarily extended transport

Figure 10.6 Circular routing alone is correct but inefficient   *Based on Rowstron and Druschel [2001]*

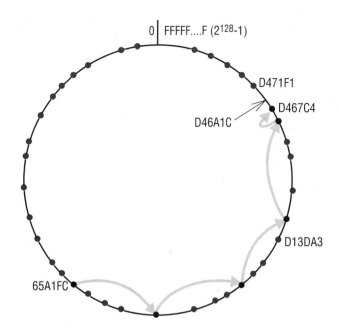

The dots depict live nodes. The space is considered as circular: node 0 is adjacent to node $(2^{128}-1)$. The diagram illustrates the routing of a message from node 65A1FC to D46A1C using leaf set information alone, assuming leaf sets of size 8 ($l = 4$). This is a degenerate type of routing that would scale very poorly; it is not used in practice.

paths, Pastry uses a locality metric based on network distance in the underlying network (such as a hop counts or round trip latency measurements) to select appropriate neighbours when setting up the routing tables used at each node.

Thousands of hosts located at widely-dispersed sites can participate in a Pastry overlay; it is fully self organizing; when new nodes join the overlay they obtain the data needed to construct a routing table and other required state from existing members in *O(log N)* messages, where *N* is the number of hosts participating in the overlay. In the event of a node failure or departure, the remaining nodes can detect its absence and cooperatively reconfigure to reflect the required changes in the routing structure in a similar number of messages.

Routing algorithm ◊   The full routing algorithm involves the use of a routing table at each node to route messages efficiently, but for the purposes of explanation, we describe the routing algorithm in two stages. The first stage describes a simplified form of the algorithm which routes messages correctly but inefficiently without a routing table and the second stage describes the full routing algorithm which routes a request to any node in *O(log N)* messages.

Figure 10.7   First four rows of a Pastry routing table

$p =$	GUID prefixes and corresponding nodehandles n															
0	0	1	2	3	4	5	6	7	8	9	A	B	C	D	E	F
	n	n	n	n	n	n		n	n	n	n	n	n	n	n	n
1	60	61	62	63	64	65	66	67	68	69	6A	6B	6C	6F	6E	6F
	n	n	n	n	n		n	n	n	n	n	n	n	n	n	n
2	650	651	652	653	654	655	656	657	658	659	65A	65B	65C	65D	65E	65F
	n	n	n	n	n	n	n	n	n	n		n	n	n	n	n
3	65A0	65A1	65A2	65A3	65A4	65A5	65A6	65A7	65A8	65A9	65AA	65AB	65AC	65AD	65AE	65AF
	n		n	n	n	n	n	n	n	n	n	n	n	n	n	n

The routing table is located at a node whose GUID begins 65A1. Digits are in hexadecimal. The n's represent [GUID, IP address] pairs specifying the next hop to be taken by messages addressed to GUIDs that match each given prefix. Grey-shaded entries indicate that the prefix matches the current GUID up to the given value of p: the next row down or the leaf set should be examined to find a route. Although there are a maximum of 128 rows in the table, only $\log_{16} N$ rows will be populated on average in a network with N active nodes.

Stage I. Each active node stores a leaf set – a vector L (of size $2l$) containing the GUIDs and IP addresses of the nodes whose GUIDs are numerically closest on either side of its own (l above and l below). Leaf sets are maintained by Pastry as nodes join and leave. Even after a node failure they will be corrected within a short time. (Fault recovery is discussed below.) It is therefore an invariant of the Pastry system that the leaf sets reflect a recent state of the system and that they converge on the current state in the face of failures up to some maximum rate of failure.

The GUID space is treated as circular: GUID 0's lower neighbour is $2^{128}-1$. Figure 10.6 gives a view of active nodes distributed in this circular address space. Since every leaf set includes the GUIDs and IP addresses of the current node's immediate neighbours, a Pastry system with correct leaf sets of size at least 2 can route messages to any GUID trivially as follows.

Any node A that receives a message M with destination address D routes the message by comparing D with its own GUID A and with each of the GUIDs in its leaf set and forwarding M to the node amongst them that is numerically closest to D. Figure 10.6 illustrates this for a Pastry system with $l = 4$. (In typical real installations of Pastry $l = 8$.) Based on the definition of leaf sets we can conclude that at each step M is forwarded to a node that is closer to D than the current node and that this process will eventually deliver M to the active node closest to D. But

Figure 10.8   Pastry routing example   *Based on Rowstron and Druschel [2001]*

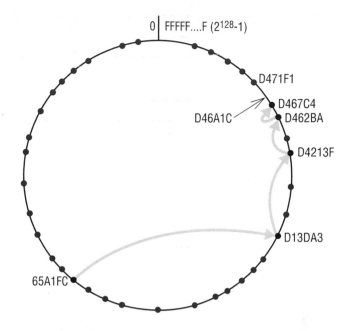

0 | FFFFF....F (2^{128}-1)

D471F1

D467C4

D46A1C

D462BA

D4213F

D13DA3

65A1FC

Routing a message from node 65A1FC to D46A1C. With the aid of a well-populated routing table the message can be delivered in ~ $\log_{16}(N)$ hops.

such a routing scheme is clearly very inefficient, requiring ~ $N/2l$ hops to deliver a message in a network with N nodes.

Stage II. The second part of our explanation describes the full Pastry algorithm and shows how efficient routing is achieved with the aid of routing tables.

Each Pastry node maintains a tree-structured routing table giving GUIDs and IP addresses for a set of nodes spread throughout the entire range of 2^{128} possible GUID values, with increased density of coverage for GUIDs numerically close to its own.

Figure 10.7 shows the structure of the routing table for a specific node and Figure 10.8 illustrates the actions of the routing algorithm. The routing table is structured as follows: GUIDs are viewed as hexadecimal values and the table classifies GUIDs based on their hexadecimal prefixes. The table has as many rows as there are hexadecimal digits in a GUID, so for the prototype Pastry system that we are describing, there are 128/4 = 32 rows. Any row n contains 15 entries – one for each possible value of the nth hexadecimal digit excluding the value in the local node's GUID. Each entry in the table points to one of the potentially many nodes whose GUIDs have the relevant prefix.

The routing process at any node A uses the information in its routing table R and leaf set L to handle each request from an application and each incoming message from another node according to the algorithm shown in Figure 10.9.

Figure 10.9   Pastry's routing algorithm

To handle a message M addressed to a node D (where $R[p,i]$ is the element at column i, row p of the routing table):

1. If $(L_{-l} < D < L_l)$ { // the destination is within the leaf set or is the current node.
2.   Forward M to the element L_i of the leaf set with GUID closest to D or the current node A.
3. } else { // use the routing table to despatch M to a node with a closer GUID
4.   find p, the length of the longest common prefix of D and A. and i, the $(p+1)^{th}$ hexadecimal digit of D.
5.   If $(R[p,i] \neq null)$ forward M to $R[p,i]$ // route M to a node with a longer common prefix.
6.   else { // there is no entry in the routing table
7.   Forward M to any node in L or R with a common prefix of length p, but a GUID that is numerically closer.
    }
  }

We can be sure that the algorithm will succeed in delivering M to its destination because lines 1, 2 and 7 perform the actions described in Stage I of our description above, and we have shown this to be a complete, although inefficient routing algorithm. The remaining steps are designed to use the routing table to improve the algorithm's performance by reducing the number of hops required.

Lines 4–5 come into play whenever D does not fall within the numeric range of the current node's leaf set and relevant routing table entries are available. The selection of a destination for the next hop involves comparing the hexadecimal digits of D with those of A (the GUID of the current node) from left to right to discover the length, p of their longest common prefix. This length is then used as a row offset, together with the first non-matching digit of D as a column offset, to access the required element of the routing table. The construction of the table ensures that this element (if not empty) contains the IP address of a node whose GUID has $p+1$ prefix digits in common with D.

Line 7 is used when D falls outside the numeric range of the leaf set and there isn't a relevant routing table entry. This case is rare; it arises only when nodes have recently failed and the table hasn't yet been updated. The routing algorithm is able to proceed by scanning both the leaf set and the routing table and forwarding M to another node whose GUID has p matching prefix digits but is numerically closer to D. If that node is in L then we are following the Stage I procedure illustrated in Figure 10.6. If it is in R then it must be closer to D than any node in L, hence we are improving on Stage I.

Host integration ◊ New nodes use a joining protocol in order to acquire their routing table and leaf set contents and notify other nodes of changes they must make to their tables. First, the new node computes a suitable GUID (typically by applying the SHA-1 hash function to the node's public key), then it makes contact with a nearby Pastry node. (Here we use the term *nearby* to refer to network distance; i.e. a small number of network hops or low transmission delay; see the box entitled *Nearest neighbour algorithm* below.)

Suppose that the new node's GUID is X and the nearby node it contacts has GUID A. Node X sends a special *join* request message to A, giving X as its destination. A despatches the *join* message via Pastry in the normal way. Pastry will route the *join* message to the existing node whose GUID is numerically closest to X; let us call this destination node Z.

A, Z and all the nodes (B, C,...) through which the *join* message is routed on its way to Z add an additional step to the normal Pastry routing algorithm which results in the transmission of the contents of the relevant part of their routing tables and leaf sets to X, which examines them and constructs its own routing table and leaf set from them, requesting some additional information from other nodes if necessary.

To see how X builds its routing table, note that the first row of the table depends on the value of X's GUID and to minimize routing distances, the table should be constructed to route messages via neighbouring nodes whenever possible. But A is a neighbour of X, so the first row of A's table is a good initial choice for the first row of X's table, X_0. On the other hand, A's table is probably not relevant for the second row X_1, because X's and A's GUIDs may not share the same first hexadecimal digit. But the routing algorithm ensures that X's and B's GUIDs do share the same first digit and this implies that the second row of B's routing table, B_1 is a suitable initial value for X_1. Similarly C_2 is suitable for X_2 and so on.

Furthermore, recalling the properties of leaf sets, note that since Z's GUID is numerically closest to X's, X's leaf set should be similar to Z's. In fact X's ideal leaf set will differ from Z's by just one member. Z's leaf set is therefore taken as an adequate initial approximation which will eventually be optimized through interaction with its neighbours as described under the Fault Tolerance heading below.

Finally, once X has constructed its leaf set and routing table in the manner outlined above, it sends their contents to all the nodes identified in the leaf set and the routing table and they adjust their own tables to incorporate the new node. The entire task of incorporating a new node into the Pastry infrastructure requires the transmission of $O(\log N)$ messages.

Host failure or departure ◊   Nodes in the Pastry infrastructure may fail or depart without warning. A Pastry node is considered failed when its immediate neighbours (in GUID space) can no longer communicate with it. When this occurs, it is necessary to repair the leaf sets that contain the failed node's GUID.

To repair its leaf set L, the node that discovers the failure looks for a live node close to the failed node in L and requests a copy of that node's leaf set, L'. L' will contain a sequence of GUIDs that partly overlap those in L, including one with an appropriate

---

Nearest neighbour algorithm

The new node should have the address of at least one existing Pastry node, but it might not be nearby. To ensure that nearby nodes are known Pastry includes a 'nearest neighbour' algorithm to find a nearby node by recursively measuring the round-trip delay for a probe message sent periodically to each member of the leaf set of the nearest currently known Pastry node.

value to replace the failed node. Other neighbouring nodes are then informed of the failure and they perform a similar procedure. This repair procedure guarantees that leaf sets will be repaired unless *l* adjacently-numbered nodes fail simultaneously.

Repairs to routing tables are made on a 'when discovered' basis. The routing of messages can proceed with some routing table entries that are no longer live – failed routing attempts result in the use of a different entry from the same row of a routing table.

Locality ◊ The Pastry routing structure is highly redundant: there are many routes between each pair of nodes. The construction of the routing tables aims to take account of this redundancy to reduce actual message transmission times by exploiting the locality properties of nodes in the underlying transport network (which is normally a subset of nodes in the Internet).

We recall that each row in a routing table contains sixteen entries. The entries in the ith row give the addresses of sixteen nodes with GUIDs with i-1 initial hexadecimal digits that match the current node's GUID and an ith digit that takes each of the possible hexadecimal values. A well-populated Pastry overlay will contain many more nodes than can be contained in an individual routing table and whenever a new routing table is being constructed a choice is made for each position between several candidates (taken from routing information supplied by other nodes) based on a Proximity Neighbour Selection algorithm [Gummadi *et al.* 2003]. A locality metric (number of IP hops or measured latency) is used to compare candidates and the closest available node is chosen. Since the information available is not comprehensive, this mechanism cannot produce globally optimal routings, but simulations have shown that it results in routes that are on average only about 30–50% longer than the optimum.

Fault tolerance ◊ As described above, the Pastry routing algorithm assumes that all entries in routing tables and leaf sets refer to live, correctly-functioning nodes. All nodes send '*heartbeat' messages* (i.e. messages sent at fixed time intervals to indicate that the sender is alive) to neighbouring nodes in their leaf sets, but information about failed nodes detected in this manner may not be disseminated sufficiently rapidly to eliminate routing errors. Nor does it account for malicious nodes that may attempt to interfere with correct routing. To overcome these problems, clients that depend upon reliable message delivery are expected to employ an 'at-least-once' delivery mechanism (see Section 5.2.4) and repeat several times in the absence of a response. This will allow Pastry a longer time window to detect and repair node failures.

To deal with any remaining failures or malicious nodes, a small degree of randomness is introduced into the route selection algorithm described in Figure 10.9. Essentially, the step in line 5 of Figure 10.9 is modified in a randomly-selected small proportion of cases to yield a common prefix that is less than the maximum length. This results in the use of a routing taken from an earlier row of the routing table producing less optimal but different routing than the standard version of the algorithm. With this random variation in the routing algorithm, client re-transmissions should eventually succeed even in the presence of a small number of malicious nodes.

Dependability ◊ The authors of Pastry have developed an updated version called MSPastry [Castro *et al.* 2003] that uses the same routing algorithm and similar host management methods, but it includes some additional dependability measures and some performance optimizations in the host management algorithms.

Dependability measures include the use of acknowledgements at each hop in the routing algorithm. If the sending host does not receive an acknowledgement after a specified timeout, it selects an alternative route and retransmits the message. The node that failed to send an acknowledgement is then noted as a suspected failure.

To detect failed nodes each Pastry node periodically sends a heartbeat message to its immediate neighbour to the left (i.e. with a lower GUID) in the leaf set. Each node also records the time of the last heartbeat message received from its immediate neighbour on the right (with a higher GUID). If the interval since the last heartbeat exceeds a timeout threshold, the detecting node starts a repair procedure that involves contacting the remaining nodes in the leaf set with a notification about the failed node and a request for suggested replacements. Even in the case of multiple simultaneous failures, this procedure terminates with all nodes on the side of the failed node having leaf sets that contain the l live nodes with the closest GUIDs.

We have seen that the routing algorithm can function correctly using leaf sets alone; but the maintenance of the routing tables is important for performance. Suspected failed nodes in routing tables are probed in a similar manner to the leaf set and if they fail to respond, their routing table entries are replaced with a suitable alternative, obtained from a nearby node. In addition, a simple gossip protocol (Section 14.4.1) is used to periodically exchange routing table information between nodes in order to repair failed entries and prevent slow deterioration of the locality properties. The gossip protocol is run about every 20 minutes.

Evaluation work ◊ Castro and his colleagues have carried out an exhaustive performance evaluation of MSPastry, aimed at determining the impact on performance and dependability of the host join/leave rate and the associated dependability mechanisms [Castro *et al.* 2003].

The evaluation was performed by running the MSPastry system under control of a simulator running on a single machine that simulates a large network of hosts, with message passing replaced by simulated transmission delays. The simulation realistically modelled the join/leave behaviour of hosts and IP transmission delays based on parameters from real installations.

All of the dependability mechanisms of MSPastry were included, with realistic intervals for probe and heartbeat messages. The simulation work was validated by comparison with measurements taken with MSPastry running a real application load across an internal network with 52 nodes.

Here we summarize only their key results.

Dependability: With an assumed IP message loss rate of 0% MSPastry failed to deliver 1.5 in 100,000 requests (presumably due to the non-availability of destination hosts) and all requests that were delivered arrived at the correct node.

With an assumed IP message loss rate of 5% MSPastry lost about 3.3 in 100,000 requests and 1.6 in 100,000 requests were delivered to the wrong node. The use of per-hop acknowledgements in MSPastry ensures that all lost or misdirected messages are eventually retransmitted and reach the correct node.

Performance: The metric used to evaluate the performance of MSPastry is called *relative delay penalty* (RDP) [Chu *et al.* 2000] or *stretch*. RDP is a direct measure of the extra cost incurred in employing an overlay routing layer. It is the ratio between

Figure 10.10   Tapestry routing   *From [Zhao et al. 2004]*

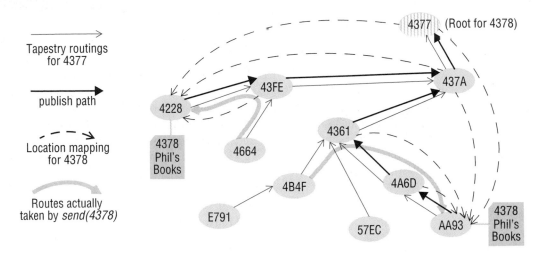

Replicas of the file *Phil's Books* (G=4378) are hosted at nodes 4228 and AA93. Node 4377
is the root node for object 4378. The Tapestry routings shown are some of the entries in
routing tables. The publish paths show routes followed by the publish messages laying down
cached location mappings for object 4378. The location mappings are subsequently used to
route messages sent to 4378.

the average delay in delivering a request by the routing overlay and in delivering a
similar message between the same two nodes via UDP/IP. The RDP values observed
for MSPastry under simulated loads ranged from ~1.8 with zero network message
loss to ~2.2 with 5% network message loss.

Overheads: The extra network load generated by *control traffic* – messages involved
in maintaining leaf sets and routing tables – was less than 2 messages per minute per
node. The RDP and control traffic were both increased significantly for session
lengths less than about 60 minutes due to initial setup overheads.

Overall these results show that overlay routing layers can be constructed that achieve
good performance and high dependability with thousands of nodes operating in realistic
environments. Even with mean session lengths shorter than 60 minutes and high
network error rates the system degrades gracefully, continuing to provide an effective
service.

10.5.2 Tapestry

Tapestry implements a distributed hash table and routes messages to nodes based on
GUIDs associated with resources using prefix routing in a manner similar to Pastry. But

Tapestry's API conceals the distributed hash table from applications behind a DOLR interface like the one shown in Figure 10.5. Nodes that hold resources use the *publish(GUID)* primitive to make them known to Tapestry, the holders of resources remain responsible for storing them. Replicated resources are published with the same GUID by each node that holds a replica, resulting in multiple entries in the Tapestry routing structure.

This gives Tapestry applications additional flexibility: they can place replicas close (in network distance) to frequent users of resources in order to reduce latencies and minimize network loads or to ensure tolerance of network and host failures. But this distinction between Pastry and Tapestry is not fundamental: Pastry applications can achieve similar flexibility by making the objects associated with GUIDs simply act as proxies for more complex application-level objects and Tapestry can be used to implement a distributed hash table in terms of its DOLR API [Dabek *et al.* 2003].

In Tapestry 160-bit identifiers are used to refer both to objects and to the nodes that perform routing actions. Identifiers are either *NodeIds* which refer to computers that perform routing operations or *GUIDs* which refer to the objects. For any resource with GUID G there is a unique root node with GUID R_G that is numerically closest to G. Hosts H holding replicas of G periodically invoke *publish(G)* to ensure that newly-arrived hosts become aware of the existence of G. On each invocation of *publish(G)* a publish message is routed from the invoker towards node R_G. On receipt of a publish message R_G enters (G, IP_H), the mapping between G and the sending host's IP address in its routing table and each node along the publication path caches the same mapping. This process is illustrated in Figure 10.10. When nodes hold multiple (G, IP) mappings for the same GUID, they are sorted by the network distance (round trip time) to the IP address. For replicated objects this results in the selection of the nearest available replica of the object as destination for subsequent messages sent to the object.

Zhao *et al.* [2004] give full details of the Tapestry routing algorithms and the management of Tapestry's routing tables in the face of node arrival and departure. Their paper includes comprehensive performance evaluation data based on simulation of large-scale Tapestry networks showing that its performance is similar to Pastry's. In Section 10.6.2 we describe the OceanStore file store which has been built and deployed over Tapestry.

10.6 Application case studies: Squirrel, OceanStore, Ivy

Large-scale peer-to-peer systems are not yet a mainstream technology. Their widest deployment has been in applications for file downloading by end-users in systems such as Napster, Freenet, Gnutella, Kazaa and BitTorrent. But those systems do not employ separate routing overlay layers, so evaluations of their performance are difficult to extrapolate to other applications.

The routing overlay layers described in the preceding section have been exploited in several application experiments and the resulting applications have been extensively evaluated. We have chosen three of them for further study, the Squirrel web caching service based on Pastry, and the OceanStore and Ivy file stores.

10.6.1 Squirrel web cache

The authors of Pastry have developed the Squirrel peer-to-peer web caching service for use in local networks of personal computers [Iyer *et al*. 2002]. In medium and large local networks web caching is typically performed using a dedicated server computer or cluster. The Squirrel system performs the same task by exploiting storage and computing resources already available on desktop computers in the local network. We first give a brief general description of the operation of a web caching service, then we outline the design of Squirrel and review its effectiveness.

Web caching ◊ Web browsers generate HTTP *GET* requests for Internet objects like HTML pages, images, etc. These may be serviced from a browser cache on the client machine, from a *proxy web cache* – a service running on another computer in the same local network or on a nearby node in the Internet, or from the *origin web server* – the server whose domain name is included in the parameters of the GET request – depending on which contains a fresh copy of the object. The local and proxy caches each contain a set of recently-retrieved objects organized for fast lookup by URL. Some objects are uncacheable because they are generated dynamically by the server in response to each request.

When a browser cache or proxy web cache receives a *GET* request there are three possibilities: the requested object is uncacheable, there is a cache miss or the object is found in the cache. In the first two cases the request is forwarded to the next level towards the origin web server. When the requested object is found in a cache, the cached copy must be tested for freshness.

Web objects are stored in web servers and cache servers with some additional metadata values including a timestamp giving a *date of last modification T* and possibly a *time-to-live t* or an *eTag* (a hash computed from the contents of a web page). These metadata items are supplied by the origin server whenever an object is returned to a client.

For objects that have an associated time-to-live t, the object is considered fresh if $T+t$ is later than the current real time. For objects without a time-to-live, an estimated value for t is used (often only a few seconds). If the result of this freshness evaluation is positive, the cached object is returned to the client without contacting the origin web server. Otherwise a conditional *GET* (*cGET*) request is issued to the next level for validation. There are two basic types of *cGET* requests: an *If-Modified-Since* request containing the timestamp of the last known modification, and an *If-None-Match* request containing an *eTag* representing the object contents. This *cGET* request can be serviced either by another web cache or by the origin server. A web cache that receives a *cGET* request and does not have a fresh copy of the object forwards the request towards the origin web server. The response contains either the entire object, or a *not-modified* message if the cached object is unchanged.

Whenever a newly-modified cacheable object is received from the origin server, it is added to the set of objects in the local cache (displacing older objects that are still valid if necessary) together with a timestamp, a time-to-live and *eTag* if available.

The scheme described above is the basis of operation for the centralized proxy web caching services deployed in most local networks that support large numbers of web clients. Proxy web caches are typically implemented as a multi-threaded process running on a single dedicated host or a set of processes running on a cluster of computers and require a substantial quantity of dedicated computing resources in both cases.

Squirrel ◊   The Squirrel web caching service performs the same functions using a small part of the resources of each client computer on a local network. The SHA-1 secure hash function is applied to the URL of each cached object to produce a 128-bit Pastry GUID. Since the GUID is not used to validate their contents, it need not be based on the entire object contents, as it is in other Pastry applications. The authors of Squirrel base their justification for this on the end-to-end argument (Section 2.2.1), arguing that the authenticity of a web page may be compromised at many points in its journey from the host to the client; authentication of cached pages only adds little to any overall guarantee of authenticity – the HTTPS protocol (incorporating end-to-end Transport Layer Security, Section 7.6.3) should be used to achieve a much better guarantee for those interactions that require it.

In the simplest implementation of Squirrel – which proved to be the most effective one – the node whose GUID is numerically closest to the GUID of an object becomes that object's *home node*, responsible for holding any cached copy of the object.

Client nodes are configured to include a local Squirrel proxy process which takes responsibility for both local and remote caching of web objects. If a fresh copy of a required object is not in the local cache Squirrel routes a *Get* request or a *cGet* request (when there is a stale copy of the object in the local cache) via Pastry to the home node. If the home node has a fresh copy it directly responds to the client with a *not-modified* message or a fresh copy, as appropriate. If the home node has a stale copy or no copy of the object it issues a *cGet* or a *Get* to the origin server, respectively. If the origin server may respond with a *not-modified* or a copy of the object. In the former case, the home node re-validates its cache entry and forwards a copy of the object to the client. In the latter case, it forwards a copy of the new value to the client and places a copy in its local cache if the object is cacheable.

Evaluation of Squirrel ◊   Squirrel was evaluated by simulation using modelled loads derived from traces of the activity of existing centralized proxy web caches in two real working environments within Microsoft, one with 105 active clients (in Cambridge) and the other with more than 36,000 (in Redmond). The evaluation compared the performance of a Squirrel web cache with a centralized one in three respects:

The reduction in total external bandwidth used: The total external bandwidth is inversely related to the hit ratio, since it is only cache misses that generate requests to external web servers. The hit ratios observed for centralized web cache servers were 29% (for Redmond) and 38% (for Cambridge). When the same activity logs were used to generate a simulated load for the Squirrel cache, with each client contributing 100 MB of disk storage, very similar hit ratios of 28% (Redmond) and 37% (Cambridge) were achieved. It follows that the external bandwidth would be reduced by a similar proportion.

The latency perceived by users for access to web objects: The use of a routing overlay results in several message transfers (routing hops) across the local network to transmit a request from a client to the host responsible for caching the relevant object (the home node). The mean numbers of routing hops observed in the simulation were 4.11 hops to deliver a GET request in the Redmond case and 1.8

hops in the Cambridge case whereas only a single message transfer is required to access a centralized cache service.

But local transfers take only a few milliseconds with modern Ethernet hardware, including TCP connection setup time, whereas wide-area TCP message transfers across the Internet require 10–100 ms. The Squirrel authors therefore argue that the latency for access to objects found in the cache is swamped by the much greater latency of access to objects not found in the cache, giving a similar user experience to that provided with a centralized cache.

The computational and storage load imposed on client nodes: The average number of cache requests served for other nodes by each node over the whole period of the evaluation was extremely low at only 0.31 per minute (Redmond) indicating that the overall proportion of system resources consumed is extremely low.

Based on the measurements described above, the authors of Squirrel concluded that its performance is comparable to that of a centralized cache. Squirrel achieves a reduction in the observed latency for web page access close to that achievable by a centralized cache server with a similarly-sized dedicated cache. The additional load imposed on client nodes is low and likely to be imperceptible to users. The Squirrel system was subsequently deployed as the primary web cache in a local network with 52 client machines using Squirrel and the results confirmed their conclusions.

10.6.2 OceanStore file store

The developers of Tapestry have designed and built a prototype for a peer-to-peer file store. Unlike Past, it supports the storage of mutable files. The OceanStore design [Kubiatowicz *et al.* 2000, Kubiatowicz 2003, Rhea *et al.* 2001, Rhea *et al.* 2003] aims to provide a very large scale, incrementally-scalable persistent storage facility for mutable data objects with long-term persistence and reliability in an environment of constantly changing network and computing resources. OceanStore is intended for use in a variety of applications including the implementation of an NFS-like file service, electronic mail hosting, databases and other applications involving the sharing and persistent storage of large numbers of data objects.

The design includes provision for the replicated storage of both mutable and immutable data objects. The mechanism for maintaining consistency between replicas can be tailored to application needs in a manner that was inspired by the Bayou system (Section 14.4.2). Privacy and integrity are achieved through the encryption of data and the use of a Byzantine agreement protocol (see Sections 11.5.3 and 11.5.4) for updates to replicated objects. This is needed because the trustworthiness of individual hosts cannot be assumed.

An OceanStore prototype, called Pond [Rhea *et al.* 2003] has been built. It is sufficiently complete to support applications and its performance has been evaluated against a variety of benchmarks in order to validate the OceanStore design and compare its performance with more traditional approaches. In the remainder of this section we give an overview of the OceanStore/Pond design and summarize the evaluation results.

Pond uses the Tapestry routing overlay mechanism to place blocks of data at nodes distributed throughout the Internet and to despatch requests to them.

Figure 10.11 Storage organization of OceanStore objects

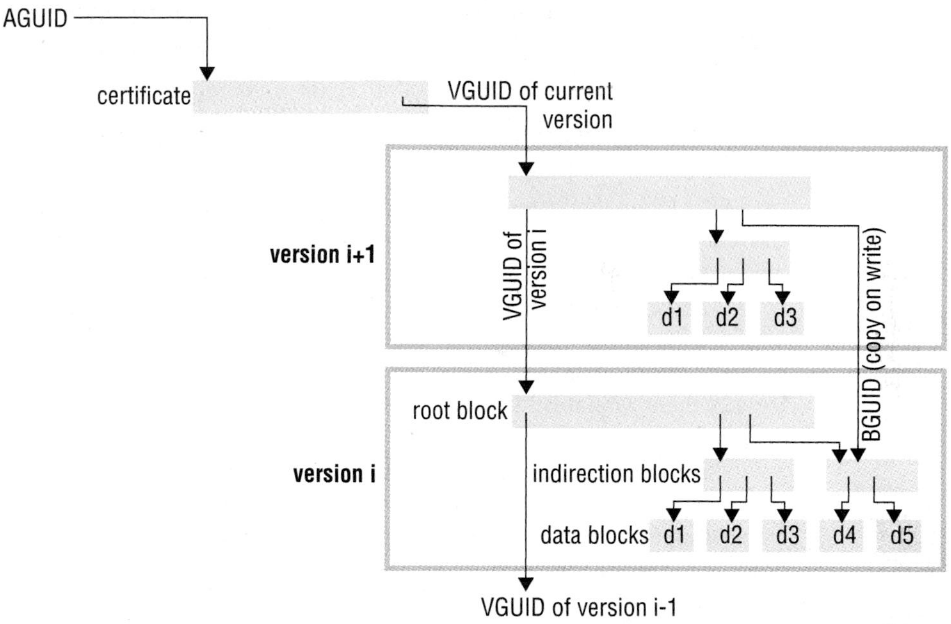

Version i+1 has been updated in blocks d1, d2 and d3. The certificate and the root blocks include some metadata not shown. All unlabelled arrows are BGUIDs.

Storage organization ◊ OceanStore/Pond data objects are analogous to files, with their data stored in a set of blocks. But each object is represented as an ordered sequence of immutable versions that are (in principle) kept for ever. Any update to an object results in the generation of a new version. The versions share any unchanged blocks, following the copy-on-write technique for creating and updating objects described in Section 6.4.2. So a small difference between versions requires only a small amount of additional storage.

Objects are structured in a manner that is reminiscent of the Unix filing system with the data blocks organized and accessed through a metadata block called the root block and additional indirection blocks if necessary (*cf.* Unix *inodes*). Another level of indirection is used to associate a persistent textual or other externally-visible name (for example the pathname for a file) with the sequence of versions of a data object. Figure 10.11 illustrates this organization. GUIDs are associated with the object (an AGUID), the root block for each version of the object (a VGUID) the indirection blocks and data blocks (BGUIDs). Several replicas of each block are stored at peer nodes selected according to locality and storage availability criteria and their GUIDs are published (using the *publish*() primitive of Figure 10.5) by each of the nodes that holds a replica so that Tapestry can be used by clients to access the blocks.

Three types of GUIDs are used, as summarized in Figure 10.12. The first two are GUIDs of the type normally assigned to objects stored in Tapestry – they are computed from the contents of the relevant block using a secure hash function so that they can be

Figure 10.12   Types of identifier used in OceanStore

Name	Meaning	Description
BGUID	block GUID	Secure hash of a data block
VGUID	version GUID	BGUID of the root block of a version
AGUID	active GUID	Uniquely identifies all the versions of an object

used later to authenticate and verify the integrity of the contents. The blocks that they reference are necessarily immutable, since any change to the contents of a block would invalidate the use of the GUID as an authentication token.

The third type of identifier used is AGUIDs. These refer (indirectly) to the entire stream of versions of an object, enabling clients to access the current version of the object or any previous version. Since the objects stored are mutable, the GUIDs used to identify them cannot be derived from their contents, because that would render GUIDs held in indexes, etc., obsolete whenever an object changed.

Instead, whenever a new storage object is created a permanent AGUID is generated by applying a secure hash function to an application-specific name (e.g. a file name) supplied by the client creating the object and a public key that represents the object's owner (see Section 7.2.5). In a filing system application, an AGUID would be stored in the directories against each file name.

The association between an AGUID and the sequence of versions of the object that it identifies is recorded in a signed certificate that is stored and replicated by a primary copy replication scheme (also called passive replication, see Section 14.3.1). The certificate includes the VGUID of the current version and the root block for every version contains the VGUID of the previous version, so their is a chain of references enabling clients that hold a certificate to traverse the entire chain of versions (Figure 10.11). A signed certificate is needed to ensure that the association is authentic and has been made by an authorized principal. Clients are expected to check this. Whenever a new version of an object is created, a new certificate is generated holding the VGUID of the new version together with a timestamp and a version sequence number.

The trust model for peer-to-peer systems requires that construction of each new certificate is agreed (as described below) amongst a small set of hosts called the *inner ring*. Whenever a new object is stored in OceanStore, a set of hosts is selected to act as the inner ring for that object. They use Tapestry's *publish*() primitive to make the AGUID for the object known to Tapestry. Clients can then use Tapestry to route requests for the object's certificate to one of the nodes in the inner ring.

The new certificate replaces the old primary copy held at each inner ring node and is disseminated to a larger number of secondary copies. It is left to clients to determine how often they check for a new version (e.g. most NFS installations operate with a consistency window of 30 seconds between client and server, see Section 8.3).

As usual in peer-to-peer systems, trust cannot be placed in any individual host. The updating of primary copies requires consensus agreement between the hosts in the inner ring. They use a version of a state-machine based Byzantine agreement algorithm described by Castro and Liskov [2000] to update the object and sign the certificate. The use of a Byzantine agreement protocol ensures that the certificate is correctly maintained

Figure 10.13 Performance evaluation of the Pond prototype emulating NFS

Phase	LAN		WAN		Predominant operations in benchmark
	Linux NFS	Pond	Linux NFS	Pond	
1	0.0	1.9	0.9	2.8	Read and write
2	0.3	11.0	9.4	16.8	Read and write
3	1.1	1.8	8.3	1.8	Read
4	0.5	1.5	6.9	1.5	Read
5	2.6	21.0	21.5	32.0	Read and write
Total	4.5	37.2	47.0	54.9	

The figures show times in seconds to run different phases of the Andrew benchmark. It has five phases: (1) creates subdirectories recursively; (2) copies a source tree; (3) examines the status of all the files in the tree without examining their data; (4) examines every byte of data in all the files; and (5) compiles and links the files.

even if some members of the inner ring fail or behave maliciously. Because the computational and communication costs of Byzantine agreement rise with the square of the number of hosts involved, the number of hosts in the inner ring is kept small and the resulting certificate is replicated more widely using the primary copy scheme already mentioned.

Performing an update also involves checking access rights and serializing the update with any other pending writes. Once the update process is completed for the primary copy, the results are disseminated to secondary replicas stored on hosts outside the inner ring using a multicast routing tree that is managed by Tapestry.

Because of their read-only nature, data blocks are replicated by a different, more storage-efficient mechanism. This is based on the division of each block into m equal-sized fragments, which are encoded using *erasure codes* [Weatherspoon and Kubiatowicz 2002] to n fragments where $n>m$. The key property of erasure coding is that it is possible to reconstruct a block from any m of its fragments. In a system that uses erasure coding all data objects remain available with the loss of up to $n-m$ hosts. In the Pond implementation $m = 16$ and $n = 32$ so for a doubling of the storage cost, the system can tolerate the failure of up to 16 hosts without loss of data. The fragments are stored in the network using Tapestry to place them and retrieve them.

This high level of fault tolerance and data availability is achieved at some cost in reconstructing blocks from erasure-coded fragments. To minimize the impact of this, the whole blocks are also stored in the network using Tapestry. Since they can be reconstructed from their fragments, these blocks are treated as a cache – they are not fault tolerant and they can be disposed of when storage space is required.

Performance ◊ Pond was developed as prototype to prove the feasibility of a scalable peer-to-peer file service rather than as a production implementation. It is implemented in Java and includes almost all of the design outlined above. It was evaluated against several purpose-designed benchmarks and in a simple emulation of an NFS client and server in terms of OceanStore objects. The developers tested the NFS emulation against the Andrew benchmark [Howard *et al.* 1988] which emulates a software development workload. The table in Figure 10.13 shows the results for the latter. They were obtained using 1 GHz Pentium III PC running Linux. The LAN tests were performed using a Gigabit Ethernet and the WAN results were obtained using two sets of nodes linked by the Internet.

The conclusions drawn by the authors are that the performance of OceanStore/Pond when operating over a wide-area network (i.e. the Internet) substantially exceeds NFS for reading and is within a factor of three of NFS for updating files and directories; the LAN results are substantially worse. Overall, the results suggest that an Internet-scale peer-to-peer file service based on the OceanStore design would be an effective solution for the distribution of files that do not change very rapidly (such as cached copies of web pages). Its potential for use as an alternative to NFS is questionable even for the wide-area and is clearly uncompetitive for purely local use.

These results were obtained with data blocks stored without erasure-code based fragmentation and replication. The use of public keys contributes substantially to the computational cost of Pond's operation. The figures shown are for 512-bit keys, whose security is good but less than perfect. The results for 1024-bit keys were substantially worse for the phases of those benchmarks that involved file updates. Other results obtained with purpose-designed benchmarks include measurement of the impact of the Byzantine agreement process on the latency of updates. These are in the range 100 ms to 10 seconds. A test of update throughput achieved a maximum of 100 updates/second.

10.6.3 Ivy file system

Like OceanStore, Ivy [Muthitacharoen *et al.* 2002] is a read/write file system supporting multiple readers and writers implemented over an overlay routing layer and a distributed hash-addressed data store. Unlike OceanStore, the Ivy file system emulates a Sun NFS server. Ivy stores the state of files as logs of the file update requests issued by Ivy clients and reconstructs the files by scanning the logs whenever it is unable to satisfy an access request from its local cache. The log records are held in the DHash distributed hash-addressed storage service [Dabek *et al.* 2001]. (Logs were first used to record file updates in the Sprite distributed operating system [Rosenblum and Ooosterhout 1992], as described briefly in Section 8.5, but there they were used simply to optimize the update performance of the file system.)

The design of Ivy resolves several previously unresolved issues arising from the need to host files in partially trusted or unreliable machines including:

- The maintenance of consistent file metadata (*cf.* inode contents in Unix/NFS file systems) with potentially concurrent file updates at different nodes. Locking is not used because the failure of nodes or network connectivity might cause indefinite blocking.

- Partial trust between participants and vulnerability to attacks of participants' machines. Recovery from integrity failures caused by such attacks is based on the notion of *views* of the file system. A view is a representation of the state constructed from logs of the updates made by a set of participants. Participants may be removed and a view re-computed without their updates. Thus a shared file

Figure 10.14 Ivy system architecture

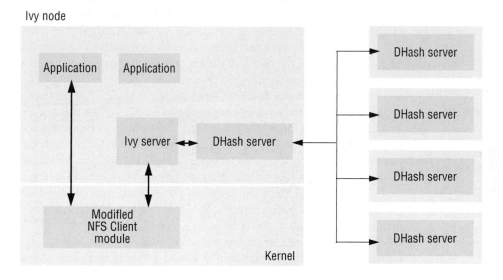

system is seen as the result of merging all the updates performed by a (dynamically selected) set of participants.

• Continued operation during partitions in the network which can result in conflicting updates to shared files. Conflicting updates are resolved using methods related to those used in the Coda file system (Section 15.4.3).

Ivy implements an API at each client node that is based on the NFS server protocol (similar to the set of operations listed in Section 8.3, Figure 8.9). Client nodes include an Ivy server process which uses DHash to store and access log records at nodes throughout a local or wide-area network based on keys (GUIDs) that are computed as the hash of the record contents (see Figure 10.14). DHash implements a programming interface like the one shown in Figure 10.4 and replicates all entries at several nodes for resilience and availability. The Ivy authors note that DHash could in principle be replaced by another distributed hash-addressed store such as Pastry, Tapestry or CAN.

An Ivy file store consists of a set of update logs, one log per participant. Each Ivy participant appends only to its own log but can read from all the logs that comprise the file system. Updates are stored in separate per-participant logs so that they can be rolled back in case of security breaches or consistency failures.

An Ivy log is a reverse time-ordered linked list of log entries. Each log entry is a timestamped record of a client request to change the contents or metadata of a file or directory. DHash uses the 160-bit SHA-1 hash of a record as a key for placing and retrieving the record. Each participant also maintains a mutable DHash block (called a log-head) that points to the participant's most recent log record. Mutable blocks are assigned a cryptographic public key pair by their owner. The contents of the block are signed with the private key and can therefore be authenticated with the corresponding public key. Ivy uses version vectors (i.e. vector timestamps, see Section 10.4) to impose a total order on log entries when reading from multiple logs.

DHash stores a log record using a SHA-1 hash of its contents as the key. Log records are chained in timestamp order using the DHash key as a link. The log-head holds the key for the most recent log entry. To store and retrieve log-heads a public key pair is computed by the owner of the log. The public key value is used as its DHash key and the private key is used by the owner to sign the log-head. Any participant that has the public key can retrieve the log-head and use it to access all of the records in the log.

Assuming a file system composed of a single log for the moment, the canonical execution method for a request to read a sequence of bytes from a file requires a sequential scan of the log to find the log records that contain updates for the relevant portion of the file. Logs are of unlimited length, but the scan terminates when the first record or records are found that cover the required sequence of bytes.

The canonical algorithm to access a multi-user, multiple-log file system involves the comparison of vector timestamps in log records and to determine the order of updates (since a global clock cannot be assumed).

The time to perform this process for an operation as simple as a *read* request is potentially very long. It is reduced to a more tolerable and predicable duration through the use of a combination of local caches and *snapshots*. Snapshots are representations of the file system computed and stored locally by each participant as a by-product of their use of the logs. They constitute a soft representation of the file system in the sense that they may be invalidated if a participant is ejected from the system.

Update consistency is *close-to-open*; that is, the updates performed on a file by an application are not visible to other processes until the file is closed. The use of a close-to-open consistency model enables *write* operations on a file to be saved at the client node until the file is closed, then the entire set of write operations is written as a single log record and a new log-head record is generated and written (an extension to the NFS protocol enables the occurrence of a *close* operation in the application to be notified to the Ivy server).

Since there is a separate Ivy server at each node and each autonomously stores its updates in a separate log without coordination with the other servers, the serialization of updates must be done at the time when logs are read in order to construct the content of files. The version vectors written into log records can be used to order most updates, but conflicting updates are possible and they must be resolved by application-specific automatic or manual methods as is done in Coda (Section 15.4.3).

Data integrity is achieved by a combination of the mechanisms that we have already mentioned: log records are immutable and their address is a secure hash of their contents; log-heads are verified by checking a public-key signature of their contents. But the trust model allows for the possibility that a malicious participant may gain access to a file system. For example, they might delete files that they own maliciously. When this is detected, the malicious participant is ejected from the view; their log is no longer used to calculate the contents of the file system and files that they have deleted are once again visible in the new view.

The Ivy authors used a modified Andrew Benchmark [Howard *et al.* 1988] to compare the performance of Ivy with a standard NFS server in local and wide-area network environments. They considered (a) Ivy using local DHash servers compared to a single local NFS server and (b) Ivy using DHash servers located at several remote

Internet sites compared to a single remote NFS server. They also considered the performance characteristics as a function of the numbers of participants in a view, the number of participants writing concurrently and the number of DHash servers used to store the logs.

They found that Ivy execution times were within a factor of two of NFS execution times for most of the tests in the benchmark and within a factor of three for all of them. The execution times for the wide-area network deployment exceeded those for the local case by a factor of 10 or more, but similar ratios obtained for a remote NFS server. Full details of the performance evaluation can be found in the Ivy paper [Muthitacharoen *et al.* 2002]. But it should be noted that NFS was not designed for wide-area use; the Andrew File System and other more recently-developed server-based systems such as xFS [Anderson *et al.* 1996] offer higher performance in wide-area deployment and they might have made better bases for the comparison. The primary contribution of Ivy is in its novel approach to the management of security and integrity in an environment of partial trust – an inevitable feature of very large distributed systems that span many organizations and jurisdictions.

10.7 Summary

Peer-to-peer architectures were first shown to support very large-scale data sharing with the Internet-wide use of Napster and its descendants for digital music sharing. The fact that much of their use conflicted with copyright laws doesn't diminish their technical significance, although they had technical drawbacks which restricted their deployment to applications in which guarantees of data integrity and availability are unimportant.

Subsequent research resulted in the development of peer-to-peer middleware platforms that deliver requests to data objects wherever they are located in the Internet. The objects are addressed using GUIDs, which are pure names containing no IP addressing information. Objects are placed at nodes according to some mapping function that is specific to each middleware system. Delivery is performed by a routing overlay in the middleware which maintains routing tables and forwards requests along a route determined by calculating distance according to the chosen mapping function.

The middleware platforms add integrity guarantees based on the use of a secure hash function to generate the GUIDs and availability guarantees based on the replication of objects at several nodes and on fault-tolerant routing algorithms.

The platforms have been deployed in several large-scale pilot applications, refined and evaluated. Recent evaluation results indicate that the technology is ready for deployment in applications involving large numbers of users sharing many data objects. The benefits of peer-to-peer systems include:

- their ability to exploit unused resources (storage, processing) in the host computers;

- their scalability to support large numbers of clients and hosts with excellent balancing of the loads on network links and host computing resources;

- the self-organizing properties of the middleware platforms results in support costs that are largely independent of the numbers of clients and hosts deployed.

Weaknesses and subjects of current research include:

- their use for the storage of mutable data is relatively costly compared to a trusted, centralized service;

- the promising basis that they provide for client and host anonymity has not yet resulted in strong guarantees of anonymity;

EXERCISES

10.1 Early file-sharing applications such as Napster were restricted in their scalability by the need to maintain a central index of resources and the hosts that hold them. What other solutions to the indexing problem can you identify?

pages 402–404, 409, Section 15.4

10.2 The problem of maintaining indexes of available resources is application-dependent. Consider the suitability of each of your answers to Exercise 10.1 for (a) music and media file sharing, (b) long-term storage of archived material such as journal or newspaper content, (c) network storage of general-purpose read-write files.

10.3 What are the main guarantees that users expect conventional servers (e.g. web servers or file servers) to offer?   *Section 1.4.5*

10.4 The guarantees offered by conventional servers may be violated as a result of:

a) physical damage to the host;

b) Errors or inconsistencies by system administrators or their managers;

c) successful attacks on the security of the system software;

d) hardware or software errors.

Give two examples of possible incidents for each type of violation. Which of them could be described as a breach of trust or a criminal act? Would they be breaches of trust if they occurred on a personal computer that was contributing some resources to a peer-to-peer service? Why is this relevant for peer-to-peer systems?   *Section 7.1.1*

10.5 Peer-to-peer systems typically depend on *untrusted* and *volatile* computer systems for most of their resources. Trust is a social phenomenon with technical consequences. Volatility (i.e. unpredictable availability) also is often due to human actions. Elaborate your answers to Exercise 10.4 by discussing the possible ways in which each of them are likely to differ according to the following attributes of the computers used:

- ownership
- geographic location
- network connectivity
- country or jurisdiction

What does this suggest about policies for the placement of data objects in a peer-to-peer storage service?

10.6 Assess the availability and trustworthiness of the personal computers in your environment. You should estimate:

> *Uptime*: hours per day when the computer is operating and connected to the Internet.

> *Software consistency*: is the software managed by a competent technician?

> *Security*: is the computer fully protected against tampering by its users or others?

Based on your assessment, discuss the feasibility of running a data sharng service on the set of computers you have assessed and outline the problems that must be addressed in a peer-to-peer data sharing service. *pages 405–406*

10.7 Explain how using the secure hash of an object to identify and route messages to it ensures that it is tamper-proof. What properties are required of the hash function? How can integrity be maintained, even if a substantial proportion of peer nodes are subverted? *pages 400, 423, Section 7.4.3*

10.8 It is often argued that peer-to-peer systems can offer anonymity for (a) clients accessing resources and (b) the hosts providing access to resources. Discuss each of these propositions. Suggest a way in which the resistance to attacks on anonymity might be improved. *page 403*

10.9 Routing algorithms choose a next hop according to an estimate of distance in some addressing space. Pastry and Tapestry both use circular linear address spaces in which a function based on the approximate numerical difference between GUIDs determines their separation. Kademlia uses the XOR of the GUIDs. How does this help in the maintenance of routing tables? Does the XOR operation provide appropriate properties for a distance metric? *pages 409, [Maymounkov and Mazieres 2002]*

10.10 When the Squirrel peer-to-peer web caching service was evaluated by simulation, 4.11 hops were required on average to route a request for a cache entry when simulating the Redmond traffic, whereas only 1.8 were required for the Cambridge traffic. Explain this and show that it supports the theoretical performance claimed for Pastry. *pages 410, 421*

11

TIME AND GLOBAL STATES

In this chapter, we introduce some topics related to the issue of time in distributed systems. Time is an important practical issue. For example, we require computers around the world to timestamp electronic commerce transactions consistently. Time is also an important theoretical construct in understanding how distributed executions unfold. But time is problematic in distributed systems. Each computer may have its own physical clock, but the clocks typically deviate, and we cannot synchronize them perfectly. We shall examine algorithms for synchronizing physical clocks approximately, and then go on to explain logical clocks, including vector clocks, which are a tool for ordering events without knowing precisely when they occurred.

The absence of global physical time makes it difficult to find out the state of our distributed programs as they execute. We often need to know what state process A is in when process B is in a certain state, but we cannot rely on physical clocks to know what is true at the same time. The second half of the chapter examines algorithms to determine global states of distributed computations despite the lack of global time.

11.1 Introduction

This chapter introduces fundamental concepts and algorithms related to monitoring distributed systems as their execution unfolds, and to timing the events that occur in their executions.

Time is an important and interesting issue in distributed systems, for several reasons. First, time is a quantity we often want to measure accurately. In order to know at what time of day a particular event occurred at a particular computer it is necessary to synchronize its clock with an authoritative, external source of time. For example, an 'e-commerce' transaction involves events at a merchant's computer and at a bank computer. It is important, for auditing purposes, that those events are timestamped accurately.

Second, algorithms that depend upon clock synchronization have been developed for several problems in distribution [Liskov 1993]. These include maintaining the consistency of distributed data (the use of timestamps to serialize transactions is discussed in Section 13.6); checking the authenticity of a request sent to a server (a version of the Kerberos authentication protocol, discussed in Chapter 7, depends on loosely synchronized clocks); and eliminating the processing of duplicate updates (see, for example, Ladin *et al.* [1992]).

Einstein demonstrated, in his Special Theory of Relativity, the intriguing consequences that follow from the observation that the speed of light is constant for all observers, regardless of their relative velocity. He proved from this assumption, among other things, that two events that are judged to be simultaneous in one frame of reference are not necessarily simultaneous according to observers in other frames of reference that are moving relative to it. For example, an observer on the Earth and an observer travelling away from the Earth in a spaceship will disagree on the time interval between events, the more so as their relative speed increases.

Moreover, the relative order of two events can even be reversed for two different observers. But this cannot happen if one event could have caused the other to occur. In that case, the physical effect follows the physical cause for all observers, although the time elapsed between cause and effect can vary. The timing of physical events was thus proved to be relative to the observer, and Newton's notion of absolute physical time was discredited. There is no special physical clock in the universe to which we can appeal when we want to measure intervals of time.

The notion of physical time is also problematic in a distributed system. This is not due to the effects of special relativity, which are negligible or non-existent for normal computers (unless one counts computers travelling in spaceships!). The problem is based on a similar limitation in our ability to timestamp events at different nodes sufficiently accurately to know the order in which any pair of events occurred, or whether they occurred simultaneously. There is no absolute, global time that we can appeal to. And yet we sometimes need to observe distributed systems and establish whether certain states of affairs occurred at the same time. For example, in object-oriented systems we need to be able to establish whether references to a particular object no longer exist – whether the object has become garbage (in which case we can free its memory). Establishing this requires observations of the states of processes (to find out whether they contain references) and of the communication channels between processes (in case messages containing references are in transit).

In the first half of this chapter, we examine methods whereby computer clocks can be approximately synchronized, using message passing. We go on to introduce logical clocks, including vector clocks, which are used to define an order of events without measuring the physical time at which they occurred.

In the second half, we describe algorithms whose purpose is to capture global states of distributed systems as they execute.

11.2 Clocks, events and process states

Chapter 2 presented an introductory model of interaction between the processes within a distributed system. We shall refine that model in order to help us to understand how to characterize the system's evolution as it executes, and how to timestamp the events in a system's execution that interest users. We begin by considering how to order and timestamp the events that occur at a single process.

We take a distributed system to consist of a collection $\wp$ of N processes $p_i, i = 1, 2, ...N$. Each process executes on a single processor, and the processors do not share memory (Chapter 18 considers the case of processes that share memory). Each process p_i in $\wp$ has a state s_i which, in general, it transforms as it executes. The process's state includes the values of all the variables within it. Its state may also include the values of any objects in its local operating system environment that it affects, such as files. We assume that processes cannot communicate with one another in any way except by sending messages through the network. So, for example, if the processes operate robot arms connected to their respective nodes in the system, then they are not allowed to communicate by shaking one another's robot hands!

As each process p_i executes it takes a series of actions, each of which is either a message Send or Receive operation, or an operation that transforms p_i's state – one that changes one or more of the values in s_i. In practice, we may choose to use a high-level description of the actions, according to the application. For example, if the processes in $\wp$ are engaged in an e-commerce application, then the actions may be ones such as 'client dispatched order message' or 'merchant server recorded transaction to log'.

We define an event to be the occurrence of a single action that a process carries out as it executes – a communication action or a state-transforming action. The sequence of events within a single process p_i can be placed in a single, total ordering, which we shall denote by the relation $\rightarrow_i$ between the events. That is, $e \rightarrow_i e'$ if and only if the event e occurs before e' at p_i. This ordering is well defined, whether or not the process is multi-threaded, since we have assumed that the process executes on a single processor.

Now we can define the *history* of process p_i to be the series of events that take place within it, ordered as we have described by the relation $\rightarrow_i$:

$$history(p_i) = h_i = <e_i^0, e_i^1, e_i^2, ...>$$

Clocks ◊ We have seen how to order the events at a process but not how to timestamp them – to assign to them a date and time of day. Computers each contain their own

Figure 11.1   Skew between computer clocks in a distributed system

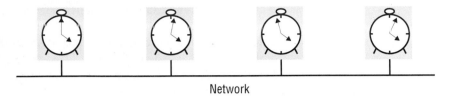

Network

physical clock. These clocks are electronic devices that count oscillations occurring in a crystal at a definite frequency, and that typically divide this count and store the result in a counter register. Clock devices can be programmed to generate interrupts at regular intervals in order that, for example, timeslicing can be implemented; however we shall not concern ourselves with this aspect of clock operation.

The operating system reads the node's hardware clock value $H_i(t)$ scales it and adds an offset so as to produce a software clock $C_i(t) = \alpha H_i(t) + \beta$ that approximately measures real, physical time t for process p_i. In other words, when the real time in an absolute frame of reference is t, $C_i(t)$ is the reading on the software clock. For example, $C_i(t)$ could be the 64-bit value of the number of nanoseconds that have elapsed at time t since a convenient reference time. In general, the clock is not completely accurate, and so $C_i(t)$ will differ from t. Nonetheless, if C_i behaves sufficiently well (we shall examine the notion of clock correctness shortly), we can use its value to timestamp any event at p_i. Note that successive events will correspond to different timestamps only if the *clock resolution* – the period between updates of the clock value – is smaller than the time interval between successive events. The rate at which events occur depends on such factors as the length of the processor instruction cycle.

Clock skew and clock drift ◊ Computer clocks, like any others, tend not to be in perfect agreement (Figure 11.1). The instantaneous difference between the readings of any two clocks is called their *skew*. Also, the crystal-based clocks used in computers are, like any other clocks, subject to *clock drift*, which means that they count time at different rates, and so diverge. The underlying oscillators are subject to physical variations, with the consequence that their frequencies of oscillation differ. Moreover, even the same clock's frequency varies with temperature. Designs exist that attempt to compensate for this variation, but they cannot eliminate it. The difference in the oscillation period between two clocks might be extremely small, but the difference accumulated over many oscillations leads to an observable difference in the counters registered by two clocks, no matter how accurately they were initialized to the same value. A clock's *drift rate* is the change in the offset (difference in reading) between the clock and a nominal perfect reference clock per unit of time measured by the reference clock. For ordinary clocks based on a quartz crystal, this is about 10^{-6} seconds/second – giving a difference of 1 second every 1,000,000 seconds, or 11.6 days. The drift rate of 'high precision' quartz clocks is about 10^{-7} or 10^{-8}.

Coordinated Universal Time ◊ Computer clocks can be synchronized to external sources of highly accurate time. The most accurate physical clocks use atomic oscillators, whose drift rate is about one part in 10^{13}. The output of these atomic clocks is used as the standard for elapsed real time, known as *International Atomic Time*. Since 1967, the standard second has been defined as 9,192,631,770 periods of transition between the two hyperfine levels of the ground state of Caesium-133 (Cs^{133}).

Seconds and years and other time units that we use are rooted in astronomical time. They were originally defined in terms of the rotation of the Earth on its axis and its rotation about the Sun. However, the period of the Earth's rotation about its axis is gradually getting longer, primarily because of tidal friction; atmospheric effects and convection currents within the Earth's core also cause short-term increases and decreases in the period. So astronomical time and atomic time have a tendency to get out of step.

Coordinated Universal Time – abbreviated as UTC (from the French equivalent) – is an international standard for timekeeping. It is based on atomic time, but a so-called leap second is inserted – or, more rarely, deleted – occasionally to keep in step with astronomical time. UTC signals are synchronized and broadcast regularly from land-based radio stations and satellites covering many parts of the world. For example, in the USA, the radio station WWV broadcasts time signals on several shortwave frequencies. Satellite sources include the *Global Positioning System* (GPS).

Receivers are available commercially. Compared with 'perfect' UTC, the signals received from land-based stations have an accuracy in the order of 0.1–10 milliseconds, depending on the station used. Signals received from GPS are accurate to about 1 microsecond. Computers with receivers attached can synchronize their clocks with these timing signals. Computers may also receive the time to an accuracy of a few milliseconds over a telephone line, from organizations such as the National Institute for Standards and Technology in the USA.

11.3 Synchronizing physical clocks

In order to know at what time of day events occur at the processes in our distributed system $\wp$ – for example, for accountancy purposes – it is necessary to synchronize the processes' clocks C_i with an authoritative, external source of time. This is *external synchronization*. And if the clocks C_i are synchronized with one another to a known degree of accuracy, then we can measure the interval between two events occurring at different computers by appealing to their local clocks – even though they are not necessarily synchronized to an external source of time. This is *internal synchronization*. We define these two modes of synchronization more closely as follows, over an interval of real time I:

> *External synchronization*: For a synchronization bound $D > 0$, and for a source S of UTC time, $|S(t) - C_i(t)| < D$, for $i = 1, 2, ...N$ and for all real times t in I. Another way of saying this is that the clocks C_i are *accurate* to within the bound D.

> *Internal synchronization*: For a synchronization bound $D > 0$, $|C_i(t) - C_j(t)| < D$ for $i, j = 1, 2, ...N$, and for all real times t in I. Another way of saying this is that the clocks C_i *agree* within the bound D.

Clocks that are internally synchronized are not necessarily externally synchronized, since they may drift collectively from an external source of time, even though they agree with one another. However, it follows from the definitions that if the system $\wp$ is externally synchronized with a bound D then the same system is internally synchronized with a bound of $2D$.

Various notions of *correctness* for clocks have been suggested. It is common to define a hardware clock H to be correct if its drift rate falls within a known bound $\rho > 0$ (a value derived from one supplied by the manufacturer, such as 10^{-6} seconds/second). This means that the error in measuring the interval between real times t and t' ($t' > t$) is bounded:

$$(1 - \rho)(t' - t) \leq H(t') - H(t) \leq (1 + \rho)(t' - t)$$

This condition forbids jumps in the value of hardware clocks (during normal operation). Sometimes we also require our software clocks to obey the condition. But a weaker condition of *monotonicity* may suffice. Monotonicity is the condition that a clock C only ever advances:

$$t' > t \Rightarrow C(t') > C(t)$$

For example, the UNIX *make* facility is a tool that is used to compile only those source files that have been modified since they were last compiled. The modification dates of each corresponding pair of source and object files are compared to determine this condition. If a computer whose clock was running fast set its clock back after compiling a source file but before the file was changed, the source file might appear to have been modified prior to the compilation. Erroneously, *make* will not recompile the source file.

We can achieve monotonicity despite the fact that a clock is found to be running fast. We need only change the rate at which updates are made to the time as given to applications. This can be achieved in software without changing the rate at which the underlying hardware clock ticks – recall that $C_i(t) = \alpha H_i(t) + \beta$, where we are free to choose the values of α and β.

A hybrid correctness condition that is sometimes applied is to require that a clock obeys the monotonicity condition, and that its drift rate is bounded between synchronization points, but to allow the clock value to jump ahead at synchronization points.

A clock that does not keep to whatever correctness conditions apply is defined to be *faulty*. A clock's *crash failure* is said to occur when the clock stops ticking altogether; any other clock failure is an *arbitrary failure*. An example of an arbitrary failure is that of a clock with the 'Y2K bug', which breaks the monotonicity condition by registering the date after 31 December 1999 as 1 January 1900 instead of 2000; another example is a clock whose batteries are very low and whose drift rate suddenly becomes very large.

Note that clocks do not have to be accurate to be correct, according to the definitions. Since the goal may be internal rather than external synchronization, the criteria for correctness are only concerned with the proper functioning of the clock's 'mechanism', not its absolute setting.

We now describe algorithms for external synchronization and for internal synchronization.

11.3.1 Synchronization in a synchronous system

We begin by considering the simplest possible case: of internal synchronization between two processes in a synchronous distributed system. In a synchronous system, bounds are known for the drift rate of clocks, the maximum message transmission delay, and the time to execute each step of a process (see Section 2.3.1).

One process sends the time t on its local clock to the other in a message m. In principle, the receiving process could set its clock to the time $t + T_{trans}$, where T_{trans} is the time taken to transmit m between them. The two clocks would then agree (since the aim is internal synchronization, it does not matter whether the sending process's clock is accurate).

Unfortunately, T_{trans} is subject to variation and is unknown. In general, other processes are competing for resources with the processes to be synchronized at their respective nodes, and other messages compete with m for the network. Nonetheless, there is always a minimum transmission time min that would be obtained if no other processes executed and no other network traffic existed; min can be measured or conservatively estimated.

In a synchronous system, by definition, there is also an upper bound max on the time taken to transmit any message. Let the uncertainty in the message transmission time be u, so that $u = (max - min)$. If the receiver sets its clock to be $t + min$, then the clock skew may be as much as u, since the message may in fact have taken time max to arrive. Similarly, if it sets its clock to $t + max$, the skew may again be as large as u. If, however, it sets its clock to the half-way point, $t + (max + min)/2$, then the skew is at most $u/2$. In general, for a synchronous system, the optimum bound that can be achieved on clock skew when synchronizing N clocks is $u(1 - 1/N)$ [Lundelius and Lynch 1984].

Most distributed systems found in practice are asynchronous: the factors leading to message delays are not bounded in their effect, and there is no upper bound max on message transmission delays. This is particularly so for the Internet. For an asynchronous system, we may say only that $T_{trans} = min + x$, where $x \geq 0$. The value of x is not known in a particular case, although a distribution of values may be measurable for a particular installation.

11.3.2 Cristian's method for synchronizing clocks

Cristian [1989] suggested the use of a time server, connected to a device that receives signals from a source of UTC, to synchronize computers externally. Upon request, the server process S supplies the time according to its clock, as shown in Figure 11.2.

Figure 11.2   Clock synchronization using a time server

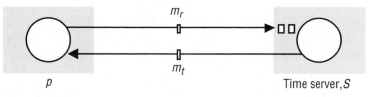

p Time server, S

Cristian observed that while there is no upper bound on message transmission delays in an asynchronous system, the round-trip times for messages exchanged between pairs of processes are often reasonably short – a small fraction of a second. He describes the algorithm as *probabilistic*: the method achieves synchronization only if the observed round-trip times between client and server are sufficiently short compared with the required accuracy.

A process p requests the time in a message m_r, and receives the time value t in a message m_t (t is inserted in m_t at the last possible point before transmission from S's computer). Process p records the total round-trip time T_{round} taken to send the request m_r and receive the reply m_t. It can measure this time with reasonable accuracy if its rate of clock drift is small. For example, the round-trip time should be in the order of 1–10 milliseconds on a LAN, over which time a clock with a drift rate of 10^{-6} seconds/second varies by at most 10^{-5} milliseconds.

A simple estimate of the time to which p should set its clock is $t + T_{round}/2$, which assumes that the elapsed time is split equally before and after S placed t in m_t. This is normally a reasonably accurate assumption, unless the two messages are transmitted over different networks. If the value of the minimum transmission time *min* is known or can be conservatively estimated, then we can determine the accuracy of this result as follows.

The earliest point at which S could have placed the time in m_t was *min* after p dispatched m_r. The latest point at which it could have done this was *min* before m_t arrived at p. The time by S's clock when the reply message arrives is therefore in the range $[t + min, t + T_{round} - min]$. The width of this range is $T_{round} - 2min$, so the accuracy is $\pm(T_{round}/2 - min)$.

Variability can be dealt with to some extent by making several requests to S (spacing the requests so that transitory congestion can clear) and taking the minimum value of T_{round} to give the most accurate estimate. The greater is the accuracy required, the smaller is the probability of achieving it. This is because the most accurate results are those in which both messages are transmitted in a time close to *min* – an unlikely event in a busy network.

Discussion of Cristian's algorithm ◊ As described, Cristian's method suffers from the problem associated with all services implemented by a single server, that the single time server might fail and thus render synchronization impossible temporarily. Cristian suggested, for this reason, that time should be provided by a group of synchronized time servers, each with a receiver for UTC time signals. For example, a client could multicast its request to all servers and use only the first reply obtained.

Note that a faulty time server that replied with spurious time values, or an imposter time server that replied with deliberately incorrect times, could wreak havoc in a computer system. These problems were beyond the scope of the work described by Cristian [1989], which assumes that sources of external time signals are self-checking. Cristian and Fetzer [1994] describe a family of probabilistic protocols for internal clock synchronization, each of which tolerates certain failures. Srikanth and Toueg [1987] first described an algorithm that is optimal with respect to the accuracy of the synchronized clocks, while tolerating some failures. Dolev *et al.* [1986] showed that if f is the number of faulty clocks out of a total of N, then we must have $N > 3f$ if the other, correct, clocks are still to be able to achieve agreement. The problem of dealing with faulty clocks is partially addressed by the Berkeley algorithm, which is described next. The problem of malicious interference with time synchronization can be dealt with by authentication techniques.

11.3.3 The Berkeley algorithm

Gusella and Zatti [1989] describe an algorithm for internal synchronization that they developed for collections of computers running Berkeley UNIX. In it, a coordinator computer is chosen to act as the *master*. Unlike Cristian's protocol, this computer periodically polls the other computers whose clocks are to be synchronized, called *slaves*. The slaves send back their clock values to it. The master estimates their local clock times by observing the round-trip times (similarly to Cristian's technique), and it averages the values obtained (including its own clock's reading). The balance of probabilities is that this average cancels out the individual clocks' tendencies to run fast or slow. The accuracy of the protocol depends upon a nominal maximum round-trip time between the master and the slaves. The master eliminates any occasional readings associated with larger times than this maximum.

Instead of sending the updated current time back to the other computers – which would introduce further uncertainty due to the message transmission time – the master sends the amount by which each individual slave's clock requires adjustment. This can be a positive or negative value.

The algorithm eliminates readings from faulty clocks. Such clocks could have a significant adverse effect if an ordinary average was taken. The master takes a *fault-tolerant average*. That is, a subset of clocks is chosen that do not differ from one another by more than a specified amount, and the average is taken of readings from only these clocks.

Gusella and Zatti describe an experiment involving 15 computers whose clocks were synchronized to within about 20–25 milliseconds using their protocol. The local clocks' drift rate was measured to be less than 2×10^{-5}, and the maximum round-trip time was taken to be 10 milliseconds.

Should the master fail, then another can be elected to take over and function exactly as its predecessor. Section 12.3 discusses some general-purpose election algorithms. Note that these are not guaranteed to elect a new master in bounded time – and so the difference between two clocks would be unbounded if they were used.

11.3.4 The Network Time Protocol

Cristian's method and the Berkeley algorithm are intended primarily for use within intranets. The Network Time Protocol (NTP) [Mills 1995] defines an architecture for a time service and a protocol to distribute time information over the Internet.

NTP's chief design aims and features are as follows.

To provide a service enabling clients across the Internet to be synchronized accurately to UTC: Despite the large and variable message delays encountered in Internet communication. NTP employs statistical techniques for the filtering of timing data and it discriminates between the quality of timing data from different servers.

Figure 11.3   An example synchronization subnet in an NTP implementation

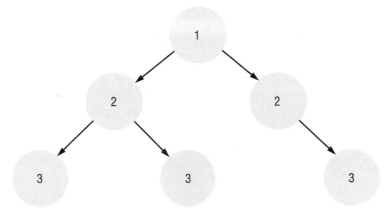

Note: Arrows denote synchronization control, numbers denote strata.

To provide a reliable service that can survive lengthy losses of connectivity: There are redundant servers and redundant paths between the servers. The servers can reconfigure so as to continue to provide the service if one of them becomes unreachable.

To enable clients to resynchronize sufficiently frequently to offset the rates of drift found in most computers: The service is designed to scale to large numbers of clients and servers.

To provide protection against interference with the time service, whether malicious or accidental: The time service uses authentication techniques to check that timing data originate from the claimed trusted sources. It also validates the return addresses of messages sent to it.

The NTP service is provided by a network of servers located across the Internet. *Primary servers* are connected directly to a time source such as a radio clock receiving UTC; *secondary servers* are synchronized, ultimately, with primary servers. The servers are connected in a logical hierarchy called a *synchronization subnet* (see Figure 11.3), whose levels are called *strata*. Primary servers occupy stratum 1: they are at the root. Stratum 2 servers are secondary servers that are synchronized directly with the primary servers; stratum 3 servers are synchronized with stratum 2 servers, and so on. The lowest-level (leaf) servers execute in users' workstations.

The clocks belonging to servers with high stratum numbers are liable to be less accurate than those with low stratum numbers, because errors are introduced at each level of synchronization. NTP also takes into account the total message round-trip delays to the root in assessing the quality of timekeeping data held by a particular server.

The synchronization subnet can reconfigure as servers become unreachable or failures occur. If, for example, a primary server's UTC source fails, then it can become

Figure 11.4   Messages exchanged between a pair of NTP peers

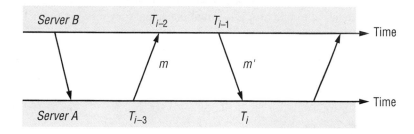

a stratum 2 secondary server. If a secondary server's normal source of synchronization fails or becomes unreachable, then it may synchronize with another server.

NTP servers synchronize with one another in one of three modes: multicast, procedure-call and symmetric mode. *Multicast mode* is intended for use on a high-speed LAN. One or more servers periodically multicasts the time to the servers running in other computers connected by the LAN, which set their clocks assuming a small delay. This mode can achieve only relatively low accuracies, but ones that nonetheless are considered sufficient for many purposes.

Procedure-call mode is similar to the operation of Cristian's algorithm, described above. In this mode, one server accepts requests from other computers, which it processes by replying with its timestamp (current clock reading). This mode is suitable where higher accuracies are required than can be achieved with multicast – or where multicast is not supported in hardware. For example, file servers on the same or a neighbouring LAN, which need to keep accurate timing information for file accesses, could contact a local server in procedure-call mode.

Finally, *symmetric mode* is intended for use by the servers that supply time information in LANs and by the higher levels (lower strata) of the synchronization subnet, where the highest accuracies are to be achieved. A pair of servers operating in symmetric mode exchange messages bearing timing information. Timing data are retained as part of an association between the servers that is maintained in order to improve the accuracy of their synchronization over time.

In all modes, messages are delivered unreliably, using the standard UDP Internet transport protocol. In procedure-call mode and symmetric mode, processes exchange pairs of messages. Each message bears timestamps of recent message events: the local times when the previous NTP message between the pair was sent and received, and the local time when the current message was transmitted. The recipient of the NTP message notes the local time when it receives the message. The four times T_{i-3}, T_{i-2}, T_{i-1} and T_i are shown in Figure 11.4 for the messages m and m' sent between servers A and B. Note that in symmetric mode, unlike Cristian's algorithm described above, there can be a non-negligible delay between the arrival of one message and the dispatch of the next. Also, messages may be lost, but the three timestamps carried by each message are nonetheless valid.

For each pair of messages sent between two servers the NTP calculates an *offset* o_i, which is an estimate of the actual offset between the two clocks, and a *delay* d_i, which is the total transmission time for the two messages. If the true offset of the clock at B relative to that at A is o, and if the actual transmission times for m and m' are t and t' respectively, then we have:

$$T_{i-2} = T_{i-3} + t + o \ and \ T_i = T_{i-1} + t' - o$$

This leads to:

$$d_i = t + t' = T_{i-2} - T_{i-3} + T_i - T_{i-1}$$

Also

$$o = o_i + (t' - t)/2, \text{ where } o_i = (T_{i-2} - T_{i-3} + T_{i-1} - T_i)/2$$

Using the fact that $t, t' \geq 0$ it can be shown that $o_i - d_i/2 \leq o \leq o_i + d_i/2$. Thus o_i is an estimate of the offset, and d_i is a measure of the accuracy of this estimate.

NTP servers apply a data filtering algorithm to successive pairs $<o_i, d_i>$, which estimates the offset o and calculates the quality of this estimate as a statistical quantity called the *filter dispersion*. A relatively high filter dispersion represents relatively unreliable data. The eight most recent pairs $<o_i, d_i>$ are retained. As with Cristian's algorithm, the value of o_j that corresponds to the minimum value d_j is chosen to estimate o.

The value of the offset derived from communication with a single source is not necessarily used by itself to control the local clock, however. In general, an NTP server engages in message exchanges with several of its peers. In addition to data filtering applied to exchanges with each single peer, NTP applies a peer-selection algorithm. This examines the values obtained from exchanges with each of several peers, looking for relatively unreliable values. The output from this algorithm may cause a server to change the peer that it primarily uses for synchronization.

Peers with lower stratum numbers are more favoured than those in higher strata because they are 'closer' to the primary time sources. Also, those with the lowest *synchronization dispersion* are relatively favoured. This is the sum of the filter dispersions measured between the server and the root of the synchronization subnet. (Peers exchange synchronization dispersions in messages, allowing this total to be calculated.)

NTP employs a phase lock loop model [Mills 1995], which modifies the local clock's update frequency in accordance with observations of its drift rate. To take a simple example, if a clock is discovered always to gain time at the rate of, say, four seconds per hour, then its frequency can be reduced slightly (in software or hardware) to compensate for this. The clock's drift in the intervals between synchronization is thus reduced.

Mills quotes synchronization accuracies in the order of tens of milliseconds over Internet paths, and one millisecond on LANs.

Figure 11.5   Events occurring at three processes

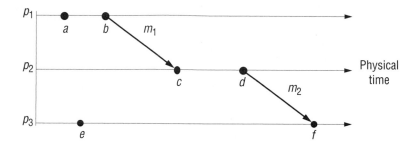

11.4 Logical time and logical clocks

From the point of view of any single process, events are ordered uniquely by times shown on the local clock. However, as Lamport [1978] pointed out, since we cannot synchronize clocks perfectly across a distributed system, we cannot in general use physical time to find out the order of any arbitrary pair of events occurring within it.

In general, we can use a scheme that is similar to physical causality, but that applies in distributed systems, to order some of the events that occur at different processes. This ordering is based on two simple and intuitively obvious points:

- If two events occurred at the same process p_i ($i = 1, 2, ..., N$), then they occurred in the order in which p_i observes them – this is the order $\rightarrow_i$ that we defined above.

- Whenever a message is sent between processes, the event of sending the message occurred before the event of receiving the message.

Lamport called the partial ordering obtained by generalizing these two relationships the *happened-before* relation. It is also sometimes known as the relation of *causal ordering* or *potential causal ordering*.

We can define the happened-before relation, denoted by $\rightarrow$, as follows:

HB1:   If $\exists$ process p_i: $e\rightarrow_i e'$, then $e \rightarrow e'$.

HB2:   For any message m, $send(m) \rightarrow receive(m)$
              – where $send(m)$ is the event of sending the message, and $receive(m)$
              is the event of receiving it.

HB3:   If e, e' and e'' are events such that $e \rightarrow e'$ and $e' \rightarrow e''$, then $e \rightarrow e''$.

Thus, if e and e' are events, and if $e \rightarrow e'$, then we can find a series of events $e_1, e_2, ..., e_n$ occurring at one or more processes such that $e = e_1$ and $e' = e_n$, and for $i = 1, 2, ..., N - 1$ either HB1 or HB2 applies between e_i and e_{i+1}. That is, either they occur in succession at the same process, or there is a message m such that $e_i = send(m)$ and $e_{i+1} = receive(m)$. The sequence of events $e_1, e_2, ..., e_n$ need not be unique.

The relation $\rightarrow$ is illustrated for the case of three processes p_1, p_2 and p_3 in Figure 11.5. It can be seen that $a \rightarrow b$, since the events occur in this order at process p_1 ($a\rightarrow_1 b$) and similarly $c \rightarrow d$. Furthermore, $b \rightarrow c$, since these events are the sending and reception of message m_1, and similarly $d \rightarrow f$. Combining these relations, we may also say that, for example, $a \rightarrow f$.

It can also be seen from Figure 11.5 that not all events are related by the relation $\rightarrow$. For example, $a \nrightarrow e$ and $e \nrightarrow a$, since they occur at different processes, and there is no chain of messages intervening between them. We say that events such as a and e that are not ordered by $\rightarrow$ are *concurrent* and write this $a \parallel e$.

The relation $\rightarrow$ captures a flow of data intervening between two events. Note, however, that in principle data can flow in ways other than by message passing. For example, if Smith enters a command to his process to send a message, then telephones Jones, who commands her process to issue another message, then the issuing of the first message clearly happened-before that of the second. Unfortunately, since no network messages were sent between the issuing processes, we cannot model this type of relationship in our system.

Another point to note is that if the happened-before relation holds between two events, then the first might or might not actually have caused the second. For example, if a server receives a request message and subsequently sends a reply, then clearly the reply transmission is caused by the request transmission. However, the relation $\rightarrow$ captures only potential causality, and two events can be related by $\rightarrow$ even though there is no real connection between them. A process might, for example, receive a message and subsequently issue another message, but one that it issues every five minutes anyway and bears no specific relation to the first message. No actual causality has been involved, but the relation $\rightarrow$ would order these events.

Logical clocks ◊ Lamport invented a simple mechanism by which the happened-before ordering can be captured numerically, called a *logical clock*. A Lamport logical clock is a monotonically increasing software counter, whose value need bear no particular relationship to any physical clock. Each process p_i keeps its own logical clock, L_i, which it uses to apply so-called *Lamport timestamps* to events. We denote the timestamp of event e at p_i by $L_i(e)$, and by $L(e)$ we denote the timestamp of event e at whatever process it occurred.

To capture the happened-before relation $\rightarrow$, processes update their logical clocks and transmit the values of their logical clocks in messages as follows:

LC1: L_i is incremented before each event is issued at process p_i:
$L_i := L_i + 1$

LC2: (a) When a process p_i sends a message m, it piggybacks on m the value $t = L_i$.

(b) On receiving (m, t), a process p_j computes $L_j := max(L_j, t)$ and then applies LC1 before timestamping the event *receive(m)*.

Although we increment clocks by 1, we could have chosen any positive value. It can easily be shown, by induction on the length of any sequence of events relating two events e and e', that $e \rightarrow e' \Rightarrow L(e) < L(e')$.

Note that the converse is not true. If $L(e) < L(e')$, then we cannot infer that $e \rightarrow e'$. In Figure 11.6 we illustrate the use of logical clocks for the example given in Figure 11.5. Each of the processes p_1, p_2 and p_3 has its logical clock initialized to 0. The clock values given are those immediately after the event to which they are adjacent. Note that, for example, $L(b) > L(e)$ but $b \parallel e$.

Figure 11.6   Lamport timestamps for the events shown in Figure 11.5.

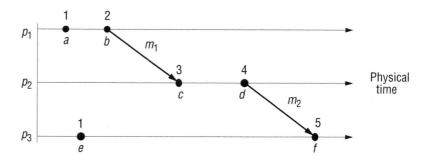

Totally ordered logical clocks ◊ Some pairs of distinct events, generated by different processes, have numerically identical Lamport timestamps. However, we can create a total order on events – that is, one for which all pairs of distinct events are ordered – by taking into account the identifiers of the processes at which events occur. If e is an event occurring at p_i with local timestamp T_i, and e' is an event occurring at p_j with local timestamp T_j, we define the global logical timestamps for these events to be (T_i, i) and (T_j, j) respectively. And we define $(T_i, i) < (T_j, j)$ if and only if either $T_i < T_j$, or $T_i = T_j$ and $i < j$. This ordering has no general physical significance (because process identifiers are arbitrary), but it is sometimes useful. Lamport used it, for example, to order the entry of processes to a critical section.

Vector clocks ◊ Mattern [1989] and Fidge [1991] developed vector clocks to overcome the shortcoming of Lamport's clocks: the fact that from $L(e) < L(e')$ we cannot conclude that $e \rightarrow e'$. A vector clock for a system of N processes is an array of N integers. Each process keeps its own vector clock V_i, which it uses to timestamp local events. Like Lamport timestamps, processes piggyback vector timestamps on the messages they send to one another, and there are simple rules for updating the clocks as follows:

VC1:   Initially, $V_i[j] = 0$, for $i, j = 1, 2..., N$.

VC2:   Just before p_i timestamps an event, it sets $V_i[i] := V_i[i] + 1$.

VC3: p_i includes the value $t = V_i$ in every message it sends.

VC4:   When p_i receives a timestamp t in a message, it sets $V_i[j] := max(V_i[j], t[j])$, for $j = 1, 2..., N$. Taking the component-wise maximum of two vector timestamps in this way is known as a *merge* operation.

For a vector clock V_i, $V_i[i]$ is the number of events that p_i has timestamped, and $V_i[j]$ ($j \neq i$) is the number of events that have occurred at p_j that p_i has potentially been affected by. (Process p_j may have timestamped more events by this point, but no information has flowed to p_i about them in messages as yet.)

Figure 11.7   Vector timestamps for the events shown in Figure 11.5

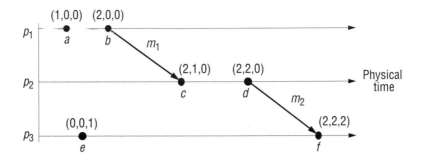

We may compare vector timestamps as follows:

$$V = V' \;\; iff \;\; V[j] = V'[j] \text{ for } j = 1, 2..., N$$

$$V \le V' \;\; iff \;\; V[j] \le V'[j] \text{ for } j = 1, 2..., N$$

$$V < V' \;\; iff \;\; V \le V' \wedge V \ne V'$$

Let $V(e)$ be the vector timestamp applied by the process at which e occurs. It is straightforward to show, by induction on the length of any sequence of events relating two events e and e', that $e \rightarrow e' \Rightarrow V(e) < V(e')$. Exercise 10.13 leads the reader to show the converse: if $V(e) < V(e')$, then $e \rightarrow e'$.

Figure 11.7 shows the vector timestamps of the events of Figure 11.5. It can be seen, for example, that $V(a) < V(f)$, which reflects the fact that $a \rightarrow f$. Similarly, we can tell when two events are concurrent by comparing their timestamps. For example, that $c \parallel e$ can be seen from the facts that neither $V(c) \le V(e)$ nor $V(e) \le V(c)$.

Vector timestamps have the disadvantage, compared with Lamport timestamps, of taking up an amount of storage and message payload that is proportional to N, the number of processes. Charron-Bost [1991] showed that, if we are to be able to tell whether or not two events are concurrent by inspecting their timestamps, then the dimension N is unavoidable. However, techniques exist for storing and transmitting smaller amounts of data, at the expense of the processing required to reconstruct complete vectors. Raynal and Singhal [1996] give an account of some of these techniques. They also describe the notion of *matrix clocks*, whereby processes keep estimates of other processes' vector times as well as their own.

11.5 Global states

In this and the next section we shall examine the problem of finding out whether a particular property is true of a distributed system as it executes. We begin by giving the examples of distributed garbage collection, deadlock detection, termination detection and debugging.

Figure 11.8   Detecting global properties

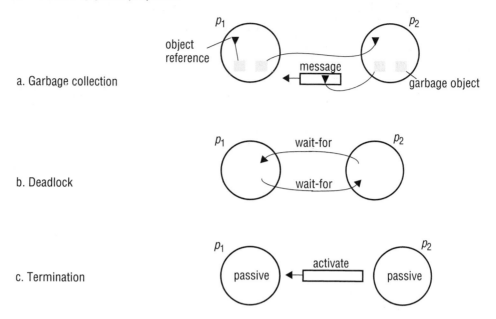

a. Garbage collection

b. Deadlock

c. Termination

Distributed garbage collection: An object is considered to be garbage if there are no longer any references to it anywhere in the distributed system. The memory taken up by that object can be reclaimed once it is known to be garbage. To check that an object is garbage, we must verify that there are no references to it anywhere in the system. In Figure 11.8a, process p_1 has two objects that both have references – one has a reference within p_1 itself, and p_2 has a reference to the other. Process p_2 has one garbage object, with no references to it anywhere in the system. It also has an object for which neither p_1 nor p_2 has a reference, but there is a reference to it in a message that is in transit between the processes. This shows that when we consider properties of a system, we must include the state of communication channels as well as the state of the processes.

Distributed deadlock detection: A distributed deadlock occurs when each of a collection of processes waits for another process to send it a message, and where there is a cycle in the graph of this 'waits-for' relationship. Figure 11.8b shows that each of processes p_1 and p_2 waits for a message from the other, so this system will never make progress.

Distributed termination detection: The problem here is to detect that a distributed algorithm has terminated. Detecting termination is a problem that sounds deceptively easy to solve: it seems at first only necessary to test whether each process has halted. To see that this is not so, consider a distributed algorithm executed by two processes p_1 and p_2, each of which may request values from the other. Instantaneously, we may find that a process is either active or passive – a passive process is not engaged in any activity of its own but is prepared to respond with a value requested by the other. Suppose we discover that p_1 is passive and that p_2 is passive (Figure 11.8c).

To see that we may not conclude that the algorithm has terminated, consider the following scenario: when we tested p_1 for passivity, a message was on its way from p_2, which became passive immediately after sending it. On receipt of the message, p_1 became active again – after we found it to be passive. The algorithm had not terminated.

The phenomena of termination and deadlock are similar in some ways, but they are different problems. First, a deadlock may affect only a subset of the processes in a system, whereas all processes must have terminated. Second, process passivity is not the same as waiting in a deadlock cycle: a deadlocked process is attempting to perform a further action, for which another process waits; a passive process is not engaged in any activity.

Distributed debugging: Distributed systems are complex to debug [Bonnaire *et al.* 1995], and care needs to be taken in establishing what occurred during the execution. For example, Smith has written an application in which each process p_i contains a variable x_i ($i = 1, 2..., N$). The variables change as the program executes, but they are required always to be within a value δ of one another. Unfortunately, there is a bug in the program, and she suspects that under certain circumstances $|x_i - x_j| > \delta$ for some i and j, breaking her consistency constraints. Her problem is that this relationship must be evaluated for values of the variables that occur at the same time.

Each of the problems above has specific solutions tailored to it; but they all illustrate the need to observe a global state, and so motivate a general approach.

11.5.1 Global states and consistent cuts

It is possible in principle to observe the succession of states of an individual process, but the question of how to ascertain a global state of the system – the state of the collection of processes – is much harder to address.

The essential problem is the absence of global time. If all processes had perfectly synchronized clocks then we could agree on a time at which each process would record its state – the result would be an actual global state of the system. From the collection of process states we could tell, for example, whether the processes were deadlocked. But we cannot achieve perfect clock synchronization, so this method is not available to us.

So we might ask whether we can assemble a meaningful global state from local states recorded at different real times. The answer is a qualified 'yes', but in order to see this we first introduce some definitions.

Let us return to our general system $\wp$ of N processes p_i ($i = 1, 2, ..., N$), whose execution we wish to study. We said above that a series of events occurs at each process, and that we may characterize the execution of each process by its history:

$$history(p_i) = h_i = <e_i^0, e_i^1, e_i^2, ...>$$

Similarly, we may consider any finite prefix of the process's history:

$$h_i^k = <e_i^0, e_i^1, ... e_i^k>$$

Figure 11.9   Cuts

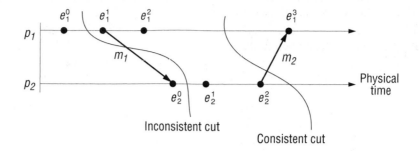

Each event is either an internal action of the process (for example, the updating of one of its variables) or it is the sending or receipt of a message over the communication channels that connect the processes.

In principle, we can record what occurred in $\wp$'s execution. Each process can record the events that take place there, and the succession of states it passes through. We denote by s_i^k the state of process p_i immediately before the kth event occurs, so that s_i^0 is the initial state of p_i. We noted in the examples above that the state of the communication channels is sometimes relevant. Rather than introducing a new type of state, we make the processes record the sending or receipt of all messages as part of their state. If we find that process p_i has recorded that it sent a message m to process $p_j (i \neq j)$, then by examining whether p_j has received that message we can infer whether or not m is part of the state of the channel between p_i and p_j.

We can also form the *global history* of $\wp$ as the union of the individual process histories:

$$H = h_0 \cup h_1 \cup ... \cup h_{N-1}$$

Mathematically, we can take any set of states of the individual processes to form a global state $S = (s_1, s_2, ... s_N)$. But which global states are meaningful – that is, which process states could have occurred at the same time? A global state corresponds to initial prefixes of the individual process histories. A *cut* of the system's execution is a subset of its global history that is a union of prefixes of process histories:

$$C = h_1^{c_1} \cup h_2^{c_2} \cup ... \cup h_N^{c_N}$$

The state s_i in the global state S corresponding to the cut C is that of p_i immediately after the last event processed by p_i in the cut – $e_i^{c_i}$ ($i = 1, 2, ..., N$). The set of events $\{ e_i^{c_i} : i = 1, 2, ..., N \}$ is called the *frontier* of the cut.

Consider the events occurring at processes p_1 and p_2 shown in Figure 11.9. The figure shows two cuts, one with frontier $<e_1^0, e_2^0>$ and another with frontier $<e_1^2, e_2^2>$. The leftmost cut is *inconsistent*. This is because at p_2 it includes the receipt of the message m_1, but at p_1 it does not include the sending of that message. This is showing an 'effect' without a 'cause'. The actual execution never was in a global state corresponding to the process states at that frontier, and we can in principle tell this by examining the $\rightarrow$ relation between events. By contrast, the rightmost cut is *consistent*.

It includes both the sending and the receipt of message m_1. It includes the sending but not the receipt of message m_2. That is consistent with the actual execution – after all, the message took some time to arrive.

A cut C is consistent if, for each event it contains, it also contains all the events that happened-before that event:

$$\text{For all events } e \in C, \; f \rightarrow e \Rightarrow f \in C$$

A *consistent global state* is one that corresponds to a consistent cut. We may characterize the execution of a distributed system as a series of transitions between global states of the system:

$$S_0 \rightarrow S_1 \rightarrow S_2 \rightarrow \dots$$

In each transition, precisely one event occurs at some single process in the system. This event is either the sending of a message, the receipt of a message, or an internal event. If two events happened simultaneously, we may nonetheless deem them to have occurred in a definite order – say ordered according to process identifiers. (Events that occur simultaneously must be concurrent: neither happened-before the other.) A system evolves in this way through consistent global states.

A *run* is a total ordering of all the events in a global history that is consistent with each local history's ordering, $\rightarrow_i$ ($i = 1, 2, \dots, N$). A *linearization* or *consistent run* is an ordering of the events in a global history that is consistent with this happened-before relation $\rightarrow$ on H. Note that a linearization is also a run.

Not all runs pass through consistent global states, but all linearizations pass only through consistent global states. We say that a state S' is *reachable* from a state S if there is a linearization that passes through S and then S'.

Sometimes we may alter the ordering of concurrent events within a linearization, and derive a run that still passes through only consistent global states. For example, if two successive events in a linearization are the receipt of messages by two processes, then we may swap the order of these two events.

11.5.2 Global state predicates, stability, safety and liveness

Detecting a condition such as deadlock or termination amounts to evaluating a *global state predicate*. A global state predicate is a function that maps from the set of global states of processes in the system $\wp$ to {*True, False*}. One of the useful characteristics of the predicates associated with the state of an object being garbage, of the system being deadlocked or the system being terminated is that they are all *stable*: once the system enters a state in which the predicate is *True*, it remains *True* in all future states reachable from that state. By contrast, when we monitor or debug an application we are often interested in non-stable predicates, such as that in our example of variables whose difference is supposed to be bounded. Even if the application reaches a state in which the bound obtains, it need not stay in that state.

We also note here two further notions relevant to global state predicates: safety and liveness. Suppose there is an undesirable property α that is a predicate of the system's global state – for example, α could be the property of being deadlocked. Let

S_0 be the original state of the system. *Safety* with respect to α is the assertion that α evaluates to *False* for all states S reachable from S_0. Conversely, let β be a desirable property of a system's global state – for example, the property of reaching termination. *Liveness* with respect to β is the property that, for any linearization L starting in the state S_0, β evaluates to *True* for some state S_L reachable from S_0.

11.5.3 The 'snapshot' algorithm of Chandy and Lamport

Chandy and Lamport [1985] describe a 'snapshot' algorithm for determining global states of distributed systems, which we now present. The goal of the algorithm is to record a set of process and channel states (a 'snapshot') for a set of processes p_i $(i = 1, 2, ..., N)$ such that, even though the combination of recorded states may never have occurred at the same time, the recorded global state is consistent.

We shall see that the state that the snapshot algorithm records has convenient properties for evaluating stable global predicates.

The algorithm records state locally at processes; it does not give a method for gathering the global state at one site. An obvious method for gathering the state is for all processes to send the state they recorded to a designated collector process, but we shall not address this issue further here.

The algorithm assumes that:

- neither channels nor processes fail; communication is reliable so that every message sent is eventually received intact, exactly once;

- channels are unidirectional and provide FIFO-ordered message delivery;

- the graph of processes and channels is strongly connected (there is a path between any two processes);

- any process may initiate a global snapshot at any time;

- the processes may continue their execution and send and receive normal messages while the snapshot takes place.

For each process p_i, let the *incoming channels* be those at p_i over which other processes send it messages; similarly, p_i's *outgoing channels* are those on which it sends messages to other processes. The essential idea of the algorithm is as follows. Each process records its state and also for each incoming channel a set of messages sent to it. The process records, for each channel, any messages that arrived after it recorded its state and before the sender recorded its own state. This arrangement allows us to record the states of processes at different times but to account for the differentials between process states in terms of messages transmitted but not yet received. If process p_i has sent a message m to process p_j, but p_j has not received it, then we account for m as belonging to the state of the channel between them.

The algorithm proceeds through use of special *marker* messages, which are distinct from any other messages the processes send, and which the processes may send and receive while they proceed with their normal execution. The marker has a dual role: as a prompt for the receiver to save its own state, if it has not already done so; and as a means of determining which messages to include in the channel state.

Figure 11.10   Chandy and Lamport's 'snapshot' algorithm

> *Marker receiving rule for process* p_i
>> On p_i's receipt of a *marker* message over channel c:
>>> *if* (p_i has not yet recorded its state) it
>>>> records its process state now;
>>>> records the state of c as the empty set;
>>>> turns on recording of messages arriving over other incoming channels;
>>> *else*
>>>> p_i records the state of c as the set of messages it has received over c
>>>> since it saved its state.
>>> *end if*
>
> *Marker sending rule for process* p_i
>> After p_i has recorded its state, for each outgoing channel c:
>>> p_i sends one marker message over c
>>> (before it sends any other message over c).

The algorithm is defined through two rules, the *marker receiving rule* and the *marker sending rule* (Figure 11.10). The marker sending rule obligates processes to send a marker after they have recorded their state, but before they send any other messages.

The marker receiving rule obligates a process that has not recorded its state to do so. In that case, this is the first marker that it has received. It notes which messages subsequently arrive on the other incoming channels. When a process that has already saved its state receives a marker (on another channel), it records the state of that channel as the set of messages it received on it since it saved its state.

Any process may begin the algorithm at any time. It acts as though it has received a marker (over a non-existent channel) and follows the marker receiving rule. Thus it records its state and begins to record messages arriving over all its incoming channels. Several processes may initiate recording concurrently in this way (as long as the markers they use can be distinguished).

We illustrate the algorithm for a system of two processes, p_1 and p_2 connected by two unidirectional channels, c_1 and c_2. The two processes trade in 'widgets'. Process p_1 sends orders for widgets over c_2 to p_2, enclosing payment at the rate of \$10 per widget. Some time later, process p_2 sends widgets along channel c_1 to p_1. The

Figure 11.11   Two processes and their initial states

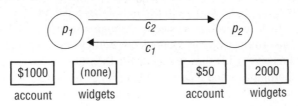

Figure 11.12 The execution of the processes in Figure 11.11

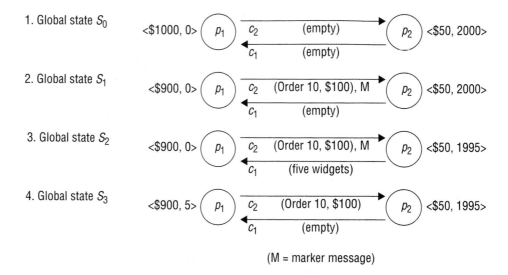

(M = marker message)

processes have the initial states shown in Figure 11.11. Process p_2 has already received an order for five widgets, which it will shortly dispatch to p_1.

Figure 11.12 shows an execution of the system while the state is recorded. Process p_1 records its state in the actual global state S_0, when p_1's state is <$1000, 0>. Following the marker sending rule, process p_1 then emits a marker message over its outgoing channel c_2 before it sends the next application-level message: (Order 10, $100) over channel c_2. The system enters actual global state S_1.

Before p_2 receives the marker, it emits an application message (five widgets) over c_1 in response to p_1's previous order, yielding a new actual global state S_2.

Now process p_1 receives p_2's message (five widgets), and p_2 receives the marker. Following the marker receiving rule, p_2 records its state as <$50, 1995> and that of channel c_2 as the empty sequence. Following the marker sending rule, it sends a marker message over c_1.

When process p_1 receives p_2's marker message, it records the state of channel c_1 as the single message (five widgets) that it received after it first recorded its state. The final actual global state is S_3.

The final recorded state is p_1: <$1000, 0>; p_2: <$50, 1995>; c_1: <(five widgets)>; c_2: < >. Note that this state differs from all the global states through which the system actually passed.

Termination of the snapshot algorithm ◊ We assume that a process that has received a marker message records its state within a finite time and sends marker messages over each outgoing channel within a finite time (even when it no longer needs to send application messages over these channels). If there is a path of communication channels and processes from a process p_i to a process p_j ($j \neq i$), then it is clear on these assumptions that p_j will record its state a finite time after p_i recorded its state. Since we are assuming the graph of processes and channels to be strongly connected, it follows

Figure 11.13   Reachability between states in the snapshot algorithm

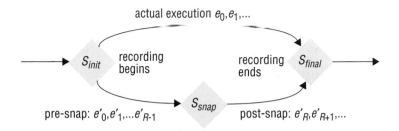

that all processes will have recorded their states and the states of incoming channels a finite time after some process initially records its state.

Characterizing the observed state ◊ The snapshot algorithm selects a cut from the history of the execution. The cut, and therefore the state recorded by this algorithm, is consistent. To see this, let e_i and e_j be events occurring at p_i and p_j, respectively, such that $e_i \rightarrow e_j$. We assert that if e_j is in the cut then e_i is in the cut. That is, if e_j occurred before p_j recorded its state, then e_i must have occurred before p_i recorded its state. This is obvious if the two processes are the same, so we shall assume that $j \neq i$. Assume, for the moment, the opposite of what we wish to prove: that p_i recorded its state before e_i occurred. Consider the sequence of H messages $m_1, m_2 ..., m_H$ ($H \geq 1$), giving rise to the relation $e_i \rightarrow e_j$. By FIFO ordering over the channels that these messages traverse, and by the marker sending and receiving rules, a marker message would have reached p_j ahead of each of $m_1, m_2 ..., m_H$. By the marker receiving rule, p_j would therefore have recorded its state before the event e_j. This contradicts our assumption that e_j is in the cut, and we are done.

We may further establish a reachability relation between the observed global state and the initial and final global states when the algorithm runs. Let $Sys = e_0, e_1, ...$ be the linearization of the system as it executed (where two events occurred at exactly the same time, we order them according to process identifiers). Let S_{init} be the global state immediately before the first process recorded its state; let S_{final} be the global state when the snapshot algorithm terminates, immediately after the last state-recording action; and let S_{snap} be the recorded global state.

We shall find a permutation of Sys, $Sys' = e'_0, e'_1, e'_2, ...$ such that all three states S_{init}, S_{snap} and S_{final} occur in Sys', S_{snap} is reachable from S_{init} in Sys', and S_{final} is reachable from S_{snap} in Sys'. Figure 11.13 shows this situation, in which the upper linearization is Sys, and the lower linearization is Sys'.

We derive Sys' from Sys by first categorizing all events in Sys as *pre-snap* events or *post-snap* events. A pre-snap event at process p_i is one that occurred at p_i before it recorded its state; all other events are post-snap events. It is important to understand that a post-snap event may occur before a pre-snap event in Sys, if the events occur at different processes. (Of course no post-snap event may occur before a pre-snap event at the same process.)

We shall show how we may order all pre-snap events before post-snap events to obtain Sys'. Suppose that e_j is a post-snap event at one process, and e_{j+1} is a pre-snap event at a different process. It cannot be that $e_j \rightarrow e_{j+1}$. For then these two events would be the sending and receiving of a message, respectively. A marker message would have to have preceded the message, making the reception of the message a post-snap event, but by assumption e_{j+1} is a pre-snap event. We may therefore swap the two events without violating the happened-before relation (that is, the resultant sequence of events remains a linearization). The swap does not introduce new process states, since we do not alter the order in which events occur at any individual process.

We continue swapping pairs of adjacent events in this way as necessary until we have ordered all pre-snap events $e'_0, e'_1, e'_2, ..., e'_{R-1}$ prior to all post-snap events $e'_R, e'_{R+1}, e'_{R+2}, ...$ with Sys' the resulting execution. For each process, the set of events in $e'_0, e'_1, e'_2, ..., e'_{R-1}$ that occurred at it is exactly the set of events that it experienced before it recorded its state. Therefore the state of each process at that point, and the state of the communication channels, is that of the global state S_{snap} recorded by the algorithm. We have disturbed neither of the states S_{init} or S_{final} with which the linearization begins and ends. So we have established the reachability relationship.

Stability and the reachability of the observed state ◊ The reachability property of the snapshot algorithm is useful for detecting stable predicates. In general, any non-stable predicate we establish as being *True* in the state S_{snap} may or may not have been *True* in the actual execution whose global state we recorded. However, if a stable predicate is *True* in the state S_{snap} then we may conclude that the predicate is *True* in the state S_{final}, since by definition a stable predicate that is *True* of a state S is also *True* of any state reachable from S. Similarly, if the predicate evaluates to *False* for S_{snap}, then it must also be *False* for S_{init}.

11.6 Distributed debugging

We now examine the problem of recording a system's global state so that we may make useful statements about whether a transitory state – as opposed to a stable state – occurred in an actual execution. This is what we require, in general, when debugging a distributed system. We gave an example above in which each of a set of processes p_i has a variable x_i. The safety condition required in this example is $|x_i - x_j| \leq \delta$ ($i, j = 1, 2, ..., N$); this constraint is to be met even though a process may change the value of its variable at any time. Another example is a distributed system controlling a system of pipes in a factory where we are interested in whether all the valves (controlled by different processes) were open at some time. In these examples, we cannot in general observe the values of the variables or the states of the valves simultaneously. The challenge is to monitor the system's execution over time – to capture 'trace' information rather than a single snapshot – so that we can establish *post hoc* whether the required safety condition was or may have been violated.

Chandy and Lamport's snapshot algorithm collects state in a distributed fashion, and we pointed out how the processes in the system could send the state they gather to a monitor process for collection. The algorithm we shall describe (due to Marzullo and Neiger [1991]) is centralized. The observed processes send their states to a process called a monitor, which assembles globally consistent states from what it receives. We consider the monitor to lie outside the system, observing its execution.

Our aim is to determine cases where a given global state predicate ϕ was definitely *True* at some point in the execution we observed, and cases where it was possibly *True*. The notion 'possibly' arises as a natural concept because we may extract a consistent global state S from an executing system and find that $\phi(S)$ is *True*. No single observation of a consistent global state allows us to conclude whether a non-stable predicate ever evaluated to *True* in the actual execution. Nevertheless, we may be interested to know whether they *might* have occurred, as far as we can tell by observing the execution.

The notion 'definitely' does apply to the actual execution and not to a run that we have extrapolated from it. It may sound paradoxical for us to consider what happened in an actual execution. However, it is possible to evaluate whether ϕ was definitely *True* by considering all linearizations of the observed events.

We now define the notions of *possibly* ϕ and *definitely* ϕ for a predicate ϕ in terms of linearizations of H, the history of the system's execution.

possibly ϕ The statement *possibly* ϕ means that there is a consistent global state S through which a linearization of H passes such that $\phi(S)$ is *True*.

definitely ϕ The statement *definitely* ϕ means that for all linearizations L of H, there is a consistent global state S through which L passes such that $\phi(S)$ is *True*.

When we use Chandy and Lamport's snapshot algorithm and obtain the global state S_{snap} we may assert *possibly* ϕ if $\phi(S_{snap})$ happens to be *True*. But in general evaluating *possibly* ϕ entails a search through all consistent global states derived from the observed execution. Only if $\phi(S)$ evaluates to *False* for all consistent global states S is it not the case that *possibly* ϕ. Note also that while we may conclude *definitely* $(\neg\phi)$ from $\neg possibly$ ϕ, we may not conclude $\neg possibly$ ϕ from *definitely* $(\neg\phi)$. The latter is the assertion that $\neg\phi$ holds at some state on every linearization: ϕ may hold for other states.

We now describe:

- how the process states are collected;

- how the monitor extracts consistent global states;

- how the monitor evaluates *possibly* ϕ and *definitely* ϕ in both asynchronous and synchronous systems.

Collecting the state $\lozenge$ The observed processes p_i ($i = 1, 2, ..., N$) send their initial state to the monitor process initially, and thereafter from time to time, in *state messages*. The monitor process records the state messages from process p_i in a separate queue Q_i, for each $i = 1, 2, ..., N$.

The activity of preparing and sending state messages may delay the normal execution of the observed processes, but it does not otherwise interfere with it. There is no need to send the state except initially and when it changes. There are two optimizations to reduce the state-message traffic to the monitor. First, the global state predicate may depend only on certain parts of the processes' states. For example, it may depend only on the states of particular variables. So the observed processes need only send the relevant state to the monitor process. Second, they need only send their state at times when the predicate ϕ may become *True* or cease to be *True*. There is no point in sending changes to the state that do not affect the predicate's value.

Figure 11.14   Vector timestamps and variable values for the execution of Figure 11.9

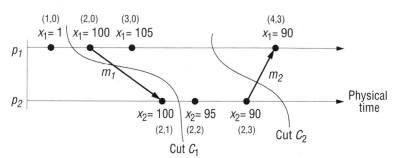

For example, in the example system of processes p_i that are supposed to obey the constraint $|x_i - x_j| \leq \delta$. ($i, j = 1, 2, ..., N$), the processes need only notify the monitor when the values of their own variable x_i changes. When they send their state, they supply the value of x_i but do not need to send any other variables.

11.6.1 Observing consistent global states

The monitor must assemble consistent global states against which it evaluates ϕ. Recall that a cut C is consistent if and only if for all events e in the cut C, $f \rightarrow e \Rightarrow f \in C$.

For example, Figure 11.14 shows two processes p_1 and p_2 with variables x_1 and x_2, respectively. The events shown on the timelines (with vector timestamps) are adjustments to the values of the two variables. Initially, $x_1 = x_2 = 0$. The requirement is $|x_1 - x_2| \leq 50$. The processes make adjustments to their variables, but 'large' adjustments cause a message containing the new value to be sent to the other process. When either of the processes receives an adjustment message from the other, it sets its variable equal to the value contained in the message.

Whenever one of the processes p_1 or p_2 adjusts the value of its variable (whether it is a 'small' adjustment or a 'large' one), it sends the value in a state message to the monitoring process. The latter keeps the state messages in the per-process queues for analysis. If the monitor processes used values from the inconsistent cut C_1 in Figure 11.14, then it would find that $x_1 = 1$, $x_2 = 100$, breaking the constraint $|x_1 - x_2| \leq 50$. But this state of affairs never occurred. On the other hand, values from the consistent cut C_2 show $x_1 = 105$, $x_2 = 90$.

In order that the monitor can distinguish consistent global states from inconsistent global states, the observed processes enclose their vector clock values with their state messages. Each queue Q_i is kept ordered in sending order, which can immediately be established by examining the ith component of the vector timestamps. Of course, the monitor process may deduce nothing about the ordering of states sent by different processes from their arrival order, because of variable message latencies. It must instead examine the vector timestamps of the state messages.

Let $S = (s_1, s_2, ..., s_N)$ be a global state drawn from the state messages that the monitor process has received. Let $V(s_i)$ be the vector timestamp of the state s_i received from p_i. Then it can be shown that S is a consistent global state if and only if:

Figure 11.15   The lattice of global states for the execution of Figure 11.14

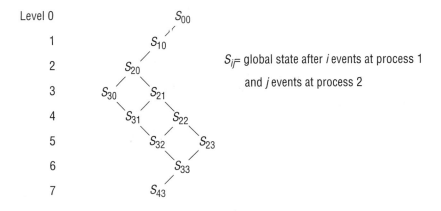

$$V(s_i)[i] \geq V(s_j)[i] \text{ for } i, j = 1, 2, ..., N - \text{(Condition } CGS)$$

This says that the number of p_i's events known at p_j when it sent s_j is no more than the number of events that had occurred at p_i when it sent s_i. In other words, if one process's state depends upon another (according to happened-before ordering), then the global state also encompasses the state upon which it depends.

In summary, we now possess a method whereby the monitor process may establish whether a given global state is consistent, using the vector timestamps kept by the observed processes and piggybacked on the state messages that they send to it.

Figure 11.15 shows the lattice of consistent global states corresponding to the execution of the two processes in Figure 11.14. This structure captures the relation of reachability between consistent global states. The nodes denote global states, and the edges denote possible transitions between these states. The global state S_{00} has both processes in their initial state; S_{10} has p_2 still in its initial state and p_1 in the next state in its local history. The state S_{01} is not consistent, because of the message m_1 sent from p_1 to p_2, so it does not appear in the lattice.

The lattice is arranged in levels with, for example, S_{00} in level 0, S_{10} in level 1. In general, S_{ij} is in level $(i + j)$. A linearization traverses the lattice from any global state to any global state reachable from it on the next level – that is, in each step some process experiences one event. For example, S_{22} is reachable from S_{20}, but S_{22} is not reachable from S_{30}.

The lattice shows us all the linearizations corresponding to a history. It is now clear in principle how a monitor process should evaluate *possibly* ϕ and *definitely* ϕ. To evaluate *possibly* ϕ, the monitor process starts at the initial state and steps through all consistent states reachable from that point, evaluating ϕ at each stage. It stops when ϕ evaluates to *True*. To evaluate *definitely* ϕ, the monitor process must attempt to find a set of states through which all linearizations must pass, and at each of which ϕ evaluates to *True*. For example, if $\phi(S_{30})$ and $\phi(S_{21})$ in Figure 11.15 are both *True* then, since all linearizations pass through these states, *definitely* ϕ holds.

Figure 11.16   Algorithms to evaluate *possibly* φ and *definitely* φ

---

1. *Evaluating possibly φ for global history H of N processes*

$L := 0;$

$States := \{ (s_1^0, s_2^0, ..., s_N^0) \};$

while $(\phi(S) = False$ for all $S \in States)$

$\quad L := L + 1;$

$\quad Reachable := \{ S': S'$ reachable in H from some $S \in States \wedge level(S') = L \};$

$\quad States := Reachable$

end while

output "*possibly* φ";

2. *Evaluating definitely φ for global history H of N processes*

$L := 0;$

if $(\phi(s_1^0, s_2^0, ..., s_N^0))$ *then* $States := \{\}$ *else* $States := \{ (s_1^0, s_2^0, ..., s_N^0) \};$

while $(States \neq \{\})$

$\quad L := L + 1;$

$\quad Reachable := \{ S': S'$ reachable in H from some $S \in States \wedge level(S') = L \};$

$\quad States := \{ S \in Reachable : \phi(S) = False \}$

end while

output "*definitely* φ";

11.6.2 Evaluating possibly φ

To evaluate *possibly* φ, the monitor process must traverse the lattice of reachable states, starting from the initial state $(s_1^0, s_2^0 ... s_N^0)$. The algorithm is shown in Figure 11.16. The algorithm assumes that the execution is infinite. It may easily be adapted for a finite execution.

The monitor process may discover the set of consistent states in level $L + 1$ reachable from a given consistent state in level L by the following method. Let $S = (s_1, s_2, ..., s_N)$ be a consistent state. Then a consistent state in the next level reachable from S is of the form $S' = (s_1, s_2, ...s_i', ..., s_N)$, which differs from S only by containing the next state (after a single event) of some process p_i. The monitor can find all such states by traversing the queues of state messages Q_i $(i = 1, 2, ..., N)$. The state S' is reachable from S if and only if:

$$\text{for } j = 1, 2, ..., N, j \neq i: V(s_j)[j] \geq V(s_i')[j]$$

This condition comes from condition CGS above and from the fact that S was already a consistent global state. A given state may in general be reached from several states at the previous level, so the monitor process should take care to evaluate the consistency of each state only once.

Figure 11.17 Evaluating *definitely* φ

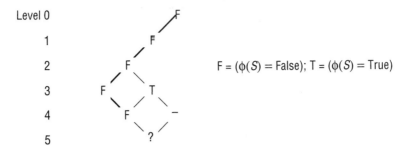

Level 0

1

2   F = (φ(S) = False); T = (φ(S) = True)

3

4

5

11.6.3 Evaluating definitely φ

To evaluate *definitely* φ, the monitor process again traverses the lattice of reachable states a level at a time, starting from the initial state $(s_1^0, s_2^0, ..., s_N^0)$. The algorithm (shown in Figure 11.16) again assumes that the execution is infinite but may easily be adapted for a finite execution. It maintains the set *States*, which contains those states at the current level that may be reached on a linearization from the initial state by traversing only states for which φ evaluates to *False*. As long as such a linearization exists, we may not assert *definitely* φ: the execution could have taken this linearization, and φ would be *False* at every stage along it. If we reach a level for which no such linearization exists, we may conclude *definitely* φ.

In Figure 11.17, at level 3 the set *States* consists of only one state, which is reachable by a linearization on which all states are *False* (marked in bold lines). The only state considered at level 4 is the one marked 'F'. (The state to its right is not considered, since it can only be reached via a state for which φ evaluates to *True*.) If φ evaluates to *True* in the state at level 5, then we may conclude *definitely* φ. Otherwise, the algorithm must continue beyond this level.

Cost ◊ The algorithms we have just described are combinatorially explosive. Suppose that k is the maximum number of events at a single process. Then the algorithms we have described entail $O(k^N)$ comparisons (the monitor process compares the states of each of the N observed processes with one another).

There is also a space cost to these algorithms of $O(kN)$. However, we observe that the monitor process may delete a message containing state s_i from queue Q_i when no other item of state arriving from another process could possibly be involved in a consistent global state containing s_i. That is, when:

$$V(s_j^{last})[i] > V(s_i)[i] \text{ for } j = 1, 2, ..., N, j \neq i$$

where s_j^{last} is the last state that the monitor process has received from process p_j.

11.6.4 Evaluating possibly ϕ and definitely ϕ in synchronous systems

The algorithms we have given so far work in an asynchronous system: we have made no timing assumptions. But the price paid for this is that the monitor may examine a consistent global state $S = (s_1, s_2, ..., s_N)$ for which any two local states s_i and s_j occurred an arbitrarily long time apart in the actual execution of the system. Our requirement, by contrast, is to consider only those global states that the actual execution could in principle have traversed.

In a synchronous system, suppose that the processes keep their physical clocks internally synchronized within a known bound, and that the observed processes provide physical timestamps as well as vector timestamps in their state messages. Then the monitor process need consider only those consistent global states whose local states could possibly have existed simultaneously, given the approximate synchronization of the clocks. With good enough clock synchronization, these will number many less than all globally consistent states.

We now give an algorithm to exploit synchronized clocks in this way. We assume that each observed process p_i ($i = 1, 2, ..., N$) and the monitor process, which we shall call p_0, keeps a physical clock C_i ($i = 0, 1, ..., N$). These are synchronized to within a known bound $D > 0$; that is, at the same real time:

$$\left| C_i(t) - C_j(t) \right| < D \text{ for } i, j = 0, 1, ..., N$$

The observed processes send both their vector time and physical time with their state messages to the monitor process. The monitor process now applies a condition that not only tests for consistency of a global state $S = (s_1, s_2, ..., s_N)$, but also tests whether each pair of states could have happened at the same real time, given the physical clock values. In other words, for $i, j = 1, 2, ..., N$:

$$V(s_i)[i] \geq V(s_j)[i] \text{ and } s_i \text{ and } s_j \text{ could have occurred at the same real time.}$$

The first clause is the condition that we used earlier. For the second clause, note that p_i is in the state s_i from the time it first notifies the monitor process, $C_i(s_i)$, to some later local time $L_i(s_i)$, say, when the next state transition occurs at p_i. For s_i and s_j to have obtained at the same real time we thus have, allowing for the bound on clock synchronization:

$$C_i(s_i) - D \leq C_j(s_j) \leq L_i(s_i) + D - \text{or } \textit{vice versa} \text{ (swapping } i \textit{ and } j).$$

The monitor process must calculate a value for $L_i(s_i)$, which is measured against p_i's clock. If the monitor process has received a state message for p_i's next state s_i', then $L_i(s_i)$ is $C_i(s_i')$. Otherwise, the monitor process estimates $L_i(s_i)$ as $C_0 - max + D$, where C_0 is the monitor's current local clock value, and max is the maximum transmission time for a state message.

11.7 Summary

This chapter began by describing the importance of accurate timekeeping for distributed systems. It then described algorithms for synchronizing clocks despite the drift between them and the variability of message delays between computers.

The degree of synchronization accuracy that is practically obtainable fulfils many requirements but is nonetheless not sufficient to determine the ordering of an arbitrary pair of events occurring at different computers. The happened-before relation is a partial order on events that reflects a flow of information between them – within a process, or via messages between processes. Some algorithms require events to be ordered in happened-before order, for example successive updates made at separate copies of data. Lamport clocks are counters that are updated in accordance with the happened-before relationship between events. Vector clocks are an improvement on Lamport clocks, because it is possible to determine by examining their vector timestamps whether two events are ordered by happened-before or are concurrent.

We introduced the concepts of events, local and global histories, cuts, local and global states, runs, consistent states, linearizations (consistent runs), and reachability. A consistent state or run is one that is in accord with the happened-before relation.

We went on to consider the problem of recording a consistent global state by observing a system's execution. Our objective was to evaluate a predicate on this state. An important class of predicates are the stable predicates. We described the snapshot algorithm of Chandy and Lamport, which captures a consistent global state and allows us to make assertions about whether a stable predicate holds in the actual execution. We went on to give Marzullo and Neiger's algorithm for deriving assertions about whether a predicate held or may have held in the actual run. The algorithm employs a monitor process to collect states. The monitor examines vector timestamps to extract consistent global states, and it constructs and examines the lattice of all consistent global states. This algorithm involves great computational complexity but is valuable for understanding and can be of some practical benefit in real systems where relatively few events change the global predicate's value. The algorithm has a more efficient variant in synchronous systems, where clocks may be synchronized.

EXERCISES

11.1   Why is computer clock synchronization necessary? Describe the design requirements for a system to synchronize the clocks in a distributed system.   *page 434*

11.2   A clock is reading 10:27:54.0 (hr:min:sec) when it is discovered to be 4 seconds fast. Explain why it is undesirable to set it back to the right time at that point and show (numerically) how it should be adjusted so as to be correct after 8 seconds has elapsed.   *page 438*

11.3   A scheme for implementing at-most-once reliable message delivery uses synchronized clocks to reject duplicate messages. Processes place their local clock value (a 'timestamp') in the messages they send. Each receiver keeps a table giving, for each sending process, the largest message timestamp it has seen. Assume that clocks are synchronized to within 100 ms, and that messages can arrive at most 50 ms after transmission.

(i)   When may a process ignore a message bearing a timestamp T, if it has recorded the last message received from that process as having timestamp T'?

(ii)   When may a receiver remove a timestamp 175,000 (ms) from its table? (Hint: use the receiver's local clock value.)

(iii)   Should the clocks be internally synchronized or externally synchronized?

page 439

11.4   A client attempts to synchronize with a time server. It records the round-trip times and timestamps returned by the server in the table below.

Which of these times should it use to set its clock? To what time should it set it? Estimate the accuracy of the setting with respect to the server's clock. If it is known that the time between sending and receiving a message in the system concerned is at least 8 ms, do your answers change?

Round-trip (ms)	Time (hr:min:sec)
22	10:54:23.674
25	10:54:25.450
20	10:54:28.342

page 439

11.5   In the system of Exercise 11.4 it is required to synchronize a file server's clock to within ±1 millisecond. Discuss this in relation to Cristian's algorithm.   *page 439*

11.6   What reconfigurations would you expect to occur in the NTP synchronization subnet?

page 442

11.7   An NTP server B receives server A's message at 16:34:23.480 bearing a timestamp 16:34:13.430 and replies to it. A receives the message at 16:34:15.725, bearing B's timestamp 16:34:25.7. Estimate the offset between B and A and the accuracy of the estimate.   *page 443*

11.8   Discuss the factors to be taken into account when deciding to which NTP server a client should synchronize its clock.   *page 444*

11.9   Discuss how it is possible to compensate for clock drift between synchronization points by observing the drift rate over time. Discuss any limitations to your method. *page 445*

11.10   By considering a chain of zero or more messages connecting events e and e' and using induction, show that $e \rightarrow e' \Rightarrow L(e) < L(e')$.   *page 446*

11.11   Show that $V_j[i] \leq V_i[i]$.   *page 447*

11.12   In a similar fashion to Exercise 10.10, show that $e \rightarrow e' \Rightarrow V(e) < V(e')$.   *page 448*

11.13   Using the result of Exercise 10.11, show that if events e and e' are concurrent then neither $V(e) \leq V(e')$ nor $V(e') \leq V(e)$. Hence show that if $V(e) < V(e')$ then $e \to e'$.
page 448

11.14   Two processes P and Q are connected in a ring using two channels, and they constantly rotate a message m. At any one time, there is only one copy of m in the system. Each process's state consists of the number of times it has received m, and P sends m first. At a certain point, P has the message and its state is 101. Immediately after sending m, P initiates the snapshot algorithm. Explain the operation of the algorithm in this case, giving the possible global state(s) reported by it.
page 453

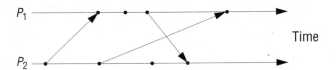

11.15   The figure above shows events occurring for each of two processes, p_1 and p_2. Arrows between processes denote message transmission.

Draw and label the lattice of consistent states (p_1 state, p_2 state), beginning with the initial state (0,0).
page 460

11.16   Jones is running a collection of processes $p_1, p_2, ..., p_N$. Each process p_i contains a variable v_i. She wishes to determine whether all the variables $v_1, v_2, ..., v_N$ were ever equal in the course of the execution.

(i)   Jones' processes run in a synchronous system. She uses a monitor process to determine whether the variables were equal. When should the application processes communicate with the monitor process, and what should their messages contain?

(ii)   Explain the statement *possibly* $(v_1 = v_2 = ... = v_N)$. How can Jones determine whether this statement is true of her execution?
page 461

12
COORDINATION AND AGREEMENT

In this chapter, we introduce some topics and algorithms related to the issue of how processes coordinate their actions and agree on shared values in distributed systems, despite failures. The chapter begins with algorithms to achieve mutual exclusion among a collection of processes, so as to coordinate their accesses to shared resources. It goes on to examine how an election can be implemented in a distributed system. That is, it describes how a group of processes can agree on a new coordinator of their activities after the previous coordinator has failed.

The second half examines the related problems of multicast communication, consensus, byzantine agreement and interactive consistency. In multicast, the issue is how to agree on such matters as the order in which messages are to be delivered. Consensus and the other problems generalize from this: how can any collection of processes agree on some value, no matter what the domain of the values in question? We encounter a fundamental result in the theory of distributed systems: that under certain conditions – including surprisingly benign failure conditions – it is impossible to guarantee that processes will reach consensus.

12.1 Introduction

This chapter introduces a collection of algorithms whose goals vary but which share an aim that is fundamental in distributed systems: for a set of processes to coordinate their actions or to agree on one or more values. For example, in the case of a complex piece of machinery such as a spaceship, it is essential that the computers controlling it agree on such conditions as whether the spaceship's mission is proceeding or has been aborted. Furthermore, the computers must coordinate their actions correctly with respect to shared resources (the spaceship's sensors and actuators). The computers must be able to do so even where there is no fixed master-slave relationship between the components (which would make coordination particularly simple). The reason for avoiding fixed master-slave relationships is that we often require our systems to keep working correctly even if failures occur, so we need to avoid single points of failure, such as fixed masters.

An important distinction for us, as in Chapter 11, will be whether the distributed system under study is asynchronous or synchronous. In an asynchronous system we can make no timing assumptions. In a synchronous system, we shall assume that there are bounds on the maximum message transmission delay, on the time to execute each step of a process, and on clock drift rates. The synchronous assumptions allow us to use timeouts to detect process crashes.

Another important aim of the chapter while discussing algorithms is to consider failures, and how to deal with them when designing algorithms. Section 2.3.2 introduced a failure model, which we shall use in this chapter. Coping with failures is a subtle business, so we begin by considering some algorithms that tolerate no failures and progress through benign failures until we consider how to tolerate arbitrary failures. We encounter a fundamental result in the theory of distributed systems. Even under surprisingly benign failure conditions, it is impossible to guarantee in an asynchronous system that a collection of processes can agree on a shared value – for example, for all of a spaceship's controlling processes to agree 'mission proceed' or 'mission abort'.

Section 12.2 examines the problem of distributed mutual exclusion. This is the extension to distributed systems of the familiar problem of avoiding race conditions in kernels and multi-threaded applications. Since much of what occurs in distributed systems is resource sharing, this is an important problem to solve. Next, Section 12.3 introduces a related but more general issue of how to 'elect' one of a collection of processes to perform a special role. For example, in Chapter 11 we saw how processes synchronized their clocks to a designated time server. If this server fails and several surviving servers can fulfil that role, then for the sake of consistency it is necessary to choose just one server to take over.

Multicast communication is the subject of Section 12.4. As Section 4.5.1 explained, multicast is a very useful communication paradigm, with applications from locating resources to coordinating the updates to replicated data. Section 12.4 examines multicast reliability and ordering semantics, and gives algorithms to achieve the variations. Multicast delivery is essentially a problem of agreement between processes: the recipients agree on which messages they will receive, and in which order they will receive them. Section 12.5 discusses the problem of agreement more generally, primarily in the forms known as consensus and byzantine agreement.

Figure 12.1   A network partition

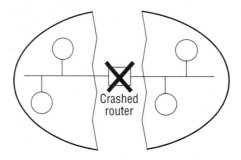

The treatment followed in this chapter involves stating the assumptions and the goals to be met, and giving an informal account of why the algorithms presented are correct. There is insufficient space to provide a more rigorous approach. For that, we refer the reader to a text that gives a thorough account of distributed algorithms, such as Attiya and Welch [1998] and Lynch [1996].

Before presenting the problems and algorithms, we discuss failure assumptions and the practical matter of detecting failures in distributed systems.

12.1.1 Failure assumptions and failure detectors

For the sake of simplicity, this chapter assumes that each pair of processes is connected by reliable channels. That is, although the underlying network components may suffer failures, the processes use a reliable communication protocol that masks these failures – for example, by retransmitting missing or corrupted messages. Also for the sake of simplicity, we assume that no process failure implies a threat to the other processes' ability to communicate. This means that none of the processes depends upon another to forward messages.

Note that a reliable channel *eventually* delivers a message to the recipient's input buffer. In a synchronous system, we suppose that there is hardware redundancy where necessary, so that a reliable channel not only eventually delivers each message despite underlying failures but it does so within a specified time bound.

In any particular interval of time, communication between some processes may succeed while communication between others is delayed. For example, the failure of a router between two networks may mean that a collection of four processes is split into two pairs, such that intra-pair communication is possible over their respective networks; but inter-pair communication is not possible while the router has failed. This is known as a *network partition* (Figure 12.1). Over a point-to-point network such as the Internet, complex topologies and independent routing choices mean that connectivity may be *asymmetric*: communication is possible from process p to process q, but not *vice versa*. Connectivity may also be *intransitive*: communication is possible from p to q and from q to r; but p cannot communicate directly with r. Thus our reliability assumption entails that eventually any failed link or router will be repaired or circumvented. Nevertheless, the processes may not all be able to communicate at the same time.

The chapter assumes, unless we state otherwise, that processes only fail by crashing – an assumption that is good enough for many systems. In Section 12.5, we shall consider how to treat the cases where processes have arbitrary (byzantine) failures. Whatever the type of failure, a *correct* process is one that exhibits no failures at any point in the execution under consideration. Note that correctness applies to the whole execution, not just to a part of it. So a process that suffers a crash failure is 'non-failed' before that point, not 'correct' before that point.

One of the problems in the design of algorithms that can overcome process crashes is that of deciding when a process has crashed. A *failure detector* [Chandra and Toueg 1996, Stelling *et al.* 1998] is a service that processes queries about whether a particular process has failed. It is often implemented by an object local to each process (on the same computer) that runs a failure-detection algorithm in conjunction with its counterparts at other processes. The object local to each process is called a *local failure detector*. We shall outline how to implement failure detectors shortly, but first we shall concentrate on some of the properties of failure detectors.

A failure 'detector' is not necessarily accurate. Most fall into the category of *unreliable failure detectors*. An unreliable failure detector may produce one of two values when given the identity of a process: *Unsuspected* or *Suspected*. Both of these results are hints, which may or may not accurately reflect whether the process has actually failed. A result of *Unsuspected* signifies that the detector has recently received evidence suggesting that the process has not failed; for example, a message was recently received from it. But of course the process can have failed since then. A result of *Suspected* signifies that the failure detector has some indication that the process may have failed. For example, it may be that no message from the process has been received for more than a nominal maximum length of silence (even in an asynchronous system, practical upper bounds can be used as hints). The suspicion may be misplaced: for example, the process could be functioning correctly, but on the other side of a network partition; or it could be running more slowly than expected.

A *reliable failure detector* is one that is always accurate in detecting a process's failure. It answers processes' queries with either a response of *Unsuspected* – which, as before, can only be a hint – or *Failed*. A result of *Failed* means that the detector has determined that the process has crashed. Recall that a process that has crashed stays that way, since by definition a process never takes another step once it has crashed.

It is important to realize that, although we speak of one failure detector acting for a collection of processes, the response that the failure detector gives to a process is only as good as the information available at that process. A failure detector may sometimes give different responses to different processes, since communication conditions vary from process to process.

We can implement an unreliable failure detector using the following algorithm. Each process p sends a 'p is here' message to every other process, and it does this every T seconds. The failure detector uses an estimate of the maximum message transmission time of D seconds. If the local failure detector at process q does not receive a 'p is here' message within $T + D$ seconds of the last one, then it reports to q that p is *Suspected*. However, if it subsequently receives a 'p is here' message, then it reports to q that p is *OK*.

In a real distributed system, there are practical limits on message transmission times. Even email systems give up after a few days, since it is likely that communication links and routers will have been repaired in that time. If we choose small values for T and D (so that they total 0.1 second, say), then the failure detector is likely to suspect non-crashed processes many times, and much bandwidth will be taken up with 'p is here' messages. If we choose a large total timeout value (a week, say) then crashed processes will often be reported as *Unsuspected*.

A practical solution to this problem is to use timeout values that reflect the observed network delay conditions. If a local failure detector receives a 'p is here' in 20 seconds instead of the expected maximum of 10 seconds, then it could reset its timeout value for p accordingly. The failure detector remains unreliable, and its answers to queries are still only hints, but the probability of its accuracy increases.

In a synchronous system, our failure detector can be made into a reliable one. We can choose D so that it is not an estimate but an absolute bound on message transmission times; the absence of a 'p is here' message within $T + D$ seconds entitles the local failure detector to conclude that p has crashed.

The reader may wonder whether failure detectors are of any practical use. Unreliable failure detectors may suspect a process that has not failed (they may be *inaccurate*); and they may not suspect a process that has in fact failed (they may be *incomplete*). Reliable failure detectors, on the other hand, require that the system is synchronous (and few practical systems are).

We have introduced failure detectors because they help us to think about the nature of failures in a distributed system. And any practical system that is designed to cope with failures must detect them – however imperfectly. But it turns out that even unreliable failure detectors with certain well-defined properties can help us to provide practical solutions to the problem of coordinating processes in the presence of failures. We return to this point in Section 12.5.

12.2 Distributed mutual exclusion

Distributed processes often need to coordinate their activities. If a collection of processes share a resource or collection of resources, then often mutual exclusion is required to prevent interference and ensure consistency when accessing the resources. This is the *critical section* problem, familiar in the domain of operating systems. In a distributed system, however, neither shared variables nor facilities supplied by a single local kernel can be used to solve it, in general. We require a solution to *distributed mutual exclusion*: one that is based solely on message passing.

In some cases shared resources are managed by servers that also provide mechanisms for mutual exclusion. Chapter 13 describes how some servers synchronize client accesses to resources. But in some practical cases a separate mechanism for mutual exclusion is required.

Consider users who update a text file. A simple means of ensuring that their updates are consistent is to allow them to access it only one at a time, by requiring the editor to lock the file before updates can be made. NFS file servers, described in Chapter 8, are designed to be stateless and therefore do not support file locking. For this reason, UNIX systems provide a separate file-locking service, implemented by the daemon *lockd*, to handle locking requests from clients.

A particularly interesting example is where there is no server, and a collection of peer processes must coordinate their accesses to shared resources amongst themselves. This occurs routinely on networks such as Ethernets, and IEEE 802.11 wireless networks in 'ad hoc' mode, where network interfaces cooperate as peers so that only one node transmits at a time on the shared medium. Consider, also, a system monitoring the number of vacancies in a car park with a process at each entrance and exit that tracks the number of vehicles entering and leaving. Each process keeps a count of the total number of vehicles within the car park and displays whether or not it is full. The processes must update the shared count of the number of vehicles consistently. There are several ways of achieving that, but it would be convenient for these processes to be able to obtain mutual exclusion solely by communicating among themselves, eliminating the need for a separate server.

It is useful to have a generic mechanism for distributed mutual exclusion at our disposal – one that is independent of the particular resource management scheme in question. We now examine some algorithms for achieving that.

12.2.1 Algorithms for mutual exclusion

We consider a system of N processes p_i, $i = 1, 2, ..., N$ that do not share variables. The processes access common resources, but they do so in a critical section. For the sake of simplicity, we assume that there is only one critical section. It is straightforward to extend the algorithms we shall present to more than one critical section.

We assume that the system is asynchronous, that processes do not fail, and that message delivery is reliable, so that any message sent is eventually delivered intact, exactly once.

The application-level protocol for executing a critical section is as follows:

enter()	// enter critical section – block if necessary
resourceAccesses()	// access shared resources in critical section
exit()	// leave critical section – other processes may now enter

Our essential requirements for mutual exclusion are as follows:

ME1: (safety)	At most one process may execute in the critical section (CS) at a time.
ME2: (liveness)	Requests to enter and exit the critical section eventually succeed.

Condition ME2 implies freedom from both deadlock and starvation. A deadlock would involve two or more of the processes becoming stuck indefinitely while attempting to enter or exit the critical section, by virtue of their mutual interdependence. But, even without a deadlock, a poor algorithm might lead to *starvation*: the indefinite postponement of entry for a process that has requested it.

The absence of starvation is a *fairness* condition. Another fairness issue is the order in which processes enter the critical section. It is not possible to order entry to the critical section by the times that the processes requested it, because of the absence of global clocks. But a useful fairness requirement that is sometimes made makes use of the happened-before ordering (Section 11.4) between messages that request entry to the critical section:

Figure 12.2   Server managing a mutual exclusion token for a set of processes

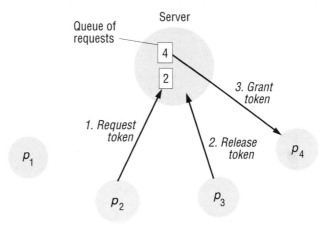

ME3: ($\rightarrow$ ordering)   If one request to enter the CS happened-before another, then entry to the CS is granted in that order.

If a solution grants entry to the critical section in happened-before order, and if all requests are related by happened-before, then it is not possible for a process to enter the critical section more than once while another waits to enter. This ordering also allows processes to coordinate their accesses to the critical section. A multi-threaded process may continue with other processing while a thread waits to be granted entry to a critical section. During this time, it might send a message to another process, which consequently also tries to enter the critical section. ME3 specifies that the first process be granted access before the second.

We evaluate the performance of algorithms for mutual exclusion according to the following criteria:

- the *bandwidth* consumed, which is proportional to the number of messages sent in each *entry* and *exit* operation;

- the *client delay* incurred by a process at each *entry* and *exit* operation;

- the algorithm's effect upon the *throughput* of the system. This is the rate at which the collection of processes as a whole can access the critical section, given that some communication is necessary between successive processes. We measure the effect using the *synchronization delay* between one process exiting the critical section and the next process entering it; the throughput is greater when the synchronization delay is shorter.

We shall not take the implementation of resource accesses into account in our descriptions. We do, however, assume that the client processes are well behaved and spend a finite time accessing resources within their critical sections.

The central server algorithm ◊ The simplest way to achieve mutual exclusion is to employ a server that grants permission to enter the critical section. Figure 12.2 shows the use of this server. To enter a critical section, a process sends a request message to

Figure 12.3   A ring of processes transferring a mutual exclusion token

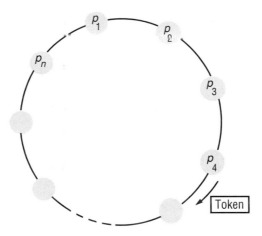

the server and awaits a reply from it. Conceptually, the reply constitutes a token signifying permission to enter the critical section. If no other process has the token at the time of the request, then the server replies immediately, granting the token. If the token is currently held by another process, then the server does not reply but queues the request. On exiting the critical section, a message is sent to the server, giving it back the token.

If the queue of waiting processes is not empty, then the server chooses the oldest entry in the queue, removes it and replies to the corresponding process. The chosen process then holds the token. In the figure, we show a situation in which p_2's request has been appended to the queue, which already contained p_4's request. p_3 exits the critical section, and the server removes p_4's entry and grants permission to enter to p_4 by replying to it. Process p_1 does not currently require entry to the critical section.

Given our assumption that no failures occur, it is easy to see that the safety and liveness conditions are met by this algorithm. The reader should check, however, that the algorithm does not satisfy property ME3.

We now evaluate the performance of this algorithm. Entering the critical section – even when no process currently occupies it – takes two messages (a *request* followed by a *grant*), and delays the requesting process by the time for this round-trip. Exiting the critical section takes one *release* message. Assuming asynchronous message-passing, this does not delay the exiting process.

The server may become a performance bottleneck for the system as a whole. The synchronization delay is the time taken for a round-trip: a *release* message to the server, followed by a *grant* message to the next process to enter the critical section.

A ring-based algorithm ◊ One of the simplest ways to arrange mutual exclusion between the N processes without requiring an additional process is to arrange them in a logical ring. This requires only that each process p_i has a communication channel to the next process in the ring, $p_{(i+1)\,mod\,N}$. The idea is that exclusion is conferred by obtaining a token in the form of a message passed from process to process in a single direction –

Figure 12.4   Ricart and Agrawala's algorithm

On initialization
   state := RELEASED;

To enter the section
   state := WANTED;
   Multicast *request* to all processes;   *Request processing deferred here*
   T := request's timestamp;
   Wait until (number of replies received = $(N-1)$);
   state := HELD;

On receipt of a request $<T_i, p_i>$ *at* p_j $(i \neq j)$
   if (state = HELD *or* (state = WANTED *and* $(T, p_j) < (T_i, p_i)))$
   then

                queue *request* from p_i without replying;
      else

                reply immediately to p_i;
   end if

To exit the critical section
   state := RELEASED;
   reply to any queued requests;

---

clockwise, say – around the ring. The ring topology may be unrelated to the physical interconnections between the underlying computers.

   If a process does not require to enter the critical section when it receives the token, then it immediately forwards the token to its neighbour. A process that requires the token waits until it receives it, but retains it. To exit the critical section, the process sends the token on to its neighbour.

   The arrangement of processes is shown in Figure 12.3. It is straightforward to verify that the conditions ME1 and ME2 are met by this algorithm, but that the token is not necessarily obtained in happened-before order. (Recall that the processes may exchange messages independently of the rotation of the token.)

   This algorithm continuously consumes network bandwidth (except when a process is inside the critical section): the processes send messages around the ring even when no process requires entry to the critical section. The delay experienced by a process requesting entry to the critical section is between 0 messages (when it has just received the token) and N messages (when it has just passed on the token). To exit the critical section requires only one message. The synchronization delay between one process's exit from the critical section and the next process's entry is anywhere from 1 to N message transmissions.

An algorithm using multicast and logical clocks ◊ Ricart and Agrawala [1981] developed an algorithm to implement mutual exclusion between N peer processes that is based upon multicast. The basic idea is that processes that require entry to a critical section multicast a request message, and can enter it only when all the other processes have

Figure 12.5   Multicast synchronization

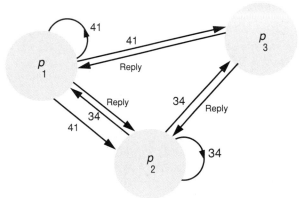

replied to this message. The conditions under which a process replies to a request are designed to ensure that conditions ME1–ME3 are met.

The processes $p_1, p_2..., p_N$ bear distinct numeric identifiers. They are assumed to possess communication channels to one another, and each process p_i keeps a Lamport clock, updated according to the rules LC1 and LC2 of Section 11.4. Messages requesting entry are of the form $<T, p_i>$, where T is the sender's timestamp and p_i is the sender's identifier.

Each process records its state of being outside the critical section (RELEASED), wanting entry (WANTED) or being in the critical section (HELD) in a variable *state*. The protocol is given in Figure 12.4.

If a process requests entry and the state of all other processes is RELEASED, then all processes will reply immediately to the request and the requester will obtain entry. If some process is in state HELD, then that process will not reply to requests until it has finished with the critical section, and so the requester cannot gain entry in the meantime. If two or more processes request entry at the same time, then whichever process's request bears the lowest timestamp will be the first to collect $N - 1$ replies, granting it entry next. If the requests bear equal Lamport timestamps, the requests are ordered according to the processes' corresponding identifiers. Note that, when a process requests entry, it defers processing requests from other processes until its own request has been sent and it has recorded the timestamp T of the request. This is so that processes make consistent decisions when processing requests.

This algorithm achieves the safety property ME1. If it were possible for two processes p_i and p_j $(i \neq j)$ to enter the critical section at the same time, then both of those processes would have to have replied to the other. But since the pairs $<T_i, p_i>$ are totally ordered, this is impossible. We leave the reader to verify that the algorithm also meets requirements ME2 and ME3.

To illustrate the algorithm, consider a situation involving three processes, p_1, p_2 and p_3 shown in Figure 12.5. Let us assume that p_3 is not interested in entering the critical section, and that p_1 and p_2 request it concurrently. The timestamp of p_1's request is 41, that of p_2 is 34. When p_3 receives their requests, it replies immediately.

When p_2 receives p_1's request, it finds its own request has the lower timestamp, and so does not reply, holding p_1 off. However, p_1 finds that p_2's request has a lower timestamp than that of its own request and so replies immediately. On receiving this second reply, p_2 can enter the critical section. When p_2 exits the critical section, it will reply to p_1's request and so grant it entry.

Gaining entry takes $2(N-1)$ messages in this algorithm: $N-1$ to multicast the request, followed by $N-1$ replies. Or, if there is hardware support for multicast, only one message is required for the request; the total is then N messages. It is thus a more expensive algorithm, in terms of bandwidth consumption, than the algorithms just described. However, the client delay in requesting entry is again a round-trip time (ignoring any delay incurred in multicasting the request message).

The advantage of this algorithm is that its synchronization delay is only one message transmission time. Both the previous algorithms incurred a round-trip synchronization delay.

The performance of the algorithm can be improved. First, note that the process that last entered the critical section and that has received no other requests for it still goes through the protocol as described, even though it could simply decide locally to re-allocate it to itself. Second, Ricart and Agrawala refined this protocol so that it requires N messages to obtain entry in the worst (and common) case, without hardware support for multicast. This is described in Raynal [1988].

Maekawa's voting algorithm ◊   Maekawa [1985] observed that in order for a process to enter a critical section, it is not necessary for all of its peers to grant it access. Processes need only obtain permission to enter from *subsets* of their peers, as long as the subsets used by any two processes overlap. We can think of processes as voting for one another to enter the critical section. A 'candidate' process must collect sufficient votes to enter. Processes in the intersection of two sets of voters ensure the safety property ME1, that at most one process can enter the critical section, by casting their votes for only one candidate.

Maekawa associated a *voting set* V_i with each process p_i ($i = 1, 2 ..., N$), where $V_i \subseteq \{p_1, p_1 ..., p_N\}$. The sets V_i are chosen so that, for all $i, j = 1, 2 ..., N$:

- $p_i \in V_i$

- $V_i \cap V_j \neq \emptyset$ – there is at least one common member of any two voting sets

- $|V_i| = K$ – to be fair, each process has a voting set of the same size

- Each process p_j is contained in M of the voting sets V_i.

Maekawa showed that the optimal solution, which minimizes K and allows the processes to achieve mutual exclusion, has $K \sim \sqrt{N}$ and $M = K$ (so that each process is in as many of the voting sets as there are elements in each one of those sets). It is non-trivial to calculate the optimal sets R_i. As an approximation, a simple way of deriving sets R_i such that $|R_i| \sim 2\sqrt{N}$ is to place the processes in a $\sqrt{N}$ by $\sqrt{N}$ matrix and let V_i be the union of the row and column containing p_i.

Maekawa's algorithm is shown in Figure 12.6. To obtain entry to the critical section, a process p_i sends *request* messages to all K members of V_i (including itself). p_i cannot enter the critical section until it has received all K *reply* messages. When a process p_j in V_i receives p_i's *request* message, it sends a *reply* message immediately,

Figure 12.6   Maekawa's algorithm

On initialization
     state := RELEASED;
     voted := FALSE;

For p_i to enter the critical section
     state := WANTED;
     Multicast *request* to all processes in V_i;
     Wait until (number of replies received = K);
     state := HELD;

On receipt of a request from p_i at p_j
     if (*state* = HELD *or voted* = TRUE)
     then
                    queue *request* from p_i without replying;
          else
                    send *reply* to p_i;
                    voted := TRUE;
     end if

For p_i to exit the critical section
     state := RELEASED;
     Multicast *release* to all processes in V_i;

On receipt of a release from p_i at p_j
     if (queue of requests is non-empty)
     then
                    remove head of queue – from p_k, say;
                    send *reply* to p_k;
                    voted := TRUE;
          else
                    voted := FALSE;
     end if

unless either its state is HELD or it has already replied ('voted') since it last received a *release* message. Otherwise, it queues the request message (in the order of its arrival) but does not yet reply. When a process receives a *release* message, it removes the head of its queue of outstanding requests (if the queue is non-empty) and sends a *reply* message (a 'vote') in response to it. To leave the critical section, p_i sends *release* messages to all the K members of V_i (including itself).

This algorithm achieves the safety property ME1. If it were possible for two processes p_i and p_j to enter the critical section at the same time, then the processes in $V_i \cap V_j \neq \emptyset$ would have to have voted for both. But the algorithm allows a process to make at most one vote between successive receipts of a *release* message – so this situation is impossible.

Unfortunately, the algorithm is deadlock-prone. Consider three processes p_1, p_2 and p_3 with $V_1 = \{p_1, p_2\}$, $V_2 = \{p_2, p_3\}$ and $V_3 = \{p_3, p_1\}$. If the three processes concurrently request entry to the critical section, then it is it is possible for p_1 to reply to itself and hold off p_2; for p_2 to reply to itself and hold off p_3; and for p_3 to reply to itself and hold off p_1. Each process has received one out of two replies, and none can proceed.

The algorithm can be adapted [Saunders 1987] so that it becomes deadlock-free. In the adapted protocol, processes queue outstanding requests in happened-before order, so that requirement ME3 is also satisfied.

The algorithm's bandwidth utilization is $2\sqrt{N}$ messages per entry to the critical section and $\sqrt{N}$ messages per exit (assuming no hardware multicast facilities). The total of $3\sqrt{N}$ is superior to the $2(N-1)$ messages required by Ricart and Agrawala's algorithm, if $N > 4$. The client delay is the same as that of Ricart and Agrawala's algorithm, but the synchronization delay is worse: a round-trip time instead of a single message transmission time.

Fault tolerance ◊ The main points to consider when evaluating the above algorithms with respect to fault tolerance are:

- What happens when messages are lost?
- What happens when a process crashes?

None of the algorithms that we have described would tolerate the loss of messages, if the channels were unreliable. The ring-based algorithm cannot tolerate a crash failure of any single process. As it stands, Maekawa's algorithm can tolerate some process crash failures: if a crashed process is not in a voting set that is required, then its failure will not affect the other processes. The central server algorithm can tolerate the crash failure of a client process that neither holds nor has requested the token. The Ricart and Agrawala algorithm as we have described it can be adapted to tolerate the crash failure of such a process, by taking it to grant all requests implicitly.

We invite the reader to consider how to adapt the algorithms to tolerate failures, on the assumption that a reliable failure detector is available. Even with a reliable failure detector, care is required to allow for failures at any point (including during a recovery procedure), and to reconstruct the state of the processes after a failure has been detected. For example, in the central-server algorithm, if the server fails then it must be established whether it held the token or whether one of the client processes held the token.

We examine the general problem of how processes should coordinate their actions in the presence of faults in Section 12.5.

12.3 Elections

An algorithm for choosing a unique process to play a particular role is called an *election algorithm*. For example, in a variant of our 'central-server' algorithm for mutual exclusion, the 'server' is chosen from among the processes p_i, $i = 1, 2..., N$ that need to use the critical section. An election algorithm is needed to choose which of the processes will play the role of server. It is essential that all the processes agree on the choice. Afterwards, if the process that plays the role of server wishes to retire, then another election is required to choose a replacement.

We say that a process *calls the election* if it takes an action that initiates a particular run of the election algorithm. An individual process does not call more than one election at a time, but in principle the N processes could call N concurrent elections. At any point in time, a process p_i is either a *participant* – meaning that it is engaged in some run of the election algorithm – or a *non-participant* – meaning that it is not currently engaged in any election.

An important requirement is for the choice of elected process to be unique, even if several processes call elections concurrently. For example, two processes could decide independently that a coordinator process has failed, and both call elections.

Without loss of generality, we require that the elected process be chosen as the one with the largest identifier. The 'identifier' may be any useful value, as long as the identifiers are unique and totally ordered. For example, we could elect the process with the lowest computational load, by having each process use $<1/load, i>$ as its identifier, where $load > 0$ and the process index i is used to order identifiers with the same load.

Each process p_i $(i = 1, 2..., N)$ has a variable $elected_i$, which will contain the identifier of the elected process. When the process first becomes a participant in an election it sets this variable to the special value '$\perp$' to denote that it is not yet defined.

Our requirements are that, during any particular run of the algorithm:

E1: (safety)	A participant process p_i has $elected_i = \perp$ or $elected_i = P$, where P is chosen as the non-crashed process at the end of the run with the largest identifier.
E2: (liveness)	All processes p_i participate and eventually set $elected_i \neq \perp$ – or crash.

Note that there may be processes p_j that are not yet participants, which record in $elected_j$ the identifier of the previous elected process.

We measure the performance of an election algorithm by its total network bandwidth utilization (which is proportional to the total number of messages sent), and by the *turnaround time* for the algorithm: the number of serialized message transmission times between the initiation and termination of a single run.

A ring-based election algorithm ◊ We give the algorithm of Chang and Roberts [1979], which is suitable for a collection of processes arranged in a logical ring. Each process p_i has a communication channel to the next process in the ring, $p_{(i+1) mod N}$, and all messages are sent clockwise around the ring. We assume that no failures occur, and that the system is asynchronous. The goal of this algorithm is to elect a single process called the *coordinator*, which is the process with the largest identifier.

Initially, every process is marked as a *non-participant* in an election. Any process can begin an election. It proceeds by marking itself as a *participant*, placing its identifier in an *election* message and sending it to its clockwise neighbour.

When a process receives an *election* message, it compares the identifier in the message with its own. If the arrived identifier is the greater, then it forwards the message to its neighbour. If the arrived identifier is smaller and the receiver is not a *participant* then it substitutes its own identifier in the message and forwards it; but it does not

Figure 12.7   A ring-based election in progress

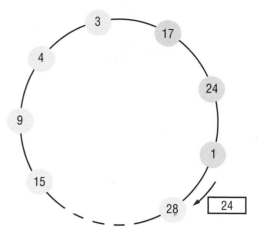

Note: The election was started by process 17. The highest process identifier encountered so far is 24. Participant processes are shown in a darker blue tint.

forward the message if it is already a *participant*. On forwarding an *election* message in any case, the process marks itself as a *participant*.

If, however, the received identifier is that of the receiver itself, then this process's identifier must be the greatest, and it becomes the coordinator. The coordinator marks itself as a *non-participant* once more and sends an *elected* message to its neighbour, announcing its election and enclosing its identity.

When a process p_i receives an *elected* message, it marks itself as a *non-participant*, sets its variable *elected$_i$* to the identifier in the message and, unless it is the new coordinator, forwards the message to its neighbour.

It is easy to see that condition E1 is met. All identifiers are compared, since a process must receive its own identifier back before sending an *elected* message. For any two processes, the one with the larger identifier will not pass on the other's identifier. It is therefore impossible that both should receive their own identifier back.

Condition E2 follows immediately from the guaranteed traversals of the ring (there are no failures). Note how the *non-participant* and *participant* states are used so that messages arising when another process starts an election at the same time are extinguished as soon as possible, and always before the 'winning' election result has been announced.

If only a single process starts an election, then the worst-performing case is when its anti-clockwise neighbour has the highest identifier. A total of $N - 1$ messages is then required to reach this neighbour, which will not announce its election until its identifier has completed another circuit, taking a further N messages. The *elected* message is then sent N times, making $3N - 1$ messages in all. The turnaround time is also $3N - 1$, since these messages are sent sequentially.

Figure 12.8   The bully algorithm

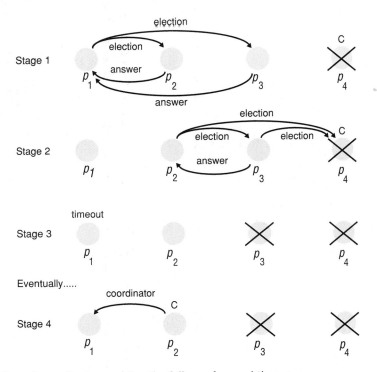

The election of coordinator p_2, after the failure of p_4 and then p_3

An example of a ring-based election in progress is shown in Figure 12.7. The *election* message currently contains 24, but process 28 will replace this with its identifier when the message reaches it.

While the ring-based algorithm is useful for understanding the properties of election algorithms in general, the fact that it tolerates no failures makes it of limited practical value. However, with a reliable failure detector it is in principle possible to re-constitute the ring when a process crashes.

The bully algorithm ◊ The bully algorithm [Garcia-Molina 1982] allows processes to crash during an election, although it assumes that message delivery between processes is reliable. Unlike the ring-based algorithm, this algorithm assumes that the system is synchronous: it uses timeouts to detect a process failure. Another difference is that the ring-based algorithm assumed that processes have minimal *a priori* knowledge of one another: each knows only how to communicate with its neighbour, and none knows the identifiers of the other processes. The bully algorithm, on the other hand, assumes that each process knows which processes have higher identifiers, and that it can communicate with all such processes.

There are three types of message in this algorithm. An *election* message is sent to announce an election; an *answer* message is sent in response to an election message; and a *coordinator* message is sent to announce the identity of the elected process – the new 'coordinator'. A process begins an election when it notices, through timeouts, that the coordinator has failed. Several processes may discover this concurrently.

Since the system is synchronous, we can construct a reliable failure detector. There is a maximum message transmission delay T_{trans} and a maximum delay $T_{process}$ for processing a message. Therefore, we can calculate a time $T = 2T_{trans} + T_{process}$ which is an upper bound on the total elapsed time from sending a message to another process to receiving a response. If no response arrives within time T, then the local failure detector can report that the intended recipient of the request has failed.

The process that knows it has the highest identifier can elect itself as the coordinator simply by sending a *coordinator* message to all processes with lower identifiers. On the other hand, a process with a lower identifier begins an election by sending an *election* message to those processes that have a higher identifier and awaits an *answer* message in response. If none arrives within time T, the process considers itself the coordinator and sends a *coordinator* message to all processes with lower identifiers announcing this. Otherwise, the process waits a further period T' for a *coordinator* message to arrive from the new coordinator. If none arrives, it begins another election.

If a process p_i receives a *coordinator* message, it sets its variable $elected_i$ to the identifier of the coordinator contained within it and treats that process as the coordinator.

If a process receives an *election* message, it sends back an *answer* message and begins another election – unless it has begun one already.

When a process is started to replace a crashed process, it begins an election. If it has the highest process identifier, then it will decide that it is the coordinator and announce this to the other processes. Thus it will become the coordinator, even though the current coordinator is functioning. It is for this reason that the algorithm is called the 'bully' algorithm.

The operation of the algorithm is shown in Figure 12.8. There are four processes p_1–p_4. Process p_1 detects the failure of the coordinator p_4, and announces an election (stage 1 in the figure). On receiving an *election* message from p_1, processes p_2 and p_3 send *answer* messages to p_1 and begin their own elections; p_3 sends an *answer* message to p_2, but p_3 receives no *answer* message from the failed process p_4 (stage 2). It therefore decides that it is the coordinator. But before it can send out the *coordinator* message, it too fails (stage 3). When p_1's timeout period T' expires (which we assume occurs before p_2's timeout expires), it deduces the absence of a *coordinator* message and begins another election. Eventually, p_2 is elected coordinator (stage 4).

This algorithm clearly meets the liveness condition E2, by the assumption of reliable message delivery. And if no process is replaced, then the algorithm meets condition E1. It is impossible for two processes to decide that they are the coordinator, since the process with the lower identifier will discover that the other exists and defer to it.

But the algorithm is *not* guaranteed to meet the safety condition E1 if processes that have crashed are replaced by processes with the same identifier. A process that replaces a crashed process p may decide that it has the highest identifier just as another process (which has detected p's crash) has decided that it has the highest identifier. Two processes will announce themselves as the coordinator concurrently. Unfortunately, there are no guarantees on message delivery order, and the recipients of these messages may reach different conclusions on which is the coordinator process.

Furthermore, condition E1 may be broken if the assumed timeout values turn out to be inaccurate – that is, if the processes' failure detector is unreliable.

Taking the example just given, suppose that p_3 either had not failed but was running unusually slowly (that is, the assumption that the system is synchronous is incorrect) or that p_3 had failed but is then replaced. Just as p_2 sends its *coordinator* message, p_3 (or its replacement) does the same. p_2 receives p_3's *coordinator* message after it sent its own and so sets $elected_2 = p_3$. Due to variable message transmission delays, p_1 receives p_2's *coordinator* message after p_3's and so eventually sets $elected_1 = p_2$. Condition E1 has been broken.

With regard to the performance of the algorithm, in the best case the process with the second highest identifier notices the coordinator's failure. Then it can immediately elect itself and send $N-2$ coordinator messages. The turnaround time is one message. The bully algorithm requires $O(N^2)$ messages in the worst case – that is, when the process with the least identifier first detects the coordinator's failure. For then $N-1$ processes altogether begin elections, each sending messages to processes with higher identifiers.

12.4 Multicast communication

Section 4.5.1 described IP multicast, which is an implementation of group communication. Group, or multicast, communication requires coordination and agreement. The aim is for each of a group of processes to receive copies of the messages sent to the group, often with delivery guarantees. The guarantees include agreement on the set of messages that every process in the group should receive and on the delivery ordering across the group members.

Group communication systems are extremely sophisticated. Even IP multicast, which provides minimal delivery guarantees, requires a major engineering effort. Time and bandwidth efficiency are important concerns, and are challenging even for static groups of processes. The problems are multiplied when processes can join and leave groups at arbitrary times.

Here we study multicast communication to groups of processes whose membership is known. Chapter 15 will expand our study to fully fledged group communication, including the management of dynamically varying groups.

Multicast communication has been the subject of many projects, including the V-system [Cheriton and Zwaenepoel 1985], Chorus [Rozier *et al.* 1988], Amoeba [Kaashoek *et al.* 1989, Kaashoek and Tanenbaum 1991], Trans/Total [Melliar-Smith *et al.* 1990], Delta-4 [Powell 1991], Isis [Birman 1993], Horus [van Renesse *et al.* 1996], Totem [Moser *et al.* 1996] and Transis [Dolev and Malki 1996] – and we shall cite other notable work in the course of this section.

The essential feature of multicast communication is that a process issues only one *multicast* operation to send a message to each of a group of processes (in Java this operation is *aSocket.send(aMessage)*) instead of issuing multiple *send* operations to individual processes. Communication to *all* processes in the system, as opposed to a sub-group of them, is known as *broadcast*.

The use of a single *multicast* operation instead of multiple *send* operations amounts to much more than a convenience for the programmer. It enables the implementation to be efficient and allows it to provide stronger delivery guarantees than would otherwise be possible.

Efficiency: The information that the same message is to be delivered to all processes in a group allows the implementation to be efficient in its utilization of bandwidth. It can take steps to send the message no more than once over any communication link, by sending the message over a distribution tree; and it can use network hardware support for multicast where this is available. The implementation can also minimize the total time taken to deliver the message to all destinations, instead of transmitting it separately and serially.

To see these advantages, compare the bandwidth utilization and the total transmission time taken when sending the same message from a computer in London to two computers on the same Ethernet in Palo Alto, (a) by two separate UDP sends, and (b) by a single IP-multicast operation. In the former case, two copies of the messages are sent independently, and the second is delayed by the first. In the latter case, a set of multicast-aware routers forward a single copy of the message from London to a router on the destination LAN. The final router then uses hardware multicast (provided by the Ethernet) to deliver the message to the destinations, instead of sending it twice.

Delivery guarantees: If a process issues multiple independent *send* operations to individual processes, then there is no way for the implementation to provide delivery guarantees that affect the group of processes as a whole. If the sender fails half-way through sending, then some members of the group may receive the message while others do not. And the relative ordering of two messages delivered to any two group members is undefined. In the particular case of IP multicast, no ordering or reliability guarantees are in fact offered. But stronger multicast guarantees can be made, and we shall shortly define some.

System model ◊   The system contains a collection of processes, which can communicate reliably over one-to-one channels. As before, processes may fail only by crashing.

The processes are members of groups, which are the destinations of messages sent with the *multicast* operation. It is generally useful to allow processes to be members of several groups simultaneously – for example, to enable processes to receive information from several sources by joining several groups. But to simplify our discussion of ordering properties, we shall sometimes restrict processes to being members of at most one group at a time.

The operation *multicast*(g, m) sends the message m to all members of the group g of processes. Correspondingly, there is an operation *deliver*(m) that delivers a message sent by multicast to the calling process. We use the term *deliver* rather than *receive* to make clear that a multicast message is not always handed to the application layer inside the process as soon as it is received at the process's node. This is explained when we discuss multicast delivery semantics shortly.

Every message m carries the unique identifier of the process *sender*(m) that sent it, and the unique destination group identifier *group*(m). We assume that processes do not lie about the origin or destinations of messages.

Figure 12.9   Open and closed groups

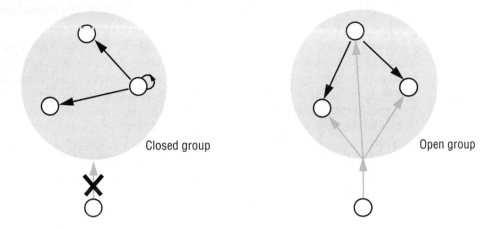

Closed group   Open group

A group is said to be *closed* if only members of the group may multicast to it (Figure 12.9). A process in a closed group delivers to itself any message that it multicasts to the group. A group is *open* if processes outside the group may send to it. (The categories 'open' and 'closed' also apply with analogous meanings to mailing lists.) Closed groups of processes are useful, for example, for cooperating servers to send messages to one another that only they should receive. Open groups are useful, for example, for delivering events to groups of interested processes.

Some algorithms assume that groups are closed. The same effect as openness can be achieved with a closed group by picking a member of the group and sending it a message (one-to-one) for it to multicast to its group. Rodrigues *et al.* [1998] discuss multicast to open groups.

12.4.1 Basic multicast

It is useful to have at our disposal a basic multicast primitive that guarantees, unlike IP multicast, that a correct process will eventually deliver the message, as long as the multicaster does not crash. We call the primitive *B-multicast* and its corresponding basic delivery primitive is *B-deliver*. We allow processes to belong to several groups, and each message is destined for some particular group.

A straightforward way to implement *B-multicast* is to use a reliable one-to-one *send* operation, as follows:

To *B-multicast*(g, m): for each process $p \in g$, *send*(p, m);

On *receive*(m) at p: *B-deliver*(m) at p.

The implementation may use threads to perform the *send* operations concurrently, in an attempt to reduce the total time taken to deliver the message. Unfortunately, such an implementation is liable to suffer from a so-called *ack-implosion* if the number of processes is large. The acknowledgments sent as part of the reliable *send* operation are liable to arrive from many processes at about the same time. The multicasting process's buffers will rapidly fill and it is liable to drop acknowledgments. It will therefore retransmit the message, leading to yet more acknowledgments and further waste of network bandwidth. A more practical basic multicast service can be built using IP multicast, and we invite the reader to show this.

12.4.2 Reliable multicast

Section 2.3.2 defined reliable one-to-one communication channels between pairs of processes. The required safety property is called *integrity* – that any message delivered is identical to one that was sent, and that no message is delivered twice. The required liveness property is called *validity*: that any message is eventually delivered to the destination, if it is correct.

Following Hadzilacos and Toueg [1994] and Chandra and Toueg [1996], we now define a *reliable multicast*, with corresponding operations *R-multicast* and *R-deliver*. Properties analogous to integrity and validity are clearly highly desirable in reliable multicast delivery. But we add another: a requirement that *all* correct processes in the group must receive a message if *any* of them does. It is important to realize that this is not a property of the *B-multicast* algorithm that is based on a reliable one-to-one send operation. The sender may fail at any point while *B-multicast* proceeds, so some processes may deliver a message while others do not.

A reliable multicast is one that satisfies the following properties; we explain the properties after stating them.

Integrity: A correct process p delivers a message m at most once. Furthermore, $p \in group(m)$ and m was supplied to a *multicast* operation by *sender(m)*. (As with one-to-one communication, messages can always be distinguished by a sequence number relative to their sender.)

Validity: If a correct process multicasts message m then it will eventually deliver m.

Agreement: If a correct process delivers message m, then all other correct processes in $group(m)$ will eventually deliver m.

The integrity property is analogous to that for reliable one-to-one communication. The validity property guarantees liveness for the sender. This may seem an unusual property, because it is asymmetric (it mentions only one particular process). But notice that validity and agreement together amount to an overall liveness requirement: if one process (the sender) eventually delivers a message m then, since the correct processes agree on the set of messages they deliver, it follows that m will eventually be delivered to all the group's correct members.

The advantage of expressing the validity condition in terms of self-delivery is simplicity. What we require is that the message be delivered eventually by *some* correct member of the group.

The agreement condition is related to atomicity, the property of 'all or nothing', applied to delivery of messages to a group. If a process that multicasts a message crashes before it has delivered it, then it is possible that the message will not be delivered to any process in the group; but if it is delivered to some correct process, then all other correct processes will deliver it. Many papers in the literature use the term 'atomic' to include a total ordering condition; we define this shortly.

Figure 12.10 Reliable multicast algorithm

On initialization
    Received := { };

For process p to R-multicast message m to group g
    B-multicast(g, m);   // $p \in g$ is included as a destination

On B-deliver(m) at process q with g = group(m)
    if (m ∉ Received)
    then
                Received := Received ∪ {m};
                if (q ≠ p) then B-multicast(g, m); end if
                R-deliver m;
    end if

Implementing reliable multicast over B-multicast ◊ Figure 12.10 gives a reliable multicast algorithm, with primitives *R-multicast* and *R-deliver*, which allows processes to belong to several closed groups simultaneously. To *R-multicast* a message, a process *B-multicast*s the message to the processes in the destination group (including itself). When the message is *B-deliver*ed, the recipient in turn *B-multicast*s the message to the group (if it is not the original sender), and then *R-deliver*s the message. Since a message may arrive more than once, duplicates of the message are detected and not delivered.

This algorithm clearly satisfies validity, since a correct process will eventually *B-deliver* the message to itself. By the integrity property of the underlying communication channels used in *B-multicast*, the algorithm also satisfies the integrity property.

Agreement follows from the fact that every correct process *B-multicast*s the message to the other processes after it has *B-deliver*ed it. If a correct process does not *R-deliver* the message, then this can only be because it never *B-deliver*ed it. That in turn can only be because no other correct process *B-deliver*ed it either; therefore, none will *R-deliver* it.

The reliable multicast algorithm that we have described is correct in an asynchronous system, since we made no timing assumptions. But the algorithm is inefficient for practical purposes. Each message is sent $|g|$ times to each process.

Reliable multicast over IP multicast ◊ An alternative realization of *R-multicast* is to use a combination of IP multicast, piggy backed acknowledgments (that is, acknowledgements attached to other messages), and negative acknowledgments. This *R-multicast* protocol is based on the observation that IP multicast communication is often successful. In the protocol, processes do not send separate acknowledgment messages; instead, they piggy back acknowledgments on the messages that they send to the group. Processes send a separate response message only when they detect that they have missed a message. A response indicating the absence of an expected message is known as a *negative acknowledgement*.

The description assumes that groups are closed. Each process p maintains a sequence number S_g^p for each group g to which it belongs. The sequence number is initially zero. Each process also records R_g^q, the sequence number of the latest message it has delivered from process q that was sent to group g.

Figure 12.11   The hold-back queue for arriving multicast messages

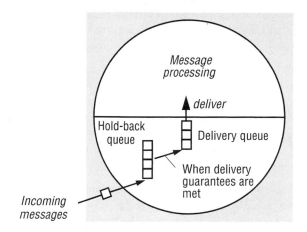

For p to *R-multicast* a message to group g, it piggy backs onto the message the value S_g^p and acknowledgments, of the form $<q, R_g^q>$. An acknowledgement states, for some sender q, the sequence number of the latest message from q destined for g that p has delivered since it last multicast a message. The multicaster p then IP-multicasts the message with its piggy backed values to g, and increments S_g^p by one.

The piggy backed values in a multicast message enable the recipients to learn about messages that they have not received. A process *R-delivers* a message destined for g bearing the sequence number S from p if and only if $S = R_g^p + 1$, and it increments R_g^p by one immediately after delivery. If an arriving message has $S \le R_g^p$, then r has delivered the message before and it discards it. If $S > R_g^p + 1$, or if $R > R_g^q$ for an enclosed acknowledgement $<q, R>$, then there are one or more messages that it has not yet received (and which are likely to have been dropped, in the first case). It keeps any message for which $S > R_g^p + 1$ in a *hold-back queue* (Figure 12.11) – such queues are often used to meet message delivery guarantees. It requests missing messages by sending negative acknowledgements – to the original sender or to a process q from which it has received an acknowledgement $<q, R_g^q>$ with R_g^q no less than the required sequence number.

The hold-back queue is not strictly necessary for reliability but it simplifies the protocol by enabling us to use sequence numbers to represent sets of delivered messages. It also provides us with a guarantee of delivery order (see Section 11.4.3).

The integrity property follows from the detection of duplicates and the underlying properties of IP multicast (which uses checksums to expunge corrupted messages). The validity property holds because IP multicast has that property. For agreement we require, first, that a process can always detect missing messages. That in turn means that it will always receive a further message that enables it to detect the omission. As this simplified protocol stands, we guarantee detection of missing messages only in the case where correct processes multicast messages indefinitely. Second, the agreement property requires that there is always an available copy of any message needed by a process that did not receive it. We therefore assume that processes retain copies of the messages they have delivered – indefinitely, in this simplified protocol.

Neither of the assumptions we made to ensure agreement is practical (see Exercise 11.14). However, agreement is practically addressed in the protocols from which ours is derived: the Psync protocol [Peterson *et al.* 1989], Trans protocol [Melliar-Smith *et al.* 1990] and scalable reliable multicast protocol [Floyd *et al.* 1997]. Psync and Trans also provide further delivery ordering guarantees.

Uniform properties ◊ The definition of agreement given above refers only to the behaviour of *correct* processes – processes that never fail. Consider what would happen in the algorithm of Figure 12.10 if a process is not correct and crashed after it had *R-deliver*ed a message. Since any process that *R-delivers* the message must first *B-multicast* it, it follows that all correct processes will still eventually deliver the message.

Any property that holds whether or not processes are correct is called a *uniform* property. We define uniform agreement as follows:

> *Uniform agreement*: If a process, whether it is correct or fails, delivers message *m*, then all correct processes in *group(m)* will eventually deliver *m*.

Uniform agreement allows a process to crash after it has delivered a message, while still ensuring that all correct processes will deliver the message. We have argued that the algorithm of Figure 12.10 satisfies this property, which is stronger than the non-uniform agreement property defined above.

Uniform agreement is useful in applications where a process may take an action that produces an observable inconsistency before it crashes. For example, consider that the processes are servers that manage copies of a bank account, and that updates to the account are sent using reliable multicast to the group of servers. If the multicast does not satisfy uniform agreement, then a client that accesses a server just before it crashes may observe an update that no other server will process.

It is interesting to note that if we reverse the lines '*R-deliver m*' and '*if (q ≠ p) then B-multicast(g, m); end if*' in Figure 12.10, then the resultant algorithm does not satisfy uniform agreement.

Just as there is a uniform version of agreement, there are also uniform versions of any multicast property, including validity and integrity and the ordering properties that we are about to define.

12.4.3 Ordered multicast

The basic multicast algorithm of Section 12.4.1 delivers messages to processes in an arbitrary order, due to arbitrary delays in the underlying one-to-one send operations. This lack of an ordering guarantee is not satisfactory for many applications. For example, in a nuclear power plant it may be important that events signifying threats to safety conditions and events signifying actions by control units are observed in the same order by all processes in the system.

The common ordering requirements are total ordering, causal ordering, FIFO ordering and the hybrids total-causal and total-FIFO. To simplify our discussion, we define these orderings under the assumption that any process belongs to at most one group. We shall later discuss the implications of allowing groups to overlap.

> *FIFO ordering*: If a correct process issues *multicast(g, m)* and then *multicast(g, m′)*, then every correct process that delivers *m′* will deliver *m* before *m′*.

Figure 12.12   Total, FIFO and causal ordering of multicast messages

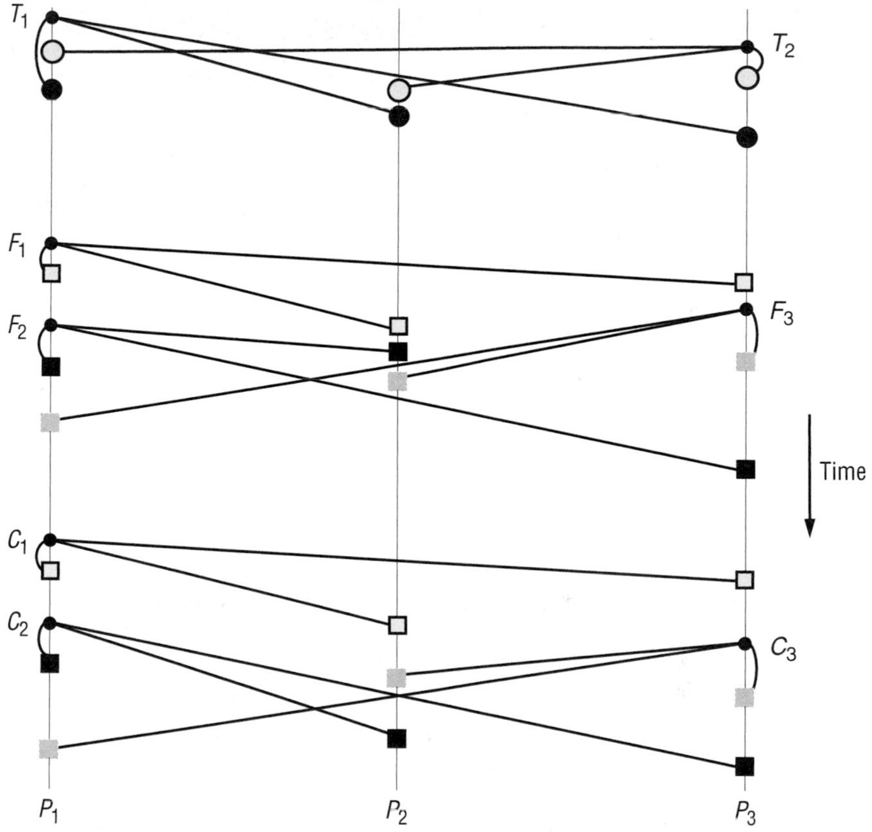

Notice the consistent ordering of totally ordered messages T_1 and T_2, the FIFO-related messages F_1 and F_2 and the causally related messages C_1 and C_3 – and the otherwise arbitrary delivery ordering of messages

Causal ordering: If $multicast(g, m) \rightarrow multicast(g, m')$, where $\rightarrow$ is the happened-before relation induced only by messages sent between the members of g, then any correct process that delivers m' will deliver m before m'.

Total ordering: If a correct process delivers message m before it delivers m', then any other correct process that delivers m' will deliver m before m'.

Causal ordering implies FIFO ordering, since any two multicasts by the same process are related by happened-before. Note that FIFO ordering and causal ordering are only partial orderings: not all messages are sent by the same process, in general; similarly, some multicasts are concurrent (not ordered by happened-before).

Figure 12.12 illustrates the orderings for the case of three processes. Close inspection of the figure shows that the totally ordered messages are delivered in the opposite order to the physical time at which they were sent. In fact, the definition of total

Figure 12.13   Display from bulletin board program

Bulletin board: *os.interesting*		
Item	From	Subject
23	A.Hanlon	Mach
24	G.Joseph	Microkernels
25	A.Hanlon	Re: Microkernels
26	T.L'Heureux	RPC performance
27	M.Walker	Re: Mach
end		

ordering allows message delivery to be ordered arbitrarily, as long as the order is the same at different processes. Since total ordering is not necessarily also a FIFO or causal ordering, we define the hybrid of *FIFO-total* ordering as one for which message delivery obeys both FIFO and total ordering; similarly, under *causal-total* ordering message delivery obeys both causal and total ordering.

The definitions of ordered multicast do not assume or imply reliability. For example, the reader should check that, under total ordering, if correct process p delivers message m and then delivers m', then a correct process q can deliver m without also delivering m' or any other message ordered after m.

We can also form hybrids of ordered and reliable protocols. A reliable totally ordered multicast is often referred to in the literature as an *atomic multicast*. Similarly, we may form reliable FIFO multicast, reliable causal multicast and reliable versions of the hybrid ordered multicasts.

Ordering the delivery of multicast messages, as we shall see, can be expensive in terms of delivery latency and bandwidth consumption. The ordering semantics that we have described may delay the delivery of messages unnecessarily. That is, at the application level, a message may be delayed for another message that it does not in fact depend upon. For this reason, some have proposed multicast systems that use the application-specific message semantics alone to determine the order of message delivery [Cheriton and Skeen 1993, Pedone and Schiper 1999].

The example of the bulletin board ◊ To make multicast delivery semantics more concrete, consider an application in which users post messages to bulletin boards. Each user runs a bulletin-board application process. Every topic of discussion has its own process group. When a user posts a message to a bulletin board, the application multicasts the user's posting to the corresponding group. Each user's process is a member of the group for the topic in which he or she is interested, so that the user will receive just the postings concerning that topic.

Reliable multicast is required if every user is to receive every posting eventually. The users also have ordering requirements. Figure 12.13 shows the postings as they appear to a particular user. At a minimum, FIFO ordering is desirable, since then every posting from a given user – 'A.Hanlon', say – will be received in the same order, and users can talk consistently about A.Hanlon's second posting.

Note that the message whose subjects are 'Re: Microkernels' (25) and 'Re: Mach' (27) appear after the messages to which they refer. A causally ordered multicast is needed to guarantee this relationship. Otherwise, arbitrary message delays could mean that, say, a message 'Re: Mach' could appear before the original message about Mach.

If the multicast delivery was totally ordered, then the numbering in the left-hand column would be consistent between users. Users could refer unambiguously, for example, to 'message 24'.

In practice, the USENET bulletin board system implements neither causal nor total ordering. The communication costs of achieving these orderings on a large scale outweighs their advantages.

Implementing FIFO ordering ◊ FIFO-ordered multicast (with operations *FO-multicast* and *FO-deliver*) is achieved with sequence numbers, much as we would achieve it for one-to-one communication. We shall consider only non-overlapping groups. The reader should verify that the reliable multicast protocol that we defined on top of IP multicast in Section 12.4.2 also guarantees FIFO ordering, but we shall show how to construct a FIFO-ordered multicast on top of any given basic multicast. We use the variables S_g^p and R_g^q held at process p from the reliable multicast protocol of Section 12.4.2: S_g^p is a count of how many messages p has sent to g and, for each q, R_g^q is the sequence number of the latest message p has delivered from process q that was sent to group g.

For p to *FO-multicast* a message to group g, it piggy backs the value S_g^p onto the message, *B-multicast*s the message to g and then increments S_g^p by 1. Upon receipt of a message from q bearing the sequence number S, p checks whether $S = R_g^q + 1$. If so, this message is the next one expected from the sender q and p *FO-deliver*s it, setting $R_g^q := S$. If $S > R_g^q + 1$, it places the message in the hold-back queue until the intervening messages have been delivered and $S = R_g^q + 1$.

Since all messages from a given sender are delivered in the same sequence, and since a message's delivery is delayed until its sequence number has been reached, the condition for FIFO ordering is clearly satisfied. But this is so only under the assumption that groups are non-overlapping.

Note that we can use any implementation of *B-multicast* in this protocol. Moreover, if we use a reliable *R-multicast* primitive instead of *B-multicast*, then we obtain a reliable FIFO multicast.

Implementing total ordering ◊ The basic approach to implementing total ordering is to assign totally ordered identifiers to multicast messages so that each process makes the same ordering decision based upon these identifiers. The delivery algorithm is very similar to the one we described for FIFO ordering; the difference is that processes keep group-specific sequence numbers rather than process-specific sequence numbers. We only consider how to totally order messages sent to non-overlapping groups. We call the multicast operations *TO-multicast* and *TO-deliver*.

We discuss two main methods for assigning identifiers to messages. The first of these is for a process called a *sequencer* to assign them (Figure 12.14). A process wishing to *TO-multicast* a message m to group g attaches a unique identifier $id(m)$ to it. The messages for g are sent to the sequencer for g, *sequencer*(g), as well as to the members of g. (The sequencer may be chosen to be a member of g.) The process *sequencer*(g) maintains a group-specific sequence number s_g, which it uses to assign increasing and consecutive sequence numbers to the messages that it *B-delivers*. It

Figure 12.14   Total ordering using a sequencer

1. Algorithm for group member p

On initialization: $r_g := 0$,

To TO-multicast message m to group g
    $B\text{-}multicast(g \cup \{sequencer(g)\}, <m, i>)$;

On B-deliver(<m, i>) with g = group(m)
    Place $<m, i>$ in hold-back queue;

On B-deliver(m_{order} = <"order", i, S>) with g = group(m_{order})
    wait until $<m, i>$ in hold-back queue and $S = r_g$;
    TO-deliver m;   // (after deleting it from the hold-back queue)
    $r_g := S + 1$;

2. Algorithm for sequencer of g

On initialization: $s_g := 0$;

On B-deliver(<m, i>) with g = group(m)
    $B\text{-}multicast(g, <"order", i, s_g>)$;
    $s_g := s_g + 1$;

---

announces the sequence numbers by *B-multicast*ing *order* messages to g (see Figure 12.14 for the details).

A message will remain in the hold-back queue indefinitely until it can be *TO-deliver*ed according to the corresponding sequence number. Since the sequence numbers are well defined (by the sequencer), the criterion for total ordering is met. Furthermore, if the processes use a FIFO-ordered variant of *B-multicast*, then the totally ordered multicast is also causally ordered. We leave the reader to show this.

The obvious problem with a sequencer-based scheme is that the sequencer may become a bottleneck and is a critical point of failure. Practical algorithms exist that address the problem of failure. Chang and Maxemchuk [1984] first suggested a multicast protocol employing a sequencer (which they called a *token site*). Kaashoek *et al.* [1989] developed a sequencer-based protocol for the Amoeba system. These protocols ensure that a message is in the hold-back queue at $f + 1$ nodes before it is delivered; up to f failures can thus be tolerated. Like Chang and Maxemchuk, Birman *et al.* [1991] also employ a token-holding site that acts as a sequencer. The token can be passed from process to process so that, for example, if only one process sends totally-ordered multicasts then that process can act as the sequencer, saving communication.

The protocol of Kaashoek *et al.* uses hardware-based multicast – available on an Ethernet, for example – rather than reliable point-to-point communication. In the simplest variant of their protocol, processes send the message to be multicast to the sequencer, one-to-one. The sequencer multicasts the message itself, as well as the identifier and sequence number. This has the advantage that the other members of the

Figure 12.15   The ISIS algorithm for total ordering

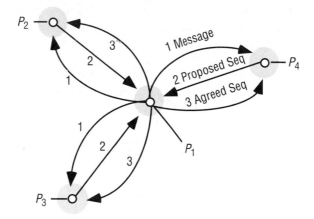

group receive only one message per multicast; its disadvantage is increased bandwidth utilization. The protocol is described in full at www.cdk4.net/coordination.

The second method that we examine for achieving totally ordered multicast is one in which the processes collectively agree on the assignment of sequence numbers to messages in a distributed fashion. A simple algorithm – similar to one that was originally developed to implement totally ordered multicast delivery for the ISIS toolkit [Birman and Joseph 1987a] – is shown in Figure 12.15. Once more, a process *B-multicasts* its message to the members of the group. The group may be open or closed. The receiving processes propose sequence numbers for messages as they arrive and return these to the sender, which uses them to generate *agreed* sequence numbers.

Each process q in group g keeps A_g^q, the largest agreed sequence number it has observed so far for group g, and P_g^q, its own largest proposed sequence number. The algorithm for process p to multicast a message m to group g is as follows:

1. p *B-multicasts* $<m, i>$ to g, where i is a unique identifier for m.

2. Each process q replies to the sender p with a proposal for the message's agreed sequence number of $P_g^q := Max(A_g^q, P_g^q) + 1$. In reality, we must include process identifiers in the proposed values P_g^q to ensure a total order, since otherwise different processes could propose the same integer value; but for the sake of simplicity we shall not make that explicit here. Each process provisionally assigns the proposed sequence number to the message and places it in its hold-back queue, which is ordered with the *smallest* sequence number at the front.

3. p collects all the proposed sequence numbers and selects the largest one a as the next agreed sequence number. It then *B-multicasts* $<i, a>$ to g. Each process q in g sets $A_g^q := Max(A_g^q, a)$ and attaches a to the message (which is identified by i). It reorders the message in the hold-back queue if the agreed sequence number differs from the proposed one. When the message at the front of the hold-back queue has been assigned its agreed sequence number, it is transferred to the tail of the delivery queue. Messages that have been assigned their agreed sequence

number but are not at the head of the hold-back queue are not yet transferred, however.

If every process agrees the same set of sequence numbers and delivers them in the corresponding order, then total ordering is satisfied. It is clear that correct processes ultimately agree on the same set of sequence numbers, but we must show that they are monotonically increasing and that no correct process can deliver a message prematurely.

Assume that a message m_1 has been assigned an agreed sequence number and has reached the front of the hold-back queue. By construction, a message that is received after this stage will and should be delivered after m_1: it will have a larger proposed sequence number and thus a larger agreed sequence number than m_1. So let m_2 be any other message that has not yet been assigned its agreed sequence number but which is on the same queue. We have that:

$$agreedSequence(m_2) \geq proposedSequence(m_2)$$

by the algorithm just given. Since m_1 is at the front of the queue:

$$proposedSequence(m_2) > agreedSequence(m_1)$$

Therefore:

$$agreedSequence(m_2) > agreedSequence(m_1)$$

and total ordering is assured.

This algorithm has higher latency than the sequencer-based multicast: three messages are sent serially between the sender and the group before a message can be delivered.

Note that the total ordering chosen by this algorithm is not also guaranteed to be causally or FIFO-ordered: any two messages are delivered in an essentially arbitrary total order, influenced by communication delays.

For other approaches to implementing total ordering, see Melliar-Smith *et al.* [1990], Garcia-Molina and Spauster [1991] and Hadzilacos and Toueg [1994].

Implementing causal ordering ◊ We give an algorithm for non-overlapping closed groups based on that developed by Birman *et al.* [1991], shown in Figure 12.16, in which the causally-ordered multicast operations are *CO-multicast* and *CO-deliver*. The algorithm takes account of the happened-before relationship only as it is established by *multicast* messages. If the processes send one-to-one messages to one another, then these will not be accounted for.

Each process p_i $(i = 1, 2, ..., N)$ maintains its own vector timestamp (see Section 11.4). The entries in the timestamp count the number of multicast messages from each process that happened-before the next message to be multicast.

To *CO-multicast* a message to group g, the process adds 1 to its entry in the timestamp, and *B-multicast*s the message along with its timestamp to g.

When a process p_i *B-deliver*s a message from p_j, it must place it in the hold-back queue before it can *CO-deliver* it: until it is assured that it has delivered any messages that causally preceded it. To establish this, p_i waits until (a) it has delivered any earlier message sent by p_j, and (b) it has delivered any message that p_j had delivered at the

Figure 12.16   Causal ordering using vector timestamps

Algorithm for group member p_i $(i = 1, 2 ..., N)$

On initialization

$$V_i^g[j] := 0 \ (j = 1, 2 ..., N);$$

To CO-multicast message m to group g

$$V_i^g[i] := V_i^g[i] + 1;$$

$$B\text{-}multicast(g, <V_i^g, m>);$$

On B-deliver($<V_j^g, m>$) from p_j ($j \neq i$), with g = group(m)

place $<V_j^g, m>$ in hold-back queue;

wait until $V_j^g[j] = V_i^g[j] + 1$ and $V_j^g[k] \leq V_i^g[k]$ $(k \neq j)$;

CO-deliver m;   // after removing it from the hold-back queue

$$V_i^g[j] := V_i^g[j] + 1 ;$$

time it multicast the message. Both of those conditions can be detected by examining vector timestamps, as shown in Figure 12.16. Note that a process can immediately *CO-deliver* to itself any message that it *CO-multicast*s, although this is not described in Figure 12.16.

Each process updates its vector timestamp upon delivering any message, to maintain the count of causally precedent messages. It does this by incrementing the *j*th entry in its timestamp by one. This is an optimization of the *merge* operation that appears in the rules for updating vector clocks in Section 11.4. We can make the optimization in view of the delivery condition in the algorithm of Figure 12.16, which guarantees that only the *j*th entry will increase.

We outline the proof of the correctness of this algorithm as follows. Suppose that $multicast(g, m) \rightarrow multicast(g, m')$. Let V and V' be the vector timestamps of m and m', respectively. It is straightforward to prove inductively from the algorithm that $V < V'$. In particular, if process p_k multicast m, then $V[k] \leq V'[k]$.

Consider what happens when some correct process p_i *B-delivers* m' (as opposed to *CO-delivering* it) without first *CO-delivering* m. By the algorithm, $V_i[k]$ can increase only when p_i delivers a message from p_k, when it increases by 1. But p_i has not received m, and therefore $V_i[k]$ cannot increase beyond $V[k] - 1$. It is therefore not possible for p_i to *CO-deliver* m', since this would require that $V_i[k] \geq V'[k]$, and therefore that $V_i[k] \geq V[k]$.

The reader should check that if we substitute the reliable *R-multicast* primitive in place of *B-multicast*, then we obtain a multicast that is both reliable and causally ordered.

Furthermore, if we combine the protocol for causal multicast with the sequencer-based protocol for totally ordered delivery, then we obtain message delivery that is both total and causal. The sequencer delivers messages according to the causal order and multicasts the sequence numbers for the messages in the order in which it receives them.

The processes in the destination group do not deliver a message until they have received an *order* message from the sequencer and the message is next in the delivery sequence.

Since the sequencer delivers message in causal order, and since all other processes deliver messages in the same order as the sequencer, the ordering is indeed both total and causal.

Overlapping groups ◊ We have considered only non-overlapping groups in the definitions and algorithms for FIFO, total and causal ordering semantics. This simplifies the problem but it is not satisfactory, since in general processes need to be members of multiple overlapping groups. For example, a process may be interested in events from multiple sources, and thus join a corresponding set of event-distribution groups.

We can extend the ordering definitions to global orders [Hadzilacos and Toueg 1994], in which we have to consider that if message m is multicast to g, and if message m' is multicast to g', then both messages are addressed to the members of $g \cap g'$.

Global FIFO ordering: If a correct process issues *multicast*(g, m) and then *multicast*(g', m'), then every correct process in $g \cap g'$ that delivers m' will deliver m before m'.

Global causal ordering: If *multicast*$(g, m) \rightarrow$ *multicast*(g', m'), where $\rightarrow$ is the happened-before relation induced by any chain of multicast messages, then any correct process in $g \cap g'$ that delivers m' will deliver m before m'.

Pairwise total ordering: If a correct process delivers message m sent to g before it delivers m' sent to g', then any other correct process in $g \cap g'$ that delivers m' will deliver m before m'.

Global total ordering: Let '<' be the relation of ordering between delivery events. We require that '<' obeys pairwise total ordering and that it is acyclic – under pairwise total ordering, '<' is not acyclic by default.

One way of implementing these orders would be to multicast each message m to the group of *all* processes in the system. Each process either discards or delivers the message according to whether it belongs to *group*(m). This would be an inefficient and unsatisfactory implementation: a multicast should involve as few processes as possible beyond the members of the destination group. Alternatives are explored in Birman *et al.* [1991], Garcia-Molina and Spauster [1991], Hadzilacos and Toueg [1994], Kindberg [1995] and Rodrigues *et al.* [1998].

Multicast in synchronous and asynchronous systems ◊ In this section, we have described algorithms for reliable unordered multicast, (reliable) FIFO-ordered multicast, (reliable) causally ordered multicast and totally ordered multicast. We also indicated how to achieve a multicast that is both totally and causally ordered. We leave the reader to devise an algorithm for a multicast primitive that guarantees both FIFO and total ordering. All the algorithms that we have described work correctly in asynchronous systems.

We did not, however, give an algorithm that guarantees both reliable and totally ordered delivery. Surprising though it may seem, while possible in a *synchronous* system, a protocol with these guarantees is *impossible* in an asynchronous distributed system – even one that at worst suffered a single process crash failure. We return to this point in the next section.

12.5 Consensus and related problems

This section introduces the problem of consensus [Pease *et al.* 1980, Lamport *et al.* 1982] and the related problems of byzantine generals and interactive consistency. We shall refer to these collectively as problems of *agreement*. Roughly speaking, the problem is for processes to agree on a value after one or more of the processes has proposed what that value should be.

For example, in Chapter 2 we described a situation in which two armies should decide consistently to attack or retreat. Similarly, we may require that all the correct computers controlling a spaceship's engines should decide 'proceed', or all of them decide 'abort', after each has proposed one action or the other. In a transaction to transfer funds from one account to another, the computers involved must consistently agree to perform the respective debit and credit. In mutual exclusion, the processes agree on which process can enter the critical section. In an election, the processes agree on which is the elected process. In totally ordered multicast, the processes agree on the order of message delivery.

Protocols exist that are tailored to these individual types of agreement. We described some of them above, and Chapters 13 and 14 examine transactions. But it is useful for us to consider more general forms of agreement, in a search for common characteristics and solutions.

This section defines consensus more precisely and relates it to three related agreement problems: byzantine generals, interactive consistency and totally ordered multicast. We go on to examine under what circumstances the problems can be solved, and sketch some solutions. In particular, we shall discuss the well-known impossibility result of Fischer *et al.* [1985], which states that in an asynchronous system a collection of processes containing only one faulty process cannot be guaranteed to reach consensus. Finally, we consider how it is that practical algorithms exist despite the impossibility result.

12.5.1 System model and problem definitions

Our system model includes a collection of processes p_i ($i = 1, 2, ..., N$) communicating by message passing. An important requirement that applies in many practical situations is for consensus to be reached even in the presence of faults. We assume, as before, that communication is reliable but that processes may fail. In this section, we shall consider byzantine (arbitrary) process failures, as well as crash failures. We shall sometimes specify an assumption that up to some number f of the N processes are faulty – that is, they exhibit some specified types of fault; the remainder of the processes are correct.

If arbitrary failures can occur, then another factor in specifying our system is whether the processes digitally sign the messages that they send (see Section 7.4). If processes sign their messages, then a faulty process is limited in the harm it can do. Specifically, during an agreement algorithm it cannot make a false claim about the values that a correct process has sent to it. The relevance of message signing will become clearer when we discuss solutions to the byzantine generals problem. By default, we assume that signing does not take place.

Figure 12.17 Consensus for three processes

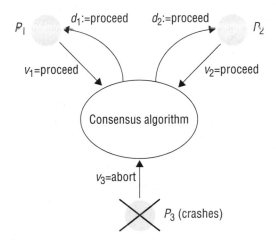

Definition of the consensus problem ◊ To reach consensus, every process p_i begins in the *undecided* state and *proposes* a single value v_i, drawn from a set D ($i = 1, 2, ..., N$). The processes communicate with one another, exchanging values. Each process then sets the value of a *decision variable* d_i. In doing so it enters the *decided* state, in which it may no longer change d_i ($i = 1, 2, ..., N$). Figure 12.17 shows three processes engaged in a consensus algorithm. Two processes propose 'proceed' and a third proposes 'abort' but then crashes. The two processes that remain correct each decide 'proceed'.

The requirements of a consensus algorithm are that the following conditions should hold for every execution of it:

Termination: Eventually each correct process sets its decision variable.

Agreement: The decision value of all correct processes is the same: if p_i and p_j are correct and have entered the *decided* state, then $d_i = d_j$ ($i, j = 1, 2, ..., N$).

Integrity: If the correct processes all proposed the same value, then any correct process in the *decided* state has chosen that value.

Variations on the definition of integrity may be appropriate, according to the application. For example, a weaker type of integrity would be for the decision value to equal a value that some correct process proposed – not necessarily all of them. We shall use the definition stated above.

To help in understanding how the formulation of the problem translates into an algorithm, consider a system in which processes cannot fail. It is then straightforward to solve consensus. For example, we can collect the processes into a group and have each process reliably multicast its proposed value to the members of the group. Each process waits until it has collected all N values (including its own). It then evaluates the function $majority(v_1, v_1, ..., v_N)$, which returns the value that occurs most often among its arguments, or the special value $\perp \notin D$ if no majority exists. Termination is guaranteed by the reliability of the multicast operation. Agreement and integrity are guaranteed by the definition of *majority*, and the integrity property of a reliable multicast. Every process receives the same set of proposed values, and every process evaluates the same function of those values. So they must all agree, and if every process proposed the same value, then they all decide on this value.

Note that *majority* is only one possible function that the processes could use to agree upon a value from the candidate values. For example, if the values are ordered then the functions *minimum* and *maximum* may be appropriate.

If processes can crash then this introduces the complication of detecting failures, and it is not immediately clear that a run of the consensus algorithm can terminate. In fact, if the system is asynchronous then it may not; we shall return to this point shortly.

If processes can fail in *arbitrary* (byzantine) ways, then faulty processes can in principle communicate random values to the others. This may seem unlikely in practice, but it is not beyond the bounds of possibility for a process with a bug to fail in this way. Moreover, the fault may not be accidental but the result of mischievous or malevolent operation. Someone could deliberately make a process send different values to different peers in an attempt to thwart the others, which are trying to reach consensus. In case of inconsistency, correct processes must compare what they have received with what other processes claim to have received.

The byzantine generals problem ◊ In the informal statement of the *byzantine generals problem* [Lamport *et al.* 1982], three or more generals are to agree to attack or to retreat. One, the commander, issues the order. The others, lieutenants to the commander, are to decide to attack or retreat. But one or more of the generals may be 'treacherous' – that is, faulty. If the commander is treacherous, he proposes attacking to one general and retreating to another. If a lieutenant is treacherous, he tells one of his peers that the commander told him to attack and another that they are to retreat.

The byzantine generals problem differs from consensus in that a distinguished process supplies a value that the others are to agree upon, instead of each of them proposing a value. The requirements are:

Termination: Eventually each correct process sets its decision variable.

Agreement: The decision value of all correct processes is the same: if p_i and p_j are correct and have entered the *decided* state, then $d_i = d_j$ $(i, j = 1, 2, ..., N)$.

Integrity: If the commander is correct, then all correct processes decide on the value that the commander proposed.

Note that, for the byzantine generals problem, integrity implies agreement when the commander is correct; but the commander need not be correct.

Interactive consistency ◊ The interactive consistency problem is another variant of consensus, in which every process proposes a single value. The goal of the algorithm is for the correct processes to agree on a *vector* of values, one for each process. We shall call this the 'decision vector'. For example, the goal could be for each of a set of processes to obtain the same information about their respective states.

The requirements for interactive consistency are:

Termination: Eventually each correct process sets its decision variable.

Agreement: The decision vector of all correct processes is the same.

Integrity: If p_i is correct, then all correct processes decide on v_i as the *i*th component of their vector.

Relating consensus to other problems ◊ Although it is common to consider the byzantine generals problem with arbitrary process failures, in fact each of the three problems – consensus, byzantine generals and interactive consistency – is meaningful in the context of either arbitrary or crash failures. Similarly, each can be framed assuming either a synchronous or an asynchronous system.

It is sometimes possible to derive a solution to one problem using a solution to another. This is a very useful property, both because it increases our understanding of the problems and because by reusing solutions we can potentially save on implementation effort and complexity.

Suppose that there exist solutions to consensus (C), byzantine generals (BG) and interactive consistency (IC) as follows:

$C_i(v_1, v_2, ..., v_N)$ returns the decision value of p_i in a run of the solution to the consensus problem, where $v_1, v_2, ..., v_N$ are the values that the processes proposed.

$BG_i(j, v)$ returns the decision value of p_i in a run of the solution to the byzantine generals problem, where p_j, the commander, proposes the value v.

$IC_i(v_1, v_2, ..., v_N)[j]$ returns the *j*th value in the decision vector of p_i in a run of the solution to the interactive consistency problem, where $v_1, v_2, ..., v_N$ are the values that the processes proposed.

The definitions of C_i, BG_i and IC_i assume that a faulty process proposes a single notional value, even though it may have given different proposed values to each of the other processes. This is only a convenience: the solutions will not rely on any such notional value.

It is possible to construct solutions out of the solutions to other problems. We give three examples:

IC from BG: We construct a solution to IC from BG by running BG N times, once with each process p_i ($i, j = 1, 2..., N$) acting as the commander:

$$IC_i(v_1, v_2..., v_N)[j] = BG_i(j, v_j) \ (i, j = 1, 2, ..., N)$$

C from IC: For the case where a majority of processes are correct, we construct a solution to C from IC by running IC to produce a vector of values at each process, then applying an appropriate function on the vector's values to derive a single value:

$$C_i(v_1, ..., v_N) = majority(IC_i(v_1, ..., v_N)[1], ..., IC_i(v_1, ..., v_N)[N])$$

($i = 1, 2...N$), where *majority* is as defined above.

BG from C: We construct a solution to BG from C as follows:

- The commander p_j sends its proposed value v to itself and each of the remaining processes;
- All processes run C with the values $v_1, v_2, ..., v_N$ that they receive (p_j may be faulty);

Figure 12.18 Consensus in a synchronous system

Algorithm for process $p_i \in g$; algorithm proceeds in $f + 1$ rounds

On initialization
  $Values_i^1 := \{v_i\}; Values_i^0 = \{\};$

In round r ($1 \leq r \leq f + 1$)
  B-multicast(g, $Values_i^r - Values_i^{r-1}$); // Send only values that have not been sent
  $Values_i^{r+1} := Values_i^r;$

  while (in round r)
  {
          On B-deliver(V_j) from some p_j
            $Values_i^{r+1} := Values_i^{r+1} \cup V_j;$
  }

After ($f + 1$) rounds
  Assign $d_i = minimum(Values_i^{f+1});$

- They derive $BG_i(j, v) = C_i(v_1, v_2, ..., v_N)$ ($i = 1, 2, ..., N$).

The reader should check that the termination, agreement and integrity conditions are preserved in each case. Fischer [1983] relates the three problems in more detail.

In systems with crash failures, consensus is equivalent to solving reliable and totally ordered multicast: given a solution to one, we can solve the other. Implementing consensus with a reliable and totally ordered multicast operation *RTO-multicast* is straightforward. We collect all the processes into a group g. To achieve consensus, each process p_i performs *RTO-multicast(g, v_i)*. Then each process p_i chooses $d_i = m_i$, where m_i is the *first* value that p_i *RTO-delivers*. The termination property follows from the reliability of the multicast. The agreement and integrity properties follow from the reliability and total ordering of multicast delivery. Chandra and Toueg [1996] demonstrate how reliable and totally ordered multicast can be derived from consensus.

12.5.2 Consensus in a synchronous system

This section describes an algorithm that uses only a basic multicast protocol to solve consensus in a synchronous system. The algorithm assumes that up to f of the N processes exhibit crash failures.

To reach consensus, each correct process collects proposed values from the other processes. The algorithm proceeds in $f + 1$ rounds, in each of which the correct processes *B-multicast* the values between themselves. At most f processes may crash, by assumption. At worst, all f crashes occurred during the rounds, but the algorithm guarantees that at the end of the rounds all the correct processes that have survived are in a position to agree.

The algorithm, shown in Figure 12.18, is based on that by Dolev and Strong [1983] and its presentation by Attiya and Welch [1998]. The variable $Values_i^r$ holds the set of proposed values known to process p_i at the beginning of round r. Each process multicasts the set of values that it has not sent in previous rounds. It then takes delivery of similar multicast messages from other processes and records any new values. Although this is not shown in Figure 12.18, the duration of a round is limited by setting a timeout based on the maximum time for a correct process to multicast a message. After $f + 1$ rounds, each process chooses the minimum value it has received as its decision value.

Termination is obvious from the fact that the system is synchronous. To check the correctness of the algorithm, we must show that each process arrives at the same set of values at the end of the final round. Agreement and integrity will then follow, because the processes apply the *minimum* function to this set.

Assume, to the contrary, that two processes differ in their final set of values. Without loss of generality, some correct process p_i possesses a value v that another correct process p_j $(i \neq j)$ does not possess. The only explanation for p_i possessing a proposed value v at the end that p_j does not possess is that any third process, p_k say, that managed to send v to p_i crashed before v could be delivered to p_j. In turn, any process sending v in the previous round must have crashed, to explain why p_k possesses v in that round but p_j did not receive it. Proceeding in this way, we have to posit at least one crash in each of the preceding rounds. But we have assumed that at most f crashes can occur, and there are $f + 1$ rounds. We have arrived at a contradiction.

It turns out that *any* algorithm to reach consensus despite up to f crash failures requires at least $f + 1$ rounds of message exchanges, no matter how it is constructed [Dolev and Strong 1983]. This lower bound also applies in the case of byzantine failures [Fischer and Lynch 1982].

12.5.3 The byzantine generals problem in a synchronous system

We discuss the byzantine generals problem in a synchronous system. Unlike the algorithm for consensus described in the previous section, here we assume that processes can exhibit arbitrary failures. That is, a faulty process may send any message with any value at any time; and it may omit to send any message. Up to f of the N processes may be faulty. Correct processes can detect the absence of a message through a timeout; but they cannot conclude that the sender has crashed, since it may be silent for some time and then send messages again.

We assume that the communication channels between pairs of processes are private. If a process could examine all the messages that other processes send, then it could detect the inconsistencies in what a faulty process sends to different processes. Our default assumption of channel reliability means that no faulty process can inject messages into the communication channel between correct processes.

Lamport *et al.* [1982] considered the case of three processes that send unsigned messages to one another. They showed that there is no solution that guarantees to meet the conditions of the byzantine generals problem if one process is allowed to fail. They generalized this result to show that no solution exists if $N \leq 3f$. We shall demonstrate these results shortly. They went on to give an algorithm that solves the byzantine generals problem in a synchronous system if $N \geq 3f + 1$, for unsigned (they call them 'oral') messages.

Figure 12.19 Three byzantine generals

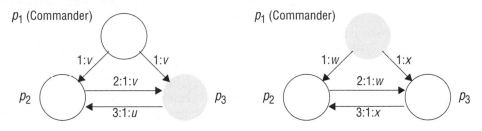

Faulty processes are shown in blue tint

Impossibility with three processes ◊ Figure 12.19 shows two scenarios in which just one of three processes is faulty. In the left configuration one of the lieutenants, p_3 is faulty; on the right the commander, p_1 is faulty. Each scenario in Figure 12.19 shows two rounds of messages: the values the commander sends, and the values that the lieutenants subsequently send to each other. The numeric prefixes serve to specify the sources of messages and to show the different rounds. Read the ':' symbol in messages as 'says'; for example, '3:1:u' is the message '3 says 1 says u'.

In the left-hand scenario, the commander correctly sends the same value v to each of the other two processes, and p_2 correctly echoes this to p_3. However, p_3 sends a value $u \neq v$ to p_2. All p_2 knows at this stage is that it has received differing values; it cannot tell which were sent out by the commander.

In the right-hand scenario, the commander is faulty and sends differing values to the lieutenants. After p_3 has correctly echoed the value x that it received, p_2 is in the same situation as it was in when p_3 was faulty: it has received two differing values.

If a solution exists, then process p_2 is bound to decide on value v when the commander is correct, by the integrity condition. If we accept that no algorithm can possibly distinguish between the two scenarios, p_2 must also choose the value sent by the commander in the right-hand scenario.

Following exactly the same reasoning for p_3, assuming that it is correct, we are forced to conclude, by symmetry, that p_3 also chooses the value sent by the commander as its decision value. But this contradicts the agreement condition (the commander sends differing values if it is faulty). So no solution is possible.

Note that this argument rests on our intuition that nothing can be done to improve a correct general's knowledge beyond the first stage, where it cannot tell which process is faulty. It is possible to prove the correctness of this intuition [Pease *et al.* 1980]. Byzantine agreement *can* be reached for three generals, with one of them faulty, if the generals digitally sign their messages.

Impossibility with N ≤ 3f ◊ Pease *et al.* generalized the basic impossibility result for three processes, to prove that no solution is possible if $N \leq 3f$. In outline, the argument is as follows. Assume that a solution exists with $N \leq 3f$. Let each of three processes p_1, p_2 and p_3 use the solution to simulate the behaviour of n_1, n_2 and n_3 generals, respectively, where $n_1 + n_2 + n_3 = N$ and $n_1, n_2, n_3 \leq N/3$. We assume, furthermore, that one of the three processes is faulty. Those of p_1, p_2 and p_3 that are correct simulate correct generals: they simulate the interactions of their own generals internally and send messages from their generals to those simulated by other processes. The faulty process's simulated generals are faulty: the messages that it sends as part of the simulation to the other two processes may be spurious. Since $N \leq 3f$ and $n_1, n_2, n_3 \leq N/3$, at most f simulated generals are faulty.

Because the algorithm that the processes run is assumed to be correct, the simulation terminates. The correct simulated generals (in the two correct processes) agree and satisfy the integrity property. But now we have a means for the two correct processes out of the three to reach consensus: each decides on the value chosen by all of their simulated generals. This contradicts our impossibility result for three processes, with one faulty.

Solution with one faulty process ◊ There is not sufficient space to describe fully the algorithm of Pease *et al.* that solves the byzantine generals problem in a synchronous system with $N \geq 3f + 1$. Instead, we give the operation of the algorithm for the case $N \geq 4$, $f = 1$ and illustrate it for $N = 4$, $f = 1$.

The correct generals reach agreement in two rounds of messages:

- In the first round, the commander sends a value to each of the lieutenants.

- In the second round, each of the lieutenants sends the value it received to its peers.

A lieutenant receives a value from the commander, plus $N - 2$ values from its peers. If the commander is faulty, then all the lieutenants are correct and each will have gathered exactly the set of values that the commander sent out. Otherwise, one of the lieutenants is faulty; each of its correct peers receives $N - 2$ copies of the value that the commander sent, plus a value that the faulty lieutenant sent to it.

In either case, the correct lieutenants need only apply a simple majority function to the set of values they receive. Since $N \geq 4$, $(N - 2) \geq 2$. Therefore, the *majority* function will ignore any value that a faulty lieutenant sent, and it will produce the value that the commander sent if the commander is correct.

We now illustrate the algorithm that we have just outlined for the case of four generals. Figure 12.20 shows two scenarios similar to those in Figure 12.19, but in this case there are four processes, one of which is faulty. As in Figure 12.19, in the left-hand configuration one of the lieutenants, p_3, is faulty; on the right, the commander, p_1, is faulty.

In the left-hand case, the two correct lieutenant processes agree, deciding on the commander's value:

p_2 decides on $majority(v, u, v) = v$

p_4 decides on $majority(v, v, w) = v$

In the right-hand case the commander is faulty, but the three correct processes agree:

p_2, p_3 and p_4 decide on $majority(u, v, w) = \perp$ (the special value $\perp$ applies where no majority of values exists).

The algorithm takes account of the fact that a faulty process may omit to send a message. If a correct process does not receive a message within a suitable time limit (the system is synchronous), it proceeds as though the faulty process had sent it the value $\perp$.

Discussion ◊ We can measure the efficiency of a solution to the byzantine generals problem – or any other agreement problem – by asking:

Figure 12.20 Four byzantine generals

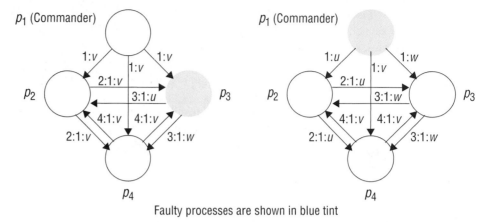

Faulty processes are shown in blue tint

- How many message rounds does it take? (This is a factor in how long it takes for the algorithm to terminate.)

- How many messages are sent, and of what size? (This measures the total bandwidth utilization and has an impact on the execution time.)

In the general case ($f \geq 1$) the Lamport *et al.* algorithm for unsigned messages operates over $f + 1$ rounds. In each round, a process sends to a subset of the other processes the values that it received in the previous round. The algorithm is very costly: it involves sending $O(N^{f + 1})$ messages.

Fischer and Lynch [1982] proved that any deterministic solution to consensus assuming byzantine failures (and hence to the byzantine generals problem, as Section 12.5.1 showed) will take at least $f + 1$ message rounds. So no algorithm can operate faster in this respect than that of Lamport *et al.* But there have been improvements in the message complexity, for example Garay and Moses [1993].

Several algorithms, such as that of Dolev and Strong [1983], take advantage of signed messages. Dolev and Strong's algorithm again takes $f + 1$ rounds, but the number of messages sent is only $O(N^2)$.

The complexity and cost of the solutions suggest that they are applicable only where the threat is great. If faulty hardware is the source of the threat, then the likelihood of truly arbitrary behaviour is small. Solutions that are based on more detailed knowledge of the fault model may be more efficient [Barborak *et al.* 1993]. If malicious users are the source of the threat, then a system to counter them is likely to use digital signatures; a solution without signatures is impractical.

12.5.4 Impossibility in asynchronous systems

We have provided solutions to consensus and the byzantine generals problem (and hence, by derivation, to interactive consistency) in synchronous systems. However, all these solutions relied upon the system being synchronous. The algorithms assume that message exchanges take place in rounds, and that processes are entitled to timeout and assume that a faulty process has not sent them a message within the round, because the maximum delay has been exceeded.

Fischer *et al.* [1985] proved that no algorithm can guarantee to reach consensus in an asynchronous system, even with one process crash failure. In an asynchronous system, processes can respond to messages at arbitrary times, so a crashed process is indistinguishable from a slow one. Their proof, which is beyond the scope of this book, involves showing that there is always some continuation of the processes' execution that avoids consensus being reached.

We immediately know from the result of Fischer *et al.* that there is no guaranteed solution in an asynchronous system to the byzantine generals problem, to interactive consistency or to totally ordered and reliable multicast. If there were such a solution then, by the results of Section 12.5.1, we would have a solution to consensus – contradicting the impossibility result.

Note the word 'guarantee' in the statement of the impossibility result. The result does not mean that processes can *never* reach distributed consensus in an asynchronous system if one is faulty. It allows that consensus can be reached with some probability greater than zero, confirming what we know in practice. For example, despite the fact that our systems are often effectively asynchronous, transaction systems have been reaching consensus regularly for many years.

One approach to working around the impossibility result is to consider *partially synchronous* systems, which are sufficiently weaker than synchronous systems to be useful as models of practical systems, and sufficiently stronger than asynchronous systems for consensus to be solvable in them [Dwork *et al.* 1988]. That approach is beyond the scope of this book. However, three other techniques for working around the impossibility result that we shall now outline are fault masking, and reaching consensus by exploiting failure detectors and by randomizing aspects of the processes' behaviour.

Masking faults ◊ The first technique is to avoid the impossibility result altogether by masking any process failures that occur (see Section 2.3.2 for an introduction to fault-masking). For example, transaction systems employ persistent storage, which survives crash failures. If a process crashes, then it is restarted (automatically, or by an administrator). The process places sufficient information in persistent storage at critical points in its program so that if it should crash and be restarted, it will find sufficient data to be able to continue correctly with its interrupted task. In other words, it will behave like a process that is correct, but which sometimes takes a long time to perform a processing step.

Of course, fault masking is generally applicable in system design. Chapter 14 discusses how transactional systems take advantage of persistent storage. Chapter 15 describes how process failures can also be masked by replicating software components.

Consensus using failure detectors ◊ Another method for circumventing the impossibility result is to employ failure detectors. Some practical systems employ 'perfect by design' failure detectors to reach consensus. No failure detector in an asynchronous system that works solely by message passing can really be perfect. However, processes can agree to *deem* a process that has not responded for more than a bounded time to have failed. An unresponsive process may not really have failed, but the remaining processes act as if it had done. They make the failure 'fail-silent' by discarding any subsequent messages that they do in fact receive from a 'failed' process.

In other words, we have effectively turned an asynchronous system into a synchronous one. This technique is used in the ISIS system [Birman 1993].

This method relies upon the failure detector usually being accurate. When it is inaccurate, then the system has to proceed without a group member that otherwise could potentially have contributed to the system's effectiveness. Unfortunately, making the failure detector reasonably accurate involves using long timeout values, forcing processes to wait a relatively long time (and not perform useful work) before concluding that a process has failed. Another issue that arises for this approach is network partitioning, which we discuss in Chapter 15.

A quite different approach is to use imperfect failure detectors, and to reach consensus while allowing suspected processes to behave correctly instead of excluding them. Chandra and Toueg [1996] analysed the properties that a failure detector must have in order to solve the consensus problem in an asynchronous system. They showed that consensus can be solved in an asynchronous system, even with an unreliable failure detector, if fewer than $N/2$ processes crash and communication is reliable. The weakest type of failure detector for which this is so is called an *eventually weak failure detector*. This is one that is:

Eventually weakly complete: each faulty process is eventually suspected permanently by some correct process;

Eventually weakly accurate: after some point in time, at least one correct process is never suspected by any correct process.

Chandra and Toueg show that we cannot implement an eventually weak failure detector in an asynchronous system by message passing alone. However, we described a message-based failure detector in Section 12.1 that adapts its timeout values according to observed response times. If a process or the connection to it is very slow, then the timeout value will grow so that cases of falsely suspecting a process become rare. In the case of many real systems, this algorithm behaves sufficiently closely to an eventually weak failure detector for practical purposes.

Chandra and Toueg's consensus algorithm allows falsely suspected processes to continue their normal operations and allows processes that have suspected them to receive messages from them and process those messages normally. This makes the application programmer's life complicated, but it has the advantage that correct processes are not wasted by being falsely excluded. Moreover, timeouts for detecting failures can be set less conservatively than with the ISIS approach.

Consensus using randomization ◊ The result of Fischer *et al.* depends on what we can consider to be an 'adversary'. This is a 'character' (actually just a collection of random events) who can exploit the phenomena of asynchronous systems so as to foil the processes' attempts to reach consensus. The adversary manipulates the network to delay messages so that they arrive at just the wrong time, and similarly it slows down or speeds up the processes just enough so that they are in the 'wrong' state when they receive a message.

The third technique that addresses the impossibility result is to introduce an element of chance in the processes' behaviour, so that the adversary cannot exercise its thwarting strategy effectively. Consensus might still not be reached in some cases, but this method enables processes to reach consensus in a finite *expected* time. A probabilistic algorithm that solves consensus even with byzantine failures can be found in Canetti and Rabin [1993].

12.6   Summary

The chapter began by discussing the need for processes to access shared resources under conditions of mutual exclusion. Locks are not always implemented by the servers that manage the shared resources, and a separate distributed mutual exclusion service is then required. Three algorithms were considered that achieve mutual exclusion: one employing a central server, a ring-based algorithm, and a multicast-based algorithm using logical clocks. None of these mechanisms can withstand failure as we described them, although they can be modified to tolerate some faults.

Then the chapter considered a ring-based algorithm and the bully algorithm, whose common aim is to elect a process uniquely from a given set – even if several elections take place concurrently. The Bully algorithm could be used, for example, to elect a new master time server, or a new lock server, when the previous one fails.

The chapter described multicast communication. It discussed reliable multicast, in which the correct processes agree on the set of messages to be delivered; and multicast with FIFO, causal and total delivery ordering. We gave algorithms for reliable multicast and for all three types of delivery ordering.

Finally, we described the three problems of consensus, byzantine generals and interactive consistency. We defined the conditions for their solution and we showed relationships between these problems – including the relationship between consensus and reliable, totally ordered multicast.

Solutions exist in a synchronous system, and we described some of them. In fact, solutions exist even when arbitrary failures are possible. We outlined part of the solution to the byzantine generals problem of Lamport *et al*. More recent algorithms have lower complexity, but in principle none can better the $f + 1$ rounds taken by this algorithm, unless messages are digitally signed.

The chapter ended by describing the fundamental result of Fischer *et al*. concerning the impossibility of guaranteeing consensus in an asynchronous system. We discussed how it is that, nonetheless, systems regularly do reach agreement in asynchronous systems.

EXERCISES

12.1   Is it possible to implement either a reliable or an unreliable (process) failure detector using an unreliable communication channel?   *page 470*

12.2   If all client processes are single-threaded, is mutual exclusion condition ME3, which specifies entry in happened-before order, relevant?   *page 473*

12.3   Give a formula for the maximum throughput of a mutual exclusion system in terms of the synchronization delay.   *page 473*

12.4 In the central server algorithm for mutual exclusion, describe a situation in which two requests are not processed in happened-before order. *page 474*

12.5 Adapt the central server algorithm for mutual exclusion to handle the crash failure of any client (in any state), assuming that the server is correct and given a reliable failure detector. Comment on whether the resultant system is fault tolerant. What would happen if a client that possesses the token is wrongly suspected to have failed? *page 474*

12.6 Give an example execution of the ring-based algorithm to show that processes are not necessarily granted entry to the critical section in happened-before order. *page 475*

12.7 In a certain system, each process typically uses a critical section many times before another process requires it. Explain why Ricart and Agrawala's multicast-based mutual exclusion algorithm is inefficient for this case, and describe how to improve its performance. Does your adaptation satisfy liveness condition ME2? *page 477*

12.8 In the Bully algorithm, a recovering process starts an election and will become the new coordinator if it has a higher identifier than the current incumbent. Is this a necessary feature of the algorithm? *page 482*

12.9 Suggest how to adapt the Bully algorithm to deal with temporary network partitions (slow communication) and slow processes. *page 484*

12.10 Devise a protocol for basic multicast over IP multicast. *page 486*

12.11 How, if at all, should the definitions of integrity, agreement and validity for reliable multicast change for the case of open groups? *page 487*

12.12 Explain why reversing the order of the lines '*R-deliver m*' and '*if* ($q \neq p$) *then B-multicast*(g, m); *end if*' in Figure 12.10 makes the algorithm no longer satisfy uniform agreement. Does the reliable multicast algorithm based on IP multicast satisfy uniform agreement? *page 488*

12.13 Explain whether the algorithm for reliable multicast over IP multicast works for open as well as closed groups. Given any algorithm for closed groups, how, simply, can we derive an algorithm for open groups? *page 488*

12.14 Consider how to address the impractical assumptions we made in order to meet the validity and agreement properties for the reliable multicast protocol based on IP multicast. Hint: add a rule for deleting retained messages when they have been delivered everywhere; and consider adding a dummy 'heartbeat' message, which is never delivered to the application, but which the protocol sends if the application has no message to send. *page 488*

12.15 Show that the FIFO-ordered multicast algorithm does not work for overlapping groups, by considering two messages sent from the same source to two overlapping groups, and considering a process in the intersection of those groups. Adapt the protocol to work for this case. Hint: processes should include with their messages the latest sequence numbers of messages sent to *all* groups. *page 493*

12.16 Show that, if the basic multicast that we use in the algorithm of Figure 12.14 is also FIFO-ordered, then the resultant totally-ordered multicast is also causally ordered. Is it the case that any multicast that is both FIFO-ordered and totally ordered is thereby causally ordered? *page 494*

12.17   Suggest how to adapt the causally ordered multicast protocol to handle overlapping groups.   *page 497*

12.18   In discussing Maekawa's mutual exclusion algorithm, we gave an example of three subsets of a set of three processes that could lead to a deadlock. Use these subsets as multicast groups to show how a pairwise total ordering is not necessarily acyclic.
page 498

12.19   Construct a solution to reliable, totally ordered multicast in a synchronous system, using a reliable multicast and a solution to the consensus problem.   *page 498*

12.20   We gave a solution to consensus from a solution to reliable and totally ordered multicast, which involved selecting the first value to be delivered. Explain from first principles why, in an asynchronous system, we could not instead derive a solution by using a reliable but not totally ordered multicast service and the 'majority' function. (Note that, if we could, then this would contradict the impossibility result of Fischer *et al*.!) Hint: consider slow/failed processes.   *page 503*

12.21   Show that byzantine agreement can be reached for three generals, with one of them faulty, if the generals digitally sign their messages.   *page 505*

12.22   Explain how to adapt the algorithm for reliable multicast over IP multicast to eliminate the hold-back queue – so that a received message that is not a duplicate can be delivered immediately, but without any ordering guarantees. Hint: use sets instead of sequence numbers to represent the messages that have been delivered so far.   *page 489*

13

TRANSACTIONS AND CONCURRENCY CONTROL

This chapter discusses the application of transactions and concurrency control to shared objects managed by servers.

A transaction defines a sequence of server operations that is guaranteed by the server to be atomic in the presence of multiple clients and server crashes. Nested transactions are structured from sets of other transactions. They are particularly useful in distributed systems because they allow additional concurrency.

All of the concurrency control protocols are based on the criterion of serial equivalence and are derived from rules for conflicts between operations. Three methods are described:

- Locks are used to order transactions that access the same objects according to the order of arrival of their operations at the objects.

- Optimistic concurrency control allows transactions to proceed until they are ready to commit, whereupon a check is made to see whether they have performed conflicting operations on objects.

- Timestamp ordering uses timestamps to order transactions that access the same objects according to their starting times.

13.1 Introduction

The goal of transactions is to ensure that all of the objects managed by a server remain in a consistent state when they are accessed by multiple transactions and in the presence of server crashes. Chapter 2 introduced a failure model for distributed systems. Transactions deal with crash failures of processes and omission failures in communication, but not any type of arbitrary (or byzantine) behaviour. The failure model for transactions is presented in Section 13.1.2.

Objects that can be recovered after their server crashes are called *recoverable* objects. In general, the objects managed by a server may be stored in volatile memory (for example, RAM) or persistent memory (for example, disk). Even if objects are stored in volatile memory, the server may use persistent memory to store sufficient information for the state of the objects to be recovered in case the server process crashes. This enables servers to make objects recoverable. A transaction is specified by a client as a set of operations on objects to be performed as an indivisible unit by the servers managing those objects. The servers must guarantee that either the entire transaction is carried out and the results recorded in permanent storage or, in the case that one or more of them crashes, its effects are completely erased. The next chapter discusses issues related to transactions that involve several servers, in particular how they decide on the outcome of a distributed transaction. This chapter concentrates on the issues for a transaction at a single server. A client's transaction is also regarded as indivisible from the point of view of other clients' transactions in the sense that the operations of one transaction cannot observe the partial effects of the operations of another. Section 13.1.1 discusses simple synchronization of access to objects, and Section 13.2 introduces transactions, which require more advanced techniques to prevent interference between clients. Section 13.3 discusses nested transactions. Sections 13.4 to 13.6 discuss three methods of concurrency control for transactions whose operations are all addressed to a single server (locks, optimistic concurrency control and timestamp ordering). Chapter 14 discusses how these methods are extended for use with transactions whose operations are addressed to several servers.

To explain some of the points made in this chapter, we use a banking example, shown in Figure 13.1. Each account is represented by a remote object whose interface *Account* provides operations for making deposits and withdrawals and for enquiring about and setting the balance. Each branch of the bank is represented by a remote object whose interface *Branch* provides operations for creating a new account, for looking up an account by name and for enquiring about the total funds at that branch.

13.1.1 Simple synchronization (without transactions)

One of the main issues of this chapter is that unless a server is carefully designed, its operations performed on behalf of different clients may sometimes interfere with one another. Such interference may result in incorrect values in the objects. In this section, we discuss how client operations may be synchronized without recourse to transactions.

Atomic operations at the server ◊ We have seen in earlier chapters that the use of multiple threads is beneficial to performance in many servers. We have also noted that the use of threads allows operations from multiple clients to run concurrently and

Figure 13.1 Operations of the *Account* interface

deposit(amount)
   deposit *amount* in the account

withdraw(amount)
   withdraw *amount* from the account

getBalance()→ amount
   return the balance of the account

setBalance(amount)
   set the balance of the account to *amount*

Operations of the *Branch* interface

create(name)→ account
   create a new account with a given name

lookUp(name)→ account
   return a reference to the account with the given name

branchTotal()→ amount
   return the total of all the balances at the branch

---

possibly access the same objects. Therefore, the methods of objects should be designed for use in a multi-threaded context. For example, if the methods *deposit* and *withdraw* are not designed for use in a multi-threaded program, then it is possible that the actions of two or more concurrent executions of the method could be interleaved arbitrarily and have strange effects on the instance variables of the account objects.

Chapter 6 explains the use of the *synchronized* keyword, which can be applied to methods in Java to ensure that only one thread at a time can access an object. In our example, the class that implements the *Account* interface will be able to declare the methods as synchronized. For example:

> *public synchronized void deposit(int amount) throws RemoteException{*
> *// adds amount to the balance of the account*
> *}*

If one thread invokes a synchronized method on an object, then that object is effectively locked, and another thread that invokes one of its synchronized methods will be blocked until the lock is released. This form of synchronization forces the execution of threads to be separated in time and ensures that the instance variables of a single object are accessed in a consistent manner. Without synchronization, two separate *deposit* invocations might read the balance before either has incremented it – resulting in an incorrect value. Any method that accesses an instance variable that can vary should be synchronized.

Operations that are free from interference from concurrent operations being performed in other threads are called *atomic operations*. The use of synchronized methods in Java is one way of achieving atomic operations. But in other programming environments for multi-threaded servers the operations on objects still need to have atomic operations in order to keep their objects consistent. This may be achieved by the use of any available mutual exclusion mechanism such as a mutex.

Enhancing client cooperation by synchronization of server operations ◊ Clients may use a server as a means of sharing some resources. This is achieved by some clients using operations to update the server's objects and other clients using operations to access them. The above scheme for synchronized access to objects provides all that is required in many applications – it prevents threads interfering with one another. However, some applications require a way for threads to communicate with each other.

For example, a situation may arise in which the operation requested by one client cannot be completed until an operation requested by another client has been performed. This can happen when some clients are producers and others are consumers – the consumers may have to wait until a producer has supplied some more of the commodity in question. It can also occur when clients are sharing a resource – clients needing the resource may have to wait for other clients to release it. We shall see later in this chapter that a similar situation arises when locks or timestamps are used for concurrency control in transactions.

The Java *wait* and *notify* methods introduced in Chapter 6 allow threads to communicate with one another in a manner that solves the above problems. They must be used within synchronized methods of an object. A thread calls *wait* on an object so as to suspend itself and to allow another thread to execute a method of that object. A thread calls *notify* to inform any thread waiting on that object that it has changed some of its data. Access to an object is still atomic when threads wait for one another: a thread that calls *wait* gives up its lock and suspends itself as a single atomic action; when a thread is restarted after being notified it acquires a new lock on the object and resumes execution from after its *wait*. A thread that calls *notify* (from within a synchronized method) completes the execution of that method before releasing the lock on the object.

Consider the implementation of a shared *Queue* object with two methods: *first* removes and returns the first object in the queue; *append* adds a given object to the end of the queue. The method *first* will test whether the queue is empty, in which case it will call *wait* on the queue. If a client invokes *first* when the queue is empty, then the client will not get a reply until another client has added something to the queue – the *append* operation will call *notify* when it has added an object to the queue. This allows one of the threads waiting on the queue object to resume and to return the first object in the queue to its client. When threads can synchronize their actions on an object by means of *wait* and *notify*, the server holds on to requests that cannot immediately be satisfied and the client waits for a reply until another client has produced whatever they need.

In the later section on locks for transactions, we discuss the implementation of a lock as an object with synchronized operations. When clients attempt to acquire a lock, they can be made to wait until the lock is released by other clients.

Without the ability to synchronize threads in this way, a client that cannot be satisfied immediately, for example, a client that invokes the *first* method on an empty queue, is told to try again later. This is unsatisfactory, because it will involve the client in polling the server and the server in carrying out extra requests. It is also potentially unfair because other clients may make their requests before the waiting client tries again.

13.1.2 Failure model for transactions

Lampson [1981] proposed a fault model for distributed transactions that accounts for failures of disks, servers and communication. In this model, the claim is that the algorithms work correctly in the presence of predictable faults, but no claims are made about their behaviour when a disaster occurs. Although errors may occur, they can be detected and dealt with before any incorrect behaviour occurs. The model states the following:

- Writes to permanent storage may fail – either by writing nothing or by writing a wrong value – for example, writing to the wrong block is a disaster. File storage may also decay. Reads from permanent storage can detect (by a checksum) when a block of data is bad.

- Servers may crash occasionally. When a crashed server is replaced by a new process, its volatile memory is first set to a state in which it knows none of the values (for example, of objects) from before the crash. After that it carries out a recovery procedure using information in permanent storage and obtained from other processes to set the values of objects including those related to the two-phase commit protocol (see Section 14.6). When a processor is faulty, it is made to crash so that it is prevented from sending erroneous messages and from writing wrong values to permanent storage – that is, it cannot produce arbitrary failures. Crashes can occur at any time – in particular, they may occur during recovery.

- There may be an arbitrary delay before a message arrives. A message may be lost, duplicated or corrupted. The recipient can detect corrupted messages (by a checksum). Both forged messages and undetected corrupt messages are regarded as disasters.

The fault model for permanent storage, processors and communications was used to design a stable system whose components can survive any single fault and present a simple failure model. In particular, *stable storage* provided an atomic *write* operation in the presence of a single fault of the *write* operation or a crash failure of the process. This was achieved by replicating each block on two disk blocks. A *write* operation was applied to the pair of disk blocks – and in the case of a single fault one good block was always available. A *stable processor* used stable storage to enable it to recover its objects after a crash. Communication errors were masked by using a reliable remote procedure calling mechanism.

13.2 Transactions

In some situations, clients require a sequence of separate requests to a server to be atomic in the sense that:

1. they are free from interference by operations being performed on behalf of other concurrent clients; and

2. either all of the operations must be completed successfully or they must have no effect at all in the presence of server crashes.

Figure 13.2   A client's banking transaction

Transaction T:
a.withdraw(100);
b.deposit(100);
c.withdraw(200);
b.deposit(200);

We return to our banking example to illustrate transactions. A client that performs a sequence of operations on a particular bank account on behalf of a user will first *lookUp* the account by name and then apply the *deposit*, *withdraw* and *getBalance* operations directly to the relevant account. In our examples, we use accounts with names A, B and C. The client looks them up and stores references to them in variables *a*, *b* and *c* of type *Account*. The details of looking up the accounts by name and the declarations of the variables are omitted from the examples.

Figure 13.2 shows an example of a simple client transaction specifying a series of related actions involving the bank accounts A, B and C. The first two actions transfer $100 from A to B and the second two transfer $200 from C to B. A client achieves a transfer operation by doing a withdrawal followed by a deposit.

Transactions originate from database management systems. In that context, a transaction is an execution of a program that accesses a database. Transactions were introduced to distributed systems in the form of transactional file servers such as XDFS [Mitchell and Dion 1982]. In the context of a transactional file server, a transaction is an execution of a sequence of client requests for file operations. Transactions on distributed objects were provided in several research systems, including Argus [Liskov 1988] and Arjuna [Shrivastava *et al.* 1991]. In this last context, a transaction consists of the execution of a sequence of client requests, as, for example, in Figure 13.2. From the client's point of view, a transaction is a sequence of operations that forms a single step, transforming the server data from one consistent state to another.

Transactions can be provided as a part of middleware. For example, CORBA provides the specification for an Object Transaction Service [OMG 2003] with IDL interfaces allowing clients' transactions to include multiple objects at multiple servers. The client is provided with operations to specify the beginning and end of a transaction. The client ORB maintains a context for each transaction, which it propagates with each operation in that transaction. In CORBA, transactional objects are invoked within the scope of a transaction and generally have some persistent store associated with them.

In all of these contexts, a transaction applies to recoverable objects and is intended to be atomic. It is often called an *atomic transaction* (see the box opposite). There are two aspects to atomicity:

All or nothing: A transaction either completes successfully, and the effects of all of its operations are recorded in the objects, or (if it fails or is deliberately aborted) it has no effect at all. This all-or-nothing effect has two further aspects of its own:

  failure atomicity: the effects are atomic even when the server crashes;

durability: after a transaction has completed successfully, all its effects are saved in permanent storage. We use the term 'permanent storage' to refer to files held on disk or another permanent medium. Data saved in a file will survive if the server process crashes.

Isolation: Each transaction must be performed without interference from other transactions; in other words, the intermediate effects of a transaction must not be visible to other transactions.

To support the requirement for failure atomicity and durability, the objects must be *recoverable*; when a server process crashes unexpectedly due to a hardware fault or a software error, the changes due to all completed transactions must be available in permanent storage so that when the server is replaced by a new process, it can recover the objects to reflect the all-or-nothing effect. By the time a server acknowledges the completion of a client's transaction, all of the transaction's changes to the objects must have been recorded in permanent storage.

A server that supports transactions must synchronize the operations sufficiently to ensure that the isolation requirement is met. One way of doing this is to perform the transactions serially – one at a time in some arbitrary order. Unfortunately, this solution would generally be unacceptable for servers whose resources are shared by multiple interactive users. In our banking example, it is desirable to allow several bank clerks to perform online banking transactions at the same time as one another.

The aim for any server that supports transactions is to maximize concurrency. Therefore transactions are allowed to execute concurrently if they would have the same effect as a serial execution – that is they are *serially equivalent* or *serializable*.

Transaction capabilities can be added to servers of recoverable objects. Each transaction is created and managed by a coordinator, which implements the *Coordinator* interface shown in Figure 13.3. The coordinator gives each transaction an identifier, or

ACID properties ◊ Härder and Reuter [1983] suggested the mnemonic 'ACID' to remember the properties of transactions as follows:

Atomicity: a transaction must be all or nothing;

Consistency: a transaction takes the system from one consistent state to another consistent state;

Isolation;

Durability.

We have not included 'consistency' in our list of the properties of transactions because it is generally the responsibility of the programmers of servers and clients to ensure that transactions leave the database consistent.

As an example of consistency, suppose that in the banking example, an object holds the sum of all the account balances and its value is used as the result of *branchTotal*. Clients can get the sum of all the account balances either by using *branchTotal* or by calling *getBalance* on each of the accounts. For consistency, they should get the same result from both methods. To maintain this consistency, the *deposit* and *withdraw* operations must update the object holding the sum of all the account balances.

Figure 13.3   Operations in *Coordinator* interface

openTransaction() → trans;
> starts a new transaction and delivers a unique TID *trans*. This identifier will be used in the other operations in the transaction.

closeTransaction(trans)→ (commit, abort);
> ends a transaction: a *commit* return value indicates that the transaction has committed; an *abort* return value indicates that it has aborted.

abortTransaction(trans);
> aborts the transaction.

TID. The client invokes the *openTransaction* method of the coordinator to introduce a new transaction – a transaction identifier or TID is allocated and returned. At the end of a transaction, the client invokes the *closeTransaction* method to indicate its end – all of the recoverable objects accessed by the transaction should be saved. If, for some reason, the client wants to abort a transaction, it invokes the *abortTransaction* method – all of its effects should be removed from sight.

A transaction is achieved by cooperation between a client program, some recoverable objects and a coordinator. The client specifies the sequence of invocations on recoverable objects that are to comprise a transaction. To achieve this, the client sends with each invocation the transaction identifier returned by *openTransaction*. One way to make this possible is to include an extra argument in each operation of a recoverable object to carry the TID. For example, in the banking service the *deposit* operation might be defined:

> *deposit(trans, amount)*
>> deposit *amount* in the account for transaction with TID *trans*

When transactions are provided as middleware, the TID can be passed implicitly with all remote invocations between *openTransaction* and *closeTransaction* or *abortTransaction*. This is what the CORBA transaction service does. We shall not show TIDs in our examples.

Normally, a transaction completes when the client makes a *closeTransaction* request. If the transaction has progressed normally the reply states that the transaction is *committed* – this constitutes an undertaking to the client that all of the changes requested in the transaction are permanently recorded and that any future transactions that access the same data will see the results of all of the changes made during the transaction.

Alternatively, the transaction may have to *abort* for one of several reasons related to the nature of the transaction itself, to conflicts with another transaction or to the crashing of a process or computer. When a transaction is aborted the parties involved (the recoverable objects and the coordinator) must ensure that none of its effects is visible to future transactions, either in the objects or in their copies in permanent storage.

A transaction is either successful or it is aborted in one of two ways – the client aborts it (using an *abortTransaction* call to the server) or the server aborts it. Figure 13.4

Figure 13.4   Transaction life histories

Successful	Aborted by client	Aborted by server	
openTransaction	openTransaction		openTransaction
operation	operation		operation
operation	operation		operation
•	•	server aborts	•
•	•	transaction $\rightarrow$	•
operation	operation		operation ERROR
			reported to client
closeTransaction	abortTransaction		

shows these three alternative life histories for transactions. We refer to a transaction as *failing* in both of these cases.

Service actions related to process crashes ◊ If a server process crashes unexpectedly, it is eventually replaced. The new server process aborts any uncommitted transactions and uses a recovery procedure to restore the values of the objects to the values produced by the most recently committed transaction. To deal with a client that crashes unexpectedly during a transaction, servers can give each transaction an expiry time and abort any transaction that has not completed before its expiry time.

Client actions related to server process crashes ◊ If a server crashes while a transaction is in progress, the client will become aware of this when one of the operations returns an exception after a timeout. If a server crashes and is then replaced during the progress of a transaction, the transaction will no longer be valid and the client must be informed as an exception to the next operation. In either case, the client must then formulate a plan, possibly in consultation with the human user, for the completion or abandonment of the task of which the transaction was a part.

13.2.1 Concurrency control

This section illustrates two well-known problems of concurrent transactions in the context of the banking example – the 'lost update' problem and the 'inconsistent retrievals' problem. This section then shows how both of these problems can be avoided by using serially equivalent executions of transactions. We assume throughout that each of the operations *deposit*, *withdraw*, *getBalance* and *setBalance* is a synchronized operation – that is, its effects on the instance variable that records the balance of an account is atomic.

The lost update problem ◊ The lost update problem is illustrated by the following pair of transactions on bank accounts *A*, *B* and *C*, whose initial balances are $100, $200 and $300, respectively. Transaction *T* transfers an amount from account *A* to account *B*.

Figure 13.5   The lost update problem

Transaction *T*:		Transaction *U*:	
balance = b.getBalance();		*balance = b.getBalance();*	
b.setBalance(balance*1.1);		*b.setBalance(balance*1.1);*	
a.withdraw(balance/10)		*c.withdraw(balance/10)*	
balance = b.getBalance();	$200		
		balance = b.getBalance();	$200
		b.setBalance(balance*1.1);	$220
b.setBalance(balance*1.1);	$220		
a.withdraw(balance/10)	$80		
		c.withdraw(balance/10)	$280

Figure 13.6   The inconsistent retrievals problem

Transaction *V*:		Transaction *W*:	
a.withdraw(100)		*aBranch.branchTotal()*	
b.deposit(100)			
a.withdraw(100);	$100		
		total = a.getBalance( )	$100
		total = total + b.getBalance()	$300
		total = total + c.getBalance()	
b.deposit(100)	$300	•	
		•	

Transaction *U* transfers an amount from account *C* to account *B*. In both cases, the amount transferred is calculated to increase the balance of *B* by 10%. The net effects on account *B* of executing the transactions *T* and *U* should be to increase the balance of account *B* by 10% twice, so its final value is $242.

Now consider the effects of allowing the transactions *T* and *U* to run concurrently, as in Figure 13.5. Both transactions get the balance of *B* as $200 and then deposit $20. The result is incorrect, increasing the balance of account *B* by $20 instead of $42. This is an illustration of the 'lost update' problem. *U*'s update is lost because *T* overwrites it without seeing it. Both transactions have read the old value before either writes the new value.

In Figure 13.5 onwards, we show the operations that affect the balance of an account on successive lines down the page, and the reader should assume that an operation on a particular line is executed at a later time than the one on the line above it.

Inconsistent retrievals ◊ Figure 13.6 shows another example related to a bank account in which transaction *V* transfers a sum from account *A* to *B* and transaction *W* invokes

Figure 13.7   A serially equivalent interleaving of *T* and *U*

Transaction *T*:		**Transaction *U*:**	
balance = b.getBalance()		*balance = b.getBalance()*	
*b.setBalance(balance*1.1)*		*b.setBalance(balance*1.1)*	
a.withdraw(balance/10)		*c.withdraw(balance/10)*	
balance = b.getBalance()	$200		
*b.setBalance(balance*1.1)*	$220		
		balance = b.getBalance()	$220
		*b.setBalance(balance*1.1)*	$242
a.withdraw(balance/10)	$80		
		c.withdraw(balance/10)	$278

the *branchTotal* method to obtain the sum of the balances of all the accounts in the bank. The balances of the two bank accounts, *A* and *B*, are both initially $200. The result of *branchTotal* includes the sum of *A* and *B* as $300, which is wrong. This is an illustration of the 'inconsistent retrievals' problem. *W*'s retrievals are inconsistent because *V* has performed only the withdrawal part of a transfer at the time the sum is calculated.

Serial equivalence ◊ If each of several transactions is known to have the correct effect when it is done on its own, then we can infer that if these transactions are done one at a time in some order the combined effect will also be correct. An interleaving of the operations of transactions in which the combined effect is the same as if the transactions had been performed one at a time in some order is a serially equivalent interleaving. When we say that two different transactions have the *same effect* as one another, we mean that the read operations return the same values and that the instance variables of the objects have the same values at the end.

The use of serial equivalence as a criterion for correct concurrent execution prevents the occurrence of lost updates and inconsistent retrievals.

The lost update problem occurs when two transactions read the old value of a variable and then use it to calculate the new value. This cannot happen if one transaction is performed before the other, because the later transaction will read the value written by the earlier one. As a serially equivalent interleaving of two transactions produces the same effect as a serial one, we can solve the lost update problem by means of serial equivalence. Figure 13.7 shows one such interleaving in which the operations that affect the shared account, *B*, are actually serial, for transaction *T* does all its operations on *B* before transaction *U* does. Another interleaving of *T* and *U* that has this property is one in which transaction *U* completes its operations on account *B* before transaction *T* starts.

We now consider the effect of serial equivalence in relation to the inconsistent retrievals problem, in which transaction *V* is transferring a sum from account *A* to *B* and transaction *W* is obtaining the sum of all the balances (see Figure 13.6). The inconsistent retrievals problem can occur when a retrieval transaction runs concurrently with an update transaction. It cannot occur if the retrieval transaction is performed before or after the update transaction. A serially equivalent interleaving of a retrieval transaction

Figure 13.8   A serially equivalent interleaving of V and W

Transaction V:		Transaction W:	
a.withdraw(100);		aBranch.branchTotal( )	
b.deposit(100)			
a.withdraw(100);	$100		
b.deposit(100)	$300		
		total = a.getBalance( )	$100
		total = total + b.getBalance()	$400
		total = total + c.getBalance()	
		...	

and an update transaction, for example as in Figure 13.8, will prevent inconsistent retrievals occurring.

Conflicting operations ◊ When we say that a pair of operations conflicts we mean that their combined effect depends on the order in which they are executed. To simplify matters we consider a pair of operations *read* and *write*. *Read* accesses the value of an object and *write* changes its value. The *effect* of an operation refers to the value of an object set by a *write* operation and the result returned by a *read* operation. The conflict rules for *read* and *write* operations are given in Figure 13.9.

For any pair of transactions, it is possible to determine the order of pairs of conflicting operations on objects accessed by both of them. Serial equivalence can be defined in terms of operation conflicts as follows:

> For two transactions to be *serially equivalent*, it is necessary and sufficient that all pairs of conflicting operations of the two transactions be executed in the same order at all of the objects they both access.

Figure 13.9   *Read* and *write* operation conflict rules

Operations of different transactions		Conflict	Reason
read	read	No	Because the effect of a pair of *read* operations does not depend on the order in which they are executed
read	write	Yes	Because the effect of a *read* and a *write* operation depends on the order of their execution
write	write	Yes	Because the effect of a pair of *write* operations depends on the order of their execution

Figure 13.10   A non-serially equivalent interleaving of operations of transactions T and U

Transaction T:	Transaction U:
$x = read(i)$	
$write(i, 10)$	
	$y = read(j)$
	$write(j, 30)$
$write(j, 20)$	
	$z = read\ (i)$

Consider as an example the transactions T and U, defined as follows:

> T: x = read(i); write(i, 10); write(j, 20);
> U: y = read(j); write(j, 30); z = read (i);

Then consider the interleaving of their executions, shown in Figure 13.10. Note that each transaction's access to objects i and j is serialized with respect to one another, because T makes all of its accesses to i before U does and U makes all of its accesses to j before T does. But the ordering is not serially equivalent, because the pairs of conflicting operations are not done in the same order at both objects. Serially equivalent orderings require one of the following two conditions:

1. T accesses i before U and T accesses j before U.

2. U accesses i before T and U accesses j before T.

Serial equivalence is used as a criterion for the derivation of concurrency control protocols. These protocols attempt to serialize transactions in their access to objects. Three alternative approaches to concurrency control are commonly used: locking, optimistic concurrency control and timestamp ordering. However, most practical systems use locking, which is discussed in Section 13.4. When locking is used, the server sets a lock, labelled with the transaction identifier, on each object just before it is accessed and removes these locks when the transaction has completed. While an object is locked, only the transaction that it is locked for can access that object; other transactions must either wait until the object is unlocked or in some cases, share the lock. The use of locks can lead to deadlock, with transactions waiting for each other to release locks, as, for example, when a pair of transactions each has an object locked that the other needs to access. We shall discuss the deadlock problem and some remedies for it in Section 13.4.1.

Optimistic concurrency control is described in Section 13.5. In optimistic schemes, a transaction proceeds until it asks to commit, and before it is allowed to commit the server performs a check to discover whether it has performed operations on any objects that conflict with the operations of other concurrent transactions, in which case the server aborts it and the client may restart it. The aim of the check is to ensure that all the objects are correct.

Timestamp ordering is described in Section 13.6. In timestamp ordering, a server records the most recent time of reading and writing each object and for each operation,

Figure 13.11   A dirty read when transaction *T* aborts

Transaction *T*:		Transaction *U*:	
a.getBalance()		*a.getBalance()*	
a.setBalance(balance + 10)		*a.setBalance(balance + 20)*	
balance = a.getBalance()	$100		
a.setBalance(balance + 10)	$110		
		balance = a.getBalance()	$110
		a.setBalance(balance + 20)	$130
		commit transaction	
abort transaction			

the timestamp of the transaction is compared with that of the object to determine whether it can be done immediately, delayed or rejected. When an operation is delayed, the transaction waits; when it is rejected, the transaction is aborted.

Basically, concurrency control can be achieved either by clients' transactions waiting for one another or by restarting transactions after conflicts between operations have been detected, or by a combination of the two.

13.2.2   Recoverability from aborts

Servers must record the effects of all committed transactions and none of the effects of aborted transactions. They must therefore allow for the fact that a transaction may abort by preventing it affecting other concurrent transactions if it does so.

This section illustrates two problems associated with aborting transactions in the context of the banking example. These problems are called 'dirty reads' and 'premature writes', and both of them can occur in the presence of serially equivalent executions of transactions. These issues are concerned with the effects of operations on objects such as the balance of a bank account. To simplify things, operations are considered in two categories: *read* operations and *write* operations. In our illustrations, *getBalance* is a *read* operation and *setBalance* a *write* operation.

Dirty reads ◊   The isolation property of transactions requires that transactions do not see the uncommitted state of other transactions. The 'dirty read' problem is caused by the interaction between a read operation in one transaction and an earlier write operation in another transaction on the same object. Consider the executions illustrated in Figure 13.11, in which *T* gets the balance of account A and sets it to $10 more, then *U* gets the balance of account A and sets it to $20 more, and the two executions are serially equivalent. Now suppose that the transaction *T* aborts after *U* has committed. Then the transaction *U* will have seen a value that never existed, since A will be restored to its original value. We say that the transaction *U* has performed a *dirty read*. As it has committed, it cannot be undone.

Figure 13.12 Overwriting uncommitted values

Transaction *T*:		Transaction *U*:	
a.setBalance(105)		*a.setBalance(110)*	
	$100		
a.setBalance(105)	$105		
		a.setBalance(110)	$110

Recoverability of transactions ◊ If a transaction (like *U*) has committed after it has seen the effects of a transaction that subsequently aborted, the situation is not recoverable. To ensure that such situations will not arise, any transaction (like *U*) that is in danger of having a dirty read delays its commit operation. The strategy for recoverability is to delay commits until after the commitment of any other transaction whose uncommitted state has been observed. In our example, *U* delays its commit until after *T* commits. In the case that *T* aborts, then *U* must abort as well.

Cascading aborts ◊ In Figure 13.11, suppose that transaction *U* delays committing until after *T* aborts. As we have said, *U* must abort as well. Unfortunately, if any other transactions have seen the effects due to *U*, they too must be aborted. The aborting of these latter transactions may cause still further transactions to be aborted. Such situations are called *cascading aborts*. To avoid cascading aborts, transactions are only allowed to read objects that were written by committed transactions. To ensure that this is the case, any *read* operation must be delayed until other transactions that applied a *write* operation to the same object have committed or aborted. The avoidance of cascading aborts is a stronger condition than recoverability.

Premature writes ◊ Consider another implication of the possibility that a transaction may abort. This one is related to the interaction between *write* operations on the same object belonging to different transactions. For an illustration, we consider two *setBalance* transactions *T* and *U* on account A, as shown in Figure 13.12. Before the transactions, the balance of account A was $100. The two executions are serially equivalent, with *T* setting the balance to $105 and *U* setting it to $110. If the transaction *U* aborts and *T* commits, the balance should be $105.

Some database systems implement the action of *abort* by restoring 'before images' of all the *Writes* of a transaction. In our example, A is $100 initially, which is the 'before image' of *T*'s *write*; similarly $105 is the 'before image' of *U*'s *write*. Thus if *U* aborts, we get the correct balance of $105.

Now consider the case when *U* commits and then *T* aborts. The balance should be $110, but as the 'before image' of *T*'s *write* is $100, we get the wrong balance of $100. Similarly, if *T* aborts and then *U* aborts, the 'before image' of *U*'s *write* is $105 and we get the wrong balance of $105 – the balance should revert to $100.

To ensure correct results in a recovery scheme that uses before images, *write* operations must be delayed until earlier transactions that updated the same objects have either committed or aborted.

Figure 13.13   Nested transactions

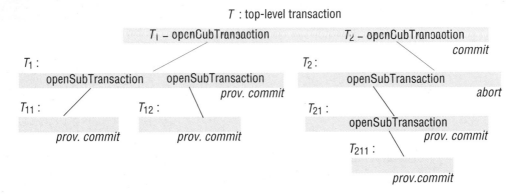

Strict executions of transactions ◊ Generally, it is required that transactions delay both their *read* and *write* operations so as to avoid both 'dirty reads' and 'premature writes'. The executions of transactions are called *strict* if the service delays both *read* and *write* operations on an object until all transactions that previously wrote that object have either committed or aborted. The strict execution of transactions enforces the desired property of isolation.

Tentative versions ◊ For a server of recoverable objects to participate in transactions, it must be designed so that any updates of objects can be removed if and when a transaction aborts. To make this possible, all of the update operations performed during a transaction are done in tentative versions of objects in volatile memory. Each transaction is provided with its own private set of tentative versions of any objects that it has altered. All the update operations of a transaction store values in the transaction's own private set. Access operations in a transaction take values from the transaction's own private set if possible, or failing that, from the objects.

The tentative versions are transferred to the objects only when a transaction commits, by which time they will also have been recorded in permanent storage. This is performed in a single step, during which other transactions are excluded from access to the objects that are being altered. When a transaction aborts, its tentative versions are deleted.

13.3 Nested transactions

Nested transactions extend the above transaction model by allowing transactions to be composed of other transactions. Thus several transactions may be started from within a transaction, allowing transactions to be regarded as modules that can be composed as required.

The outermost transaction in a set of nested transactions is called the *top-level* transaction. Transactions other than the top-level transaction are called *subtransactions*. For example in Figure 13.13, T is a top-level transaction, which starts a pair of subtransactions T_1 and T_2. The subtransaction T_1 starts its own pair of subtransactions

T_{11} and T_{22}. Also, subtransaction T_2 starts its own subtransaction T_{21} which starts another subtransaction T_{211}.

A subtransaction appears atomic to its parent with respect to transaction failures and to concurrent access. Subtransactions at the same level, such as T_1 and T_2 can run concurrently but their access to common objects is serialized, for example by the locking scheme described in Section 13.4. Each subtransaction can fail independently of its parent and of the other subtransactions. When a subtransaction aborts, the parent transaction can sometimes choose an alternative subtransaction to complete its task. For example, a transaction to deliver a mail message to a list of recipients could be structured as a set of subtransactions, each of which delivers the message to one of the recipients. If one or more of the subtransactions fails, the parent transaction could record the fact and then commit, with the result that all the successful child transactions commit. It could then start another transaction to attempt to redeliver the messages that were not sent the first time.

When we need to distinguish our original form of transaction from nested ones, we use the term *flat* transaction. It is flat because all of its work is done at the same level between an *openTransaction* and a *commit* or *abort*, and it is not possible to commit or abort parts of it. Nested transactions have the following main advantages:

1. Subtransactions at one level (and their descendants) may run concurrently with other subtransactions at the same level in the hierarchy. This can allow additional concurrency in a transaction. When subtransactions run in different servers, they can work in parallel. For example, consider the *branchTotal* operation in our banking example. It can be implemented by invoking *getBalance* at every account in the branch. Now each of these invocations may be performed as a subtransaction, in which case they can be performed concurrently. Since each one applies to a different account, there will be no conflicting operations among the subtransactions.

2. Subtransactions can commit or abort independently. In comparison with a single transaction, a set of nested subtransactions is potentially more robust. The above example of delivering mail shows that this is so – with a flat transaction, one transaction failure would cause the whole transaction to be restarted. In fact, a parent can decide on different actions according to whether a subtransaction has aborted or not.

The rules for committing of nested transactions are rather subtle:

- A transaction may commit or abort only after its child transactions have completed.

- When a subtransaction completes, it makes an independent decision either to commit provisionally or to abort. Its decision to abort is final.

- When a parent aborts, all of its subtransactions are aborted. For example, if T_2 aborts then T_{21} and T_{211} must also abort, even though they may have provisionally committed.

- When a subtransaction aborts, the parent can decide whether to abort or not. In our example, T decides to commit although T_2 has aborted.

- If the top-level transaction commits, then all of the subtransactions that have provisionally committed can commit too, provided that none of their ancestors has aborted. In our example, T's commitment allows T_1, T_{11} and T_{12} to commit, but not T_{21} and T_{211} since their parent T_2 aborted. Note that the effects of a subtransaction are not permanent until the top-level transaction commits.

In some cases, the top-level transaction may decide to abort because one or more of its subtransactions has aborted. As an example, consider the following *Transfer* transaction:

Transfer $100 from *B* to *A*
a.deposit(100)
b.withdraw(100)

This can be structured as a pair of subtransactions, one for the *withdraw* operation and the other for *deposit*. When the two subtransactions both commit, the *Transfer* transaction can also commit. Suppose that a *withdraw* subtransaction aborts whenever an account is overdrawn. Now consider the case when the *withdraw* subtransaction aborts and the *deposit* subtransaction commits – and recall that the commitment of a child transaction is conditional on the parent transaction committing. We presume that the top-level (*Transfer*) transaction will decide to abort. The aborting of the parent transaction causes the subtransactions to abort – so the *deposit* transaction is aborted and all its effects are undone.

The CORBA Object Transaction Service supports both flat and nested transactions. Nested transactions are particularly useful in distributed systems because child transactions may be run concurrently in different servers. We return to this issue in Chapter 14. This form of nested transactions is due to Moss [1985]. Other variants of nested transactions with different serializability properties have been proposed; for example, see Weikum [1991].

13.4 Locks

Transactions must be scheduled so that their effect on shared data is serially equivalent. A server can achieve serial equivalence of transactions by serializing access to the objects. Figure 13.7 shows an example of how serial equivalence can be achieved with some degree of concurrency – transactions T and U both access account B, but T completes its access before U starts accessing it.

A simple example of a serializing mechanism is the use of exclusive locks. In this locking scheme the server attempts to lock any object that is about to be used by any operation of a client's transaction. If a client requests access to an object that is already locked due to another client's transaction, the request is suspended and the client must wait until the object is unlocked.

Figure 13.14 illustrates the use of exclusive locks. It shows the same transactions as Figure 13.7, but with an extra column for each transaction showing the locking, waiting and unlocking. In this example, it is assumed that when transactions T and U start, the balances of the accounts A, B and C are not yet locked. When transaction T is about to use account B, it is locked for T. Subsequently, when transaction U is about to

Figure 13.14 Transactions *T* and *U* with exclusive locks

Transaction *T*:		Transaction *U*:	
balance = b.getBalance()		*balance = b.getBalance()*	
b.setBalance(bal*1.1)		*b.setBalance(bal*1.1)*	
a.withdraw(bal/10)		*c.withdraw(bal/10)*	
Operations	Locks	Operations	Locks
openTransaction			
bal = b.getBalance()	lock *B*		
b.setBalance(bal*1.1)		*openTransaction*	
a.withdraw(bal/10)	lock *A*	*bal = b.getBalance()*	waits for *T*'s lock on *B*
closeTransaction	unlock *A, B*	• • •	
			lock *B*
		b.setBalance(bal*1.1)	
		c.withdraw(bal/10)	lock *C*
		closeTransaction	unlock *B, C*

use *B* it is still locked for *T*, and transaction *U* waits. When transaction *T* is committed, *B* is unlocked, whereupon transaction *U* is resumed. The use of the lock on *B* effectively serializes the access to *B*. Note that if, for example, *T* had released the lock on *B* between its *getBalance* and *setBalance* operations, transaction *U*'s *getBalance* operation on *B* could be interleaved between them.

Serial equivalence requires that all of a transaction's accesses to a particular object be serialized with respect to accesses by other transactions. All pairs of conflicting operations of two transactions should be executed in the same order. To ensure this, a transaction is not allowed any new locks after it has released a lock. The first phase of each transaction is a 'growing phase', during which new locks are acquired. In the second phase, the locks are released (a 'shrinking phase'). This is called *two-phase locking*.

We saw in Section 13.2.2 that because transactions may abort, strict executions are needed to prevent dirty reads and premature writes. Under a strict execution regime, a transaction that needs to read or write an object must be delayed until other transactions that wrote the same object have committed or aborted. To enforce this rule, any locks applied during the progress of a transaction are held until the transaction commits or aborts. This is called *strict two-phase locking*. The presence of the locks prevents other transactions reading or writing the objects. When a transaction commits, to ensure recoverability, the locks must be held until all the objects it updated have been written to permanent storage.

A server generally contains a large number of objects, and a typical transaction accesses only a few of them and is unlikely to clash with other current transactions. The *granularity* with which concurrency control can be applied to objects is an important issue, since the scope for concurrent access to objects in a server will be limited severely if concurrency control (for example, locks) can only be applied to all the objects at once. In our banking example, if locks are applied to all customer accounts at a branch, only one bank clerk could perform an on-line banking transaction at any time – hardly an acceptable constraint!

The portion of the objects to which access must be serialized should be as small as possible; that is, just that part involved in each operation requested by transactions. In our banking example, a branch holds a set of accounts, each of which has a balance. Each banking operation affects one or more account balances – *deposit* and *withdraw* affect one account balance and *branchTotal* affects all of them.

The description of concurrency control schemes given below does not assume any particular granularity. We discuss concurrency control protocols that are applicable to objects whose operations can be modelled in terms of *read* and *write* operations on the objects. For the protocols to work correctly, it is essential that each *read* and *write* operation is atomic in its effects on objects.

Concurrency control protocols are designed to cope with *conflicts* between operations in different transactions on the same object. In this chapter, we use the notion of conflict between operations to explain the protocols. The conflict rules for *read* and *write* operations are given in Figure 13.9, which shows that pairs of *read* operations from different transactions on the same object do not conflict. Therefore, a simple exclusive lock that is used for both *read* and *write* operations reduces concurrency more than is necessary.

It is preferable to adopt a locking scheme that controls the access to each object so that there can be several concurrent transactions reading an object, or a single transaction writing an object, but not both. This is commonly referred to as a 'many readers/single writer' scheme. Two types of locks are used: *read locks* and *write locks*. Before a transaction's *read* operation is performed, a read lock should be set on the object. Before a transaction's *write* operation is performed, a write lock should be set on the object. Whenever it is impossible to set a lock immediately, the transaction (and the client) must wait until it is possible to do so – a client's request is never rejected.

As pairs of *read* operations from different transactions do not conflict, an attempt to set a read lock on an object with a read lock is always successful. All the transactions reading the same object share its read lock – for this reason, read locks are sometimes called *shared locks*.

The operation conflict rules tell us that:

1. If a transaction T has already performed a *read* operation on a particular object, then a concurrent transaction U must not *write* that object until T commits or aborts.

2. If a transaction T has already performed a *write* operation on a particular object, then a concurrent transaction U must not *read* or *write* that object until T commits or aborts.

To enforce (1), a request for a write lock on an object is delayed by the presence of a read lock belonging to another transaction. To enforce (2), a request for either a read lock or a write lock on an object is delayed by the presence of a write lock belonging to another transaction.

Figure 13.15   Lock compatibility

For one object		Lock requested	
		read	*write*
Lock already set	*none*	OK	OK
	read	OK	wait
	write	wait	wait

Figure 13.15 shows the compatibility of read locks and write locks on any particular object. The entries to the left of the first column in the table show the type of lock already set, if any. The entries above the first row show the type of lock requested. The entry in each cell shows the effect on a transaction that requests the type of lock given above when the object has been locked in another transaction with the type of lock on the left.

Inconsistent retrievals and lost updates are caused by conflicts between *read* operations in one transaction and *write* operations in another without the protection of a concurrency control scheme such as locking. Inconsistent retrievals are prevented by performing the retrieval transaction before or after the update transaction. If the retrieval transaction comes first, its read locks delay the update transaction. If it comes second, its request for read locks causes it to be delayed until the update transaction has completed.

Lost updates occur when two transactions read a value of an object and then use it to calculate a new value. Lost updates are prevented by making later transactions delay their reads until the earlier ones have completed. This is achieved by each transaction setting a read lock when it reads an object and then *promoting* it to a write lock when it writes the same object – when a subsequent transaction requires a read lock it will be delayed until any current transaction has completed.

A transaction with a read lock that is shared with other transactions cannot promote its read lock to a write lock, because the latter would conflict with the read locks held by the other transactions. Therefore, such a transaction must request a write lock and wait for the other read locks to be released.

Lock promotion refers to the conversion of a lock to a stronger lock – that is, a lock that is more exclusive. The lock compatibility table shows which locks are more or less exclusive. The read lock allows other read locks, whereas the write lock does not. Neither allows other write locks. Therefore, a write lock is more exclusive than a read lock. Locks may be promoted because the result is a more exclusive lock. It is not safe to demote a lock held by a transaction before it commits, because the result will be more permissive than the previous one and may allow executions by other transactions that are inconsistent with serial equivalence.

The rules for the use of locks in a strict two-phase locking implementation are summarized in Figure 13.16. To ensure that these rules are adhered to, the client has no access to operations for locking or unlocking items of data. Locking is performed when the requests for *read* and *write* operations are about to be applied to the recoverable objects, and unlocking is performed by the *commit* or *abort* operations of the transaction coordinator.

Figure 13.16   Use of locks in strict two-phase locking

1. When an operation accesses an object within a transaction:

   (a) If the object is not already locked, it is locked and the operation proceeds.

   (b) If the object has a conflicting lock set by another transaction, the transaction must wait until it is unlocked.

   (c) If the object has a non-conflicting lock set by another transaction, the lock is shared and the operation proceeds.

   (d) If the object has already been locked in the same transaction, the lock will be promoted if necessary and the operation proceeds. (Where promotion is prevented by a conflicting lock, rule (b) is used.)

2. When a transaction is committed or aborted, the server unlocks all objects it locked for the transaction.

For example, the CORBA Concurrency Control Service [OMG 2000b] can be used to apply concurrency control on behalf of transactions or to protect objects without using transactions. It provides a means of associating a collection of locks (called a *lockset*) with a resource such as a recoverable object. A lockset allows locks to be acquired or released. A lockset's *lock* method will acquire a lock or block until the lock is free; other methods allow locks to be promoted or released. Transactional locksets support the same methods as locksets, but their methods require transaction identifiers as arguments. We mentioned earlier that the CORBA transaction service tags all client requests in a transaction with the transaction identifier. This enables a suitable lock to be acquired before each of the recoverable objects is accessed during a transaction. The transaction coordinator is responsible for releasing the locks when a transaction commits or aborts.

The rules given in Figure 13.16 ensure strictness, because the locks are held until a transaction has either committed or aborted. However, it is not necessary to hold read locks to ensure strictness. Read locks need only be held until the request to commit or abort arrives.

Lock implementation ◊ The granting of locks will be implemented by a separate object in the server that we call the *lock manager*. The lock manager holds a set of locks, for example in a hash table. Each lock is an instance of the class *Lock* and is associated with a particular object. The class *Lock* is shown in Figure 13.17. Each instance of *Lock* maintains the following information in its instance variables:

- the identifier of the locked object;
- the transaction identifiers of the transactions that currently hold the lock (shared locks can have several holders);
- a lock type.

Figure 13.17   Lock class

```
public class Lock {
    private Object object;      // the object being protected by the lock
    private Vector holders;     // the TIDs of current holders
    private LockType lockType;  // the current type

    public synchronized void acquire(TransID trans,  LockType aLockType ){
        while(/*another transaction holds the lock in conflicing mode*/) {
            try {
                wait();
            }catch ( InterruptedException e){/*...*/ }
        }
        if (holders.isEmpty()) { // no TIDs  hold lock
            holders.addElement(trans);
            lockType = aLockType;
        } else if (/*another transaction holds the lock, share it*/ ) ){
            if (/* this transaction not a holder*/) holders.addElement(trans);
        } else if (/* this transaction is a holder but needs a more exclusive lock*/)
                lockType.promote();
        }
    }

    public synchronized void release(TransID trans ){
        holders.removeElement(trans);    // remove this holder
        // set locktype to none
        notifyAll();
    }
}
```

The methods of *Lock* are synchronized so that the threads attempting to acquire or release a lock will not interfere with one another. But, in addition, attempts to acquire the lock use the *wait* method whenever they have to wait for another thread to release it.

The *acquire* method carries out the rules given in Figure 13.15 and Figure 13.16. Its arguments specify a transaction identifier and the type of lock required by that transaction. It tests whether the request can be granted. If another transaction holds the lock in a conflicting mode, it invokes *wait*, which causes the caller's thread to be suspended until a corresponding *notify*. Note that the *wait* is enclosed in a *while*, because all waiters are notified and some of them may not be able to proceed. When, eventually, the condition is satisfied, the remainder of the method sets the lock appropriately:

- if no other transaction holds the lock, just add the given transaction to the holders and set the type;

Figure 13.18   *LockManager* class

```
public class LockManager {
  private Hashtable theLocks;

  public  void setLock(Object object, TransID trans,  LockType lockType){
    Lock foundLock;
    synchronized(this){
        // find the lock associated with object
        // if there isn't one, create it and add to the hashtable
      }
    foundLock.acquire(trans, lockType);
  }

  // synchronize this one because we want to remove all entries
  public synchronized void unLock(TransID trans) {
    Enumeration e = theLocks.elements();
    while(e.hasMoreElements()){
      Lock aLock = (Lock)(e.nextElement());
      if(/* trans is a holder of this lock*/ ) aLock.release(trans);
    }
  }
}
```

- else if another transaction holds the lock, share it by adding the given transaction to the holders (unless it is already a holder);

- else if this transaction is a holder but is requesting a more exclusive lock, promote the lock.

The *release* method's arguments specify the transaction identifier of the transaction that is releasing the lock. It removes the transaction identifier from the holders, sets the lock type to *none* and calls *notifyAll*. The method notifies all waiting threads in case there are multiple transactions waiting to acquire read locks, in which cases all of them may be able to proceed.

The class *LockManager* is shown in Figure 13.18. All requests to set locks and to release them on behalf of transactions are sent to an instance of *LockManager*.

- The *setLock* method's arguments specify the object that the given transaction wants to lock and the type of lock. It finds a lock for that object in its hashtable or if necessary creates one. It then invokes the *acquire* method of that lock.

- The *unLock* method's argument specifies the transaction that is releasing its locks. It finds all of the locks in the hashtable that have the given transaction as a holder. For each one, it calls the *release* method.

Some questions of policy: Note that, when several threads *wait* on the same locked item, the semantics of *wait* ensure that each transaction gets its turn. In the above program, the conflict rules allow the holders of a lock to be either multiple readers or one writer. The arrival of a request for a read lock is always granted unless the holder has a write lock. The reader is invited to consider the following:

- What is the consequence for *write* transactions in the presence of a steady trickle of requests for read locks? Think of an alternative implementation.

When the holder has a write lock, several readers and writers may be waiting. The reader should consider the effect of *notifyAll* and think of an alternative implementation. If a holder of a read lock tries to promote the lock when the lock is shared, it will be blocked. Is there any solution to this difficulty?

Locking rules for nested transactions ◊ The aim of a locking scheme for nested transactions is to serialize access to objects so that:

1. each set of nested transactions is a single entity that must be prevented from observing the partial effects of any other set of nested transactions;

2. each transaction within a set of nested transactions must be prevented from observing the partial effects of the other transactions in the set.

The first rule is enforced by arranging that every lock that is acquired by a successful subtransaction is *inherited* by its parent when it completes. Inherited locks are also inherited by ancestors. Note that this form of inheritance passes from child to parent! The top-level transaction eventually inherits all of the locks that were acquired by successful subtransactions at any depth in a nested transaction. This ensures that the locks can be held until the top-level transaction has committed or aborted, which prevents members of different sets of nested transactions observing one another's partial effects.

The second rule is enforced as follows:

- parent transactions are not allowed to run concurrently with their child transactions. If a parent transaction has a lock on an object, it *retains* the lock during the time that its child transaction is executing. This means that the child transaction temporarily acquires the lock from its parent for its duration;

- subtransactions at the same level are allowed to run concurrently, so when they access the same objects, the locking scheme must serialize their access.

The following rules describe lock acquisition and release:

- for a subtransaction to acquire a read lock on an object, no other active transaction can have a write lock on that object, and the only retainers of a write lock are its ancestors;

- for a subtransaction to acquire a write lock on an object, no other active transaction can have a read or write lock on that object, and the only retainers of read and write locks on that object are its ancestors;

- when a subtransaction commits, its locks are inherited by its parent, allowing the parent to retain the locks in the same mode as the child;

Figure 13.19   Deadlock with write locks

Transaction T		Transaction U	
Operations	Locks	Operations	Locks
a.deposit(100);	write lock A		
		b.deposit(200)	write lock B
b.withdraw(100)			
•••	waits for U's	a.withdraw(200);	waits for T's
	lock on B	•••	lock on A
•••		•••	
•••		•••	

- when a subtransaction aborts, its locks are discarded. If the parent already retains the locks it can continue to do so.

Note that subtransactions at the same level that access the same object will take turns to acquire the locks retained by their parent. This ensures that their access to a common object is serialized.

As an example, suppose that subtransactions T_1, T_2 and T_{11} in Figure 13.13 all access a common object, which is not accessed by the top-level transaction T. Suppose that subtransaction T_1 is the first to access the object and successfully acquires a lock, which it passes on to T_{11} for the duration of its execution, getting it back when T_{11} completes. When T_1 completes its execution, the top-level transaction T inherits the lock, which it retains until the set of nested transactions completes. The subtransaction T_2 can acquire the lock from T for the duration of its execution.

13.4.1 Deadlocks

The use of locks can lead to deadlock. Consider the use of locks shown in Figure 13.19. Since the *deposit* and *withdraw* methods are atomic, we show them acquiring write locks – although in practice they read the balance and then write it. Each of them acquires a lock on one account and then gets blocked when it tries to access the account that the other one has locked. This is a deadlock situation – two transactions are waiting, and each is dependent on the other to release a lock so it can resume.

Deadlock is a particularly common situation when clients are involved in an interactive program, for a transaction in an interactive program may last for a long period of time, resulting in many objects being locked and remaining so, thus preventing other clients using them.

Note that the locking of sub-items in structured objects can be useful for avoiding conflicts and possible deadlock situations. For example, a day in a diary could be structured as a set of time slots, each of which can be locked independently for updating. Hierarchic locking schemes are useful if the application requires a different granularity of locking for different operations. See Section 13.4.2.

Figure 13.20   The wait-for graph for Figure 13.19

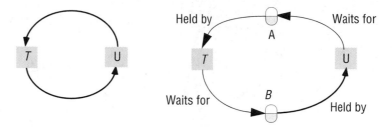

Figure 13.21   A cycle in a wait-for graph

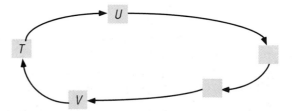

Definition of deadlock ◊ Deadlock is a state in which each member of a group of transactions is waiting for some other member to release a lock. A *wait-for graph* can be used to represent the waiting relationships between current transactions. In a wait-for graph the nodes represent transactions and the edges represent wait-for relationships between transactions – there is an edge from node T to node U when transaction T is waiting for transaction U to release a lock. See Figure 13.20, which illustrates the wait-for graph corresponding to the deadlock situation illustrated in Figure 13.19. Recall that the deadlock arose because transactions T and U both attempted to acquire an object held by the other. Therefore T waits for U and U waits for T. The dependency between transactions is indirect – via a dependency on objects. The diagram on the right shows the objects held by and waited for by transactions T and U. As each transaction can wait for only one object, the objects can be omitted from the wait-for graph – leaving the simple graph on the left.

Suppose that as in Figure 13.21, a wait-for graph contains a cycle $T \rightarrow U \rightarrow \dots \rightarrow V \rightarrow T$, then each transaction is waiting for the next transaction in the cycle. All of these transactions are blocked waiting for locks. None of the locks can ever be released, and the transactions are deadlocked. If one of the transactions in a cycle is aborted, then its locks are released and that cycle is broken. For example, if transaction T in Figure 13.21 is aborted, it will release a lock on an object that V is waiting for – and V will no longer be waiting for T.

Now consider a scenario in which the three transactions T, U and V share a read lock on an object C, transaction W holds a write lock on object B on which transaction V is waiting to obtain a lock, as shown on the right in Figure 13.22. The transactions T and W then request write locks on object C and a deadlock situation arises in which T

Figure 13.22   Another wait-for graph

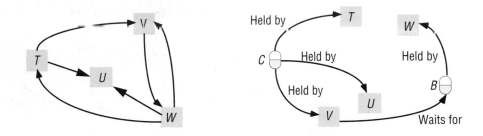

waits for U and V, V waits for W, and W waits for T, U and V, as shown on the left in Figure 13.22. This shows that although each transaction can wait for only one object at a time, it may be involved in several cycles. For example, transaction V is involved in cycles: $V \rightarrow W \rightarrow T \rightarrow V$ and $V \rightarrow W \rightarrow V$.

In this example, suppose that transaction V is aborted. This will release V's lock on C and the two cycles involving V will be broken.

Deadlock prevention ◊ One solution is to prevent deadlock. An apparently simple but not very good way to overcome deadlock is to lock all of the objects used by a transaction when it starts. This would need to be done as a single atomic step so as to avoid deadlock at this stage. Such a transaction cannot run into deadlock with other transactions, but it unnecessarily restricts access to shared resources. In addition, it is sometimes impossible to predict at the start of a transaction which objects will be used. This is generally the case in interactive applications, for the user would have to say in advance exactly which objects they were planning to use, which is inconceivable in browsing-style applications, which allow users to find objects they do not know about in advance. Deadlock can also be prevented by requesting locks on objects in a predefined order, but this can result in premature locking and a reduction in concurrency.

Upgrade locks ◊ CORBA's Concurrency Control Service introduces a third type of lock, called *upgrade,* the use of which is intended to avoid deadlock. Deadlock is often caused by two conflicting transactions first taking read locks and then attempting to promote them to write locks. A transaction with an upgrade lock on a data item is permitted to read that data item, but this lock conflicts with any upgrade locks set by other transactions on the same data item. This type of lock cannot be set implicitly by the use of a *read* operation, but must be requested by the client.

Deadlock detection ◊ Deadlocks may be detected by finding cycles in the wait-for graph. Having detected a deadlock, a transaction must be selected for abortion to break the cycle.

The software responsible for deadlock detection can be part of the lock manager. It must hold a representation of the wait-for graph so that it can check it for cycles from time to time. Edges are added to the graph and removed from the graph by the lock manager's *setLock* and *unLock* operations. At the point illustrated by Figure 13.22 on the left it will have the following information:

Transaction	Waits for transaction
T	U, V
V	W
W	T, U, V

An edge $T \rightarrow U$ is added whenever the lock manager blocks a request by transaction T for a lock on an object that is already locked on behalf of transaction U. Note that when a lock is shared, several edges may be added. An edge $T \rightarrow U$ is deleted whenever U releases a lock that T is waiting for and allows T to proceed. See Exercise 13.14 for a more detailed discussion of the implementation of deadlock detection. If a transaction shares a lock, the lock is not released, but the edges leading to a particular transaction are removed.

The presence of cycles may be checked each time an edge is added, or less frequently to avoid unnecessary overhead. When a deadlock is detected, one of the transactions in the cycle must be chosen and then be aborted. The corresponding node and the edges involving it must be removed from the wait-for graph. This will happen when the aborted transaction has its locks removed.

The choice of the transaction to abort is not simple. Some factors that may be taken into account are the age of the transaction and the number of cycles it is involved in.

Timeouts ◊ Lock timeouts are a method for resolution of deadlocks that is commonly used. Each lock is given a limited period in which it is invulnerable. After this time, a lock becomes vulnerable. Provided that no other transaction is competing for the object that is locked, an object with a vulnerable lock remains locked. However, if any other transaction is waiting to access the object protected by a vulnerable lock, the lock is broken (that is, the object is unlocked) and the waiting transaction resumes. The transaction whose lock has been broken is normally aborted.

There are many problems with the use of timeouts as a remedy for deadlocks: the worst problem is that transactions are sometimes aborted due to their locks becoming vulnerable when other transactions are waiting for them, but there is actually no deadlock. In an overloaded system, the number of transactions timing out will increase, and transactions taking a long time can be penalized. In addition, it is hard to decide on an appropriate length for a timeout. In contrast, if deadlock detection is used, transactions are aborted because deadlocks have occurred and a choice can be made as to which transaction to abort.

Using lock timeouts, we can resolve the deadlock in Figure 13.19 as shown in Figure 13.23, in which the write lock for T on A becomes vulnerable after its timeout period. Transaction U is waiting to acquire a write lock on A. Therefore, T is aborted and it releases its lock on A, allowing U to resume and complete the transaction.

When transactions access objects located in several different servers, the possibility of distributed deadlocks arises. In a distributed deadlock, the wait-for graph can involve objects at multiple locations. We return to this subject in Section 14.5.

Figure 13.23   Resolution of the deadlock in Figure 13.19

Transaction T		Transaction U	
Operations	Locks	Operations	Locks
a.deposit(100);	write lock A		
		b.deposit(200)	write lock B
b.withdraw(100)			
•••	waits for U's	*a.withdraw(200);*	waits for T's
	lock on B	•••	lock on A
	(timeout elapses)	•••	
T's lock on A becomes vulnerable, unlock A, abort T			
		a.withdraw(200);	write locks A
			unlock A, B

13.4.2 Increasing concurrency in locking schemes

Even when locking rules are based on the conflicts between *read* and *write* operations and the granularity at which they are applied is as small as possible, there is still some scope for increasing concurrency. We shall discuss two approaches that have been used. In the first approach (two-version locking), the setting of exclusive locks is delayed until a transaction commits. In the second approach (hierarchic locks), mixed-granularity locks are used.

Two-version locking ◊ This is an optimistic scheme that allows one transaction to write tentative versions of objects while other transactions read from the committed version of the same objects. *Read* operations only wait if another transaction is currently committing the same object. This scheme allows more concurrency than read-write locks, but writing transactions risk waiting or even rejection when they attempt to commit. Transactions cannot commit their *write* operations immediately if other uncompleted transactions have read the same objects. Therefore, transactions that request to commit in such a situation are made to wait until the reading transactions have completed. Deadlock may occur when transactions are waiting to commit. Therefore, transactions may need to be aborted when they are waiting to commit, to resolve deadlocks.

This variation on strict two-phase locking uses three types of lock: a read lock, a write lock and a commit lock. Before a transaction's *read* operation is performed, a read lock must be set on the object – the attempt to set a read lock is successful unless the object has a commit lock, in which case the transaction waits. Before a transaction's *write* operation is performed, a write lock must be set on the object – the attempt to set a write lock is successful unless the object has a write lock or a commit lock, in which case the transaction waits.

Figure 13.24 Lock compatibility (*read*, *write* and *commit* locks)

For one object		*Lock to be set*		
		read	*write*	*commit*
Lock already set	*none*	OK	OK	OK
	read	OK	OK	wait
	write	OK	wait	–
	commit	wait	wait	–

When the transaction coordinator receives a request to commit a transaction, it attempts to convert all that transaction's write locks to commit locks. If any of the objects have outstanding read locks, the transaction must wait until the transactions that set these locks have completed and the locks are released. The compatibility of read, write and commit locks is shown in Figure 13.24.

There are two main differences in performance between the two-version locking scheme and an ordinary read-write locking scheme. On the one hand, *read* operations in the two-version locking scheme are delayed only while the transactions are being committed rather than during the entire execution of transactions – in most cases, the commit protocol takes only a small fraction of the time required to perform an entire transaction. On the other hand, *read* operations of one transaction can cause delay in committing other transactions.

Hierarchic locks ◊ In some applications, the granularity suitable for one operation is not appropriate for another operation. In our banking example, the majority of the operations require locking at the granularity of an account. The *branchTotal* operation is different – it reads the values of all the account balances and would appear to require a read lock on all of them. To reduce locking overhead, it would be useful to allow locks of mixed granularity to coexist.

Gray [1978] proposed the use of a hierarchy of locks with different granularities. At each level, the setting of a parent lock has the same effect as setting all the equivalent child locks. This economizes on the number of locks to be set. In our banking example, the branch is the parent and the accounts are children (see Figure 13.25).

Mixed-granularity locks could be useful in a diary system in which the data could be structured with the diary for a week being composed of a page for each day and the latter subdivided further into a slot for each time of day, as shown in Figure 13.26. The operation to view a week would cause a read lock to be set at the top of this hierarchy, whereas the operation to enter an appointment would cause a write lock to be set on a time slot. The effect of a read lock on a week would be to prevent write operations on any of the substructures, for example, the time slots for each day in that week.

In Gray's scheme, each node in the hierarchy can be locked – giving the owner of the lock explicit access to the node and implicit access to its children. In our example, in Figure 13.25 a read/write lock on the branch implicitly read/write locks all the accounts. Before a child node is granted a read/write lock, an intention to read/write lock

Figure 13.25 Lock hierarchy for the banking example

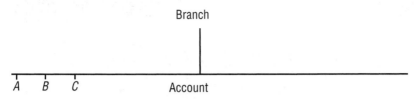

Figure 13.26 Lock hierarchy for a diary

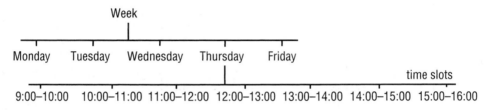

is set on the parent node and its ancestors (if any). The intention lock is compatible with other intention locks but conflicts with read and write locks according to the usual rules. Figure 13.27 gives the compatibility table for hierarchic locks. Gray also proposed a third type of intention lock – one that combines the property of a read lock with an intention to write lock.

In our banking example, the *branchTotal* operation requests a read lock on the branch, which implicitly sets read locks on all the accounts. A *deposit* operation needs to set a write lock on a balance, but first it attempts to set an intention to write lock on the branch. These rules prevent these operations running concurrently.

Hierarchic locks have the advantage of reducing the number of locks when mixed-granularity locking is required. The compatibility tables and the rules for promoting locks are more complex.

The mixed granularity of locks could allow each transaction to lock a portion whose size is chosen according to its needs. A long transaction that accesses many objects could lock the whole collection, whereas a short transaction can lock at finer granularity.

The CORBA Concurrency Control Service supports variable granularity locking with intention to read and intention to write lock types. These can be used as described above to take advantage the opportunity to apply locks at differing granularities in hierarchically structured data.

Figure 13.27 Lock compatibility table for hierarchic locks

For one object		Lock to be set			
		read	*write*	*I-read*	*I-write*
Lock already set	*none*	OK	OK	OK	OK
	read	OK	wait	OK	wait
	write	wait	wait	wait	wait
	I-read	OK	wait	OK	OK
	I-write	wait	wait	OK	OK

13.5 Optimistic concurrency control

Kung and Robinson [1981] identified a number of inherent disadvantages of locking and proposed an alternative optimistic approach to the serialization of transactions that avoids these drawbacks. We can summarize the drawbacks of locking:

- Lock maintenance represents an overhead that is not present in systems that do not support concurrent access to shared data. Even read-only transactions (queries), which cannot possibly affect the integrity of the data, must, in general, use locking in order to guarantee that the data being read is not modified by other transactions at the same time. But locking may be necessary only in the worst case.

  For example, consider two client processes that are concurrently incrementing the values of n objects. If the client programs start at the same time and run for about the same amount of time, accessing the objects in two unrelated sequences and using a separate transaction to access and increment each item, the chances that the two programs will attempt to access the same object at the same time are just 1 in n on average, so locking is really needed only once in every n transactions.

- The use of locks can result in deadlock. Deadlock prevention reduces concurrency severely, and therefore deadlock situations must be resolved either by the use of timeouts or by deadlock detection. Neither of these is wholly satisfactory for use in interactive programs.

- To avoid cascading aborts, locks cannot be released until the end of the transaction. This may reduce significantly the potential for concurrency.

The alternative approach proposed by Kung and Robinson is 'optimistic' because it is based on the observation that, in most applications, the likelihood of two clients' transactions accessing the same object is low. Transactions are allowed to proceed as though there were no possibility of conflict with other transactions until the client completes its task and issues a *closeTransaction* request. When a conflict arises, some transaction is generally aborted and will need to be restarted by the client. Each transaction has the following phases:

Working phase: During the working phase, each transaction has a tentative version of each of the objects that it updates.This is a copy of the most recently committed version of the object. The use of tentative versions allows the transaction to abort (with no effect on the objects), either during the working phase or if it fails validation due to other conflicting transactions. *Read* operations are performed immediately – if a tentative version for that transaction already exists, a *read* operation accesses it, otherwise it accesses the most recently committed value of the object. *Write* operations record the new values of the objects as tentative values (which are invisible to other transactions). When there are several concurrent transactions, several different tentative values of the same object may coexist. In addition, two records are kept of the objects accessed within a transaction: a *read set* containing the objects read by the transaction; and a *write set* containing the objects written by the transaction. Note that as all *read* operations are performed on committed versions of the objects (or copies of them), dirty reads cannot occur.

Validation phase: When the *closeTransaction* request is received, the transaction is validated to establish whether or not its operations on objects conflict with operations of other transactions on the same objects. If the validation is successful, then the transaction can commit. If the validation fails, then some form of conflict resolution must be used and either the current transaction, or in some cases those with which it conflicts, will need to be aborted.

Update phase: If a transaction is validated, all of the changes recorded in its tentative versions are made permanent. Read-only transactions can commit immediately after passing validation. Write transactions are ready to commit once the tentative versions of the objects have been recorded in permanent storage.

Validation of transactions ◊ Validation uses the read-write conflict rules to ensure that the scheduling of a particular transaction is serially equivalent with respect to all other *overlapping* transactions – that is, any transactions that had not yet committed at the time this transaction started. To assist in performing validation, each transaction is assigned a transaction number when it enters the validation phase (that is, when the client issues a *closeTransaction*). If the transaction is validated and completes successfully it retains this number; if it fails the validation checks and is aborted, or if the transaction is read only, the number is released for reassignment. Transaction numbers are integers assigned in ascending sequence; the number of a transaction therefore defines its position in time – a transaction always finishes its working phase after all transactions with lower numbers. That is, a transaction with the number T_i always precedes a transaction with the number T_j if i < j. (If the transaction number were to be assigned at the beginning of the working phase, then a transaction that reached the end of the working phase before one with a lower number would have to wait until the earlier one had completed before it could be validated.)

The validation test on transaction T_v is based on conflicts between operations in pairs of transaction T_i and T_v. For a transaction T_v to be serializable with respect to an overlapping transaction T_i, their operations must conform to the following rules:

T_v	T_i	Rule	
write	read	1.	T_i must not read objects written by T_v.
read	write	2.	T_v must not read objects written by T_i.
write	write	3.	T_i must not write objects written by T_v and T_v must not write objects written by T_i.

As the validation and update phases of a transaction are generally short in duration compared with the working phase, a simplification can be achieved by making the rule that only one transaction may be in the validation and update phase at one time. When no two transactions may overlap in the update phase, rule 3 is satisfied. Note that this restriction on *write* operations, together with the fact that no dirty reads can occur, produces strict executions. To prevent overlapping, the entire validation and update phases can be implemented as a critical section so that only one client at a time can execute it. In order to increase concurrency, part of the validation and updating may be implemented outside the critical section, but it is essential that the assignment of transaction numbers is performed sequentially. We note that at any instant, the current transaction number is like a pseudo-clock that ticks whenever a transaction completes successfully.

The validation of a transaction must ensure that the rules 1 and 2 are obeyed by testing for overlaps between the objects of pairs of transactions T_v and T_i. There are two forms of validation – backward and forward [Härder 1984]. Backward validation checks the transaction undergoing validation with other preceding overlapping transactions – those that entered the validation phase before it. Forward validation checks the transaction undergoing validation with other later transactions, which are still active.

Backward validation ◊ As all the *read* operations of earlier overlapping transactions were performed before the validation of T_v started, they cannot be affected by the *writes* of the current transaction (and rule 1 is satisfied). The validation of transaction T_v checks whether its read set (the objects affected by the *read* operations of T_v) overlaps with any of the write sets of earlier overlapping transactions T_i (rule 2). If there is any overlap, the validation fails.

Let *startTn* be the biggest transaction number assigned (to some other committed transaction) at the time when transaction T_v started its working phase and *finishTn* be the biggest transaction number assigned at the time when T_v entered the validation phase. The following program describes the algorithm for the validation of T_v:

```
boolean valid = true;
for (int Ti = startTn+1; Ti <= finishTn; Ti++){
    if (read set of Tv intersects write set of Ti) valid = false;
}
```

Figure 13.28 shows overlapping transactions that might be considered in the validation of a transaction T_v. Time increases from left to right. The earlier committed transactions are T_1, T_2 and T_3. T_1 committed before T_v started. T_2 and T_3 committed before T_v finished its working phase. *StartTn* $+ 1 = T_2$ and *finishTn* $= T_3$. In backward validation, the read set of T_v must be compared with the write sets of T_2 and T_3.

Figure 13.28   Validation of transactions

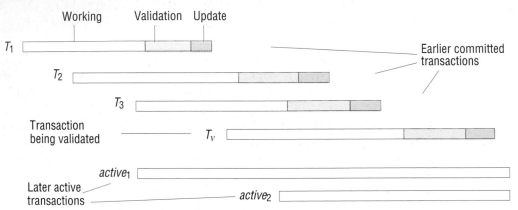

In backward validation, the read set of the transaction being validated is compared with the write sets of other transactions that have already committed. Therefore, the only way to resolve any conflicts is to abort the transaction that is undergoing validation.

In backward validation, transactions that have no *read* operations (only *write* operations) need not be checked.

Optimistic concurrency control with backward validation requires that the write sets of old committed versions of objects corresponding to recently committed transactions are retained until there are no unvalidated overlapping transactions with which they might conflict. Whenever a transaction is successfully validated, its transaction number, *startTn* and write set are recorded in a preceding transactions list that is maintained by the transaction service. Note that this list is ordered by transaction number. In an environment with long transactions, the retention of old write sets of objects may be a problem. For example, in Figure 13.28 the write sets of T_1, T_2, T_3 and T_v must be retained until the active transaction *active*$_1$ completes. Note that the although the active transactions have transaction identifiers, they do not yet have transaction numbers.

Forward validation ◊   In forward validation of the transaction T_v, the write set of T_v is compared with the read sets of all overlapping active transactions – those that are still in their working phase (rule 1). Rule 2 is automatically fulfilled because the active transactions do not write until after T_v has completed. Let the active transactions have (consecutive) transaction identifiers *active*$_1$ to *active*$_N$, then the following program describes the algorithm for the forward validation of T_v:

```
boolean valid = true;
for (int Tid = active1; Tid <= activeN; Tid++){
    if (write set of Tv intersects read set of Tid) valid = false;
}
```

In Figure 13.28, the write set of transaction T_v must be compared with the read sets of the transactions with identifiers *active*$_1$ and *active*$_2$. (Forward validation should allow for the fact that read sets of active transactions may change during validation and writing.) As the read sets of the transaction being validated are not included in the check, read-only transactions always pass the validation check. As the transactions being compared with the validating transaction are still active, we have a choice of whether to abort the validating transaction or to take some alternative way of resolving the conflict. Härder [1984] suggests several alternative strategies:

- Defer the validation until a later time when the conflicting transactions have finished. However, there is no guarantee that the transaction being validated will fare any better in the future. There is always the chance that further conflicting active transactions may start before the validation is achieved.

- Abort all the conflicting active transactions and commit the transaction being validated.

- Abort the transaction being validated. This is the simplest strategy but has the disadvantage that future conflicting transactions may be going to abort, in which case the transaction under validation has aborted unnecessarily.

Comparison of forward and backward validation ◊ We have already seen that forward validation allows flexibility in the resolution of conflicts, whereas backward validation allows only one choice – to abort the transaction being validated. In general, the read sets of transactions are much larger than the write sets. Therefore, backward validation compares a possibly large read set against the old write sets, whereas forward validation checks a small write set against the read sets of active transactions. We see that backward validation has the overhead of storing old write sets until they are no longer needed. On the other hand, forward validation has to allow for new transactions starting during the validation process.

Starvation ◊ When a transaction is aborted, it will normally be restarted by the client program. But in schemes that rely on aborting and restarting transactions, there is no guarantee that a particular transaction will ever pass the validation checks, for it may come into conflict with other transactions for the use of objects each time it is restarted. The prevention of a transaction ever being able to commit is called starvation.

Occurrences of starvation are likely to be rare, but a server that uses optimistic concurrency control must ensure that a client does not have its transaction aborted repeatedly. Kung and Robinson suggest that this could be done if the server detects a transaction that has been aborted several times. They suggest that when the server detects such a transaction it should be given exclusive access by the use of a critical section protected by a semaphore.

13.6 Timestamp ordering

In concurrency control schemes based on timestamp ordering, each operation in a transaction is validated when it is carried out. If the operation cannot be validated, the transaction is aborted immediately and can then be restarted by the client. Each transaction is assigned a unique timestamp value when it starts. The timestamp defines its position in the time sequence of transactions. Requests from transactions can be totally ordered according to their timestamps. The basic timestamp ordering rule is based on operation conflicts and is very simple:

- A transaction's request to write an object is valid only if that object was last read and written by earlier transactions. A transaction's request to read an object is valid only if that object was last written by an earlier transaction.

This rule assumes that there is only one version of each object and restricts access to one transaction at a time. If each transaction has its own tentative version of each object it accesses, then multiple concurrent transactions can access the same object. The timestamp ordering rule is refined to ensure that each transaction accesses a consistent set of versions of the objects. It must also ensure that the tentative versions of each object are committed in the order determined by the timestamps of the transactions that made them. This is achieved by transactions waiting, when necessary, for earlier transactions to complete their writes. The *write* operations may be performed after the *closeTransaction* operation has returned, without making the client wait. But the client must wait when *read* operations need to wait for earlier transactions to finish. This cannot lead to deadlock, since transactions only wait for earlier ones (and no cycle could occur in the wait-for graph).

Timestamps may be assigned from the server's clock or, as in the previous section, a 'pseudo-time' may be based on a counter that is incremented whenever a timestamp value is issued. We defer until Chapter 14 the problem of generating timestamps when the transaction service is distributed and several servers are involved in a transaction.

We will now describe a form of timestamp-based concurrency control following the methods adopted in the SDD-1 system [Bernstein *et al*. 1980] and described by Ceri and Pelagatti [1985].

As usual, the *write* operations are recorded in tentative versions of objects and are invisible to other transactions until a *closeTransaction* request is issued and the transaction is committed. Every object has a write timestamp and a set of tentative versions, each of which has a write timestamp associated with it; and a set of read timestamps. The write timestamp of the (committed) object is earlier than that of any of its tentative versions, and the set of read timestamps can be represented by its maximum member. Whenever a transaction's *write* operation on an object is accepted, the server creates a new tentative version of the object with write timestamp set to the transaction timestamp. A transaction's *read* operation is directed to the version with the maximum write timestamp less than the transaction timestamp. Whenever a transaction's *read* operation on an object is accepted, the timestamp of the transaction is added to its set of read timestamps. When a transaction is committed, the values of the tentative versions become the values of the objects, and the timestamps of the tentative versions become the timestamps of the corresponding objects.

In timestamp ordering, each request by a transaction for a *read* or *write* operation on an object is checked to see whether it conforms to the operation conflict rules. A request by the current transaction T_c can conflict with previous operations done by other transactions, T_i, whose timestamps indicate that they should be later than T_c. These rules are shown in Figure 13.29, in which $T_i > T_c$ means T_i is later than T_c and $T_i < T_c$ means T_i, is earlier than T_c.

Figure 13.29 Operation conflicts for timestamp ordering

Rule	T_c	T_i	
1.	write	read	T_c must not *write* an object that has been *read* by any T_i where $T_i > T_c$ this requires that $T_c \geq$ the maximum read timestamp of the object.
2.	write	write	T_c must not *write* an object that has been *written* by any T_i where $T_i > T_c$ this requires that $T_c >$ write timestamp of the committed object.
3.	read	write	T_c must not *read* an object that has been *written* by any T_i where $T_i > T_c$ this requires that $T_c >$ write timestamp of the committed object.

Timestamp ordering write rule: By combining rules 1 and 2 we have the following rule for deciding whether to accept a *write* operation requested by transaction T_c on object D:

```
if (T_c ≥ maximum read timestamp on D &&
    T_c > write timestamp on committed version of D)
        perform write operation on tentative version of D with write timestamp T_c
else /* write is too late */
    Abort transaction T_c
```

If a tentative version with write timestamp T_c already exists, the *write* operation is addressed to it, otherwise a new tentative version is created and given write timestamp T_c. Note that any *write* that 'arrives too late' is aborted – it is too late in the sense that a transaction with a later timestamp has already read or written the object.

Figure 13.30 illustrates the action of a *write* operation by transaction T_3 in cases where $T_3 \geq$ maximum read timestamp on the object (the read timestamps are not shown). In cases (a) to (c) $T_3 >$ write timestamp on the committed version of the object and a tentative version with write timestamp T_3 is inserted at the appropriate place in the list of tentative versions ordered by their transaction timestamps. In case (d), $T_3 <$ write timestamp on the committed version of the object and the transaction is aborted.

Timestamp ordering read rule: By using rule 3 we have the following rule for deciding whether to accept immediately, to wait or to reject a *read* operation requested by transaction T_c on object D:

```
if ( T_c > write timestamp on committed version of D) {
        let D_selected be the version of D with the maximum write timestamp ≤ T_c
        if (D_selected is committed)
            perform read operation on the version D_selected
        else
                Wait until the transaction that made version D_selected commits or aborts
                then reapply the read rule
} else
        Abort transaction T_c
```

Figure 13.30   Write operations and timestamps

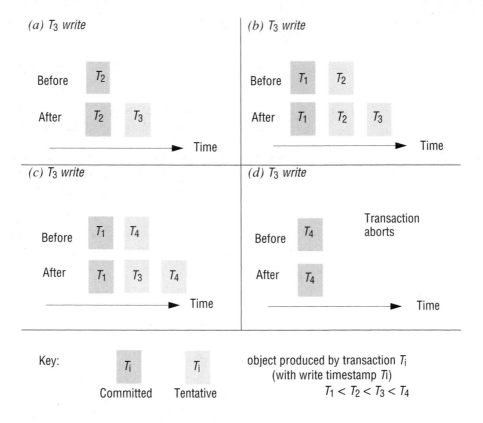

(a) T_3 write

Before T_2

After T_2 T_3

→ Time

(b) T_3 write

Before T_1 T_2

After T_1 T_2 T_3

→ Time

(c) T_3 write

Before T_1 T_4

After T_1 T_3 T_4

→ Time

(d) T_3 write

Transaction aborts

Before T_4

After T_4

→ Time

Key:

T_i Committed T_i Tentative   object produced by transaction T_i
(with write timestamp T_i)
$T_1 < T_2 < T_3 < T_4$

Note:

- If transaction T_c has already written its own version of the object, this will be used.

- A *read* operation that arrives too early waits for the earlier transaction to complete. If the earlier transaction commits, then T_c will read from its committed version. If it aborts, then T_c will repeat the read rule (and select the previous version). This rule prevents dirty reads.

- A *read* operation that 'arrives too late' is aborted – it is too late in the sense that a transaction with a later timestamp has already written the object.

Figure 13.31 illustrates the timestamp ordering read rule. It includes four cases labelled (a) to (d), each of which illustrates the action of a *read* operation by transaction T_3. In each case, a version whose write timestamp is less than or equal to T_3 is selected. If such a version exists, it is indicated with a line. In cases (a) and (b) the *read* operation is directed to a committed version – in (a) it is the only version, whereas in (b) there is a tentative version belonging to a later transaction. In case (c) the *read* operation is directed to a tentative version and must wait until the transaction that made it commits or aborts. In case (d) there is no suitable version to read and transaction T_3 is aborted.

Figure 13.31   *Read* operations and timestamps

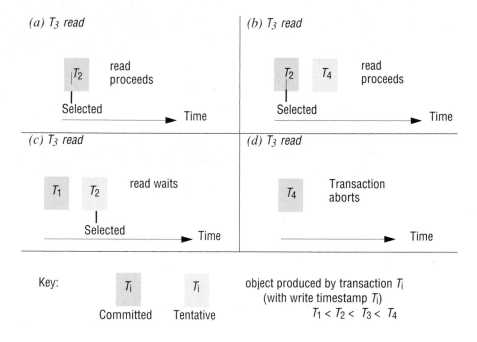

When a coordinator receives a request to commit a transaction, it will always be able to do so because all the operations of transactions are checked for consistency with those of earlier transactions before being carried out. The committed versions of each object must be created in timestamp order. Therefore, a coordinator sometimes needs to wait for earlier transactions to complete before writing all the committed versions of the objects accessed by a particular transaction, but there is no need for the client to wait. In order to make a transaction recoverable after a server crash, the tentative versions of objects and the fact that the transaction has committed must be written to permanent storage before acknowledging the client's request to commit the transaction.

Note that this timestamp ordering algorithm is a strict one – it ensures strict executions of transactions (see Section 13.2). The timestamp ordering read rule delays a transaction's *read* operation on any object until all transactions that had previously written that object have committed or aborted. The arrangement to commit versions in order ensures that the execution of a transaction's *write* operation on any object is delayed until all transactions that had previously written that object have committed or aborted.

In Figure 13.32, we return to our illustration concerning the two concurrent banking transactions T and U introduced in Figure 13.7. The columns headed A, B and C refer to information about accounts with those names. Each account has an entry RTS that records the maximum read timestamps and an entry WTS that records the write timestamp of each version – with timestamps of committed versions in bold. Initially, all accounts have committed versions written by transaction S, and the set of read

Figure 13.32   Timestamps in transactions *T* and *U*

		Timestamps and versions of objects					
T	*U*	*A*		*B*		*C*	
		RTS	*WTS*	*RTS*	*WTS*	*RTS*	*WTS*
		{}	*S*	{}	*S*	{}	*S*
openTransaction							
bal = b.getBalance()				{*T*}			
	openTransaction						
b.setBalance(bal*1.1)					*S, T*		
	bal = b.getBalance()						
	wait for T						
a.withdraw(bal/10)	•••		*S, T*				
commit	•••		*T*		*T*		
	bal = b.getBalance()			{*U*}			
	b.setBalance(bal*1.1)				*T, U*		
	c.withdraw(bal/10)						*S, U*

timestamps is empty. We assume $S < T < U$. The example shows that when transaction *U* is ready to get the balance of *B* it will be wait for *T* to complete so that it can read the value set by *T* if it commits.

The timestamp method just described does avoid deadlock, but, is quite prone to restarts. A modification known as 'ignore obsolete write' rule is an improvement. This is a modification to the timestamp ordering write rule:

• If a write is too late it can be ignored instead of aborting the transaction, because if it had arrived in time its effects would have been overwritten anyway. However, if another transaction has read the object, the transaction with the late write fails due to the read timestamp on the item.

Multiversion timestamp ordering   ◊   In this section, we have shown how the concurrency provided by basic timestamp ordering is improved by allowing each transaction to write its own tentative versions of objects. In multiversion timestamp ordering, which was introduced by Reed [1983], a list of old committed versions as well as tentative versions is kept for each object. This list represents the history of the values of the object. The benefit of using multiple versions is that *read* operations that arrive too late need not be rejected.

Each version has a read timestamp recording the largest timestamp of any transaction that has read from it in addition to a write timestamp. As before, whenever a *write* operation is accepted, it is directed to a tentative version with the write timestamp of the transaction. Whenever a *read* operation is carried out it is directed to the version with the largest write timestamp less than the transaction timestamp. If the transaction

Figure 13.33 Late *write* operation would invalidate a *read*

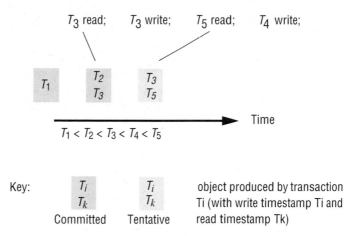

Key:

T_i	T_i
T_k	T_k
Committed	Tentative

object produced by transaction
Ti (with write timestamp Ti and
read timestamp Tk)

timestamp is larger than the read timestamp of the version being used, the read timestamp of the version is set to the transaction timestamp.

When a read arrives late, it can be allowed to read from an old committed version, so there is no need to abort late *read* operations. In multiversion timestamp ordering, *read* operations are always permitted, although they may have to *Wait* for earlier transactions to complete (either commit or abort), which ensures that executions are recoverable. See Exercise 13.22 for a discussion of the possibility of cascading aborts. This deals with rule 3 in the conflict rules for timestamp ordering.

There is no conflict between *write* operations of different transactions, because each transaction writes its own committed version of the objects it accesses. This removes rule 2 in the conflict rules for timestamp ordering, leaving us with:

Rule 1. T_c must not *write* objects that have been *read* by any T_i where $T_i > T_c$.

This rule will be broken if there is any version of the object with read timestamp $> T_c$, but only if this version has a write timestamp less than or equal to T_c. (This write cannot have any effect on later versions.)

Multiversion timestamp ordering write rule: As any potentially conflicting *read* operation will have been directed to the most recent version of an object, the server inspects the version $D_{\text{maxEarlier}}$ with the maximum write timestamp less than or equal to T_c. We have the following rule for performing a *write* operation requested by transaction T_c on object D:

if (read timestamp of $D_{\text{maxEarlier}} \leq T_c$)
        perform *write* operation on a tentative version of D with write timestamp T_c
    else Abort transaction T_c

Figure 13.33 illustrates an example where a *write* is rejected. The object already has committed versions with write timestamps T_1 and T_2. The object receives the following sequence of requests for operations on the object:

T_3 read; T_3 write; T_5 read; T_4 write.

1. T_3 requests a *read* operation, which puts a read timestamp T_3 on T_2's version;

2. T_3 requests a *write* operation, which makes a new tentative version with write timestamp T_3;

3. T_5 requests a *read* operation, which uses the version with write timestamp T_3 (the highest timestamp that is less than T_5);

4. T_4 requests a *write* operation, which is rejected because the read timestamp T_5 of the version with write timestamp T_3 is bigger than T_4. (If it were permitted, the write timestamp of the new version would be T_4. If such a version were allowed, then it would invalidate T_5's *read* operation, which should have used the version with timestamp T_4.)

When a transaction is aborted, all the versions that it created are deleted. When a transaction is committed, all the versions that it created are retained, but to control the use of storage space, old versions must be deleted from time to time. Although it has the overhead of storage space, multiversion timestamp ordering does allow considerable concurrency, does not suffer from deadlocks and always permits *read* operations. For further information about multiversion timestamp ordering, see Bernstein *et al.* [1987].

13.7 Comparison of methods for concurrency control

We have described three separate methods for controlling concurrent access to shared data: strict two-phase locking, optimistic methods and timestamp ordering. All of the methods carry some overheads in the time and space they require, and they all limit to some extent the potential for concurrent operation.

The timestamp ordering method is similar to two-phase locking in that both use pessimistic approaches in which conflicts between transactions are detected as each object is accessed. On the one hand, timestamp ordering decides the serialization order statically – when a transaction starts. On the other hand, two-phase locking decides the serialization order dynamically – according to the order in which objects are accessed. Timestamp ordering and in particular multiversion timestamp ordering is better than strict two-phase locking for read-only transactions. Two-phase locking is better when the operations in transactions are predominantly updates.

Some work uses the observation that timestamp ordering is beneficial for transactions with predominantly *read* operations and that locking is beneficial for transactions with more *writes* than *reads* as an argument for allowing hybrid schemes in which some transactions use timestamp ordering and others use locking for concurrency control. Readers who are interested in the use of mixed methods should read Bernstein *et al.* [1987].

The pessimistic methods differ in the strategy used when a conflicting access to an object is detected. Timestamp ordering aborts the transaction immediately, whereas locking makes the transaction wait – but with a possible later penalty of aborting to avoid deadlock.

When optimistic concurrency control is used, all transactions are allowed to proceed, but some are aborted when they attempt to commit, or in forward validation transactions are aborted earlier. This results in relatively efficient operation when there are few conflicts, but a substantial amount of work may have to be repeated when a transaction is aborted.

Locking has been in use for many years in database systems, but timestamp ordering has been used in the SDD-1 database system. Both methods have been used in file servers. However, the predominant method of concurrency control of access to data in distributed systems is by locking, for example as mentioned earlier, the CORBA Concurrency Control Service is based entirely on the use of locks. In particular, it provides hierarchic locking, which allows for mixed granularity locking on hierarchically structured data.

Several research distributed systems, for example Argus [Liskov 1988] and Arjuna [Shrivastava *et al.* 1991], have explored the use of semantic locks, timestamp ordering and new approaches to long transactions.

Work in two application areas has shown that the above concurrency control mechanisms are not always adequate. One of these areas concerns multi-user applications in which all users expect to see common views of objects being updated by any of the users. Such applications require their data to be atomic in the presence of concurrent updates and server crashes; and transaction techniques appear to offer an approach to their design. However, these applications have two new requirements relating to concurrency control: (1) users require immediate notification of changes made by other users – which is contrary to the idea of isolation; and (2) users need to be able to access objects before other users have completed their transactions, which has led to the development of new types of lock that trigger actions when objects are accessed. Work in this area has suggested many schemes that relax isolation and provide notification of changes. For a review of this work, see Ellis *et al.* [1991]. The second application area concerns what are sometimes described as advanced database applications – such as cooperative CAD/CAM and software development systems. In such applications, transactions last for a long time, and users work on independent versions of objects that are checked out from a common database and checked in when the work is finished. The merging of versions requires cooperation between users. For a review of this work, see Barghouti and Kaiser [1991].

13.8 Summary

Transactions provide a means by which clients can specify sequences of operations that are atomic in the presence of other concurrent transactions and server crashes. The first aspect of atomicity is achieved by running transactions so that their effects are serially equivalent. The effects of committed transactions are recorded in permanent storage so that the transaction service can recover from process crashes. To allow transactions the ability to abort, without having harmful side effects on other transactions, executions must be strict – that is, reads and writes of one transaction must be delayed until other transactions that wrote the same objects have either committed or aborted. To allow transactions the choice of either committing or aborting, their operations are performed in tentative versions that cannot be accessed by other transactions. The tentative versions of objects are copied to the real objects and to permanent storage when a transaction commits.

Nested transactions are formed by structuring transactions from other sub-transactions. Nesting is particularly useful in distributed systems because it allows concurrent execution of subtransactions in separate servers. Nesting also has the advantage of allowing independent recovery of parts of a transaction.

Operation conflicts form a basis for the derivation of concurrency control protocols. Protocols must not only ensure serializability but also allow for recovery by using strict executions to avoid problems associated with transactions aborting, such as cascading aborts.

Three alternative strategies are possible in scheduling an operation in a transaction. They are (1) to execute it immediately, (2) to delay it, or (3) to abort it.

Strict two-phase locking uses the first two strategies, resorting to abortion only in the case of deadlock. It ensures serializability by ordering transactions according to when they access common objects. Its main drawback is that deadlocks can occur.

Timestamp ordering uses all three strategies to ensure serializability by ordering transactions' accesses to objects according to the time transactions start. This method cannot suffer from deadlocks and is advantageous for read-only transactions. However, transactions must be aborted when they arrive too late. Multiversion timestamp ordering is particularly effective.

Optimistic concurrency control allows transactions to proceed without any form of checking until they are completed. Transactions are validated before being allowed to commit. Backward validation requires the maintenance of multiple write sets of committed transactions, whereas forward validation must validate against active transactions and has the advantage that it allows alternative strategies for resolving conflicts. Starvation can occur due to repeated aborting of a transaction that fails validation in optimistic concurrency control and even in timestamp ordering.

EXERCISES

13.1   The TaskBag is a service whose functionality is to provide a repository for 'task descriptions'. It enables clients running in several computers to carry out parts of a computation in parallel. A *master* process places descriptions of sub-tasks of a computation in the TaskBag, and *worker* processes select tasks from the TaskBag and carry them out, returning descriptions of results to the TaskBag. The *master* then collects the results and combines them to produce the final result.

The TaskBag service provides the following operations:

    setTask   allows clients to add task descriptions to the bag;

    takeTask   allows clients to take task descriptions out of the bag.

A client makes the request *takeTask*, when a task is not available but may be available soon. Discuss the advantages and drawbacks of the following alternatives:

(i)   the server can reply immediately, telling the client to try again later;

(ii)   make the server operation (and therefore the client) wait until a task becomes available;

(iii) use callbacks.   *page 516*

13.2   A server manages the objects $a_1, a_2, ... a_n$. The server provides two operations for its clients:

>   *read (i)* returns the value of a_i;
>   *write(i, Value)* assigns *Value* to a_i.

The transactions T and U are defined as follows:

> T: $x = read(j); y = read (i); write(j, 44); write(i, 33);$
> U: $x = read(k); write(i, 55); y = read (j); write(k, 66).$

Give three serially equivalent interleavings of the transactions T and U.   *page 523*

13.3   Give serially equivalent interleavings of T and U in Exercise 13.2 with the following properties: (1) that is strict; (2) that is not strict but could not produce cascading aborts; (3) that could produce cascading aborts.   *page 527*

13.4   The operation *create* inserts a new bank account at a branch. The transactions T and U are defined as follows:

> T: *aBranch.create("Z")*;
> U: *z.deposit(10); z.deposit(20).*

Assume that Z does not yet exist. Assume also that the *deposit* operation does nothing if the account given as argument does not exist. Consider the following interleaving of transactions T and U:

T	U
	z.deposit(10);
aBranch.create(Z);	
	z.deposit(20);

State the balance of Z after their execution in this order. Are these consistent with serially equivalent executions of T and U?   *page 523*

13.5   A newly created object like Z in Exercise 13.4 is sometimes called a *phantom*. From the point of view of transaction U, Z is not there at first and then appears (like a ghost). Explain, with an example, how a phantom could occur when an account is deleted.

13.6   The 'transfer' transactions T and U are defined as:

> T: a.withdraw(4); b.deposit(4);
> U: c.withdraw(3); b.deposit(3);

Suppose that they are structured as pairs of nested transactions:

> T_1:   a.withdraw(4); T_2: b.deposit(4);
> U_1:   c.withdraw(3); U_2: b.deposit(3);

Compare the number of serially equivalent interleavings of T_1, T_2, U_1 and U_2 with the number of serially equivalent interleavings of T and U. Explain why the use of these nested transactions generally permits a larger number of serially equivalent interleavings than non-nested ones.   *page 523*

13.7   Consider the recovery aspects of the nested transactions defined in Exercise 13.6. Assume that a *withdraw* transaction will abort if the account will be overdrawn and that in this case the parent transaction will also abort. Describe serially equivalent interleavings of T_1, T_2, U_1 and U_2 with the following properties: (i) that is strict; (ii) that is not strict. To what extent does the criterion of strictness reduce the potential concurrency gain of nested transactions?   *page 523*

13.8   Explain why serial equivalence requires that once a transaction has released a lock on an object, it is not allowed to obtain any more locks.

A server manages the objects $a_1, a_2, ... a_n$. The server provides two operations for its clients:

      read(i) returns the value of a_i

      write(i, Value) assigns *Value* to a_i

The transactions *T* and U are defined as follows:

      T: x = read(i); write(j, 44);

      U: write(i, 55); write(j, 66);

Describe an interleaving of the transactions *T* and *U* in which locks are released early with the effect that the interleaving is not serially equivalent.   *page 531*

13.9   The transactions *T* and *U* at the server in Exercise 13.8 are defined as follows:

      T: x = read(i); write(j, 44);

      U: write(i, 55); write(j, 66);

Initial values of a_i and a_j are 10 and 20, respectively. Which of the following interleavings are serially equivalent, and which could occur with two-phase locking?

(a)

T	U
x= read (i);	
	write(i, 55);
write(j, 44);	
	write(j, 66);

(b)

T	U
x= read (i);	
write(j, 44);	
	write(i, 55);
	write(j, 66);

(c)

T	U
	write(i, 55);
	write(j, 66);
x= read (i);	
write(j, 44);	

(d)

T	U
	write(i, 55);
x= read (i);	
	write(j, 66);
write(j, 44);	

page 531

13.10   Consider a relaxation of two-phase locks in which read-only transactions can release read locks early. Would a read-only transaction have consistent retrievals? Would the objects become inconsistent? Illustrate your answer with the following transactions *T* and *U* at the server in Exercise 13.8:

      T: x = read (i); y= read(j);

      U: write(i, 55); write(j, 66);

in which initial values of a_i and a_j are 10 and 20.   *page 528*

13.11 The executions of transactions are strict if *read* and *write* operations on an object are delayed until all transactions that previously wrote that object have either committed or aborted. Explain how the locking rules in Figure 13.16 ensure strict executions.

page 534

13.12 Describe how a non-recoverable situation could arise if write locks are released after the last operation of a transaction but before its commitment. *page 528*

13.13 Explain why executions are always strict, even if read locks are released after the last operation of a transaction but before its commitment. Give an improved statement of rule 2 in Figure 13.16. *page 528*

13.14 Consider a deadlock detection scheme for a single server. Describe precisely when edges are added to and removed from the wait-for-graph.

Illustrate your answer with respect to the following transactions T, U and V at the server of Exercise 13.8.

T	U	V
	write(i, 66)	
write(i, 55)		
		write(i, 77)
	commit	

When U releases its write lock on a_i, both T and V are waiting to obtain write locks on it. Does your scheme work correctly if T (first come) is granted the lock before V? If your answer is 'No', then modify your description. *page 540*

13.15 Consider hierarchic locks as illustrated in Figure 13.26. What locks must be set when an appointment is assigned to a time slot in week w, day d, at time t? In what order should these locks be set? Does the order in which they are released matter?

What locks must be set when the time slots for every day in week w are viewed? Can this be done when the locks for assigning an appointment to a time slot are already set? *page 543*

13.16 Consider optimistic concurrency control as applied to the transactions T and U defined in Exercise 13.9. Suppose that transactions T and U are active at the same time as one another. Describe the outcome in each of the following cases:

(i) T's request to commit comes first and backward validation is used;

(ii) U's request to commit comes first and backward validation is used;

(iii) T's request to commit comes first and forward validation is used;

(iv) U's request to commit comes first and forward validation is used.

In each case describe the sequence in which the operations of T and U are performed, remembering that writes are not carried out until after validation. *page 545*

13.17   Consider the following interleaving of transactions T and U:

T	U
openTransaction	openTransaction
y = read(k);	
	write(i, 55);
	write(j, 66);
	commit
x = read(i);	
write(j, 44);	

The outcome of optimistic concurrency control with backward validation is that T will be aborted because its *read* operation conflicts with U's *write* operation on a_i, although the interleavings are serially equivalent. Suggest a modification to the algorithm that deals with such cases.   *page 545*

13.18   Make a comparison of the sequences of operations of the transactions T and U of Exercise 13.8 that are possible under two-phase locking (Exercise 13.9) and under optimistic concurrency control (Exercise 13.16).

13.19   Consider the use of timestamp ordering with each of the example interleavings of transactions T and U in Exercise 13.9. Initial values of a_i and a_j are 10 and 20, respectively, and initial read and write timestamps are t_0. Assume that each transaction opens and obtains a timestamp just before its first operation; for example, in (a) T and U get timestamps t_1 and t_2 respectively, where $t_0 < t_1 < t_2$. Describe in order of increasing time the effects of each operation of T and U. For each operation, state the following:

(i)   whether the operation may proceed according to the write or read rule;

(ii)   timestamps assigned to transactions or objects;

(iii)   creation of tentative objects and their values.

What are the final values of the objects and their timestamps?   *page549*

13.20   Repeat Exercise 13.19 for the following interleavings of transactions T and U:

T	U		T	U
openTransaction			openTransaction	
	openTransaction			openTransaction
	write(i, 55);			write(i, 55);
	write(j, 66);			write(j, 66);
x = read (i);				commit
write(j, 44);			x = read (i);	
	commit		write(j, 44);	

page 549

13.21   Repeat Exercise 13.20 using multiversion timestamp ordering.

page 554

13.22   In multiversion timestamp ordering, *read* operations can access tentative versions of objects. Give an example to show how cascading aborts can happen if all *read* operations are allowed to proceed immediately.   *page 554*

13.23   What are the advantages and drawbacks of multiversion timestamp ordering in comparison with ordinary timestamp ordering.   *page 554*

13.24   Make a comparison of the sequences of operations of the transactions T and U of Exercise 13.8 that are possible under two-phase locking (Exercise 13.9) and under optimistic concurrency control (Exercise 13.16)   *page 545*

14

DISTRIBUTED TRANSACTIONS

This chapter introduces distributed transactions – those that involve more than one server. Distributed transactions may be either flat or nested.

An atomic commit protocol is a cooperative procedure used by a set of servers involved in a distributed transaction. It enables the servers to reach a joint decision as to whether a transaction can be committed or aborted. This chapter describes the two-phase commit protocol, which is the most commonly used atomic commit protocol.

The section on concurrency control in distributed transactions discusses how locking, timestamp ordering and optimistic concurrency control may be extended for use with distributed transactions.

The use of locking schemes can lead to distributed deadlocks. Distributed deadlock detection algorithms are discussed.

Servers that provide transactions include a recovery manager whose concern is to ensure that the effects of transactions on the objects managed by a server can be recovered when it is replaced after a failure. The recovery manager saves the objects in permanent storage together with intentions lists and information about the status of each transaction.

14.1 Introduction

In Chapter 13, we discussed flat and nested transactions that accessed objects at a single server. In the general case, a transaction, whether flat or nested, will access objects located in several different computers. We use the term *distributed transaction* to refer to a flat or nested transaction that accesses objects managed by multiple servers.

When a distributed transaction comes to an end, the atomicity property of transactions requires that either all of the servers involved commit the transaction or all of them abort the transaction. To achieve this, one of the servers takes on a coordinator role, which involves ensuring the same outcome at all of the servers. The manner in which the coordinator achieves this depends on the protocol chosen. A protocol known as the 'two-phase commit protocol' is the most commonly used. This protocol allows the servers to communicate with one another to reach a joint decision as to whether to commit or abort.

Concurrency control in distributed transactions is based on the methods discussed in Chapter 13. Each server applies local concurrency control to its own objects, which ensures that transactions are serialized locally. Distributed transactions must be serialized globally. How this is achieved varies as to whether locking, timestamp ordering or optimistic concurrency control is in use. In some cases, the transactions may be serialized at the individual servers, but at the same time a cycle of dependencies between the different servers may occur and a distributed deadlock arise.

Transaction recovery is concerned with ensuring that all the objects involved in transactions are recoverable. In addition to that, it guarantees that the values of the objects reflect all the changes made by committed transactions and none of those made by aborted ones.

14.2 Flat and nested distributed transactions

A client transaction becomes distributed if it invokes operations in several different servers. There are two different ways that distributed transactions can be structured: as flat transactions and as nested transactions.

In a flat transaction, a client makes requests to more than one server. For example, in Figure 14.1(a), transaction T is a flat transaction that invokes operations on objects in servers X, Y and Z. A flat client transaction completes each of its requests before going on to the next one. Therefore, each transaction accesses servers' objects sequentially. When servers use locking, a transaction can only be waiting for one object at a time.

In a nested transaction, the top-level transaction can open subtransactions, and each subtransaction can open further subtransactions down to any depth of nesting. Figure 14.1(b) shows a client's transaction T that opens two subtransactions T_1 and T_2, which access objects at servers X and Y. The subtransactions T_1 and T_2 open further subtransactions T_{11}, T_{12}. T_{21} and T_{22}, which access objects at servers M, N and P. In the nested case, subtransactions at the same level can run concurrently, so T_1 and T_2 are concurrent, and as they invoke objects in different servers, they can run in parallel. The four subtransactions T_{11}, T_{12}, T_{21} and T_{22} also run concurrently.

Figure 14.1   Distributed transactions

(a) Flat transaction   (b) Nested transactions

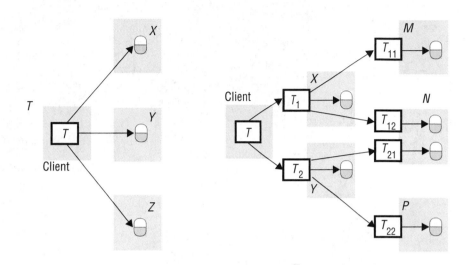

Consider a distributed transaction in which a client transfers $10 from account A to C and then transfers $20 from B to D. Accounts A and B are at separate servers X and Y and accounts C and D are at server Z. If this transaction is structured as a set of four nested transactions, as shown in Figure 14.2, the four requests (two *deposit* and two *withdraw*) can run in parallel and the overall effect can be achieved with better performance than a simple transaction in which the four operations are invoked sequentially.

Figure 14.2   Nested banking transaction

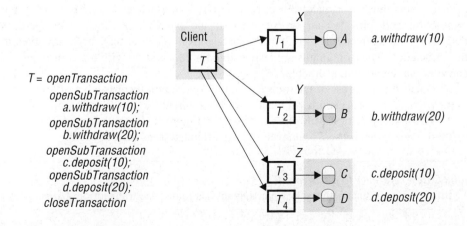

Figure 14.3   A distributed banking transaction

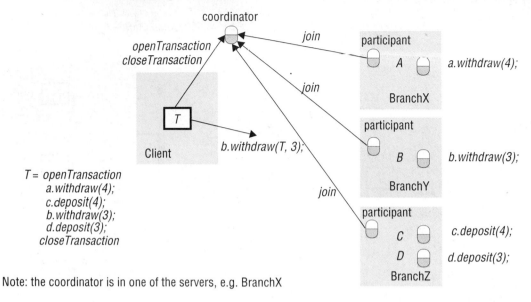

Note: the coordinator is in one of the servers, e.g. BranchX

14.2.1 The coordinator of a distributed transaction

Servers that execute requests as part of a distributed transaction need to be able to communicate with one another to coordinate their actions when the transaction commits. A client starts a transaction by sending an *openTransaction* request to a coordinator in any server, as described in Section 13.2. The coordinator that is contacted carries out the *openTransaction* and returns the resulting transaction identifier to the client. Transaction identifiers for distributed transactions must be unique within a distributed system. A simple way to achieve this is for a TID to contain two parts: the server identifier (for example, an IP address) of the server that created it and a number unique to the server.

The coordinator that opened the transaction becomes the *coordinator* for the distributed transaction and at the end is responsible for committing or aborting it. Each of the servers that manages an object accessed by a transaction is a participant in the transaction and provides an object we call the *participant*. Each participant is responsible for keeping track of all of the recoverable objects at that server involved in the transaction. The participants are responsible for cooperating with the coordinator in carrying out the commit protocol.

During the progress of the transaction, the coordinator records a list of references to the participants, and each participant records a reference to the coordinator.

The interface for *Coordinator* shown in Figure 13.3 provides an additional method, *join*, which is used whenever a new participant joins the transaction:

---

join(Trans, reference to participant)
   Informs a coordinator that a new participant has joined the transaction *Trans*.

The coordinator records the new participant in its participant list. The fact that the coordinator knows all the participants and each participant knows the coordinator will enable them to collect the information that will be needed at commit time.

Figure 14.3 shows a client whose (flat) banking transaction involves accounts *A*, *B*, *C* and *D* at servers BranchX, BranchY and BranchZ. The client's transaction, *T*, transfers $4 from account *A* to account *C* and then transfers $3 from account *B* to account *D*. The transaction described on the left is expanded to show that *openTransaction* and *closeTransaction* are directed to the coordinator, which would be situated in one of the servers involved in the transaction. Each server is shown with a *participant*, which joins the transaction by invoking the *join* method in the coordinator. When the client invokes one of the methods in the transaction, for example *b.withdraw(T, 3)*, the object receiving the invocation (*B* at BranchY in this case) informs its participant object that the object belongs to the transaction *T*. If it has not already informed the coordinator, the participant object uses the *join* operation to do so. In this example, we show the transaction identifier being passed as an additional argument so that the recipient can pass it on to the coordinator. By the time the client calls *closeTransaction*, the coordinator has references to all of the participants.

Note that it is possible for a participant to call *abortTransaction* in the coordinator if for some reason it is unable to continue with the transaction.

14.3 Atomic commit protocols

Transaction commit protocols were devised in the early 1970s, and the two-phase commit protocol appeared in Gray [1978]. The atomicity of transactions requires that when a distributed transaction comes to an end, either all of its operations are carried out or none of them. In the case of a distributed transaction, the client has requested the operations at more than one server. A transaction comes to an end when the client requests that a transaction be committed or aborted. A simple way to complete the transaction in an atomic manner is for the coordinator to communicate the commit or abort request to all of the participants in the transaction and to keep on repeating the request until all of them have acknowledged that they had carried it out. This is an example of a *one-phase atomic commit protocol*.

This simple one-phase atomic commit protocol is inadequate because, in the case when the client requests a commit, it does not allow a server to make a unilateral decision to abort a transaction. Reasons that prevent a server from being able to commit its part of a transaction generally relate to issues of concurrency control. For example, if locking is in use, the resolution of a deadlock can lead to the aborting of a transaction without the client being aware unless it makes another request to the server. If optimistic concurrency control is in use, the failure of validation at a server would cause it to decide to abort the transaction. The coordinator may not know when a server has crashed and been replaced during the progress of a distributed transaction – such a server will need to abort the transaction.

The *two-phase commit protocol* is designed to allow any participant to abort its part of a transaction. Due to the requirement for atomicity, if one part of a transaction is aborted, then the whole transaction must also be aborted. In the first phase of the protocol, each participant votes for the transaction to be committed or aborted. Once a participant has voted to commit a transaction, it is not allowed to abort it. Therefore, before a participant votes to commit a transaction, it must ensure that it will eventually be able to carry out its part of the commit protocol, even if it fails and is replaced in the interim. A participant in a transaction is said to be in a *prepared* state for a transaction if it will eventually be able to commit it. To make sure of this, each participant saves in permanent storage all of the objects that it has altered in the transaction, together with its status – prepared.

In the second phase of the protocol, every participant in the transaction carries out the joint decision. If any one participant votes to abort, then the decision must be to abort the transaction. If all the participants vote to commit, then the decision is to commit the transaction.

The problem is to ensure that all of the participants vote and that they all reach the same decision. This is fairly simple if no errors occur, but the protocol must work correctly even when some of the servers fail, messages are lost or servers are temporarily unable to communicate with one another.

Failure model for the commit protocols ◊ Section 13.1.2 presents a failure model for transactions that applies equally to the two-phase (or any other) commit protocol. Commit protocols are designed to work in an asynchronous system in which servers may crash and messages may be lost. It is assumed that an underlying request-reply protocol removes corrupt and duplicated messages. There are no byzantine faults – servers either crash or else they obey the messages they are sent.

The two-phase commit protocol is an example of a protocol for reaching a consensus. Chapter 12 asserts that consensus cannot be reached in an asynchronous system if processes sometimes fail. However, the two-phase commit protocol does reach consensus under those conditions. This is because crash failures of processes are masked by replacing a crashed process with a new process whose state is set from information saved in permanent storage and information held by other processes.

14.3.1 The two-phase commit protocol

During the progress of a transaction, there is no communication between the coordinator and the participants apart from the participants informing the coordinator when they join the transaction. A client's request to commit (or abort) a transaction is directed to the coordinator. If the client requests *abortTransaction*, or if the transaction is aborted by one of the participants, the coordinator informs the participants immediately. It is when the client asks the coordinator to commit the transaction that two-phase commit protocol comes into use.

In the first phase of the two-phase commit protocol the coordinator asks all the participants if they are prepared to commit; and in the second, it tells them to commit (or abort) the transaction. If a participant can commit its part of a transaction, it will agree as soon as it has recorded the changes and its status in permanent storage – and is prepared to commit. The coordinator in a distributed transaction communicates with the participants to carry out the two-phase commit protocol by means of the operations summarized in Figure 14.4. The methods *canCommit*, *doCommit* and *doAbort* are

Figure 14.4 Operations for two-phase commit protocol

canCommit?(trans)→ Yes / No
> Call from coordinator to participant to ask whether it can commit a transaction. Participant replies with its vote.

doCommit(trans)
> Call from coordinator to participant to tell participant to commit its part of a transaction.

doAbort(trans)
> Call from coordinator to participant to tell participant to abort its part of a transaction.

haveCommitted(trans, participant)
> Call from participant to coordinator to confirm that it has committed the transaction.

getDecision(trans) → Yes / No
> Call from participant to coordinator to ask for the decision on a transaction after it has voted *Yes* but has still had no reply after some delay. Used to recover from server crash or delayed messages.

methods in the interface of the participant. The methods *haveCommitted* and *getDecision* are in the coordinator interface.

The two-phase commit protocol consists of a voting phase and a completion phase as shown in Figure 14.5. By the end of step (2) the coordinator and all the participants that voted *Yes* are prepared to commit. By the end of step (3) the transaction is effectively completed. At step (3a) the coordinator and the participants are committed, so the coordinator can report a decision to commit to the client. At (3b) the coordinator reports a decision to abort to the client.

At step (4) participants confirm that they have committed so that the coordinator knows when the information it has recorded about the transaction is no longer needed.

This apparently straightforward protocol could fail due to one or more of the servers crashing or due to a breakdown in communication between the servers. To deal with the possibility of crashing, each server saves information relating to the two-phase commit protocol in permanent storage. This information can be retrieved by a new process that is started to replace a crashed server. The recovery aspects of distributed transactions are discussed in Section 14.6.

The exchange of information between the coordinator and participants can fail when one of the servers crashes, or when messages are lost. Timeouts are used to avoid processes blocking for ever. When a timeout occurs at a process, it must take an appropriate action. To allow for this the protocol includes a timeout action for each step at which a process may block. These actions are designed to allow for the fact that in an asynchronous system, a timeout may not necessarily imply that a server has failed.

Timeout actions in the two-phase commit protocol ◊ There are various stages in the protocol at which the coordinator or a participant cannot progress its part of the protocol until it receives another request or reply from one of the others.

Figure 14.5   The two-phase commit protocol

Phase 1 (voting phase):

1. The coordinator sends a *canCommit?* request to each of the participants in the transaction.

2. When a participant receives a *canCommit?* request it replies with its vote (*Yes* or *No*) to the coordinator. Before voting *Yes*, it prepares to commit by saving objects in permanent storage. If the vote is *No* the participant aborts immediately.

Phase 2 (completion according to outcome of vote):

3. The coordinator collects the votes (including its own).

   (a) If there are no failures and all the votes are *Yes* the coordinator decides to commit the transaction and sends a *doCommit* request to each of the participants.

   (b) Otherwise the coordinator decides to abort the transaction and sends *doAbort* requests to all participants that voted *Yes*.

4. Participants that voted *Yes* are waiting for a *doCommit* or *doAbort* request from the coordinator. When a participant receives one of these messages it acts accordingly and in the case of commit, makes a *haveCommitted* call as confirmation to the coordinator.

Consider first the situation where a participant has voted *Yes* and is waiting for the coordinator to report on the outcome of the vote by telling it to commit or abort the transaction. See step (2) in Figure 14.6. Such a participant is *uncertain* of the outcome and cannot proceed any further until it gets the outcome of the vote from the coordinator. The participant cannot decide unilaterally what to do next, and meanwhile the objects used by its transaction cannot be released for use by other transactions. The participant makes a *getDecision* request to the coordinator to determine the outcome of the transaction. When it gets the reply it continues the protocol at step (4) in Figure 14.5. If

Figure 14.6   Communication in two-phase commit protocol

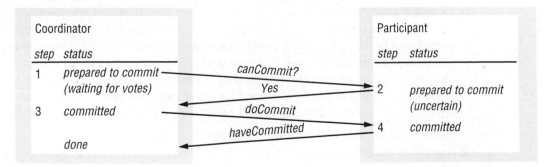

the coordinator has failed, the participant will not be able to get the decision until the coordinator is replaced, which can result in extensive delays for participants in the uncertain state.

Other alternative strategies are available for the participants to obtain a decision cooperatively instead of contacting the coordinator. These strategies have the advantage that they may be used when the coordinator has failed. See Exercise 14.5 and Bernstein *et al.* [1987] for details. However, even with a cooperative protocol, if all the participants are in the *uncertain* state, they will be unable to get a decision until the coordinator or a participant with the knowledge is available.

Another point at which a participant may be delayed is when it has carried out all its client requests in the transaction but has not yet received a *canCommit?* call from the coordinator. As the client sends the *closeTransaction* to the coordinator, a participant can only detect such a situation if it notices that it has not had a request in a particular transaction for a long time, for example by a timeout period on a lock. As no decision has been made at this stage, the participant can decide to *abort* unilaterally after some period of time.

The coordinator may be delayed when it is waiting for votes from the participants. As it has not yet decided the fate of the transaction it may decide to abort the transaction after some period of time. It must then announce *doAbort* to the participants who have already sent their votes. Some tardy participants may try to vote *Yes* after this, but their votes will be ignored and they will enter the *uncertain* state as described above.

Performance of the two-phase commit protocol ◊ Provided that all goes well – that is, that the coordinator and participants and the communication between them do not fail, the two-phase commit protocol involving N participants can be completed with N *canCommit?* messages and replies, followed by N *doCommit* messages. That is, the cost in messages is proportional to $3N$, and the cost in time is three rounds of messages. The *haveCommitted* messages are not counted in the estimated cost of the protocol, which can function correctly without them – their role is to enable servers to delete stale coordinator information.

In the worst case, there may be arbitrarily many server and communication failures during the two-phase commit protocol. However, the protocol is designed to tolerate a succession of failures (server crashes or lost messages) and is guaranteed to complete eventually, although it is not possible to specify a time limit within which it will be completed.

As noted in the section on timeouts, the two-phase commit protocol can cause considerable delays to participants in the *uncertain* state. These delays occur when the coordinator has failed and cannot reply to *getDecision* requests from participants. Even if a cooperative protocol allows participants to make *getDecision* requests to other participants, delays will occur if all the active participants are *uncertain*.

Three-phase commit protocols have been designed to alleviate such delays. They are more expensive in the number of messages and the number of rounds required for the normal (failure-free) case. For a description of three-phase commit protocols, see Exercise 14.2 and Bernstein *et al.* [1987].

Figure 14.7   Operations in coordinator for nested transactions

openSubTransaction(trans) $\rightarrow$ *subTrans*
> Opens a new subtransaction whose parent is *trans* and returns a unique subtransaction identifier.

getStatus(trans) $\rightarrow$ *committed, aborted, provisional*
> Asks the coordinator to report on the status of the transaction *trans*. Returns values representing one of the following: *committed, aborted, provisional*.

14.3.2 Two-phase commit protocol for nested transactions

The outermost transaction in a set of nested transactions is called the *top-level transaction*. Transactions other than the top-level transaction are called *subtransactions*. In Figure 14.1(b), T is the top-level transaction, T_1, T_2, T_{11}, T_{12}, T_{21} and T_{22} are subtransactions. T_1 and T_2 are child transactions of T, which is referred to as their parent. Similarly, T_{11} and T_{12} are child transactions of T_1, and T_{21} and T_{22} are child transactions of T_2. Each subtransaction starts after its parent and finishes before it. Thus, for example, T_{11} and T_{12} start after T_1 and finish before it.

When a subtransaction completes, it makes an independent decision either to commit provisionally or to abort. A provisional commit is different from being prepared to commit: it is not backed up on permanent storage. If the server crashes subsequently, its replacement will not be able to commit. After all subtransactions have completed, the provisionally committed ones participate in a two-phase commit protocol, in which servers of provisionally committed subtransactions express their intention to commit and those with an aborted ancestor will abort. A prepared commit guarantees a subtransaction will be able to commit, whereas a provisional commit only means it has finished correctly – and will probably agree to commit when it is subsequently asked to.

A coordinator for a subtransaction will provide an operation to open a subtransaction, together with an operation enabling the coordinator of a subtransaction to enquire whether its parent has yet committed or aborted, as shown in Figure 14.7.

A client starts a set of nested transactions by opening a top-level transaction with an *openTransaction* operation, which returns a transaction identifier for the top-level transaction. The client starts a subtransaction by invoking the *openSubTransaction* operation, whose argument specifies its parent transaction. The new subtransaction automatically *joins* the parent transaction, and a transaction identifier for a subtransaction is returned.

An identifier for a subtransaction must be an extension of its parent's TID, constructed in such a way that the identifier of the parent or top-level transaction of a subtransaction can be determined from its own transaction identifier. In addition, all subtransaction identifiers should be globally unique. The client makes a set of nested transactions come to completion by invoking *closeTransaction* or *abortTransaction* on the coordinator of the top-level transaction.

Meanwhile, each of the nested transactions carries out its operations. When they are finished, the server managing a subtransaction records information as to whether the

Figure 14.8   Transaction *T* decides whether to commit

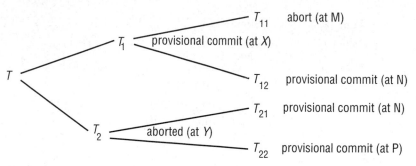

subtransaction committed provisionally or aborted. Note that if its parent aborts, then the subtransaction will be forced to abort too.

Recall from Chapter 13 that a parent transaction – including a top-level transaction – can commit even if one of its child subtransactions has aborted. In such cases, the parent transaction will be programmed to take different actions according to whether a subtransaction has committed or aborted. For example, consider a banking transaction that is designed to perform all the 'standing orders' at a branch on a particular day. This transaction is expressed as several nested *Transfer* subtransactions, each of which consists of nested *deposit* and *withdraw* subtransactions. We assume that when an account is overdrawn, *withdraw* aborts and then the corresponding *Transfer* aborts. But there is no need to abort all the standing orders just because one *Transfer* subtransaction aborts. Instead of aborting, the top-level transaction will note the *Transfer* subtransactions that aborted and take appropriate actions.

Consider the top-level transaction *T* and its subtransactions shown in Figure 14.8, which is based on Figure 14.1(b). Each subtransaction has either provisionally committed or aborted. For example, T_{12} has provisionally committed and T_{11} has aborted, but the fate of T_{12} depends on its parent T_1 and eventually on the top-level transaction, *T*. Although T_{21} and T_{22} have both provisionally committed, T_2 has aborted and this means that T_{21} and T_{22} must also abort. Suppose that *T* decides to commit in spite of the fact that T_2 has aborted, also that T_1 decides to commit in spite of the fact that T_{11} has aborted.

When a top-level transaction completes, its coordinator carries out a two-phase commit protocol. The only reason for a participant subtransaction being unable to complete is if it has crashed since it completed its provisional commit. Recall that when each subtransaction was created, it *joined* its parent transaction. Therefore, the coordinator of each parent transaction has a list of its child subtransactions. When a nested transaction provisionally commits, it reports its status and the status of its descendants to its parent. When a nested transaction aborts, it just reports abort to its parent without giving any information about its descendants. Eventually, the top-level transaction receives a list of all the subtransactions in the tree, together with the status of each. Descendants of aborted subtransactions are actually omitted from this list.

The information held by each coordinator in the example shown in Figure 14.8 is shown in Figure 14.9. Note that T_{12} and T_{21} share a coordinator as they both run at server N. When subtransaction T_2 aborted, it reported the fact to its parent, *T*, but without

Figure 14.9   Information held by coordinators of nested transactions:

Coordinator of transaction	Child transactions	Participant	Provisional commit list	Abort list
T	T_1, T_2	yes	T_1, T_{12}	T_{11}, T_2
T_1	T_{11}, T_{12}	yes	T_1, T_{12}	T_{11}
T_2	T_{21}, T_{22}	no (aborted)		T_2
T_{11}		no (aborted)		T_{11}
T_{12}, T_{21}		T_{12} but not T_{21}	T_{21}, T_{12}	
T_{22}		no (parent aborted)	T_{22}	

passing on any information about its subtransactions T_{21} and T_{22}. A subtransaction is an *orphan* if one of its ancestors aborts, either explicitly or because its coordinator crashed. In our example, subtransactions T_{21} and T_{22} are orphans because their parent aborted without passing information about them to the top-level transaction. Their coordinator can however, make enquiries about the status of their parent by using the *getStatus* operation. A provisionally committed subtransaction of an aborted transaction should be aborted, irrespective of whether the top-level transaction eventually commits.

The top-level transaction plays the role of coordinator in the two-phase commit protocol, and the participant list consists of the coordinators of all the subtransactions in the tree that have provisionally committed but do not have aborted ancestors. By this stage, the logic of the program has determined that the top-level transaction should try to commit whatever is left, in spite of some aborted subtransactions. In Figure 14.8, the coordinators of T, T_1 and T_{12} are participants and will be asked to vote on the outcome. If they vote to commit, then they must *prepare* their transactions by saving the state of the objects in permanent storage. This state is recorded as belonging to the top-level transaction of which it will form a part. The two-phase commit protocol may be performed in either a hierarchic manner or in a flat manner.

The second phase of the two-phase commit protocol is the same as for the non-nested case. The coordinator collects the votes and then informs the participants as to the outcome. When it is complete, coordinator and participants will have committed or aborted their transactions.

Hierarchic two-phase commit protocol ◊ In this approach, the two-phase commit protocol becomes a multi-level nested protocol. The coordinator of the top-level transaction communicates with the coordinators of the subtransactions for which it is the immediate parent. It sends *canCommit?* messages to each of the latter, which in turn pass them on to the coordinators of their child transactions (and so on down the tree). Each participant collects the replies from its descendants before replying to its parent. In our example, T sends *canCommit?* messages to the coordinator of T_1 and then T_1 sends *canCommit?* messages to T_{12} asking about descendants of T_1. The protocol does not include the coordinators of transactions such as T_2, which has aborted. Figure 14.10 shows the arguments required for *canCommit?* The first argument is the TID of the top-level transaction, for use when preparing the data. The second argument is the TID of

Figure 14.10 *canCommit?* for hierarchic two-phase commit protocol

canCommit?(trans, subTrans) → *Yes / No*
Call a coordinator to ask coordinator of child subtransaction whether it can commit a subtransaction *subTrans*. The first argument *trans* is the transaction identifier of top-level transaction. Participant replies with its vote *Yes / No*.

Figure 14.11 *canCommit?* for flat two-phase commit protocol

canCommit?(trans, abortList) → *Yes / No*
Call from coordinator to participant to ask whether it can commit a transaction. Participant replies with its vote *Yes / No*.

the participant making the *canCommit?* call. The participant receiving the call looks in its transaction list for any provisionally committed transaction or subtransaction matching the TID in the second argument. For example, the coordinator of T_{12} is also the coordinator of T_{21}, since they run in the same server, but when it receives the *canCommit?* call, the second argument will be T_1 and it will deal only with T_{12}.

If a participant finds any subtransactions that match the second argument, it prepares the objects and replies with a *Yes* vote. If it fails to find any, then it must have crashed since it performed the subtransaction and it replies with a *No* vote.

Flat two-phase commit protocol ◊ In this approach, the coordinator of the top-level transaction sends *canCommit?* messages to the coordinators of all of the subtransactions in the provisional commit list. In our example, to the coordinators of T_1 and T_{12}. During the commit protocol, the participants refer to the transaction by its top-level TID. Each participant looks in its transaction list for any transaction or subtransaction matching that TID. For example, the coordinator of T_{12} is also the coordinator of T_{21}, since they run in the same server (N).

Unfortunately, this does not provide sufficient information to enable correct actions by participants such as the coordinator at server N that have a mix of provisionally committed and aborted subtransactions. If N's coordinator is just asked to commit T it will end up by committing both T_{12} and T_{21}, because, according to its local information, both have provisionally committed. This is wrong in the case of T_{21}, because its parent, T_2, has aborted. To allow for such cases, the *canCommit?* operation for the flat commit protocol has a second argument that provides a list of aborted subtransactions, as shown in Figure 14.11. A participant can commit descendants of the top-level transaction unless they have aborted ancestors. When a participant receives a *canCommit?* request, it does the following:

- If the participant has any provisionally committed transactions that are descendants of the top-level transaction, *trans*:

      – check that they do not have aborted ancestors in the *abortList*. Then prepare to commit (by recording the transaction and its objects in permanent storage);

      – those with aborted ancestors are aborted;

      – send a *Yes* vote to the coordinator.

- If the participant does not have a provisionally committed descendent of the top-level transaction, it must have failed since it performed the subtransaction and it sends a *No* vote to the coordinator.

A comparison of the two approaches ◊ The hierarchic protocol has the advantage that at each stage, the participant only need look for subtransactions of its immediate parent, whereas the flat protocol needs to have the abort list in order to eliminate transactions whose parents have aborted. Moss [1985] preferred the flat algorithm because it allows the coordinator of the top-level transaction to communicate directly with all of the participants, whereas the hierarchic variant involves passing a series of messages down and up the tree in stages.

Timeout actions ◊ The two-phase commit protocol for nested transactions can cause the coordinator or a participant to be delayed at the same three steps as in the non-nested version. There is a fourth step at which subtransactions can be delayed. Consider provisionally committed child subtransactions of aborted subtransactions: they do not necessarily get informed of the outcome of the transaction. In our example, T_{22} is such a subtransaction – it has provisionally committed, but as its parent T_2 has aborted, it does not become a participant. To deal with such situations, any subtransaction that has not received a *canCommit?* message will make an enquiry after a timeout period. The *getStatus* operation in Figure 14.7 allows a subtransaction to enquire whether its parent has committed or aborted. To make such enquiries possible, the coordinators of aborted subtransactions need to survive for a period. If an orphaned subtransaction cannot contact its parent, it will eventually abort.

14.4 Concurrency control in distributed transactions

Each server manages a set of objects and is responsible for ensuring that they remain consistent when accessed by concurrent transactions. Therefore, each server is responsible for applying concurrency control to its own objects. The members of a collection of servers of distributed transactions are jointly responsible for ensuring that they are performed in a serially equivalent manner.

    This implies that if transaction T is before transaction U in their conflicting access to objects at one of the servers then they must be in that order at all of the servers whose objects are accessed in a conflicting manner by both T and U.

14.4.1 Locking

In a distributed transaction, the locks on an object are held locally (in the same server). The local lock manager can decide whether to grant a lock or make the requesting transaction wait. However, it cannot release any locks until it knows that the transaction has been committed or aborted at all the servers involved in the transaction. When locking is used for concurrency control, the objects remain locked and are unavailable for other transactions during the atomic commit protocol, although an aborted transaction releases its locks after phase 1 of the protocol.

As lock managers in different servers set their locks independently of one another, it is possible that different servers may impose different orderings on transactions. Consider the following interleaving of transactions T and U at servers X and Y:

T			U		
Write(A)	at X	locks A			
			Write(B)	at Y	locks B
Read(B)	at Y	waits for U			
			Read(A)	at X	waits for T

The transaction T locks object A at server X and then transaction U locks object B at server Y. After that, T tries to access B at server Y and waits for U's lock. Similarly, transaction U tries to access A at server X and has to wait for T's lock. Therefore, we have T before U in one server and U before T in the other. These different orderings can lead to cyclic dependencies between transactions and a distributed deadlock situation arises. The detection and resolution of distributed deadlocks is discussed in the next section of this chapter. When a deadlock is detected, a transaction is aborted to resolve the deadlock. In this case, the coordinator will be informed and will abort the transaction at the participants involved in the transaction.

14.4.2 Timestamp ordering concurrency control

In a single server transaction, the coordinator issues a unique timestamp to each transaction when it starts. Serial equivalence is enforced by committing the versions of objects in the order of the timestamps of transactions that accessed them. In distributed transactions, we require that each coordinator issue globally unique timestamps. A globally unique transaction timestamp is issued to the client by the first coordinator accessed by a transaction. The transaction timestamp is passed to the coordinator at each server whose objects perform an operation in the transaction.

The servers of distributed transactions are jointly responsible for ensuring that they are performed in a serially equivalent manner. For example, if the version of an object accessed by transaction U commits after the version accessed by T at one server, then if T and U access the same object as one another at other servers, they must commit them in the same order. To achieve the same ordering at all the servers, the coordinators must agree as to the ordering of their timestamps. A timestamp consists of a pair <*local timestamp, server-id*>. The agreed ordering of pairs of timestamps is based on a comparison in which the server-id part is less significant.

The same ordering of transactions can be achieved at all the servers even if their local clocks are not synchronized. However, for reasons of efficiency it is required that the timestamps issued by one coordinator be roughly synchronized with those issued by the other coordinators. When this is the case, the ordering of transactions generally corresponds to the order in which they are started in real time. Timestamps can be kept roughly synchronized by the use of synchronized local physical clocks (see Chapter 11).

When timestamp ordering is used for concurrency control, conflicts are resolved as each operation is performed. If the resolution of a conflict requires a transaction to be aborted, the coordinator will be informed and it will abort the transaction at all the participants. Therefore, any transaction that reaches the client request to commit should always be able to commit. Therefore, a participant in the two-phase commit protocol will normally agree to commit. The only situation in which a participant will not agree to commit is if it had crashed during the transaction.

14.4.3 Optimistic concurrency control

Recall that with optimistic concurrency control, each transaction is validated before it is allowed to commit. Transaction numbers are assigned at the start of validation and transactions are serialized according to the order of the transaction numbers. A distributed transaction is validated by a collection of independent servers, each of which validates transactions that access its own objects. The validation at all of the servers takes place during the first phase of the two-phase commit protocol.

Consider the following interleavings of transactions T and U, which access objects A and B at servers X and Y, respectively.

T		U	
Read(A)	at X	Read(B)	at Y
Write(A)		Write(B)	
Read(B)	at Y	Read(A)	at X
Write(B)		Write(A)	

The transactions access the objects in the order T before U at server X and in the order U before T at server Y. Now suppose that T and U start validation at about the same time, but server X validates T first and server Y validates U first. Recall that Section 13.5 recommends a simplification of the validation protocol that makes a rule that only one transaction may perform validation and update phases at a time. Therefore each server will be unable to validate the other transaction until the first one has completed. This is an example of commitment deadlock.

The validation rules in Section 13.5 assume that validation is fast, which is true for single-server transactions. However, in a distributed transaction, the two-phase commit protocol may take some time and will delay other transactions from entering validation until a decision on the current transaction has been obtained. In distributed optimistic transactions, each server applies a parallel validation protocol. This is an extension of either backward or forward validation to allow multiple transactions to be in the validation phase at the same time. In this extension, rule 3 must be checked as well as rule 2 for backward validation. That is, the write set of the transaction being validated must be checked for overlaps with the write set of earlier overlapping transactions. Kung and Robinson [1981] describe parallel validation in their paper.

If parallel validation is used, transactions will not suffer from commitment deadlock. However, if servers simply perform independent validations, it is possible that different servers of a distributed transaction may serialize the same set of transactions in different orders, for example with T before U at server X and U before T at server Y in our example.

The servers of distributed transactions must prevent this happening. One approach is that after a local validation by each server, a global validation is carried out [Ceri and Owicki 1982]. The global validation checks that the combination of the orderings at the individual servers is serializable; that is, that the transaction being validated is not involved in a cycle.

Another approach is that all of the servers of a particular transaction use the same globally unique transaction number at the start of the validation [Schlageter 1982]. The coordinator of the two-phase commit protocol is responsible for generating the globally unique transaction number and passes it to the participants in the *canCommit?* messages. As different servers may coordinate different transactions, the servers must (as in the distributed timestamp ordering protocol) have an agreed order for the transaction numbers they generate.

Agrawal *et al.* [1987] have proposed a variation of Kung and Robinson's algorithm that favours read-only transactions, together with an algorithm called MVGV (multi-version generalized validation). MVGV is a form of parallel validation that ensures that transaction numbers reflect serial order, but it requires that the visibility of some transactions be delayed after having committed. It also allows the transaction number to be changed so as to permit some transactions to validate that otherwise would have failed. The paper also proposes an algorithm for committing distributed transactions. It is similar to Schlageter's proposal in that a global transaction number has to be found. At the end of the read phase, the coordinator proposes a value for the global transaction number and each participant attempts to validate their local transactions using that number. However, if the proposed global transaction number is too small, some participants may not be able to validate their transaction and they negotiate with the coordinator for an increased number. If no suitable number can be found, then that participants will have to abort its transaction. Eventually, if all of the participants can validate their transactions the coordinator will have received proposals for transaction numbers from each of them. If common numbers can be found then the transaction will be committed.

14.5 Distributed deadlocks

The discussion of deadlocks in Section 13.4 shows that deadlocks can arise within a single server when locking is used for concurrency control. Servers must either prevent or detect and resolve deadlocks. Using timeouts to resolve possible deadlocks is a clumsy approach – it is difficult to choose an appropriate timeout interval, and transactions are aborted unnecessarily. With deadlock detection schemes, a transaction is aborted only when it is involved in a deadlock. Most deadlock detection schemes

Figure 14.12   Interleavings of transactions *U*, *V* and *W*

U		V		W	
d.deposit(10)	lock D				
		b.deposit(10)	lock B		
a.deposit(20)	lock A		at Y		
	at X				
				c.deposit(30)	lock C
b.withdraw(30)	wait at Y				at Z
		c.withdraw(20)	wait at Z		
				a.withdraw(20)	wait at X

operate by finding cycles in the transaction wait-for graph. In a distributed system involving multiple servers being accessed by multiple transactions, a global wait-for graph can in theory be constructed from the local ones. There can be a cycle in the global wait-for graph that is not in any single local one – that is, there can be a *distributed deadlock*. Recall that the wait-for graph is a directed graph in which nodes represent transactions and objects, and edges represent either an object held by a transaction or a transaction waiting for an object. There is a deadlock if and only if there is a cycle in the wait-for graph.

Figure 14.12 shows the interleavings of the transactions *U*, *V* and *W* involving the objects *A* and *B* managed by servers *X* and *Y* and objects *C* and *D* managed by server *Z*.

The complete wait-for graph in Figure 14.13(a) shows that a deadlock cycle consists of alternate edges, which represent a transaction waiting for an object and an object held by a transaction. As any transaction can only be waiting for one object at a time, objects can be left out of wait-for graphs, as shown in Figure 14.13(b).

Detection of a distributed deadlock requires a cycle to be found in the global transaction wait-for graph that is distributed among the servers that were involved in the transactions. Local wait-for graphs can be built by the lock manager at each server, as discussed in Chapter 13. In the above example, the local wait-for graphs of the servers are:

> server *Y*: $U \rightarrow V$ (added when *U* requests *b.withdraw(30)*)
> server *Z*: $V \rightarrow W$ (added when *V* requests *c.withdraw(20)*)
> server *X*: $W \rightarrow U$ (added when *W* requests *a.withdraw(20)*)

As the global wait-for graph is held in part by each of the several servers involved, communication between these servers is required to find cycles in the graph.

A simple solution is to use centralized deadlock detection. in which one server takes on the role of global deadlock detector. From time to time, each server sends the latest copy of its local wait-for graph to the global deadlock detector, which amalgamates the information in the local graphs in order to construct a global wait-for

Figure 14.13   Distributed deadlock

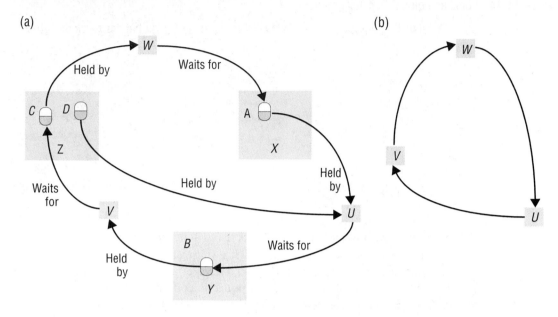

graph. The global deadlock detector checks for cycles in the global wait-for graph. When it finds a cycle, it makes a decision on how to resolve the deadlock and informs the servers as to the transaction to be aborted to resolve the deadlock.

Centralized deadlock detection is not a good idea, because it depends on a single server to carry it out. It suffers from the usual problems associated with centralized solutions in distributed systems – poor availability, lack of fault tolerance and no ability to scale. In addition, the cost of the frequent transmission of local wait-for graphs is high. If the global graph is collected less frequently, deadlocks may take longer to be detected.

Phantom deadlocks ◊   A deadlock that is 'detected' but is not really a deadlock is called a phantom deadlock. In distributed deadlock detection, information about wait-for relationships between transactions is transmitted from one server to another. If there is a deadlock, the necessary information will eventually be collected in one place and a cycle will be detected. As this procedure will take some time, there is a chance that one of the transactions that holds a lock will meanwhile have released it, in which case the deadlock will no longer exist.

Consider the case of a global deadlock detector that receives local wait-for graphs from servers X and Y, as shown in Figure 14.14. Suppose that transaction U then releases an object at server X and requests the one held by V at server Y. Suppose also that the global detector receives server Y's local graph before server X's. In this case, it would detect a cycle $T \rightarrow U \rightarrow V \rightarrow T$, although the edge $T \rightarrow U$ no longer exists. This is an example of a phantom deadlock.

The observant reader will have realized that if transactions are using two-phase locks, they cannot release objects and then obtain more objects, and phantom deadlock

Figure 14.14   Local and global wait-for graphs

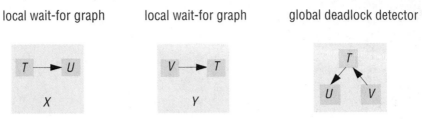

cycles cannot occur in the way suggested above. Consider the situation in which a cycle $T \rightarrow U \rightarrow V \rightarrow T$ is detected: either this represents a deadlock or each of the transactions T, U and V must eventually commit. It is actually impossible for any of them to commit, because each of them is waiting for an object that will never be released.

A phantom deadlock could be detected if a waiting transaction in a deadlock cycle aborts during the deadlock detection procedure. For example, if there is a cycle $T \rightarrow U \rightarrow V \rightarrow T$ and U aborts after the information concerning U has been collected, then the cycle has been broken already and there is no deadlock.

Edge chasing ◊ A distributed approach to deadlock detection uses a technique called edge chasing or path pushing. In this approach, the global wait-for graph is not constructed, but each of the servers involved has knowledge about some of its edges. The servers attempt to find cycles by forwarding messages called *probes*, which follow the edges of the graph throughout the distributed system. A probe message consists of transaction wait-for relationships representing a path in the global wait-for graph.

The question is: when should a server send out a probe? Consider the situation at server X in Figure 14.13. This server has just added the edge $W \rightarrow U$ to its local wait-for graph and at this time, transaction U is waiting to access object B, which transaction V holds at server Y. This edge could possibly be part of a cycle such as $V \rightarrow T_1 \rightarrow T_2 \rightarrow \ldots \rightarrow W \rightarrow U \rightarrow V$ involving transactions using objects at other servers. This indicates that there is a potential distributed deadlock cycle, which could be found by sending out a probe to server Y.

Now consider the situation a little earlier when server Z added the edge $V \rightarrow W$ to its local graph: at this point in time, W is not waiting. Therefore, there would be no point in sending out a probe.

Each distributed transaction starts at a server (called the coordinator of the transaction) and moves to several other servers (called participants in the transaction), which can communicate with the coordinator. At any point in time, a transaction can be either active or waiting at just one of these servers. The coordinator is responsible for recording whether the transaction is active or is waiting for a particular object, and participants can get this information from their coordinator. Lock managers inform coordinators when transactions start waiting for objects and when transactions acquire objects and become active again. When a transaction is aborted to break a deadlock, its coordinator will inform the participants and all of its locks will be removed, with the

Figure 14.15   Probes transmitted to detect deadlock

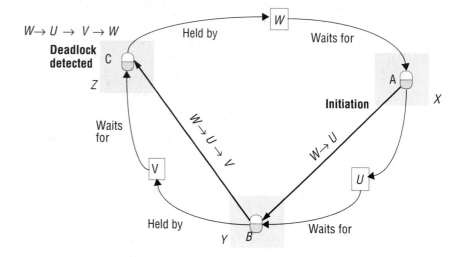

effect that all edges involving that transaction will be removed from the local wait-for graphs.

Edge-chasing algorithms have three steps – initiation, detection and resolution.

Initiation: When a server notes that a transaction T starts waiting for another transaction U, where U is waiting to access an object at another server, it initiates detection by sending a probe containing the edge $< T \rightarrow U >$ to the server of the object at which transaction U is blocked. If U is sharing a lock, probes are sent to all the holders of the lock. Sometimes further transactions may start sharing the lock later on, in which case probes can be sent to them too.

Detection: Detection consists of receiving probes and deciding whether deadlock has occurred and whether to forward the probes.

For example, when a server of an object receives a probe $< T \rightarrow U >$ (indicating that T is waiting for a transaction U that holds a local object), it checks to see whether U is also waiting. If it is, the transaction it waits for (for example, V) is added to the probe (making it $< T \rightarrow U \rightarrow V >$), and if the new transaction (V) is waiting for another object elsewhere, the probe is forwarded.

In this way, paths through the global wait-for graph are built one edge at a time. Before forwarding a probe, the server checks to see whether the transaction (for example, T) it has just added has caused the probe to contain a cycle (for example, $< T \rightarrow U \rightarrow V \rightarrow T >$). If this is the case, it has found a cycle in the graph and deadlock has been detected.

Resolution: When a cycle is detected, a transaction in the cycle is aborted to break the deadlock.

In our example, the following steps describe how deadlock detection is initiated and the probes that are forwarded during the corresponding detection phase.

- Server X initiates detection by sending probe $< W \rightarrow U >$ to the server of B (Server Y).

- Server Y receives probe $< W \rightarrow U >$, notes that B is held by V and appends V to the probe to produce $< W \rightarrow U \rightarrow V >$. It notes that V is waiting for C at server Z. This probe is forwarded to server Z.

- Server Z receives probe $< W \rightarrow U \rightarrow V >$ and notes C is held by W and appends W to the probe to produce $< W \rightarrow U \rightarrow V \rightarrow W >$.

This path contains a cycle. The server detects a deadlock. One of the transactions in the cycle must be aborted to break the deadlock. The transaction to be aborted can be chosen according to transaction priorities, which are described shortly.

Figure 14.15 shows the progress of the probe messages from the initiation by the server of A to the deadlock detection by the server of C. Probes are shown as heavy arrows, objects as circles and transaction coordinators as rectangles. Each probe is shown as going directly from one object to another. In reality, before a server transmits a probe to another server, it consults the coordinator of the last transaction in the path to find out whether the latter is waiting for another object elsewhere. For example, before the server of B transmits the probe $<W \rightarrow U \rightarrow V>$ it consults the coordinator of V to find out that V is waiting for C. In most of the edge-chasing algorithms, the servers of objects send probes to transaction coordinators, which then forward them (if the transaction is waiting) to the server of the object the transaction is waiting for. In our example, the server of B transmits the probe $<W \rightarrow U \rightarrow V>$ to the coordinator of V, which then forwards it to the server of C. This shows that when a probe is forwarded, two messages are required.

The above algorithm should find any deadlock that occurs, provided that waiting transactions do not abort and there are no failures such as lost messages or servers crashing. To understand this, consider a deadlock cycle in which the last transaction, W, starts waiting and completes the cycle. When W starts waiting for an object, the server initiates a probe that goes to the server of the object held by each transaction that W is waiting for. The recipients extend and forward the probes to the servers of objects requested by all waiting transactions they find. Thus every transaction that W waits for directly or indirectly will be added to the probe unless a deadlock is detected. When there is a deadlock, W is waiting for itself indirectly. Therefore, the probe will return to the object that W holds.

It might appear that large numbers of messages are sent in order to detect deadlock. In the above example, we see two probe messages to detect a cycle involving three transactions. Each of the probe messages is in general two messages (from object to coordinator and then from coordinator to object).

A probe that detects a cycle involving N transactions will be forwarded by $(N-1)$ transaction coordinators via $(N-1)$ servers of objects, requiring $2(N-1)$ messages. Fortunately, the majority of deadlocks involve cycles containing only two transactions, and there is no need for undue concern about the number of messages involved. This observation has been made from studies of databases. It can also be argued by considering the probability of conflicting access to objects. See Bernstein *et al.* [1987].

Transaction priorities ◊ In the above algorithm, every transaction involved in a deadlock cycle can cause deadlock detection to be initiated. The effect of several transactions in a

Figure 14.16 Two probes initiated

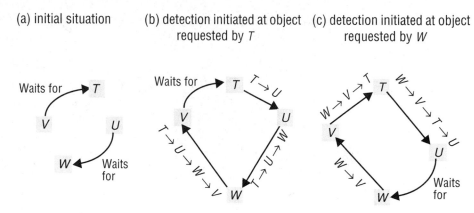

(a) initial situation   (b) detection initiated at object   (c) detection initiated at object
                                  requested by *T*   requested by *W*

cycle initiating deadlock detection is that detection may happen at several different servers in the cycle with the result that more than one transaction in the cycle is aborted.

In Figure 14.16(a), consider transactions T, U, V and W, where U is waiting for W and V is waiting for T. At about the same time, T requests the object held by U and W requests the object held by V. Two separate probes $< T \rightarrow U >$ and $< W \rightarrow V >$ are initiated by the servers of these objects and are circulated until deadlock is detected by each of two different servers. See in Figure 14.16(b), where the cycle is $< T \rightarrow U \rightarrow W \rightarrow V \rightarrow T >$, and (c), where the cycle is $< W \rightarrow V \rightarrow T \rightarrow U \rightarrow W >$.

In order to ensure that only one transaction in a cycle is aborted, transactions are given *priorities* in such a way that all transactions are totally ordered. Timestamps for example, may be used as priorities. When a deadlock cycle is found, the transaction with the lowest priority is aborted. Even if several different servers detect the same cycle, they will all reach the same decision as to which transaction is to be aborted. We write $T > U$ to indicate that T has higher priority than U. In the above example, assume $T > U > V > W$. Then the transaction W will be aborted when either of the cycles $< T \rightarrow U \rightarrow W \rightarrow V \rightarrow T >$ or $< W \rightarrow V \rightarrow T \rightarrow U \rightarrow W >$ is detected.

It might appear that transaction priorities could also be used to reduce the number of situations that cause deadlock detection to be initiated, by using the rule that detection is initiated only when a higher-priority transaction starts to wait for a lower-priority one. In our example in Figure 14.16, as $T > U$ the initiating probe $< T \rightarrow U >$ would be sent, but as $W < V$ the initiating probe $< W \rightarrow V >$ would not be sent. If we assume that when a transaction starts waiting for another transaction it is equally likely that the waiting transaction has higher or lower priority than the waited-for transaction, then the use of this rule is likely to reduce the number of probe messages by about half.

Transaction priorities could also be used to reduce the number of probes that are forwarded. The general idea is that probes should travel 'downhill' – that is, from transactions with higher priorities to transactions with lower priorities. To do this, servers use the rule that they do not forward any probe to a holder that has higher priority than the initiator. The argument for doing this is that if the holder is waiting for another

Figure 14.17   Probes travel downhill

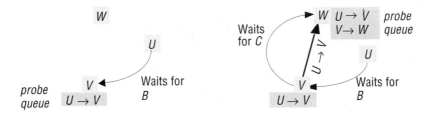

(a) V stores probe when U starts waiting   (b) Probe is forwarded when V starts waiting

transaction then it must have initiated detection by sending a probe when it started waiting.

However, there is a pitfall associated with these apparent improvements. In our example in Figure 14.15 transactions U, V and W are executed in an order in which U is waiting for V and V is waiting for W when W starts waiting for U. Without priority rules, detection is initiated when W starts waiting by sending a probe $< W \rightarrow U>$. Under the priority rule, this probe will not be sent, because $W < U$ and deadlock will not be detected.

The problem is that the order in which transactions start waiting can determine whether or not deadlock will be detected. The above pitfall can be avoided by using a scheme in which coordinators save copies of all the probes received on behalf of each transaction in a *probe queue*. When a transaction starts waiting for an object, it forwards the probes in its queue to the server of the object, which propagates the probes on downhill routes.

In our example in Figure 14.15, when U starts waiting for V, the coordinator of V will save the probe $< U \rightarrow V >$. See Figure 14.17(a). Then when V starts waiting for W, the coordinator of W will store $<V \rightarrow W>$ and V will forward its probe queue $< U \rightarrow V >$ to W. See Figure 14.17(b), in which W's probe queue has $< U \rightarrow V >$ and $<V \rightarrow W>$. When W starts waiting for A it will forward its probe queue $< U \rightarrow V \rightarrow W >$ to the server of A, which also notes the new dependency $W \rightarrow U$ and combines it with the information in the probe received to determine that $U \rightarrow V \rightarrow W \rightarrow U$. Deadlock is detected.

When an algorithm requires probes to be stored in probe queues, it also requires arrangements to pass on probes to new holders and to discard probes that refer to transactions that have been committed or aborted. If relevant probes are discarded, undetected deadlocks may occur, and if outdated probes are retained, false deadlocks may be detected. This adds much to the complexity of any edge-chasing algorithm. Readers who are interested in the details of such algorithms should see Sinha and Natarajan [1985] and Choudhary *et al.* [1989], who present algorithms for use with exclusive locks. But they will see that Choudhary *et al.* showed that Sinha and Natarajan's algorithm is incorrect and fails to detect all deadlocks and may even report false deadlocks. Kshemkalyani and Singhal [1991] corrected the algorithm of Choudhary *et al.* (which fails to detect all deadlocks and may report false deadlocks) and provide a proof of correctness for the corrected algorithm. In a subsequent paper, Kshemkalyani and Singhal [1994] argue that distributed deadlocks are not very well understood because there is no global state or time in a distributed system. In fact, any cycle that has been collected may contain sections recorded at different times. In addition, sites may hear about deadlocks but may not hear that they have been resolved until after random delays. The paper describes distributed deadlocks in terms of the contents of distributed memory, using causal relationships between events at different sites.

14.6 Transaction recovery

The atomic property of transactions requires that the effects of all committed transactions and none of the effects of incomplete or aborted transactions are reflected in the objects they accessed. This property can be described in terms of two aspects: durability and failure atomicity. Durability requires that objects are saved in permanent storage and will be available indefinitely thereafter. Therefore, an acknowledgment of a client's commit request implies that all the effects of the transaction have been recorded in permanent storage as well as in the server's (volatile) objects. Failure atomicity requires that effects of transactions are atomic even when the server crashes. Recovery is concerned with ensuring that a server's objects are durable and that the service provides failure atomicity.

Although file servers and database servers maintain data in permanent storage, other kinds of servers of recoverable objects need not do so except for recovery purposes. In this chapter, we assume that when a server is running it keeps all of its objects in its volatile memory and records its committed objects in a *recovery file* or files. Therefore, recovery consists of restoring the server with the latest committed versions of its objects from permanent storage. Databases need to deal with large volumes of data. They generally hold the objects in stable storage on disk with a cache in volatile memory.

The two requirements for durability and for failure atomicity are not really independent of one another and can be dealt with by a single mechanism – the *recovery manager*. The task of a recovery manager is:

- to save objects in permanent storage (in a recovery file) for committed transactions;

- to restore the server's objects after a crash;

- to reorganize the recovery file to improve the performance of recovery;

- to reclaim storage space (in the recovery file).

In some cases, we require the recovery manager to be resilient to media failures – failures of its recovery file so that some of the data on the disk is lost, either by being corrupted during a crash, by random decay or by a permanent failure. In such cases, we need another copy of the recovery file. This can be in stable storage, which is implemented so as to be very unlikely to fail by using mirrored disks or copies at a different location.

Intentions list ◊ Any server that provides transactions needs to keep track of the objects accessed by clients' transactions. Recall from Chapter 13 that when a client opens a transaction, the server first contacted provides a new transaction identifier and returns it to the client. Each subsequent client request within a transaction up to and including the *commit* or *abort* request includes the transaction identifier as an argument. During the progress of a transaction, the update operations are applied to a private set of tentative versions of the objects belonging to the transaction.

At each server, an *intentions list* is recorded for all of its currently active transactions – an intentions list of a particular transaction contains a list of the references and the values of all the objects that are altered by that transaction. When a transaction is committed, that transaction's intentions list is used to identify the objects it affected. The committed version of each object is replaced by the tentative version made by that transaction, and the new value is written to the server's recovery file. When a transaction aborts, the server uses the intentions list to delete all the tentative versions of objects made by that transaction.

Recall also that a distributed transaction must carry out an atomic commit protocol before it can be committed or aborted. Our discussion of recovery is based on the two-phase commit protocol, in which all the participants involved in a transaction first say whether they are prepared to commit and then, later on if all the participants agree, they all carry out the actual commit actions. If the participants cannot agree to commit, they must abort the transaction.

At the point when a participant says it is prepared to commit a transaction, its recovery manager must have saved both its intentions list for that transaction and the objects in that intentions list in its recovery file, so that it will be able to carry out the commitment later on, even if it crashes in the interim.

When all the participants involved in a transaction agree to commit it, the coordinator informs the client and then sends messages to the participants to commit their part of the transaction. Once the client has been informed that a transaction has committed, the recovery files of the participating servers must contain sufficient information to ensure that the transaction is committed by all of the servers, even if some of them crash between preparing to commit and committing.

Entries in recovery file ◊ To deal with recovery of a server that can be involved in distributed transactions, further information in addition to the values of the objects is stored in the recovery file. This information concerns the *status* of each transaction – whether it is *committed*, *aborted* or *prepared* to commit. In addition, each object in the recovery file is associated with a particular transaction by saving the intentions list in the recovery file. Figure 14.18 shows a summary of the types of entry included in a recovery file.

The transaction status values relating to the two-phase commit protocol are discussed in Section 14.6.4 on recovery of the two-phase commit protocol. We shall now describe two approaches to the use of recovery files: logging and shadow versions.

14.6.1 Logging

In the logging technique, the recovery file represents a log containing the history of all the transactions performed by a server. The history consists of values of objects,

Figure 14.18 Types of entry in a recovery file

Type of entry	Description of contents of entry
Object	A value of an object.
Transaction status	Transaction identifier, transaction status (*prepared*, *committed*, *aborted*) – and other status values used for the two-phase commit protocol.
Intentions list	Transaction identifier and a sequence of intentions, each of which consists of <identifier of object>, <position in recovery file of value of object>.

transaction status entries and intentions lists of transactions. The order of the entries in the log reflects the order in which transactions have prepared, committed and aborted at that server. In practice, the recovery file will contain a recent snapshot of the values of all the objects in the server followed by a history of transactions after the snapshot.

During the normal operation of a server, its recovery manager is called whenever a transaction prepares to commit, commits or aborts a transaction. When the server is prepared to commit a transaction, the recovery manager appends all the objects in its intentions list to the recovery file, followed by the current status of that transaction (*prepared*) together with its intentions list. When a transaction is eventually committed or aborted, the recovery manager appends the corresponding status of the transaction to its recovery file.

It is assumed that the append operation is atomic in the sense that it writes one or more complete entries to the recovery file. If the server fails, only the last write can be incomplete. To make efficient use of the disk, several subsequent writes can be buffered and then written as a single write to disk. An additional advantage of the logging technique is that sequential writes to disk are faster than writes to random locations.

After a crash, any transaction that does not have a *committed* status in the log is aborted. Therefore, when a transaction commits, its *committed* status entry must be *forced* to the log – that is, written to the log together with any other buffered entries.

The recovery manager associates a unique identifier with each object so that the successive versions of an object in the recovery file may be associated with the server's objects. For example, a durable form of a remote object reference such as a CORBA persistent reference will do as an object identifier.

Figure 14.19 illustrates the log mechanism for the banking service transactions T and U in Figure 13.7. The log was recently reorganized, and entries to the left of the double line represent a snapshot of the values of A, B and C before transactions T and U started. In this diagram, we use the names A, B and C as unique identifiers for objects. We show the situation when transaction T has committed and transaction U has prepared but not committed. When transaction T prepares to commit, the values of objects A and B are written at positions P_1 and P_2 in the log, followed by a prepared transaction status entry for T with its intentions list ($< A, P_1 >, < B, P_2 >$). When transaction T commits, a

Figure 14.19   Log for banking service

P_0			P_1	P_2	P_3	P_4	P_5	P_6	P_7
Object:A	Object:B	Object:C	Object:A	Object:B	Trans:T	Trans:T	Object:C	Object:B	Trans:U
100	200	300	80	220	prepared	committed	278	242	prepared
					$<A, P_1>$				$<C, P_5>$
					$<B, P_2>$				$<B, P_6>$
					P_0	P_3			P_4

Checkpoint   End of log

committed transaction status entry for T is put at position P_4. Then when transaction U prepares to commit, the values of objects C and B are written at positions P_5 and P_6 in the log, followed by a prepared transaction status entry for U with its intentions list $(< C, P_5 >, < B, P_6 >)$.

Each transaction status entry contains a pointer to the position in the recovery file of the previous transaction status entry to enable the recovery manager to follow the transaction status entries in reverse order through the recovery file. The last pointer in the sequence of transaction status entries points to the checkpoint.

Recovery of objects ◊ When a server is replaced after a crash, it first sets default initial values for its objects and then hands over to its recovery manager. The recovery manager is responsible for restoring the server's objects so that they include all the effects of all the committed transactions performed in the correct order and none of the effects of incomplete or aborted transactions.

The most recent information about transactions is at the end of the log. There are two approaches to restoring the data from the recovery file. In the first, the recovery manager starts at the beginning and restores the values of all of the objects from the most recent checkpoint. It then reads in the values of each of the objects, associates them with their intentions lists and for committed transactions replaces the values of the objects. In this approach, the transactions are replayed in the order in which they were executed and there could be a large number of them. In the second approach, the recovery manager will restore a server's objects by 'reading the recovery file backwards'. The recovery file has been structured so that there is a backwards pointer from each transaction status entry to the next. The recovery manager uses transactions with committed status to restore those objects that have not yet been restored. It continues until it has restored all of the server's objects. This has the advantage that each object is restored once only.

To recover the effects of a transaction, a recovery manager gets the corresponding intentions list from its recovery file. The intentions list contains the identifiers and positions in the recovery file of values of all the objects affected by the transaction.

If the server fails at the point reached in Figure 14.19, its recovery manager will recover the objects as follows. It starts at the last transaction status entry in the log (at P_7) and concludes that transaction U has not committed and its effects should be ignored. It then moves to the previous transaction status entry in the log (at P_4) and concludes that transaction T has committed. To recover the objects affected by transaction T, it moves to the previous transaction status entry in the log (at P_3) and finds the intentions list for T ($< A, P_1 >, < B, P_2 >$). It then restores objects A and B from the values at P_1 and P_2. As it has not yet restored C, it moves back to P_0, which is a checkpoint, and restores C.

To help with subsequent reorganization of the recovery file, the recovery manager notes all the prepared transactions it finds during the process of restoring the server's objects. For each prepared transaction, it adds an aborted transaction status to the recovery file. This ensures that in the recovery file, every transaction is eventually shown as either committed or aborted.

The server could fail again during the recovery procedures. It is essential that recovery be idempotent in the sense that it can be done any number of times with the same effect. This is straightforward under our assumption that all the objects are restored to volatile memory. In the case of a database, which keeps its objects in permanent storage, with a cache in volatile memory, some of the objects in permanent storage will be out of date when a server is replaced after a crash. Therefore, its recovery manager has to restore the objects in permanent storage. If it fails during recovery, the partially restored objects will still be there. This makes idempotence a little harder to achieve.

Reorganizing the recovery file ◊ A recovery manager is responsible for reorganizing its recovery file so as to make the process of recovery faster and to reduce its use of space. If the recovery file is never reorganized, then the recovery process must search backwards through the recovery file until it has found a value for each of its objects. Conceptually, the only information required for recovery is a copy of the committed versions of all the objects in the server. This would be the most compact form for the recovery file. The name *checkpointing* is used to refer to the process of writing the current committed values of a server's objects to a new recovery file, together with transaction status entries and intentions lists of transactions that have not yet been fully resolved (including information related to the two-phase commit protocol). The term *checkpoint* is used to refer to the information stored by the checkpointing process. The purpose of making checkpoints is to reduce the number of transactions to be dealt with during recovery and to reclaim file space.

Checkpointing can be done immediately after recovery but before any new transactions are started. However, recovery may not occur very often. Therefore, checkpointing may need to be done from time to time during the normal activity of a server. The checkpoint is written to a future recovery file, and the current recovery file remains in use until the checkpoint is complete. Checkpointing consists of 'adding a mark' to the recovery file when the checkpointing starts, writing the server's objects to the future recovery file and then copying (1) entries before the mark that relate to as yet unresolved transactions and (2) all entries after the mark in the recovery file to the future recovery file. When the checkpoint is complete, the future recovery file becomes the recovery file.

The recovery system can reduce its use of space by discarding the old recovery file. When the recovery manager is carrying out the recovery process, it may encounter a checkpoint in the recovery file. When this happens, it can restore immediately all outstanding objects from the checkpoint.

Figure 14.20   Shadow versions

	Map at start				Map when T commits		
	$A \rightarrow P_0$				$A \rightarrow P_1$		
	$B \rightarrow P_0'$				$B \rightarrow P_2$		
	$C \rightarrow P_0''$				$C \rightarrow P_0''$		

	P_0	P_0'	P_0''	P_1	P_2	P_3	P_4
Version store	100	200	300	‖ 80	220	278	242

Checkpoint

14.6.2 Shadow versions

The *logging* technique records transaction status entries, intentions lists and objects all in the same file – the log. The *shadow versions* technique is an alternative way to organize a recovery file. It uses a *map* to locate versions of the server's objects in a file called a *version store*. The map associates the identifiers of the server's objects with the positions of their current versions in the version store. The versions written by each transaction are shadows of the previous committed versions. The transaction status entries and intentions lists are dealt with separately. Shadow versions are described first.

When a transaction is prepared to commit, any of the objects changed by the transaction are appended to the version store, leaving the corresponding committed versions unchanged. These new as yet tentative versions are called *shadow* versions. When a transaction commits, a new map is made by copying the old map and entering the positions of the shadow versions. To complete the commit process, the new map replaces the old map.

To restore the objects when a server is replaced after a crash, its recovery manager reads the map and uses the information in the map to locate the objects in the version store.

This technique is illustrated with the same example involving transactions T and U in Figure 14.20. The first column in the table shows the map before transactions T and U, when the balances of the accounts A, B and C are \$100, \$200 and \$300, respectively. The second column shows the map after transaction T has committed.

The version store contains a checkpoint, followed by the versions of A and B at P_1 and P_2 made by transaction T. It also contains the shadow versions of B and C made by transaction U, at P_3 and P_4.

The map must always be written to a well-known place (for example, at the start of the version store or a separate file) so that it can be found when the system needs to be recovered.

The switch from the old map to the new map must be performed in a single atomic step. To achieve this it is essential that stable storage is used for the map – so that there is guaranteed to be a valid map even when a file write operation fails. The shadow versions method provides faster recovery than logging because the positions of the current committed objects are recorded in the map, whereas recovery from a log requires searching throughout the log for objects. Logging should be faster than shadow versions during the normal activity of the system. This is because logging requires only a sequence of append operations to the same file, whereas shadow versions requires an additional stable storage write (involving two unrelated disk blocks).

Shadow versions on their own are not sufficient for a server that handles distributed transactions. Transaction status entries and intentions lists are saved in a file called the transaction status file. Each intentions list represents the part of the map that will be altered by a transaction when it commits. The transaction status file may, for example, be organized as a log.

The figure below shows the map and the transaction status file for our current example when T has committed and U is prepared to commit.

Transaction status file (stable storage)

Map		T	T	U
$A \rightarrow P_1$		prepared	committed	prepared
$B \rightarrow P_2$		$A \rightarrow P_1$		$B \rightarrow P_3$
$C \rightarrow P_0"$		$B \rightarrow P_2$		$C \rightarrow P_4$

There is a chance that a server may crash between the time when a committed status is written to the transaction status file and the time when the map is updated – in which case the client will not have been acknowledged. The recovery manager must allow for this possibility when the server is replaced after a crash, for example by checking whether the map includes the effects of the last committed transaction in the transaction status file. If it does not, then the latter should be marked as aborted.

14.6.3 The need for transaction status and intentions list entries in a recovery file

It is possible to design a simple recovery file that does not include entries for transaction status items and intentions lists. This sort of recovery file may be suitable when all transactions are directed to a single server. The use of transaction status items and intentions lists in the recovery file is essential for a server that is intended to participate in distributed transactions. This approach can also be useful for servers of non-distributed transactions for various reasons, including the following:

- Some recovery managers are designed to write the objects to the recovery file early – under the assumption that transactions normally commit.

- If transactions use a large number of big objects, the need to write them contiguously to the recovery file may complicate the design of a server. When objects are referenced from intentions lists, they can be found wherever they are.

- In timestamp ordering concurrency control, a server sometimes knows that a transaction will eventually be able to commit and acknowledges the client – at this time the objects are written to the recovery file (see Chapter 13) to ensure their permanence. However, the transaction may have to wait to commit until earlier transactions have committed. In such situations, the corresponding transaction status entries in the recovery file will be *waiting to commit* and then *committed* to ensure timestamp ordering of committed transactions in the recovery file. On

Figure 14.21 Log with entries relating to two-phase commit protocol

Trans:*T*	Coord'r:*T* •	• Trans:*T*	Trans:*U*	•	• Part'pant:*U*	Trans:*U*	Trans:*U*
prepared	part'pant list: . . .	committed	prepared		Coord'r: . . .	uncertain	committed
intentions list			intentions list				

recovery, any waiting-to-commit transactions can be allowed to commit, because the ones they were waiting for have either just committed or if not have to be aborted due to failure of the server.

14.6.4 Recovery of the two-phase commit protocol

In a distributed transaction, each server keeps its own recovery file. The recovery management described in the previous section must be extended to deal with any transactions that are performing the two-phase commit protocol at the time when a server fails. The recovery managers use two new status values: *done*, *uncertain*. These status values are shown in Figure 14.6. A coordinator uses *committed* to indicate that the outcome of the vote is *Yes* and *done* to indicate that the two-phase commit protocol is complete. A participant uses *uncertain* to indicate that it has voted *Yes* but does not yet know the outcome. Two additional types of entry allow a coordinator to record a list of participants and a participant to record its coordinator:

Type of entry	Description of contents of entry
Coordinator	Transaction identifier, list of participants
Participant	Transaction identifier, coordinator

In phase 1 of the protocol, when the coordinator is prepared to commit (and has already added a prepared status entry to its recovery file), its recovery manager adds a *coordinator* entry to its recovery file. Before a participant can vote *Yes*, it must have already prepared to commit (and must have already added a prepared status entry to its recovery file). When it votes *Yes*, its recovery manager records a *participant* entry and adds an *uncertain* transaction status to its recovery file as a forced write. When a participant votes *No*, it adds an *abort* transaction status to its recovery file.

In phase 2 of the protocol, the recovery manager of the coordinator adds either a *committed* or an *aborted* transaction status to its recovery file, according to the decision. This must be a forced write. Recovery managers of participants add a *commit* or *abort* transaction status to their recovery files according to the message received from the coordinator. When a coordinator has received a confirmation from all of its participants, its recovery manager adds a *done* transaction status to its recovery file - this need not be forced. The *done* status entry is not part of the protocol but is used when the recovery file is reorganized. Figure 14.21 shows the entries in a log for transaction *T*, in which the

Figure 14.22 Recovery of the two-phase commit protocol

Role	Status	Action of recovery manager
Coordinator	*prepared*	No decision had been reached before the server failed. It sends *abortTransaction* to all the servers in the participant list and adds the transaction status *aborted* in its recovery file. Same action for state *aborted*. If there is no participant list, the participants will eventually timeout and abort the transaction.
Coordinator	*committed*	A decision to commit had been reached before the server failed. It sends a *doCommit* to all of the participants in its participant list (in case it had not done so before) and resumes the two-phase protocol at step 4 (see Figure 14.5).
Participant	*committed*	The participant sends a *haveCommitted* message to the coordinator (in case this was not done before it failed). This will allow the coordinator to discard information about this transaction at the next checkpoint.
Participant	*uncertain*	The participant failed before it knew the outcome of the transaction. It cannot determine the status of the transaction until the coordinator informs it of the decision. It will send a *getDecision* to the coordinator to determine the status of the transaction. When it receives the reply it will commit or abort accordingly.
Participant	*prepared*	The participant has not yet voted and can abort the transaction.
Coordinator	*done*	No action is required.

server played the coordinator role, and for transaction U, in which the server played the participant role. For both transactions, the *prepared* transaction status entry comes first. In the case of a coordinator it is followed by a coordinator entry, and a *committed* transaction status entry. The *done* transaction status entry is not shown in Figure 14.21. In the case of a participant, the *prepared* transaction status entry is followed by a participant entry whose state is *uncertain* and then a *committed* or *aborted* transaction status entry.

When a server is replaced after a crash, the recovery manager has to deal with the two-phase commit protocol in addition to restoring the objects. For any transaction where the server has played the coordinator role, it should find a coordinator entry and a set of transaction status entries. For any transaction where the server played the participant role, it should find a participant entry and a set of transaction status entries. In both cases, the most recent transaction status entry – that is, the one nearest the end of the log – determines the transaction status at the time of failure. The action of the recovery manager with respect to the two-phase commit protocol for any transaction depends on whether the server was the coordinator or a participant and on its status at the time of failure, as shown in Figure 14.22.

Reorganization of recovery file ◊ Care must be taken when performing a checkpoint to ensure that *coordinator* entries of transactions without status *done* are not removed from the recovery file. These entries must be retained until all the participants have confirmed that they have completed their transactions. Entries with status *done* may be discarded. Participant entries with transaction state *uncertain* must also be retained.

Recovery of nested transactions ◊ In the simplest case, each subtransaction of a nested transaction accesses a different set of objects. As each participant prepares to commit during the two-phase commit protocol, it writes its objects and intentions lists to the local recovery file, associating them with the transaction identifier of the top-level transaction. Although nested transactions use a special variant of the two-phase commit protocol, the recovery manager uses the same transaction status values as for flat transactions.

However, abort recovery is complicated by the fact that several subtransactions at the same and different levels in the nesting hierarchy can access the same object. Section 13.4 describes a locking scheme in which parent transactions inherit locks and subtransactions acquire locks from their parents. The locking scheme forces parent transactions and subtransactions to access common data objects at different times and ensures that accesses by concurrent subtransactions to the same objects must be serialized.

Objects that are accessed according to the rules of nested transactions are made recoverable by providing tentative versions for each subtransaction. The relationship between the tentative versions of an object used by the subtransactions of a nested transaction is similar to the relationship between the locks. To support recovery from aborts, the server of an object shared by transactions at multiple levels provides a stack of tentative versions – one for each nested transaction to use.

When the first subtransaction in a set of nested transactions accesses an object, it is provided with a tentative version that is a copy of the current committed version of the object. This is regarded as being at the top of the stack, but unless any other subtransactions access the same object, the stack will not materialize.

When one of its subtransactions does access the same object, it copies the version at the top of the stack and pushes it back on the stack. All of that subtransaction's updates are applied to the tentative version at the top of the stack. When a subtransaction provisionally commits, its parent inherits the new version. To achieve this, both the subtransaction's version and its parent's version are discarded from the stack and then the subtransaction's new version is pushed back on to the stack (effectively replacing its parent's version). When a subtransaction aborts, its version at the top of the stack is discarded. Eventually, when the top-level transaction commits, the version at the top of the stack (if any) becomes the new committed version.

For example, in Figure 14.23, suppose that transactions T_1, T_{11}, T_{12} and T_2 all access the same object, A, in the order T_1; T_{11}; T_{12}; T_2. Suppose that their tentative versions are called A_1, A_{11}, A_{12} and A_2. When T_1 starts executing, A_1 is based on the committed version of A and is pushed on the stack. When T_{11} starts executing, it bases its version A_{11} on A_1 and pushes it on the stack, when it completes, it replaces its parent's

Figure 14.23 Nested transactions

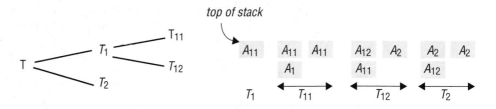

version on the stack. Transactions T_{12} and T_2 act in a similar way, finally leaving the result of T_2 at the top of the stack.

14.7 Summary

In the most general case, a client's transaction will request operations on objects in several different servers. A distributed transaction is any transaction whose activity involves several different servers. A nested transaction structure may be used to allow additional concurrency and independent committing by the servers in a distributed transaction.

The atomicity property of transactions requires that the servers participating in a distributed transaction either all commit it or all abort it. Atomic commit protocols are designed to achieve this effect, even if servers crash during their execution. The two-phase commit protocol allows a server to decide to abort unilaterally. It includes timeout actions to deal with delays due to servers crashing. The two-phase commit protocol can take an unbounded amount of time to complete but is guaranteed to complete eventually.

Concurrency control in distributed transactions is modular – each server is responsible for the serializability of transactions that access its own objects. However, additional protocols are required to ensure that transactions are serializable globally. Distributed transactions that use timestamp ordering require a means of generating an agreed timestamp ordering between the multiple servers. Those that use optimistic concurrency control require global validation or a means of forcing a global ordering on committing transactions.

Distributed transactions that use two-phase locking can suffer from distributed deadlocks. The aim of distributed deadlock detection is to look for cycles in the global wait-for graph. If a cycle is found, one or more transactions must be aborted to resolve the deadlock. Edge chasing is a non-centralized approach to the detection of distributed deadlocks.

Transaction-based applications have strong requirements for the long life and integrity of the information stored, but they do not usually have requirements for immediate response at all times. Atomic commit protocols are the key to distributed transactions, but they cannot be guaranteed to complete within a particular time limit. Transactions are made durable by performing checkpoints and logging in a recovery file, which is used for recovery when a server is replaced after a crash. Users of a transaction service would experience some delay during recovery. Although it is assumed that the servers of distributed transactions exhibit crash failures and run in an asynchronous system, they are able to reach consensus about the outcome of transactions because crashed servers are replaced with new processes that can acquire all the relevant information from permanent storage or from other servers.

EXERCISES

14.1   In a decentralized variant of the two-phase commit protocol the participants communicate directly with one another instead of indirectly via the coordinator. In phase 1, the coordinator sends its vote to all the participants. In phase 2, if the coordinator's vote is *No*, the participants just abort the transaction; if it is *Yes*, each participant sends its vote to the coordinator and the other participants, each of which decides on the outcome according to the vote and carries it out. Calculate the number of messages and the number of rounds it takes. What are its advantages or disadvantages in comparison with the centralized variant?   *page 570*

14.2   A three-phase commit protocol has the following parts:

> *Phase 1*: is the same as for two-phase commit.

> *Phase 2*: the coordinator collects the votes and makes a decision; if it is *No*, it *aborts* and informs participants that voted *Yes*; if the decision is *Yes*, it sends a *preCommit* request to all the participants. Participants that voted *Yes* wait for a *preCommit* or *doAbort* request. They acknowledge *preCommit* requests and carry out *doAbort* requests.

> *Phase 3*: the coordinator collects the acknowledgments. When all are received, it *Commits* and sends *doCommit* to the participants. Participants wait for a *doCommit* request. When it arrives they *Commit*.

Explain how this protocol avoids delay to participants during their 'uncertain' period due to the failure of the coordinator or other participants. Assume that communication does not fail.   *page 573*

14.3   Explain how the two-phase commit protocol for nested transactions ensures that if the top-level transaction commits, all the right descendants are committed or aborted.
                                page 574

14.4   Give an example of the interleavings of two transactions that is serially equivalent at each server but is not serially equivalent globally.   *page 578*

14.5   The *getDecision* procedure defined in Figure 14.4 is provided only by coordinators. Define a new version of *getDecision* to be provided by participants for use by other participants that need to obtain a decision when the coordinator is unavailable.

Assume that any active participant can make a *getDecision* request to any other active participant. Does this solve the problem of delay during the 'uncertain' period? Explain your answer. At what point in the two-phase commit protocol would the coordinator inform the participants of the other participants' identities (to enable this communication)?   *page 570*

14.6 Extend the definition of two-phase locking to apply to distributed transactions. Explain how this is ensured by distributed transactions using strict two-phase locking locally.
page 578, Chapter 13

14.7 Assuming that strict two-phase locking is in use, describe how the actions of the two-phase commit protocol relate to the concurrency control actions of each individual server. How does distributed deadlock detection fit in? *pages 570, 578*

14.8 A server uses timestamp ordering for local concurrency control. What changes must be made to adapt it for use with distributed transactions? Under what conditions could it be argued that the two-phase commit protocol is redundant with timestamp ordering?
pages 570, 579

14.9 Consider distributed optimistic concurrency control in which each server performs local backward validation sequentially (that is, with only one transaction in the validate and update phase at one time), in relation to your answer to Exercise 14.4. Describe the possible outcomes when the two transactions attempt to commit. What difference does it make if the servers use parallel validation? *Chapter 13, page 580*

14.10 A centralized global deadlock detector holds the union of local wait-for graphs. Give an example to explain how a phantom deadlock could be detected if a waiting transaction in a deadlock cycle aborts during the deadlock detection procedure. *page 583*

14.11 Consider the edge-chasing algorithm (without priorities). Give examples to show that it could detect phantom deadlocks. *page 584*

14.12 A server manages the objects a_1, a_2 ,.... a_n. It provides two operations for its clients:

> *Read(i)* returns the value of a_i
> *Write(i, Value)* assigns *Value* to a_i

The transactions *T*, *U* and *V* are defined as follows:

> *T: x = Read(i); Write(j, 44);*
> *U: Write(i, 55); Write(j, 66);*
> *V: Write(k, 77); Write(k, 88);*

Describe the information written to the log file on behalf of these three transactions if strict two-phase locking is in use and *U* acquires a_i and a_j before *T*. Describe how the recovery manager would use this information to recover the effects of *T*, *U* and *V* when the server is replaced after a crash. What is the significance of the order of the commit entries in the log file? *pages 590–592*

14.13 The appending of an entry to the log file is atomic, but append operations from different transactions may be interleaved. How does this affect the answer to Exercise 14.12?
pages 590–592

14.14   The transactions T, U and V of Exercise 14.12 use strict two-phase locking and their requests are interleaved as follows:

T	U	V
$x = Read(i);$		
		$Write(k, 77);$
	$Write(i, 55)$	
$Write(j, 44)$		
		$Write(k,88)$
	$Write(j, 66)$	

Assuming that the recovery manager appends the data entry corresponding to each *Write* operation to the log file immediately instead of waiting until the end of the transaction, describe the information written to the log file on behalf of the transactions T, U and V. Does early writing affect the correctness of the recovery procedure? What are the advantages and disadvantages of early writing?   *pages 590–592*

14.15   Transactions T and U are run with timestamp ordering concurrency control. Describe the information written to the log file on behalf of T and U, allowing for the fact that U has a later timestamp than T and must wait to commit after T. Why is it essential that the commit entries in the log file be ordered by timestamps? Describe the effect of recovery if the server crashes (i) between the two *Commits* and (ii) after both of them.

T	U
$x= Read(i);$	
	$Write(i, 55);$
	$Write(j, 66);$
$Write(j, 44);$	
	Commit
Commit	

What are the advantages and disadvantages of early writing with timestamp ordering?
page 595

14.16   The transactions T and U in Exercise 14.15 are run with optimistic concurrency control using backward validation and restarting any transactions that fail. Describe the information written to the log file on their behalf. Why is it essential that the commit entries in the log file be ordered by transaction numbers? How are the write sets of committed transactions represented in the log file?   *pages 590–592*

14.17   Suppose that the coordinator of a transaction crashes after it has recorded the intentions list entry but before it has recorded the participant list or sent out the *canCommit?* requests. Describe how the participants resolve the situation. What will the coordinator do when it recovers? Would it be any better to record the participant list before the intentions list entry?   *page 596*

15

REPLICATION

Replication is a key to providing high availability and fault tolerance in distributed systems. High availability is of increasing interest with the tendency towards mobile computing and consequently disconnected operation. Fault tolerance is an abiding concern for services provided in safety-critical and other important systems.

The first part of the chapter considers systems that apply a single operation at a time to collections of replicated objects. The chapter begins with a description of architectural components and a system model for services that employ replication. We describe the integration of group membership management as part of group communication, which is particularly important for fault-tolerant services.

The chapter then describes approaches to achieving fault tolerance. It introduces the correctness criteria of linearizability and sequential consistency. Then two approaches are introduced and discussed: passive (primary-backup) replication, in which clients communicate with a distinguished replica; and active replication, in which clients communicate by multicast with all replicas.

Case studies of three systems for highly available services are considered. In the gossip and Bayou architectures, updates are lazily propagated between replicas of shared data. In Bayou, the technique of operational transformation is used to enforce consistency. Coda is an example of a highly available file service.

The chapter ends by considering transactions – sequences of operations – upon replicated objects. It considers the architectures of replicated transactional systems and how these systems handle server failures and network partitions.

15.1 Introduction

In this chapter, we study the replication of data: the maintenance of copies of data at multiple computers. Replication is a key to the effectiveness of distributed systems in that it can provide enhanced performance, high availability and fault tolerance. Replication is used widely. For example, the caching of resources from web servers in browsers and web proxy servers is a form of replication, since the data held in caches and at servers are replicas of one another. The DNS naming service, described in Chapter 9, maintains copies of name-to-attribute mappings for computers and is relied on for day-to-day access to services across the Internet.

Replication is a technique for enhancing *services*. The motivations for replication are to improve a service's performance, to increase its availability, or to make it fault-tolerant.

Performance enhancement: The caching of data at clients and servers is by now familiar as a means of performance enhancement. For example, Chapter 2 pointed out that browsers and proxy servers cache copies of web resources to avoid the latency of fetching resources from the originating server. Furthermore, data are sometimes replicated transparently between several originating servers in the same domain. Workload is shared between the servers by binding all the server IP addresses to the site's DNS name, say *www.aWebSite.org*. A DNS lookup of *www.aWebSite.org* results in one of the several servers' IP address being returned, in a round-robin fashion (see Section 9.2.3). Replication of immutable data is trivial: it increases performance with little cost to the system. Replication of changing data, such as that of the Web, incurs overheads in the form of protocols designed to ensure that clients receive up-to-date data (see Section 2.2.5). Thus there are limits to the effectiveness of replication as a performance-enhancement technique.

Increased availability: Users require services to be highly available. That is, the proportion of time for which the service is accessible with reasonable response times should be close to 100%. Apart from delays due to pessimistic concurrency control conflicts (data locking), the factors that are relevant to high availability are:

- server failures;

- network partitions and disconnected operation: communication disconnections that are often unplanned and are a side effect of user mobility.

To take the first of these, replication is a technique for automatically maintaining the availability of data despite server failures. If data are replicated at two or more failure-independent servers then client software may be able to access data at an alternative server should the default server fail or become unreachable. That is, the percentage of time during which the *service* is available can be enhanced by replicating server data. If each of n servers has an independent probability p of failing or becoming unreachable, then the availability of an object stored at each of these servers is:

$$1 - probability(all\ managers\ failed\ or\ unreachable) = 1 - p^{n}$$

For example, if there is a 5% probability of any individual server failure over a given time period and if there are two servers, then the availability is $1 - 0.05^2 = 1 - 0.0025 = 99.75\%$. An important difference between caching systems and server replication is that caches do not necessarily hold collections of objects such as files in their entirety. So caching does not necessarily enhance availability at the application level – a user may have one needed file but not another.

Network partitions (see Section 12.1) and disconnected operation are the second factor that militate against high availability. Mobile users deliberately disconnect their computers or may become unintentionally disconnected from a wireless network as they move around. For example, a user on a train with a laptop may have no access to networking (wireless networking may be interrupted, or they may have no such capability). In order to be able to work in these circumstances – so-called *disconnected working* or *disconnected operation* – the user will often prepare by copying heavily used data, such as the contents of a shared diary, from their usual environment to the laptop. But there is often a trade-off to availability during such a period of disconnection: when the user consults or updates the diary, they risk reading data that someone else has altered in the meantime. For example, they may make an appointment in a slot that has since been occupied. Disconnected working is only feasible if the user (or the application, on the user's behalf) can cope with stale data and can later resolve any conflicts that arise.

Fault tolerance: Highly available data is not necessarily strictly correct data. It may be out of date, for example; or two users on opposite sides of a network partition may make updates that conflict and need to be resolved. A fault-tolerant service, by contrast, always guarantees strictly correct behaviour despite a certain number and type of faults. The correctness concerns the freshness of data supplied to the client and the effects of the client's operations upon the data. Correctness sometimes also concerns the timeliness of the service's responses – as, for example, in the case of a system for air traffic control, where correct data is needed on short timescales.

The same basic technique used for high availability – of replicating data and functionality between computers – is also applicable for achieving fault tolerance. If up to f of $f + 1$ servers crash, then in principle at least one remains to supply the service. And if up to f servers can exhibit byzantine failures, then in principle a group of $2f + 1$ servers can provide a correct service, by having the correct servers outvote the failed servers (who may supply spurious values). But fault tolerance is subtler than this simple description makes it seem. The system must manage the coordination of its components precisely to maintain the correctness guarantees in the face of failures, which may occur at any time.

A common requirement when data are replicated is for *replication transparency*. That is, clients should not normally have to be aware that multiple *physical* copies of data exist. As far as clients are concerned, data are organized as individual *logical* objects (or objects) and they identify only one item in each case when they request an operation to be performed. Furthermore, clients expect operations to return only one set of values. This is despite the fact that operations may be performed upon more than one physical copy in concert.

The other general requirement for replicated data – one that can vary in strength between applications – is that of consistency. This concerns whether the operations

Figure 15.1   A basic architectural model for the management of replicated data

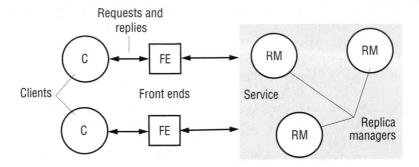

performed upon a collection of replicated objects produce results that meet the specification of correctness for those objects.

We saw in the example of the diary that during disconnected operation data may be allowed to become inconsistent, at least temporarily. But when clients remain connected it is often not acceptable for different clients (using different physical copies of data) to obtain inconsistent results when they make requests affecting the same logical objects. That is, it is not acceptable if the results break the application's correctness criteria.

We now examine in more detail the design issues raised when we replicate data to achieve highly available and fault-tolerant services. We also examine some standard solutions and techniques for dealing with those issues. First, Sections 15.2 to 15.4 cover the case where clients make individual invocations upon shared data. Section 15.2 presents a general architecture for managing replicated data and it introduces group communication as an important tool. Group communication is particularly useful for achieving fault tolerance, which is the subject of Section 15.3. Section 15.4 describes techniques for high availability, including disconnected operation. It includes case studies of the gossip architecture, Bayou and the Coda file system. Section 15.5 examines how to support transactions on replicated data. As Chapters 13 and 14 explained, transactions are made up of sequences of operations, rather than single operations.

15.2 System model and group communication

The data in our system consist of a collection of items that we shall call objects. An 'object' could be a file, say, or a Java object. But each such *logical* object is implemented by a collection of *physical* copies called *replicas*. The replicas are physical objects, each stored at a single computer, with data and behaviour that are tied to some degree of consistency by the system's operation. The 'replicas' of a given object are not necessarily identical, at least not at any particular point in time. Some replicas may have received updates that others have not received.

In this section, we provide a general system model for managing replicas and then describe group communication systems, which are particularly useful for achieving fault tolerance through replication.

15.2.1 System model

We assume an asynchronous system in which processes may fail only by crashing. Our default assumption is that network partitions may not occur, but we shall sometimes consider what happens if they do occur. Network partitions make it harder to build failure detectors, which we use to achieve reliable and totally ordered multicast.

For the sake of generality, we describe architectural components by their roles and do not mean to imply that they are necessarily implemented by distinct processes (or hardware). The model involves replicas held by distinct *replica managers* (see Figure 15.1), which are components that contain the replicas on a given computer and perform operations upon them directly. This general model may be applied in a client-server environment, in which case a replica manager is a server. We shall sometimes simply call them servers instead. Equally, it may be applied to an application and application processes can in that case act as both clients and replica managers. For example, the user's laptop on a train may contain an application that acts as a replica manager for their diary.

We shall always require that a replica manager applies operations to its replicas recoverably. This allows us to assume that an operation at a replica manager does not leave inconsistent results if it fails part-way through. We sometimes require each replica manager to be a *state machine* [Lamport 1978, Schneider 1990]. Such a replica manager applies operations to its replicas atomically (indivisibly), so that its execution is equivalent to performing operations in some strict sequence. Moreover, the state of its replicas is a deterministic function of their initial states and the sequence of operations that it applies to them. Other stimuli, such as the reading on a clock or an attached sensor, have no bearing on these state values. Without this assumption, consistency guarantees between replica managers that accept update operations independently could not be made. The system can only determine which operations to apply at all replica managers and in what order – it cannot reproduce non-deterministic effects. The assumption implies that it may not be possible, depending upon the threading architecture, for the servers to be multi-threaded.

Often each replica manager maintains a replica of every object and we assume this is so unless we state otherwise. But in general the replicas of different objects may be maintained by different sets of replica managers. For example, one object may be needed mostly by clients on one network and another by clients on another network. There is little to be gained by replicating them at managers on the other network.

The set of replica managers may be static or dynamic. In a dynamic system, new replica managers may appear (for example, a second secretary copies a diary onto their laptop); this is not allowed in a static system. In a dynamic system, replica managers may crash, and they are then deemed to have left the system (although they may be replaced). In a static system, replica managers do not crash (crashing implies *never* executing another step), but they may cease operating for an indefinite period. We return to the issue of failure in Section 15.4.2.

The general model of replica management is shown in Figure 15.1. A collection of replica managers provides a service to clients. The clients see a service that gives them access to objects (for example, diaries or bank accounts), which in fact are replicated at the managers. Clients each request a series of operations – invocations upon one or more of the objects. An operation involves a combination of reads of objects and updates to objects. Requested operations that involve no updates are called *read-only requests*; requested operations that update an object are called *update requests* (these may also involve reads).

Each client's requests are first handled by a component called a *front end*. The role of the front end is to communicate by message passing with one or more of the replica managers, rather than forcing the client to do this itself explicitly. It is the vehicle for making replication transparent. A front end may be implemented in the client's address space, or it may be a separate process.

In general, five phases are involved in the performance of a single request upon the replicated objects [Wiesmann *et al.* 2000]. The actions in each phase vary according to the type of system, as will become clear in the next two sections. For example, a service that supports disconnected operation behaves differently from one that provides a fault-tolerant service. The phases are as follows:

The front end issues the request to one or more replica managers. The first possibility is for the front end to communicate with a single replica manager, which in turn communicates with other replica managers. The second is for the front end to multicast the request to the replica managers.

Coordination: The replica managers coordinate in preparation for executing the request consistently. They agree, if necessary at this stage, on whether the request is to be applied (it might not be applied at all if failures occur at this stage). They also decide on the ordering of this request relative to others. All of the types of ordering defined for multicast in Section 12.4.3 also apply to request handling and we define those orders again for this context:

FIFO ordering: If a front end issues request r then request r', then any correct replica manager that handles r' handles r before it.

Causal ordering: If the issue of request r happened-before the issue of request r', then any correct replica manager that handles r' handles r before it.

Total ordering: If a correct replica manager handles r before request r', then any correct replica manager that handles r' handles r before it.

Most applications require FIFO ordering. We discuss the requirements for causal and total ordering – and the hybrid orderings that are both FIFO and total, or both causal and total – in the next two sections.

Execution: The replica managers execute the request – perhaps *tentatively*: that is, in such a way that they can undo its effects later.

Agreement: The replica managers reach consensus on the effect of the request – if any – that will be committed. For example, in a transactional system the replica managers may collectively agree to abort or commit the transaction at this stage.

Response: One or more replica managers responds to the front end. In some systems, one replica manager sends the response. In others, the front end receives responses from a collection of replica managers and it selects or synthesizes a single response to pass back to the client. For example, it could pass back the first response to arrive, if high availability is the goal. If tolerance of byzantine failures is the goal, then it could give the client the response that a majority of the replica managers provides.

Different systems may make different choices about the ordering of the phases, as well as their contents. For example, in a system that supports disconnected operation, it is important to give the client (the application on the user's laptop, say) as early a response as possible. The user does not want to wait until the replica manager on the laptop and the replica manager back in the office can coordinate. By contrast, in a fault-tolerant system the client is not given the response until the end, when the correctness of the result can be guaranteed.

15.2.2 Group communication

In Section 12.4 we discussed multicast communication, which is also known as group communication because process groups are the destinations of multicast messages. Groups are useful for managing replicated data and in other systems where processes cooperate towards a common goal by receiving and processing the same set of multicast messages. They are equally useful where the group members independently consume one or more common streams of messages, such as messages carrying events to which the processes react independently.

Section 12.4 took the membership of groups to be statically defined, although group members may crash. Practical systems often require dynamic membership, however: processes join and leave the group as the system executes. In a service that manages replicated data, for example, users may add or withdraw a replica manager, or a replica manager may crash and thus need to be withdrawn from the system's operation. A full implementation of group communication incorporates a *group membership service* to manage the dynamic membership of groups, in addition to multicast communication.

Multicast and group membership management are strongly interrelated. Figure 15.2 shows an open group, in which a process outside the group sends to the group without knowing the group's membership. The group communication service has to manage changes in the group's membership while multicasts take place concurrently.

Role of the group membership service ◊ A group membership service has four main tasks, as follows:

Providing an interface for group membership changes: The membership service provides operations to create and destroy process groups and to add or withdraw a process to or from a group. In most systems, a single process may belong to several groups at the same time. This is true of IP multicast, for example.

Implementing a failure detector: The service incorporates a failure detector (see Section 12.1). The service monitors the group members not only in case they should crash but also in case they should become unreachable because of a communication failure. The detector marks processes as *Suspected* or *Unsuspected*. The service uses

Figure 15.2   Services provided for process groups

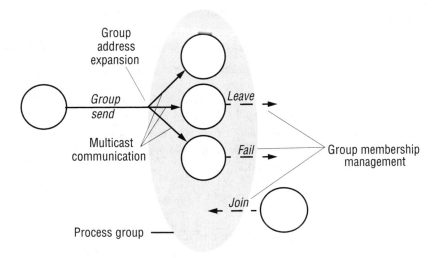

Group
address
expansion

Group
send

Leave

Multicast
communication

Fail

Group membership
management

Join

Process group

the failure detector to reach a decision about the group's membership: it excludes a process from membership if it is suspected to have failed or to have become unreachable.

Notifying members of group membership changes: The service notifies the group's members when a process is added, or when a process is excluded (through failure or when the process is deliberately withdrawn from the group).

Performing group address expansion: When a process multicasts a message, it supplies the group identifier rather than a list of processes in the group. The membership management service expands the identifier into the current group membership for delivery. The service can coordinate multicast delivery with membership changes by controlling address expansion. That is, it can decide consistently where to deliver any given message, even though the membership may be changing during delivery. We discuss *view-synchronous* communication below.

Note that IP multicast is a weak case of a group membership service, with some but not all of these properties. It does allow processes to join or leave groups dynamically and it performs address expansion, so that senders need only provide a single IP multicast address as the destination for a multicast message. But IP multicast does not itself provide group members with information about current membership and multicast delivery is not coordinated with membership changes.

Systems that can adapt as processes join, leave and crash – fault-tolerant systems, in particular – require the more advanced features of failure detection and notification of membership changes. A full group membership service maintains *group views*, which are lists of the current group members, identified by their unique process identifiers. The list is ordered, for example, according to the sequence in which the members joined the group. A new group view is generated when processes are added or excluded.

It is important to understand that a group membership service may exclude a process from a group because it is *Suspected*, even though it may not have crashed. A communication failure may have made the process unreachable, while it continues to execute normally. A membership service is always free to exclude such a process. The effect of exclusion is that no messages will be delivered to that process henceforth. Moreover, in the case of a closed group, if that process becomes connected again, any messages it attempts to send will not be delivered to the group members. That process will have to rejoin the group (as a 'reincarnation' of itself, with a new identifier), or abort its operations.

A false suspicion of a process and the consequent exclusion of the process from the group may reduce the group's effectiveness. The group has to manage without the extra reliability or performance that the withdrawn process could potentially have provided. The design challenge, apart from designing failure detectors to be as accurate as possible, is to ensure that a system based on group communication does not behave *incorrectly* if a process is falsely suspected.

An important consideration is how group management service treats network partitions. Disconnection or the failure of components such as a router in a network may split a group of processes into two or more subgroups, such that communication between subgroups is impossible. Group management services differ in whether they are *primary-partition* or *partitionable*. In the first case, the management service allows at most one subgroup (a majority) to survive a partition; the remaining processes are informed that they should suspend operations. This arrangement is appropriate for cases where the processes manage important data and the costs of inconsistencies between two or more subgroups outweigh any advantage of disconnected working.

On the other hand, in some circumstances it is acceptable for two or more subgroups to continue to operate and a partitionable group membership service allows this. For example, in an application in which users hold an audio or video conference to discuss some issues, it may be acceptable for two or more subgroups of users to continue their discussions independently despite a partition. They can merge their results when the partition heals and the subgroups are connected again.

View delivery ◊ Consider the task of a programmer writing an application that runs in each process in a group that must cope with new and lost members. The programmer needs to know that the system treats each member in a consistent way when the membership changes. It would be awkward if the programmer had to query the state of all the other members and reach a global decision whenever a membership change occurred, rather than being able to make a local decision on how to respond to the change. The programmer's life is made harder or easier according to the guarantees that apply when the system delivers views to the group members.

For each group g the group management service delivers to any member process $p \in g$ a series of views $v_0(g)$, $v_1(g)$, $v_2(g)$, etc. For example, a series of views could be $v_0(g) = (p)$, $v_1(g) = (p, p')$ and $v_2(g) = (p) - p$ joins an empty group, then p' joins the group, then p' leaves it. Although several membership changes may occur concurrently, such as when one process joins the group just as another leaves, the system imposes an order on the sequence of views given to each process.

We shall speak of a member *delivering a view* when a membership change occurs and the application is notified of the new membership – just as we speak of a process delivering a multicast message. As with multicast delivery, delivering a view is distinct from receiving a view. Group membership protocols keep proposed views on a hold-back queue until all extant members can agree to their delivery.

We also speak of an event as occurring *in a view* $v(g)$ at process p if, at the time of the event's occurrence, p has delivered $v(g)$ but has not yet delivered the next view $v'(g)$.

Some basic requirements for view delivery are as follows:

Order: If a process p delivers view $v(g)$ and then view $v'(g)$, then no other process $q \neq p$ delivers $v'(g)$ before $v(g)$.

Integrity: If process p delivers view $v(g)$ then $p \in v(g)$.

Non-triviality: If process q joins a group and is or becomes indefinitely reachable from process $p \neq q$, then eventually q is always in the views that p delivers. Similarly, if the group partitions and remains partitioned, then eventually the views delivered in any one partition will exclude any processes in another partition.

The first of these requirements goes some way to giving the programmer a consistency guarantee by ensuring that view changes always occur in the same order at different processes. The second requirement is a 'sanity check'. The third guards against trivial solutions. For example, a membership service that tells every process, regardless of its connectivity, that it is in a group all by itself is not of great interest. The non-triviality condition states that if two processes that have each joined the same group can eventually communicate indefinitely, then they should each be deemed members of that same group. Similarly, it requires that, when a partition occurs, the membership service should eventually reflect the partition. The condition does not state how the group membership service should behave in the problematic case of intermittent connectivity.

View-synchronous group communication ◊ A *view-synchronous* group communication system makes guarantees additional to those above about the delivery ordering of view notifications with respect to the delivery of multicast messages. View-synchronous communication extends the reliable multicast semantics that we described in Chapter 12 to take account of changing group views. For the sake of simplicity, we restrict our discussion to the case where partitions may not occur. The guarantees provided by view-synchronous group communication are as follows.

Agreement: Correct processes deliver the same sequence of views (starting from the view in which they join the group), and the same set of messages in any given view. That is, if a correct process delivers message m in view $v(g)$, then all other correct processes that deliver m also do so in the view $v(g)$.

Integrity: If a correct process p delivers message m, then it will not deliver m again. Furthermore, $p \in group(m)$ and the process that sent m is in the view in which p delivers m.

Validity (closed groups): Correct processes always deliver the messages that they send. If the system fails to deliver a message to any process q, then it notifies the surviving processes by delivering a new view with q excluded, immediately after the view in which any of them delivered the message. That is, let p be any correct process

Figure 15.3   View-synchronous group communication

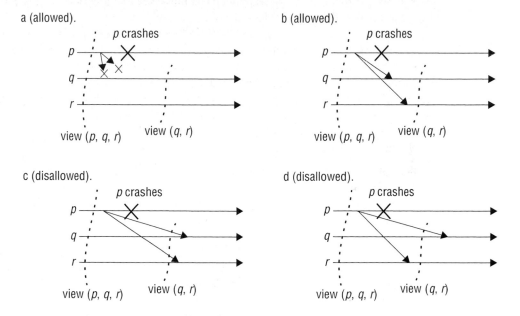

that delivers message m in view $v(g)$. If some process $q \in v(g)$ does not deliver m in view $v(g)$, then the next view $v'(g)$ that p delivers has $q \notin v'(g)$.

Consider a group with three processes p, q and r (see Figure 15.3). Suppose that p sends a message m while in view (p, q, r) but that p crashes soon after sending m, while q and r are correct. One possibility is that p crashes before m has reached any other process. In this case, q and r each deliver the new view (q, r), but neither ever delivers m (Figure 15.3a). The other possibility is that m has reached at least one of the two surviving processes when p crashes. Then q and r both deliver first m and then the view (q, r) (Figure 15.3b). It is not allowed for q and r to deliver first the view (q, r) and then m (Figure 15.3c), since then they would deliver a message from a process that they have been informed has failed; nor can the two deliver the message and the new view in opposite orders (Figure 15.3d).

In a view-synchronous system, the delivery of a new view draws a conceptual line across the system and every message that is delivered at all is consistently delivered on one side or the other of that line. This enables the programmer to draw useful conclusions about the set of messages that other correct processes have delivered when it delivers a new view, based only on the local ordering of message delivery and view delivery events.

An illustration of the usefulness of view-synchronous communication is how it can be used to achieve *state transfer* – the transfer of the working state from a current member of a process group to a new member of the group. For example, if the processes are replica managers that each hold the state of a diary, then a replica manager that joins the group for that diary needs to acquire the diary's current state when it joins. But the diary may be updated concurrently while the state is being captured. It is important that the replica manager does not miss any update messages that are not reflected in the state it acquires and that it does not reapply update messages that are already reflected in the state (unless those updates are idempotent).

To achieve this state transfer we can use view-synchronous communication in a simple scheme such as the following. Upon delivery of the first view containing the new process, some distinct process from the pre-existing members – say the oldest – captures its state, sends it one-to-one to the new member and suspends its execution. All other pre-existing processes suspend their execution. Note that precisely the set of updates reflected in this state has, by definition, been applied at all other members. Upon receipt of the state, the new process integrates it and multicasts a 'commence!' message to the group, at which point all proceed once more.

Discussion ◊ The notion of view-synchronous group communication that we have presented is a formulation of the 'virtually synchronous' communication paradigm originally developed in the ISIS system [Birman 1993, Birman *et al.* 1991, Birman and Joseph 1987b]. Schiper and Sandoz [1993] describe a protocol for achieving view-synchronous (or as they call it, *view-atomic*) communication. Note that a group membership service achieves consensus, but it does so without flouting the impossibility result of Fischer *et al.* [1985]. As we discussed in Section 12.5.4, a system can circumvent that result by using an appropriate failure detector.

Schiper and Sandoz also provide a uniform version of view-synchronous communication in which the agreement condition covers the case of processes that crash. This is similar to uniform agreement for multicast communication, which we described in Section 12.4.2. In the uniform version of view-synchronous communication, even if a process crashes after it delivers a message, all correct processes are forced to deliver the message in the same view. This stronger guarantee is sometimes needed in fault-tolerant applications, since a process that has delivered a message may have had an effect on the outside world before crashing. For the same reason, Hadzilacos and Toueg [1994] consider uniform versions of the reliable and ordered multicast protocols described in Chapter 12.

The V system [Cheriton and Zwaenepoel 1985] was the first system to include support for process groups. After ISIS, process groups with some type of group membership service have been developed in several other systems, including Horus [van Renesse *et al.* 1996], Totem [Moser *et al.* 1996] and Transis [Dolev and Malki 1996].

Variations on view synchrony have been proposed for partitionable group membership services, including support for partition-aware applications [Babaoglu *et al.* 1998] and extended virtual synchrony [Moser *et al.* 1994].

Finally, Cristian [1991b] discusses a group membership service for *synchronous* distributed systems.

Object groups ◊ Object groups provide an object-oriented approach to group computing. An object group is a collection of objects (normally instances of the same class) that process the same set of invocations concurrently and each returns responses. Client objects need not be aware of the replication. They invoke operations on a single, local object, which acts as a proxy for the group. The proxy uses a group communication system to send the invocations to the members of the object group.

Electra [Maffeis 1995] is a CORBA-compliant system that supports object groups. An Electra group can be interfaced to any CORBA-compliant application.

Electra was originally built on top of the Horus group communication system, which it uses to manage the membership of the group and to multicast invocations. In 'transparent mode', the local proxy returns the first available response to a client object. In 'non-transparent mode', the client object can access all the responses returned by the group members. Electra uses an extension of the standard CORBA ORB interface, with functions for creating and destroying object groups and managing their membership.

Eternal [Moser et al. 1998] and the Object Group Service [Guerraoui et al. 1998] also provide CORBA-compliant support for object groups.

15.3 Fault-tolerant services

In this section, we examine how to provide a service that is correct despite up to f process failures, by replicating data and functionality at replica managers. For the sake of simplicity, we assume that communication remains reliable and that no partitions occur.

Each replica manager is assumed to behave according to a specification of the semantics of the objects it manages, when they have not crashed. For example, a specification of bank accounts would include an assurance that funds transferred between bank accounts can never disappear, and that only deposits and withdrawals affect the balance on any particular account.

Intuitively, a service based on replication is correct if it keeps responding despite failures and if clients cannot tell the difference between the service they obtain from an implementation with replicated data and one provided by a single correct replica manager. Care is needed in meeting this criterion. If precautions are not taken, then anomalies can arise when there are several replica managers – even bearing in mind that we are considering the effects of individual operations, not transactions.

Consider a naive replication system, in which two replica managers at computers A and B each maintain replicas of two bank accounts x and y. Clients read and update the accounts at their local replica manager but try another replica manager if that one fails. Replica managers propagate updates to one another in the background after responding to the client. Both accounts initially have a balance of $0.

Client 1 updates the balance of x at its local replica manager B to be $1 and then attempts to update y's balance to be $2 but discovers that B has failed. Client 1 therefore applies the update at A instead. Now client 2 reads the balances at its local replica manager A and finds first that y has $2 and then that x has $0 – the update to bank account x from B has not arrived, since B failed. The situation is shown below, where the operations are labelled by the computer at which they first took place and lower operations happen later:

Client 1:	Client 2:
$setBalance_B(x, 1)$	
$setBalance_A(y, 2)$	
	$getBalance_A(y) \rightarrow 2$
	$getBalance_A(x) \rightarrow 0$

This execution does not match a common-sense specification for the behaviour of bank accounts: client 2 should have read a balance of $1 for x, given that it read the balance of $2 for y, since y's balance was updated after that of x. The anomalous behaviour in the replicated case could not have occurred if the bank accounts had been implemented by a single server. We can construct systems that manage replicated objects without the anomalous behaviour produced by the naive protocol in our example. First, we need to understand what counts as correct behaviour for a replicated system.

Linearizability and sequential consistency ◊ There are various correctness criteria for replicated objects. The most strictly correct systems are *linearizable* and this property is called *linearizability*. In order to understand linearizability, consider a replicated service implementation with two clients. Let the sequence of read and update operations that client i performs in some execution be $o_{i0}, o_{i1}, o_{i2}, \ldots$. Each operation o_{ij} in these sequences is specified by the operation type and the arguments and return values as they occurred at run time. We assume that every operation is synchronous. That is, clients wait for one operation to complete before requesting the next.

A single server managing a single copy of the objects would serialize the operations of the clients. In the case of an execution with only client 1 and client 2, this interleaving of the operations could be $o_{20}, o_{21}, o_{10}, o_{22}, o_{11}, o_{12}, \ldots$, say. We define our correctness criteria for replicated objects by referring to a *virtual* interleaving of the clients' operations, which does not necessarily physically occur at any particular replica manager but which establishes the correctness of the execution.

A replicated shared object service is said to be linearizable if *for any execution* there is some interleaving of the series of operations issued by all the clients that satisfies the following two criteria:

- The interleaved sequence of operations meets the specification of a (single) correct copy of the objects.

- The order of operations in the interleaving is consistent with the real times at which the operations occurred in the actual execution.

This definition captures the idea that for any set of client operations there is a virtual canonical execution – the interleaved operations that the definition refers to – against a virtual single image of the shared objects. And each client sees a view of the shared objects that is consistent with that single image: that is, the results of the client's operations make sense as they occur within the interleaving.

The service that gave rise to the execution of the bank account clients in the example is not linearizable. Even ignoring the real time at which the operations took place, there is no interleaving of the two clients' operations that would satisfy any correct bank account specification: for auditing purposes, if one account update occurred after another, then the first update should be observed if the second has been observed.

Note that linearizability concerns only the interleaving of individual operations and is not intended to be transactional. A linearizable execution may break application-specific notions of consistency if concurrency control is not applied.

The real-time requirement in linearizability is desirable in an ideal world, because it captures our notion that clients should receive up-to-date information. But, equally, the presence of real time in the definition raises the issue of linearizability's practicality, because we cannot always synchronize clocks to the required degree of accuracy. A weaker correctness condition is *sequential consistency*, which captures an essential requirement concerning the order in which requests are processed without appealing to real time. The definition keeps the first criterion from the definition for linearizability but modifies the second as follows:

A replicated shared object service is said to be sequentially consistent if *for any execution* there is some interleaving of the series of operations issued by all the clients which satisfies the following two criteria:

- The interleaved sequence of operations meets the specification of a (single) correct copy of the objects.

- The order of operations in the interleaving is consistent with the program order in which each individual client executed them.

Note that absolute time does not appear in this definition. Nor does any other *total* order on all operations. The only notion of ordering that is relevant is the order of events at each separate client – the program order. The interleaving of operations can shuffle the sequence of operations from a set of clients in any order, as long as each client's order is not violated and the result of each operation is consistent, in terms of the objects' specification, with the operations that preceded it. This is similar to shuffling together several packs of cards so that they are intermingled in such a way as to preserve the original order of each pack.

Every linearizable service is also sequentially consistent, since real-time order reflects each client's program order. The converse does not hold. An example execution for a service that is sequentially consistent but not linearizable follows:

Client 1:	Client 2:
$setBalance_B(x, 1)$	
	$getBalance_A(y) \rightarrow 0$
	$getBalance_A(x) \rightarrow 0$
$setBalance_A(y, 2)$	

This execution is possible under a naive replication strategy even if neither of the computers A or B fails but if the update of x that client 1 made at B has not reached A when client 2 reads it. The real-time criterion for linearizability is not satisfied, since $getBalance_A(x) \rightarrow 0$ occurs later than $setBalance_B(x, 1)$; but the following interleaving satisfies both criteria for sequential consistency: $getBalance_A(y) \rightarrow 0$, $getBalance_A(x) \rightarrow 0$, $setBalance_B(x, 1)$, $setBalance_A(y, 2)$.

Lamport conceived of both sequential consistency [1979] and linearizability [1986] in relation to shared memory registers (although he used the term 'atomicity' instead of 'linearizability'). Herlihy and Wing [1990] generalized the idea to cover arbitrary shared objects. Chapter 18, which examines distributed shared memory, defines and discusses some weaker consistency properties.

Figure 15.4   The passive (primary-backup) model for fault tolerance

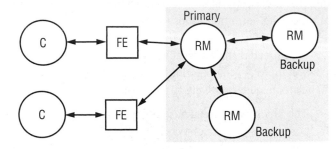

15.3.1 Passive (primary-backup) replication

In the *passive* or *primary-backup* model of replication for fault tolerance (Figure 15.4), there is at any one time a single primary replica manager and one or more secondary replica managers – 'backups' or 'slaves'. In the pure form of the model, front ends communicate only with the primary replica manager to obtain the service. The primary replica manager executes the operations and sends copies of the updated data to the backups. If the primary fails, one of the backups is promoted to act as the primary.

The sequence of events when a client requests an operation to be performed is as follows:

1. *Request*: The front end issues the request, containing a unique identifier, to the primary replica manager.

2. *Coordination*: The primary takes each request atomically, in the order in which it receives it. It checks the unique identifier, in case it has already executed the request and if so it simply re-sends the response.

3. *Execution*: The primary executes the request and stores the response.

4. *Agreement*: If the request is an update then the primary sends the updated state, the response and the unique identifier to all the backups. The backups send an acknowledgement.

5. *Response*: The primary responds to the front end, which hands the response back to the client.

This system obviously implements linearizability if the primary is correct, since the primary sequences all the operations upon the shared objects. If the primary fails, then the system retains linearizability if a single backup becomes the new primary and if the new system configuration takes over exactly where the last left off:

- the primary is replaced by a unique backup (if two clients began using two backups, then the system could perform incorrectly); and

- the replica managers that survive agree on which operations had been performed at the point when the replacement primary takes over.

Both of these requirements are met if the replica managers (primary and backups) are organized as a group and if the primary uses view-synchronous group communication to send the updates to the backups. The first of the above two requirements is then easily satisfied. When the primary crashes, the communication system eventually delivers a new view to the surviving backups, one that excludes the old primary. The backup that replaces the primary can be chosen by any function of that view. For example, the backups can choose the first member in that view as the replacement. That backup can register itself as the primary with a name service that the clients consult when they suspect that the primary has failed (or when they require the service in the first place).

The second requirement is also satisfied, by the ordering property of view-synchrony and the use of stored identifiers to detect repeated requests. The view-synchronous semantics guarantee that either all the backups or none of them will deliver any given update before delivering the new view. Thus the new primary and the surviving backups all agree on whether any particular client's update has or has not been processed.

Consider a front end that has not received a response. The front end retransmits the request to whichever backup takes over as the primary. The primary may have crashed at any point during the operation. If it crashed before the agreement stage (4), then the surviving replica managers cannot have processed the request. If it crashed during the agreement stage, then they may have processed the request. If it crashed after that stage, then they have definitely processed it. But the new primary does not have to know what stage the old primary was in when it crashed. When it receives a request, it proceeds from stage 2 above. By view-synchrony, no consultation with the backups is necessary, because they have all processed the same set of messages.

Discussion of passive replication ◊ The primary-backup model may be used even where the primary replica manager behaves in a non-deterministic way, for example due to multi-threaded operation. Since the primary communicates the updated state from the operations rather than a specification of the operations themselves, the backups slavishly record the state determined by the primary's actions alone.

To survive up to f process crashes, a passive replication system requires $f+1$ replica managers (such a system cannot tolerate byzantine failures). The front end requires little functionality to achieve fault tolerance. It needs to be able to look up the new primary when the current primary does not respond.

Passive replication has the disadvantage of providing relatively large overheads. View-synchronous communication requires several rounds of communication per multicast, and if the primary fails then yet more latency is incurred while the group communication system agrees upon and delivers the new view.

In a variation of the model as presented here, clients may be able to submit read requests to the backups, thus off-loading work from the primary. The guarantee of linearizability is thereby lost but the clients receive a sequentially consistent service.

Passive replication is used in the Harp replicated file system [Liskov *et al.* 1991]. The Sun Network Information Service (NIS, formerly Yellow Pages) uses passive replication to achieve high availability and good performance, although with weaker guarantees than sequential consistency. The weaker consistency guarantees are still satisfactory for many purposes, such as storing certain types of system administration records. The replicated data is updated at a master server and propagated from there to slave servers using one-to-one (rather than group) communication. Clients may

Figure 15.5   Active replication

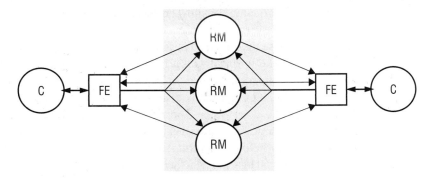

communicate with either a master or a slave server to retrieve information. In NIS, however, clients may not request updates: updates are made to the master's files.

15.3.2 Active replication

In the *active* model of replication for fault tolerance (see Figure 15.5), the replica managers are state machines that play equivalent roles and are organized as a group. Front ends multicast their requests to the group of replica managers and all the replica managers process the request independently but identically and reply. If any replica manager crashes, then this need have no impact upon the performance of the service, since the remaining replica managers continue to respond in the normal way. We shall see that active replication can tolerate byzantine failures, because the front end can collect and compare the replies it receives.

Under active replication, the sequence of events when a client requests an operation to be performed is as follows:

1. *Request*: The front end attaches a unique identifier to the request and multicasts it to the group of replica managers, using a totally ordered, reliable multicast primitive. The front end is assumed to fail by crashing at worst. It does not issue the next request until it has received a response.

2. *Coordination*: The group communication system delivers the request to every correct replica manager in the same (total) order.

3. *Execution*: Every replica manager executes the request. Since they are state machines and since requests are delivered in the same total order, correct replica managers all process the request identically. The response contains the client's unique request identifier.

4. *Agreement*: No agreement phase is needed, because of the multicast delivery semantics.

5. *Response*: Each replica manager sends its response to the front end. The number of replies that the front end collects depends upon the failure assumptions and on the multicast algorithm. If, for example, the goal is to tolerate only crash failures and the

multicast satisfies uniform agreement and ordering properties, then the front end passes the first response to arrive back to the client and discards the rest (it can distinguish these from responses to other requests by examining the identifier in the response).

This system achieves sequential consistency. All correct replica managers process the same sequence of requests. The reliability of the multicast ensures that every correct replica manager processes the same set of requests and the total order ensures that they process them in the same order. Since they are state machines, they all end up with the same state as one another after each request. Each front end's requests are served in FIFO order (because the front end awaits a response before making the next request), which is the same as 'program order'. This ensures sequential consistency.

If clients do not communicate with other clients while waiting for responses to their requests, then their requests are processed in happened-before order. If clients are multi-threaded and can communicate with one another while awaiting responses from the service, then to guarantee request processing in happened-before order we would have to replace the multicast with one that is both causally and totally ordered.

The active replication system does not achieve linearizability. This is because the total order in which the replica managers process requests is not necessarily the same as the real-time order in which the clients made their requests. Schneider [1990] describes how, in a synchronous system with approximately synchronized clocks, the total order in which the replica managers process requests can be based on the order of physical timestamps that the front ends supply with their requests. This does not guarantee linearizability, because the timestamps are not perfectly accurate; but it approximates it.

Discussion of active replication ◊ We have assumed a solution to totally ordered and reliable multicast. As Chapter 12 pointed out, solving reliable and totally ordered multicast is equivalent to solving consensus. Solving consensus in turn requires either that the system is synchronous or that a technique such as employing failure detectors is used in an asynchronous system, to work around the impossibility result of Fischer *et al.* [1985].

Some solutions to consensus, such as that of Canetti and Rabin [1993], work even with the assumption of byzantine failures. Given such a solution, and therefore a solution to totally ordered and reliable multicast, the active replication system can mask up to f byzantine failures, as long as the service incorporates at least $2f + 1$ replica managers. Each front end waits until it has collected $f + 1$ identical responses and passes that response back to the client. It discards other responses to the same request. To be strictly sure of which response is really associated with which request (given byzantine behaviour), we require that the replica managers digitally sign their responses.

It may be possible to relax the system that we have described. First, we have assumed that all updates to the shared replicated objects must occur in the same order. However, in practice some operations may commute: that is, the effect of two operations performed in the order $o_1;o_2$ is the same as in the reverse order $o_2;o_1$. For example, any two read-only operations (from different clients) commute; and any two operations that do not perform reads but update distinct objects commute. An active replication system may be able to exploit knowledge of commutativity in order to avoid the expense of ordering all the requests. We pointed out in Chapter 12 that some have proposed application-specific multicast ordering semantics [Cheriton and Skeen 1993, Pedone and Schiper 1999].

Finally, front ends may send read-only requests only to individual replica managers. In doing so, they lose the fault tolerance that comes with multicasting requests but the service remains sequentially consistent. Moreover, the front end can easily mask the failure of a replica manager in this case, simply by submitting the read-only request to another replica manager.

15.4 Case studies of highly available services: the gossip architecture, Bayou and Coda

In this section, we consider how to apply replication techniques to make services highly available. Our emphasis now is on giving clients access to the service – with reasonable response times – for as much of the time as possible, even if some results do not conform to sequential consistency. For example, the user on the train at the beginning of this chapter may be willing to cope with temporary inconsistencies between copies of data such as diaries if they can continue to work while disconnected and fix any problems later.

In Section 15.3, we saw that fault-tolerant systems transmit updates to the replica managers in an 'eager' fashion: all correct replica managers receive the updates as soon as possible and they reach collective agreement before passing control back to the client. This behaviour is undesirable for highly available operation. Instead, the system should provide an acceptable level of service using a minimal set of replica managers connected to the client. And it should minimize how long the client is tied up while replica managers coordinate their activities. Weaker degrees of consistency generally require less agreement and so allow shared data to be more available.

We now examine the design of three systems that provide highly available services: the gossip architecture, Bayou and Coda.

15.4.1 The gossip architecture

Ladin *et al.* [1992] developed what we shall call the *gossip architecture* as a framework for implementing highly available services by replicating data close to the points where groups of clients need it. The name reflects the fact that the replica managers exchange 'gossip' messages periodically in order to convey the updates they have each received from clients (see Figure 15.6). The architecture is based upon earlier work on databases by Fischer and Michael [1982] and Wuu and Bernstein [1984]. It may be used, for example, to create a highly available electronic bulletin board or diary service.

A gossip service provides two basic types of operation: *queries* are read-only operations and *updates* modify but do not read the state (the latter is a more restricted definition than the one we have been using). A key feature is that front ends send queries and updates to any replica manager they choose – any that is available and can provide reasonable response times. The system makes two guarantees, even though replica managers may be temporarily unable to communicate with one another:

Figure 15.6   Query and update operations in a gossip service

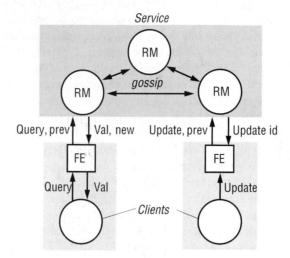

Each client obtains a consistent service over time: In answer to a query, replica managers only ever provide a client with data that reflects at least the updates that the client has observed so far. This is even though clients may communicate with different replica managers at different times – and therefore could in principle communicate with a replica manager that is 'less advanced' than one they used before.

Relaxed consistency between replicas: All replica managers eventually receive all updates and they apply updates with ordering guarantees that make the replicas sufficiently similar to suit the needs of the application. It is important to realize that while the gossip architecture can be used to achieve sequential consistency, it is primarily intended to deliver weaker consistency guarantees. Two clients may observe different replicas even though the replicas include the same set of updates; and a client may observe stale data.

To support relaxed consistency, the gossip architecture supports *causal* update ordering, as we defined it in Section 14.2.1. It also supports stronger ordering guarantees in the form of *forced* (total and causal) and *immediate* ordering. Immediate-ordered updates are applied in a consistent order relative to *any* other update at all replica managers, whether the other update ordering is specified as causal, forced or immediate. Immediate ordering is provided in addition to forced ordering, because a forced-order update and a causal-order update that are not related by the happened-before relation may be applied in different orders at different replica managers.

The choice of which ordering to use is left to the application designer and reflects a trade-off between consistency and operation costs. Causal updates are considerably less costly than the others and are expected to be used whenever possible. Note that queries, which can be satisfied by any single replica manager, are always executed in causal order with respect to other operations.

Consider an electronic bulletin board application, in which a client program (which incorporates the front end) executes on the user's computer and communicates with a local replica manager. The client sends the user's postings to the local replica manager and the replica manager sends new postings in gossip messages to other replica managers. Readers of bulletin boards experience slightly out-of-date lists of posted items but this does not usually matter if the delay is in the order of minutes or hours rather than days. Causal ordering could be used for posting items. This would mean that in general postings could appear in different orders at different replica managers but that, for example, a posting whose subject is 'Re: oranges' will always be posted after the message about 'oranges' to which it refers. Forced ordering could be used for adding a new subscriber to a bulletin board, so that there is an unambiguous record of the order in which users joined. Immediate ordering could be used for subtracting a user from a bulletin board's subscription list, so that messages could not be retrieved by that user via some tardy replica manager, once the deletion operation had returned.

The front end for a gossip service handles operations that the client makes using an application-specific API and turns them into gossip operations. In general, client operations can either read the replicated state, modify it or both. Since in gossip updates purely modify the state, the front end converts an operation that both reads and modifies the state into a separate query and update.

In terms of our basic replication model, an outline of how a gossip service processes queries and update operations is as follows.

1. *Request*: The front end normally sends requests to only a single replica manager at a time. However, a front end will communicate with a different replica manager when the one it normally uses fails or becomes unreachable, and it may try one or more others if the normal manager is heavily loaded. Front ends, and thus clients, may be blocked on query operations. The default arrangement for update operations, on the other hand, is to return to the client as soon as the operation has been passed to the front end; the front end then propagates the operation in the background. Alternatively, for increased reliability, clients may be prevented from continuing until the update has been delivered to $f + 1$ replica managers, and so will be delivered everywhere despite up to f failures.

2. *Update response*: If the request is an update then the replica manager replies as soon as it has received the update.

3. *Coordination*: The replica manager that receives a request does not process it until it can apply the request according to the required ordering constraints. This may involve receiving updates from other replica managers, in gossip messages. No other coordination between replica managers is involved.

4. *Execution*: The replica manager executes the request.

5. *Query response*: If the request is a query then the replica manager replies at this point.

6. *Agreement*: The replica managers update one another by exchanging *gossip messages*, which contain the most recent updates they have received. They are said to update one another in a *lazy* fashion, in that gossip messages may be exchanged only occasionally, after several updates have been collected, or when a replica

Figure 15.7   Front ends propagate their timestamps whenever clients communicate directly

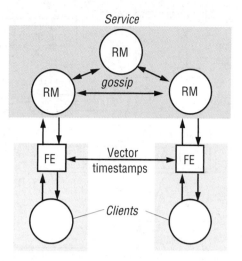

manager finds out that it is missing an update sent to one of its peers that it needs to process a request.

We now describe the gossip system in more detail. We begin by considering the timestamps and data structures that front ends and replica managers maintain in order to maintain update ordering guarantees. Then, in terms of these, we explain how replica managers process queries and updates. Much of the processing of vector timestamps needed to maintain causal updates is similar to the causal multicast algorithm of Section 12.4.3.

The front end's version timestamp ◊ In order to control the ordering of operation processing, each front end keeps a vector timestamp that reflects the version of the latest data values accessed by the front end (and therefore accessed by the client). This timestamp, denoted *prev* in Figure 15.6, contains an entry for every replica manager. The front end sends it in every request message to a replica manager, together with a description of the query or update operation itself. When a replica manager returns a value as a result of a query operation, it supplies a new vector timestamp (*new* in Figure 15.6), since the replicas may have been updated since the last operation. Similarly, an update operation returns a vector timestamp (*update id* in Figure 15.6) that is unique to the update. Each returned timestamp is merged with the front end's previous timestamp to record the version of the replicated data that has been observed by the client. (See Section 11.4 for a definition of vector timestamp merging.)

Clients exchange data by accessing the same gossip service and by communicating directly with one another. Since client-to-client communication can also lead to causal relationships between operations applied to the service, it also occurs via the clients' front ends. That way, the front ends can piggy back their vector timestamps on messages to other clients. The recipients merge them with their own timestamps in

Figure 15.8   A gossip replica manager, showing its main state components

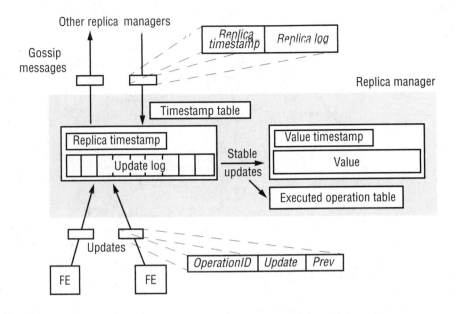

order that causal relationships can be inferred correctly. The situation is shown in Figure 15.7

Replica manager state ◊ Regardless of the application, a replica manager contains the following main state components (Figure 15.8):

Value: This is the value of the application state as maintained by the replica manager. Each replica manager is a state machine, which begins with a specified initial value and which is thereafter solely the result of applying update operations to that state.

Value timestamp: This is the vector timestamp that represents the updates that are reflected in the value. It contains one entry for every replica manager. It is updated whenever an update operation is applied to the value.

Update log: All update operations are recorded in this log as soon as they are received. A replica manager keeps updates in a log for one of two reasons. The first is that the replica manager cannot yet apply the update because it is not yet *stable*. A stable update is one that may be applied consistently with its ordering guarantees (causal, forced or immediate). An update that is not yet stable must be held back and not yet processed. The second reason for keeping an update in the log is that, even though the update has become stable and has been applied to the value, the replica manager has not received confirmation that this update has been received at all other replica managers. In the meantime, it propagates the update in gossip messages.

Replica timestamp: This vector timestamp represents those updates that have been accepted by the replica manager – that is, placed in the manager's log. It differs from the value timestamp in general, of course, because not all updates in the log are stable.

Executed operation table: The same update may arrive at a given replica manager from a front end and in gossip messages from other replica managers. To prevent an update being applied twice, the 'executed operation' table is kept, containing the unique front-end-supplied identifiers of updates that have been applied to the value. The replica managers check this table before adding an update to the log.

Timestamp table: This table contains a vector timestamp for each other replica manager, filled with timestamps that arrive from them in gossip messages. Replica managers use the table to establish when an update has been applied at all replica managers.

The replica managers are numbered 0, 1, 2, .., and the ith element of a vector timestamp held by replica manager i corresponds to the number of updates received from front ends by i; and the jth component ($j \neq i$) equals the number of updates received by j and propagated to i in gossip messages. So, for example, in a three-manager gossip system a value timestamp of (2,4,5) at manager 0 would represent the fact that the value there reflects the first two updates accepted from front ends at manager 0, the first four at manager 1 and the first five at manager 2. The following looks in more detail at how the timestamps are used to enforce the ordering.

Query operations ◊ The simplest operation to consider is that of a query. Recall that a query request q contains a description of the operation and a timestamp $q.prev$ sent by the front end. The latter reflects the latest version of the value that the front end has read or submitted as an update. Therefore the task of the replica manager is to return a value that is at least as recent as this. If *valueTS* is the replica's value timestamp, then q can be applied to the replica's value if:

$$q.prev \leq valueTS$$

The replica manager keeps q on a list of pending query operations (that is, a hold-back queue) until this condition is fulfilled. It can either wait for the missing updates, which should eventually arrive in gossip messages; or it can request the updates from the replica managers concerned. For example, if *valueTS* is (2,5,5) and $q.prev$ is (2,4,6), it can be seen that just one update is missing – from replica manager 2. (The front end that submitted q must have contacted a different replica manager previously for it to have seen this update, which the replica manager has not seen.)

Once the query can be applied, the replica manager returns *valueTS* to the front end as the timestamp *new* shown in Figure 15.6. The front end then merges this with its timestamp: *frontEndTS* := *merge(frontEndTS, new)*. The update at replica manager 1 that the front end has not seen before the query in the example just given ($q.prev$ has 4 where the replica manager has 5) will be reflected in the update to *frontEndTS* (and potentially in the value returned, depending on the query).

Processing update operations in causal order ◊ A front end submits an update request to one or more replica managers. Each update request u contains a specification of the update (its type and parameters) $u.op$, the front end's timestamp $u.prev$, and a unique identifier that the front end generates, $u.id$. If the front end sends the same request u to several replica managers, it uses the same identifier in u each time – so that it will not be processed as several different but identical requests.

When replica manager i receives an update request from a front end it checks that it has not already processed this request by looking up its operation identifier in the executed operation table and in the records in its log. The replica manager discards the update if it has already seen it; otherwise, it increments the ith element in its replica timestamp by one, to keep count of the number of updates it has received directly from front ends. Then the replica manager assigns to the update request u a unique vector timestamp whose derivation is given shortly, and a record for the update is placed in the replica manager's log. If ts is the unique timestamp that the replica manager assigns to the update, then the update record is constructed and stored in the log as the following tuple:

$$logRecord := <i, ts, u.op, u.prev, u.id>$$

Replica manager i derives the timestamp ts from $u.prev$ by replacing $u.prev$'s ith element by the ith element of its replica timestamp (which it has just incremented). This action makes ts unique, thus ensuring that all system components will correctly record whether or not they have observed the update. The remaining elements in ts are copied from $u.prev$, since it is these values sent by the front end that must be used to determine when the update is stable. The replica manager then immediately passes ts back to the front end, which merges it with its existing timestamp. Note that a front end can submit its update to several replica managers and receive different timestamps in return, all of which have to be merged into its timestamp.

The stability condition for an update u is similar to that for queries:

$$u.prev \leq valueTS$$

This condition states that all the updates on which this update depends – that is, all the updates that had been observed by the front end that issued the update – have already been applied to the value. If this condition is not met at the time the update is submitted, it will be checked again when gossip messages arrive. When the stability condition has been met for an update record r, the replica manager applies the update to the value and updates the value timestamp and the executed operation table $executed$:

$$value := apply(value, r.u.op)$$
$$valueTS := merge(valueTS, r.ts)$$
$$executed := executed \cup \{r.u.id\}$$

The first of these three statements represents the application of the update to the value. In the second statement, the update's timestamp is merged with that of the value. In the third, the update's operation identifier is added to the set of identifiers of operations that have been executed – which is used to check for repeated operation requests.

Forced and immediate update operations ◊ Forced and immediate updates require special treatment. Recall that forced updates are totally as well as causally ordered. The basic method for ordering forced updates is for a unique sequence number to be appended to the timestamps associated with them, and to process them in order of this sequence number. As Chapter 12 explained, a general method for generating sequence numbers is to use a single sequencer process. But reliance upon a single process is inadequate in the context of a highly available service. The solution is to designate a so-called *primary replica manager* as the sequencer at any one time but to ensure that another replica manager can be elected to take over consistently as the sequencer should the primary fail. What is required is for a majority of replica managers (including the primary) to record which update is next in sequence before the operation can be applied. Then, as long as a majority of replica managers survive failure, this ordering decision will be honoured by a new primary elected from among the surviving replica managers.

Immediate updates are ordered with respect to forced updates by using the primary replica manager to order them in this sequence. The primary also determines which causal updates are deemed to have preceded an immediate update. It does this by communicating and synchronizing with the other replica managers in order to reach agreement on this. Further details are in Ladin *et al.* [1992].

Gossip messages ◊ Replica managers send gossip messages containing information concerning one or more updates so that other replica managers can bring their state up to date. A replica manager uses the entries in its timestamp table to estimate which updates any other replica manager has not yet received (it is an estimate because that replica manager may have received more updates by now).

A gossip message m consists of two items sent by the source replica manager: its log *m.log* and its replica timestamp *m.ts* (see Figure 15.8). The replica manager that receives a gossip message has three main tasks:

- To merge the arriving log with its own (it may contain updates not seen by the receiver before).

- To apply any updates that have become stable and have not been executed before (stable updates in the arrived log may in turn make pending updates become stable).

- To eliminate records from the log and entries in the executed operation table when it is known that the updates have been applied everywhere and for which there is no danger of repeats. Clearing redundant entries from the log and from the executed operation table is an important task, since they would otherwise grow without limit.

Merging the log contained in an arrived gossip message with the receiver's log is straightforward. Let *replicaTS* denote the recipient's replica timestamp. A record r in *m.log* is added to the receiver's log unless $r.ts \leq replicaTS$ – in which case it is already in the log or it has been applied to the value and then discarded.

The replica manager merges the timestamp of the incoming gossip message with its own replica timestamp *replicaTS*, so that it corresponds to the additions to the log:

$$replicaTS := merge(replicaTS, m.ts)$$

When new update records have been merged into the log, the replica manager collects the set S of any updates in the log that are now stable. These can be applied to the value but care must be taken over the order in which they are applied so that the happened-before relation is observed. The replica manager sorts the updates in the set according to the partial order '≤' between vector timestamps. It then applies the updates in this order, smallest first. That is, each $r \in S$ is applied only when there is no $s \in S$ such that $s.prev < r.prev$.

The replica manager then looks for records in the log that can be discarded. If the gossip message was sent by replica manager j and if *tableTS* is the table of replica timestamps of the replica managers, then the replica manager sets

$$tableTS[j] := m.ts$$

The replica manager can now discard any record r in the log for an update that has been received everywhere. That is, if c is the replica manager that created the record, then we require for all replica managers i:

$$tableTS[i][c] \geq r.ts[c]$$

The gossip architecture also defines how replica managers can discard entries in the executed operation table. It is important not to discard these entries too early, otherwise a much-delayed operation could mistakenly be applied twice. Ladin *et al.* [1992] provide details of the scheme. In essence, front ends issue acknowledgements to the replies to their updates, so replica managers know when a front end will stop sending the update. They assume a maximum update propagation delay from that point.

Update propagation ◊ The gossip architecture does not specify when replica managers exchange gossip messages, or how a replica manager picks other replica managers to send gossip to. A robust update-propagation strategy is needed if all replica managers are to receive all updates in an acceptable time.

The time it takes for all replica managers to receive a given update depends upon three factors:

- The frequency and duration of network partitions.
- The frequency with which replica managers send gossip messages.
- The policy for choosing a partner with which to exchange gossip.

The first factor is beyond the system's control, although users can to some extent determine how often they work disconnectedly.

The desired gossip-exchange frequency may be tuned to the application. Consider a bulletin board system shared between several sites. It seems unnecessary for every item to be dispatched immediately to all sites. But what if gossip is only exchanged after long periods, say once a day? If only causal updates are used, then it is quite possible for clients at each site to have their own consistent debates over the same bulletin board, oblivious to the discussions at the other sites. Then at, say, midnight, all the debates will be merged; but debates on the same topic are likely to be incongruous, when it would have been preferable for them to take account of one another. A gossip-exchange period of minutes or hours seems more appropriate in this case.

There are several types of partner-selection policy. Golding and Long [1993] consider *random*, *deterministic* and *topological* policies for their 'timestamped anti-entropy protocol', which uses a gossip-style update propagation scheme.

Random policies choose a partner randomly but with weighted probabilities so as to favour some partners over others – for example, near partners over far partners. Golding and Long found that such a policy works surprisingly well under simulations. Deterministic policies utilize a simple function of the replica manager's state to make the choice of partner. For example, a replica manager could examine its timestamp table and choose the replica manager that appears to be the furthest behind in the updates it has received.

Topological policies arrange the replica managers into a fixed graph. One possibility is a mesh: replica managers send gossip messages to the four replica managers it is connected to. Another is to arrange the replica managers in a circle, with each passing on gossip only to its neighbour (in the clockwise direction, say), so that updates from any replica manager eventually traverse the circle. There are many other possible topologies, including trees.

Different partner-seclection policies such as these trade off the amount of communication against higher transmission latencies and the possibility that a single failure will affect other replica managers. The choice depends in practice on the relative importance of these factors. For example, the circle topology produces relatively little communication but is subject to high transmission latencies since gossip generally has to traverse several replica managers. Moreover, if one replica manager fails then the circle cannot function and needs to be reconfigured. By contrast, the random selection policy is not susceptible to failures but it may produce more variable update propagation times.

Discussion of the gossip architecture ◊ The gossip architecture is aimed at achieving high availability for services. In its favour, clients can continue to obtain a service even when they are partitioned from the rest of the network, as long as at least one replica manager continues to function in the partition. But this type of availability is achieved at the expense of enforcing only relaxed consistency guarantees. For objects such as bank accounts, where sequential consistency is required, a gossip architecture can do no better than the fault-tolerant systems studied in Section 15.3 and supply the service only in a majority partition.

Its lazy approach to update propagation makes a gossip-based system inappropriate for updating replicas in near-real time, such as when users take part in a 'real-time' conference and update a shared document. A multicast-based system would be more appropriate for that case.

The scalability of a gossip system is another issue. As the number of replica managers grows, so does the number of gossip messages that have to be transmitted and the size of the timestamps used. If a client makes a query, then this normally takes two messages (between front end and replica manager). If a client makes a causal update operation and if each of the R replica managers normally collects G updates into a gossip message, then the number of messages exchanged is $2 + (R-1)/G$. The first term represents communication between the front end and replica manager and the second is the update's share of a gossip message sent to the other replica managers. Increasing G improves the number of messages; but it worsens the delivery latencies, because the replica manager waits for more updates to arrive before propagating them.

One approach to making gossip-based services scalable is to make most of the replicas read-only. In other words, these replicas are updated by gossip messages but do not receive updates directly from front ends. This arrangement is potentially useful where the *update/query* ratio is small. Read-only replicas can be situated close to client groups and updates can be serviced by relatively few central replica managers. Gossip traffic is reduced, since read-only replicas have no gossip to propagate. And vector timestamps need only contain entries for the updateable replicas.

15.4.2 Bayou and the operational transformation approach

The Bayou system [Terry *et al.* 1995, Petersen *et al.* 1997] provides data replication for high availability with weaker guarantees than sequential consistency, like the gossip architecture and the timestamped anti-entropy protocol. As in those systems, Bayou replica managers cope with variable connectivity by exchanging updates in pairs, in what the designers also call an anti-entropy protocol. But Bayou adopts a markedly different approach in that it enables domain-specific conflict detection and conflict resolution to take place.

Consider the user who needs to update a diary while working disconnectedly. If strict consistency is required then, in the gossip architecture, updates would have to be performed using a forced (totally ordered) operation. But then only users in a majority partition could update the diary. The users' access to the diary may thus be limited – regardless of whether they in fact need to make updates that would break the diary's integrity. Users who want to fill in a non-conflicting appointment are treated the same as users who may have unwittingly double-booked a time slot.

In Bayou, by contrast, the users on the train and at work may make any updates they like. All the updates are applied and recorded at whatever replica manager they reach. When updates received at any two replica managers are merged during an anti-entropy exchange, however, the replica managers detect and resolve conflicts. Any domain-specific criterion of conflict between operations may be applied. For example, if an executive and her secretary had added appointments in the same time slot, then a Bayou system detects this after the executive has reconnected their laptop. Moreover, it resolves the conflict according to a domain-specific policy. In this case, it could, for example, confirm the executive's appointment and remove the secretary's booking in the slot. Such an effect, in which one or more of a set of conflicting operations is undone or altered in order to resolve them, is called an *operational transformation*.

The state that Bayou replicates is held in the form of a database, supporting queries and updates (that may insert, modify or delete items in the database). Although we shall not concentrate on this aspect here, a Bayou update is a special case of a transaction. It consists of a single operation, an invocation of a 'stored procedure', which affects several objects within each replica manager but which is carried out with the ACID guarantees. Bayou may undo and redo updates to the database as execution proceeds.

The Bayou guarantee is that, eventually, every replica manager receives the same set of updates and it eventually applies those updates in such a way that the replica managers' databases are identical. In practice, there may be a continuous stream of updates and the databases may never become identical; but they would become identical if the updates ceased.

Figure 15.9   Committed and tentative updates in Bayou

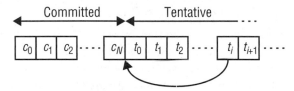

Tentative update t_i becomes the next committed update
and is inserted after the last committed update c_N.

Committed and tentative updates ◊ Updates are marked as *tentative* when they are first applied to a database. Bayou arranges that tentative updates are eventually placed in a canonical order and marked as *committed*. While updates are tentative, the system may undo and reapply them as it produces a consistent state. Once committed, they remain applied in their allotted order. In practice, the committed order can be achieved by designating some replica manager as the *primary* replica manager. In the usual way, this decides the committed order as that in which it receives the tentative updates and it propagates that ordering information to other replica managers. For the primary, users can choose, for example, a fast machine that is usually available; equally, it could be the replica manager on the executive's laptop, if that user's updates take priority.

At any one time, the state of a database replica derives from a (possibly empty) sequence of committed updates followed by a (possibly empty) sequence of tentative updates. If the next committed update arrives, or if one of the tentative updates that has been applied becomes the next committed update, then a reordering of the updates must take place. In Figure 15.9, t_i has become committed. All tentative updates after c_N need to be undone; t_i is then applied after c_N and t_0 to t_{i-1} and t_{i+1} etc. reapplied after t_i.

Dependency checks and merge procedures ◊ An update may conflict with some other operation that has already been applied. Because of this possibility, every Bayou update contains a *dependency check* and a *merge procedure* in addition to the operation's specification (the operation type and parameters). All these components of an update are domain-specific.

A replica manager calls the dependency check procedure before applying the operation. It checks whether a conflict would occur if the update was applied and it may examine any part of the database to do that. For example, consider the case of booking an appointment in a diary. The dependency check could, most simply, test for a *write-write* conflict: that is, whether another client has filled the required slot. But the dependency check could also test for a read-write conflict. For example, it could test that the desired slot is empty and that the number of appointments on that day is fewer than six.

If the dependency check indicates a conflict, then Bayou invokes the operation's merge procedure. That procedure alters the operation that will be applied so that it achieves something similar to the intended effect but avoids a conflict. For example, in the case of the diary the merge procedure could choose another slot at a nearby time instead or, as we mentioned above, it could use a simple priority scheme to decide which appointment is more important and impose that one. The merge procedure may fail to find a suitable alteration of the operation, in which case the system indicates an error. The effect of a merge procedure is deterministic, however – Bayou replica managers are state machines.

Discussion ◊ Bayou differs from the other replication schemes that we have considered in that it makes replication non-transparent to the application. It exploits knowledge of the application's semantics in order to increase the availability of data while maintaining a replicated state that is what we might call *eventually sequentially consistent*.

The disadvantages of this approach are, first, the increased complexity for the application programmer, who must supply dependency checks and merge procedures. Both may be complex to produce, given a large number of possible conflicts that need to be detected and resolved. The second disadvantage is the increased complexity for the user. Not only are users expected to deal with data that are read while they are still tentative but also with the fact that the operation that a user specified may turn out to have been altered. For example, the user booked a slot in a diary, only to find later that the booking has 'jumped' to a nearby slot. It is very important that the user be given a clear indication of which data are tentative and which are committed.

The operational transformation approach used by Bayou appears particularly in systems to support computer supported cooperative working (CSCW), where conflicting updates between geographically separated users may occur [Kindberg *et al.* 1996], [Sun and Ellis 1998]. The approach is limited, in practice, to applications where conflicts are relatively rare; where the underlying data semantics are relatively simple; and where users can cope with tentative information.

15.4.3 The Coda file system

The Coda file system is a descendent of AFS (see Section 8.4) that aims to address several requirements that AFS does not meet, particularly the requirement to provide high availability despite disconnected operation. It has been developed in a research project undertaken by Satyanarayanan and his co-workers at Carnegie-Mellon University [Satyanarayanan *et al.* 1990; Kistler and Satyanarayanan 1992]. The design requirements for Coda were derived from experience with AFS at CMU and elsewhere involving its use in large-scale distributed systems on both local- and wide-area communication networks.

While the performance and ease of administration of AFS were found to be satisfactory under the conditions of use at CMU, it was felt that the limited form of replication (restricted to read-only volumes) offered by AFS was bound to become a limiting factor at some scale, especially for accessing widely shared files such as electronic bulletin boards and other system-wide databases.

In addition, there was room for improvement in the availability of the service offered by AFS. The most common difficulties experienced by users of AFS arose from the failure (or scheduled interruption) of servers and network components. The scale of the system at CMU was such that a few service failures occurred every day and they could seriously inconvenience many users for periods ranging from a few minutes to many hours.

Finally, a mode of computer use was emerging that AFS did not cater for – the mobile use of portable computers. This led to a requirement to make all of the files needed for a user to continue their work available while disconnected from the network without resorting to manual methods for managing the locations of files.

Coda aims to meet all three of these requirements under the general heading of *constant data availability*. The aim was to provide users with the benefits of a shared file repository but to allow them to rely entirely on local resources when the repository is partially or totally inaccessible. In addition to these aims, Coda retains the original goals of AFS with regard to scalability and the emulation of UNIX file semantics.

In contrast to AFS, where read-write volumes are stored on just one server, the design of Coda relies on the replication of file volumes to achieve a higher throughput of file access operations and a greater degree of fault tolerance. In addition, Coda relies on an extension of the mechanism used in AFS for caching copies of files at client computers to enable those computers to operate when they are not connected to the network.

We shall see that Coda is like Bayou (see Section 15.4.2) in so far as it follows an optimistic strategy. That is, it allows clients to update data while the system is partitioned, on the basis that conflicts are relatively unlikely and that they can be fixed if they do occur. Like Bayou, it detects conflicts but, unlike Bayou, it performs this check without regard to the semantics of the data stored in files. And unlike Bayou it provides only limited system support for resolving conflicting replicas.

The Coda architecture ◊ Coda runs what it calls 'Venus' processes at the client computers and 'Vice' processes at file server computers, adopting the AFS terminology. The Vice processes are what we have called replica managers. The Venus processes are a hybrid of front ends and replica managers. They play the front end's role of hiding the service implementation from local client processes; but, since they manage a local cache of files, they are also replica managers, although of a different type to the Vice processes.

The set of servers holding replicas of a file volume is known as the *volume storage group* (*VSG*). At any instant, a client wishing to open a file in such a volume can access some subset of the VSG, known as the *available volume storage group* (AVSG). The membership of the AVSG varies as servers become accessible or are made inaccessible by network or server failures.

Normally, Coda file access proceeds in a similar manner to AFS, with cached copies of files being supplied to the client computers by any one of the servers in the current AVSG. As in AFS, clients are notified of changes via a *callback promise* mechanism but this now depends on an additional mechanism for the distribution of updates to each replica. On *close*, copies of modified files are broadcast in parallel to all of the servers in the AVSG.

In Coda, disconnected operation is said to occur when the AVSG is empty. This may be due to network or server failures, or it may be a consequence of the deliberate disconnection of the client computer, as in the case of a laptop. Effective disconnected operation relies on the presence in the client computer's cache of *all* of the files that are required for the user's work to proceed. To achieve this, the user must cooperate with Coda to generate a list of files that should be cached. A tool is provided that records a historical list of file usage while connected and this serves as a basis for predicting usage while disconnected.

It is a principle of the design of Coda that the copies of files residing on servers are more reliable than those residing in the caches of client computers. Although it might be possible logically to construct a file system that relies entirely on cached copies of files in client computers, it is unlikely that a satisfactory quality of service would be achieved. The Coda servers exist to provide the necessary quality of service. The copies of files residing in client computer caches are regarded as useful only as long as their currency can be periodically revalidated against the copies residing in servers. In the case of disconnected operation, revalidation occurs when disconnected operation ceases and the cached files are reintegrated with those in the servers. In the worst case, this may require some manual intervention to resolve inconsistencies or conflicts.

The replication strategy ◊ Coda's replication strategy is optimistic – it allows modification of files to proceed when the network is partitioned or during disconnected operation. It relies on the attachment to each version of a file of a *Coda version vector* (CVV). A CVV is a vector timestamp with one element for each server in the relevant VSG. Each element of the CVV is an estimate of the number of modifications performed on the version of the file that is held at the corresponding server. The purpose of the CVVs is to provide sufficient information about the update history of each file replica to enable potential conflicts to be detected and submitted for manual intervention and for stale replicas to be updated automatically.

If the CVV at one of the sites is greater than or equal to all the corresponding CVVs at the other sites (Section 11.4 defines the meaning of $v_1 \geq v_2$ for vector timestamps v_1 and v_2), then there is no conflict. Older replicas (with strictly smaller timestamps) include all the updates in a newer replica and they can automatically be brought up to date with it.

When this is not the case, that is when neither $v_1 \geq v_2$ nor $v_2 \geq v_1$ holds for two CVVs, then there is a conflict: each replica reflects at least one update that the other does not reflect. Coda does not, in general, resolve conflicts automatically. The file is marked as 'inoperable' and the owner of the file is informed of the conflict.

When a modified file is closed, each site in the current AVSG is sent an update message by the Venus process at the client, containing the current CVV and the new contents for the file. The Vice process at each site checks the CVV and, if it is greater than the one currently held, stores the new contents for the file and returns a positive acknowledgement. The Venus process then computes a new CVV with modification counts increased for the servers that responded positively to the update message and distributes the new CVV to the members of the AVSG.

Since the message is sent only to the members of the AVSG and not the VSG, servers that are not in the current AVSG do not receive the new CVV. Any CVV will therefore always contain an accurate modification count for the local server but the counts for non-local servers will in general be lower bounds, since they will be updated only when the server receives an update message.

The box opposite contains an example illustrating the use of CVVs to manage the updating of a file replicated at three sites. Further details on the use of CVVs for the management of updates can be found in Satyanarayanan *et al.* [1990]. CVVs are based on the replication techniques used in the Locus system [Popek and Walker 1985].

In normal operation, the behaviour of Coda appears similar to AFS. A cache miss is transparent to users and only imposes a performance penalty. The advantages deriving from the replication of some or all file volumes on multiple servers are:

- The files in a replicated volume remain accessible to any client that can access at least one of the replicas.

- The performance of the system can be improved by sharing some of the load of servicing client requests on a replicated volume between all of the servers that hold replicas.

In disconnected operation (when none of the servers for a volume can be accessed by the client) a cache miss prevents further progress and the computation is suspended until the connection is resumed or the user aborts the process. It is therefore important to load the cache before disconnected operation commences so that cache misses can be avoided.

In summary, compared with AFS, Coda enhances availability both by the replication of files across servers and by the ability of clients to operate entirely out of their caches. Both methods depend upon the use of an optimistic strategy for the detection of update conflicts in the presence of network partitions. The mechanisms are

Example: Consider a sequence of modifications to a file F in a volume that is replicated at 3 servers, S_1, S_2 and S_3. The VSG for F is $\{S_1, S_2, S_3\}$. F is modified at about the same time by two clients C_1, C_2. Because of a network fault, C_1 can access only S_1 and S_2 (C_1's AVSG is $\{S_1, S_2\}$) and C_2 can access only S_3 (C_2's AVSG is $\{S_3\}$).

1. Initially, the CVVs for F at all 3 servers are the same, say [1,1,1].

2. C_1 runs a process that opens F, modifies it and then closes it. The Venus process at C_1 broadcasts an update message to its AVSG, $\{S_1, S_2\}$, finally resulting in new versions of F and a CVV [2,2,1] at S_1 and S_2 but no change at S_3.

3. Meanwhile, C_2 runs two processes each of which opens F, modifies it and then closes it. The Venus process at C_2 broadcasts an update message to its AVSG, $\{S_3\}$ after each modification, finally resulting in a new version of F and a CVV [1,1,3] at S_3.

4. At some later time, the network fault is repaired, and C_2 makes a routine check to see whether the inaccessible members of the VSG have become accessible (the process by which such checks are made is described later) and discovers that S_1 and S_2 are now accessible. It modifies its AVSG to $\{S_1, S_2, S_3\}$ for the volume containing F and requests the CVVs for F from all members of the new AVSG. When they arrive, C_2 discovers that S_1 and S_2 each have CVVs [2,2,1] whereas S_3 has [1,1,3]. This represents a *conflict* requiring manual intervention to bring F up-to-date in a manner that minimizes the loss of update information.

On the other hand, consider a similar but simpler scenario that follows the same sequence of events as the one above, but omitting item (3), so that F is not modified by C_2. The CVV at S_3 therefore remains unchanged as [1,1,1], and when the network fault is repaired, C_2 discovers that the CVVs at S_1 and S_2 ([2,2,1]) *dominate* that at S_3. The version of the file at S_1 or S_2 should replace that at S_3.

complementary and independent of each other. For example, a user can exploit the benefits of disconnected operation even though the required file volumes are stored on a single server.

Update semantics ◊ The currency guarantees offered by Coda when a client opens a file are weaker than for AFS, reflecting the optimistic update strategy. The single server S referred to in the currency guarantees for AFS is replaced by a set of servers $\overline{S}$ (the file's VSG) and the client C can access a subset of servers $\overline{s}$ (the AVSG for the file seen by C).

Informally, the guarantee offered by a successful *open* in Coda is that it provides the most recent copy of F from the current AVSG, and if no server is accessible, a locally cached copy of F is used if one is available. A successful *close* guarantees that the file has been propagated to the currently accessible set of servers, or if no server is available, the file has been marked for propagation at the earliest opportunity.

A more precise definition of these guarantees, taking into account the effect of lost callbacks, can be made using an extension of the notation used for AFS. In each definition except the last there are two cases: the first, beginning $\overline{s} \neq \emptyset$, refers to all situations in which the AVSG is not empty; and the second deals with disconnected operation:

after a successful *open*:	$(\overline{s} \neq \emptyset$ and $(latest(F, \overline{s}, 0)$
	or $(latest(F, \overline{s}, T)$ and $lostCallback(\overline{s}, T)$ and $inCache(F))))$
	or $(\overline{s} = \emptyset$ and $inCache(F))$
after a failed *open*:	$(\overline{s} \neq \emptyset$ and $conflict(F, \overline{s}))$
	or $(\overline{s} = \emptyset$ and $\neg inCache(F))$
after a successful *close*:	$(\overline{s} \neq \emptyset$ and $updated(F, \overline{s}))$
	or $(\overline{s} = \emptyset)$
after a failed *close*:	$\overline{s} \neq \emptyset$ and $conflict(F, \overline{s})$

This model assumes a synchronous system: T is the longest time for which a client can remain unaware of an update elsewhere to a file that is in its cache; $latest(F, \overline{s}, T)$ denotes the fact that the current value of F at C was the latest across all the servers in $\overline{s}$ at some instant in the last T seconds and that there were no conflicts among the copies of F at that instant; $lostCallback(\overline{s}, T)$ means that a callback was sent by some member of $\overline{s}$ in the last T seconds and was not received at C, and $conflict(F, \overline{s})$ means that the values of F at some servers in $\overline{s}$ are currently in conflict.

Accessing replicas ◊ The strategy used on *open* and *close* to access the replicas of a file is a variant of the *read-one/write-all* approach. On *open*, if a copy of the file is not present in the local cache the client identifies a preferred server from the AVSG for the file. The preferred server may be chosen at random, or on the basis of performance criteria such as physical proximity or server load. The client requests a copy of the file attributes and contents from the preferred server, and on receiving it, it checks with all the other members of the AVSG to verify that the copy is the latest available version. If not, a member of the AVSG with the latest version is made the preferred site, the file contents are refetched and the members of the AVSG are notified that some members have stale replicas. When the fetch has been completed, a callback promise is established at the preferred server.

When a file is closed at a client after modification, its contents and attributes are transmitted in parallel to all the members of the AVSG using a multicast remote procedure calling protocol. This maximizes the probability that every replication site for a file has the current version at all times. It doesn't guarantee it, because the AVSG does not necessarily include all the members of the VSG. It minimizes the server load by giving clients the responsibility for propagating changes to the replication sites in the normal case (servers are involved only when a stale replica is discovered on *open*).

Since maintaining callback state in all the members of an AVSG would be expensive, the callback promise is maintained only at the preferred server. But this introduces a new problem: the preferred server for one client need not be in the AVSG of another client. If this is the case, an update by the second client will not cause a callback to the first client. The solution adopted to this problem is discussed in the next subsection.

Cache coherence ◊ The Coda currency guarantees stated above mean that the Venus process at each client must detect the following events within T seconds of their occurrence:

- enlargement of an AVSG (due to the accessibility of a previously inaccessible server);

- shrinking of an AVSG (due to a server becoming inaccessible);

- a lost callback event.

To achieve this, Venus sends a probe message to all the servers in VSGs of the files that it has in its cache every T seconds. Responses will be received only from accessible servers. If Venus receives a response from a previously inaccessible server it enlarges the corresponding AVSG and drops the callback promises on any files that it holds from the relevant volume. This is done because the cached copy may no longer be the latest version available in the new AVSG.

If it fails to receive a response from a previously accessible server Venus shrinks the corresponding AVSG. No callback changes are required unless the shrinkage is caused by the loss of a preferred server, in which case all callback promises from that server must be dropped. If a response indicates that a callback message was sent but not received, the callback promise on the corresponding file is dropped.

We are now left with the problem, mentioned above, of updates that are missed by a server because it is not in the AVSG of a different client that performs an update. To deal with this case, Venus is sent a *volume version vector* (*volume CVV*) in response to each probe message. The volume CVV contains a summary of the CVVs for all of the files in the volume. If Venus detects any mismatch between the volume CVVs then some members of the AVSG must have some file versions that are not up to date. Although the outdated files may not be the ones that are in its local cache, Venus makes a pessimistic assumption and drops the callback promises on all of the files that it holds from the relevant volume.

Note that Venus only probes servers in the VSGs of files for which it holds cached copies and that a single probe message serves to update the AVSGs and check the callbacks for all of the files in a volume. This, combined with a relatively large value for

T (in the order of 10 minutes in the experimental implementation), means that the probes are not an obstacle to the scalability of Coda to large numbers of servers and wide-area networks.

Disconnected operation ◊ During brief disconnections, such as those that may occur because of unexpected service interruptions, the least recently used cache replacement policy normally adopted by Venus may be sufficient to avoid cache misses on the disconnected volumes. But it is unlikely that a client could operate in disconnected mode for extended periods without generating references to files or directories that are not in the cache unless a different policy is adopted.

Coda therefore allows users to specify a prioritized list of files and directories that Venus should strive to retain in the cache. Objects at the highest level are identified as *sticky* and these must be retained in the cache at all times. If the local disk is large enough to accommodate all of them, the user is assured that they will remain accessible. Since it is often difficult to know exactly what file accesses are generated by any sequence of user actions, a tool is provided that enables the user to bracket a sequence of actions; Venus notes the file references generated by the sequence and flags them with a given priority.

When disconnected operation ends, a process of *reintegration* begins. For each cached file or directory that has been modified, created or deleted during disconnected operation, Venus executes a sequence of update operations to make the AVSG replicas identical to the cached copy. Reintegration proceeds top-down from the root of each cached volume.

Conflicts may be detected during reintegration due to updates to AVSG replicas by other clients. When this occurs, the cached copy is stored in a temporary location on the server, and the user that initiated the reintegration is informed. This approach is based on the design philosophy adopted in Coda, which assigns priority to server-based replicas over cached copies. The temporary copies are stored in a *covolume*, which is associated with each volume on a server. Covolumes resemble the *lost+found* directories found in conventional UNIX systems. They mirror just those parts of the file directory structure needed to hold the temporary data. Little additional storage is required, because the covolumes are almost empty.

Performance ◊ Satyanarayanan *et al.* [1990] compare the performance of Coda with AFS under benchmark loads designed to simulate user populations ranging from five to fifty typical AFS users.

With no replication, there is no significant difference between the performance of AFS and that of Coda. With three-fold replication, the time for Coda to perform a benchmark load equivalent to 5 typical users exceeds that of AFS without replication by only 5%. However, with three-fold replication and a load equivalent to 50 users, the time to complete the benchmark is increased by 70%, whereas that for AFS without replication is increased by only 16%. This difference is attributed only in part to the overheads associated with replication – differences in the tuning of the implementation are said to account for part of the difference in performance.

Discussion ◊ We pointed out above that Coda is similar to Bayou in that it also employs an optimistic approach to achieving high availability (although they differ in several other ways, not least because one manages files and the other databases). We also described how Coda uses CVVs to check for conflicts, without regard to the semantics of the data stored in files. The approach can detect potential write-write conflicts but not read-write conflicts. These are 'potential' write-write conflicts because at the level of the application semantics there may be no actual conflict: clients may have updated different objects in the file compatibly and a simple automatic merge would be possible.

Coda's overall approach of semantics-free conflict detection and manual resolution is sensible in many cases, especially in applications that require human judgment or in systems with no knowledge of the data's semantics.

Directories are a special case in Coda. Automatically maintaining the integrity of these key objects through conflict resolution is sometimes possible, since their semantics are relatively simple: the only changes that can be made to directories are the insertion or deletion of directory entries. Coda incorporates its own method for resolving directories. It has the same effect as Bayou's approach of operational transformation but Coda merges the state of conflicting directories directly, since it has no record of the operations that clients performed.

15.5 Transactions with replicated data

So far in this chapter we have considered systems in which clients request single operations at a time on replicated sets of objects. Chapters 13 and 14 explained that transactions are *sequences* of one or more operations, applied in such a way as to enforce the ACID properties. As with the systems in Section 15.4, objects in transactional systems may be replicated to increase both availability and performance.

From a client's viewpoint, a transaction on replicated objects should appear the same as one with non-replicated objects. In a non-replicated system, transactions appear to be performed one at a time in some order. This is achieved by ensuring a serially equivalent interleaving of clients' transactions. The effect of transactions performed by clients on replicated objects should be the same as if they had been performed one at a time on a single set of objects. This property is called *one-copy serializability*. It is similar to, but not to be confused with, sequential consistency. Sequential consistency considers valid executions without any notion of aggregating the client operations into transactions.

Each replica manager provides concurrency control and recovery of its own objects. In this section, we assume that two-phase locking is used for concurrency control.

Recovery is complicated by the fact that a failed replica manager is a member of a collection and that the other members continue to provide a service during the time that it is unavailable. When a replica manager recovers from a failure, it uses information obtained from the other replica mangers to restore its objects to their current values, taking into account all the changes that have occurred during the time it was unavailable.

This section first introduces the architecture for transactions with replicated data. Architectural questions are whether a client request can be addressed to any of the replica managers; how many replica managers are required for the successful completion of an operation; whether the replica manager contacted by a client can defer the forwarding of requests until a transaction is committed; and how to carry out a two-phase commit protocol.

The implementation of one-copy serializability is illustrated by *read one/write all* – a simple replication scheme in which *Read* operations are performed by a single replica manager and *write* operations are performed by all of them.

The section then discusses the problems of implementing replication schemes in the presence of server crashes and recovery. It introduces available copies replication – a variant of the read-one/write-all replication scheme in which *read* operations are performed by any single replica manager and *write* operations are performed by all of those that are available.

Finally, the section presents three replication schemes that work correctly when the collection of replica managers is divided into subgroups by a network partition:

- *Available copies with validation*: available copies replication is applied in each partition and when a partition is repaired, a validation procedure is applied and any inconsistencies are dealt with.

- *Quorum consensus*: a subgroup must have a quorum (meaning that it has sufficient members) in order to be allowed to continue providing a service in the presence of a partition. When a partition is repaired (and when a replica manager restarts after a failure) replica managers get their objects up-to-date by means of recovery procedures.

- *Virtual partition*: a combination of quorum consensus and available copies. If a virtual partition has a quorum, it can use available copies replication.

15.5.1 Architectures for replicated transactions

As with the range of systems we have already considered in previous sections, a front end may either multicast client requests to groups of replica managers or it may send each request to a single replica manager, which is then responsible for processing the request and responding to the client. Wiesmann *et al.* [2000] and Schiper and Raynal [1996] consider the case of multicast requests and we shall not deal with it here. Henceforth, we assume that a front end sends client requests to one of the group of replica managers of a logical object. In the *primary copy* approach, all front ends communicate with a distinguished 'primary' replica manager to perform an operation, and that replica manager keeps the backups up to date. Alternatively, front ends may communicate with any replica manager to perform an operation – but coordination between the replica managers is consequently more complex.

The replica manager that receives a request to perform an operation on a particular object is responsible for getting the cooperation of the other replica managers in the group that have copies of that object. Different replication schemes have different rules as to how many of the replica managers in a group are required for the successful completion of an operation. For example, in the read-one/write-all scheme, a *read* request can be performed by a single replica manager, whereas a *write* request must be performed by all the replica managers in the group, as shown in Figure 15.10 (there can be different numbers of replicas of the various objects). Quorum consensus schemes are designed to reduce the number of replica managers that must perform update operations,

Figure 15.10   Transactions on replicated data

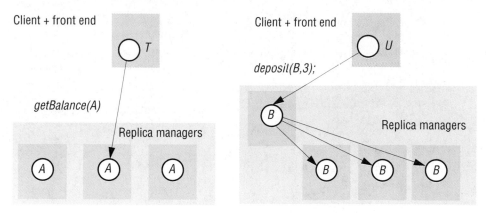

but at the expense of increasing the number of replica managers required to perform *read-only* operations.

Another issue is whether the replica manager contacted by a front end should defer the forwarding of update requests to other replica managers in the group until after a transaction commits – the so-called *lazy* approach to update propagation; or, conversely, whether replica managers should forward each update request to all the necessary replica managers within the transaction and before it commits – the *eager* approach. The lazy approach is an attractive alternative because it reduces the amount of communication between the replica managers that takes place before responding to the updating client. However, concurrency control must also be considered. The lazy approach is sometimes used in primary copy replication (see below), where a single primary replica manager serializes the transactions. But if several different transactions may attempt to access the same objects at different replica managers in a group then, to ensure that the transactions are correctly serialized at all the replica managers in the group, each replica manager needs to know about the requests performed by the others. The eager approach is the only one available in that case.

The two-phase commit protocol ◊ The two-phase commit protocol becomes a two-level nested two-phase commit protocol. As before, the coordinator of a transaction communicates with the workers. But if either the coordinator or a worker is a replica manager it will communicate with the other replica managers to which it passed requests during the transaction.

That is, in the first phase, the coordinator sends the *canCommit?* to the workers, which pass it on to the other replica managers and collect their replies before replying to the coordinator. In the second phase, the coordinator sends the *doCommit* or *doAbort* request, which is passed on to the members of the groups of replica managers.

Primary copy replication ◊ Primary copy replication may be used in the context of transactions. In this scheme, all client requests (whether or not they are read-only) are directed to a single primary replica manager (see Figure 15.4). For primary copy replication, concurrency control is applied at the primary. To commit a transaction, the primary communicates with the backup replica managers and then, in the eager

Figure 15.11 Available copies

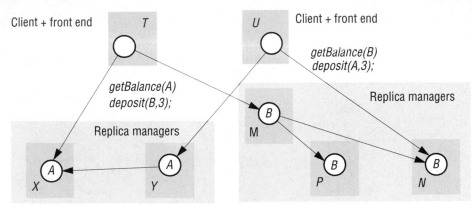

approach, replies to the client. This form of replication allows a backup replica manager to take over consistently if the primary fails. In the lazy alternative, the primary responds to front ends before it has updated its backups. In that case, a backup that replaces a failed front end will not necessarily have the latest state of the database.

Read-one / write-all ◊ We use this simple replication scheme to illustrate how two-phase locking at each replica manager can be used to achieve one-copy serializability, where front ends may communicate with any replica manager. Every *write* operation must be performed at all of the replica managers, each of which sets a write lock on the object affected by the operation. Each *read* operation is performed by a single replica manager, which sets a read lock on the object affected by the operation.

Consider pairs of operations of different transactions on the same object: any pair of *write* operations will require conflicting locks at all of the replica managers; a *read* operation and a *write* operation will require conflicting locks at a single replica manager. Thus one-copy serializability is achieved.

15.5.2 Available copies replication

Simple read-one/write-all replication is not a realistic scheme, because it cannot be carried out if some of the replica managers are unavailable, either because they have crashed or because of a communication failure. The available copies scheme is designed to allow for some replica managers being temporarily unavailable. The strategy is that a client's *read* request on a logical object may be performed by any available replica manager but that a client's update request must be performed by all available replica managers in the group with copies of the object. The idea of the 'available members of a group of replica managers' is similar to Coda's available volume storage group described in Section 15.4.3.

In the normal case, client requests are received and performed by a functioning replica manager. *Read* requests can be performed by the replica manager that receives them. *Write* requests are performed by the receiving replica manager and all the other available replica managers in the group. For example, in Figure 15.11, the *getBalance* operation of transaction *T* is performed by *X*, whereas its *deposit* operation is performed by *M*, *N* and *P*. Concurrency control at each replica manager affects the operations performed locally. For example, at *X*, transaction *T* has read *A* and therefore transaction *U* is not allowed to update *A* with the *deposit* operation until transaction *T* has completed. So long as the set of available replica managers does not change, local concurrency control achieves one-copy serializability in the same way as in read-one/write-all replication. Unfortunately, this is not the case if a replica manager fails or recovers during the progress of the conflicting transactions.

Replica manager failure ◊ We assume that replica managers fail benignly by crashing. However, a crashed replica manager is replaced by a new process, which recovers the committed state of the objects from a recovery file. Front ends use timeouts to decide that a replica manager is not currently available. When a client makes a request to a replica manager that has crashed, the front end times out and retries the request at another replica manager in the group. If the request is received by a replica manager at which the object is out of date because the replica manager has not completely recovered from failure, the replica manager rejects the request and the front end retries the request at another replica manager in the group.

One-copy serializability requires that crashes and recoveries be serialized with respect to transactions. According to whether it can access an object or not, a transaction observes that a failure occurs after it finished or before it started. One-copy serializability is not achieved when different transactions make conflicting failure observations.

Consider the case in Figure 15.11 where the replica manager *X* fails just after *T* has performed *getBalance* and replica manager *N* fails just after *U* has performed *getBalance*. Assume that both of these replica managers fail before *T* and *U* have performed their *deposit* operations. This implies that *T*'s *deposit* will be performed at replica managers *M* and *P* and *U*'s *deposit* will be performed at replica manager *Y*. Unfortunately, the concurrency control on *A* at replica manager *X* does not prevent transaction *U* from updating *A* at replica manager *Y*. Neither does concurrency control on *B* at replica manager *N* prevent transaction *T* updating *B* at replica managers *M* and *P*.

This is contrary to the requirement for one-copy serializability. If these operations were to be performed on single copies of the objects, they would be serialized either with transaction *T* before *U* or with transaction *U* before *T*. This ensures that one of the transactions will read the value set by the other. Local concurrency control on copies of objects is not sufficient to ensure one-copy serializability in the available copies replication scheme.

As *write* operations are directed to all available copies, local concurrency control does ensure that conflicting writes on an object are serialized. In contrast, a *read* by one transaction and a *write* by another do not necessarily affect the same copy of an object. Therefore, the scheme requires additional concurrency control to prevent the dependencies between a *read* operation of one transaction and a *write* operation of another transaction forming a cycle. Such dependencies cannot arise if the failures and recoveries of replicas of objects are serialized with respect to transactions.

Local validation ◊ We refer to the additional concurrency control procedure as local validation. The local validation procedure is designed to ensure that any failure or recovery event does not appear to happen during the progress of a transaction. In our

Figure 15.12   Network partition

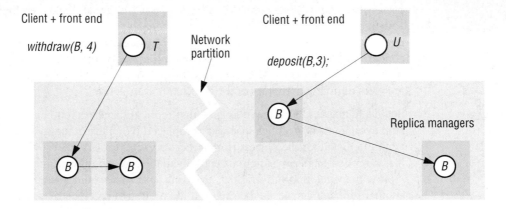

example, as T has read from an object at X, X's failure must be after T. Similarly, as T observes the failure of N when it attempts to update the object, N's failure must be before T. That is:

N fails $\rightarrow$ T reads object A at X; T writes object B at M and P $\rightarrow$ T commits $\rightarrow$ X fails

It can also be argued for transaction U that:

X fails $\rightarrow$ U reads object B at N; U writes object A at Y $\rightarrow$ U commits $\rightarrow$ N fails

The local validation procedure ensures that two such incompatible sequences cannot both occur. Before a transaction commits it checks for any failures (and recoveries) of replica managers of objects it has accessed. In the example, transaction T would check that N is still unavailable and X, M and P are still available. If this is the case, T can commit. This implies that X fails after T validated and before U validated. In other words, U's validation is after T's validation. U's validation fails because N has already failed.

Whenever a transaction has observed a failure, the local validation procedure attempts to communicate with the failed replica managers to ensure that they have not yet recovered. The other part of the local validation, which is testing that replica managers have not failed since objects were accessed, can be combined with the two-phase commit protocol.

Available copies algorithms cannot be used in environments in which functioning replica managers are unable to communicate with one another.

15.5.3 Network partitions

Replication schemes need to take into account the possibility of network partitions. A network partition separates a group of replica managers into two or more subgroups in such a way that the members of one subgroup can communicate with one another but members of different subgroups cannot communicate with one another. For example, in Figure 15.12, the replica managers receiving the *deposit* request cannot send it to the replica managers receiving the *withdraw* request.

Replication schemes are designed with the assumption that partitions will eventually be repaired. Therefore, the replica managers within a single partition must ensure that any requests that they execute during a partition will not make the set of replicas inconsistent when the partition is repaired.

Davidson *et al.* [1985] discuss many different approaches, which they categorize as being either optimistic or pessimistic as to whether inconsistencies are likely to occur. The optimistic schemes do not limit availability during a partition, whereas pessimistic schemes do.

The optimistic approaches allow updates in all partitions – this can lead to inconsistencies between partitions, which must be resolved when the partition is repaired. An example of this approach is a variant of the available copies algorithm in which updates are allowed in partitions and, after the partition has been repaired, the updates are validated – any updates that break the one-copy serializability criterion are aborted.

The pessimistic approach limits availability even when there are no partitions, but it prevents any inconsistencies occurring during partitions. When a partition is repaired, all that need be done is to update the copies of the objects. The quorum consensus approach is pessimistic. It allows updates in a partition that has the majority of replica managers and propagates the updates to the other replica managers when the partition is repaired.

15.5.4 Available copies with validation

The available copies algorithm is applied within each partition. This optimistic approach maintains the normal level of availability for *read* operations, even during partitions. When a partition is repaired, the possibly conflicting transactions that took place in the separate partitions are validated. If the validation fails, then some steps must be taken to overcome the inconsistencies. If there had been no partition, one of a pair of transactions with conflicting operations would have been delayed or aborted. Unfortunately, as there has been a partition, pairs of conflicting transactions have been allowed to commit in different partitions. The only choice after the event is to abort one of them. This requires making changes in the objects and in some cases, compensating effects in the real world, such as dealing with overdrawn bank accounts. The optimistic approach is only feasible with applications where such compensating actions can be taken.

Version vectors can be used to validate conflicts between pairs of *write* operations. These are used in the Coda file system and are described in Section 15.4.3. This approach cannot detect read-write conflicts but works well in file systems where transactions tend to access a single file and read-write conflicts are unimportant. It is not suitable for applications such as our banking example where read-write conflicts are important.

Davidson [1984] used *precedence graphs* to detect inconsistencies between partitions. Each partition maintains a log of the objects affected by the *read* and *write* operations of transactions. This log is used to construct a precedence graph whose nodes are transactions and whose edges represent conflicts between the *read* and *write* operations of transactions. Such a graph will not contain any cycles, since concurrency control has been applied within the partition. The validation procedure takes the precedence graphs from the partitions and adds edges, representing conflicts, between transactions in different partitions. If the resulting graph contains cycles, then the validation fails.

15.5.5 Quorum consensus methods

One way of preventing transactions in different partitions from producing inconsistent results is to make a rule that operations can be carried out within only one of the partitions. As the replica managers in different partitions cannot communicate with one another, the subgroup of replica managers within each partition must be able to decide independently whether they are allowed to carry out operations. A quorum is a subgroup of replica managers whose size gives it the right to carry out operations. For example, if having a majority is the criterion, a subgroup that has the majority of the members of a group would form a quorum because no other subgroup could have a majority.

In quorum consensus replication schemes an update operation on a logical object may be completed successfully by a subgroup of its group of replica managers. The other members of the group will therefore have out-of-date copies of the object. Version numbers or timestamps may be used to determine whether copies are up to date. If versions are used, the initial state of an object is the first version, and after each change we have a new version. Each copy of an object has a version number, but only the copies that are up to date have the current version number, whereas out-of-date copies have earlier version numbers. Operations should be applied only to copies with the current version number.

Gifford [1979] developed a file replication scheme in which a number of 'votes' is assigned to each physical copy at a replica manager of a single logical file. A vote can be regarded as a weighting related to the desirability of using a particular copy. Each *read* operation must first obtain a read quorum of R votes before it can proceed to read from any up-to-date copy, and each *write* operation must obtain a write quorum of W votes before it can proceed with an update operation. R and W are set for a group of replica managers such that

$W >$ half the total votes

$R + W >$ total number of votes for the group

This ensures that any pair, consisting of a read quorum and a write quorum or two write quora, must contain common copies. Therefore, if there is a partition, it is not possible to perform conflicting operations on the same copy, but in different partitions.

To perform a *read* operation, a read quorum is collected by making sufficient version number enquiries to find a set of copies, the sum of whose votes is not less than R. Not all of these copies need be up to date. Since each read quorum overlaps with every write quorum, every read quorum is certain to include at least one current copy. The read operation may be applied to any up-to-date copy.

To perform a *write* operation, a write quorum is collected by making sufficient version number enquiries to find a set of replica managers with up-to-date copies, the sum of whose votes is not less than W. If there are insufficient up-to-date copies, then a non-current file is replaced with a copy of the current file, to enable the quorum to be established. The updates specified in the *write* operation are then applied by each replica manager in the write quorum, the version number is incremented and completion of the write is reported to the client.

The files at the remaining available replica managers are then updated by performing the *write* operation as a background task. Any replica manager whose copy of the file has an older version number than the one used by the write quorum updates it by replacing the entire file with a copy obtained from a replica manager that is up to date.

Two-phase read-write locking may be used for concurrency control in Gifford's replication scheme. The preliminary version number enquiry to obtain the read quorum, R, causes read locks to be set at each replica manager contacted. When a *write* operation is applied to the write quorum, W, a write lock is set at each replica manager involved. (Locks are applied with the same granularity as version numbers.) The locks ensure one-copy serializability, as any read quorum overlaps with any write quorum and any two write quora overlap.

Configurability of groups of replica managers ◊ An important property of the weighted voting algorithm is that groups of replica managers can be configured to provide different performance or reliability characteristics. Once the general reliability and performance of a group of replica managers is established by its voting configuration, the reliability and performance of *write* operations may be increased by decreasing W and similarly for *reads* by decreasing R.

The algorithm can also allow for the use of copies of files on local disks at client computers as well as those at file servers. The copies of files in client computers are regarded as *weak representatives* and are always allocated zero votes. This ensures that they are not included in any quorum. A *read* operation may be performed at any up-to-date copy, once a read quorum has been obtained. Therefore a *read* operation may be carried out on the local copy of the file if it is up to date. Weak representatives can be used to speed up *read* operations.

An example from Gifford ◊ Gifford gives three examples showing the range of properties that can be achieved by allocating weights to the various replica managers in a group and assigning R and W appropriately. We now reproduce Gifford's examples, which are based on the table on the next page. The blocking probabilities give an indication of the probability that a quorum cannot be obtained when a *read* or *write* request is made. They are calculated assuming that there is a 0.01 probability that any single replica manager will be unavailable at the time of a request.

Example 1 is configured for a file with a high read-to-write ratio in an application with several weak representatives and a single replica manager. Replication is used to enhance the performance of the system, not the reliability. There is one replica manager on the local network that can be accessed in 75 milliseconds. Two clients have chosen to make weak representatives on their local disks, which they can access in 65 milliseconds, resulting in lower latency and less network traffic.

Example 2 is configured for a file with a moderate read-to-write ratio, which is accessed primarily from one local network. The replica manager on the local network is assigned two votes and the replica managers on the remote networks are assigned one vote apiece. Reads can be satisfied from the local replica manager, but writes must access the local replica manager and one remote replica manager. The file will remain available in read-only mode if the local replica manager fails. Clients could create local weak representatives for lower read latency.

		Example 1	Example 2	Example 3
Latency	Replica 1	75	75	75
(milliseconds)	Replica 2	65	100	750
	Replica 3	65	750	750
Voting	Replica 1	1	2	1
configuration	Replica 2	0	1	1
	Replica 3	0	1	1
Quorum	R	1	2	1
sizes	W	1	3	3

Derived performance of file suite:				
Read	Latency	65	75	75
	Blocking probability	0.01	0.0002	0.000001
Write	Latency	75	100	750
	Blocking probability	0.01	0.0101	0.03

Example 3 is configured for a file with a very high read-to-write ratio, such as a system directory in a three-replica-manager environment. Clients can read from any replica manager, and the probability that the file will be unavailable is small. Updates must be applied to all copies. Once again, clients could create weak representatives on their local machines for lower read latency.

The main disadvantage of quorum consensus is that the performance of *read* operations is degraded by the need to collect a read quorum from R replica managers.

Herlihy [1986] proposed an extension of the quorum consensus method for abstract data types. This method allows the semantics of operations to be taken into account and thereby to increase the availability of objects. Herlihy's method uses timestamps instead of version numbers. This has the advantage that there is no need to make version number enquiries in order to get a new version number before performing a write operation. The main advantage claimed by Herlihy is that the use of semantic knowledge can increase the number of choices for a quorum.

15.5.6 Virtual partition algorithm

This algorithm, which was proposed by El Abbadi *et al.* [1985], combines the quorum consensus approach with the available copies algorithm. Quorum consensus works correctly in the presence of partitions but available copies is less expensive for *read* operations. A *virtual partition* is an abstraction of a real partition and contains a set of replica managers. Note that the term 'network partition' refers to the barrier that divides replica managers into several parts, whereas the term 'virtual partition' refers to the parts

Figure 15.13 Two network partitions

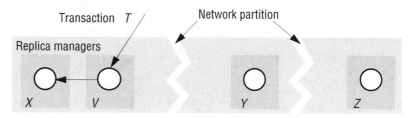

themselves. Although they are not connected with multicast communication, virtual partitions are similar to group views, which we introduced in Section 15.2.2. A transaction can operate in a virtual partition if it contains sufficient replica managers to have a read quorum and a write quorum for the objects accessed. In this case, the transaction uses the available copies algorithm. This has the advantage that *read* operations need only ever access a single copy of an object and may enhance performance by choosing the 'nearest' copy. If a replica manager fails and the virtual partition changes during a transaction, then the transaction is aborted. This ensures one-copy serializability of transactions because all transactions that survive see the failures and recoveries of replica managers in the same order.

Whenever a member of a virtual partition detects that it cannot access one of the other members – for example, when a *write* operation is not acknowledged – it attempts to create a new virtual partition with a view to obtaining a virtual partition with read and write quora.

Suppose, for example, that we have four replica managers V, X, Y and Z, each of which has one vote, and that the read and write quora are $R = 2$ and $W = 3$. Initially, all the managers can contact one another. So long as they remain in contact, they can use the available copies algorithm. For example, a transaction T consisting of a *read* followed by a *write* operation will perform the *read* at a single replica manager (for example, V) and the *write* operation at all four of them.

Suppose that transaction T starts by performing its *read* at V at a time when V is still in contact with X, Y and Z. Now suppose that a network partition occurs as in Figure 15.13 in which V and X are in one part and Y and Z are in different ones. Then when transaction T attempts to apply its *write*, V will notice that it cannot contact Y and Z.

When a replica manager cannot contact managers that it could previously contact, it keeps on trying until it can create a new virtual partition. For example, V will keep on trying to contact Y and Z until one or both of them replies, as, for example, in Figure 15.14 when Y can be accessed. The group of replica managers V, X and Y comprise a virtual partition because they are sufficient to form read and write quora.

When a new virtual partition is created during a transaction that has performed an operation at one of the replica managers (such as transaction T), the transaction must be aborted. In addition, the replicas within a new virtual partition must be brought up to date by copying them from other replicas. Version numbers can be used as in Gifford's algorithm to determine which copies are up to date. It is essential that all replicas be up to date, because *read* operations are performed on any single replica.

Figure 15.14 Virtual partition

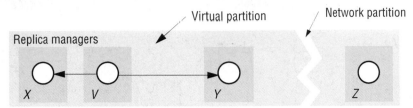

Implementation of virtual partitions ◊ A virtual partition has a creation time, a set of potential members and a set of actual members. Creation times are logical timestamps. The actual members of a particular virtual partition have the same idea as to its creation time and membership (a shared *view* of the replica managers with which they can communicate). For example, in Figure 15.14 the potential members are V, X, Y, Z and the actual members are V, X and Y.

The creation of a new virtual partition is achieved by a cooperative protocol carried out by those of the potential members that can be accessed by the replica managers that initiated it. Several replica managers may attempt to create a new virtual partition simultaneously. For example, suppose that the replica managers Y and Z shown in Figure 15.13 keep making attempts to contact the others and after a while the network partition is partially repaired so that Y cannot communicate with Z but the two groups V, X, Y and V, X, Z can communicate among themselves. Then there is a danger that two overlapping virtual partitions such as V_1 and V_2 shown in Figure 15.15 might both be created.

Consider the effect of executing different transactions in the two virtual partitions. The *read* operation of the transaction in V, X, Y might be applied at the replica manager Y, in which case its read lock will not conflict with write locks set by a *write* operation of a transaction in the other virtual partition. Overlapping virtual partitions are contrary to one-copy serializability.

Figure 15.15 Two overlapping virtual partitions

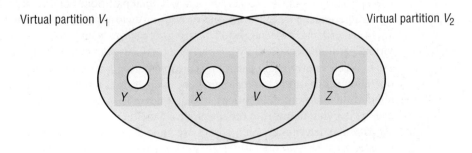

Figure 15.16   Creating a virtual partition

Phase 1:

- The initiator sends a *Join* request to each potential member. The argument of *Join* is a proposed logical timestamp for the new virtual partition.

- When a replica manager receives a *Join* request, it compares the proposed logical timestamp with that of its current virtual partition.

    - If the proposed logical timestamp is greater it agrees to join and replies *Yes*;

    - If it is less, it refuses to join and replies *No*.

Phase 2:

- If the initiator has received sufficient *Yes* replies to have *read* and *write* quora, it may complete the creation of the new virtual partition by sending a *Confirmation* message to the sites that agreed to join. The creation timestamp and list of actual members are sent as arguments.

- Replica managers receiving the *Confirmation* message join the new virtual partition and record its creation timestamp and list of actual members.

The aim of the protocol is to create new virtual partitions consistently, even if real partitions occur during the protocol. The protocol for creating a new virtual partition has two phases as shown in Figure 15.16.

A replica manager that replies *Yes* in Phase 1 does not belong to a virtual partition until it receives the corresponding *Confirmation* message in Phase 2.

In our example above, the replica managers Y and Z shown in Figure 15.13 each attempt to create a virtual partition, and whichever one has the higher logical timestamp will be the one that is used in the end.

This is an effective method when partitions are not a common occurrence. Each transaction uses the available copies algorithm within a virtual partition.

15.6 Summary

Replicating objects is an important means of achieving services with good performance, high availability and fault tolerance in a distributed system. We described architectures for services in which replica managers hold replicas of objects, and in which front ends make this replication transparent. Clients, front ends and replica managers may be separate processes or exist in the same address space.

The chapter began by describing a system model in which each logical object is implemented by a set of physical replicas. Often, updates to these replicas can be made conveniently by group communication. We expanded our account of group communication to include group membership services and view-synchronous communication.

We defined linearizability and sequential consistency as correctness criteria for fault-tolerant services. These criteria express how the services must provide the equivalent of a single image of the set of logical objects, even though those objects are replicated. The most practically significant of the criteria is sequential consistency.

In passive (primary-backup) replication, fault tolerance is achieved by directing all requests through a distinguished replica manager and having a backup replica manager take over if this fails. In active replication, all replica managers process all requests independently. Both forms of replication can be conveniently implemented using group communication.

Next we considered highly available services. Gossip and Bayou both allow clients to make updates to local replicas while partitioned. In each system, replica managers exchange updates with one another when they become reconnected. Gossip provides its highest availability at the expense of relaxed, causal consistency. Bayou provides stronger eventual consistency guarantees, employing automatic conflict detection, and the technique of operational transformation to resolve conflicts. Coda is a highly available file system that uses version vectors to detect potentially conflicting updates.

Finally, we considered the performance of transactions against replicated data. Both primary-backup architectures and architectures in which front ends may communicate with any replica manager exist for this case. We discussed how transactional systems allow for replica manager failures and network partitions. The techniques of available copies, quorum consensus and virtual partitions enable operations within transactions to make progress even in some circumstances where not all replicas are reachable.

EXERCISES

15.1   Three computers together provide a replicated service. The manufacturers claim that each computer has a mean time between failure of five days; a failure typically takes four hours to fix. What is the availability of the replicated service?   *page 604*

15.2   Explain why a multi-threaded server might not qualify as a state machine.   *page 607*

15.3   In a multi-user game, the players move figures around a common scene. The state of the game is replicated at the players' workstations and at a server, which contains services controlling the game overall, such as collision detection. Updates are multicast to all replicas.

(i)   The figures may throw projectiles at one another and a hit debilitates the unfortunate recipient for a limited time. What type of update ordering is required here? Hint: consider the 'throw', 'collide' and 'revive' events.

(ii)   The game incorporates magic devices which may be picked up by a player to assist them. What type of ordering should be applied to the pick-up-device operation?

page 608

15.4   A router separating process *p* from two others, *q* and *r*, fails immediately after *p* initiates the multicasting of message *m*. If the group communication system is view-synchronous, explain what happens to *p* next.   *page 612*

15.5   You are given a group communication system with a totally ordered multicast operation, and a failure detector. Is it possible to construct view-synchronous group communication from these components alone?   *page 612*

15.6   A *sync-ordered* multicast operation is one whose delivery ordering semantics are the same as those for delivering views in a view-synchronous group communication system. In a *thingumajig* service, operations upon thingumajigs are causally ordered. The service supports lists of users able to perform operations on each particular thingumajig. Explain why removing a user from a list should be a sync-ordered operation. *page 612*

15.7   What is the consistency issue raised by state transfer?   *page 613*

15.8   An operation *X* upon an object *o* causes *o* to invoke an operation upon another object *o′*. It is now proposed to replicate *o* but not *o′*. Explain the difficulty that this raises concerning invocations upon *o′*, and suggest a solution.   *page 614*

15.9   Explain the difference between linearizability and sequential consistency, and why the latter is more practical to implement, in general.   *page 616*

15.10   Explain why allowing backups to process read operations leads to sequentially consistent rather than linearizable executions in a passive replication system. *page 619*

15.11   Could the gossip architecture be used for a distributed computer game as described in Exercise 15.3?   *page 622*

15.12   In the gossip architecture, why does a replica manager need to keep both a 'replica' timestamp and a 'value' timestamp?   *page 626*

15.13   In a gossip system, a front end has vector timestamp $(3, 5, 7)$ representing the data it has received from members of a group of three replica managers. The three replica managers have vector timestamps $(5, 2, 8)$, $(4, 5, 6)$ and $(4, 5, 8)$, respectively. Which replica manager(s) could immediately satisfy a query from the front end and what is the resultant time stamp of the front end? Which could incorporate an update from the front end immediately?   *page 627*

15.14   Explain why making some replica managers read-only may improve the performance of a gossip system.   *page 631*

15.15   Write pseudocode for dependency checks and merge procedures (as used in Bayou) suitable for a simple room-booking application.   *page 633*

15.16   In the Coda file system, why is it sometimes necessary for users to intervene manually in the process of updating the copies of a file at multiple servers?   *page 640*

15.17   Devise a scheme for integrating two replicas of a file system directory that underwent separate updates during disconnected operation. Use either Bayou's operational transformation approach, or supply a solution for Coda.   *page 641*

15.18 Available copies replication is applied to data items A and B with replicas A_x, A_y and B_m, B_n. The transactions T and U are defined as:

T: $Read(A)$; $Write(B, 44)$. U: $Read(B)$; $Write(A, 55)$.

Show an interleaving of T and U, assuming that two-phase locks are applied to the replicas. Explain why locks alone cannot ensure one copy serializability if one of the replicas fails during the progress of T and U. Explain with reference to this example, how local validation ensures one copy serializability. *page 644*

15.19 Gifford's quorum consensus replication is in use at servers X, Y and Z which all hold replicas of data items A and B. The initial values of all replicas of A and B are 100 and the votes for A and B are 1 at each of X, Y and Z. Also $R = W = 2$ for both A and B. A client reads the value of A and then writes it to B.

(i)   At the time the client performs these operations, a partition separates servers X and Y from server Z. Describe the quora obtained and the operations that take place if the client can access servers X and Y.

(ii) Describe the quora obtained and the operations that take place if the client can access only server Z.

(iii) The partition is repaired and then another partition occurs so that X and Z are separated from Y. Describe the quora obtained and the operations that take place if the client can access servers X and Z. *page 649*

MOBILE AND UBIQUITOUS COMPUTING

This chapter surveys the fields of mobile and ubiquitous computing, which have come about due to device miniaturization and wireless connectivity. Broadly speaking, mobile computing is concerned with exploiting the connectedness of portable devices; ubiquitous computing is about exploiting the increasing integration of computing devices with our everyday physical world.

The chapter introduces a common system model that stresses the volatility of mobile and ubiquitous systems: the set of users, devices and software components in any given environment is liable to change frequently. The chapter then surveys some of the chief areas of research that come about because of volatility and the physical bases for volatility, including: how software components come to associate and interoperate with one another as entities move, fail or spontaneously appear; how systems become integrated with the physical world through sensing and context awareness; the security and privacy issues that arise in volatile, physically integrated systems; and techniques for adapting to small devices' lack of computational and I/O resources. The chapter ends with a case study of the Cooltown project, which devised a human-oriented, web-based architecture for mobile and ubiquitous computing.

16.1 Introduction

Mobile and ubiquitous computing have come about due to device miniaturization and wireless connectivity. Broadly speaking, mobile computing is concerned with exploiting the connectedness of devices that move around in the everyday physical world; ubiquitous computing is about exploiting the increasing integration of computing devices with our everyday physical world. As devices become smaller, we are better able to carry them around with us or wear them, and we can embed them into many parts of the physical world – not just on the familiar desktop or in a server rack. And as wireless connectivity becomes more prevalent, we are better able to connect these new small devices to one another, and to conventional personal and server computers.

This chapter surveys aspects of mobile computing (a subject already touched upon in Chapter 15's treatment of disconnected operation) and ubiquitous computing. The chapter concentrates on their common properties, and on the differences they share from more conventional distributed systems. Given progress to date, the chapter is more about open issues than solutions.

The chapter first outlines the beginnings of mobile and ubiquitous computing, and introduces the subfields known as wearable, handheld and context-aware computing. But after that point it describes a system model that encompasses all of those fields and subfields through their volatility: the set of users, devices and software components in any given environment is liable to change frequently. The chapter then surveys some of the chief areas of research that come about because of volatility and the physical bases for volatility, including: how software components come to associate and interoperate with one another as entities move, fail or spontaneously appear in environments; how systems become integrated with the physical world through sensing and context awareness; the security and privacy issues that arise in volatile, physically integrated systems; and techniques for adapting to small devices' lack of computational and I/O resources. The chapter ends with a case study of the Cooltown project, which devised a human-oriented, web-based architecture for mobile and ubiquitous computing.

Mobile computing ◊ Mobile computing arose as a paradigm in which users could carry their personal computers and retain some connectivity to other machines. About 1980 it became possible to build personal computers that were just about light enough to carry, and which could be connected to other computers over telephone lines via a modem. Technological evolution has led to more or less the same idea but with far better functionality and performance: the present-day equivalent is a laptop or the smaller notebook type of computer, with combinations of wireless connectivity including infrared, WiFi, Bluetooth and GPRS or 3G telecommunications technologies.

A different path of technological evolution has led to *handheld computing*: the use of devices that fit in the hand, including personal digital assistants (PDAs), mobile phones and other more specialized hand-operated devices. PDAs are general-purpose computers capable of running many different types of applications, but compared to laptops and notebooks they trade off their smaller size and battery capacity against correspondingly limited processing power, a smaller screen, and other resource restrictions. Manufacturers increasingly equip PDAs with the same range of wireless connectivity as laptops and notebooks.

An interesting trend in handheld computing has been the blurring of distinctions between PDAs, mobile phones and purpose-built handheld devices such as cameras. Several types of mobile phone have PDA-like computing functionality by virtue of running the Linux, Symbian or Microsoft Smartphone operating systems. PDAs and mobile phones can be equipped with cameras, barcode-readers and other types of specialized attachment, making them an alternative to purpose-built handheld devices. For example, a user who wants to take digital photographs can use a purpose-built camera; a PDA with a camera attachment; or a camera-phone. All of the above come with, or can be purchased with, a form of short- or long-range wireless connectivity.

Stojmenovic [2002] covers principles and protocols for wireless communication, including coverage of two major network-layer problems that need to be solved for the systems studied in this chapter. The first problem is how to provide continuous connectivity for mobile devices that pass in and out of range of *base stations*, which are infrastructure components that provide regions of wireless coverage. The second problem is how to enable collections of devices to wirelessly communicate with one another in places where there is no infrastructure (see the brief treatment of *ad hoc networks* in Section 16.4.2). Both problems arise because direct wireless connectivity is often not available between two given devices. Communication then has to be achieved over several wireless or wired network segments. Two main factors lead to this subdivided wireless coverage. First, the greater the range of a wireless network, the more devices will compete for its limited bandwidth. Second, energy considerations apply: the energy needed to transmit a wireless signal is proportional to the square of its range; but many of the devices we shall consider have limited energy capacity.

Ubiquitous computing ◊ Mark Weiser coined the term ubiquitous computing in 1988 [Weiser 1991]. Ubiquitous computing is also sometimes known as pervasive computing, and in the two terms are usually taken to be synonymous. 'Ubiquitous' means 'to be found everywhere'. Weiser saw the increasing prevalence of computing devices as leading to revolutionary shifts in the way we would use computers.

First, each person in the world would utilize many computers. We can compare this to the personal computing revolution before it, which saw one computer to each person. Although it sounds simple, that change had a dramatic effect on the way we use computers compared to the mainframe era before it, when there was one computer to many people. Weiser's idea of 'one person, many computers' means something very different to the common situation in which we each have several computers more or less alike – one at work, one at home, a laptop and perhaps a PDA we carry with us. Rather, in ubiquitous computing, computers multiply in form and function, not just in number, to suit different tasks.

For example, suppose that all the inert display and writing surfaces in a room – whiteboards, books, pieces of paper, post-it notes, etc. – were replaced by tens or hundreds of individual computers with electronic displays. Whiteboards could assist people in drawing, organizing and archiving their ideas; books could become devices that allow readers to search their text, look up the meaning of words, search for related ideas on the web and see linked multimedia content. Now embed computing functionality in all the writing implements. For example, pens and markers become able to store what the user has written and drawn, and to collect, copy and move multimedia content between the many computers lying around. That scenario raises usability and

Figure 16.1   A room responding to a user wearing an active badge

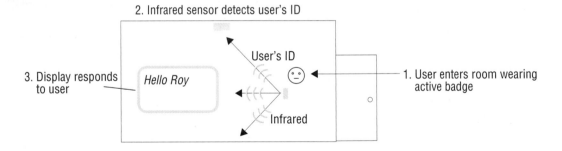

economic issues, and it touches on only one small part of our lives; but it gives us an idea of what 'computing everywhere' might be like.

The second shift that Weiser predicted was that computers would 'disappear' – that they would 'weave themselves into the fabric of everyday life until they are indistinguishable from it'. This is largely a psychological notion, comparable to how people take furniture for granted and barely notice it. It reflects the idea that computing will become embedded in what we think of as everyday items – ones we don't normally think of as having computational capabilities, any more than we think of washing machines or vehicles as 'computing devices', even though embedded microprocessors control them – about 100 microprocessors in the case of some cars.

While the invisibility of certain devices is appropriate – in cases such as the computer systems embedded in a car – it is not true of all the devices we shall consider, particularly the devices that mobile users typically carry. For example, mobile phones are some of the most pervasive devices at the time of writing but their computational ability is hardly invisible and neither, arguably, should it be.

Wearable computing ◊ Users carry wearable computing devices on their person, either attached to or within the fabric of their clothes, or worn like watches, jewellery or spectacles on their body. Unlike the handheld devices we mentioned above, these devices often operate without the user having to manipulate them. They typically have specialized functionality. An early example is the 'active badge', a small computing device clipped to the user that regularly broadcasts the badge's identity (associated with a user) via an infrared transmitter [Want *et al*. 1992; Harter and Hopper 1994]. The point of the badge is for devices in the environment to respond to the badge's transmissions, and so respond to the presence of a user; the infrared transmissions have a limited range and so they will be picked up only if the user is nearby. For example, an electronic display could adapt to the presence of a user by customizing its behaviour according to that user's preferences, such as the default drawing colour and line thickness (Figure 16.1). A room could adapt the air conditioning and lighting settings according to the person within it.

Context-aware computing ◊ The active badge – or rather, other devices' reactions to its presence – exemplifies context-aware computing, which is an important subfield of mobile and ubiquitous computing. This is where computer systems automatically adapt their behaviour according to physical circumstances. Those circumstances can in principle be anything physically measurable or detectable, such as the presence of a user, the time of day, or atmospheric conditions. Some of the dependent conditions are relatively straightforward to determine, such as whether it is night-time (from the time, day of the year and geographic position). But others require sophisticated processing to detect them. For example, consider a context-aware mobile phone, which is to ring only when it is appropriate. In particular, it should automatically switch itself to 'vibrate' instead of 'ring' when it is in the cinema. But detecting that the user is watching a film inside a cinema, as opposed to standing in the cinema lobby, is non-trivial given the inaccuracies in position sensor measurements. Section 16.4 examines context in more detail.

16.1.1 Volatile systems

From the point of view of distributed systems, there is no essential difference between mobile and ubiquitous computing or the subfields we have introduced (or indeed the subfields we have left out, such as tangible computing [Ishii and Ullmer 1997], and augmented reality as exemplified by Wellner's digital desk [Wellner 1991]). In this subsection we give a model of what we shall call *volatile systems* that encompasses the essential distributed systems features of all of them.

We call the systems described in this chapter volatile because, unlike most of the systems described elsewhere in this book, certain changes are common rather than exceptional. The set of users, hardware and software in mobile and ubiquitous systems is highly dynamic and changes unpredictably. Another word we shall sometimes use for these systems is *spontaneous*, which appears in the literature in the phrase *spontaneous networking*. The relevant forms of volatility include:

- failures of devices and communication links;

- changes in the characteristics of communication such as bandwidth;

- the creation and destruction of *associations* – logical communication relationships – between software components resident on the devices.

Here the term 'component' encompasses any software unit such as objects or processes, regardless of whether it interoperates as a client or server or peer.

Chapter 15 has already provided ways of dealing with some of those changes, namely processing failures and disconnected operation. But the solutions considered there were predicated on processing and communication failures being the exception rather than the rule, and on the existence of redundant processing resources. Volatile systems not only break those assumptions but they also add yet more change phenomena, notably the frequent changes in associations between components.

It is worth clearing up a possible misunderstanding before we go further. Volatility is not a *defining* property of mobile and ubiquitous systems: there are other types of system that demonstrate one or more forms of volatility but which are neither mobile nor ubiquitous. A good example is peer-to-peer computing such as file-sharing applications (Chapter 10), in which the set of participating processes and the associations between them are subject to high rates of change. What is different about mobile and ubiquitous computing is that they exhibit *all* of the above forms of volatility, due to the way they are integrated with the physical world. We shall have much to say about this physical integration and how it causes volatility. But physical integration is not itself a distributed systems property whereas volatility is. Hence that is the term we adopt.

In the remainder of this section we'll describe smart spaces, which are environments within which volatile systems subsist; then we'll characterize mobile and ubiquitous devices, their physical and logical connectivity, and the consequences in lowered trust and privacy.

Smart spaces ◊ Physical spaces are important in that they form the background to mobile and ubiquitous computing. Mobility takes place between physical spaces; ubiquitous computing is embedded in physical spaces. A *smart space* is any physical place with embedded services – that is, services provided only or principally within that physical space. It is possible to introduce computing devices into the wild, where no infrastructure exists, to perform an application such as environmental monitoring. But more typically mobile devices and ubiquitous systems exist at any one time in a computationally enhanced part of the built or vehicular environment such as a room, building, town square or train carriage. In those cases, the smart space typically contains a relatively stable computing infrastructure, which may include conventional server computers; devices such as printers and displays; sensors; and a wireless networking infrastructure, including a connection to the Internet.

There are several types of movement or 'appearance and disappearance' that can occur in smart spaces. First, there is *physical mobility*. Smart spaces act as environments for devices that visit and leave them. Users bring in and depart with devices they carry or wear; robotic devices may even move themselves into and out of the space. Second, there is *logical mobility*. A mobile process or agent may move into or out of a smart space, or to or from a user's personal device. Also, a device's physical movement may cause the logical movement of components within it. However, whether or not a component moves due to its device's physical movement, logical mobility has not occurred in any interesting sense unless the component changes some of its associations with other components as a result. Third, users may add relatively static devices such as media players as longer-term additions to the space, and correspondingly withdraw older devices from it. Consider, for example, the evolution of a *smart home* whose occupants vary the set of devices within it [Edwards and Grinter 2001] in a relatively unplanned way over time. Fourth and finally, devices may fail and thus 'disappear' from a space.

Some of those phenomena seem similar from the distributed systems perspective. In each case, either a software component *appears* in a pre-existing smart space and, if anything of interest is to result, becomes integrated, at least temporarily, into that space; or a component *disappears* from the space through mobility or because it is simply switched off or fails. It may or may not be possible for any particular component to distinguish 'infrastructure' devices from 'visiting' devices.

However, there are significant distinctions to be drawn when designing a system. An important difference that may arise between volatile systems is the rate of change. Algorithms that have to cope with a handful of appearing or disappearing components a day (e.g. in a smart home) may be very differently designed to those for which there is at least one such change occurring at any one time (e.g. a system implemented using Bluetooth communication between mobile phones in a crowded city). Moreover, while all the above appearance and disappearance phenomena appear similar to a first approximation, there are of course important differences. For example, from the security point of view, it is one thing for a user's device to enter a smart space and another for an outside software component to move to an infrastructure device belonging to the space.

Device model ◊ With the rise of mobile and ubiquitous computing, a new class of computing device is becoming a part of distributed systems. This device is limited in its energy supply and computing resources; and it may have ways of interfacing with the physical world: sensors such as light detectors, and/or actuators such as a programmable means of movement.

Limited energy: A device that is portable or embedded in the physical world typically has to run on batteries, and the smaller and lighter the device needs to be, the lower will be its battery capacity. Replacing or re-charging those batteries is liable to be inconvenient in terms of time (there may be hundreds of such devices per user) and physical access. Computation, access to memory and other forms of storage all consume precious energy. Wireless communication is particularly energy-intensive. Moreover, the energy consumed by receiving a message can amount to a substantial fraction of that required to transmit it; even 'standby' mode, in which a network interface is ready to receive a message, can require appreciable power consumption [Shih *et al.* 2002]. So, if a device is to last as long as possible on a given level of battery charge, algorithms need to be sensitive to the energy they consume, especially in terms of their message complexity. But ultimately, the probability of device failure is increased because of battery discharge.

Resource constraints: Mobile and ubiquitous devices have limited computational resources in terms of processor speed, storage capacity and network bandwidth. This is in part because energy consumption increases as we improve those characteristics. But also, making devices portable or embedding them into everyday physical objects entails making them physically small which, given limitations imposed by manufacturing processes, restricts the number of transistors in the nodes. Two issues spring from this: how to design algorithms that can execute on the node in reasonable time despite the resource limitations; and how to augment the node's meagre resources using resources in its environment.

Sensors and actuators: To enable their integration with the physical world – in particular, to make them context-aware – devices are equipped with *sensors* and *actuators*. Sensors are devices that measure physical parameters and supply their values to software. Conversely, actuators are software-controllable devices that affect the physical world. A wide variety of each type of component exists. On the sensor side, for example, there are sensors that measure position, orientation, load, and light and sound levels. Actuators include programmable air-conditioning controllers and motors. An important issue for sensors is accuracy, which is quite limited and so can lead to spurious behaviour, such as an inappropriate response to what turns out to be the wrong location. Inaccuracy is likely to remain a characteristic of devices that are cheap enough to deploy ubiquitously.

The devices described above sound somewhat exotic. However, not only are they commercially available but they are even mass-produced. Two examples are motes and camera phones.

Motes: Motes [Hill *et al*. 2000; www.xbow.com] are devices intended for autonomous operation in applications such as environmental sensing. They are designed to be embedded in an environment, programmed so that they wirelessly discover one another and transfer sensed values amongst themselves. If, for example, there is a forest fire, then one or more motes scattered around the forest could sense abnormally high temperatures and communicate those, via their peers, to a more high-powered device capable of communicating the situation to the emergency services. The most basic form of motes has a low-power processor (a microcontroller) that runs the TinyOS operating system [Culler *et al*. 2001] on internal flash memory; memory for data-logging; and a short-range, two-way 'Industrial, Scientific and Medical' (ISM) band radio transceiver. A variety of sensor modules may be added. Motes are also known as 'smart dust', reflecting the tiny size ultimately intended for these devices, although their size at the time of writing is around 6×3×1 cm, excluding battery pack and sensors. Smart-its provide similar functionality to motes in a similar form-factor [www.smart-its.org]. Section 16.4.2 discusses the uses of mote-like devices in wireless sensor networks.

Camera phones: Camera phones are a quite different example of a device in the systems we are considering. Their principal functions are human communication and imaging. But, running an operating system such as Symbian, they are programmable for quite a wide variety of applications. In addition to their wide-area data connectivity, they often have infrared (IrDA) or Bluetooth short-range wireless network interfaces that enable them to connect to one another, to PCs, and to sensing devices, such as GPS or other satellite navigation units for determining their location. Moreover, they may run software to recognize symbols such as barcodes from their camera images, making them sensors of 'coded-values' on physical objects such as products, which can be used to access associated services. For example, a user could use their camera phone to discover the specifications of a product in a shop from the barcode on its box [Kindberg 2002].

Volatile connectivity ◊ The devices of interest in this chapter all have some form of wireless connectivity, and may have several. The connection technologies (whether Bluetooth, WiFi, GPRS, etc.) vary in their nominal bandwidth and latency, in their energy costs, and in whether there are financial costs to communication. But the volatility of connectivity – the variability at runtime of the state of connection or disconnection between devices, and the quality of service between them – also has a strong impact on system properties.

Disconnection: Wireless disconnections are far more likely than wired disconnections. Many of the devices we have described are mobile, and so may exceed their operating distance from other devices or encounter radio occlusions between them, e.g. from buildings. Even when the devices are static, there may be moving users and vehicles that cause disconnection by occlusion. There is also the question of multi-hop wireless routing between devices. In *ad hoc routing*, a collection of devices communicate with one another without reliance on any other device: they collaborate to route all packets between themselves. Taking our example of motes in a forest, a mote might continue to be able to communicate with all other motes in immediate radio range, but fail to be able to communicate its

Figure 16.2 Examples of pre-configured versus spontaneous association

Pre-configured	Spontaneous
Service-driven: *email client and server*	Human-driven: *web browser and web servers* Data-driven: *P2P file-sharing applications* Physically-driven: *mobile and ubiquitous systems*

high-temperature reading to the emergency services, because of the failure of more distant motes through which all packets had to pass.

Variable bandwidth and latency: The factors that can lead to complete disconnection can also lead to highly varying bandwidth and latency, because they entail changing error rates. As the error rate increases, more and more packets are dropped. That leads intrinsically to low throughput rates. But the situation may be exacerbated by timeouts in higher-layer protocols. Timeout values are difficult to adapt to dramatically changing conditions. If they are too big compared to current error conditions, latency and throughput suffers. If they are too small, they may increase congestion and waste energy.

Spontaneous interoperation ◊ In a volatile system, components routinely change the set of components they communicate with, as they move or as other components appear in their environment. We use the term *association* for the logical relationship formed when at least one of a given pair of components communicates with the other over some well-defined period of time, and *interoperation* for their interactions during their association. Note that association is distinct from connectivity: two components (e.g. an email client on a laptop and an email server) may be currently disconnected while they remain associated.

In a smart space, associations change because components take advantage of opportunities to interact with local components. A simple example of such an opportunity is for a device to use a local printer wherever the device happens to be. Similarly, a device may want to offer services to clients in its local environment – such as a 'personal server' [Want *et al.* 2002] that the user wears (for example, on their belt), which supplies anonymized attributes about the user to an air-conditioning unit. That unit is then able to adjust the room conditions according to the user's preferences. Of course, certain static associations still make sense even in a volatile system; we have given the example of a laptop computer that travels with its owner around the world, but which only ever communicates with a fixed email server.

To place this type of association into a bigger picture of services on the Internet, Figure 16.2 shows examples of three types of spontaneous association (on the right), as compared with pre-configured associations (on the left).

Pre-configured associations are service-driven: that is, clients have a long-term need to use a specific service, and so they are pre-configured to be associated with it.

The effort of configuring the clients (including setting them up with the address of the required service) is small compared to the long-term value of using the particular service.

On the right-hand side of the figure are types of association that vary routinely, driven by a human operator, by the need for specific data, or by changing physical circumstances. We can regard associations between a web browser and web services as spontaneous and *human-driven*: the user makes dynamic and (from the system's point of view) unpredictable choices of link to click on and thus service instance to access. The web is a truly volatile system and important to its success is the fact that changing the associations typically involves negligible effort – the authors of web pages have done the configuration work.

Peer-to-peer applications on the Internet such as file-sharing programs are also volatile systems, but they are primarily *data-driven*. That data often originates from the human (e.g. the name of the content to be sought), but it is the value of the data provided to it that causes a peer to make associations with a peer it may never have associated with before and whose address was not formerly stored by it, via a data-based distributed discovery algorithm.

The mobile and ubiquitous systems in this chapter are distinguished by exhibiting largely *physically driven* spontaneity of associations. The associations are made and broken – sometimes by humans – according to the current physical circumstances of the components, in particular their proximity.

Lowered trust and privacy ◊   As Chapter 7 explained, security in distributed systems is ultimately based on trusted hardware and software – the trusted computing base. But trust in volatile systems is problematic because of spontaneous interoperation: what basis of trust can there be between components that are able to associate spontaneously? Components moving between smart spaces may belong to disparate individuals or organizations and have little or no prior knowledge of one another or of a trusted third party.

Privacy is a major issue for users, who may distrust systems because of their sensing capabilities. The presence of sensors in smart spaces means that it becomes possible to track users electronically on a potentially massive scale not seen before. In benefiting from context-aware services – as in the example of rooms that set the air conditioning according to the preferences of users within them – users may enable others to learn where they were and what they were doing there. To make matters worse, they may not always be aware that they are being sensed. Even if the user does not disclose their identity, it may be possible for others to learn it and so find out what a particular individual does – for example, by observing regular journeys between a home and a place of work, and correlating those with the use of a credit card somewhere in between.

16.2 Association

As explained above, devices are liable to appear in and disappear from smart spaces unpredictably. Despite this, volatile components need to interoperate – preferably without user intervention. In other words, a device that appears in a smart space needs to be able to bootstrap itself on the local network to enable communication with other devices, and associate appropriately in the smart space:

- Network bootstrapping. Typically, communication takes place over a local network. The device must first acquire an address on the local network (or register a pre-existing address such as a mobile IP address); it may also acquire or register a name.

- Association. Components on the device either associate to services in the smart space or provide services to components elsewhere in the smart space, or both.

Network bootstrapping ◊ There are well-established solutions to this problem of integrating a device on the network. Some of those solutions rely on servers accessible within the smart space. For example, a DHCP server (see Section 3.4.3) can supply an IP address and other networking and DNS parameters, which the device obtains by issuing a query to a well-known broadcast address. Servers in the smart space may also assign a unique domain name to the device; or if there is access to the open Internet then the device can use a dynamic DNS update service to register its new IP address against a static domain name.

A more interesting case is to assign networking parameters in the absence of any service infrastructure in the smart space or beyond it. That is desirable both to simplify the smart space and to avoid dependencies on services that might fail. The IPv6 standard includes a protocol for serverless address assignment. The Zero Configuration Networking working group of the IETF [www.zeroconf.org] is developing standards for serverless address assignment, domain name lookup, multicast address assignment, and discovery of services (see the next subsection). Apple's Rendezvous [www.apple.com] is a commercial implementation of much of that functionality. As with DHCP access, all such methods utilize broadcasts or multicasts over the local network using a well-known address. Any device can listen on or transmit to such an address, and only the devices' own network interfaces are involved.

The association problem and the boundary principle ◊ Once a device can communicate in the smart space, it is faced with the *association problem*: of how to associate appropriately within it. Solutions to the association problem must address two main aspects: scale and scope. First, there may be tens or even hundreds of devices per cubic metre within the smart space, and perhaps orders of magnitude more software components on those devices; with which of these, if any, should components on the appearing device interoperate, and how can the choice be made efficiently?

Second, how can we constrain the *scope* when solving that problem, so as to consider only components from the smart space – and *all* the components in the smart space – rather than the potential trillions of components that lie beyond? Scoping is partly but not only a type of scaling issue. A smart space typically has administrative and territorial boundaries, which can make a large difference to users and administrators. For example, if a device is to discover a service such as a printer in a hotel room, it must find a printer in its user's room, and not the room next door. Equally, if there is an appropriate printer in the user's room, then a solution should include it as a candidate for association.

The *boundary principle* is that smart spaces need to have system boundaries that correspond accurately to meaningful spaces as they are normally defined territorially and administratively [Kindberg and Fox 2001]. Those 'system boundaries' are system-defined criteria that scope but do not necessarily constrain association.

One attempt at a solution to the association problem is to use a discovery service, described next, with an account of Jini's discovery service. Discovery services are normally based on subnet multicast, which has the disadvantage that the subnet's reach may not coincide with the services that are available in a smart space – that they break the boundary principle – as we shall explain. Section 16.2.2 then describes some solutions that provide more accurately scoped associations by relying on physical parameters and human input.

16.2.1 Discovery services

Clients find out about the services provided in a smart space using a **discovery service**. A discovery service is a directory service (see Section 9.3) in which services in a smart space are registered and looked up by their attributes, but one whose implementation takes account of volatile system properties. First, the directory data required by a particular client – i.e., the set of service attributes against which queries are to be run – is determined at run time. The directory data is dynamically determined as a function of the client's context – in this case, the particular smart space where the queries take place. Second, there may be no infrastructure in the smart space to host a directory server. Third, services registered in the directory may spontaneously disappear. Fourth, the protocols used for accessing the directory need to be sensitive to the energy and bandwidth they consume.

Both *device discovery* and *service discovery* services exist; Bluetooth includes both. With device discovery, clients discover the names and addresses of co-present devices. Typically, they then choose an individual device on the basis of out-of-band information (such as selection by a human) and query it for the services it offers. On the other hand, a service discovery service is used where clients are not concerned with which device provides the service they need, but on the attributes of the service alone. This description will concentrate on service discovery services and, unless stated otherwise, that is what we mean by discovery services henceforth.

A discovery service has an interface for automatically registering and de-registering the services that are available for association, as well as an interface for clients to look up services from those that are currently available, so as to go on to associate with an appropriate service. Figure 16.3 gives a fictitious, simplified example of those interfaces. First, there are calls to register a service's availability with given address and attributes, and to manage its registration subsequently. Then there is a call to look up the services that match a specification of required attributes. Zero or more services may match the specification; each is returned with its address and attributes. Note that a discovery service does not enable association by itself: *service selection* – the choice of one service from the returned set – is also required. That may occur programatically, or by listing the matching services for a user to choose from.

Developments in discovery services include the Jini discovery service (see below), the service location protocol [Guttman 1999], the Intentional Naming System [Adjie-Winoto *et al.* 1999], the simple service discovery protocol, which is at the heart of the Universal Plug and Play initiative [www.upnp.org] and the Secure Service

Figure 16.3   The interface to a discovery service

Methods for service de/registration	Explanation
lease := register(address, attributes)	Register the service at the given address with the given attributes; a lease is returned
refresh(lease)	Refresh the lease returned at registration
deregister(lease)	Remove the service record registered under the given lease
Method invoked to look up a service	
serviceSet := *query(attributeSpecification)*	Return a set of registered services whose attributes match the given specification

Discovery Service [Czerwinski *et al.* 1999]. There are also link-layer discovery services such as that of Bluetooth.

The issues to be dealt with in the design of a discovery service are as follows:

- Low-effort, appropriate association. Ideally, appropriate associations would be made without any human effort. First, the set of services returned by the *query* operation (Figure 16.3) would be appropriate – they would be precisely the services existing in the smart space that matched the query. Second, service selection could be made programatically or with minimal human input so as to meet the users' needs.

- Service description and query language. The overall goal is to match services to clients' requests for services. That presupposes a language for describing available services, and one for expressing service requirements. The query and description languages have to agree (or be translatable); and their expressiveness has to keep pace with the development of new devices and services.

- Smart-space-specific discovery. We require a mechanism for devices to access an instance (or scope) of the discovery service that is appropriate to their current physical circumstances – a mechanism that doesn't rely on the device knowing the particular name or address for that service *a priori*. In practice, discovery services are related to a particular smart space only through the limited reach of multicast over a subnet that intersects with it, as we shall explain.

- Directory implementation. Logically, each instance of a discovery service involves a queryable directory of available services. There are several ways of implementing such a directory, with varying implications for network bandwidth, timeliness of service discovery, and energy consumption.

- Service volatility. Any service in a volatile system has to efficiently and gracefully handle the disappearance of a client. A discovery service has services as clients, and it needs to handle service disappearance appropriately.

As an example of association by discovery, consider an occasional or first-time visitor to a host organization or a hotel, who needs to print a document from a laptop. The user cannot reasonably be expected to have the names of particular local printers configured in their laptop, or to guess their names (such as *myrtle**titus*, and *lionel**frederick*). Rather than forcing the user to configure their machine while they visit, it would be preferable for the laptop to use the *query* call of a discovery service to find the set of available network printers that match the user's needs. A particular printer can be selected via interaction with the user or by consulting a record of the user's preferences.

The required attributes of the printing service may, for example, specify whether it is 'laser' or 'inkjet'; whether or not it provides colour printing; and its physical location with respect to the user (for example, the room number).

Correspondingly, services provide their address and attributes to the discovery service with the *register* call. For example, a printer (or a service that manages it) may register its address and attributes with the discovery service as follows:

> *serviceAddress=http://www.hotelDuLac.com/services/printer57; resource-Class=printer, type=laser, colour=yes, resolution=600dpi, location=room101*

The usual way to bootstrap access to the local discovery service at runtime without manual configuration is to use the reach of the local subnet; specifically, to multicast (or broadcast) queries to a well-known IP multicast address over the local subnet. The well-known IP multicast address is known *a priori* by all devices that need to access the discovery service. Discovery services based only on network reach are sometimes explicitly known as *network discovery services*.

Note that some networks such as Bluetooth use frequency-hopping and cannot communicate with all neighbouring devices simultaneously at a physical level. Bluetooth achieves discovery using a counterpart to 'well-known address': a well-known frequency-hopping sequence. Discoverable devices cycle through the frequencies more slowly than devices attempting to discover them, so that senders (discoverers) and receivers eventually coincide in frequency and establish communication.

There are several design choices when implementing a discovery service, which can have a considerable effect on the ways it can be used.

The first is whether the discovery service should be implemented by a *directory server*, or be serverless. A directory server holds a set of descriptions of services that have registered with it, and responds to clients issuing queries for services. Any component (server or client) wanting to use the local directory service issues a multicast request to locate it, and the directory server responds with its unicast address. The component then communicates with it point-to-point – saving the interruption of uninvolved devices that occurs with multicast communication. This works well in smart spaces that provide infrastructure. The directory service can often be run from mains power on a robust machine. But in simpler smart spaces such as basic meeting rooms, there may be no facilities for a directory server. In principle it would be possible to elect a server from whatever devices happened to be present (Section 12.3), but any such server might disappear spontaneously. This would lead to complexity in the implementation of clients of the discovery service, which then have to adapt to a changing registry server. Moreover, the overheads due to re-election may be great in a highly volatile system.

An alternative is *serverless discovery*, where the participating devices collaborate to implement a distributed discovery service, in lieu of a directory server. As with any distributed directory, there are two main implementation variants. In the *push* model, services multicast ('advertise') their descriptions regularly. Clients listen for the multicasts and run their queries against them, possibly caching descriptions in case they are needed later. In the *pull* model, clients multicast their queries. Devices providing services run the queries against their descriptions, and only respond with any descriptions that match. Clients repeat their queries at intervals if there is no response.

Both push and pull models have implications for bandwidth and energy usage. Every time a device issues a multicast message, bandwidth is consumed and all listening devices expend energy receiving the message. In a pure push model, devices need to advertise their services regularly so that appearing clients can discover them. But this is wasteful of bandwidth and energy if there are no clients needing to discover a particular service. And the time that an appearing client waits to hear about services has to be traded off against the bandwidth and energy costs, which increase with the frequency of advertisements.

In a pure pull model, a client can discover available services as soon as it appears. And there are no wasted multicasts if there are no discovery needs in a given interval. But the client may receive several responses when a single response would do. And no advantage is taken, by default, of requests bearing the same query – for frequently required services.

It is possible to design hybrid protocols that address the above shortcomings, and Exercise 16.2 deals with this.

A service may invoke the *deregister* call (Figure 16.3) before it disappears, but equally it may disappear spontaneously. Service volatility is handled in different ways according to the architecture of the directory implementation. A directory server needs to become aware as soon as possible after a registered service disappears, so that it does not give out its description misleadingly. That is normally accomplished using a general mechanism called *leases*. A lease is a temporary allocation of some resource by a server to a client, which can only be renewed by a further request from the client before the lease's deadline has expired. If the client fails to renew it (for example, with the *refresh* call of Figure 16.3), the server withdraws (and may reallocate) the resource. We introduced leases as part of Jini in Section 5.2.6; also DHCP servers use leases when allocating IP addresses. A directory server maintains a service's registration only if the service periodically communicates with the directory server to renew its lease on the entry. Here we see a similar trade-off of timeliness against bandwidth and energy consumption – the shorter the lease period, the faster will a service's disappearance be noticed, but the more networking and energy resources will be required. In a serverless architecture, no steps need be taken (except to clear stale entries in devices that cache services), since a service that has disappeared will no longer advertise itself; and a client using a pull-based protocol can only discover present services.

Jini ◊ Jini [Waldo 1999; Arnold *et al.* 1999] is a system designed to be used for mobile and ubiquitous systems. It is entirely Java-based – it assumes that Java virtual machines run in all of the computers, allowing them to communicate with one another by means

Figure 16.4   Service discovery in Jini

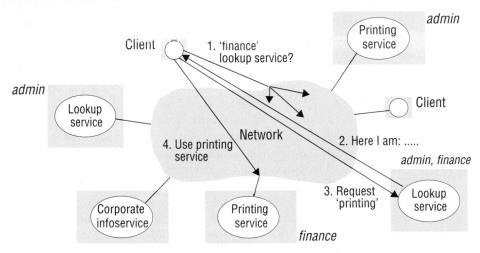

of RMI or events (see Chapter 5) and to download code as necessary. Here we describe Jini's discovery system.

The discovery-related components in a Jini system are *lookup* services, Jini services and Jini clients (see Figure 16.4). The *lookup* service implements what we have termed a discovery service, although Jini uses the term 'discovery' only for discovering the lookup service itself. The lookup service allows Jini services to register the services they offer, and Jini clients to request services that match their requirements. A Jini service, such as a printing service, may be registered with one or more lookup services. A Jini service provides, and the lookup services store, an object that provides the service, as well as the attributes of the service. Jini clients query lookup services to find Jini services that match their requirements; if a match is found, they download an object that provides access to the service from the lookup service. The matching of service offers to clients' requests can be based on attributes or on Java typing, for example allowing a client to request a colour printer for which it has the corresponding Java interface.

When a Jini client or service starts up, it sends a request to a well-known IP multicast address. Any lookup service that receives the request and can respond to it sends its address, enabling the requester to perform a remote invocation to look up or register a service with it (registration is called *joining* in Jini). Lookup services also announce their existence in datagrams sent to the same multicast address. Jini clients and services may also listen on the multicast address so that they learn about new lookup services.

There may be several instances of the lookup service reachable by multicast communication from a given Jini client or service. Every such service instance is configured with one or more *group* names such as 'admin', 'finance' and 'sales', which act as scoping labels. Figure 16.4 shows a Jini client discovering and using a printing service. The client requires a lookup service in the 'finance' group, so it multicasts a request bearing that group name (message 1 in the figure). Only one lookup service is bound to the 'finance' group (the service that is also bound to the 'admin' group), and that service responds (2). The lookup service's response includes its address, and the client communicates directly with it by RMI to locate all services of type 'printing' (3). Only one printing service has registered itself with that lookup service under the 'finance' group, and an object to access that particular service is returned. The client then uses the printing service directly, using the returned object (4). The figure also shows another printing service, one that is in the 'admin' group. There is also a corporate information service that is not bound to any particular group (and which may be registered with all lookup services).

Discussion of network discovery services ◊ The discovery services based only on network reach that we have just described – network discovery services – go some way toward solving the association problem. Efficient directory implementations exist, including ones that do not rely on infrastructure. In many cases, the number of clients and services that can be reached over a subnet is manageable in terms of computation and network costs, so scale is often not a problem. We have described measures to cope with system volatility.

But network discovery services raise two difficulties when looked at from the perspective of the boundary principle: the use of a subnet, and inadequacies in the way services are described.

The subnet may be a poor approximation to a smart space. First, network discovery may mistakenly include services that are not in the smart space. Consider a hotel room, for example. Transmissions based on radio-frequency (RF) signals such as 802.11 or Bluetooth will typically penetrate the walls to other guests' rooms. Following the Jini example, services could be logically partitioned by groups – one group per hotel room. But that begs the question of how the user's hotel room is to become a parameter for the discovery service. Second, network discovery may mistakenly discount services that are 'in' the smart space in the sense of being eligible for discovery there, but which are hosted beyond its subnet. The Cooltown case study (see Section 16.7.1) illustrates how non-electronic entities such as printed documents in a smart space may be associated with services hosted outside the smart space.

Moreover, network discovery services do not always lead to appropriate associations because the language used to describe services may be inadequate in two respects. First, discovery may be *brittle*: even slight variations in the service-description vocabulary used by disparate organizations could cause it to fail. For example, the hotel room has a service called 'Print' whereas the guest's laptop searches for 'Printing'. Variations in which human language is used for the vocabulary tend to exacerbate that problem. Second, there may be *lost opportunities* for service access. For example, there is a 'digital picture frame' on the hotel room's wall, which will display holiday snaps in JPEG format. The guest's camera has a wireless connection and produces images in that format but it has no description for the service – it has not been upgraded with that relatively recent development. So the camera is incapable of taking advantage of it.

16.2.2 Physical association

The shortcomings of network discovery systems can be solved to some extent using physical means, although the solutions often require a greater degree of human involvement. The following techniques have been developed.

Human input to scope discovery: ◊ This case is where a human provides input to the device to set the scope of discovery. A simple example of this would be to type in or select the smart space's identifier, such as the room number in the case of the hotel guest. The device can then use the identifier as an extra service 'group' attribute (as in Jini).

Sensing and physically constrained channels to scope discovery ◊ A less laborious possibility is for the user to employ a sensor on their device. For example, the smart space might have an identifier presented in identifier-encoding symbols called *glyphs* on documents and surfaces in the space – e.g. displayed on the TV screen in the guest's hotel room. The guest uses their camera phone or other imaging device to decode such a symbol, and the device uses the resultant identifier in the way we described for direct human input. Another possibility, for use with smart spaces where satellite navigation signals are available, is to use a sensor to obtain the position of the smart space in latitude and longitude coordinates, and to send those coordinates to a well-known wide-area service which returns the address of the local discovery service. However, given the inaccuracies in satellite navigation, that method may be less precise in identifying the smart space if there are other spaces close by.

Another technique that avoids human input is to use a *physically constrained channel* (see also Section 16.5.2) – communication channel that, to some degree of approximation, permeates only the physical span of the smart space. For example, in the guest room the TV could be playing background music at low volume, with a digital encoding of the room's identifier superimposed as an inaudible perturbation of the signal [Madhavapeddy *et al.* 2003]; or there could be an infrared transmitter (a beacon) in the room that propagates the identifier [Kindberg *et al.* 2002a]. Both of those channels are significantly attenuated by the materials at the boundaries of the room (assuming the doors and windows are closed).

Direct association ◊ The final set of techniques we shall consider here is for the human to use a physical mechanism to directly associate two devices, without using a discovery service. Typically, this is where the devices involved offer just one or a small set of human-selectable services. In each of the following techniques, the human enables the device they are carrying to learn the network address (e.g. Bluetooth or IP address) of a 'target' device.

Address-sensing: Using one device to sense the network address of the target device directly. Possibilities include: reading a glyph on the device that encodes its network address; or bringing one device very close to the other and using a short-range wireless channel to read its address. Two examples of those short-range channels are (1) Near Field Communication [www.nfc-forum.org] – a standard for bidirectional radio communication that spans several short ranges but has a variant for only up to about 3 centimetres; or (2) very short-range infrared transmissions.

Physical stimulus: Using a physical stimulus to cause the target device to send its address. An example here is to shine a digitally modulated laser beam (another physically constrained channel) onto the target device [Patel and Abowd 2003], thus transmitting its address to the target, which responds with its address.

Temporal or physical correlation: Using temporally or physically correlated stimuli to associate devices. The SWAP-CA specification [SWAP-CA 2002] for wireless networking in a home environment introduced a protocol, sometimes referred to as the two-button protocol, for humans to associate two wireless devices with each other. Each device listens on a well-known multicast address. The users press buttons on their respective devices more or less simultaneously, at which point the devices send their network address to the multicast address. It is unlikely that another round of this protocol will occur at the same time in the same subnet. The devices therefore associate using any address that arrives within a small interval of the button press. There is an interesting, if rarely practical, physical counterpart to this approach in which a user holds two devices in the same hand and shakes them together [Holmquist *et al.* 2001]. Each device has an accelerometer for sensing its state of motion. The device records the shaking pattern, computes an identifier from it, and multicasts that identifier together with its unicast address to a well-known multicast address. Only the two devices experiencing exactly that acceleration pattern – and within direct communication range – will recognize each other's identifier and hence learn each other's address.

16.2.3 Summary and perspective

This section has described the association problem for components in volatile systems, and some attempts at solving that problem ranging from network discovery to more human-supervised techniques. Mobile and ubiquitous systems raise unique difficulties because they are integrated with our everyday, messy physical world of spaces such as domestic rooms and offices, making it hard to scope the solutions. Humans tend to have strong territorial and administrative considerations in mind when they consider what is in a particular smart space and what is outside it. The boundary principle says that solutions to the association problem need to match the underlying physical spaces to a degree that is acceptable to humans. We have seen that some degree of human supervision is often entailed, because of the deficiencies of network discovery systems. The Cooltown case study (Section 16.7) describes a particular model of human involvement.

We have largely ignored scale as a factor in solutions to the association problem, on the basis that the world is broken up into smart spaces which, typically, are of manageable size. However, there is research into scalable discovery services – after all, some applications might consider the entire planet to be a smart space. An example is INS/Twine [Balazinska *et al.* 2002], which divides directory data between a collection of peer resolvers.

16.3 Interoperation

We have described ways in which two or more components in a volatile system come to be associated and now turn to the question of how they interoperate. Components associate on the basis of certain attributes or data that one or both of them possesses. But that leaves the questions of what protocol they use to communicate and, at a higher level, what programming model is best suited for interaction between them. This section deals with those questions.

Chapters 4 and 5 describe models for interoperation including various forms of inter-process communication, method invocation and procedure invocation. An implicit assumption underlying some of those models is that the interoperating components are designed to work together in a specific system or application, and that changes to the set of interoperating components are either a long-term configuration issue or a runtime error condition to be handled occasionally. But those assumptions are invalid in mobile and ubiquitous systems. Fortunately, as we explain in this section, some of the methods for interoperation from Chapters 4 and 5, in addition to some new methods, are better suited to those volatile systems.

Ideally, a component in a mobile or ubiquitous system could associate with varying classes of services, and not just a varying set of instances of the same service class. That is, it is best to avoid the 'lost opportunity' problem described in the previous section where, for example, a digital camera is unable to send its images to a digital picture frame, because it cannot interoperate with the frame's picture-consuming service.

Put another way, one goal for ubiquitous and mobile computing is that a component should have a reasonable chance of interoperating with a functionally compatible component, even if the latter is in a different type of smart space from the one for which it was originally developed. That entails some global agreement between software developers. Given the effort needed to reach agreement, it is best to minimize what needs to be agreed upon.

The main difficulty that stands in the way of volatile interoperation is software interface incompatibility. If, for example, a digital camera expects to invoke an operation *pushImage* and there is no such operation in the digital picture frame's interface, then they cannot interoperate – at least, not directly.

There are two main approaches to this problem. The first is to allow interfaces to be heterogeneous, but to adapt interfaces to one another. For example, if the digital picture frame were to have an operation *sendImage* with the same parameters and semantics as *pushImage*, then it would be straightforward to construct a component that acted as a proxy for the digital picture frame, converting the camera's *pushImage* invocation into a *sendImage* invocation for the picture frame.

However, it is very hard to realize this approach. Often the semantics of operations may vary as well as the syntax, and overcoming semantic incompatibility is in general difficult and error prone. Then there is the scale of the problem: if there are N interfaces, then potentially N^2 adaptors have to be written – and more and more interfaces will be created over time. Moreover, there is the question of how components are to acquire suitable interface adaptors as they re-associate in a volatile system. Components (or the devices that host them) cannot come pre-loaded with all possible N^2 adaptors, so the correct adaptor has to be determined and loaded at runtime. Despite all of these difficulties, there is research into how to make interface adaptation practical. See, for example, Ponnekanti and Fox [2004].

Another approach to interoperability is to constrain interfaces to be identical in syntax across as wide a class of components as possible. That may sound unrealistic at first but in fact it has been widely and successfully practised for several decades. The simplest example is pipes in UNIX. A pipe has only two operations, *read* and *write*, for the transport of data between components (processes) at its two ends. Over the years, UNIX programmers have created many programs that can read data from a pipe and/or write data to a pipe. Because of their standardized interfaces and generic text-processing functionalities, the output of any of those programs can be fed into the input of another; users and programmers have found many useful ways of combining programs in that way – programs that were written independently, without knowledge of the specific functionality of the other programs.

A yet more successful example of a system that achieves a high degree of interoperability through a fixed interface is the web. The set of methods defined by the HTTP specification (see Section 4.4) is small and fixed; typically, a web client uses only the GET and POST operations to access a web server. The consequence of the fixed interface is that a relatively stable piece of software – often the browser – is able to interoperate with an evolving set of services. What changes between services is the type and values of the content that is exchanged, and the server's processing semantics. But every interaction is still a GET or POST operation.

16.3.1 Data-oriented programming for volatile systems

We shall call systems that use an unvarying service interface, such as UNIX pipes and the web, *data-oriented* (or, equivalently, *content-oriented*). The term is chosen in distinction to *object-oriented*. A component in a data-oriented system can be invoked by any other component that knows the fixed interface. An object or collection of procedures, on the other hand, has one of a widely varying set of possible interfaces and can only be invoked by just those components that know its particular interface. Distributing and exploiting an indefinite number of specialized interface definitions is a much more problematic proposition than publishing and using one interface specification, such as the HTTP specification. That helps explain why the most widely used, heterogeneous distributed system we have known is the web, rather than a similarly scaled collection of, say, CORBA objects.

But the flexibility of data-oriented systems is traded off against robustness. It does not always make sense for two particular components to interoperate, and yet there is little basis for programs to check for compatibility. In an object- or procedure-oriented system, programs can at least check that their particular interface signatures match. But a data-oriented component can enforce compatibility only by verifying the type of data that is sent to it. It must either do that through standardized data-type descriptors supplied as metadata (such as MIME types for web content), or by checking the data values passed to it; for example, JPEG data begins with recognizable header information.

We now examine some programming models that have been used for volatile systems because of their data-oriented interoperability features. We begin with two models for interoperation between indirectly associated components: event systems and tuple spaces. We go on to describe two designs for interoperation between directly associated devices: JetSend and Speakeasy.

Event systems ◊ We introduced event systems [Bates *et al.* 1996] in Section 5.4. Event systems provide instances of event services. Each system offers a fixed, generic interface by which components called *publishers* publish structured data known as events and, correspondingly, components called *subscribers* receive events. Each event service is associated with some physical or logical scope of event delivery. Subscribers only receive ('handle') events that (1) are published at the same event service and (2) match their registered specifications of which events they are interested in.

Events are a natural programming paradigm for announcing and handling the changes experienced by components while they are in a volatile system or when they move between volatile systems. Events can be constructed to specify new states of affairs, such as changes in a device's location. A recent example of a system that uses events for ubiquitous computing is *one.world* [Grimm 2004]. But events have been used in ubiquitous systems from early in their development. In the Active Badge system [Harter and Hopper 1994], applications could subscribe to location-change events that occur when users move around. Location events also present the issue of detecting patterns of events that occur together or in close succession, also known as *composite events*. For example, consider the problem of detecting when two users are co-located, when all that is known is when individual users enter or leave a particular location. A location system does not detect such occurrences by itself: there is a need for rules that specify, in terms of primitive events such as 'Arrive(user, location, time)' and 'Leave(user, location, time)', when composite events such as co-location occur.

Although the publishing, subscription and handling interface for event is a given (with relatively minor variations between event systems), publishers and subscribers can interoperate correctly only if they agree on the event service they use (there may be many instances) and the types and attributes of events – their syntax and semantics. Thus, event systems shift rather than solve the problem of ubiquitous interoperability. For a given component to interoperate in a wide variety of smart spaces would require standards for event types, and events would ideally be described in a programming-language-independent markup language such as XML.

On the other hand, event producers and consumers do not need to identify one another. That can be an advantage in a volatile system, where keeping track of which other components are present could be difficult. Two components come to communicate by virtue of publishing and subscribing to matching events, and by agreement on the scope of event delivery – in other words, they associate indirectly.

The scope of event delivery is itself an interesting topic in mobile and ubiquitous systems. As with service discovery, the question arises of how the scope of an event service is related to the physical extent of the smart space. This point is the topic of Exercise 16.7.

Tuple spaces ◊ Like event systems, tuple spaces are also a mature programming paradigm that has found application in volatile systems. Components use a fixed, generic interface to add and retrieve structured data called tuples to and from a tuple space (see also Section 18.2.1). Tuple space systems allow application-specific tuples to be exchanged, and the basis for association and interoperation is the components' agreement about structures for tuples and values contained within them.

As an example, a digital camera could discover the tuple space for the local smart space – a hotel room, say – and place its images in the tuple space using a tuple such as:

< 'The leaning tower', 'image/jpeg', <jpeg data>>

The designers of the camera software have a model only of a tuple space into which images may be placed in a certain format, and no model of the particular forms of processing to which those images will be subject.

Correspondingly, an image-consuming device such as a digital picture frame could be programmed to discover its local tuple space and to attempt to retrieve from it tuples with the form of the following template, in which '*' represents a wildcard value:

<*, 'image/jpeg', *>

The camera's tuple matches the template required by the picture frame – it has three fields and its second field contains the required MIME type string. The picture frame will thus retrieve the camera's tuple and can display the image and associated title. As another example, the user could have activated a printer to consume the image from the tuple space and print it.

Several programming systems based on tuple spaces have been developed specifically for mobile and ubiquitous systems. Despite its name, the *event heap* [Johanson and Fox 2004] is a tuple-based programming system developed for a type of smart space known as the 'iRoom', which contains multiple large displays and other infrastructure devices. To each iRoom there is a corresponding event heap, which components in the iRoom – including those on mobile devices brought into the room – can discover or can be configured to use. Components interoperate by exchanging tuples via the event heap, and it provides a level of indirection that facilitates dynamic association between the devices. An example is where a remote control device kept in the iRoom can be associated dynamically to different displays. For example, a video can be presented on any of several large displays. When a user presses the 'pause' button on the remote control, the control places a 'pause' tuple in the event heap. Whatever device is displaying the video is programmed to look for and retrieve 'pause' tuples, and thus respond. The remote control could be made to work with an audio output device in exactly the same way, without reprogramming it.

The LIME system (Linda in a Mobile Environment) [Murphy *et al.* 2001] was developed as a programming model for mobile systems. In LIME, participating devices host tuple spaces and there is no reliance on infrastructure. Each device hosts its own tuple space. LIME shares the individual tuple spaces when their host devices become associated, forming the union of the sets of tuples in the aggregate of shared spaces. This could be used for service discovery, for example. A component that requires a service could be programmed to attempt to retrieve a tuple describing an instance of the service it requires; a device implementing a corresponding service would be programmed to place a descriptive tuple in its local tuple space. When the two became connected, LIME would establish the match and the would-be client would obtain the service's details.

While the LIME model is simple to state, it is non-trivial to implement suitable consistency semantics in the face of arbitrary connections and disconnections. LIME's implementors made arguably unrealistic assumptions to simplify their design, including: that multicast connectivity holds uniformly between the devices whose tuple spaces are aggregated; and that connections and disconnections to and from an aggregated set are serialized and orderly.

Comparing event systems and tuple spaces: If we identify 'event' with 'tuple' and 'specification of interest' with 'tuple-matching template', there is a correspondence between the two models of interoperation. Both provide a level of indirection that is useful for volatile systems since the identity of the components that produce and consume events or tuples are hidden from one another by default. The set of components can thus change transparently. However, there are important differences. First, the event model is exclusively asynchronous, whereas tuple space systems supply a synchronous operation to retrieve a matching tuple. It can be easier to program with synchronous operations. On the other hand, it is a bad idea to expect that a particular component (for example, an image-producing device that has been dynamically encountered) will eventually supply a matching tuple, since disconnection may occur at any time.

The second important difference is the lifetime of events and tuples. By default, an event does not outlast its propagation between publishers and subscribers. A tuple in a tuple space, however, may outlast the component that placed it there – and any component that reads (as opposed to destructively consumes) it. That persistence can be an advantage; for example, the batteries in a user's camera might fail after they have uploaded pictures to a hotel room's tuple space but before they have assigned them to another device. At the same time, persistence can be a disadvantage: what if an uncontrollable set of devices places tuples in a space, but they are never consumed because the components expected to consume them have become disconnected? The set of tuples in such a space might grow uncontrollably. Without global knowledge of a volatile set of components, it would be impossible to determine which tuples were garbage.

The designers of the event heap recognized the persistence problem for iRooms. They chose to allow tuples to expire (that is, to be garbage-collected) after being in an event heap for a specified time, which is usually chosen to correspond with a human interaction timespan. That prevents, for example, an unconsumed *pause* event from a remote control to cause a nuisance when a user tries to play a video the next day.

Direct device interoperation ◊ The previous programming models were for interoperation between indirectly associated components. JetSend and Speakeasy are systems designed for interoperation between two devices that a human has brought into direct association.

JetSend: The JetSend protocol [Williams 1998] was designed for interaction between appliances such as cameras, printers, scanners and TVs. JetSend was explicitly designed to be data-oriented, so that no appliance had to be loaded with specialized drivers according to the specific devices it would interact with. For example, a JetSend camera can send an image to a JetSend image-consuming device such as a printer or TV, regardless of the specific functionality of the consumer. The central generic operation between connected JetSend devices is to *synchronize* the state that one presents to the other. That means transferring the state, in a format over which the devices negotiate. For example, an image-producing device such as a scanner could synchronize with an image-consuming device such as a digital picture frame by consuming an image from the producer in JPEG format, chosen from several image formats that the producer could provide. The same scanner might equally synchronize with a TV, perhaps using a different image format.

JetSend's designers recognized that their synchronization operation benefited only simple interoperation – essentially, data transfer – between heterogeneous devices. That begs the question of how to achieve more complex interactions between specific devices. For example, how should a choice be made between monochrome and colour when transferring an image to be printed? By assumption, the source device has no driver for a specific printer. And it is not possible for that device to be programmed *a priori* with the semantics of any arbitrary device (including devices yet to be invented) that it might connect with. The JetSend answer to that problem was to rely on a human to select the specific functions of the target device (say a printer), using a user interface specified by the target device but rendered on her source device (say a camera). That is how interoperation happens routinely on the web, as users interact with highly heterogeneous services via their browser: each service they interact with sends its interface in the form of mark-up script to the browser, which renders it to the user as a generic set of widgets, and without knowledge of the service's specific semantics. Web services (see Chapter 19) are an attempt to replace the human by programs even for complex interactions.

Speakeasy: The Speakeasy project [Edwards *et al.* 2002] later applied the same design principles as JetSend to device-device interoperation, but with one difference: they utilize mobile code. There are two motivations for using mobile code. The first is that a device such as a printer can send any user interface to a user of another device such as a PDA. A mobile-code implementation of a user interface can perform local processing such as input validation; and it can provide interaction modes not available in user interfaces that have to be specified in a mark-up language. However, against this advantage has to be set the implications for security of executing mobile code, which requires sophisticated protection mechanisms against trojan horses; and the resource implications of running mobile code on a virtual machine as opposed to processing much more restricted mark-up script.

The second motivation for mobile code in device interoperation is optimization of data transfer. While Speakeasy's mobile code has to work within the constraints of the host device's API, it may perform arbitrary interactions with the remote device that sent it. Thus, for example, the mobile code can implement an optimized protocol for transferring content that is specific to the type of content – e.g. video could be compressed on the fly before transmission. By contrast, JetSend can use only predefined content transfer protocols.

16.3.2 Indirect associations and soft state

When a service is resourced well enough to be highly available (such as an infrastructure service), then it makes sense for components to associate with it explicitly – that is, to learn its address. When components later use that address to interoperate with the service – say, ten minutes after association – then they can reasonably expect it to be reachable still and to respond. However, in general, system volatility makes it undesirable to rely on a service provided by a particular component since that component could leave or fail at any time. One lesson from that distinction is that it is useful for programmers to be told which services are highly available, and which are volatile. In addition, to cope with volatility, they need to be provided with programming techniques that do not involve reliance on a specific component.

Some of the above examples of data-oriented programming systems involved indirect, anonymous associations. Specifically, components that interoperate via an event system or tuple space do not necessarily know one another's names or addresses. As long as the event service or the tuple space persist, the individual components can come and go and be replaced. Care is needed to maintain the correct operation of the system overall, but at least the programmers of the components do not have to manage individual associations with routinely disappearing peers.

An example of a client-server system that uses indirect association is the Intentional Name System (INS) [Adjie-Winoto *et al.* 1999]. Components issue requests that specify the attributes of the required service, the operation to be invoked and its parameters. The components do not need to specify the name or address of an instance of the required service, because the INS automatically routes the operation and parameters to an appropriate – e.g. local – service instance that matches the required attributes. Since successive operations directed to the same attribute specification could be handled by different server components, the INS assumes that those servers are stateless, or replicate their state using one of the techniques described in Chapter 15.

That leads to a general question: how are programmers supposed to manage state in a volatile system? The replication techniques from Chapter 15 assume a redundancy of resources, which may not be available in a volatile system – at least, not continuously. The replication techniques also entail extra communication that may not be practical because of the associated energy consumption and performance degradation.

Lamport's 'Part-time Parliament' algorithm [1998] provides a way of reaching distributed agreement despite volatility – the participating processes are assumed to disappear and reappear regularly and independently. However, the algorithm depends on each process having access to its own persistent store.

By contrast, some implementations use *soft state* to provide more relaxed but still useful consistency guarantees, even in the absence of continuously available persistent storage. Clark [Clark 1988] introduced the notion of soft state as a way of managing the configuration of Internet routers despite failures. The collection of routers is a volatile system that has to continue to function even though no routers in the system can be assumed always to be available. The definition of soft state has been the subject of debate [Raman and McCanne 1999], but broadly speaking it is data that provides a hint (that is, it might be stale and should not be relied upon for its strict currency) and, most importantly, the sources of soft state automatically update it. Some discovery systems (Section 16.2) exemplify the use of soft state to manage the collection of service registration entries. First, the entries are only hints – there may be an entry for a service that has disappeared. Second, the entries are automatically updated by multicasts from services – to add new entries and keep existing entries current.

16.3.3 Summary and perspective

This section has described models of interoperation between components in volatile systems. If each smart space was to develop its own programming interface, then the benefits of mobility would be limited. If a component did not originate in a given smart space but moved there, the only way it could interoperate with services within the smart space would be via a way of adapting its interface spontaneously to that of its new surroundings. Achieving that would require very sophisticated runtime support, which is as yet unrealized outside a few examples in the laboratory.

A different approach, described through several examples above, is data-oriented programming. On the one hand, the Web has shown the extensibility and mass applicability of that paradigm. On the other hand, there is no 'silver bullet' that will solve all of the problems of interoperation for volatile systems. Data-oriented systems trade agreement on the set of functions in an interface against agreement on the types of data that are passed as arguments to those functions. While XML (see Section 4.3.3) is sometimes touted as a way of facilitating data interoperation by enabling data to be 'self-describing', in fact it merely provides a framework for expressing structure and vocabulary. Of itself, XML has nothing to contribute to what is a semantic problem. Some authors consider the 'Semantic Web' [www.w3.org XX] to be a possible place holder for a future solution.

16.4 Sensing and context-awareness

The foregoing sections have concentrated on aspects of the volatility of mobile and ubiquitous systems. This section will concentrate on the other chief characterization of those systems: that of being integrated with the physical world. Specifically, it will consider architectures for processing data collected from sensors, and context-aware systems that can respond to their (sensed) physical circumstances. The sensing of location, an important physical parameter, will be examined in more detail.

Since users and the devices we are considering are often mobile, and since the physical world presents different opportunities for rich interactions across locations and times, their physical circumstances are often relevant as a determinant of system behaviour. The Active Badge system provides a historical example: the location of a user – that is, the location of the badge they wore – was used to identify which phone their calls should be routed to [Want *et al.* 1992], in the days before mobile phones. The context-aware braking system of a car could adjust its behaviour according to whether the road conditions are icy. A personal device could automatically harness resources detected in its environment, such as a large display.

The **context** of an entity (person, place or thing, whether electronic or otherwise) is an aspect of its physical circumstances of relevance to system behaviour. That includes relatively simple values such as the location; the time; the temperature; the identity of an associated user, e.g. one operating a device, or of users nearby; the presence and state of an object such as another device, e.g. a display. Context can be codified and acted upon through rules, such as 'If the user is Fred and he is in an IQ Labs meeting room, and if there is a display within 1m, then show information from the device on the display – unless a non-IQ Labs employee is present'. Context is also taken to include more complex attributes such as the user's activity. For example, a context-aware phone that has to decide whether to ring requires answers to questions such as: Is the user in a cinema watching a film or are they chatting to their friends before the screening?

16.4.1 Sensors

The determination of a contextual value begins with sensors, which are combinations of hardware and/or software used to measure contextual values. Some examples are:

Location, velocity and orientation. satellite navigation (for example, GPS) units for providing global coordinates and velocities; accelerometers to detect movement; magnetometers and gyroscopes to provide orientation data.

Ambient conditions: thermometers; sensors that measure light intensity; microphones for sound intensity.

Presence: sensors that measure physical load, e.g. to detect the presence of a person on a chair or walking across a floor; devices that read electronic identifiers on tags brought near to them, such as *RFID* (Radio Frequency IDentification) readers [Want 2004], or infrared readers such as those used to sense active badges; software used to detect key presses on a computer.

The above categories are meant only as examples of sensor use for particular purposes. A given sensor may be put to various purposes. For example, the presence of humans could be detected using microphones in a meeting room; an object's location could be determined by detecting the presence of its active badge in a known place.

An important aspect of a sensor is its error model. All sensors produce values with some degree of error. Some sensors, e.g. thermometers, can be manufactured so that the errors fall within the bounds of a fairly well known tolerance, and with a known (e.g. Gaussian) distribution. Others, such as satellite navigation units, have complicated error modes that depend on their current circumstances. First, they may fail to produce a value at all in certain circumstances. Satellite navigation units are dependent on the set of satellites currently visible. They may not work at all inside buildings, whose walls may attenuate the satellite signals too much for the unit to operate. Second, the calculation of the unit's location depends on dynamic factors including satellite positions, the existence of nearby occlusions, and ionospheric conditions. Even outside buildings, a unit will typically provide different values at different times for the same location, with only a best-effort estimate of the current accuracy. Near to buildings or other tall objects that occlude or reflect radio signals, just enough satellites may be visible to produce a reading, but the accuracy may be low and the reading may even be entirely spurious.

A useful way to state a sensor's error behaviour is to quote an accuracy that it reaches for a specified proportion of measurements, for example: 'Within the given area, the satellite navigation unit was found to be accurate to within 10m for 90% of measurements'. Another approach is to state a *confidence* value for a particular measurement – a number (usually between 0 and 1) chosen according to uncertainties encountered in deriving the measurement.

16.4.2 Sensing architectures

Salber *et al.* [1999] identify four functional challenges to be overcome in designing context-aware systems:

Integration of idiosyncratic sensors. Some of the sensors needed for context-aware computing are unusual in their construction and programming interfaces. Specialized knowledge may be needed to correctly deploy them in the physical scenario of interest (e.g. where should accelerometers be attached to measure the user's arm gestures?); and there may be system issues such as the availability of drivers for standard operating systems.

Abstracting from sensor data. Applications require abstractions of contextual attributes, to avoid concern with the peculiarities of individual sensors. The problem is that even sensors that can be put to similar purposes typically provide different raw data. For example, a given location may either be sensed as a latitude/longitude pair by a satellite navigation sensor, or sensed as the string 'Joe's Café' read from a nearby infrared source. Either, both or neither might be what the application needs to function. There needs to be agreement on the meaning of contextual attributes, and software to infer those attributes from raw sensor values.

Sensor outputs may need to be combined. Reliably sensing a phenomenon may entail combining values from several error-prone sources. For example, detecting the presence of a person might require each of: a microphone (to detect voice – but nearby sounds might interfere), floor pressure sensors (to detect human movement – but different users' patterns are hard to distinguish), and video (to detect human forms – but facial features are hard to distinguish). Combining sensor sources to reduce errors is known as *sensor fusion*. Equally, an application may require output from sensors of different types in order to gather several contextual attributes that it needs to operate. For example, a context-aware PDA that decides whether to project its data on a nearby display requires data from different sensor sources, including ones to detect who and which devices are present, and one or more to sense the location.

Context is dynamic. A context-aware application typically needs to respond to changes in context, and not simply to read a snapshot of it. For example, the context-aware PDA needs to blank its data from the room's display if a non-employee enters, or if Fred (the device's owner) leaves the room.

Researchers have devised various software architectures to support context-aware applications while dealing with some or all of the above issues. We give examples of architectures for situations in which the set of available sensors is more or less known and static, and architectures for determining contextual attributes from volatile collections of sensors – where non-functional requirements such as energy-saving also become prominent.

Sensing in the infrastructure ◊ Active badge sensors were originally deployed in the laboratory of Olivetti Research in Cambridge, England, at known, fixed locations in the building. One of the original context-aware applications was as an aid for a telephone receptionist. If someone called for, say, Roy Want, the receptionist would look for Roy's room location on the screen, and thus put the call through to an appropriate extension. The system determined Roy's location from information about where the badge he wore was last sensed, and displayed that information to the receptionist. Systems for processing active badge data and other contextual data were refined at Olivetti Research Labs and at Xerox PARC. Harter and Hopper [1994] describe an entire system for processing location events. Schilit *et al.* [1994] also describe a system that can process

Figure 16.5   The *IdentityPresence* widget class of the Context Toolkit

Attributes (accessible by polling)	Explanation
Location	Location the widget is monitoring
Identity	ID of the last user sensed
Timestamp	Time of the last arrival
Callbacks	
PersonArrives(location, identity, timestamp)	Triggered when a user arrives
PersonLeaves(location, identity, timestamp)	Triggered when a user leaves

active badge sensing events, through what they call *context-triggered actions*. For example, the specification:

> *Coffee   Kitchen   arriving   'play -v 50 /sounds/rooster.au'*

would cause a sound to be played whenever a badge was sensed arriving at the sensor mounted by the coffee machine in the kitchen.

The Context Toolkit [Salber *et al.* 1999] is an example of a system architecture for more general context-aware applications than those based around a specific technology such as active badges. It was the designers of the Context Toolkit who stated the four challenges for context-aware systems listed above. Their architecture follows the model of how graphical user interfaces are constructed from re-usable widget libraries, which hide most of the concerns of dealing with the underlying hardware – and much of the interaction management – from the application developer. The context toolkit defines *context widgets*. Those re-usable software components present an abstraction of some type of context attribute while hiding the complexity of the actual sensors used. For example, Figure 16.5 shows the interface to an *IdentityPresence* widget. It provides contextual attributes to software polling the widget and it also raises callbacks when the contextual information changes (a user arrives or leaves). As indicated above, the presence information could be derived from any of several combinations of sensors in a given implementation; the abstraction enables the application writer to ignore those details.

Widgets are constructed from distributed components. *Generators* acquire raw data from sensors such as floor pressure sensors, and provide that data to widgets. Widgets use the services of *interpreters*, which abstract contextual attributes from the generator's low-level data, deriving higher-level values such as the identity of a person who is present from their distinctive footsteps. Finally, widgets called *servers* provide further levels of abstraction by collecting, storing and interpreting contextual attributes from other widgets. For example, a *PersonFinder* widget for a building could be constructed from the *IdentityPresence* widgets for each room in the building (Figure 16.6), which in turn could be implemented using footstep interpretation from floor

Figure 16.6   A *PersonFinder* widget constructed using *IdentityPresence* widgets

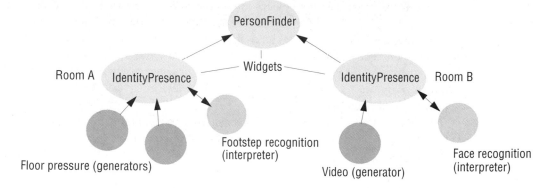

pressure readings or face recognition from video capture. The *PersonFinder* widget encapsulates the complexity of a building for the application writer.

Looked at in relation to the four challenges presented above that the Context Toolkit's designers stated, their architecture does accommodate a variety of sensor types; it is geared towards the production of abstract contextual attributes from raw sensor data; and, through polling or call-backs, a context-aware application can learn about changes in its context. However, the toolkit goes only a limited way towards a practical solution. It does not of itself help users and programmers to integrate idiosyncratic sensors; neither does it solve any of the hard problems inherent in the processes of interpretation and combination for a specific case.

Wireless sensor networks ◊   We have discussed architectures for applications in which the set of sensors is relatively stable – for example, the sensors are installed in rooms in a building, often with external power and wired network connections. We now turn to cases where the set of sensors forms a volatile system. A **wireless sensor network** consists of a (typically large) number of small, low-cost devices or *nodes*, each with facilities for sensing, computing and wireless communication [Culler *et al.* 2004]. It is a special case of an **ad hoc network**: the nodes are physically arranged more or less randomly, but they can communicate over multiple wireless hops between their peers. An important design goal for these networks is to function without any global control; each node bootstraps itself by discovering its wireless neighbours and communicating via them alone. Section 3.5.2 describes *ad hoc* configurations of 802.11 networks; but lower-power technologies such as ZigBee (IEEE 802.15.4) are more relevant here.

One reason why nodes do not communicate in a single hop to all other nodes, but instead communicate directly only with nodes nearby, is that wireless communication is costly in power consumption, which increases as the square of radio range. The other main reason for restricting the range of individual radios is to reduce network contention.

Wireless sensor networks are designed to be added to an existing natural or built environment, and to function independently of it, i.e. without reliance on infrastructure. Given their limited radio and sensing range, the nodes are installed at a sufficient density to make it probable both that multihop communication will be possible between any pair of nodes, and that significant phenomena can be sensed.

For example, consider devices placed throughout a forest, whose job is to monitor for fires and perhaps other environmental conditions such as the presence of animals. These nodes are very much the devices introduced in Section 16.1.1. They each have sensors attached, e.g. for temperature, sound and light; they run on batteries; and they communicate with other devices in a peer-to-peer fashion via short-range radio communication. The volatility stems from the fact that these devices can fail due to battery exhaustion or accidents such as fires; and their connectivity may change due to node failures (nodes relay packets between other nodes) or environmental conditions affecting radio propagation.

Another example is where the nodes are attached to vehicles to monitor traffic and road conditions. A node that has observed a poor condition can relay information about it via nodes on passing vehicles. With sufficient overall connectivity, this system can warn other nearby drivers headed in the direction of the problem. Here the volatility arises principally because of the nodes' movement, which rapidly changes each node's state of connectivity with other nodes. This is an example of a *mobile ad hoc network*.

In general, wireless sensor networks are dedicated to an application-specific purpose that amounts to detecting certain *alarms* – conditions of interest such as fires or poor road conditions. At least one more powerful device, a *root node*, is usually included in the network, for longer-range communication with a conventional system that reacts to the alarms, for example by calling the emergency services when there is a fire.

One approach to software architectures for sensor networks is to treat them similarly to conventional networks by separating the network layer from higher layers. In particular, it is possible to adapt existing routing algorithms to the graph of nodes as they dynamically discover themselves to be connected by their direct radio links, with each node able to act as a router for communications from other nodes. Adaptive routing, which attempts to accommodate the volatility of the network, has been the subject of much study and Milanovic *et al.* [2004] provide an overview of some techniques.

However, limiting concern to the network layer raises issues. First, adaptive routing algorithms are not necessarily tuned to low energy (and bandwidth) consumption. Second, volatility undermines some of the assumptions in traditional layers *above* the network layer. An alternative, first-principles approach to software architectures for wireless sensor networks is driven by two main requirements: energy conservation, and continuous operation despite volatility. Those two factors lead to three main architectural features: in-network processing, disruption-tolerant networking, and data-oriented programming models.

In-network processing: Not only is wireless communication absolutely costly in energy consumption, but it is relatively expensive compared to processing. Pottie and Kaiser [2000] calculated energy consumption and found that a general-purpose processor could execute 3 million instructions for the same amount of energy (3J) used to transmit 1 Kbit of data 100m by radio. So, in general, processing is preferable to communication: it is better to spend some processor cycles determining whether communication is (yet) necessary, rather than to blindly transmit sensed data. Indeed, that is why the nodes in sensor networks have a processing capability – otherwise, they could have consisted simply of sensing and communication modules that would send sensed values to root nodes for processing.

The phrase *in-network* processing refers to processing within the sensor network; that is, on the network nodes. The nodes in a sensor network perform tasks such as: aggregating or averaging values from nearby nodes so as to examine values for an area rather than a single sensor; filtering out data of no interest or repeated data; examining data to detect alarms; and switching sensors on or off according to the values being sensed. For example, if low-power light sensors indicate the possible presence of animals (due to the casting of shadows), then the nodes near to where the shadows were cast could switch on their higher-power sensors such as microphones to try to detect animal sounds. That scheme enables the microphones to be turned off otherwise, to conserve energy.

Disruption-tolerant networking: The end-to-end argument (Section 2.2.1) has been an important architectural principle for distributed systems. However, in volatile systems such as sensor networks, it may be that no end-to-end path exists continuously for long enough to achieve an operation such as the movement of data in bulk across a system. The terms *Disruption Tolerant Networking* and *Delay Tolerant Networking* are used for protocols to achieve higher-layer transfers across volatile (and typically heterogeneous) networks [www.dtnrg.org]. The techniques are intended not only for sensor networks but also other volatile networks such as interplanetary communication systems needed for space research [www.ipnsig.org]. Rather than relying on continuous connectivity between two fixed endpoints, communication becomes opportunistic: data are transferred as and when they can be, and nodes take on successive responsibilities to move data in a store-and-forward fashion until an end-to-end goal such as bulk transport has been attained. The unit of transfer between nodes is known as a *bundle* [Fall 2003], which contains a source's application data and data describing how to manage and process it both at the endpoint and at intermediate nodes. For example, a bundle might be transferred with hop-by-hop reliable transports; once a bundle has been handed over, the recipient node assumes responsibility for its subsequent delivery over the next hop – and so on. This procedure does not rely on any continuous route; also resource-poor nodes are relieved from storing the data as soon as they have transferred it to the next hop. To guard against failure, data can be forwarded redundantly to several neighbouring nodes.

Data-oriented programming models: Turning to interoperation in the application layers, data-oriented techniques including *directed diffusion* and *distributed query processing*, described shortly, have been developed for applications of sensor networks. These techniques recognise the need for in-network processing by incorporating methods for distributing the processing across the nodes. Moreover, the techniques recognize the volatility of sensor networks by eliminating node identities – and any other names for components such as processes or objects associated with a node. As we discussed in Section 16.3.2, any program that relies on the continuous existence of a node or a component will not work robustly in a volatile system, since there is a significant chance that communication with that node or component will become impossible.

In *directed diffusion* [Heidemann *et al.* 2001], the programmer specifies *interests*, which are declarations of tasks injected into the system at certain nodes called *sinks*. For example, a node might express an interest in the presence of animals. Each interest contains attribute-value pairs, which are the 'names' of the nodes that will perform the task. Thus, nodes are referred to not through their identity but through characteristics

Figure 16.7   Directed diffusion

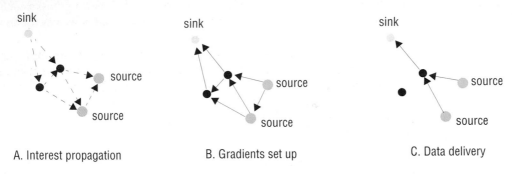

A. Interest propagation   B. Gradients set up   C. Data delivery

required to perform the required task, such as values in a certain range that are being sensed there.

The runtime system propagates interests from a sink through the network in a process called *diffusion* (Figure 16.7A). The sink forwards the interest to neighbouring nodes. Any node that receives an interest stores a record of it, along with information needed to pass data back to the sink node, before propagating it further in the search for nodes that match the interest. A *source* node is one that matches an interest by virtue of characteristics that match the attribute-value pairs specified in the interest – for example, it may be equipped with appropriate sensors. There may be several source nodes for a given interest (just as there may be several sinks at which the interest was injected). When the runtime system finds a matching source node, it passes the interest to the application, which turns on its sensors as required and generates the data needed by the sink node. The runtime system ferries that data back to the sink along a reverse path made up of nodes that forwarded the interest from the sink.

Since, in general, no node has *a priori* knowledge of which other node can act as a source, directed diffusion may involve considerable redundant communication. At worst, the entire network may be flooded with an interest. However, sometimes the interest concerns only a certain physical region, such as a specific area in a forest. If sensor nodes know their locations, then the interest need be propagated only to the target area. In principle, nodes could be equipped with satellite navigation receivers for that purpose, although natural coverage such as dense trees may obstruct readings.

The flow of data back from source to sink is controlled by *gradients*, which are (*direction, value*) pairs between nodes that are set up for each particular interest as it diffuses through the network (Figure 16.7B). The *direction* is that in which the data is to flow, and the *value* is application-specific but can be used to control the rate of flow. For example, the sink might require data about animal sightings only a certain number of times per hour. There may be several paths from a given source to a given sink. The system can apply various strategies for choosing among them, including using paths redundantly in case of failure, or applying heuristics to find a path of minimum length (Figure 16.7C).

The application programmer can also supply software called *filters* that run on each of the nodes to intercept the flow of matching data passing through the node. For example, a filter could suppress duplicate animal-detection alarms that derive from different nodes sensing the same animal (possibly the node between the sources and sink in Figure 16.7C).

Another data-oriented approach to programming sensor networks is distributed query processing [Gehrke and Madden 2004]. In this case, however, an SQL-like language is used to declare queries that will be executed collectively by the nodes. The optimum plan for executing a query is typically processed on the user's PC or *base station* outside the network, taking into account any known costs associated with the use of particular sensor nodes. The base station distributes the optimized query to the nodes in the network along dynamically discovered routes, taking into account the communication patterns that processing the query entails, such as sending data to collection points for averaging. As with directed diffusion, data can be aggregated in the network to amortize communication costs. The results flow back to the base station for further processing.

16.4.3 Location-sensing

Of all the types of sensing used in ubiquitous computing, location sensing has received the most attention. Location is an obvious parameter for mobile, context-aware computing. It seems natural to make applications and devices behave in a way that depends on where the user is, such as the context-aware phone. But location sensing has many other uses, from assisting users in navigating through urban or rural areas to determining network routes by geography [Imielinski and Navas 1999].

Location-sensing systems are designed to obtain data about the position of objects (living or otherwise) within some type of region of interest. Here we shall concentrate on objects' locations, but some technologies also derive values for their orientation and higher-order values such as their velocities.

An important distinction, especially when it comes to privacy, is whether an object or user determines its own location, or whether something else determines its location. The latter case is known as *tracking*.

Figure 16.8 (based on a similar figure in [Hightower and Borriello 2001]) shows some types of location technologies, and some of their principle characteristics. One characteristic is the mechanism used to derive a location. That mechanism sometimes imposes limitations on where the technology can be deployed, such as whether the technology works indoors or outdoors, and what installations are required in the local infrastructure. The mechanism is also associated with an accuracy, given in Figure 16.8 to an order of magnitude. Next, different technologies yield different types of data about an object's location. Finally, technologies differ in what information, if any, is supplied about the entity being located, which is relevant to users' concerns about privacy. Additional technologies are surveyed in Hightower and Borriello [2001].

The US Global Positioning System (GPS) is the most well-known instance of a satellite navigation system – a system for determining the approximate position of a *receiver* or *unit* from satellite signals. Other satellite navigation systems are the Russian GLONASS system, and the planned European Galileo system. GPS, which only functions outdoors because of signal attenuation inside buildings, is used routinely in vehicles and in handheld form for navigation, and increasingly for less conventional applications such as the delivery of location-dependent media to people in urban areas [Hull *et al.* 2004]. The receiver's position is calculated with respect to a subset of 24

Figure 16.8   Some location-sensing technologies

Type	Mechanism	Limitations	Accuracy	Type of location data	Privacy
GPS	Multilateration from satellite radio sources	Outdoors only (satellite visibility)	1–10m	Absolute geographic coordinates (latitude, longitude, altitude)	Yes
Radio beaconing	Broadcasts from wireless base stations (GSM, 802.11, Bluetooth)	Areas with wireless coverage	10m–1km	Proximity to known entity (usually semantic)	Yes
Active Bat	Multilateration from radio and ultrasound	Ceiling mounted sensors	10cm	Relative (room) coordinates.	Bat identity disclosed
Ultra Wide Band	Multilateration from reception of radio pulses	Receiver installations	15cm	Relative (room) coordinates	Tag identity disclosed
Active badge	Infrared sensing	Sunlight or fluorescent light	Room size	Proximity to known entity (usually semantic)	Badge identity disclosed
Automatic identification tag	RFID, Near Field Communication, visual tag (e.g. barcode)	Reader installations	1cm–10m	Proximity to known entity (usually semantic)	Tag identity disclosed
Easy Living	Vision, triangulation	Camera installations	Variable	Relative (room) coordinates	No

satellites orbiting the Earth in six planes, four per plane. Each satellite orbits the Earth about twice per day. Each satellite broadcasts the current time from an on-board atomic clock, and information about its locations over a range of times (as judged by observations from ground stations). The receiver, whose location is to be determined, calculates its distance from each of several visible satellites using the difference between the time of arrival of the signal and the time it was broadcast – that is, the time encoded in the signal – and an estimate of the speed of radio propagation from the satellite to Earth. The reader then calculates its position using a trigonometrical calculation known as *multilateration*. At least three satellites visible from the receiver are required to obtain a position. The reader can calculate only its latitude and longitude if just three satellites are visible; with more visible satellites, altitude can also be calculated.

Another positioning method that potentially works over a wide area, at least in highly populated regions, is to listen for identifiers that are *beaconed* (that is, broadcast periodically) from wireless base stations with a limited range. Devices can compare signal strengths as a measure of which station is nearest. GSM base stations for mobile phones each have a *cell ID*; 802.11 access points have a Basic Service Set Identifier (BSSID). Base stations beacon their identifiers unless configured not to, for security

Figure 16.9   Locating an active bat within a room

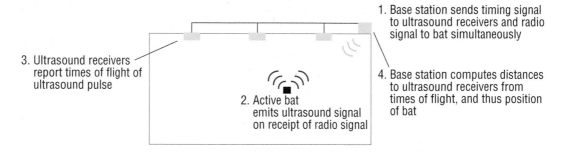

3. Ultrasound receivers report times of flight of ultrasound pulse

1. Base station sends timing signal to ultrasound receivers and radio signal to bat simultaneously

2. Active bat emits ultrasound signal on receipt of radio signal

4. Base station computes distances to ultrasound receivers from times of flight, and thus position of bat

reasons. A Bluetooth 'beacon' is a device that provides its identifier upon discovery by another device; it does not actually broadcast its identifier.

Radio beaconing does not determine an entity's position *per se*, but only its proximity to another entity. If the beaconing entity's position is known, then the target entity's position is known to within the range of the radio. Absolute positioning therefore requires looking up the beaconed identifier in a database. The organizations that manage the radio sources, such as telecommunication providers, usually do not (or will not) disclose the details of their locations. But some community projects exist whereby users provide the location details themselves.

Proximity can be a useful property in itself. For example, using proximity it is possible to create location-aware applications that are triggered by the return to a location visited before. For example, a user waiting at a train station could create an alert reminding them to buy a new monthly train ticket when they enter the proximity of the train station (that is, when their device receives the same beaconed identifier) on the first of the month. Bluetooth, an alternative radio technology, has the interesting property that some radio beacons – for example, ones integrated with mobile phones – are themselves mobile. This can still be useful. For example, train commuters could receive data that people they frequently travel with – 'familiar strangers' – provide via their mobile phones.

Turning back to more definite forms of positioning, GPS derives an object's *absolute* (that is, global) coordinates outdoors. By contrast, the Active Bat system [Harter *et al.* 2002] was designed to produce an object's or human's location indoors, in *relative* coordinates – that is, with respect to the room that contains the object (Figure 16.9). The Active Bat system is accurate to about 10cm. Relatively accurate indoor location is useful for applications such as detecting which screen a mobile user is near to, and 'teleporting' their PC's desktop to it using the VNC protocol (see 'Thin client implementations' in Section 2.2.3). A *bat* is a device attached to a user or object whose location is to be found, and which receives radio signals and emits ultrasound signals. The system relies on a grid of ultrasound receivers at known locations in the ceiling, wired to a *base station*. To locate a bat, the base station simultaneously emits a radio signal to the bat containing its identifier, and a wired signal to the ceiling-mounted ultrasound receivers. When the bat with the given identifier receives the base station's signal, it emits a short ultrasound pulse. When a receiver in the ceiling receives the base station's signal, it starts a timer. Since the speed of electromagnetic propagation is so much greater than the speed of sound, the emission of the ultrasound pulse and the start of the timer are effectively simultaneous. When a ceiling receiver receives the corresponding ultrasound pulse (from the bat), it reads the elapsed time and forwards it to the base station, which uses an estimate of the speed of sound to deduce the receiver's distance from the bat. If the base station receives distances from at least three non-colinear ultrasound receivers, it can compute the bat's position in 3D space.

Ultra Wide Band (UWB) is a technique for propagating data at high bit rates (100Mbps or more) over short ranges (up to 10m). The bits are propagated at very low power but over a very wide frequency spectrum, using thin pulses – in the order of 1ns in width. Given the size and shape of the pulse, it is possible to measure times of flight to great accuracy. By arranging receivers in the environment and using multilateration as with the above technologies, it is possible to determine a UWB tag's coordinates to an accuracy of about 15cm. Unlike the above technologies, UWB signals propagate through walls and other typical objects found in the built environment. Its low power consumption is another advantage.

GPS, Active Bats and UWB all provide data about an object's *physical location*: its coordinates in a physical region. One advantage of knowing a physical location is that, through databases including *geographical information systems* (GIS) and *world models* of built spaces, a single location can be related to many types of information about the object or its relationship to other objects. However, the disadvantage is the effort required to produce and maintain those databases, which might experience high rates of change.

By contrast, the Active Badge system (Section 16.1) produces an object's *semantic location*: the location's name or description. For example, if a badge is sensed by the infrared receiver in room '101', then the location of that badge is determined to be 'Room 101'. (Unlike most radio signals, building materials strongly attenuate infrared signals so the badge is unlikely to be outside the room.) That data tells us nothing explicitly about the location in space, but it does provide users with information that relates to their knowledge of the world they live in. By contrast, the latitude and longitude of the same place *51° 27.010 N 002° 37.107 W* is useful for, say, calculating distances to other places; but it is difficult for humans to work with. Note that radio beacons – which invert Active Badge technologies by placing the receiver on the target to be located rather than in the infrastructure – can be used to provide either semantic or (very approximate) physical locations.

Active Badges are a specialized form of *automatic identification tags*: electronically readable identifiers designed typically for mass industrial applications. Automatic identification tags include RFID [Want 2004], Near Field Communication (NFC) [www.nfc-forum.org], and glyphs or other visual symbols such as barcodes – especially those designed to be readable at a distance by cameras [de Ipiña *et al.* 2002]. These tags are attached to the object whose location is to be determined. When read by a reader with a limited range and at a known location, the target object's location becomes known.

Finally, the Easy Living project [Krumm *et al.* 2000] used vision algorithms to locate an object such as a human viewed by several cameras. A target object can be located if it can be recognized by a camera at a known location. With several cameras at known locations, in principle the differences between the object's appearances in their images can be used to determine the object's physical location.

As demonstrated in the Cooltown case study (Section 16.7.2), some of the above location technologies – especially automatic identification tags and infrared beacons – can also be used to provide access to information and services concerning the entity to which they are attached, through the identifiers they make available.

Comparing the above technologies with respect to privacy, the GPS solution provides absolute privacy: at no point in the GPS's operation is information about the receiving device transmitted elsewhere. Radio beaconing can provide absolute privacy but it depends on how it is used. If a device simply listens for beacons and never otherwise communicates with the infrastructure, then it maintains privacy. By contrast, the other technologies are tracking technologies. Active Bats, UWB, Active Badges and automatic identification methods each yield an identifier to the infrastructure as present in a known location at a known time. Even if the associated user does not disclose their identity, it might be possible to infer it. Easy Living's vision techniques rely on recognising users in order to locate them and so the user's identity is much more directly disclosed.

Architectures for location-sensing ◊ Two of the key characteristics required for location systems are: (1) generality with respect to the types of sensor used for location-sensing, and (2) scalability with respect to the number of objects to be located and the rate of location update events occurring when mobile objects such as people and vehicles change their locations. Researchers and developers have produced architectures for location-sensing in the small – in individual smart spaces such as rooms, buildings, or natural environments covered by sensor networks; and for highly scalable geographic information systems, intended to cover large areas and include the locations of very many objects.

The *location stack* [Hightower *et al.* 2002, Graumann *et al.* 2003] is aimed at meeting the requirement for generality. It divides location-sensing systems for individual smart spaces into layers. The *sensor layer* contains drivers for extracting raw data from a variety of location sensors. The *measurements layer* then turns that raw data into common measurement types including distance, angle and velocity. The *fusion layer* is the lowest layer available to applications. It combines the measurements from different sensors (typically of different types), to infer the location of an object and provide it through a uniform interface. Since sensors produce uncertain data, the inferences of the fusion layer are probabilistic. Fox *et al.* [2003] survey some of the Bayesian techniques available. The *arrangements layer* deduces relationships between objects, such as whether they are co-located. Above those are layers for combining location data with data from other types of sensors, to determine more complex contextual attributes, such as whether a group of people located in a house are all asleep.

Scalability is a major concern in geographic information systems. *Spatio-temporal* queries such as 'Who has been in this building in the last 60 days?' or 'Is someone following me?' or 'Which moving objects in this region are most in danger of colliding?' illustrate the need for scalability. The number of objects – in particular, the number of mobile objects – to be located and the number of concurrent queries may be large. Moreover, in the last of those example queries, real-time responsiveness is required.The obvious approach to making location systems scalable is to divide the region of interest recursively into sub-regions, using data structures such as quadtrees. Such indexing of spatial and temporal databases is an active area of research.

16.4.4 Summary and perspective

This section has described some of the infrastructures that have been devised for context-aware computing. Mostly we have concentrated on the ways in which sensors are harnessed to produce the contextual attributes on which applications depend for their behaviour. We looked at both architectures for relatively static collections of sensors, and architectures for highly volatile sensor networks. Finally, we described some technologies for the particularly important case of location-sensing.

Through context awareness, we integrate the everyday physical world with computer systems. A key problem remaining is that, compared to the subtle understanding that humans have of their physical world, the systems we have described are quite crude. Not only are sensors (at least, those cheap enough to deploy widely) inevitably inaccurate, but the final stage of producing semantically rich information accurately from raw sensor data is extremely difficult. The world of robotics (which involves actuation, a topic we have ignored, in addition to sensing) has been tackling this difficulty for many years. In tightly restricted domains such as domestic vacuum-cleaning or industrial production, robots can perform reasonably well. But generalization from those domains remains elusive.

16.5 Security and privacy

Volatile systems raise many new issues for both security and privacy. First, users and administrators of volatile systems require security for their data and resources (confidentiality, integrity and availability). However, as we pointed out when describing the model of volatile systems in Section 16.1, trust – the basis for all security – is often lowered in volatile systems. Trust is lowered because the principals whose components interact spontaneously may have little if any prior knowledge of one another, and may not have a trusted third party in common. Second, many users are concerned about their *privacy* – roughly speaking, their ability to control the accessibility of information about themselves. But privacy is potentially more threatened than ever before due to sensing in the smart spaces users pass through.

Despite those challenging factors, measures to ensure people's security and privacy must be lightweight – partly to preserve the spontaneity of interactions, and partly because of the restricted user interfaces of many devices. People will not want, for example, to 'log in' to a smart pen before they use it in their host's office!

In this section we outline some of the main security and privacy problems for volatile systems. Stajano [2002] gives a more detailed treatment of some of these issues. Langheinrich [2001] examines the topic of privacy in ubiquitous computing starting from its historical and legal context.

16.5.1 Background

Security and privacy are complicated in volatile systems by hardware-related issues such as resource poverty, and because their spontaneity leads to new types of resource sharing.

Hardware-related issues ◊ Conventional security protocols tend to make assumptions about devices and connectivity that often do not hold in volatile systems. First, portable devices such as PDAs, phones and sensor nodes can, in general, be more easily stolen and tampered with than devices such as PCs in locked rooms. A security design for volatile systems should not rely on the integrity of any subset of devices that could be feasibly compromised. For example, if a smart space spans a large enough physical area, then one way to help protect the system's overall integrity is to make it necessary for an attacker to visit many locations within it at more or less the same time if their attack is to succeed [Anderson *et al.* 2004].

Second, devices in volatile systems sometimes do not have sufficient computing resources for asymmetric (public-key) cryptography – even when using elliptic curve cryptography (Section 7.3.2). SPINS [Perrig *et al.* 2002] provides security guarantees for the data that low-power nodes in wireless sensor networks exchange in a potentially hostile environment. Their protocols use only symmetric-key cryptography which, unlike asymmetric-key cryptography, is feasible on such low-power devices. However, that begs the question of which nodes in a wireless sensor network should share the same symmetric key. At one extreme, if all nodes share the same key then a successful attack on one node will compromise the entire system. At the other extreme, if each node shares a distinct key with every other node, then there may be too many keys for nodes with limited memory to store. A compromise position is for nodes to share keys only with their nearest neighbours, and to rely on chains of mutually trusting nodes that encrypt messages hop-by-hop, rather than using end-to-end encryption.

Third, as always, energy is an issue. Not only must security protocols be designed to minimize communication overheads to preserve battery life, but in addition limited energy is the basis for a new type of denial of service attack. Stajano and Anderson [1999] describe the 'sleep deprivation torture attack' on battery-powered nodes: an attacker can deny service by sending spurious messages to cause the devices to run their batteries down as they waste energy receiving them. Martin *et al.* [2004] describe further 'sleep deprivation' attacks, including more covertly providing devices with code or data that causes them to waste energy through processing. For example, an attacker could provide an animated GIF image that appears static to the user but actually causes constant re-rendering.

Finally, disconnected operation means that it is preferable to avoid security protocols that rely on continuous online access to a server. For example, suppose that vending machines at rest stops are to dispense certain refreshments for free but only to *bona fide* passengers of a specific bus company. Rather than assuming such a machine is always connected to the company headquarters to verify authorization, it is better to design a protocol whereby the user's device (such as a phone) is given a certificate enabling the vending machine to verify authorization using only Bluetooth or other short-range communication [Zhang and Kindberg 2002]. Unfortunately, the absence of an online server also means that a certificate cannot be revoked and can only be constructed to expire by a given time – begging the question of how offline devices are to keep securely accurate time.

New types of resource-sharing: example problems ◊ Volatile systems give rise to new types of resource sharing which require new security designs, such as the following examples.

- The administrators of a smart space expose a service accessible to visitors over a wireless network – such as sending slides to the projection service in a seminar room or using a printer in a café.

- Two employees of the same company who encounter one another at a conference wirelessly exchange a document between their mobile phones or other portable devices.

- A nurse takes a wireless heart-rate monitor from a box of similar devices, attaches it to a patient and associates it to the clinical data-logging service for that patient.

Each of those cases is an example of spontaneous interoperation; each raises security and/or privacy issues. None is quite like the resource-sharing patterns normally encountered within firewall-protected intranets or on the open Internet.

The projection and printing services are intended only for visitors but the wireless network may go beyond the building's boundaries, from where attackers could eavesdrop, disrupt presentations or send bogus print jobs. So the services require protection, similarly to a web server intended only for members of a club. But logging in – typing a username and password – and the registration procedure that preceded it would be too much effort; additionally, users may object on privacy grounds.

The document exchange between two employees is similar in some ways to sending an email within a corporate intranet. And yet the interaction took place over a public wireless network in a place filled mostly with unknown people. A trusted third party (their company) exists in principle, but in practice it may not be reachable (they may not be able to obtain a good enough wireless telecommunications signal for their phone in the conference hall) or it may not be configured in all the users' devices.

What the nurse does is in some ways similar to the first example: she appropriates a trusted device temporarily but securely, as a visitor might appropriate a projector or printer. But the example is intended to show more emphatically the issue of reuse. There may be a confusing number of wireless sensors used for different patients at different times, and it is essential to securely make and break associations between the devices and the respective patient logs.

16.5.2 Some solutions

We now examine some attempts to solve the problems of providing security and privacy in volatile systems: secure spontaneous device association, location-based authentication, and privacy protection. The security techniques we shall describe depart markedly from standard approaches in distributed systems. They exploit the fact that the systems we are considering are integrated into our everyday physical world, by using physical evidence rather than cryptographic evidence to bootstrap security properties.

Secure spontaneous device association ◊ An important question raised by the foregoing examples is how to secure a spontaneous association between two devices connected by a wireless radio network W such as Bluetooth or 802.11. This is the *secure spontaneous device association* problem, also known as the *secure transient association* problem. The goal is to create a secure channel between two devices by securely exchanging a session key between those two devices and using it to encrypt their communication over W. The starting assumptions are that, since the association is spontaneous, neither device

Figure 16.10 Secure device association using physical contact

1. Fresh secret key *K* exchanged by physical contact

2. Devices communicate using secure channel constructed over *W* using *K*

(or its user) shares a secret with the other; neither possesses the other's public key; and the devices do not have access to a trusted third party. Even if a trusted third party exists, it may be offline. An attacker can attempt to eavesdrop on *W* and to replay and synthesize messages. In particular, an attacker may attempt to launch a man-in-the-middle attack (Section 7.1.1).

A solution to this problem would enable a visitor to make a secure connection to a projector or printer service; the colleagues at a conference could securely exchange a document between their portable devices; the nurse could securely connect a wireless heart-rate monitor to a data-logging unit by the patient's bed.

No amount of communication over *W* will enable secure key exchange by itself so out-of-band communication is required. In particular, the standard method for establishing a link-level key between two devices connected by Bluetooth relies on the out-of-band actions of one or more users. A digit string chosen on one device must be entered by a user at the other device. But this method is often not carried out securely, since simple, short digit strings such as '0000' tend to be used, which attackers can learn by exhaustive search.

Another approach to solving the secure association problem is to use a side channel with certain physical properties. Specifically, the propagation of signals over this side channel is constrained in angle, range or timing (or a combination of those). To a first degree of approximation, we can infer properties about the sender or receiver of messages on such channels that enable us to establish secure association with a physically demonstrable device, as we shortly show. Kindberg *et al.* [2002b] call them *physically constrained channels*, the term we shall use here; Balfanz *et al.* [2002] refer to *location-limited channels*; Stajano and Anderson [1999] first exploited such a side channel in the form of physical contact. We introduced some examples of these channels for the purposes of physical device association in Section 16.2.2.

In one scenario, one of the devices generates a fresh session key and sends it to the other over a *receive-constrained* channel that provides a degree of secrecy – that is, it constrains which devices can receive the key. Some examples of technologies for receive-constrained channels are:

- Physical contact. Each device has terminals for direct electrical connection [Stajano and Anderson 1999]. See Figure 16.10.

- Infrared. Infrared beams can be made directional to within about 60 degrees and are largely attenuated by walls and windows. A user can 'beam' a key to the required receiver device over a distance of up to about a metre [Balfanz *et al.* 2002].

- Audio. Data can be transmitted as modulations of an audio signal such as music playing softly throughout a room, but with little reach beyond it [Madhavapeddy *et al.* 2003]

- Laser. One user points their device's narrow data-carrying laser beam onto a receiver on the other device [Kindberg and Zhang 2003a]. This method allows for more precision than the other long-range techniques.

- Barcode and camera. One device displays the secret key as a barcode (or other decodable image) on its display, which the other device – equipped with a camera, such as a camera phone – reads and decodes. This method's precision is inversely related to the distance between the devices.

In general, physically constrained channels provide only a limited degree of security. An attacker with a sufficiently sensitive receiver can eavesdrop on infrared or audio; an attacker with a powerful camera may be able to read a barcode even on a small display. Laser light is subject to atmospheric scattering, although quantum modulation techniques can make the scattered signal useless to an eavesdropper [Gibson *et al.* 2004]. However, when the technologies are deployed in appropriate circumstances, the attacks entail considerable effort and the security obtained may be good enough for everyday purposes.

A second approach for securely exchanging a session key is to use a constrained channel to physically authenticate one device's public key, which it sends to the other device. The devices then engage in a standard protocol to exchange a session key using the authenticated public key. Of course, this method assumes that the devices are powerful enough to perform public-key cryptography.

The simplest way of authenticating the public key is for the device to send it over a *send-constrained* channel, which enables a user to authenticate the key as deriving from that physical device. There are several ways to implement suitable send-constrained channels. For example, physical contact provides a send-constrained channel since only a directly connected device can send on the channel. Exercise 16.14 invites the reader to consider which of the other techniques for receive-constrained channels described above also provide send-constrained channels. Moreover, it is possible to implement a send-constrained channel using a receive-constrained channel, or *vice versa*. See Exercise 16.15.

A third approach utilizing physically constrained channels is for the devices to exchange a session key optimistically but insecurely, and then to use a physically constrained channel to *validate* the key – that is, to use a physically constrained channel to verify that the key is possessed solely by the required physical source.

First we consider how to exchange a session key spontaneously but possibly with the wrong principal, and go on to examine some technologies for validating the exchange. If validation fails, then the process can be repeated.

In Section 16.2.2 we described physical and human-mediated techniques for associating two devices, such as the two-button protocol in which devices exchange their network addresses when humans press buttons on them more or less simultaneously. It is straightforward to adapt that protocol so that the devices also

Figure 16.11 Detecting a man-in-the-middle

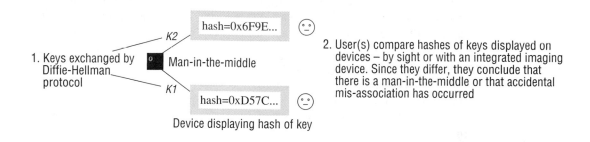

1. Keys exchanged by Diffie-Hellman protocol

Man-in-the-middle

Device displaying hash of key

2. User(s) compare hashes of keys displayed on devices – by sight or with an integrated imaging device. Since they differ, they conclude that there is a man-in-the-middle or that accidental mis-association has occurred

exchange session keys using the Diffie–Hellman protocol [Diffie and Hellman 1976]. But, as it stands, that method is not secure: it is still possible for separate groups of users to accidentally mis-associate devices by running the protocol concurrently, and for malicious parties to launch man-in-the-middle attacks.

The following techniques enable us to validate a key before using it. They involve send-constrained channels although receive-constrained channels could also be used (see Exercise 16.15). It is a property of the Diffie–Hellman protocol that a man in the middle cannot (except with negligible probability) exchange the same key with each device, so we can validate the association by comparing the secure hashes of the keys obtained by the two devices after running the Diffie–Hellman protocol (Figure 16.11).

- Displayed hashes. Stajano and Anderson pointed out that each device could display the hash of its public key as hexadecimal characters or in some other form that humans can compare. However, they argued that this type of human involvement is too error-prone. The barcode method above would be more reliable. That method is another example of using a send-constrained channel: the optical path between the display of one device and the camera of the other brought close to it securely propagates the secure hash from the required device.

- Ultrasound. An ultrasound signal, in combination with a radio signal, can be used to infer the distance and direction of the device that sent a hash, using techniques similar to those used for the Active Bat described in Section 16.4.3 [Kindberg and Zhang 2003b].

Turning to consideration of all the above methods, they vary in the degree of security they provide because of the properties of the constrained channels, but all are suitable for spontaneous association. None requires online access to any other component. None requires users to authenticate themselves or to find out electronic names or identifiers for the devices – instead, the users are provided with physical evidence about which devices have been securely associated. By assumption, the users have established trust in those devices (and their users). Of course, the security that has been achieved is only as good as the trustworthiness of the devices involved: it is possible to 'securely associate' a device to another that in fact launches an attack.

Stajano and Anderson [1999, Stajano 2002] used physically constrained channels in the context of the 'resurrecting duckling' protocol. That protocol is relevant to the example of the wireless heart-rate monitor, where several identical devices are to be associated and re-associated securely between patients. The name of the protocol refers to the fact that (actual) ducklings begin life in the *imprintable* state and come under the control of whatever entity they first recognize (ideally, their biological mothers!) – a process known as *imprinting*. In our case, the 'duckling' device comes under the control of the first device associated with it and then refuses requests from any other entity – that is, any principal that does not know the secret key that the 'duckling' exchanged with its 'mother' at the point of imprinting. Re-association can only occur by first 'killing the duckling's soul' – for example, when the 'mother' instructs the 'duckling' to re-assume the imprintable state, in which its memory is securely wiped. From that point, the 'duckling' is prepared to be controlled by the next device that associates with it.

Location-based authentication ◊ The examples of the visitor using a seminar room's projection service and a user printing documents in a café can be looked at from both the visitors' and the administrators' perspectives. From the visitors' point of view, they can securely associate their device to the projector or printer using one of the foregoing physically constrained channels, so as to protect the privacy and integrity of their data (although printing a sensitive document in a café may be unwise).

But the administrators of each of those smart spaces has an additional requirement: as well as wanting their visitors to enjoy security, they need to implement access control. Only people physically in their spaces (speakers in their seminar room, people drinking the café's coffee) should be able to use their services. And yet, as we have explained, authenticating users' identities may be inappropriate because of the visitors' requirements for privacy, and the administrators' need to integrate a stream of users and devices that spontaneously appear and disappear.

An approach to authorization that meets those requirements is to base access control on the *location* of the services' clients, rather than their identity. Kindberg *et al.* [2002b] describe a protocol for authenticating the clients' locations using a physically constrained channel that pervades the smart space but does not reach beyond it. For example, that channel could be constructed using music playing in a café or infrared in a meeting room. There is also a *location authentication proxy* embedded in the corresponding smart space – that is, directly connected to the same constrained channel – which the location-specific services trust. For example, the Acme café company might want to reward their customers throughout their chain with free media downloads but it wants to ensure that no-one outside an Acme café can access the media, even though the download service is centralized and connected to the Internet. The protocol assumes that users access services through a web browser and uses web re-direction so that the visitors' devices transparently obtain proof from the location authentication proxy that the client device is where it claims it is, and forwards it to the target service.

Sastry *et al.* [2003] use temporally constrained channels implemented using ultrasound to verify location claims. The basis of their protocol is that, since the speed of sound is physically constrained, only a device that is where it claims to be can transmit a message quickly enough by ultrasound to a destination at the location, when echoing a nonce contained in a request packet.

As with secure device association, location authentication only secures a system to a limited extent. Even though a service has verified a client to be in a *bona fide* location, that client could nonetheless be malicious and act as a proxy for clients at other locations.

Privacy protection ◊ Location-based authentication demonstrates a trade-off that makes it difficult to protect privacy in volatile systems: even though the user withholds their identity, he or she discloses a location that may be unwittingly associated with other types of potentially identifying information. Safeguards are needed on all channels through which information about the user may flow. For example, even if a user accesses an electronic service anonymously in a café, their privacy may be destroyed if a camera captures them. And if a user needs to pay for a service then they have to supply electronic payment details, even if they do so via a third party. They may also buy goods that have to be physically delivered to their address.

At the system level, the basic threat is that, wittingly or unwittingly, users provide identifiers of various kinds to smart spaces when they visit them and access services there. First, they may provide names and addresses in service accesses. Second, the Bluetooth or IEEE 802.11 network interfaces on their personal devices each maintain a constant MAC-level address that is visible to other devices such as access points. Third, if users carry tags such as RFID tags (for example, ones embedded in their clothes so that their smart washing machines can automatically choose an appropriate washing cycle), then smart spaces could potentially sense those tags at doorways and other 'pinch-points'. The RFIDs are globally unique and may be used both to identify what the user has with them (such as the type of clothes they wear) as well as for tracking purposes.

Whatever their source, identifiers can become associated with a location and an activity at a given time, and thus may potentially be linked to the user's personal information. Users in a smart space may eavesdrop and gather the identifiers. If smart spaces (or services embedded in smart spaces) collude, then they could track identifiers across locations and infer movements, all potentially leading to loss of privacy.

Research is underway into how to make what are currently hard-wired identifiers (such as wireless MAC addresses and RFIDs) into 'soft' addresses, that may be replaced from time to time to inhibit tracking. The difficulty with MAC addresses (as well as higher level network addresses such as IP addresses) is that changing them causes disruptions to communication, which has to be traded off against privacy [Gruteser and Grunwald 2003]. The difficulty with RFIDs is that, while an RFID-bearing user does not want to be tracked by the 'wrong' sensors, in general, the user does want their RFID tag to be read by certain 'right' sensors (such as the one in their washing machine). A technique to address that problem is for the tag to use (one-way) hash functions both to replace the stored identifier and to generate the emitted identifier each time it is read [Ohkubo *et al*. 2003]. Only a trusted party that knows the tag's original unique identifier can use an emitted identifier to verify which tag was read. Moreover, since tags pass their stored identifier through a one-way hash function before emitting them, attackers are unable (unless they can tamper with the tag) to learn the stored identifier and thus spoof the tag – for example, with the intention of falsely claiming that a tagged user was present at the scene of a crime.

Turning to the software identifiers that clients provide to services, an obvious approach to help safeguard privacy is to substitute either an anonymous identifier – one randomly chosen for every service request – or a *pseudonym*: a false identifier that is nonetheless used consistently for the same client principal for some period of time. The advantage of a pseudonym over an anonymous identifier is that it enables a client to build a relationship of trust or a good reputation with a given service but without necessarily disclosing a true identity.

It would be far too laborious for a user to manage anonymous or pseudonymous identifiers so that is normally done by a system component called a *privacy proxy*. The privacy proxy is a component that the user trusts to forward all service requests anonymously. Each of the user's devices has a secure, private channel to the privacy proxy. That proxy substitutes anonymous identifiers or pseudonyms for all of the true identifiers in service requests.

One problem with a privacy proxy is that it is a central point of vulnerability: if the proxy is successfully attacked then all of the client's service usage becomes disclosed. Another problem is that proxies do not hide which services the user accesses. An eavesdropper or a colluding set of eavesdroppers could employ *traffic analysis*: that is, they could observe correlations in traffic between messages flowing to or from a particular user's device and messages flowing to or from a particular service – examining such factors as the timing and sizes of the messages.

Mixing is a statistical technique for combining communications from many users in such a way that attackers cannot easily disentangle one user's actions from another, and thus helping to safeguard the users' privacy. One application of mixing is to construct an overlay network of proxies that encrypt, aggregate, re-order and forward messages between themselves for several hops after they have entered the network, in a way that makes it hard to correlate any message entering the network from a client or service with any message leaving it, respectively to a service or client [Chaum 1981]. Each proxy trusts and shares keys only with its neighbours. It would be difficult to compromise the network without the collusion of all proxies. Al-Muhtadi *et al.* [2002] describe an architecture for anonymously routing messages from a client in a smart space to services.

Another application of mixing is to obscure users' locations by exploiting the presence of many users in each location. Beresford and Stajano [2003] describe a system for obscuring users' locations through the use of *mix zones*, which are regions where users do *not* access location-aware services, such as hallways between smart rooms. The idea is that users change their pseudonymous identities in mix zones, where no user's location is known. If mix zones are sufficiently small and if enough people pass through them, then mix zones can plays a role akin to a mix network of anonymizing proxies. Exercise 16.16 considers mix zones in more depth.

16.5.3 Summary and perspective

This section has provided an introduction to the problems of providing security and privacy in volatile systems, and a brief look at some attempts at solutions, including secure spontaneous association, location-based authentication, and various techniques aimed at privacy protection. Widespread sensing, hardware-related issues such as resource poverty, and spontaneous association are at the root of the difficulties. Sensing heightens users' privacy concerns since not only can their service accesses be monitored but such basic information as their locations can, too; and hardware-related issues and spontaneity challenge our ability to provide security solutions. This is an important area of research: security and, especially, privacy may turn out to be barriers to the use of volatile systems.

16.6 Adaptation

The devices in the volatile systems studied in this chapter are much more heterogeneous than PCs in processing power, I/O capabilities such as screen size, network bandwidth, memory, and energy capacity. Heterogeneity is unlikely to ease significantly because of the multiple purposes we have for devices. The demands of carrying and embedding devices mean that the devices that are poorest and richest in resources such as energy and screen size are likely to continue to differ by orders of magnitude. (The only overall positive trend in resources is in increasingly dense but affordable persistent storage [Want and Pering 2003].) And what is certain not to alter, looking forward, is the presence of runtime change itself: runtime conditions such as the available bandwidth and energy are prone to change dramatically.

This section introduces *adaptive* systems: ones that are based on a model of varying resources, and which adapt their runtime behaviour to the current resource availability. The aim of adaptive systems is to accommodate heterogeneity by allowing software reuse across contexts that vary in factors such as device capabilities and user preferences, and to accommodate changing runtime resource conditions by adapting application behaviour without sacrificing crucial application properties. But achieving those goals can be extremely difficult. This section gives a flavour of both those areas of adaptation.

16.6.1 Context-aware adaptation of content

In Section 16.3.1 we saw that some devices in volatile systems supply multimedia content to one another. Multimedia applications (see Chapter 17) operate by exchanging or streaming multimedia data such as images, audio and video.

A simple approach to exchanging content would be for content producers to send the same content regardless of the content-consuming device, and for that device to render the content appropriately for its needs and limitations. Indeed, that approach sometimes works, as long as the content can be specified sufficiently abstractly that the recipient device can always find a concrete representation to fit its needs.

However, it turns out that factors such as bandwidth limitations and device heterogeneity make that approach impractical in general. Unlike PCs, the capabilities of devices in volatile systems to receive, process, store and display multimedia content vary widely. Their screen sizes vary – some do not even have screens – so sending fixed-size images and text in a fixed font size, all in a fixed layout, will often lead to unsatisfactory results. The devices may or may not have all of the other forms of I/O that are taken for granted on PCs: keyboards, microphones, audio output, etc. Even if a device has I/O hardware to render a form of content such as video, it may not have the software needed for a given encoding (for example, MPEG or Quicktime) or it may have insufficient memory or processing resources to render media at full fidelity, such as video at full resolution or frame rate. Finally, a device may have all the resources to render given content, but if the bandwidth to the device is too low, then it cannot be sent to it unless it is suitably compressed.

More generally, the content that a service needs to deliver to a given device is a function of the *context*: the media producer should take account not only of the consuming device's capabilities, but also such factors as the preferences of the device's user, and the nature of his or her task. For example, one particular user might prefer text to images on a small screen; another might prefer audio output to visual output. Moreover, the items that the service delivers within a piece of content may need to be a function of the user's task. For example, the features required in a map of a given region will depend on whether the user is a tourist looking for attractions or a worker looking for infrastructure access points [Chalmers *et al.* 2004]. On a screen-limited device, the map is more likely to be legible if it contains just one type of feature.

It would be too much effort for multimedia content authors to hand-craft individual solutions for many different contexts. The alternative is to adapt the original data programatically into a suitable form, by selecting from it, generating content from it, or transforming it – or any combination of those three processes. Sometimes the original data is expressed independently of how it should be presented – for example, data might be held in XML form, and scripts in the eXtensible Style Language Transformations (XSLT) used to create renderable forms for a given context. In other cases, the original data is already a type of multimedia data, such as images; in that case, the process of adapting it is known as *transcoding*. Adaptation can occur within media types (for example, selecting from map data or reducing the resolution of an image) and across media types (for example, converting text to speech or *vice versa*, according to the user's preferences or according to whether the consuming device has a display or audio output).

The problem of content adaptation has received a lot of attention for client-server systems on the Internet, especially the Web. The web model is for adaptation to take place in the resource-rich infrastructure – either in the service itself or in a proxy – and not in the resource-poor client. The HTTP protocol allows a type of content negotiation (Section 4.4): a client specifies preferences for the MIME types of the content it can accept in its request headers, and the server can try to match those preferences in the content it returns. But that mechanism is too limited for context-aware adaptation – for example, the client can specify acceptable image-encodings but not the device's screen size. The World Wide Web Consortium (W3C), through its Device Independence working group [www.w3 XIX], and the Open Mobile Alliance (OMA) [www.openmobilealliance.org] are developing standards whereby device capabilities and configurations can be expressed in some detail. The W3C produced the Composite Capabilities/Preferences profile (CC/PP) to enable devices of different classes to specify their capabilities and configurations such as screen size and bandwidth. OMA's *user agent profile* specification provides a CC/PP vocabulary for mobile phones. It can be so detailed for a given device as to extend to over 10 KB. Such a profile would be too expensive in bandwidth and energy to send along with requests, so a mobile phone sends only the URI of its profile in a request header. The server retrieves the specification to provide matching content, and caches the specification for future use.

An important type of adaptation for bandwidth-limited devices is type-specific compression. Fox *et al.* [1998] describe an architecture in which proxies perform compression on the fly between services (which may or may not be part of the web) and clients. They argue for three main features in their architecture:

- To accommodate limited bandwidth, compression should be lossy but specific to the media type, so that semantic information can be used to decide which media features it is important to retain. For example, an image can be compressed by throwing away colour information.

- Transcoding should be performed on the fly because statically pre-prepared content forms will not provide sufficient flexibility to cope with dynamic data and an increasing set of permutations of clients and services.

- Transcoding should be performed in proxy servers so that both clients and services are transparently separated from transcoding concerns. No code has to be re-written, and the compute-intensive transcoding activity can be run on suitably scalable hardware such as clusters of rack-mounted computers, to keep latencies within acceptable bounds.

When it comes to volatile systems such as smart spaces, we have to revisit some of the assumptions made for web and other Internet-scale adaptation. Volatile systems are more demanding in that they may require adaptation between any pair of dynamically associated devices, and so adaptation is not restricted to clients of particular services in the infrastructure. There are now potentially many more providers whose content needs to be adapted. Moreover, those providers may also be too resource-poor to perform certain types of adaptation themselves.

One implication is for smart spaces to provide proxies in their infrastructure for adapting content between the volatile components they host [Kiciman and Fox 2000; Ponnekanti *et al.* 2001]. The second implication is the need to look more closely at which types of content adaptation can and should be performed on small devices – in particular, compression is an important example.

Even if there is a powerful adaptation proxy in the infrastructure, a device still has to send its data to that proxy. We discussed above how communication is expensive compared to processing. In principle, it may be most energy-efficient to compress data prior to transmission. However, the pattern of memory accesses made during compression has a strong effect on energy consumption. Barr and Asanovic [2003] show that it may cost more energy to first compress data using default implementations, but that careful optimization of compression and decompression algorithms, especially with respect to memory accesses patterns, can lead to overall energy savings compared to transmission of uncompressed data.

16.6.2 Adapting to changing system resources

While hardware resources such as screen size are heterogeneous across devices, they are at least stable and well known. By contrast, applications also rely on resources that are subject to change at runtime and which may be hard to predict, such as available energy and network bandwidth. In this subsection we discuss techniques for dealing with those changes to resource levels at runtime. We discuss operating system support for applications running in volatile systems, and support in the smart space infrastructure for enhancing the resources available to applications.

OS support for adaptation to volatile resources ◊ Satyanarayanan [2001] describes three approaches to adaptation. One approach is for applications to request and obtain resource reservations. While resource reservation can be convenient for applications (Chapter 17), satisfactory QoS guarantees are sometimes difficult to achieve in volatile systems and are even impossible in cases such as energy depletion. A second approach is to notify the user of changed levels of resource availability, so that they can act according to the application. For example, if bandwidth becomes low, the user of a video player could operate a slider in the application to switch the frame rate or resolution. The third approach is for the OS to notify the application of changing resource conditions, and for the application to adapt according to its particular needs.

Odyssey [Noble and Satyanarayanan 1999] provides operating system support for applications that adapt to changes in the available levels of resources such as the network bandwidth. For example, if the bandwidth drops then a video player could switch to a video stream with fewer colours, or adjust the resolution or frame rate. In the Odyssey architecture, applications manage data types such as video or images, and as resource conditions change they adjust the *fidelity* – the type-specific quality – with which those data are rendered. A system component called the *viceroy* divides the device's total resources between each of several applications running on it. At any time, each application runs with a *window of tolerance* to changes in resource conditions. The window of tolerance is an interval of resource levels that is chosen to be wide enough to be realistic in terms of actual resource variations, but narrow enough for the application to behave more or less consistently within those limits. When the viceroy has to change resource levels to a value outside the window of tolerance, it makes an upcall into the application, which then reacts accordingly. For example, a video player might change to black and white if bandwidth hits a very low level; above that, it might smoothly adjust the frame rate and/or resolution.

Taking advantage of smart space resources ◊ *Cyber foraging* [Satyanarayanan 2001; Goyal and Carter 2004; Balan *et al.* 2003] is where a processing-limited device discovers a compute server in a smart space and offloads some of its processing load to it. For example, converting the user's speech to text is a processing-intensive activity, and one which portable devices are barely able to carry out satisfactorily. One aim is to increase application responsiveness for the user – a computer in the infrastructure can have many times the processing power of a portable device. But this is also an example of *energy-aware adaptation*: the other aim is to save the portable device's batteries by allocating work to the mains-powered compute server.

There are challenging requirements associated with cyber foraging. The application needs to be decomposed in such a way that part of it can be processed efficiently on a compute server, but the application should still function correctly (albeit more slowly or with reduced fidelity) if no compute server is available. The compute server should run a part of the application that involves relatively little communication with the portable device – otherwise the time taken by communication over a low-bandwidth connection could outweigh the processing gains. Moreover, the overall energy consumption for the portable device must be satisfactory. Since communication is energy-intensive, it does not automatically follow that energy will be saved by using a compute server; it may be that the energy costs of communication with the compute server outweigh the energy savings from offloading processing.

Balan *et al.* [2003] discuss the problem of partitioning an application to meet the foregoing challenges, and describe a system for monitoring resource levels (such as compute server availability, bandwidth and energy) and consequently adapting the application's partitioning between the portable device and compute servers using one of a small set of decomposition options. For example, consider a situation in which a user speaks into a mobile device to dictate text, which is then translated into a foreign language (that of the country they are visiting). There are various ways of splitting this application between the mobile device and compute servers, with different implications for resource utilization. If several compute servers are available, then the various stages of recognition and translation could be split between them; if only one compute server is available, then they could be run together at that machine or between the mobile device and the compute server.

Goyal and Carter [2004] take a more static approach to dividing up the application, which is assumed to have been decomposed into separate communicating programs. For example, a mobile device could perform speech recognition in two ways. In the first mode, the application runs entirely – and very slowly – on the mobile device. In the second mode, the mobile device runs only the user interface, which ships the digital audio of the user's voice to a program running on a compute server; that program sends the recognized text back for the mobile device to display. It would be very costly in energy for the mobile device to send the recognition program to a computer server, so the device sends the URL of the program instead, which the compute server downloads from an external source and runs.

16.6.3 Summary and perspective

This section has described two main categories of adaptation in volatile systems, which are motivated by their heterogeneity and the volatility of their runtime conditions. There is adaptation of multimedia data to the context of the media consumer, such as the characteristics of the device and the task of the device's user. And there is adaptation to the dynamic levels of system resources such as energy and bandwidth.

We argued that, in principle, it would be better to produce adaptive software that can accommodate varying conditions according to a well understood model of variation, than to evolve software and hardware in an *ad hoc* fashion as the need presses. However, making such adaptive software is difficult and there is no general agreement on how to do so. First, the models of variation themselves – of how resourcing levels change and of how to react when they change – can be hard to derive with any generality. Second, there are software engineering challenges. Finding suitable points of adaptation in existing software requires intimate knowledge of its workings and may not always be successful. However, when creating new adaptive software from scratch, there are techniques from the software engineering community such as aspect-oriented programming [Elrad *et al.* 2001] to help programmers manage adaptation.

Figure 16.12 Cooltown layers

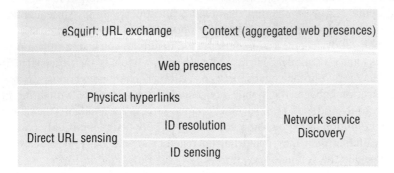

16.7 Case study of Cooltown

The goal of Hewlett-Packard's Cooltown project [Kindberg *et al*. 2002a; Kindberg and Barton 2001] was to provide infrastructure for *nomadic computing*, a term the project used for human-oriented mobile and ubiquitous computing. 'Nomadic' refers to humans moving between places such as home, work and shops as they go about their everyday lives. 'Computing' refers here to services provided to those nomadic users – not just services such as email that can be provided anywhere there is connectivity, but more particularly services integrated with entities in the everyday physical world through which the users move. To access those services, humans are assumed to carry or wear wirelessly connected and sensor-equipped devices such as phones, PDAs or smart watches.

More specifically, the project's aim was to apply lessons learned from the success of the Web to nomadic computing, via two objectives. First, since the Web provides a rich and extensible set of resources in the virtual world, much can potentially be gained by extending the Web's architecture and the Web's existing resources to the physical world. One objective for the Cooltown design was expressed in the maxim 'everything has a web page': each entity in our physical world, whether electronic or not, is to have an associated web resource called a *web presence*., which the user is to be able to access conveniently when in the presence of that entity. A web presence could simply be a web page containing information about the entity; but it could be any service provided in association with the entity. For example, the web presence of a physical product could be a service for obtaining replacement parts.

The second objective was to achieve the Web's high degree of interoperability for interactions with devices. Nomadic users may need to interact in places they have never visited before, with web presences they have never encountered before. It would not be acceptable for the user to have to load new software or reconfigure existing software on their portable devices in order to benefit from those services.

The aspects of the Cooltown architecture that we shall concentrate on here (Figure 16.12) are: web presences; *physical hyperlinks*, which are links from physical entities to web presences and thus to the hyperlinked resources of the Web; and *eSquirt*, a protocol for interoperation with web present devices.

16.7.1 Web presences

Cooltown considers physical entities to be divided into three categories: people, places, and things. The web presence of a person, place or thing is potentially any web resource chosen to suit a specific application; but Cooltown adopts certain roles for the web presences of people and places. The web presences of things and people are collected in the web presences of places, so the description follows that order.

Things. A 'thing' is either a device or a non-electronic physical entity. Things become web-present by embedding web-servers in them or by hosting their web-presence within a web server. If the thing is a device, then its URL is that of the service it implements. For example, an 'Internet radio' is a music-playing device that hosts its own web presence. A user who has discovered the URL of an Internet radio retrieves a web page with controls that enables them to 'tune' it to an Internet broadcasting source, adjust its settings such as the volume, or upload the user's own sound file. But even non-electronic things may have a web presence – a web resource associated with the thing but hosted by a web server somewhere else. For example, a printed document's web presence could be its electronic document counterpart: instead of having to photocopy the printed document (with a consequent reduction in quality), a user can discover its web presence from the physical artefact – as we explain in Section 16.7.2 – and request a new print. The web presence of a music CD could be some associated digital content such as extra music clips and photographs, hosted in its owner's personal media collection.

People. People become web present by offering global web home pages with services to facilitate communications with them and by offering information about their current context. For example, users without mobile phones could make the local phone number available via their web presence – a value that their web presence automatically updates as they move around. But they might also choose for their web presence to register their current location explicitly – through a link to the web-presence of the place in which they are physically present.

Places. Places are smart spaces, to use the terminology of this chapter. Places become web present by registering the web presences of people and things within them – and even the web presences of nested or otherwise related places – with a place-specific directory service (Section 9.3). A place's directory also contains relatively static information such as a description of the place's physical properties and function. The directory service enables components to discover and thus interact with the dynamic set of web presences within the place. It is also used as a source of information about the place and its contents to be presented to humans, in the form of web pages.

The directory entries for the web presences within a place can be established in two main ways. First, a network discovery service (Section 16.2.1) can be used to automatically register any web presences that are implemented by devices within the place's subnet – devices that have wirelessly connected within the place, or the place's infrastructure servers. However, while network discovery services are useful, they suffer from the problem that not all web presences are hosted by devices in the place's subnet. The web presences of non-electronic physical entities such as humans, printed documents and music CDs that move into the place or are brought into it may be hosted anywhere. Those web presences have to be registered there manually or via sensing mechanisms, in a process called *physical registration* [Barton *et al*. 2002] – for example, by sensing their RFID tags.

A service called a *web presence manager* [Debaty and Caswell 2001] manages web present places – for example, for all the rooms within a building – and it can also manage the web presences of people and things. Places are a particular instance of the Cooltown abstraction of a *context*: a set of related web-present entities linked together for purposes such as browsing. The web presence manager relates each web-present entity to the web presences of entities in its context. For example, if the entity is a thing, its related entities could be the person who carries it and the place where it is located. If the entity is a person, its related entities could be the things carried by the person, the place where the person is currently located and possibly the directly surrounding persons.

16.7.2 Physical hyperlinks

Web presences are web resources like any other, so web pages can contain text or image links to web presences like any other links. But in that standard web-linking model the user comes across the web presence of a person, place or thing via an *information* source: the web page. The Cooltown design enables humans additionally to go directly to web presences from their *physical* source: namely, the specific physical person, place or thing that they have encountered in their everyday movements through the physical world.

A *physical hyperlink* is any means by which a user can retrieve the URL of an entity's web presence from the physical entity itself or its immediate surroundings. We now consider ways of implementing physical hyperlinks. First, consider the HTML markup for a typical link in a web page, say:

<a href="http://cdk4.net/ChopSuey.html">Hopper's painting Chop Suey</a>.

That links the text 'Hopper's painting Chop Suey' in a web page to a page at *http://cdk4.net/Hopper.html* about the Edward Hopper painting *Chop Suey* that is being referred to. Now, consider the question of how a visitor to a museum who encounters the painting there could 'click on' the painting to obtain information about it in the browser on their mobile phone, PDA or other portable device. That would require a way of discovering the URL of the painting from the physical configuration of the painting itself. One way would be to write the URL on the wall by the painting so that the user could type it into their device's browser. But that would be inelegant and laborious.

Instead, Cooltown utilizes the fact that users have sensors integrated with their devices, and investigated two main approaches to discovering the URLs of entities via those sensors: *direct sensing* and *indirect sensing*.

Direct sensing: In this model, the user's device senses a URL directly from a tag (an 'automatic identification' tag) or beacon attached to the entity of interest or next to it (see Section 16.4.3). A relatively large entity such as a room could have several tags or beacons located in highly visible places. A tag is a passive device or artefact that presents the URL when the user places their device's sensor near it. For example, a camera phone could in principle perform optical character recognition against the URL written on a sign or it could read the URL encoded in a two-dimensional barcode. A

Figure 16.13 Capturing and printing the web presence of a painting

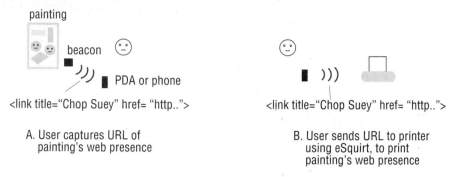

A. User captures URL of painting's web presence

B. User sends URL to printer using eSquirt, to print painting's web presence

beacon, on the other hand, regularly emits the entity's URL, typically over (directional) infrared rather than radio, which is typically omnidirectional and thus can lead to ambiguity as to which URL belongs to which entity.

In particular, the Cooltown project developed beacons in the form of small devices (a few centimetres across) that emit a string every few seconds over infrared using a one-shot, connectionless protocol (Figure 16.13A). The emitted string is an XML-like document consisting of the URL of the entity's web presence and a short title. Many portable devices such as mobile phones and PDAs have integrated infrared transceivers and so are capable of receiving those strings. When a client program receives the string, it can, for example, either cause the device's browser to go to the received URL directly or it can create a hyperlink from the received title to the received URL and add that hyperlink to a list of received hyperlinks, which the user can click on when they choose.

Indirect sensing: Indirect sensing is where the user's device obtains an identifier from a tag or beacon, which is looked up to obtain a URL. The sensing device knows the URL of a *resolver* – a name server that maintains a collection of bindings from identifiers to URLs (a naming context, in the terminology of Chapter 9) and which returns the URL bound to the given identifier [Kindberg 2002]. Ideally, the name space used for entity identifiers would be sufficiently large to enable every physical entity to have a unique identifier and thus remove the possibility for ambiguity. However, in principle, local identifiers could be used as long as they were only ever looked up using a local resolver – otherwise, spurious results might be obtained since someone else might have used the same identifier for a different entity.

Indirect sensing is sometimes used because constraints in the tag technology mean that direct URL sensing is impossible. For example, linear barcodes do not have sufficient capacity to store an arbitrary URL; cheap RFID tags store only a fixed-length binary identifier. In each case, the stored identifier has to be looked up to obtain the web presence's URL.

But there is also a positive reason to use indirect sensing: it allows a given physical entity to have a set of web presences instead of just one. Just as the same phrase 'Hopper's painting Chop Suey' could appear in several web pages but be linked to different web pages in them, so a given physical painting could lead to different web presences according to the choice of resolver. For example, one web presence of the painting could be a link to a service that prints a copy on a nearby printer in the museum;

another web presence for the same painting could be a page providing information about the painting from an independent third party with no connection to the museum.

The implementation of resolution follows the web architecture in that each resolver is an independent web site. The client software is a browser augmented by a simple plug-in. Resolvers provide web forms that contain a field which the client fills as a side-effect of sensing, rather than presenting the field to the user for manual entry. When the user, say, scans a barcode, the resultant identifier is automatically filled into the form and the client posts the form to the resolver. The resolver returns the corresponding URL, if such exists.

Since resolvers are themselves web resources, the user navigates to them as they would any other web page [Kindberg 2002], and updates the client with which resolver it is to use. In particular, the user may pick up the URL of a local resolver using a local physical hyperlink. For example, the museum's administrators could set up Cooltown beacons emitting the local resolver's URL, so that the visitors could use that resolver to obtain locally relevant web presences for the paintings within the museum. Equally, if the identifiers of the paintings are well known and globally established, then the visitors could utilize other resolvers anywhere on the Web – for example, a Spanish visitor might utilize the bookmarked resolver of a Spanish art commentary site while visiting a museum in North America.

Finally, although we have pointed out some advantages of indirect sensing over direct sensing, its main disadvantage is the client's extra round-trip to a resolver, and the consequences for latency and energy consumption.

16.7.3 Interoperation and the 'eSquirt' protocol

One method for interoperation between a web-present target device and the user's portable device is to use standard web protocols. The user's portable device issues an HTTP GET or POST operation; the target device responds with a user interface in the form of a web page, which the portable device renders for the user. Returning to a previous example, a web-present Internet radio can present the URL of its web service via a beacon facing out to its users. The user walks in front of the radio and points the infrared receiver on their portable device – say their PDA – at it; the client on their PDA receives the URL from the radio and passes the URL to its browser. The result is the radio's 'home' page on the PDA, with controls to adjust its volume, upload and play sound files from the PDA, etc.

A web-present printer in a museum could behave similarly. The user obtains the printer's home page via its beacon, and thus can upload content to the printer and specify the printer's settings via the web page. Of course, devices such as printers may have physical user interfaces; but simpler appliances such as digital picture frames may not, and a virtual user interface is then essential.

The above form of interoperation is data-oriented and thus device-independent, like the Web in general. Since the target device provides its own user interface, a user can control the device through their browser without requiring target-specific software. For example, a user with an image file on her PDA can render it on an arbitrary image-rendering device, whether it be a printer or a digital picture frame, say; and a user with a sound file on her PDA can hear it on an arbitrary audio-consuming device, whether it be, for example, an Internet radio or a 'smart' HiFi system.

A problem with those scenarios is that the user's relatively resource-poor portable device, which may have a low-bandwidth wireless connection, is in the content pathway between the content's source and sink. Suppose that the user has obtained an image of a painting in a Cooltown-enhanced museum, or has obtained an audio clip of someone talking about the painting. In each case, the adaptation techniques of Section 16.6 may have been applied because of limited resources such as screen size and bandwidth, resulting in somewhat low fidelity versions of the image or sound clip on the portable device. When the user passes the image to a printer in the museum, or the sound clip to the Internet radio in their hotel room, they will be presented with low-quality versions even though those devices are capable of high-quality rendering and may have a high-bandwidth wired network connection.

Cooltown's *eSquirt* protocol for interoperation between devices removes the low-fidelity problem – and avoids precious bandwidth and energy consumption – by passing the *URL* of the content from one device to another, instead of the content itself. In fact, the protocol is identical to the one used to send a URL (and title) from a Cooltown beacon to a device over infrared (Figure 16.13B). The devices pass that small amount of data over the low-energy infrared medium, and that is the only network operation in which each device is involved during the eSquirt protocol itself. However, the recipient device can then act as a web client to retrieve the content using the URL, and perform an operation such as rendering the resultant data.

For example, a user who has obtained the URL of an image of a Hopper painting from a beacon beside the painting sends that URL to a printer using her eSquirt-capable PDA. The protocol that eSquirt uses is unreliable but, as with a TV remote control, if transmission fails then the user presses the 'squirt' button again until feedback at the printer confirms success. The printer (rather, the printing service, which may be implemented in the infrastructure) then acts as a web client to retrieve the content from the URL – in its full-fidelity form – and prints it.

The user's portable device thus can act like a device-independent clipboard for URLs, similar to an application-independent clipboard for data in copy-and-paste operations on a desktop user interface. The user employs the device to 'copy and paste' URLs between sources and sinks to transfer content between them.

Device-independence is the most important advantage of the eSquirt paradigm. The eSquirt protocol always works the same way; what differs is the processing of the URL by the recipient. However, the user has to have a reasonable idea of what combinations of squirted URLs and receiving devices make sense. The receiving device's designer must expect some mistakes: a user may mistakenly squirt a URL of an audio file into a printer. However, it is still inadvisable to design away such mistakes in advance. The prevention measures, such as type-checking, may lead to the phenomena of lost opportunities and brittle interoperation that we identified in Section 16.2.2.

While simplicity is a strength of the eSquirt protocol, a disadvantage is that it relies on using default settings in the recipient device, or using physical controls to input its settings. That is, eSquirt does not enable the interoperation paradigm with which we began this subsection, in which a client device obtains a virtual user interface for controlling the settings of a target device. For example, after squirting the URL of a sound file or a streaming radio station to an Internet radio, how does the user control the volume from their portable device? Exercise 16.19 explores this issue.

16.7.4 Summary and perspective

We have outlined the main features of the Cooltown architecture. The goal of that project was to benefit nomadic users by extending the Web, a virtual collection of hyperlinked content, to entities in their physical world, regardless of whether those entities have electronic functionality of their own. The architecture considered physical entities, including people, places and things, to be associated with web presences. Next are the physical hyperlinks – the mechanisms for sensing the web presence's URL from a physical entity. The project implemented physical hyperlinks using infrared beacons, tags such as barcodes and RFID tags, and resolvers to turn identifiers into URLs. Finally, eSquirt is a device-independent interoperation protocol, which relieves low-powered portable devices from the need to be in the content pathway between sources and sinks of content.

Cooltown largely achieved its objectives but only on the assumption that the human is very much 'in the loop'. Humans physically discover the services associated with the entities they encounter, via physical hyperlinks. Humans may also have to physically register the web presences of tagged non-electronic entities such as music CDs when they are placed in the context of a web-present place such as a house, so that they become electronically discoverable there. Finally, humans not only associate their portable devices to web-present entities by 'clicking' on physical hyperlinks but, via the eSquirt protocol, they also bring about device-independent interoperation. The involvement of the human makes for great flexibility, and eliminates the problem of lost opportunities for interaction. However, the simple eSquirt interoperation model does not give users control over what a recipient device does with a URL that they have squirted into it.

An alternative development would be for automated association and interoperation of web-present entities. Each physical entity could have an instance of a uniform type of web presence, which would record details of that entity's semantics (perhaps using semantic web technologies), including relationships between that entity and others – in particular, the relationship between a web-present person or thing and the web-presence of the place that contains them. Thus, all web presences within a given place could discover one another and interoperate. For example, the web presence of the secretary in a meeting could discover documents within a meeting room that needed to be printed, discover which members were present, discover a nearby printer, and cause the requisite number of a copies to be printed. Cooltown's web presence manager [Debaty and Caswell 2001] made a start at realizing that vision, through uniform management not just of places but of web-present things and people that have links to related entities such as the web-present place they are in. For example, when an entity enters a new place and is registered there, the entity is automatically updated with a link to the web presence of its new host place. Ideally, entity relationships would all be programatically established, instead of the limited support available today. But the complicated semantics of our everyday world make it likely that realizing an application such as automated meeting support in a practically useful rather than error-prone way is still a long way off. In the meantime, involving humans in the loop enables progress to be made.

16.8 Summary

This chapter has presented the main challenges raised by mobile and ubiquitous computer systems, and rather fewer solutions since not many are available. Most of the challenges stem from the fact that those systems are volatile, which in turn is largely due to the fact that they are integrated with our everyday physical world. The systems are volatile in that the set of users, hardware and software components in a given smart space is subject to unpredictable change. Components tend to make and break associations routinely, either as they move from smart space to smart space or because of failure. Connection bandwidth can vary widely over time. Components can fail as batteries die or for other reasons. Sections 16.1 to 16.3 discussed those aspects of volatility in full, and some techniques for associating components and enabling them to interoperate despite the difficulties of 'constant change'.

The integration of devices with our physical world involves sensing and context awareness (Section 16.4), and we have described some architectures for processing sensed data. But there remains a challenge that we might describe as *physical fidelity*: how accurately can a system with sensing and computation behave in accordance with the subtle semantics we humans associate with the physical world in which we live? Does a 'context aware phone' really behave as we would want in inhibiting rings appropriately as we move between places? Does the web presence of a place such as a hotel room in Cooltown actually record all the web-present entities that a human would say were in that place – and not, for example, some in an adjacent room?

Security and privacy (Section 16.5) feature strongly in research on mobile and ubiquitous systems. Volatility complicates security because it begs the question of what basis there can be for trust between components that wish to establish a secure channel. Fortunately, the existence of physically constrained channels goes some way to enabling secure channels where there is a human present. Physical integration has implications for privacy: if the user is being tracked to provide them with context aware services, then there may be a severe loss of privacy. We described some approaches to identifier management and outlined statistical techniques aimed at reducing that problem.

Physical integration also means new degrees of constraint in terms of such factors as device energy capacity, wireless bandwidth and user interfaces – a node in a sensor network has little of the first two and none of the last; a mobile phone has more of all three, but still much less than a desktop machine. Section 16.6 discussed some of the architectures by which components can adapt to resource constraints.

Section 16.7 described the architecture of the Cooltown project as a case study. The architecture is distinctive in that it applies lessons learned from the Web to ubiquitous computing. The advantage is a high degree of interoperability. But as a result, the Cooltown design applies mainly to situations in which humans supervise interactions.

Finally, this chapter has concentrated on the *differences* between mobile and ubiquitous systems and the more conventional distributed systems that appear elsewhere in this book – on aspects of volatility and physical integration. Exercise 16.20 invites the reader to list some of the similarities, and to consider the extent to which conventional distributed systems solutions apply.

EXERCISES

16.1   What is a volatile system? List the main types of changes that occur in a ubiquitous system.   *page 661*

16.2   Discuss whether it is possible to improve upon the 'pull' model of service discovery by multicasting (or broadcasting) and caching replies to queries.   *page 671*

16.3   Explain the use of leases in a discovery service to cope with the problem of service volatility.   *page 671*

16.4   The Jini lookup service matches service offers to client requests based on attributes or on Java typing. Explain with examples the difference between these two methods of matching. What is the advantage of allowing both sorts of matching?   *page 672*

16.5   Describe the use of IP multicast and group names in the Jini 'discovery' service which allows clients and servers to locate lookup servers.   *page 672*

16.6   What is data-oriented programming and how does it differ from object-oriented programming?   *page 677*

16.7   Discuss the issue of how the scope of an event system can and should be related to the physical extent of a smart space in which it is used.   *page 678*

16.8   Compare and contrast the persistence requirements associated with event systems and tuple spaces in the infrastructure of smart spaces.   *page 679*

16.9   Describe three ways of sensing the presence of a user beside a display and thus motivate some features required in an architecture for context-aware systems.   *page 684*

16.10   Explain and motivate in-network processing for wireless sensor networks.   *page 688*

16.11   In the Active Bat location system, only three ultrasound receivers are used by default to obtain a 3D position whereas four satellites are required to obtain a 3D position in satellite navigation. Why is there a difference?   *page 693*

16.12   In some location systems, tracked objects give up their identifiers to the infrastructure. Explain how this may give rise to concerns about privacy, even if the identifiers are anonymous.   *page 695*

16.13   Many sensor nodes are to be scattered throughout a region. The nodes are to communicate securely. Explain the problem of key distribution and outline a probabilistic strategy for distributing keys.   *page 697*

16.14   We described several technologies that provide receive-constrained channels for use in secure spontaneous device association. Which of those technologies also provide send-constrained channels?   *page 699*

16.15   Show how to construct a send-constrained channel from a receive-constrained channel, and *vice versa*. Hint: use a trusted node connected to the given channel.   *page 699*

16.16   A group of smart spaces are connected only by a space between them such as a hallway or square. Discuss the factors that determine whether that intervening space can act as a mix zone.   *page 704*

16.17 Explain the contextual factors to be taken into account when adapting multimedia content.   *page 705*

16.18 Assume that a device can execute 3 million instructions for the same amount of energy (3J) used to transmit or receive 1 Kbit of data a distance of 100m by radio. The device has the option of sending a 100 Kbyte binary program to a compute server 100m away, which when run will execute 60 billion instructions and exchange 10,000 1 Kbit messages with the device. If energy is the only consideration, should the device offload the computation or execute it itself? Assume computation on the device is negligible in the offloaded case.   *page 708*

16.19 A Cooltown user squirts the URL of a sound file or a streaming radio station to an Internet radio. Suggest a modification to the eSquirt protocol that would enable the user to control the volume from their portable device. Hint: consider what extra data the squirting device should provide.   *page 715*

16.20 Discuss the applicability to mobile and ubiquitous systems of techniques drawn from the areas of (a) peer-to-peer systems (Chapter 10); (b) coordination and agreement protocols (Chapter 12); and (c) replication (Chapter 15).   *page 717*

17

DISTRIBUTED MULTIMEDIA SYSTEMS

Multimedia applications generate and consume continuous streams of data in real time. They contain large quantities of audio, video and other time-based data elements, and the timely processing and delivery of the individual data elements (audio samples, video frames) is essential. Elements delivered late are of no value and are normally dropped.

A flow specification for a multimedia stream is expressed in terms of acceptable values for the rate at which data passes from a source to a destination (the bandwidth), the delivery delay for each element (latency) and the rate at which elements are lost or dropped. The latency is particularly important in interactive applications. Some small degree of data loss from multimedia streams is often acceptable provided that the application can resynchronize the elements following those that are lost.

The planned allocation and scheduling of resources to meet the needs of multimedia and other applications is referred to as quality of service management. The allocation of processing capacity, network bandwidth and memory (for the buffering of data elements that are delivered early) are all important. They are allocated in response to quality of service requests from applications. A successful QoS request delivers a QoS guarantee to the application and results in the reservation and subsequent scheduling of the resources requested.

This chapter draws substantially on a tutorial paper by Ralf Herrtwich [1995] and we are grateful to him for permission to use his material.

17.1 Introduction

Modern computers can handle streams of continuous, time-based data such as digital audio and video. This capability has led to the development of distributed multimedia applications such as networked video libraries, Internet telephony and videoconferencing. Such applications are viable with current general-purpose networks and systems, although the quality of the resulting audio and video is often less than satisfactory. More demanding applications such as large-scale videoconferencing, digital TV production, interactive TV and video surveillance systems are beyond the capabilities of current networking and distributed system technologies.

Multimedia applications demand the timely delivery of streams of multimedia data to end-users. Audio and video streams are generated and consumed in real time, and the timely delivery of the individual elements (audio samples, video frames) is essential to the integrity of the application. In short, multimedia systems are real-time systems: they must perform tasks and deliver results according to a schedule that is externally determined. The degree to which this is achieved by the underlying system is known as the *quality of service* (QoS) enjoyed by an application.

Although the problems of real-time system design had been studied before the advent of multimedia systems, and many successful real-time systems were developed (see, for example, Kopetz and Verissimo [1993]), they have not generally been integrated into more general-purpose operating systems and networks. The nature of the tasks performed by these existing real-time systems, such as avionics, air traffic control, manufacturing process control and telephone switching, differs from those performed in multimedia applications. The former generally deal with relatively small quantities of data and have relatively infrequent *hard deadlines*, but failure to meet any deadline can have serious or even disastrous consequences. In such cases, the solution adopted has been to over-specify the computing resources and to allocate them on a fixed schedule that ensures that worst-case requirements are always met.

The planned allocation and scheduling of resources to meet the needs of multimedia and other applications is referred to as *quality of service management*. Most current operating systems and networks do not include the QoS management facilities needed to support multimedia applications.

The consequences of failure to meet deadlines in multimedia applications can be serious, especially in commercial environments such as video-on-demand services, business conferencing applications and remote medicine, but the requirements differ significantly from those of other real-time applications:

- Multimedia applications are often highly distributed and operate within general-purpose distributed computing environments. They therefore compete with other distributed applications for network bandwidth and for computing resources at users' workstations and servers.

- The resource requirements of multimedia applications are dynamic. A videoconference will require more or less network bandwidth as the number of participants grows or shrinks. Its use of computing resources at each user's workstation will also vary, since, for example, the number of video streams that have to be displayed varies. Multimedia applications may involve other variable

Figure 17.1 A distributed multimedia system

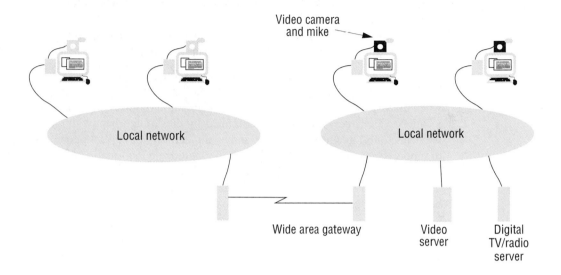

or intermittent loads. For example, a multimedia lecture might include a processor-intensive simulation activity.

- Users often wish to balance the resource costs of a multimedia application with other activities. Thus they may be willing to reduce their demands for video bandwidth in a conferencing application in order to allow a separate voice conversation to proceed, or they may wish a program development or a word-processing activity to proceed while they are participating in a conference.

QoS management systems are intended to meet all of these needs, managing the available resources dynamically and varying the allocations in response to changing demands and user priorities. A QoS management system must manage all of the computing and communication resources needed to acquire, process and transmit multimedia data streams, especially where the resources are shared between applications.

Figure 17.1 illustrates a typical distributed multimedia system capable of supporting a variety of applications, such as desktop conferencing or providing access to stored video sequences, broadcast digital TV and radio. The resources for which QoS management is required include network bandwidth, processor cycles and memory capacity. Disk bandwidth at the video server may also be included. We shall adopt the generic term *resource bandwidth* to refer to the capacity of any hardware resource (network, central processor, disk subsystem) to transmit or process multimedia data.

In an open distributed system, multimedia applications can be started up and used without prior arrangement. Several applications may coexist in the same network and even on the same workstation. The need for QoS management therefore arises regardless of the *total quantity* of resource bandwidth or memory capacity in the system. QoS management is needed in order to *guarantee* that applications will be able to obtain the necessary quantity of resources at the required times, even when other applications are competing for the resources.

Some multimedia applications have been deployed even in today's QoS-less, best-efforts computing and network environments. These include:

Web-based multimedia: These are applications that provide best-effort access to streams of audio and video data published via the Web. They have been successful when there is little or no need for the synchronization of the data streams at different locations. Their performance is constrained by the limited bandwidth and variable latencies found in current networks and by the inability of current operating systems to support real-time resource scheduling. For audio and low-quality video sequences, the use of extensive buffering at the destination to smooth out the variations in bandwidth and latency results in continuous and smooth display of video sequences but with a source-to-destination delay that may reach several seconds.

Network phone and audio conferencing: This application has relatively low bandwidth requirements, especially when efficient compression techniques are used. But its interactive nature demands low round-trip delays, and these cannot always be achieved.

Video-on-demand services: These supply video information in digital form, retrieving the data from large online storage systems and delivering them to the end-user's display. These are successful where sufficient dedicated network bandwidth is available and where the video server and the receiving stations are dedicated. They also employ considerable buffering at the destination.

Highly interactive applications pose much greater problems. Many multimedia applications are cooperative (involving several users) and synchronous (requiring the users' activities to be closely coordinated). They span a wide spectrum of application contexts and scenarios. For example:

- Internet telephony. See box on the adjacent page.

- A simple videoconference involving two or more users, each using a workstation equipped with a digital video camera, microphone, sound output and video display capability. Application software to support simple teleconferencing is widely available (for example: *CU-SeeMe* [Dorcey 1995], *NetMeeting* [www.microsoft.com III], *iChat AV* [Apple Computer 2004]), but its performance is often limited by bandwidth and latency constraints.

- A music rehearsal and performance facility enabling musicians at different locations to perform in an ensemble [Konstantas *et al.* 1997]. This is a particularly demanding multimedia application because the synchronization constraints are so tight.

Applications such as these require:

Low-latency communication: Round trip delays of 100–300 ms, so that interaction between users appears to be synchronous.

Synchronous distributed state: If one user stops a video on a given frame, the other users should see it stopped at the same frame.

Media synchronization: All participants in a music performance should hear the performance at approximately the same time (Konstantas *et al.* [1997] identified a requirement for synchronization within 50 ms). Separate soundtrack and video streams should maintain 'lip sync', e.g. for a user commenting live on a video playback, or a distributed *karaoke* session.

External synchronization: In conferencing and other cooperative applications, there may be active data in other formats, such as computer-generated animations, CAD data, electronic whiteboards and shared documents. Updates to these must be

Internet telephony – VoIP

The Internet was not designed for real-time interactive applications such as telephony, but it has become possible to use it for that purpose as a result of the increases in the capacity and performance of the Internet's core components – its backbone of network links run at 10–40 Gbps and the routers that interconnect them have comparable performance. These components typically run at low load factors (< 10% bandwidth utilization) and IP traffic is therefore seldom delayed or dropped as a result of contention for resources.

   This has resulted in the feasibility of building telephony applications over the public Internet by transmitting streams of digitized voice samples from source to destination as UDP packets with no special provision for quality of service. Voice-over-IP (VoIP) applications such as Skype and Vonage rely on this technique, as do the voice features of instant-messaging applications such as AOL Instant Messaging, Apple iChat AV and Microsoft NetMeeting.

   Of course these are real-time interactive applications and latency remains an issue. As discussed in Chapter 3, the routing of IP packets incurs an inevitable delay at each router they pass through. For long routes these delays can easily total in excess of 150 ms and users will observe this in the form of delays in conversational interaction. For this reason, long-distance (especially intercontinental) Internet telephone calls suffer from delays to a much greater extent than those using the conventional telephone network.

   Nevertheless, much voice traffic is carried on the Internet and integration with the conventional telephone network is underway. SIP (Session Initiation Protocol, defined in RFC 2543 [Handley *et al.* 1999]) is an application-level protocol for the establishment of voice calls (as well as other services such as instant messaging) over the Internet. Gateways to the conventional telephone network exist in many locations throughout the world, enabling calls to be initiated from Internet-connected devices that are routed over the Internet and terminate at conventional telephones or personal computers.

Figure 17.2   The window of scarcity for computing and communication resources

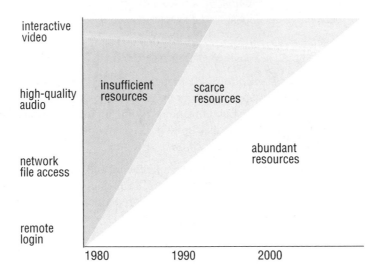

distributed and acted upon in a manner that appears at least approximately synchronized with the time-based multimedia streams.

Such applications will run successfully only in systems that include rigorous QoS management schemes.

The window of scarcity ◊ Many of today's computer systems provide some capacity to handle multimedia data, but the necessary resources are very limited. Especially when dealing with large audio and video streams, many systems are constrained in the quantity and quality of streams they can support. This situation has been depicted as the *window of scarcity* [Anderson *et al.* 1990b]. While a certain class of applications lies within this window, a system needs to allocate and schedule its resources carefully in order to provide the desired service (see Figure 17.2). Before the window of scarcity is reached, a system has insufficient resources to execute the relevant applications. This was the situation for multimedia applications before the mid-1980s. Once an application class has left the window of scarcity, system performance will be sufficient to provide the service even under adverse circumstances and without customized mechanisms.

Advances in system performance are likely to be used to improve the quality of multimedia data to include higher frame rates and greater resolution for video streams or to support many media streams concurrently, for example, in a videoconferencing system. But more demanding applications, including virtual reality and real-time stream manipulation ('special effects'), can extend the window of scarcity almost indefinitely.

In Section 17.2 we review the characteristics of multimedia data. Section 17.3 describes approaches to the allocation of scarce resources in order to achieve QoS, and Section 17.4 discusses methods for scheduling them. Section 17.5 discusses methods for optimizing the flow of data in multimedia systems. Section 17.6 describes the Tiger video file server, a low-cost scalable system for the delivery of stored video streams to large numbers of clients concurrently.

Figure 17.3   Characteristics of typical multimedia streams

	Data rate (approximate)	Sample or frame size	frequency
Telephone speech	64 kbps	8 bits	8000/sec
CD-quality sound	1.4 Mbps	16 bits	44,000/sec
Standard TV video (uncompressed)	120 Mbps	up to 640 × 480 pixels × 16 bits	24/sec
Standard TV video (MPEG-1 compressed)	1.5 Mbps	variable	24/sec
HDTV video (uncompressed)	1000–3000 Mbps	up to 1920 × 1080 pixels × 24 bits	24–60/sec
HDTV video (MPEG-2 compressed)	10–30 Mbps	variable	24–60/sec

17.2 Characteristics of multimedia data

We have referred to video and audio data as continuous and time-based. How can we define these characteristics more precisely? The term 'continuous' refers to the user's view of the data. Internally, continuous media are represented as sequences of discrete values that replace each other over time. For example, the value of an image array is replaced 25 times per second to give the impression of a TV-quality view of a moving scene; a sound amplitude value is replaced 8000 times per second to convey telephone-quality speech.

Multimedia streams are said to be *time-based* (or *isochronous*) because timed data elements in audio and video streams define the semantics or 'content' of the stream. The times at which the values are played or recorded affect the validity of the data. Hence systems that support multimedia applications need to preserve the timing when they handle continuous data.

Multimedia streams are often bulky. Hence systems that support multimedia applications need to move data with greater throughput than conventional systems. Figure 17.3 shows some typical data rates and frame/sample frequencies. We note that the resource bandwidth requirements for some are very large. This is especially so for video of reasonable quality. For example, a standard TV video stream requires more than 120 Mbps, which exceeds the capacity of a 100 Mbps Ethernet network. CPU capacities are also stretched; a program that copies or applies a simple data transformation to each frame of a standard TV video stream requires at least 10% of the CPU capacity of a 400 MHz PC. The figures for high-definition television streams are even higher, and in many applications, such as videoconferencing, there is a need to handle multiple video and audio streams concurrently. The use of compressed representations is therefore essential, although transformations such as video mixing are difficult to accomplish with compressed streams.

Compression can reduce bandwidth requirements by factors between 10 and 100, but the timing requirements of continuous data are unaffected. There is intensive research and standardization activity aimed at producing efficient, general-purpose representations and compression methods for multimedia data streams. This work has resulted in various compressed data formats, such as GIF, TIFF and JPEG for still images and MPEG-1, MPEG-2 and MPEG-4 for video sequences. We do not detail these here; several other sources, such as Buford [1994] and Gibbs and Tsichritzis [1994], provide reviews of media types, representations and standards, and the web site [Multimedia Directory] is a useful source of references to documentation on current multimedia standards and other resources.

Although the use of compressed video and audio data reduces bandwidth requirements in communication networks, it imposes substantial additional loads on processing resources at the source and destination. This has often been supplied through the use of special-purpose hardware to process and dispatch video and audio information – the video and audio coders/decoders (*codecs*) found on video cards manufactured for personal computers. But the increasing power of personal computers and multiprocessor architectures are likely to enable them to perform much of this work in software using software coding and decoding filters. This approach offers greater flexibility, with better support for application-specific data formats, special-purpose application logic and the simultaneous handling of multiple media streams.

The compression method used for the MPEG video formats is asymmetric, with a complex compression algorithm and simpler decompression. This tends to help its use in desktop conferencing, where compression is often performed by a hardware codec but decompression of the several streams arriving at each user's computer is performed in software, enabling the number of conference participants to vary without regard to the number of codecs in each user's computer.

17.3 Quality of service management

When multimedia applications run in networks of personal computers, they compete for resources at the workstations running the applications (processor cycles, bus cycles, buffer capacity) and in the networks (physical transmission links, switches, gateways). Workstations and networks may have to support several multimedia and conventional applications. There is competition between the multimedia and conventional applications, between different multimedia applications and even between the media streams within individual applications.

The concurrent use of physical resources for a variety of tasks has long been possible with multi-tasking operating systems and shared networks. In multi-tasking operating systems, the central processor is allocated to individual tasks (or processes) in a round-robin or other scheduling scheme that shares the processing resources on a *best-efforts* basis among all of the tasks currently competing for the central processor.

Networks are designed to enable messages from different sources to be interleaved, allowing many virtual communication channels to exist on the same

Figure 17.4 Typical infrastructure components for multimedia applications

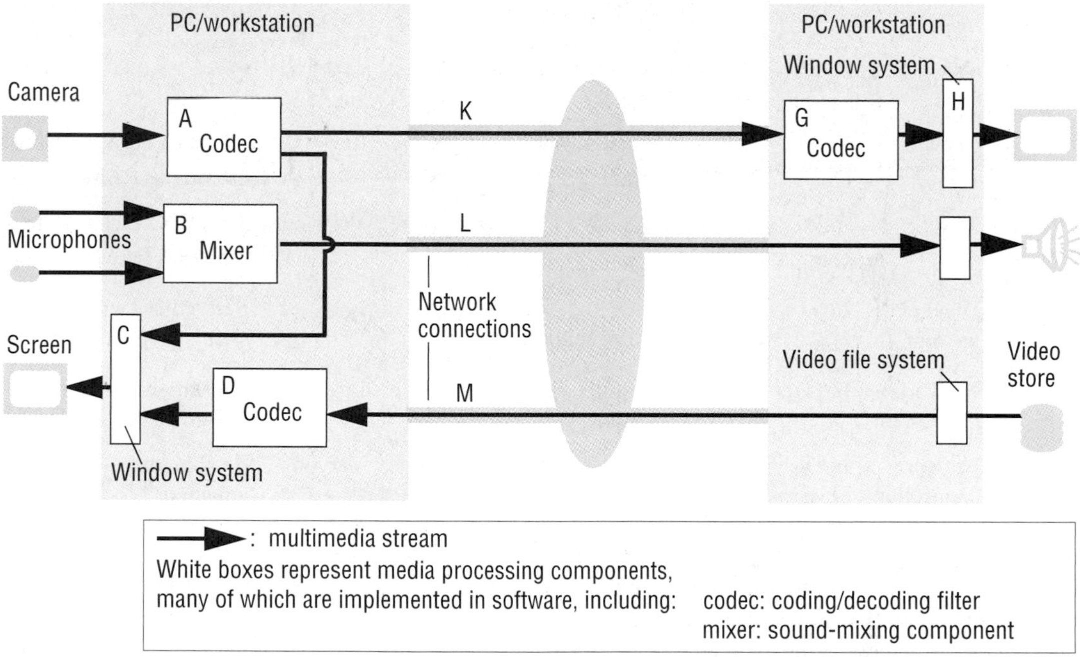

physical channels. The predominant local-area network technology, Ethernet, manages a shared transmission medium in a *best-efforts* manner. Any node may use the medium when it is quiet. But packet collisions can occur, and when they do, sending nodes wait for random backoff periods in order to prevent repeated collisions. Collisions are likely to occur when the network is heavily loaded, and this scheme cannot provide any guarantees regarding the bandwidth or latency in such situations.

The key feature of these resource allocation schemes is that they handle increases in demand by spreading the available resources more thinly between the competing tasks. Round-robin and other best-efforts methods for sharing processor cycles and network bandwidth cannot meet the needs of multimedia applications. As we have seen, the timely processing and transmission of multimedia streams is crucial for them. Late delivery is valueless. In order to achieve timely delivery, applications need guarantees that the necessary resources will be allocated and scheduled at the required times.

The management and allocation of resources to provide such guarantees is referred to as *quality of service management*. Figure 17.4 shows the infrastructure components for a simple multimedia conferencing application running on two personal computers, using software data compression and format conversion. The white boxes represent software components whose resource requirements may affect the quality of service of the application.

The figure shows the most commonly used abstract architecture for multimedia software, in which continuously flowing *streams* of media data elements (video frames, audio samples) are processed by a collection of processes and transferred between the

Figure 17.5   QoS specifications for components of the application shown in Figure 17.4

Component		Bandwidth	Latency	Loss rate	Resources required
Camera	Out:	10 frames/sec, raw video 640x480x16 bits	–	Zero	–
A Codec	In: Out:	10 frames/sec, raw video MPEG-1 stream	Interactive	Low	10 ms CPU each 100 ms; 10 Mbytes RAM
B Mixer	In: Out:	2 × 44 kbps audio 1 × 44 kbps audio	Interactive	Very low	1 ms CPU each 100 ms; 1 Mbytes RAM
H Window system	In: Out:	various 50 frame/sec framebuffer	Interactive	Low	5 ms CPU each 100 ms; 5 Mbytes RAM
K Network connection	In/Out:	MPEG-1 stream, approx. 1.5 Mbps	Interactive	Low	1.5 Mbps, low-loss stream protocol
L Network connection	In/Out:	Audio 44 kbps	Interactive	Very low	44 kbps, very low-loss stream protocol

processes by interprocess connections. The processes produce, transform and consume continuous streams of multimedia data. The connections link the processes in a sequence from a *source* of media elements to a *target,* at which it is rendered or consumed. The connections between the processes may be implemented by networked connections or by in-memory transfers when processes reside on the same machine. For the elements of multimedia data to arrive at their target on time, each process must be allocated adequate CPU time, memory capacity and network bandwidth to perform its designated task and must be scheduled to use the resources sufficiently frequently to enable it to deliver the data elements in its stream to the next process on time.

In Figure 17.5, we set out resource requirements for the main software components and network connections in Figure 17.4 (note the corresponding letters against components in these two figures). Clearly, the required resources can be guaranteed only if there is a system component responsible for the allocation and scheduling of those resources. We shall refer to that component as the *quality of service manager.*

Figure 17.6 shows the QoS manager's responsibilities in the form of a flowchart. In the next two subsections we describe the QoS manager's two main subtasks:

Quality of service negotiation: The application indicates its resource requirements to the QoS manager. The QoS manager evaluates the feasibility of meeting the requirements against a database of the available resources and current resource commitments and gives a positive or negative response. If it is negative, the application may be reconfigured to use reduced resources, and the process is repeated.

Admission control: If the result of the resource evaluation is positive, the requested resources are reserved and the application is given a *resource contract*, stating the resources that have been reserved. The contract includes a time limit. The application is then free to run. If it changes its resource requirements it must notify the QoS manager. If the requirements decrease, the resources released are returned to the database as available resources. If they increase, a new round of negotiation and admission control is initiated.

In the remainder of this section we describe techniques for performing these subtasks in further detail. Of course, while an application is running, there is a need for fine-grained scheduling of resources such as processor time and network bandwidth to ensure that real-time processes receive their allocated resources on time. Techniques for this are discussed in Section 17.4.

17.3.1 Quality of service negotiation

To negotiate QoS between an application and its underlying system, an application must specify its QoS requirements to the QoS manager. This is done by the transmission of a set of parameters. Three parameters are of primary interest when it comes to processing and transporting multimedia streams: *bandwidth*, *latency* and *loss rate*.

Bandwidth: The bandwidth of a multimedia stream or component is the rate at which data flows through it.

Latency: Latency is the time required for an individual data element to move through a stream from the source to the destination.This may vary depending on the volume of other data in the system and other characteristics of the system load. This variation is termed *jitter* – formally, jitter is the first derivative of the latency.

Loss rate: Since the late delivery of multimedia data is of no value, data elements will be dropped when it is impossible to deliver them before their scheduled delivery time. In a perfectly managed QoS environment, this should never happen, but as yet, few such environments exist, for reasons outlined earlier. Furthermore, the resource cost of guaranteeing on-time delivery for every media element is often unacceptable – it is likely to involve the reservation of resources far exceeding the average requirement in order to deal with occasional peaks. The alternative that is adopted is to accept a certain rate of data loss – dropped video frames or audio samples. The acceptable ratios are usually kept low – seldom more than 1% and much lower for quality-critical applications.

The three parameters can be used:

1. To describe the characteristics of a multimedia stream in a particular environment. For example, a video stream may require an average bandwidth of 1.5 Mbps, and because it is used in a conferencing application it needs to be transferred with at most 150 ms delay to avoid conversation gaps. The decompression algorithm used at the target may still yield acceptable pictures with a loss rate of one frame out of 100.

2. To describe the capabilities of resources to transport a stream. For example, a network may provide connections of 64 kbps bandwidth, its queuing algorithms guarantee delays of less than 10 ms, and the transmission system may guarantee a loss rate smaller than 1 in 10^6.

The parameters are interdependent. For example:

Figure 17.6   The QoS manager's task

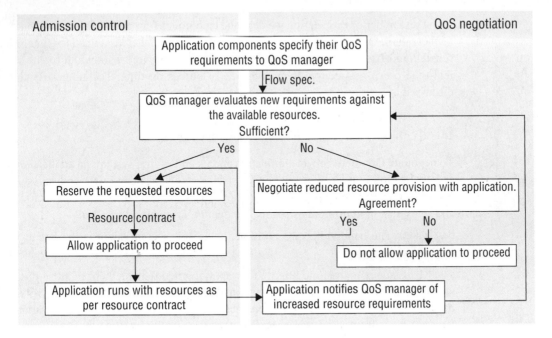

- Loss rate in modern systems rarely depends on actual bit errors due to noise or malfunction; it results from buffer overflow and from time-dependent data arriving too late. Hence, the larger bandwidth and delay can be, the more likely is a low loss rate.

- The smaller the overall bandwidth of a resource is compared with its load, the more messages will accumulate in front of it and the larger the buffers for this accumulation need to be to avoid loss. The larger the buffers become, the more likely it is that messages need to wait for other messages in front of them to be serviced – that is, the larger the delay will become.

Specifying the QoS parameters for streams ◊   The values of QoS parameters can be stated explicitly (e.g. for the camera output stream in Figure 17.4 we might require *bandwidth*: 50 Mbps, *delay*: 150 ms, *loss*: < 1 frame in 10^3) or implicitly (e.g. the bandwidth of the input stream to the network connection K is the result of applying MPEG-1 compression to the camera output).

But the more usual case is that we need to specify a value and a range of permissible variation. Here we consider this requirement for each of the parameters:

Bandwidth: Most video compression techniques produce a stream of frames of differing sizes depending on the original content of the raw video. For MPEG, the average compression ratio is between 1:50 and 1:100, but this will vary dynamically depending on content; for example, the required bandwidth will be highest when the content is changing most rapidly. Because of this, it is often useful to quote QoS parameters as maximum, minimum or average values, depending on the type of QoS management regime that will be used.

Another problem that arises in the specification of the bandwidth is the characterization of *burstiness*. Consider three streams of 1 Mbps. One stream transfers a single frame of 1 Mbit every second, the second is an asynchronous stream of computer-generated animation elements with an average bandwidth of 1 Mbps, and the third sends a 100-bit sound sample every microsecond. Whereas all three streams require the same bandwidth, their traffic patterns are very different.

One way to take care of irregularities is to define a burst parameter in addition to rate and frame size. The burst parameter specifies the maximum number of media elements that may arrive early – that is, before they should arrive according to the regular arrival rate. The model of *linear-bounded arrival processes* (LBAP) used in Anderson [1993] defines the maximum number of messages in a stream during any time interval t as $Rt + B$, where R is the rate and B is the maximum size of burst. The advantage of using this model is that it nicely reflects the characteristics of multimedia sources: multimedia data read from disks is usually delivered in large blocks, and data received from networks often arrives in the form of sequences of smaller packets. In this case, the burst parameter defines the amount of buffer space required to avoid loss.

Latency: Some timing requirements in multimedia result from the stream itself: if a frame of a stream does not get processed with the same rate at which frames arrive, backlog builds up and buffer capacity may be exceeded. If this is to be avoided, a frame must on average not remain in a buffer for longer than $1/R$, where R is the frame rate of a stream, or a backlog will occur. If backlogs do occur, the number and size of the backlogs will affect the maximum end-to-end delay of a stream, in addition to the processing and propagation times.

Other latency requirements arise from the application environment. In conferencing applications, the need for apparently instantaneous interaction between the participants makes it necessary to achieve absolute end-to-end delays of no more than 150 ms to avoid problems in the human perception of the conversation, whereas for the replay of stored video, to ensure a proper system response to commands such as *Pause* and *Stop*, the maximum latency should be in the order of 500 ms.

A third consideration for the delivery time of multimedia messages is jitter – variation in the period between the delivery of two adjacent frames. Whereas most multimedia devices make sure that they present data at its regular rate without variation, software presentations (for example, in a software decoder for video frames) need to take extra care to avoid jitter. Jitter is essentially solved by buffering, but the scope for jitter removal is limited, because total end-to-end delay is constrained by the consideration mentioned above, so the playback of media sequences also requires media elements to arrive before fixed deadlines.

Loss rate: Loss rate is the most difficult QoS parameter to specify. Typical loss rate values result from probability calculations about overflowing buffers and delayed messages. These calculations are either based on worst-case assumptions or on standard distributions. Neither of these is necessarily a good match for practical situations. However, loss rate specifications are necessary to qualify the bandwidth and latency parameters: two applications may have the same bandwidth and latency characteristics;

Figure 17.7   Traffic shaping algorithms

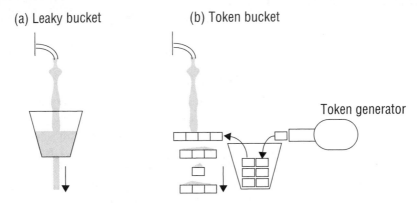

they will look dramatically different when one application loses every fifth media element and the other loses only one in a million.

As with bandwidth specifications, where not just the volume of data sent in a time interval but its distribution over the time interval is important, a loss rate specification needs to determine the time interval during which to expect a certain loss. In particular, loss rates given for infinite time spans are not useful, as any loss over a short time may exceed the long-term rate significantly.

Traffic shaping ◊ Traffic shaping is the term used to describe the use of output buffering to smooth the flow of data elements. The bandwidth parameter of a multimedia stream typically provides an idealistic approximation of the actual traffic pattern that will occur when the stream is transmitted. The closer the actual traffic pattern matches the description, the better a system will be able to handle the traffic, in particular when it uses scheduling methods that are designed for periodic requests.

The LBAP model of bandwidth variations calls for regulation of the burstiness of multimedia streams. Any stream can be regulated by inserting a buffer at the source and by defining a method by which data elements leave the buffer. A good illustration of this method is the image of a leaky bucket (Figure 17.7(a)): the bucket can be filled arbitrarily with water until it is full; through a leak at the bottom of the bucket water will flow continuously. The leaky bucket algorithm ensures that a stream will never flow with a rate higher than R. The size of the buffer B defines the maximum burst a stream can incur without losing elements. B also bounds the time for which an element will remain in the bucket.

The leaky bucket algorithm completely eliminates bursts. Such elimination is not always necessary as long as bandwidth is bounded over any time interval. The token bucket algorithm achieves this while allowing larger bursts to occur when a stream has been idle for a while (Figure 17.7(b)). It is a variation of the leaky bucket algorithm in which tokens to send data are generated at a fixed rate R. They are collected in a bucket of size B. Data of size S can be sent only if at least S tokens are in the bucket. The send process then removes these S tokens. The token bucket algorithm ensures that over any interval t the amount of data sent is not larger than $Rt + B$. It is, hence, an implementation of the LBAP model.

Figure 17.8   The RFC 1363 Flow Spec

	Protocol version
	Maximum transmission unit
Bandwidth:	Token bucket rate
	Token bucket size
	Maximum transmission rate
Delay:	Minimum delay noticed
	Maximum delay variation
	Loss sensitivity
Loss:	Burst loss sensitivity
	Loss interval
	Quality of service guarantee

High peaks of size B can only occur in a token bucket system when a stream has been idle for a while. To avoid these bursts, a simple leaky bucket can be placed behind the token bucket. The flow rate F of this bucket needs to be significantly larger than R for this scheme to make sense. Its only purpose is to break up really large bursts.

Flow specifications ◊ A collection of QoS parameters is typically known as a flow specification, or *flow spec* for short. Several examples of flow specs exist and are all similar. In Internet RFC 1363 [Partridge 1992], a flow spec is defined as eleven 16-bit numeric values (Figure 17.8), which reflect the QoS parameters discussed above in the following way:

- The maximum transmission unit and maximum transmission rate determine the maximum bandwidth required by the stream.

- The token bucket size and rate determine the burstiness of the stream.

- The delay characteristics are specified by the minimum delay that an application can notice (since we wish to avoid over-optimization for short delays) and maximum jitter it can accept.

- The loss characteristics are defined by the total acceptable number of losses over a certain interval and the maximum number of consecutive losses.

There are many alternatives for expressing each parameter group. In SRP [Anderson *et al.* 1990a], the burstiness of a stream is given by a maximum workahead parameter, which defines the number of messages a stream may be ahead of its regular arrival rate at any point in time. In Ferrari and Verma [1990], a worst-case delay bound is given: if the system cannot guarantee to transport data within this timespan, the data transport will be useless for the application. In RFC 1190, the specification of the ST-II protocol [Topolcic 1990], loss is represented as the probability of each packet being dropped.

All the above examples provide a continuous spectrum of QoS values. If the set of applications and streams to be supported is limited, it may be sufficient to define a discrete set of QoS classes: for example, telephone-quality and high-fidelity audio, live and playback video, etc. The requirements of all classes must be implicitly known by all system components; the system may even be configured for a certain traffic mix.

Negotiation procedures ◊ For distributed multimedia applications, the components of a stream are likely to be located in several nodes. There will be a QoS manager at each node. A straightforward approach to QoS negotiation is to follow the flow of data along each stream from the source to the target. A source component initiates the negotiation by sending out a flow spec to its local QoS manager. The manager can check against its database of available resources whether the requested QoS can be provided. If other systems are involved in the application, the flow spec is forwarded to the next node where resources are required. The flow spec traverses all the nodes until the final target is reached. Then the information on whether the desired QoS can be provided by the system is passed back to the source. This simple approach to negotiation is satisfactory for many purposes, but it does not consider the possibilities for conflict between concurrent QoS negotiations starting at different nodes. A distributed transactional QoS negotiation procedure would be required for a full solution to this problem.

Applications rarely have fixed QoS requirements. Instead of returning a boolean value on whether a certain QoS can be provided or not, it is more appropriate for the system to determine what kind of QoS it can provide and let the application decide on whether it is acceptable. In order to avoid over-optimized QoS or to abort the negotiation when it becomes clear that the desired quality is not achievable, it is common to specify a desired and worst value for each QoS parameter. An application may specify that it desires a bandwidth of 1.5 Mbps but would also be able to handle 1 Mbps, or that delay should be 200 ms, but 300 ms would be the worst case that is still acceptable. As only one parameter can be optimized at a time, Systems such as HeiRAT [Vogt *et al.* 1993], expects the user to define values for only two parameters and leaves it to the system to optimize the third.

If a stream has multiple sinks, the negotiation path forks according to the data flow. As a straightforward extension to the above scheme, intermediate nodes can aggregate QoS feedback messages from the targets to produce worst-case values for the QoS parameters. The available bandwidth then becomes the smallest available bandwidth of all targets, the delay becomes the longest of all targets, and the loss rate becomes the largest of all targets. This is the procedure practised by sender-initiated negotiation protocols such as SRP, ST-II and RCAP [Banerjea and Mah 1991].

In situations with heterogeneous targets, it is usually inappropriate to assign a common worst-case QoS to all targets. Instead, each target should receive the best possible QoS. This calls for a receiver-initiated negotiation process rather then a sender-oriented one. RSVP [Zhang *et al.* 1993] is an alternative QoS negotiation protocol in which targets connect to streams. Sources communicate the existence of streams and their inherent characteristics to all targets. Targets can then connect to the closest node through which the stream passes and derive data from there. In order for them to obtain data with the appropriate QoS, they may need to use techniques such as filtering (discussed in Section 17.5).

17.3.2 Admission control

Admission control regulates access to resources to avoid resource overload and to protect resources from requests that they cannot fulfil. It involves turning down service requests should the resource requirements of a new multimedia stream violate existing QoS guarantees.

An admission control scheme is based on some knowledge of both the overall system capacity and the load generated by each application. The bandwidth requirement specification for an application may reflect the maximum amount of bandwidth that an application will ever require, the minimum bandwidth it will need to function, or some average value in between. Correspondingly, an admission control scheme may base its resource allocation on any of these values.

For resources that have a single allocator, admission control is straightforward. Resources that have distributed access points, such as many local area networks, require either a centralized admission control entity or some distributed admission control algorithm that avoids conflicting concurrent admissions. Bus arbitration within workstations falls into this category; however, even multimedia systems that perform bandwidth allocation extensively do not control bus admission, as bus bandwidth is not considered to be in the window of scarcity.

Bandwidth reservation ◊ A common way to ensure a certain QoS level for a multimedia stream is to reserve some portion of resource bandwidth for its exclusive use. In order to fulfil the requirements of a stream at all times, a reservation needs to be made for its maximum bandwidth. This is the only possible way to provide guaranteed QoS to an application – at least as long as no catastrophic system failures occur. It is used for applications that cannot adapt to different QoS levels or become useless when quality drops occur. Examples include some medical applications (a symptom may appear in an x-ray video just at the time when video frames are dropped) and video recording (where dropped frames will result in a flaw in the recording that is visible every time the video is played).

Reservation based on maximum requirements can be straightforward: when controlling access to a network of a certain bandwidth B, multimedia streams s of a bandwidth b_s can be admitted as long as $\Sigma b_s <= B$. Thus a token ring of 16 Mb/s may support up to ten digital video streams of 1.5 Mb/s each.

Unfortunately, capacity calculations are not always as simple as in the network case. To allocate CPU bandwidth in the same way requires the execution profile of each application process to be known. Execution times, however, depend on the processor used and often cannot be determined precisely. While several proposals for automatic execution time calculation exist [Mok 1985, Kopetz et al. 1989], none of them has achieved widespread use. Execution times are usually determined through measurements that often have wide error margins and limited portability.

For typical media encodings such as MPEG, the actual bandwidth consumed by an application may be significantly lower than its maximum bandwidth. Reservations based on maximum requirements may then lead to wasted resource bandwidth: requests for new admissions are turned down although they could be satisfied with the bandwidth that is reserved for, but not actually used by existing applications.

Statistical multiplexing ◊ Because of the potential under-utilization that can occur, it is common to overbook resources. The resulting guarantees, often called statistical or soft guarantees to distinguish them from the deterministic or hard guarantees introduced before, are only valid with some (usually very high) probability. Statistical guarantees tend to provide better resource utilization as they do not consider the worst case. But just as when resource allocation is based on minimum or average requirements, simultaneous peak loads can cause drops in service quality; applications have to be able to handle these drops.

Statistical multiplexing is based on the hypothesis that for a large number of streams the aggregate bandwidth required remains nearly constant regardless of the bandwidth of individual streams. It assumes that when one stream sends a large quantity of data, there will also be another stream that sends a small quantity and overall the requirements will balance out. This, however, is only the case for uncorrelated streams.

As experiments show [Leland *et al.* 1993], multimedia traffic in typical environments does not obey this hypothesis. Given a larger number of bursty streams, the aggregate traffic still remains bursty. The term *self-similar* has been applied to this phenomenon, meaning that the aggregate traffic shows similarity to the individual streams of which it is composed.

17.4 Resource management

To provide a certain QoS level to an application, not only does a system need to have sufficient resources (performance), it also needs to make these resources available to an application when they are needed (scheduling).

17.4.1 Resource scheduling

Processes need to have resources assigned to them according to their priority. A resource scheduler determines the priority of processes based on certain criteria. Traditional CPU schedulers in time-sharing systems often base their priority assignments on responsiveness and fairness: I/O-intensive tasks get high priority to guarantee fast response to user requests, CPU-bound tasks get lower priorities and overall, processes in the same class are treated equally.

Both criteria remain valid for multimedia systems, but the existence of deadlines for the delivery of individual multimedia data elements changes the nature of the scheduling problem. Real-time scheduling algorithms can be applied to this problem as discussed below. As multimedia systems have to handle both discrete and continuous media, it becomes a challenge to provide sufficient service to time-dependent streams without causing starvation of discrete-media access and other interactive applications.

Scheduling methods need to be applied to (and coordinated for) all resources that affect the performance of a multimedia application. In a typical scenario, a multimedia stream would be retrieved from disk and then sent through a network to a target station, where it is synchronized with a stream coming from another source and finally displayed. The resources required in this example include disk, network and CPUs as well as memory and bus bandwidth on all systems involved.

Fair scheduling ◊ If several streams compete for the same resource, it becomes necessary to consider fairness and to prevent ill-behaved streams taking too much bandwidth. A straightforward approach ensuring fairness is to apply round-robin scheduling to all streams in the same class. Whereas in Nagle [1987] such a method was introduced on a packet-by-packet basis, in Demers *et al.* [1989] the method is used on a bit-by-bit basis, which provides more fairness with respect to varying packet sizes and packet arrival times. These methods are known as fair queuing.

Packets cannot actually be sent on a bit-by-bit basis, but given a certain frame rate it is possible to calculate for each packet when it should have been sent completely. If packet transmissions are ordered based on this calculation, one achieves almost the same behaviour as with actual bit-by-bit round robin, except that when a large packet is sent, it may block the transmission of a smaller packet, which would have been preferred under the bit-by-bit scheme. However, no packet is delayed for longer than the maximum packet transmission time.

All basic round-robin schemes assign the same bandwidth to each stream. To take the individual bandwidth of streams into account, the bit-by-bit scheme can be extended so that for certain streams a larger number of bits can be transmitted per cycle. This method is called weighted fair queuing.

Real-time scheduling ◊ Several real-time scheduling algorithms have been developed to meet the CPU scheduling needs of applications such as avionics industrial process control. Assuming that the CPU resources have not been over-allocated (which is the task of the QoS manager), they assign CPU time slots to a set of processes in a manner that ensures that they complete their tasks on time.

Traditional real-time scheduling methods suit the model of regular continuous multimedia streams very well. Earliest-deadline-first (EDF) scheduling has almost become a synonym for these methods. An EDF scheduler uses a deadline that is associated with each of its work items to determine the next item to be processed: the item with the earliest deadline goes first. In multimedia applications, we identify each media element arriving at a process as a work item. EDF scheduling is proven to be optimal for allocating a single resource based on timing criteria: if there is a schedule that fulfils all timing requirements, EDF scheduling will find it [Dertouzos 1974].

EDF scheduling requires one scheduling decision per message (i.e. per multimedia element). It would be more efficient to base scheduling on elements that exist for a longer time. Rate-monotonic (RM) scheduling is a prominent technique for real-time scheduling of periodic processes that achieves just this. Streams are assigned priorities according to their rate: the higher the rate of work items on a stream, the higher the priority of a stream. RM scheduling has been shown to be optimal for situations that only utilize a given bandwidth by less than 69% [Liu and Layland 1973]. Using such an allocation scheme, the remaining bandwidth could be given to non-real-time applications.

To cope with bursty real-time traffic, the basic real-time scheduling methods should be adjusted to distinguish between time-critical and non-critical continuous-media work items. In Govindan and Anderson [1991], deadline/workahead scheduling is introduced. It allows messages in a continuous stream to arrive ahead of time in bursts but applies EDF scheduling to a message only at its regular arrival time.

17.5 Stream adaptation

Whenever a certain QoS cannot be guaranteed or can be guaranteed only with a certain probability, an application needs to adapt to changing QoS levels, adjusting its performance accordingly. For continuous-media streams, the adjustment translates into different levels of media presentation quality.

The simplest form of adjustment is to drop pieces of information. This is easily done in audio streams, where samples are independent of each other, but it can be noticed immediately by the listener. Dropouts in a video stream encoded in Motion JPEG, where each frame is freestanding, are more tolerable. Encoding mechanisms such as MPEG, where the interpretation of a frame depends on the values of several adjacent frames, are less robust against omissions: it takes a longer time to recover from errors, and the encoding mechanism may in fact amplify errors.

If there is insufficient bandwidth and data is not dropped, the delay of a stream will increase over time. For non-interactive applications this may be acceptable, although it can eventually lead to buffer overflows as data is accumulated between the source and sink. For conferencing and other interactive applications, increasing delays are not acceptable, or must exist only for a short period. If a stream is behind its assigned playout time, its playout rate should be increased until it gets back on schedule: while a stream is delayed, frames should be output as soon as they are available.

17.5.1 Scaling

If adaptation is performed at the target of a stream, the load on any bottleneck in the system is not decreased and the overload situation persists. It is useful to adapt a stream to the bandwidth available in the system before it enters a bottleneck resource in order to resolve contention. This is known as scaling.

Scaling is best applied when live streams are sampled. For stored streams, it depends on the encoding method how easy it is to generate a downgraded stream. Scaling may be too cumbersome if the entire stream has to be decompressed and encoded again just for scaling purposes. Scaling algorithms are media-dependent, although the overall scaling approach is the same: to subsample a given signal. For audio information, such subsampling can be achieved by reducing the rate of audio sampling. It can also be achieved by dropping a channel in a stereo transmission. As this example shows, different scaling methods can work at different granularities.

For video, the following scaling methods are appropriate:

Temporal scaling: reduces the resolution of the video stream in the time domain by decreasing the number of video frames transmitted within an interval. Temporal scaling is best suited for video streams in which individual frames are self-contained and can be accessed independently. Delta compression techniques are more difficult to handle as not all frames can be easily dropped. Hence, temporal scaling is more suitable for Motion JPEG than for MPEG streams.

Spatial scaling: reduces the number of pixels of each image in a video stream. For spatial scaling, hierarchical arrangement is ideal because the compressed video is immediately available in various resolutions. Therefore, the video can be transferred

Figure 17.9   Filtering

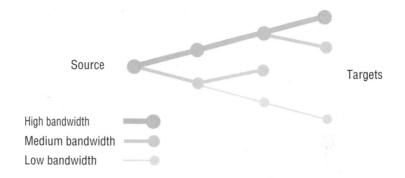

Source

Targets

High bandwidth
Medium bandwidth
Low bandwidth

over the network using different resolutions without recoding each picture before finally transmitting it. JPEG and MPEG-2 support different spatial resolutions of images and are well-suited for this kind of scaling.

Frequency scaling: modifies the compression algorithm applied to an image. This results in some loss of quality, but in a typical picture, compression can be increased significantly before a reduction of image quality becomes visible.

Amplitudinal scaling: reduces the colour depths for each image pixel. This scaling method is in fact used in H.261 encodings to arrive at a constant throughput as image content varies.

Colour space scaling: reduces the number of entries in the colour space. One way to realize colour space scaling is to switch from colour to grey-scale presentation.

Combinations of these scaling methods can be used if necessary.

A system to perform scaling consists of a monitor process at the target and a scaler process at the source. The monitor keeps track of the arrival times of messages in a stream. Delayed messages are an indication of a bottleneck in the system. The monitor then sends a *scale-down* message to the source and the source reduces the bandwidth of the stream. After some period of time, the source scales the stream up again. Should the bottleneck still exist, the monitor will again detect a delay and scale the stream down [Delgrossi *et al.* 1993]. A problem for the scaling system is to avoid unnecessary *scale-up* operations and to prevent the system from oscillating.

17.5.2 Filtering

As scaling modifies a stream at the source, it is not always suitable for applications that involve several receivers: when a bottleneck occurs on the route to one target, this target sends a *Scale-Down* message to the source and all targets receive the degraded quality, although some would have no problem in handling the original stream.

Filtering is a method that provides the best possible QoS to each target by applying scaling at each relevant node on the path from the source to the target (Figure 17.9). RSVP [Zhang *et al.* 1993] is an example of a QoS negotiation protocol that supports

Figure 17.10   Tiger video file server hardware configuration

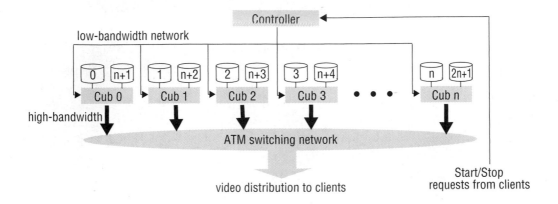

filtering. Filtering requires that a stream be partitioned into a set of hierarchical sub-streams, each adding a higher level of quality. The capacity of nodes on a path determines the number of sub-streams a target receives. All other sub-streams are filtered out as close to the source as possible (perhaps even at the source) to avoid transfer of data that is later thrown away. A sub-stream is not filtered at an intermediate node if somewhere downstream a path exists that can carry the entire sub-stream.

17.6 Case study: the Tiger video file server

A video storage system that supplies multiple real-time video streams simultaneously is seen as an important system component to support consumer-oriented multimedia applications. Several prototype systems of this type have been developed, and some have evolved into products (see [Cheng 1998]). One of the most advanced of these is the Tiger video file server developed at the Microsoft Research Labs [Bolosky *et al.* 1996].

Design goals ◊ The main design goals for the system were as described below:

Video-on-demand for a large number of users: The typical application is a service that supplies movies to paying clients. The movies are selected from a large stored digital movie library. Clients should receive the first frames of their selected movies within a few seconds of issuing a request, and they should be able to perform pause, rewind and fast-forward operations at will. Although the library of available movies is large, a few movies may be very popular and they will be the subject of multiple unsynchronized requests, resulting in several concurrent but time-shifted playings of them.

Quality of service: Video streams must be supplied at a constant rate with a maximum jitter that is determined by the (assumed small) amount of buffering available at the clients and a very low loss rate.

Scalable and distributed: The aim was to design a system with an architecture that is extensible (by the addition of computers) to support up to 10,000 clients simultaneously.

Low-cost hardware: The system was to be built using low-cost hardware ('commodity' PCs with standard disk drives).

Fault tolerant: The system should continue to operate without noticeable degradation after the failure of any single server computer or disk drive.

Taken together, these requirements demand a radical approach to the storage and retrieval of video data and an effective scheduling algorithm that balances the workload across a large number of similar servers. The primary task is the transfer of high-bandwidth streams of video data from disk storage to a network, and it is this load that has to be shared between the servers.

Architecture ◊ The Tiger hardware architecture is shown in Figure 17.10. All of the components are off-the-shelf products. The *cub* computers shown in the figure are identical PCs with the same number of standard hard disk drives (typically between 2 and 4) attached to each. They are also equipped with Ethernet and ATM network cards. The *controller* is another PC. It is not involved in the handling of multimedia data and is responsible only for the handling of client requests and the management of the work schedules of the cubs.

Storage organization ◊ The key design issue is the distribution of the video data among the disks attached to cubs in order to enable them to share the load. Since the load may involve the supply of multiple streams from the same movie as well as the supply of streams from many different movies, any solution based on the use of a single disk to store each movie is unlikely to achieve the goal. Instead, movies are stored in a striped representation across all disks. This leads to a failure model in which the loss of a disk or a cub results in a gap in the sequence of every movie. This is dealt with by a storage mirroring scheme that replicates the data and a fault tolerance mechanism, as described below.

Striping: A movie is divided into *blocks* (chunks of video of equal play time, typically around 1 second, occupying about 0.5 Mbytes), and the set of blocks that make up a movie (typically about 7000 of them for a two-hour movie) is stored on disks attached to different cubs in a sequence indicated by the disk numbers shown in Figure 17.10. A movie can start on any disk. Whenever the highest-numbered disk is reached, the movie is 'wrapped around' so that the next block is stored on disk 0 and the process continues.

Mirroring: The mirroring scheme divides each block into several portions, called *secondaries*. This ensures that when a cub fails, the extra workload of supplying data for blocks on the failed cub falls on several of the remaining cubs and not just one of them. The number of secondaries per block is determined by a *decluster factor*, d, with typical values in the range 4 to 8. The secondaries for a block stored on disk i are stored on disks $i+1$ to $i+d$. Note that, provided that there are more than d cubs, none of these disks is attached to the same cub as disk i. With a decluster factor of 8, approximately 7/8ths of the processing capacity and disk bandwidth of cubs can be allocated to fault-free tasks. The remaining 1/8th of its resources should be enough to serve secondaries when needed.

Figure 17.11   Tiger schedule

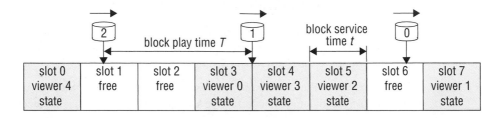

Distributed schedule ◊ The heart of Tiger's design is the scheduling of the workload for the cubs. The schedule is organized as a list of *slots*, where each slot represents the work that must be done to play one block of a movie – that is, to read it from the relevant disk and transfer it to the ATM network. There is exactly one slot for each potential client receiving a movie (called a *viewer*), and each occupied slot represents one viewer receiving a real-time video data stream. The viewer state is represented in the schedule by:

- the address of the client computer;

- the identity of the file being played;

- the viewer's position in the file (the next block to be delivered in the stream);

- the viewer's play sequence number (from which a delivery time for the next block can be calculated);

- some bookkeeping information.

The schedule is illustrated in Figure 17.11. The *block play time T* is the time that will be required for a viewer to display a block on the client computer, typically about 1 second and assumed to be the same for all the stored movies. Tiger must therefore maintain a time interval T between the delivery times of the blocks in each stream, with a small allowable jitter that is determined by the available buffering at the client computers.

Each cub maintains a pointer into the schedule for each disk that it controls. During each block play time it must process all of the slots with block numbers that fall on the disks it controls and delivery times that fall within the current block play time. The cub steps through the schedule in real-time processing slots as follows:

1. Read the next block into buffer storage at the cub.

2. Packetize the block and deliver it to the cub's ATM network controller with the address of the client computer.

3. Update viewer state in the schedule to show the new next block and play sequence number and pass the updated slot to the next cub.

These actions are assumed to occupy a maximum time t, which is known as the *block service time*. As can be seen in Figure 17.11, t is substantially less than the block play time. The value of t is determined by the disk bandwidth or the network bandwidth, whichever is smaller. (The processing resources in a cub are adequate to perform the scheduled work for all the attached disks.) When a cub has completed the schedule tasks for the current block play time it is available for unscheduled tasks until the start of the next play time. In practice, disks do not provide blocks with a fixed delay, and to accommodate their uneven delivery the disk read is initiated at least one block service time before the block is needed for packetizing and delivery.

A disk can handle the work to service T/t streams, and the values of T and t typically result in a value > 4 for this ratio. This and the number of disks in the entire system determines the number of viewers that a Tiger system can service. For example, a Tiger system with five cubs and three disks attached to each can deliver approximately 70 video streams simultaneously.

Fault tolerance ◊ Because of the striping of all the movie files across all of the disks in a Tiger system, failure of any component (a disk drive or a cub) would result in a disruption of service to all clients. The Tiger design remedies this by retrieving data from the mirrored secondary copies when a primary block is unavailable because of the failure of a cub or a disk drive. Recall that secondary blocks are smaller than primary blocks in the ratio of the decluster factor d and that the secondaries are distributed so that they fall on several disks that are attached to different cubs.

When a cub or a disk fails, the schedule is modified by an adjacent cub to show several *mirror viewer states*, representing workload for the d disks that hold the secondaries for those movies. A mirror viewer state is similar to a normal viewer state but with different block numbers and timing requirements. Because this extra workload is shared among d disks and d cubs, it can be accommodated without disrupting the tasks in other slots, provided that there is a small amount of spare capacity in the schedule. The failure of a cub is equivalent to the failure of all of the disks attached to it and is handled in a similar manner.

Network support ◊ The blocks of each movie are simply passed to the ATM network by the cubs that hold them, together with the address of the relevant client. The QoS guarantees of ATM network protocols (Section 3.5.3) are relied upon to deliver blocks to client computers in sequence and in time. The client needs sufficient buffer storage to hold two primary blocks, the one that is currently playing on the client's screen and one that is arriving from the network. When primary blocks are being served, the client need only check the sequence number of each arriving block and pass it to the display handler. When secondaries are being served, the d cubs responsible for a declustered block deliver their secondaries to the network in sequence, and it is the client's responsibility to collect and assemble them in its buffer storage.

Other functions ◊ We have described the time-critical activities of a Tiger server. The design requirements called for the provision of fast-forward and rewind functions. These functions call for the delivery of some fraction of the blocks in the movie to the client in order to give the visual feedback typically provided by video recorders. This is done on a best-effort basis by the cubs in unscheduled time.

The remaining tasks include the management and distribution of the schedule and the management of the database of movies, deleting old and writing new movies onto the disks, and maintaining an index of movies.

In the initial Tiger implementation, schedule management and distribution were handled by the controller computer. Because this constitutes a single point of failure and a potential performance bottleneck, schedule management was subsequently redesigned as a distributed algorithm [Bolosky *et al*. 1997]. Management of the movie database is performed by cubs in unscheduled time in response to commands from the controller.

Performance and scalability ◊ The initial prototype was developed in 1994 and used five 133MHz Pentium PCs, each equipped with 48 Mbytes of RAM and three 2-Gbyte SCSI disk drives and an ATM network controller, running over Windows NT. This configuration was measured under a simulated client load. When serving movies to 68 clients with no faults in the Tiger system the delivery of the data was perfect – no blocks were lost or delivered to clients late. With one cub failed (and hence three disks) the service was maintained with a data loss rate of only 0.02%, well within the design goal.

Another measurement that was taken was the startup latency to deliver the first block of a movie after receipt of a client request. This will be highly dependent on the number and the position of free slots in the schedule. The algorithm used for this initially would place a client request in the nearest free slot to the disk holding block 0 of the requested movie. This resulted in measured values for the startup latency in the range 2 to 12 seconds. Recent work has resulted in a slot allocation algorithm that reduces clustering of occupied slots in the schedule, leaving free slots distributed more evenly in the schedule and improving average startup latency [Douceur and Bolosky 1999].

Although the initial experiments were made with a small configuration, later measurements were made with a fourteen-cub, 56-disk configuration and the distributed scheduling scheme described by Bolosky *et al*. [1997]. The load that could be serviced by this system scaled successfully to deliver 602 simultaneous 2-Mbps data streams with a loss rate of less than one block in 180,000 when all cubs were functioning. With one cub failed, less than 1 in 40,000 blocks was lost. These results are impressive and appear to bear out the claim that a Tiger system could be configured with up to 1000 cubs servicing up to 30,000–40,000 simultaneous viewers.

17.7 Summary

Multimedia applications require new system mechanisms to enable them to handle large volumes of time-dependent data. The most important of these mechanisms are concerned with quality of service management. They must allocate bandwidth and other resources in a manner that ensures that application resource requirements can be met, and they must schedule the use of the resources so that the many fine-grained deadlines of multimedia applications are met.

Quality of service management handles QoS requests from applications, specifying the bandwidth, latency and loss rates acceptable for multimedia streams, and it performs admission control, determining whether sufficient unreserved resources are available to meet each new request and negotiating with the application if necessary. Once a QoS request is accepted, the resources are reserved and a guarantee is issued to the application.

The processor capacity and network bandwidth allocated to an application must then be scheduled to meet the application's needs. A real-time processor scheduling algorithm such as earliest-deadline-first or rate-monotonic is required to ensure that each stream element is processed in time.

Traffic shaping is the name given to algorithms that buffer real-time data to smooth out the timing irregularities that inevitably arise. Streams can be adapted to utilize fewer resources by reducing the bandwidth of the source (scaling) or at points along the way (filtering).

The Tiger video file server is an excellent example of a scalable system that provides stream delivery on a potentially very large scale with strong quality of service guarantees. Its resource scheduling is highly specialized, and it offers an excellent example of the changed design approach that is often required for such systems.

EXERCISES

17.1 Outline a system to support a distributed music rehearsal facility. Suggest suitable QoS requirements and a hardware and software configuration that might be used.

pages 724, 730

17.2 The Internet does not currently offer any resource reservation or quality of service management facilities. How do the existing Internet-based audio and video streaming applications achieve acceptable quality? What limitations do the solutions they adopt place on multimedia applications? *pages 724, 734, 740*

17.3 Explain the distinctions between the three forms of synchronization (synchronous distributed state, media synchronization and external synchronization) that may be required in distributed multimedia applications. Suggest mechanisms by which each of them could be achieved, for example in a videoconferencing application. *page 725*

17.4 Outline the design of a QoS manager to enable desktop computers connected by an ATM network to support several concurrent multimedia applications. Define an API for your QoS manager, giving the main operations with their parameters and results.

pages 730–732

17.5 In order to specify the resource requirements software components that process multimedia data, we need estimates of their processing loads. How can this information be obtained without undue effort? *pages 730–732*

17.6 How does the Tiger system cope with a large number of clients all requesting the same movie at random times? *pages 742–746*

17.7 The Tiger schedule is potentially a large data structure that changes frequently, but each cub needs an up-to-date representation of the portions it is currently handling. Suggest a mechanism for the distribution of the schedule to the cubs. *pages 742–746*

17.8 When Tiger is operating with a failed disk or cub, secondary data blocks are used in place of missing primaries. Secondary blocks are n times smaller than primaries (where n is the decluster factor), how does the system accommodate this variability in block size? *page 745*

18

DISTRIBUTED SHARED MEMORY

This chapter describes distributed shared memory (DSM), an abstraction used for sharing data between processes in computers that do not share physical memory. The motivation for DSM is that it allows a shared memory programming model to be employed, which has some advantages over message-based models. For example, programmers do not have to marshal data items in DSM.

A central problem in implementing DSM is how to achieve good performance that is retained as systems scale to large numbers of computers. Accesses to DSM involve potential underlying network communication. Processes competing for the same or neighbouring data items may cause large amounts of communication to occur. The amount of communication is strongly related to the consistency model of a DSM – the model that determines which of possibly many written values will be returned when a process reads from a DSM location.

The chapter discusses DSM design issues such as the consistency model and implementation issues such as whether copies of the same data item are invalidated or updated when one copy is written. It goes on to discuss invalidation protocols in more detail. Finally, it describes release consistency – a relatively weak consistency model that is adequate for many purposes and relatively cheap to implement.

18.1 Introduction

Distributed shared memory (DSM) is an abstraction used for sharing data between computers that do not share physical memory. Processes access DSM by reads and updates to what appears to be ordinary memory within their address space. However, an underlying runtime system ensures transparently that processes executing at different computers observe the updates made by one another. It is as though the processes access a single shared memory, but in fact the physical memory is distributed (see Figure 18.1).

The main point of DSM is that it spares the programmer the concerns of message passing when writing applications that might otherwise have to use it. DSM is primarily a tool for parallel applications or for any distributed application or group of applications in which individual shared data items can be accessed directly. DSM is in general less appropriate in client-server systems, where clients normally view server-held resources as abstract data and access them by request (for reasons of modularity and protection). However, servers can provide DSM that is shared between clients. For example, memory-mapped files that are shared and for which some degree of consistency is maintained are a form of DSM. (Mapped files were introduced with the MULTICS operating system [Organick 1972].)

Message passing cannot be avoided altogether in a distributed system: in the absence of physically shared memory, the DSM runtime support has to send updates in messages between computers. DSM systems manage replicated data: each computer has a local copy of recently accessed data items stored in DSM, for speed of access. The problems of implementing DSM are related to those discussed in Chapter 15, as well as those of caching shared files discussed in Chapter 8.

One of the first notable examples of a DSM implementation was the Apollo Domain file system [Leach *et al.* 1983], in which processes hosted by different workstations share files by mapping them simultaneously into their address spaces. This example shows that distributed shared memory can be persistent. That is, it may outlast the execution of any process or group of processes that accesses it and be shared by different groups of processes over time.

Figure 18.1 The distributed shared memory abstraction

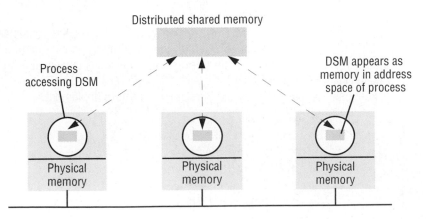

The significance of DSM first grew alongside the development of shared-memory multiprocessors (see Section 6.3). Much research has gone into investigating algorithms suitable for parallel computation on these multiprocessors. At the hardware architectural level, developments include both caching strategies and fast processor-memory inter-connections, aimed at maximizing the number of processors that can be sustained while achieving fast memory access latency and throughput [Dubois *et al.* 1988]. Where processes are connected to memory modules over a common bus, the practical limit is in the order of 10 processors before performance degrades drastically due to bus conten-tion. Processors sharing memory are commonly constructed in groups of four, sharing a memory module over a bus on a single circuit board. Multiprocessors with up to 64 processors in total are constructed from such boards in a *Non-Uniform Memory Access (NUMA)* architecture. This is a hierarchical architecture in which the four-processor boards are connected using a high-performance switch or higher-level bus. In a NUMA architecture, processors see a single address space containing all the memory of all the boards. But the access latency for on-board memory is less than that for a memory module on a different board – hence the name of this architecture.

In *distributed memory multiprocessors* and clusters of off-the-shelf computing components (see Section 6.3), the processors do not share memory but are connected by a very high-speed network. These systems, like general-purpose distributed systems, can scale to much greater numbers of processors than a shared-memory multiprocessor's 64 or so. A central question that has been pursued by the DSM and multiprocessor research communities is whether the investment in knowledge of shared memory algorithms and the associated software can be directly transferred to a more scalable distributed memory architecture.

18.1.1 Message passing versus DSM

As a communication mechanism, DSM is comparable with message passing rather than with request-reply-based communication, since its application to parallel processing, in particular, entails the use of asynchronous communication. The DSM and message passing approaches to programming can be contrasted as follows:

Programming model: Under the message passing model, variables have to be marshalled from one process, transmitted and unmarshalled into other variables at the receiving process. By contrast, with shared memory the processes involved share variables directly, so no marshalling is necessary – even of pointers to shared variables – and thus no separate communication operations are necessary. Most implementations allow variables stored in DSM to be named and accessed similarly to ordinary unshared variables. In favour of message passing, on the other hand, is that it allows processes to communicate while being protected from one another by having private address spaces, whereas processes sharing DSM can, for example, cause one another to fail by erroneously altering data. Furthermore, when message passing is used between heterogeneous computers, marshalling takes care of differences in data representation; but how can memory be shared between computers with, for example, different integer representations?

Synchronization between processes is achieved in the message model through message passing primitives themselves, using techniques such as the lock server implementation discussed in Chapter 13. In the case of DSM, synchronization is via normal constructs for shared-memory programming such as locks and semaphores (although these require different implementations in the distributed memory environment). Chapter 6 briefly discussed such synchronization objects in the context of programming with threads.

Finally, since DSM can be made persistent, processes communicating via DSM may execute with non-overlapping lifetimes. A process can leave data in an agreed memory location for the other to examine when it runs. By contrast, processes communicating via message passing must execute at the same time.

Efficiency: Experiments show that certain parallel programs developed for DSM can be made to perform about as well as functionally equivalent programs written for message passing platforms on the same hardware [Carter *et al.* 1991] – at least in the case of relatively small numbers of computers (ten or so). However, this result cannot be generalized. The performance of a program based on DSM depends upon many factors, as we shall discuss below – particularly the pattern of data sharing (such as whether an item is updated by several processes).

There is a difference in the visibility of costs associated with the two types of programming. In message passing, all remote data accesses are explicit and therefore the programmer is always aware of whether a particular operation is in-process or involves the expense of communication. Using DSM, however, any particular read or update may or may not involve communication by the underlying runtime support. Whether it does or not depends upon such factors as whether the data have been accessed before and the sharing pattern between processes at different computers.

There is no definitive answer as to whether DSM is preferable to message passing for any particular application. DSM is a promising tool whose ultimate status depends upon the efficiency with which it can be implemented.

18.1.2 Implementation approaches to DSM

Distributed shared memory is implemented using one or a combination of specialized hardware, conventional paged virtual memory or middleware:

Hardware: Shared-memory multiprocessor architectures based on a NUMA architecture (for example, Dash [Lenoski *et al.* 1992] and PLUS [Bisiani and Ravishankar 1990]) rely on specialized hardware to provide the processors with a consistent view of shared memory. They handle memory LOAD and STORE instructions by communicating with remote memory and cache modules as necessary to store and retrieve data. This communication is over a high-speed interconnection which is analogous to a network. The prototype Dash multiprocessor has 64 nodes connected in a NUMA architecture.

Paged virtual memory: Many systems, including Ivy [Li and Hudak 1989], Munin [Carter *et al.* 1991], Mirage [Fleisch and Popek 1989], Clouds [Dasgupta *et al.* 1991] (see www.cdk4.net/oss), Choices [Sane *et al.* 1990], COOL [Lea *et al.* 1993] and Mether [Minnich and Farber 1989], implement DSM as a region of virtual memory occupying the same address range in the address space of every participating process.

Figure 18.2   Mether system program

```
        #include "world.h"
        struct shared { int a, b; };

Program Writer:
    main()
    {
        struct shared *p;
        methersetup();                      /* Initialize the Mether runtime */
        p = (struct shared *)METHERBASE;
                                            /* overlay structure on METHER segment */
        p->a = p->b = 0;                    /* initialize fields to zero */
        while(TRUE){                        /* continuously update structure fields */
            p ->a = p ->a + 1;
            p ->b = p ->b - 1;
        }
    }

Program Reader:
    main()
    {
        struct shared *p;
        methersetup();
        p = (struct shared *)METHERBASE;
        while(TRUE){                        /* read the fields once every second */
            printf("a = %d, b = %d\n", p ->a, p ->b);
            sleep(1);
        }
    }
```

This type of implementation is normally only suited to a collection of homogeneous computers, with common data and paging formats.

Middleware: Some languages such as Orca [Bal *et al.* 1990], and middleware such as Linda [Carriero and Gelernter 1989] and its derivatives JavaSpaces [Bishop and Warren 2003] and TSpaces [Wyckoff *et al.* 1998], support forms of DSM without any hardware or paging support, in a platform-neutral way. In this type of implementation, sharing is implemented by communication between instances of the user-level support layer in clients and servers. Processes make calls to this layer when they access data items in DSM. The instances of this layer at the different computers access local data items and communicate as necessary to maintain consistency.

This chapter concentrates on the use of software to implement DSM on standard computers. Even with hardware support, high-level software techniques may be used to minimize the amount of communication between components of a DSM implementation.

The page-based approach has the advantage of imposing no particular structure on the DSM, which appears as a sequence of bytes. In principle, it enables programs designed for a shared-memory multiprocessor to run on computers without shared memory, with little or no adaptation. Microkernels such as Mach and Chorus provide native support for DSM (and other memory abstractions – the Mach virtual memory facilities are described in www.cdk4.net/mach). Page-based DSM is more usually implemented largely at user level to take advantage of the flexibility that that provides. The implementation utilizes kernel support for user-level page fault handlers. UNIX and some variants of Windows provide this facility. Microprocessors with 64-bit address spaces widen the scope for page-based DSM by relaxing constraints on address space management [Bartoli *et al.* 1993].

The example in Figure 18.2 is of two C programs, *Reader* and *Writer*, which communicate via the page-based DSM provided by the Mether system [Minnich and Farber 1989]. *Writer* updates two fields in a structure overlaid upon the beginning of the Mether DSM segment (beginning at address *METHERBASE*) and *Reader* periodically prints out the values it reads from these fields.

The two programs contain no special operations; they are compiled into machine instructions that access a common range of virtual memory addresses (starting at *METHERBASE*). Mether ran over conventional Sun workstation and network hardware.

The middleware approach is quite different to the use of specialized hardware and paging in that it is not intended to utilize existing shared-memory code. Its significance is that it enables us to develop higher-level abstractions of shared objects, rather than shared memory locations.

18.2 Design and implementation issues

This section discusses design and implementation options concerning the main features that characterize a DSM system. These are the structure of data held in DSM; the synchronization model used to access DSM consistently at the application level; the DSM consistency model, which governs the consistency of data values accessed from different computers; the update options for communicating written values between computers; the granularity of sharing in a DSM implementation; and the problem of thrashing.

18.2.1 Structure

In Chapter 15, we considered systems that replicate a collection of objects such as diaries and files. Those systems enable client programs to perform operations upon the objects as though there was only one copy of each object, but in reality they may be accessing different physical replicas. The systems make guarantees about the extent to which the replicas of the objects are allowed to diverge.

A DSM system is just such a replication system. Each application process is presented with some abstraction of a collection of objects, but in this case the 'collection' looks more or less like memory. That is, the objects can be addressed in some fashion or other. Different approaches to DSM vary in what they consider to be an 'object' and in how objects are addressed. We consider three approaches, which view DSM as being composed respectively of contiguous bytes, language-level objects or immutable data items.

Byte-oriented ◊ This type of DSM is accessed as ordinary virtual memory – a contiguous array of bytes. It is the view illustrated above by the Mether system. It is also the view of many other DSM systems, including Ivy, which we discuss in Section 18.3. It allows applications (and language implementations) to impose whatever data structures they want on the shared memory. The shared objects are directly addressible memory locations (in practice, the shared locations may be multi-byte words rather than individual bytes). The only operations upon those objects are *read* (or LOAD) and *write* (or STORE). If x and y are two memory locations, then we denote instances of these operations as follows:

$R(x)a$ – a *read* operation that reads the value a from location x.

$W(x)b$ – a *write* operation that stores value b at location x.

An example execution is $W(x)1$, $R(x)2$. This process writes the value 1 to location x and then reads the value 2 from it. Some other process must have written the value 2 to that location meanwhile.

Object-oriented ◊ The shared memory is structured as a collection of language-level objects with higher-level semantics than simple *read/write* variables, such as stacks and dictionaries. The contents of the shared memory are changed only by invocations upon these objects and never by direct access to their member variables. An advantage of viewing memory in this way is that object semantics can be utilized when enforcing consistency. Orca views DSM as a collection of shared objects and automatically serializes operations upon any given object.

Immutable data ◊ Here DSM is viewed as a collection of immutable data items that processes can read, add to and remove from. Examples include Agora [Bisiani and Forin 1988] and, more significantly, Linda and its derivatives, TSpaces and JavaSpaces.

Linda-type systems provide the programmer with collections of tuples called a *tuple space* (see Section 16.3.1). Tuples consist of a sequence of one or more typed data fields such as <"fred", 1958>, <"sid", 1964> and <4, 9.8, "Yes">. Any combination of types of tuples may exist in the same tuple space. Processes share data by accessing the same tuple space: they place tuples in tuple space using the *write* operation and read or extract them from tuple space using the *read* or *take* operation. The *write* operation adds a tuple without affecting existing tuples in the space. The *read* operation returns the value of one tuple without affecting the contents of the tuple space. The *take* operation also returns a tuple, but in this case it also removes the tuple from the tuple space.

When reading or taking a tuple from tuple space, a process provides a tuple specification and the tuple space returns any tuple that matches that specification – this is a type of associative addressing. To enable processes to synchronize their activities, the *read* and *take* operations both block until there is a matching tuple in the tuple space. A tuple specification includes the number of fields and the required values or types of the fields. For example, *take*(<String, integer>) could extract either <"fred", 1958> or <"sid", 1964>; *take*(<String, 1958>) would extract only <"fred", 1958> of those two.

In Linda, no direct access to tuples in tuple space is allowed and processes have to replace tuples in the tuple space instead of modifying them. Suppose, for example, that a set of processes maintains a shared counter in tuple space. The current count (say 64) is in the tuple <"counter", 64>. A process must execute code of the following form in order to increment the counter in a tuple space *myTS*:

```
<s, count> := myTS.take(<"counter", integer>);
myTS.write(<"counter", count+1>);
```

The reader should check that race conditions cannot arise, because *take* extracts the counter tuple from tuple space.

18.2.2 Synchronization model

Many applications apply constraints concerning the values stored in shared memory. This is as true of applications based on DSM as it is of applications written for shared-memory multiprocessors (or indeed for any concurrent programs that share data, such as operating system kernels and multi-threaded servers). For example, if *a* and *b* are two variables stored in DSM, then a constraint might be that $a = b$ always. If two or more processes execute the following code:

```
a := a + 1;
b := b + 1;
```

then an inconsistency may arise. Suppose *a* and *b* are initially zero and that process 1 gets as far as setting *a* to 1. Before it can increment *b*, process 2 sets *a* to 2 and *b* to 1. The constraint has been broken. The solution is to make this code fragment into a critical section: to synchronize processes to ensure that only one may execute it at a time.

In order to use DSM, then, a distributed synchronization service needs to be provided, which includes familiar constructs such as locks and semaphores. Even when DSM is structured as a set of objects, the implementors of the objects have to be concerned with synchronization. Synchronization constructs are implemented using message passing (see Chapter 13 for a description of a lock server). Special machine instructions such as *testAndSet*, which are used for synchronization in shared-memory multiprocessors, are applicable to page-based DSM, but their operation in the distributed case may be very inefficient. DSM implementations take advantage of application-level synchronization to reduce the amount of update transmission. The DSM then includes synchronization as an integrated component.

18.2.3 Consistency model

As we described in Chapter 15, the issue of consistency arises for a system such as DSM, which replicates the contents of shared memory by caching it at separate computers. In the terminology of Chapter 15, each process has a local replica manager, which holds cached replicas of objects. In most implementations, data is read from local replicas for efficiency, but updates have to be propagated to the other replica managers.

The local replica manager is implemented by a combination of middleware (the DSM runtime layer in each process) and the kernel. It is usual for middleware to perform the majority of DSM processing. Even in a page-based DSM implementation, the kernel usually provides only basic page mapping, page-fault handling and communication

Figure 18.3   Two processes accessing shared variables

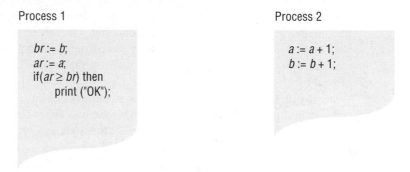

Process 1

$br := b$;
$ar := a$;
if$(ar \geq br)$ then
    print ("OK");

Process 2

$a := a + 1$;
$b := b + 1$;

mechanisms and middleware is responsible for implementing the page-sharing policies. If DSM segments are persistent, then one or more storage servers (for example, file servers) will also act as replica managers.

In addition to caching, a DSM implementation may buffer updates and thus amortize communication costs by spreading them over multiple updates. We saw a similar approach to amortizing communication costs in the gossip architecture of Chapter 15.

A *memory consistency* model [Mosberger 1993] specifies the consistency guarantees that a DSM system makes about the values that processes read from objects, given that they actually access a replica of each object and that multiple processes may update the objects. Note that this is different from the higher-level, application-specific notion of consistency discussed under the heading of application synchronization above.

Cheriton [1985] describes how forms of DSM can be envisaged for which a considerable degree of inconsistency is acceptable. For example, DSM might be used to store the loads of computers on a network in order that clients can select the least-loaded computers for running applications. Since such information is by its nature liable to become inaccurate on relatively small timescales, it would be a waste of effort to keep it consistent at all times for all computers in the system.

Most applications do, however, have stronger consistency requirements. Care must be taken to give programmers a model that conforms to reasonable expectations of the way memory should behave. Before describing memory consistency requirements in more detail, it is helpful first to look at an example.

Consider an application in which two processes access two variables, a and b (Figure 18.3), which are initialized to zero. Process 2 increments a and b, in that order. Process 1 reads the values of b and a into local variables br and ar, in that order. Note that there is no application-level synchronization. Intuitively, process 1 should expect to see one of the following combinations of values, depending upon the points at which the read operations applied to a and b (implied in the statements $br := b$ and $ar := a$) occur with respect to process 2's execution: $ar = 0$, $br = 0$; $ar = 1$, $br = 0$; $ar = 1$, $br = 1$. In other words, the condition $ar \geq br$ should always be satisfied and process 1 should print 'OK'. However, a DSM implementation might deliver the updates to a and b out of order to the replica manager for process 1, in which case the combination $ar = 0$, $br = 1$ could occur.

The reader's immediate reaction to the example just given is probably that the DSM implementation, which reverses the order of two updates, is incorrect. If process 1 and process 2 execute together at a single-processor computer, we would assume that the memory subsystem was malfunctioning. However, it may be a correct implementation, in the distributed case, of a consistency model that is weaker than what many of us would intuitively expect, but that nonetheless can be useful and is relatively efficient.

Mosberger [1993] delineates a range of models that have been devised for shared-memory multiprocessors and software DSM systems. The main consistency models that can be practically realized in DSM implementations are sequential consistency and models that are based on weak consistency.

The central question to be asked in order to characterize a particular memory consistency model is this: when a read access is made to a memory location, which write accesses to the location are candidates whose values could be supplied to the read? At the weakest extreme, the answer is: any write that was issued before the read. This model would be obtained if replica managers could delay propagating updates to their peers indefinitely. It is too weak to be useful.

At the strongest extreme, all written values are instantaneously available to all processes: a read returns the most recent write at the time that the read takes place. This definition is problematic in two respects. First, neither writes nor reads take place at a single point in time, so the meaning of 'most recent' is not always clear. Each type of access has a well-defined point of issue, but they complete at some later time (for example, after message passing has taken place). Second, Chapter 11 showed that there are limits to how closely clocks can be synchronized in a distributed system. So it is not always possible to determine accurately whether one event occurred before another.

Nonetheless, this model has been specified and studied. The reader may already have recognized it: it is what we called linearizability in Chapter 15. Linearizability is more usually called *atomic consistency* in the DSM literature. We now restate the definition of linearizability from Chapter 15.

A replicated shared object service is said to be linearizable if *for any execution* there is some interleaving of the series of operations issued by all the clients that satisfies the following two criteria:

L1:   The interleaved sequence of operations meets the specification of a (single) correct copy of the objects.

L2:   The order of operations in the interleaving is consistent with the real times at which the operations occurred in the actual execution.

This definition is a general one that applies to any system containing shared replicated objects. We can be more specific now, since we know that we are dealing with a shared memory. Consider the simple case where the shared memory is structured as a set of variables that may be read or written. The operations are all reads and writes, which we introduced a notation for in Section 18.2.1: a read of value a from variable x is denoted $R(x)a$; a write of value b to variable x is denoted $W(x)b$. We can now express the first criterion L1 in terms of variables (the shared objects) as follows:

L1':   The interleaved sequence of operations is such that if $R(x)a$ occurs in the sequence, then either the last write operation that occurs before it in the interleaved sequence is $W(x)a$, or no write operation occurs before it and a is the initial value of x.

This criterion states our intuition that a variable can only be changed by a write operation. The second criterion for linearizability, L2, remains the same.

Sequential consistency ◊ Linearizability is too strict for most practical purposes. The strongest memory model for DSM that is used in practice is *sequential consistency* [Lamport 1979], which we introduced in Chapter 15. We adapt Chapter 15's definition for the particular case of shared variables as follows.

A DSM system is said to be sequentially consistent if *for any execution* there is some interleaving of the series of operations issued by all the processes that satisfies the following two criteria:

SC1: The interleaved sequence of operations is such that if $R(x)a$ occurs in the sequence, then either the last write operation that occurs before it in the interleaved sequence is $W(x)a$, or no write operation occurs before it and a is the initial value of x.

SC2: The order of operations in the interleaving is consistent with the program order in which each individual client executed them.

Criterion SC1 is the same as L1'. Criterion SC2 refers to program order rather than temporal order, which is what makes it possible to implement sequential consistency.

The condition can be restated as follows: there is a virtual interleaving of all the processes' *read* and *write* operations against a single virtual image of the memory; the program order of every individual process is preserved in this interleaving and each process always reads the latest value written within the interleaving.

In an actual execution, memory operations may be overlapped and some updates may be ordered differently at different processes, as long as the definition's constraints are not thereby broken. Note that memory operations upon the entire DSM have to be taken into account to satisfy the conditions of sequential consistency – and not just the operations on each individual location.

The combination $ar = 0$, $br = 1$ in the above example could not occur under sequential consistency, because process 1 would be reading values that conflict with process 2's program order. An example interleaving of the processes' memory accesses in a sequentially consistent execution is shown in Figure 18.4. Once more, while this shows an actual interleaving of the read and write operations, the definition only stipulates that the execution should take place *as though* such a strict interleaving takes place.

Sequentially consistent DSM could be implemented by using a single server to hold all the shared data and by making all processes perform reads or writes by sending requests to the server, which globally orders them. This architecture is too inefficient for a DSM implementation and practical means of achieving sequential consistency are described below. Nonetheless, it remains a costly model to implement.

Coherence ◊ One reaction to the cost of sequential consistency is to settle for a weaker model with well-defined properties. *Coherence* is an example of a weaker form of consistency. Under coherence, every process agrees on the order of *write* operations to the same location, but they do not necessarily agree on the ordering of *write* operations

Figure 18.4   Interleaving under sequential consistency

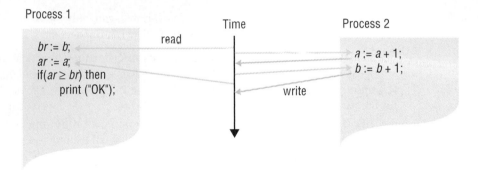

to different locations. We can think of coherence as sequential consistency on a location-by-location basis. Coherent DSM can be implemented by taking a protocol for implementing sequential consistency and applying it separately to each unit of replicated data – for example, each page. The saving comes from the fact that accesses to two different pages are independent and need not delay one another, since the protocol is applied separately to them.

Weak consistency ◊ Dubois *et al.* [1988] developed the weak consistency model in an attempt to avoid the costs of sequential consistency on multiprocessors, while retaining the *effect* of sequential consistency. This model exploits knowledge of synchronization operations in order to relax memory consistency, while appearing to the programmer to implement sequential consistency (at least, under certain conditions that are beyond the scope of this book). For example, if the programmer uses a lock to implement a critical section, then a DSM system can assume that no other process may access the data items accessed under mutual exclusion within it. It is therefore redundant for the DSM system to propagate updates to these items until the process leaves the critical section. While items are left with 'inconsistent' values some of the time, they are not accessed at those points; the execution appears to be sequentially consistent. Adve and Hill [1990] describe a generalization of this notion called weak ordering: '(A DSM system) is weakly ordered with respect to a synchronization model if and only if it appears sequentially consistent to all software that obeys the synchronization model.' Release consistency, which is a development of weak consistency, is described in Section 18.4.

18.2.4 Update options

Two main implementation choices have been devised for propagating updates made by one process to the others: write-update and write-invalidate. These are applicable to a variety of DSM consistency models, including sequential consistency. In outline, the options are as follows:

Write-update: The updates made by a process are made locally and multicast to all other replica managers possessing a copy of the data item, which immediately modify the data read by local processes (Figure 18.5). Processes read the local copies of data items, without the need for communication. In addition to allowing multiple readers,

Figure 18.5 DSM using write-update

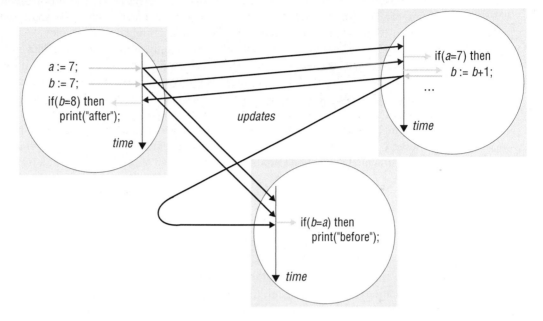

several processes may write the same data item at the same time; this is known as *multiple-reader/multiple-writer sharing*.

The memory consistency model that is implemented with write-update depends on several factors, mainly the multicast ordering property. Sequential consistency can be achieved by using multicasts that are totally ordered (see Chapter 12 for a definition of totally ordered multicast), which do not return until the update message has been delivered locally. All processes then agree on the order of updates. The set of reads that take place between any two consecutive updates is well defined and their ordering is immaterial to sequential consistency.

Reads are cheap in the write-update option. However, Chapter 12 showed that ordered multicast protocols are relatively expensive to implement in software. Orca uses write-update and employs the Amoeba multicast protocol [Kaashoek and Tanenbaum 1991] (see www.cdk4.net/coordination), which uses hardware support for multicast. Munin supports write-update as an option. A write-update protocol is used with specialized hardware support in the PLUS multiprocessor architecture.

Write-invalidate: This is commonly implemented in the form of multiple-reader/ single-writer sharing. At any time, a data item may either be accessed in read-only mode by one or more processes, or it may be read and written by a single process. An item that is currently accessed in read-only mode can be copied indefinitely to other processes. When a process attempts to write to it, a multicast message is first sent to all other copies to invalidate them and this is acknowledged before the write can take place; the other processes are thereby prevented from reading stale data (that is, data that are not up to date). Any processes attempting to access the data item are blocked if a writer exists. Eventually, control is transferred from the writing process, and other accesses may take place once the update has been sent. The effect is to process all accesses to the item on a first-come, first-served basis. By the proof given by Lamport [1979], this scheme achieves sequential consistency. We shall see in Section 18.4 that invalidations may be delayed under release consistency.

Under the invalidation scheme, updates are only propagated when data are read and several updates can take place before communication is necessary. Against this must be placed the cost of invalidating read-only copies before a write can occur. In the multiple-reader/single-writer scheme described, this is potentially expensive. But if the read/write ratio is sufficiently high, then the parallelism obtained by allowing multiple simultaneous readers offsets this cost. Where the read/write ratio is relatively small, a single-reader/single-writer scheme can be more appropriate: that is, one in which at most one process may be granted read-only access at a time.

18.2.5 Granularity

An issue that is related to the structure of DSM is the granularity of sharing. Conceptually, all processes share the entire contents of a DSM. As programs sharing DSM execute, however, only certain parts of the data are actually shared and then only for certain times during the execution. It would clearly be very wasteful for the DSM implementation always to transmit the entire contents of DSM as processes access and update it. What should be the unit of sharing in a DSM implementation? That is, when a process has written to DSM, which data does the DSM runtime send in order to provide consistent values elsewhere?

We focus here on page-based implementations, although the granularity issue does arise in other implementations (see Exercise 18.11). In a page-based DSM, the hardware supports alterations to an address space efficiently in units of pages – essentially by the placement of a new page frame pointer in the page table (see, for example, Bacon [2002] for a description of paging). Page sizes can typically range up to 8 kilobytes, so this is an appreciable amount of data that must be transmitted over a network to keep remote copies consistent when an update occurs. By default, the price of the whole page transfer must be paid whether the entire page has been updated, or just one byte of it.

Using a smaller page size – 512 bytes or 1 kilobyte say – does not necessarily lead to an improvement in overall performance. First, in cases where processes do update large amounts of contiguous data, it is better to send one large page rather than several smaller pages in separate updates, because of the fixed software overheads per network packet. Second, using a small page as the unit of distribution leads to a large number of units that must be administered separately by the DSM implementation.

To complicate matters further, processes tend to contend more for pages when the page size is large, because the likelihood that the data they access will lie within the same page increases with the page size. Consider, for example, two processes, one of which accesses only data item A while the other accesses only data item B, which lie within the same page (Figure 18.6). For the sake of concreteness, let us assume that one process reads A and the other updates B. There is no contention at the application level. However, the entire page must be transmitted between the processes, since the DSM runtime does not by default know which locations in the page have been altered. This phenomenon is known as *false sharing*: two or more processes share parts of a page, but

Figure 18.6   Data items laid out over pages

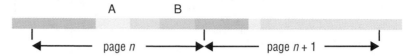

only one in fact accesses each part. In write-invalidate protocols, false sharing can lead to unnecessary invalidations. In write-update protocols, when several writers falsely share data items they may cause them to be overwritten with older versions.

In practice, the choice of the unit of sharing has to be made based on the physical page sizes available, although a unit of several contiguous pages may be taken if the page size is small. The layout of data with respect to page boundaries is an important factor in determining the number of page transfers made when a program executes.

18.2.6 Thrashing

A potential problem with write-invalidate protocols is thrashing. Thrashing is said to occur where the DSM runtime spends an inordinate amount of time invalidating and transferring shared data compared with the time spent by application processes doing useful work. It occurs when several processes compete for the same data item, or for falsely shared data items. If, for example, one process repeatedly reads a data item that another is regularly updating, then this item will be constantly transferred from the writer and invalidated at the reader. This is an example of a sharing pattern for which write-invalidate is inappropriate and write-update would be better. The next section describes the Mirage approach to thrashing, in which computers 'own' pages for a minimum period; Section 18.4 describes how Munin allows the programmer to declare access patterns to the DSM system so that it can choose appropriate update options for each data item and avoid thrashing.

18.3 Sequential consistency and Ivy case study

This section describes methods for implementing sequentially consistent, page-based DSM. It draws upon Ivy [Li and Hudak 1989] as a case study.

18.3.1 The system model

The basic model to be considered is one in which a collection of processes shares a segment of DSM (Figure 18.7). The segment is mapped to the same range of addresses in each process, so that meaningful pointer values can be stored in the segment. The processes execute at computers equipped with a paged memory management unit. We shall assume that there is only one process per computer that accesses the DSM segment. There may in reality be several such processes at a computer. However, these could then share DSM pages directly (the same page frame can be used in the page tables used by the different processes). The only complication would be to coordinate fetching and

Figure 18.7   System model for page-based DSM

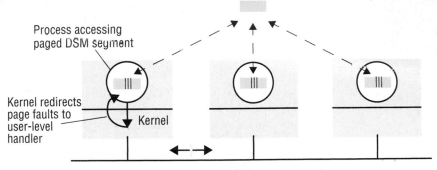

propagating updates to a page when two or more local processes access it. This description ignores such details.

Paging is transparent to the application components within processes; they can logically both read and write any data in DSM. However, the DSM runtime restricts page access permissions in order to maintain sequential consistency when processing reads and writes. Paged memory management units allow the access permissions to a data page to be set to *none*, *read-only* or *read-write*. If a process attempts to exceed the current access permissions, then it takes a read or write page fault, according to the type of access. The kernel redirects the page fault to a handler specified by the DSM runtime layer in each process. The page fault handler – which runs transparently to the application – processes the fault in a special way, to be described below, before returning control to the application. In the original DSM systems such as Ivy, the kernel itself performs much of the processing that we describe here. We shall speak of the processes themselves performing page-fault handling and communication handling. In actuality, some combination of the DSM runtime layer in the process and the kernel performs these handling functions. Usually, the in-process DSM runtime contains the most significant functionality in order than this can be reimplemented and fine-tuned without the problems associated with altering a kernel.

This description will ignore the page-fault processing that takes place as part of the normal virtual memory implementation. Apart from the fact that DSM segments compete with other segments for page frames, the implementations are independent.

The problem of write-update ◊ The previous section outlined the general implementation alternatives of write-update and write-invalidation. In practice, if the DSM is page-based, then write-update is used only if writes can be buffered. This is because standard page-fault handling is unsuited to the task of processing every single write update to a page.

To see this, suppose that every update has to be multicast to the remaining replicas. Suppose that a page has been write-protected. When a process attempts to write upon the page, it takes a page fault and a handler routine is called. This handler could, in principle, examine the faulting instruction to determine the value and address being written and multicast the update before restoring write access and returning to complete the faulting instruction.

But now that write access has been restored, subsequent updates to the page will not cause a page fault. To make every write access produce a page fault, it would be necessary for the page fault handler to set the process into TRACE mode, whereby the processor generates a TRACE exception after each instruction. The TRACE exception handler would turn off write permissions to the page and turn off TRACE mode once more. The whole exercise would be repeated when a write fault next occurred. It is clear that this method is liable to be very expensive. There would be many exceptions caused during the execution of a process.

In practice, write-update is used with page-based implementations, but only where the page is left with write permissions after an initial page fault and several writes are allowed to occur before the updated page is propagated. Munin uses this write-buffering technique. As an extra efficiency measure, Munin tries to avoid propagating the whole page – only a small part of which may have been updated. When a process first attempts to write to the page, Munin handles the page fault by taking a copy of the page and setting the copy aside before enabling write access. Later, when Munin is ready to propagate the page, it compares the updated page with the copy that it took and encodes the updates as a set of differences between the two pages. The differences often take up much less space than an entire page. Other processes generate the updated page from the pre-update copy and the set of differences.

18.3.2 Write invalidation

Invalidation-based algorithms use page protection to enforce consistent data sharing. When a process is updating a page, it has read and write permissions locally; all other processes have no access permissions to the page. When one or more processes are reading the page, they have read-only permission; all other processes have no access permissions (although they may acquire read permissions). No other combinations are possible. A process with the most up-to-date version of a page p is designated as its *owner* – referred to as *owner*(p). This is either the single writer, or one of the readers. The set of processes that have a copy of a page p is called its *copy set* – referred to as *copyset*(p).

The possible state transitions are shown in Figure 18.8. When a process P_w attempts to write a page p to which it has no access or read-only access, a page fault takes place. The page-fault handling procedure is as follows:

- The page is transferred to P_w, if it does not already have an up-to-date read-only copy.

- All other copies are invalidated: the page permissions are set to no access at all members of *copyset*(p).

- *copyset*(p) := { P_w }.

- *owner*(p) := P_w.

- The DSM runtime layer in P_w places the page with read-write permissions at the appropriate location in its address space and restarts the faulting instruction.

Figure 18.8   State transitions under write-invalidation

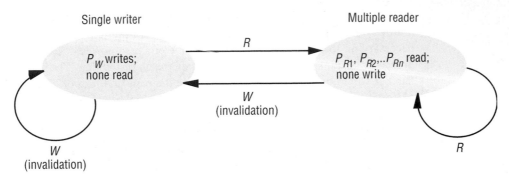

Note: R = read fault occurs; *W* = write fault occurs.

Note that two or more processes with read-only copies may take write faults at more or less the same time. A read-only copy of a page may be out-of-date when ownership is eventually granted. To detect whether a current read-only copy of a page is out-of-date, each page can be associated with a sequence number, which is incremented whenever ownership is transferred. A process requiring write access encloses the sequence number of its read-only copy, if it possesses one. The current owner can then tell whether the page has been modified and therefore needs to be sent. This scheme is described by Kessler and Livny [1989] as the 'shrewd algorithm'.

When a process P_R attempts to read a page p for which it has no access permissions, a read page fault takes place. The page-fault handling procedure is as follows:

- The page is copied from *owner(p)* to P_R.

- If the current owner is a single writer, then it remains as p's owner and its access permission for p is set to read-only access. Retaining read access is desirable in case the process attempts to read the page subsequently – it will have retained an up-to-date version of the page. However, as the owner it will have to process subsequent requests for the page even if it does not access the page again. So it might turn out to have been more appropriate to reduce permission to no access and transfer ownership to P_R.

- *copyset(p)* := *copyset(p)* $\cup$ {P_R}.

- The DSM runtime layer in P_R places the page with read-only permissions at the appropriate location in its address space and restarts the faulting instruction.

It is possible for a second page fault to occur during the transition algorithms just described. In order that transitions take place consistently, any new request for the page is not processed until after the current transition has completed.

The description just given has only explained *what* must be done. The problem of *how* to implement page fault handling efficiently is now addressed

Figure 18.9   Central manager and associated messages

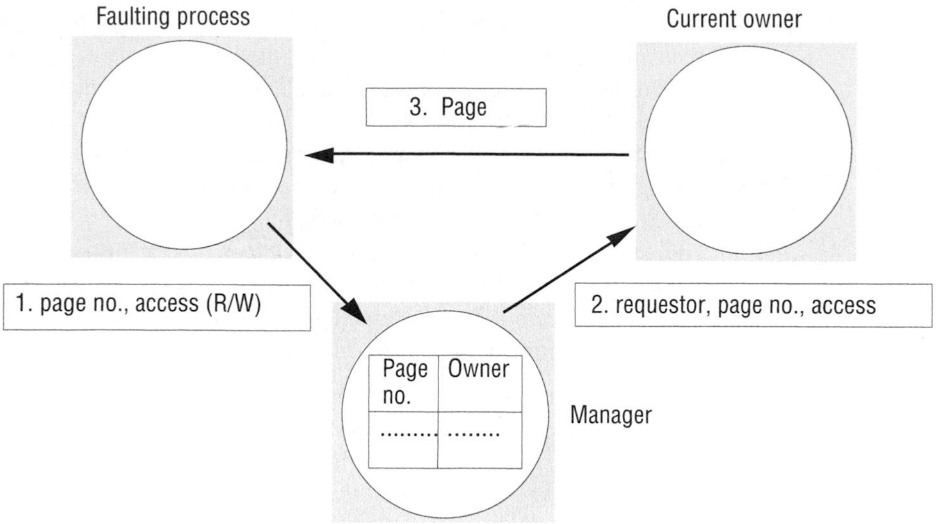

18.3.3 Invalidation protocols

Two important problems remain to be addressed in a protocol to implement the invalidation scheme:

1. How to locate *owner*(*p*) for a given page *p*.

2. Where to store *copyset*(*p*).

For Ivy, Li and Hudak [1989] describe several architectures and protocols that take varying approaches to these problems. The simplest we shall describe is their improved centralized manager algorithm. In it, a single server called a manager is used to store the location (transport address) of *owner*(*p*) for every page *p*. The manager could be one of the processes running the application, or it could be any other process. In this algorithm, the set *copyset*(*p*) is stored at *owner*(*p*). That is, the identifiers and transport addresses of the members of *copyset*(*p*) are stored.

As shown in Figure 18.9, when a page fault occurs the local process (which we shall refer to as the *client*) sends a message to the manager containing the page number and the type of access required (read or read-write). The client awaits a reply. The manager handles the request by looking up the address of *owner*(*p*) and forwarding the request to the owner. In the case of a write fault, the manager sets the new owner to be the client. Subsequent requests are thus queued at the client until it has completed the transfer of ownership to itself.

The previous owner sends the page to the client. In the case of a write fault, it also sends the page's copy set. The client performs the invalidation when it receives the copy set. It sends a multicast request to the members of the copy set, awaiting acknowledgement from all the processes concerned that invalidation has taken place. The multicast need not be ordered. The former owner need not be included in the list of destinations, since it invalidates itself. The details of copy set management are left to the reader, who should consult the general invalidation algorithms given above.

The manager is a performance bottleneck and a critical point of failure. Li and Hudak suggested three alternatives that allow the load of page management to be divided between computers: fixed distributed page management, multicast-based distributed management and dynamic distributed management. In the first, multiple managers are used, each functionally equivalent to the central manager just described, but the pages are divided statically between them. For example, each manager could manage just those pages whose page numbers hash to a certain range of values. Clients calculate the hash number for the needed page and use a predetermined configuration table to look up the address of the corresponding manager.

This scheme would ameliorate the problem of load in general, but it has the disadvantage that a fixed mapping of pages to managers may not be suitable. When processes do not access the pages equally, some managers will incur more load than others. We now describe multicast-based and dynamic distributed management.

Using multicast to locate the owner ◊ Multicast can be used to eliminate the manager completely. When a process faults, it multicasts its page request to all the other processes. Only the process that owns the page replies. Care must be taken to ensure correct behaviour if two clients request the same page at more or less the same time: each client must obtain the page eventually, even if its request is multicast during transfer of ownership.

Consider two clients C_1 and C_2, which use multicast to locate a page owned by O. Suppose that O receives C_1's request first and transfers ownership to it. Before the page arrives, C_2's request arrives at O and at C_1. O will discard C_2's request because it no longer owns the page. Li and Hudak pointed out that C_1 should defer processing C_2's request until after it has obtained the page – otherwise it would discard the request because it is not the owner and C_2's request would be lost altogether. However, a problem still remains. C_1's request has been queued at C_2 meanwhile. After C_1 has eventually given C_2 the page, C_2 will receive and process C_1's request – which is now obsolete!

One solution is to use totally ordered multicast, so that clients can safely discard requests that arrive before their own (requests are delivered to themselves as well as to other processes). Another solution, which uses a cheaper unordered multicast but which consumes more bandwidth, is to associate each page with a vector timestamp, with one entry per process (see Chapter 11 for a description of vector timestamps). When page ownership is transferred, so is the timestamp. When a process obtains ownership, it increments its entry in the timestamp. When a process requests ownership, it encloses the last timestamp it held for the page. In our example, C_2 could discard C_1's request, because C_1's entry in the request's timestamp is lower than that which arrived with the page.

Whether an ordered multicast or unordered multicast is used, this scheme has the usual disadvantage of multicast schemes: processes that are not the owners of a page are interrupted by irrelevant messages, wasting processing time.

18.3.4 A dynamic distributed manager algorithm

Li and Hudak suggested the dynamic distributed manager algorithm, which allows page ownership to be transferred between processes but which uses an alternative to multicast as its method of locating a page's owner. The idea is to divide the overheads of locating pages between those computers that access them. Every process keeps, for every page p, a hint as to the page's current owner – the probable owner of p, or $probOwner(p)$. Initially, every process is supplied with accurate page locations. In general, however, these values are *hints*, because pages can be transferred elsewhere at any time. As in previous algorithms, ownership is transferred only when a write fault occurs.

The owner of a page is located by following chains of hints that are set up as ownership of the page is transferred from computer to computer. The length of the chain – that is, the number of forwarding messages necessary to locate the owner – threatens to increase indefinitely. The algorithm overcomes this by updating the hints as more up-to-date values become available. Hints are updated and requests are forwarded as follows:

- When a process transfers ownership of page p to another process, it updates $probOwner(p)$ to be the recipient.

- When a process handles an invalidation request for a page p, it updates $probOwner(p)$ to be the requester.

- When a process that has requested read access to a page p receives it, it updates $probOwner(p)$ to be the provider.

- When a process receives a request for a page p that it does not own, it forwards the request to $probOwner(p)$ and resets $probOwner(p)$ to be the requester.

The first three updates follow simply from the protocol for transferring page ownership and providing read-only copies. The rationale for the update when forwarding requests is that, for write requests, the requester will soon be the owner, even though it is not currently. In fact, in Li and Hudak's algorithm, assumed here, the $probOwner$ update is made whether the request is for read access or write access. We return to this point shortly.

Figure 18.10 ((a) and (b)) illustrates $probOwner$ pointers before and after process A takes a write page fault. A's $probOwner$ pointer for the page initially points to B. Processes B, C and D forward the request to E by following their own $probOwner$ pointers; thereafter, all are set to point to A as a result of the update rules just described. The arrangement after fault handling is clearly better than that which preceded it: the chain of pointers has collapsed.

If, however, A takes a read fault, then process B is better off (two steps instead of three to E), C's situation is the same as it was before (two steps), but D is worse off, with two steps instead of one (Figure 18.10(c)). Simulations are required to investigate the overall effect of this tactic on performance.

The average length of pointer chains can further be controlled by periodically broadcasting the current owner's location to all processes. This has the effect of collapsing all chains to length 1.

Li and Hudak describe the results of simulations that they carried out to investigate the efficacy of their pointer updates. With faulting processes chosen at random, for 1024 processors they found that the average number of messages taken to reach the owner of a page was 2.34 if broadcasts announcing the owner's location are made every 256 faults and 3.64 if broadcasts are made every 1024 faults. These figures are given only as illustrations: a complete set of results is given by Li and Hudak [1989].

Figure 18.10   Updating *probOwner* pointers

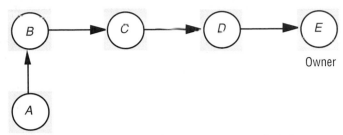

(a) *probOwner* pointers just before process *A* takes a page fault for a page owned by *E*

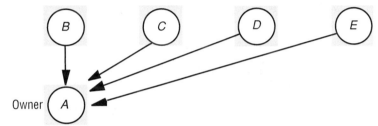

(b) Write fault: *probOwner* pointers after *A*'s write request is forwarded

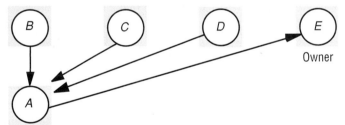

(c) Read fault: *probOwner* pointers after *A*'s read request is forwarded

Note that a DSM system that uses a central manager requires two messages to reach the owner of a page.

Finally, Li and Hudak describe an optimization that potentially both makes invalidation more efficient and reduces the number of messages required to handle a read page fault. Instead of having to obtain a page copy from the owner of a page, a client can obtain a copy from any process with a valid copy. There is a chance that a client attempting to locate the owner will encounter such a process before the owner on the pointer chain.

This is done with the proviso that processes keep a record of clients that have obtained a copy of a page from them. The set of processes that possess read-only copies of a page thus forms a tree rooted at the owner, with each node pointing to the child nodes below, which obtained copies from it. The invalidation of a page begins at the owner and works down through the tree. On receiving an invalidation message, a node forwards it to its children in addition to invalidating its own copy. The overall effect is that some invalidations occur in parallel. This can reduce the overall time taken to invalidate a page – especially in an environment without hardware support for multicast.

18.3.5 Thrashing

It can be argued that it is the programmer's responsibility to avoid thrashing. The programmer could annotate data items in order to assist the DSM runtime in minimizing page copying and ownership transfers. The latter approach is discussed in the next section in the context of the Munin DSM system.

Mirage [Fleisch and Popek 1989] takes an approach to thrashing that is intended to be transparent to programmers. Mirage associates each page with a small time interval. Once a process has access to a page, it is allowed to retain access for the given interval, which serves as a type of timeslice. Other requests for the page are held off in the meantime. An obvious disadvantage of this scheme is that it is very difficult to choose the length of the timeslice. If the system uses a statically chosen length of time, it is liable to be inappropriate in many cases. A process might, for example, write a page only once and thereafter not access it; nonetheless, other processes are prevented from accessing it. Equally, the system might grant another process access to the page before it has finished using it.

A DSM system could choose the length of the timeslice dynamically. A possible basis for this is observation of accesses to the page (using the memory management unit's *referenced* bits). Another factor that could be taken into account is the length of the queue of processes waiting for the page.

18.4 Release consistency and Munin case study

The algorithms in the previous section were designed to achieve sequentially consistent DSM. The advantage of sequential consistency is that DSM behaves in the way that programmers expect shared memory to behave. Its disadvantage is that it is costly to implement. DSM systems often require the use of multicasts in their implementations, whether they are implemented using write-update or write-invalidation – although unordered multicast suffices for invalidation. Locating the owner of a page tends to be expensive: a central manager that knows the location of every page's owner acts as a bottleneck; following pointers involves more messages, on average. In addition, invalidation-based algorithms may give rise to thrashing.

Release consistency was introduced with the Dash multiprocessor, which implements DSM in hardware, primarily using a write-invalidation protocol [Lenoski *et al.* 1992]. Munin and Treadmarks [Keleher *et al.* 1992] have adopted a software implementation of it. Release consistency is weaker than sequential consistency and cheaper to implement, but it has reasonable semantics that are tractable to programmers.

The idea of release consistency is to reduce DSM overheads by exploiting the fact that programmers use synchronization objects such as semaphores, locks and barriers. A DSM implementation can use knowledge of accesses to these objects to allow memory to become inconsistent at certain points, while the use of synchronization objects nonetheless preserves application-level consistency.

18.4.1 Memory accesses

In order to understand release consistency – or any other memory model that takes synchronization into account – we begin by categorizing memory accesses according to their role, if any, in synchronization. Furthermore, we shall discuss how memory accesses may be performed asynchronously to gain performance and give a simple operational model of how memory accesses take effect.

As we said above, DSM implementations on general-purpose distributed systems may use message passing rather than shared variables to implement synchronization, for reasons of efficiency. But it may help to bear shared-variable-based synchronization in mind in the following discussion. The following pseudocode implements locks using the *testAndSet* operation on variables. The function *testAndSet* sets the lock to 1 and returns 0 if it finds it zero; otherwise it returns 1. It does this atomically.

```
acquireLock(var int lock):      // lock is passed by-reference
       while (testAndSet(lock) = 1)
              skip;
releaseLock(var int lock):      // lock is passed by-reference
       lock := 0;
```

Types of memory access ◊ The main distinction is between *competing* accesses and *non-competing* (*ordinary*) accesses. Two accesses are competing if:

- they may occur concurrently (there is no enforced ordering between them) and

- at least one is a *write*.

So two *read* operations can never be competing; a *read* and a *write* to the same location made by two processes that synchronize between the operations (and so order them) are non-competing.

We further divide competing accesses into *synchronization* and *non-synchronization* accesses:

- synchronization accesses are *read* or *write* operations that contribute to synchronization;

- non-synchronization accesses are *read* or *write* operations that are concurrent but that do not contribute to synchronization.

The *write* operation implied by '*lock* := 0' in *releaseLock* (above) is a synchronization access. So is the *read* operation implicit in *testAndSet*.

Synchronization accesses are competing, because potentially synchronizing processes must be able to access synchronization variables concurrently and they must update them: *read* operations alone could not achieve synchronization. But not all competing accesses are synchronization accesses – there are classes of parallel algorithms in which processes make competing accesses to shared variables just to update and read one another's results and not to synchronize.

Figure 18.11 Timeline for performing a DSM *read* or *write* operation

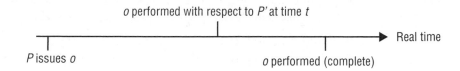

o performed with respect to *P'* at time *t*

Real time

P issues *o*   *o* performed (complete)

Synchronization accesses are further divided into *acquire* accesses and *release* accesses, corresponding to their role in potentially blocking the process making the access, or in unblocking some other process.

Performing asynchronous operations ◊ As we saw when discussing implementations of sequentially consistent DSM, memory operations may incur significant delays. Several forms of asynchronous operation are available to increase the rate at which processes execute, despite these delays. First, *write* operations may be implemented asynchronously. A written value is buffered before being propagated and the effects of the *write* are observed later by other processes. Second, DSM implementations may pre-fetch values in anticipation of reading them, to avoid stalling a process at the time it needs the values. Third, processors may perform instructions out of order. While awaiting completion of the current memory access, they may issue the next instruction, as long as it does not depend on the current instruction.

In view of the asynchronous operation that we have outlined, we distinguish between the point at which a *read* or *write* operation is issued – when the process first commences execution of the operation – and the point when the instruction is *performed* or completed.

We shall assume that our DSM is at least coherent. As Section 18.2.3 explained, this means that every process agrees on the order of *write* operations to the same location. Given this assumption, we may speak unambiguously of the ordering of *write* operations to a given location.

In a distributed shared memory system, we can draw a timeline for any memory operation *o* that process *P* executes (see Figure 18.11).

We say that a *write* operation $W(x)v$ has *performed* with respect to a process *P* if from that point *P*'s *read* operations will return *v* as written by that *write* operation, or the value of some subsequent write to *x* (note that another operation may write the same value *v*).

Similarly, we say that a *read* operation $R(x)v$ has performed with respect to process *P* when no subsequent *write* issued to the same location could possibly supply the value *v* that *P* reads. For example, *P* may have pre-fetched the value it needs to *read*.

Finally, the operation *o* has *performed* if it has performed with respect to all processes.

18.4.2 Release consistency

The requirements that we wish to meet are:

- to preserve the synchronization semantics of objects such as locks and barriers;

- to gain performance, we allow a degree of asynchronicity for memory operations;

- to constrain the overlap between memory accesses in order to guarantee executions that provide the equivalent of sequential consistency.

Release-consistent memory is designed to satisfy these requirements. Gharachorloo *et al.* 1990 define release consistency as follows:

RC1: before an ordinary *read* or *write* operation is allowed to perform with respect to any other process, all previous *acquire* accesses must be performed.

RC2: before a *release* operation is allowed to perform with respect to any other process, all previous ordinary *read* and *write* operations must be performed.

RC3: *acquire* and *release* operations are sequentially consistent with respect to one another.

RC1 and RC2 guarantee that, when a release has taken place, no other process acquiring a lock can read stale versions of data modified by the process that performs the release. This is consistent with the programmer's expectation that a release of a lock, for example, signifies that a process has finished modifying data within a critical section.

The DSM runtime can only enforce the release consistency guarantee if it is aware of synchronization accesses. In Munin, for example, the programmer is forced to use Munin's own *acquireLock*, *releaseLock* and *waitAtBarrier* primitives. (A barrier is a synchronization object that blocks each of a set of processes until all have waited on it; all processes then continue.) A program must use synchronization to ensure that updates are made visible to other processes. Two processes that share DSM but never use synchronization objects may never see one another's updates if the implementation strictly applies the sole guarantee given above.

Note that the release consistency model does allow an implementation to employ some asynchronous operations. For example, a process need not be blocked when it makes updates within a critical section. Nor do its updates have to be propagated until it leaves the critical section by releasing a lock. Furthermore, updates can then be collected and sent in a single message. Only the final update to each data item need be sent.

Consider the processes in Figure 18.12, which acquire and release a lock in order to access a pair of variables a and b (a and b are initialized to zero). Process 1 updates a and b under conditions of mutual exclusion, so that process 2 cannot read a and b at the same time and so will find $a = b = 0$ or $a = b = 1$. The critical sections enforce consistency – equality of a and b – *at the application level*. It is redundant to propagate updates to the variables affected during the critical section. If process 2 tried to access a, say, outside a critical section, then it might find a stale value. That is a matter for the application writer.

Let us assume that process 1 acquires the lock first. Process 2 will block and not cause any activity related to DSM until it has acquired the lock and attempts to access a and b. If the two processes were to execute on a sequentially consistent memory, then process 1 would block when it updates a and b. Under a write-update protocol, it would block while all versions of the data are updated; under a write-invalidation protocol, it would block while all copies are invalidated.

Figure 18.12 Processes executing on a release-consistent DSM

Process 1:
        acquireLock();   // enter critical section
        $a := a + 1$;
        $b := b + 1$;
        releaseLock();   // leave critical section

Process 2:
        acquireLock();   // enter critical section
        print ("The values of a and b are: ", a, b);
        releaseLock();   // leave critical section

Under release consistency, process 1 will not block when it accesses a and b. The DSM runtime system notes which data have been updated but need take no further action at that time. It is only when process 1 has released the lock that communication is required. Under a write-update protocol, the updates to a and b will be propagated; under a write-invalidation protocol, the invalidations should be sent.

The programmer (or a compiler) is responsible for labelling read and write operations as *release*, *acquire* or *non-synchronization* accesses – other instructions are assumed to be ordinary. To label the program is to direct the DSM system to enforce the release consistency conditions.

Gharachorloo *et al.* [1990] describe the concept of a *properly labelled* program. They prove that such a program cannot distinguish between a release-consistent DSM and a sequentially consistent DSM.

18.4.3 Munin

The Munin DSM design [Carter *et al.* 1991] attempts to improve the efficiency of DSM by implementing the release consistency model. Furthermore, Munin allows programmers to annotate their data items according to the way in which they are shared, so that optimizations can be made in the update options selected for maintaining consistency. It is implemented upon the V kernel [Cheriton and Zwaenepoel 1985], which was one of the first kernels to allow user-level threads to handle page faults and manipulate page tables.

The following points apply to Munin's implementation of release consistency:

- Munin sends update or invalidation information as soon as a lock is released.

- The programmer can make annotations that associate a lock with particular data items. In this case, the DSM runtime can propagate relevant updates in the same message that transfers the lock to a waiting process – ensuring that the lock's recipient has copies of the data it needs before it accesses them.

Keleher *et al.* [1992] describe an alternative to Munin's *eager* approach of sending update or invalidation information at the time of a release. Instead, this *lazy* implementation does so only when the lock in question is next acquired. Furthermore, it sends this information only to the process acquiring the lock and piggy backs it onto the message granting the lock. It is unnecessary to make the updates visible to other processes until they in turn acquire the lock.

Sharing annotations ◊ Munin implements a variety of consistency protocols, which are applied at the granularity of individual data items. The protocols are parameterized according to the following options:

- whether to use a write-update or write-invalidate protocol;

- whether several replicas of a modifiable data item may exist simultaneously;

- whether or not to delay updates or invalidations (for example, under release consistency);

- whether the item has a fixed owner, to which all updates must be sent;

- whether the same data item may be modified concurrently by several writers;

- whether the data item is shared by a fixed set of processes;

- whether the data item may be modified.

These options are chosen according to the nature of the data item and the pattern of its sharing between processes. The programmer can make an explicit choice of which parameter options to use for each data item. However, Munin supplies a small, standard set of annotations for the programmer to apply to data items, each of which implies a convenient choice of the parameters, suitable for a variety of applications and data items. These are as follows:

Read-only: No updates may be made after initialization and the item may be freely copied.

Migratory: Processes typically take turns in making several accesses to the item, at least one of which is an update. For example, the item might be accessed within a critical section. Munin always gives both read and write access together to such an object, even when a process takes a read fault. This saves subsequent write-fault processing.

Write-shared: Several processes update the same data item (for example, an array) concurrently, but this annotation is a declaration from the programmer that the processes do not update the same parts of it. This means that Munin can avoid false sharing but must propagate only those words in the data item that are actually updated at each process. To do this, Munin makes a copy of a page (inside a write-fault handler) just before it is updated locally. Only the differences between the two versions are sent in an update.

Producer-consumer: The data object is shared by a fixed set of processes, only one of which updates it. As we explained when discussing thrashing above, a write-update protocol is most suitable here. Moreover, updates may be delayed under the model of release consistency, assuming that the processes use locks to synchronize their accesses.

Reduction: The data item is always modified by being locked, read, updated and unlocked. An example of this is a global minimum in a parallel computation, which must be fetched and modified atomically if it is greater than the local minimum. These items are stored at a fixed owner. Updates are sent to the owner, which propagates them.

Result: Several processes update different words within the data item; a single process reads the whole item. For example, different 'worker' processes might fill in different elements of an array, which is then processed by a 'master' process. The point here is that the updates need only be propagated to the master and not to the workers (as would occur under the 'write-shared' annotation just described).

Conventional: The data item is managed under an invalidation protocol similar to that described in the previous section. No process may therefore read a stale version of the data item.

Carter *et al.* [1991] detail the parameter options used for each of the annotations we have given. This set of annotations is not fixed. Others may be created as sharing patterns that require different parameter options are encountered.

18.5 Other consistency models

Models of memory consistency can be divided into *uniform models*, which do not distinguish between types of memory access, and *hybrid models*, which do distinguish between ordinary and synchronization accesses (as well as other types of access).

Several uniform models exist that are weaker than sequential consistency. We introduced coherence in Section 18.2.3, in which the memory is sequentially consistent on a location-by-location basis. Processors agree on the order of all writes to a given location, but they may differ on the order of writes from different processors to different locations [Goodman 1989, Gharachorloo *et al.* 1990].

Other uniform consistency models include:

Causal consistency: Reads and writes may be related by the happened-before relationship (see Chapter 11). This is defined to hold between memory operations when either (a) they are made by the same process; (b) a process reads a value written by another process; or (c) there exists a sequence of such operations linking the two operations. The model's constraint is that the value returned by a read must be consistent with the happened-before relationship. This is described by Hutto and Ahamad [1990].

Processor consistency: The memory is both coherent and adheres to the pipelined RAM model (see below). The simplest way to think of processor consistency is that the memory is coherent and that all processes agree on the ordering of any two write accesses made by the same process – that is, they agree with its program order. This was first defined informally by Goodman [1989] and later formally defined by Gharachorloo *et al.* [1990] and Ahamad *et al.* [1992].

Pipelined RAM: All processors agree on the order of writes issued by any given processor [Lipton and Sandberg 1988].

In addition to release consistency, hybrid models include:

Entry consistency: Entry consistency was proposed for the Midway DSM system [Bershad *et al*. 1993]. In this model, every shared variable is bound to a synchronization object such as a lock, which governs access to that variable. Any process that first acquires the lock is guaranteed to read the latest value of the variable. A process wishing to write the variable must first obtain the corresponding lock in 'exclusive' mode – making it the only process able to access the variable. Several processes may read the variable concurrently by holding the lock in non-exclusive mode. Midway avoids the tendency to false sharing in release consistency, but at the expense of increased programming complexity.

Scope consistency: This memory model [Iftode *et al*. 1996] attempts to simplify the programming model of entry consistency. In scope consistency, variables are associated with synchronization objects largely automatically instead of relying on the programmer to associate locks with variables explicitly. For example, the system can monitor which variables are updated in a critical section.

Weak consistency: Weak consistency [Dubois *et al*. 1988] does not distinguish between *acquire* and *release* synchronization accesses. One of its guarantees is that all previous ordinary accesses complete before *either* type of synchronization access completes.

Discussion ◊ Release consistency and some of the other consistency models weaker than sequential consistency appear to be the most promising for DSM. It does not seem to be a significant disadvantage of the release consistency model that synchronization operations need to be known to the DSM runtime – as long as those supplied by the system are sufficiently powerful to meet the needs of programmers.

It is important to realize that, under the hybrid models, most programmers are not forced to consider the particular memory consistency semantics used as long as they synchronize their data accesses appropriately. But there is a general danger in DSM designs of asking the programmer to perform many annotations to his or her program in order to make its execution efficient. This includes both annotations identifying data items with synchronization objects and the sharing annotations such as those of Munin. One of the advantages of shared-memory programming over message passing is supposed to be its relative convenience.

18.6 Summary

This chapter has described and motivated the concept of distributed shared memory as an abstraction of shared memory that is an alternative to message-based communication in a distributed system. DSM is primarily intended for parallel processing and data sharing. It has been shown to perform as well as message passing for certain parallel applications, but it is difficult to implement efficiently, and its performance varies with applications.

The chapter has concentrated on software implementations of DSM – particularly those using the virtual memory subsystem – but it has been implemented with hardware support.

The main design and implementation issues are the DSM structure, the means by which applications synchronize, the memory consistency model, the use of write-update or write-invalidation protocols, the granularity of sharing, and thrashing.

The DSM is structured either as a series of bytes, a collection of shared objects, or a collection of immutable data items such as tuples.

Applications using DSM require synchronization in order to meet application-specific consistency constraints. They use objects such as locks for this purpose, implemented using message passing for efficiency.

The most common strict type of memory consistency implemented in DSM systems is sequential consistency. Because of its cost, weaker consistency models have been developed, such as coherence and release consistency. Release consistency enables the implementation to exploit the use of synchronization objects to achieve greater efficiency without breaking application-level consistency constraints. Several other consistency models were outlined, including entry, scope and weak consistency, which all exploit synchronization.

Write-update protocols are those in which updates are propagated to all copies as data items are updated. These are usually implemented in hardware, although software implementations using totally ordered multicast exist. Write-invalidation protocols prevent stale data being read by invalidating copies as data items are updated. These are more suited to page-based DSM, for which write-update may be an expensive option.

The granularity of DSM affects the likelihood of contention between processes that falsely share data items because they are contained in the same unit of sharing (for example, page). It also affects the cost per byte of transferring updates between computers.

Thrashing may occur when write-invalidation is used. This is the repeated transfer of data between competing processes at the expense of application progress. This may be reduced by application-level synchronization, by allowing computers to retain a page for a minimum time, or by labelling data items so that both read and write access are always granted together.

The chapter has described Ivy's three main write-invalidate protocols for page-based DSM, which address the problems of managing the copy set and locating the owner of a page. These were the central manager protocol, in which a single process stores the current owner's address for each page; the protocol that uses multicast to locate the current owner of a page; and the dynamic distributed manager protocol, which uses forwarding pointers to locate the current owner of a page.

Munin is an example implementation of release consistency. It implements eager release consistency in that it propagates update or invalidation messages as soon as a lock is released. Alternative, lazy implementations exist, which propagate those messages only when they are required. Munin allows programmers to annotate their data items in order to select the protocol options that are best suited to them, given the way in which they are shared.

EXERCISES

18.1   Explain in which respects DSM is suitable or unsuitable for client-server systems.

page 750

18.2   Discuss whether message passing or DSM is preferable for fault-tolerant applications.

page 751

18.3   How would you deal with the problem of differing data representations for a middleware-based implementation of DSM on heterogeneous computers? How would you tackle the problem in a page-based implementation? Does your solution extend to pointers?   *page 753*

18.4   Why should we want to implement page-based DSM largely at user-level, and what is required to achieve this?   *page 754*

18.5   How would you implement a semaphore using a tuple space?   *page 755*

18.6   Is the memory underlying the following execution of two processes sequentially consistent (assuming that, initially, all variables are set to zero)?

P_1: $R(x)1; R(x)2; W(y)1$

P_2: $W(x)1; R(y)1; W(x)2$ *page 759*

18.7   Using the $R()$, $W()$ notation, give an example of an execution on a memory that is coherent but not sequentially consistent. Can a memory be sequentially consistent but not coherent?   *page 759*

18.8   In write-update, show that sequential consistency could be broken if each update were to be made locally before asynchronously multicasting it to other replica managers, even though the multicast is totally ordered. Discuss whether an asynchronous multicast can be used to achieve sequential consistency. (Hint: consider whether to block subsequent operations.)   *page 760*

18.9   Sequentially consistent memory can be implemented using a write-update protocol employing a synchronous, totally ordered multicast. Discuss what multicast ordering requirements would be necessary to implement coherent memory.   *page 760*

18.10   Explain why, under a write-update protocol, care is needed to propagate only those words within a data item that have been updated locally.

Devise an algorithm for representing the differences between a page and an updated version of it. Discuss the performance of this algorithm.   *page 760*

18.11   Explain why granularity is an important issue in DSM systems. Compare the issue of granularity between object-oriented and byte-oriented DSM systems, bearing in mind their implementations.

Why is granularity relevant to tuple spaces, which contain immutable data?

What is false sharing? Can it lead to incorrect executions?   *page 762*

18.12   What are the implications of DSM for page replacement policies (that is, the choice of which page to purge from main memory in order to bring a new page in)?   *page 763*

18.13 Prove that Ivy's write-invalidate protocol guarantees sequential consistency. *page 765*

18.14 In Ivy's dynamic distributed manager algorithm, what steps are taken to minimize the number of lookups necessary to find a page? *page 768*

18.15 Why is thrashing an important issue in DSM systems and what methods are available for dealing with it? *page 771*

18.16 Discuss how condition RC2 for release consistency could be relaxed. Hence distinguish between eager and lazy release consistency. *page 774*

18.17 A sensor process writes the current temperature into a variable t stored in a release-consistent DSM. Periodically, a monitor process reads t. Explain the need for synchronization to propagate the updates to t, even though none is otherwise needed at the application level. Which of these processes needs to perform synchronization operations? *page 773*

18.18 Show that the following history is not causally consistent:

P_1: $W(a)0; W(a)1$

P_2: $R(a)1; W(b)2$

P_3: $R(b)2; R(a)0$ *page 777*

18.19 What advantage can a DSM implementation obtain from knowing the association between data items and synchronization objects? What is the disadvantage of making the association explicit? *page 778*

WEB SERVICES

A web service provides a service interface enabling clients to interact with servers in a more general way than web browsers do. Clients access the operations in the interface of a web service by means of requests and replies formatted in XML and usually transmitted over HTTP. Web services can be accessed in a more *ad hoc* manner than Corba-based services, enabling them to be more easily used in Internet-wide applications.

Like CORBA and Java, the interfaces of web services can be described in an IDL. But for web services, additional information including the encoding and communication protocols in use and the service location need to be described.

Users require a secure means for creating, storing and modifying documents and exchanging them over the Internet. The secure channels of TLS do not provide all of the necessary requirements. XML security is intended to breach this gap.

The Grid is the name used to refer to a middleware platform based on web services and designed for use by large dispersed groups of users with massive data resources that require substantial processing. The astronomers' World-Wide Telescope is a typical grid application for scientific collaboration. The characteristics of data-intensive scientific applications are derived from a study of the World-Wide Telescope. These characteristics lead to a set of requirements for a grid architecture.

19.1 Introduction

The growth of the Web in the last five years (see Figure 1.6) proves the effectiveness of using simple protocols over the Internet as the basis for a large number of wide-area services and applications. In particular, the HTTP request-reply protocol (Section 4.4), allows general-purpose clients called browsers to view web pages and other resources with reference to their URLs. See the box below for a note on URIs, URLs and URNs.

However, the use of a general-purpose browser as client, even with the enhancements provided by downloaded application-specific applets, restricts the potential scope of applications. In the original client-server model, both client and server were functionally specialized. Web services return to this model, in which an application-specific client interacts with a service with a functionally-specialized interface over the Internet.

Thus, web services provide an infrastructure for maintaining a richer and more structured form of interoperability between clients and servers. They provide a basis whereby a client program in one organization may interact with a server in another organization without human supervision. In particular, web services allow complex applications to be developed by providing services that integrate several other services. Due to the generality of their interactions, web services cannot be accessed directly by browsers.

The provision of web services as an addition to web servers is based on the ability to use an HTTP request to cause the execution of a program. Recall that, when a URL in an HTTP request refers to an executable program, for example, a search, then the result is produced by that program and returned. In a similar way, web services are an extension of the Web and can be provided by web servers. However, their servers need not be web servers. The terms 'web server' and 'web services' should not be confused: a web server provides a basic HTTP service, whereas a web service provides a service based on the operations defined in its interface.

External data representation and marshalling of messages exchanged between clients and web services is done in XML, which is described in Section 4.3.3. To recap, XML is a textual representation that, although more bulky than alternative representations, has been adopted for its readability and the consequent ease of debugging.

The SOAP protocol (Section 19.2.1) specifies the rules for using XML to package messages, for example to support a request-reply protocol.

Figure 19.1 summarizes the main points about the communication architecture in which web services operate: a web service is identified by a URI and can be accessed by clients using messages formatted in XML. SOAP is used to encapsulate these

URI, URL and URN ◊ The Uniform Resource Identifier (URI) is a general resource identifier, whose value may be either a URL or a URN. A URL, which includes resource location information, such as the domain name of the server of a resource being named, is well known to all web users. Uniform Resource Names (URNs) are location independent – they rely on a lookup service to map them onto the URLs of resources. URNs are discussed in more detail in Section 9.1.

Figure 19.1   Web services infrastructure and components

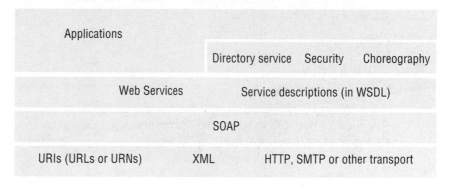

messages and transmit them over HTTP or another protocol, for example, TCP or SMTP. A web service deploys service descriptions to specify the interface and other aspects of the service for the benefit of potential clients.

The top layer of the figure illustrates the following:

- Web services and applications may be built on top of other web services.

- Some particular web services provide general functionality required for the operation of a large number of other web services. They include directory services, security and choreography, all of which are discussed later in this chapter.

A web service generally provides a *service description*, which includes an interface definition and other information, such as the server's URL. This is used as the basis for a common understanding between client and server as to the service on offer. Section 19.3 presents WSDL (Web Services Description Language).

Another common need in middleware is for a naming or directory service to allow clients to find out about services. Clients of web services have similar needs, but frequently manage without directory services. For example, they often find out about services from information on a web page, for example as the result of a Google search. However, some work has been done to provide a directory service that is suitable for use within organizations. This is discussed in Section 19.4.

XML Security is introduced in Section 19.5. In this approach to security, documents or parts of documents may be signed or encrypted. A document that has signed or encrypted elements may then be transmitted or stored; later additions may be made and these too may be signed or encrypted.

Web services provide access to resources for remote clients, but they do not provide a means for coordinating their operations with one another. Section 19.7 discusses choreography of web services, which is intended to allow one web service to use predefined patterns of access in using a set of other web services.

The last section of this chapter contains a case study of the Grid – an application based on web services. The Grid is an infrastructure that is intended to provide access to large-scale sharing of resources including programs, files, data, computers, sensors and networks. The Web was originally created to satisfy the needs of teams of physicists at different sites wanting to share the documentation of their experiments. More recently, the grid concept has developed amongst scientists with a need for a more general distributed computing environment in the Internet.

19.2 Web services

A web service interface generally consists of a collection of operations that can be used by a client over the Internet. The operations in a web service may be provided by a variety of different resources, for example, programs, objects or databases. A web service may either be managed by a web server along with web pages; or it may be a totally separate service.

The key characteristic of most web services is they it can process XML-formatted SOAP messages (see Section 19.2.1). An alternative is the REST approach which is outlined in the box on page 788. Each web service uses its own service description to deal with the service-specific characteristics of the messages it receives. For a good account of many more-detailed aspects of web services, see Newcomer [2002].

Many well-known commercial web servers including Amazon, Yahoo, Google and eBay offer web service interfaces that allow clients to manipulate their web resources. As an example, the web service offered by Amazon.com provides operations to allow clients to get information about products, to add an item to a shopping cart or to check the status of a transaction. The Amazon web services [associates.amazon.com] may be accessed either by SOAP (Section 19.2.1) or by REST. This enables third-party applications to build value-added services over those provided by Amazon.com. For example, an inventory control and purchasing application might order supplies of various commodities as they are needed from Amazon.com and automatically keep track of the changing status of each order. Over 50,000 developers have registered to use these web services in the two years since they were introduced [Greenfield and Dornan 2004].

Another interesting example of an application that requires the presence of a web service is the application that implements 'sniping' in eBay auctions. Sniping means placing a bid during the last few seconds before an auction closes. Although humans can perform the same actions by direct interaction with the web page, they cannot do it as quickly.

Combination of web services ◊ The provision of a service interface allows its operations to be combined with those of other services to provide new functionality. In fact, the above purchasing application might be using other suppliers as well. As another example of the benefits of combining several services: consider the fact that people currently use their browsers to book flights, hotels and car hire with a selection of different web sites. However, if each of these web sites were to provide a standard web service interface, then a 'Travel Agent Service' could use their operations in order to provide a traveller with a combination of these services. This point is illustrated in Figure 19.2.

Communication patterns ◊ The 'travel agent' service illustrates the possible use of the two alternative communication patterns available in web services:

Figure 19.2   The 'travel agent service' combines other web services

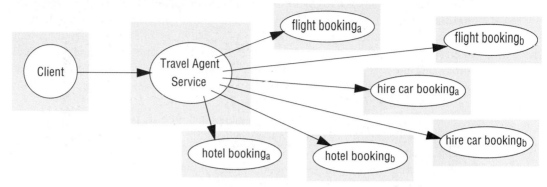

- the processing of a booking takes a long time to complete and could well be supported by an asynchronous exchange of documents, starting with the details of the dates and destinations, followed by a return of status information from time to time and eventually the details of completion. Performance is not an issue here.

- whereas the checking of credit card details and the interactions with the client should be supported by a request-reply protocol.

In general, web services use either a synchronous request-reply pattern of communication with their clients or they communicate by means of asynchronous messages. The latter style of communication may be used even when requests require replies, in which case, the client sends a request and then later receives the reply asynchronously. An event-style pattern can also be used: for example, clients of a directory service may register for events of interest – and they will be notified whenever certain events occur. For example, an event could be the arrival or departure of a service.

To allow for a variety of patterns of communication, the SOAP protocol (Section 19.2.1) is based on the packaging of single one-way messages. Its supports request-reply interactions by using pairs of single messages and specifying how to represent operations, their arguments and results.

No particular programming model ◊ Web services are designed to support distributed computing in the Internet, in which a multitude of different programming languages are used. They are independent of any particular programming paradigm. The main differences from the distributed object model are the following:

- remote objects cannot be instantiated – effectively a web service consists of a single remote object and therefore:

  – garbage collection is irrelevant;

  – remote object references are irrelevant.

We return to the comparison of web services with distributed objects in Section 19.2.2. The REST approach advocates that web services should have very little variety in their interface as explained in the box on page 788. According to Greenfield and Dornan [2004], 80% of the requests to the web services at amazon.com are via the REST interface, the remaining 20% make use of SOAP.

Representation of messages ◊ Both SOAP and the data it carries are represented in XML – a textual self-describing format introduced in Section 4.3.3. Textual representations take up more space than binary ones and require more time to process. In document-style interactions speed is not an issue, but it is important in request-reply interactions. However, it can be argued that there is an advantage in a human-readable format that allows for the easy construction of simple messages and for debugging more complex ones. It can also allow a user to see the text in a message before it. But there are situations in which it is too slow.

Each item in an XML description is annotated with its type and the meaning of each type is defined by a schema referenced within the description. This makes the format extensible, enabling any type of data to be transported. There is no limit on the potential richness and complexity of documents formatted in XML, but there could be a problem in interpreting those that become unduly complex.

Service references ◊ In general, each web service has a URI, which clients use to refer to it. The URL is the most frequently used form of URI. Because a URL contains the domain name of a computer, the service to which it refers will always be accessed at that computer. However, the access point of a web service with a URN can depend on context and can change from time to time – its current URL can be obtained from a URN lookup service.

Activation of services ◊ A web service will be accessed via the computer whose domain name is included in its current URL. That computer may run the web service itself or it may run it on another server computer. For example, a service provider with tens of thousands of clients will need to deploy hundreds of computers to provide that service. A web service may run continuously or it may be activated on demand. The URL is a persistent reference – meaning that it will continue to refer to the service for as long as that server exists.

Transparency ◊ A major task of many middleware platforms is to protect the programmer from the details of data representation and marshalling and sometimes with making remote invocations look like local ones. None of these things are provided as a part of an infrastructure or middleware platform for web services. At the simplest level, clients and servers may read and write their messages directly in SOAP, using XML.

But for convenience, the details of SOAP and XML are generally hidden by a local API in a programming language such as Java, Perl, Python or C++. In this case,

---

REST (representational state transfer) ◊ REST [Fielding 2000] is an approach with a very constrained style of operation, in which clients use URLs and the HTTP operations GET, PUT, DELETE and POST to manipulate resources that are represented in XML. The emphasis is on the manipulation of data resources rather than on interfaces. Clients are supplied the entire state of a resource instead of calling an operation to provide some part of it. Fielding believes that in the context of the Internet, the proliferation of different service interfaces will not be as useful as a simple minimum uniform set of operations. When a new resource is created, then it has a new URL by which it can be accessed or updated.

the service description may be used as a basis for automatically generating the necessary marshalling and unmarshalling procedures.

Proxies: It is an option to hide the difference between local and remote calls by providing a client proxy or a set of stub procedures. Section 19.2.3 explains how this is done in Java. Client proxies or stubs provide a static form of invocation in which the framework for each call and the marshalling procedures are generated before any invocations are made.

Dynamic invocation: An alternative to proxies is to provide clients with a generic operation to be used irrespective of the remote procedure to be called, similar to the *DoOperation* procedure defined in Figure 4.15 (but without the first argument). In this case, the client specifies the name of an operation and its arguments and they are converted to SOAP and XML on the fly. The asynchronous communication of single messages can be achieved in a similar way by providing clients with generic operations for sending and receiving messages.

19.2.1 SOAP

SOAP is designed to enable both client-server and asynchronous interaction over the Internet. It defines a scheme for using XML to represent the contents of request and reply messages (see Figure 4.16) as well as a scheme for the communication of documents. Originally SOAP was based only on HTTP, but the current version is designed to use a variety of transport protocols including SMTP, TCP or UDP. The description in this section is based on SOAP version 1.2 [www.w3.org IX], which is a World Wide Web Consortium (W3C) recommendation. SOAP is an extension of Userland's XML-RPC [Winer 1999].

The SOAP specification states:

- how XML is to be used to represent the contents of individual messages;

- how a pair of single messages can be combined to produce a request-reply pattern;

- the rules as to how the recipients of messages should process the XML elements that they contain;

- how HTTP and SMTP should be used to communicate SOAP messages. It is expected that future versions of the specification will define how to use other transport protocols, for example, TCP.

This section describes how SOAP uses XML to represent messages and HTTP to communicate them. However, the programmer does not normally need to be concerned with these details, since SOAP APIs have been implemented in many programming languages, including Java, Javascript, Perl, Python,.NET, C, C++, C# and Visual Basic.

To support client-server communication, SOAP specifies how to use the HTTP *POST* method for the request message and its response for the reply message. The combined use of XML and HTTP provides a standard protocol for client-server communication over the Internet.

It is intended that a SOAP message can be passed via intermediaries on the way to the computer that manages the resource to be accessed and that higher-level

Figure 19.3   SOAP message in an envelope

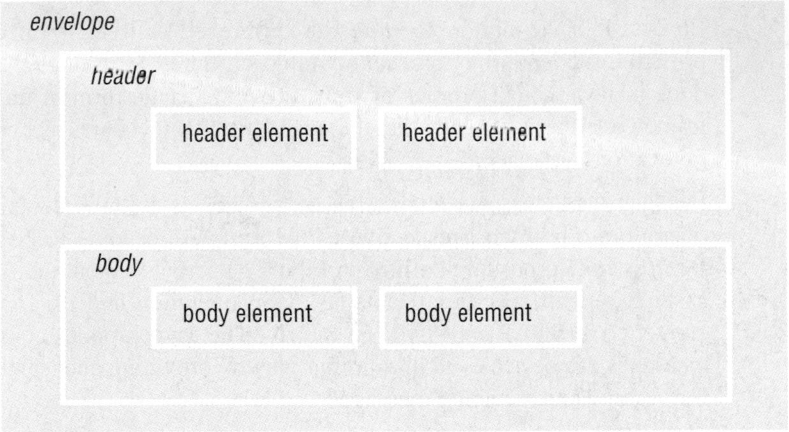

middleware services such as transactions or security may use these intermediaries to perform processing.

SOAP messages ◊ A SOAP message is carried in an 'envelope'. Inside the envelope there is an optional header and a body as shown in Figure 19.3. Message headers can be used for establishing the necessary context for a service or for keeping a log or audit of operations. An intermediary may interpret and act on the information in the message headers, for example by adding, altering or removing information. The message body carries an XML document for a particular web service.

The XML elements *envelope*, *header* and *body*, together with other attributes and elements of SOAP messages are defined as a schema in the SOAP XML namespace. The definition of this schema can be found on the W3C web site [www.w3.org]. Since they use a textual encoding, XML schemas can be viewed with the 'view source' option of a browser. Both the header and the body contain inner elements.

The previous section explained that service descriptions contain information that is to be shared by clients and servers. Message senders use these descriptions to generate the *body* and to ensure that it contains the correct contents and message recipients use them to parse and check the validity of the contents.

A SOAP message may be used either to convey a document or to support client-server communication:

- A document to be communicated is placed directly inside the *body* element, together with a reference to an XML schema containing the service description – which defines the names and types used in the document. This sort of SOAP message may be sent either synchronously or asynchronously.

- For client-server communication, the *body* element contains either a *Request* or a *Reply*. These two cases are illustrated in Figure 19.4 and Figure 19.5.

Figure 19.4 shows an example of a simple request message without a header. The *body* encloses an element with the name of the procedure to be called and the URI of the namespace (the file containing the XML schema) for the relevant service description,

Figure 19.4   Example of a simple request without headers

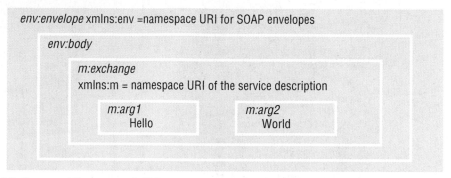

In this figure and the next, each XML element is represented by a shaded box with its name in italic, followed by any attributes and its content

Figure 19.5   Example of a reply corresponding to the request in Figure 19.4

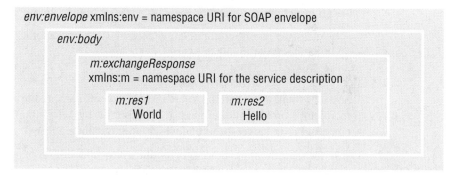

which is denoted by *m*. The inner elements of a request message contain the arguments of the procedure. This request message provides two strings to be returned in the opposite order by the procedure at the server. The XML namespace denoted by *env* contains the SOAP definitions for an *envelope*. Figure 19.5 shows the corresponding successful reply message, which contains the two output arguments. Note that the name of the procedure has 'Response' added to it. If a procedure has a return value, then it may be denoted as an element called *rpc:result*. Note that the reply message uses the same two XML schemas as the request message, the first defining the SOAP envelope and the second, the application-specific procedure and argument names.

Soap faults: If a request fails in some way, the fault descriptions are conveyed in the body of a reply message in a *fault* element. This element contains information about the fault, including a code and an associated string, together with application specific details.

SOAP headers ◊ Message headers are intended to be used by intermediaries to add to the service that deals with the message carried in the corresponding body. However, two aspects of this usage are left unclear in the SOAP specification:

Figure 19.6   Use of HTTP POST Request in SOAP client-server communication

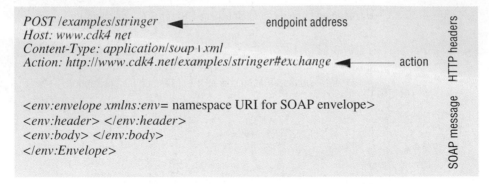

1. how the headers will be used by any particular higher middleware service. For example, a header might contain:

   – a transaction identifier for use with a transaction service;

   – a message identifier for relating messages to one another, for example, for implementing reliable delivery;

   – a user name, a digital signature or a public key.

2. how the messages will be routed via a set of intermediaries to the ultimate recipient. For example, a message transported by HTTP could be routed via a chain of proxy servers, some of which might assume a SOAP role.

However, the specification does specify the roles and duties of intermediaries. An attribute called role can specify whether every intermediary, none of them, or just the ultimate recipient must process the element (see [www.w3.org]). The particular actions to be carried out are defined by applications, for example, an action might be to log the contents of an element.

Transport of SOAP messages ◊ A transport protocol is required to send a SOAP message to its destination. SOAP messages are independent of the type of transport used – their envelopes contain no reference to the destination address. HTTP (or whatever protocol is used to transport a SOAP message) is left to specify the destination address.

Figure 19.6 illustrates how the HTTP *POST* method is used to transmit a SOAP message. The HTTP headers and body are used as follows:

- the HTTP headers specify the endpoint address (the URI of the ultimate receiver) and the action to be carried out. The *Action* parameter is intended to optimize dispatching – by revealing the name of the operation without the need to analyse the SOAP message in the body of the HTTP message;

- the HTTP body carries the SOAP message.

As HTTP is a synchronous protocol, it is used to return a reply containing the SOAP reply, for example the one shown in Figure 19.5. Section 4.4 details the status codes and reasons returned by HTTP for successful and failing requests.

If a SOAP *Request* is just a request for information to be returned, has no arguments and does not alter data in the server, then the HTTP *GET* method can be used to carry it out.

The above point about the *Action* header and dispatching applies to any service that performs a variety of different actions for clients, even if it does not offer operations as such. For example, a web service may be able to deal with a variety of different types of documents, such as purchase orders and enquiries, which are dealt with by different software modules. The *Action* header enables the correct module to be chosen without inspecting the SOAP message. This header can be used if the HTTP content type is specified as *application/soap+xml*.

The separation of the definition of the SOAP envelope from the information as to how and where it is to be sent makes it possible to use a variety of different underlying protocols. The SOAP specification states how SMTP can be used as an alternative way for transmitting documents encoded as SOAP messages.

But this strength is also a weakness. It implies that the developer must be involved in the details of the specific transport protocol chosen. In addition, it makes it difficult to use different protocols for different parts of the route followed by a particular message.

Advances in SOAP addressing and routing ◊ Two problems were mentioned above:

- how to make SOAP independent of the underlying transport used;

- and how to specify a route to be followed by a SOAP message via a set of intermediaries.

Early work in this area called WS-Routing by Nielsen and Thatte [2001] suggests that the endpoint address and the dispatching information should be specified in SOAP headers. This effectively separates the message destination from the underlying protocol. They suggested specifying the path to be followed by giving the address of the endpoint and the 'next hop'. Each of the intermediaries would update the 'next hop' information.

More recent work reported by Box and Curbera *et al.* [2004] and described as WS-Addressing suggests that having intermediaries alter the headers could lead to breaches of security. They propose an alternative in which the headers specify the endpoint address and an underlying SOAP infrastructure provides the 'next hop' information. In addition, they propose using SOAP headers for the return address and a message identifier.

Reliable communication ◊ Web services lack a protocol that delivers messages reliably in the presence of failures. SOAP's usual protocol, HTTP runs over TCP, whose failure model is discussed in Section 4.2.4. To summarize: TCP does not guarantee to deliver messages in the face of all difficulties – and when it reaches a timeout on waiting for acknowledgements, it declares that the connection is broken, at which point the communicating processes are left without any idea as to whether the messages they sent recently have been received or not.

Some work has been done on the provision of reliable communication of SOAP messages with guaranteed delivery, no duplicates, and guaranteed message ordering. Two competing specifications have been provided by Ferris and Langworthy [2004] and Evans *et al.* [2003].

It will be interesting to see whether established fault-tolerance measures, such as acknowledgements, retransmission of requests, duplicate filtering and sequence numbers will be effective for the very large-scale and heterogeneous Internet environment. In particular, the choice of timeout periods may be a challenge.

Traversing firewalls ◊ Web services are intended to be used by clients in one organization accessing servers in another organization over the Internet. Most organizations use a firewall to protect the resources on their own networks and the transport protocols such as those used by Java RMI or CORBA would not normally be able to pass through a firewall. However, firewalls do normally allow both HTTP and SMTP messages to pass through them. Therefore it is convenient to use one of these protocols for transporting SOAP messages.

19.2.2 A comparison of web services with the distributed object model

A web service has a service interface which can provide operations for accessing and updating the data resources it manages. At a superficial level, the interaction between client and server is very similar to RMI, where a client uses a remote object reference to invoke an operation in a remote object. For a web service the client uses a URI to invoke an operation in the resource named by that URI. For arguments about the similarities and differences between web services and distributed objects, see Birman [2004], Vinoski [2002] and Vogels [2003]. We shall attempt to show that there are limits to the above analogy, by making use of the shared whiteboard example used in Section 5.5 for Java RMI and Section 20.2. for CORBA.

Remote object references are not very similar to URIs ◊ The URI of a web service can be compared with the remote object reference of a single object. However, in the distributed object model, objects can create remote objects dynamically and return remote references to them. The recipient of these remote references can use them to invoke operations in the objects to which they refer. In the shared whiteboard example, an invocation of the *newShape* factory method causes a new instance of *Shape* to be created and a remote references to it is returned. Nothing like this can be done with web services which cannot create instances of remote objects.

Web services model ◊ The users of the Java web services toolkit (JAX-RPC) [java.sun.com VII] must model their web services programs to allow for the fact that they are not using transparent Java-to-Java remote invocation, but are using the web services model, in which remote objects cannot be instantiated. This is taken into account by JAX-RPC, which does not permit remote object references to be passed as arguments or returned as results.

Figure 19.7 shows a version of the interface given in Figure 5.12 which has been modified as follows to become a web services interface:

- in the original (distributed object) version of the program, instances of *Shape* are created in the server and remote references to them returned by *newShape*, whose modified (web service) version is shown in line 1. To avoid the instantiation of remote objects and the consequent use of remote object references, the *Shape* interface is removed and its operations (*getAllState* and *getGOVersion* – originally *getVersion*) are added to the *ShapeList* interface;

Figure 19.7   Java web service interface *ShapeList*

```
import java.rmi.*;
public interface ShapeList extends Remote {
        int newShape(GraphicalObject g) throws RemoteException;                    1
        int numberOfShapes()throws RemoteException;
        int getVersion() throws RemoteException;
        int getGOVersion(int i)throws RemoteException;
        GraphicalObject getAllState(int i) throws RemoteException;
}
```

- in the original (distributed object) version of the program, the server stored a vector of *Shape*. This will be changed to a vector of *GraphicalObject*. The new (web service) version of the method *newShape* returns an integer that gives the offset of the *GraphicalObject* in that vector.

This change to the method *newShape* means that it is no longer a factory method – that is, it does not create instances of remote objects.

Servants ◊ In the distributed object model, the server program is generally modelled as a collection of servants (potentially remote objects). For example, the shared whiteboard application used one servant for the list of shapes and one servant for each graphical object created. These servants were created as instances of servant classes *ShapeList* and *Shape* respectively. When the server started, its *main* function created the instance of *ShapeList* and each time the client called the *newShape* method, the server created an instance of *Shape*.

In contrast, web services do not support servants. Therefore web services applications cannot create servants as and when they are needed to handle different server resources. To enforce this situation, the implementations of web service interfaces must not have either constructors or main methods.

19.2.3 The use of SOAP with Java

The Java API for developing web services and clients over SOAP is called JAX-RPC. It is described in the Java web services tutorial [java.sun.com VII]. This API hides all the details of SOAP from the programmers of both clients and the services.

JAX-RPC maps some of the types in the Java language to definitions in XML used both in SOAP messages and service descriptions. The permitted types include *Integer*, *String*, *Date* and *Calendar*, as well as *java.net.uri*, which allows URIs to be passed as arguments or returned as results. It supports some of the collection types (including *Vector*) as well as the primitive types of the language and arrays.

In addition, instances of some classes may be passed as arguments and results of remote calls, provided that:

- each of their instance variables is one of the permitted types;
- they have a public default constructor;
- they do not implement the *Remote* interface.

Figure 19.8   Java implementation of the *ShapeList* server

```
import java.util.Vector;
public class ShapeListImpl implements ShapeList{
    private Vector theList = new Vector();
    private int version = 0;
    private Vector theVersions = new Vector();

    public int newShape(GraphicalObject g) throws RemoteException{
        version++;
        theList.addElement(g);
        theVersions.addElement(new Integer(version));
        return theList.size();
    }
    public int numberOfShapes(){}
    public int getVersion() {}
    public int getGOVersion(int i){  }
    public GraphicalObject getAllState(int i) {}
}
```

In general, as mentioned in the previous section, values of types that are remote references (that is, they implement the *Remote* interface) cannot be passed as arguments or returned as results of remote calls.

The service interface ◊ The Java interface of a web service must conform to the following rules, some of which are illustrated in Figure 19.7:

- It must extend the *Remote* interface.

- It must not have constant declarations, such as *public final static*.

- The methods must throw the *java.rmi.RemoteException* or one of its subclasses.

- Method parameters and return types must be permitted JAX-RPC types.

The server program ◊ The class that implements the interface *ShapeList* is shown in Figure 19.8. As explained above, there is no *main* method, and the implementation of the *ShapeList* interface does not have a constructor. In effect, a web service is a single object that offers a set of procedures. The source of the programs shown in Figure 19.7, Figure 19.8 and Figure 19.9 is available on the book's web site at www.cdk4.net/webs.

The service interface and its implementation are compiled as usual. A pair of tools called *wscompile* and *wsdeploy* can be used to generate the skeleton class and the service description (in WSDL), using information concerning the URL of the service, its name and description from a configuration file written in XML. The name of the service (in this case, *MyShapeListService*) is used to generate the name of the class used in the client program to access it. That is, *MyShapeListService_Impl*.

Servlet container ◊ The service implementation is run as a servlet inside a *servlet container* whose role is to load, initialize, and execute servlets. The servlet container includes a dispatcher and skeletons (see Section 5.2.5). When a request arrives, the dispatcher maps it to a particular skeleton which translates it into Java and passes on the request to the appropriate method in the servlet, which carries out the request and produces a reply which the skeleton translates back into a SOAP reply. The URL of a service consists of a concatenation of the URL of the servlet container and the service category and name, for example, *http://localhost:8080/ShapeList-jaxrpc/ShapeList*.

Tomcat [Apache 2004] is a commonly used servlet container. When Tomcat is running, its management interface is available at a URL for viewing with a browser. This interface shows the names of servlets that are currently deployed and provides operations for managing them and for accessing information about each one, including its service description. Once a servlet is deployed in Tomcat, clients may access it and the combined effects of their operations will be stored in its instance variables. In our example, a list of *GraphicalObjects* will be built up as each one is added as the result of a client request to the *newShape* operation. If a servlet is stopped by Tomcat's management interface, then the values of the instance variables are reset when it is restarted.

Tomcat also provides access to a service description of each of the services that it contains, to enable programmers to design client programs and to facilitate the automatic compilation of the proxies required by client code. The service description is human readable since it is expressed in XML notation.

The client program ◊ The client program may use static proxies, dynamic proxies or a dynamic invocation interface. In all cases, the relevant service description may be used to obtain any information required by client code. In our example, the service description can be obtained from Tomcat.

Static proxies: Figure 19.9 shows the *ShapeList* client making a call through a proxy – a local object which passes on messages to the remote service. The code for the proxy is generated by *wscompile* from the service description. The class name for the proxy is formed by adding '*_Impl*' to the name of the service – in this case, the proxy class is called *MyShapeListService_Impl*. This name is implementation-specific, since the SOAP specification does not give a rule for naming proxy classes.

At line 1, the *createProxy* method is called. This method is shown at line 5, where it goes on to line 6 to create a proxy, using the class *MyShapeListService_Impl;* and then returns the proxy (note that proxies are sometimes called stubs, hence the name of the class *Stub*). At line 2, the URL of the service is supplied to the proxy via the argument given on the command line. At line 3, the type of the *proxy* is narrowed to suit the type of the interface – *ShapeList*. Line 4 makes a call to the remote procedure *getAllState*, asking the service to return the object at element 0 in the vector of *GraphicalObject*s.

Because the proxy is created at compile time, it is called a static proxy. The service description of the service from which it was generated will not necessarily have been generated from a Java interface, but may have been made by any one of a variety of tools associated with various different language systems. It may even have been written directly in XML.

Dynamic proxies: Instead of using a precompiled static proxy, the client uses a dynamic proxy whose class is created at runtime from the information in the service description and the interface of the service. This method avoids the need for involving an implementation-specific name for the proxy class.

Figure 19.9   Java implementation of the *ShapeList* client

```
package staticstub;
import javax.xml.rpc.Stub;
public class ShapeListClient {
    public static void main(String[] args) { /* pass URL of service */
        try {
            Stub proxy = createProxy();                                        1
            proxy._setProperty                                                 2
                (javax.xml.rpc.Stub.ENDPOINT_ADDRESS_PROPERTY, args[0]);
            ShapeList aShapeList = (ShapeList)proxy;                           3
            GraphicalObject g = aShapeList.getAllState(0);                    4
        } catch (Exception ex) { ex.printStackTrace(); }
    }

    private static Stub createProxy() {                                        5
        return
            (Stub) (new MyShapeListService_Impl().getShapeListPort());        6
    }
}
```

Dynamic invocation interface: This allows a client to call a remote procedure, even if its signature or the name of the service is unknown until runtime. In contrast to the above alternatives, the client does not require a proxy. Instead, it has to use a series of operations to set the name of the server operation, the return value and each of the parameters before making the procedure call.

Implementation of Java SOAP ◊ The way the Java API is implemented can be explained with reference to Figure 5.7. The following paragraphs explain the roles of the various components in a Java/SOAP environment – the interactions between the components are the same as before. There is no remote reference module.

Communication modules: The tasks of these modules are carried out by a pair of HTTP modules. The HTTP module in the server selects the dispatcher according to the URL given in the *action* header to the POST request.

Client proxy: A proxy (or stub) method knows the URL of the service and marshals its own method name and its arguments, together with a reference to the XML schema for the service into a SOAP request envelope. Unmarshalling the reply consists of analysing a SOAP envelope in order to extract the results, return value or fault report. The client's request method call is sent to the service as an HTTP request.

Dispatcher and skeleton: As mentioned above, the dispatcher and skeletons live in the servlet container. The dispatcher extracts the name of the operation from the *action* header in the HTTP request and invokes the corresponding method in the appropriate skeleton, passing the SOAP envelope to it. A skeleton method carries out the following tasks: it analyses the SOAP envelope in the request message and extracts its arguments, calls the corresponding method and assembles a SOAP reply envelope containing the results.

Errors, faults and correctness in SOAP/XML: Faults may be reported by the HTTP module, the dispatcher, the skeleton or the service itself. The service can report its errors via a return value or by means of fault parameters specified in the service description. The skeleton is responsible for checking that the SOAP envelope contains a request and the XML in which it is written well-formed. Having established that the XML is valid, the skeleton will use the XML namespace in the envelope to check that the request corresponds to the service on offer and that the operation and its arguments are appropriate. If the validation of the request fails at either of these levels, then an error is returned to client. Similar checks are made by the proxy when it receives the SOAP envelope containing the result.

19.2.4 Comparison of web services with CORBA

The main difference between web services and CORBA or other similar middleware is the context in which they are intended to be used. CORBA was designed for use within a single organization or between a small number of collaborating organizations. This resulted in certain aspects of the design being too centralized for collaborative use by independent organizations or for *ad hoc* use without prior arrangements, as will now be explained.

Naming issues ◊ In CORBA, each remote object is referenced by means of a name that is managed by an instance of the CORBA naming service (Section 20.3.1). This service, like DNS provides a mapping from a name to a value to be used as an address (an IOR in CORBA). But unlike DNS, the CORBA Naming Service is designed for use within an organization, instead of throughout the Internet.

In the CORBA naming service, each server manages a graph of names with an initial naming context and is initially independent of any other servers. Although separate organizations may federate their naming services, this is not automatic. Before a server can federate with another, it needs to know the initial naming context of the latter. Thus, the design of the CORBA naming service effectively restricts the sharing of CORBA objects to within a small set of organizations that have federated their naming services.

Reference issues ◊ We now consider whether a CORBA remote object reference, which is called an IOR (Section 20.2.4) could be used as an Internet-wide object reference in the same way as a URL. Each IOR contains a slot that specifies the type identifier of the interface of the object it references. However, this type identifier is understood only by the interface repository that stores the definition of the corresponding type. This has the implication that client and server need to use the same interface repository, which is not really practical on a global scale.

In contrast, in the web services model, a service is identified by means of a URL, enabling a client anywhere in the Internet to make a request to a service that may belong to any organization anywhere else. That is, a web service can be shared by clients throughout the Internet. The DNS is the only service required for URL access – and is designed to work effectively Internet-wide.

Separation of activation and location ◊ The tasks of locating and activating web services are neatly separated. In contrast, a CORBA persistent reference refers to a component of the platform (the implementation repository) which activates the corresponding object on demand on any suitable computer and is also responsible for locating the object once it has been activated.

Ease of use ◊ The HTTP and XML infrastructure for web services is well-understood and convenient to use and is already installed on all of the most commonly used operating systems, although the user does require a convenient programming language API to SOAP. In contrast, the CORBA platform is a large and complex piece of software requiring installation and support.

Efficiency ◊ CORBA has been designed to be efficient: CORBA CDR (Section 4.3.1) is binary, whereas XML is textual. A study by Olson and Ogbuji [2002] compares the performance of CORBA with that of SOAP and XML-RPC. They found that SOAP request messages are 14 times as large as the equivalent ones in CORBA and that a SOAP request took 882 times as long as an equivalent CORBA invocation. But the message overhead and slower performance of SOAP is not noticed in some applications and its effects are made less obvious by the availability of cheap bandwidth, processors, memory and disk space.

The W3C and others have been investigating the possibility of allowing binary data to be included in XML elements so as to increase efficiency. Discussions of this topic can be found at www.w3.org. Note that XML does already provide for both hexadecimal and base64 representations of binary data. The base64 representation is used in conjunction with XML encryption (see Section 19.5). There is a considerable time and space overhead when binary data is converted to base64 or hexadecimal. Therefore, what is really needed is to be able to a include a binary representation of a pre-parsed sequence of data items as, for example, produced by CORBA CDR or *gzip*. Another approach, which is also under investigation is to take a SOAP message, together with attachments, some of which may be binary and use a multipart MIME document to transport it. However, this last approach does not conform to the SOAP model.

The strengths of CORBA ◊ The availability of CORBA services for transactions, concurrency control, security and access control, events and persistent objects makes it a desirable choice for use in many applications that are intended for use within an organization or a related group of organizations. In general, it is a good choice for those applications that require very complex interactions. In addition, the distributed object model is an attractive one for the design of complex applications and worth the extra learning effort needed to understand the details of the relationship between the CORBA object model (Section 20.2) and the particular programming language in use.

19.3 Service descriptions and IDL for web services

Interface definitions are needed to allow clients to communicate with services. For web services, interface definitions are provided as part of a more general *service description*, which specifies two other additional characteristics – how the messages are to be

Figure 19.10   The main elements in a WSDL description

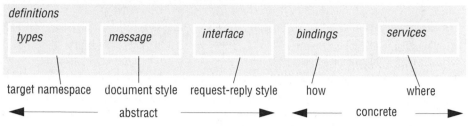

communicated (for example, by SOAP over HTTP) and the URI of the service. To cater for use in a multi-language environment, service descriptions are written in XML.

A service description forms the basis of an agreement between a client and a server as to the service on offer. It assembles all of the facts concerning the service that are relevant to its clients. Service descriptions are generally used to generate client stubs which automatically implement the correct behaviour for the client.

The IDL-like component of a service description is more flexible than other IDLs, in that a service may be specified either in terms of the types of messages that it will send and receive or in terms of the operations it supports, to allow for both document exchange and the request-reply style of interactions.

A variety of different methods of communication can be used by web services and their clients. Therefore the method of communication is left to be decided by the service provider and specified in the service description, rather than built into the system, as in CORBA, for example.

The ability to specify the URI of a service as a part of the service description avoids the need for the separate binder or naming service used by most other middleware. It has the implication that the URI cannot be changed once the service description has been made available to potential clients. But the URN scheme does cater for a change of location by allowing for an indirection at the reference level.

In contrast, in the binder approach, the client uses a name to look up the service reference at runtime, allowing the service references to change over time. But this approach requires an indirection from a name to a service reference for all services even though many of them may always remain at the same location.

In the web services context, Web Services Description Language (or WSDL), is commonly used for service descriptions. At the time of writing, WSDL 2.0 [www.w3.org XI] is a W3C working draft. It defines an XML schema for representing the components of a service description, which include, for example, the element names *definitions*, *types*, *message*, *interface*, *bindings* and *services*.

WSDL separates the abstract part of a service description from the concrete part as shown in Figure 19.10.

The abstract part of the description includes a set of definitions of the types used by the service, in particular the types of the values exchanged in messages. The Java example from Section 19.2.3, whose Java interface is shown in Figure 19.7, uses the Java types *int* and *GraphicalObject*. The former (like any basic type) can be translated directly into the XML equivalent. But *GraphicalObject* is defined in Java in terms of the types *int*, *String* and *boolean*. *GraphicalObject* is represented in XML, for common use

Figure 19.11 WSDL request and reply messages for the *newShape* operation

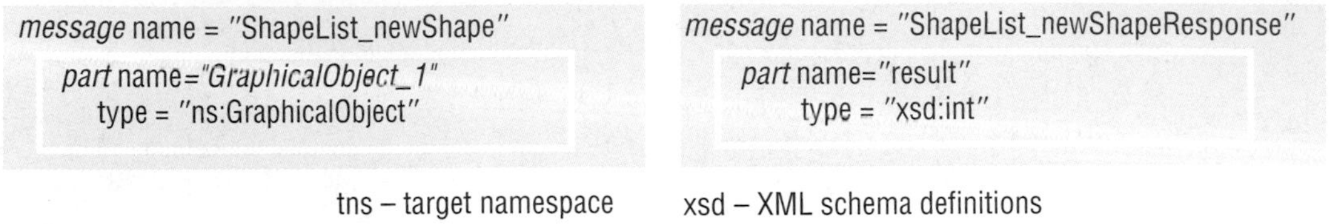

message name = "ShapeList_newShape"

 part name="GraphicalObject_1"
   type = "ns:GraphicalObject"

message name = "ShapeList_newShapeResponse"

 part name="result"
   type = "xsd:int"

tns – target namespace   xsd – XML schema definitions

by heterogeneous clients, as a *complexType* consisting of a *sequence* of named XML types including, for example:

<element name="isFilled" type="boolean"/>
<element name="originx" type="int"/>

The set of names defined within the *types* section of a WSDL definition is called its *target namespace*. The *message* section of the abstract part contains a description of the set of messages exchanged. For the document style of interaction, these messages will be used directly. For the request-reply style of interaction, there are two messages for each operation, which are used to describe the operations in the *interface* section. The concrete part specifies how and where the service may be contacted.

The inherent modularity of a WSDL definition allows its components to be combined in different ways, for example, the same interface may be used with different bindings or locations. The types may be defined inside the *types* element or they may be defined in a separate document referenced by a URI from the *types* element. In the latter case, the type definitions can be referenced from several different WSDL documents.

Messages or operations ◊ In web services, all that the client and the server need, is to have a common idea about the messages to be exchanged. For a service based on the exchange of a small number of different types of document, WSDL just describes the types of the different messages to be exchanged. When a client sends one of these messages to a web service, the latter decides what operation to perform and what type of message to send back to the client, on the basis of the type of the message it received. In our Java example, two messages will be defined for each of the operations in the interface – one for the request and one for the reply. For example, Figure 19.11 shows the request and reply messages for the operation *newShape* operation which has a single input argument of type *GraphicalObject* and a single output argument of type *int*.

But for services that support several different operations, it is more effective to specify the messages exchanged as requests for operations with arguments and their corresponding replies, allowing the service to dispatch each request to the appropriate operation. However, in WSDL an operation is a construct for relating request and reply messages, rather than the definition of an operation in a service interface.

Interface ◊ The collection of operations belonging to a web service are grouped together in an XML element named *interface* (sometimes called *portType*). Each operation must specify the message exchange pattern between client and server. The available options include those shown in Figure 19.12. The first one, *In-Out* is the commonly used RR form of client-server communication. In this pattern, the reply message may be replaced with a fault message. *In-Only* is for one-way messages with *Maybe* semantics and *Out-*

Figure 19.12   Message exchange patterns for WSDL operations

Name	Messages sent by		Delivery	Fault message
	Client	*Server*	*Delivery*	*Fault message*
In-Out	*Request*	*Reply*		may replace *Reply*
In-Only	*Request*			no fault message
Robust In-Only	*Request*		guaranteed	may be sent
Out-In	*Reply*	*Request*		may replace *Reply*
Out-Only		*Request*		no fault message
Robust Out-Only		*Request*	guaranteed	may send fault

Only is for oneway messages from server to client; fault messages cannot be sent with either. *Robust-In-Only* and *Robust Out-Only* are the corresponding messages with guaranteed delivery; and fault messages may be exchanged. *Out-In* is a request-response interaction initiated by the server.

Returning to our Java example, each of the operations is defined to have an *In-Out* pattern. The operation *newShape* is shown in Figure 19.13, using the messages defined in Figure 19.11. This definition, together with definitions of the four other operations will be enclosed in an XML *interface* element. An operation may also specify the fault messages that can be sent.

But if for example, an operation has two arguments, say an integer and a string, then there is no need to define a new datatype, since these types are defined for XML schemas. However it will be necessary to define a message that has these two parts. This message can then be used as an input or output in the definition for operation.

Inheritance: Any WSDL interface may extend one or more other WSDL interfaces. This is a simple form of inheritance in which an interface supports the operations of any interfaces it extends in addition to those it defines itself. Recursive definition of interfaces is not allowed; that is, if interface B extends interface A, then interface A cannot extend interface B.

Figure 19.13   WSDL operation *newShape*

operation name = "newShape"
    pattern = In-Out

input message = "tns:ShapeList_newShape"

output message = "tns:ShapeList_newShapeResponse"

tns – target namespace   xsd – XML schema definitions

The names *operation*, pattern, *input* and *output* are defined in the XML schema for WSDL

Figure 19.14   SOAP binding and service definitions

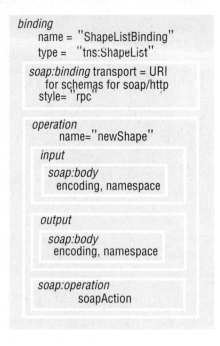

the service URI is:
"http://localhost:8080/ShapeList-jaxrpc/ShapeList"

Concrete part ◊ The remaining (concrete) part of a WSDL document consists of the *binding* (the choice of protocols) and the *service* (the choice of endpoint or server address). The two are related, since the form of address depends on the type of protocol in use. For example, a SOAP endpoint will use a URI whereas a CORBA endpoint would use a CORBA-specific object identifier.

Binding: The *binding* section in a WSDL document says which message formats and form of external data representation are to be used. For example, web services frequently use SOAP, HTTP and MIME. But they should eventually be able to use, for example, GIOP (Section 20.1) to access instances of CORBA objects. Bindings may be associated with particular operations or interfaces or they may be left free for use by a variety of different web services.

Figure 19.14 shows an example of a *binding* enclosing a *soap:binding* that specifies the URL of a particular protocol for transmitting SOAP envelopes: the HTTP binding for SOAP. Optional attributes of this element may also specify the following:

- the message exchange pattern, which may be either *rpc* (request-reply) or *document* exchange. The default value is *document*;

- the XML schema for the message formats. The default is the SOAP *envelope*;

- the XML schema for the external data representation. The default is the SOAP encoding of XML.

Figure 19.14 also shows the details of the bindings for one of the operations (*newShape*), specifying that both the *input* and the *output* message should travel in a soap body, using a particular encoding style and in addition that the operation should be transmitted as a soap *Action*.

Service: Each *service* element in a WSDL document specifies the name of the service and one or more *endpoints* (or ports) where an instance of the service may be contacted. Each of the *endpoint* elements refers to the name of the binding in use and, in the case of a SOAP binding, uses a *soap:address* element to specify the URI of the service location.

Documentation ◊ Both human and machine readable information may be inserted in a *documentation* element at most points within a WSDL document. This information may be removed before WSDL is used for automatic processing, for example, by stub compilers.

WSDL use ◊ Complete WSDL documents can be accessed via their URIs by clients and servers, either directly or indirectly via a directory service such as UDDI. Tools are available for generating WSDL definitions from information provided via a graphical user interface, removing the need for users to be involved in the complex details and structure of WSDL. For example, the Web Services Description Language for Java toolkit allows the creation, representation, and manipulation of WSDL documents describing services [WSDL4J 2003]. WSDL definitions can also be generated from interface definitions written in other languages such as Java JAX-RPC discussed earlier in Section 19.2.1.

19.4 A directory service for use with web services

There are many ways in which clients can obtain service descriptions, for example anyone providing a higher-level web service like the Travel Agent service discussed in Section 19.1 would almost certainly make a web page advertising the service and potential clients would come across the web page when searching for services of that type.

However, any organization that plans to base its applications on web services will find it more convenient to use a directory service to make these services available to clients. This is the purpose of the Universal Directory and Discovery Service (UDDI) [Bellwood *et al.* 2003], which provides both a name service and a directory service (see Section 9.3. That is, WSDL service descriptions may be looked up by name (a white pages service) or by attribute (a yellow pages service). They may also be accessed directly via their URLs, which is convenient for developers who are designing client programs that use the service.

Clients may use the yellow pages approach to look up a particular category of service such as travel agent or bookseller, or they may use the white pages approach to look up a service with reference to the organization that provides it.

Data structures ◊ The data structures supporting UDDI are designed to allow all the above styles of access and can incorporate any amount of human-readable information. The data is organized in terms of the four structures shown in Figure 19.15, each of which can be accessed individually by means of an identifier called a *key* (apart from *tModel*, which can be accessed by a URL):

Figure 19.15   The main UDDI data structures

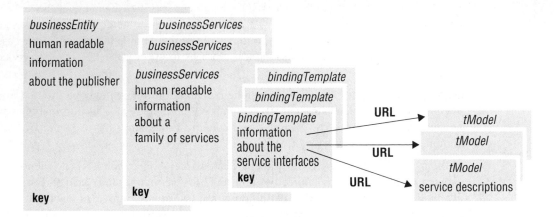

businessEntity: describes the organization that provides these web services, giving its name, address and activities etc.;

businessServices: stores information about a set of instances of a web service, such as its name and a description of its purpose, for example, travel agent or bookseller;

bindingTemplate: holds the address of a web service instance and references to service descriptions;

tModel: holds service descriptions, usually WSDL documents, stored outside the database and accessed by means of URLs.

Lookup ◊ UDDI provides an API for looking up services based on two sets of query operations:

- the *get_xxx* set of operations includes *get_BusinessDetail*, *get_ServiceDetail*, *get_bindingDetail* and *get_tModelDetail*; they retrieve an entity corresponding to a given key;

- the *find_xxx* set of operations includes *find_business*, *find_service*, *find_binding* and *find_tModel*; they retrieve the set of entities that matches a particular set of search criteria, providing a summary of names, descriptions, keys and URLs.

Thus, clients in possession of a particular key may use a *get_xxx* operation to retrieve the corresponding entity directly. Other clients may use browsing to assist with searches – starting with a large set of results and gradually narrowing it down. For example, they may start by using the *find_business* operation in order to get a list containing a summary of information on matching providers. From this summary, the user may use the *find_service* operation to narrow the search by matching the sort of service required. In both cases, they will find the key of a suitable *bindingTemplate* and thereby find the URL for retrieving the WSDL document for a suitable service.

In addition, UDDI provides a notify/subscribe interface by which clients register interest in a particular set of entities in a UDDI registry and get change notifications, either synchronously or asynchronously.

Publication ◊ UDDI provides an interface for publishing and updating information about web services. The first time that a data structure (see Figure 19.15) is published at a UDDI server, it is given a kcy in the form of a URI, for example, *uddi:cdk4.net:213* and that server becomes its owner.

Registries ◊ The UDDI service is based on replicated data stored in registries. A UDDI registry consists of one or more UDDI servers, each of which has a copy of the same set of data. The data is replicated between the members of a registry. Each of them may respond to queries and publish information. Changes to a data structure must be submitted to its owner – that is, the server at which it was first published. It is possible for an owner to pass on the ownership to another UDDI server in the same registry.

Replication scheme: The members of a registry propagate copies of data structures to one another as follows: a server that has made changes notifies the other servers in the registry, which then request the changes. A form of vector timestamp is used to determine which of the changes should be propagated and applied. The scheme is simple in comparison with other replication schemes that use vector timestamps such as Gossip (Section 15.4.1) or Coda (Section 15.4.3) because:

1. all changes to a particular data structure are made at the same server;

2. updates from a particular server are received in sequential order by the other members, but no particular ordering is imposed between update operations made by different servers.

Interaction between servers: As described above, servers interact with one another to carry out the replication scheme. They can also interact in order to transfer ownership of data structures. However, the response to a look up operation is performed by a single server without any interaction with other servers in the registry, unlike the X.500 directory service (Section 9.5) in which data is partitioned between servers that cooperate with one another in finding the relevant server for a particular request.

19.5 XML security

XML security consists of a set of related W3C designs for signing, key management and encryption. It is intended for use in cooperative work over the Internet involving documents whose contents may need to be authenticated or encrypted. Typically the documents are created, exchanged, stored and then exchanged again, possibly after being modified by a series of different users.

WS-Security [Kaler 2002] is another approach to security that is concerned with applying message integrity, message confidentiality, and single message authentication to SOAP.

As an example of a context in which XML security would be useful, consider a document containing a patient's medical records. Different parts of this document are used at the local doctor's surgery and at the various special clinics and hospitals visited by the patient. It will be updated by doctors, nurses and consultants making notes on conditions and treatment, by administrators making appointments and by pharmacists providing medicine. Different parts of the document will be viewable by the different roles mentioned above and possibly the patient as well. It is essential that certain parts of the document, for example, recommendations as to treatment, can be attributed to the person that made them and can be guaranteed not to have been altered.

These needs cannot be met by TLS (previously known as SSL, Section 7.6.3) which is used to create a secure channel for the communication of information. It allows the processes at the two ends of the channel to negotiate as to the need for authentication or encryption and the keys and algorithms to be used, both when a channel is set up and during its lifetime. For example, data about a financial transaction might be signed and sent in the clear until sensitive information such as credit card details are to be given, at which point encryption will be applied.

To allow for the new type of usage outlined above, the security must be specified within the document itself and applied to the document rather than as a property of the channel that will convey it from one user to another.

This is possible in XML or other structured document formats, in which metadata can be used. XML tags can be used to define the properties of the data in the document. In particular, XML security depends on new tags that can be used to indicate the beginning and end of sections of encrypted or signed data and of signatures. Once the necessary security has been applied within a document, it may be sent to a variety of different users, even by means of multicast.

Basic requirements ◊ XML security should provide at least the same level of protection as TLS. That is:

To be able to encrypt either an entire document or just some selected parts of it: For example, consider the information about a financial transaction, which includes a person's name, the type of transaction, and details about the credit or debit card being used. In one case, just the card details could be hidden, making it possible to identify the transaction before decrypting the record. In another case, the type of transaction could also be hidden, so that outsiders cannot tell whether it is, for example, an order or a payment.

To be able to sign either an entire document or just some selected parts of it: When a document is intended to be used for cooperative work by a group of people, there can be some critical parts of the document that should be signed in order to guarantee that they were made by a particular person or that they have not been changed. But it is also useful to be able to have other parts that can be altered during the use of the document – these should not be signed.

Additional basic requirements ◊ Further requirements arise from the need to store documents, possibly to modify them and then to send them on to a variety of different recipients:

To add to a document that is already signed and to sign the result: For example, Alice may sign a document and pass it on to Bob who 'witnesses her signature' by adding a remark to that effect and then signing the entire document.

To add to a document that already contains encrypted sections and to encrypt part of the new version, possibly including some of the already encrypted sections.

To authorize various different users to view different parts of a document: In the case of a medical record, a researcher can view some particular section of the medical data, an administrator can view personal details and a doctor can view both.

The flexibility and structuring capabilities of the XML notation makes it possible do all of the above, without any additions to the scheme derived from the basic requirements.

Requirements concerning algorithms ◊ XML secure documents are signed and/or encrypted well in advance of any consideration as to who will be accessing them. If the originator is no longer involved, it is not possible to negotiate the protocols and whether to use authentication or encryption. Therefore:

The standard should specify a suite of algorithms to be provided in any implementation of XML security: At least one encryption and one signature algorithm should be mandatory, to enable the widest possible interoperability. Other optional algorithms should be provided for use within smaller groups.

The algorithms used for encryption and authentication of a particular document must be selected from that suite and the names of the algorithms in use must be referenced within the XML document itself: If the places where the document will be used cannot be predicted, then one of the required protocols should be used.

XML security defines the names of elements that can be used to specify the URI of the algorithm in use for signing or encryption. So as to be able to select a variety of algorithms within the same XML document, an element that specifies an algorithm is generally nested inside an element containing signed information or encrypted data.

Requirements for finding keys ◊ When a document is created and each time that it is updated, appropriate keys must be chosen, without any negotiation with those parties that may access the document in the future. This leads to the following requirements:

To help the users of secure documents with finding the necessary keys: For example, a document that includes signed data should contain information as to the public key to be used to validate the signature, such as a name that can be used to obtain the key, or a certificate. A *KeyInfo* element can be used for this purpose.

To make it possible for cooperating users to help one another with keys: Provided that the *KeyInfo* element is not cryptographically bound to the signature itself then information may be added without breaking the digital signature. For example, Alice signs a document and sends it to Bob with a *KeyInfo* element that specifies only the name of the key. When Bob receives the document he retrieves information needed to validate the signature and adds this to the *KeyInfo* element when he passes the document to Carol.

The KeyInfo element ◊ XML security specifies a *KeyInfo* element for indicating the key to be used to validate a signature or to decrypt some data. It may contain, for example, certificates, the names of keys or key agreement algorithms. Its use is optional: the signer may not want to reveal any key information to all of the parties that access the document and in some cases, the application using XML security may already have access to the keys in use.

Figure 19.16   Algorithms required for XML signature

Type of algorithm	Name of algorithm	Required	reference
Message digest	SHA-1	Required	Section 7.4.3
Encoding	base64	Required	[Freed and Borenstein 1996]
Signature	DSA with SHA-1	Required	[NIST 1994]
(asymmetric)	RSA with SHA-1	Recommended	Section 7.3.2
MAC signature	HMAC-SHA-1	Required	Section 7.4.2 and
(symmetric)			Krawczyk *et al.* [1997]
Canonicalization	Canonical XML	Required	Page 810

Canonical XML ◊   Some applications may make changes that have no effect on the actual information content of an XML document. This arises because there is a variety of different ways of representing what is logically the same XML document. For example, attributes may be in different orders and differing character encodings may be used, yet the information content is equivalent. Canonical XML [www.w3.org X] was designed for use with digital signatures, which are used to guarantee that the information content of a document has not been changed. XML elements are canonicalized before being signed and the name of the canonicalization algorithm is stored, together with the signature. This enables the same algorithm to be used when the signature is validated.

The canonical form is a standard serialization of XML as a stream of bytes. It adds default attributes and removes superfluous schemas, putting the attributes and schema declarations in lexicographic order in each element. It uses a standard form for line breaks and the UTF-8 encoding for characters. Any two equivalent XML documents have the same canonical form.

When a subset of an XML document, say an element is canonicalized, the canonical form includes the ancestor context, that is, the namespaces declared and the values of attributes. Thus when canonical XML is used in conjunction with digital signatures, the signature of an element will not pass its validation if that element is placed in a different context.

A variation of this algorithm, called Exclusive Canonical XML, omits the context from the serialization. This could be used if the application intends a particular signed element to be used in different contexts.

Use of digital signatures in XML ◊   The specification for digital signatures in XML [www.w3.org XII] is a W3C recommendation that defines new XML element types to hold signatures, the names of algorithms, keys and references to signed information. The names provided in this specification are defined in the XML signature schema which includes the elements *Signature*, *SignatureValue*, *SignedInfo* and *KeyInfo*. Figure 19.16 shows the algorithms that must be available in an implementation of XML signature.

Key management service ◊   The specification of the XML key management service [www.w3.org XIII] contains protocols for distributing and registering public keys for use in XML signatures. Although it does not require any particular public key infrastructure, the service is designed to be compatible with existing ones, for example,

Figure 19.17 Algorithms required for encryption (the algorithms in Figure 19.16 are also required)

Type of algorithm	Name of algorithm	Required	reference
Block cipher	TRIPLEDES, AES-128, AES-256	required	Section 7.3.1
	AES-192	optional	
Encoding	base64	required	[Freed and Borenstein 1996]
Key transport	RSA-v1.5,	required	Section 7.3.2
	RSA-OAEP		[Kaliski and Staddon 1998]
Symmetric key wrap (signature by shared key)	TRIPLEDES KeyWrap, AES-128 KeyWrap, AES-256KeyWrap	required	[Housley 2002]
	AES-192 KeyWrap	optional	
Key agreement	Diffie-Hellman	optional	[Rescorla, 1999]

X.509 certificates (Section 7.4.4), SPKI (simple public key infrastructure, Section 7.4.4) or PGP key identifiers (pretty good privacy, Section 7.5.2).

Clients can use this service to find the public key of a person. For example, if Alice wants to send an encrypted email to Bob, she can use this service to obtain his public key. In another example, Bob receives a signed document from Alice containing her X.509 certificate and then asks the key information service to extract the public key.

XML encryption ◊ The standard for encryption in XML is defined in [www.w3.org XIV], a W3C recommendation that specifies both the way to represent encrypted data in XML and the process for encrypting and decrypting it. It introduces an *EncryptedData* element for enclosing portions of encrypted data.

Figure 19.17 specifies the encryption algorithms that should be included in an implementation of XML encryption. Block cipher algorithms are used for encrypting the data; and base64 encoding is used in XML for representing digital signatures and encrypted data. Key transport algorithms are public key encryption algorithms designed for use in encrypting and decrypting the keys themselves.

Symmetric key wrap algorithms are shared secret key encryption algorithms designed for encrypting and decrypting symmetric keys by means of another key. This could be used if a key were to be included in a *KeyInfo* element.

A Key agreement algorithm allows a shared secret key to be derived from a computation on a pair of public keys. This algorithm is made available for use by applications that need to agree a shared key without any exchange. It is not applied by the XML security system itself.

19.6 Coordination of web services

The SOAP infrastructure supports single request-response interactions between clients and web services. However, many useful applications involve several requests that need to be done in a particular order. For example, when booking a flight, the price and availability information is collected before the reservations are made. When a user interacts with web pages by means of a browser, for example, to book a flight or to make a bid in an auction, the interface provided by the browser, which is based on the information provided by the server, controls the sequence in which the operations are performed.

However, if it is a web service that is making reservations, like the travel agent service shown in Figure 19.2, then that web service needs to work from a description of the appropriate way to proceed when interacting with other services that perform, for example, car hire and hotel booking as well as flight booking. Figure 19.18 shows an example of such a description.

These examples illustrate the need for web services as clients to be provided with a description of a particular protocol to follow when interacting with other web services. But there is also the issue of maintaining consistency in the server data when it is receiving and responding to requests from multiple clients. Chapters 13 and 14 discuss transactions, illustrating the issues by means of a series of banking transactions. As a

Figure 19.18   Travel agent scenario

1. The client asks the travel agent service for information about a set of services; for example, flights, car hire and hotel bookings.

2. The travel agent service collects prices and availability information and sends it to the client, which chooses one of the following on behalf of the user:

    (a) refine the query, possibly involving more providers to get more information, then repeat step 2;

    (b) make reservations;

    (c) quit.

3. The client requests a reservation and the travel agent service checks availability.

4. *Either* all are available;

    or for services that are not available;

    either alternatives are offered to the client who goes back to step 3;

    or the client goes back to step 1.

5. Take deposit.

6. Give the client a reservation number as a confirmation.

7. During the period until the final payment, the client may modify or cancel reservations.

simple example, in a transfer of money between two bank accounts, consistency requires that both the deposit in one account and the withdrawal from the other must be performed. Chapter 14 presents the two-phase commit protocol that is used by cooperating servers to ensure consistency of transactions.

In some cases, atomic transactions suit the requirements of applications using web services. However, activities such as those of the travel agent take a long time to complete and it would be impractical to use a two-phase commit protocol to carry them out because it involves keeping resources locked for long periods of time. An alternative is to use a more relaxed protocol in which each participant makes changes to persistent state as they occur. In the case of failure, an application-level protocol is used to undo these actions.

In conventional middleware, the infrastructure provides a simple request-reply protocol, leaving other services such as transactions, persistency and security to be implemented as separate higher-level services that can be used when they are needed. The same is true for web services, where W3C and others have been putting in effort towards the definition of higher-level services.

Work has been done on a general model for coordination of web services, which is similar to the distributed transaction model described in Section 14.2, in that it has coordinator and participant roles that are able to act out particular protocols, for example, to carry out a distributed transaction. This work, which is called WS-Coordination, is described by Langworthy [2004]. The same group has also shown how transactions may be carried out within this model. For a comprehensive study of web services coordination protocols, see Alonso *et al.* [2004].

In the remainder of this section, we outline the ideas behind web service choreography. Consider the fact that it would be possible to describe all of the possible valid alternative paths through the set of interactions between pairs of web services working together in a joint task such as the travel agent scenario. If such a description were available, it could be used as an aid to the coordination of joint tasks. It could also be used as a specification to be followed by new instances of a service, such as a new flight booking service wishing to join a collaboration.

W3C use the term *choreography* to refer to a language based on WSDL for defining coordination. For example, the language might specify constraints on the order and the conditions in which messages are exchanged by participants. A choreography is intended to provide a global description of a set of interactions, showing the behaviour of each member of a set of participants, with a view to enhancing interoperability.

Requirements for choreography ◊ Choreography is intended to support interactions between web services which are generally managed by different companies and organizations. A collaboration involving multiple web services and clients should be described in terms of the sets of observable interactions between pairs of them. Such a description might be seen as a contract between the participants: it could be put to the following uses:

- to generate code outlines for a new service that wants to participate;

- as a basis for generating test messages for a new service;

- to promote a common understanding of the collaboration;

- to analyse the collaboration, for example to identify possible deadlock situations.

The use of a common choreography description by a set of collaborating web services should result in more robust services with better interoperability. In addition, it should be easier to develop and to introduce new services, making the overall service more useful.

The W3C working draft document at [www.w3.org XV] suggests that a choreography language should include the following features:

- hierarchical and recursive composition of choreographies;

- the ability to add new instances of an existing service and new services;

- concurrent paths, alternative paths and the ability to repeat a section of a choreography;

- variable timeouts – for example, different periods for holding reservations;

- exceptions, for example, to deal with messages arriving out of sequence and user actions such as cancellations;

- asynchronous interactions (callbacks);

- reference passing, for example, to allow a car hire company to consult a bank for a credit check on behalf of a user;

- marking of the boundaries of the separate transactions that take place, for example, to allow for recovery;

- the ability to include human-readable documentation.

A model based on these requirements is described in another W3C working draft document [www.w3.org XVI].

Languages for choreography ◊ The intention is to produce a declarative, XML-based language for defining choreographies that can make use of WSDL definitions. The early stages of the work on Choreography Definition Language are reported in [www.w3.org XVII]. Prior to this, a group of companies submitted to W3C a specification for the web services choreography interface [www.w3.org XVIII].

19.7 Case study: the Grid

The name 'Grid' is used to refer to middleware that is designed to enable the sharing of resources such as files, computers, software, data and sensors on a very large scale. The resources are shared typically by groups of users in different organizations who are collaborating on the solution of problems requiring large numbers of computers to solve them, either by the sharing of data or by the sharing of computing power. These resources are necessarily supported by heterogeneous computer hardware, operating systems, programming languages and applications. Management is needed to coordinate the use of resources to ensure that clients get what they need and that services can afford to supply it. In some cases, sophisticated security techniques are required to ensure that the correct use is made of resources in this type of environment.

Section 19.7.1 introduces the World-Wide Telescope, a data-intensive application that is an example of the type of problem solving for which the Grid is designed. It illustrates a typical pattern of sharing and geographic distribution of users from which can be derived the characteristics of a family of scientific applications, which suggest a set of requirements for a Grid (see Section 19.7.2). We use these requirements, to motivate the architecture, which specifies a Grid that runs over web services (see Section 19.7.3). The last section introduces the Globus toolkit, which is an implementation of the grid architecture.

19.7.1 The World-Wide Telescope – a grid application

This project is concerned with deploying the data resources shared by the astronomy community. It is described in the work of Szalay and Gray [2004], Szalay and Gray [2001] and Gray and Szalay [2002]. Astronomy data consists of archives of observations, each of which covers a particular period of time, a part of the electromagnetic spectrum (optical, x-ray, radio) and a particular area of the sky. These observations are made by different instruments deployed at various places throughout the world.

A study of how astronomers share their data is useful for deriving the characteristics of a typical grid application, because astronomers freely share their results with one another and issues of security can be omitted, making this discussion simpler.

Astronomers make studies that need to combine data on the same celestial objects but involve several different periods of time and multiple parts of the spectrum. The ability to use independent observations of data is important to research. Visualization allows astronomers to see the data as 2D or 3D scatter plots.

The teams gathering the data store it in immense archives (currently terabytes) which are managed locally by each team that gathers data. The instruments used in gathering data are subject to Moore's law. Hence the amount of data gathered grows exponentially. As it is gathered, the data is analysed by a pipeline process and stored as derived data for use by astronomers throughout the world. But before data can be used by other researchers, scientists working in a particular field need to agree on a common way of labelling their data.

Szalay and Gray [2004] point out that in the past, scientific research data was included by authors in articles and published in journals which lived in libraries. But nowadays, the quantity of data is too great to be included in a publication. This applies not only to astronomy, but also in the fields of particle physics, genome and biology research. The role of author now belongs to the collaborations, which take 5–10 years to build their experiment before producing the data that is published to the world in web-based archives. Thus, the scientists working on the projects become data publishers and librarians as well as authors.

This additional role requires any project that manages a data archive to make it accessible to other researchers. This implies a considerable overhead in addition to the original task of data analysis. To make such sharing possible, the raw data requires metadata to describe, for example, the time it was collected, the part of the sky and the instrument used. In addition, the derived data needs to be accompanied by metadata describing the parameters of the pipelines through which it was processed.

The calculation of derived data requires heavy computational support. It often has to be recalculated as techniques improve. All of this is a considerable expense for the project that owns the data.

The aim of the World-Wide Telescope is to unify the world's astronomy archives into a giant database containing astronomy literature, images, raw data, derived datasets and simulation data.

19.7.2 The characteristics of a family of data-intensive scientific applications

In this section we refer to the study of the World-Wide Telescope in presenting the defining characteristics of a family of similar scientific applications, and then go on to outline the requirements for supporting them. The characteristics are as follows:

- data is collected by means of scientific instruments;

- the data is stored in archives on a set of separate sites whose locations can be in different sites anywhere in the world;

- the data is managed by teams of scientists belonging to separate organizations;

- an immense and increasing quantity (terabytes or petabytes) of raw data is generated from the instruments;

- computer programs will be used to analyse and make summaries of the raw data, for example, to classify, calibrate and catalogue the raw data representing celestial objects.

The Internet makes all of these data archives potentially available to scientists throughout the world. They will be able to get data from different instruments taken at different times and at different sites. However, a particular scientist using this data for their own research will be interested in just a subset of the objects in the archives.

The immense quantity of data in an archive makes it infeasible to transfer it to the location of the user before processing it to extract the objects of interest, due to considerations of the transmission time and the local disk space required. Therefore, it is not appropriate to use ftp or web access in this context. The processing of the raw data should take place at the location where it is collected and stored in a database. Then when a scientist makes a query about particular objects, the information in each database should be analysed and if necessary, visualizations produced before returning the results to the remote query.

The fact that data is processed at many different sites provides an inbuilt parallelism that effectively divides the immense task being undertaken.

From the above characteristics, the following requirements are derived:

R1: Remote access to resources – that is, to the required information in the archives.

R2: Processing of data at the site where it is stored and managed, either when it is gathered or in response to a request. A typical query might result in a visualisation based on data collected for one region of sky recorded by different instruments at different times. It will involve selecting a small quantity of data from each massive data archive.

R3: The resource manager of a data archive should be able to create service instances dynamically to deal with the particular section of data required, just as in the distributed object model, where servants are created whenever they are needed to handle different resources managed by a service.

R4: Metadata to describe:

- characteristics of the data in an archive, for example, for astronomy: the area of the sky, the date and time collected and the instruments used;

- the characteristics of a service managing that data, for example, its cost, its geographic location, its publisher or its load or space available.

R5: Directory services based on the above metadata.

R6: Software to manage queries, data transfers and advance reservation of resources, taking into account that the resources are generally managed by the projects that generate the data and that access to them may need to be rationed.

Web services can deal with the first two requirements by providing a convenient way for allowing scientists to access operations on data in remote archives. This will require that each particular application provides a service description that includes a set of methods for accessing its data. The grid middleware deals with the remaining requirements.

Although the World-Wide Telescope is a typical data-intensive application, Grids are also used for computationally-intensive applications such as image analysis and other examples discussed in Section 19.7.4. Where computationally-intensive applications are deployed on a Grid, resource management will be concerned with allocating computing resources and balancing loads.

Finally, security will be needed for many grid applications. For example, the Grid is in use for medical research and for business applications. Even when the privacy of data is not an issue, it will be important to establish the identity of the people who created the data.

19.7.3 Open grid services architecture

The open grid services architecture (OGSA) is a standard for grid-based applications [Foster *et al.* 2002 and 2001]. It provides a framework within which the above requirements can be met. It is based on web services. Resources are managed by application-specific grid services. The Globus toolkit, which implements the architecture is discussed in Section 19.7.5.

Figure 19.19 shows the main components of the grid architecture. It illustrates two important aspects of *application-level grid services*:

1. They are web services that implement standard grid-service interfaces in addition to their application-specific interfaces. Specifically, they implement the following grid-service interfaces and additional functionality:

- an interface to a set of data (called *service data*) that contains metadata about the service. Metadata includes, for example, the time to be terminated, but can

Figure 19.19   Open grid services architecture

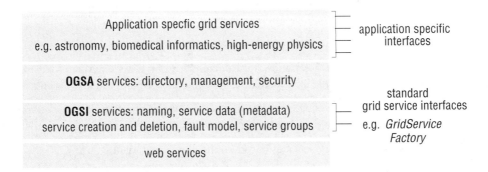

include any of the items mentioned in requirement R4 above, as well as application values such as sets of recent results or average values;

– the context in which a service runs must provide a *factory* with the ability to create new service instances and to stop them when their time runs out, as suggested by requirement R3. The factory relies on the naming facilities of the OGSI layer to manage the names of the service instances it creates.

2. They make use of the standard grid services which are provided as two separate layers, called OGSI and OGSA, above web services. The OGSA services layer includes:

– directory service – allowing client software to select service instances suitable for its needs, based on the metadata collected from service instances that have registered with the directory service. This deals with requirement R5;

– management service – to monitor services from information in their service data, to deal with failures; and to control the lifetimes of service instances by setting values in the service data. This deals with requirement R6;

– security services – providing single logins and delegation as well as authentication and data encryption.

The open grid services infrastructure (OGSI) layer includes the following:

– the implementation of a scheme for the naming of service instances;

– the definition of standard *service data* elements which must be implemented by every application-level grid service instance, together with operations to set and get their values. These elements include, for example, names of the interfaces supported, a reference to the factory that created the instance or the termination time;

– definitions of the interface to the factory for creating new service instances and operations to set their termination times or to destroy them;

– a fault model for use by all grid services;

- notification services – to enable services to become publishers of information about service data; and other services to become subscribers;

- service groups – operations for adding and removing members, for use by cooperating groups providing a service.

The above definitions and services are provided in the *GridService*, *Factory* and other interfaces of the OGSI layer.

Open grid services infrastructure ◊ We now introduce the two-level naming scheme that relates the high-level names of service instances to low-level names and then present further details of the other services in the OGSI layer.

Two-level naming scheme: Grid services can be created dynamically. Therefore to fulfil the need to distinguish one instance from another, the infrastructure includes a naming scheme that provides each instance with a long-lived and globally unique identifier called a grid service handle (GSH). When an instance of a service is restarted with the same state as before, the same GSH may be used.

A GSH is represented by a URI, which can be mapped onto a short-lived name called a grid service reference (GSR), which is used to refer to the destination of an invocation. The infrastructure includes a handle-resolution service to perform this mapping. The GSR is a name whose structure depends on the request-reply mechanism in use, for example, in the case of SOAP, the GSR will refer to a WSDL document containing *<service>* and *<binding>* elements. A GSR becomes invalid when the service instance it refers to fails.

If a URN is used for the GSH, it may be resolved to different service instances at different times, allowing the latter to be migrated or even replicated at different resources.

Service Data (metadata): The idea is that clients can request an instance of a service to return information about its current state, for example, its capacity, free space, load or current errors or even its recent results. This requires that each instance of an application-level grid service must implement storage for service data and a set of operations to access it.

A standard set of operations is provided in the *GridService* interface – these include operations to access the names of the interfaces supported by the service, the names of the service data elements, the identity of the factory that created it, its GSH and GSR and its termination time. Every grid service must support the *GridService* interface, but may also include OGSI interfaces for notification or for service groups.

Service creation and deletion: This part of the infrastructure defines a standard *Factory* interface that specifies operations for creating transient service instances on demand with new names in the form of a GSH and GSR pair. The *Factory* interface must be implemented by any container for running application-level grid services.

A typical request to create a new service instance is made by an application which specifies as arguments its service description and the end of its lifetime. In response, the factory creates a new service instance and registers it with a handle resolution service, finally returning the GSH and the current GSR to the client.

A service instance will end, either when its task is completed or on the request of the client that created it. Each service instance is given a lifetime to prevent it from surviving for ever, in the event that messages are lost. But the creator can request extensions of the lifetime by sending 'keep alive' messages. In the event that the client fails, there will be no more keep alive messages and the service instance will eventually terminate. To provide service autonomy, an instance can decide to change its own lifetime. All the resources used by a service instance are recovered when its lifetime expires. Service instances may be shared by clients.

Fault model: The infrastructure defines a common approach to the reporting of faults, which is used by all the OGSI-level services and is recommended for use by the application-level grid services. It is defined as an XML schema which requires at least two elements to specify the originating service and a timestamp. It offers optional elements for describing a fault in plain language, its cause and a fault code. There is scope for extending the fault report to include information specific to an OGSI or application service.

WSDL interface extensions: Since standard WSDL does not include mechanisms for defining service data, OGSI has provided an extension to WSDL for associating definitions of the names and types of service data elements with a particular interface in a service description. The data elements might, for example, hold its capacity, free space, load, or current error indications.

OGSA services ◊ Higher level services are built over the OGSI services. According to Foster *et al.* [2004] different developers will provide a variety of different OGSA services to meet the specific requirements of application-level services. They list those OGSA components that are sufficiently widely-applicable to be included in any grid system, for example, directory services, management and monitoring; and security. The availability of standard interfaces for these services is a basis for ensuring that different implementations can work with one another. We defer a discussion of directory and security services until Section 19.7.5, in which we present them in the context of the Globus toolkit.

Management services: Management in the Grid is concerned with any kind of resource that can be shared or exploited. This amounts to the management of services, which is concerned with arranging for them to be used and monitoring their state. Issues that it addresses include task submission, agreement to provide some particular quality of service and advanced reservation of resources. These can be provided with the help of *service-level agreement*s (SLAs) [Hauch and Reiser 2000] which give the client of a resource a guarantee as to the type of service being provided, and allow the owner of the resource to maintain control as to how it is used and how much information is exposed to the client.

Three different sorts of SLA are proposed: task level, which is used to agree on the performance of an activity; resource level, which is used to agree on the right to consume a resource, for example by advance reservation; and binding, which is used to agree on the use of a resource in a task.

19.7.4 Some examples of grid applications

Figure 19.20 shows some examples of applications that are using grid technology. The first three of these have characteristics similar to the World-Wide Telescope in that data is collected by scientific instruments and stored at the site where it is collected. In

Figure 19.20 A selection of the grid projects presented in Foster and Kesselman [2004]

Description of the project	Reference
1. Aircraft engine maintenance using fault histories and sensors for predictive diagnostics	www.cs.york.ac.uk/dame
2. Telepresence for predicting the effects of earthquakes on buildings, using simulations and test sites	www.neesgrid.org
3. Bio-medical informatics network providing researchers with access to experiments and visualizations of results	nbcr.sdsc.edu
4. Analysis of data from the CMS high energy particle detector at CERN by physicists world-wide over 15 years	www.uscms.org
5. Testing the effects of candidate drug molecules for their effect on the activity of a protein, by performing parallel computations using idle desktop computers	[Taufer *et al.* 2003] [Chien 2004]
6. Use of the Sun Grid Engine to enhance aerial photographs by using spare capacity on a cluster of web servers	www.globexplorer.com
7. The butterfly Grid supports multiplayer games for very large numbers of players on the internet over the Globus toolkit	www.butterfly.net
8. The Access Grid supports the needs of small group collaboration, for example by providing shared workspaces	www.accessgrid.org

example 1, vibration data is collected by means of a sensor on an aircraft engine. In example 2, data is collected from test structures that are being subjected to violent shaking to simulate an earthquake. In example 3, instruments such as MRI or CT are used to collect brain images. In all cases, the quantity of raw data grows over time, as more measurements are made. In addition, the quantity of processed data grows as analyses are carried out.

In these three examples, the data is managed by teams of scientists or engineers belonging to separate organizations. Analyses of the raw data and simulations are made locally and are available to co-workers throughout the world.

These examples confirm that the World-Wide Telescope is a typical data-intensive application. However, grid applications are also used for computationally-intensive applications such as:

- Example 4 refers to the new detector at CERN that will become operational in 2007. Prior to this, teams of physicists are carrying out simulations of the expected results from the detector. This is a computationally intensive task which is being carried out by multiple cooperating computers.

- Example 5 is about virtual screening – the testing of a database of millions of drug molecules to see whether they block the activity of each of a large number of potential proteins. Spare computing power is used on a set of desktop computers running grid software. The task is performed in parallel by each of the computers testing the effect of a particular drug molecule on a particular protein. It uses spare capacity on idle desktop computers.

- Example 6 is about image analysis. The company GlobeExplorer provides good quality satellite images and aerial photographs, derived from an archive of thousands of raw images, each of which requires enhancement. It uses spare capacity on a cluster of web servers.

A common feature of examples 5 and 6 is the use of spare computing capacity and the partitioning of the task to be performed. They may be compared to the SETI@home project (see Section 10.1), whose task is to search for extra-terrestrial intelligence in radio telescope data. SETI@home uses peer-to-peer software to solve a computationally intensive problem by using spare computing power on end-user computers. The large database is partitioned so that the task may be carried out in parallel.

   Examples 7 and 8 are included because they illustrate two different uses of the Grid that are outside of the realms of science and engineering. Each of them requires the management of distributed state; in the first case, the state of the game and the second a shared workspace.

19.7.5 The Globus toolkit

The Globus Project started in 1994 with a view to providing software that integrates and standardizes the functions required by a family of scientific applications. These functions include directory services, security and resource management. The first Globus toolkit appeared in 1997. The OGSA evolved from the second version of the toolkit (called GT2), which is described in Foster and Kesselman [2004].

   The third version appeared in 2002. It is called GT3 and is based on OGSA and is therefore built on web services. It was developed by the Globus Alliance (www.globus.org) and others and is available as open-source software.

   The core of GT3 is described by Sandholm and Gawor [2003]. It includes all of the interfaces in the OGSI layer as Java classes which implement interfaces such as *GridService* and *Factory* and are compatible with JAX-RPC (see Section 19.2.3). The simplest way to add this functionality to existing web services is to make their classes subclasses of the OGSI classes. In fact, application-level grid services may be configured to include whatever grid service functionality is required. For example, notification services or service group operations may be added as desired.

   Grid service instances and factories are deployed in a runtime environment called a grid-service *container*. A grid-service container is similar in some respects to a CORBA POA (Section 20.2.2) in that it can do dispatching, but it also deals with:

- the dynamic creation and management of service instances with global names;

- simple access to the state of service instances by means of the *FindServiceData* operation of the *GridService* interface, or alternatively by means of notification;

- security, including delegation of credentials, signing of messages, encryption and authorization.

A service instance may be created inside the same container as its factory or it may be deployed elsewhere. A container may, for example, be based on a servlet container (see page 796). When a container is started up, the service instances do not become active until the first time they are used. Containers may deactivate idle service instances such as those in use for notification or service groups.

Security service ◊ The security service in GT3 provides for the protection of SOAP messages. It is based on WS-Security [Kaler 2002], XML-Signature, and XML-Encryption (see Section 19.5). Authentication uses X.509 certificates as credentials, which are supplied in the usual manner by a trusted certification authority. It uses an extension to X.509 to provide for proxy certificates that may be used by services acting on behalf of users.

Directory service ◊ GT3 does not use the UDDI because its data structures and hence its search criteria contain the wrong sort of information, for example, technical details about protocols (see Figure 19.15), whereas clients of grid services need to find out about the particular characteristics of service instances. For example, management clients may be interested in the load on the service and astronomers may be interested in information about when, where and how the data was collected.

Instead, GT3 provides an *index service* which is intended to be used for finding out which instance of a service matches a set of particular requirements. The index service collects information based on the service data of the group of service instances that registers with it. It could use the *FindServiceData* operation to collect information, but for variable service data, it would be more appropriate to use the notification interface so as to be informed whenever data values change.

The index service can respond to queries by carrying out algorithms to decide on the service instance most suitable for a particular client. For example, it might base this on the type of processor used by a service instance, its speed, the clients it supports or the cost of using it. Index services support notification interfaces in addition to responding to queries.

Index services can be combined together in various ways in order to provide an information service for use within a large community.

An implementation of the index service needs to include fault-tolerance measures to deal with situations such as the case when it is left holding stale data in its indexes when a service instance stops running without notifying it.

Management and reliable file transfer service ◊ The management service in GT3 is concerned with monitoring and managing the container and the service instances inside it, for example, monitoring the current state or load and activating or deactivating instances.

GT3 also provides a reliable file transfer service to allow for bulk transfer of data between grid services.

Future relation with web services ◊ There has been some discussion of the possibility of integrating OGSI features into web services – under the heading of the WS-Resource framework [Globus 2004]. The Globus Alliance suggests that the ability to create service instances and to make use of service state could be used more widely than in the context of grid applications. However, its distributed object approach may not be successful for many of the sort of loosely-coupled applications commonly running as web services.

19.8 Summary

In this chapter we have shown that web services have arisen from the need to provide an infrastructure to support interworking between different organizations. This infrastructure generally uses the widely-used HTTP protocol to transport messages between clients and servers over the Internet and is based on the use of URIs to refer to resources. XML, a textual format, is used for data representation and marshalling.

Two separate influences led to the emergence of web services. One of these is the addition of service interfaces to web servers with a view to allowing the resources on a site to be accessed by client programs other than browsers and using a richer form of interaction. The other is the desire to provide something like RPC over the Internet, based on the existing protocols. The resulting web services provide interfaces with sets of operations that can be called remotely. Like any other form of service, a web service can be the client of another web service, thus allowing a web service to integrate or combine a set of other web services.

SOAP is the communication protocol that is generally used by web services and their clients. It can be used to transmit request messages and their replies between client and server, either by the asynchronous exchange of documents or by a form of request-reply protocol based on a pair of asynchronous message exchanges. In both cases, the request or reply message is enclosed in an XML-formatted document called an envelope. The SOAP envelope is generally transmitted over the synchronous HTTP protocol, although other transports can be used.

XML and SOAP processors are available for all of the widely used programming languages and operating systems. This enables web services and their clients to be deployed almost anywhere. This form of interworking is enabled by the facts that web services are neither tied to any particular programming language nor do they support the distributed object model.

In conventional middleware services, interface definitions provide clients with the details of services. However, in the case of web services, service descriptions are used. A service description specifies the communication protocol to be used (for example, SOAP) and the URI of the service, as well as describing its interface. The interface may be described either as a set of operations or as a set of messages to be exchanged between client and server.

XML security was designed to provide the necessary protection for the contents of a document exchanged by members of a group of people, who have different tasks to perform on that document. Different parts of the document will be available to different people, some with the ability to add or alter the content and others to read it. To enable a complete flexibility in its future use, the security properties are defined within the document itself. This is achieved by means of XML, which is a self-describing format. XML elements are used to specify document parts that are encrypted or signed as well as details of the algorithms used and information to help with finding keys.

The grid middleware runs over web services, in order to support collaborations between scientists or engineers in organizations in different parts of the world. Their work is very often based on the use of raw data collected by instruments at different sites and then processed locally. The provision of web service interfaces enables this data to be accessed remotely. However, the requirement to start processing data on behalf of remote clients leads to the need to create instances of services on demand and to manage their lifetimes. The grid architecture adds factories to web services, together with a two-level naming scheme for referencing service instances. In addition it provides support for metadata that describes the characteristics of service instances. It also specifies directory, management and security services. The Globus toolkit is an implementation of the architecture that has been used in a variety of data-intensive and computationally-intensive applications.

EXERCISES

19.1   Compare the request reply protocol as described in Section 4.4 with the implementation of client-server communication in SOAP. State two reasons why the use of asynchronous messages by SOAP is more appropriate for use over the Internet. To what extent does the use of HTTP by SOAP reduce the difference between the two approaches?   *page 790*

19.2   Compare the structure of URLs as used for web services with that of remote object references as specified in Section 4.3.4. State in each case how they are used to get a client request executed.   *page 794*

19.3   Illustrate the contents of a SOAP Request message and corresponding Reply message in the *Election* service example of Exercise 5.1, using the pictorial version of XML as shown in Figure 19.4 and Figure 19.5.   *page 791*

19.4   Outline the five main elements of a WSDL service description. In the case of the *Election* service defined in Question 5.1, state the type of information to be used by the request and reply messages – docs any of this need to be included in the target namespace? For the *vote* operation, draw diagrams similar to Figure 19.11 and Figure 19.13.   *page 803*

19.5   Continuing with the example of the *Election* service, explain why the part of the WSDL defined in Question 19.4 is referred to as 'abstract'. What would need to be added to the service description to make it completely concrete?   *page 800*

19.6   Define a Java interface for the *Election* service suitable for use as a web service. State why you think the interface you defined is suitable. Explain how a WSDL document for the service is generated and how it is made available to clients.   *page 796*

19.7   Describe the contents of a Java client proxy for the *Election* service. Explain how the appropriate marshalling and unmarshalling methods can be obtained for a static proxy.
                                                                                      page 797

19.8   Explain the role of a servlet container in the deploying of a web service and the execution of a client request.   *page 796*

19.9   In the Java example illustrated in Figure 19.8 and Figure 19.9, both client and server are dealing with objects, although web services do not support distributed objects. How can this be the case? What are the limitations imposed on the interfaces of Java web services?   *page 796*

19.10   Outline the replication scheme used in UDDI. Supposing that vector timestamps are used to support this scheme, define a pair of operations for use by registries needing to exchange data.   *page 807*

19.11   Explain why UDDI can be described as being both a name service and a directory service, mentioning the types of enquiries that can be made. The second 'D' in the name UDDI refers to 'discovery' – is UDDI really a discovery service?

Chapter 9 and *page 805*

19.12   Outline the main difference between TLS and XML security. Explain why XML is particularly suitable for the role it plays, in terms of these differences.   *page 807*

19.13   Documents protected by XML security may be signed or encrypted long before anyone can predict who will be the ultimate recipients. What measures are taken to ensure that the latter have access to the algorithms used by the former?   *page 807*

19.14   Explain the relevance of canonical XML to digital signatures. What contextual information can be included in the canonical form? Give an example of a breach of security where the context is omitted from canonical form.   *page 810*

19.15   A coordination protocol could be carried out in order to coordinate the actions of web services. Outline an architecture for (i) a centralized and (ii) a distributed coordination protocol. In each case, describe the interactions needed to establish coordination between a pair of web services.   *page 812*

19.16   To what extent do web services satisfy the requirements for supporting the Grid? Outline how the OGSI services add the functionality that web services do not provide.

page 822

19.17   Outline the function of the Index service in the Globus toolkit. State why UDDI was not regarded as suitable for use as a directory service for the Grid.   *page 822*

20

CORBA CASE STUDY

CORBA is a middleware design that allows application programs to communicate with one another irrespective of their programming languages, their hardware and software platforms, the networks they communicate over and their implementors.

Applications are built from CORBA objects, which implement interfaces defined in CORBA's interface definition language, IDL. Clients access the methods in the IDL interfaces of CORBA objects by means of RMI. The middleware component that supports RMI is called the Object Request Broker or ORB.

The specification of CORBA has been sponsored by members of the Object Management Group (OMG). Many different ORBs have been implemented from the specification, supporting a variety of programming languages including Java and C++.

CORBA services provide generic facilities that may be of use in a wide variety of applications. They include the Naming Service, the Event and Notification Services, the Security Service, the Transaction and Concurrency Services and the Trading Service.

20.1 Introduction

The OMG (Object Management Group) was formed in 1989 with a view to encouraging the adoption of distributed object systems in order to gain the benefits of object-oriented programming for software development and to make use of distributed systems, which were becoming widespread. To achieve its aims, the OMG advocated the use of open systems based on standard object-oriented interfaces. These systems would be built from heterogeneous hardware, computer networks, operating systems and programming languages.

An important motivation was to allow distributed objects to be implemented in any programming language and to be able to communicate with one another. They therefore designed an interface language that was independent of any specific implementation language.

They introduced a metaphor, the *object request broker* (or ORB), whose role is to help a client to invoke a method on an object. This role involves locating the object, activating the object if necessary and then communicating the client's request to the object, which carries it out and replies.

In 1991, a specification for an object request broker architecture known as CORBA (Common Object Request Broker Architecture) was agreed by a group of companies. This was followed in 1996 by the CORBA 2.0 specification, which defined standards enabling implementations made by different developers to communicate with one another. These standards are called the General Inter-ORB protocol or GIOP. It is intended that GIOP can be implemented over any transport layer with connections. The implementation of GIOP for the Internet uses the TCP protocol and is called the Internet Inter-ORB Protocol or IIOP [OMG 2004a]. CORBA 3 first appeared in late 1999 and a component model has been added recently.

The main components of CORBA's language-independent RMI framework are the following:

- An interface definition language known as IDL, which is illustrated early in Section 20.2 and described more fully in Section 20.2.3.

- An architecture, which is discussed in Section 20.2.2.

- The GIOP defines an external data representation, called CDR, which is described in Section 4.3. It also defines specific formats for the messages in a request-reply protocol. In addition to request and reply messages, it specifies messages for enquiring about the location of an object, for cancelling requests and for reporting errors.

- The IIOP, an implementation of GIOP defines a standard form for remote object references, which is described in Section 20.2.4.

The CORBA architecture also allows for CORBA services – a set of generic services that can be useful for distributed applications. These are introduced in Section 20.3 which includes a more detailed discussion of the Naming Service, the Event Service, the Notification Service and the Security Service. For an interesting collection of articles on CORBA, see the *CACM* special issue [Seetharamanan 1998].

Before discussing the above components of CORBA, we introduce CORBA RMI from a programmer's point of view.

20.2 CORBA RMI

Programming in a multi-language RMI system such as CORBA RMI requires more of the programmer than programming in a single-language RMI system such as Java RMI. The following new concepts need to be learned:

- the object model offered by CORBA;

- the interface definition language and its mapping onto the implementation language.

Other aspects of CORBA programming are similar to those discussed in Chapter 5. In particular, the programmer defines remote interfaces for the remote objects and then uses an interface compiler to produce the corresponding proxies and skeletons. But in CORBA, proxies are generated in the client language and skeletons in the server language. We will use the shared whiteboard example introduced in Section 5.5 to illustrate how to write an IDL specification and to build server and client programs.

CORBA's object model ◊ The CORBA object model is similar to the one described in Section 5.2, but clients are not necessarily objects – a client can be any program that sends request messages to remote objects and receives replies. The term *CORBA object* is used to refer to remote objects. Thus, a CORBA object implements an IDL interface, has a remote object reference and is able to respond to invocations of methods in its IDL interface. A CORBA object can be implemented by a language that is not object-oriented, for example without the concept of class. Since implementation languages will have different notions of class or even none at all, the class concept does not exist in CORBA. Therefore classes cannot be defined in CORBA IDL, which means that instances of classes cannot be passed as arguments. However, data structures of various types and arbitrary complexity can be passed as arguments.

CORBA IDL ◊ A CORBA IDL interface specifies a name and a set of methods that clients can request. Figure 20.1 shows two interfaces named *Shape* (line 3) and *ShapeList* (line 5), which are IDL versions of the interfaces defined in Figure 5.12. These are preceded by definitions of two *structs*, which are used as parameter types in defining the methods. Note in particular that *GraphicalObject* is defined as a *struct*, whereas it was a class in the Java RMI example. A component whose type is a *struct* has a set of fields containing values of various types like the instance variables of an object, but it has no methods. There is more about IDL in Section 20.2.3.

Parameters and results in CORBA IDL: Each parameter is marked as being for input or output or both, using the keywords *in*, *out* or *inout*. Figure 5.2 illustrates a simple example of the use of those keywords. In Figure 20.1, line 7, the parameter of *newShape* is an *in* parameter to indicate that the argument should be passed from client to server in the request message. The return value provides an additional *out* parameter – it can be indicated as *void* if there is no *out* parameter.

Figure 20.1   IDL interfaces *Shape* and *ShapeList*

```
struct Rectangle{                                                          1
    long width,
    long height;
    long x;
    long y;
} ;
struct GraphicalObject {                                                   2
    string type;
    Rectangle enclosing;
    boolean isFilled;
};
interface Shape {                                                          3
    long getVersion() ;
    GraphicalObject getAllState() ;     // returns state of the GraphicalObject
};
typedef sequence <Shape, 100> All;                                         4
interface ShapeList {                                                      5
    exception FullException{ };                                            6
    Shape newShape(in GraphicalObject g) raises (FullException);           7
    All allShapes();              // returns sequence of remote object references  8
    long getVersion() ;
};
```

The parameters may be any one of the primitive types such as *long* and *boolean* or one of the constructed types such as *struct* or *array*. Primitive and structured types are described in more detail in Section 20.2.3. Our example shows the definitions of two *structs* in lines 1 and 2. Sequences and arrays are defined in *typedefs*, as shown in line 4, which shows a sequence of elements of type *Shape* of length 100. The semantics of parameter passing are as follows:

Passing CORBA objects: Any parameter whose type is specified by the name of an IDL interface, such as the return value *Shape* in line 7, is a reference to a CORBA object and the value of a remote object reference is passed.

Passing CORBA primitive and constructed types: Arguments of primitive and constructed types are copied and passed by value. On arrival, a new value is created in the recipient's process. For example, the *struct GraphicalObject* passed as argument (in line 7) produces a new copy of this *struct* at the server.

These two forms of parameter passing are combined in the method *allShapes* (in line 8), whose return type is an array of type *Shape* – that is, an array of remote object references. The return value is a copy of the array in which each of the elements is a remote object reference.

Type *Object*. *Object* is the name of a type whose values are remote object references. It is effectively a common supertype of all of IDL interface types such as *Shape* and *ShapeList*.

Exceptions in CORBA IDL. CORBA IDL allows exceptions to be defined in interfaces and thrown by their methods. To illustrate this point, we have defined our list of shapes in the server as a sequence of a fixed length (line 4) and have defined *FullException* (line 6), which is thrown by the method *newShape* (line 7) if the client attempts to add a shape when the sequence is full.

Invocation semantics. Remote invocation in CORBA has *at-most-once* call semantics as the default. However, IDL may specify that the invocation of a particular method has *maybe* semantics by using the *oneway* keyword. The client does not block on *oneway* requests, which can be used only for methods without results. For an example of a *oneway* request, see the example on callbacks at the end of Section 20.2.1.

The CORBA Naming service. The CORBA Naming Service is discussed in Section 20.3.1. It is a binder that provides operations including *rebind* for servers to register the remote object references of CORBA objects by name and *resolve* for clients to look them up by name. The names are structured in a hierarchic fashion, and each name in a path is inside a structure called a *NameComponent*. This makes access in a simple example seem rather complex.

CORBA pseudo objects. Implementations of CORBA provide interfaces to the functionality of the ORB that programmers need to use. In particular, they include interfaces to two of the components shown in Figure 20.6: the *ORB core* and the *Object Adaptor*. The roles of these two components are explained in Section 20.2.2

The objects representing these components are called *pseudo-objects* because they cannot be used like CORBA objects; for example, they cannot be passed as arguments in RMIs. They have IDL interfaces and are implemented as libraries. Those relevant to our simple example (which uses Java 2 version 1.4) are:

- The Object Adaptor, which has been portable since CORBA 2.2, is known as the Portable Object Adaptor (POA). Its interface includes: one method for activating a *POAmanager* and another method *servant_to_reference* for registering a CORBA object.

- The ORB, whose interface includes: the method *init*, which must be called to initialize the ORB; the method *resolve_initial_references*, which is used to find services such as the Naming Service and the root POA; and other methods, which enable conversions between remote object references and strings.

20.2.1 CORBA client and server example

This section outlines the steps necessary to produce client and server programs that use the IDL *Shape* and *ShapeList* interfaces shown in Figure 20.1. This is followed by a discussion of callbacks in CORBA. We use Java as the client and server languages, but the approach is similar for other languages. The interface compiler *idlj* can be applied to the CORBA interfaces to generate the following items:

Figure 20.2   Java interfaces generated by *idlj* from CORBA interface *ShapeList*.

```
public interface ShapeListOperations {
    Shape newShape(GraphicalObject g) throws ShapeListPackage.FullException;
    Shape[] allShapes();
    int getVersion();
}
```

```
public interface ShapeList extends ShapeListOperations, org.omg.CORBA.Object,
    org.omg.CORBA.portable.IDLEntity { }
```

- The equivalent Java interfaces – two per IDL interface. The name of the first Java interface ends in *Operations* – this interface just defines the operations in the IDL interface. The Java second interface has the same name as the IDL interface and implements the operations in the first interface as well as those in an interface suitable for a CORBA object. For example, the IDL interface *ShapeList* results in two Java interfaces *ShapeListOperations* and *ShapeList* as shown in Figure 20.2.

- The server skeletons for each *idl* interface. The names of skeleton classes end in *POA*, for example *ShapeListPOA*.

- The proxy classes or client stubs, one for each IDL interface. The names of these classes end in *Stub*, for example _*ShapeListStub*.

- A Java class to correspond to each of the *structs* defined with the IDL interfaces. In our example, classes *Rectangle* and *GraphicalObject* are generated. Each of these classes contains a declaration of one instance variable for each field in the corresponding *struct* and a pair of constructors, but no other methods.

- Classes called helpers and holders, one for each of the types defined in the IDL interface. A helper class contains the *narrow* method, which is used to cast down from a given object reference to the class to which it belongs, which is lower down the class hierarchy. For example, the *narrow* method in *ShapeHelper* casts down to class *Shape*. The holder classes deal with *out* and *inout* arguments, which cannot be mapped directly onto Java. See Exercise 20.9 for an example of the use of holders.

Server program ◊ The server program should contain implementations of one or more IDL interfaces. For a server written in an object-oriented language such as Java or C++, these implementations are implemented as servant classes. CORBA objects are instances of servant classes.

When a server creates an instance of a servant class, it must register it with the POA, which makes the instance into a CORBA object and gives it a remote object reference. Unless this is done, the CORBA object will not be able to receive remote invocations. Readers who studied Chapter 5 carefully may realize that registering the object with the POA causes it to be recorded in the CORBA equivalent of the remote object table.

In our example, the server contains implementations of the interfaces *Shape* and *ShapeList* in the form of two servant classes, together with a server class that contains a *initialization* section (see Section 5.2.5) in its *main* method.

Figure 20.3   *ShapeListServant* class of the Java server program for CORBA interface *ShapeList*

```
import org.omg.CORBA.*;
import org.omg.PortableServer.POA;
class ShapeListServant extends ShapeListPOA {
    private POA theRootpoa;
    private Shape theList[];
    private int version;
     private static int n=0;
    public ShapeListServant(POA rootpoa){
        theRootpoa = rootpoa;
        // initialize the other instance variables
    }
    public Shape newShape(GraphicalObject g) throws ShapeListPackage.FullException {1
        version++;
        Shape s = null;
        ShapeServant shapeRef = new ShapeServant( g, version);
        try {
            org.omg.CORBA.Object ref = theRoopoa.servant_to_reference(shapeRef);  2
            s = ShapeHelper.narrow(ref);
        } catch (Exception e) {}
         if(n >=100) throw new ShapeListPackage.FullException();
        theList[n++] = s;
        return s;
    }
    public  Shape[] allShapes(){ ... }
    public int getVersion() { ... }
}
```

The servant classes: Each servant class extends the corresponding skeleton class and implements the methods of an IDL interface using the method signatures defined in the equivalent Java interface. The servant class that implements the *ShapeList* interface is named *ShapeListServant*, although any other name could have been chosen. Its outline is shown in Figure 20.3. Consider the method *newShape* in line 1, which is a factory method because it creates *Shape* objects. To make a *Shape* object a CORBA object, it is registered with the POA by means of its *servant_to_reference* method, as shown in line 2, which makes use of the reference to the root POA which was passed on via the constructor when the servant was created. Complete versions of the IDL interface and the client and server classes in this example are available at www.cdk4.net/corba.

The server: The *main* method in the server class *ShapeListServer* is shown in Figure 20.4. It first creates and initializes the ORB (line 1). It gets a reference to the root POA and activates the POAManager (lines 2 & 3). Then it creates an instance of *ShapeListServant,* which is just a Java object (line 4) and in doing this, passes on a reference to the root POA. It then makes it into a CORBA object by registering it with

Figure 20.4   Java class *ShapeListServer*

```
import org.omg.CosNaming.*;
 import org.omg.CosNaming.NamingContextPackage.*;
import org.omg.CORBA.*;
import org.omg.PortableServer.*;
public class ShapeListServer {
    public static void main(String args[]) {
        try{
            ORB orb = ORB.init(args, null);                                              1
            POA rootpoa = POAHelper.narrow(orb.resolve_initial_references("RootPOA"));   2
            rootpoa.the_POAManager().activate();                                         3
            ShapeListServant SLSRef = new ShapeListServant(rootpoa);                     4
            org.omg.CORBA.Object ref = rootpoa.servant_to_reference(SLSRef);             5
            ShapeList SLRef = ShapeListHelper.narrow(ref);
            org.omg.CORBA.Object objRef = orb.resolve_initial_references("NameService");
            NamingContext ncRef = NamingContextHelper.narrow(objRef);                    6
            NameComponent nc = new NameComponent("ShapeList", "");                       7
            NameComponent path[] = {nc};                                                 8
            ncRef.rebind(path, SLRef);                                                   9
            orb.run();                                                                  10
        } catch (Exception e) { ... }
    }
}
```

the POA (line 5). After this, it registers the server with the Naming Service. It then waits for incoming client requests (line 10).

Servers using the Naming Service first get a root naming context (line 6), then make a *NameComponent* (line 7), define a path (line 8) and finally use the *rebind* method (line 9) to register the name and remote object reference. Clients carry out the same steps but use the *resolve* method as shown in Figure 20.5, line 2.

The client program ◊ An example client program is shown in Figure 20.5. It creates and initializes an ORB (line 1), then contacts the Naming Service to get a reference to the remote *ShapeList* object by using its *resolve* method (line 2). After that it invokes its method *allShapes* (line 3) to obtain a sequence of remote object references to all the *Shapes* currently held at the server. It then invokes the *getAllState* method (line 4), giving as argument the first remote object reference in the sequence returned; the result is supplied as an instance of the *GraphicalObject* class.

The *getAllState* method seems to contradict our earlier statement that objects cannot be passed by value in CORBA, because both client and server deal in instances of the class *GraphicalObject*. However, there is no contradiction: the CORBA object returns a *struct*, and clients using a different language might see it differently. For example, in the C++ language the client would see it as a *struct*. Even in Java, the generated class *GraphicalObject* is more like a *struct* because it has no methods.

Figure 20.5   Java client program for CORBA interfaces *Shape* and *ShapeList*

```
import org.omg.CosNaming.*;
import org.omg.CosNaming.NamingContextPackage.*;
import org.omg.CORBA.*;
public class ShapeListClient{
    public static void main(String args[]) {
        try{
            ORB orb = ORB.init(args, null);                                    1
            org.omg.CORBA.Object objRef =
            orb.resolve_initial_references("NameService");
            NamingContext ncRef = NamingContextHelper.narrow(objRef);
            NameComponent nc = new NameComponent("ShapeList", "");
            NameComponent path [] = { nc };
            ShapeList shapeListRef =
            ShapeListHelper.narrow(ncRef.resolve(path));                       2
            Shape[] sList = shapeListRef.allShapes();                          3
            GraphicalObject g = sList[0].getAllState();                        4
        } catch(org.omg.CORBA.SystemException e) {...}
    }
}
```

Client programs should always catch CORBA *SystemExceptions*, which report on errors due to distribution (see line 5). Client programs should also catch the exceptions defined in the IDL interface, such as the *FullException* thrown by the *newShape* method.

This example illustrates the use of the *narrow* operation: the *resolve* operation of the Naming Service returns a value of type *Object*; this type is narrowed to suit the particular type required – *ShapeList*.

Callbacks ◊ Callbacks can be implemented in CORBA in a manner similar to the one described for Java RMI in Section 5.5.1. For example, the *WhiteboardCallback* interface may be defined as follows:

```
interface WhiteboardCallback {
    oneway void callback(in int version);
};
```

This interface is implemented as a CORBA object by the client, enabling the server to send the client a version number whenever new objects are added. But before the server can do this, the client needs to inform the server of the remote object reference of its object. To make this possible, the *ShapeList* interface requires additional methods such as *register* and *deregister*, as follows:

```
int register(in WhiteboardCallback callback);
void deregister(in int callbackId);
```

After a client has obtained a reference to the *ShapeList* object and created an instance of *WhiteboardCallback*, it uses the *register* method of *ShapeList* to inform the server that

Figure 20.6   The main components of the CORBA architecture

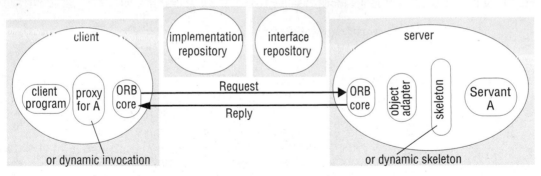

it is interested in receiving callbacks. The *ShapeList* object in the server is responsible for keeping a list of interested clients and notifying all of them each time its version number increases when a new object is added. The *callback* method is declared as *oneway* so that the server may use asynchronous calls to avoid delay as it notifies each client.

20.2.2 The architecture of CORBA

The architecture is designed to support the role of an object request broker that enables clients to invoke methods in remote objects, where both clients and servers can be implemented in a variety of programming languages. The main components of the CORBA architecture are illustrated in Figure 20.6.

This figure should be compared with Figure 5.7, in which case it will be noted that the CORBA architecture contains three additional components: the object adapter, the implementation repository and the interface repository.

CORBA provides for both static and dynamic invocations. Static invocations are used when the remote interface of the CORBA object is known at compile time, enabling client stubs and server skeletons to be used. If the remote interface is not known at compile time, dynamic invocation must be used. Most programmers prefer to use static invocation because it provides a more natural programming model.

We now discuss the components of the architecture, leaving those concerned with dynamic invocation until last.

ORB core ◊   The role of the ORB core is similar to that of the communication module of Figure 5.7. In addition, an ORB core provides an interface that includes the following:

- operations enabling it to be started and stopped;

- operations to convert between remote object references and strings;

- operations to provide argument lists for requests using dynamic invocation.

Object adapter ◊   The role of an *object adapter* is to bridge the gap between CORBA objects with IDL interfaces and the programming language interfaces of the corresponding servant classes. This role also includes that of the remote reference and dispatcher modules in Figure 5.7. An object adapter has the following tasks:

- it creates remote object references for CORBA objects (see Section 20.2.4);

- it dispatches each RMI via a skeleton to the appropriate servant;

- it activates and deactivates servants.

An object adapter gives each CORBA object a unique *object name*, which forms part of its remote object reference. The same name is used each time an object is activated. The object name may be specified by the application program or generated by the object adapter. Each CORBA object is registered with its object adapter, which may keep a remote object table that maps the names of CORBA objects to their servants.

Each object adapter has its own name, which also forms part of the remote object references of all of the CORBA objects it manages. This name may either be specified by the application program or generated automatically.

Portable object adapter ◊ The CORBA 2.2 standard for object adapters is called the Portable Object Adapter. It is called portable because it allows applications and servants to be run on ORBs produced by different developers [Vinoski 1998]. This is achieved by means of the standardization of the skeleton classes and of the interactions between the POA and the servants.

The POA supports CORBA objects with two different sorts of lifetimes:

- those whose lifetimes are restricted to that of the process their servants are instantiated in;

- and those whose lifetimes can span the instantiations of servants in multiple processes.

The former have transient object references and the latter have persistent object references (see Section 20.2.4).

The POA allows CORBA objects to be instantiated transparently; and in addition, it separates the creation of CORBA objects from the creation of the *servants* that implement those objects. Server applications such as databases with large numbers of CORBA objects can create servants on demand, only when the objects are accessed. In this case, they may use database keys for the object names, Alternatively, they may use a single servant to support all of these objects.

In addition, it is possible to specify policies to the POA, for example, as to whether it should provide a separate thread for each invocation, whether the object references should be persistent or transient and whether there should be a separate servant for each CORBA object. The default is that a single servant can represent all of the CORBA objects for its POA.

Skeletons ◊ Skeleton classes are generated in the language of the server by an IDL compiler. As before, remote method invocations are dispatched via the appropriate skeleton to a particular servant, and the skeleton unmarshals the arguments in request messages and marshals exceptions and results in reply messages.

Client stubs/proxies ◊ These are in the client language. The class of a proxy (for object-oriented languages) or a set of stub procedures (for procedural languages) is generated from an IDL interface by an IDL compiler for the client language. As before, the client stubs/proxies marshal the arguments in invocation requests and unmarshal exceptions and results in replies.

Implementation repository ◊   An implementation repository is responsible for activating registered servers on demand and for locating servers that are currently running. The object adapter name is used to refer to servers when registering and activating them.

An implementation repository stores a mapping from the names of object adapters to the pathnames of files containing object implementations. Object implementations and object adapter names are generally registered with the implementation repository when server programs are installed. When object implementations are activated in servers, the hostname and port number of the server are added to the mapping.

Implementation repository entry:

object adapter name	pathname of object implementation	hostname and port number of server

Not all CORBA objects need to be activated on demand. Some objects, for example callback objects created by clients, run once and cease to exist when they are no longer needed. They do not use the implementation repository.

An implementation repository generally allows extra information to be stored about each server, for example access control information as to who is allowed to activate it or to invoke its operations. It is possible to replicate information in implementation repositories in order to provide availability or fault tolerance.

Interface repository ◊   The role of the interface repository is to provide information about registered IDL interfaces to clients and servers that require it. For an interface of a given type it can supply the names of the methods and for each method, the names and types of the arguments and exceptions. Thus, the interface repository adds a facility for reflection to CORBA. Suppose that a client program receives a remote reference to a new CORBA object. Also suppose that the client has no proxy for it; then it can ask the interface repository about the methods of the object and the types of parameter each of them requires.

When an IDL compiler processes an interface, it assigns a type identifier to each IDL type it encounters. For each interface registered with it, the interface repository provides a mapping between the type identifier of that interface and the interface itself. Thus, the type identifier of an interface is sometimes called the *repository ID* because it may be used as a key to IDL interfaces registered in the interface repository.

Every CORBA remote object reference includes a slot that contains the type identifier of its interface, enabling clients that hold it to enquire of its type with the interface repository. Those applications that use static (ordinary) invocation with client proxies and IDL skeletons do not require an interface repository. Not all ORBs provide an interface repository.

Dynamic invocation interface ◊   As suggested in Section 5.5, in some applications, it may be necessary to construct a client program without knowing all the proxy classes it will need in the future. For example, an object browser might need to display information about all the CORBA objects available in the various servers in a distributed system. It is not feasible that such a program should have to include proxies for all of these objects, particularly as new objects may be added to the system as time passes. CORBA does not allow classes for proxies to be downloaded at run time as in Java RMI. The dynamic invocation interface is CORBA's alternative.

The dynamic invocation interface allows clients to make dynamic invocations on remote CORBA objects. It is used when it is not practical to employ proxies. The client can obtain from the interface repository the necessary information about the methods available for a given CORBA object. The client may use this information to construct an invocation with suitable arguments and send it to the server.

Dynamic skeletons ◊ Again, as explained in Section 5.5, it may be necessary to add to a server a CORBA object whose interface was unknown when the server was compiled. If a server uses dynamic skeletons, then it can accept invocations on the interface of a CORBA object for which it has no skeleton. When a dynamic skeleton receives an invocation, it inspects the contents of the request to discover its target object, the method to be invoked and the arguments. It then invokes the target.

Legacy code ◊ The term *legacy code* refers to existing code that was not designed with distributed objects in mind. A piece of legacy code may be made into a CORBA object by defining an IDL interface for it and providing an implementation of an appropriate object adapter and the necessary skeletons.

20.2.3 CORBA Interface Definition Language

The CORBA Interface Definition Language, IDL, provides facilities for defining modules, interfaces, types, attributes and method signatures. We have shown examples of all of the above, apart from modules, in Figures 5.2 and 20.1. IDL has the same lexical rules as C++ but has additional keywords to support distribution, for example *interface*, *any*, *attribute*, *in*, *out*, *inout*, *readonly*, *raises*. It also allows standard C++ pre-processing facilities. See, for example, the *typedef* for *All* in Figure 20.7. The grammar of IDL is a subset of ANSI C++ with additional constructs to support method signatures. We give here only a brief overview of IDL. A useful overview and many examples are given in Baker [1997] and Henning and Vinoski [1999]. The full specification is available in on the OMG website [OMG 2002a].

IDL modules ◊ The module construct allows interfaces and other IDL type definitions to be grouped in logical units. A *module* defines a naming scope, which prevents names defined within a module clashing with names defined outside it. For example, the definitions of the interfaces *Shape* and *ShapeList* could belong to a module called *Whiteboard*, as shown in Figure 20.7.

IDL interfaces ◊ As we have seen, an IDL interface describes the methods that are available in CORBA objects that implement that interface. Clients of a CORBA object may be developed just from the knowledge of its IDL interface. From a study of our examples, readers will see that an interface defines a set of operations and attributes and generally depends on a set of types defined with it. For example, the *PersonList* interface in Figure 5.2 defines an attribute and three methods and depends on the type *Person*.

Figure 20.7   IDL module *Whiteboard*.

```
module Whiteboard {
    struct Rectangle{
    ...} ;
    struct GraphicalObject {
    ...};
    interface Shape {
    ...};
    typedef sequence <Shape, 100> All;
    interface ShapeList {
    ...};
};
```

IDL methods ◊ The general form of a method signature is:

[oneway] <return_type> <method_name> (parameter1,..., parameterL)
[raises (except1,..., exceptN)] [context (name1,..., nameM)]

where the expressions in square brackets are optional. For an example of a method signature that contains only the required parts, consider:

void getPerson(in string name, out Person p);

As explained in the introduction to Section 20.2, the parameters are labelled as *in, out* or *inout*, where the value of an *in* parameter is passed from the client to the invoked CORBA object and the value of an *out* parameter is passed back from the invoked CORBA object to the client. Parameters labelled as *inout* are seldom used, but they indicate that the parameter value may be passed in both directions. The return type may be specified as *void* if no value is to be returned.

The optional *oneway* expression indicates that the client invoking the method will not be blocked while the target object is carrying out the method. In addition, *oneway* invocations are executed once or not at all – that is, with *maybe* invocation semantics. We saw the following example in Section 20.2.1:

oneway void callback(in int version);

In this example, where the server calls a client each time a new shape is added, an occasional lost request is not a problem to the client, because the call just indicates the latest version number and subsequent calls are unlikely to be lost.

The optional *raises* expression indicates user-defined exceptions that can be raised to terminate an execution of the method. For example, consider the following example from Figure 20.1:

exception FullException{ };
Shape newShape(in GraphicalObject g) raises (FullException);

The method *newShape* specifies with the *raises* expression that it may raise an exception called *FullException*, which is defined within the *ShapeList* interface. In our example, the exception contains no variables. However, exceptions may be defined to contain variables, for example:

exception FullException {GraphicalObject g };

When an exception that contains variables is raised, the server may use the variables to return information to the client about the context of the exception.

CORBA can also produce system exceptions relating to problems with servers, such as their being too busy or unable to be activated, problems with communication and client-side problems. Client programs should handle user-defined and system exceptions. The optional *context* expression is used to supply mappings from string names to string values. See Baker [1997] for an explanation of context.

IDL types ◊   IDL supports fifteen primitive types, which include *short* (16-bit), *long* (32-bit), *unsigned short*, *unsigned long*, *float* (32-bit), *double* (64-bit), *char*, *boolean* (TRUE, FALSE), *octet* (8-bit), and *any* (which can represent any primitive or constructed type). Constants of most of the primitive types and constant strings may be declared, using the *const* keyword. IDL provides a special type called *Object*, whose values are remote object references. If a parameter or result is of type *Object*, then the corresponding argument may refer to any CORBA object.

IDL's constructed types are described in Figure 20.8, all of which are passed by value in arguments and results. All arrays or sequences used as arguments must be defined in *typedefs*. None of the primitive or constructed data types can contain references.

Attributes ◊   IDL interfaces can have attributes as well as methods. Attributes are like public class fields in Java. Attributes may be defined as *readonly* where appropriate. The attributes are private to CORBA objects, but for each attribute declared, a pair of accessor methods is generated automatically by the IDL compiler, one to retrieve the value of the attribute and the other to set it. For *readonly* attributes, only the getter method is provided. For example, the *PersonList* interface defined in Figure 5.2 includes the following definition of an attribute:

readonly attribute string listname;

Inheritance ◊   IDL interfaces may be extended. For example, if interface *B* extends interface *A*, this means that it may add new types, constants, exceptions, methods and attributes to those of *A*. An extended interface can redefine types, constants and exceptions, but is not allowed to redefine methods. A value of an extended type is valid as the value of a parameter or result of the parent type. For example, the type *B* is valid as the value of a parameter or result of the type *A*.

interface A { };
interface B: A{ };
interface C {};
interface Z : B, C {};

In addition, an IDL interface may extend more than one interface. For example, interface *Z* extends both *B* and *C*. This means that *Z* has all of the components of both B and *C* (apart from those it redefines) as well as those it defines as an extension.

Figure 20.8   IDL constructed types.

Type	Examples	Use
sequence	typedef sequence <Shape, 100> All; typedef sequence <Shape> All bounded and unbounded sequences of Shapes	Defines a type for a variable-length sequence of elements of a specified IDL type. An upper bound on the length may be specified.
string	string name; typedef string<8> SmallString; unbounded and bounded sequences of characters	Defines a sequences of characters, terminated by the null character. An upper bound on the length may be specified.
array	typedef octet uniqueId[12]; typedef GraphicalObject GO[10][8]	Defines a type for a multi-dimensional fixed-length sequence of elements of a specified IDL type.

record	struct GraphicalObject {
	    string type;
	    Rectangle enclosing;
	    boolean isFilled;
	};
		Defines a type for a record containing a group of related entities. Structs are passed by value in arguments and results.

enumerated	enum Rand (Exp, Number, Name);	The enumerated type in IDL maps a type name onto a small set of integer values.

union	union Exp switch (Rand) {
	    case Exp: string vote;
	    case Number: long n;
	    case Name: string s;
	};
		The IDL discriminated union allows one of a given set of types to be passed as an argument. The header is parameterized by an enum, which specifies which member is in use.

When an interface such as Z extends more than one interface, there is a possibility that it may inherit a type, constant or exception with the same name from two different interfaces. For example, suppose that both B and C define a type called Q; then the use of Q in the Z interface is ambiguous unless a scoped name such as B::Q or C::Q is given. IDL does not permit an interface to inherit methods or attributes with common names from two different interfaces.

All IDL interfaces inherit from the type *Object*, which implies that all IDL interfaces are compatible with the type *Object*. This makes it possible to define IDL operations that can takes as argument or return as a result a remote object reference of any type. The *bind* and *resolve* operations in the Naming Service are examples.

IIDL type identifiers ◊ Section 20.2.2 mentioned that type identifiers are generated by the IDL compiler for each type in an IDL interface. For example, the IDL type for the interface *Shape* type (Figure 20.7) might be:

IDL:Whiteboard/Shape:1.0

This example shows that an IDL type name has three parts – the IDL prefix, a type name and a version number. Since interface identifiers are used as keys for accessing interface definitions in the interface repository, programmers must ensure that they provide a unique mapping to the interfaces themselves. A programmer may use the IDL prefix pragma to prefix an additional string to the type name in order to distinguish their own types from those of others.

IDL pragma directives: These allow additional, non-IDL properties to be specified for components in an IDL interface (see Henning and Vinoski [1999]). These properties include, for example, specifying that an interface will be used only locally, or supplying the value of an interface repository ID. Each pragma is introduced by *#pragma* and specifies its type, for example:

#pragma version Whiteboard 2.3

Extensions to CORBA ◊ Some new features were added in version 2.3 of the CORBA specification. These include the ability to pass non-CORBA objects by value and an asynchronous variant of RMI. Both of these are discussed in the *CACM* article by Vinoski [1998].

Objects that can be passed by value: As we have seen above, IDL arguments and results of constructed and primitive types are passed by value, whereas those that refer to CORBA objects are passed by reference. Support for passing non-CORBA objects by value is now part of CORBA [OMG 2002c]. These non-CORBA objects are object-like in the sense that they possess both attributes and methods. However, they are purely local objects in that their operations cannot be invoked remotely. The pass-by-value facility provides the ability to pass a copy of a non-CORBA object between client and server.

This is achieved by the addition to IDL of a type called *valuetype* for representing non-CORBA objects. A *valuetype* is a *struct* with additional method signatures (like those of an interface). *Valuetype* arguments and results are passed by value; that is, the state is passed to the remote site and used to produce a new object at the destination.

The methods of this new object may be invoked locally, causing its state to diverge from the state of the original object. Passing the implementation of the methods is not so straightforward, since client and server may use different languages. However, if client and server are both implemented in Java, the code can be downloaded. For a common implementation in C++, the necessary code would need to be present at both client and server.

This facility is useful when it is beneficial to place a copy of an object in the client process to enable it to receive local invocations. However, it does not get us any nearer to passing CORBA objects by value.

Asynchronous RMI: CORBA now provides a form of asynchronous RMI which allows clients to make non-blocking invocation requests on CORBA objects [OMG 2004e]. It is intended to be implemented in the client. Therefore a server is generally unaware as to whether it is invoked synchronously or asynchronously. (One exception is the Transaction Service which would need to be aware of the difference.)

Asynchronous RMI adds two new variants to the invocation semantics of RMIs:

- *callback*, in which a client uses an extra parameter to pass a reference to a callback with each invocation, so that the server can call back with the results;

- and *polling*, in which the server returns a *valuetype* object that can be used to poll or wait for the reply.

The architecture of asynchronous RMI allows an intermediate agent to be deployed to make sure that the request is carried out and if necessary to store the reply. Thus it is appropriate for use in environments where clients may become temporarily disconnected – as, for example, a client using a laptop in a train.

20.2.4 CORBA remote object references

CORBA 2.0 specifies a format for remote object references that is suitable for use, whether or not the remote object is to be activated by an implementation repository. References using this format are called interoperable object references (IORs). The following figure is based on Henning [1998], which contains a more detailed account of IORs:

IOR format

IDL interface type id	Protocol and address details			Object key	
interface repository identifier	IIOP	host domain name	port number	adapter name	object name

- The first field of an IOR specifies the type identifier of the IDL interface of the CORBA object. Note that if the ORB has an interface repository, this type name is also the interface repository identifier of the IDL interface, which allows the IDL definition for the interface to be retrieved at runtime.

- The second field specifies the transport protocol and the details required by that particular transport protocol to identify the server. In particular, the Internet Inter-ORB protocol (IIOP) uses TCP, in which the server address consists of a host domain name and a port number.

- The third field is used by the ORB to identify a CORBA object. It consists of the name of an object adapter in the server and the object name of a CORBA object specified by the object adapter.

Transient IORs for CORBA objects last only as long as the process that hosts those objects, whereas *persistent IORs* last between activations of the CORBA objects. A transient IOR contains the address details of the server hosting the CORBA object, whereas a persistent IOR contains the address details of the implementation repository with which it is registered. In both cases, the client ORB sends the request message to the server whose address details are given in the IOR. We now discuss how the IOR is used to locate the servant representing the CORBA object in the two cases.

Transient IORs: The server ORB core receives the request message containing the object adapter name and object name of the target. It uses the object adapter name to locate the object adapter, which uses the object name to locate the servant.

Persistent IORs: An implementation repository receives the request. It extracts the object adapter name from the IOR in the request. Provided that the object adapter name is in its table, it attempts if necessary to activate the CORBA object at the host address specified in its table. Once the CORBA object has been activated, the implementation repository returns its address details to the client ORB, which uses them as the destination for RMI request messages, which include the object adapter name and the object name. These enable the server ORB core to locate the object adapter, which uses the object name to locate the servant, as before.

The second field of an IOR may be repeated, so as to specify the host domain name and port number of more than one destination, to allow for an object or an implementation repository to be replicated at several different locations.

The reply message in the request-reply protocol includes header information that enables the procedure for persistent IORs to be carried out. In particular, it includes a status entry that can indicate whether the request should be forwarded to a different server, in which case the body of the reply includes an IOR that contains the address of the server of the newly activated object.

20.2.5 CORBA language mappings

We have seen from our examples that the mapping from the types in IDL to Java types is quite straightforward. The primitive types in IDL are mapped to the corresponding primitive types in Java. *Structs, enums* and *unions* are mapped to Java classes; sequences and arrays in IDL are mapped to arrays in Java. An IDL exception is mapped to a Java class that provides instance variables for the fields of the exception and constructors. The mappings in C++ are similarly straightforward.

However, we have seen that some difficulties arise with mapping the parameter passing semantics of IDL onto those of Java. In particular, IDL allows methods to return several separate values via output parameters, whereas Java can have only a single result. The *Holder* classes are provided to overcome this difference, but this requires the programmer to make use of them, which is not altogether straightforward. For example, the method *getPerson* in Figure 5.2 is defined in IDL as follows:

> *void getPerson(in string name, out Person p);*

and the equivalent method in the Java interface would be defined as:

> *void getPerson(String name, PersonHolder p);*

and the client must provide an instance of *PersonHolder* as the argument of its invocation. The holder class has an instance variable that holds the value of the argument for the client to access when the invocation returns. It also has methods to transmit the argument between server and client.

Although C++ implementations of CORBA can handle *out* and *inout* parameters quite naturally, C++ programmers suffer from a different set of problems with parameters, related to storage management. These difficulties arise when object references and variable-length entities such as strings or sequences are passed as arguments.

For example, in Orbix [Baker 1997] the ORB keeps reference counts to remote objects and proxies and releases them when they are no longer needed. It provides programmers with methods for releasing or duplicating them. Whenever a server method has finished executing, the *out* arguments and results are released and the programmer must duplicate them if they will still be needed. For example, a C++ servant implementing the *ShapeList* interface will need to duplicate the references returned by the method *allShapes*. Object references passed to clients must be released when they are no longer needed. Similar rules apply to variable-length parameters.

In general, programmers using IDL not only have to learn the IDL notation itself but also have an understanding of how its parameters are mapped onto the parameters of the implementation language.

20.2.6 Integration of CORBA and Web Services

CORBA was already well established and widely used within organizations, when web services started to emerge, early in the twenty-first century. Chapter 19 argues that web services are very suitable for use for interworking between organizations over the Internet. Section 19.2.4 makes a comparison of web services and CORBA, showing that although CORBA is not suited to inter-organizational distributed applications, its main benefits are efficiency and the fact that it provides a set of services for transactions, concurrency control, security and so forth (see Section 20.3).

Many organizations rely on CORBA applications, with their associated benefits of reliability and good performance. But there could be considerable additional advantages from integrating CORBA services with web services. A useful approach would be to provide a WSDL service description (Section 19.3) to existing CORBA services. The IDL definition of a CORBA object would be expressed in XML in the abstract part of a WSDL service description and the communication protocol (for example, IIOP) would be specified in the concrete part of the description.

This would allow a CORBA object to be accessed by clients as though it were any other web service. Once that is possible, new web services may be built by combining CORBA services with web service interfaces with other web services. This would enable the users of CORBA services to benefit from the advantages of the flexibility and lightweight infrastructure associated with web services.

In autumn 2004, the OMG called for proposals for a set of CORBA bindings to WSDL, which will require:

- the mapping of CORBA interfaces defined in IDL into WSDL descriptions;

- the mapping of IDL types into XML schema types;

- a mechanism for making instances of CORBA objects accessible as web services via the communication mechanism required by those CORBA objects.

Once this work is completed, it should be possible to advertise the interfaces of existing CORBA services in WSDL. Clients will be able to access these interfaces as though they are web services, without being aware of the actions of the underlying CORBA middleware. Client programs will be compiled to use the message format, data representation and communication protocols specified in the WSDL binding. They will appear to address CORBA objects by means of URLs but these will be translated into IORs.

20.3 CORBA services

CORBA includes specifications for services that may be required by distributed objects. In particular, the Naming Service is an essential addition to any ORB, as we saw in our programming example in Section 20.2. An index to documentation on all of the services can be found at OMG's web site at [www.omg.org]. Many of the CORBA services are described in Orfali *et al.* [1996 and 1997]. The CORBA services include the following:

Naming Service: The CORBA naming service is detailed in Section 20.3.1.

Event Service and Notification Service: The CORBA event service is discussed in 20.3.2 and the notification service in 20.3.3.

Security service: The CORBA security service is discussed in Section 20.3.4.

Trading service: In contrast to the Naming Service which allows CORBA objects to be located by name, the Trading Service [OMG 2000a] allows them to be located by attribute – that is, it is a directory service. Its database contains a mapping from service types and their associated attributes onto remote object references of CORBA objects. The service type is a name, and each attribute is a name-value pair. Clients make queries by specifying the type of service required, together with other arguments specifying constraints on the values of attributes, and preferences for the order in which to receive matching offers. Trading servers can form federations in which they not only use their own databases but also perform queries on behalf of one anothers' clients. For a detailed description of the Trading Service, see Henning and Vinoski [1999].

Transaction service and concurrency control service: The object transaction service [OMG 2003] allows distributed CORBA objects to participate in either flat or nested transactions. The client specifies a transaction as a sequence of RMI calls, which are introduced by *begin* and terminated by *commit* or *rollback* (*abort*). The ORB attaches a transaction identifier to each remote invocation and deals with *begin*, *commit* and *rollback* requests. Clients can also suspend and resume transactions. The transaction service carries out a two-phase commit protocol. The concurrency control service [OMG 2000b] uses locks to apply concurrency control to the access of CORBA objects. It may be used from within transactions or independently.

Persistent state service: Section 5.2.5 explained that persistent objects can be implemented by storing them in a passive form in a persistent object store while they are not in use and activating them when they are needed. Although ORBs activate CORBA objects with persistent object references, getting their implementations from the implementation repository, they are not responsible for saving and restoring the state of CORBA objects.

The CORBA Persistent State Service is intended to be suitable for use as a persistent object store for CORBA objects [OMG 2002d]. It replaces an earlier

Figure 20.9   Naming graph in CORBA Naming Service

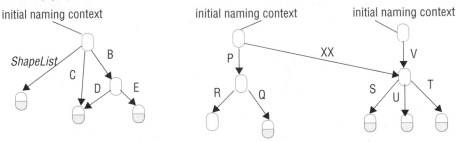

service called the Persistent Object Service. It is based on an architecture in which servants have access to a datastore, for example a database or a file system, via an internal interface. Servants that are to represent persistent objects are called *storage objects* and they are kept in *storage homes* both within the server process and the datastore. Each storage home contains only storage objects of a particular type. A Java-like language is provided for specifying the interfaces of storage objects and associating them with storage homes. The servants can create and access storage objects within their storage homes. Storage objects may also be used transparently via programming languages including Java and C++. For transparent persistence, a pre-processor inserts operations to transfer objects between the servants and the datastore. The Persistent State Service is designed to be used in the context of transactions in the Transaction Service.

Life cycle service   The life cycle service defines conventions for creating, deleting, copying and moving CORBA objects. It specifies how clients can use factories to create objects in particular locations, allowing persistent storage to be used if required. It defines an interface that allows clients to delete CORBA objects or to move or copy them to a specified location. Strategies for making shallow and deep copies are discussed [OMG 2002e].

20.3.1 CORBA Naming Service

The CORBA Naming Service is a sophisticated example of the binder described in Chapter 5. It allows names to be bound to the remote object references of CORBA objects within naming contexts.

As explained in Section 9.2, a *naming context* is the scope within which a set of names applies – each of the names within a context must be unique. A name can be associated with either an object reference for a CORBA object in an application or with another context in the naming service. Contexts may be nested so as to provide a hierarchic name space, as shown in Figure 20.9, in which CORBA objects are shown in the normal way, but naming contexts are shown as plain ovals. The graph on the left shows an entry for the *ShapeList* object described in the programming example in Section 20.2.1.

An *initial naming context* provides a root for a set of bindings. Note that more than one initial naming context can point into the same naming graph. In practice, each instance of an ORB has a single initial naming context, but name servers associated with different ORBs can form federations, as described later in this section. Client and server programs request the initial naming context from the ORB, as shown in Figure 20.5, by invoking its method *resolve_initial_references*, giving *"NameService"* as argument. The ORB returns a reference to an object of type *NamingContext* – see Figure 20.10. This refers to the initial context of the name server for that ORB. Since there can be several initial contexts, objects do not have absolute names – names are always interpreted relative to an initial naming context.

A name with one or more components can be resolved, starting in any naming context. To resolve a name with several components, the naming service looks in the starting context for a binding that matches the first component. If one exists, it will be either a remote object reference or a reference to another naming context. If the result is a naming context, the second component of the name is resolved in that context. This procedure is repeated until all the components of a name have been resolved and a remote object reference obtained, unless the matching fails on the way.

The names used by the CORBA Naming Service are two-part names, called *NameComponent*s, each of which consists of two strings, one for the *name* and the other for the *kind* of the object. The *kind* field provides a single attribute that is intended for use by applications and may contain any useful descriptive information; it is not interpreted by the Naming Service.

Although CORBA objects are given hierarchic names by the Naming Service, these names cannot be expressed as pathnames like those of UNIX files. So, in Figure 20.9, we cannot refer to the object on the far right as /V/T. This is because names can include any characters, which precludes the possibility of having a delimiter.

Figure 20.10 shows the main operations provided by the *NamingContext* class of the CORBA Naming Service, defined in CORBA IDL. The full specification may be obtained from OMG [OMG2004b]. For simplicity, our figure does not describe the exceptions raised by the methods. For example, the *resolve* method can throw a *NotFound* exception, and *bind* can throw an *AlreadyBound* exception.

Clients use the *resolve* method to look up object references by name. Its return type is *Object*, so it can return references to any type of object belonging to applications. The result must be narrowed before it can be used to invoke a method in an application remote object, as shown in Figure 20.5, line 2. The argument of *resolve* is of type *Name*, which is defined as a sequence of name components. This means that the client must construct a sequence of name components before making the call. Figure 20.5 showed a client making an array called *path* consisting of a single name component, which it used as argument to *resolve*. This does not seem a very convenient alternative to using a normal pathname.

Servers of remote objects use the *bind* operation to register names for their objects and *unbind* to remove them. The *bind* operation binds a given name and remote object reference and is invoked on the context in which the binding is to be added. See Figure 20.4, in which the name *ShapeList* was bound in the initial naming context. In that example, the method *rebind* is used because the *bind* operation throws an exception if it is called with a name that already has a binding, whereas *rebind* allows bindings to be replaced.

The *bind_new_context* operation is used to create a new context and to bind it with the given name in the context on which it was invoked. Another method called

Figure 20.10   Part of the CORBA Naming Service *NamingContext* interface in IDL

struct NameComponent { string id; string kind; };

typedef sequence <NameComponent> Name;

interface NamingContext {

    void bind (in Name n, in Object obj);
       binds the given name and remote object reference in my context.

    void unbind (in Name n);
       removes an existing binding with the given name.

    void bind_new_context(in Name n);
       creates a new naming context and binds it to a given name in my context.

    Object resolve (in Name n);
       looks up the name in my context and returns its remote object reference.

    void list (in unsigned long how_many, out BindingList bl, out BindingIterator bi);
       returns the names in the bindings in my context.

};

bind_context binds a given naming context to a given name in the context on which it was invoked. The *unbind* method can be used to remove contexts as well as names.

The operation *list* is intended to be used for browsing the information available from a context in the Naming Service. It returns a list of bindings from a target *NameContext*. Each binding consists of a name and a type – an object or a context. Sometimes, a naming context may contain a very large number of bindings, in which case it would be undesirable to return them all as the result of a single invocation. For this reason, the *list* method returns some maximum number of bindings as a result of a call to *list*, and if further bindings remain to be sent, it arranges to return the results in batches. This is achieved by returning an iterator as a second result. The client uses the iterator to retrieve the remainder of the results a few at a time.

The method *list* is shown in Figure 20.10, but the definitions of the types of its arguments are omitted for the sake of simplicity. The type *BindingList* is a sequence of bindings, each of which contains a name and its type, which is either a context or remote object reference. The type *BindingIterator* provides a method *next_n* for accessing its next set of bindings; its first argument specifies how many bindings are wanted and its second argument receives a sequence of bindings. The client calls the method *list* giving as first argument the maximum number of bindings to be obtained immediately via the second argument. The third argument is an iterator, which can be used to obtain the remainder of the bindings, if any.

The CORBA name space allows for the federation of Naming Services, using a scheme in which each server provides a subset of the name graph. For example, in Figure 20.9, the initial naming contexts in the graphs in the middle and on the right are managed by different servers. The graph in the middle has a binding labelled 'XX' to a context in the graph on the right by which clients may access objects named in the remote graph. To complete the federation, the graph on the right would need to add a binding to a node in the middle graph. An organization can provide access to some or all of the contexts in its name space by providing remote name servers with remote references to them.

The Java implementation of the CORBA Naming Service is very simple and is called transient because it stores all of its bindings in volatile memory. Any serious implementation would at least keep copies of its naming graph in files. As we have seen in the DNS study, replication can be used to provide better availability.

20.3.2 CORBA Event Service

The CORBA Event Service specification defines interfaces allowing objects of interest, called *suppliers*, to communicate notifications to subscribers, called *consumers*. The notifications are communicated as arguments or results of ordinary synchronous CORBA remote method invocations. Notifications may be propagated either by being *pushed* by the supplier to the consumer or *pulled* by the consumer from the supplier. In the first case, the consumers implement the *PushConsumer* interface which includes a method *push* that takes any CORBA data type as argument. Consumers register their remote object references with the suppliers. The supplier invokes the *push* method, passing a notification as argument. In the second case, the supplier implements the *PullSupplier* interface, which includes a method *pull* that receives any CORBA data type as its return value. Suppliers register their remote object references with the consumers. The consumers invoke the *pull* method and receive a notification as result.

The notification itself is transmitted as an argument or result whose type is *any*, which means that the objects exchanging notifications must have an agreement about the contents of notifications. Application programmers, however, may define their own IDL interfaces with notifications of any desired type.

Event channels are CORBA objects that may be used to allow multiple suppliers to communicate with multiple consumers in an asynchronous manner. An event channel acts as a buffer between suppliers and consumers. It can also multicast the notifications to the consumers. Communication via an event channel may use either the push or pull style. The two styles may be mixed; for example, suppliers may push notifications to the channel and consumers may pull notifications from it.

When a distributed application needs to use asynchronous notifications, it creates an event channel, which is a CORBA object whose remote object reference may be supplied to the components of the application via the Naming Service or by means of an RMI. The suppliers in the application make themselves available for subscription by getting *proxy consumers* from the event channel and connecting the suppliers to them by passing them their remote object references. The consumers in the application subscribe to notifications by getting *proxy suppliers* from the notification channel and connecting the consumers to them. The proxy suppliers and consumers are available in both push and pull styles. When a supplier generates a notification using the push style of interaction, it calls the *push* method of a push proxy consumer. The notification passes through the channel and is given to the proxy suppliers, which pass them on to the consumers, as shown in Figure 20.11. If the consumers use the pull style of interaction, they will call the *pull* method of a pull proxy supplier.

Figure 20.11 CORBA event channels

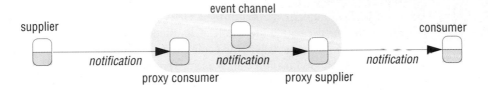

The presence of the proxy suppliers and proxy consumers makes it possible to construct chains of event channels in which each channel supplies notifications to be consumed by the following channel. The event channels in the CORBA model are similar to the observers defined in Figure 5.11. They may be programmed to carry out some of the roles of observers discussed in Section 5.4. However, notifications do not carry any form of identifiers, and therefore the recognition of patterns or the filtering of notifications will need to be based on type information put in the notifications by the application.

A fuller explanation of the CORBA Event Service and an outline of its main interfaces is given in Farley [1998]. The full specification of the CORBA Event service is in [OMG 2004c]. However, the specification does not state how to create an event channel nor how to request the reliability required from it.

20.3.3 CORBA Notification Service

The CORBA Notification Service [OMG 2004d] extends the CORBA Event Service, retaining all of its features including event channels, event consumers and event suppliers. The event service provides no support for filtering events or for specifying delivery requirements. Without the use of filters, all the consumers attached to a channel have to receive the same notifications as one another. And without the ability to specify delivery requirements, all of the notifications sent via a channel are given the delivery guarantees built into the implementation.

The notification service adds the following new facilities:

- Notifications may be defined as data structures. This is an enhancement of the limited utility provided by notifications in the event service, whose type could only be either *any* or a type specified by the application programmer.

- Event consumers may use filters that specify exactly which events they are interested in. The filters may be attached to the proxies in a channel. The proxies will forward notifications to event consumers according to constraints specified in filters in terms of the contents of each notification.

- Event suppliers are provided with a means of discovering the events the consumers are interested in. This allows them to generate only those events that are required by the consumers.

- Event consumers can discover the event types offered by the suppliers on a channel, which enables them to subscribe to new events as they become available.

- It is possible to configure the properties of a channel, a proxy or a particular event. These properties include the reliability of event delivery, the priority of events, the ordering required (for example, FIFO or by priority) and the policy for discarding stored events.

- An event type repository is an optional extra. It will provide access to the structure of events, making it convenient to define filtering constraints.

The Structured Event type introduced by the notification service provides a data structure into which a wide variety of different types of notification can be mapped. Filters can be defined in terms of the components of the Structured Event type. A structured event consists of an event header and an event body. The following example illustrates the contents of the header:

domain type	*event type*	*event name*	*requirements*
"home"	*"burglar alarm"*	*"21 Mar at 2pm"*	*"priority"*, 1000

The domain type refers to the defining domain (for example, *"finance"*, *"hotel"* or *"home"*). The event type categorizes the type of event uniquely within the domain (for example, *"stock quote"*, *"breakfast time"*, *"burglar alarm"*). The event name uniquely identifies the specific instance of the event being transmitted. The remainder of the header contains a list of <name, value> pairs, which are intended to be used to specify reliability and other requirements on event delivery.

The following example illustrates the information in the body of a structured event:

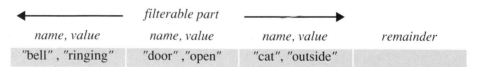

name, value	*name, value*	*name, value*	*remainder*
"bell" , *"ringing"*	*"door"* ,*"open"*	*"cat"*, *"outside"*	

The first part of the event body contains a sequence of <name, value> pairs which are intended for use by the filters. It is expected that different industry domains will define standards for the <name, value> pairs that are used in the filterable part of the event body – the same names and values will be used when defining filters. Perhaps when the burglar alarm goes off, the event may include the state of the alarm bell, whether the front door is open and the location of the cat. The remainder of the event body is intended for transmitting data relating to the particular event; for example, when the burglar alarm goes off, it might contain a digital photograph of the interior of the premises.

Filter objects are used by proxies in making decisions as to whether to forward each notification. A filter is designed as a collection of constraints, each of which is a data structure with two components:

- A list of data structures, each of which indicates an event type in terms of its domain name and event type, for example, *"home"*, *"burglar alarm"*. The list includes all of the event types to which the constraint should apply.

- A string containing a boolean expression involving the values of the event types listed above. For example:

("domain type" == "home" && "event type" == "burglar alarm") &&
    ("bell" != "ringing" !! "door" == "open")

Our example uses an informal syntax. The notification service specification includes the definition of a constraint language, which is an extension of the constraint language used by the trading service.

20.3.4 CORBA Security Service

The CORBA Security Service [Blakley 1999, Baker 1997, <u>OMG 2002b</u>] includes the following:

- Authentication of principals (users and servers); generating credentials for principals (that is, certificates stating their rights); delegation of credentials is supported as described in Section 7.2.5.

- Access control can be applied to CORBA objects when they receive remote method invocations. Access rights may for example be specified in access control lists (ACLs).

- Security of communication between clients and objects, protecting messages for integrity and confidentiality.

- Auditing by servers of remote method invocations.

- Facilities for non-repudiation. When an object carries out a remote invocation on behalf of a principal, the server creates and stores credentials that prove that the invocation was done by that server on behalf of the requesting principal.

To guarantee that security is applied correctly to remote method invocations, the security service requires cooperation on behalf of the ORB. To make a secure remote method invocation, the client's credentials are sent in the request message. When the server receives a request message, it validates the client's credentials to see, for example, if they are fresh and signed by an acceptable authority. If the credentials are valid, they are used to make a decision as to whether the principal has the right to access the remote object using the method in the request message. This decision is made by consulting an object containing information about which principal is allowed to access each method of the target object (possibly in the form of an ACL). If the client has sufficient rights, the invocation is carried out and the result returned to the client, together with the server's credentials if needed. The target object may also record details about the invocation in an audit log or store non-repudiation credentials.

CORBA allows a variety of security policies to be specified according to requirements. A message-protection policy states whether client or server (or both) must be authenticated, and whether messages must be protected against disclosure and/or modification. Policies may also be specified with respect to auditing and non-repudiation; for example, a policy might state which methods and arguments they should be applied to.

Access control takes into account that many applications have large numbers of users and even larger numbers of objects, each with its own set of methods. Users are supplied with a special type of credential called a *privilege* according to their roles. Objects are grouped into *domains*. Each domain has a single access control policy specifying the access rights for users with particular privileges to objects within that domain. To allow for the unpredictable variety of methods, each method is classified in terms of one of four generic methods (*get*, *set*, *use* and *manage*). *Get* methods just return parts of the object state, *set* methods alter the object state, *use* methods cause the object to do some work, and *manage* methods perform special functions that are not intended to be available for general use. Since CORBA objects have a variety of different interfaces, the access rights must be specified for each new interface in terms of the above generic methods. This involves application designers being involved in the application of access control, the setting of appropriate privilege attributes (for example, groups or roles) and in helping the user to acquire the appropriate privileges for their task.

In its simplest form, security may be applied in a manner that is transparent to applications. It includes applying the required protection policy to remote method invocations, together with auditing. The security service allows users to acquire their individual credentials and privileges in return for supplying authentication data such as a password.

20.4 Summary

The main component of CORBA is the Object Request Broker or ORB, which allows clients written in one language to invoke operations in remote objects (called CORBA objects) written in another language. CORBA addresses other aspects of heterogeneity as follows:

- The CORBA General Inter-ORB protocol (GIOP) includes an external data representation called CDR, which makes it possible for clients and servers to communicate irrespective of their hardware. It also specifies a standard form for remote object references.

- GIOP also includes a specification for the operations of a request-reply protocol that can be used irrespective of the underlying operating system.

- The Internet Inter-ORB Protocol (IIOP) implements the request-reply protocol over TCP. IIOP remote object references include the domain name and port number of a server.

A CORBA object implements the operations in an IDL interface. All that clients need to know to access a CORBA object is the operations available in its interface. The client program accesses CORBA objects via proxies or stubs, which are generated automatically from their IDL interfaces in the language of the client. Server skeletons for CORBA objects are generated automatically from their IDL interfaces in the language of the client. The object adapter is an important component of CORBA servers. Its roles include activating and deactivating servants, creating remote object references and forwarding request messages to the appropriate servants.

The CORBA architecture allows CORBA objects to be activated on demand. This is achieved by a component called the implementation repository, which keeps a database of implementations indexed by their object adapter names. When a client invokes a CORBA object, it can be activated if necessary in order to carry out the invocation.

An interface repository is a database of IDL interface definitions indexed by repository IDs. Since the IOR of a CORBA object contains the repository ID of its interface, the appropriate interface repository can be used to get the information about the methods in its interface which is required for dynamic method invocations.

CORBA services provide functionality above RMI, which may be required by distributed applications, allowing them to use additional services such as naming and directory services, event notifications, transactions or security as required.

EXERCISES

20.1   The Task Bag is an object that stores pairs of (key and value). A key is a string and a value is a sequence of bytes. Its interface provides the following remote methods:

pairOut: with two parameters through which the client specifies a *key* and a *value* to be stored.

pairIn: whose first parameter allows the client to specify the *key* of a pair to be removed from the Task Bag. The *value* in the pair is supplied to the client via a second parameter. If no matching pair is available, an exception is thrown.

readPair: is the same as *pairIn* except that the pair remains in the Task Bag.

Use CORBA IDL to define the interface of the Task Bag. Define an exception that can be thrown whenever any one of the operations cannot be carried out. Your exception should return an integer indicating the problem number and a string describing the problem. The Task Bag interface should define a single attribute giving the number of tasks in the bag.   *page 839*

20.2   Define an alternative signature for the methods *pairIn* and *readPair*, whose return value indicates when no matching pair is available. The return value should be defined as an enumerated type whose values can be *ok* and *wait*. Discuss the relative merits of the two alternative approaches. Which approach would you use to indicate an error such as a key that contains illegal characters?   *page 840*

20.3   Which of the methods in the Task Bag interface could have been defined as a *oneway* operation? Give a general rule regarding the parameters and exceptions of *oneway* methods. In what way does the meaning of the *oneway* keyword differ from the remainder of IDL?   *page 840*

20.4   The IDL *union* type can be used for a parameter that will need to pass one of a small number of types. Use it to define the type of a parameter that is sometimes empty and sometimes has the type *Value*.   *page 842*

20.5   In Figure 20.1 the type *All* was defined as a sequence of a fixed length.   Redefine this as an array of the same length. Give some recommendations as to the choice between arrays and sequences in an IDL interface.   *page 842*

20.6   The Task Bag is intended to be used by cooperating clients, some of which add pairs (describing tasks) and others remove them (and carry out the tasks described). When a client is informed that no matching pair is available, it cannot continue with its work until a pair becomes available. Define an appropriate callback interface for use in this situation.   *page 835*

20.7   Describe the necessary modifications to the Task Bag interface to allow callbacks to be used.   *page 835*

20.8   Which of the parameters of the methods in the TaskBag interface are passed by value and which are passed by reference?   *page 830*

20.9   Use the Java IDL compiler to process the interface you defined in Exercise 20.1. Inspect the definition of the signatures for the methods *pairIn* and *readPair* in the generated Java equivalent of the IDL interface. Look also at the generated definition of the holder method for the value argument for the methods *pairIn* and *readPair*. Now give an example showing how the client will invoke the *pairIn* method, explaining how it will acquire the value returned via the second argument.   *page 845*

20.10   Give an example to show how a Java client will access the attribute giving the number of tasks in the Task bag object. In what respects does an attribute differ from an instance variable of an object?   *page 841*

20.11   Explain why the interfaces to remote objects in general and CORBA objects in particular do not provide constructors. Explain how CORBA objects can be created in the absence of constructors.   *Chapter 5 and page 833*

20.12   Redefine the Task Bag interface from Exercise 20.1 in IDL so that it makes use of a *struct* to represent a *Pair*, which consists of a *Key* and a *Value*. Note that there is no need to use a *typedef* to define a *struct*.   *page 842*

20.13   Discuss the functions of the implementation repository from the point of view of scalability and fault tolerance.   *page 838, page 844*

20.14   To what extent may CORBA objects be migrated from one server to another?

page 838, page 844

20.15   Discuss the benefits and drawbacks of the two-part names or *NameComponents* in the CORBA naming service.   *page 848*

20.16   Give an algorithm that describes how a multipart name is resolved in the CORBA naming service. A client program needs to resolve a multipart name with components "A", "B" and "C", relative to an initial naming context. How would it specify the arguments for the *resolve* operation in the naming service?   *page 848*

20.17   A virtual enterprise consists of a collection of companies who are cooperating with one another to carry out a particular project. Each company wishes to provide the others with access to only those of its CORBA objects relevant to the project. Describe an appropriate way for the group to federate their CORBA Naming Services.   *page 850*

20.18   Discuss how to use directly connected suppliers and consumers of the CORBA event
        service in the context of the shared whiteboard application. The *PushConsumer* and
        PushSupplier interfaces are defined in IDL as follows:

> *interface PushConsumer {*
>
> > *void push(in any data) raises (Disconnected);*
> > *void disconnect_push_consumer();*
>
> *}*
>
> *interface PushSupplier {*
>
> > *void disconnect_push_supplier();*
>
> *}*

Either the supplier or the consumer may decide to terminate the event communication
by calling *disconnect_push_supplier*() or *disconnect_push_consume*r() respectively.

page 851

20.19   Describe how to interpose an Event Channel between the supplier and the consumers in
        your solution to Exercise 20.18. An event channel has the following IDL interface:

> *interface EventChannel {*
>
> > *ConsumerAdmin for_consumers();*
> > *SupplierAdmin for_suppliers();*
>
> *};*

where the interfaces *SupplierAdmin* and *ConsumerAdmin*, which allow the supplier and
the consumer to get proxies are defined in IDL as follows:

> *interface SupplierAdmin {*
>
> > *ProxyPushConsumer obtain_push_consumer();*
> > *---*
>
> *};*
>
> *interface ConsumerAdmin {*
>
> > *ProxyPushSupplier obtain_push_supplier();*
> > *---*
>
> *};*

The interface for the proxy consumer and procy supplier are defined in IDL as follows:

> *interface ProxyPushConsumer : PushConsumer{*
>
> > *void connect_push_supplier (in PushSupplier supplier)*
> > > *raises (AlreadyConnected);*
>
> *};*
>
> *interface ProxyPushSupplier : PushSupplier{*
>
> > *void connect_push_consumer (in PushConsumer consumer)*
> > > *raises (AlreadyConnected);*
>
> *};*

What advantage is gained by the use of the event channel?   *page 851*

REFERENCES

Online references

This reference list is available on the Web at www.cdk4.net/refs. It provides clickable links for those documents that exist only on the Web. In this printed list, they are identified by an underlined tag, for example, www.omg.org or Linux AFS. Links go to the document itself or to an index page containing a link to the document.

The references to RFCs refer to the series of Internet standards and specifications called 'requests for comments' that are available from the Internet Engineering Task Force, at www.ietf.org/rfc/ and several other well-known sites.

The online reference list may also be used as an aid to searching for web copies of other documents by searching for authors or titles with Google or Citeseer at citeseer.ist.psu.edu.

Online material written or edited by the authors to supplement the book is referenced in the book by a www.cdk4.net tag, but is not included in the reference list. For example, www.cdk4.net/ipc refers to the additional material about interprocess communication on our web pages.

Abadi and Gordon 1999   Abadi, M. and Gordon, A.D. (1999). A calculus for cryptographic protocols: The spi calculus. *Information and Computation*, Vol. 148, No. 1, pp. 1–70, January.

Abadi *et al.* 1998   Abadi, M., Birrell, A.D., Stata, R. and Wobber, E.P. (1998). Secure Web tunneling. In *Proceedings 7th International World Wide Web Conference*, pp. 531–9. Elsevier, in *Computer Networks and ISDN Systems*, Volume 30, Nos 1–7.

Abrossimov *et al.* 1989   Abrossimov, V., Rozier, M. and Shapiro, M. (1989). Generic virtual memory management for operating system kernels. *Proceedings of 12th ACM Symposium on Operating System Principles*, pp. 123–36, December.

Accetta *et al.* 1986   Accetta, M., Baron, R., Golub, D., Rashid, R., Tevanian, A. and Young, M. (1986). Mach: A new kernel foundation for UNIX development. In *Proceedings Summer 1986 USENIX Conference*, pp. 93–112.

Adjie-Winoto *et al.* 1999   Adjie-Winoto, W., Schwartz, E., Balakrishnan, H. and Lilley, J. (1999). The design and implementation of an intentional naming system. In *Proceedings 17th ACM Symposium on Operating System Principles*, published as *Operating Systems Review*, Vol. 34, No. 5, pp. 186–201.

Adve and Hill 1990   Adve, S. and Hill, M. (1990). Weak ordering – a new definition. In *Proceedings 17th. Annual Symposium on Computer Architecture*, IEEE, pp. 2–14.

Agrawal *et al.* 1987   Agrawal, D., Bernstein, A., Gupta, P. and Sengupta, S. (1987). Distributed optimistic concurrency control with reduced rollback. *Distributed Computing*, Vol. 2: pp. 45–59. Springer-Verlag.

Ahamad *et al.* 1992   Ahamad, M., Bazzi, R., John, R., Kohli, P. and Neiger, G. (1992). *The Power of Processor Consistency*. Technical report GIT-CC-92/34, Georgia Institute of Technology, Atlanta.

Al-Muhtadi *et al.* 2002   Al-Muhtadi, J., Campbell, R., Kapadia, A., Mickunas, D. and Yi, S. (2002). Routing Through the Mist: Privacy Preserving Communication in Ubiquitous Computing Environments. *Proceedings of the 22nd International Conference on Distributed Computing Systems (ICDCS'02)*, Vienna, Austria, July, pp. 74–83.

Alonso *et al.* 2004   Alonso, G., Casata, C., Kuno, H. and Machiraju, V. (2004) *Web Services, Concepts, Architectures and Application*s. Berlin, Heidelberg: Springer-Verlag.

Anderson 1993   Anderson, D.P. (1993). Meta-scheduling for distributed continuous media. *ACM Transactions on Computer Systems*, Vol. 11, No. 3.

Anderson 1996   Anderson, R. J. (1996). The Eternity Service. In *Proceedings of Pragocrypt '96*.

Anderson 2001   Anderson, R.J. (2001). *Security Engineering*. John Wiley & Sons.

Anderson *et al.* 1990a   Anderson, D.P., Herrtwich, R.G. and Schaefer, C. (1990). *SRP – A Resource Reservation Protocol for Guaranteed-Performance Communication in the Internet*. Technical report 90-006, International Computer Science Institute, Berkeley, CA.

Anderson *et al.* 1990b   Anderson, D.P., Tzou, S., Wahbe, R., Govindan, R. and Andrews, M. (1990). Support for continuous media in the DASH System. *Tenth International Conference on Distributed Computing Systems*, Paris.

Anderson *et al.* 1991   Anderson, T., Bershad, B., Lazowska, E. and Levy, H. (1991). Scheduler activations: efficient kernel support for the user-level management of parallelism. In *Proceedings 13th ACM Symposium on Operating System Principles*, pp. 95–109.

Anderson *et al.* 1995   Anderson, T., Culler, D., Patterson, D. and the NOW team. (1995). A case for NOW (Networks Of Workstations), *IEEE Micro*, Vol. 15, No. 1.

Anderson *et al.* 1996	Anderson, T.E., Dahlin, M.D., Neefe, J.M., Patterson, D.A., Roselli, D.S. and Wang, R.Y. (1996). Serverless Network File Systems. *ACM Trans. on Computer Systems*, Vol. 14, No. 1, pp. 41–79. February.
Anderson et al. 2002	Anderson, D.P., Cobb, J., Korpela, E., Lebofsky, M. and Werthimer, D. (2002). SETI@home: An experiment in public-resource computing. *Communications of the ACM*, Nov. 2002, Vol. 45, No. 11, pp. 56–61.
Anderson *et al.* 2004	Anderson, R., Chan, H. and Perrig, A. (2004). Key Infection: Smart Trust for Smart Dust. *Proceedings of IEEE 12th International Conference on Network Protocols* (ICNP 2004), Berlin, Germany, October, pp. 206–215.
ANSA 1989	ANSA (1989). *The Advanced Network Systems Architecture (ANSA) Reference Manual*. Castle Hill, Cambridge, England: Architecture Project Management.
ANSI 1985	American National Standards Institute (1985). *American National Standard for Financial Institution Key Management*, Standard X9.17 (revised).
Apache 2004	The Apache foundation (2004). *Apache Tomcat*.
Apple Computer 2004	Apple Computer (2004). iChat AV *Video conferencing for the rest of us*.
Armand *et al.* 1989	Armand, F., Gien, M., Herrman, F. and Rozier, M. (1989). Distributing UNIX brings it back to its original virtues. *Proc.Workshop on Experiences with Building Distributed and Multiprocessor Systems*, pp. 153–174, October.
Arnold *et al.* 1999	Arnold, K., O'Sullivan, B., Scheifler, R.W., Waldo, J. and Wollrath, A. (1999). *The Jini Specification*, Reading, MA: Addison-Wesley.
associates.amazon.com	Amazon Web Service FAQs.
Attiya and Welch1998	Attiya, H. and Welch, J. (1998). *Distributed Computing – Fundamentals, Simulations and Advanced Topics*. McGraw-Hill.
Babaoglu *et al.* 1998	Babaoglu, O., Davoli, R., Montresor, A. and Segala, R. (1998). System support for partition-aware network applications. In *Proceedings 18th InternationalConference on Distributed Computing Systems* (ICDCS '98), pp. 184–191.
Bacon 2002	Bacon, J. (2002). *Concurrent Systems*, third edition. Harlow, England: Addison-Wesley.
Baghwan *et al.* 2003	Bhagwan, R., Savage, S. and Voelker, G. (2003). Understanding availability. In *Proc. 2nd International Workshop on Peer-to-Peer Systems (IPTPS '03)*, Berkeley, CA, Feb. 2003.
Baker 1997	Baker, S. (1997). *CORBA Distributed Objects Using Orbix*. Harlow, England: Addison-Wesley.

Bal *et al.* 1990   Bal, H.E., Kaashoek, M.F. and Tanenbaum, A.S. (1990). Experience with distributed programming in Orca. In *Proceedings International Conference on Computer Languages '90*, IEEE, pp. 79–89.

Balakrishnan *et al.* 1995   Balakrishnan, H., Seshan, S. and Katz, R.H. (1995). Improving reliable transport and hand-off performance in cellular wireless networks. In *Proceedings ACM Mobile Computing and Networking Conference*, ACM, pp. 2–11.

Balakrishnan *et al.* 1996   Balakrishnan, H., Padmanabhan, V., Seshan, S. and Katz, R. (1996). A Comparison of Mechanisms for Improving TCP Performance over Wireless Links. *Proceedings of the ACM SIGCOMM '96 Conference*, pp. 256–69.

Balan *et al.* 2003   Balan, R.K., Satyanarayanan, M., Park, S., Okoshi, T. (2003). Tactics-Based Remote Execution for Mobile Computing. *Proceedings First USENIX International Conference on Mobile Systems, Applications, and Services (MobiSys 2003)*, San Francisco, CA, USA, May, pp. 273–286.

Balazinska *et al.* 2002   Balazinska, M., Balakrishnan, H. and Karger, D. (2002). INS/Twine: A Scalable Peer-to-Peer Architecture for Intentional Resource Discovery. *Proceedings Pervasive 2002 – International Conference on Pervasive Computing*, Zurich, Switzerland, August, pp. 195–210.

Balfanz *et al.* 2002   Balfanz, D., Smetters, D.K., Stewart, P. and Wong, H.C. (2002). Talking to strangers: authentication in ad-hoc wireless networks. Proceedings Network and Distributed System Security Symposium, San Diego, CA, USA, February.

Banerjea and Mah 1991   Banerjea, A. and Mah, B.A. (1991). The real-time channel administration protocol. *Second International Workshop on Network and Operating System Support for Digital Audio and Video*, Heidelberg.

Baran 1964   Baran, P. (1964). *On Distributed Communications*. Research Memorandum RM-3420-PR, Rand Corporation.

Barborak *et al.* 1993   Barborak, M., Malek, M. and Dahbura, A. (1993). The consensus problem in fault-tolerant computing. *ACM Computing Surveys*, Vol. 25, No. 2, pp. 171–220.

Barghouti and Kaiser 1991   Barghouti, N.S. and Kaiser, G.E. (1991). Concurrency control in advanced database applications. *Computing Surveys*, Vol. 23, No. 3, pp. 269–318.

Barham *et al.* 2003   Barham, P., Dragovic, B., Fraser, K., Hand, S., Harris, T., Ho, A., Neugebauer, R., Pratt, I. and Warfield, A. (2003). Xen and the art of virtualization. *Proceedings nineteenth ACM Symposium on Operating Systems Principles*, Bolton Landing, NY, USA, October, pp. 164–177.

Barr and Asanovic 2003	Barr, K. and Asanovic, K. (2003). Energy Aware Lossless Data Compression. *Proceedings First USENIX International Conference on Mobile Systems, Applications, and Services (MobiSys 2003)*, San Francisco, CA, USA, May, pp. 231–244.
Bartoli *et al.* 1993	Bartoli, A., Mullender, S.J. and van der Valk, M. (1993). Wide-address spaces – exploring the design space. *ACM Operating Systems Review*, Vol. 27, No. 1, pp. 11–17.
Barton *et al.* 2002	Barton, J., Kindberg, T. and Sadalgi, S. (2002). Physical Registration: Configuring Electronic Directories using Handheld Devices. *IEEE Wireless Communications*, Vol. 9, No. 1, February, pp. 30–38.
Bates *et al.* 1996	Bates, J., Bacon, J., Moody, K. and Spiteri, M. (1996). Using events for the scalable federation of heterogeneous components, *European SIGOPS Workshop*.
Bell and LaPadula 1975	Bell, D.E. and LaPadula, L.J. (1975). *Computer Security Model: Unified Exposition and Multics Interpretation*. Mitre Corporation, 1975.
Bellman 1957	Bellman, R.E. (1957). *Dynamic Programming*. Princeton, NJ: Princeton University Press.
Bellovin and Merritt 1990	Bellovin, S.M. and Merritt, M. (1990). Limitations of the Kerberos authentication system. *ACM Computer Communications Review*, Vol. 20, No. 5, pp. 119–32.
Bellwood et al. 2003	Bellwood, T., Clément, L. and von Riegen, C. (eds) (2003). *UDDI Version 3.0.1*. Oasis Corporation.
Beresford and Stajano 2003	Beresford, A. and Stajano, F. (2003). Location Privacy in Pervasive Computing. *IEEE Pervasive Computing*, Vol. 2, No. 1, Jan.–Mar., pp. 46–55.
Berners-Lee 1991	Berners-Lee, T. (1991). World Wide Web Seminar.
Berners-Lee 1999	Berners-Lee, T. (1999). *Weaving The Web*. HarperCollins.
Berners-Lee et al. 2005	Berners Lee, T., Fielding, R. and Masinter, L. (2005). Uniform Resource Identifiers (URI): Generic Syntax, August. Internet RFC 3986.
Bernstein *et al.* 1980	Bernstein, P.A., Shipman, D.W. and Rothnie, J.B. (1980). Concurrency control in a system for distributed databases (SDD-1). *ACM Transactions Database Systems*, Vol. 5, No. 1, pp. 18–51.
Bernstein et al. 1987	Bernstein, P., Hadzilacos, V. and Goodman, N. (1987). *Concurrency Control and Recovery in Database Systems*. Reading, MA: Addison-Wesley. Text available online.
Bershad *et al.* 1990	Bershad, B., Anderson, T., Lazowska, E. and Levy, H. (1990). Lightweight remote procedure call. *ACM Transactions Computer Systems*, Vol. 8, No. 1, pp. 37–55.

Bershad *et al.* 1991	Bershad, B., Anderson, T., Lazowska, E. and Levy, H. (1991). User-level interprocess communication for shared memory multiprocessors. *ACM Transactions Computer Systems*, Vol. 9, No. 2, pp. 175–198.
Bershad *et al.* 1993	Bershad, B., Zekauskas, M. and Sawdon, W. (1993). The Midway distributed shared memory system. In *Proceedings IEEE COMPCON Conference, IEEE*, pp. 528–37.
Bershad *et al.* 1995	Bershad, B., Savage, S., Pardyak, P., Sirer, E., Fiuczynski, M., Becker, D., Chambers, C. and Eggers, S. (1995). Safety and performance in the SPIN operating system. *Proceedings of the 15th ACM Symposium on Operating Systems Principles*, pp. 267–84.
Bhatti and Friedrich 1999	Bhatti, N. and Friedrich, R. (1999). *Web Server Support for Tiered Services*. Hewlett-Packard Corporation Technical Report HPL-1999-160.
Birman 1993	Birman, K.P. (1993). The process group approach to reliable distributed computing. *Comms. ACM*, Vol. 36, No. 12, pp. 36–53.
Birman 1996	Birman, K.P. (1996). *Building Secure and Reliable Network Applications*. Greenwich, CT: Manning.
Birman 2004	Birman, K.P. (2004). Like it or not, Web Services are Distributed Objects! *Comm. of the ACM*. Vol. 47, No. 12, pp. 60–62. December.
Birman and Joseph 1987a	Birman, K.P. and Joseph, T.A. (1987). Reliable communication in the presence of failures. *ACM Transactions Computer Systems*, Vol. 5, No. 1, pp. 47–76.
Birman and Joseph 1987b	Birman, K. and Joseph, T. (1987). Exploiting virtual synchrony in distributed systems. In *Proceedings 11th ACM Symposium on Operating Systems Principles*, pp. 123–38.
Birman *et al.* 1991	Birman, K.P., Schiper, A. and Stephenson, P. (1991). Lightweight causal and atomic group multicast. *ACM Transactions Computer Systems*, Vol. 9, No. 3, pp. 272–314.
Birrell and Needham 1980	Birrell, A.D. and Needham, R.M. (1980). A universal file server. *IEEE Transactions Software Engineering*, Vol. SE-6, No. 5, pp. 450–3.
Birrell and Nelson 1984	Birrell, A.D. and Nelson, B.J. (1984). Implementing remote procedure calls. *ACM Transactions Computer Systems*, Vol. 2, pp. 39–59.
Birrell *et al.* 1982	Birrell, A.D., Levin, R., Needham, R.M. and Schroeder, M.D. (1982). Grapevine: an exercise in distributed computing. *Comms. ACM*, Vol. 25, No. 4, pp. 260–73.
Birrell *et al.* 1995	Birrell, A., Nelson, G. and Owicki, S. (1993). Network objects. In *Proceedings 14th ACM Symposium on Operating Systems Principles*, pp. 217–30.

Bishop and Warren 2003   Bishop, P. and Warren, N. (2003). *JavaSpaces in Practice*. Pearson Education.

Bisiani and Forin 1988   Bisiani, R. and Forin, A. (1988). Multilanguage parallel programming of heterogeneous machines. *IEEE Transactions Computers*, Vol. 37, No. 8, pp. 930–45.

Bisiani and Ravishankar 1990   Bisiani, R. and Ravishankar, M. (1990). Plus: a distributed shared memory system. In *Proceedings 17th International Symposium on Computer Architecture*, pp. 115–24.

Black 1990   Black, D. (1990). Scheduling support for concurrency and parallelism in the Mach operating system, *IEEE Computer*, Vol. 23, No. 5, pp. 35–43.

Black and Artsy 1990   Black, A. and Artsy, Y. (1990). Implementing location independent invocation, *IEEE Transactions Parallel and Distributed Systems*, Vol. 1, No. 1.

Blair and Stefani 1997   Blair, G.S. and Stefani, J.-B. (1997). *Open Distributed Processing and Multimedia*. Harlow, England: Addison-Wesley.

Blakley 1999   Blakley, R. (1999). *CORBA Security – An Introduction to Safe Computing with Objects*. Reading, MA: Addison-Wesley.

Bolosky *et al.* 1996   Bolosky, W., Barrera, J., Draves, R., Fitzgerald, R., Gibson, G., Jones, M., Levi, S., Myhrvold, N. and Rashid, R. (1996). The Tiger video fileserver, *6th NOSSDAV Conference*, Zushi, Japan, April.

Bolosky *et al.* 1997   Bolosky, W., Fitzgerald, R. and Douceur, J. (1997). Distributed schedule management in the Tiger video fileserver, *16th ACM Symposium on Operating System Principles*, pp. 212–23, St Malo, France, October.

Bolosky *et al.* 2000   Bolosky, W.J., Douceur, J.R., Ely, D. and Theimer, M. (2000). Feasibility of a Serverless Distributed File System Deployed on an Existing Set of Desktop PCs, in *Proceedings of the International Conference on Measurement and Modeling of Computer Systems*, 2000, pp. 34–43.

Bonnaire *et al.* 1995   Bonnaire, X., Baggio, A. and Prun, D. (1995). Intrusion free monitoring: an observation engine for message server based applications. In *Proceedings of the 10th International Symposium on Computer and Information Sciences* (ISCIS X), pp. 541–48.

Borisov *et al.* 2001   Borisov, N., Goldberg, I. and Wagner, D. (2001) Intercepting mobile communications: The insecurity of 802.11. In *Proceedings of MOBICOM 2001*.

Bowman *et al.* 1990   Bowman, M., Peterson, L. and Yeatts, A. (1990). Univers: an attribute-based name server. *Software–Practice and Experience*, Vol. 20, No. 4, pp. 403–24.

Box 1998   Box, D. (1998). *Essential COM*. Reading, MA: Addison-Wesley.

Box and Curbera 2004   Box, D. and Curbera, F. (2004). *Web Services Addressing (WS-Addressing)*, BEA Systems, IBM and Microsoft. August.

Boykin *et al.* 1993   Boykin, J., Kirschen, D., Langerman, A. and LoVerso, S. (1993). *Programming under Mach*. Reading, MA: Addison-Wesley.

Bray and Sturman 2002   Bray, J. and Sturman. C.F. (2002). *Bluetooth: Connect Without Cables*, 2nd edn, Prentice Hall.

Buford 1994   Buford, J.K. (1994). *Multimedia Systems*. Addison-Wesley.

Burns and Wellings 1998   Burns, A. and Wellings, A. (1998). *Concurrency in Ada*, Cambridge University Press.

Burrows *et al.* 1989   Burrows, M., Abadi, M. and Needham, R. (1989). *A logic of authentication*. Technical Report 39, Palo Alto, CA: Digital Equipment Corporation Systems Research Center.

Burrows *et al.* 1990   Burrows, M., Abadi, M. and Needham, R. (1990). A logic of authentication. *ACM Transactions Computer Systems*, Vol. 8, pp. 18–36.

Bush 1945   Bush, V. (1945). As we may think. *The Atlantic Monthly*, July.

Callaghan 1996a   Callaghan, B. (1996). *WebNFS Client Specification*, Internet RFC 2054, October.

Callaghan 1996b   Callaghan, B. (1996). *WebNFS Server Specification*, Internet RFC 2055, October.

Callaghan 1999   Callaghan, B. (1999). *NFS Illustrated*, Reading, MA: Addison-Wesley.

Callaghan et al. 1995   Callaghan, B., Pawlowski, B. and Staubach, P. (1995). *NFS Version 3 Protocol Specification, Internet RFC 1813*, Sun Microsystems, June.

Campbell 1997   Campbell, R. (1997). *Managing AFS: The Andrew File System*, Prentice-Hall.

Campbell *et al.* 1993   Campbell, R., Islam, N., Raila, D. and Madany, P. (1993). Designing and implementing Choices: an object-oriented system in C++. *Comms. ACM*, Vol. 36, No. 9, pp. 117–26.

Canetti and Rabin 1993   Canetti, R. and Rabin, T. (1993). Fast asynchronous byzantine agreement with optimal resilience. In *Proceedings 25th ACM Symposium on Theory of Computing*, pp. 42–51.

Carriero and Gelernter 1989   Carriero, N. and Gelernter, D. (1989). Linda in context. *Comms. ACM*, Vol. 32, No. 4, pp. 444–58.

Carter *et al.* 1991   Carter, J.B., Bennett, J.K. and Zwaenepoel, W. (1991). Implementation and performance of Munin. In *Proceedings 13th ACM Symposium on Operating System Principles*, pp. 152–64.

Carter *et al.* 1998   Carter, J., Ranganathan, A. and Susarla, S. (1998). Khazana, An Infrastructure for Building Distributed Services. In *Proceedings of ICDCS '98*. Amsterdam, The Netherlands.

Castro and Liskov 2000
Castro, M. and Liskov, B. (2000). Proactive Recovery in a Byzantine-Fault-Tolerant System, *Proceedings of the Fourth Symposium on Operating Systems Design and Implementation (OSDI '00)*, San Diego, USA, October 2000.

Castro *et al.* 2002
Castro, M., Druschel, P., Hu, Y.C. and Rowstron, A. (2002). Topology-aware routing in structured peer-to-peer overlay networks. *Technical Report MSR-TR-2002-82*, Microsoft Research, 2002.

Castro *et al.* 2003
Castro, M., Costa, M. and Rowstron, A. (2003). Performance and dependability of structured peer-to-peer overlays. *Technical Report MSR-TR-2003-94*, Microsoft Research, 2003.

CCITT 1988a
CCITT (1988). *Recommendation X.500: The Directory – Overview of Concepts, Models and Service*. International Telecommunications Union, Place des Nations, 1211 Geneva, Switzerland.

CCITT 1988b
CCITT (1988). *Recommendation X.509: The Directory – Authentication Framework*. International Telecommunications Union, Place des Nations, 1211 Geneva, Switzerland.

CCITT 1990
CCITT (1990). *Recommendation I.150: B-ISDN ATM Functional Characteristics*. International Telecommunications Union, Place des Nations, 1211 Geneva, Switzerland.

Ceri and Owicki 1982
Ceri, S. and Owicki, S. (1982). On the use of optimistic methods for concurrency control in distributed databases. In *Proceedings 6th Berkeley Workshop on Distributed Data Management and Computer Networks*, Berkeley, CA. pp. 117–30.

Ceri and Pelagatti 1985
Ceri, S. and Pelagatti, G. (1985). *Distributed Databases – Principles and Systems*. McGraw-Hill.

Chalmers *et al.* 2004
Chalmers, D., Dulay, N. and Sloman, M. (2004). Meta Data to Support Context Aware Mobile Applications. *Proceedings IEEE Intl. Conference on Mobile Data Management (MDM2004)*, Berkeley, CA, USA, January, pp. 199–210.

Chandra and Toueg 1996
Chandra, T. and Toueg, S. (1996). Unreliable failure detectors for reliable distributed systems. *Journal of the ACM*, Apr., pp. 374–82.

Chandy and Lamport 1985
Chandy, K. and Lamport, L. (1985). Distributed snapshots: determining global states of distributed systems. *ACM Transactions on Computer Systems*, Vol. 3, No. 1, pp. 63–75.

Chang and Maxemchuk 1984
Chang, J. and Maxemchuk, N. (1984). Reliable Broadcast Protocols, *ACM Transactions on Computer Systems*. Vol. 2. No. 3. pp. 251–75.

Chang and Roberts 1979
Chang, E.G. and Roberts, R. (1979). An improved algorithm for decentralized extrema-finding in circular configurations of processors. *Comms. ACM*, Vol. 22, No. 5, pp. 281–3.

Charron-Bost 1991	Charron-Bost, B. (1991). Concerning the size of logical clocks in distributed systems. *Information Processing Letters*, Vol. 39, July, pp. 11–16.
Chaum 1981	Chaum, D. (1981). Untraceable Electronic Mail, Return Addresses and Digital Pseudonyms. *Comms ACM*, Vol. 24, No. 2, February, pp. 84–88.
Chen *et al.* 1994	Chen, P., Lee, E., Gibson, G., Katz, R. and Patterson, D. (1994). RAID: High-Performance, Reliable Secondary Storage. ACM Computing Surveys, Vol. 26, No. 2, June, pp. 145–188.
Cheng 1998	Cheng, C.K. (1998). *A survey of media servers*. Hong Kong University CSIS, November.
Cheriton 1984	Cheriton, D.R. (1984). The V kernel: a software base for distributed systems. *IEEE Software*, Vol. 1 No. 2, pp. 19–42.
Cheriton 1985	Cheriton, D.R. (1985). Preliminary thoughts on problem-oriented shared memory: a decentralized approach to distributed systems. *ACM Operating Systems Review*, Vol. 19, No. 4, pp. 26–33.
Cheriton 1986	Cheriton, D.R. (1986). VMTP: A protocol for the next generation of communication systems.In *Proceedings SIGCOMM '86 Symposium on Communication Architectures and Protocols*, ACM, pp. 406–15.
Cheriton and Mann 1989	Cheriton, D. and Mann, T. (1989). Decentralizing a global naming service for improved performance and fault tolerance. *ACM Transactions Computer Systems*, Vol. 7, No. 2, pp. 147–83.
Cheriton and Skeen 1993	Cheriton, D. and Skeen, D. (1993). Understanding the limitations of causally and totally ordered communication. In *Proceedings 14th ACM Symposium on Operating System Principles*, Dec., pp. 44–57.
Cheriton and Zwaenepoel 1985	Cheriton, D.R. and Zwaenepoel, W. (1985). Distributed process groups in the V kernel. *ACM Transactions Computer Systems*, Vol. 3, No. 2, pp. 77–107.
Cheswick and Bellovin 1994	Cheswick, E.R. and Bellovin, S.M. (1994). *Firewalls and Internet Security*. Reading, MA: Addison-Wesley.
Chien 2004	Chien, A. (2004). Massively Distributed Computing: Virtual Screening on a Desktop Grid. In Foster, I. and Kesselman, C. (eds), *The Grid 2*. San Francisco, CA: Morgan Kauffman.
Choudhary *et al.* 1989	Choudhary, A., Kohler, W., Stankovic, J. and Towsley, D. (1989). A modified priority based probe algorithm for distributed deadlock detection and resolution. *IEEE Transactions Software Engineering*, Vol. 15, No. 1.
Chu *et al.* 2000	Chu,Y.-H., Rao, S.G. and Zhang, H. (2000). A case for end system multicast. In *Proc. of ACM Sigmetrics*, June 2000, pp. 1–12.

<u>Clark 1982</u>	Clark, D.D. (1982). *Window and Acknowledgement Strategy in TCP*, Internet RFC 813.
Clark 1988	Clark, D.D. (1988). The Design Philosophy of the DARPA Internet Protocols. *ACM SIGCOMM Computer Communication Review*, Vol. 18, No. 4, August, pp. 106–114.
Clarke *et al.* 2000	Clarke, I., Sandberg, O., Wiley, B. and Hong, T. (2000). Freenet: A Distributed Anonymous Information Storage and Retrieval System. In *Proc. of the ICSI Workshop on Design Issues in Anonymity and Unobservability*, Berkeley, CA, 2000.
<u>Cohen 2003</u>	Cohen, B. (2003). Incentives Build Robustness in BitTorrent, May 2003, Internet publication.
Comer 2000a	Comer, D.E. (2000). *Internetworking with TCP/IP, Volume 1: Principles, Protocols and Architecture*, 4th edn. Upper Saddle River, NJ: Prentice-Hall.
Comer 2000b	Comer, D.E. (2000). *The Internet Book*, 3rd edn. Upper Saddle River, NJ: Prentice-Hall.
Condict *et al.* 1994	Condict, M., Bolinger, D., McManus, E., Mitchell, D. and Lewontin, S. (1994). *Microkernel modularity with integrated kernel performance.* Technical report, OSF Research Institute, Cambridge, MA, April.
<u>Coulouris et al. 1998</u>	Coulouris, G.F., Dollimore, J. and Roberts, M. (1998). Role and task-based access control in the PerDiS groupware platform. *Third ACM Workshop on Role-Based Access Control*, George Mason University, Washington DC, October 22–23.
Cristian 1989	Cristian, F. (1989). Probabilistic clock synchronization. *Distributed Computing*, Vol. 3, pp. 146–58.
Cristian 1991a	Cristian, F. (1991). Understanding fault-tolerant distributed systems. *Comms. ACM*, Vol. 34, No. 2.
Cristian 1991b	Cristian, F. (1991). Reaching agreement on processor group membership in synchronous distributed systems. *Distributed Computing*, Springer Verlag, Vol. 4, pp. 175–87.
Cristian and Fetzer 1994	Cristian, F. and Fetzer, C. (1994). Probabilistic Internal Clock Synchronization. In *Proceedings 13th Symposium on Reliable Distributed Systems*, IEEE Computer Society Press, October 25–27, pp. 22–31.
Crow *et al.* 1997	Crow, B., Widjaja, I., Kim, J. and Sakai, P. (1997). IEEE 802.11 Wireless local area networks. *IEEE Communications Magazine*, Sept. 1997, pp. 116–26.
<u>cryptography.org</u>	*North American Cryptography Archives.*

Culler *et al*. 2001   Culler, D.E., Hill, J., Buonadonna, P., Szewczyk, R. and Woo, A. (2001). A Network-Centric Approach to Embedded Software for Tiny Devices. *Proceedings of the First International Workshop on Embedded Software*, Tahoe City, CA, USA, October, pp. 114–130.

Culler *et al*. 2004   Culler, D., Estrin, D. and Srivastava, M. (2004). Overview of Sensor Networks. *IEEE Computer*, Vol. 37, no. 8, August, pp. 41–49.

Curtin and Dolske 1998   Kurtin, M. and Dolski, J. (1998). A brute force search of DES Keyspace. *;login: – the Newsletter of the USENIX Association*, May.

Custer 1998   Custer, H. (1998). *Inside Windows NT*, second edition. Microsoft Press.

Czerwinski *et al*. 1999   Czerwinski, S., Zhao, B., Hodes, T., Joseph, A. and Katz, R. (1999). An architecture for a secure discovery service. In *Proceedings Fifth Annual International Conference on Mobile Computing and Networks*.

Dabek *et al*. 2001   Dabek, F., Kaashoek, M.F., Karger, D., Morris, R. and Stoica, I. (2001). Wide-area cooperative storage with CFS. In *Proc. of the ACM Symposium on Operating System Principles*, October 2001.

Dabek *et al*. 2003   Dabek, F., Zhao, B., Druschel, P. and Kubiatowicz, J. (2003). Ion Stoica, Towards a Common API for Structured Peer-to-Peer Overlays, In *Proceedings of the 2nd International Workshop on Peer-to-Peer Systems (IPTPS '03)*, Berkeley, CA, February 2003.

Daemen and Rijmen 2000   Daemen, J. and Rijmen, V. (2000). The Block Cipher Rijndael, Smart Card Research and Applications, LNCS 1820, J.-J. Quisquater and B. Schneier, (eds). Springer-Verlag, 2000, pp. 288–296.

Daemen and Rijmen 2002   Daemen, J. and Rijmen, V. (2002). *The Design of Rijndael: AES – The Advanced Encryption Standard*, Springer-Verlag.

Dasgupta *et al*. 1991   Dasgupta, P., LeBlanc Jr, R.J., Ahamad, M. and Ramachandran, U. (1991). The Clouds distributed operating system. *IEEE Computer*, Vol. 24, No. 11, pp. 34–44.

Davidson 1984   Davidson, S.B. (1984). Optimism and consistency in partitioned database systems. *ACM Transactions Database Systems*, Vol. 9, No. 3, pp. 456–81.

Davidson *et al*. 1985   Davidson, S.B., Garcia-Molina, H. and Skeen, D. (1985). Consistency in partitioned networks. *Computing Surveys*, Vol. 17, No. 3, pp. 341–70.

Davies *et al*. 1998   Davies, N., Friday, A., Wade, S. and Blair, G. (1998). L2imbo: a distributed systems platform for mobile computing. *Mobile Networks and Applications*, Vol. 3, No. 2, August, pp. 143–156.

de Ipiña *et al*. 2002   de Ipiña, D.L., Mendonça, P. and Hopper, A. (2002). TRIP: a Low-Cost Vision-Based Location System for Ubiquitous Computing. *Personal and Ubiquitous Computing*, Vol. 6, No. 3, May, pp. 206–219.

Debaty and Caswell 2001   Debaty, P. and Caswell, D. (2001). Uniform Web Presence Architecture for People, Places, and Things. IEEE Personal Communications, Vol. 8, No. 4, August, pp. 6–11.

DEC 1990   Digital Equipment Corporation (1990). *In Memoriam: J. C. R. Licklider 1915–1990*, Technical Report 61, DEC Systems Research Center.

Delgrossi *et al.* 1993   Delgrossi, L., Halstrick, C., Hehmann, D., Herrtwich, R.G., Krone, O., Sandvoss, J. and Vogt, C. (1993). Media scaling for audiovisual communication with the Heidelberg transport system. *ACM Multimedia '93*, Anaheim, CA.

Demers *et al.* 1989   Demers, A., Keshav, S. and Shenker, S. (1989). Analysis and simulation of a fair queueing algorithm. *ACM SIGCOMM '89*.

Denning and Denning 1977   Denning, D. and Denning, P. (1977). Certification of programs for secure information flow. *Comms. ACM*, Vol. 20, No. 7, pp. 504–13.

Dertouzos 1974   Dertouzos, M.L. (1974). Control robotics – the procedural control of physical processes. *IFIP Congress*.

Dierks and Allen 1999   Dierks, T. and Allen, C. (1999). *The TLS Protocol Version 1.0*, Internet RFC 2246.

Diffie 1988   Diffie, W. (1988). The first ten years of public-key cryptography. *Proceedings of the IEEE*, Vol. 76, No. 5, May 1988, pp. 560–77.

Diffie and Hellman 1976   Diffie, W. and Hellman, M.E. (1976). New directions in cryptography. *IEEE Transactions Information Theory*, Vol. IT-22, pp. 644–54.

Diffie and Landau 1998   Diffie, W. and Landau, S. (1998). *Privacy on the Line*. Cambridge, MA: MIT Press.

Dijkstra 1959   Dijkstra, E.W. (1959). A note on two problems in connection with graphs. *Numerische Mathematic*, Vol. 1, pp. 269–71.

Dingledine *et al.* 2000   Dingledine, R., Freedman, M.J. and Molnar, D. (2000). The Free Haven project: Distributed anonymous storage service. In *Proc. Workshop on Design Issues in Anonymity and Unobservability*, Berkeley, CA, July 2000.

Dolev and Malki 1996   Dolev, D. and Malki, D. (1996). The Transis approach to high availability cluster communication. *Comms. ACM*, Vol. 39, No. 4, pp. 64–70.

Dolev and Strong 1983   Dolev, D. and Strong, H. (1983). Authenticated algorithms for byzantine agreement. *SIAM Journal of Computing*, Vol. 12, No. 4, pp. 656–66.

Dolev *et al.* 1986   Dolev, D., Halpern, J., and Strong, H. (1986). On the possibility and impossibility of achieving clock synchronization. *Journal of Computing Systems Science*, 32, 2 (Apr.), pp. 230–50.

Dorcey 1995   Dorcey, T. (1995). CU-SeeMe Desktop Video Conferencing Software, *Connexions*, vol. 9, no. 3 (March).

Douceur and Bolosky 1999   Douceur, J.R. and Bolosky, W. (1999). Improving responsiveness of a stripe-scheduled media server. *SPIE Proceedings*, Vol. 3654. *Multimedia Computing and Networking*. pp. 192–203.

Douglis and Ousterhout 1991   Douglis, F. and Ousterhout, J. (1991). Transparent process migration: design alternatives and the Sprite implementation, *Software – Practice and Experience*, Vol. 21, No. 8, pp. 757–89.

Draves 1990   Draves, R. (1990). A revised IPC interface, In *Proceedings USENIX Mach Workshop*, pp. 101–21, October.

Draves *et al.* 1989   Draves, R.P., Jones, M.B. and Thompson, M.R. (1989). *MIG - the Mach Interface Generator*. Technical Report, Dept. of Computer Science, Carnegie-Mellon University.

Druschel and Peterson 1993   Druschel, P. and Peterson, L. (1993). Fbufs: a high-bandwidth cross-domain transfer facility. In *Proceedings 14th ACM Symposium on Operating System Principles*, pp. 189–202.

Druschel and Rowstron 2001   Druschel, P. and Rowstron, A. (2001). PAST: A large-scale, persistent peeer-to-peer storage utility. In *Proceedings of the Eighth Workshop on Hot Topics in Operating Systems (HotOS-VIII)*. Schloss Elmau, Germany, May 2001.

Dubois *et al.* 1988   Dubois, M., Scheurich, C. and Briggs, F.A. (1988). Synchronization, coherence and event ordering in multiprocessors. *IEEE Computer*, Vol. 21, No. 2, pp. 9–21.

Dwork *et al.* 1988   Dwork, C., Lynch, N. and Stockmeyer, L. (1988). Consensus in the presence of partial synchrony. *Journal of the ACM*, Vol. 35, No. 2, pp. 288–323.

Eager *et al.* 1986   Eager, D., Lazowska, E. and Zahorjan, J. (1986). Adaptive load sharing in homogeneous distributed systems. *IEEE Transactions on Software Engineering*, Vol. SE-12, No. 5, pp. 662–675.

Edney and Arbaugh 2003   Edney, J. and Arbaugh, W. (2003). *Real 802.11 Security: Wi-Fi Protected*. Pearson Education.

Edwards and Grinter 2001   Edwards, W.K. and Grinter, R. (2001). At Home with Ubiquitous Computing: Seven Challenges. *Proceedings Third International Conference on Ubiquitous Computing (Ubicomp 2001)*, Atlanta, GA, USA, Sep.–Oct., Springer-Verlag, pp. 256–272.

Edwards *et al.* 2002   Edwards, W.K., Newman, M.W., Sedivy, J.Z., Smith, T.F. and Izadi, S. (2002). Challenge: Recombinant Computing and the Speakeasy Approach. *Proceedings of the Eighth ACM International Conference on Mobile Computing and Networking (MobiCom 2002)*, Atlanta, GA. September, pp. 279–286.

EFF 1998   Electronic Frontier Foundation (1998). *Cracking DES, Secrets of Encryption Research, Wiretap Politics & Chip Design*. Sebastapol, CA: O'Reilly & Associates.

Egevang and Francis 1994	Egevang, K. and Francis, P. (1994), *The IP Network Address Translator (NAT)*, Internet RFC 1631, May.
Eisler et al. 1997	Eisler, M., Chiu, A. and Ling, L. (1997). *RPCSEC_GSS Protocol Specification*. Sun Microsystems. Internet RFC 2203. September.
El Abbadi *et al.* 1985	El Abbadi, A., Skeen, D. and Cristian, C. (1985). An efficient fault-tolerant protocol for replicated data management. In *4th Annual ACM SIGACT/SIGMOD Symposium on Principles of Data Base Systems*, Portland, OR.
Ellis *et al.* 1991	Ellis, C., Gibbs, S. and Rein, G. (1991). Groupware – some issues and experiences. *Comms. ACM*, Vol. 34, No. 1, pp. 38–58.
Ellison 1996	Ellison, C. (1996). Establishing identity without certification authorities. In *6th USENIX Security Symposium*, San Jose, July 22–25.
Ellison et al. 1999	Ellison, C., Frantz, B., Lampson, B., Rivest, R., Thomas, B. and Ylonen, T. (1999). *SPKI Certificate Theory*. Internet RFC 2693, September.
Elrad *et al.* 2001	Elrad, T., Filman, R. and Bader A. (eds) (2001). Theme Section on Aspect-Oriented Programming, *Comms. ACM*, Vol. 44, No. 10.
Evans et al. 2003	Evans, C. and 15 other authors (2003). *Web Services Reliability (WS-Reliability)*, Fujitsu, Hitachi, NEC, Oracle Corporation, Sonic Software, and Sun Microsystems. January.
Fall 2003	Fall, K. (2003). A delay-tolerant network architecture for challenged internets. *Proceedings of the ACM 2003 conference on Applications, technologies, architectures, and protocols for computer communications (SIGCOMM 2003)*, Karlsruhe, Germany, August, pp. 27–34.
Farley 1998	Farley, J. (1998). *Java Distributed Computing*. Cambridge, MA: O'Reilly.
Farrow 2000	Farrow, R. (2000). Distributed denial of service attacks – how Amazon, Yahoo, eBay and others were brought down. *Network Magazine*, April.
Ferguson and Schneier 2003	Ferguson, N. and Schneier, B. (2003). *Practical Cryptography*, John Wiley & Sons.
Ferrari and Verma 1990	Ferrari, D. and Verma, D. (1990). A scheme for real-time channel establishment in wide-area networks, *IEEE Journal on Selected Areas in Communications*, Vol. 8, No. 4.
Ferreira *et al.* 2000	Ferreira, P., Shapiro, M., Blondel, X., Fambon, O., Garcia, J., Kloostermann, S., Richer, N., Roberts, M., Sandakly, F., Coulouris, G., Dollimore, J., Guedes, P., Hagimont, D. and Krakowiak, S. (2000). PerDiS: Design, Implementation, and Use of a PERsistent DIstributed Store. In *LNCS 1752: Advances in Distributed Systems*. Berlin, Heidelberg, New York: Springer-Verlag. pp. 427–53.

<u>Ferris and Langworthy 2004</u>	Ferris, C. and Langworthy, D. (eds), Bilorusets, R. and 22 other authors (2004). *Web Services Reliable Messaging Protocol (WS-Reliable Messaging)*. BEA, IBM,Microsoft and TibCo. March.
Fidge 1991	Fidge, C. (1991), Logical Time in Distributed Computing Systems. *IEEE Computer*, Vol. 24, No. 8, pp. 28–33.
<u>Fielding 2000</u>	Fielding, R. (2000). *Architectural Styles and the Design of Network-based Software Architecture*s, PhD. Dissertation.
<u>Fielding et al. 1999</u>	Fielding, R., Gettys, J., Mogul, J.C., Frystyk, H., Masinter, L. , Leach, P. and Berners-Lee, T. (1999). *Hypertext Transfer Protocol – HTTP/1.1*. Internet RFC 2616.
Fischer 1983	Fischer, M. (1983). The Consensus Problem in Unreliable Distributed Systems (a Brief Survey). In Karpinsky, M. (ed.), *Foundations of Computation Theory*, Vol. 158 of *Lecture Notes in Computer Science*, Springer-Verlag, pp. 127–140. Yale University Technical Report YALEU/DCS/TR-273.
Fischer and Lynch 1982	Fischer, M. and Lynch, N. (1982). A lower bound for the time to assure interactive consistency. *Inf. Process. Letters*, Vol. 14, No. 4, June, pp. 183–6.
Fischer and Michael 1982	Fischer, M.J. and Michael, A. (1982). Sacrificing Serializability to Attain High Availability of Data in an Unreliable Network. In *Proceedings Symposium on Principles of Database Systems*, ACM, pp. 70–5.
Fischer *et al*. 1985	Fischer, M., Lynch, N. and Paterson, M. (1985). Impossibility of distributed consensus with one faulty process. *Journal of the ACM*, Vol. 32, No. 2, Apr., pp. 374–82.
Fitzgerald and Rashid 1986	Fitzgerald, R. and Rashid, R.F. (1986). The integration of virtual memory management and interprocess communication in Accent. *ACM Transactions Computer Systems*, Vol. 4, No. 2, pp. 147–77.
Flanagan 2002	Flanagan, D. (2002). *Java in a Nutshell*. 4th edn. Cambridge, England: O'Reilly.
Fleisch and Popek 1989	Fleisch, B. and Popek, G. (1989). Mirage: a coherent distributed shared memory design. In *Proceedings 12th ACM Symposium on Operating System Principles*, December, pp. 211–23.
Floyd 1986	Floyd, R. (1986). *Short term file reference patterns in a UNIX environment*. Technical Rep. TR 177, Rochester, NY: Dept of Computer Science, University of Rochester.
Floyd and Jacobson 1993	Floyd, S. and Jacobson, V. (1993). The Synchronization of Periodic Routing Messages. *ACM Sigcomm '93 Symposium*.

Floyd *et al.* 1997 Floyd, S., Jacobson, V., Liu, C., McCanne, S. and Zhang, L. (1997). A Reliable Multicast Framework for Lightweight Sessions and Application Level Framing. *IEEE/ACM Transactions on Networking*, Vol. 5, No. 6, pp. 784–803.

Fluhrer *et al.* 2001 Fluhrer, S., Mantin, I. and Shamir, A. (2001). Weaknesses in the Key Scheduling Algorithm of RC4, in *Proceedings of the 8th annual workshop on Selected Areas of Cryptography (SAC)*, Toronto, Canada.

Ford and Fulkerson 1962 Ford, L.R. and Fulkerson, D.R. (1962). *Flows in Networks*. Princeton, NJ: Princeton University Press.

Foster and Kesselman 2004 Foster, I. and Kesselman, C. (eds) (2004). *The Grid 2*. San Francisco, CA: Morgan Kauffman.

Foster *et al.* 2001 Foster, I., Kesselman, C. and Tuecke, S. (2001). The Anatomy of the Grid: enabling scalable virtual organisations. *Intl. J. Supercomputer Applications*. Vol. 15, No. 3, pp. 200–222.

Foster *et al.* 2002 Foster, I., Kesselman, C., Nick, J. and Tuecke, S. (2002). Grid services for distributed systems integration. *IEEE Computer*, Vol. 35, No. 6, pp. 37–46.

Foster *et al.* 2004 Foster, I., Kesselman, C. and Tuecke, S. (2004). T*he Open Grid Services Architecture*. In Foster, I. and Kesselman, C. (eds), *The Grid 2*. San Francisco, CA: Morgan Kauffman.

Fox *et al.* 1997 Fox, A., Gribble, S., Chawathe, Y., Brewer, E. and Gauthier, P. (1997). Cluster-based scalable network services. *Proceedings of the 16th ACM Symposium on Operating Systems Principles*, pp. 78–91.

Fox *et al.* 1998 Fox, A., Gribble, S.D., Chawathe, Y. and Brewer, E.A. (1998). Adapting to Network and Client Variation Using Active Proxies: Lessons and Perspectives. *IEEE Personal Communications*, Vol. 5, No. 4, August, pp. 10–19.

Fox *et al.* 2003 Fox, D., Hightower, J., Liao, L., Schulz, D. and Borriello, G. (2003). Bayesian Filtering for Location Estimation. *IEEE Pervasive Computing*, Vol. 2, No. 3, July–September, pp. 24–33.

Freed and Borenstein 1996 Freed, N. and Borenstein, N. (1996). *MIME (Multipurpose Internet Mail Extensions) Part One: Mechanisms for Specifying and Describing the Format of Internet Message Bodies. September*. Internet RFC 1521.

Freenet 2004 The Free Network Project (2004).

FreePastry project 2004 FreePastry project (2004). Pastry: A substrate for peer-to-peer applications.

Garay and Moses 1993 Garay, J. and Moses, Y. (1993). Fully polynomial Byzantine agreement in *t*+1 rounds. In *Proceedings 25th ACM symposium on theory of computing*, ACM Press, pp. 31–41, May.

Garcia-Molina 1982	Garcia-Molina, H. (1982). Elections in Distributed Computer Systems. *IEEE Transactions on Computers*, Vol. C-31, No. 1, pp. 48–59.
Garcia-Molina and Spauster 1991	Garcia-Molina, H. and Spauster, A. (1991). Ordered and Reliable Multicast Communication. *ACM Transactions Computer Systems*, Vol. 9, No. 3, pp. 242–71.
Garfinkel 1994	Garfinkel, S. (1994). *PGP: Pretty Good Privacy*. O'Reilly.
Gehrke and Madden 2004	Gehrke, J. and Madden, S. (2004). Query processing in sensor networks. *IEEE Pervasive Computing*, Vol. 3, No. 1, Jan–Mar, pp. 46–55.
Gharachorloo *et al.* 1990	Gharachorloo, K., Lenoski, D., Laudon, J., Gibbons, P., Gupta, A. and Hennessy, J. (1990). Memory Consistency and Event Ordering in Scalable Shared-Memory Multiprocessors. In *Proceedings 17th. Annual International Symposium on Computer Architecture*, May, pp. 15–26.
Gibbs and Tsichritzis 1994	Gibbs, S.J. and Tsichritzis, D.C. (1994). *Multimedia Programming*. Addison-Wesley.
Gibson *et al.* 2004	Gibson, G., Courtial, J., Padgett, M.J., Vasnetsov, M., Pas'ko, V., Barnett, S.M. and Franke-Arnold, S. (2004). Free-space information transfer using light beams carrying orbital angular momentum. *Optics Express*, Vol. 12, No. 22, November, pp. 5448–5456.
Gifford 1979	Gifford, D.K. (1979). Weighted voting for replicated data. In *Proceedings 7th Symposium on Operating Systems Principles*, ACM, pp. 150–62.
Globus 2004	The Globus Alliance (2004). *WS-Resource framework*.
Gokhale and Schmidt 1996	Gokhale, A. and Schmidt, D. (1996). Measuring the Performance of Communication Middleware on High-Speed Networks. *Proceedings of SIGCOMM '96*, ACM, pp. 306–17.
Golding and Long 1993	Golding, R. and Long, D. (1993). *Modeling replica divergence in a weak-consistency protocol for global-scale distributed databases*. Technical report UCSC-CRL-93-09, Computer and Information Sciences Board, University of California, Santa Cruz.
Goldschlag *et al.* 1999	Goldschlag, D., Reed, M. and Syverson, P. (1999). Onion routing for anonymous and private internet connections. *Communications of the ACM*, Vol. 42, No. 2, pp. 39–41.
Golub et al. 1990	Golub, D., Dean, R., Forin, A. and Rashid, R. (1990). *UNIX as an application program. Proc. USENIX Summer Conference*, pp. 87–96.
Gong 1989	Gong, L. (1989). A Secure Identity-Based Capability System. In *Proceedings of the IEEE Symposium on Security and Privacy*, Oakland, CA, May, pp. 56–63.
Goodman 1989	Goodman, J. (1989). *Cache Consistency and Sequential Consistency*. Technical Report 61, SCI Committee.

Gordon 1984

Gordon, J. (1984). *The Story of Alice and Bob.*

Govindan and Anderson 1991

Govindan, R. and Anderson, D.P. (1991). Scheduling and IPC Mechanisms for Continuous Media. *ACM Operating Systems Review,* Vol. 25, No. 5, pp. 68–80.

Goyal and Carter 2004

Goyal, S. and Carter, J. (2004). A Lightweight Secure Cyber Foraging Infrastructure for Resource-Constrained Devices. Proceedings Sixth IEEE Workshop on Mobile Computing Systems and Applications (WMCSA 2004), December, pp. 186–195.

Graumann *et al.* 2003

Graumann, D., Lara, W., Hightower, J. and Borriello, G. (2003). Real-world implementation of the Location Stack: The Universal Location Framework. *Proceedings of the 5th IEEE Workshop on Mobile Computing Systems & Applications (WMCSA 2003)*, Monterey, CA, USA, October, pp. 122–128.

Gray 1978

Gray, J. (1978). Notes on database operating systems. In *Operating Systems: an Advanced Course. Lecture Notes in Computer Science*, Vol. 60, pp. 394–481, Springer-Verlag.

Gray and Szalay 2002

Gray, J. and Szalay, A. (2002). *The World-Wide Telescope, an Archetype for Online Science*. Technical Report. MSR-TR-2002-75. Microsoft Research.

Greenfield and Dornan 2004

Greenfield, D. and Dornan, A. (2004). *Amazon: Web Site to Web Services*, Network Magazine. October.

Grimm 2004

Grimm, R. (2004). One.world: Experiences with a pervasive computing architecture. *IEEE Pervasive Computing*, Vol. 3, No. 3, Jul.–Sep., pp. 22–30.

Gruteser and Grunwald 2003

Gruteser, M. and Grunwald, D. (2003). Enhancing location privacy in wireless LAN through disposable interface identifiers: a quantitative analysis. *Proceedings of the 1st ACM international workshop on Wireless mobile applications and services on WLAN hotspots (WMASH '03)*, San Diego, CA, USA, September, pp. 46–55.

Guerraoui *et al.* 1998

Guerraoui, R., Felber, P., Garbinato, B. and Mazouni, K. (1998). System support for object groups. *In Proceedings of the ACM Conference on Object Oriented Programming Systems, Languages and Applications (OOPSLA'98).*

Gummadi *et al.* 2003

Gummadi, K.P., Gummadi, R., Gribble, S.D., Ratnasamy, S., Shenker, S. and Stoica, I. (2003). The impact of dht routing geometry on resilience and proximity. In *ACM SIGCOMM 2003.*

Gusella and Zatti 1989

Gusella, R. and Zatti, S. (1989). The accuracy of clock synchronization achieved by TEMPO in Berkeley UNIX 4.3BSD. *IEEE Transactions Software Engineering*, Vol. 15, pp. 847–53.

Guttman 1999	Guttman, E. (1999). Service Loocation Protocol: Automatic Discovery of IP Network Services. *IEEE Internet Computing*, Vol. 3, No. 4, pp. 71–80.
Haartsen *et al.* 1998	Haartsen, J., Naghshineh, M., Inouye, J., Joeressen, O.J. and Allen, W. (1998). Bluetooth: Vision, Goals, and Architecture, *ACM Mobile Computing and Communications Review*, Oct., vol. 2, no. 4, pp. 38–45.
Hadzilacos and Toueg 1994	Hadzilacos, V. and Toueg, S. (1994). *A Modular Approach to Fault-tolerant Broadcasts and Related Problems*, Technical report, Dept of Computer Science, University of Toronto.
Handley 1998	Handley, M. (1998). Session Directories and Scalable Internet Multicast Address Allocation. *Proceedings of ACM SIGCOMM*, September.
Handley *et al.* 1999	Handley, M., Schulzrinne, H., Schooler, E., Rosenberg, J. (1999). *SIP: Session Initiation Protocol*, Internet RFC 2543.
Harbison 1992	Harbison, S. P. (1992). *Modula-3*. Prentice Hall.
Härder 1984	Härder, T. (1984). Observations on Optimistic Concurrency Control Schemes. *Information Systems*, Vol. 9, No. 2, pp. 111–20.
Härder and Reuter 1983	Härder, T. and Reuter, A. (1983). Principles of Transaction-Oriented Database Recovery. *Computing Surveys*, Vol. 15, No. 4.
Harrenstien et al. 1985	Harrenstien, K., Stahl, M. and Feinler, E. (1985). *DOD Internet Host Table Specification*. Internet RFC 952.
Harter and Hopper 1994	Harter, A. and Hopper, A. (1994). A distributed location system for the active office. *IEEE Network*, Vol. 8, No. 1, January/February 1994, pp. 62–70.
Harter *et al.* 2002	Harter, A., Hopper, A., Steggles, P., Ward, A. and Webster, P. (2002). The Anatomy of a Context-Aware Application. Wireless Networks, Vol. 8, No. 2–3, Mar–May, pp. 187–197.
Härtig *et al.* 1997	Härtig, H., Hohmuth, M., Liedtke, J., Schönberg, S., and Wolter, J. (1997). The performance of kernel-based systems. In *Proceedings 16th ACM Symposium on Operating System Principles*, pp. 66–77.
Hartman and Ousterhout 1995	Hartman, J. and Ousterhout, J. (1995). The Zebra Striped Network File System. *ACM Trans. on Computer Systems*, Vol. 13 , No. 3, August, pp. 274–310.
Hauch and Reiser 2000	Hauch, R. and Reiser, H. (2000). Monitoring Quality of Service across Organisational Boundaries. In *Trends in Distributed Systems: Towards a Universal Service Market*. Proc. third Intl. IFIP/HGI Working conference, USM. September.
Hayton *et al.* 1998	Hayton, R., Bacon, J. and Moody, K. (1998). OASIS: Access Control in an Open, Distributed Environment. In *Proceedings IEEE Symposium on Security and Privacy*, Oakland, CA, pp. 3–14, May.
Hedrick 1988	Hedrick, R. (1988). *Routing Information Protocol*, Internet RFC 1058.

Heidemann *et al.* 2001 Heidemann, J., Silva, F., Intanagonwiwat, C., Govindan, R., Estrin, D. and Ganesan, D. (2001). Building efficient wireless sensor networks with low-level naming. *Proceedings of the 18th ACM Symposium on Operating Systems Principles*, Banff, Alberta, Canada, October, pp. 146–159.

Henning 1998 Henning, M. (1998). Binding, Migration and Scalability in CORBA, *Comms. ACM*, October, Vol. 41, No. 10. pp. 62–71.

Henning and Vinoski 1999 Henning, M. and Vinoski, S. (1999). *Advanced CORBA Programming with C++*. Reading, MA: Addison-Wesley.

Herlihy 1986 Herlihy, M. (1986). A Quorum-Consensus Replication Method for Abstract Data Types. *ACM Transactions Computer Systems*, Vol. 4, No. 1, pp. 32–53.

Herlihy and Wing 1990 Herlihy, M. and Wing, J. (1990). On Linearizability: a correctness condition for concurrent objects. *ACM Transactions on programming languages and systems*, Vol. 12, No. 3, (July), pp. 463–92.

Herrtwich 1995 Herrtwich, R.G. (1995). Achieving Quality of Service for Multimedia Applications. *ERSADS '95, European Research Seminar on Advanced Distributed Systems*, l'Alpe d'Huez, France, April.

Hightower and Borriello 2001 Hightower, J. and Borriello, G. (2001). Location Systems for Ubiquitous Computing. *IEEE Computer*, Vol. 34, No. 8, August, pp. 57–66.

Hightower *et al.* 2002 Hightower, J., Brumitt, B. and Borriello, G. (2002). The Location Stack: A Layered Model for Location in Ubiquitous Computing. *Proceedings of the 4th IEEE Workshop on Mobile Computing Systems & Applications (WMCSA 2002)*, Callicoon, NY, USA, June, pp. 22–28.

Hill *et al.* 2000 Hill, J., Szewczyk, R., Woo, A., Hollar, S., Culler, D. and Pister, K. (2000). System architecture directions for networked sensors. *Proceedings of the ninth ACM international conference on Architectural support for programming languages and operating systems (ASPLOS-IX)*, Cambridge, MA, USA, November, pp. 93–104.

Hirsch 1997 Hirsch, F.J. (1997). Introducing SSL and Certificates using SSLeay. *World Wide Web Journal*, Vol. 2, No. 3, Summer.

Holmquist *et al.* 2001 Holmquist, L.E., Mattern, F., Schiele, B., Alahuhta, P., Beigl, M. and Gellersen, H.-W. (2001). Smart-Its Friends: A Technique for Users to Easily Establish Connections between Smart Artefacts. *Proceedings Third International Conference on Ubiquitous Computing (Ubicomp 2001)*, Atlanta, GA, USA, September 30–October 2, Springer-Verlag, pp. 116–122.

Housley 2002 Housley, R. (2002). *Cryptographic Message Syntax (CMS) Algorithms*. Internet RFC 3370.

Howard *et al.* 1988
Howard, J.H., Kazar, M.L., Menees, S.G, Nichols, D.A., Satyanarayanan, M., Sidebotham, R.N. and West, M.J. (1988). Scale and Performance in a Distributed File System. *ACM Transactions Computer Systems*, Vol. 6, No. 1, pp. 51–81.

Huang *et al.* 2000
Huang, A., Ling, B., Barton, J. and Fox, A. (2000). Running the Web backwards: appliance data services. *Proceedings 9th international World Wide Web conference.*

Huitema 1998
Huitema, C. (1998). *IPv6 – the New Internet Protocol.* Upper Saddle River, NJ: Prentice-Hall.

Huitema 2000
Huitema, C. (2000). *Routing in the Internet*, 2nd edn. Englewood Cliffs, NJ: Prentice-Hall.

Hull *et al.* 2004
Hull, R., Clayton, B. and Melamad, T. (2004). Rapid Authoring of Mediascapes. *Proceedings Sixth International Conference on Ubiquitous Computing (Ubicomp 2004)*, Nottingham, England, September, Springer-Verlag, pp. 125–142.

Hunter and Crawford 1998
Hunter, J. and Crawford, W. (1998). *Java Servlet Programming.* O'Reilly.

Hutchinson and Peterson 1991
Hutchinson, N. and Peterson, L. (1991). The x-kernel: An architecture for implementing network protocols. *IEEE Transactions on Software Engineering*, Vol. 17, No. 1, pp. 64–76.

Hutchinson *et al.* 1989
Hutchinson, N.C., Peterson, L.L., Abbott, M.B. and O'Malley, S.W. (1989). RPC in the x-Kernel: Evaluating New Design Techniques. In *Proc. 12th ACM Symposium on Operating System Principles*, pp. 91–101.

Hutto and Ahamad 1990
Hutto, P. and Ahamad, M. (1990). Slow memory: weakening consistency to enhance concurrency in distributed shared memories. In *Proceedings 10th International Conference on Distributed Computer Systems*, IEEE, pp. 302–11.

Hyman *et al.* 1991
Hyman, J., Lazar, A.A. and Pacifici, G. (1991). MARS – The MAGNET-II Real-Time Scheduling Algorithm. *ACM SIGCOM '91*, Zurich.

IEEE 1985a
Institute of Electrical and Electronic Engineers (1985). *Local Area Network – CSMA/CD Access Method and Physical Layer Specifications.* American National Standard ANSI/IEEE 802.3, IEEE Computer Society.

IEEE 1985b
Institute of Electrical and Electronic Engineers (1985). *Local Area Network – Token Bus Access Method and Physical Layer Specifications.* American National Standard ANSI/IEEE 802.4, IEEE Computer Society.

IEEE 1985c   Institute of Electrical and Electronic Engineers (1985). *Local Area Network – Token Ring Access Method and Physical Layer Specifications*. American National Standard ANSI/IEEE 802.5, IEEE Computer Society.

IEEE 1990   Institute of Electrical and Electronic Engineers (1990). *IEEE Standard 802: Overview and Architecture*. American National Standard ANSI/IEEE 802, IEEE Computer Society.

IEEE 1994   Institute of Electrical and Electronic Engineers (1994). *Local and metropolitan area networks – Part 6: Distributed Queue Dual Bus (DQDB) access method and physical layer specifications*. American National Standard ANSI/IEEE 802.6, IEEE Computer Society.

IEEE 1999   Institute of Electrical and Electronic Engineers (1999). *Local and metropolitan area networks – Part 11: Wireless LAN Medium Access Control (MAC) and Physical Layer (PHY) Specifications*, American National Standard ANSI/IEEE 802.11, IEEE Computer Society.

IEEE 2002   Institute of Electrical and Electronic Engineers (2002). *Wireless Medium Access Control (MAC) and Physical Layer (PHY) Specifications for Wireless Personal Area Networks (WPANs)*, American National Standard ANSI/IEEE 802.15.1, IEEE Computer Society.

IEEE 2003   Institute of Electrical and Electronic Engineers (2003). *Part 15.4: Wireless Medium Access Control (MAC) and Physical Layer (PHY) Specifications for Low-Rate Wireless Personal Area Networks (LR-WPANs)*, American National Standard ANSI/IEEE 802.15.4, IEEE Computer Society.

IEEE 2004a   Institute of Electrical and Electronic Engineers (2004). IEEE Standard for Local and Metropolitan Area Networks – Part 16: *Air Interface for Fixed Broadband Wireless Access Systems*. American National Standard ANSI/IEEE 802.16, IEEE Computer Society.

IEEE 2004b   Institute of Electrical and Electronic Engineers (2004). *Wireless LAN Medium Access Control (MAC) and Physical Layer (PHY) Specifications: Medium Access Control (MAC) Security Enhancement*, American National Standard ANSI/IEEE 802.11i, IEEE Computer Society.

Iftode *et al.* 1996   Iftode, L., Singh, J. and Li, K. (1996). Scope consistency: a bridge between release consistency and entry consistency. In *Proceedings 8th annual ACM symposium on Parallel algorithms and architectures*. pp. 277–87.

Imielinski and Navas 1999   Imielinski, T. and Navas, J.C. (1999). GPS-based geographic addressing, routing, and resource discovery. *Comms. ACM*, Vol. 42, No. 4, pp. 86–92.

international pgp	*The International PGP Home Page.*
Internet World Stats 2004	Internet World Stats.
Ishii and Ullmer 1997	Ishii, H. and Ullmer, B., (1997). Tangible Bits: Towards Seamless Interfaces between People, Bits and Atoms. *Proceedings of ACM Conference on Human Factors in Computing Systems (CHI '97)*, Atlanta, GA, USA, March, pp. 234–241.
ISO 1992	International Organization for Standardization (1992). *Basic Reference Model of Open Distributed Processing, Part 1: Overview and guide to use.* ISO/IEC JTC1/SC212/WG7 CD 10746-1, International Organization for Standardization.
ISO 8879	International Organization for Standardization (1986). Information Processing – Text and Office Systems – Standard Generalized Markup Language (SGML), 1986.
ITU/ISO 1997	ITU/ISO (1997). Recommendation X.500 (08/97): *Open Systems Interconnection – The Directory: Overview of concepts, models and services.* International Telecommunication Union.
Iyer *et al.* 2002	Iyer, S., Rowstron, A. and Druschel, P. (2002). Squirrel: A decentralized peer-to-peer web cache. In *12th ACM Symposium on Principles of Distributed Computing (PODC 2002)*, July.
java.sun.com I	Sun Microsystems. *Java Remote Method Invocation.*
java.sun.com II	Sun Microsystems. *Java Object Serialization Specification.*
java.sun.com III	Sun Microsystems. *Servlet Tutorial.*
java.sun.com IV	Jordan, M. and Atkinson, M. (1999). *Orthogonal Persistence for the Java Platform - Draft Specification.* Sun Microsystems Laboratories. Palo Alto, CA.
java.sun.com V	Sun Microsystems, *Java Security API.*
java.sun.com VI	Sun Microsystems (1999). *JavaSpaces technology.*
java.sun.com VII	Sun Microsystems. *The Java Web Services Tutorial.*
java.sun.com VIII	Sun Microsystems (2003). *Java Data Objects (JDO).*
java.sun.com IX	Sun Microsystems. *Java Remote Object Activation Tutorial.*
Johanson and Fox 2004	Johanson, B. and Fox, A. (2004). Extending Tuplespaces For Coordination in Interactive Workspaces. *Journal of Systems and Software*, Vol. 69, No. 3, January, pp. 243–266.
Johnson and Zwaenepoel 1993	Johnson, D. and Zwaenepoel, W. (1993). The Peregrine High-performance RPC System. S*oftware–Practice and Experience*, Vol. 23, No. 2, pp. 201–21.
Jordan 1996	Jordan, M. (1996). Early Experiences with Persistent Java. In *Proceedings first international workshop on persistrence and Java.* Glasgow, Scotland.

Joseph *et al.* 1997	Joseph, A., Tauber, J. and Kaashoek, M. (1997). Mobile Computing with the Rover Toolkit. *IEEE Transactions on Computers: Special issue on Mobile Computing*, Vol. 46, No. 3, pp. 337–52.
Jul *et al.* 1988	Jul, E., Levy, H., Hutchinson, N. and Black, A. (1988). Fine-grained Mobility in the Emerald System. *ACM Transactions Computer Systems*, Vol. 6, No. 1, pp. 109–33.
Kaashoek and Tanenbaum 1991	Kaashoek, F. and Tanenbaum, A. (1991). Group Communication in the Amoeba Distributed Operating System. In *Proceedings 11th International Conference on Distributed Computer Systems*, pp. 222–30.
Kaashoek *et al.* 1989	Kaashoek, F., Tanenbaum, A., Flynn Hummel, S. and Bal, H. (1989). An Efficient Reliable Broadcast Protocol. *Operating Systems Review*, Vol. 23, No. 4, pp. 5–20.
Kaashoek *et al.* 1997	Kaashoek, M., Engler, D., Ganzer, G., Briceño, H., Hunt, R., Mazières, D., Pinckney, T., Grimm, R., Jannotti, J. and Mackenzie, K. (1997). Application performance and flexibility on exokernel systems. *Proceedings of the 16th ACM Symposium on Operating Systems Principles*, pp. 52–65.
Kahn 1967	Kahn, D. (1967). *The Codebreakers: The Story of Secret Writing*. New York: Macmillan.
Kahn 1983	Kahn, D. (1983). *Kahn on Codes*. New York: Macmillan.
Kahn 1991	Kahn, D. (1991). *Seizing the Enigma*. Boston: Houghton Mifflin.
Kaler 2002	Kaler, C. (ed.) (2002). *Specification: Web Services Security (WS-Security)*.
Kaliski and Staddon 1998	Kaliski, B. and Staddon, J. (1998). *RSA Cryptography Specifications*, Version 2.0. Internet RFC 2437.
Kantor and Lapsley 1986	Kantor, B. and Lapsley, P. (1986). Ne*twork News Transfer Protocol: A Proposed Standard for the Stream-Based Transmission of News*, Internet RFC 977, February.
Kehne *et al.* 1992	Kehne, A., Schonwalder, J. and Langendorfer, H. (1992). A Nonce-based Protocol for Multiple Authentications. *ACM Operating Systems Review*, Vol. 26, No. 4, pp. 84–9.
Keith and Wittle 1993	Keith, B.E. and Wittle, M. (1993). LADDIS: The Next Generation in NFS File Server Benchmarking, *Summer USENIX Conference Proceedings*. USENIX Association, Berkeley, CA, June.
Keleher *et al.* 1992	Keleher, P., Cox, A. and Zwaenepoel, W. (1992). Lazy consistency for software distributed shared memory. In *Proceedings 19th Annual International Symposium on Computer Architecture*. pp. 13–21, May 1992.

Kessler and Livny 1989   Kessler, R.E. and Livny, M. (1989). An Analysis of Distributed Shared Memory Algorithms, In *Proceedings 9th International Conference Distributed Computing Systems*. IEEE, pp. 98–104.

Kiciman and Fox 2000   Kiciman, E. and Fox, A. (2000). Using Dynamic Mediation to Integrate COTS Entities in a Ubiquitous Computing Environment. *Proceedings Second International Symposium on Handheld and Ubiquitous Computing (HUC2K)*, Bristol, England, September, pp. 211–226.

Kille 1992   Kille, S. (1992). *Implementing X.400 and X.500: The PP and QUIPU Systems*. Artech House.

Kindberg 1995   Kindberg, T. (1995). A Sequencing Service for Group Communication (abstract), In *Proceedings 14th annual ACM Symposium on Principles of Distributed Computing*, p. 260. Technical Report No. 698, Queen Mary and Westfield College Dept. of CS, 1995.

Kindberg 2002   Kindberg, T. (2002). Implementing Physical Hyperlinks Using Ubiquitous Identifier Resolution. *Proceedings Eleventh International World Wide Web Conference (WWW2002)*, Honolulu, HI, USA, May pp. 191–199.

Kindberg and Barton 2001   Kindberg, T. and Barton, J. (2001). A Web-Based Nomadic Computing System. *Computer Networks*, Vol. 35, No. 4, pp. 443–456.

Kindberg and Fox 2001   Kindberg, T. and Fox, A. (2001). System Software for Ubiquitous Computing. *IEEE Pervasive Computing*, Vol. 1, No. 1, Jan.–Mar., pp. 70–81.

Kindberg and Zhang 2003a   Kindberg, T. and Zhang, K. (2003). Secure Spontaneous Device Association. *Proceedings Fifth International Conference on Ubiquitous Computing (Ubicomp 2003)*, Seattle, WA, USA, October, pp. 124–131.

Kindberg and Zhang 2003b   Kindberg, T. and Zhang, K. (2003). Validating and Securing Spontaneous Associations between Wireless Devices. *Proceedings 6th Information Security Conference (ISC'03)*, Bristol, England, October, Springer-Verlag, pp. 44–53.

Kindberg *et al.* 1996   Kindberg, T., Coulouris, G., Dollimore, J. and Heikkinen, J. (1996). Sharing objects over the Internet: the Mushroom approach. In *Proceedings IEEE Global Internet 1996*, London, Nov., pp. 67–71.

Kindberg *et al.* 2002a   Kindberg, T., Barton, J., Morgan, J., Becker, G., Bedner, I., Caswell, D., Debaty, P., Gopal, G., Frid, M., Krishnan, V., Morris, H., Pering, C., Schettino, J. and Serra, B. (2002). People, Places, Things: Web Presence for the Real World. *Mobile Networks and Applications (MONET)*, Vol. 7, No. 5, October, pp. 365–376.

Kindberg *et al.* 2002b   Kindberg, T., Zhang, K. and Shanka, N. (2002). Context Authentication Using Constrained Channels. *Proceedings of the 4th IEEE Workshop on Mobile Computing Systems & Applications (WMCSA 2002)*, Callicoon, NY, USA, June, pp. 14–21.

Kistler and Satyanarayanan 1992   Kistler, J.J. and Satyanarayanan, M. (1992). Disconnected Operation in the Coda File System. *ACM Transactions on Computer Systems*, Vol. 10, No. 1, pp. 3–25.

Kleinrock 1961   Kleinrock, L. (1961). *Information Flow in Large Communication Networks*, MIT, RLE Quarterly Progress Report, July.

Kleinrock 1997   Kleinrock, L. (1997). Nomadicity: anytime, anywhere in a disconnected world. *Mobile Networks and Applications*, Vol. 1, No. 4, pp. 351–7.

Kohl and Neuman 1993   Kohl, J. and Neuman, C. (1993). *The Kerberos Network Authentication Service (V5)*, Internet RFC 1510, September.

Konstantas *et al.* 1997   Konstantas, D., Orlarey, Y., Gibbs, S. and Carbonel, O. (1997). Distributed Music Rehearsal. In *Proceedings International Computer Music Conference* 97.

Kopetz and Verissimo 1993   Kopetz, H. and Verissimo, P. (1993). Real Time and Dependability Concepts. In Mullender (ed.), *Distributed Systems*, 2nd edn. Addison-Wesley.

Kopetz *et al.* 1989   Kopetz, H., Damm, A., Koza, C., Mulazzani, M., Schwabl, W. Senft, C. and Zainlinger, R. (1989). Distributed Fault-Tolerant Real-Time Systems – The MARS Approach. *IEEE Micro*, Vol. 9, No. 1.

Krawczyk et al. 1997   Krawczyk, H., Bellare, M. and Canetti, R. (1997). *HMAC: Keyed-Hashing for Message Authentication.* Internet RFC 2104.

Krumm *et al.* 2000   Krumm, J., Harris, S., Meyers, B., Brumitt , B., Hale, M. and Shafer, S. (2000). Multi-Camera Multi-Person Tracking for EasyLiving. *Proceedings of the Third IEEE International Workshop on Visual Surveillance (VS'2000)*, Dublin, Ireland, July, pp. 3–10.

Kshemkalyani and Singhal 1991   Kshemkalyani, A. and Singhal, M. (1991). Invariant-Based Verification of a Distributed Deadlock Detection Algorithm. *IEEE Transactions on Software Engineering*, Vol. 17, No. 8. August.

Kshemkalyani and Singhal 1994   Kshemkalyani, A. and Singhal, M. (1994). On Characterisation and Corrrectness of Distributed Deadlock detection, *Journal of Parallel and Distributed Computing*, Vol. 22, pp. 44–59.

Kubiatowicz 2003   Kubiatowicz, J. (2003). Extracting Guarantees from Chaos, *Communications of the ACM*, pp. 33–38, vol. 46, No. 2, February.

Kubiatowicz *et al.* 2000   Kubiatowicz, J., Bindel, D., Chen, Y., Czerwinski, S., Eaton, P., Geels, D., Gummadi, R., Rhea, S., Weatherspoon, H., Weimer, W., Wells, C. and Zhao, B. (2000). OceanStore: an architecture for global-scale persistent storage. *In ASPLOS 2000*, pp. 190–201, November.

Kung and Robinson 1981   Kung, H.T. and Robinson, J.T. (1981). Optimistic methods for concurrency control. *ACM Transactions on Database Systems*, Vol. 6, No. 2, pp. 213–26.

Kurose and Ross 2000   Kurose, J.F. and Ross, K.W. (2000). *Computer Networking: A Top-Down Approach Featuring the Internet*. Addison Wesley Longman.

Ladin *et al.* 1992   Ladin, R., Liskov, B., Shrira, L. and Ghemawat, S. (1992). Providing Availability Using Lazy Replication. *ACM Transactions on Computer Systems*, Vol. 10, No. 4, pp. 360–91.

Lai 1992   Lai, X. (1992). On the Design and Security of Block Ciphers, *ETH Series in Information Processing*, Vol. 1, Konstanz: Hartung-Gorre Verlag.

Lai and Massey 1990   Lai, X. and Massey, J. (1990). A proposal for a new Block Encryption Standard. *Advances in Cryptology–Eurocrypt '90*. In *Proceedings*, Springer-Verlag, pp. 389–404.

Lamport 1978   Lamport, L. (1978). Time, clocks and the ordering of events in a distributed system. *Comms. ACM*, Vol. 21, No. 7, pp. 558–65.

Lamport 1979   Lamport, L. (1979). How to Make a Multiprocessor Computer that Correctly Executes Multiprocess Programs. *IEEE Transactions Computers*, Vol. C-28, No. 9, pp. 690–1.

Lamport 1986   Lamport, L. (1986). On interprocess communication, parts I and II. *Distributed Computing*, Vol. 1, No. 2, pp. 77–101.

Lamport 1989   Lamport, L. (1989). The part-time parliament. Technical Report 49, DEC SRC, Palo Alto. (Also in *ACM Transactions on Computer Systems*, vol. 16, no. 2, pp. 133–169, 1998.)

Lamport 1998   Lamport, L. (1998). The part-time parliament. *ACM Transactions on Computer Systems (TOCS)*, Vol. 16, No. 2, May, pp. 133–69.

Lamport *et al.* 1982   Lamport, L., Shostak, R. and Pease, M. (1982). Byzantine Generals Problem. *ACM Transactions Programming Languages and Systems*, Vol. 4, No. 3, pp. 382–401.

Lampson 1971   Lampson, B. (1971). Protection. In *Proceedings 5th Princeton Conference on Information Sciences and Systems*, Princeton, p. 437. Reprinted in *ACM Operating Systems Review*. Vol. 8, No. 1, January, p. 18.

Lampson 1981   Lampson, B.W. (1981). Atomic Transactions. In *Distributed systems: Architecture and Implementation. Lecture Notes in Computer Science 105*, pp. 254–9. Berlin: Springer-Verlag.

Lampson 1986   Lampson, B.W. (1986). Designing a Global Name Service. In *Proceedings 5th ACM Symposium Principles of Distributed Computing*, pp. 1–10, August.

Lampson *et al.* 1992   Lampson, B.W., Abadi, M., Burrows, M. and Wobber, E. (1992). Authentication in Distributed Systems: Theory and Practice. *ACM Transactions on Computer Systems*, Vol. 10, No. 4, pp. 265–310.

Langheinrich 2001   Langheinrich, M. (2001). Privacy by design – principles of privacy-aware ubiquitous systems. *Proceedings Third International Conference on Ubiquitous Computing (Ubicomp 2001)*, Atlanta, GA, USA, Sep.–Oct., Springer-Verlag, pp. 273–291.

Langworthy 2004   Langworthy, D. (ed.) (2004) *Web Services Coordination (WS-Coordination)*, IBM, Microsoft, BEA. November.

Lea *et al.* 1993   Lea, R., Jacquemot, C. and Pillevesse, E. (1993). COOL: system support for distributed programming. *Comms. ACM*, Vol. 36, No. 9, pp. 37–46.

Leach *et al.* 1983   Leach, P.J., Levine, P.H., Douros, B.P., Hamilton, J.A., Nelson, D.L. and Stumpf, B.L. (1983). The architecture of an integrated local network. *IEEE J. Selected Areas in Communications*, Vol. SAC-1, No. 5, pp. 842–56.

Lee and Thekkath 1996   Lee, E.K. and Thekkath, C.A. (1996). Petal: Distributed Virtual Disks, In *Proc. 7th Intl. Conf. on Architectural Support for Prog. Langs. and Operating Systems*, October, pp. 84–96.

Lee *et al.* 1996   Lee, C., Rajkumar, R. and Mercer, C. (1996). Experiences with Processor Reservation and Dynamic QOS in Real-Time Mach. In *Proceedings Multimedia Japan '96*.

Leffler *et al.* 1989   Leffler, S., McKusick, M., Karels, M. and Quartermain, J. (1989). *The Design and Implementation of the 4.3 BSD UNIX Operating System*. Reading, MA: Addison-Wesley.

Leibowitz *et al.* 2003   Leibowitz, N., Ripeanu, M. and Wierzbicki, A. (2003). Deconstructing the Kazaa Network. in *3rd IEEE Workshop on Internet Applications (WIAPP'03)*. Santa Clara, CA.

Leiner 1997   Leiner, B.M., Cerf, V.G., Clark, D.D., Kahn, R.E., Kleinrock, L., Lynch, D.C., Postel, J., Roberts, L.G. and Wolff, S. (1997). A Brief History of the Internet, *Comms. ACM*, Vol. 40, No. 1, Feb., pp. 102–108.

Leland *et al.* 1993   Leland, W.E., Taqqu, M.S., Willinger, W. and Wilson, D.V. (1993). On the Self-Similar Nature of Ethernet Traffic. *ACM SIGCOMM '93*, San Francisco.

Lenoski *et al.* 1992   Lenoski, D., Laudon, J., Gharachorloo, K., Weber, W.D., Gupta, A., Hennessy, J., Horowitz, M. and Lam, M.S. (1992). The Stanford Dash multiprocessor, *IEEE Computer*, Vol. 25, No. 3, pp. 63–79.

Leslie *et al.* 1996   Leslie, I., McAuley, D., Black, R., Roscoe, T., Barham, P., Evers, D., Fairbairns, R. and Hyden, E. (1996). The design and implementation of an operating system to support distributed multimedia applications, *ACM Journal of Selected Areas in Communication*, Vol. 14, No. 7, pp. 1280–97.

Li and Hudak 1989   Li, K. and Hudak, P. (1989). Memory Coherence in Shared Virtual Memory Systems. *ACM Transactions on Computer Systems*, Vol. 7, No. 4, pp. 321–59.

Liedtke 1996	Liedtke, J. (1996). Towards real microkernels, *Comms. ACM*, Vol. 39, No. 9, pp. 70–7.
Linux AFS	*The Linux AFS FAQ.*
Lipton and Sandberg 1988	Lipton, R. and Sandberg, J. (1988). *PRAM: A scalable shared memory.* Technical Report CS-TR-180-88, Princeton University.
Liskov 1988	Liskov, B. (1988). Distributed programming in Argus. *Comms. ACM*, Vol. 31, No. 3, pp. 300–12.
Liskov 1993	Liskov, B. (1993). Practical uses of synchronized clocks in distributed systems, *Distributed Computing*, Vol. 6, No. 4, pp. 211–19.
Liskov and Scheifler 1982	Liskov, B. and Scheifler, R.W. (1982). Guardians and actions: linguistic support for robust, distributed programs. *ACM Transactions Programming Languages and Systems*, Vol. 5, No. 3, pp. 381–404.
Liskov and Shrira 1988	Liskov, B. and Shrira, L. (1988). Promises: Linguistic Support for Efficient Asynchronous Procedure Calls in Distributed Systems. In *Proceedings SIGPLAN '88 Conference Programming Language Design and Implementation*. Atlanta.
Liskov *et al.* 1991	Liskov, B., Ghemawat, S., Gruber, R., Johnson, P., Shrira, L., Williams, M. (1991). Replication in the Harp File System. In *Proceedings 13th ACM Symposium on Operating System Principles*, pp. 226–38.
Liu and Albitz 1998	Liu, C. and Albitz, P. (1998). *DNS and BIND*, third edition. O'Reilly.
Liu and Layland 1973	Liu, C.L. and Layland, J.W. (1973). Scheduling Algorithms for Multiprogramming in a Hard Real-Time Environment. *Journal of the ACM*, Vol. 20, No. 1.
Loepere 1991	Loepere, K. (1991). *Mach 3 Kernel Principles*. Open Software Foundation and Carnegie-Mellon University.
Lundelius and Lynch 1984	Lundelius, J. and Lynch, N. (1984). An Upper and Lower Bound for Clock Synchronization. *Information and Control* 62, 2/3 (Aug./Sep.), pp. 190–204.
Lynch 1996	Lynch, N. (1996). *Distributed Algorithms*. Morgan Kaufmann.
Ma 1992	Ma, C. (1992). *Designing a Universal Name Service*. Technical Report 270, University of Cambridge.
Macklem 1994	Macklem, R. (1994). Not Quite NFS: Soft Cache Consistency for NFS. *Proceedings of the Winter '94 USENIX Conference*, San Francisco, CA, January, pp. 261–278.
Madhavapeddy *et al.* 2003	Madhavapeddy, A., Scott, D., Sharp, R. (2003). Context-aware computing with sound. *Proceedings Fifth International Conference on Ubiquitous Computing (Ubicomp 2003)*, Seattle, WA, USA, October, pp. 315–332.

Maekawa 1985 — Maekawa, M. (1985). A $\sqrt{N}$ Algorithm for Mutual Exclusion in Decentralized Systems. *ACM Transactions on Computer System*s, Vol. 3, No. 2, pp. 145–159.

Maffcis 1995 — Maffeis, S. (1995). Adding group communication and fault tolerance to CORBA. In *Proceedings of the 1995 USENIX conference on object-oriented technologies*. Monterey, CA, USA. pp. 135–146.

Malkin 1993 — Malkin, G. (1993). *RIP Version 2 – Carrying Additional Information*, Internet RFC 1388.

Marsh *et al.* 1991 — Marsh, B., Scott, M., LeBlanc, T. and Markatos, E. (1991). First-class User-level Threads. In *Proceedings 13th ACM Symposium on Operating System Principles*, pp. 110–21.

Martin *et al.* 2004 — Martin, T., Hsiao, M., Ha, D. and Krishnaswami, J. (2004). Denial-of-Service Attacks on Battery-powered Mobile Computers. *Proceedings 2nd IEEE Pervasive Computing Conference*, Orlando, FL, USA, March, pp. 309–318.

Marzullo and Neiger 1991 — Marzullo, K., and Neiger, G. (1991). Detection of global state predicates, In Toug, S., Spirakis, P. and Kirousis, L. (eds), *Proceedings 5th International Workshop on Distributed Algorithms*. Springer-Verlag, pp. 254–72.

Mattern 1989 — Mattern, F. (1989). Virtual Time and Global States in Distributed Systems. In Cosnard, M. *et al.* (eds), *Proceedings Workshop on Parallel and Distributed Algorithm*s. Amsterdam: North-Holland, pp. 215–26.

Maymounkov and Mazieres 2002 — Maymounkov, P. and Mazieres, D. (2002). Kademlia: A peer-to-peer information system based on the xor metric. In *Proceedings of IPTPS02*, Cambridge, USA, March.

mbone — *BIBs: Introduction to the Multicast Backbone.*

McGraw and Felden 1999 — McGraw, G. and Felden, E. (1999). *Securing Java*. John Wiley & Sons.

Melliar-Smith *et al.* 1990 — Melliar-Smith, P., Moser, L. and Agrawala, V. (1990). Broadcast Protocols for Distributed Systems. *IEEE Transactions on Parallel and Distributed Systems*, Vol. 1, No. 1, pp. 17–25.

Menezes 1993 — Menezes, A. (1993). *Elliptic Curve Public Key Cryptosystems*. Kluwer Academic Publishers.

Menezes *et al.* 1997 — Menezes, A., van Oorschot, O. and Vanstone, S. (1997). *Handbook of Applied Cryptography*. CRC Press.

Metcalfe and Boggs 1976 — Metcalfe, R.M. and Boggs, D.R. (1976). Ethernet: distributed packet switching for local computer networks. *Comms. ACM*, Vol. 19, pp. 395–403.

Milanovic *et al.* 2004   Milanovic, N., Malek, M., Davidson, A. and Milutinovic, V. (2004). Routing and Security in Mobile Ad Hoc Networks. *IEEE Computer*, Vol. 37, No. 2, February, pp. 69–73.

Mills 1995   Mills, D. (1995). Improved Algorithms for Synchronizing Computer Network Clocks, *IEEE Transactions Networks*, June, pp. 245–54.

Milojicic *et al.* 1999   Milojicic, J., Douglis, F. and Wheeler, R. (1999). *Mobility, Processes, Computers and Agents*. Reading: Addison-Wesley.

Minnich and Farber 1989   Minnich, R. and Farber, D. (1989). The Mether System: a Distributed Shared Memory for SunOS 4.0. In *Proceedings Summer 1989 Usenix Conference*.

Mitchell and Dion 1982   Mitchell, J.G. and Dion, J. (1982). A comparison of two network-based file servers. *Comms. ACM*, Vol. 25, No. 4, pp. 233–45.

Mitchell *et al.* 1992   Mitchell, C.J., Piper, F. and Wild, P. (1992). Digital Signatures. In Simmons, G.J. (ed.), *Contemporary Cryptology*. New York: IEEE Press.

Mockapetris 1987   Mockapetris, P. (1987). *Domain names – concepts and facilities*. Internet RFC 1034. November.

Mogul 1994   Mogul, J.D. (1994). Recovery in Spritely NFS, *Computing Systems*, Vol. 7, No. 2.

Mok 1985   Mok, A.K. (1985). SARTOR – A Design Environment for Real-Time Systems. *Ninth IEEE COMP-SAC*.

Morin 1997   Morin, R. (ed.) (1997). *MkLinux: Microkernel Linux for the Power Macintosh*. Prime Time Freeware.

Morris *et al.* 1986   Morris, J., Satyanarayanan, M., Conner, M.H., Howard, J.H., Rosenthal, D.S. and Smith, F.D. (1986). Andrew: a distributed personal computing environment. *Comms. ACM*, Vol. 29, No. 3, pp. 184–201.

Mosberger 1993   Mosberger, D. (1993). *Memory Consistency Models*. Technical Report 93/11, University of Arizona.

Moser *et al.* 1994   Moser, L., Amir, Y., Melliar-Smith, P. and Agarwal, D. (1994). Extended Virtual Synchrony. In *Proceedings 14th International Conference on Distributed Computing Systems*, IEEE Computer Society Press, pp. 56–65.

Moser *et al.* 1996   Moser, L., Melliar-Smith, P., Agarwal, D., Budhia, R., and Lingley-Papadopoulos, C. (1996). Totem: a Fault-Tolerant Multicast Group Communication System. *Comms. ACM*, Vol. 39, No. 4, pp. 54–63.

Moser *et al.* 1998   Moser, L., Melliar-Smith, P. and Narasimhan, P. (1998). Consistent object replication in the Eternal system. *Theory and practice of object systems*, Vol. 4, No. 2.

Moss 1985	Moss, E. (1985). *Nested Transactions, An Approach to Reliable Distributed Computing*. MIT Press.
Multimedia Directory 2005	Multimedia Directory (2005). Scala Inc.
Murphy *et al.* 2001	Murphy, A.L., Picco, G.P. and Roman, G.-C. (2001). Lime: A Middleware for Physical and Logical Mobility. *Proceedings 21st International Conference on Distributed Computing Systems (ICDCS-21)*, Phoenix, AZ, USA, April, pp. 524–233.
Muthitacharoen *et al.* 2002	Muthitacharoen, A., Morris, R., Gil, T.M. and Chen, B. (2002). Ivy: A Read/Write Peer-to-peer File System. In *Fifth Symposium on Operating Systems Design and Implementation (OSDI)*. Boston, MA. December.
Myers and Liskov 1997	Myers, A.C. and Liskov, B. (1997). A Decentralized Model for Information Flow Control, *ACM Operating Systems Review*, Vol. 31, No. 5, pp. 129–42, December.
Nagle 1984	Nagle, J. (1984). Congestion Control in TCP/IP Internetworks, *Computer Communications Review*, Vol. 14, pp. 11–17, October.
Nagle 1987	Nagle, J. (1987). On Packet Switches with Infinite Storage. *IEEE Transactions on Communications*, Vol. 35, No. 4.
National Bureau of Standards 1977	National Bureau of Standards (1977). *Data Encryption Standard (DES)*. Federal Information Processing Standards No. 46, Washington DC: US National Bureau of Standards.
nbcr.sdsc.edu	National Biomedical Computation Resource, University of California, San Diego.
Needham 1993	Needham, R. (1993). Names. In Mullender, S. (ed.), *Distributed Systems, an Advanced Course*, 2nd edn. Wokingham, England: ACM Press/Addison-Wesley. pp. 315–26.
Needham and Schroeder 1978	Needham, R.M. and Schroeder, M.D. (1978). Using encryption for authentication in large networks of computers. *Comms. ACM*, Vol. 21, pp. 993–9.
Nelson *et al.* 1988	Nelson, M.N., Welch, B.B. and Ousterhout, J.K. (1988). Caching in the Sprite Network File System, *ACM Transactions on Computer Systems*, Vol. 6, No. 1, pp. 134–154.
Netscape 1996	Netscape Corporation (1996). *SSL 3.0 Specification*.
Neuman et al. 1999	Neuman, B.C., Tung, B. and Wray, J. (1999). *Public Key Cryptography for Initial Authentication in Kerberos*, Internet Draft ietf-cat-kerberos-pk-init-09, July.
Neumann and Ts'o 1994	Neuman, B.C. and Ts'o, T. (1994). Kerberos: An Authentication Service for Computer Networks, *IEEE Communications*, vol. 32, no. 9, pp. 33–38. Sept.
Newcomer 2002	Newcomer, E. (2002). *Understanding Web Services XML, WSDL, SOAP and UDDI*. Boston: Pearson.

<u>Nielsen and Thatte 2001</u>	Nielsen, H.F. and Thatte, S. (2001). *Web Services Routing Protocol (WS-Routing)*. Microsoft Corporation. October.
Nielson *et al.* 1997	Nielsen, H., Gettys, J., Baird-Smith, A., Prud'hommeaux, E., Lie, H. and Lilley, C. (1997). Network Performance Effects of HTTP/1.1, CSS1, and PNG. *Proceedings SIGCOMM '97*.
<u>NIST 1994</u>	National Institute for Standards and Technology (1994). *Digital Signature Standard*, NIST FIPS 186. US Department of Commerce.
<u>NIST 1999</u>	National Institute for Standards and Technology (1999). *AES – a Crypto Algorithm for the Twenty-first Century*, US Department of Commerce.
<u>NIST 2002</u>	National Institute for Standards and Technology (2002). *Secure Hash Standard*. NIST FIPS 180-2 + Change Notice to include SHA-224, US Department of Commerce.
<u>NIST 2004</u>	National Institute for Standards and Technology (2004). *NIST Brief Comments on Recent Cryptanalytic Attacks on Secure Hashing Functions and the Continued Security Provided by SHA-1*, US Department of Commerce, August.
Noble and Satyanarayanan 1999	Noble, B. and Satyanarayanan, M. (1999). Experience with Adaptive Mobile Applications in Odyssey. *Mobile Networks and Applications*, Vol. 4 , No. 4, December, pp. 245–254.
<u>now.cs.berkeley.edu</u>	*The Berkeley NOW project home page.*
Oaks and Wong 1999	Oaks, S. and Wong, H. (1999). *Jave Threads*, 2nd edn., O'Reilly.
Ohkubo *et al.* 2003	Ohkubo, M., Suzuki, K. and Kinoshita, S. (2003). Cryptographic approach to 'privacy-friendly' tags. *Proceedings RFID Privacy Workshop*, MIT, USA.
<u>Olson and Ogbuji 2002</u>	Olson, M. and Ogbuji, U. (2002) *Choose the best tool for the task at hand.*
<u>OMG 2000a</u>	Object Management Group (2000). *Trading Object Service Specification*,Vn. 1.0. Needham, MA: OMG.
<u>OMG 2000b</u>	Object Management Group (2000). *Concurrency Control Service Specification*, Needham, MA: OMG.
<u>OMG 2002a</u>	Object Management Group (2002). *The CORBA IDL Specification.* Needham, MA: OMG.
<u>OMG 2002b</u>	Object Management Group (2002). *CORBA Security Service Specification* Vn. 1.8. Needham, MA: OMG.
<u>OMG 2002c</u>	Object Management Group (2002). *Value Type Semantics*. Needham, MA: OMG.
<u>OMG 2002d</u>	Object Management Group (2002). *Life Cycle Service*, Vn. 1.2. Needham, MA: OMG.
<u>OMG 2002e</u>	Object Management Group (2002). *Persistent State Service*, Vn. 2.0. Needham, MA: OMG.

OMG 2003   Object Management Group, (2003). *Object Transaction Service Specification. Version 1.4*. Needham, MA: OMG.

OMG 2004a   Object Management Group (2004). *CORBA/IIOP 3.0.3 Specification*. Needham, MA: OMG.

OMG 2004b   Object Management Group (2004). *Naming Service Specification*. Needham, MA: OMG.

OMG 2004c   Object Management Group (2004). *Event Service Specification*. Vn. 1.2. Needham, MA: OMG.

OMG 2004d   Object Management Group (2004). *Notification service Specification*. Vn. 1.1. Needham, MA: OMG. Technical report telecom/98-06-15.

OMG 2004e   Object Management Group (2004). *CORBA Messaging*. Needham, MA: OMG.

Omidyar and Aldridge 1993   Omidyar, C.G. and Aldridge, A. (1993). Introduction to SDH/SONET. *IEEE Communications Magazine*, Vol. 31, pp. 30–3, Sept.

OpenNap 2001   OpenNap: Open Source Napster Server, Beta release 0.44, September 2001.

Oppen and Dalal 1983   Oppen, D.C. and Dalal Y.K. (1983). The Clearinghouse: a decentralized agent for locating named objects in a distributed environment. *ACM Trans. on Office Systems*, Vol. 1, pp. 230–53.

Oram 2001   Oram, A. (2001). *Peer-to-Peer: Harnessing the Benefits of Disruptive Technologies*, O'Reilly, Sebastapol, CA.

Orfali *et al.* 1996   Orfali, R., Harkey, D. and Edwards, J. (1996). *The Essential Distributed Objects Survival Guide*. New York: Wiley.

Orfali *et al.* 1997   Orfali, R., Harkey, D., and Edwards, J. (1997) *Instant CORBA*. New York: Wiley.

Organick 1972   Organick, E.I. (1972). *The MULTICS System: An Examination of its Structure*. Cambridge, MA: MIT Press.

Orman *et al.* 1993   Orman, H., Menze, E., O'Malley, S. and Peterson, L. (1993). A fast and general implementation of Mach IPC in a Network. In *Proceedings Third USENIX Mach Conference*, April.

OSF 1997   *Introduction to OSF DCE*. The Open Group.

Ousterhout *et al.* 1985   Ousterhout, J., Da Costa, H., Harrison, D., Kunze, J., Kupfer, M. and Thompson, J. (1985). A Trace-driven analysis of the UNIX 4.2 BSD file system. In *10th ACM Symposium Operating System Principles*.

Ousterhout *et al.* 1988   Ousterhout, J., Cherenson, A., Douglis, F., Nelson, M. and Welch, B. (1988). The Sprite Network Operating System. *IEEE Computer,* Vol. 21, No. 2, pp. 23–36.

Parker 1992   Parker, B. (1992). *The PPP AppleTalk Control Protocol (ATCP)*. Internet RFC 1378.

Parrington *et al.* 1995
Parrington, G.D., Shrivastava, S.K., Wheater, S.M. and Little, M.C. (1995). The Design and Implementation of Arjuna, *USENIX Computing Systems Journal*, Vol. 8, No. 3.

Partridge 1992
Partridge, C. (1992). *A Proposed Flow Specification*. Internet RFC 1363.

Patel and Abowd 2003
Patel, S.N. and Abowd, G.D. (2003). A 2-way Laser-assisted Selection Scheme for Handhelds in a Physical Environment. *Proceedings Fifth International Conference on Ubiquitous Computing (Ubicomp 2003)*, Seattle, WA, USA, October, pp. 200–207.

Patterson *et al.* 1988
Patterson, D., Gibson, G. and Katz, R. (1988). A Case for Redundant Arrays of Interactive Disks, ACM *International Conf. on Management of Data (SIGMOD)*, pp. 109–116, May.

Pease *et al.* 1980
Pease, M., Shostak, R. and Lamport, L. (1980). Reaching agreement in the presence of faults. *Journal of the ACM*, Vol. 27, No. 2, April, pp. 228–34.

Pedone and Schiper 1999
Pedone, F. and Schiper, A. (1999). Generic Broadcast. In *Proceedings of the 13th International Symposium on Distributed Computing* (DISC '99), September.

Perrig *et al.* 2002
Perrig, A., Szewczyk, R., Wen, V., Culler, D. and Tygar, D. (2002). SPINS: Security Protocols for Sensor Networks. *Wireless Networks*, Vol. 8, No. 5, September, pp. 521–534.

Petersen *et al.* 1997
Petersen, K., Spreitzer, M., Terry, D., Theimer, M. and Demers, A. (1997). Flexible update propagation for weakly consistent replication. *Proceedings of the 16th ACM Symposium on Operating Systems Principles*, pp. 288–301.

Peterson 1988
Peterson, L. (1988). The Profile Naming Service. *ACM Transactions Computer Systems*, Vol. 6, No. 4, pp. 341–64.

Peterson *et al.* 1989
Peterson, L.L., Buchholz, N.C. and Schlichting, R.D. (1989). Preserving and Using Context Information in Interprocess Communication. *ACM Transactions on Computer Systems*, Vol. 7, No. 3, pp. 217–46.

Pike *et al.* 1993
Pike, R., Presotto, D., Thompson, K., Trickey, H. and Winterbottom, P. (1993). The Use of Name Spaces in Plan 9. *Operating Systems Review*, Vol. 27, No. 2, April 1993, pp. 72–76.

Plaxton *et al.* 1997
Plaxton, C.G., Rajaraman, R. and Richa, A.W. (1997). Accessing nearby copies of replicated objects in a distributed environment. *ACM Symposium on Parallel Algorithms and Architectures*, pp. 311–320.

Ponnekanti and Fox 2004
Ponnekanti, S. and Fox, A. (2004). Interoperability among Independently Evolving Web Services. *Proceedings ACM/Usenix/IFIP 5th International Middleware Conference*, Toronto, Canada, September.

Ponnekanti *et al.* 2001	Ponnekanti, S.R., Lee, B., Fox, A., Hanrahan, P. and Winograd, T. (2001). ICrafter: A Service Framework for Ubiquitous Computing Environments. *Proceedings Third International Conference on Ubiquitous Computing (Ubicomp 2001)*, Atlanta, GA, USA, Sep.–Oct., Springer-Verlag, pp. 56–75.
Popek and Walker 1985	Popek, G. and Walker, B. (eds) (1985). *The LOCUS Distributed System Architecture*. Cambridge, MA: MIT Press.
Postel 1981a	Postel, J. (1981). *Internet Protocol*. Internet RFC 791.
Postel 1981b	Postel, J. (1981). *Transmission Control Protocol*. Internet RFC 793.
Pottie and Kaiser 2000	Pottie, G.J. and Kaiser, W.J. (2000). Embedding the internet: wireless integrated network sensors. *Comms. ACM*, Vol. 43, No. 5, May, pp. 51–58.
Powell 1991	Powell, D. (ed.) (1991). *Delta-4: a Generic Architecture for Dependable Distributed Computing*. Berlin and New York: Springer-Verlag.
Pradhan and Chiueh 1998	Pradhan, P. and Chiueh, T. (1998). Real-Time Performance Guarantees over Wired and Wireless LANS, in *IEEE Conference on Real-Time Applications and Systems*, RTAS'98, June.
Preneel *et al.* 1998	Preneel, B., Rijmen, V. and Bosselaers, A. (1998). Recent developments in the design of conventional cryptographic algorithms. In *Computer Security and Industrial Cryptography, State of the Art and Evolution*, Lecture Notes in Computer Science, No. 1528, Springer-Verlag, pp. 106–131.
privacy.nb.ca	*International Cryptography Freedom*.
Radia *et al.* 1993	Radia, S., Nelson, M. and Powell, M. (1993). *The Spring Naming Service*. Technical Report 93–16, Sun Microsystems Laboratories, Inc.
Raman and McCanne 1999	Raman, S. and McCanne, S. (1999). A model, analysis, and protocol framework for soft state-based communication. *Proceedings ACM SIGCOMM*, Cambridge, MA, USA, September, pp. 15–25.
Randall and Szydlo 2004	Randall, J. and Szydlo, M. (2004). Collisions for SHA0, MD5, HAVAL, MD4, and RIPEMD, but SHA1 still secure, *RSA Laboratories Technical Note*, August 31.
Rashid 1985	Rashid, R.F. (1985). Network operating systems. In *Local Area Networks: An Advanced Course, Lecture Notes in Computer Science*, 184, Springer-Verlag, pp. 314–40.
Rashid 1986	Rashid, R.F. (1986). From RIG to Accent to Mach: the evolution of a network operating system. In *Proceedings of the ACM/IEEE Computer Society Fall Joint Conference*, ACM, November.

Rashid and Robertson 1981	Rashid, R. and Robertson, G. (1981). Accent: a communications oriented network operating system kernel. *ACM Operating Systems Review*, Vol. 15, No. 5, pp. 64–75.
Rashid *et al.* 1988	Rashid, R., Tevanian Jr, A., Young, M., Golub, D., Baron, R., Black, D., Bolosky, W.J. and Chew, J. (1988). Machine-Independent Virtual Memory Management for Paged Uniprocessor and Multiprocessor Architectures. *IEEE Transactions Computers*, Vol. 37, No. 8, pp. 896–907.
Ratnasamy *et al.* 2001	Ratnasamy, S., Francis, P., Handley, M., Karp, R. and Shenker, S. (2001). A scalable content-addressable network. In *Proc. ACM SIGCOMM 2001*, August.
Raynal 1988	Raynal, M. (1988). *Distributed Algorithms and Protocols*. Wiley.
Raynal 1992	Raynal, M. (1992). About Logical Clocks for Distributed Systems. *ACM Operating Systems Review*, Vol. 26, No. 1, pp. 41–8.
Raynal and Singhal 1996	Raynal, M. and Singhal, M. (1996). Capturing Causality in Distributed Systems. *IEEE Computer*, February, pp. 49–56.
Redmond 1997	Redmond, F.E. (1997). *DCOM: Microsoft Distributed Component Model*. IDG Books Worldwide.
Reed 1983	Reed, D.P. (1983). Implementing atomic actions on decentralized data. *ACM Transactions on Computer Systems*, Vol. 1, No. 1, pp. 3–23.
Rescorla 1999	Rescorla, E. (1999). *Diffie-Hellman Key Agreement Method*. Internet RFC 2631.
Rether	Rether: A Real-Time Ethernet Protocol.
Rhea *et al.* 2001	Rhea, S., Wells, C., Eaton, P., Geels, D., Zhao, B., Weatherspoon, H. and Kubiatowicz, J. (2001). Maintenance-Free Global Data Storage, *IEEE Internet Computing*, Vol 5, No 5, September/October, pp. 40–49.
Rhea *et al.* 2003	Rhea, S., Eaton, P., Geels, D., Weatherspoon, H., Zhao, B. and Kubiatowicz, J. (2003). Pond: the OceanStore Prototype, *Proceedings of the 2nd USENIX Conference on File and Storage Technologies (FAST '03)*.
Ricart and Agrawala 1981	Ricart, G. and Agrawala, A.K. (1981). An optimal algorithm for mutual exclusion in computer networks. *Comms. ACM*, Vol. 24, No. 1, pp. 9–17.
Richardson *et al.* 1998	Richardson, T., Stafford-Fraser, Q., Wood, K.R. and Hopper, A. (1998). Virtual Network Computing, *IEEE Internet Computing*. Vol. 2, No. 1, Jan/Feb, pp. 33–8.
Ritchie 1984	Ritchie, D. (1984). A Stream Input Output System. *AT&T Bell Laboratories Technical Journal*, Vol. 63, No. 8, pt 2, pp. 1897–910.
Rivest 1992	Rivest, R. (1992). *The MD5 Message-Digest Algorithm*. Internet RFC 1321.

Rivest 1992a	Rivest, R. (1992). The RC4 Encryption Algorithm, RSA Data Security Inc.
Rivest *et al.* 1978	Rivest, R.L., Shamir, A. and Adelman, L. (1978). A method of obtaining digital signatures and public key cryptosystems. *Comms. ACM*, Vol. 21, No. 2, pp. 120–6.
Rodrigues *et al.* 1998	Rodrigues, L., Guerraoui, R. and Schiper, A. (1998). Scalable Atomic Multicast. In *Proceedings IEEE IC3N '98*. Technical Report 98/257. École polytechnique fédérale de Lausanne.
Rose 1992	Rose, M.T. (1992). *The Little Black Book: Mail Bonding with OSI Directory Services*. Englewood Cliffs, NJ: Prentice-Hall.
Rosenblum and Ousterhout 1992	Rosenblum, M. and Ousterhout, J. (1992). The Design and Implementation of a Log-Structured File System, *ACM Transactions on Computer Systems*, Vol. 10, No. 1, February, pp. 26–52.
Rosenblum and Wolf 1997	Rosenblum, D.S. and Wolf, A.L. (1997). A Design Framework for Internet-Scale Event Observation and Notification. In *Proceedings sixth European Software Engineering Conference/ACM SIGSOFT Fifth Symposium on the Foundations of Software Engineering*, Zurich, Switzerland.
Rowley 1998	Rowley, A. (1998). *A Security Architecture for Groupware*, Doctoral Thesis, Queen Mary and Westfield College, University of London.
Rowstron and Druschel 2001	Rowstron, A. and Druschel, P. (2001). Pastry: Scalable, distributed object location and routing for large-scale peer-to-peer systems. In *Proc. IFIP/ACM Middleware 2001*, Heidelberg, Germany, Nov.
Rozier *et al.* 1988	Rozier, M., Abrossimov, V., Armand, F., Boule, I., Gien, M., Guillemont, M., Herrman, F., Kaiser, C., Langlois, S., Leonard, P. and Neuhauser, W. (1988). Chorus Distributed Operating Systems. *Computing Systems Journal*, Vol. 1, No. 4, pp. 305–70.
Rozier *et al.* 1990	Rozier, M., Abrossimov, V., Armand, F., Boule, I., Gien, M., Guillemont, M., Herrman, F., Kaiser, C., Langlois, S., Leonard, P. and Neuhauser, W. (1990). *Overview of the Chorus Distributed Operating System*. Technical Report CS/TR-90-25.1, Chorus Systèmes, France.
RTnet	RTnet: Hard Real-Time Networking for Linux/RTAI.
Salber *et al.* 1999	Salber, D., Dey, A.K. and Abowd, G.D. (1999). The Context Toolkit: Aiding the Development of Context-Enabled Applications. *Proceedings of the 1999 Conference on Human Factors in Computing Systems (CHI '99)*, Pittsburgh, PA, May, pp. 434–441.
Saltzer *et al.* 1984	Saltzer, J.H., Reed, D.P. and Clarke, D. (1984). End-to-End Arguments in System Design, *ACM Transactions on Computer Systems* Vol. 2, No. 4, pp. 277–88.

Sandberg 1987   Sandberg, R. (1987). *The Sun Network File System: Design, Implementation and Experience*. Technical Report. Mountain View, CA: Sun Microsystems.

Sandberg *et al.* 1985   Sandberg, R., Goldberg, D., Kleiman, S., Walsh, D. and Lyon, B. (1985). The Design and Implementation of the Sun Network File System. In *Proceedings Usenix Conference*, Portland, OR.

Sandholm and Gawor 2003   Sandholm, T. and Gawor, J. (2003). *Globus Toolkit 3 Core – A Grid Service Container Framework*. July.

Sandhu *et al.* 1996   Sandhu, R., Coyne, E., Felstein, H. and Youman, C. (1996). Role-Based Access Control Models, *IEEE Computer*, Vol. 29, No. 2, February.

Sane *et al.* 1990   Sane, A., MacGregor, K. and Campbell, R. (1990). Distributed Virtual Memory Consistency Protocols: Design and Performance. *Second IEEE Workshop on Experimental Distributed Systems*, pp. 91–6, October.

Sansom *et al.* 1986   Sansom, R.D., Julin, D.P. and Rashid, R.F. (1986). *Extending a capability based system into a network environment*. Technical Report CMU-CS-86-116, Carnegie-Mellon University.

Santifaller 1991   Santifaller, M. (1991). *TCP/IP and NFS, Internetworking in a Unix Environment*. Reading, MA: Addison-Wesley.

Saroiu *et al.* 2002   Saroiu, S., Gummadi, P. and Gribble, S. (2002). A Measurement Study of Peer-to-Peer File Sharing Systems, In *Proc. Multimedia Computing and Networking (MMCN)*, 2002.

Sastry *et al.* 2003   Sastry, N., Shankar, U. and Wagner, D. (2003). Secure Verification of Location Claims. *Proceedings ACM Workshop on Wireless Security (WiSe 2003)*, September, pp. 1–10.

Satyanarayanan 1981   Satyanarayanan, M. (1981). A study of file sizes and functional lifetimes. In *Proceedings 8th ACM Symposium on Operating System Principles*, Asilomar, CA.

Satyanarayanan 1989a   Satyanarayanan, M. (1989). Distributed File Systems. In Mullender, S. (ed.), *Distributed Systems, an Advanced Course*, 2nd edn, Wokingham: ACM Press/Addison-Wesley. pp. 353–83.

Satyanarayanan 1989b   Satyanarayanan, M. (1989). Integrating Security in a Large Distributed System. *ACM Transactions on Computer Systems*, Vol. 7, No. 3, pp. 247–80.

Satyanarayanan 2001   Satyanarayanan, M. (2001). Pervasive computing: Vision and challenges. *IEEE Personal Communications*, Vol. 8, No. 4, August, pp. 10–17.

Satyanarayanan *et al.* 1990   Satyanarayanan, M., Kistler, J.J., Kumar, P., Okasaki, M.E., Siegel, E.H. and Steere, D.C. (1990). Coda: A Highly Available File System for a Distributed Workstation Environment. *IEEE Transactions on Computers*, Vol. 39, No. 4, pp. 447–59.

Saunders 1987	Saunders, B. (1987). The Information Structure of Distributed Mutual Exclusion Algorithms. *ACM Transactions on Computer Systems*, Vol. 3, No. 2, pp. 145–59.
Scheifler and Gettys 1986	Scheifler, R.W. and Gettys, J. (1986). The X window system. *ACM Transactions on Computer Graphics*, Vol. 5, No. 2, pp. 76–109.
Schilit *et al.* 1994	Schilit, B.N., Adams, N.I. and Want, R. (1994). Context-Aware Computing Applications. *Proceedings of the IEEE Workshop on Mobile Computing Systems and Applications*, Santa Cruz, CA, December, pp. 85–90.
Schiper and Raynal 1996	Schiper, A. and Raynal, M. (1996). From Group Communication to Transactions in Distributed Systems. *Comms. ACM*, Vol. 39, No. 4, pp. 84–7.
Schiper and Sandoz 1993	Schiper, A. and Sandoz, A. (1993). Uniform reliable multicast in a virtually synchronous environment. *Proceedings 13th International Conference on Distributed Computing Systems*, IEEE Computer Society Press, pp. 561–8.
Schlageter 1982	Schlageter, G. (1982). Problems of Optimistic Concurrency Control in Distributed Database Systems, *SigMOD Record,* Vol. 13, No. 3, pp. 62–6.
Schmidt 1998	Schmidt, D. (1998). Evaluating architectures for multithreaded object request brokers, *Comms. ACM*, Vol. 44, No. 10, pp. 54–60.
Schneider 1990	Schneider, F.B. (1990). Implementing Fault-tolerant Services Using the State Machine Approach: A Tutorial. *ACM Computing Surveys*, Vol. 22, No. 4, pp. 300–19.
Schneider 1996	Schneider, S. (1996). Security properties and CSP. In *IEEE Symposium, on Security and Privacy*, pp. 174–187.
Schneier 1996	Schneier, B. (1996). *Applied Cryptography*, second edition. New York: John Wiley.
Schroeder and Burrows 1990	Schroeder, M. and Burrows, M. (1990). The Performance of Firefly RPC. *ACM Transactions on Computer Systems*, Vol. 8, No. 1. pp. 1–17.
Schroeder *et al.* 1984	Schroeder, M.D., Birrell, A.D. and Needham, R.M. (1984). Experience with Grapevine: The growth of a distributed system, *ACM Transactions on Computer Systems*, Vol. 2, No. 1.
Schulzrinne et al. 1996	Schulzrinne, H., Casner, S., Frederick, D. and Jacobson, V. (1996). *RTP:A Transport Protocol for Real-Time Applications*, Internet RFC 1889, January.
Seetharamanan 1998	Seetharamanan, K. (ed.) (1998). Special Issue: The CORBA Connection, *Comms. ACM*, October, Vol. 41, No. 10.
session directory	*User Guide to sd (Session Directory).*

Shannon 1949	Shannon, C.E. (1949). Communication Theory of Secrecy Systems, *Bell System Technical Journal*, Vol. 28, No. 4, pp. 656–715.
Shepler 1999	Shepler, S. (1999). *NFS Version 4 Design Considerations*, Internet RFC 2624, Sun Microsystems, June.
Shih *et al.* 2002	Shih, E., Bahl, P. and Sinclair, M. (2002). Wake on Wireless: An Event Driven Energy Saving Strategy for Battery Operated Devices. *Proceedings of the Eighth Annual ACM Conference on Mobile Computing and Networking*, Altanta, GA, USA, September, pp. 160–171.
Shirky 2000	Shirky, C. (2000). What's P2P and What's Not, 11/24/2000. Internet publication.
Shoch and Hupp 1980	Shoch, J.F. and Hupp, J.A. (1980). Measured performance of an Ethernet local network. *Comms. ACM*, Vol. 23, No. 12, pp. 711–21.
Shoch and Hupp 1982	Shoch, J.F. and Hupp, J.A. (1982). The 'Worm' programs – early experience with a distributed computation. *Comms. ACM*, Vol. 25, No. 3, pp. 172–80.
Shoch *et al.* 1982	Shoch, J.F., Dalal, Y.K. and Redell, D.D. (1982). The evolution of the Ethernet local area network. *IEEE Computer*, Vol. 15, No. 8, pp. 10–28.
Shoch *et al.* 1985	Shoch, J.F., Dalal, Y.K., Redell, D.D. and Crane, R.C. (1985). The Ethernet. In *Local Area Networks: an Advanced Course, Lecture Notes in Computer Science*. No. 184, Springer-Verlag, pp. 1–33.
Shrivastava *et al.* 1991	Shrivastava, S., Dixon, G.N. and Parrington, G.D. (1991). An Overview of the Arjuna Distributed Programming System. *IEEE Software*, January, pp. 66–73.
Singh 1999	Singh, S. (1999). *The Code Book*. London: Fourth Estate.
Sinha and Natarajan 1985	Sinha, M. and Natarajan, N. (1985). A Priority Based Distributed Deadlock Detection Algorithm. *IEEE Transactions on Software Engineering*. Vol. 11, No. 1, pp. 67–80.
Spafford 1989	Spafford, E.H. (1989). The Internet Worm: Crisis and Aftermath. *Comms. ACM*, Vol. 32, No. 6, pp. 678–87.
Spasojevic and Satyanarayanan 1996	Spasojevic, M. and Satyanarayanan, M. (1996). An Empirical Study of a Wide-Area Distributed File System, *ACM Transactions on Computer Systems*, Vol. 14, No. 2, May, pp. 200–222.
Spector 1982	Spector, A.Z. (1982). Performing remote operations efficiently on a local computer network. *Comms. ACM*, Vol. 25, No. 4, pp. 246–60.
Spurgeon 2000	Spurgeon, C.E. (2000). *Ethernet: The Definitive Guide*. O'Reilly.
Srikanth and Toueg 1987	Srikanth, T. and Toueg, S. (1987). Optimal Clock Synchronization. *Journal ACM*. 34, 3 (July), pp. 626–45.

Srinivasan 1995a	Srinivasan, R. (1995). RPC: *Remote Procedure Call Protocol Specification Version 2*. Sun Microsystems. Internet RFC 1831. August.
Srinivasan 1995b	Srinivasan, R. (1995). *XDR: External Data Representation Standard*. Sun Microsystems. RFC 1832. Network Working Group. August.
Srinivasan and Mogul 1989	Srinivasan, R. and Mogul, J.D. (1989). Spritely NFS: Experiments with Cache-Consistency Protocols, 12th ACM Symposium on Operating System Principles, Litchfield Park, AZ, December, pp. 45–57.
Srisuresh and Holdrege 1999	Srisuresh, P. and Holdrege, M. (1999), I*P Network Address Translator (NAT) Terminology and Considerations*, Internet RFC 2663, August.
Stajano 2002	Stajano, F. (2002). *Security for ubiquitous computing*. Wiley.
Stajano and Anderson 1999	Stajano, F. and Anderson, R. (1999). The Resurrecting Duckling: Security Issues for Adhoc Wireless Networks. *Proceedings 7th International Workshop on Security Protocols*, Springer-Verlag, pp. 172–194.
Stallings 1998a	Stallings, W. (1998). *High Speed Networks – TCP/IP and ATM Design Principles*. Upper Saddle River, NJ: Prentice-Hall.
Stallings 1998b	Stallings, W. (1998). *Operating Systems*, third edition. Prentice-Hall International.
Stallings 1999	Stallings, W. (1999). *Cryptography and Network Security – Principles and Practice*, second edition. Upper Saddle River, NJ: Prentice-Hall.
Steiner *et al.* 1988	Steiner, J., Neuman, C. and Schiller, J. (1988). Kerberos: an authentication service for open network systems. In *Proceedings Usenix Winter Conference*, Berkeley: CA.
Stelling *et al.* 1998	Stelling, P., Foster, I., Kesselman, C., Lee, C. and von Laszewski, G. (1998). A Fault Detection Service for Wide Area Distributed Computations, *Proceedings 7th IEEE Symposium on High Performance Distributed Computing*, pp. 268–78.
Stoica *et al.* 2001	Stoica, I., Morris, R., Karger, D., Kaashoek, F. and Balakrishnan, H. (2001). Chord: A scalable Peer-To-Peer lookup service for internet applications. In *ACM SIGCOMM*, August.
Stojmenovic 2002	Stojmenovic, I. (ed.) (2002). *Handbook of Wireless Networks and Mobile Computing*. Wiley.
Stoll 1989	Stoll, C. (1989). *The Cuckoo's Egg: Tracking a Spy Through a Maze of Computer Espionage*. New York: Doubleday.
Stone 1993	Stone, H. (1993). *High-performance Computer Architecture*, third edition. Addison-Wesley.
Sun 1989	Sun Microsystems Inc. (1989). *NFS: Network File System Protocol Specification*. Internet RFC 1094.

Sun and Ellis 1998 — Sun, C. and Ellis, C. (1998). Operational transformation in real-time group editors: issues, algorithms, and achievements. *Proceedings Conference on Computer Supported Cooperative Work Systems*, ACM Press, pp. 59–68.

SWAP-CA 2002 — Shared Wireless Access Protocol (Cordless Access) Specification (SWAP-CA), Revision 2.0,1 The HomeRF Technical Committee, July 2002.

Szalay and Gray 2001 — Szalay, A. and Gray, J. (2001) The World-Wide Telescope, *Science*, Vol. 293, pp. 2037–2040.

Szalay and Gray 2004 — Szalay, A. and Gray, J. (2004). *Scientific Data Federation: The World-Wide Telescope*. In Foster, I. and Kesselman, C. (eds), *The Grid 2*. San Francisco, CA: Morgan Kauffman.

Tanenbaum 2001 — Tanenbaum, A.S. (2001). *Modern Operating Systems*, second edition. Englewood Cliffs, NJ: Prentice-Hall.

Tanenbaum 2003 — Tanenbaum, A.S. (2003). *Computer Networks*, fourth edition. Prentice-Hall International.

Tanenbaum and van Renesse 1985 — Tanenbaum, A. and van Renesse, R. (1985). Distributed Operating Systems, *Computing Surveys, ACM*, Vol. 17, No. 4, pp. 419–70.

Tanenbaum et al. 1990 — Tanenbaum, A.S., van Renesse, R., van Staveren, H., Sharp, G., Mullender, S., Jansen, J. and van Rossum, G. (1990). Experiences with the Amoeba Distributed Operating System. *Comms. ACM*, Vol. 33, No. 12, pp. 46–63.

Taufer et al. 2003 — Taufer, M., Crowley, M., Karanicolas, J., Cicotti, P., Chien, A. and Brooks, L. (2003). *Moving towards desktop Grid solutions for large scale modelling in Computational Chemistry*. University of California, San Diego.

Terry et al. 1995 — Terry, D., Theimer, M., Petersen, K., Demers, A., Spreitzer, M. and Hauser, C. (1995). Managing update conflicts in Bayou, a weakly connected replicated storage system. *Proceedings of the 15th ACM Symposium on Operating Systems Principles*, pp. 172–183.

TFCC — *IEEE Task Force on Cluster Computing*.

Thayer 1998 — Thayer, R. (1998). *IP Security Document Roadmap*, Internet RFC 2411, November.

Thekkath et al. 1997 — Thekkath, C.A., Mann, T. and Lee, E.K. (1997). Frangipani: A Scalable Distributed File System, in *Proc. 16th ACM Symposium on Operating System Principles*, St Malo, France, October, pp. 224–237.

Tokuda et al. 1990 — Tokuda, H., Nakajima, T. and Rao, P. (1990). Real-time Mach: towards a predictable real-time system. In *Proceedings USENIX Mach Workshop*, pp. 73–82, October.

<u>Topolcic 1990</u>	Topolcic, C. (ed.) (1990). *Experimental Internet Stream Protocol, Version 2.* Internet RFC 1190.
Tzou and Anderson 1991	Tzou, S.-Y. and Anderson, D. (1991). The performance of message-passing using restricted virtual memory remapping. *Software–Practice and Experience*, Vol. 21, pp. 251–67.
van Renesse *et al.* 1989	van Renesse, R., van Staveran, H. and Tanenbaum, A. (1989). The Performance of the Amoeba Distributed Operating System. *Software – Practice and Experience*, Vol. 19, No. 3, pp. 223–34.
van Renesse *et al.* 1995	van Renesse, R., Birman, K., Friedman, R., Hayden, M. and Karr, D. (1995). A Framework for Protocol Composition in Horus. *Proceedings PODC 1995*, pp. 80–9.
van Renesse *et al.* 1996	van Renesse, R., Birman, K. and Maffeis, S. (1996). Horus: a Flexible Group Communication System. *Comms. ACM*, Vol. 39, No. 4, pp. 54–63.
van Steen *et al.* 1998	van Steen, M., Hauck, F., Homburg, P. and Tanenbaum, A. (1998). Locating objects in wide-area systems. *IEEE Communication*, Vol. 36, No. 1, pp. 104–109.
Vinoski 1998	Vinoski, S. (1998). New Features for CORBA 3.0, *Comms. ACM*, October 1998, Vol. 41, No. 10. pp. 44–52.
Vinoski 2002	Vinoski, S. (2002). Putting the 'Web' into Web Services. *IEEE Internet Computing*. July–August.
Vogels 2003	Vogels, W. (2003). Web Services are not Distributed objects. *IEEE Internet Computing*. Nov–Dec 2003.
Vogt *et al.* 1993	Vogt, C., Herrtwich, R.G. and Nagarajan, R. (1993). HeiRAT – The Heidelberg Resource Administration Technique: Design Philosophy and Goals. *Kommunikation in verteilten Systemen*, Munich, Informatik aktuell, Springer.
Volpano and Smith 1999	Volpano, D. and Smith, G. (1999). Language Issues in Mobile Program Security. To appear in *Lecture Notes in Computer Science*, Vol. 1419, pp. 25–43. Springer.
von Eicken *et al.* 1995	von Eicken, T., Basu, A., Buch, V. and Vogels, V. (1995). U-Net: a user-level network interface for parallel and distributed programming. *Proceedings of the 15th ACM Symposium on Operating Systems Principles*, pp. 40–53.
<u>Wahl et al. 1997</u>	Wahl, M., Howes, T. and Kille, S. (1997). *The Lightweight Directory Access Protocol (v3)*. Internet RFC 2251.
Waldo 1999	Waldo, J. (1999). The Jini Architecture for Network-centric Computing. *Comms. ACM*. Vol. 42, No. 7, pp. 76–82.
Waldo *et al.* 1994	Waldo, J., Wyant, G., Wollrath, A. and Kendall, S. (1994). A Note on Distributed Computing. In Arnold *et al.* 1999, pp. 307–26.

Waldspurger *et al.* 1992   Waldspurger, C., Hogg, T., Huberman, B., Kephart, J. and Stornetta, W. (1992). Spawn: A Distributed Computational Economy. *Transactions on Software Engineering*, Vol. 18, No. 2, pp. 103–17.

Want 2004   Want, R. (2004). Enabling ubiquitous sensing with RFID. *IEEE Computer*, Vol. 37, No. 4, April, pp. 84–86.

Want and Pering 2003   Want, R. and Pering, T. (2003). New Horizons for Mobile Computing. *Proceedings First IEEE International Conference on Pervasive Computing and Communication (PerCom'03)*, Dallas-Fort Worth, USA, March, pp. 3–8.

Want *et al.* 1992   Want, R., Hopper, A., Falcao, V. and Gibbons, V. (1992). The Active Badge Location System. *ACM Transactions on Information Systems*, Vol. 10, No.1, January, pp. 91–102.

Want *et al.* 2002   Want, R., Pering, T., Danneels, G., Kumar, M., Sundar, M. and Light, J. (2002). The Personal Server: changing the way we think about ubiquitous computing. *Proceedings Fourth International Conference on Ubiquitous Computing (Ubicomp 2002)*, Goteborg, Sweden, Sep.–Oct., Springer-Verlag, pp.194–209.

Weatherspoon and Kubiatowicz 2002   Weatherspoon, H. and Kubiatowicz, J.D. (2002). Erasure Coding vs. Replication: A Quantitative Comparison, *1st International Workshop on Peer-'to-Peer Systems (IPTPS '02)*, Cambridge, MA, March.

web.mit.edu I   *Kerberos: The Network Authentication Protocol.*

web.mit.edu II   *The Three Myths of Firewalls.*

Weikum 1991   Weikum, G. (1991). Principles and Realization Strategies of Multilevel Transaction Management. *ACM Transactions Database Systems*, Vol. 16, No. 1, pp. 132–40.

Weiser 1991   Weiser, M. (1991). The Computer for the 21st Century. *Scientific American*, Vol. 265, No. 3, September, pp. 94–104.

Weiser 1993   Weiser, M. (1993). Some computer science issues in ubiquitous computing. *Comms. ACM*, Vol. 36, No. 7, pp. 74–84.

Wellner 1991   Wellner, P.D. (1991). The DigitalDesk calculator – tangible manipulation on a desk-top display. *Proceedings of the 4th annual ACM symposium on User interface software and technology*, Hilton Head, SC, USA, November, pp. 27–33.

Wheeler and Needham 1994   Wheeler, D.J. and Needham, R.M. (1994). TEA, a Tiny Encryption Algorithm. Technical Report 355, *Two Cryptographic Notes*, Computer Laboratory, University of Cambridge, December, pp. 1–3.

Wheeler and Needham 1997   Wheeler, D.J. and Needham, R.M. (1997). *Tea Extensions*, October 1994, pp. 1–3.

Wiesmann *et al.* 2000	Wiesmann, M., Pedone, F., Schiper, A., Kemme, B. and Alonso, G. (2000). Understanding replication in databases and distributed systems. In *Proceedings 20th International Conference on Distributed Computing Systems (ICDCS '2000)*, Taipei, Republic of China, IEEE.
Williams 1998	Williams, P. (1998). JetSend: An Appliance Communication Protocol. *Proceedings IEEE International Workshop on Networked Appliances, (IEEE IWNA '98)*, Kyoto, Japan, November 1998.
Winer 1999	Winer, D. (1999). *The XML-RPC specification.*
Wobber *et al.* 1994	Wobber, E., Abadi, M., Burrows, M. and Lampson, B. (1994). Authentication in the Taos operating system. *ACM Transactions Computer Systems*. 12, 1 (Feb.), pp. 3–32.
Wright *et al.* 2002	Wright, M., Adler, M., Levine, B.N. and Shields, C. (2002). An Analysis of the Degradation of Anonymous Protocols, *In the Proceedings of the Network and Distributed Security Symposium – NDSS '02*, February.
WSDL4J 2003	*The Web Services Description Language for Java Toolkit (WSDL4J).*
Wulf *et al.* 1974	Wulf, W., Cohen, E., Corwin, W., Jones, A., Levin, R., Pierson, C. and Pollack, F. (1974). HYDRA: the kernel of a multiprocessor operating system. *Comms. ACM*, Vol. 17, No. 6, pp. 337–345.
Wuu and Bernstein 1984	Wuu, G.T. and Bernstein, A.J. (1984). Efficient Solutions to the Replicated Log and Dictionary Problems. *ACM Proceedings Third Annual Symposium Principles of Distributed Computing*, pp. 233–42.
www.accessgrid.org	*The Access Grid Project.*
www.apple.com	Apple Computer Corp. Rendezvous technical resources.
www.bluetooth.com	The Official Bluetooth SIG Website.
www.butterfly.net	Butterfly.net, *The scalable, reliable and high performance online game platform, GoGrid.*
www.bxa.doc.gov	Bureau of Export Administration, US Department of Commerce, *Commercial Encryption Export Controls.*
www.cdk4.net	Coulouris, G., Dollimore, J. and Kindberg, T. (eds), *Distributed Systems, Concepts and Design: Supporting material.*
www.citrix.com	Citrix Corporation. *Server-based Computing White Paper.*
www.cren.net	Corporation for Research and Educational Networking, *CREN Certificate Authority.*
www.cryptopp.com	Crypto++® Library 5.2.1.
www.cs.york.ac.uk/dame	*Distributed Aircraft Maintenance Environment (DAME).*
www.cuseeme.com	CU-SeeMe Networks Inc. *Home page.*
www.doi.org	International DOI Foundation. *Pages on digital object identifiers.*
www.dtnrg.org	Delay Tolerant Networking Research Group. *Home page.*

www.globexplorer.com	*Globexplorer, the world's largest online library of aerial and satellite imagery.*
www.handle.net	Handle system. *Home page.*
www.iana.org	Internet Assigned Numbers Authority. *IANA Home page.*
www.ietf.org	Internet Engineering Task Force. *Internet RFC Index page.*
www.iona.com	Iona Technologies, *Orbix.*
www.ipnsig.org	InterPlaNetary Internet Project. *Home page.*
www.isoc.org	Robert Hobbes Zakon. *Hobbes' Internet Timeline.*
www.microsoft.com I	Microsoft Corporation. *Active Directory Services.*
www.microsoft.com II	Microsoft Corporation. *Windows 2000 Kerberos Authentication*, White Paper.
www.microsoft.com III	Microsoft Corporation. *NetMeeting Home page.*
www.neesgrid.org	*NEES Grid, Building the National Virtual Collaboratory for Earthquake Engineering.*
www.nfc-forum.org	Near Field Communication (NFC). *Forum Home page.*
www.omg.org	Object Management Group, *Index to CORBA services.* OMG: Needham, MA.
www.opengroup.org	Open Group. *Portal to the World of DCE.*
www.openmobilealliance. org	Open Mobile Alliance. *Home page.*
www.openssl.org	OpenSSL Project. *OpenSSL: The Open Source toolkit for SSL/TLS.*
www.pgp.com	PGP. *Home page.*
www.reed.com	Read, D.P. (2000). *The End of the End-to-End Argument.*
www.rsasecurity.com	RSA Security Inc. *Home page.*
www.rsasecurity.com I	RSA Corporation (1997). *DES Challenge.*
www.rsasecurity.com II	RSA Corporation (2004). *RSA Factoring Challenge.*
www.rtj.org	*Real-Time for Java TM Experts Group.*
www.secinf.net	Network Security Library.
www.smart-its.org	The Smart-Its Project. *Home page.*
www.spec.org	*SPEC SFS97 Benchmark.*
www.upnp.org	Universal Plug and Play. *Home page.*
www.uscms.org	USCMS, *The Compact Muon Solenoid.*
www.verisign.com	Verisign Inc. *Home page.*
www.w3.org I	World Wide Web Consortium. *Home page.*
www.w3.org II	World Wide Web Consortium. *Pages on the HyperText Markup Language.*

www.w3.org III	World Wide Web Consortium. *Pages on Naming and Addressing.*
www.w3.org IV	World Wide Web Consortium. *Pages on the HyperText Transfer Protocol.*
www.w3.org V	World Wide Web Consortium. *Pages on the Resource Description Framework and other metadata schemes.*
www.w3.org VI	World Wide Web Consortium. *Pages on the Extensible Markup Language.*
www.w3.org VII	World Wide Web Consortium. *Pages on the Extensible Stylesheet Language.*
www.w3.org VIII	*XML Schemas.*W3C Recommendation. (2001)
www.w3.org IX	World Wide Web Consortium. *Pages on SOAP.*
www.w3.org X	World Wide Web Consortium. *Pages on Canonical XML, Version 1.0.* W3C Recommendation. March.
www.w3.org XI	World Wide Web Consortium. *Pages on Web Services Description Language (WSDL).*
www.w3.org XII	World Wide Web Consortium. *Pages on XML Signature Syntax and Processing.*
www.w3.org XIII	World Wide Web Consortium. *Pages on.XML key management specification XKMS.*
www.w3.org XIV	World Wide Web Consortium. *Pages on XML Encryption Syntax and Processing.*
www.w3.org XV	World Wide Web Consortium. *Pages on Web Services Choreography Requirements.* W3C Working Draft.
www.w3.org XVI	Burdett, D. and Kavantsas, N. (2004). *WS Choreography Model Overview*, W3C Working Draft.
www.w3.org XVII	World Wide Web Consortium. *Pages on Web Services Choreography Description Language Version 1.0.*
www.w3.org XVIII	World Wide Web Consortium. *Pages on Web Services Choreography Interface (WSCI).*
www.w3.org XIX	World Wide Web Consortium. *Pages on Device Independence.*
www.w3.org XX	World Wide Web Consortium. *Pages on the Semantic Web.*
www.wapforum.org	WAP Forum. *White Papers and Specifications.*
www.wlana.com	*The IEEE 802.11 Wireless LAN Standard.*
www.xbow.com	Crossbow Technology Inc. *Pages on wireless sensor networks.*
www.zeroconf.org	IETF Zeroconf Working Group. *Home page.*
Wyckoff *et al.* 1998	Wyckoff, P., McLaughry, S., Lehman, T. and Ford, D. (1998). T Spaces. *IBM Systems Journal*, Vol. 37, No. 3.
zakon.org	Zakon, R.H. Hobbes' Internet Timeline v7.0,

Zhang and Kindberg 2002   Zhang, K. and Kindberg, T. (2002). An authorization infrastructure for nomadic computing. *Proceedings Seventh ACM Symposium on Access Control Models and Technologies*, Monterey, CA, USA, June, pp. 107–113.

Zhang *et al.* 1993   Zhang, L., Deering, S.E., Estrin, D., Shenker, S. and Zappala, D. (1993). RSVP – A New Resource Reservation Protocol. *IEEE Network Magazine*, Vol. 9, No. 5.

Zhao *et al.* 2004   Zhao, B.Y., Huang, L., Stribling, J., Rhea, S.C., Joseph, A.D. and Kubiatowicz, J.D. (2004). Tapestry: A Resilient Global-Scale Overlay for Service Deployment, *IEEE Journal on Selected Areas in Communications*, Vol. 22, No. 1, January.

Zimmermann 1995   Zimmermann, P.R. (1995). *The Official PGP User's Guide*. Cambridge, MA: MIT Press.

INDEX